A HISTORY
of the
PHILADELPHIA THEATRE
1835 to 1855

A HISTORY
of the
PHILADELPHIA THEATRE
1835 to 1855

By

ARTHUR HERMAN WILSON

Professor of English
Susquehanna University

GREENWOOD PRESS, PUBLISHERS
NEW YORK   1968

FOREWORD

THIS third volume in the history of the Philadelphia theatre hardly needs a foreword, since Professor Wilson's own introduction gives to the reader all the necessary information. But since there has apparently been a change of plan in the arrangement of the material, a word may perhaps be in order. In planning the series, it was decided that usefulness and interest should never be sacrificed to mere uniformity. In Professor Pollock's *The Philadelphia Theatre in the Eighteenth Century* it was possible to give complete casts in the daily record and, owing to the small number of theatres, to preface these with a chronological introduction dealing with all matters connected with the stage. In the second volume, Professor James had an opportunity to reprint exactly the unique manuscript of William Wood, the manager of the Chesnut Street Theatre, and consequently his record from 1800 to 1835 took a somewhat different shape. From this point, the increasing number of theatres has made it necessary to present the daily record in a more condensed form, giving casts only as indicated by Professor Wilson when the play is first performed in Philadelphia and, instead of a chronological record, chapters on the Plays, the Players, and the Theatres will furnish a general survey. Complete indices will make easy references for any play, playwright, or actor who took part in the Philadelphia theatre during the years from 1835 to 1855. These dates are not accidental. In planning the series, each volume brings the history of the Philadelphia theatre to a certain logical climax. This section of the history ends with the year in which Boker's *Francesca da Rimini* brought the romantic tragedy in America to its height. The record of Charles Durang, never published in book form, ends with this year, and the problems of the historian change somewhat when this mine of information, invaluable but always in need of verification, ceases. It was a very significant period in the history of the stage in Philadelphia and deserves the scholarly treatment it has received, not only as a new volume in the series, but for its intrinsic interest.

ARTHUR HOBSON QUINN

ACKNOWLEDGMENTS

It is with the keenest pleasure that the present researcher acknowledges his supreme debt to Dr. Arthur Hobson Quinn, distinguished student of the American drama and theatre. Without his guiding inspiration, expert technical direction, and unselfish human spirit of friendliness, this research would have been impossible.

Gratitude is due, also, to Dr. Reese D. James and Dr. Thomas Pollock, friends and co-workers, for their coöperation through constructive criticism.

For all our pleasant and instructive talks concerning the Philadelphia drama and theatre of fifty and sixty years ago, the present writer wishes to remember Mr. Arthur Ehrlinger, whose memory of great actors, managers, and theatres has helped to recapture the living atmosphere of the old times.

A record of appreciation is also gladly ascribed to the Misses Elizabeth and Mary Britton and Mrs. W. G. Phillips for their laborious accuracy in the preparation of manuscript.

In addition, the writer wishes to thank the staff of the Historical Society of Pennsylvania, and particularly Mr. George Fairchild.

The generous aid of the American Council of Learned Societies is also deeply appreciated by the author.

ARTHUR HERMAN WILSON

CONTENTS

INTRODUCTION

THE year of 1835 marks an epoch in the dramatic history of Philadelphia since it brings to a close the account book or diary of William B. Wood, famous actor-manager, and also witnesses the end of his active years of service in our city.

The year of 1855 also records a turning point in the history of the footlights in Philadelphia. At that time, three major events took place to affect the three departments of our history, namely: the theatres, the plays, and the actors. The Chesnut Street Theatre, known as "Old Drury," ended sixty-two years of active service in 1855, and was demolished. With its disappearance, the ghosts of its greenroom were laid and the romantic age became a memory. At this time, also, appeared an epochmaking play, George Henry Boker's *Francesca da Rimini,* which came as a crowning glory to the romantic age of tragedy. And, as a third event, Dion Boucicault first appeared upon the boards of the legitimate stage in Philadelphia in the year of 1855. It was his influence which was to break up the splendid old stock companies of actors and substitute the complete traveling companies that occupy a theatre building by engagement as they do today.

A detailed account of the earliest theatrical history in Philadelphia has been written by Dr. Thomas C. Pollock in his book, *The Philadelphia Theatre in the Eighteenth Century.* And a minute record of the years between 1800 and 1835 has been made a subject of exacting research by Dr. Reese Davis James, in *Old Drury of Philadelphia.* Dr. James has edited the account book of William B. Wood, the actor-manager, whose career runs throughout those years.

BIBLIOGRAPHY OF NEWSPAPERS

THIS list contains only Philadelphia newspapers and the dates (between 1835 and 1855) when they serve as reference for the Philadelphia theatres.

Cummings' Evening Telegraphic Bulletin: Published by Cummings and Peacock, 46 South Third Street; Vol. XXXVIII, new series No. 1070, 1850.

The (Daily) Pennsylvanian: Published by Mifflin and Parry, 99 South Second Street; 1833–1855.

National Gazette and Literary Register: 1835–1840.

North American and United States Gazette: Published by M'Michael and Bird, 66 South Third Street; incorp. 1847–1855.

Pennsylvania Inquirer and Daily Courier: Printed and published by Jesper Harding, 74 South Second Street; 1835–1855.

Philadelphia Recorder: 1835–1848.

Poulson's American Daily Advertiser: Printed by Zachariah Poulson, 106 Chesnut Street; 1835–1839.

Public Ledger (and Daily Transcript): Published by Swain, Abell, and Simmons, Second and Dock Streets; 1836–1855.

The Quaker City: December 30, 1848–December 30, 1849.

The Spirit of the Times: Published by A. H. Smith and Company, 42 South Third Street; Vol. XXIV, No. 5362, 1850.

The Daily Sun: Published by Wallace and Fletcher, 64 South Third Street; Vol. XII, No. 84, 1850.

The Sunday Dispatch: Containing Charles Durang's articles about the Philadelphia stage between the years of 1749 and 1855, First Series, 1749–1821, starting in the paper of May 7, 1854; Second Series, 1822–1830, starting June 29, 1856; Third Series, embracing the period between the season of 1830–31 and the demolition of the Chesnut Street Theatre, April, 1855, starting in the paper of July 8, 1860.

United States Gazette: Published by Joseph R. Chandler, 66 Dock Street; 1835–1847.

THE THEATRES

CHAPTER I

THE THEATRES

1835

THE three theatres which were the mainstay of Philadelphia theatrical entertainment in 1835 were the Arch, on the north side of Arch Street above Sixth, the Walnut, at the northeast corner of Ninth and Walnut Streets, and the Chesnut, above Sixth Street on the north side of Chesnut Street.

In 1835, Maywood and Company had become the lessees of the Chesnut and the Arch, while the Walnut was without a lessee for a short period. Maywood himself was busy in London, beating around for recruits, star and stock, to supply his Philadelphia theatres.

The campaign for 1834 and 1835 commenced at the Arch under the management of Messrs. Maywood, Rowbotham, and Pratt. The house was repainted and decorated in an elegant manner by Henry Warren. The lobbies were laid with new matting. The orchestra, selected from some of the best talent in the city, was under the direction of Ben. C. Cross, Jr. The prices were: boxes, seventy-five cents; pit, thirty-seven and a-half cents; gallery, twenty-five cents.

Francis C. Wemyss returned to Philadelphia from an unsuccessful Pittsburgh venture to take over the Walnut with the backing of his good angel, George A. Cook. The rent at this theatre was four thousand, one hundred and fifty dollars a year, exclusive of the rooms occupied as bar saloons. Wemyss declined to have anything to do with the bars and their accessories, as a recent law prohibiting the granting of tavern licenses to theatres was in force at that moment. However, the law did not last long and, it is said by Durang, the stockholders received the sum of three thousand dollars a year for the bars, making a rental of upwards of seven thousand dollars for the theatre.

When Wemyss leased the Walnut this season, the house was to be redecorated and thoroughly painted according to plans furnished by him. He signed the lease, paid one thousand dollars in advance, returned to the Iron City, closed his campaign there, and with his dramatic corps recrossed the Alleghenies to the eastward. The bills of the Walnut for this year were headed "American Theatre," with the cut of a large spread-eagle, and a large scroll in his talons inscribed with "Walnut Street Theatre." The prices of admission were: boxes, fifty cents; pit, twenty-five cents; gallery, twenty-five cents. C. Porter was acting manager; W. Barrymore, stage manager; J. G. Clemens, leader of the orchestra; and Landers, stage carpenter.

A large sum of money had been expended on the decorations at the Walnut, which represented the celebrated events in American history from the Declaration of Independence to the closing of the late war following the glorious battle of New Orleans. Each tier of boxes was decorated with paintings representing some celebrated battle in the history of the United States. Around the dress circle were placed medallions of the heads of all the presidents, around the second tier the heads of celebrated generals, and around the third tier the heads of naval heroes. Between each medallion and its corresponding painting was a large gold star, the whole forming a pink ground—a most novel and beautiful interior. A new drop scene was painted by Harry Williams and an additional scene by Coyle. The proscenium and the general decorations were painted by W. Russell Smith, a young artist of Pittsburgh. Designs so original and perfect had never been offered to a Philadelphia audience, Durang assures us.

It was stated that the receipts of this season taken by Wemyss amounted to $27,925, giving an average for ninety-six nights of $291 a night. Wemyss was induced to reopen the theatre for a summer season which he subsequently regretted, losing about twelve hundred dollars in the fifty-six nights it was open.

Maywood and Company kept the Chesnut opened until Monday, February 23, 1835, when they opened the Arch in place of the other theatre. However, on Monday, April 6, 1835, the Chesnut was again in use and the Arch was closed. The Walnut, which had been open all winter, was made dark with its last performance on Saturday, April 11, 1835, the last part of the week in which the Chesnut reopened. For the rest of April, the Chesnut had the field to itself, until the Walnut reopened for a summer season beginning Saturday, May 2. Both theatres closed for a summer recess starting at the close of performances, Saturday, July 4. A special benefit for Mrs. Cook was held at the Walnut, July 6, with the combined companies of both houses. Both the Walnut and the Chesnut again resumed performances, Saturday, August 22, and continued uninterruptedly for the remainder of the year.

[6]

Tradition is a word which has always meant much to Philadelphia, in theory as well as in practice. And one of America's own stage traditions was that of giving timely plays upon the occasions of memorial days. Washington's birthday was remembered usually by the performance of *Gustavus Vasa* (otherwise known as *The Hero of the North, or The Liberator of His Country*). Independence Day was celebrated by such native dramas as *The Liberty Tree, or The Boston Boys of '76,* and *The Star-Spangled Banner.* And even famous American battle-days were given occasional memorial attention.

Another tradition of the stage was that of literally knocking together an occasional play of allusion to topics of the day. Usually, the play was in the nature of a farce, but not necessarily so. Two Philadelphia farces which sprang up mushroom-like in 1835 owe their origin to the mild furor created in the city by Sir John Herschel, astronomical scientist, whose articles anent lunar discoveries were appearing in the United States Gazette. *Discoveries in the Moon, or Herschel Out-Herscheled,* by T. D. Rice of Jim Crow fame appeared at the Walnut, September 5, and the Chesnut followed, September 7, with *Moonshine, or Lunar Caustic,* by Wm. E. Burton.

1836

The Chesnut, when opened by Maywood and Company, after the summer recess, was repainted and redecorated by Carr. A new drop curtain was painted by Henry Warren, the subject taken from Sully's historical picture of Washington crossing the Delaware in the Revolutionary War.

The Pennsylvania Theatre, Coates Street, was now in operation, but not flourishing. Cornelius Logan, the ostensible lessee and manager, withdrew early from the venture. The establishment belonged to F. C. Wemyss, who built it by way of experiment. It was one of the principal rocks upon which his management subsequently was wrecked.

This new theatre, as Wemyss built it, was situated on Coates Street not far from Second Street, on the north side. The architect was Sera; the scene painter, a very ingenious French artist. He did all he could, with the means allowed, to give this edifice a respectable aspect and an air of taste; but it had quite a shanty, makeshift appearance, and as suddenly sunk as it rose. It opened on November 7, under the auspices of Cornelius A. Logan, from the management of which he retired on the ensuing January. Originally the house was converted from a church into a theatre, and from that into a vendue shop of second-hand furniture; afterwards to a lager beer saloon and concert saloon.

Wemyss likewise remained the lessee of the Walnut, which he ran regularly. And Maywood and Company continued in their practice of employing the Arch as an early-summer theatre, after their closing of the Chesnut. The Walnut and the Chesnut both entertained the playgoers of Philadelphia during January and February of 1836 until Maywood and Company closed the Chesnut to open the Arch, Saturday, February 27, when the Walnut and Arch continued together. This arrangement persisted until Monday, June 13, 1836, when the Chesnut was reopened and the Arch closed.

The Walnut entered upon the summer intermission with the performance on Monday, July 4, but the Chesnut remained open for one week longer, closing on Monday, July 11, 1836. Likewise, following the warm weather, the Chesnut began its activities on Saturday, August 20, one week before the opening of the Walnut on Saturday, August 27.

The Pennsylvania Theatre, on Coates Street, entered the field Monday, November 7, and continued with the other two theatres for the remainder of the year.

Another, and more fascinating, tradition of the stage was that of the Christmas pantomimes. Thackeray has much to say for the subject in that Roundabout paper of his called "Round about the Christmas Tree." Anyone who is skeptical about the importance of old-fashioned harlequinades will kindly read the words of the master and be converted. Philadelphia, with its roots so deep in eighteenth-century tradition, usually followed the ancient and respected custom of the English Christmas week with the amusing capers of Pantaloon, Clown, and Columbine.

The reader can locate all of the actual titles of these pantomimes under the heading of Harlequin in the Play-List, such as: *Harlequin and Mother Goose, Harlequin and the Fairy of the Rose, Harlequin and the Magic Trumpet, Harlequin Hurry Scurry, Harlequin Shipwreck,* and *Harlequin Tom the Piper's Son.*

1837

F. C. Wemyss, in 1837, had a dispute with the stockholders of the Walnut because he wanted them to install gas. The stockholders agreed, provided they were given one thousand dollars in advance rent. Then, following this incident, when Cooke wanted to bring his circus to Philadelphia, he offered to sublet the Walnut from Wemyss, but the stockholders flatly refused. So Cooke erected the Chesnut Street Circus, at Ninth and Chesnut, which, in 1840, was altered into the New National Theatre by W. E. Burton.

The gas fixtures at the Chesnut (which precipitated the whole discussion and unfriendliness between Wemyss and the stockholders at the Walnut) were installed by C. Cornelius and Son. The gas, which was introduced from the public works, with all the modern improvements, imparted a new phase to everything dramatic, particularly in the scenic illusions, since it aided in a remarkable degree the lights and shadows of painting.

The Chesnut at this time was adorned with a species of decorative painting then new to the public: the superb paintings of classical subjects by Signor Monachesi, particularly his painting of "The Hours," after the great Italian master, Guido.

The rent of the house was advanced to nine thousand dollars a year. The stockholders, this year, had been offered ten thousand dollars from a New York applicant, but, in consideration of Maywood and Company's early exertions and honesty of action, they continued that firm. The original rent of the Chesnut, according to Durang, was twenty-five hundred dollars to three thousand dollars a year, the stockholders being entitled to a season ticket. On the dissolution of Warren and Wood's partnership in 1826, the rent was three thousand dollars on which they held a lease for sixteen years.

The Pennsylvania Theatre continued through January to February 18, 1837, when Wemyss closed it and left the field to the Walnut and Chesnut alone. The Walnut itself ceased performances on the night of Monday, April 3, 1837. The Chesnut carried along in solitude for the rest of April, but gave way to the Arch on Monday, May 1. The Walnut reopened for a summer season and fell into stride with the Arch on Saturday, June 17. On Saturday, July 8, the Arch closed and left the Walnut sole center of entertainment. The Walnut continued through the hot months of summer and there was, therefore, no summer recess with theatres closed this year as there had been for the two preceding years. The Chesnut itself started up again Saturday, August 19.

The Walnut finally succumbed to the heat of the weather Saturday, September 2, and left the Chesnut in solitary sway until Wednesday,

November 15, when it reopened, and the two continued for the remaining months of the year.

The name of Charles Durang deserves special mention and must be discussed here in a place where there is room to give particular notice to it. As an actor, Durang does not stand out in any individual prominence, but as stage-manager for the Walnut (1837) he directed considerable personal influence upon the actors appearing there, and himself took occasional parts. For his benefit night, Feb. 6th, he played the part of Lubin in the sketch of *Little Red Riding Hood.*

In 1836, for the opening of the legendary drama of *The Maid of Cashmere* we find reference to the fact that he had charge of the dances arranged for that play. He himself occasionally danced the specialty number of Rickett's hornpipe (June 24, 1835). And he appeared also, in the Christmas pantomime of that year, *Harlequin Hurry Scurry* (Dec. 25, 1835). From time to time he adapted plays for the stage of the Walnut, noticeably Byron's tragedy of *Sardanapalus,* at its Philadelphia premier on Nov. 23, 1836. And for April 9, 1842, we find that he translated a play from the French of Alexander Dumas for E. S. Conner, called *The Warrior of the Wave.* But, as a writer, his real importance lies in the achievement of his history of the Philadelphia Stage (1749 to 1855, inclusive).

The versatility of his character can be seen through the scope of the many activities that were his: actor, manager, dancer, play-fashioner, pantomimist, theatrical historian, and writer; and the public acceptance of him in these various rôles attests his good craftsmanship.

1838

F. C. Wemyss had a very unsatisfactory year at the Walnut and it was only following the summer recess that he met any degree of financial success in the grand, spectacular procession of *The Coronation of Queen Victoria,* modeled after Elliston's famous *Coronation of George the Fourth,* in London, 1820.

The lengthy season at the Walnut of sixty-four weeks and one night brought many reverses to Wemyss. By October, he had lost five hundred dollars, but by the summer he retrieved the entire deficiency and made so much money that it was the best season, probably, asserts Durang, that he ever had during his managerial reign.

The Chesnut commenced the fall and winter season with the advertisement that:

In consequence of the enormous expenses attending the establishment, the prices of admission are fixed upon the following scale: boxes, one dollar; pit, fifty cents. The gallery, during the recess, has been entirely removed.

The reasons set forth for the advance in prices were several, namely: the advance in rents; the expense attending the engagements; the outlay in new scenery, repainting, and wardrobes.

W. T. Russell Smith, who was called "our native artist," had produced a novel classic drop curtain for the Chesnut. The subject was Thespis on his cart at Athens, surrounded by a group of actors.

The stock company at the Chesnut was truly more effective this season than it had been for years, but it was unfortunately oppressed by the presence of stars on engagement. The extravagant sums extorted by the stars gradually sank Maywood and Company into ruin.

The Walnut and the Chesnut continued to hold the attention of the theatre-going public until the Walnut closed on Thursday, March 22, to be reopened again on Monday, April 2, by Cooke's traveling company for an engagement which lasted until Saturday, May 5, when the Chesnut was again in sole possession of Philadelphia's theatrical entertainment.

The Walnut reopened on Monday, July 2 (one week before the Chesnut closed on Saturday, July 7), and continued as a summer theatre for the rest of the season with the production on Friday, August 10, of *The Coronation of Queen Victoria,* keeping the field to itself until the relighting of the Chesnut on Saturday, August 25. So, we must say again, that at no time this summer (as in the last summer, likewise) did Philadelphia's theatres completely desert the city. And the two theatres, Walnut and Chesnut, remained in step together without intermission during September, October, November, and December.

William E. Burton, the comedian and playwright, who two years later became the unsurpassed man of the hour in Philadelphia theatricals, already at a date even earlier than 1838 gave promise of the timeliness and accuracy of his judgment as an entertainer. His ingenuity and ability to know how to please is very adequately suggested in the advertisement included in the *United States Gazette* for July 7, 1838, the last night of season for the Chesnut and likewise the occasion of Burton's own benefit.

Mr. Burton requests the attention of his Friends to the nature of the entertainments which are selected to suit the season, being of a light and airy nature, and particularly adapted to warm weather. . . . Les Vaudevilles are now considered a Fashionable night's entertainment, superior to the dullness of a long tragedy or the heaviness of a five-act comedy. This arrangement presents the visitors with continued amusement, without compelling them to remain the whole evening to see the end of a piece.

The vaudevilles alluded to are found to be "The Dancing Barber," "Does Your Mother Know You Are Out?", "The Original," and "The Spitfire."

1839

F. C. Wemyss was surprised to be informed that, on signing the new lease for 1839–40, a stipulation would be inscribed by the stockholders as to the prices of admittance into their theatre. The notice thus given was that the Board of Agents had come to the conclusion not to renew Wemyss' lease unless he agreed to raise the price of admission to the pit to thirty-seven and a-half cents. To this Wemyss demurred, reasoning with the Board of Agents upon the fatal effects which would attend so injurious a measure as increasing upon the most popular branch of the audience one-third of the long established rates. At half price, he argued, he had offered more successful novelties than the Chesnut (surnamed the aristocratic theatre, or "Old Drury"), and, in spite of their foreign stars, had equaled them in popular attractions. And, certainly, he had satisfied the popular voice in cultivating and producing native talent.

G. H. Freeman, who was the president of the Board, demanded compliance with the terms or vacation of the theatre by Wemyss at the end of the lease. Wemyss was compelled to surrender, although he realized the ultimate folly of the step. Maywood at the Chesnut, also, it is to be remembered, raised the prices. The public, however, refused to support such prices.

In due course of time, after E. A. Marshall became lessee of the Walnut, circumstances had changed. The country had become remarkably prosperous. Commerce and our manufactories were flourishing, and fashion had assumed a patronizing air in the cause of art.

In Wemyss' endeavor to stem the tide and to avoid the calamity ahead, he altered his old system of strategy and, on Saturday, September 14, brought the season of 1838–39 to a close, having kept the theatre open for a whole year.

On Saturday he closed; Sunday intervened; and on Monday, September 16, the auditorium was entirely renovated: newly painted, seats recovered, every department apparently renewed, and all points even to mouldings regilt and burnished. Wemyss had prepared appropriate decorations by his new artist, Hielge, on canvas, so that they could be tacked on during a few hours of labor over the front boxes and the proscenium. The affair was very ingenious and was rapidly and cleverly executed. The curtain rose just half an hour beyond its time. It had the effect of magic; and the audience, for three nights, were struck with wonder at the effect so miraculously produced.

However, the result of the raise in price ultimately supported Wemyss' prediction of failure. On January 25, 1840, he graciously received permission from the Board of Agents to do as he liked with regard to the prices. But it was too late. The pit could not be coaxed back. In 114 nights, he lost six thousand dollars. In the whole season of 261 nights, 155 produced less than half the amount of the nightly expenses necessary to keep the doors open. Wemyss, from that time forth, never recovered himself.

Maywood and Company at the Chesnut were likewise fighting a losing battle with their advance in prices. They had not been able to open their Arch for two seasons.

The next year was to see many changes. Through the dreary year from January to June, the Walnut and the Chesnut kept open, and, when the Chesnut closed with the performance of Saturday, June 22, the Walnut continued alone through the dull summer until it was rejoined by the Chesnut on Saturday, August 24, 1839. And then, the two of them pushed along for the remaining months, sinking deeper and deeper into financial failure.

Benefit nights were a regular part of the life of the early stage. Every actor appearing by engagement was given his benefit on the night following the last night of his engagement. Every stock-actor received one benefit each season. Even the doorkeepers, the prompters, treasurers, orchestra leaders and house police force received their benefits. Voluntary benefits were awarded to people distressed by sectional calamity; to the Floridans harassed by the Indians, to the Texans oppressed by their neighbors, to victims of fire, flood, and famine. And no theatre was more ready to help the needy than the Walnut under the direction of Francis C. Wemyss, the man of good heart.

One wonders how much the Walnut was responsible for the efficiency of the Philadelphia fire fighters of the time. In three months of 1839, there were twenty-four benefits for the firemen, three at the Chesnut, the rest at Wemyss' Walnut. The fire companies needed equipment, and needed houses, for many of them were newly organized. The following is a list of these benefits and the early engine companies:

APRIL

W. 9. Niagara Hose Co.
W. 10. Hibernia Fire Co.
W. 11. America Fire Co.
C. 12. Reliance Fire Co.
W. 13. Weccacoe Fire Co.
W. 15. Columbia Hose Co.
W. 16. Marion Hose Co.
W. 17. Hand In Hand Engine Co.
W. 19. Delaware Fire Engine Co.
W. 20. Firemen's Complimentary Benefit to F. C. Wemyss.

MAY

C. 7. Northern Liberty Hose Co.
W. 7. Neptune Hose Co.
W. 8. Good Will Fire Co.
W. 9. Columbia Engine Co.
W. 14. Southward Fire Co.
W. 15. Fair Mount Fire Co.
W. 16. La Fayette Hose Co.
W. 17. Globe Engine Co.
W. 21. Robert Morris Hose Co.
C. 21. Humane Hose Co.
W. 22. Hope Fire Engine Co.
W. 24. Western Hose Co.

JUNE

W. 5. United States Hose Co.
W. 21. East Kensington Fire Engine Co.

1840

In regard to renewing the lease for 1840–41 at the Walnut, Wemyss addressed the Board of Agents, making a detailed statement of his grievances, of his losses, of his expenditures for repairs, and giving cogent reasons why he thought himself entitled to expect from their hands some consideration. His accounts were:

For canvas, lumber, paints, cordage, tinware, extra carpenters' wages (not including his regular weekly bill for carpenter work of $42) upwards of $7,000, independent of rent, which, in six years has amounted to $27,900. The stockholders have received during the same time, for bar rents, viz.: twenty-five weeks for the first seven months, say $50 per week, $1,250; forty-five weeks for the second year, at $50 per week, $2,250; thirty-five weeks for the third year, at $50, $1,100; thirty-three weeks for the fourth year, at $50, $1,650; fifty-two weeks for the fifth year, at $70, $3,640; forty-eight weeks for the sixth year, at $70, $3,560. Total, $13,250. $13,250, in addition to the $27,900, making the gross amount of $41,150 for the five years and seven months of the lease— nearly fifteen percent per year, reckoning one hundred and seventy-five shares at $275 each.

Durang gives us these figures in his history.

Wemyss had twice decorated the house, and the stockholders had decorated it but once, in order to lease it in 1834. Wemyss had also paid for half of the papering and painting of the lobbies, paying five months' rent before the theatre was ready for performance. He then offered to take the lease for the ensuing year of 1840–41 if the stockholders would not require any payment from him in advance, and if they would be satisfied to receive two hundred dollars a week from the usual time of opening, in this way making a difference of five weeks in the time of the payment of the whole rent. Then he asked them to repaint and paper the vestibules and lobbies, to put up a new dome, and to decorate the panels of the boxes, from designs which he would furnish for their approval, so as to give the house a fresh look. The proposition was never answered by the stockholders.

The Arch Street Theatre was then to let, Maywood and Company having abandoned it as unprofitable. Wemyss took it and abandoned the Walnut to its new lessees, W. Dinneford and E. A. Marshall, with William Rufus Blake as stage director. This new dynasty opened it at the low prices of twelve and a-half cents for the pit, and twenty-five cents for the second tier of boxes.

December 30, 1839, R. C. Maywood, in a valedictory address to the public at the Chesnut, announced his withdrawal from the firm of Maywood and Company. He had exhausted his energies, his purse, and all the talent of both hemispheres, in the service of the public, so he said. He had done his best to resuscitate the drama, but he feared that it was a forlorn hope. Actually, Maywood had become very unpopular, principally because he was himself a mass of foreign prejudices against our "native graces."

Newspaper advertisement, for January 1, 1840, recorded the dissolution of partnership existing between R. C. Maywood and Lewis T. Pratt under the firm of Maywood and Company. And Lewis T. Pratt informed his friends and the public generally that the Chesnut Street Theatre would be under his sole management. The prices were to be: boxes, seventy-five cents; pit, thirty-seven and a-half cents. William B. Wood was to be the acting manager, and G. F. Jervis the stage manager.

The New National Theatre, under William E. Burton, opened Monday, August 31, 1840. The house was situated upon the site of Cooke's Circus, Chesnut Street east of Ninth, south side. Burton, both here and subsequently at New York, most successfully established the old system of public and managerial reliance upon excellent stock companies in which stars rarely appeared or, when they did, were worthy of being wondered at. But after he had in a most extraordinary manner established a nonpareil theatre and stock corps, he threw a wet blanket over his whole good intent and destroyed at once the rising popularity of his excellent stock company by falling back upon the star system.

At the Walnut this year William Dinneford and E. A. Marshall became estranged and did not resume partnership in the lease of the theatre for the ensuing year. Both of them made application to the stockholders for the new lease, but Marshall won.

The Walnut and the Chesnut were playing regularly at the opening of the year of 1840, with the exception of the last week in January, when the newspapers carry no advertisement for the Walnut. A German company performed at the Arch occasionally during January and February. By the tenth of July, the Chesnut was closed for the season and the Walnut followed suit on the twenty-fifth of the month. The Coates Street Theatre was opened for a few nights in August by T. Placide.

Saturday, August 29, 1840, the Chesnut reopened, and was joined

[16]

by the New National Theatre on Monday. One week later, September 7, lights were on in the Arch, which, however, succumbed to darkness again after the performance of Saturday, September 19. The Walnut joined the Chesnut and the National on October 14, Wednesday, and the Arch came back on Tuesday, December 1. The four theatres then remained open for the rest of the year.

The reader may be interested to know that the year 1840 marks a definite change in theatrical Philadelphia by the passing of the old régime of Francis C. Wemyss, veteran actor-manager. This year his stronghold at the Walnut which he held for so many years was closed to him. He was beginning to lose his foothold and his place of active prominence. Nothing is more indicative of the new order of things than Wemyss' own advertisement in the *Inquirer* of Sept. 7, on the eve of his unsuccessful first venture of the season at the Arch:

Dinna Forget "Auld Lang Syne." The stars, being all engaged elsewhere, can only twinkle here occasionally.

1841

Since William Dinneford could not have the Walnut for 1841, as the stockholders awarded the lease to E. A. Marshall, the former took the lease of the Arch (August 10, 1841, opening night), where he had a certain amount of small success at the beginning, but he was finally compelled to close the doors before the year was out.

Lewis T. Pratt announced the opening of the Chesnut under his management by saying that, during the summer recess, various alterations had been made: the panels of the boxes and proscenium altered and embellished by Gibson and Company, ornamental painters; added private boxes designed and executed by Messrs. Cowperthwaite, upholsterers; stage supplied with new appointments of fashionable drawing-room furniture by Messrs. Cowperthwaite; the scenic department carefully revised under the superintendence of the well-known artist, Charles Lehr.

William E. Burton was still holding on to his New National in 1841. On June 12, Mitchell's Olympic Company from New York started an engagement there which was unsuccessful. The Arch was again to let, as it was frequently for many years, but in March, William Rufus Blake and William Jones took it over. E. A. Marshall continued at the Walnut.

January 1, 1841, found the four theatres running: the Walnut, the Arch, the National, and the Chesnut. The Arch dropped out with the performance of Tuesday, February 2, and during this same week the Chesnut, which was playing opera, was dark for several nights. Finally, it did close on Monday, March 2, leaving the field to the Walnut and the National.

The Arch opened on Monday, April 5, and continued through the summer. The National closed on Saturday, April 24, in preparation for the melodrama of *The Seven Champions of Christendom,* with which it opened on Saturday, May 8, but only remained open for the ensuing week. The Chesnut again opened, with opera, on Saturday, May 1.

The Walnut, the Chesnut, and the Arch continued alone until they were joined by the National on Saturday, June 12, with Mitchell's Olympic Company from New York. However, the opera season at the Chesnut was over on Monday, June 21, and the theatre closed for the summer. Likewise, Mitchell's Olympic Company left the National on Monday, July 5, and that theatre closed. On the same night, the Arch finished out its season. These two theatres may have closed on the succeeding night, July 6. The date is not certain because no newspapers were published for July 6, 1841. But it is certain that the Walnut continued along by itself until Wednesday, July 21, when it, too, was darkened for the season.

The Arch began the new fall season on Tuesday, August 10, to be joined by the National on Saturday, August 21. The Walnut and the Chesnut both reopened the week afterward, Saturday, August 28. However, the Chesnut again closed on Wednesday, October 27, but it came to light in the last month, Thursday, December 2, and all four houses continued together during the remaining weeks of the year.

In the seven years from 1835 to 1841, the most popular play on the Philadelphia stage was Shakespeare's *Richard III,* with eighty-three performances. No other play approached the record of *Richard III,* and its nearest competitors are *Othello* with fifty-seven presentations and *Hamlet* with fifty-three. It is to be remembered that at this time in the history of our Philadelphia stage, even the most popular new play (like *London Assurance,* for instance) never ran for more than two weeks, or three weeks, as a record performance, and was seldom revived. If a new play was revived months later in the same year, it ran only for a few nights.

Following is a tabular arrangement to show the distribution of the performances of *Richard III* in the Philadelphia theatres over the period of seven years.

RICHARD III

83 Performances in 7 Years

Theatres	1835	1836	1837	1838	1839	1840	1841	Total
W.	12	12	8	8	5	8	3	5υ
C.	2		3	4	2	2		13
A.		1	1			3	3	8
P.		2	2					4
N.						1	1	2
Total	14	15	14	12	7	14	7	83

1842

In the spring of 1842, the Arch was again in the market. Many more times it was so, in those days, and thus was conveniently open to any adventurer who could advance fifty dollars. Charles S. Porter, who had not been so pleasantly situated as he could have desired in any engagement after Wemyss' failure, this time took the Arch, expecting to benefit not only himself but also his son and daughter, both aspiring young professionals.

Charles Durang, in the sixty-ninth chapter of his history, third series, tells us that the Arch

was christened "The American" [by Porter] in contradistinction to the Walnut which did not then employ the title "the" as a prefix; at least, Wemyss says it was a fling at the Walnut's title, which was then called "American Theatre." The old "South Street Theatre," after the "New Theatre" in Chesnut Street had been built in 1793, received the appellation of the "Old American Theatre," and its company the "Old American" in contradistinction to the new one. This phrase, after it had died out by time, was again revived (not by the management, but by public sentiment) when Jones, Duffy, and W. Forrest became the lessees of the Arch Street Theatre in 1832. The managers and the entire company, with one or two exceptions, being all native-born Americans. In the case of Porter, it was intended as a sneer upon those who had used the term, and had no claim to its application; but Porter soon withdrew the name from the head of his bill, as his corps was composed of ming ed nationalities of the four nations. The stage had English, Scotch, Irish, and natives, while the orchestra was composed of Germans and Italians.

The Arch, after a season of a few weeks, was closed to make new arrangements. C. S. Porter associated with him Lewis T. Pratt when Hield was introduced as a leading tragedian and stage manager of the Arch. The new organization of management under the rule of L. T. Pratt and C. Porter proved, in a very short period, also visionary, as all the preceding managerial attempts at this theatre did at this time. The present season did not continue long and was divided into two periods of anarchy, intrigue, and tribulations, ending in dissolution.

After the Porter (and Pratt) régime at the Arch, Thomas B. Russell secured the theatre for fifty dollars paid to Lacour, President of the Board of Agents. It was considered madness for Russell to take the house, but the result astonished everyone, for, in September, the public made a run on the theatre and pushed it to the pinnacle of success. Suddenly, when he had at least two thousand dollars in cash in his hands, Russell absconded like a thief, filching the actors' salaries.

The National Theatre, under Burton, closed on January 29, 1842, which was his last exit from this temple of his own rearing and his fond hopes. The old Chesnut struggled on under Pratt. The Walnut seemed to float best through this turbulent sea of hard times. The season there, however, was brought to a close on May 7.

E. A. Marshall, about this time, was induced to form a coalition with L. T. Pratt: a union of the forces at the Walnut and the Chesnut that, it was thought, no doubt would prove advantageous to both parties. Whatever the motives, the union was effected and as readily dissolved, presumably because the money advanced by Marshall was soon swallowed up by the losses sustained. A general suspension of theatricals seemed then to be the order of the day.

On March 23, L. T. Pratt announced that he had formed a coalition with W. E. Burton, who with their double company would open "Old Drury" with the play of *Money*. The alliance might have availed both parties if it had been made sooner, but both men were doomed to lose by the arrangement. P. Richings was their stage manager, and the prices were: boxes, seventy-five cents; pit, thirty-seven and a-half cents; colored gallery, twenty-five cents. The old policy was pursued. A host of stars entered perforce and cleaned the treasury of the little money that was floated into it. The National passed into the hands of General Welch and Mann who converted it into a magnificent circus amphitheatre which for a series of years they conducted with a great spirit, truly garnering Burton's harvest.

The Chesnut Street Theatre, following the summer, was without a tenant. It had bankrupted the manager, L. T. Pratt. The stockholders had attributed the failures and reverses to Maywood's previous mismanagement and unpopular course. But of this conclusion they seemed to repent, and they invited Maywood at this time to renew his direction over the theatre. Their changed feelings toward Maywood must have come as a balm to his wounds. However, he wisely declined all responsibility and proposed his daughter, Mary E. Maywood, who had been in London with him, to be placed as its manager, he only assuming the business management. Peter Richings was appointed the stage manager.

And this same year, on September 22, Miss Charlotte Cushman took over the management of E. A. Marshall's Walnut. Although Miss Maywood fell to rise no more before the season half expired, Miss Cushman reigned a season with a varied prestige and, in the ensuing season, divided managerial honors with the august William Rufus Blake.

Durang makes the comment that the curse of this season, as of seasons that followed, was the vast multiplicity of stars, the majority of whom were not above mediocrity of talent: excellent stock people whose only effects as stars were to impoverish the treasury and injure the interests of those called stock performers.

On January 1, 1842, the four theatres were all open, but the Arch dropped out on Saturday, January 8. The National likewise dropped out on Saturday, January 29, and left the field to the Chesnut and the Walnut, which continued alone until the Arch reopened on Monday, March 28. The Chesnut then closed on Tuesday, May 10, leaving the Arch and Walnut to continue until Tuesday, July 26, when the Walnut closed for the season. The Arch, however, remained open during the entire summer.

The Chesnut began the fall season on Saturday, September 17, and the Walnut on Thursday, September 22. All three houses remained open through October and November. During the first week of December, the performances at the three houses are uncertain, but, by the second week, the Arch had dropped out for the month, and the Walnut and the Chesnut had resumed regular performances for the remaining weeks of the year.

It is to be remembered that our early native playwrights had to fight hard to be recognized in the face of the Anglomania from which our country suffered. It seemed to be felt that even our plays needed to be stamped with a British trademark to assure them certain success. There is the famous case of the new American play which was, at its opening, falsely represented as the latest work of a well-known British dramatist. And it was not until days later, when the success of the piece had been established, that the producer had the temerity to announce that the play was actually written by a new and native artist.

We catch the undercurrent of this spirit in the way that dramas were frequently advertised. For instance, many times a program announces a new play in the fashion that we find under date of October 24, 1842, for the Chesnut: *"The Banker,* a new and original comedy written by the author of *Abduction, Kate Kearney,* and *The Queen's Jewels."* Or, again, from time to time, we have the announcement, "Benefit Night For The Author Of The Last New Play."

1843

The Olympic Theatre, formerly Burton's National, was opened on September 13, 1843, with F. C. Wemyss and John H. Oxley as lessees.

E. A. Marshall, who defeated Pratt and Wemyss in their attempt to obtain the Chesnut in partnership this year, opened the house in September for the purpose of playing the great stars, and closed after a short season on December 25, repairing to his Walnut Street Theatre, which had been occupied for a period by Howe's Equestrian Troupe.

E. A. Marshall this year controlled both the Walnut and the Chesnut. He had the interior of the latter theatre redecorated and painted. New proscenium boxes were added to those already erected and fashionable furniture was placed in them. A superior new drop curtain was painted by Peter Grain, Jr. William Rufus Blake was appointed stage manager; and Miss Charlotte Cushman, acting manager. The prices to the boxes were seventy-five cents and to the pit fifty cents. Frank Cline was the leader of the orchestra, and Cunnington the conductor. Marshall opened his campaign with a series of the old English comedies and played until September 14, when he opened the Walnut with his dramatic company. The French opera troupe commenced at the Chesnut on September 20. On Wednesday, November 1, the Walnut was closed and the entire dramatic company returned to the Chesnut Street Theatre for the winter season. The Walnut was then arranged for a circus arena and opened on Saturday, November 4, with N. Howe's equestrian troupe.

The Arch Street Theatre, after the flight of T. B. Russell in 1842, remained for some time in the market under the lesseeship of Richard O. R. Lovett, a stockholder of the theatre. However, in the winter of 1843, William A. Deverna became its lessee and opened it on Monday, December 11. The prices were: for dress circle, fifty cents; second and third tiers, twenty-five cents; pit, twelve and a-half cents; gallery, twelve and a-half cents. The opening was not very flattering. The company wanted strength in talent and numbers, although there were some few old favorites among the rank and file. The season did not last any length of time.

E. A. Marshall, this year, lost heavily through his speculations with opera companies which he brought to the Chesnut on engagement.

The Chesnut and the Walnut began the theatrical year on January 1, and to them was added the Olympic on Monday, January 9. But the Olympic dropped out, as a legitimate playhouse, with the performance of Wednesday, January 18. The Walnut and the Chesnut both continued performances until Friday, February 17, when the end of the operatic engagement at the Chesnut brought that theatre to a close.

The Arch Street Theatre opened on Saturday, March 4, and this gave a bit of opposition to the Walnut, which had been having things completely to itself since the close of the Chesnut. But the Arch was finally darkened by Tuesday, May 9. The Walnut continued along in its *pas seul* until opera again opened the Chesnut on Saturday, July 15, but the opera was over and the theatre shut down at the end of the month.

The Arch again opened on Thursday, August 10, and the Walnut closed on Saturday, August 12, so the Arch had the field entirely unmolested until September. The Chesnut reopened Thursday, September 7, and the Walnut on Thursday, September 14. The National joined the others on Saturday, September 23, and the four theatres continued until the end of October. By the first of November, the Arch dropped out, and one week later the Walnut. On Monday, December 11, the Arch started up again, and the Chesnut, the National, and the Arch finished out the year.

Particular attention in 1843 should be called to the two complete opera companies which came to the Chesnut for long engagements this year: The Italian Opera Company and the French Opera Company.

The program of the first included the production of *Lucia Di Lammermoor, Il Puritani, Norma, Belisario,* and *Gemma Di Vergy,* and of the latter, *Les Diamans De La Couronne, Le Domino Noir, Le Grace De Dieu, La Fille Du Regiment, Le Postillion De Lonjumeau,* and *Anna Bolena.*

Occasionally in the district of Northern Liberties, that is, outside the central theatre belt of the city, a German company spasmodically produced an opera, and the Chesnut frequently included opera as a part of its regular entertainment, with visiting leads, but the year of 1843 brings us two foreign companies that are entities in themselves, and the season might well be called the year for the opera.

1844

The season of Wemyss and Oxley's management of the National was brought to a close April 27, 1844, the theatre being open 185 performing nights. The only persons who derived any benefit from its operations were the original lessees, Welch and Mann. One wonders why Wemyss and Oxley failed. The theatre was splendid and the location excellent, but the current of public favor is hard to fathom. Perhaps there were more amusements than Philadelphians could support at that time.

John Oxley relinquished his share in the management at the close of the season, while Wemyss continued his lesseeship. He made strenuous exertions for another season, but the reopening in May was blighted by the unfortunate riots which occurred in Kensington and Southwark, where bloodshed and murder seemed to reign madly triumphant. The military were called out and these districts placed under martial law. The city heard the booming of midnight cannon. On the very day that Wemyss announced the opening of his theatre, the proclamation of military rule went into effect, and, in consequence, no person could think of public amusements during the next two weeks. After order was restored, Wemyss struggled on for some time to miserable houses, but at last yielded to stern necessity and closed his doors. He surrendered the theatre to General Welch and Co., who subsequently established, with their large means, a most splendid amphitheatre wherein first-class circus and stage performances were given for many successful seasons, until it was destroyed by fire, with the Chinese Museum, on the evening of July 5, 1854.

On June 1, 1844, William E. Burton opened the Arch for the summer season. Many thought that this was a perilous undertaking: to saddle oneself with a theatre that seemed doomed. The prices were: boxes, fifty cents; second tier, twenty-five cents; colored gallery, twenty-five cents; but it did not pay. Burton commenced his campaign with a very meager corps, and no vaunting promises. He gradually expanded his operations as his strength of talent accumulated, but his final success depended upon, and was triumphantly gained, by playing burlettas with a small, select company.

When E. A. Marshall retired from the Chesnut in 1844, L. T. Pratt was again induced to take the house and associated F. C. Wemyss with him. John Sefton was the stage manager. The prices were: boxes, fifty cents; pit, twenty-five cents; colored gallery, twenty-five cents. The venture, however, was not successful.

A serious event occurred early in the season and almost closed the doors of the Chesnut. George Lippard had written a book called *The Monks of Monk Hall,* which was an exposé of the profligacy of the "powerful wealthy" in Philadelphia. The book created a sensation and, at the suggestion of Ashbel Green, Deputy Attorney-General, Wemyss agreed to produce it. Lippard made his own dramatization of it into a play called *The Quaker City.* And then the fun began. The "powerful wealthy," such as Singleton, Mercer, Judge Conrad, and others, made a tremendous demonstration against the presentation of it. Matters became so embroiled that Wemyss was beset on all sides: with his stockholders, Mayor Peter McCall of Philadelphia, the "powerful wealthy" themselves, and law and order in general.

Any possible success that the season might have brought to Wemyss and Pratt was forestalled by the untimely fate of *The Quaker City,* on whose preparation they lost much money. And the subsequent disfavor of the public caused the houses to thin out, since the press took up the matter over the whole country and accused Wemyss of trying to force an immoral and objectionable play upon the public.

January 1844 fostered three theatres: the Walnut, the National, and the Arch. At the beginning of February, the Arch discontinued for two weeks, and by the end of the month it closed down, not to reopen for months.

The dramatic field was left to the Walnut and the National, which were joined on Monday, April 1, by the Chesnut with opera. The opera lasted until Tuesday, April 23. Several nights later the National, also, was darkened, but reopened again in the middle of May for a short season which only endured the rest of the month.

Opera again came to the Chesnut on Saturday, May 25. Lights were on in the Arch, Saturday, June 1. Therefore, the beginning of June furnished Philadelphia theatre-goers with a choice of three theatres: the Walnut, the Chesnut, or the Arch. Opera at the Chesnut was once more finished, however, on June 4. The Walnut and the Arch carried through the entire summer and were not joined by another theatre until the Chesnut opened on Monday, October 14. From then until the end of the year, performances at the three theatres continued regularly.

William E. Burton, upon opening the Arch in June, made the following announcement of unusual interest:

To render the Arch St. Theatre in every way worthy a liberal support, the Third Tier Nuisance will be abolished; improper characters will be prevented from obtaining admission to any part of the house; and the sale of alcohol, in any shape, will be discontinued in the saloons. In sacrificing the large profits attending these usual practices of all other theatres, now attempted for the first time in the United States, W. E. Burton looks for a compensation in the more frequent attendance of families, who may depend upon experiencing at the Arch St. Theatre a wholesome entertainment of the highest character, without the possibility of witnessing an impropriety either on or off the stage.

1845

Burton, in 1845, became the lessee of both the Arch and the Chesnut, and kept them open at the same time. The members of his two companies played alternately, as circumstances required, at either the one or the other house. E. A. Marshall retained the Walnut, with his well organized forces, under the stage guidance of William Rufus Blake.

Burton commenced the winter campaign at the Chesnut, August 30, announcing that the house was entirely renovated and brilliantly decorated in every part. The dress circle lobby was carpeted, newly papered and painted. All the other lobbies were also thus improved. Burnished gold ornaments of chaste appropriate designs were placed around the three tiers of boxes. The proscenium ornaments were of the most gorgeous patterns, profusely decorated with arabesque devices in green and gold. Stage doors were added, new draperies were placed over the private boxes, to move at pleasure. A new drop curtain, representing the city and bay of Naples, with a view of Vesuvius, was painted by

George Heilge. The orchestra at the Chesnut, under Signor La Manna, contained the following solo performers: Pazzaglia, Capuano, Le Bianco, Rallo, Stolto, Dueckle, and others of equal merit. The medallion of Shakespeare, over the proscenium, was painted by Thomas Sully, Jr. This was preserved, by the direction of Burton, when the theatre was torn down, and formed one of the items of his library sale. The property man was Andrew Welsh; stage machinist, Cadwallader Griffiths; scenic artists, George Heilge and Hackurt.

Burton deserved much praise in those disjointed theatrical times for his efforts to restore the drama through the instrumentality of good stock companies. He made his first effort at the New National Theatre, and failed. The charm of the old regular system seemed irrevocably gone. He became the lessee of the Chesnut in 1845–46, only to retire from it and fall back upon the Arch with light pieces and burlesques, played by a small, carefully chosen company. Pursuing this course for some time with energy, despite the rise and fall in his career, he finally succeeded in realizing some eight or ten thousand dollars, which led him to New York to Palmer's Opera House and to high fortune, Durang tells us.

The Walnut Street Theatre, having closed a very long season on September 6, reopened for the fall and winter season on Wednesday, October 1. E. A. Marshall continued as lessee. The prices of admission were: pit, twenty-five cents; dress circle, fifty cents; second and third tiers, twenty-five cents; orchestra, seventy-five cents.

The Arch was open for the first week of January, but no longer in that month. When it closed, the Walnut and the Chesnut carried Philadelphia's theatrical honors alone. However, Thursday, February 13, the Chesnut apparently closed also. The Walnut continued singly until Saturday, March 22, when it was joined by the Arch. The Chesnut reopened on Saturday, April 26, and the National on Monday, April 28. The National withdrew its performances on Saturday, May 10.

The Arch took an intermission from its performance on Wednesday, June 18, until it opened for a summer season on Friday, July 4, but the Walnut and the Chesnut continued during the intermission at the Arch. However, on Saturday, July 5, the Chesnut gave its last showing for the summer.

The Walnut and the Arch continued through the summer and were joined by the Chesnut again in the fall, Saturday, August 30. One week later, the Walnut took an intermission with the performance of Saturday, September 6, until the house was lighted again on Wednesday, October 1. The three theatres then performed their dramas regularly through October and November to the middle of December, when the Chesnut inaugurated the practice of forsaking the legitimate drama occasionally for legerdemain, which it introduced upon its boards spasmodically during the remainder of the month.

An interesting side-light is thrown upon the life in the old theatre buildings by an advertisement in the *Public Ledger* for Monday, December 29, 1845. It reads:

> Chesnut street theatre—To let, the Pit Bar, Oyster and Fruit Stands, in said theatre—also, the Third Tier Bar.

Intimate knowledge is thus given to us of the specific manner in which our ancestors regaled themselves during the intermissions: they not only drank intoxicating beverages, but they also gulped oysters and munched fruit.

To those of us who take our theatre seriously, the gentle art of eating during a play is very disconcerting. Somehow the indiscriminate consumption of ineffable confections by the noisy mandibles of our neighbors slightly disturbs the intellectual morale which we like to preserve in justice to the play in progress,—to say nothing of what it does to the illusion of the play-world which the actors struggle so hard to create. For instance, oranges are delightful for breakfast, but the present writer does not think that even the person of Nell Gwynn herself selling them in the theatre could compensate for the odorous curtain which they would throw up between the stage and the spectators. We have traveled far from those days when theatres were also lunch rooms, but we are still disturbed occasionally by hawkers of candy. May their tribe decrease!

1846

The Arch closed its season suddenly on January 24, 1846, but Burton announced that it would soon be reopened for a short season, prior to its being closed for the purpose of extensive alterations since he intended to place the theatre in the first rank of dramatic establishments. The company there was excellent, with J. M. Scott as acting manager and Stevens as stage manager. The prices were: dress circle, fifty cents; second and third tiers, twenty-five cents; pit, twelve and a-half cents; and gallery, twelve and a-half cents.

The Arch Street Theatre, during the summer recess of 1846, underwent the most expensive repairs, alterations, and improvements in its various parts. The exterior of the edifice had been newly painted, the interior renovated, and a new roof had been placed over the entire building. The stage had been considerably enlarged, with the proscenium newly constructed and ornamented. Private and stage boxes had been erected, while a new pit had been formed, extending partly under the boxes. This was a new feature of extension. The flooring and seats were entirely new. Thus it was made equal to the capacity of the largest pit in the city. The boxes and lobbies had been papered and painted, and the seats newly stuffed and covered. A splendid dome of architectural design had been painted by George Hielge. New draperies of novel style, and gold ornaments of Louis Quatorze pattern, decorated the fronts of the three tiers of boxes. They were designed and executed in papier maché by Messrs. C. and W. Long, and burnished in gold. There were paintings in oil in front of the proscenium and boxes, by Thomas Glessing, from designs furnished by the life and plays of Shakespeare. The State arms, in carved relief, formed the keystone of the arch, designed and executed by the Messrs. Long. The national flag draped the stage boxes. The carpenter work was done by Jackson and McClay. A new drop scene was painted by George Hielge. The leader of the orchestra and composer of music was Sandie Jamieson; stage manager, J. M. Scott; and treasurer, Edmonds.

Concerning the present season at the Arch, Durang gives the following account in the eighty-fifth chapter of his history, third series:

The same policy continued of managers outbidding each other for the élite of the stars which had characterized the several late seasons—a most ruinous policy, that always left the treasury empty. The renovating and thoroughly redecorating of the theatres at the beginning of every new season was really a very questionable outlay of money. It seldom proved very attractive after a few nights. The best bower anchor ahead, in our opinion, was a good stock company, with one or two of the prominent fashionable actors. As the managers ran after the stars, so did they in the same ratio enhance their demands. This star system, after having been carried out to its tether in all our cities, began to show symptoms of a decline. The Park Theatre, the grand metropolitan theatre of the country, which originally had imported these kinds of theatrical goods, now became hopelessly embarrassed from these heedless importations, but pertinaciously adhered to its course. To add to managerial burthens, large rents were required from them by the proprietors of the theatres—this, too, when the prices of admission were relatively reduced. It would seem that Mr. E. A. Marshall had secured the principal stars this season, and that Burton relied more upon his resources of a very good working company, and new attractive dramas of the scenic kind, with the novelty of the clever Ravels and extra amusements not to be legitimately included in the dramatic category. It must be admitted also that Burton was "a host" within himself, and his leading people were good and great favorites with his audience.

At this time, a temporary theatre had been erected in the grand dancing saloon of the old Masonic Hall, Chesnut Street, which had been occupied as Peale's Museum, wherein numerous theatrical pieces had been given from time to time by disengaged performers from the other theatres. At the present season, farces and vaudevilles formed the backbone of the programs at Peale's. The price of admission was twenty-five cents.

Peale's Museum, at the Masonic Hall, Chesnut Street, or "The Academy of Fine Arts" as it was called after the Museum ceased to be exhibited at that location, this year was opened as a regular theatre. Durang gives us some information concerning it in the eighty-fifth chapter of his history, third series:

They performed light comedies and singing dramas with great cleverness, there being some of the best stock talent in the country concentrated on the effort. The patronage was of the respectable classes. The pieces were well put upon the stage, and "local habitation and name," on the fashionable promenade of Chesnut Street, was not without its advantages. The nature of the organization we are not conversant with. Mr. John Sefton seemed ostensibly its index and minute hand. Under many adverse circumstances, prolonged its season to an unexpected duration. As a minor temple it was far beyond anything of the sort since offered to public attention. In its neat, clever, and respectable conduct, the names that appeared in their casts are guarantee for our assertion.

E. A. Marshall continued as lessee of the Walnut, where he engaged actors of much talent. The Chesnut was unoccupied this year, after Burton's failure in the previous year to make it run, except for a short season of opera. The Walnut, Arch, and Chesnut opened the theatrical year together, but the Chesnut closed down as a failure on Tuesday, January 20. The Walnut and Arch continued alone until they were joined by Peale's Philadelphia Museum on Monday, March 9. The Chesnut opened with opera, Monday, April 27; closed on Monday, May 18; reopened Monday, June 1, with one performance of legitimate drama. The Arch ended its season on Saturday, July 25, and reopened Monday,

August 26, but the Walnut and Peale's Museum persisted in their performances through the summer. The three theatres remained open regularly for the rest of the year.

One of the amusements of the day was the circus or, more definitely, the hippodrome. Certain theatres were manned by equestrian troupes who performed in as many ways as possible with their horses, even presenting occasional dramas that permitted equestrian processions, combats, and feats of skill.

And on October 5, 1846, the National Theatre, which Burton initiated so gloriously several years earlier as the finest house of legitimate drama in the United States, became a circus. The *Public Ledger* for this date bears the following program:

CIRCUS AND NATIONAL THEATRE—Under The Management Of Messrs. Welch And Mann—Doors open 7¼, and commence at a quarter before 8 o'clock—THIS EVENING, October 5th, will commence with the Union Of Chivalry And Beauty; Finished Equestrian Act, by Master R. Rivers; Arena Gymnastics; Le Festin De Polichinel, by Master Chambers; Cry Of Liberty, by Howard; Enchanted Ladder, by Master R. Rivers; Equestrianism, by Mrs. Howard; Display On The Floating Cord, by William Day; Professional Act, without saddle or bridle, by Mr. Glenroy, Jr.; classic poses of the three Brothers Rivers. To conclude with the Extravaganza Of The Hunted Tailor.

1847

The Chesnut Street Theatre had been lying fallow, after Burton's unsuccessful attempt to resuscitate its decayed status. It had been renovated with some new painting and brushing up, and thus put again in the theatrical market through the exertions of J. R. Pollock, a stockholder of the theatre, and James Quinlan, the proprietor of the saloons. A young American magician appeared in the renascent Chesnut three times a week.

The Chesnut Street Theatre had been leased to Messrs. Seguin and Frazer for their presentations of opera. During their starring excursion to the South, it was left under the agency of William R. Dinmore, their treasurer, who let it by the night, or week, to wandering persons who might want to exhibit themselves temporarily. The Seguins opened it for an opera season on Monday, April 5, 1847, styling it "The Opera House." Prices of tickets: dress circle and parquet, fifty cents; family circle, twenty-five cents. The first week of June saw the dissolution of partnership between the Seguins and Frazer, and the Chesnut was now let to anybody and everybody. Negro minstrels and heel-and-toe, double-shuffle dancers now adorned the stage of "Old Drury."

W. E. Burton continued at the Arch, and E. A. Marshall remained as lessee of the Walnut. Peale's Museum, the Walnut, and the Arch opened the year and extended their performances through January and part of February when, with Tuesday, February 16, the Arch closed its doors. The other two theatres kept the field to themselves until the Arch reopened on Thursday, March 25. The Chesnut, with Seguin and Frazer's opera company, opened its doors on Monday, April 5. With the performance of Saturday, April 24, Peale's Museum closed in prep-aration for a series of new dramas which were introduced to the theatre-goers of Philadelphia on Monday, May 3. On Saturday, June 5, Seguin and Frazer closed the Chesnut and dissolved partnership. Peale's Mu-seum discontinued the performance of legitimate drama after Saturday, July 17. The Arch and the Walnut now carried through the summer by themselves, and met no new rival in their theatrical field for the entire remainder of the year, through August to the end of December.

The lively spirit of competition which existed among the theatres is very amusingly and very humanly shown in the following series of four advertisements appearing in the daily newspapers during 1847:

Feb. 16. U. S. G.

LES DANSEUSES VIENNOISES
Mr. W. E. Burton

Having made a positive arrangement with Madame Weiss for the performances of these children at Philadelphia and Baltimore, the public is assured that they will appear at the ARCH STREET THEATRE, all announcements to the contrary, notwithstanding. Preparations of an extensive nature have been making for sometime. Every Divertisement of the Danseuses will be ornamented with new and beautiful Scenery, new Stage Properties and Decorations. The audience part of the house will also undergo some essential alterations, for which purpose the Theatre will close for a short period.

———

Feb. 18. U. S. G.

LES DANSEUSES VIENNOISES
New York, 16 Wall St.

Feb. 16th, 1847.

To the Editor of the New York Herald:—

DEAR SIR—In your columns of yesterday, and of the day previous, I noticed among the Theatrical Items, a statement to the effect that "Les Danseuses Viennoises" are engaged at the Walnut Street Theatre, Philadelphia. This, I beg leave to state, is erroneous, as Madame Weiss long since engaged the services of "Les Danseuses Viennoises" to Mr. Burton, of the Arch Street Theatre, at which place they are shortly to appear.

Yours, &c.,

JOHN K. HACKETT,

Attorney and Counsel for Madame Weiss.

March 15. P. L.

ARCH STREET THEATRE—The management of the Park Theatre, New York, having interfered with the arrangement of Madame Weiss, the Directress of

LES DANSEUSES VIENNOISES,

These interesting performers can not appear at the Arch Street Theatre during the whole of the present week.

The manager deeply regrets the present disappointment of his patrons, but feels assured that many days will not elapse before he shall have the honor of presenting the children to their notice. Those persons wishing to withdraw their certificates can have their money returned.

March 22. P. L.

WALNUT STREET THEATRE—Lessee, Mr. E. A. Marshall—Manager, Mr. W. R. Blake—Dress Circle, $1; 2d and 3d tiers, 50 cts; Private Boxes and Orchestra Seats, $1; Pit, 50 cts.—Doors open at 7; Commence at 7½ o'clock—First appearance of the DANSEUSES VIENNOISES—THIS EVENING, March 22d, the comedy of the WIND MILL—Sampson Low—Mr. Chapman. Forty-two DANSEUSES VIENNOISES will appear in a Grand Divertisement. After which, the TWO THOMPSONS. After which, another Grand Divertisement. Together with many other Entertainments.

It seems, therefore, that the Viennese dancers went to the Walnut after all, and that E. A. Marshall succeeded in outwitting W. E. Burton, a difficult thing to do, one might conjecture.

1848

The Chesnut Street Theatre was occupied as an opera house in February. The Italian troupe from New York opened this season on Saturday,

[33]

February 19, with something of a brilliant prospect. This opera speculation was effected through subscription. Some of our fashionable, wealthy citizens created a fund to carry out the object for a limited period. Charles Kuhn was to receive the subscriptions at his office, 66 South Sixth Street. The opera nights were Monday, Wednesday, and Friday. First tier and second tier, with parquet, one dollar; upper boxes, fifty cents—the gallery being arranged as boxes.

At the opening of the Walnut Street Theatre for the fall season of 1848, under E. A. Marshall as lessee, Peter Richings was the stage manager. The opposition of rival theatres was now rife. The Arch was open, the opera was at the Chesnut, Welch's Circus was going, the Museum Theatre (Peale's) was still at work, and Swaim's new Athenaeum preparing to open.

The newly named Athenaeum and National Museum opened its doors for public entertainment during the Christmas holidays. It was situated at the southeast corner of Seventh and Chesnut Streets. This theatre, built by Swaim, from designs and drawings by G. Parker Cummings, architect, was one of the earliest palatial store buildings in our city. The original proprietors of the building were Messrs. Taber and J. S. Silsbee, who, since their theatrical project fell through, neglected to pay for the building. The prices of admission were lowered to twenty-five cents to all parts of the house in an attempt to keep the theatre going. The whole proved a dead failure, and Barnum subsequently entered the premises.

Burton still remained at his Arch Street Theatre, but at the close of the year migrated to New York and deserted Philadelphia theatricals permanently. The Arch and the Walnut were the two open theatres that heralded the new year of 1848. On Wednesday, February 1, the New York opera under Max Maretzek appeared at the Chesnut and remained until Friday, March 24. Peale's Museum recommenced the performance of legitimate drama on Thursday, March 16, but discontinued again with Saturday, May 20. On Monday, May 22, the Olympic gave one week of legitimate drama and then disappeared.

The Walnut and the Arch were lighted nightly from the beginning of the year and, following the spasmodic burst of activity at Peale's and at the Olympic, continued undisturbed until the Chesnut again became a rival for theatrical favor with opera on Tuesday, June 6. On Saturday, July 1, Peale's Museum again began to give plays, but once more discontinued on Wednesday, July 10. By the end of July, the Chesnut was again closed, and the Walnut and the Arch were left to finish the summer. Opera again opened the Chesnut on Wednesday, October 4, but only remained until Saturday, October 28. The opera flashed across the lights of the Chesnut once more on Tuesday, December 5, to last for the rest of the year. Swaim's new Athenaeum opened on Monday, December 25, and increased the number of theatres to four.

The man whom we have to reckon with is William E. Burton. We recall his initiative, his forward-looking enterprise. We recall that he is the man who attempts to do things, although he sometimes fails, as in his vainglorious effort to foist the New National upon the Philadelphia theatre-goers. Financially, the New National was too great a proposition for him at the time, so he went back to the Arch to recuperate his fortunes, and he succeeded. In 1848, we find him again at the peak of prominence with Burton's Arch as the leading Philadelphia theatre.

He was alert. There is no question about that. Witness the activity of the Arch Street Theatre for the year of 1848. First, he brought both new actors and new plays to Philadelphia in greater numbers than all the other Philadelphia theatres combined. In 1848, he had practically a monopoly upon the new visiting players of long and short engagements. The reader has only to look at the chapter of text which enumerates the additional actors for 1848, and he will find proof of Burton's monopoly. He will also see that the preceding year bears witness to the same monopoly. And then, also, Burton brought twice as many new plays to the Philadelphia stage in 1848, as did all the other Philadelphia theatres combined. Indubitably, it is important that new plays shall be given a hearing, and Burton was doing this. He is the figure that stands at the keystone of the Philadelphia theatre through the fifth decade of the Nineteenth Century.

1849

After the regular dramatic companies had ceased to perform at the Chesnut Street Theatre for lack of patronage from a fashionable public, the several opera corps of Italians and the Seguin English troupe occupied it for brief seasons of four and six weeks, as circumstances required. It then was occupied in portions of 1848, and in the winter and spring of 1849, by the Virginia Serenaders and other black-faced comedians. In the summer, J. Sandford and J. Lewis presented their minstrels there. W. Horn was the lessee. At this time, also, Sandford and Lewis brought out a dramatic company. Vaudevilles and farces were acted: *The Day After the Wedding, A Glance at Philadelphia,* and others.

On September 1, 1849, the Chesnut Street Theatre opened for a regular season, under the stage and acting management of Joseph Foster. The lessee was supposed to be James Quinlan, acting silently. The prices were very low: first tier and parquet, twenty-five cents; second and third tiers, twelve and a-half cents; colored gallery, twenty-five cents. This was done to make a select place for the colored people, but they never gave it any support. The Chesnut Street Theatre drew its slow length along under the Foster régime and the Quinlan silent direction until it gave up the ghost some time in March or April. No advertisements appeared at all at that time.

The year of 1849 was the last for William E. Burton at the Arch. He left for New York where he continued to produce successfully and perhaps more profitably. Ethelbert A. Marshall continued as lessee of the Walnut which, under his direction, was the prime theatrical house in Philadelphia.

The year of 1849 began with four theatres open: the Arch, the Walnut, the Athenaeum, and the Chesnut, but the Chesnut closed with the performance on January 3, and the Athenaeum discontinued legitimate performance, Saturday, January 27. The Arch and the Walnut then had the theatrical field to themselves until Peale's Philadelphia Museum started on Wednesday, April 25, 1849, but Peale's Museum ceased to play legitimate drama after Wednesday, June 6. The Arch dropped out after the performance of Wednesday, June 20, and the Walnut closed for the season on Saturday, June 23. Therefore there was no advertised theatre playing legitimate drama in Philadelphia until Wednesday, June 27, when Peale's Philadelphia Museum presented a dramatic company for the summer.

Peale's Museum had no competitor and closed its season on Saturday, July 28. There was, then, no advertised legitimate house open in Philadelphia until the middle of the next month, when the Arch and the Chesnut both opened on Wednesday, August 15, 1849. The Chesnut, however, only enjoyed a short run, for it closed again in two weeks, on Tuesday, August 28. The Arch continued alone until the first of September, when a new dramatic company appeared at the Chesnut. A week later, Monday, September 10, the Walnut also opened. The national was lighted for five nights, beginning Monday, October 8, with an engagement of Chanfrau. Lights continued brightly in the Arch, the Walnut and the Chesnut during October and November. However, by Tuesday, December 11, the Chesnut became dark for the rest of the year.

Is it worth while or is it even interesting to raise the question: What was a "Free and Easy?" The following advertisements historically chronicle the "Free and Easy" under the heading of Amusements:

Jan. 5, 1849—Public Ledger—E. A. BEEBE respectfully informs his friends and the public that there will be a Free and Easy in the large hall of the Mammoth Bowling Saloon, 100 by 23 feet, No. 457 North Third Street, on SATURDAY EVENING, Jan. 6, 1849, under the direction of R. WILLIAMS, to commence at 7 o'clock.

Apr. 14, 1849—Public Ledger—FREE AND EASY—AT BROWN'S, Third and Chesnut Sts., THIS (Saturday) EVENING, 14th inst.; and each Saturday evening hereafter.

The first advertisement certainly recorded a grand occasion (with 2,300 square feet to move around in), but the second comes to a closer approximation of the normal or domestic variety of "Free and Easy."

I have been told by men whose memory is coeval with the early years of the "Free and Easy" in Philadelphia, that it was a custom English in origin. Certain saloons, perhaps one evening a week, served as the centers for song. In their back rooms gathered men who could sing, and men who could listen. Sometimes a singer of mild fame was present as the celebrity of the evening. Usually, after one man had presented his favorite song to his audience of jovial listeners, someone else volunteered a song of his own choosing and his own singing. Everyone sang what he wished; everyone sang when he wished. However, there was a certain orderliness, because every man was duly heard and given the floor for his vocal outburst. Each took his turn in supplying music for the general entertainment. Frequently young singers (and old) trying to get a foothold on the stage or before the public made their debut in the "Free and Easy." And many a famous ballad first rang out its tale of sentimentality in the "Free and Easy," and, with its soul-stirring words, bedimmed the eyes of men with tears.

A very pleasant evening was spent in singing, and in wetting one's lips so that one could sing again.

1850

With Burton's departure from the Arch Street Theatre, E. S. Conner became its lessee and advertised for a company to open on March 4, 1850. The prices were: boxes, fifty cents; pit, twelve and a-half cents; colored gallery, twelve and a-half cents. Conner made it a rule to admit no one behind the scenes except a member of the company. The house had fallen into much disrepute at the period when Conner became the lessee, in consequence of the indecorous behavior of the audience. The pit especially was unruly, and too often the upper tier of boxes. Through stringent police power, order was comparatively obtained.

During May, on the occasion of Miss Charlotte Cushman's appearance, Conner made public the following card:

Mr. E. S. Conner presents his compliments to the stockholders of the theatre and to the gentlemen of the Press, and respectfully requests, as a personal favor, that they will occupy the boxes appropriated to their use. The enormous expense attending Miss Cushman's engagement renders it necessary that all possible room be given for the accommodation of the public at large; and the manager feels assured that his friends will comply with his request, and not leave their own boxes empty to occupy seats in the front which otherwise would add to the treasury. He would further add, that notwithstanding the collection of a sterling, expensive stock corps and the engagement of first rate, celebrated auxiliaries, he has not advanced the terms of admission, though urged to do so. He therefore begs to remind his friends and patrons of this fact, and hopes for their coöperation in this arduous endeavor to maintain a popular house, one adapted to all classes of the community. It is therefore necessary to announce that the free list must be suspended entirely.

Charles Durang, in the ninety-eighth chapter of his history, third series, assures us that it was bad policy for Conner to suggest a modification in the free use of privileges or the moderate exercise of them as exerted by the stockholders, and that it was the first wrong direction of his management, finally losing his theatre for him in 1851.

E. S. Conner did fall into difficulties with the stockholders of the Arch Street Theatre this year. He issued proposals, then, for a new theatre to be located somewhere above Sixth Street, in Callowhill; and another suggestion was made to locate it in Spring Garden Street, near Eighth, or at the corner of those streets. A prospectus was issued for "Conner's Lyceum," and G. Parker Cummings, an architect of Philadelphia, furnished a plan for him, which was exhibited in one of the picture stores in Chesnut Street for some time. The design seemed feasible and beautiful, but the project finally was abandoned.

On September 7, the new theatre in Coates Street was opened under the management of Cornelius Logan, with Francis C. Wemyss as the silent partner. On Monday, August 19, Barnum's Museum opened with a dramatic company. Charles Durang tells us in the one hundred and third chapter of his history of the Philadelphia stage, third series, that on July 20, 1850, Barnum announced that his own interest in the Museum had ceased. C. Spooner became the proprietor. At the beginning of the autumn of 1850, no regular plan had been adopted to organize a theatrical company at the Chesnut for the season of 1850–51. A Mr. Whipples occupied the house for a time with an exhibition of dissolving views—a diorama.

In November 1850 a splendid scheme of presenting the Italian opera was offered to the Philadelphia public by Max Maretzek, the great opera and concert meister. The following was the operatic proposal:

November 15th.—*Italian opera.*—Max Maretzek proposes to open in December a series of Italian operas, in the same style of grandeur and magnificence as they are produced at the Astor Opera House at New York. The programme will show that the Director's determination is not to establish a mere branch in a neighboring city, but to avail himself of the existing facility of communication, in a manner that all the operatic novelties brought out in New York may be represented in succession, and with the aid of all the artistes, and all other accessories that have been given so successfully at New York. It is the Director's intention to establish a regular *permanent* opera in Philadelphia. He therefore proposes, and trusts to realize those well founded hopes, through the well known musical taste and liberal patronage ever elicited and extended to opera in this city. He now proposes a series of fifteen nights, to which this first season is limited. . . .

The prices will be the same as at New York.

Secured seats, $1.50; box and parquette seats, $1; on Mlle. Parodi's nights, secured seats $2.50; evening's performances, $2. Prices of subscription, to afford facilities to those persons who regularly wish to attend the opera, the Director has fixed the price of admission to subscribers at $20 for the fifteen nights.

The above notice by M. Maretzek appeared in the newspapers of the day for November 15.

These Italian arrangements, however, underwent a slight change. The subscriptions did not fill up as advantageously as anticipated, so Edward

L. Walker stepped in as business agent and finally arranged satisfactorily for the operatic season.

Lessees seemed to come and go at the Arch and at the Chesnut, but E. A. Marshall seemed to go on forever at the Walnut, where he remained during 1850 and during many years thereafter. The Arch, the Walnut, and the Chesnut began the year of 1850, but the Arch was closed after the performance of Wednesday, January 2. The Chesnut and the Walnut continued alone until they were again joined by the Arch on Monday, March 4. All three theatres remained in active service during March, April, May, and June. It was not until Thursday, July 4, that the Walnut brought its season to a close. At the end of the month, Wednesday, July 31, the Chesnut also closed for the summer.

The Arch was the only summer theatre running until Monday, August 19, when the Walnut and Barnum's Museum opened with legitimate drama. The Chesnut opened on Monday, September 9. However, the operatic season at the Chesnut was finished by Tuesday, September 24, and the other three theatres continued without the Chesnut through October and November. On Tuesday, December 10, the Chesnut reopened for another run of opera on several evenings every week during the month.

The *United States Gazette and North American,* daily paper, for September 4, 1850, tells us that there swept down through the Schuylkill Valley, on the night of September 2, 1850, the worst freshet in the history of Philadelphia. The morning of September 3 found the flood of serious proportions, following a torrential storm, which had spread over the upper Schuylkill and Lehigh valleys.

All through the third September day, the water continued to rise until, at the peak of the flood, it was almost eleven feet above the top of Fairmount Dam. Roads and bridges had been wiped out, the Falls and Manayunk bridges swept away, the Norristown Railroad put out of service, the Schuylkill Canal wrecked, and the banks of the lower river washed out.

East and west of the river many householders found themselves marooned, but the most striking effect of the flood was that it plunged the city into darkness. At this period of our history, people who did not use candles to light their homes were dependent upon the gas supplied from the city works at the Market Street crossing of the river. The flood suspended operation of the works and the gas left in the mains was soon used up, for the reserve supply was small.

On the night of September 3, the streets were left in blackness, since the oil lamps had been removed. Only one light burned on Chesnut Street and that was the Drummond light which P. T. Barnum, the enterprising showman, had set up in front of his Museum. Inside his theatre there was an oasis of brilliance. He must have purchased the entire contents of a camphene lamp establishment, because he had lights burning in profusion all over the house. The other centers of amusement, like the Walnut Street Theatre and the Circus, had to be closed. And Conner presented his company at the Arch under the feeble glow of the tallow candle.

1851

During the season of 1851–52, the Chesnut Street Theatre launched forth boldly under the Quinlan dynasty. The acting manager was W. Fredericks, and the stage manager, Henry Wallack. The prices were: for dress circle and parquet, fifty cents; second tier, called the family circle, twenty-five cents; the third tier, twenty-five cents; and the gallery, twenty-five cents. During the recess of two or three months, the theatre had undergone many alterations and improvements.

July 31, 1851, saw the last of E. S. Conner in his managerial career on the boards of the Arch Street Theatre. Thomas J. Hemphill, a citizen of Philadelphia, succeeded him in the management of the Arch, which opened for the season of 1851–52 on Saturday evening, August 30, 1851. Charles Burke was the stage manager. The prices of admission were: dress circle, fifty cents; family circle, twenty-five cents; private boxes, from three dollars to four dollars; pit, twelve and a-half cents.

E. A. Marshall still continued at the Walnut. Dr. Cunnington was the orchestra leader; Peter Grain, Jr., the scenic atrist; A. Wilson, machinist; Denby, prompter; Robinson, property man. The prices of admission were: dress circle and parquet, fifty cents; second and third circles, twenty-five cents; orchestra box seats, seventy-five cents. W. H. Stuart was the treasurer.

The Walnut, the Arch, the Chesnut, and Barnum's Museum began the theatrical year of 1851, but the performances at the Chesnut were only occasional, occurring several times a week, and, by the second week of April, they ceased entirely. With the performance of Saturday, July 5, the Walnut closed for the summer. It is certain that the Chesnut was closed one week later. The Arch, then, continued singly for the summer until it was joined by the National on Tuesday, July 15, 1851. At the end of the month, the Arch also was closed.

The National was the only legitimate house advertised in the papers during the first two weeks of August. On Monday, August 18, lights were on at the Chesnut for the fall season and at the Arch on Saturday, August 30, one month after its closing. On Monday, August 18, the Walnut opened and the National was dark. On Monday, September 1, Barnum's Museum was again active. Therefore, the first of September saw the four theatres of the Walnut, the Chesnut, the Arch, and Barnum's Museum harnessed together for the fall entertainment of the city of Philadelphia. These four theatres continued in uninterrupted performances during the remaining months of September, October, November, and December.

The *Public Ledger* for July 10, 1851, bears the following very interesting announcement which is testimony to the early and spasmodic efforts of actors to give protection to their own:

AMERICAN DRAMATIC FUND ASSOCIATION—Incorporated April 16th, 1848—open alike to every Actor or Actress in the United States, without restriction from age or length of services in any particular THEATRE, TOWN OR CITY. Present invested Capital $10,000.

THE PRESIDENT

Trustees and Directors respectfully announce to the citizens of Philadelphia, that, by the kindness of E. S. Conner, Esq.,

A BENEFIT IN AID OF THIS FUND

The object of which is to provide for the support of all Actors and Actresses, Members thereof, rendered incapable, from age, sickness or infirmity, from pursuing their professional labors, and also to assist the Widows and Orphans, who may be thrown friendless upon the world, will take place at the

ARCH STREET THEATRE

on MONDAY, July 14

The following Ladies and Gentlemen have volunteered their services on the occasion; and the Pieces will be cast so as to embrace all the talent that can be made available:

MR. WALKER

the celebrated Young American Actor, now playing with great success, at the Broadway Theatre, New York.

(His First Appearance In Philadelphia)

Miss Anderton,
Miss C. Wemyss,
Miss M. J. Brougham,
Mr. Thos. B. Johnston,
Miss J. Gougenheim,
Mr. H. E. Stephens,
Mr. E. L. Tilton,
Mr. J. E. Shaw,
Mr. F. C. Wemyss,

Madame Ponisi,
Miss C. Chapman,
Mr. Hadaway,
Mr. Lynne,
Miss A. Gougenheim,
Mr. W. R. Goodall,
Mr. H. C. Jordan,
Mr. N. B. Clarke,
Mr. James C. Dunn,

Mr. and Mrs. Conner,

And other Ladies and Gentlemen of the profession, now in this City, whose names will be announced hereafter, making an unequalled concentration of talent.

The present writer also recalls an announcement in the *Public Ledger* of the year previous pointing attention to the Grand Fancy and Citizens' Dress Ball, to be given at the Chinese Museum, April 22, 1850, by "The Actors' Order of Friendship," tickets at three dollars to admit one gentleman and two ladies.

1852

The National Theatre, known at this time as Welch's National Circus and Theatre, was supplied this year with a dramatic company, as well as an equestrian troupe. The treasurer was C. H. Russell; stage manager, S. E. Harris (Wesley Barmore), the original Uncle Tom; equestrian manager, J. M. Nixon; director of equestrian spectacles, S. P. Stickney; scenic artist, John Wiser; prompter, J. B. Addis. The prices of admission were: parquet and dress circle, fifty cents; family circle, twenty-five cents; gallery, twelve and a-half cents; seats in private boxes, seventy-five cents; full private boxes, six to nine dollars. After a long winter and spring season, the National closed for six weeks, to reopen as a dramatic, operatic, and pantomimic theatre only.

During the summer of 1852, C. Logan was the acting manager of the Chesnut Street Theatre, but James Quinlan was still the lessee, although his name did not appear on any of the bills. The season was successful and the theatre only closed for one night to prepare for the fall and winter activities.

During the winter, W. S. Fredericks was again acting manager; Mueller, leader of the orchestra; Lingard, prompter and deputy stage director; C. Long, property man. The prices of admission were: dress circle and parquet, fifty cents; second tier and family circle, twenty-five cents; third tier, twenty-five cents; proscenium boxes, five dollars; private boxes, holding twelve persons, nine dollars; single seats in private boxes, seventy-five cents.

The Arch Street Theatre commenced its regular fall and winter season on Saturday, August 21, 1852, with Thomas J. Hemphill as lessee, A. W. Fenno as stage manager, and J. Ingles Matthias as treasurer.

During the summer the house had been much altered. The formation of the old pit seats had been changed into the parquet style, at that time being introduced in the foreign theatres. It was thereby spaciously enlarged, rendering it capable of seating over five hundred persons. The interior had been painted; the lobby walls and boxes papered; the fronts of the boxes decorated with classical devices, and the paneling regilded. The orchestra boxes were furnished with new lounges of crimson damask, and the seats stuffed and covered with Brussels carpeting. The stock scenery was repainted with several new scenes and there was a drop curtain by Heister.

E. A. Marshall reopened the Walnut for the fall and winter season on Monday, August 30, 1852. During the long summer recess, the theatre had undergone complete and extensive alterations under the supervision of the celebrated architect, R. Hoxie. The principal feature of its interior reconstruction was the very commodious and comfortable enlargement of the parquet, which was extended beneath the dress circle to the foundation walls. There were two large stairways leading from the lobby of the first tier to the parquet on both sides. Rich and magnificent orchestral arrangements were constructed in the nature of stalls, as in the London theatres, with cushioned seats. The proscenium was considerably widened, assisting the perspective qualities of the stage. There were also introduced novel facilities for heating the entire building during the winter. The enlargement of the upper tier, with new and extensive appliances for ventilation, promenading avenues, exit and entrance passages to seats, a thorough repainting, papering and decorating, an entire refitting of the gas pipes and fixtures, which were set off with new and brilliant chandeliers, offered to the public, as was claimed in the play-bill, "an establishment of capacity, elegance, sound, and ventilation unapproachable by any other in the United States, except the Broadway Theatre of New York [which was Marshall's also]—the entire expense of this elaborate alteration having amounted to the immense sum of upwards of ten thousand dollars."

The first of January, 1852, found the three theatres of the Walnut, the Chesnut, and the Arch giving performances, but the third of January was the last night for legitimate drama at the Arch during the engagement of Macallister, the magician.

The Walnut and the Chesnut continued without the Arch until the latter theatre again reverted to regular drama on Saturday, February 28, 1852. The Arch again withdrew after Saturday, May 15, but its place was taken for several nights during the ensuing week by the National.

The Chesnut brought its season to a close on Saturday, June 19, and the Walnut on Saturday, June 26. It was not until Monday, July 12, that the summer theatres began to play legitimate drama once more. At that time, the Chesnut and the National opened and continued alone until they were joined by the Arch on Saturday, August 21, and by the Walnut on Monday, August 30.

The first of September, therefore, discovered the four theatres of the National, the Arch, the Chesnut, and the Walnut in full swing for the fall season. With the night of Monday, October 25, the National dropped out, and left the other three theatres to run along undisturbed during November and December.

Between the play and the farce, a song or a dance was sometimes given. Frequently these interludes were featured if the dance happened to be a *pas seul* by Miss Clemens, or a character-song by William E. Burton or Jim Crow Rice.

The ballet and interpretative dancing frequently displaced the play proper, particularly when a troupe like the Ravel family was engaged to perform its repertoire of such "ballets d'action" like *Godenski, La Fête Champêtre, Mons. de Chalumeau,* and the *Venetian Carnival.* When such a troupe occupied the theatre, usually only one farce constituted the legitimate drama for the evening, and at the most, two farces, since there was not time for full-length drama.

On Memorial days, an historical recitation often served as the interlude, and at other times, legerdemain and feats of contortion when Signor Somebody-or-other would profess to be a human fly or the ninth wonder of the world.

1853

It is a matter of difficulty at this period of the history of the Chesnut Street Theatre to give anything like a connected account of its seasons.

Sometimes it was closed and sometimes it was opened, quite spasmodically. However, it may be said never to have closed in regular seasons during the Quinlan régime, which expired in 1854. Occasionally it was open during the summer of 1853 without any advertisements, even in the *Ledger*. We have authority for this statement in the one hundred and ninth chapter of Charles Durang's history, third series.

T. J. Hemphill continued as lessee of the Arch, and with the spring season in March announced W. Wheatley as acting manager and W. Fredericks as stage manager of the theatre.

By August 20, 1853, Wm. Wheatley and John Drew became lessees of the Arch. W. S. Fredericks was the acting and stage manager; Wm. Reed, the prompter and stage director; George Wunderlich, the scenic artist; F. Johnston, the costumer; John Scott, the machinist; Alfred King, the property man; and J. Ingles Matthias, the treasurer. The prices of admission were: boxes and parquet, seventy-five cents; orchestra stalls, fifty cents; seats in private boxes, seventy-five cents; gallery, twelve and a-half cents; gallery boxes for colored people, thirty-seven and a-half cents; and the colored gallery, twenty-five cents.

E. A. Marshall continued as lessee of the Walnut Street Theatre.

The Chesnut, the Arch, and the Walnut were running with the beginning of the year of 1853. The Arch closed with the performance of Saturday, January 15, but reopened on Saturday, January 29. The three theatres continued regularly during February, March, and April, but the advertisements for the Walnut are sparse during the month of May.

The Arch was closed for the summer with the performance of Saturday, June 11, 1853, although an occasional performance was given there during July and August. With the performance of Saturday, June 25, the Walnut brought its season to a close. The Chesnut proceeded alone during July until it was joined by the National for several nights during the last week of the month.

By Tuesday, August 30, 1853, the Arch, Chesnut, and Walnut were again running regularly and continued to run regularly during September, October, November, and December.

There were many newspaper advertisements of amusements which do not come within the province of a history of the theatre. Advertisements for the "Free and Easy," for concerts, for feats of skill and magic, all helped to make the newspaper section headed "Amusements" into a half-column every day. Let us take any day, say August 27, 1853, (as of the *Public Ledger*) and note the nature of the Amusements scheduled:

GRAND RECEPTION BALL, to be given by the INDEPENDENT ORDER OF ODD FELLOWS, in FULL REGALIA, in honor of THE GRAND LODGE OF THE UNITED STATES, the Members of which will be present on the occasion,
ON TUESDAY EVENING, Sept. 6, 1853, in both saloons of the CHINESE MUSEUM. Tickets $3. each, admitting a Gentleman and two Ladies, including Ladies' Refreshments, can be had at the Odd Fellows Hall, North Sixth Street; office of Public Ledger; and Blood's Despatch, Arcade.

DANCING—COTILLION PARTY, THIS (Saturday) EVENING, at the Saloon, FIFTH and CALLOWHILL Streets
GEO. W. COLEMAN, Prop'r.

A FREE AND EASY, at the Columbia House, SECOND and RACE Sts., on SATURDAY EVENING.
T. S. GOODWIN, Chair'n.

MR. FRED'K WADE, having returned from Europe, will be happy to see his old friends at his FREE AND EASY, held every Saturday EVENING, at the Star Hotel, SPRUCE ST., above Second. Chair taken at 8 o'clock.

RURAL FESTIVAL ON LEMON HILL—The NINTH ANNIVERSARY FESTIVAL of the LIEDERTAFEL VOCAL MUSICAL SOCIETY, takes place on
MONDAY, August 29th,
ON LEMON HILL.
All the Vocal, Musical Societies and Gymnastic Associations of the City will participate in the Festival. Tickets, 50 cents admitting one Gentleman and two Ladies. To be had of M. R. Muckle, Ledger Office, or at the Gates on the day.
THE COMMITTEE.

SANFORD'S OPERA HOUSE—SEATS can be secured in advance for LA SONNAMBULA NIGHTS. Houses crowded to excess, and hundreds turned away nightly. Tickets limited. Sanford performs nightly.

[47]

CONCERT HALL—GRAND COMBINATION CONCERT—By Miss Rosina Collins and Sister, and the Tournaire Family. Commencing MONDAY, Aug. 29th, and every evening during the week.

THOS. A. ANDREWS.

SMITH'S ISLAND—5000 Visitors are expected every AFTERNOON this week, to listen to the following great and highly popular Artists:

C. JENKINS
The unrivalled Comedian and Vocalist.

MR. JOHNSON
The renowned Comedian and Delineator of
Eccentric Character, and

MR. THIODON
The justly acknowledged Prince of Violinists.
Concerts Free. To commence at 3½ o'clock, precisely.

1854

In 1854 James Quinlan, a hotel keeper at the northwest corner of Ninth and Market Streets, had to relinquish the Chesnut. "Old Drury," after about sixty years of life, was falling upon evil days and losing its prestige. On June 3, 1854, the National Theatre being to let, Quinlan became its lessee. He had also, for many years, been a renter of the Walnut Street Theatre saloons, and other theatrical bars about the city, whereby he had accumulated a comfortable fortune. He had also been a lessee of the Chesnut for about five years during its last days. Charles Durang, in the one hundred and thirtieth chapter of his history, third series, tells us that Quinlan's chief interest in any theatre was the sale of liquor, and that the dramatic entertainment took second place to the liquid entertainment. Quinlan opened the National Theatre for a summer season in 1854. Thomas McKeon was stage manager; John Addis, stage director; and Professor Mueller, musical director. One month after Quinlan opened the National this summer, the theatre was totally destroyed by fire. Charles Durang gives us a very interesting account of this fire (c. 130, 3d series):

The Circus took fire after the performance of *Putnam,* and was soon burned down, together with the Chinese Museum, at the corner of Ninth and Sansom streets, and several houses in the row on the north side of Sansom street. The roof of the new Girard Hotel caught fire, but was soon extinguished, although some of the engines could not reach the top of the edifice. The catastrophe was awful, as it embraces a vast extent of property in the various courses which the conflagration oddly took. The old Blue Bell Tavern on Eighth street, very strangely, although surrounded by flames, escaped their fury. It had been a dram shop for many years.

How the Circus caught fire was a matter of conjecture. It was said that the wadding of the muskets fired by the soldiery at Putnam during his descent had lodged in the scenery and ignited its combustible materials. Again it was said that some of the supernumeraries engaged in these show plays had not been paid their nightly stipends, and they had revolted several times in consequence. One of them, it was rumored, was overheard to say that he "would be revenged," and also said something about making "a blazing last scene." The place where the fire was first discovered would seem to confirm the latter surmise, it being in the carpenter-shop, away from the stage, on the east side of the main building, over the stable for the horses, and next to Earle's store. The "supers" dressed there, and it would have been almost impossible for the wadding of the guns to have taken a zig-zag course to reach that remote region of the building.

E. A. Marshall again held forth at the Walnut this year. He kept his theatre open for the entire year without a recess. W. Wheatley and J. Drew began the year at the Arch. This season with them was not very conspicuous for extraordinary innovations in melodramas or spectacles, but it was generally good and sound in its programs of favorite plays.

On Tuesday, September 12, 1854, a new theatre called the City Museum, on Callowhill Street below Fifth, opened under the proprietorship of S. M. Zulich.

The Arch, the Walnut, and the Chesnut began the new theatrical year, January 2, 1854. They continued without interruption through January, February, March, and April, and up to the last week in May. On Monday, May 29, the Chesnut closed its season at the end of the nightly performance.

The Arch and the Walnut were joined by the National on June 3, and again by the Chesnut on Monday, June 12. One month later, as we have noted, July 4, the National was destroyed by fire, and the site at Ninth and Chesnut was next occupied by the Continental Hotel which in turn was torn down in the second decade of the twentieth century to give place to the Benjamin Franklin Hotel.

This famous Tuesday night, when the National burned down—the

Fourth of July—was also the closing of the season for the Walnut and the Arch.

The Chesnut continued alone through the summer until the Arch reopened on Monday, August 21, 1854. The Walnut started for the fall season, Tuesday, August 29, one week before the Arch. On Tuesday, September 12, 1854, the City Museum added a dramatic company to those already entertaining theatrical Philadelphia at the Arch, the Walnut, and the Chesnut. These four theatres continued until the Chesnut failed to play legitimate drama from the performance of Tuesday, December 19, until the New Year, during the change from James Quinlan to S. E. Harris as lessee at that time.

A new theatre opened this year when the City Museum began to play legitimate drama. The building was on Callowhill Street below Fifth. No new theatre had opened since Peale's Philadelphia Museum in 1846. Before that time, Burton had built a new theatre, the National, in 1840.

It is to be remembered that we are speaking of permanent and legitimate dramatic houses, for in the fourteen years just mentioned, one can find several new amusement houses, and many old theatres under new names. On Coates Street, now Fairmount Avenue, spasmodic theatrical ventures broke forth occasionally, but never lasted long. And, in the center of the theatrical district of the City, itself, circus buildings began to crop up. But these are not what we understand as houses either of permanent or of legitimate drama. Even Barnum's Museum did not play legitimate drama long.

The City Museum, on the other hand, belongs within our definition, although it was a house of melodrama predominantly and, in 1854, does not rank artistically with the Arch, the Walnut, and the Chesnut.

1855

William Wheatley and John Drew this year dissolved partnership at the Arch. Wheatley continued alone as lessee of the theatre, and John Drew with his wife returned as stock actors to the Walnut, which first gave them footlights in Philadelphia. E. A. Marshall was as ever lessee of the Walnut. In this our short record of the Philadelphia stage, we have recorded him as lessee of that theatre for thirteen years, from 1842 to 1855 inclusive.

James Quinlan, who was not able to carry the Chesnut through the entire year of 1854, released his hold upon the theatre, December 9. And on December 28, 1854, S. E. Harris, the noted comedian of *Uncle Tom's Cabin,* took the lease of the theatre and opened "Old Drury" with the original Wood and Christy's band of Ethiopian Minstrels from New York on New Year's Eve. He also attempted to introduce a dramatic company.

In April, S. E. Harris was succeeded by C. H. Griffiths and J. Wayne Olwine as lessees of the Chesnut. The company was considerably curtailed and the bills provided only farces and interludes for the most part. On the first day of May, the formal closing of the theatre took place with somewhat sad and sentimental exercises.

After a long life of sixty-two years of active service, "Old Drury" was demolished, and upon its ruins rose clothing bazaars, billiard saloons and, in the basement, negro concerts.

Charles Durang rings down the final curtain upon the stage of "Old Drury" with the following quotation, in the one hundred and thirty-sixth chapter of his history, third series:

> Our revels now are ended. These, our actors,
> As I foretold you, were all spirits, and
> Are melted into thin air:
> And, like the baseless fabric of this vision,
> The cloud capp'd towers, the gorgeous palaces,
> The solemn temples, the great globe itself,
> Yea, all which it inherit, shall dissolve;
> And, like this unsubstantial pageant, faded,
> Leave not a rack behind.

The Arch, the Walnut, and the City Museum opened the year of 1855. The Chesnut, under S. E. Harris, exhibited a dramatic company, beginning Monday, January 15. The four other theatres played without interruption during January, February and up to the last week in March, when the Chesnut discontinued with the performance of Tuesday, March 27. On Thursday, April 5, C. H. Griffiths and J. Wayne Olwine reopened "Old Drury" only to close it at the end of the month —for all time.

The other three theatres played from the beginning of the year until the Fourth of July. With that date the Arch closed its season and the Walnut forsook the legitimate drama, although it remained open with an engagement of the Ravel family in ballet. The City Museum also closed.

The Arch alone began its fall season the next month, Saturday, August 18. There were also spasmodic performances at the German National Theatre during August, September, and October. The Walnut reopened Thursday, September 5, and the City Museum on Saturday, September 8. And the three theatres remained open for the rest of the year.

The year of 1855 is assuredly one with which to bring to a close an epoch in the history of the theatres of Philadelphia, for the passing of "Old Drury," the Chesnut Street Theatre, is definitely sufficient to mark an era, just as in the history of the plays the production of *Francesca da Rimini* comes as the climax to the rise of the romantic tragedy. For, during our twenty-one years of dramatic development under discussion, the romantic tragedy appears as the form most characteristic and most worth while, while *Francesca* itself is the most significant play. In the realm of the actors, we have no startling events to correspond with the demolition of a theatre or the first night of an epoch-climaxing play. Yet we do have the appearance of an actor in 1855 who should absorb our attention, since he himself was to make this period the beginning of a new epoch in acting. Dion Boucicault appeared for the first time on the stage of Philadelphia at the Walnut, June 16, 1855, in his own comedy of *Used Up*. He was the man who was to sign the death warrant of the fine old stock companies by instituting the system of the complete traveling company, emanating from New York, and bringing their own new play with which they toured the provinces for many, many weeks.

Appended to the newspaper advertisement concerning the bill at the Walnut for June 23, 1855, there is this curious note:

> Mr. Barry's Patent Cool Air Machine maintains the temperature of the theatre under 70 degrees.

Might we not, then, call the Walnut the first summer theatre in Philadelphia to be artificially cooled by a mechanical invention?

The year of 1853 was the first year that John Drew leased the Arch Street Theatre in partnership with William Wheatley. The advent of John Drew as a lessee of the Arch is unequivocally important to Philadelphia theatrical history. But, to the present writer, another fact of importance was the dramatic program which, from its frequency, seemed to be the bill of first choice in the mind of John Drew himself. The two comedies, *The Comedy of Errors* and *The Serious Family,* appear and reappear constantly paired together during John Drew's first years at the Arch. Apparently Drew was tremendously popular in these two comedies that occupied first place in his program. When he and Wheatley dissolved partnership, the latter no longer put them on.

But the "first" which is of prime importance for 1855 was the Philadelphia première of Boker's *Francesca Da Rimini* with E. L. Davenport as Lanciotto, A. H. Davenport as Paolo, and Mrs. John Drew as Francesca. The play, which is Philadelphia's own, comes as the grand climax to the steady growth of the romantic tragedy in verse during our period, and as a fitting climax to our account of twenty-one years in the history of the Philadelphia theatre.

THE PLAYS

CHAPTER II
THE PLAYS

1835

THE plays which are naturally of most concern to us in detail are the new plays as Philadelphia receives them for the first time. But, for a well-rounded picture of the theatre of the time, we must remember that the Philadelphia theatres annually gave many performances of those old plays which have come into our drama to stay.

Among these old favorites in 1835, there were principally the more frequently acted and popular plays of Shakespeare: *As You Like It* (3 performances), *Hamlet* (7), *King John* (1), *King Lear* (6), *Macbeth* (7), *Merchant of Venice,* (6), *Merry Wives of Windsor* (1), *Much Ado About Nothing* (5), *Othello* (7), *Katharine and Petruchio* (2), *Richard III* (14), *Romeo and Juliet* (6), *The Tempest* (2), and the *Winter's Tale* (1). Massinger also appears out of the past with his *New Way To Pay Old Debts* (6).

Among the regularly recurring Restoration plays were Sheridan's *Rivals* (2), *School for Scandal* (6), and *The Critic* (2), Rowe's *Jane Shore* (4), and Otway's *Venice Preserved* (6).

The English dramatists of the eighteenth century were represented most frequently by the plays of Cumberland, Lillo, E. Moore, and O'Keefe; of the nineteenth century, by Holcroft, Knowles, Moncrieff, Morton, and Webster. Other and current plays by English dramatists were those of Banim, Diamond, Dibdin, Home, Millman, Milner, Murphy, Poole, and Reynolds.

Among the plays on the stage at the time were those by our native playwrights: J. S. Jones, S. H. Rowson, H. J. Conway, W. G. Simms, Wm. Dunlap, J. H. Payne, J. Stokes, S. Woodworth, W. E. Burton, B. H. Brewster, R. T. Conrad, T. S. Rice, R. Tyler, H. J. Finn, and J. K. Paulding.

In discussing the new plays for each year, we are going to make an attempt at unity by dividing them into their type-groups. However, when we are under the necessity of discussing plays which are now unknown or little known, we may err by calling a play a comedietta when it is really a burletta or a farce; or again, by calling a play a melodrama when others insist that it is a romantic drama or a domestic drama. Therefore, the present writer wishes to state that the reader may call any of these plays by any name that he prefers.

A new tragedy was produced at the Chesnut, April 22, 1835, called *Ugolino, or the Innocent Condemned.* It was supposed to be an adaptation of the *Ugolino, or Blood for Blood,* of 1825, by Junius Brutus Booth, but Charles Durang tells us that Booth would never acknowledge the authorship. *Jack Cade, or the Noble Yeoman,* a play in five acts, by R. T. Conrad, was another new tragedy, produced at the Walnut, December 7, 1835.

B. H. Brewster's *The Infidel,* a romantic play, was introduced to Philadelphia theatre-goers on October 24, 1835, at the Walnut. Other new romantic dramas this year were: *Mary Stewart, Shadow on the Wall, Robber's Wife, Gipsy of Ashburnham Dell,* and *Uda and Magnus.*

The new domestic dramas for this year, including W. E. Burton's *The Intemperate,* were *Henriette, Rake's Progress, Deserter of Naples, Deserted Village, Woman's Life,* and the *Note Forger.*

There were usually a number of new plays representing different types of American character. These new plays for 1835 included: *Beulah Spa; Knight of the Golden Fleece; Lion of the East; Man with the Carpet Bag; Congress Hall; Spirit of '76; Kaspar Hauser;* and *Adventure.*

Many and various were the new melodramas put on each year. One of the most spectacular of the new melodramas for 1835 was *Zanthe,* built by W. Barrymore of the Walnut from Kenney's tragedy of *Hernani,* as an expedient for the elaborate *Gustavus III* production which the Chesnut presented before the Walnut could bring forth its own version. Thus the Walnut had to turn to, and unearth another play. *Zanthe* was the result. It necessitated a full military brass band and six drummers nightly, costing twenty-five dollars; one hundred and thirty-two supernumeraries, thirty-two dollars and fifty cents; and wax candles, red, blue, and green fires, sixty or seventy dollars. H. J. Conway, the American playwright, contributed three new melodramas to the Philadelphia stage this year: *Fatal Prophecies; Arab Chief;* and *Spanish Pirates.*

Other melodramas of the year were: *Mary; Old Man's Curse; Last Days of Pompeii; Seventeen Hundred Years Ago; Ardeschi; Schinder-*

hannes; Wild Woman of Our Village; Wild Boy; Black Angus of the Evil Eye; Gray Man of Tottenham; and *Fieschi.*

There were also the melodramatic sketches of Mlle. Celeste: *Wizard Skiff; Moorish Page; Spirit Bride; Victoire;* and the *Death Plank;* and the dog or monkey extravagances with Cony and Blanchard: *Cherokee Chief; Ourang Outang; Monkeyana; Planter and His Dogs; Love Me Love My Dog; Hyder Ali; Murder of the Blind Boy; Zenocles and the Greek Chief;* and the *Dumb Savoyard and His Monkey.*

The new comedies for the year included: *My Uncle John; Blind Beggar of Bethnal Green; Old Gentleman; Pet of the Petticoats; My Friend the Governor; Miser's Daughter; Patrician and Parvenu; Skeleton Witness; Biena; Hazard of the Die; Lo Zingaro; Secret Service; Seven Clerks; Second Thoughts; I'll Be Your Second; Win Her and Wear Her; Matchmaking;* and the *Climbing Boy.*

Among the new farces for 1835 was one called *Queer Neighbors, or the Party Wall,* a translation of Kotzebue's German farce, *Gefahrliche Nachbarschaff.*

Other new farces for the year were: *Deep, Deep Sea; In the Wrong Box; Ladies' Man; Pay for Peeping; Damp Beds; Welsh Girl; Tristram Shandy; Cupid; Unfinished Gentleman; Zoological Gardens; My Wife's Mother; Personation; Affair of Honour; Fighting By Proxy; My Neighbor's Wife; Young Reefer; My Fellow Clerk; Miser's Miseries;* and *One, Two, Three, Four, Five.*

The two topical farces, *Discoveries in the Moon, or Herschel Out-Herscheled,* by T. D. Rice; and *Moonshine, or Lunar Caustic,* by W. E. Burton, bear witness to the mild furore caused this year by the presence and ideas of Sir John Herschel, British astronomical scientist, in Philadelphia.

The two principal new operettas this year were: *Gustavus III, or the Masked Ball,* a grand musical and historical drama, and *The White Lady, or the Spirit of Avenel,* the celebrated opera from Borieldrius' *Dame Blanche.* T. D. (Jim Crow) Rice this year contributed an "Ethiopian opera," called *Bone Squash Diavolo,* which took a permanent place in his repertoire.

1836

An interesting tragedy produced in 1836 was *Sardanapalus,* by Lord Byron, adapted to the Philadelphia stage by Charles Durang. Durang tells us in his history that the play ran smoothly. The alterations necessary to render it an acting piece, Durang says, impaired the unities of the classic drama, the purity of which the genius of Byron well preserved. The celebrated dream scene at the beginning of the fourth act was transposed to the second, leaving the last act more effectively divested of dull recitation, and thus invested with more stage action. It was telling in its acting and was repeated. Under the influence of E. S. Conner's acting and popularity, it drew the large receipt of $929.

Other new tragedies of the year were: *Caradora, Caswallon,* and *Ion.*

The new romantic d   f *The Maid of Cashmere* was produced by Wemyss as a matter of managerial expedience. The success of Mlle. Celeste in *La Bayadere* at the rival theatre made it necessary for Wemyss to produce a counter attraction. So he made a drama of his own adaptation from *Lurline, or the Spirit of the Rhine,* which he called *The Maid of Cashmere.*

Conway, the prompter at the Walnut, also wrote a romantic drama this year, called *Ida Stephanoff,* but it did not prove successful. Other romantic dramas for the year were: *Lestocq, Actress of Padua, Bleeding Nun, Broken Heart, Marie de Montville, The Minerali, Passion and Repentance, Dream at Sea, Rinaldo Rinaldini, Skeleton Robber,* and *Walter Brandt.*

Wemyss also dramatized the popular novel of *Norman Leslie* this year into a domestic drama of the same name. Other new domestic dramas for 1836 were: *Lucille, Paul Ulric, Provost of Bruges, Ransom, Spirit of the Black Mantle,* and *Yelva.*

The plays of American types this year included: *Job Fox, The Yankee Pedlar; Fall of the Alamo; Mob, the Outlaw;* and *Liberty Tree.*

Again, numerous and spectacular were the new melodramas for the year. Wemyss himself contributed one, called *The Jewess,* altered from the drama of *Esther, the Jewess.* Durang tells us that it was a very showy piece, and gives us an account of it. This particular biblical story of a very notable woman was calculated to draw attention. The plot was simplicity itself. In truth, it had no other merit than its picturesque accessories: its Egyptian and Assyrian scenery which the brush of Russell Smith made impressively beautiful, costumes, and magnificent pageantry. The principal feature in it was what may be termed an allegorical procession uniquely contrived. Instead of entering from the back or sides of the stage, this procession entered from the back of the pit under a wide entrance made under the center box, whence issued the pageant from the pit saloon and lobby, crossing over a platform laid over the pit about eight feet wide, going over the center of the orchestra, and so to the stage.

The scene set on the stage was only in the second grooves, so that the procession, as it reached the first entrance, countermarched and made its exit as the people came up at the prompter's side. And, to economize room for two hundred persons in the ranks, they were kept constantly countermarching behind the scenes until the entire procession had passed over the pit and the front of the stage and all had disappeared behind the scenes from the eyes of the spectators. The front flats were then drawn off, and the entire depth of the stage discovered, when the head of the procession was again seen advancing down the stage to lead the ranks to assigned positions, where they were to take their stand. The effect was novel and striking. On the left of the stage was a superb throne, composed of variegated marble, resting on the backs of numerous recumbent sphinxes.

La Fitte, another new melodrama, was originally dramatized for Hamblin by Miss L. H. Medina, but in Philadelphia, according to Wemyss, it was patched together by a youth named Percival who played in it at New York, and did it well. Durang, in the forty-eighth chapter of his anecdotal account of the Philadelphia stage, third series, gives an interesting and lengthy historical record of the pirate figure, La Fitte.

A most singularly successful melodrama was *The Bronze Horse, or the Spell of the Cloud King,* advertised as a Chinese Romance. It ran for thirty-one days. Other new melodramas for 1836 were: *Andreas Zell, Brian Boroihme, Council of the Inquisition, The Demon Statue, Children of Chittigong, King O'Neil, The Last Nail, Murder at the Black Farm, Prince Le Boo, Vow of Silence,* and *Who Owns the Hand?*

New comedies for the year included: *Circumstantial Evidence, Court of Love, The Duddlestones, My Poll and My Partner Joe, Stag Hall, Farmer's Story,* and *Military Execution.*

The new farces for the year were legion. All we can do is to catalogue them because most of them were either rather impromptu pieces improvised by an actor and belonging to his repertoire, or carefully guarded by the manager to prevent their theft by another house. The titles of the new farces for 1836 included: *All at Coventry, Borrowed Feathers, Call Again To-Morrow, Comfortable Service, Everybody's Husband, Forty and Fifty, Freaks and Follies, A Gentleman in Difficulties, Hide and Seek, How Do You Manage?, Hunting a Turtle,*

Make Your Wills, Man About Town, Married Rake, Mrs. White and Mrs. Peter White, My Husband's Ghost, Othello Travestie, The Picnic, Quite at Home, Removing the Deposites, Scapegoat, Scotch Cooper, The Sledge Driver, State Secrets, Swiss Cottage, Twa Ghaists, The Widow's Victim, and *Yellow Kids.* Reference to the Play List will reveal the identity of the dramatists if known to the present writer.

This year saw the Philadelphia première of Auber's grand legendary ballet opera, *The Maid of Cashmere, or le Dieu et la Bayadere,* of Bellini's opera, *La Sonnambula,* and of the opera called *The Mountain Sylph.*

Three new pantomimes came to enliven Philadelphia's Christmas this year: *Harlequin Tom the Piper's Son, Pongo,* and *The Three Gladiators.*

1837

Nathaniel Parker Willis' *Bianca Visconti, or the Heart Overtasked,* was, this year of 1837, a new and successful tragedy of considerable poetic feeling. It was written in competition for a prize offered by Miss Josephine Clifton for the best play adapted to her abilities, and was brought by her to Philadelphia, December 27, 1837, at the Chesnut. Other new tragedies for the year were Knowles' *Wrecker's Daughter,* and *The Saxon Girl, or Walter Tyrrel.*

The new romantic drama for 1837 included: *Crichton, or the Admirable Scot,* first time on any stage, by Coleman of Philadelphia, a grand historical drama; Bulwer's *Duchess de la Valliere;* Lord Byron's *Marino Faliero, or the Doge of Venice,* adapted by Charles Durang; *The Lady of the Lake, or the Knight of Snowden,* announced as an original romantic drama with music; *Brothers of the Pyrenees,* advertised as a new drama adapted to the stage from Miss Pardoe's tale of the same name; and *The Beggar of Cripplegate.*

Among the new domestic dramas for the year were: a one-act sketch, called *Arabella, or the Discarded Child; The Daughter; Julie, or the Forced Marriage,* advertised as a new pathetic drama in three acts; *Lilian, the Show Girl,* which was peculiarly announced to be a new domestic drama, never acted in America, forwarded by the approval of "Mr. E. Forrest to Mr. Rufus Welsh, and consigned by him to Mr. [W.] Barrymore"; *Mother's Dream; Paul, the Reprobate, or the Midnight Assassin;* and *Infidelity.*

The new plays of American character for 1837 were: *The Star Spangled Banner, or the American Tar's Fidelity,* announced as the first performance in Philadelphia after considerable success in New York; *A Down East Bargain, or Love in New York,* written by Moncrieff especially for Hill, the Yankee comedian; C. A. Logan's *Yankee Land;* and *Yankee Tar.*

One of the most pretentious melodramas for 1837 was N. H. Bannister's *Destruction of Jerusalem.* Durang gives us a good account of it. He tells us that this drama, which was so magnificently produced and ingenious in the novelty of its dramatic effects, seemed to be beyond the comprehension of the audience. The Evil Spirit, so opposed to the Good Spirit, as the theme of the play, was a mythical antithesis or a metaphysical distinction which the many-headed play-going public did not understand. Although Milton's poetical conception of Satan was an angel of beauty and light, and Goethe's Evil Spirit was fascinating to poor Margaret, still Durang claims that a like spiritual treatment of Evil in Bannister's play did not meet the popular conception of the vulgar mind that demanded a devil with horns, hoofs, and tail, with a serpent's head, and a hissing, forked tongue. Durang goes on to say that in this historical drama of events related in biblical as well as in profane history, no incident or reference was made to any particularized religious tenets, such as those of the Greeks, the Romans, the Hebrews, or the Christians. Yet a hue and cry was made against the drama as insulting to religion, a sacrilege, a profanity on the stage, and a contempt of all religious rites and ceremonies. All the press joined in the nonsensical halloo about the piece in a most stupid, fanatical chase. Such were the thoughtless denunciations upon the ill-fated *Destruction of Jerusalem* play, that Wemyss was forced to withdraw it after the sixth night.

Well, the comment of the present writer is that six nights did not constitute a bad run for a new play—for any play, in fact, in those days —and we wonder how much in money those six nights meant to Wemyss. Probably a good deal, probably a very respectable, successful amount. It is too bad for our curiosity, that we do not know the receipts, but, if scandalous advertisement affected the theatre-going public in those days in the same way that it does in the present age, one might suppose that the notoriety given to *Jerusalem* by the Church militant and the press scurrilous brought in very acceptable golden returns to Wemyss.

No, Durang in his account gives undue sympathy to Bannister—"Poor Bannister," as he calls the man. It is not everyone, you see, who can write a play to produce such grand free advertising.

Another new melodrama by Bannister this year was one called *Gaulantus, or the Last of the Gauls*. Another melodrama of the year was *The Prophet of St. Paul* in five acts, by David Paul Brown. Durang says the piece was butchered in production, but was acted to a receipt of $728. Other new melodramas for 1837 were: *The Battle of Sedgemoor, or the Days of Kirk and Monmouth; Faith and Falsehood, or the Fate of a Bushranger;* Mrs. H. Siddons' *Father and Son, or the Convent Ruins; The Fire-Raiser, or the Prophet of the Haunted Moor; Koeuba, or the Pirate of the Capes; North Pole, or a Tale of the Frozen Sea; Robber Chieftain; Siege of Missolonghi, or the Greek Patriots; Thalaba, or the Burning Sword;* and *Trial by Battle*.

The new comedies for the year included: *Confusion; Bravo of Venice; John Buzzby; Old English Gentleman; Pickwick Club; Rural Felicity;* and *Speculations*.

The new farces for the year included: *Barbers at Court; Barrack Room; Black and White; House Room; Ion Travestie; Jim Crow in London; Joe Miller; Middy Ashore; My Own Ghost; One Hour; Peculiar Position; Pleasant Neighbors; Rival Pages; Set a Beggar on Horseback; Ship Launch; La Sonnambula Travestie; Twice Killed;* and *Za Ze Zi Zo Zu*.

Tyrone Power, the Irish actor and playwright, appeared this year in a new musical fairy drama in three acts (as performed at the Theatre Covent Garden), called *O'Flannigan and the Fairies, or a Midsummer Night's Dream—not Shakespeare's*. The advertisement for it (from the *United States Gazette*), contains the following most fascinating explanation of the play:

There is hardly a lonely valley or wild mountain range in all Ireland that is not characterized by names denoting the residence of the Good People or Fairies; and the belief that those eflin inhabitants of earth and air occasionally condescend to interfere with mortals, either in mirth or in malice, still lingers amongst the peasantry; one of the most poetical of our national superstitions, and highly congenial to the temperament of an imaginative people. This drama, however, presents the Good People in dream only; the action of the piece from the time the Fairies appear, until the sleeping Flannigan awakes once more to a working world existing only in the creations of a wild fellow's brain, fired by whiskey, and disordered by hard blows. His imaginary perils and sufferings being at once the consequence of his intemperance, and the moral punishment of the relapsed whiskey lover.

Other new musical plays were: first time in America, *Don Juan,* a faithful translation of Mozart's opera; first time in America, a new grand operatic, legendary and romantic drama, called *One O'clock, or the Knight and the Wood Demon,* by Monk Lewis; *Pirate Boy,* a new melodramatic opera in three acts, written by J. B. Phillips, and musically arranged by J. Watson, director and composer at Covent Garden; and the *Two Figaros,* a new comic opera.

The new pantomimes for 1837 included; *Harlequin and the Magic Trumpet; Farmer's Son;* and *Grenadier.*

1838

N. H. Bannister contributed two new tragedies to the Walnut in 1838, one called *Caius Silius, or the Slave of Carthage,* advertised as a tragedy written expressly for Parsons, the actor; and the other, *Syracusan Brothers,* announced as a new tragedy written by several literary gentlemen of Philadelphia, but actually a play by Bannister. A third new tragedy for 1838 was one called *Velasco, or Castilian Honor,* by Epes Sargent of Boston.

The principal new romantic dramas for the year were: Bulwer's *Lady of Lyons;* Knowles' *Maid of Mariendorpt;* and S. S. Steele's *Clandare, or the Robber Clans of the Lochs.* Bannister also wrote one called the *Gentleman of Lyons,* but Durang says that it did not reap a fair profit. Other new romantic plays for the year were: *Child of Air; King's Command; Leila, or the Siege of Granada; Maiden's Vow;* and *Margaret's Ghost.*

The new domestic dramas for 1838 were: *The Mother; Law of the Land;* and *St. Mary's Eve.*

For the new melodramas, we have: *The Avenger of Blood, or Richard Hurdis and the Idiot Girl,* announced as a play from the book, a work by W. G. Simms; *The Battle of Poictiers, or the Knights of the Garter,* W. Barrymore's new historical drama written expressly for the Walnut; N. H. Bannister's *The Bush Whacker,* written expressly for Marble, the Yankee Comedian; *Friar's Oak; Henri and Louise, or the Two Murderers,* advertised as the first time in this country, a melodramatic sketch in one act, founded on a thrilling event registered in the *Causes Célèbres* of France, and departing in a very trifling degree from its awful termination; Lord Byron's *Mazeppa, and the Wild Horse;* and *Zameo, or the White Warrior.*

The new comedy of *Weak Points, or the Nice Young Man* by Buckstone was advertised as more successful in England than any piece of the season and as produced in Philadelphia from the only copy in this country, as the advertisement for it claims. Other new comedies of the season were: Knowles' *Love Chase; Boat Builder's Hovel; Good Husbands Make Good Wives; Love and Murder; Two Queens;* and *The White Horse of the Peppers.*

The new farces for the year of 1838 included the long list of: *Dancing Barber; Does Your Mother Know You're Out?; Impulse; Irish Lion; Life in Philadelphia; Manager's Daughter; A Match in the Dark; My Young Wife and My Old Umbrella; The Original; Patter versus Clatter; A Quiet Day; The Strange Gentleman; Tom Noddy's Secret; Trick for Trick; U and I; Will Watch;* and *The Yankee Duellist.*

Other new dramas of the year included the operettas of *Amilie, or the Love Test,* and *Dew Drop;* the national drama of *The Jesuit's Colony, or the Indian's Doom,* announced as written by a gentleman of Philadelphia; and the silent-action play of *Samuel Slick, or Love in the Far, Far West,* a comic ballet; *Soldier's Wife and Soldier's Widow;* and Wemyss' grand successful pageant and spectacle of the *Coronation of Queen Victoria,* which was modeled after Elliston's famous *Coronation of George the Fourth in London, 1820.*

1839

The new tragedies for 1839 included Isaac C. Pray's *Julietta Gordini, or the Miser's Daughter,* and Nathaniel Parker Willis' *Tortesa the Usurer.*

For the new romantic drama of the year, we have *Blanche of Navarre,* announced as a dramatization of James' novel of *Love.* Then there is Knowles' new yearly contribution, this time, *Love; Romanzo, or the Exile of Naples,* whose authorship is unknown; and *Gaspardo the Gondolier.*

For the new domestic drama of 1839, there is the dramatization of Charles Dickens' novel into the play of *Oliver Twist, or the Alms House Boy.* Dickens' novels were quickly dramatized. Apparently, since this process continued over several years, these dramatizations were successful. Usually there were many different dramatic versions for each book, done by men at the different theatres. Take, for example, *David Copperfield;* many tried a hand at dramatizing it, but the version of John Brougham is considered the best. Still, for the distant commentator, it is difficult to know whose dramatic version was being played when no name is given. It is the opinion of the present researcher that Wemyss dramatized the particular version of *Oliver Twist* which appeared at his Walnut, since he has many other dramatizations to his credit, such as *Norman Leslie, Captain Kyd,* and *The Jewess.* Another novelist who had numerous dramatizations was Sir Walter Scott. A glance at the Play-List will reveal many of his titles.

The new melodrama of the year was Bulwer's *Richelieu.* Durang has much to say about Wemyss' lavish production of it. No old stock scenes were used. The interior of the house of Madame de l'Orme was not set out with the usual mode in furniture of the eighteen thirties, but with that appropriate to the period of 1641. The room of the cardinal was splendidly painted and decorated with the heavy arras of gold-tissue figures used in that luxurious age. The gardens of the Louvre were taken from the facsimiles of the proper period. The Bastille and its corridors were painted from accurate views. All these historic localities were appropriately attended to, to make a play of admirable exactitude. This generous effort (to produce a play as it should be) cost Wemyss six hundred dollars in costumes alone, but the performances did not pay.

Jacques Strop (a *Robert Macaire* play) was also announced as an entirely new melodrama in three acts. And this year Wemyss produced, according to his statement, a new melodrama called *Captain Kyd, or the Wizard of the Sea,* which he claims that he dramatized from Ingraham's novel of that name. It succeeded well, and may be the play of J. S. Jones, originally produced in 1830.

Among the new comedies for 1839 were: *Evil Day; A Lesson for Ladies; Rafael the Libertine; The Scholar; Whigs and Democrats;* and *A Wife for a Day.* The only farce which the present writer is willing to advance as an entirely new play for 1839 was the one called *Jack's the Lad,* announced as a new nautical drama, adapted to the stage expressly for E. S. Conner, by C. Ferrars of New York. The new play of American Character in 1839 was Hill's vehicle of *Seth Slope, or Done for a Hundred.* W. R. Blake's *The Last Man* was also a new play this year. And the only new musical play for the year was a simple burletta by the name of *Souter Johnnie,* announced as its first production on any stage.

One should call particular attention to the singular production of Shakespeare's *Titus Andronicus* at the Walnut, January 30, 1839. The *United States Gazette,* in its theatrical column of the day, announces the performance as the first on any stage—the world première. Durang, in his account of the season, tells us that the hand of N. H. Bannister turned this work of Shakespeare into a beautiful play. What are we to believe from these two statements? It is the opinion of the present writer that the newspaper blurb which called this particular performance the world première was certainly wrong. No one will dispute that correction. Further, we offer this date of January 30, 1839, as the first professional performance of *Titus Andronicus* within the confines of Philadelphia.

It is with a tempering judgment that we must consider the statement of Durang concerning N. H. Bannister's alteration of *Titus* into a beautiful play. Not even Bannister could turn this singularly horrendous play into something akin to beauty, without changing and losing the identity of the original. However, Bannister at least succeeded in softening the Shakespearean horrors into a drama that ran for four nights.

1840

The first year of the new decade saw a profusion of new melodramas (which certainly usurped the stage for 1840) but no new tragedy.

Knowles contributed to our boards his yearly play, a romantic drama entitled *John Di Procida, or the Bridal of Messina.* The year gave us three national dramas: *The Frontier Maid,* written by Major Noah expressly for Mlle. Celeste; *The Lion of the Sea, or Our Infant Navy,* by Silas S. Steele; and *The Battle of Tippecanoe,* by S. S. Steele. W. E. Burton, this year, wrote a new domestic drama which was produced under the name of *Emigration, or the Progress of an Intemperate.*

Among the most spectacular of the melodramas for 1840 was *The Naiad Queen, or the Mystery of Lurlei Berg,* produced by Burton at his National. It was a play in three acts extremely well concocted from a melodrama called *Lurline, or the Spirit of the Rhine,* out of which Wemyss had made a new drama to oppose Celeste's *La Bayadere,* some seasons before, which he christened *The Maid of Cashmere.*

John Russell Smith painted a vast quantity of new scenes for *The*

Naiad Queen, all very beautiful. The Gothic halls were finely executed. The landscapes of the Rhine River were accurate and handsomely painted. One scene especially was truly magnificent and unique in conception, so Durang tells us. This was the Lurlie Grotto Baths. All the wings at the sides of the stage were removed entirely, and the stage, to the very side walls and back, was made to represent a circular Grotto. A staging ran around, close to this boundary, representing shelving coral and variegated golden and silver shells, whereon the nymphs reclined and thence plunged into the silvery waters, which occupied the center of the stage. It was like a lake, or an amphitheatre of stalactical forms. Around the margin of the waters, whereon these real nymphs or naiads gracefully floated, arose pyramids of red and other colored coral substances.

Other new melodramas for 1840 were: *The Dark Lady of Doona, or the Bride's Revenge,* in two acts, by W. E. Burton; *The Death Token, or the Murderer's Fate; The Ice Witch and the Sun Spirit, or the Frozen Hand; Peter Bell the Wagoner; The Provost of Paris, or the Truand Chief; Sadak and Kalasrade, or the Waters of Oblivion;* and *The Sixes, or the Devil's in the Dice.*

The new comedies for 1840 numbered: *Ben the Boatswain, or Sailors' Sweethearts; Le Preux Chevalier; Poor Jack; Romantic Widow; Ups and Downs, or Felix in Search of a Wife; Yankee Bill Sticker;* J. H. Payne's *Love in Humble Life;* and J. D. Burke's *The Inn at Abbeville.*

Among the farces, we have: *Curiosity Cured, or Powder for Peeping; Humbug; Is the Philadelphian Dead, or Is He Alive and Merry?; The Little Back Parlor;* and *Solomon Smink.*

Opera brings to us this year, *Die Brilleninsel* (The Isle of Spectacles), advertised as the first in this country, a German Opera written by Kotzebue, especially composed for the Philadelphia German Theatre (occupying the Arch, February 10) by Ferdinand Riemann; the German Opera of *The Swiss Family,* music by Weigh; and *The Postillion of Lonjumeau.* The comic ballet of *La Tarentule* in two acts, was also introduced to Philadelphia this year.

1841

Dion Boucicault's comedy of *London Assurance* made its appearance in Philadelphia in 1841, under striking conditions. The play came to Philadelphia, according to advertisement, after seventy-three nights at the Covent Garden, London, and four weeks at the Park, New York. Burton was preparing to produce it first, to assure himself the priority over the other Philadelphia theatres, and, in this plan, he did not expect any competition since his preparations were well under way. However, Flynn, the manager at the Walnut, was cunning enough to deceive Burton. Flynn advertised the fact that the Walnut was making elaborate preparations to produce *The Naiad Queen,* and Burton believed him— until November 6, 1841, when *The Naiad Queen* turned out to be *London Assurance.* Burton's own production at his National did not occur until November 15. Managerial strategy is apparently a many-headed Hydra.

Flynn announced *London Assurance* in an elaborate fashion. The stage was set with costly ottomans, cushions, chairs, superior imperial carpets with different and splendid patterns for each scene. The upholstery and draperies were of the finest and most expensive kind. Perfect and correct statuary was secured, and the garden scene was laid out with natural flowers, grass plots, with orange and lemon trees from the gardens of the first horticulturists of the city of Philadelphia.

But Burton still went Flynn one better. The furnishings for the stage of the National were even more gorgeous. The drawing room was illuminated by a splendid cut-glass chandelier, lighted with gas. The furniture supposedly manufactured expressly for this piece, was of the most costly description, of gold pattern with white, arabesque ornaments, according to the use of European palaces. The ottomans and lounges were covered with damask satin. The courtyard, park, and gardens were ornamented with a marble fountain of real water. An aviary of living birds, flower parterres, statues from the antiques, busts, vases, porcelain seats, and a tesselated pavement, completed the arrangements. The present cast was advertised by Burton as infinitely superior to that either of London or of New York, where its success established a new era in dramatic history. At the National (Burton's) in Philadelphia, the players were Browne, Conner, Buckstone, W. Jones, J. Wallack, Burton, Mrs. A. Sefton, Mrs. Fitzwilliam, and Miss Clifton.

London Assurance was followed, a month later, by a burlesque called *Philadelphia Assurance.* Another farce of the year, probably by Burton, was called *The New President.* H. H. Weld's comedy, *Easy Joe Bruce,* was new this year.

In melodrama, this year, we have the spectacular *Water Queen, or the*

Sprites of Donau, with splendid new scenery by P. Grain, Jr., and J. Wiser. It was supposed to be an old English melodrama of German origin, concocted out of the incidents of *Undine, Naiad Queen, Lurline,* and perhaps others of the same nature. One imposing scene in this drama came in the last act: a transparent sea. It was called on the bills, "A Tremendous Conflict Of The Adverse Elements," and was really a grand display of fairy illusion. There were five thousand jets of real water and six thousand jets of liquid fire, all at one time played in opposite directions in varied hues.

Other new melodramas for 1841 were *The Ocean Child; Rookwood,* by N. H. Bannister (so Durang tells us), adapted from Ainsworth's book; and *The Bank Monster* by S. S. Steele.

The new domestic dramas included: *Barnaby Rudge,* by Boz; *Sixteen Years Ago,* from the French; *Bill Stickers and the Jersey Girl;* and *Werner, or the Inheritance.*

For the new national dramas, there are the titles of *The First Fleet and the First Flag, or Our Navy in '76,* and J. S. Jones' *Siege of Boston, or the Sons of the Soil.*

1842

The two new tragedies that came to Philadelphia in 1842 were both foreign: *Nina Sforza,* advertised as its first performance in America, and *Walter Lynch, or the Warden of Galway,* likewise announced as a first appearance in America.

The two new domestic dramas for the year were *The Drunkard's Progress,* and *Marie du Cange,* a play with Mlle. Celeste.

The new national dramas included: *Washington, or the Hero of Valley Forge,* a military drama by James Rees of Philadelphia; and *Red Gauntlet.*

The new melodramas for 1842 were: *Amaldi, or the Brigand's Daughter,* first in America; *Mungo Park, or the Arab of the Niger;* and *Foreign Affairs, or the Court of Queen Anne.*

For the comedies, we have: *Charles O'Malley, or the Irish Dragoon; Ten Thousand a Year, or the History of Tittlebat Titmouse,* announced as a new play in four parts from the celebrated novel of that name, probably by Burton; *Something Original; The Banker, or a Friend in Need;* and *Peter and Paul, or the Mechanic and His Brother,* first time in America.

The new farces were: *Hobbs, Dobbs, and Stubs, or the Three Temperance Grocers,* a new farce never acted in America before; *My Wife's Dentist;* and the *Rise of the Rothschilds.*

A very spectacular, costly, and unique introduction this year was the new pantomime of *The Black Raven of the Tombs.* Its story hinged upon the adventures of the lovers, Flodoardo and Marie. The Signor Montano, a notorious roué, attempts to gain the affections of Marie and, for this purpose, makes a pretended visit of condolence to the chamber of her sick mother, Alice. Alice, however, on perceiving the drift of his visit, indignantly orders him and his valet, Noucum, from the house; then, exhausted by the exertion, blesses her child and dies. Determined to gain possession of the lovely maiden, Montano takes the opportunity when, with filial affection, Marie is strewing flowers over her mother's grave, to have her seized and conveyed to his castle. Flodoardo, hearing of the outrage, charges Montano and his valet with it. They overpower him, and shut him up in the cemetery behind locked gates. The Black Raven flies to his relief, presents him with a magic branch and instructs him how to proceed. The remainder of the piece is composed of numerous escapes by the lovers from the continued persecutions of Montano, until, at length, a dreadful punishment overtakes him.

The scenes of the pantomime were twelve, as follows: (1) Chamber of Alice, (2) Cemetery and Mysterious Tombs, the haunt of the Black Raven, (3) Magnificent Gothic Ball Room, brilliantly illuminated, (4) Outside of a Restaurant, (5) Market Place, (7) Exterior of a Turkish Harem! Mummies! Statues! and Flight of Brazen Dragon! (9) A Street, (10) Inside of a Hotel, (11) Rocky Mountain Pass! Mysterious Appearance of the Black Raven! (12) Pandemonium! Last scene—Magnificent Cloud Palace of the Black Raven. Dreadful punishment of the guilty on a Revolving Wheel of Fire! Grand Tableau!

1843

A new domestic drama of great interest in 1843 was *Gabrielle or a Night's Hazards,* translated from the French of Dumas' *Mademoiselle de Belle-Isle* and adapted to the English stage by J. M. Field. It was announced as a French piece full of the effective claptraps of the stage, natural and unnatural. In such dramas felicity of language in phrases, playfulness in application to passing events, and repartee caused piquant and telling points to be made. The piece was quite a success, abounding in vivid and racy characters, blended with the heroics of French sentiment.

The prime new melodrama for 1843 was the *Mysteries of Paris*. The novel of the same name had just come out and was in every reader's hand from youth to age. All were struck with the vivid painted language of the horrible, thrilling scenes of Parisian society among princes and canaille. As usual, the managers were not unmindful of the excitement thus produced in the reading world. Wemyss dramatized the *Mysteries of Paris* to the stage in the form of a melodrama of the romantic kind, where thunder roared, lightning flashed, and mock human blood flowed in the kennel. By a curious device, the moon's rays were made at night to reflect the blood of humanity mantling the waters of the Seine. We are told that the multitude gaped at it in wonder.

In order that Wemyss might not be forestalled by the other theatrical managers in the dramatization of the new novel, three persons were secretly employed to do it into a drama in twenty-four hours, and it was thus produced by sleight of hand in three days. Actors studied their parts; scenery was painted and ready. It proved successful. F. C. Wemyss dramatized the first act, James Gann the second, and John Sefton, the third.

Other new melodramas of the year were the *Gold Bug* and the *Ruby Ring*. J. M. Field's *The Artful Dodger* and J. P. Addams' *Redwood* made their appearance. The new plays of American character for 1843 included: *Nick of Time: Sam Patch in France;* and *The Market Street Merchant. The Boston Tea Party* was a new anonymous play this year. A new pantomime is to be mentioned: *Harlequin and the Ocean Nymph.*

1844

Just as the prime melodrama for 1843 had Paris as its background, so did the most interesting melodrama of 1844 have Paris for its locale. *The Bohemians, or the Rogues of Paris* was a drama by E. Sterling, author of *Nicholas Nickleby*. The following is Durang's account of it from the seventy-third chapter of his history, third series:

There are many "Bohemians" in Paris. "Bohemians" is the name applied to that class of individuals whose existence is a problem, their conditions and their fortunes an enigma, having no resting place—who are never to be found, and yet to be seen everywhere—who have no trade, yet live in professions, the greater number of whom rise without knowing where they shall dine—rich today and dying tomorrow with hunger—ready to live honestly, if they can, and otherwise, if they can not. It is estimated that there are ten thousand of them in Paris.

The time of action was 1842; the place Paris. The unities of the classic drama are most decidedly outraged in these revolting melodramas. What says Voltaire on the unities? What is a dramatic piece? The representation of one action. Why of one and not of two or three? Because the human mind cannot take in so many objects at once; because the interest which is divided is soon destroyed. In a picture two different events offend the sight. Nature has taught us the sense which ought to be as immutable as herself. The unity of place is essential for the same reason, for one single action cannot be transacting in many places at the same time. If the personages we see are at Athens in the first act, how can they be in Persia in the second? Has Le Brun painted Alexander at Arbella and in the Indies on the same canvas? The unity of time is naturally joined to the two others, *par example:* A conspiracy is formed against Augustus at Rome. I wish to know what is about to happen to Augustus and the conspirators. If the poet makes the action continue fifteen days, he ought to inform us what has passed during that time. We want to be informed of what passes. The unity of time is often extended to twenty-four hours, and the unity of place to the circumference of a place, etc. We do not wish to dwell upon this to any length. However, Dr. Johnson, in his preface to Shakespeare, answers these objections to the violation of the unities by the Bard of Avon with very cogent reasons of a common sense nature. The construction of *Julius Caesar,* for instance, assumes great latitude as to time, to place, etc. Brutus and Cassius are at Rome in the first act, and and in Thessaly in the fifth act.

In *The Bohemians,* some very well painted scenes were given by Grain, Jr., of Paris and its environs, from accurate views. They embraced the Pont Marie; the River Seine with all its stereotyped architectural historical objects; the home of the Bohemians, "Those spiders of civilization, who spread their nets to catch dupes," was a very graphic representation of these dens of mixed up miseries and bacchanalian carousal. The quarries of Montmarte; the heights overlooking Paris; the bivouac of the Bohemians, etc.; were all very effective scenes, and helped the piece in its many-colored illustrations of Parisian life.

Another new melodrama of the year was of the *El-Hyder* variety. It was called *Yara the Gypsy* and receives an account from Durang in the seventieth chapter of his history, third series:

We remember this piece contained several very beautiful landscape scenes, one especially painted in detached scenes, with a very fine terminating view of mountain ranges, occupying the entire depth of the stage. This scene was designed and painted by John Wiser, then a young artist. It deserves a record.

It was a battle scene by moonlight, after a bloody struggle, picturing piles of slaughtered soldiers strewed over the plain and the sloping hills in various positions, with horses lying dead by their wounded riders. The débris of arms, the cannon dismounted from their carriages, broken wheels, with the camps in the distance in smouldering ashes. These presented a pictorial war scene of repose, after a terrible contest of a most thrilling nature. The effect of the moon's beams falling on the dead and their arms, tinging out each group and objects with its silvery light, imparted to the picture, and therefore to the spectator's eye, a most impressive view of battle subjects under such a phase. The awful silence and dread repose that succeeds after an engagement of great carnage, viewed, too, under the benign light of the Heavenly bodies in their calmest state, most deeply impresses the mind and heart of man with the horrors of war, and irresistibly makes him deprecate the rash causes, however justified, which lead and urge to such demoniac demonstrations.

Other new melodramas for 1844 were the *Dancing Feather, or Secrets of Life in New York,* and T. D. English's *The Doom of the Drinker.*

New romantic dramas of the year were *Lochinvar,* and S. S. Steele's *The Grecian Queen.* The new national dramas were *Putnam, or the Eagle Eye and the Hand of Steel,* and *Mad Anthony, or the Pennsylvania Line.* Comedy was served by the new plays of *Handy Andy, The Love Gift,* and T. D. English's *Gammon and Galvinism.* And pantomime was represented by *Munchausen,* first time in America, so announced.

1845

New plays this year included the romantic drama of *Eva, The Page,* the domestic dramas of *Oregon, or the Emigrant's Dream* and S. S. Steele's *Emilie Plater,* and the melodrama of Burke's *Murrell the Land Pirate.* Among the new historical dramas we must place the following for 1845: *The Battle of Germantown, or a Tale of Tracy's Rangers; A Veteran;* W. M. Leman's *Freedom's Last Martyr; The Declaration of Independence;* and General Harlon's *The Fall of Kessichack.*

The comedy of greatest significance this year was Mrs. Mowatt's s cial satire of *Fashion, or Life in New York,* which pointed a finger of scorn at people who try to ape the outward forms of high society without knowing the inward reasons and values for them. In this comedy, a wealthy American family, or, principally the mother of that family, apes the modes and mannerisms of Paris. It is interesting to note that in our first social satire, *The Contrast,* the people imitated the modes and mannerisms of London. By the time of Barker's *Tears and Smiles* in

1817, America had shifted from Anglomania to Francomania in its search for the latest word which is fashion.

Just as a literary imitator so frequently reproduces only the foibles and eccentricities of the writer whom he imitates, so also the social imitator usually reproduces imperfectly the customs which he seeks to imitate. In her *Autobiography,* Mrs. Mowatt laments this imperfect reproduction of French manners by American would-be's when she speaks of the custom of abolishing formal introductions at large social assembles:

The custom is intended to obviate the ceremoniousness of formal introductions. Every one is expected to talk to his neighbor, and if mutual pleasure is received from the intercourse, an acquaintance is formed. The same fashion in vogue with us renders society cold and stiff. Few persons feel at liberty to address strangers. Little contracted circles of friends herd in clannish groups together and mar the true object of society.

Also in her *Autobiography,* Mrs. Mowatt says: "The critics who condemned *Fashion* seemed to hold my Country responsible for its short comings. Those who awarded the meed of praise, in turn bestowed their eulogiums upon America, as due to her through one of her children."

Edgar A. Poe, in one of his pungent, queer, critical remarks, said of *Fashion* that "it resembled *The School for Scandal* in the same degree that the shell of a locust resembles the living locust." Charles Durang, in the eighty-sixth chapter of his history, third series, comments upon this remark of Poe's by saying: "Then, as the authoress accounts for its success, the performers must have infused their spirit into the shell, and gave it the life of that chirping insect."

Other new comedies for 1845 were: Dion Boucicault's *Old Heads and Young Hearts; Change Makes Change* (in which Mrs. Mowatt herself acted); *Monseigneur, or the Paris Robbers in 1720;* and D. W. Jerrold's *Time Works Wonders.*

A farce of interest was W. E. Burton's *Fashion, or How to Write a Comedy,* in which he scored a tremendous hit at the expense of Mrs. Mowatt.

1846

The period of 1846 was a slim year in the production of new plays of any account. *The King of the Commons* was a new play for 1846, probably a romantic drama. The author, James White, a Scottish clergyman, was the writer of other dramas, but they were not adapted for stage representation. Romantic also was George Hielge's *Montezuma*.

For the national drama, we have Walter M. Leman's *Prairie Bird, or a Child of the Delawares,* and the play of *Swamp Fox, or Marion and His Merry Men.* Among the farces and comedies we must note the new ones of *Arcade; Crimson Crimes;* E. Fitzball's *Home Again;* J. B. Buckstone's *The Bear Hunters; Did You Ever Send Your Wife to Germantown?;* and *Did You Ever Send Your Wife to Burlington?* The *Germantown* farce originated with Burton at his Arch Street Theatre, where it won popular applause. (Burton was playing farces almost exclusively at the Arch this year.) And the Burlington farce was very likely an attempt at the Walnut to cash in on the popularity of the *Germantown* farce which had appeared at the Arch a week before.

Balfé's new operatic, scenic drama, *The Enchantress,* in three acts came to Philadelphia for the first time in 1846, and received the plaudits of the theatre-goers.

1847

The year of 1847 was again a period of comparative dearth in the production of new plays in Philadelphia. *The Cavalier,* with C. D. Pitt and Mrs. Burke, was a new play of the year, probably a romantic drama. *The Secret Pamphlet, or the Ups and Downs of a Printer,* and *Who's the Composer?* formed the extent of the new comedies for 1847. The new farces were *Cerro Gordo; Actor and Heiress; Wrong Passenger;* and *Native Nobility.*

There was considerable operatic activity this year, with the Seguins and Frazer at the Chesnut where several seasons of opera were given. The new operas launched in Philadelphia this year were: Vincent Wallace's *Maritana;* and Adolph Adam's *Brewer of Preston;* and *The Chalet.* Another new play this year was *The Crock of Gold* by H. M. Ward.

1848

The year of 1848 saw renewed theatrical activity in the production of new plays. For tragedy, we have the three new plays of *Genevieve; Octavia Bragaldi;* and *Love's Martyr.* For domestic drama, the new plays of *John Savile of Haysted; Dombey and Son;* and *The Fireman's Daughter* were introduced.

[77]

The year of 1848 brought to Philadelphia the new national drama of *The Forest Princess, or Two Centuries Ago,* by Mrs. C. B. Conner. It was an historical drama in three acts, of blank verse, founded on the life of Pocahontas. The historical characters were well preserved and graphically delineated. There follows a brief outline of the scenes: Part I. Scene—America, in Wingandocoa, the land of Powhatan, named Virginia by Sir Walter Raleigh. Time, 1607. Part II. Scene—America, in the country of Powhatan. Time 1609. Part III. Scene—England, in London and at Gravesend. Time 1609. The death of Pocahontas, exclaiming—

> I lose thee now,
> My eyes behold Virginia's grassy turf—
> I hear my father. Husband, fare thee well!
> We part—but we shall meet above!

Another new national drama for 1848 was called *Three Eras in Washington's Life.*

Anent the production of the new classical play, *Horatii and the Curiatii,* by Burton, March 21, 1848, Charles Durang tells us a very interesting story in the ninetieth chapter of his history, third series:

There was a lady of Philadelphia who wrote a play upon this subject of Roman history, with the combat of the brothers introduced. This play was given to Mr. Burton, some months before, to peruse and to accept. The lady's play was kept for some time before any opinion or decision was given by Burton, although he was urged to do so; the answer being the usual one from theatrical cabinets: "Not having leisure to finish the reading." But to the authoress' astonishment, one day she saw the subject announced for performances on March 22d [really March 21st], as written or dramatized by Burton himself (of course, *sub rosa*). The lady seated herself in the theatre on the first night, and she had the mortification to see her principal stage incidents taken— or those of her play; all the effective points called, with various scenes, and speeches almost literally taken from Knowles' *William Tell.* The play that was thus offered in good faith to Mr. Burton was a very effective drama, and well written. Certainly, it did not deserve the cavalier fate it received from the autocracy of a manager's tribunal whence there is no appeal. He had the right to refuse the play as the great Garrick refused the tragedy of *Douglass* before him; but it was a gross injustice to take the idea, the plot, and its general composition, by the lady, and then serve it up as a melodramatic rehash, with plagiarized condiments. Her labors deserved at least courtesy. We suppose he did the deed upon the principle that "Heaven sends good meat, but the devil sends cooks." Therefore, the meat being good, the thought struck him, he would dress it himself.

The new comedies for the year included: *Pride of the Market; Exiles of Erin; O'Donoghue; Romance and Reality; Volunteers; Departure and Return; The Millionaire; Old Honesty;* and *Philadelphia in Spots.*

The most interesting farce of the year was William E. Burton's *A Glance at Philadelphia* which he fashioned from B. A. Baker's *A Glance at New York.* Charles Durang in the ninety-first chapter of his history, third series, gives us a timely account of it:

Burton in this matter adapted the piece to the racy, vulgar character of our Jakey classes with much *gout.* He, therefore, rehashed or boiled it in his own witty cauldron, although the various spices which gave a pungent flavor to this coarse dish of "all sorts" may have been sprinkled over it by J. Owens, T. Johnson, and others *incog.* Be this as it may, it proved a merry standing repast for the Arch Street Theatre for an entire season. It proved a fortunate *Glance* of attraction to "Billy" Burton, and led him soon to Palmo's [i.e., Palmer's] Opera House at New York.

There was new scenery of a local character painted for the piece by George Hielge: View of the State House; and the Court Houses; Chesnut Street Wharf; the old Market Houses; noted places in Southwark, and the Northern Liberties; Moyamensing Prison; Barrett's Gymnasium in Market Street; Prosser's Restaurant; and the United States Hotel.

Other new farces for the year of 1848 included: *Box and Cox; Box, Cox and Knox; Sprigs of Laurel; Down among the Dead Men; Some Things can be Done as Well as Others; Mose's Visit to Philadelphia; Poor Pillicoddy;* and *The Eighth of January.*

This year there was produced a new melodramatic opera in three acts, called *Il Giuramento* [The Oath], with music by Mercadante and words by Gaetano Rossi. Others new plays were *Jacob Leisler* by Cornelius Mathews, and two plays about a visiting foreign actress, *Lola Montez or Catching a Governor,* and *Lola Montez or Countess for an Hour.*

1849

The new tragedies of 1849 were *Walter Raymond* and *Strathmore.* The new romantic dramas for the year included: *Flowers of the Forest; Wardock Kennilson;* and *Orange Girl of Venice. Madelaine; Time Tries All;* and *Mary Melwyn* constituted the new domestic dramas for 1849. The new historical drama for the year was *Benjamin Franklin, or the Days of 1776.*

The most important melodrama for the year was *The Count of Monte Cristo,* dramatized by George H. Andrews of New York from the novel by Alexander Dumas. The melodramatic music was supplied by Roberts of the Broadway Theatre; the glees by Dr. W. P. Cunnington; the dances by Schmidt, ballet master of the Arch; the scenery by Peter Grain, Jr.; the machinery by A. Wilson; appointments by Robinson; and costumes by H. Watson.

Other melodramas of the year were: *The Venetian; Twin Brothers of the Blood Red Cross; Eagle Eye; Horse of the Prairie; Idiot of the Mill;* and *Hand of Cards.*

This year there was a profusion of one certain kind of American-type drama: the *Mose and Jakey* melodramas. Among these was *New York As It Is,* by B. A. Baker. As much of an idea of it as any one of us today would desire to have can be obtained from a short sketch of the scenes, to wit: A view of Chatham Square Theatre, interior of a soup house, a boxing scene à la Tom and Jerry, Catharine Street Fish and Clam Market, Chatham Street, a Ladies' Gymnasium, and the grand finale of the Old Brewery in flames. Mose and his fire company arrive. He dashes into the building and appears at the window with a child in his arms. "My chee-ild! She is saved! Thank God!" Grand tableaux. Curtain.

The Mysteries and Miseries of New York came to Philadelphia, also, this year. It was an adaptation by H. P. Grattan of "Ned Buntline's" novel of the same name (see Ireland, II, 533), and was another of the many attempts to apotheosize the darling of the gods and the firemen, Mose, the home-town boy. Of course, every city had its own Mose, and these plays went the whole gamut of the cities and were easily adapted to local surroundings by the mere substitution of different place names.

Mose and Jakey (In Philadelphia), or the United Fire Boys, by T. B. Johnston, was rather low in moral content or rather, more strongly, immoral. Moral content was never a high feature in the *Mose and Jakey* plays, but in this one particularly it was totally absent. The Bowery boys visit the Philadelphia Jakeys, consisting of fast men, genteel and low loafers, pickpockets, and men leaving their wives to live with "the gals." The company was certainly not very choice.

Fistimania, or the Man who Saw the Fight was a new Jakey sketch by William E. Burton this year and, according to Durang, netted him ten thousand dollars. Other *Mose and Jakey* plays for the year were *Mose in China; Mose in California; Mose and Jakey's Visit to the Chesnut;* and *Jakey's Visit to California.*

The new comedies for 1849 included *Court and City; Lavater; Delusion; Three Wives of Madrid; The Miser of Philadelphia; O'Grady; Knight of Arva; Matchwoman of Philadelphia;* and *The Serious Family.*

One of the extravaganzas of the year was called *The Empire of Hayti, or King Craft in 1852.* It was written by Thomas Dunn English and was, presumably, a farce. One of the characters in it, "Victoria the Last," was announced on the program as "sensible but severe, who is not felt when she reigns, but is mist when she mizzles."

Other new farces were: *Slasher and Crasher; Monte Cristy; Chloroform; Mr. and Mrs. Macbeth; Where's Barnum?; Pierre Gamouche; John Dobbs; Taken in and Done for; A Wonderful Woman; Mammon and Gammon; Irish Secretary; Philadelphia Directory;* and *Mental Electricity.*

1850

The year of 1850, the beginning of the new decade, again found considerable activity in the theatres in the production of new plays. *Virginia* was the new tragedy of the year, with Miss Davenport in the title rôle. Romantic drama was represented this year by three new plays.

The Duke's Wager was announced as an adaptation from M. Emile Augier's play of *Gabrielle* and A. Dumas' *Maid of Belle Isle,* being the same popular story as the recently successful drama of Mrs. Frances Ann Kemble.

King René's Daughter seemed to be a romantic drama of note, and the story of it is interesting, for King René's daughter is a blind girl, who, purposely kept in seclusion by her father, has been ignorant of her infirmity until a strange cavalier, who falls in love with her, makes her acquainted with it. The following speech, delivered in reply to a question concerning the use of her eyes is representative of the poetic quality of the piece:

> You ask of what avail—how can you ask?
> And yet I ne'er have given the matter thought.
> My eyes! My Eyes! 'Tis easy to perceive,
> At eve, when I am weary, slumber first
> Droops heavy on my eyes, and thence it spreads
> O'er all my body, with no thought of mine.
> Thus, then, I know my eyes avail me much.
> When I had pined for many tedious days
> Because my father was detained from home,
> I wept for very gladness when he came!

[81]

Through tears I gave my bursting heart relief,
And at my eyes, I found a gushing vent.
Then never ask me unto what avail
Omnipotence hath gifted me with eyes.
Through them, when I am weary, comes repose;
Through them, my sorrow lightened, and through them
My joy is raised to rapture!

When her father tries to explain to her the nature of sight, she says:

Oh, father! these are wondrous words to me!
Incomprehensible! Explain one thing to me!
I, with my eyes, it seems, should grasp the world.
Yon stranger, too, who lately was with me,
And whose strange words are stamped so deeply here,
He spoke of sight. What is it, then, to see?
Can I, oh! father, *see* his *voice*, which touch'd
My soul with joy and sadness? Can I see
With these, mine eyes the nightingale's thick note,
Whereon I've *mused* so oft, and vainly striven
To follow it in thought, away, away?
Or is her song a flower, whose fragrant breath
I know, but not its root, and stem and leaves?

A most important romantic drama of the year was the play in five acts by G. H. Boker, called *The Betrothal*. The newspaper advertisement announced it as a piece "wherein he [Boker] has moulded the Dramatis Personae for the express capabilities of each representative." For an excellent critical account of this play, see Dr. Arthur Hobson Quinn's book, *A History of the American Drama from the Beginning to the Civil War*.

The new national dramas of the year were *Eddystone Elf, or the Fiend of the Rock, General Washington,* and *Oua Cousta, the Lion of the Forest,* founded on events during the French and English Wars in America, by N. H. Bannister. It was a *Metamora* painting throughout, and thought by many to be superior to that drama.

The melodramas for 1850 were numerous. *Democracy and Aristocracy, or the Rich and Poor of New York* gave representations of a number of the low dens of vice and immorality in the city. The last scene portrayed the poor man's cottage showing the rich man's oppression and the eventual conquest of the right. The keynote of the play may be expressed in the sentence: "The rich may be exceeding poor, and the poor exceeding rich."

The Mysteries and Miseries of Philadelphia was another *Mose and*

Jakey melodrama fashioned after *The Mysteries and Miseries of New York.*

Other new melodramas for 1850 were: *Morgan the Jersey Wagoner; Kit Karson, or the Hero of the Prairie; Zindel, or the Brothers of the Burning Belt; El Melechor; Struggle for Life and Death; Knight of the Lion Heart, or Golden Days of Chivalry; Rose of Ettrick Vale, or the Bridal on the Border; Pride of Birth;* and *Roman Tribute, or Attilla the Hun; Life in Alabama;* and John Brougham's *David Copperfield.*

The new comedies for 1850 included: *The Philadelphia Fireman, or the Chesnut Street Heiress; Leap Year, or the Ladies' Privilege; Extremes; Grub, Mudge and Company; The Trumpeter's Wedding; Changes; Delicate Ground,* announced as the most successful drama that has been written for ten years; *Adrienne the Actress; Catspaw; Irish Honor; Retribution; Irish Fortune Hunter; Giralda;* and S. D. Johnson's *In and Out of Place.*

Another *Mose and Jakey* farce for 1850 was *The Ship['s] Carpenter of Kensington.* Other farces for the year were: *Paddy's Trip to America; High life in Philadelphia; No. 333 Locust Street; Maharajah Surovy Seing, or the Irish M. D.; Tipperary Legacy; Live Indian; Platonic Attachment; Nettlewig Hall;* and *Family Ties.*

The Captive was a very pathetic musical drama adapted to music and to the stage by Mrs. C. B. Conner. The scene of it passes in a private madhouse where the captive lady is confined by a tyrannical husband who, in order to gain possession of her estates, has induced her relatives to believe she is in reality insane.

1851

Among the new tragedies produced on the Philadelphia stage in 1851 was Boker's *Calaynos,* which is Spanish in setting. *Valeria, or the Roman Sisters,* was another tragedy of the year, adapted, according to Durang, to the stage for Miss Davenport by an American author. Other new tragedies of the year were *Caecinna* and *The Indian Queen.*

Harvest Home was a new domestic drama in 1851, and *Philip de France and Marie de Meranie,* a new historical play.

Mrs. Mowatt's romantic drama of *Armand, or the Peer and the Peasant* reached Philadelphia for the first time in 1851, with Mrs. Mowatt herself playing the part of the heroine, Blanche. Another new romantic piece, *Ingomar the Barbarian* came to America for the first time in 1851. It was a German play translated by Mrs. Lovell. Another new romantic play of the year was E. Forrester's *Student of Morlaix.*

A new play this year in which Mrs. Conner had a hand was *Charlotte Corday,* translated and adapted by her from Lamartine's *Histoire des Girondins* and the French drama of *Charlotte Corday,* by M. M. Dumanoir and Clairville, the performance of which was prohibited by Louis Napoleon on account of its advocacy of liberty and republicanism.

The new comedies for the year included: *The Old Love and the New; Love in a Maze; Major Jones' Courtship;* and *The World a Mask,* this last play being a social satire by George Henry Boker. Boker's forte was romantic tragedy, and not social satire. For an account of this play, see Dr. Arthur Hobson Quinn's book, *A History of the American Drama from the Beginning to the Civil War.*

The new farces for the year were: *My Friend in the Straps; Sent to the Tower; School for Tigers; The Teacher Taught; The Chisel;* and *Three Cuckoos.* Additional news plays were *Brian O'Lynn* by S. D. Johnson, and *Shandy Maguire* by James Pilgrim.

1852

A tragedy of importance for 1852 was the new historical and romantic play of *De Soto,* written expressly for J. E. Murdoch by G. H. Miles of Baltimore. Part of the manuscript of this play is in the library of the University of Pennsylvania. Philadelphia gave the play its first performance on any stage. Charles Durang in the one hundred and sixth chapter of his history of the Philadelphia stage, third series, quotes the following passage from a Spanish historian, apropos of the play:

Ye shall sheath me in my mail, with my helmet on my head, and my spur on my heel! With my sword in my hand shall ye bury me, and with a banner of Castile for my shroud! In the depths of the river— of my river—shall ye bury me, with lighted torch and volleyed musketry at the midnight hour.

Scenery for the play was provided by J. Parker and R. Smith, and costumes by F. Johnson. There were some fifteen new scenes painted for the drama, principally views of the Floridas and the Mississippi River. The dénouement—the last scene—was very imposing and solemnly grand. The view of the Mississippi, painted by R. Smith, and the *Te Deum* and grand tableaux illustrating Powell's great natural picture, *The Burial of De Soto,* excited much approbation.

Another new tragedy of the year was *Helos the Helot.*

The Painter of Brienne was a new romantic play in three acts, written expressly for the Walnut Street Theatre, by a gentleman of Philadelphia. This piece was founded upon events which graphically illustrated many of the famous people who figured during the dynasty of the first Napoleon in the most thrilling and interesting times of his life, in 1804 and 1805. This new drama had a successive and successful run of four nights.

Among other new plays for 1852 were the national drama of *Scott and Pierce* and the domestic drama of *Edith.* The new comedies included: *The Custom of the Country; Ladies' Battle; The Fast Man;* and *The Fireman's Bride.* The new farces were: *I've Eaten My Friend; A Duel in the Dark; Who Stole the Pocket Book?; Our Clerks; The Youth who Never Saw a Woman;* and *A Row at the Chesnut.*

1853

A new tragedy of importance, in 1853, was Boker's *Leonor de Guzman,* a play with a Spanish setting. *Camille, or the Fate of a Coquette,* was played for the first time in America in our city this year. It was taken from a French drama which had an unprecedented run in Paris for more than a year. It was adapted to the stage in English perhaps by (but certainly for) Miss Jean Margaret Davenport, or by John Wilkins, author of the comedy of *Civilization.* The version of the play in English was entirely divested of all the immoral, objectionable features of the French drama and so modified as to become an entertainment of virtuous instruction. *Myrna Alwynn,* a play in five acts, was another new tragedy this year.

Bleak House and *The Curate's Daughter* were new domestic dramas for 1853. But the play which overshadowed everything else this year was a melodrama that caught the tide of public favor and swept along for decades.

On September 26, 1853, the Chesnut Street Theatre opened, one might say, with a new dramatic epoch for Philadelphia in the first performance of the great original drama of *Uncle Tom's Cabin, or Life among the Lowly,* dramatized from Mrs. Harriet Beecher Stowe's world-renowned work, by G. L. Aiken. It was composed of six acts, ten tableaux, and thirty scenes. The new scenery was by Joseph Parker; overture and new music by Mueller; stage direction and production, by Addis.

The following scenes, taken from southern scenes and painted by Joseph Parker, were particularly effective: 1, Uncle Tom's Cabin by moonlight; 2, Rocky Pass near the Ohio; 3, The Ohio filled with ice; 4, St. Clair's Mansion and Garden; 5, Little Eva's Bower; 6, The Slave Mart; 7, Uncle Tom's Shed; 8, Allegory—Eva in Heaven.

Its success was unbounded. For twenty-five successive nights the houses were filled to capacity, and this one play did, perhaps, as much as any other instrument of antislavery tendency to stimulate public sentiment against the abuses of the southern system of captive labor.

At this writing (1934), the play has been a part of American life for almost eighty years, since, during all those years, some company somewhere in the United States has been playing the famous old drama. Generations after generations of Americans have been acquainted with *Uncle Tom's Cabin* as the first of their dramatic fare. Countrymen in the far provinces who never heard of Broadway and the current drama of their day, received their only knowledge of the theatre from *Uncle Tom's Cabin* as presented to them by some barnstorming company in some little tank town.

Many an actor of note today recalls fondly that one of his first and small rôles was that of a minor character in *Uncle Tom's Cabin*. *Uncle Tom's Cabin* is the universal example of a popularly accepted propaganda play that has become a classic in theatrical history, despite the fact that it is merely a thesis play full of sentimentality. By some marvel of time and quirk of circumstance, its word has become life and its story has become legend.

The White Slave of England, or the Age We Live In was another new melodrama of 1853. It professed to be an answer to *Uncle Tom's Cabin*.

The new comedies for the year included: *Sea and Land; Drumming; Dick the Newsboy; Nationalities;* and *A Cure for Coquettes*. The new farces for 1853 were *Madame Anna Bishop in the Provinces; Irish Americans; Going to the Races;* and *Whitebait at Greenwich*. There was this year a new dramatic opera, called *Florentine, or the Pride of the Canton,* in two acts. The libretto was written by Mrs. Sheridan Mann expressly for Miss Caroline Richings. Other new plays were *Masks and Faces* by Charles Reade, *Our Jemima* by H. J. Conway, and the anonymous compositions of *The Battle of Buena Vista, The Black Rangers,* and *Irish Assurance and Yankee Modesty*.

1854

A curious new melodrama in 1854 was *Hot Corn, or Little Katy,* a story by Solon Robinson based upon low life in New York. The book became sensational and was read avidly. C. W. Tayleure dramatized it and retained its original title. The play was (so-called) "a religious and moral drama," and had some twenty-four characters. It was full of thrilling scenes of low life, dissipation, crime, and death. Little Katy's death was painfully affecting. There was a Grand Allegory attached to it. The spirit of little Katy ascended to Heaven in a cloud of light, attended by groups of seraphs floating upwards to realms of bliss, attended by strains of melody. The play was what actors call a gag piece.

Cabin and Parlor, or a Picture on the Other Side of Jordan to Uncle Tom's Cabin, another new melodrama, was dramatized by B. Young from the popular novel of that name. Its purpose was to reflect the opposite opinions to those contained in *Uncle Tom's Cabin.* Other new melodramas in 1854 were *The Irish Sibyl and the Rebel Chief,* founded on a story of the rebellion of 1798, and *Plot and Passion.* John Wilkins' play of *St. Marc,* which came to Philadelphia in 1854, was also probably a melodrama.

There were several new American comedies this year. J. Austin Sperry's *Life in the West, or Playing False* was a new American comedy in five acts. This year, also, saw the Philadelphia production of *The Game of Life,* another comedy in five acts, by John Brougham. Buckstone's new comedy, in one act, *The Maid with the Milking Pail, or the Speaking Likeness* received its first Philadelphia performance in 1854. *Colombe's Birthday* was another new comedy of the year.

Kenneth, or the Weird Woman of the Glen, was a new romantic play, dramatized by N. B. Clark from W. M. Reynolds' celebrated romance. *A Legend of the Chesnut Street Theatre,* a new play for 1854, might have been a romantic play, but it is very difficult to tell from the title alone.

The domestic drama of *Griselda, or the Patient Woman* was new to Philadelphia. It was advertised as a play taken from the German of Halm by Auguste Waldauer, and adapted to the English stage by J. M. Field. *The Irish Yankee, or the Birthday of Freedom,* by John Brougham, was advertised as a new national drama. A new Christmas pantomime for the year, *Fortunio and His Seven Gifted Servants,* was a fairy extravaganza in two acts, founded on a popular nursery tale by the Countess D'Anois, and dramatized by J. R. Planche. The new farces included: *Trying It On;* *A Storm in a Tea Cup;* and *The Recusant.* D. Boucicault's *Love and Money* appeared this year as a new play.

1855

The new comedies for 1855 included: *A New Comedy of Errors; Take That Girl Away; Still Waters Run Deep; The Man of Many Friends;* and *Apollo in New York.* There was a new Indian Legendary drama in three acts, this year, called *Magnolia, or the Child of the Flower.* The *Egyptian,* a new play by John Wilkins, was probably a melodrama. *Annie Blake* was a new domestic drama, and the new play of *Charity's Love* apparently a romantic comedy.

However, the crowning event of the year and the major occurrence of twenty-one years was the advent to the American stage of George Henry Boker's *Francesca da Rimini.* The story of those two lovers of thirteenth-century Italy, Francesca and Paolo, first entered literature in Dante's *Inferno.* Many pens since then have recorded the history of this tragic love: Boccaccio, Johann Ludwig Uhland, Silvio Pellico, Martin Greif, D'Annunzio, Marian Crawford, Leigh Hunt, Stephen Phillips, and George Henry Boker. With the exception of those versions by Dante, Boccaccio, and Hunt, literature has placed the story in dramatic form.

Boker's play was the first English version and the greatest of them all. He motivated his drama most powerfully through the use of contrast by presenting to us the picture of a hideous, love-starved man mad for the affection of a young and beautiful woman who loves the shapely and gracious brother. It is, among other factors, the art of contrast, so excellently handled, which makes this play good stage as well as great literature. And Boker succeeded in introducing into his drama the very breath of the middle ages. The character of Pepe, for one, is a concrete example of how well Boker understood the structure of medieval court society.

Boker's *Francesca da Rimini* was really the last and the greatest of American romantic tragedies in verse. American playwrights, and particularly the Philadelphia group of writers, had made the romantic verse tragedy their own province and particular endeavor. With them, the form grew in beauty and power until it developed into the masterpiece of the age, Boker's *Francesca.*

This play alone is sufficient to mark an epoch and to make the year of

1855 a turning point in dramatic history. Actually *Francesca da Rimini* came at the very time when Dion Boucicault began to exert a strong force in bringing about the transition from the old romantic drama to the new realistic plays that became the medium of dramatic expression for the next age.

THE ACTORS

CHAPTER III

THE ACTORS

1835

It is to be remembered that, one hundred years ago, our city still had stock companies in its theatres—in fact, they lasted until 1878. And to these stock companies came featured players chiefly from New York and abroad. The traveling-star system was at work, but it did not overwhelm the general excellence of the city stock companies, nor did it give unfair publicity to one actor and total oblivion to another. One is impressed by the records to see how featured players come and go, causing, it is true, an enthusiastic ripple, but not a maelstrom to engulf the veterans who remained at their posts year in and year out, supported by public favor.

In the Philadelphia of 1835, there were two stock companies playing excellent drama nightly. The American (which we shall call the Walnut Street) Theatre had upon its boards in this year approximately seventy players, not including the prominent visiting stars, while the Chesnut Street Theatre (or the Arch when this company occasionally used that building) had thirty-four. It might appear from these figures that there was an appreciable difference in the strength of the two companies, but the ultimate statistics speak for almost equal rank between them, for the backbone of the programs was made up of twenty-two players at the Walnut and twenty-four at the Chesnut. These figures are, of course, estimates only and may vary from reality by the margin of several players. They are, however, fairly accurate, the writer hopes, and also significant. And they show that the Walnut admitted a large number of visiting artists. One is amazed at the number of actors who came apparently unheralded, remained for a short stay, and left, leaving us only a passing, unknown name to conjure with.

The twenty-two players at the Walnut, then, formed the official family of the stock company. Of them, eleven were men and eleven women. At the Chesnut there were about thirteen men and eleven women in the inner circle. The players at the Walnut were Mr. and Mrs. (J. P.) Knight, Mr. and Mrs. Kent, Mr. and Mrs. Muzzy, Mrs. (F. B.) Conway, Mrs. Duff, Misses Anderson, Charnock, Mary Duff, Alexina

Fisher, Waring, Eliza Riddle, and Messrs. E. S. Connor, Hadaway, C. S. Porter, J. G. Porter, D. Reed, J. Sefton, (E. N.) Thayer, and F. C. Wemyss; and at the Chesnut, Mr. and Mrs. (W. G.) Jones, Mr. and Mrs. Maywood, Mr. and Mrs. Rowbotham, Mr. and Mrs. Walstein, Mr. and Mrs. (C.) Watson, Mrs. Conduit, Mrs. (E. N.) Thayer, Misses Elphinstone, Pelham, Watson, (Emma) Wheatley, and Messrs. W. E. Burton, T. S. Cline, Faulkner, (R.) Hamilton, J. E. Murdoch, Thoman, Walton, and Wood.

Among those who occasionally appeared at the two theatres as players featured to a certain degree were, at the Walnut, M. and Mme. Gouffe, Mrs. Pritchard, Mrs. Maeder, Miss Meadows, and Messrs. C. H. Eaton, Frimbley, Ingersoll, J. H. Oxley, Wm. B. Wood, and Masters Bowers, Jackson, and Roberts; and at the Chesnut, Messrs. Hathwell, Hunt, T. Power, and J. R. Scott.

The members of the two companies from whom we hear infrequently as well as the names of passing people were, at the Walnut, Mr. and Mrs. J. M. Brown, Mrs. Barrett, Mrs. Cooke, Mrs. Thorne, Misses Booth, Brittenham, Ruth, Ann Sefton, and Messrs. Allen, Blaike, Brittenham, (N. B.) Clarke, Collingbourne, J. H. Colline, Delarue, Derivage, Durang, C. Faurrest, Huntley, Jackson, Kelley, E. B. Kraft, Lyne, J. Mestayer, J. Reed, (T. B.) Russel, W. Sefton, Senior, Stanley, W. Vache, J. Wallace, Ward, W. Warren, and (C.) Webb; and at the Chesnut, Messrs, Bateman, (D.) Eberle, Jervis, T. Placide, (J. H.) Taylor, and (C.) Webb.

This list of players completes the number of sixty-nine for the Walnut and thirty-four for the Chesnut.

In a day when visiting stars often came to a distant theatre to play leads in their own individual repertoires with which they were completely familiar, the members of the stock companies seldom played the character of Hamlet, Othello, Lear, and other great tragic rôles. Comedy, then, frequently became the province of the stock-players during the intervals when the great and near great were in absentia. In the year of 1835, Mary Duff was the lovely and principal young comedienne at the Walnut. J. Sefton was the popular young comedian who was paired with her, and they appeared together in such pieces as *The Good-Looking Fellow, He Is Not A-Miss, The Deep, Deep Sea, The Golden Farmer, The Dumb Belle* and others, some of them only farces. The Misses Anderson, Charnock, Fisher, and Riddle frequently alternated with Mary Duff, and the Messrs. Connor, Hadaway, and J. G. Porter with J. Sefton.

Mr. and Mrs. Kent, Mr. and Mrs. Knight, and Mr. and Mrs. Muzzy took the supporting rôles of parents, friends, relatives, and enemies to the young lovers, and were always in demand.

There was also in the company at the Walnut, in January of 1835, a veteran comedian, W. Sefton, of 295 Walnut Street, the older brother of J. Sefton. Both were very popular. But W. Sefton was summarily dismissed for drunkenness by Francis C. Wemyss, lessee and manager of the theatre. The present writer does not wish to disturb the mold of a dusty scandal, nor malign the fair reputation of a good comedian long dead, but he does wish to point out how significant a proof this case really is of the dignified and orderly conduct of Wemyss' theatre, for considerable public comment was caused by the dismissal of the favorite, but Wemyss was adamant. On February 18, 1835, at the time of the dismissal, Wemyss published an open letter of a whole column in length in the *United States Gazette* and gave the reasons for his action. Shortly afterward, W. Sefton replied with an open letter of protest and of equal length. Even J. Sefton tried to have his brother reinstated in the company, but to no avail. And, when the young man's benefit came, on April 10, it was announced by him that W. Sefton would appear, but there was no appearance of that gentleman. And, after this time, we do not hear any more of J. Sefton —the rising and popular comedian—for several years. Perhaps, his eagerness to appease injured innocence and his staunch loyalty to family spelt temporary disaster to him. At all events, he was gone. At his benefit, also, he introduced his sister, Ann Sefton, to the stage as Elizabeth Stanton in *Tom Cringle*.

At the Chesnut, Burton was the popular comedian. Not only was he a player, but also a singer and a playwright. A great many of the farces produced on the boards of that theatre were by him, such as *Forty Winks, or Blunders in a Bed Room, The Ladies' Man, The Mummy, or the Liquor of Life,* and a domestic play like *The Intemperate, or a Sister's Love.* In fact, so prolific was his creation of farces and light comedies that one wonders how many unidentified farces at the Chesnut were really by him.

Another veteran and popular comedian at the Chesnut was J. E. Murdoch, who lived at 101 N. Seventh Street. He took his farewell of the company at his benefit on October 14, 1835, to go on the southern and western circuit for his health. Incidentally this occasion was his first appearance as Young Rapid in *A Cure for the Heartache.*

Playing opposite these actors were usually the Misses Phillips, Elphinstone, Pelham, Watson, and Wheatley, and the usual surrounding cast made up of Mr. and Mrs. Jones, Mr. and Mrs. Maywood, Mr. and Mrs. Rowbotham, Mr. and Mrs. Walstein, and Mr. and Mrs. Watson.

Many were the ambitious and extravagant operettas given at this time, and the make-up of the company at the Chesnut in particular reflects this popular demand. In the year of 1835, approximately sixty performances of operettas were given at the Chesnut, and only twenty at the Walnut. Furthermore, the latter were usually slight musical burlettas, because the company at the Walnut did not have the talent for full-fledged operettas. Of the twenty-four regularly appearing actors at the Chesnut, about fourteen sang in the operettas, in name, Mr. and Mrs. Rowbotham, Mrs. Maywood, Mrs. Watson, Miss Pelham, Miss Watson, Messrs. Walstein, Burton, Faulkner, Hamilton, Thoman, Walton, Wood, and Hunt; of these at the Walnut only four: Miss Meadows and the Messrs. (T. D.) Rice, Hadaway, and J. Reed. And, of these four, Miss Meadows was really a singer and not an actress, since she appeared in a dramatic rôle only several times during the year, and Mr. Rice was a specialty actor who took no rôles that one could call legitimately dramatic, and only appeared with the company occasionally as Jim Crow, his own act built around the famous song of the same time.

Excellent were the visting stars and featured players who came to Philadelphia in 1835, including at the Walnut Mr. and Mrs. J. Jefferson, Mr. and Miss Priscilla Cooper, Mrs. E. Knight, Mrs. S. Chapman, Miss Virginia Monier, and Messrs. A. A. Addams, E. Booth, Forbes, J. Hackett, G. H. Hill, J. S. Knowles, and Sol. Smith; and at the Chesnut Mr. and Mrs. J. S. Balls, Mr. and Mrs. Ternan, Mrs. Austen, Mrs. Rogers, Mlle. Celeste, Misses Phillips and Vos, and Messrs. Booth, G. H. Hill, Hows, J. S. Knowles, John Reeve, and James Wallack.

J. Jefferson, J. Hackett, G. H. Hill, and Sol. Smith (the latter advertised as the Liston of the South) were famous for their portrayal of American character, and the Yankee in particular. Addams, Booth, Forbes, and Hows were excellent tragedians. Knowles, that great "purifier of the modern drama," was more of a dramatist than an actor, although he was popularly received as a player in his own creations. His benefit night, April 9, 1835, on which occasion Mrs. S. Chapman of the Park Theatre appeared, was a gala performance with the combined companies of both theatres.

Mr. and Mrs. Ternan usually acted as lovers in romantic plays. In the first of the year, Mrs. Ternan was the well-known Fanny Jarman, but when the two of them returned for an engagement later in the year, they came back married.

Mlle. Celeste is an interesting person. She was French in fact as well as in name, and usually appeared in the most extravagant melodramatic sketches in which she sustained three or four characters. Her immense popularity is witnessed by this singularly human quotation, taken from the editorial page of the *United States Gazette* for November 19, 1835:

> Mademoiselle Celeste, the dancer, will receive about $70,000 for her services at the different theatres this year. The editor of the "New York American," with very proper feelings, compares those wages with the salary of a professor in any one of our colleges, and he might have have added the income of any other profession or trade. But, after all, ". . . is the reward of virtue bread?" When the year closes, the *professor* in a college is satisfied that he is a professor, and Mademoiselle Celeste must content herself that she is only a *danseuse*. The inequality of compensation is one of the events of life that have been matters for complaint or philosophical endurance from the time of the "monarch minstrel" of Israel to the present day. David found his solution in the sanctuary, and Pope in philosophy. The accomplished editor of the "American" doubtless can avail himself of both of these.

James Wallack and John Reeve were two young actors, the one usually appearing as the dashing hero or man of adventure, and the other as a versatile comedian.

At this day in the life of our theatres, there were very often interspersed between the play and the farce special numbers, such as displays of strength and skill, character dances, and songs. Of the eighteen variety-actors who appeared at the Walnut in the course of 1835, seven were dancers and three singers. The others were such as Signor Sciarra, the ninth wonder of the world, and Cony and his dogs with Master Blanchard, the ape-boy. Of the fourteen special artists who appeared during the interludes at the Chesnut, nine were vocal and instrumental performers. And in this entertainment, also, we see the further policy of the Chesnut to give the public high-grade musical performances.

1836

For 1836 in the stock companies, we must first note the absence of Mrs. Duff from the Walnut. She left at the close of the season, July 6, 1835, to go to Lancaster, for an engagement. And in the spring of 1836, her daughter, Mary Duff, also dropped out of the ranks at the Walnut.

Mr. and Mrs. Kent did not appear at the Walnut in this year, at all, and only very infrequently in 1837. And both Mrs. Conway and Miss Eliza Riddle failed to occupy a place in the stock company at the Walnut for 1836. At the Chesnut J. E. Murdoch was absent, since he was still on the southern and western circuit, and Mr. and Mrs. Watson left to go to the new Pennsylvania Theatre when it opened November 7, 1836.

The names of unfeatured, occasional actors, that appeared once or twice a year, are so many that the reader is referred to the Player-List which records the name of every advertised actor. Reference to the Player-List through comparison with the names in the groupings included at the beginning of this section will indicate to the reader both the reappearance of actors who were not members of the stock companies, as well as the continuity in the careers of those who were.

In 1836, the additions to the regular stock companies included at the Walnut Mr. and Mrs. Preston, Mrs. Willis, and Mr. (F. S.) Myers; and at the Chesnut Mrs. Broad, Miss Morgan, and Messrs. Brunton, Lindsay, (Sidney) Pearson, and (E.) Thompson.

None of these ladies and gentlemen were, in the term of the stage, heavies. They varied from high comedy to sentimental and romantic drama. Again, reference to the Player-List will give dates of certain performances in the Play-List and Chronological Record from which a judgment of their range of acting may be made.

The names of those who appeared infrequently with the stock companies for 1836, included at the Walnut Mrs. Cuvillier, Mrs. Dunham, Mrs. C. Durang, Mrs. Hamblin, Mrs. Scott, Mrs. W. H. Smith, Miss Polly Hadaway, and Messrs. Bathgate, (J. H.) Boswell, Clemens, Chappell, (J. S.) Charles, Crouta, Germon, Joseph, Morton, Newton, Percival, C. Raffile, and Woodhull; and at the Chesnut, Mrs. Wood, and Messrs. Andrews, Darley, Sharpe, and (G. B. S.) Wilks.

The list for the Walnut shows the continued number of transients on its boards: actors like Woodhull, an old stager at the Walnut; and Clemens, the dance-director there; and Charles, who appeared but one night at the benefit of Mrs. Hamblin, who herself returned the one night to the stage to take a benefit and a farewell. The Player-List will give an indication of the status of these people by recording after their names a single date or two, (1) a single date marks the first yearly appearance of the actor and signifies that there were no more than two or three performances by him the whole year—(2) a date starred with an asterisk points the way

[98]

to an actual cast in the Chronological Record and signifies that there were occasional performances throughout the year.

The visiting stars and featured players who came to the Philadelphia stage on engagements usually returned year after year. An actual check-up of their return engagements can be gotten from the Player-List by noting their names as additions appear in this chapter annually. The additions of this year over the List for 1836 included at the Walnut Mr. and Mrs. J. Barnes, Miss Barnes, and Messrs. J. Cowell, Denvil, and (H. J.) Finn; and at the Chesnut Mr. and Mrs. Checkini, Mr. and Mrs. Keeley, Mrs. Shaw, Mlle. Arreline, Miss J. Clifton, and Messrs. Brough, Dowton, E. Forrest, and the Ravel family.

E. Forrest and Denvil were classic tragedians; Dowton, a comedian of the Restoration play in particular; H. J. Finn, a specialist in the American character type, like Hill and Hackett, and an American playwright besides; "Old Joe" Cowell, a veteran comedian, and long the manager of the Walnut and acting manager of the Chesnut; Mr. and Mrs. Barnes, comedians, and their daughter, always a heroine; likewise Miss Clifton, a heroine brought by James Wallack as support; Mr. and Mrs. Keeley, sparkling comedians; and Mrs. Shaw, a lady who did Hamlet. Brough sang in the colorful operas given at the Chesnut. Mr. and Mrs. Checkini with Mlle. Arreline were brought to the Chesnut by the inimitable Mlle. Celeste as support in her melodramas. And the Ravel Family performed ballet pantomimes, with an occasional rope ascension for a grand finale. Definite information of the rôles taken by these people can be found under their names in the Player-List.

The Pennsylvania Theatre on Coates Street, which opened November 7, 1836, with Logan as owner, had for its visiting star J. R. Scott, the classic tragedian. The players who supported the performance there were regularly Mr. and Mrs. Herbert, Mr. and Mrs. Jackson, Mr. and Mrs. Logan, Mr. and Mrs. (W. H.) Smith, Mr. and Mrs. Watson, Mrs. Herring, Mrs. J. Sefton, and Mr. Bateman; and occasionally, Mrs. O'Grath, Miss Chester, and Messrs. Freemont, J. H. Kirby, Stanley, W. S. Vache, W. Warren, and F. C. Wemyss.

1837

In 1837, Mr. and Mrs. Muzzy dropped out of the company at the Walnut. The company at the Chesnut lost no actor this year, and added

Mrs. Broad to the ranks of the regular stock players. Also, we include Mrs. R. Hamilton, wife of one of the stock players, who appeared to gain considerable importance as the year went on.

The addition to the regular company at the Walnut for 1837 included Mr. and Mrs. N. H. Bannister, Mr. and Mrs. Herbert, Mr. and Mrs. (J.) Proctor, Misses E. Packard and White, and Messrs. (J.) Addams, (J. B.) Rice, and W. A. Vache.

Mr. and Mrs. Bannister appear to be the most valuable acquisition, because they not only actually performed in plays, but also provided their own, since the husband was the author of such pieces as *The Destruction of Jerusalm, Gaulantus,* and *Caius Silius.* They made their appearance on July 28, in Bannister's own play of *Infidelity, or the Husband's Return.*

Mr. and Mrs. Herbert, it is to be remembered, had been in the company at the Pennsylvania Theatre, but came to the Walnut, at the closing of the other theatre. Mr. and Mrs. (J.) Proctor came from the circuit of the western theatres. The Misses E. Packard and White were heroines, and the Messrs. (J.) Addams and (J. B.) Rice were stately actors of heavy and serious parts.

The occasional actors at the two theatres for 1837 were at the Walnut Mr. and Mrs. (J. S.) Parker, Mr. and Mrs. Watson, Misses Angelica, Chester, Hichie, Honey, S. Packard, Parker, M. W. Warren, and Messrs. F. Brown, Joe Buts, S. Collingbourne, Cunningham, Dickenson, Mc-Conachy, Steel, and R. Thorne; and at the Chesnut Mrs. Gibbs, Mrs. E. A. Hamilton, Mrs. R. Hamilton, Mrs. Lee, Misses Armstrong, Brown, Fox, Grove, Hancker, Lee, Lopez, Nelson, and Messrs. Anderson, Carnes, Craddock, Harrington, Kelly, Plumer, and Master Leavitt.

The additional visiting stars for the two companies in 1837 included at the Walnut Mr. and Mrs. John Greene, Mrs. Meer, Mr. W. E. Burton, Mr. Dan Marble, and Masters R. and J. Meer; and at the Chesnut Mrs. Flynn, Misses Horton, Ellen Tree, Turpin, St. Luke, Augusta Maywood, Messrs. Browne, E. S. Connor, C. E. Horn, H. G. Pearson, Henry Wallack, G. Vanderhoff, Walbourne, Davis Jackson, and Taylor, and Master St. Luke.

Mr. and Mrs. John Greene were comedians, as also were William E. Burton of the Chesnut, who appeared as a visitor on the boards of the Walnut for July 29, while the Chesnut was closed during summer recess. Marble, like Hill, Hackett, and Finn, was a specialist in the portrayal of American character parts. Mrs. Lewis apparently was a lady of prodigious ability. A glance at the Player-List will reveal her as Othello, Richard

III, and Virginius. Mrs. Meer evidently was a mother first and an actress second, for to her belonged that child prodigy, the Infant Apollo, Master R. Meer.

Miss Horton and C. E. Horn came in the company of Brough as support in his operatic repertoire. Mrs. Flynn supported H. G. Pearson, the classic tragedian. The Messrs. Vanderhoff, H. G. Pearson, and E. S. Conner were tragedians, and the Messrs. Browne and Henry Wallack were comedians. The troupe of four actors, Messrs. Walbourne, Davis, Jackson, and Taylor, were laugh-provokers and pantomimists. Walbourne's performance of Bob in *Tom and Jerry,* July 17, was announced as his one thousand, nine hundred and ninety-sixth repetition of that rôle. Miss Ellen Tree was a Shakespearean actress in particular, and Miss Turpin was primarily a vocalist.

The St. Lukes, brother and sister, were children who attempted to do Shakespeare, and La Petite Augusta was the offspring of the Maywoods, stock players at the Chesnut. Apparently the child could sing the leads in operas like *Maid of Cashmere* and *Dewdrop.*

The Pennsylvania Theatre lasted until February 18, because the Walnut was closed until February 19. Consequently, many of the players in the company at the Walnut appeared from time to time at the Pennsylvania. The occasional players included Mrs. Willis, Miss E. Packard, and Messrs. Berresford, Blanchard, F. Brown, Clarke, Connor, Conolly, Cony, Drummond, Duncan, Hadaway, Jones, M'Cutchen, McGuire, (W.) Myers, J. Proctor, Roland, J. Sefton, Slack, J. Wallace, Master Bowers, and the Watson twins.

It is interesting to note that the name of J. Sefton appears at the Pennsylvania for the date of February 3d, in the rôle of Jemmy in *The Golden Farmer,* the melodrama in which he used to play at the Walnut two years before. Also it is to be noted that Mrs. J. Sefton was a member of the company at the Pennsylvania.

We must make mention of the German Company which occupied the Arch Street Theatre for one week during the summer and played Kotzebue's dramas. Their numbers included Miss Rottenhaus, and Messrs. Hirsh, Sachse, Gerharding, and Wilhelm.

1838

In 1838 so many changes took place in the ranks of the veteran actors at the Walnut that we find a growing number of new names usurping the

[101]

programs. Noticeably, Connor, the favorite stock player at the Walnut, is missed, and also J. G. Porter. The additions to the regulars for the two theatres this year comprised at the Walnut Mr. and Mrs. La Forest, Mr. and Mrs. Hield, Mrs. J. B. Rice, and Messrs. Burgess and Pickering; and at the Chesnut Mrs. Sharpe, Miss De Barr, and Messrs. E. L. Davenport and J. E. Murdoch.

Mr. and Mrs. La Forest played the comedies and Mr. and Mrs. Hield the tragedies, with Burgess a supporting comedian, and Pickering a supporting tragedian. Mrs. J. B. Rice came to join her husband, who rose to the position of regular player in the company during the previous year. Mrs. Sharpe was a tragedienne, Davenport a villain; and J. E. Murdoch this year returned as a stock actor to the Chesnut.

The new occasional players for the year at the two theatres were at the Walnut Mr. and Mrs. Kemble, Mme. La Trust, Mrs. Wilks, Misses Hamblin, A. Porter, A. Packard, and Messrs. T. Bishop, H. A. Curfew, T. E. Garson, J. H. Hall, Harbord, Johnson, McCormick, Morley, Needham, Wills, and Winnan; and at the Chesnut Misses Bunjie, Oceana Fisher, Pearson, and Mr. Crowley.

The visiting actors at the Walnut and Chesnut for 1838 included at the Walnut Mrs. W. Barrymore, Mrs. Davenport, Mrs. Cole, Mrs. Herring, Mrs. A. Knight, Mrs. J. B. Phillips, Mrs. Thayer, Mme. Augusta, Misses Davenport, Gannon, Lee, Kerr, and Messrs. H. J. Amherst, (D. L.) Carpenter, T. S. Cline, Cooke, Jr., Foster, Gates, Horncastle, J. E. Murdoch, Parsons, Porter, Rodney, Russell, J. Sefton, and Woolford; and at the Chesnut, Mr. and Mrs. George Jones, Mr. and Mrs. C. Mathews, Mrs. H. Cramer, Mesdames Caradori Allan, Le Compte, Otto, and Master and Miss Wells.

In Cooke's traveling company which came to the Walnut to give an engagement of melodramas appeared Mrs. Cole, Mrs. Herring, and the Messrs. Amherst, Foster, Rodney, Gates, Woolford and Cooke, Jr.

Madame Augusta, supported by Mrs. J. B. Phillips, Miss Kerr, and the Messrs. Horncastle and Russell, entertained the Walnut with the opera of *La Bayadere.*

Other visitors were: Mrs. W. Barrymore with (D. L.) Carpenter, comedians; Parsons, classic tragedian; Miss Lee, dancer; Miss Gannon and Porter, the Lilliputian Wonder and the Kentucky Giant, respectively; Mrs. A. Knight in the character of Mrs. Haller in *The Stranger;* and Mrs. Davenport, another mother with a prodigious girl-child who attempted the mature masculine rôles of Richard III and Shylock. Mrs. Thayer and the Messrs. T. S. Cline and J. E. Murdoch from the Chesnut visited the boards of the Walnut during the summer. And J. Sefton returned to the Walnut in an engagement of the old rôle which he played there as the stock actor of 1836.

At the Chesnut appeared Mr. and Mrs. George Jones, tragedians; Mme. Caradori Allan, Madame Le Compte, and Madame Otto, all visiting leads for the favorite operas; Mrs. H. Cramer, heroine; and Master and Miss Wells, the latter appearing in opera, and the former in solo dances. Mr. and Mrs. C. Mathews are of particular note since the husband wrote most of the farces which made up their repertoire—such as, *He Would Be An Actor* and *Patter versus Clatter*. Both were well known, and Mrs. C. Mathews was loudly announced as the former Madame Vestris. At the time of their appearance at the Chesnut, the *U. S. Gazette* for Oct. 15, 1838, carried an advertisement by Turner and Fisher, booksellers, 11 North Sixth Street, to the effect that "Nearly all the pieces in which these celebrated artists appear . . . also, portraits of Madame Vestris and Mr. Mathews and the Memoirs Of The Public And Private Life Of Mrs. Mathews" were on sale.

1839

The year 1839 saw several major changes in the stock companies at the Walnut and Chesnut. Mr. and Mrs. J. Proctor were gone from the Walnut; William E. Burton transferred his allegiance from the Chesnut where he was a stock actor to the Walnut where he became a featured star, appearing by engagement; Mr. and Mrs. J. B. Rice, regular performers at the Walnut, took their farewell benefit on April 26; and J. G. Porter, favorite actor at the Walnut, also was absent from its boards this year. Mrs. Hield remained at the Walnut and incidentally suffered a severe accident during the performance of *The Cataract of the Ganges,* but her husband returned to play at the Park Theatre, New York.

As additions to the two companies, we have Mrs. W. Sefton (wife of the W. Sefton in controversy with Wemyss in 1835) coming to the Walnut. The lady could play the dark rôles of Queen Gertrude and Lady Macbeth. At the Walnut, also, as regular players this year were Messrs. Neafie and Mossop, comedians. To the Chesnut as a stock actress, Miss Anderson returned under the new name of Mrs. Thoman, wife of the singer. And Mrs. H. Cramer, portrayer of heroines, in 1839 appeared as a regular member of the company at the Chesnut. At the same theatre this year regularly appeared T. Placide and W. F. Johnson, comedians.

The new occasional actors at the two theatres for 1839 included at the Walnut Mr. and Mrs. Bennie, Mr. and Mrs. Hautonville, Mr. and Mrs. J. Herbert, Mrs. (W. R.) Blake, Misses (H.) Mathews, Murray, Reynolds, La Petite Bertha, and Messrs. J. S. Bonsall, Yankee Bowman, Carter, Chippendale, J. Field, Grierson, Harrison, Hudson, Lennox, T. Mathews, H. Nicholls, J. F. O'Connell, Powell, Whitney, and (B.) Williams; and at the Chesnut Mesdames Faulkner, Hunt, Misses Ellis, E. Wood, and Messrs. Latham and J. McDowel.

The additional actors visiting the two theatres by engagement during 1839 were at the Walnut Mesdames Fitzwilliam, Hazard, Seguin, Misses Emma Ince, Stephan, and Messrs. W. E. Burton, Morley, T. C. Parsloe, and W. Wood; and at the Chesnut Mr. and Mrs. Martin, Mr. and Mrs. Sloman, Misses Hildreth, Pool, Shireff, Vandenhoff, and Messrs. Giubeli, Charles Kean, Manvers, Mulligan, Seguin, Wells, (B.) Williams, and Wilson.

The operas were well represented this year by singers engaged to appear in musical repertoires. Noticeably, the Walnut began to call more and more of the operatic stars to its boards. In 1839, Mme. Hazard, Mlle. Stephan, and Morley appeared for an operatic engagement at the Walnut, as did Mrs. Seguin, whose husband was engaged in an operatic repertoire at the Chesnut with Miss Shireff and Wilson. Mr. and Mrs. Martyn, Miss Pool, and the Messrs. Giubeli and Manvers formed another visiting troupe of opera singers at the Chesnut.

At the Walnut also this year were: Mrs. Fitzwilliam, comedienne; Miss Emma Ince, featured dancer in operatic ballets; William E. Burton, the famous comedian formerly of the Chesnut; Parsloe, a character actor of contortive proclivities (he was "the monkey who has seen the world" in the play of the same name); and W. Wood and his dog, both acting.

At the Chesnut in 1839 were several excellent visiting players: Mr. and Mrs. Sloman, the wife a heroine, the husband, a light comedian; Miss Hildreth, a heroine; Miss Vandenhoff, who played rôles opposite her father; and Charles Kean, the classic tragedian. At Christmas time, a troupe composed of Messrs. Wells, Williams, and Mulligan appeared in a time-honored and seasonal harlequinade.

1840

The year of 1840 requires the patience of Job and the resourcefulness of a commercial genealogist to follow the peregrinations of the players from one Philadelphia theatre to another, for a bombshell was exploded in September of this year by William E. Burton with his newly built and owned National Theatre.

But first, for the earlier half of the year, when theatrical life was still moving serenely, we must notice the addition of Mrs. Hunt, Mrs. W. Sefton and Lennox to the rank of regular players at the Walnut. And, also, we must remark Mrs. Sharpe's farewell to the stage on May 5th at the Chesnut.

And now we may come to the significant occurrence of the year: William E. Burton appeared to be the most enterprising theatrical spirit in Philadelphia. From 1835 to 1838, we remember him as the popular comedian, playwright, and acting manager of Pratt and Dinmore's Chesnut Street Theatre. Then in 1839 he became a visiting star to the Walnut. Finally, in September, 1840, he eclipsed the thespian lights of both these houses by erecting and opening a theatre, the New National which he was pleased to call "the first in the Union," and which the newspapers of the day seemed to feel, likewise, was the best theatre that had yet come to our city. The reader is asked to follow the daily programs to note the variety of entertainment offered, and also, to notice carefully the names which make up Burton's list of regular players at the New National: Mrs. Herbert, Misses C. Cushman, S. Cushman, Lee, Eliza Petrie, and Messrs. Boulard, W. E. Burton, Ferrers, Graham, Neafie, Oakey, T. Placide, (C. S.) Porter, P. Richings, J. R. Scott, Shaw, Stafford, James Thorne, Whiting, and Woodbury.

Pratt and Dinmore's Chesnut also opened in the Fall, August 29th, with James E. Murdoch as acting manager. And Francis C. Wemyss opened the Arch one week later with a company that was not very strong. Actually with the best of the players at the other two houses, he had no material to work with, and after two weeks closed the Arch to prepare to turn it into a melodramatic theatre, as he announced. Two and a half months later, he again opened with a different set of actors, who (if the present writer may venture to suggest) were not very impressive. Following are the two companies which Wemyss had at the Arch: for September 7 to 18, Mesdames Hunt and La Forest, Miss Hudson, and Messrs. Hunt, J. M. Kirby, T. Mathews, and F. C. Wemyss; and for December 1 to 31,

Mesdames Judah, Cantor, and Messrs. Crane, Flynn, Isherwood, H. Lewis, Mills, Vanstavoreen, and F. C. Wemyss.

Wm. Dinneford opened the Walnut on November 14th, with a large company. Four of his players came to the Philadelphia stock company for the first time: Miss Mitchell and Messrs. Fredericks, Charles, Howard, and N. Porter. By this time of this year, players were pouring into Philadelphia from the whole length of the Atlantic theatrical seaboard. Dinneford recruited many from Boston, New York, Baltimore, and Washington. His company at the Walnut included Mesdames J. S. Charles, Flynn, La Forest, Misses A. Kinlock, Mitchell, Murray, Rock, and Messrs. W. R. Blake, (J. H.) Hall, Hadaway, (J. S.) Charles, (W. S.) Fredericks, Charles Howard, Logan, N. Porter, and B. Williams.

T. Placide opened the Coates Street Theatre (which Logan ran in 1836–37 as the Pennsylvania) during the summer of 1840 for three advertised nights, Aug. 19, 20, 21, to play the national drama of *The Battle of Tippecanoe*. His company comprised Mesdames La Forest, Thoman, and Messrs. (D.) Eberle, H. Eberle, Kelly, Pickering, T. Placide, and Thoman.

The new occasional players at the theatres for 1840 included at the Walnut Mesdames Hutchings, Barry, Messrs. Hutchings, Behin, Booth, Jr., Brydges, Edwards, Ferrers, S. Johnston, McBride, Murray Pearman, C. S. Risley, J. Sandford. Vanstavoreen, and Masters Diamond and C. Foster; at the Chesnut Mesdames Ophelia Anderson, Blake, Plumer, Miss E. Vallee, and Messrs. Creswick, Fleming, and Howard; and at the National Messrs. G. F. Cooke, Jamison, and Quayle.

The additional stars appearing at the theatres for 1840 included at the Walnut Messrs. Freer and Klishing; at the National, Mrs. Bailey, Miss J. Clifton, and Messrs. Buckstone, Braham, and J. Hackett; and at the Chesnut Mesdames Alfred, Lecomte, Scheidler, Misses Pauline des Jardins, Fanny Elssler, Lorch, S. Cushman, and Messrs. Boll, B. Grenich, Buckstone, Gohr, Kaiffer, Leffler, Meyer, Ranger, Rischler, Runeg, and Silvain.

Opera was represented in 1840 by the German Company, composed of Mme. Alfred, Mme. Scheidler, Mlle. Lorch, and Messrs. Boll, Gohr, Meyer, Runeg, and Rischler, who appeared at the Chesnut and gave *Der Freischütz* in German. At the Chesnut also this year appeared Mme. Le Comte, Mlle. Pauline des Jardins and Messrs. Kaiffer and B. Grenich to sing *La Sonnambula*. At the Chesnut in addition to these singers, were Mlle. Fanny Elssler and Mons. Silvain, in ballet opera;

Leffler, appearing with Mr. and Mrs. Wood and Brough in opera; Ranger, the comedian; Buckstone, the comedian and playwright who appeared in his own plays of *Married Life, Single Life, Weak Points,* and *A Kiss in the Dark;* and Miss S. Cushman, who acted with Buckstone for a short engagement.

To the Walnut came Freer in the part of Elgard the Idiot, in the play of the same name, and as Gaston in *The Man in the Iron Mask;* and Klishing who acted Mammoc in *The Sorcerer.*

At the New National Theatre, Mrs. Bailey (née Watson), the singer, and Messrs. Hackett and Buckstone were not new in the sense that their first appearance in Philadelphia occurred there, but they were among the first to appear by engagement at the new theatre. And Braham, the tenor, sang with Mrs. Bailey in opera this season at the New National.

The year of 1840, the beginning of a new decade, brought many new names to the Philadelphia stage, and definitely marks a point of increased theatrical activity in our city.

1841

The enterprising spirit which prompted Burton to build his New National in 1840, seemed to develop into a spirit of unrest in 1841, because even the casual observer can see that the New National performances for 1841 did not warrant superlative praise. Burton had promised too much, and could not go on in the blaze of glory in which he had started his theatre. In fact, he leased it for a month or two during the season of 1841, to Mitchell's Vaudeville Company from the Olympic in New York. And after he did resume occupation of it himself, he no longer commanded the services of all those imported actors from North, South, and West with whom he had opened his doors in 1840.

The regular stock actors (names with which we have come in contact for seven years) switched about alarmingly from theatre to theatre in this year of 1841; also, because the company from the Chesnut took up quarters in the Arch by the month of April, with Blake and Jones as lessees; and in May, Pratt opened up the Chesnut with Peter Richings as acting manager, while Wemyss was inactive in Philadelphia theatricals this year.

The company at the Chesnut was composed for the most part of actors with singing voices, since the theatres continued to produce operas. In addition to the veteran singers and stock players, the Chesnut in 1841 included Mrs. Lambert, Miss Ayres, and S. Chapman as regular performers. The new visiting actors were Messrs. Butler, classic tragedian; H. Placide, comedian; Charles Mason who played the title rôle of *Werner;* and Fitzgerald Tasistro, classic tragedian.

The regular company at the Arch can be judged by the cast for the production of *Philadelphia Assurance,* Dec. 6, 1841. In addition to the old familiar names are those of Mr. and Mrs. Bennie and Mrs. Harrison as stock players. The new visiting actors included Miss Melton, Messrs. Sinclair, Latham, Lewellen, J. S. Silsbee, J. W. Smith, Picanniny Coleman, Tuthill, Wood, and Master Wood, his son.

The cast for Nov. 6, 1841, at the opening of *London Assurance* gives us a list of the actors at the Walnut. Mrs. Flynn, Miss Harrison, and Messrs. Haines, Henckins, and Lambert were the new stock players for the year, with Messrs. Gann, J. S. Jones, and H. Placide as the new visiting players, and Mrs. Mossop as an occasional performer.

At the National, Messrs. E. S. Conner and Sherman entered the ranks of the regular players. Mrs. Seymour, Miss E. Randolph, and W. H. Williams were added to the list of actors appearing by engagement at the theatre. And Mr. and Mrs. C. Hiel, Miss Elvins, Miss Collingbourne, and Messrs. Archer, Larkins, and Plucker appeared occasionally.

During the time that Mitchell leased the National and produced vaudeville with his Olympic Company from New York, the actors whom he brought with him were Mrs. Timm, Miss Turnbull, and Messrs. Edwin, Horncastle, Graham, Roberts, Maharg, and Nickinson.

1842

Burton's National closed its doors at the end of January, 1842, and did not open them the rest of the year. Instead, L. T. Pratt of the Chesnut and Burton combined their two companies and played at the Chesnut. The following list gives the make-up of the two companies which combined: prior to the summer recess at the Chesnut, Mesdames A. Sefton, (E. N.) Thayer, Misses Hildreth, Kneas, and Messrs. (J. S.) Charles, Drummond, Faulkner, Gann, Jarvis, Mulliken, P. Richings, and Wood; and at the Walnut, Mesdames Cantor, G. Jones, and Messrs. E. S. Conner, W. Jones, E. Shaw, and J. Wallack.

On March 23, 1842, the two companies joined forces and, at that time, the Misses Grove and Collingbourne appear as regular stock players under the new arrangement at the Chesnut.

The year of 1842 brings us an innovation in the establishment of women as managers at two of Philadelphia's leading theatres, the Chesnut and the Walnut. Following the summer recess, Mary Elizabeth Maywood leased the Chesnut in her own name and opened there with a strong company including Mr. and Mrs. Maywood, Mesdames, English, J. G. Porter, Rogers, Thoman, Misses Ayres, Mary Elizabeth Maywood, George, Jones, Mathews, Norman, Seele, Thompson, and Messrs. Andrews, Bowers, (J. S.) Charles, (D.) Eberle, Henrie, Hines, Jervis, Kelley, Mathews, Perring, P. Richings, Stanly, Watson, and Wood.

Just as the Maywood family seemed to occupy the Chesnut *en masse* during the fall and winter season of 1842, so also during the spring season of that year did the Porter family appear to conduct the Arch. C. S. and J. G. Porter, from whom we have not heard for several years, came to the Arch, together with the latter's wife, Mrs. J. G. Porter, and Miss Porter, presumably a sister. The company included Mr. and Mrs. J. G. Porter, Mr. and Mrs. Thoman, Mesdames, Cappelle, J. S. Charles, (E. N.) Thayer, Miss Porter, and Messrs. Collingbourne, E. S. Conner, Gann, C. S. Porter, and Raffile.

And when E. A. Marshall, lessee, opened the Walnut, following the summer recess, Charlotte Cushman came to direct activities there. A parallel list will show the relative composition of the company at the Walnut before and after the advent of Miss Cushman. It included before summer Mesdames Flynn, Kinlock, La Forest, Marsden, Miss A. Kinlock, and Messrs. Burnes, E. S. Conner, (E. L.) Davenport, Hadaway, Haines, Henkins, Myers, J. Proctor, (T. B.) Russell, and (B.) Young; and after summer Mr. and Mrs. A'Becket, Mesdames Kinlock, Maeder, Radcliffe, (E. N.) Thayer, Misses Brown, Collingbourne, C. Cushman, S. Cushman, Reed, Smith, Tyte, Messrs. Conover, (E. L.) Davenport, George, Hackurt, Hadaway, Henkins, Oakey, (D.) Reed, (T. B.) Russell, W. Vache, B. Young, and Master Reed.

Mr. and Mrs. John Brougham are perhaps the new visiting stars of greatest brilliancy for the year of 1842. Brougham played the same repertoire as that of his countryman, Tyrone Power: comedies and farces built around an Irishman, such as *Irish Valet, Irish Tutor, Irish Attorney,* and the like, as well as the Restoration comedies in which Mrs. Brougham appeared with him. Other new artists appearing by engagement this year were Beckett, comedian; Drisback, a gentleman of melo-drama; and Shrival, Mrs. Bourlard, Miss Coad and Miss Horton in the company at the Chesnut during the operatic month of December.

There might be the virtue of exactitude in giving at this time a list of the additional players appearing during 1842, either as regular or occasional actors. These new names included—in the order of their appearance—J. B. Price, Miss Flannigan, Miss Kneas, Mulliken, Mrs. Kinlock, Mrs. Marsden, Young, Burnes, Mrs. Cappelle, Miss Durang, J. H. White, Miss C. Price, Mrs. Altemus, Jewell, Miss Raymond, Brittingham, Mrs. A'Becket, Miss Jones, Bowers, Godden, Hines, Henrie, Perring, Misses Thompson, Norman, Seele, and George; Mrs. English, Conover, George, Hackurt, Mrs. Penson, Mrs. Radcliffe, Misses Smith, Tyte, and Reed, and Mrs. Western.

1843

January 9, 1843, Charles R. Thorne, manager of the Chatham Theatre, N. Y., opened the Olympic Theatre, corner of Ninth and Chesnut Streets, late the Olympic Circus, and played legitimate drama there for about two weeks. His company, under the stage directorship of Thomas Flynn, included Mesdames (G.) Jones, (J. S.) Charles, Miss A. Fisher, and Messrs. W. E. Burton, J. S. Charles, J. Mestayer, Myers, Stevens, (E. N.) Thayer, and J. Thorne.

Several futile attempts were made this year to keep the Arch open, but a month or two brought the theatre to the end of its run after each effort. In March it opened and again, in August, with T. B. Russell as lessee. The companies to be found there for these two openings were in March Mr. and Mrs. Flynn, Mr. and Mrs. A. Phillips, Mr. and Mrs. H. Lewis, Misses Ayres, Porter, and Messrs. Altemus, (J. S.) Charles, Gann, Hamilton, James Harbord, C. S. Porter, P. Richings, Roberts, Thoman, E. Thompson, and C. Watson; and in August Mr. and Mrs. (J. S.) Charles, Mr. and Mrs. T. B. Russell, Mesdames A'Becket, Cappelle, Greene, La Forest, A. Knight, Town, Misses A. Fisher, Porter, and Messrs. Altemus, (D.) Eberle, (J. E.) Owens, Philips, C. S. Porter, J. G. Porter, J. Proctor, P. Richings, Roberts, E. N. Thayer, and E. Thompson.

Following the summer recess, we find a very strong company at the Chesnut, including excellent additions like J. M. Field, the comedian, from the Tremont, Boston, and Messrs. Leman and Spear, also from the same place. The full company comprised: Mesdames (G.) Jones, Mossop, (E. N.) Thayer, Misses Baker, C. Cushman, S. Cushman, A. Fisher, Price, and Messrs. W. R. Blake, Curtis, (E. L.) Davenport, (D.) Eberle, J. M. Field, Hackurt, Hadaway, Henkins, Leman, Radcliffe, Spear, and (B.) Young.

Wemyss and Oxley leased the National in September, and opened it with the following actors: Mr. and Mrs. A'Becket, Mr. and Mrs. H. Lewis, Mesdames Abbott, Cantor, Madison, Miss H. Matthews, and Messrs. Faulkner, Fleming, Matthews, Mossop, J. H. Oxley, E. Shaw, and F. C. Wemyss.

The Arch opened again in December, this time with Wm. S. Deverna as lessee. The actors were Mr. and Mrs. J. Greene, Mr. and Mrs. (James) Anderson, Mrs. Penson, Miss Kirby, and Messrs. Henry, Jamieson, A. J. Phillips, M. S. Phillips, Vanstavoreen, and Wareham.

The Chesnut this year had several operatic seasons composed of two engagements with an Italian Opera Company and one with a French Opera Company. Since Marshall leased both Chesnut and Walnut this year, he allowed the opera companies to sing at the Chesnut and moved his dramatic company over to the Walnut during the operatic engagement, moving back to the Chesnut again and closing the Walnut each time the operatic visitation was concluded. However, immediately following the run of the French Opera Company, in October, Marshall divided his dramatic company and kept both houses open until November 13, the opening date of the return engagement of the Italian Opera Company. These opera companies were, in personnel for the Italian, Mesdames M. Albertazzi, E. Corsini, A. Majocchi, L. Marozzi, and Messrs. J. Guissinier, L. Perozzi, B. Thornes, and A. Valtellina; and for the French Mesdames Barneck, Calvé, Lecourt, and Messrs. Bernard, Lecourt, and Richer.

In the order of their appearance during the year, the following actors comprise the new visiting players for 1843: Philips, the comedian; Barnes, the pantomimist, supported by Miss Walters; R. E. Graham, playing *Virginius* and *The Stranger;* Macready, the classic tragedian, supported by Ryder; and the Elssler Brothers, strong men, in their play of *The Hercules of Brittany.*

To the ranks of regular stock actors in 1843, came Stevens, Radcliffe, Jas. Hasbord, Altemus, Miss Baker, Mrs. Madison, Mrs. Town, Spear, Leman, Curtis, Mrs. Abbott, A. J. and M. S. Phillips, Miss Kirby, Wareham, and Mrs. J. Anderson.

Among the occasional players are the new names of Mrs. Forbes (appearing once with her husband, the star), Mrs. F. S. Myers, and Miss Julia Bell.

1844

The Walnut retained its company of the year previous, and added to its stock company the actor William Wheatley.

The National likewise retained its full company of 1843, and added to its stock company Mrs. Hautonville and Messrs. Gallagher Byrne, Brookes, Brown, and T. Steele. The new actors occasionally appearing on its boards in 1844 were Messrs. G. Smith, T. V. Turner, and L. G. Thomas. The theatre closed in May, not to reopen for the rest of the year.

In June, Burton leased the Arch and opened with the following company: Mr. and Mrs. C. Burke, Mesdames J. B. Booth, Jr., Hughes, Misses Cadell, Kirby, Wilson, and Messrs. G. Barrett, W. E. Burton, E. S. Conner, Faulkner, Graham, Grierson, Hawks, Hichman, Jervis, N. Johnson, W. G. Jones, H. Russell, Smith, Walters, and Weston.

Messrs. Neville, Morris, and Addis were the additional occasional players at the Arch in 1844.

In October Pratt and Wemyss opened the Chestnut with a large company which included Mr. and Mrs. Forest, Mr. and Mrs. (H. C.) Jordon, Mr. and Mrs. C. Mestayer, Mesdames (A.) Knight, Hautonville, Misses Archer, Bryant, Cornish, Downes, Ferrai, Mack, McBride, Nelson, Palmer, St. Clair, Smith, Wagstaff, Wilson, and Messrs. Bernard, Brunton, W. Chapman, Dawes, Grierson, C. Howard, Jamieson, Mason, T. Mathews, Mossop, J. Sefton, (C. J.) Smith, Solomon, Stafford, Sullivan, and F. C. Wemyss.

C. Moore, at his first appearance in America, played at the Chestnut for the one night, November 6, in the rôle of Claude Melnotte from the *Lady of Lyons.*

The year of 1844 brought to the Philadelphia stage among the new visiting stars: Mrs. Wilkinson, Mrs. Maclure, and Miss Zann, heroines; Anderson, tragedian; W. H. Crisp, and Jno. Dunn, portrayers of low comedy.

1845

During the year of 1845, the Walnut added six excellent players to its list of stock actors: Mr. and Mrs. Sloman, Mrs. W. R. Blake, Mrs.

W. H. Smith, and Messrs. W. B. Chapman and (W. S.) Fredericks.

On January 22d, actors from the Park Theatre, N. Y., came to the Chesnut, to form a double company with the regular troupe of the latter theatre. This arrangement lasted for about one month. Among the actors who came from New York were: Mr. and Mrs. Dyott, Miss Clara Ellis, and Messrs. Chippendale, Crocker, and John Fisher.

An attempt was made to open the National this year, April 28, but the theatre only remained open for several weeks of legitimate drama. Months later, it was converted into a circus. But during its brief legitimate run, beginning April 28, the following actors made up the important part of the company there: Mesdames (J.) Green, McLean, Preston, and Messrs. Freer, Marsh, N. Johnson, and S. Johnson.

Besides leasing and running the Arch Street Theatre, Burton also put a company of his into the Chesnut, August 30th, and kept them there until October 6th, when he brought them back to swell the numbers at the Arch. The Company at the Chesnut included Mr. and Mrs. J. Greene, Mr. and Mrs. C. Mestayer, Mesdames Bell, Capell, Davis, Hughes, Jamar, Mason, W. H. Smith, McLean, Ribas, Misses Coad, Rogers, Messrs. J. Barrett, Brazier, W. E. Burton, Duff, J. Dunn, D. Eberle, (W. S.) Fredericks, James, (E. N.) Thayer, Mulholland, Rea, (E.) Shaw, C. Smith, and Wright.

The French Opera Company again came to the Chesnut in 1845 for an engagement of about twelve nights, beginning September 29. The company included Mesdames Casini, Stephen Coeuriot, Richer, Mlle. Calvé, and Messrs. Armand, Donory, and Garry.

The additional occasional players this year were: Messrs. Brian O'Flagherty and Milnor at the Chesnut, Mrs. Drake at the Walnut, and Mrs. Dunn and Messrs. Keller and McDougal at the Arch.

Among the new visiting players this year were: Mrs. Mowatt, heroine, whose significant comedy of *Fashion* received its first Philadelphia performance April 16, 1845; J. Fest, the tragedian; and Miss Logan, heroine.

1846

On March 9, 1846, there opened a new theatre of legitimate drama in the city: Peale's Philadelphia Museum, and Gallery of Fine Arts, late Masonic Hall, Chesnut Street. The place had been in existence a long time as a hall for exhibits and variety performances, but the month of March saw the beginning of acceptable legitimate drama there.

Peale's Museum remained open constantly throughout the year, and invited to its boards the following actors: Mr. and Mrs. C. Burke, Mr. and Mrs. C. Howard, Mesdames Gibbons, Henry, (T. B.) Russell, Thompson, Misses Mary A. Gannon, Fanny Ludlow, Mary Taylor, E. Wood, and Messrs. Bowers, Byrnes, Cunningham, Duff, Holland, Kemble, J. Sefton, C. J. Smith, B. Williams, and Wright.

In 1846, Burton announced the following people as members of his company at the Arch, August 26: Mr. and Mrs. J. Wallack, Sr., Mr. and Mrs. C. Howard, Mesdames Hughes, H. Lewis, McLean, Mossop, Rogers, Miss Caroline Chapman, and Messrs. Arnold, Blankman, C. Burke, W. E. Burton, Faulkner, (R.) Hamilton, Hickman, Jervis, Marsh, Martin, Philips, J. R. Scott, Walters, Wood, and Wright.

And, following the summer recess, the Walnut opened with the following players as announced in the newspapers for August 29: Mr. and Mrs. R. Blake, Mesdames C. Burke, Gibbons, (E. N.) Thayer, A. Fisher, Wilks, Coad, Crocker, Petrie, and Messrs. A'Becket, Boswell, Brunton, W. Chapman, Denby, Duff, (D.) Eberle, G. Jamison, D. Reed, Leman, Perry, P. Richings, Radcliffe, Stevens, Warden, and (B.) Young.

Among the visiting actors new to the Philadelphia stage this year were Becom, who played the leading male rôle in *The Stranger, Oranaska,* and *The Golden Farmer;* Mr. and Mrs. C. Thorne appearing as supporting players with Becom in *Ernest Maltravers;* Miss Kate Ludlow, comedienne; G. F. Browne as Dick Turpin in the melodrama of *Rookwood;* Leonard, comedian; and Miss Julia Dean, heroine.

1847

Among the additional actors appearing at Peale's Philadelphia Museum for 1847 were Mrs. Penson, Misses E. Eberle, E. Wood, and Messrs. Elssler, Gallagher, (N.) Johnson, W. F. Johnston, Macklin, J. O. Sefton, Stuart, and (E. N.) Thayer.

This year to the regular stock company of performers the Arch added Mrs. Hilson and Mrs. Wilkinson, and the Walnut added Mrs. Bowers.

The Italian Opera Company from Havana appeared for an engagement at the Walnut and was announced to consist of seventy-two people. The outstanding singers in this company included Mesdames T. Gerli, S. Marini, F. Tedesco, and Messrs. L. Bataglini, P. Candi, J. Perozzi, and J. Piamontesi.

Particularly numerous were the new visiting stars for the year of 1847:

Mrs. Coleman Pope appeared in an engagement of nine performances at the Arch, beginning January 13th, in the rôle of Jane Shore, Julia in *The Hunchback,* and Pauline in *The Lady of Lyons.*

De Bar, the comedian, likewise played at the Arch in the character of Old Dodge from *The Artful Dodger,* and Satisfaction Skunk in *The Indian Girl.* With him, appeared Mlle. H. Vallee in the latter play as Narramattah, a part frequently taken by Mlle. Celeste.

Miss C. Wemyss, presumably the daughter of Francis C. Wemyss, fulfilled an engagement at the Arch in the parts of Jane Shore, Julie in *Richelieu,* and Bianca in *Fazio.* Her father appeared twice during her engagement.

J. B. Roberts, the tragedian, with the support of Mrs. Ada Stetson, acted for five nights at the Arch in *Pizarro,* as well as in *Romeo and Juliet* and other Shakespearean tragedies.

Mrs. Farren came to the Arch for sixteen performances, as Evadne, Lucrece Borgia, Mary Tudor, and Adelgitha.

A comedian of considerable proportions was Captain Harvey Tucket whose engagement of five nights began October 25th, first as Falstaff in *Henry IV* and then as Dazzle in *London Assurance.*

Walter Shelley, Shakespearean actor, appeared four times at the Arch, on each occasion in the different part of Hamlet, Beverly in *The Gamester,* Richelieu and Shylock.

Chas. D. Pitt and Elder G. J. Adams, both Shakespearean players, also fulfilled engagements at the Arch this year.

It appears from the records that the Arch, to the exclusion of all other Philadelphia theatres, had the monopoly in bringing new visitors to its boards in the year of 1847, and it is to be remembered that William E. Burton was the lessee, manager, and enterprising spirit behind the operation of this theatre.

Also the Arch had the monopoly upon the ranks of new occasional actors appearing upon the Philadelphia stage this year. In the following list, McKeon alone was at the Walnut and all the rest were at the Arch: Misses Clarke, Hill, Jefferson, H. Vallee, and Messrs. Garretson, McKeon, Moorhouse, J. Scott, and Tellings.

1848

The year of 1848 witnesses on our record a great increase in the list of new names appearing upon the Philadelphia stage, not only in engagements, but also in stock. William E. Burton, with his accustomed enterprising spirit, invited many new players to the Arch in this year. His stock company for the year included, besides himself, Mr. and Mrs. C. Howard, Mesdames J. B. Booth, Jr., (T. B.) Russell, Misses Hill, Petrie, and Messrs. D. P. Bowers, Henkins, J. Owens, J. H. Robinson, and (E. N.) Thayer.

At E. A. Marshall's Walnut this year, the following regular players appeared: Mr. and Mrs. J. Wallack, Jr., Misses Julia Daly, A. Fisher, and Messrs. A'Becket, W. Chapman, W. Leman, Nagle, Radcliffe, P. Richings, and W. Wheatley.

And, for the short season at Peale's Philadelphia Museum, the stock company there comprised Mr. and Mrs. F. S. Myers, Mesdames J. B. Booth, Jr., C. Burke, T. B. Russell, Misses Clark, Van Pelt, and Messrs. Allen, Daws, (N.) Johnson, (J. A.) Leonard, Martine, Moorhouse, Richardson, and Walcot.

A new theatre opened in 1848. December 25, 1848, J. S. Silsbee, owner and acting manager, opened the Athenaeum National Museum at the corner of Seventh and Chesnut Streets. D. P. Bowers was the stage manager. Silsbee himself is to be remembered as the visiting comedian and portrayer of Yankee rôles who appeared on the Philadelphia stage by engagement. His company at the Athenaeum included Mr. and Mrs. D. P. Bowers, Mr. and Mrs. J. S. Silsbee, Misses E. Eberle, Hall, Jenny West, Young, and Messrs. Bamford, Crocker, E. Dean, (J. M.) Field, (J. R.) Hall, R. Johnson, McMinn, E. Thompson, Walters, and West.

The Italian Opera Company from Havana, Cuba, appeared at the Chesnut for four engagements, which totaled almost sixty performances. The names of the principals were Mesdames Boulard, Biscaccianti, Morra, Amalia Patti, Barili Patti, Teresa Truffi, and Messrs. Arnoldi, Benedetti, Rossicorsi, Morra, Salvator Patti, Rosi, and A. Valtellina.

The new visiting actors were exceedingly many this year and, with few exceptions, appeared at Burton's Arch. They were Lover, Mortimer, T. B. Johnston, H. H. Paul, light comedians; Maurice Power, the Irish comedian; Miss Fanny Wallack, comedienne; Miss Mary Ann Heron and J. Weaver, with the Heron Children, appearing in light comedies and farces; Mrs. Winstanley, in comedy repertoire as support for Mr. and Mrs. J. Brougham; H. Grattan and W. Marshall, tragedians; Mrs. E. S. Conner, tragedienne, appearing with her husband; Fenno, tragedian, appearing with Mrs. Farren; and Brandon in tragedy repertoire as support for Macready.

Among the occasional players who appeared in 1848 for the first time on the Philadelphia stage were: Mrs. Frary, Miss Sinclair, Messrs. A. J. Adams, Atkinson, J. Baker, Bradshaw, Grosvenor, Johns, J. E. McDonough, and Siple.

1849

At Burton's Arch Street Theatre in 1849, the following names formed the backbone of his company: Mr. and Mrs. N. B. Clarke, Mesdames H. Cramer, H. Nicholls, W. H. Smith, Winstanley, Misses F. Wallack, E. Wood, and Messrs. J. Baker, J. Dunn, W. Marshall, and (E. N.) Thayer.

Burton brought Chanfrau, the Yankee comedian, to the Arch this year for an engagement. At the end of his engagement, Chanfrau with J. Owens opened the National for six nights to give the new play of the *Mysteries and Miseries of New York,* beginning October 8, but Burton hurried and produced the same play on October 3, in anticipation of their plans.

During the short season at Peale's Philadelphia Museum, from April to July, the actors who appeared were Mr. and Mrs. D. P. Bowers, Mesdames J. B. Booth, Jr., M. S. Fogg, C. Howard, J. Russell, Thompson, Misses M. Gannon, Mortimer, E. Wood, and Messrs. Belford, George F. Browne, De Bar, (D.) Eberle, J. Jefferson, Kaimes, McDonough, and Tidmarsh.

Following the summer recess, W. E. Horn, as lessee, opened the Chesnut with a stock company, which included Mesdames (C.) Burke, Hackurt, G. Jones, M. Jones, F. S. Myers, Misses A. Fisher, Logan, and Messrs. C. Foster, R. Johnson, Kaimes, J. A. Leonard, Logan, B. Rogers, and J. R. Scott.

The additional visiting actors to our theatres in 1849 were: in comedy, Mr. and Mrs. Sloan, Messrs. J. Ollier, Worrel, Seymour, and C. W. Hunt. In the repertoire of Irish comedy, in particular, Messrs. Redmond, Ryan, Belford, and Hudson as new visiting actors bear witness to the constant popularity of that one phase of our theatre, and take their places with Collins and Power, and the other Irish comedians. In the Yankee comedy, we have the new name of Mrs. J. P. Addams, who appeared with her husband, the actor and writer of Yankee comedies and farces (among them, *Sam Patch in France*); also, there is Chanfrau, who acted in the "Mose" plays.

For the serious play, we have the new name of Couldock, an actor appearing with Miss Charlotte Cushman. There is also Farren, accompanying Mrs. Farren, and Mrs. Charles Dibdin Pitt, the comedienne, playing the leading comedy rôle on the same nights that her husband took the lead in tragedy.

In melodrama, Canfield and J. H. Hall appeared, the latter in the equestrian spectacles of *Eagle Eye, or the Steed of the Delawares,* and the *Horse of the Prairie,* where King Horse was really the hero.

Littell, a heavy, played the part of Washington in *Putnam,* and Bayley took the part of Washington in the new historical drama of *Benj. Franklin, or the Days of 1776,* with Cartlick in the title rôle of the same play.

There is one event in particular, which the present writer wishes to chronicle: the return of Miss Jean Margaret Davenport to the Philadelphia stage after an absence of eleven years. In 1838, under the tutelage of her mother, she was a child actress, attempting the Shakespearean rôles of Richard III and Shylock. But now, a woman, she comes back to Philadelphia as a gracious heroine.

There is another absence of eleven years that must be noted in the reappearance of J. P. Addams.

Among the new occasional names for the year are those of Miss Barber, Messrs. Frank Bowes, Vincent, Watkins, and Rogers—the latter known as the Stammering Tragedian, who stuttered through the rôle of Shylock.

1850

The company at the Chesnut for 1850 included Mr. and Mrs. (N. B.) Clarke, Mrs. F. Myers, Miss E. Wood, and Messrs J. Baker, Ellsler, C. Foster, B. Rogers, and McMillan.

February 13, 1850, E. S. Conner took over Burton's Arch Street Theatre. Burton dropped from sight at this time, going to New York, and his theatre changed its name to Conner's Arch. The actors playing there under the new régime were Mr. and Mrs. E. S. Conner, Mr. and Mrs. I. B. Phillips, Mesdames Altemus, J. B. Booth, Jr., H. Cramer, Ellwell, Misses F. Cramer, Fanny Gordon, Rose Merrifield, Wheeler, and Messrs. Bland, J. P. Brelsford, Kellogg, Keenan, Macleis, Joseph Megary, B. G. Rogers, George Spencer, Stites, and C. Webb.

At the Walnut this year, in the regular stock company there appeared Mrs. Stephens, Misses A. Fisher, F. Wallack, and Messrs. A'Becket,

W. Chapman, Couldock, J. Dunn, (W. S.) Fredericks, P. Richings, and W. Wheatley.

Two Italian Opera Companies came to the Chesnut in 1850, one from Havana, and one from New York, under the baton of Max Maretzek. The principals in the first company were Mesdames L. Bellini, Elisa Costini, Balbina Steffenone, and Messrs. F. Badiali, D. Lorini, and I. Marini; and in the second, the leads were Mesdames Bertucca, Truffi, A. Patti, N. Fitzjames, T. Parodi, and Messrs. Airgnone, Benevantano, Forti, Rosi, and Sanquirico.

This year, P. T. Barnum's Museum, at the corner of Seventh and Chesnut Streets, offered legitimate drama under the management of Henry Sanford. The actors regularly appearing at this theatre included Mr. and Mrs. (E. N.) Thayer, Mesdames Rogers, Mueller, Misses Mortimer, A. Fisher, and Messrs. Ashmer, J. Baker, B. Rogers, and Germon.

Among the additional occasional actors at the Philadelphia theatres in 1850 were Mrs. Couldock (wife of the stock actor); Mrs. Walker; the Misses F. Mowbray, Stewart, A. Eberle, Chippendale, K. Horn, Millington, Miles, and Adderton; and Messrs. S. L. Sanford, Kingsmore, Harvey Ellis, Beechley, C. Montgomery, Sheble, E. W. Jones, Smead, Hemple, Ryer, and Reynolds.

Among the new visiting players this year were Kate and Ellen Bateman, four and six years of age respectively, who attempted Shakespeare. Mrs. Barney Williams made her appearance this year with her husband, the comedian. Other additional comedians were Sir William Don in farces, Macarthy in Irish plays, H. Linden, in the "Jakey" farces, and T. G. Booth.

To melodrama was added the name of W. R. Derr. J. P. Brelsford and Conway as leading men, Buchanan as a tragedian, and Madame Ponisi and Miss E. Maria Duret as leading ladies, complete the list of new names for the year, with one exception: we must not forget that Mademoiselle Jenny Lind, the Swedish Nightingale, made her initial Philadelphia appearance in a concert at the Chesnut for one night, October 17, 1850, with tickets selling at seven dollars, six dollars and five dollars a seat. A week or so later, the famous singer appeared at the Musical Fund Hall for two evenings, with the lowest seats at four dollars. Jenny Lind's début in America had long been promised. Witness the effect of this promise in the titles of several dramatic sketches given in our theatres for a year or so before her advent. Barnum did not fail to keep his word that he would bring Jenny Lind to America.

1851

A complimentary benefit was given to Miss Virginia Howard at the Chesnut, February 22, 1851, and provides us with the mention of many new names. Those actors taking part in the benefit were Mrs. Howard, Miss Virginia Howard, and Messrs. W. A. Baker, C. Bussard, Cartmel, Coffee, E. Hedings, Highman, J. Irvin, J. R. Mason, Myers, S. Pancoast, W. Rohrman, Shepherd, S. Siple, J. Stewart, H. L. Thomas, and H. C. Wertz.

Miss Davenport took over the Chesnut for an engagement, beginning March 1. She was supported by her own company including Messrs. John Gilbert, Mason, Savage and Ward, and had A. W. Fenno for her stage manager.

The regular stock company which followed Miss Davenport's extended stay at the Chesnut included Mr. and Mrs. Ellsler, Miss Fanny Wallack, Messrs. McDonough, (J. H.) Taylor, C. Moorhouse, G. C. Ryan, J. Owens, Lindon, Hildreth, (R.) Johnston and W. F. Wood. Two months later (when the theatre opened on August 18) after the summer recess, the Chesnut was under the new direction of Fredericks as acting manager and Henry Wallack as stage manager, with the addition of Miss Anderton, and Messrs. Taylor, Dawson, and Scharf to the regular company.

The National was opened for the summer, July 15, 1851, with W. K. Johnston as stage manager, W. T. McKeon as acting manager. W. W. Hamblin was the treasurer and Denby the prompter.

The company included Mr. and Mrs. J. Ellsler, Mr. and Mrs. Y. Leonard, Mesdames W. Gladstone, Mueller, Stephens, and Messrs. G. F. Browne, Brunton, Carson, Denby, Fisher, Fitzgerald, Hamblin, R. Johnston, Hildreth, G. Kamers, Langdon, McDonough, McKeon, D. McMillan, Nagle, J. Proctor, B. Rogers, Savage, and T. J. Worrell.

Early in the year of 1851 the Walnut added Mrs. Germon and Messrs. Worrell, Browne, W. R. Goodall, and C. J. Smith to the stock company. When the theatre was opened, on August 18, following the summer, the actors at the Walnut were Mr. and Mrs. Couldrock, Mr.

and Mrs. Seguin, Mesdames Bailey, Kinlock, J. S. Silsbee, Misses Chippendale, A. Goughenheim, J. Goughenheim, Millington, E. Reed, Wemyss, and Messrs. A'Becket, Bishop, W. Chapman, Brunton, (E. L.) Davenport, D. Eberle, Fitzgerald, (R.) Johnston, Langdon, McGowan, McKeon, William Reed, P. Richings, B. Rogers, B. Young, and Terry.

When the Arch opened on August 30, T. J. Hemphill was the lessee and Charles Burke, the stage manager. The following actors made up the company: Mr. and Mrs. Lewis Baker, Mr. and Mrs. W. G. Jones, Mr. and Mrs. D. Da Costa, Mr. and Mrs. J. Herbert, Mr. and Mrs. R. Morrell, Mr. and Mrs. A. Parker, Miss Cornelia Jefferson, Mrs. M. Burke, and Messrs. W. Anderson, J. H. Boswell, P. Brown, C. Burke, J. H. Calladine, W. S. Clifford, J. English, J. S. Fannin, B. Jackson, J. Jefferson, N. Johnston, (G. C.) Ryan, and T. J. Worrell.

The actors playing at Barnum's Museum after the summer recess, were: Mr. and Mrs. D. P. Bowers, Mr. and Mrs. E. N. Thayer, Mrs. Cooper, Mrs. Hackurt, Mrs. Wilkes, Miss Mortimer, and Messrs. J. H. Robinson, Savage, Carson, Stearns, J. A. Leonard, Quayle, and Williams.

The new visiting players for the year of 1851, included Mrs. Warner and the Misses Julia Bennett, Susan Denin, and Heron, heroines; Madame Anna Thillon, lead in opera; and Messrs. G. F. Marchant, and McVickers, comedians.

1852

In 1852, Mr. and Mrs. D. P. Bowers were added to the regular stock company at the Walnut. To the regular players at James Quinlan's Chesnut were added J. H. Taylor and Mr. and Mrs. John Drew. Husband and wife came this year to the Philadelphia stage, which they were later to captivate, and where they were to become the recognized leaders of the theatrical world in their family theatre, the Arch. To the regulars at the Arch, this year of 1852, were added Mr. and Mrs. Ward, and Brand, and when the theatre was reopened on August 21 by T. J. Hemphill, lessee, it had A. W. Fenno for stage manager, J. Ingles Matthias for treasurer, and the following company: Mesdames Da Costa, J. Gilbert, M. Jones, Wilkinson, Miss (Virginia) Howard, and Messrs. Cunningham, A. W. Fenno, Fisher, and D. S. Palmer.

The National opened on May 22nd with the following players: Mr.

and Mrs. (Y.) Leonard, and Messrs. (T. B.) Johnston, E. N. Thayer, C. F. Wood, W. F. Wood, Sr., and W. F. Wood, Jr.

And, on July 12th, Joseph C. Foster, as lessee and manager took over the National with eighty-six performers, promising a series of magnificent spectacles. The principals of the company included Mr. and Mrs. J. C. Foster, Mesdames Ellsler, Gladstone, (I. B.) Phillips, Place, and Messrs. Bayley, Brunton, Charles Foster, Burnett, N. Johnston, M. L. B. Richardson, (B. G.) Rogers, Shephard, and B. Young.

The new visiting featured players for 1852 included: G. V. Brooke, Shakespearean tragedian; Caroline Richings, lead in opera; Lola Montez, the Countess of Lansfeldt, a famous dancer; Mrs. Sinclair in support of G. Vandenhoff, the tragedian; and Kate Denin in support of her sister, Susan Denin, the heroine. B. Hill and G. E. Locke, comedians, constitute the two principal occasional players for the year.

1853

During the year of 1853, the following players appeared regularly upon the boards at the Chesnut: Mr. and Mrs. J. Gilbert, Mr. and Mrs. Tyrrell, Mesdames Cappell, Rose Merrifield, Miss Lizzie Weston, and Messrs. H. A. Davenport, Eytinge, A. W. Fenno, J. Jefferson, McFarland, and Roys.

From the first of the year to the summer closing, the additions to the stock company at the Walnut included: Mrs. Hall, Miss Emma Fitzpatrick, and Messrs. Couldock and Jordan.

With the reopening of the Walnut, September 6, 1853, Joseph O. Sefton supplanted Peter Richings as manager, and directed the following company: Mr. and Mrs. France, Mrs. Duffield, Miss A. Ince, and Messrs. A'Becket, (A. J.) Adams, W. Chapman, McDonough, J. O. Sefton, Wheatleigh, and B. Young.

From January 29, 1852, until the summer recess, Thomas J. Hemphill was the lessee of the Arch, with William S. Fredericks as manager, and J. I. Matthias as treasurer. The players were Mr. and Mrs. Conrad Clarke, Mr. and Mrs. John Drew, Mesdames J. Herbert, Place, Wilks, Misses Matilda Heron, L. Steele, William, Wilson, and Messrs. Bradley, Dolman, Hall, Hamilton, H. P. Hickey, D. P. Palmer, Paullin, Roberts, Savage, Stone, Vanhorn, and W. Wheatley.

In August, William Wheatley and John Drew took over the lease of the Arch. At this time the principal players were Mr. and Mrs. D.

P. Bowers, Mr. and Mrs. John Drew, Mr. and Mrs. (F. D.) Nelson, and Messrs. McBride, E. N. Thayer, and William Wheatley.

Among the new visiting players for 1853 were Madame Marietta Alboni in opera, and Mr. and Mrs. W. J. Florence in Irish Comedy. Fanny Morant, a new lead in heroine rôles, appeared on engagement supported by James Anderson. And for a period of several weeks in December, S. S. Sanford brought his burlesque opera company to the Chesnut. Sanford's troupe regularly occupied the building at the Southwest corner of Twelfth and Chesnut Streets, known as S. S. Sanford's Opera House. Here they played burlesque opera exclusively.

1854

The year of 1854 brings a great many new names to the ranks of the stock players in the Philadelphia theatres. To the Arch this year, Wm. S. Fredericks came as stage-and-acting manager. Messrs. Shewell and F. Nelson Drew, and Miss Olive Logan were the additions to the regular company at the Arch this year.

The following names comprised the principals in the company at the Walnut: Mr. and Mrs. Bellamy, Mr. and Mrs. D. P. Bowers, Mesdames J. Brougham, F. Nelson Drew, Maddox, Miss Laura Mowbray, and Messrs. Donaldson, G. H. Griffiths, Harris, W. F. Johnson, J. E. Nagle, O'Brien, and John Owens.

At the Walnut, under the management of John Sefton, the additional numbers of the company in 1854 were Mr. and Mrs. J. Sefton, Mesdames Hackurt, Louisa Howard, Langdon, and Messrs. H. Farren, Perry, and Wallis.

The National opened June 3, 1854, for the summer, with a company composed of Mesdames Deering, (Y.) Leonard, Miss E. Deering, and Messrs. Ashmer, Chippendale, W. R. Derr, W. R. Goodall, Lomas, McBride, McKeon, Shepard, and John Weaver.

Two different troupes of English opera came to the Philadelphia theatres in 1854, one at the Chesnut for a week, beginning June 6th, and the other at the Walnut for sixteen days, beginning October 30th. The opera company at the Chesnut, consisted of Mme. De Marguerittes, Mrs. Altemus, Mrs. King, Mlle. Lovarnay, and Messrs. A. Granville, Ferdinand Mayer, and E. Warden. The opera troupe at the Walnut had for its principals the Misses Pyne and Louisa Pyne, and Messrs. Borani and W. Harrison. In addition, there was an Italian Company at the Chesnut for a week beginning August 28th, under the direction of Max Maretzek. The singers were Mme. Bertucca Maretzek, Signora Martini D'Ormy, Signor Neri Beraldi, and Signor Graziani.

A new theatre opened its doors September 12, 1854: The City Museum, Callowhill Street below Fifth, with the following players: Mr. and Mrs. Ryner, Mesdames F. N. Drew, E. N. Thayer, Miss Hood, and Messrs. J. L. Gallagher, Hemple, J. E. McDonough, Langdon, Nagle, B. J. Rogers, and (T. J.) Worrell.

For 1854, the new visiting stars were Miss Agnes Robertson, comedienne; Lysander Thompson, comedian; Charles Henderson, tragedian; Garry Demotte, a player of melodrama; and George W. Kemble, also a player of melodrama.

1855

An abundance of new players came to Philadelphia in 1855, also, as a careful study of the stock companies will show.

Perhaps, the greatest change in the stock companies was the transfer of Mr. and Mrs. John Drew from the Arch to the Walnut for 1855. Apparently William Wheatley and John Drew dissolved the partnership which they had maintained for two years. For, in 1855, the Arch was known simply as Wheatley's Arch Street Theatre.

The company at the Walnut for 1855 included Mr. and Mrs. John Drew, Mesdames Duffield, Muzzy, Miss Bernard, and Messrs. H. A. Davenport, Perry, Shewell, and B. Young.

During the week beginning November 19, 1855, a French Company appeared at the Walnut in plays of their own tongue, from writers as different as Corneille and Molière. The players were Misses Raphael, Sarah Felix, Lia Felix, Dinah Felix, and Messrs. L. Beauvallet, Cheri, Jr., Dieudonne, Latouche, and Randoux.

The principal actors at the Arch for the year were Mr. and Mrs. F. B. Conway, Mr. and Mrs. F. N. Drew, Mr. and Mrs. E. N. Thayer, and Messrs. J. S. Clarke, (J. R.) Hall, and William Wheatley.

S. E. Harris was the sole lessee and manager of the Chesnut in 1855, and, under his direction the following players appeared: Mr. and Mrs. G. H. Griffiths, Mr. and Mrs. J. J. Prior, Mesdames (N. H.) Bannister, Rose Merrifield, Langdon, Estelle Potter, Misses Julia Daly, Gertrude Dawes, Little Lavinia Bishop, and Messrs. Edwards, S. E. Harris, Macarthy, (Charles) Mestayer, W. Olwine, Stone, and Studley.

At S. M. Zulich's City Museum, the following players acted under the management of D. P. Bowers: Mr. and Mrs. D. P. Bowers, Mesdames W. H. Hough, (C.) Watson, Misses Anna Cruise, Annie Lee, Wells, and Messrs. W. H. Bailey, C. Clarke, Byrne, Hemple, T. B. Johnston, Lingham, (C.) Mestayer, S. K. Murdock, and Page.

Beginning with the month of August, a German Company played at the Melodeon, a variety hall at 201 Chesnut Street. During their occupancy the place was known as the German National Theatre. Their performances were infrequent, and their advertising did not note the names of the players.

Among the visiting players in Philadelphia in 1855 were Miss Fanny Vining, who played opposite her husband, E. L. Davenport; S. W. Glenn, an actor in Dutch comedy; Mr. and Mrs. W. H. Rees, Miss Rosalie A. Durrand, and F. Lyster, English opera singers; Boucicault, the comedian and writer of farces (see *Used Up,* a farce of his in which he appeared); and G. E. Charles with his daughter, Miss M. A. Charles, actors in Irish comedy. For ten performances beginning October 15, 1855, Marsh's Juvenile Comedians occupied the Walnut. This was a company of "fourteen girls, three youths, and twelve ballet children," whose feature play was *Beauty and the Beast.*

ANNUAL CHRONOLOGICAL RECORDS

CHAPTER IV
ANNUAL CHRONOLOGICAL RECORDS

THE following hundreds of pages give the day-by-day record of the plays in the Philadelphia theatres from 1835 to 1855 inclusive. In this list, the title of a play is starred with an asterisk (*) whenever the newspapers advertise that the given performance was the first Philadelphia production of the play. Whenever possible, the cast of players for a first-night performance is printed in full after the title of the play. But no cast of actors is included for regularly recurrent performances of old favorite plays, since space forbids.

Semicolons serve to separate the two or three pieces played at a theatre in one evening, such as the curtain-raiser, the play proper, and the after-piece. The titles of plays and the names of actors are printed in Roman type; the rôles of characters are signified by *italics*.

The following abbreviations for the theatres have been used:

W.—Walnut Street or American Theatre
C.—Chesnut Street Theatre
A.—Arch Street Theatre
P.—Pennsylvania or Coates Street Theatre
N.—New National or National Theatre
O.—Olympic Theatre
P. M.—Peale's Philadelphia Museum
Ath.—Athenaeum National Museum
B.—Barnum's Museum
C. M.—City Museum
G. N.—German National Theatre
Mam. C.—Mammoth Circus Building.

JANUARY 1835

1. *Thursday:*
   W.—Lover's Quarrels; Deep, Deep Sea! ! *: *American Sea Serpent*—J. Sefton, *Neptune*—J. M. Brown, *Cepheus*—W. Sefton, *Venus*—Mary Duff; Night Hag.
   C.—Venice Preserved; Esmerelda.

2.   W.—The Stranger; Deep, Deep Sea! !
     C.—The Stranger; Comfortable Lodgings.

3.   W.—Night Hag; Golden Farmer; In the Wrong Box *: *D'r. Plympton*—Porter, *Godfrey Fairfax*—Wemyss, *Isabella*—Mrs. Thorne.
     C.—The Wife; Forty Winks.

5. *Monday:*
     W.—Hamlet; Dumb Belle.
     C.—Hunchback; In the Wrong Box.

6.   W.—Macbeth; In the Wrong Box.
     C.—Jane Shore; The Mummy.

7.   W.—Virginius; Amazon Sisters.
     C.—Gustavus III.*: *Gustavus*—Wood, *Baron B'Jelk*—Hamilton, *Capt. Ankarstorm*—Walstein, *Oscar*—Mrs. Rowbotham, *Christian Engleheart*—Burton, *Madame Ankarstrom*—Miss Pelham; Haunted Inn.

8.   W.—Uncle Sam; Douglass; American Sea Serpent.
     C.—Jealous Wife; Sleeping Draught.

9.   W.—Damon and Pythias; In the Wrong Box.
     C.—Provoked Husband; Matrimony; Modern Antiques.

10. W.—Pizarro; The Rake's Progress *: *Tom Rakewell*—Jackson, *Harry Markham*—Wemyss, *Sam Slop*—J. Sefton, *Ned Nokes*—Connor, *Fanny Moreland*—Mary Duff.
     C.—Gustavus III; Secret; John Jones.

12. *Monday:*
     W.—Town and Country; Bohemian Mother.
     C.—Fazio; Ladies' Man *: *Mr. Daffodil Twod*—Burton, *Brigadier Bounce*—Jones, *Widow Wiggins*—Mrs. Jones.

13. W.—Macbeth; The Rake's Progress.
     C.—Gustavus III; My Uncle John *: *Uncle John*—Burton, *Nephew Hawk*—Hamilton, *Niece Hawk*—Mrs. Maywood.

14. W.—Hunchback; The Rake's Progress.
     C.—Virginius; Ladies' Man.

15. W.—Wm. Tell; Good Looking Fellow; In the Wrong Box.
     C.—Hunchback; My Uncle John.

16. W.—Romeo and Juliet; Oh! Hush! !; Good Looking Fellow.
     C.—Stranger; Hundred-Pound Note.

17. W.—Damon and Pythias; Mary *: *Arthur Morris*—Connor, *Young Langley*—Wemyss, *Simon Scentwell*—J. M. Brown, *Jemmy Miggleby*—J. Sefton, *Mary*—Mary Duff.
     C.—Gustavus III; Ladies' Man.

19. *Monday:*
     W.—Othello; He is not A-Miss *: *Mr. Prettyman*—J. Sefton, *Fitzallan*—Wemyss, *Mrs. Aldgate*—Mary Duff.
     C.—The Wife; Katharine and Petruchio.

20.   W.—The Wife; Mary.
      C.—Blind Beggar of Bethnal Green *: *Bess*—Emma Wheatly, *Lord Wilford*—Knowles, *Albert*—Maywood, *Ralph*—Rowbotham; My Uncle John.
21.   W.—Virginius; The Golden Farmer.
      C.—Wild Oats; Gustavus III.
22.   W.—Stranger; He is not A-Miss; The Good Looking Fellow.
      C.—Blind Beggar of Bethnal Green; Comfortable Lodgings.
23.   W.—Iron Chest; Uncle Sam; He is not A-Miss.
      C.—Blind Beggar of Bethnal Green; The Review.
24.   W.—Othello; Kill or Cure!
      C.—Wm. Tell; Gustavus III.
26.   *Monday:*
      W.—Brutus; Kill or Cure!
      C.—Wild Oats; Kill or Cure!
27.   W.—Damon and Pythias; He is not A-Miss.
      C.—Point of Honour; Gustavus III.
28.   W.—Zanthe *: *Carlos*—Connor, *Don Leo*—Jackson, *Cosmo*—Jones, *Gonza*—Huntley, *Zanthe*—Miss Duff, *Felix*—Mrs. Kent, *Lenora*—Miss Charnock, *Francesca*—Miss Ruth; Kill or Cure!
      C.—As You Like It; Kill or Cure!
29.   W.—Zanthe; Nature and Philosophy.
      C.—Cinderella; John Jones.
30.   W.—Zanthe; Kill or Cure!
      C.—Wives as they Were; No Song No Supper.
31.   W.—Zanthe; Voice of Nature.
      C.—The Tempest; Luke the Laborer.

FEBRUARY

2.   *Monday:*
      W.—Somnambulist; Zanthe.
      C.—A Bold Stroke for a Husband; Modern Antiques.
3.   W.—Zanthe; Uncle Sam.
      C.—Wedding Gown; Gustavus III.
4.   W.—Zanthe; Kill or Cure!
      C.—Belle's Stratagem; John of Paris.
5.   W.—Pay for Peeping *: Mary Duff to sustain three characters; Zanthe.
      C.—White Lady *: *Gaveston*—Walton, *Sandy M'Phear*—Rowbotham, *George Brown*—Hunt, *Alie M'Phear*—Mrs. Rowbotham, *Louise*—Mrs. Austen; Ladies' Man.
6.   W.—Zanthe; He is not A-Miss.
      C.—Fazio; Perfection.

7.   W.—Zanthe; Damp Beds*: *Capt. Racket*—Wemyss, *Maria Fairlove*—Mary Duff.
   C.—White Lady; The Mummy.

9. *Monday:*
   W.—Tom and Jerry; Spoil'd Child.
   C.—Winter's Tale; Kill or Cure!

10. W.—Kill or Cure! Tom and Jerry.
   C.—White Lady; John Jones.

11. W.—Spoil'd Child; Zanthe.
   C.—All in the Wrong; Sleeping Draught.

12. W.—Married Life; Tom and Jerry.
   C.—Married Life; White Lady.

13. W.—Charles II; Popping the Question; Therese.
   C.—Soldier's Daughter; Clari.

14. W.—Golden Farmer; Siamese Twins; Tom Cringle.
   C.—Married Life; White Lady; Luke the Laborer, last act.

16. *Monday:*
   W.—Zanthe; Married Life.
   C.—The Tempest; Abon Hassan.

17. W.—Married Life; Zanthe.
   C.—Married Life; Gustavus III.

18. W.—Foundling of the Forest; Siamese Twins.
   C.—All in the Wrong; Turn Out.

19. W.—A New Way To Pay Old Debts; Married Life.
   C.—Masaniello; Cinderella, last act; Master's Rival.

20. W.—The Apostate; Siamese Twins.
   C.—Soldier's Daughter; The Rent Day.

21. W.—Richard III; Welsh Girl*: *Alfred*—Connor, *Julia*—Mrs. Kent.
   C.—Fazio; Young Widow. Last night of present season.

23. *Monday:*
   W.—Stranger; Uncle Sam.
   A.—Hero of the North; Sprigs of Laurel.

24. W.—Hamlet; Welsh Girl.
   A.—Wife; My Uncle John.

25. W.—Fazio; Zanthe.
   A.—Romeo and Juliet; Hundred-Pound Note.

26. W.—Romeo and Juliet; Siamese Twins.
   A.—Virginius; Pleasant Dreams.

27. W.—Soldier's Daughter; Zanthe.
   A.—Hero of the North; Deep, Deep Sea; John Jones.

28. W.—Old Man's Curse*: *Blanche*—Miss Monier, *Francis*—Connor, *Friboulet*—Jackson, *De Bercy*—Senior, *Melchoir*—Kent; Good Looking Fellow; Tom Thumb.
   A.—Beggar of Bethnal Green; Deep, Deep Sea.

MARCH

2. *Monday:*
   W.—Hunchback; Old Man's Curse.
   A.—Wm. Tell; Deep, Deep Sea.
3. W.—She Would and She Would Not; Tom Thumb.
   A.—Guy Mannering; Old and Young.
4. W.—Tom Thumb.
   A.—Charles II; Spoil'd Child; Mummy.
5. W.—Amazon Sisters; Weathercock; Beulah Spa *: *Sidney Beauchamp*—Thayer, *Caroline Grantley*—Miss Duff.
   A.—Poor Soldier; Deep, Deep Sea.
6. W.—Richard III; Beulah Spa.
   A.—Jane Shore; Old Gentleman *: *Nicholas Oldham*—Jones, *Bell*—Mrs. Rowbotham; Pleasant Dreams.
7. W.—Richard III, fifth act; Pet of the Petticoats *: *Paul*— Mrs. Kent, *Col. Belair*—Jackson, *Capt. Cannonade*— Connor, *Mons. Zephyr*—J. Sefton, *Job*—J. M. Brown; Zanthe.
   A.—Clari; Actress of all Work; Deep, Deep Sea.
9. *Monday:*
   W.—Macbeth; Somnambulist.
   A.—A Bold Stroke for a Husband; Poor Soldier.
10. W.—The Convent; Zanthe.
    A.—Jealous Wife; Gretna Green.
11. W.—Damon and Pythias; Welsh Girl; Tristram Shandy *: *Charles Mortram*—Miss Meadows, *Villars*—Connor, *Redtape*—J. Sefton.
    A.—Much Ado about Nothing; My Friend the Governor *: *Pequillo*—Burton, *Filissia*—Mrs. Thayer; Actress of All Work.
12. W.—Pet of the Petticoats; Major Jack Downing; High Life below Stairs.
    A.—Home, Sweet Home; Old Gentleman; A Husband at Sight.
13. W.—Evadne; Tristram Shandy.
    A.—Clari; My Friend the Governor; Dead Shot.
14. W.—Virginius; The Executioner.
    A.—The Intemperate *: *Ned Briggles*—Burton, *Reynolds*— Walton, *Edward Boyce*—Hamilton, *Mary Boyce*—Mrs. Maywood; Cupid *: *Cupid*—Burton, *Mars*—Walstein, *Psyche*—Mrs. Rowbotham; Mummy.
16. *Monday:*
    W.—Lear; Unfinished Gentleman *: *Lord Totterly*—Porter, *Chas. Danvers*—Warren, *Billy Downey*—J. Sefton,

[133]

Hon. Frisk Flammer—Blaike, *Mary Chintz*—Mrs. Kent.

A.—Wizard Skiff *: *Alexa, Alexis, Agata*—three rôles—Mlle. Celeste, *Constantine*—Wood; Old Gentleman; Pleasant Dreams.

17. W.—Venice Preserved; Tristram Shandy.
A.—Wizard Skiff; Cupid; Ladies' Man.

18. W.—Julius Caesar; Unfinished Gentleman.
A.—Wizard Skiff; Kill or Cure; Wept of Wish-Ton-Wish.

19. W.—King John; Siamese Twins.
A.—Wept of Wish-Ton-Wish; Deep, Deep Sea; Wizard Skiff.

20. W.—Apostate; Four Mowbrays.
A.—Wept of Wish-Ton-Wish; My Friend the Governor; Wizard Skiff.

21. W.—Richard III; Welsh Girl.
A.—Moorish Page *: *Adhel*—Mlle. Celeste, *Clodimir*—Murdoch; John Jones; Forty Winks.

23. *Monday:*
W.—Uncle Sam; Last Days of Pompeii *: *Arbaces*—Jackson, *Glaucus*—Connor, *Lydon*—Blaike, *Socia*—J. Sefton, *Burbo*—J. M. Brown, *Nydia*—Mary Duff, *Ione*—Miss Fisher.
A.—Moorish Page; Sprigs of Laurel; The Mummy.

24. W.—Unfinished Gentleman; Last Days of Pompeii.
A.—Moorish Page; Sleeping Draught; Deep, Deep Sea.

25. W.—Siamese Twins; Last Days of Pompeii.
A.—French Spy; My Uncle John; Ladies' Man.

26. W.—Welsh Girl; Last Days of Pompeii.
A.—French Spy; Old Gentleman; Wizard Skiff.

27. W.—Good Looking Fellow; Last Days of Pompeii.
A.—Wept of Wish-Ton-Wish; Popping the Question; Moorish Page.

28. W.—Regent of France; Last Days of Pompeii.
A.—Death Plank *: *Antonio*—Mlle. Celeste; John Jones; French Spy.

30. *Monday:*
W.—Zanthe; Yard Arm and Yard Arm; Beulah Spa.
A.—Merry Wives of Windsor; Forty Thieves.

31. W.—Married Life; Zanthe.
A.—Masaniello; The Zoological Gardens *: *Dick Snapall*—Walton, *Peter Puddyfoot*—Burton, *Zadie*—Mrs. Conduit.

APRIL

1. *Wednesday:*
W.—Regent of France; Popping the Question; Unfinished

Gentleman; Siamese Twins; Somnambulist.
A.—Dramatist; Deserter of Naples *: *Henry*—Murdoch, *Simpkin*—Burton, *Skirmish*—Maywood, *Louise*—Mrs. Rowbotham.

2. W.—Aethiop; Judgment of Solomon! ! !
A.—Married Life; Wreck Ashore.

3. W.—Old Man's Curse; Pet of the Petticoats; Harlequin Shipwreck *: *Harlequin*—Rasimi, *Columbine*—Mrs. Kent.
A.—Education; Bombastes Furioso; Honest Thieves.

4. W.—Beulah Spa; Forest of Rosenwald; Simpson and Company.
A.—Damon and Pythias; Happiest Day of my Life. Last night of present season.

6. *Monday:*
W.—Rent Day; Two Gregories; Inn Keeper's Daughter.
C.—Jealous Wife; Ladies' Man.

7. W.—Aethiop; Wandering Boys.
C.—Venice Preserved; Sleeping Draught.

8. W.—Ardeschi *: *Marquis Girotti*—Thayer, *Ardeschi*—Connor, *Emma Frielsperg*—Mary Duff, *Annia*—Mrs. Kent; Therese.
C.—Wives as they Were; Clari.

9. W.—Gamester; Lady of the Lake.
C.—Soldier's Daughter; Gustavus III.

10. W.—Lottery Ticket; Wandering Piper; Tom Cringle.
C.—Belle's Stratagem; Tam O'Shanter.

11. W.—School for Scandal; Merchant of Venice, the trial scene; Schinderhannes *: *Schinderhannes*—Connor, *Peter the Black*—Jackson, *Hag of the Tomb*—Mary Duff. Last night of the season.
C.—Hunchback; The Mummy.

13. *Monday:*
C.—Honeymoon; Personation *: *Lord Henry-Mons. La Roche*—two rôles—Ternan, *Lady Julia, Mme. La Gouvernasite*—two rôles—Fanny Jarman; Somnambulist.

14. C.—Stranger; Pleasant Dreams.

15. C.—Bride of Lammermoor; Somnambulist.

16. C.—Provoked Husband; My Friend the Governor.

17. C.—School for Scandal; John Jones.

18. C.—Heart of Midlothian; My Wife's Mother *: *Mr. Felix Bud*—Wood.

20. *Monday:*
C.—Merchant of Venice; Personation; Irish Widow.

21. C.—Richard III; My Wife's Mother.

22. C.—Ugolino *: *Ugolino*—J. R. Scott, *Angelica*—Eliza Riddle, *Serassi*—Hamilton, *Olympia*—Mrs. Walstein; My Friend the Governor; Kill or Cure.

[135]

23.   C.—Virginius; Hunter of the Alps.
24.   C.—Mogul Tale; Ugolino; My Wife's Mother.
25.   C.—Ugolino; Family Jars; Tom Cringle.
27. *Monday:*
    C.—Rendezvous; Born to Good Luck; Midnight Hour.
28.   C.—Pleasant Dreams; Nervous Man and Man of Nerve; Irish Tutor.
29.   C.—Point of Honour; Gustavus III.
30.   C.—My Friend the Governor; Irish Ambassador; Omnibus.

MAY

1. *Friday:*
    C.—Spectre Bridegroom; Married Life; My Uncle John.
2.   W.—Jacob Faithful; Day in Paris.
    C.—Rivals; Teddy the Tiler.
4. *Monday:*
    W.—Jacob Faithful; Loan of a Lover.
    C.—Fortune's Frolic; St. Patrick's Eve; Irishman in London.
5.   W.—Jacob Faithful; Day in Paris.
    C.—Sleeping Draught; Etiquette Run Mad.
6.   W.—Loan of a Lover; Jonathan in England; Day in Paris.
    C.—As You Like It; Charles II.
7.   W.—Green Mountain Boy; Loan of a Lover.
    C.—Nervous Man and Man of Nerve; More Blunders than One; Family Jars.
8.   W.—Yankee Pedlar; Tom Cringle; Lovers' Quarrels.
    C.—Comfortable Lodgings; Born to Good Luck; Animal Magnetism.
9.   W.—Virginius; Forest Rose; Hypocrite, last scene.
    C.—Wild Oats; Irish Ambassador.
11. *Monday:*
    W.—Knight of the Golden Fleece *: *Sy*—Hill, *De Luna*—Conner, *Blabastro*—Hadaway, *Donna Constantia*—Miss Fisher, *Victoria*—Mary Duff; Obid and Ovid; Green Mountain Boy.
    C.—Heart of Midlothian; Unfinished Gentleman.
12.   W.—Knight of the Golden Fleece; Jonathan in England.
    C.—Merchant of Venice; Bold Dragoons.
13.   W.—Knight of the Golden Fleece; Jonathan Doubikins.
    C.—Deserted Village *: *Morden*—Murdoch, *Mark*—Wood, *Grevious*—Burton, *Annette*—Mrs. Rowbotham; Unfinished Gentleman; Rendezvous.
14.   W.—Knight of the Golden Fleece; Forest Rose.
    C.—The Jew; Inkle and Yarico.
15.   W.—Lion of the East *: *Major Downing*—Hill, *Titler*—Had-

away, *Sarah*—Miss A. Fisher, *Nabby*—Miss Duff; Day in Paris.

C.—Haunted Inn; Deserted Village; Popping the Question.

16. W.—Lion of the East; Knight of the Golden Fleece.

C.—Iron Chest; Old Gentleman.

18. *Monday:*

W.—Wives as they Were; Somnambulist.

C.—Jew; Deserted Village.

19. W.—Golden Farmer; Young Widow.

C.—Speed the Plough; Inkle and Yarico.

20. W.—Hunchback; Loan of a Lover.

C.—Gamester; Forty Winks.

21. W.—Lear; Therese.

C.—Stranger; Chimney Piece.

22. W.—Gamester; Gretna Green.

C.—Venice Preserved; Mummy.

23. W.—Honeymoon; Luke the Laborer.

C.—Jealous Wife; Happiest Day of my Life.

25. *Monday:*

W.—Virginius; Married Life.

C.—Provoked Husband; Child of Nature.

26. W.—Zanthe; Loan of a Lover.

C.—Englishmen in India; Napoleon.

27. W.—Much Ado about Nothing; Catharine and Petruchio.

C.—Haunted Inn; Napoleon; Chimney Piece.

28. W.—Fazio; Fortune's Frolic.

C.—Knowles' Benefit, the companies of both theatres, Married Life; The Wife. Advanced prices: boxes, two dollars; pit, one dollar; gallery, fifty cents.

29. W.—Romeo and Juliet; Review.

C.—Englishmen in India; Napoleon; John Jones.

30. W.—Henriette *: *De Monval*—Connor, *Deronz*—D. Reed, *Pionette*—Thayer, *Henriette*—Emma Wheatly; Turnpike Gate.

C.—School of Reform; Wreck Ashore.

JUNE

1. *Monday:*

W.—Henriette; Hunchback, last three acts.

C.—Henri Quatre; Queer Neighbors *: *Barnaby*—Burton; Day after the Fair.

2. W.—Richard III; Affair of Honour *: *Major Linkey*—Hadaway, *Mad. Tourville*—Mary Duff.

C.—Guy Mannering; Raymond and Agnes.

3. W.—New Way to Pay Old Debts; Seventeen Hundred Years

Ago *: *Egyptian*—Jackson, *Athenian*—Connor, *Blind Girl*—Miss Duff, *Sage*—Miss A. Fisher.

C.—Road to Ruin; The Duel.

4.   W.—Iron Chest; Seventeen Hundred Years Ago.

C.—Hamlet; 102!

5.   W.—Merchant of Venice, first four acts; Seventeen Hundred Years Ago.

C.—Foundling of the Forest; Somnambulist.

6.   W.—Richard III; Affair of Honour.

C.—Married Life; Napoleon, first part; The Duel.

8. *Monday:*

W.—Cherokee Chief *: *European Dogs*—Hector and Bruin, *Cherokee Chief*—Cony, *Matilda*—Mrs. Kent; Affair of Honour; Ourang Outang *: *Ourang Outang*—Master Blanchard.

C.—Wept of Wish-Ton-Wish; John Jones; Wizard Skiff.

9.   W.—Cherokee Chief; Loan of a Lover; Ourang Outang.

C.—Sleeping Draught; Wizard Skiff; Chimney Piece.

10.   W.—Cherokee Chief; Lover's Quarrels; Ourang Outang.

C.—Death Plank; 23 John St.; French Spy.

11.   W.—Forest of Bondy; Affair of Honour; Ourang Outang.

C.—Death Plank; Queen Neighbors; French Spy.

12.   W.—Affair of Honour; Forest of Bondy; Ourang Outang.

C.—Wept of Wish-Ton-Wish; My Friend the Governor; Wizard Skiff.

13.   W.—Forest of Bondy; Fighting by Proxy *: *Flinch*—Hadaway; Monkeyana *: *Monkey*—Master Blanchard, *Strappo*—Reed, *Philader*—Hadaway, *Dellora*—Miss A. Fisher.

C.—Death Plank; Spirit Bride *: *Zelia, Alcazes, Tofak*— three rôles—Mlle. Celeste.

15. *Monday:*

W.—Hermit's Prophecy; Monkeyana.

C.—Pleasant Dreams; Spirit Bride; Kill or Cure.

16.   W.—Richard of the Lion-Heart; Monkeyana.

C.—Forty Winks; Spirit Bride; Popping the Question.

17.   W.—Richard of the Lion-Heart; Monkey who has Seen the World.

C.—Comfortable Lodgings; Moorish Page; Rendezvous.

18.   W.—Cherokee Chief; Fighting by Proxy; Monkey who has Seen the World.

C.—Mogul Tale; Spirit Bride; John Jones.

19.   W.—Planter and his Dogs *: *Dogs*—Hector and Bruin, *Cato*— Cony, *Aura*—Mrs. Cooke; Fighting by Proxy; Ourang Outang.

C.—Sleeping Draught; Moorish Page; Queer Neighbors.

20. W.—Planter and his Dogs; Don Juan.
     C.—Wept of Wish-Ton-Wish, first act; French Spy, second
         act; Mummy; Wizard Skiff, first act.
22. *Monday:*
     W.—Miser's Daughter *: *Isaac*—Jackson, *Charles*—Connor,
         Ann—Miss Duff; Maid and Magpie; My Neighbor's
         Wife *: *Somerton*—Connor, *Brown*—Hadaway, *Mrs.
         Somerton*—Miss Duff.
     C.—Brutus; Bold Dragoons.
23. W.—Othello; My Neighbor's Wife.
     C.—Town and Country; Happiest Day in my Life.
24. W.—Hunting Park Jockey; From Six to Six; Don Juan.
     C.—Housekeeper; Napoleon, first part; Tom and Jerry, first
         part.
25. W.—Richard III, fourth and fifth acts; Welsh Girl; Don Juan.
     C.—Mountaineers; Virginius, fourth act; Gretna Green.
26. W.—Richard III; Luke the Laborer.
     C.—Henri Quatre; Duel.
27. W.—Damon and Pythias; Man with the Carpet Bag *: *Wrangle*
         —Connor, *Harriet*—Miss A. Fisher; Oh, Hush.
     C.—Iron Chest; Flying Dutchman.
29. *Monday:*
     W.—King Lear; Oh, Hush.
     C.—New Way To Pay Old Debts; Henriette.
30. W.—Virginius; Virginia Mummy.
     C.—Hamlet; Chimney Piece.

JULY

1. *Wednesday:*
    W.—Macbeth; Promissory Note.
    C.—King Lear; Forty Winks.
2. W.—Wm. Tell; Turnpike Gate.
    C.—Town and Country; 23 John St.
3. W.—Pizarro; Virginia Mummy.
    C.—Othello; Colonel's Come.
4. W.—My Neighbor's Wife; Merchant of Venice, fourth act;
        Virginia Mummy; Oh, Hush. Last night of season.
    C.—Richard III; John Jones. Last night of season.
6. *Monday:*
    W.—Special performance for the benefit of Mrs. Cooke who
        is confined by severe indisposition, combined companies of
        both houses: Popping the Question; Damon and Pythias,
        fourth and fifth acts; Married Life.
7. To August 21, inclusive, summer recess.

AUGUST

22. *Saturday:*
  W.—Richard III; My Neighbor's Wife.
  C.—Married Life; Ladies' Man.
24. *Monday:*
  W.—New Way to Pay Old Debts; Maid and Magpie.
  C.—Henri Quatre; Mummy.
25. W.—Hamlet; Affair of Honor.
  C.—She Stoops to Conquer; Comfortable Lodgings.
26. W.—Brutus; My Neighbor's Wife.
  C.—Bride of Lammermoor; John Jones.
27. W.—Richard III; Siamese Twins.
  C.—Soldier's Daughter; Bold Dragoons.
28. W.—Virginius; Congress Hall *: *Frederick*—Ward, *Sir John*—
    Collingbourne, *Miss Constant*—Mrs. Conway, *Maria*—
    Mrs. Knight.
  C.—Sweethearts and Wives; Gustavus III.
29. W.—Othello; Affair of Honor.
  C.—Deserted Village; Kill or Cure.
31. *Monday:*
  W.—King Lear; Congress Hall.
  C.—Hunchback; Forty Winks.

SEPTEMBER

1. *Tuesday:*
  W.—Julius Caesar; Mayor of Garrat.
  C.—School for Scandal; 23 John St.
2. W.—Wm. Tell; In the Wrong Box.
  C.—Deserted Village; Mummy.
3. W.—Damon and Pythias; Virginia Mummy.
  C.—Fazio; Forty Winks.
4. W.—Macbeth; Young Reefer *: *Barney*—Reed, *Julian*—Mary
    Duff; Oh, Hush.
  C.—Wives as they Were; Somnambulist.
5. W.—Woman's Life *: *Eugene*—Connor, *Bajazat*—Hadaway,
    Isabelle—Mme. La Marc—Mme. *Eugene*—three rôles—
    Mary Duff; Discoveries in the Moon *: *Jim Crow*—Rice,
    Dr. Herschel—Hadaway, *Mrs. Fancy*—Mrs. Knight,
    Nova—Miss Anderson.
  C.—Patrician and Parvenu *: *De Mowbray*—Walstein, *Percy*
    —Murdoch, *Stillton*—Jones, *Dick*—Burton, *Ellen*—Mrs.
    Walstein, *Mary*—Mrs. Thayer; Gustavus III.
7. *Monday:*
  W.—Pizarro; Discoveries in the Moon.

C.—Married Life; Moonshine *: *Skysail*—Walstein, *Cag*—Murdoch, *Twag*—Burton, *Tabitha*—Mrs. Walstein; Old Gentleman.

8. W.—Woman's Life; Discoveries in the Moon.
C.—Jonathan in England; Moonshine; Forest Rose.

9. W.—Stranger; Woman's Life.
C.—Green Mountain Boy; Jonathan Doubikins; Moonshine.

10. W.—Romeo and Juliet; Discoveries in the Moon.
C.—Patrician and Parvenu; Jonathan Doubikins.

11. W.—Fazio; Woman's Life; Virginia Mummy.
C.—Knight of the Golden Fleece; Moonshine; Hypocrite.

12. W.—Skeleton Witness *: *Danvers*—Connor. *Dormer*—Porter, *Waterleg*—Reed, *Celia*—Mary Duff; Oh, Hush; Woman's Life.
C.—Green Mountain Boy; Lion of the East, first act; Forest Rose, first act; Knight of the Golden Fleece.

14. *Monday:*
W.—Alexander the Great; Dead Shot.
C.—Pizarro; My Aunt.

15. W.—Hypocrite; Pitcairn's Island.
C.—Rent Day; Brigand.

16. W.—Biena *: *O'Fetterem*—Reed, *Boan*—Connor, *Groggylust*—Muzzy, *Mrs. Boan*—Mrs. Knight; Pitcairn's Island.
C.—Rendezvous; Spring and Autumn; Brigand.

17. W.—Biena; Dumb Savoyard and his Monkey *: *Monkey*—Gouffe, *Maldechina*—Porter, *Pepino*—Mad. Gouffe, *Countess Maldechina*—Mrs. Knight.
C.—Mogul Tale; Hazard of the Die *: *David*—J. Wallack, *Charles*—Murdoch, *Violette*—Mrs. Walstein; My Aunt.

18. W.—Illustrious Stranger; The Secret; Jocko.
C.—Rent Day; Adopted Child; John Jones.

19. W.—Wild Woman of our Village *: *Richard*—Connor, *Barleycorn*—Hadaway, *Alice*—Mrs. Knight; Dumb Savoyard and his Monkey.
C.—Hazard of the Die; Spring and Autumn.

21. *Monday:*
W.—Pitcairn's Island; Lying Valet; Jocko.
C.—The Wife; The Turn Out.

22. W.—102!; Secret; Three and Deuce.
C.—School for Scandal; The Secret.

23. W.—Spirit of '76 *: *Washington*—Porter, *Lafayette*—J. G. Porter, *Cornwallis*—Wemyss, *Andre*—Connor, *O'Clinker* Reed, *Columbia*—Mary Duff; My Neighbor's Wife.
C.—Gamester; Ladies' Man.

24. W.—Spirit of '76; Skeleton Witness.
C.—Wife; Sleeping Draught.

25.   W.—Spirit of '76; Wild Woman of our Village.
      C.—Macbeth; Three Weeks after Marriage.
26.   W.—Spirit of '76; Lo Zingaro *: *Lo Zingaro*—Connor, *Baron*
      —Reed, *Constanzo*—Mary Duff.
      C.—Bertram; Children in the Wood.
28. *Monday:*
      W.—Spirit of '76; Young Widow; Lo Zingaro.
      C.—Fazio; Personation; Animal Magnetism.
29.   W.—Spirit of '76; Secret Service *: *Fouche*—Reed, *Bernard*—
      Connor, *Therese*—Mrs. Knight.
      C.—All in the Wrong; Luke the Laborer.
30.   W.—Spirit of '76; Lo Zingaro.
      C.—Stranger; My Fellow Clerk *: *Tactic*—Burton, *Victim*—
      Thoman, *Fanny*—Mrs. Walstein; American Tar.

OCTOBER

1. *Thursday:*
      W.—Wild Woman of our Village; Lying Valet; Lo Zingaro.
      C.—Hunchback; My Fellow Clerk.
2.   W.—Merchant of Venice; Cherokee Chief; Sylvester Dagger-
      wood.
      C.—As You Like It; 23 John St.
3.   W.—Seven Clerks *: *Adolphe*—Connor, *Gustavus*—Muzzy,
      Claude—Reed, *Victorine*—Mrs. Knight; Cherokee Chief.
      C.—Secret; Shadow on the Wall *: *Evelyn*—Ternan, *Norris*—
      Walton, *Walton*—Walstein, *Billy*—Burton, *Cicely*—
      Mrs. Ternan; Perfection.
5. *Monday:*
      W.—Four Sisters; Love Me, Love My Dog *: *Breaker*—Cony,
      Seaforth—Connor, *Sadluck*—Knight, *Mary*—Mrs. Con-
      way; Perfection.
      C.—Wonder!; Shadow on the Wall.
6.   W.—Seven Clerks; Ourang Outang; Love Me, Love My Dog.
      C.—Heart of Midlothian; My Fellow Clerk.
7.   W.—The Exile; Forest of Bondy.
      C.—Soldier's Daughter; Black Ey'd Susan.
8.   W.—Exile; Cherokee Chief.
      C.—Jane Shore; Mummy.
9.   W.—Damon and Pythias; Gretna Green; Love Me, Love My
      Dog.
      C.—Somnambulist; Mary Stewart *: *Mary*—Mrs. Ternan,
      Douglass—Ternan, *Lindsay*—Walton, *M'Donald*—May-
      wood, *Lady Douglass*—Miss Pelham; John Jones.
10.   W.—Hyder Ali *: *Selim*—Cony, *Kaloch*—Master Blanchard,
      Hyder Ali—Reed, *Fatima*—Mrs. Conway; Ourang Ou-

tang; Wild Boy *: *Wild Boy*—Connor, *Karwinki*—Porter, *Carl*—Hadaway, *Countess*—Mrs. Muzzy.
C.—Honeymoon; Blind Boy.

12. *Monday:*
W.—Aladdin; Ourang Outang.
C.—Wives as they Were; Crossing the Line.

13. W.—Aladdin; Wild Boy.
C.—Othello; Turnpike Gate.

14. W.—Hyder Ali; Perfection; Forest of Bondy.
C.—Cure for the Heartache; Mummy.

15. W.—Englishmen in India; Loan of a Lover; Murder of the Blind Boy *: *Rufus*—Cony, *Juliet*—Mrs. Conway, *Dog*—Hector.
C.—Damon and Pythias; Crossing the Line.

16. W.—Forest of Bondy; My Neighbor's Wife.
C.—Honeymoon; My Fellow Clerk.

17. W.—Zenocles and the Greek Chief *: *Zenocles*—Cony, *Simon*—Hadaway, *Selim*—J. G. Porter, *Old Malek*—Mestayer, *Abdallah*—Reed, *Hazarah*—Brittenham, *Korak*—Stanley, *Zerasmin*—Miss Brittenham, *Elimra*—Mrs. Knight, *Zelima*—Mrs. Muzzy, *Dogs*—Hector and Bruin; Mountain Devil; Secret; Jack Robinson and his Monkey.
C.—Romeo and Juliet; Rhyme and Reason.

19. *Monday:*
W.—Knight of the Golden Fleece; Lo Zingaro.
C.—Hamlet; Turnpike Gate.

20. W.—Seven Clerks; Green Mountain Boy; Lying Valet.
C.—Hunchback; Kill or Cure.

21. W.—Jonathan in England; Knight of the Golden Fleece.
C.—School for Scandal; Hunter of the Alps.

22. W.—Lion of the East; Wild Woman of our Village.
C.—School for Scandal; Ladies' Man.

23. W.—Jonathan Doubikins; Lion of the East.
C.—Venice Preserved; Rhyme and Reason.

24. W.—Infidel *: *Lerma*—Connor, *Cortez*—Muzzy, *Guatimozin*—J. G. Porter, *Argana*—Hadaway, *Magdelina*—Mary Duff, *Zellabualla*—Mrs. Knight; Note Forger *: *John*—Porter, *Cressfield*—Reed, *Watty*—Hadaway, *Diana*—Mrs. Muzzy, *Phillis*—Mrs. Conway.
C.—Rule a Wife and Have a Wife; Mummy.

26. *Monday:*
W.—Isabella; Infidel.
C.—Much Ado about Nothing; Day after the Wedding; John Jones.

27. W.—Gamester; Note Forger.
C.—Wheel of Fortune; 23 John St.

[143]

28.   W.—Jane Shore; Botheration; Arab Chief *: *Ismael*—Connor, *Ali Beg*—Muzzy, *Snaggs*—Hadaway, *Lanyard*—Mrs. Conway.

      C.—Gamester; Second Thoughts *: *Sudden*—Burton, *Jabber*—Walton, *Cecil*—Cline, *Isadora*—Mrs. Maywood.

29.   W.—Adelgitha; Robber's Wife *: *Redland*—Connor, *Briarly*—Porter, *Penfuddle*—Collingbourne, *O'Gig*—Reed, *Rose*—Mrs. Duff.

      C.—Exile; Second Thoughts.

30.   W.—Infidel; Young Reefer.

      C.—Exile; Mary Stuart.

31.   W.—Gipsy of Ashburnham Dell *: *Mowbray*—Connor, *Montgomery*—Porter. *Burtle*—Hadaway, *Lovel*—Reed, *Rose*—Mrs. Conway; Arab Chief.

      C.—King's Fool critic.

NOVEMBER

2. *Monday:*

      W.—Brigand; Gipsy of Ashburnham Dell.

      C.—French Spy; John Jones; Kill or Cure.

3.   W.—French Washerwoman; Secret; Brigand.

      C.—Wizard Skiff; Gretna Green; French Spy.

4.   W.—Spoil'd Child; Lying Valet; Brigand.

      C.—Death Plank; Lovers' Quarrels; Wizard Skiff.

5.   W.—Tower de Nesle *: *Buriden*—Connor, *D'Aulnay*—Muzzy, *Orisini*—Reed, *Savois*—Hadaway, *Margaret*—Mrs. Pritchard; My Neighbor's Wife.

      C.—Death Plank; Sleeping Draught; French Spy.

6.   W.—Tower de Nesle; Arab Chief.

      C.—Wept of Wish-Ton-Wish; John Jones; Wizard Skiff.

7.   W.—Richard III; French Washerwoman.

      C.—Wept of Wish-Ton-Wish; Spirit Bride.

9. *Monday:*

      W.—I'll be your Second *: *Placid*—Knight, *O'Bryan*—Reed, *Emma*—Miss Charnock; Tour de Nesle; Miser's Miseries *: *Weazle Wideawake*—Hadaway, *Jenny Ferretout*—Mrs. Conway.

      C.—French Spy, first act; Spirit Bride.

10.   W.—Note Forger; Wild Woman of our Village; Miser's Miseries.

      C.—Devil's Daughter; Rendezvous; Kill or Cure.

11.   W.—Seven Clerks; Miser's Miseries; Fieschi *: *Gerard*—Porter, *Liverwort*—Knight, *Madini*—Mrs. Muzzy.

      C.—Devil's Daughter; Midnight Hour.

12.   W.—Fieschi; Miser's Miseries; Wreckers.

C.—Devil's Daughter; Fish out of Water.

13.   W.—Wreckers; Review; Cherry Bounce.

C.—Wept of Wish-Ton-Wish; Lovers' Quarrels; Devil's Daughter.

14.   W.—Miller and his Men; Turnpike Gate; Spanish Pirates *: *Michael*—Muzzy, *Pedro*—Reed, *Snaggs*—Hadaway, *Bob* —Mrs. Conway.

C.—Victoire *: *Victoire*—*Pierre*—*Clarisse,* three rôles—Mlle. Celeste, *Washington*—Walstein, *Lavender*—Burton; Spirit Bride.

16. *Monday:*

W.—Damon and Pythias; Spanish Pirates.

C.—Dramatist; Three and the Deuce.

17.   W.—Virginius; Cherry Bounce.

C.—Laugh when you Can; Day after the Wedding; Raising the Wind.

18.   W.—Jonathan in England, second act; Kentuckian, first act; Mons. Tonson; Catching an Heiress.

C.—Wild Oats; Young Widow.

19.   W.—Macbeth; Catching an Heiress.

C.—Busy Body; Englishmen in India.

20.   W.—Catching an Heiress; Siamese Twins; Spanish Pirates.

C.—Cure for the Heartache; Three and the Deuce.

21.   W.—Richard III; Black Angus of the Evil Eye *: *Muchardus* —Muzzy, *Angus*—Reed, *Dusty*—Hadaway, *Marion*— Mrs. Knight.

C.—Wept of Wish-Ton-Wish; French Spy.

23. *Monday:*

W.—Othello; Lo Zingaro.

C.—The Way to get Married; The Critic.

24.   W.—Pizarro.

C.—Laugh when you Can; Where shall we Dine; John Jones.

25.   W.—Brutus; Wreckers.

C.—Poor Gentleman; Weathercock.

26.   W.—New Way To Pay Old Debts; Oh, Hush!!

C.—Secrets Worth Knowing; Englishmen in India.

27.   W.—Infidel; Golden Farmer.

C.—Way to get Married; Hunter of the Alps.

28.   W.—New Way To Pay Old Debts; Oh, Hush.

C.—Win Her and Wear Her *: six characters by Mr. Balls, *Freeman*—Cline, *Modelove*—Jones, *Prim*—Burton, *Anne* —Miss Wheatley; Three and the Deuce; Match-Making *: *Shuffle*—Balls, *Emily*—Miss Pelham.

30. *Monday:*

W.—King Lear; Therese.

C.—Pizarro; My Aunt.

[145]

DECEMBER

1. *Tuesday:*
   W.—Bone Squash Diavolo *: *Diavolo*—Rice; *Switchel*—Hadaway, *Ducklegs*—Reed; Gipsy of Ashburnham Dell.
   C.—Hazard of the Die; Spring and Autumn.

2. W.—Bone Squash Diavolo; Miller and his Men.
   C.—Carib Chief; Second Thoughts.

3. W.—Bone Squash Diavolo; Black Angus.
   C—Bertram; The Wolf and the Lamb.

4. W.—Virginius; Bone Squash Diavolo.
   C.—Virgin of the Sun.

5. W.—Fatal Prophecies; Is He Jealous; Ambrose Gurnett.
   C.—Hamlet; Wolf and the Lamb.

7. *Monday:*
   W.—Jack Cade *: *Cade*—Addams, *Say*—Connor, *Henry*—Watson, *Lacy*—Porter, *Helen*—Mary Duff; Luke the Laborer.
   C.—Marriage of Figaro; No Song No Supper.

8. W.—Botheration; Nature and Philosophy; Raising the Wind.
   C.—Guy Mannering; Old and Young.

9. W.—Jack Cade; Weathercock.
   C.—A School for Grown Children; Illustrious Stranger.

10. W.—Venice Preserved; Agreeable Surprise.
    C.—Cabinet; Spoil'd Child.

11. W.—Jack Cade; Perfection.
    C.—Lord of the Manor; Old and Young.

12. W.—Jack Cade; Agreeable Surprise.
    C.—Marriage of Figaro; No!

14. *Monday:*
    W.—Two Gregories; Kaspar Hauser *: *Whittle*—Hill, *Grippswault*—Connor, *Danmer*—Porter, *Kaspar*—Miss Waring; Jonathan in England, last two acts.
    C.—Cinderella; Bombastes Furioso.

15. W.—Crowded Houses; Kaspar Hauser; Green Mountain Boy.
    C.—Rob Roy; No Song No Supper.

16. W.—Adventure *: *Abner*—Hill, *Jack*—Connor, *Mulieka*—Mrs. Conway; Forest Rose.
    C.—Cinderella, third act; Pet of the Petticoats; John Jones.

17. W.—Adventure; Yankee Pedlar.
    C.—Rivals; One, Two, Three, Four, Five *: *Harry, Teazle, Dr. Endall, Sam, an Actor*—five rôles—John Reeve.

18. W.—Kaspar Hauser; Adventure, first act; Forest Rose, first act; Knight of the Golden Fleece, second act.
    C.—Sweethearts and wives; Catching an Heiress.

19. W.—Gray Man of Tottenham *: *Prince*—Connor, *Mark*—Derivage, *Willy*—Hadaway, *Rosamond*—Miss Waring;

Crowded Houses; Love Laughs at Locksmiths.
    C.—Wreck Ashore; One, Two, Three, Four, Five.
21. *Monday:*
    W.—Gray Man of Tottenham; O-I-E-O-E; Crowded Houses.
    C.—Paul Pry; Catching an Heiress.
22.   W.—George Barnwell; Note Forger.
    C.—Sweethearts and Wives; One, Two, Three, Four, Five.
23.   W.—Idiot Witness; Nature and Philosophy; Poor Soldier.
    C.—Hypocrite; Catching an Heiress.
24.   W.—Lodoiska; Cherry Bounce.
    C.—Married Bachelor; Climbing Boy *: *Jack*—Reeve, *Buzzard*—Hamilton, *Rebecca*—Miss Pelham.
25.   W.—Uda and Magnus *: *Carlmilhan*—Porter, *Magnus*—Muzzy, *Fompey*—Hadaway, *Heist*—Clarke, *Uda*—Miss Waring, *Nora*—Mrs. Conway; Harlequin Hurry Scurry; Secret.
    C.—Wreck Ashore; Mummy; Bombastes Furioso.
26.   W.—Uda and Magnus.
    C.—Paul Pry; Cupid; One, Two, Three, Four, Five.
28. *Monday:*
    W.—Damon and Pythias; Uda and Magnus.
    C.—Deserted Daughter; Mummy.
29.   W.—Wm. Tell; Uda and Magnus.
    C.—Way to get Married; Englishmen in India.
30.   W.—Pizarro; Uda and Magnus.
    C.—Laugh when you Can; Children in the Wood.
31.   W.—Virginius; Uda and Magnus.
    C.—Bold Stroke for a Husband; Falls of Clyde.

JANUARY 1836

1. *Friday:*
    W.—Ida Stephanoff *: *Graf*—Porter, *Cassimer*—Connor, *Molan*—Hadaway, *Aberto*—Clarke, *Ida*—Miss Waring, *Miriam*—Mrs. Muzzy; Weathercock.
    C.—Columbus; Gretna Green.
2.   W.—Ida Stephanoff; Black Eyed Susan.
    C.—Deserted Daughter; Call Again Tomorrow *: *Dick*—Balls. *Melville*—Thoman, *Caroline*—Mrs. Walstein.
4. *Monday:*
    W.—Ida Stephanoff; Miser's Miseries; Arab Chief.
    C.—Secrets Worth Knowing; All at Coventry *: *Timothy*—Balls, *Bramble*—Jones, *Lively*—Walton, *Dora*—Mrs. Rowbotham.
5.   W.—Cherry Bounce; Uda and Magnus; My Neighbor's Wife.
    C.—Rent Day; Three and the Deuce.

6.   W.—Weathercock; Black Eyed Susan; Uda and Magnus.
        C.—Blind Bargain; Call Again Tomorrow; 23 John Street.

7.   W.—Douglass; Purse; Tom Thumb the Great.
        C.—Romeo and Juliet; All at Coventry.

8.   W.—Maid of Orleans; Purse.
        C.—Blind Bargain; A Roland for an Oliver.

9.   W.—Fish out of Water; Passion and Repentance *: *Greenwell*—
        Porter, *John*—Connor, *Lubin*—Hadaway, *Susan*—Miss
        Waring; Diamond Arrow.
        C.—Poor Gentleman; Colonel's Come.

11. *Monday:*
        W.—Richard III; Nature and Philosophy.
        C.—Three and the Deuce; Venice Preserved, fourth act; John
        of Paris; How to Die for Love.

12.   W.—Hamlet; Diamond Arrow.
        C.—Virgin of the Sun; Brigand.

13.   W.—New Way To Pay Old Debts; Hunting a Turtle *: *Mal-
        ler*—Connor, *Levison*—Wemyss, *Timothy*—Hadaway,
        Mrs. Turtle—Miss Waring.
        C.—Macbeth; Ladies' Man.

14.   W.—Iron Chest; Hunting a Turtle; No!
        C.—Much Ado about Nothing; Rent Day.

15.   W.—Apostate; Hunting a Turtle; Maid of Orleans.
        C.—Richard III; Forty Winks.

16.   W.—Richard III; Hunting a Turtle.
        C.—Alexander the Great; Wolf and the Lamb; My Friend the
        Governor.

18. *Monday:*
        W.—Richard III; Cherokee Chief; Maid of Orleans.
        C.—Maid of Judah; My Uncle John.

19.   W.—Mountaineer; Love Me, Love My Dog; Hunting a Turtle.
        C.—Massaniello; The Mummy.

20.   W.—Othello; Murder of the Blind Boy.
        C.—Road to Ruin; Kill or Cure.

21.   W.—Harlequin Tom the Piper's Son *: *Apollo*—Mrs. Conway,
        Tom—Collingbourne, *Roger*—Master Blanchard, *Kilder-
        kin*—Cony, *Patty*—Miss Charnock; Diamond Arrow;
        Cherry Bounce.
        C.—Maid of Judah; 23 John Street.

22.   W.—Wild Boy; Harlequin Tom the Piper's Son.
        C.—Fra Diavolo; John Jones.

23.   W.—Forest of Bondy; Harlequin Tom the Piper's Son.
        C.—Massaniello; Second Thoughts.

25. *Monday:*
        W.—Woman's Life; The Children of Chittigong *: *Harry*
        —Connor, *Chittigong*—Hadaway, *Tom Cringle*—Myers.

C.—Cinderella; Forty Winks.

26. W.—Yellow Kids *: *Capt. Rocket*—Porter, *Twins*—Hadaway, *Mrs. Rocket*—Mrs. Muzzy; Children of Chittigong.

C.—Barber of Seville; Pleasant Dreams.

27. W.—Henriette the Forsaken; Diamond Arrow.

C.—School for Grown Children; Illustrious Stranger.

28. W.—Virginius; Yellow Kids.

C.—Mountain Sylph *: *Donald*—Wood, *Hela*—Brough, *Christie*—Walton, *Eolia*—Mrs. Wood, *Jessie*—Mrs. Rowbotham; Sleeping Draught.

29. W.—Pizarro; Yellow Kids.

C.—Fra Diavolo; The Quaker.

30. W.—Macbeth;

C.—Mountain Sylph; My Friend the Governor.

FEBRUARY

1. *Monday:*

W.—Jack Cade; My Poll and my Partner Joe *: *Black Beard*—Muzzy, *Sculler*—Porter, *Henry*—Connor, *Mary*—Miss Duff.

C.—Maid of Judah; Happiest Day of my Life.

2. W.—Jack Cade; My Poll and my Partner Joe.

C.—Love in a Village; Gretna Green.

3. W.—Jack Cade; Hunting a Turtle.

C.—Barber of Seville; Second Thoughts.

4. W.—Damon and Pythias; Hunting a Turtle.

C.—Rob Roy Macgregor; Party Wall.

5. W.—William Tell.

C.—Cinderella; Secret.

6. W.—Yellow Kids; Passion and Repentance; Three Hunchbacks.

C.—Fra Diavolo; Freaks and Follies *: *Ned*—Hamilton, *Tom*—Barton, *Rowland*—Cline, *Ellen*—Mrs. Walstein.

8. *Monday:*

W.—Hamlet; My Neighbor's Wife.

C.—Mountain Sylph; Mummy.

9. W.—Passion and Repentance; Maid of Orleans;

C.—Guy Mannering; The Waterman.

10. W.—Who Owns the Hand? *: *Fillipo*—Connor, *Manfredoni*—Muzzy, *Luponi*—Clarke, *Giovanni*—Reed, *Rosalvina*—Miss Waring; Ladies' Man.

C.—No performance in consequence of preparation for Thursday Evening.

11. W.—My Poll and my Partner Joe; Who Owns the Hand?

C.—La Sonnambula *; Freaks and Follies.

12. W.—Who Owns the Hand?; Uda and Magnus.

C.—La Sonnambula; Forty Winks.

13.   W.—Who Owns the Hand?; Maid of Orleans.

C.—La Sonnambula; Ladies' Man.

15.   *Monday:*

W.—Rienzi; Diamond Arrow.

C.—La Sonnambula; Illustrious Stranger.

16.   W.—Yellow Kids; Maid of Orleans; Three Hunchbacks.

C.—La Sonnambula; Sleeping Draught.

17.   W.—Rent Day; Brigand.

C.—La Sonnambula; Popping the Question.

18.   W.—Wonder; Ambrose Gwinnett.

C.—La Sonnambula; My Friend the Governor.

19.   W.—Pizarro; My Aunt.

C.—La Sonnambula; Secret Service.

20.   W.—Hazard of the Die; Wolf and the Lamb; Nature and Philosophy.

C.—La Sonnambula; John Jones.

22.   *Monday:*

W.—Hazard of the Die; Wolf and the Lamb.

C.—La Sonnambula; The Twa Ghaists *: *Sir Alexander*—Jones, *Spout*—Burton, *Donald*—Maywood, *Harriet*—Mrs. Walstein.

23.   W.—Maid of Orleans; Ambrose Gwinnett.

C.—La Sonnambula; Secret Service.

24.   W.—Hazard of the Die; My Aunt; Cherry Bounce.

C.—La Sonnambula; Twa Ghaists.

25.   W.—William Tell; Hunting a Turtle.

C.—La Sonnambula; Illustrious Stranger.

26.   W.—Rienze; Purse.

C.—La Sonnambula; Twa Ghaists. Last night of the season.

27.   W.—Spring and Autumn; Adopted Child; Hazard of the Die.

A.—The Exile; Weathercock.

29.   *Monday:*

W.—The Jewess *: *King*—Muzzy, *Haman*—Connor, *Mordecai*—Porter, *Levi*—Hadaway, *Vashti*—Mrs. Muzzy, *Esther*—Miss Waring, *Zaide*—Miss Charnock; Hunting a Turtle.

A.—King's Fool; Second Thoughts.

MARCH

1.   *Tuesday:*

W.—The Jewess; My Neighbor's Wife.

A.—Hamlet; Popping the Question.

2.   W.—The Jewess; Fish out of Water.

A.—Gamester; Hunter of the Alps.

3. W.—The Jewess; The Agreeable Surprise.
   A.—King's Fool; Illustrious Stranger.
4. W.—The Jewess; My Poll and my Partner Joe.
   A.—Hunchback, third, fourth, and fifth acts; Henriette.
5. W.—The Jewess; Passion and Repentance.
   A.—Gamester of Milan; John Jones; The Critic.
7. *Monday:*
   W.—The Jewess; Perfection.
   A.—Julius Caesar; Mummy.
8. W.—The Jewess; Raising the Wind.
   A.—Romeo and Juliet; Wolf and the Lamb.
9. W.—The Jewess; Dumb Belle.
   A.—The Wife; The Weathercock.
10. W.—The Jewess; Turnpike Gate.
    A.—Hunchback; The Critic.
11. W.—The Jewess; Golden Farmer.
    A.—Merchant of Venice, trial scene; Much Ado about Nothing,
       second act; Othello, second and third acts; Everybody's
       Husband *: *Alexis*—Abbott, *Miss Tomkins*—Mrs. Balls.
12. W.—Wild Oats; Broken Heart *: *Alfred*—Connor, *Oliver*—
       Hadaway, *Agnes*—Miss Duff.
    A.—Pizarro; Brigand.
14. *Monday:*
    W.—Norman Leslie *: *Leslie*—Connor, *Judge*—Clarke, *More-
       land*—Wemyss, *Germaine*—Porter, *Grey*—Collins, *Crier*
       —Stanley, *Morton*—Hadaway, *Romaine*—Crouta, *Clair-
       mont*—Muzzy, *Loring*—Gibson, *Foreman*—Morton,
       Jailor—Germon, *Kreutzer*—Russel, *Louise*—Miss Duff,
       Rosalie—Miss Waring, *Mrs. Temple*—Mrs. Muzzy, *Miss
       Leslie*—Miss Charnock, *Mrs. Hamilton*—Miss Anderson,
       Flora Temple—Mrs. Cuvillier; Fish out of Water.
    A.—Rivals; Critic.
15. W.—Norman Leslie; Cure for the Heart Ache.
    A.—Second Thoughts; Deep, Deep Sea.
16. W.—Norman Leslie; Broken Heart.
    A.—School for Grown Children; Deep, Deep Sea.
17. W.—Laugh when you Can; The Jewess.
    A.—Paul Pry; Cupid.
18. W.—Perfection; My Aunt; Norman Leslie.
    A.—Sweethearts and Wives; Catching an Heiress.
19. W.—Barbarossa; Norman Leslie.
    A.—Married Life; One, Two, Three, Four, Five.
21. *Monday:*
    W.—Henry IV, first part; The Jewess.
    A.—The Wreck Ashore; One, Two, Three, Four, Five.
22. W.—The Jewess; Norman Leslie.

[151]

A.—Married Bachelor; Cupid; Catching an Heiress.
23. W.—Venice Preserved; Tom and Jerry.
A.—Deserted Daughter; Secret Service.
24. W.—Macbeth; The Jewess.
A.—Tom and Jerry; Unfinished Gentleman.
25. W.—The Spirit of the Black Mantle *: *Wolf*—Connor, *Ossa*—
Collingbourne, *Wittle*—Collins, *Rowena*—Mrs. Muzzy;
Comfortable Service *: *Admiral*—Porter, *Simon*—Had-
away, *Mary*—Miss Waring; Norman Leslie, Carnival
Scene.
A.—Bold Dragoons; One, Two, Three, Four, Five; Quad-
rupeds.
26. W.—The Jewess; Norman Leslie.
A.—The Court of Love *: *Carlos*—Wood, *Pacomo*—Burton,
Eugenia—Miss Wheatly; Actor of all Work; The Devil
to Pay.
28. *Monday:*
W.—Jonathan in England; Kentuckian, first act; Comfortable
Service.
A.—Pleasant Dreams; French Spy.
29. W.—Busybody; Job Fox, The Yankee Valet *; Monsieur Ton-
son.
A.—Fortune's Frolic; French Spy; Matrimony.
30. W.—Richard III; Fortune's Frolic.
A.—My Fellow Clerk; Wizard Skiff; Sleeping Draught.
31. W.—Rip Van Winkle; Monsieur Mallet, post office scene; Job
Fox, The Yankee Valet; Kentuckian, first act.
A.—Wept of Wish-Ton-Wish; Wizard Skiff.

APRIL

1. *Friday:*
W.—Caswallon; Comfortable Service.
A.—Wept of Wish-Ton-Wish; Wizard Skiff.
2. W.—Caswallon; Spirit of the Black Mantle.
A.—Moorish Page; French Spy.
4. *Monday:*
W.—Henry IV; Sledge Driver *: *Ivan*—Scott, *Grand Duke*—
Connor, *Alexis*—Hadaway, *Foedova*—Miss Waring.
A.—I'll be your Second; Moorish Page; The Actor of all Work.
5. W.—Who Owns the Hand?; Maid of Orleans.
A.—I'll be your Second; Spirit Bride; The Devil to Pay.
6. W.—The Widow's Victim *: *Twitter*—Porter, *Clipp, John,
Strappado*—three rôles—Hadaway, *Jane*—Miss Waring;
The Youthful Queen; Alberti Contradine.

A.—A Gentleman in Difficulties *: *Sedley*—Burton, *Piminey* —Mrs. Rowbotham; Spirit Bride; Gretna Green.

7. W.—Tour de Nesle; The Widow's Victim.
A.—Death Plank; A Gentleman in Difficulties; Moorish Page.

8. W.—Soldier's Daughter; Who Owns the Hand?
A.—Wept of Wish-Ton-Wish; Death Plank.

9. W.—Tour de Nesle; French Washerwoman; 23 John Street.
A.—Prince Lee Boo *: *Lee Boo*—Mlle. Celeste, *Pelewki*— Cline, *Mattley*—Walton, *Cherokah*—Miss Pelham; Wizard Skiff.

11. *Monday:*
W.—Disowned; French Tutor; Military Execution *: *Colonel* —Porter, *Henry*—Connor, *Francois*—Hadaway, *Maria*— Miss Waring.
A.—Prince Lee Boo; Wizard Skiff.

12. W.—Heart of Midlothian; Tekeli.
A.—Moorish Page; French Spy.

13. W.—Heir at Law; Hamlet, third act; Mummy.
A.—Spirit Bride; Death Plank.

14. W.—Who Owns the Hand?; Fortune's Frolic.
A.—Yelva *: *Yelva*—Mlle. Celeste, *Countess*—Mrs. Maywood, *Mina*—Mrs. Thayer; The Scotch Cooper *: *Duncan* —Maywood, *Sandy*—Burton, *Lizzy*—Mrs. Rowbotham; Moorish Page.

15. W.—No performance in consequence of preparation for the *Council of the Inquisition.*
A.—Yelva; Scotch Cooper; Moorish Page.

16. W.—Council of the Inquisition *: *Cardinal*—Muzzy, *Eleazer*— Connor, *Prince*—J. G. Porter, *John*—Hadaway, *Rachel*— Miss Waring; Cherry Bounce.
A.—Marie de Montville *: *Marie, Hugh, Chevalier*—three rôles—Mlle. Celeste, *Charles II.*—Cline, *Cromwell*— Wood, *Grinshaw*—Rowbotham, *Spandyke*—Burton; Spirit Bride.

18. *Monday:*
W.—Council of the Inquisition; Popping the Question.
A.—Paul Pry; Cupid.

19. W.—Council of the Inquisition; Yellow Kids.
A.—Sweethearts and Wives; Catching an Heiress.

20. W.—Council of the Inquisition; Cherry Bounce.
A.—Married Bachelor; One, Two, Three, Four, Five; Bold Dragoons.

21. W.—Council of the Inquisition; Diamond Arrow.
A.—Wreck Ashore; Quadrupeds.

22. W.—Council of the Inquisition; No!

  A.—Bold Dragoons; One, Two, Three, Four, Five; Quadrupeds.

23. W.—Council of the Inquisition; Old Gentleman.
  A.—Climbing Boy; Quadrupeds.

25. *Monday:*
  W.—Dream at Sea *: *Launce*—Connor, *Ralph*—Muzzy, *Alley*
   —Porter, *Tom*—Hadaway, *Anne*—Miss Waring; Mili-
   tary Execution.
  A.—Fra Diavolo; Matrimony.

26. W.—Council of the Inquisition; Old Gentleman.
  A.—Masaniello; Mummy.

27. W.—Council of the Inquisition; Comfortable Service.
  A.—Court of Love; Pleasant Dreams.

28. W.—Dream at Sea; Popping the Question; Somnambulist.
  A.—Maid of Judah; John Jones.

29. W.—Circumstantial Evidence *: *Ozzrand*—Conner, *Baron*—
   Muzzy, *Clauson*—Porter, *Tyrtillo*—Hadaway, *Louise*—
   Mrs. Willis; Council of the Inquisition.
  A.—Barber of Seville; Kill or Cure.

30. W.—Paul Ulric *: *Paul*—Conner, *Richard*—Porter, *Despard*—
   Muzzy, *Borel*—Hadaway, *Emily*—Mrs. Willis, *Mrs. Fife*
   —Mrs. Muzzy; Gretna Green.
  A.—Cinderella; Party Wall.

MAY

2. *Monday:*
  W.—Wenlock of Wenlock; May Queen.
  A.—La Sonnambula; I'll be your Second.

3. W.—Paul Ulric; Lady and the Devil.
  A.—Fra Diavolo; Happiest Day of my Life.

4. W.—Paul Ulric; May Queen.
  A.—The Exile; Hunter of the Alps.

5. W.—Jonathan in England; Green Mountain Boy.
  A.—La Sonnambula; My Fellow Clerk.

6. W.—Knight of the Golden Fleece; Forest Rose.
  A.—Love in a Village; Sleeping Draught.

7. W.—Kaspar Hauser; Jonathan Doubikins.
  A.—La Sonnambula; Chimney Piece.

9. *Monday:*
  W.—Yankee Pedlar; Knight of the Golden Fleece.
  A.—La Sonnambula; Crossing the Line.

10. W.—Maid of Orleans; Circumstantial Evidence.
  A.—La Sonnambula; No Song No Supper.

11. W.—The Adventure(ʳ) ; Forest Rose, one act; Honest Thieves.
  A.—No performance, so that orchestra might assist Mr. and

Mrs. Wood in their rendition of "La Sonnambula" at the Musical Fund Hall.

12. W.—Kaspar Hauser; The Adventure(ʳ).
    A.—La Sonnambula; John Jones.

13. W.—Knight of the Golden Fleece; Green Mountain Boy.
    A.—La Sonnambula; Mr. and Mrs. Jenkins.

14. W.—Yankee Pedlar; Hypocrite, two acts.
    A.—Court of Love; Married Life.

16. *Monday:*
    W.—Jonathan Doubikins, first act; Old Gentleman; Is He Jealous?; Jonathan in England, second act; Hypocrite, last act; Forest Rose, first act.
    A.—Richard III; Chimney Piece.

17. W.—Pizarro; Virginia Mummy.
    A.—Hazard of the Die; Spring and Autumn.

18. W.—Town and Country; Married Rake *: *Flighty*—Murdoch, *Mrs. Trick track*—Miss Waring; Lottery Ticket.
    A.—School for Scandal; Personation; I'll be your Second.

19. W.—Venice Preserved; Bone Squash Diavolo.
    A.—School for Grown Children; Pleasant Dreams.

20. W.—Dream at Sea; Married Rake; Bone Squash Diavolo.
    A.—The Wonder; Second Thoughts.

21. W.—The Daughter; Bone Squash Diavolo, first act; Virginia Mummy.
    A.—Belle's Stratagem; Forest Rose.

23. *Monday:*
    W.—Caradora *: *Caradora*—Murdoch, *Ambrosia*—Porter, *Leonardo*—Conner, *Montargio*—J. G. Porter, *Bianca*—Mrs. Willis; Oh! Hush! !
    A.—Jonathan Doubikins; Green Mountain Boy.

24. W.—Caradora; Bone Squash Diavolo.
    A.—Knight of the Golden Fleece; Forest Rose.

25. W.—Othello; Perfection.
    A.—All in the Wrong; Green Mountain Boy, first act; Luke the Laborer.

26. W.—Richard III; My Neighbor's Wife.
    A.—Fall of the Alamo *: *Peleg*—Hill, *Travis*—Walton, *Plympton*—Rowbotham, *Crockett*—Hathwell, *Santa Anna*—Darley, *Cos*—Wilks, *Mary*—Mrs. Walstein; Knight of the Golden Fleece; Mr. and Mrs. Jenkins.

27. W.—Brutus; The Daughter.
    A.—Wild Oats; Jonathan Doubikins.

28. W.—Brian Boroihme; 23 John Street.
    A.—Poor Gentleman; Kaspar Hauser.

30. *Monday:*
    W.—Hamlet; 23 John Street.

[155]

A.—Secrets Worth Knowing; Englishmen in India.
31. W.—New Way To Pay Old Debts; Lady and the Devil.
A.—Way to get Married; Call Again Tomorrow.

JUNE

1. *Wednesday:*
   W.—Apostate; 23 John Street.
   A.—Laugh when you Can; Matrimony.
2. W.—King Lear; Comfortable Service.
   A.—Dramatist; Three and the Deuce.
3. W.—Richard III; Forty and Fifty *: *White*—Hadaway, *Mrs. White*—Miss Waring.
   A.—Gambler's Fate; Fortune's Frolic.
4. W.—Othello; Mayor of Garratt.
   A.—Hunter of the Alps; French Spy; Fire and Water.
6. *Monday:*
   W.—Iron Chest; Tom and Jerry, one scene.
   A.—Brutus; Mummy.
7. W.—Hamlet; Forty and Fifty.
   A.—My Fellow Clerk; Ugolino; Ladies' Man.
8. W.—Julius Caesar; Comfortable Service.
   A.—Othello; Chimney Piece.
9. W.—Richard III; Forty and Fifty.
   A.—Iron Chest; Sleeping Draught.
10. W.—Merchant of Venice; Married Rake.
    A.—Crossing the Line; Ugolino; Comfortable Service.
11. W.—Othello; Mayor of Garratt.
    A.—Provost of Bruges *: *Berthulphe*—J. R. Scott. *Charles*—Rowbotham, *Bouchard*—Wood, *Constance*—Miss Pelham, *Ursula*—Mrs. Walstein; The Review. Last night of the present season.
13. *Monday:*
    W.—Actress of Padua *: *Angelo*—Conner, *Homodei*—Muzzy, *Rodolpho*—J. G. Porter, *Thisbe*—Miss Waring; Brian Boroihme.
    C.—Jealous Wife; Happiest Day of my Life.
14. W.—Actress of Padua; Brian Boroihme.
    C.—Crossing the Line; Napoleon, second part; Comfortable Service.
15. W.—Actress of Padua, Author's benefit; Brian Boroihme.
    C.—Borrowed Feathers *: *Frank*—Walton, *Tom*—Burton, *Rosamond*—Mrs. Walstein, *Lucy*—Mrs. Rowbotham; Napoleon, second part; Tom Cringle.
16. W.—Actress of Padua; Brian Boroihme.

C.—Laugh when you Can; Old Maid; The Mummy.

17.   W.—Dream at Sea; Brian Boroihme.

C.—Second Thoughts; Gustavus III; John Jones.

18.   W.—Point of Honor; Norman Leslie.

C.—The Duddlestones *: *Prince*—Wood, *Duddlestone*—Burton, *Queen Ann*—Miss Pelham, *Dame Duddlestone*—Mrs. Jones; The Wandering Minstrel.

20. *Monday:*

W.—Black Eyed Susan; Frank Fox Phipps; The Last Nail *: *Stark*—Connor, *Segismund*—J. G. Porter, *Rodolpho*—Muzzy, *Olfinger*—Collingbourne, *Lady Emmeline*—Mrs. Muzzy, *Agatha*—Mrs. Willis, *Cherubini*—Miss Waring.

C.—Fire and Water; French Spy; Borrowed Feathers.

21.   W.—Tom and Jerry; The Last Nail.

C.—Fortune's Frolic; Wizard Skiff; Wandering Minstrel.

22.   W.—Lucille *: *St. Cyr*—Connor, *Vernet*—Porter, *Schuyp*—Hadaway, *Lucille*—Miss Waring, *Julie*—Mrs. Willis; William Tell, fourth act; Hunting a Turtle.

C.—Wept of Wish-Ton-Wish; Wizard Skiff.

23.   W.—The Last Nail; Lucille.

C.—Wept of Wish-Ton-Wish; Devil's Daughter.

24.   W.—Lucille; The Last Nail.

C.—French Spy; Devil's Daughter.

25.   W.—Pocahontas; Hunting a Turtle.

C.—Yelva; Prince Lee Boo.

27. *Monday:*

W.—Wood Demon; Young Widow.

C.—Yelva; Prince Lee Boo.

28.   W.—Forty and Fifty; Wood Demon; 23 John Street.

C.—Moorish Page; Devil's Daughter.

29.   W.—Caradora; Dick the Apprentice.

C.—Crossing the Line; Spirit Bride; Comfortable Service.

30.   W.—Wood Demon; A Husband at Sight.

C.—Death Plank; Wandering Minstrel.

JULY

1. *Friday:*

W.—Pocahontas; A Husband at Sight.

C.—Wizard Skiff; My Fellow Clerk; Moorish Page.

2.   W.—Judgment of Solomon; Is He Jealous?; Dick the Apprentice.

C.—Escape of King Charles the Second; Devil's Daughter.

4. *Monday:*

W.—Liberty Tree *: *Gordon*—Porter, *Nat*—Conner, *Bill*—Hadaway, *Worston*—Muzzy, *Sally*—Miss Charnock, *Esther*—Miss Waring; Black Eyed Susan. Last night of the season.

C.—Second Thoughts; Napoleon, second act; Sprigs of Laurel.

6.   C.—Duddlestones; Valentine and Orson.

7.   C.—Napoleon; Tom Thumb the Great; Botheration; The Quadrupeds of Quidlemberg.

8.   C.—Crossing the Line; Married Life; Chimney Piece.

9.   C.—Botheration; The Gnome King; Quadrupeds of Quidlemberg.

11. *Monday:*

C.—Poor Gentleman; Perfection. Last night of the season.

July 12, 1836 to August 19, 1836, inclusive. Theatres closed during summer recess.

AUGUST

20. *Saturday:*

C.—Married Life; Gnome King.

22. *Monday:*

C.—Rent Day; Gnome King.

23.   C.—Rob Roy; Comfortable Lodgings.

24.   C.—Point of Honor; Masaniello, second and third acts.

25.   C.—Speed the Plough; Rosina.

26.   C.—Mountaineers; Othello, Travestie *: *Othello*—Burton, *Iago*—Rowbotham, *Roderigo*—Brunton, *Cassio*—Walton, *Desdemona*—Mrs. Rowbotham.

27.   W.—Fate of Calas; May Queen.

C.—Soldier's Daughter; Othello, Travestie.

29. *Monday:*

W.—Fate of Calas; Somnambulist.

C.—Hunchback; Othello, Travestie.

30.   W.—Fate of Calas; Lady and the Devil.

C.—Stranger; Comfortable Service.

31.   W.—The Bronze Horse *: *Statue of King of China*—D. Reed, *Prince*—Conner, *Tojan*—Wilks, *Ping Sing*—Hadaway, *Tchin Kao*—Porter, *Koyan*—J. G. Porter, *Cloud King*—Clark, *Margelia*—Miss Charnock, *Peki*—Mrs. Willis, *Kod Jan*—Mrs. Durang, *Lo Mangli*—Miss Scott; Man about Town *: *Skirts*—Hadaway, *Aubrey*—Conner, *Topps*—Wemyss, *St. Ledger*—Morton, *Mowbray*—J. G. Porter, *Dr. Mandible*—Mestayer, *Lady Aubrey*—Miss Charnock, *Fanny*—Mrs. Willis.

C.—Jealous Wife; Cheap Boarding.

SEPTEMBER

1. *Thursday:*
   W.—Bronze Horse; Man about Town.
   C.—The Wife; Cheap Boarding.
2. W.—Bronze Horse; Man about Town.
   C.—Wonder!; No Song No Supper.
3. W.—Bronze Horse; Ransom *: *Duvalle*—Porter, *Edward*—
   Conner, *Le Blanc*—Reed, *Philippe*—Hadaway, *Pauline*—
   Mrs. Willis, *Gertrude*—Mrs. Smith.
   C.—Merchant of Venice; Mummy.
5. *Monday:*
   W.—Bronze Horse; Ransom.
   C.—Damon and Pythias; Cheap Boarding.
6. W.—Stranger; Bronze Horse.
   C.—Othello; No Song No Supper.
7. W.—Hamlet; Bronze Horse.
   C.—Gladiator; Comfortable Service.
8. W.—Murder at the Black Farm *: *Stafford*—Clarke, *Lookout*—
   Porter, *Reynolds*—Conner, *Whitesand*—Hadaway, *Ellen*
   —Mrs. Willis, *Janet*—Miss Charnock; Bronze Horse.
   C.—Gladiator; Raising the Wind.
9. W.—Richard III; Bronze Horse.
   C.—Gladiator; John Jones.
10. W.—Macbeth; Bronze Horse.
    C.—Belle's Stratagem; Turn Out.
12. *Monday:*
    W.—New Way To Pay Old Debts; Bronze Horse.
    C.—Wept of Wish-Ton-Wish; French Spy.
13. W.—Richard III; Bronze Horse.
    C.—Wizard Skiff; French Spy.
14. W.—Apostate; Bronze Horse.
    C.—Devil's Daughter; Wept of Wish-Ton-Wish.
15. W.—Macbeth; Bronze Horse.
    C.—Moorish Page; Devil's Daughter.
16. W.—Much Ado about Nothing; Bronze Horse.
    C.—Prince Lee Boo; Wizard Skiff.
17. W.—Mob, the Out-Law *: *Mob*—Conner, *Jemmy*—Hadaway,
    Pierre—Wemyss, *Jerome*—Preston, *Agatha*—Mrs. Pres-
    ton; Bronze Horse.
    C.—Andreas Zell *: *Andreas, Guiseppe, Henrico*—three rôles
    —Mlle Celeste, *Isala*—Miss Fisher; Devil's Daughter.
19. *Monday:*
    W.—Wives as they Were; Bronze Horse.
    C.—Andreas Zell; Devil's Daughter.
20. W.—Bronze Horse; Mob, the Outlaw.

C.—The Dumb Sailor Boy; Comfortable Service; Andreas Zell.

21.   W.—Othello; Bronze Horse.

C.—Dumb Sailor Boy; Cheap Boarding; Andreas Zell.

22.   W.—Mob, the Outlaw; Bronze Horse.

C.—Flying Dutchman; Moorish Page.

23.   W.—Honey Moon; Bronze Horse.

C.—Flying Dutchman; Devil's Daughter.

24.   W.—Walter Brandt *: *Audley*—Conner, *Brandt*—Reed, *Buddle* —Hadaway, *Una*—Mrs. Preston, *Margery*—Mrs. Willis; Bronze Horse.

C.—Orphan of Russia; Man about Town; Spirit Bride.

26. *Monday:*

W.—Rule a Wife and Have a Wife; Scene in a Mad House; Bronze Horse.

C.—Second Thoughts; Irish Ambassador; Rosina.

27.   W.—Walter Brandt; Bronze Horse.

C.—John Bull; Mummy.

28.   W.—Hunchback; Bronze Horse.

C.—Nervous man and Man of Nerves; Comfortable Service; Irishman in London.

29.   W.—Walter Brandt; Bronze Horse.

C.—The Rivals; Irish Tutor.

30.   W.—Walter Brandt; Mob, the Outlaw.

C.—Hamlet; How do you Manage? *: *Popjoy*—Burton, *Snooks*—Faulkner, *Mrs. Popjoy*—Mrs. Rowbotham, *Mrs. Snooks*—Mrs. Thayer.

OCTOBER

1. *Saturday:*

W.—Skeleton Robber *: *Henrico*—Conner, *Rodolph*—Porter, *Shabrico*—Reed, *Roda*—Mrs. Willis, *Adriana*—Mrs. Preston; Mob, the Outlaw.

C.—St. Patrick's Eve, Omnibus.

3. *Monday:*

W.—Clandestine Marriage; My Master's Rival.

C.—Irish Ambassador; Irishman in London.

4.   W.—Paul Pry; Legion of Honor.

C.—Born to Good Luck; Teddy the Tiler; Young Widow.

5.   W.—Tecumseh; My Master's Rival.

C.—Nervous Man and Man of Nerve; Omnibus; Raising the Wind.

6.   W.—Heir at Law; Hundred-Pound Note.

C.—St. Patrick's Eve; Irish Tutor.

7.   W.—Married and Single; Hypocrite, second and fifth acts.

C.—John Bull; Is He Jealous?

8.   W.—Richard III; Mob, the Outlaw.
     C.—Irish Ambassador; Omnibus.

10. *Monday:*
     W.—Kill or Cure; Falls of Clyde; Removing the Deposites *:
       Turning the Tables.
     C.—The West Indian; Paddy Carey.

11.   W.—Skeleton Robber; Mob, the Outlaw.
     C.—The Rivals; Irishman in London.

12.   W.—Hunchback; Bronze Horse.
     C.—Rob Roy; Mummy.

13.   W.—Fazio; Personation; Man about Town.
     C.—Born to Good Luck; The Review; Waterman.

14.   W.—Macbeth; Perfection.
     C.—Etiquette; Teddy the Tiler; Is He Jealous?

15.   W.—Jane Shore; Swiss Cottage *: *Teik*—Hadaway, *Max*—
       Conner, *Lisette*—Mrs. Willis.
     C.—Lucille; Loan of a Lover; Young Widow.

17. *Monday:*
     W.—Winter's Tale; Somnambulist.
     C.—Lucille; Loan of a Lover; No!

18.   W.—Othello; Swiss Cottage.
     C.—Maid and Magpie; My Master's Rival.

19.   W.—Venice Preserved; Swiss Cottage.
     C.—Lucille; Loan of a Lover; Purse.

20.   W.—Castle Spectre; Three Weeks after Marriage; Personation.
     C.—She Stoops to Conquer; Swiss Cottage.

21.   W.—Mob, the Outlaw; Swiss Cottage; Bronze Horse.
     C.—Love in a Village; Swiss Cottage.

22.   W.—Paul Pry; Turnpike Gate.
     C.—Ransom; Comfortable Service; Swiss Cottage.

24. *Monday:*
     W.—School for Scandal; Somnambulist.
     C.—Ransom; Comfortable Service; Loan of a Lover.

25.   W.—Jane Shore; May Queen.
     C.—Lucille; My Husband's Ghost *: *Gilks*—Keeley, *Musket*
       —Walton, *Fanny*—Mrs. Rowbotham; 'Twas I.

26.   W.—Scapegoat *: *Pops*—Barnes, *Eustace*—Porter, *Molly*—
       Mrs. Preston; Pizarro; Sprigs of Laurel.
     C.—Ransom; My Husband's Ghost; Swiss Cottage.

27.   W.—Youthful Queen; Henriette; Comedy of Errors.
     C.—Farmer's Story; 'Twas I.

28.   W.—La Fitte *: *La Fitte*—Conner, *Martinez*—Clarke, *Gethe-*
       dana—Crouta, *Solomon*—Hadaway, *Reeado*—Thompson,
       Sabastian—Myers, *Theodore*—Mrs. Willis, *Cudgoe*—
       Percival, *Velasques*—Morton, *Alphonso*—Woodhull, *Con-*
       stanza—Mrs. Preston, *English Captain*—Raffile, *Locker*—

Newton, *Jackson*—Porter, *Governor*—Durang, *Johnston* —Boswell, *Barney*—Josephs, *Sergeant*—Clemens, *Officer* Wilks, *Soldier*—Chappell, *Oula*—Mrs. Smith; Swiss Cottage.

C.—Farmer's Story; Loan of a Lover.

29.   W.—La Fitte; Turning the Tables.

C.—Lucille; Hide and Seek *: *Moses*—Keeley, *Mrs. Mordaunt*—Mrs. Keeley; Swiss Cottage.

31. *Monday:*

W.—La Fitte; Turnpike Gate.

C.—The Wife; Man about Town.

NOVEMBER

1. *Tuesday:*

W.—La Fitte; My Wife and I.

C.—The Stranger; Spring and Autumn.

2.   W.—La Fitte; The Hotel.

C.—Pizarro; My Aunt.

3.   W.—La Fitte; Turning the Tables.

C.—The Gamester; Dead Shot.

4.   W.—La Fitte; Mrs. White, and Mrs. Peter White *: *Pepper*— Porter, *Brown*—Wemyss, *White*—Hadaway, *Kitty*— Mrs. Willis.

C.—Wonder; Second Thoughts.

5.   W.—La Fitte; Mrs. White, and Mrs. Peter White.

C.—Hunchback; The Wolf and the Lamb.

7. *Monday:*

W.—La Fitte: Cherokee Chief.

C.—Poor Gentleman; Of Age Tomorrow.

P.—Raising the Wind; Charles II; Affair of Honor.

8.   W.—La Fitte; Hyder Ali.

C.—Rivals; Wandering Minstrel.

P.—Heir at Law; Man about Town.

9.   W.—La Fitte; Cherokee Chief.

C.—Henry IV; Mummy.

P.—Rent Day; Secret; Two Gregories.

10.   W.—Wallace; La Fitte.

C.—School for Scandal; John Jones.

P.—Luke the Laborer; Kill or Cure; Lottery Ticket.

11.   W.—Zenocles; La Fitte; Ourang Outang.

C.—Road to Ruin; Wandering Minstrel.

P.—Therese; Rendezvous; Husband at Sight.

12.   W.—Wallace; La Fitte.

C.—Hypocrite; Scotch Cooper; Three Weeks after Marriage.

P.—Wreck Ashore; Fortune's Frolic.

14. *Monday:*
    W.—Wallace; Bronze Horse.
    C.—Macbeth; Dead Shot.
    P.—Gambler's Fate; Intrigue; Mrs. White, and Mrs. Peter White.
15.   W.—Lestocq *: *Lestocq*—Conner, *Goloffkin*—Woodhull, *Demetrius*—J. G. Porter, *Elizabeth*—Mrs. Preston, *Catharine*—Mrs. Willis; Mrs. White, and Mrs. Peter White.
    C.—Honeymoon; Rent Day.
    P.—Wreck Ashore; Midnight Hour.
16.   W.—Biena; Lestocq.
    C.—Nervous Man; Omnibus; Waterman.
    P.—Rinaldo Rinaldini *: *Rinaldo*—Jackson, *Hobbs*—Logan, *Peter*—Watson, *Ermeldine*—Mrs. Watson; Kill or Cure; Loan of a Lover.
17.   W.—Wallace; La Fitte.
    C.—Irish Ambassador; Irish Tutor; Happiest Day of my Life.
    P.—Rinaldo Rinaldini; Gambler's Fate.
18.   W.—La Fitte; Mob, the Outlaw.
    C.—John Bull; Teddy the Tiler.
    P.—Lo Zingaro; Rinaldo Rinaldini.
19.   W.—Mrs. White, and Mrs. Peter White; La Fitte; Make your Wills *: *Ireton*—Porter, *Septimus*—Conner, *Clara*—Miss Charnock.
    C.—Born to Good Luck; Omnibus; Comfortable Service.
    P.—Rinaldo Rinaldini; Bleeding Nun.
21. *Monday:*
    W.—Lestocq; Make your Wills.
    C.—King O'Neil *: *O'Neil*—Power, *Major*—Walton, *Count*—Rowbotham, *Countess*—Mrs. Maywood, *Marchioness* Mrs. Rowbotham; Is He Jealous?; Crossing the Line.
    P.—Alonzo the Brave and the Fair Imogine; No!; Lo Zingaro.
22.   W.—Wallace; Hunt a Turtle.
    C.—King O'Neil; Paddy Carey; Young Widow.
    P.—Idiot Witness; Two Gregories; Bleeding Nun.
23.   W.—Sardanapalus *: *Sardanapalus*—Conner, *Salemenes*—Porter, *Pania*—Morton, *Belises*—Clarke, *Zarina*—Mrs. Preston, *Myrrha*—Mrs. Willis; The Pilot.
    C.—Irish Ambassador; Review; John Jones.
    P.—Jonathan Bradford; No!; Idiot Witness.
24.   W.—Maid of Cashmere *; Make your Wills.
    C.—King O'Neil; Teddy the Tiler; Comfortable Service.
    P.—Jonathan Bradford; Hide and Seek; Miller's Maid.
25.   W.—Maid of Cashmere; Make your Wills; Mrs. White, and Mrs. Peter White.
    C.—Nervous Man; More Blunders than One.

[163]

P.—Ambrose Gwinett; Husband at Sight; Miller's Maid.

26. W.—Maid of Cashmere; The Pilot.
    C.—St. Patrick's Eve; More Blunders than One.
    P.—Jonathan Bradford; Touch and Take; Miller and his Men.

28. *Monday:*
    W.—Maid of Cashmere; Quite at Home *: *Easy*—Wemyss;
        Vow of Silence *: *Baron*—Clarke, *Rodolph*—Conner,
        Edith—Mrs. Willis.
    C.—Maid of Cashmere, the opera *: *Zelica*—Mlle. Celeste,
        Fatima—Mlle. Arreline, *Haidef*—Mad. Checkini, *Zoh-*
        rah—Mons. Checkini, *The Schop Dar*—Brinton, *Alma-*
        zaide—Mrs. Walstein; Man about Town; Wandering
        Minstrel.
    P.—Maid and Magpie; My Neighbor's Wife; Miller and his
        Men.

29. W.—Sardanapalus; Vow of Silence.
    C.—Maid of Cashmere; Happiest Day of my Life; Sleeping
        Draught.
    P.—Iron Chest; Christine of Sweden; Gretna Green.

30. W.—La Fitte; Vow of Silence.
    C.—Maid of Cashmere; No!; Deaf as a Post.
    P.—Floating Beacon; Two Gregories; Therese.

DECEMBER

1. *Thursday:*
    W.—La Fitte; Maid of Cashmere.
    C.—Maid of Cashmere; Kill or Cure; Make your Wills.
    P.—Gambler's Fate; Secret; Miller and his Men.

2. W.—Mrs. White, and Mrs. Peter White; Therese; Siamese
        Twins.
    C.—Maid of Cashmere; Turning the tables; My Fellow Clerk.
    P.—Poor Gentleman; Charles II.

3. W.—Zanthe; Make your Wills.
    C.—Maid of Cashmere; Make your Wills.
    P.—Broken Sword; Christine of Sweden; Sandy and Jenny;
        Bath Road.

5. *Monday:*
    W.—Gilderoy; State Secrets *: *Hal*—Conner, *Gregory*—Had-
        away, *Maud*—Mrs. Durang; Mrs. White, and Mrs. Peter
        White.
    C.—Maid of Cashmere; Cramond Brig; Day after the Fair.
    P.—School of Reform; Spectre Bridegroom.

6. W.—Ion *: *Ion*—Mrs. Ternan, *Adrastus*—Ternan, *Ctsesiphon*
        —Conner, *Clemanthe*—Mrs. Preston; Make your Wills.
    C.—Maid of Cashmere; Scotch Cooper; Make your Wills.

P.—Richard III; State Secrets.

7. W.—Ion; Swiss Cottage.
C.—Wept of Wish-Ton-Wish; Maid of Cashmere.
P.—Virginius; Hunting a Turtle; Christine of Sweden.

8. W.—Ion; Personation.
C.—Wept of Wish-Ton-Wish; Maid of Cashmere.
P.—Damon and Pythias; Sandy and Jenny; Crossing the Line.

9. W.—Ion; Perfection.
C.—Wept of Wish-Ton-Wish; Maid of Cashmere.
P.—William Tell.

10. W.—Winter's Tale; Mary Stuart.
C.—Maid of Cashmere; French Spy.
P.—New Way To Pay Old Debts; Love in a Mist; Lottery Ticket.

12. *Monday:*
W.—Ion; Heart of Midlothian.
C.—Wizard Skiff; Moorish Page.
P.—Othello; Young Widow.

13. W.—The Minerali *: *Martello*—Denvil, *Nicolo*—Clarke, *Marco*—Percival, *Pietro*—Hadaway, *Leila*—Mrs. Preston, *Annette*—Mrs. Willis; Gilderoy.
C.—Maid of Cashmere; Moorish Page.
P.—Ugolino; Love in a Mist; Fortune's Frolic.

14. W.—State Secrets; The Minerali; Hunting a Turtle.
C.—Maid of Cashmere; Mummy.
P.—Hamlet; Adopted Child.

15. W.—The Minerali; Wallace.
C.—Flying Dutchman; French Spy.
P.—Soldier's Daughter; Two Gregories; Gretna Green.

16. W.—Merchant of Venice; The Minerali.
C.—Maid of Cashmere; Wizard Skiff.
P.—Pizarro; Is He Jealous?; Intrigue.

17. W.—Richard III; Mrs. White, and Mrs. Peter White.
C.—Masaniello; Devil's Daughter.
P.—Brigand; Touch and Take; Children in the Wood.

19. *Monday:*
W.—New Way To Pay Old Debts; Quite at Home.
C.—Stag Hall *: *Melford*—Wood, *Welling*—Thayer, *Giles*—Burton, *Lady Melford*—Mrs. Maywood, *Lady Linton*—Mrs. Rowbotham; The Picnic *: *Fluid*—Burton, *Mrs. Deputy*—Mrs. Rowbotham.
P.—Macbeth; Turn Out.

20. W.—La Fitte; Bronze Horse.
C.—Stag Hall; The Three Gladiators, first time in this country, Gabriel, Antoine, and Jerome Ravel; Vol-Au-Vent.
P.—Brutus; Mischief Making.

21.   W.—Skeleton Robber; Turning the Tables.
      C.—The Picnic; The Three Gladiators; Vol-Au-Vent.
      P.—Richard III; Family Jars.

22.   W.—Soldier's Daughter; The Minerali.
      C.—Happiest Day of my Life; Weathercock; The First Fratricide!
      P.—Rob Roy; Black Ey'd Susan.

23.   W.—Mob, the Outlaw; Bronze Horse.
      C.—Turning the Tables; Comfortable Service; The First Fratricide.
      P.—Broken Sword; Is He Jealous?; Turn Out.

24.   W.—The Demon Statue *: *Wolfgang*—J. G. Porter, *Stormo*—Porter, *Hans*—Hadaway, *Denny*—Conner, *Lestelle*—Mrs. Preston, *Barbara*—Mrs. Willis; Black Ey'd Susan.
      C.—Married Life; Godenski.
      P.—Abaellino; Perfection; Mischief Making.

26. *Monday:*
      W.—Demon Statue; Forty Thieves.
      C.—Tam O'Shanter; Whirligig Hall; Bedouin Arabs.
      P.—Abaellino; Loan of a Lover; Matheo Falcone.

27.   W.—Virginius; Make your Wills.
      C.—Stag Hall; Godenski.
      P.—Abaellino; Clari.

28.   W.—Mountaineers; Robinson Crusoe.
      C.—Green Man; Vol-Au-Vent.
      P.—George Barnwell; Crossing the Line; Gretna Green.

29.   W.—La Fitte; Savage of the Forest.
      C.—Point of Honor; La Fete Champetre; Italian Brigands.
      P.—Perfection; Black Ey'd Susan; Mischief Making; Loan of a Lover.

30.   W.—Demon Statue; Robinson Crusoe.
      C.—Cramond Brig; Pongo *: by the Ravel family; John Jones; Bedouin Arabs.
      P.—Wreck Ashore; Hide and Seek; Fortune's Frolic.

31.   W.—George Barnwell; Zembrica.
      C.—Riever's Ransom; Pongo; Bedouin Arabs; All the World's a Stage.
      P.—Gambler's Fate; Secret; Affair of Honour.

JANUARY 1837

2. *Monday:*
      W.—Brothers of the Pyrenees *: *Arrego*—Conner, *Joachim*—Conner, *Pedro*—J. G. Porter, *Gaspard*—Porter, *Matteo*—Clarke, *Conrado*—Myers, *Beatrice*—Mrs. Preston; Zembuca.

C.—Hunchback; Make your Wills.

P.—Rinaldo Rinaldini; Bleeding Nun.

3. W.—Brother of the Pyrenees; Zembuca.

C.—As You Like It; Ransom.

P.—Miller and his Men; My Neighbor's Wife; Touch and Take.

4. W.—Damon and Pythias; Paul, the Reprobate *: *Paul*—Clarke, *Groggy*—Porter, *Lucy*—Mrs. Preston.

C.—Provoked Husband; Ransom.

P.—Yankee Land *: *Sago*—Logan, *Ostrand*—Jackson, *Matson*—Watson, *Mrs. Ashton*—Mrs. Sefton; Young Widow.

5. W.—Othello; Mrs. White, and Mrs. Peter White.

C.—Second Thoughts; Gnome King.

P.—Ambrose Gwinett; Therese.

6. W.—Paul, the Reprobate; Swiss Cottage; Black Ey'd Susan.

C.—Belle's Stratagem; Youthful Queen.

P.—Crossing the Line; Hunting a Turtle; Rinaldo Rinaldini.

7. W.—Bravo of Venice *: *Bravo*—Conner, *Duke*—Porter, *Palozzi*—J. G. Porter, *Contatino*—Clarke, *Memmo*—Hadaway, *Stephano*—Wemyss, *Rosabello*—Mrs. Willis; Paul, the Reprobate.

C.—Stranger; Wandering Minstrel.

P.—Vampire; previous to play, an Introductory Vision; Mountaineers.

9. *Monday:*

W.—Bride of Abydos; Beggars of Cripplegate *: *Henry VIII*—Wemyss, *Lambert*—Conner, *Osgood*—Clarke, *Lorell*—Hadaway, *Marion*—Mrs. Preston, *Millicent*—Miss Charnock.

C.—The Wife; Cheap Boarding.

P.—Village Phantom; Day after the Wedding; Iron Chest.

10. W.—Bravo of Venice; Beggar of Cripplegate.

C.—Much Ado about Nothing; Animal Magnetism.

P.—Curfew; Vampire, with Introductory Vision.

11. W.—Bravo of Venice; Bride of Abydos.

C.—Romeo and Juliet; High Life below Stairs.

P.—Vampire, with Introductory Vision; Irish Tutor; Innkeeper's Daughter.

12. W.—Lowena of Tobolska; Budget of Blunders.

C.—Hunchback; Ladies' Man.

P.—Othello; Vampire; Introductory Vision.

13. W.—Bride of Abydos; Bravo of Venice.

C.—School for Scandal; Happiest Day of my Life.

P.—Matrimony; Vampire, with Introductory Vision; Day after the Wedding.

14. W.—The Shadow; Budget of Blunders; Lowena of Tobolska.

C.—Merchant of Venice; Perfection.

P.—A Cure for the Heart Ache; Ruffian Boy! !

16. *Monday:*

W.—Wallace; Cherokee Chief.

C.—Jealous Wife; Animal Magnetism.

P.—Blue Beard; Lover's Quarrels.

17. W.—Mountain Devil; Budget of Blunders; Jack Robinson and his Monkey.

C.—Wonder; Youthful Queen.

P.—Blue Beard; Irish Tutor; Sprigs of Laurel.

18. W.—Knights of the Cross; Ourang Outang.

C.—Honey Moon; A Roland for an Oliver.

P.—Raising the Wind; Blue Beard; Secret.

19. W.—Valentine and Orson; Knights of the Cross.

C.—Stranger; Scapegoat.

P.—Charles II; Blue Beard; Bath Road.

20. W.—Mountain Devil; Turning the Tables; Valentine and Orson.

C.—Bold Stroke for a Husband; Scapegoat.

P.—Two Friends; Blue Beard; Matrimony.

21. W.—Trial by Battle *: *Ambrose*—Porter, *Rufus*—Cony, *Henry* —Blanchard, *Geralda*—Miss Packard; Mrs. White, and Mrs. Peter White; Don Juan.

C.—Belle's Stratagem; Perfection.

P.—Vampire; Nature and Philosophy; Blue Beard.

23. *Monday:*

W.—Shakespeare's Early Days; Christine of Poland; Dramatist.

C.—Twelfth Night; The Daughter *: *Mary*—Miss Tree, *Wilson*—Maywood, *Fitzfaddle*—Burton, *Mrs. Delmore* —Mrs. Thayer.

P.—Forest of Bondy; Ourang Outang.

24. W.—Forest of Bondy; Richard III, scenes; Wild Boy.

C.—Duddlestones; The Picnic.

P.—Othello; Review.

25. W.—Damon and Pythias; The Pilot.

C.—Cinderella; State Secrets.

P.—Hyder Ali; Two Friends; Monkeyana.

26. W.—La Fitte; Shadow.

C.—Duddlestones; Vol-Au-Vent.

P.—Zenocles; Crossing the Line; Monkeyana.

27. W.—La Fitte; Shadow.

C.—John of Paris; Brother and Sister.

P.—Valentine and Orson; Knights of the Cross.

28. W.—Julius Caesar; Mayor of Garrett.

C.—Picnic; Godenski; Bedouin Arabs; State Secrets.

P.—Trial by Battle; Cherokee Chief; Ourang Outang.

30. *Monday:*
    W.—Woodman's Hut; Savage of the Forest.
    C.—Romeo and Juliet; La Fete Champetre.
    P.—Timour the Tartar; Actor of all Work; Blue Beard.
31.   W.—Woodman's Hut; Make your Wills; Shadow.
    C.—Stag Hall; The First Fratricide; The Four Lovers.
    P.—Richard III; Sprigs of Laurel.

FEBRUARY

1. *Wednesday:*
    W.—Gilderoy; Woodman's Hut.
    C.—Clari; The Four Lovers; Bedouin Arabs; State Secrets.
    P.—Review; Turnpike Gate; Blind Boy.
2.   W.—Golden Farmer; Fortune's Frolic.
    C.—Point of Honor; Pongo.
    P.—Othello; Fortune's Frolic.
3.   W.—New Way To Pay Old Debts; The Intrigue.
    C.—Apostate; Godenski.
    P.—Dramatist; Golden Farmer.
4.   W.—Cataline; Hunting a Turtle.
    C.—Fazio; Harlequin and the Magic Trumpet *: by Ravel
        family.
    P.—Evil Eye; Peter White; Mummy.
6. *Monday:*
    W.—Hofer; Little Red Riding Hood; Mob, the Outlaw.
    C.—Ravel Family in Une Passion, Vol-Au-Vent and Bedouin
        Arabs; State Secrets; The Scapegoat.
    P.—Othello; Adeline.
7.   W.—Closed in preparation for new piece of Thalaba.
    C.—Fazio; Clari.
    P.—Damon and Pythias; Irish Tutor.
8.   W.—Closed.
    C.—No!; Mons. Mallet; Kentuckian; Wandering Minstrel.
    P.—Iron Chest; Weathercock.
9.   W.—Closed.
    C.—Henry IV; Man about Town.
    P.—Heir at Law; Swiss Cottage.
10.   W.—Closed.
    C.—Rip Van Winkle; Scapegoat; Job Fox.
    P.—Mountaineers; The Dumb Belle; Agreeable Surprize.
11.   W.—Closed.
    C.—Mons. Mallet; Jonathan in England; Kentuckian.
    P.—Hofer; Mummy; Ambrose Gwinett.
13. *Monday:*
    W.—Closed.

C.—Born to Good Luck; Omnibus; Make your Wills.

P.—Paul Pry; Loan of a Lover.

14. W.—Closed.

C.—Monsieur Mallet; Rip Van Winkle; Job Fox.

P.—The Robber's Wife; Triumph of Greece.

15. W.—Closed.

C.—Nervous Man; Paddy Carey; Waterman.

P.—Sweethearts and Wives; Why don't she Marry?; Turnpike Gate.

16. W.—Closed.

C.—Irish Ambassador; Irish Tutors; State Secrets.

P.—Perfection; Tom Cringle; Turning the Tables.

17. W.—Closed.

C.—John Bull; Mummy.

P.—Golden Farmer; Day after the Wedding.

18. W.—Closed.

C.—West Indian; Teddy the Tiler.

P.—Golden Farmer; Day after the Wedding. Last night of the season.

20. *Monday:*

W.—Thalaba *: *Hareb*—Proctor, *Moath*—Porter, *Sambo*—Hadaway, *Hafna*—Cunningham, *Zalem*—Warren, *Ali*—Vache, *Markalla*—Wilks, *Thalaba*—Conner, *Obka*—Clemens, *Abdalaa*—Clarke, *Olak*—Myers, *Friend of Fire*—Chappel, *Moadin*—J. G. Porter, *Giafter*—Watson, *Zobi*—Jackson, *Zuliman*—McConachy, *Elchee*—Mestayer, *Soorah*—Thompson, *Shahnameh*—Kirby, *Onneah* Stanley, *Oneiza*—Mrs. Willis, *Marmima*—Miss Packard, *Rawla*—Mrs. Greene, *Zeinah*—Mrs. Watson, *Acratoon*—Miss S. Packard, *Johohk*—Miss Chester, *Abusheher*—Miss Hichie; Irishman in London.

C.—King O'Neil; Omnibus; No!

21. W.—Thalaba; Crowded Houses.

C.—Nervous Man; Paddy Carey; Man about Town.

22. W.—Thalaba; Review.

C.—Born to Good Luck; Review; State Secrets.

23. W.—Thalaba; Hundred-Pound Note.

C.—Scape Goat; Richard III, first act; Tempest.

24. W.—Thalaba; Honest Thieves.

C.—Irish Ambassador; Omnibus; Wandering Minstrel.

25. W.—Thalaba; Ruffian Boy.

C.—John Buzzby *: *John*—Burton, *Anderson*—Hamilton, —*Greville*—Wood, *Jingle*—Faulkner, *Mrs. Anderson*—Miss Fisher, *Cicelia*—Mrs. Walstein; Forty Winks.

27. *Monday:*

W.—Thalaba; Lilian, the Show Girl *: *Maynard*—Porter, *Ev-*

erard—Conner, *Diggs*—Hadaway, *Morris*—Procter, *Lilian*—Mrs. Willis.

C.—O'Flannigan and the Fairies *: *O'Flannigan*—Power, *Ned* —Hamilton, *Jack*—Walton, *White*—Pearson, *O'Hara*— Brunton, *Cook*—Watson, *Doran*—Lindsay, *Pedlar*— Thompson, *Mary*—Mrs. Rowbotham, *Kate*—Miss Fisher, *Widow*—Mrs. Brood, *Nancy*—Miss Armstrong, *Mrs. Flynn*—Mrs. Walstein, *Fairies*—Misses Morgan, Lee and Mew, Eberle, and Mast. Watson, *Characters in the dream* —Hathwell, Watson, Carnes, Raffile, Jones and Craddock, Mrs. Lee, Misses Fox, Brown, Stone and Lopez; High Life below Stairs.

28.   W.—Thalaba; Lilian, the Show Girl.
     C.—Green Man; Tempest.

MARCH

1. *Wednesday:*
    W.—Thalaba; Lilian, the Show Girl.
    C.—O'Flannigan and the Fairies; Married Bachelor.
2.   W.—Thalaba; Lilian, the Show Girl.
    C.—O'Flannigan and the Fairies; Turn Out.
3.   W.—Thalaba; Mother's Dream *: *Angelo*—Conner, *Fortune*— Porter, *Gobbo, Sr.*—Hadaway, *Gobbo, Jr.*—Watson, *Ida* —Mrs. Watson, *Verina*—Mrs. Greene.
    C.—Weathercock; Arabella *: *Arabella, Harry, Bridget, Travers*—four rôles—Miss St. Luke; Yankee Tar *: *Harvey* —Master St. Luke, *Eaton*—Hamilton, *Hamet*—Pearson, *Eugenia*—Miss Fisher.
4.   W.—Thalaba; Mother's Dream.
    C.—O'Flannigan and the Fairies; Irish Tutor; Fire and Water.
6. *Monday:*
    W.—Wrecker's Daughter *: *Robert*—Conner, *Morris*—Proctor, *Edward*—J. G. Porter, *Stephen*—Master Jackson, *Marian*—Mrs. Greene; Thalaba.
    C.—O'Flannigan and the Fairies; Omnibus; No!
7.   W.—Wrecker's Daughter; Thalaba.
    C.—O'Flannigan and the Fairies; Teddy the Tiler.
8.   W.—Wrecker's Daughter; Thalaba.
    C.—O'Flannigan and the Fairies; Irishman in London; Fire and Water.
9.   W.—Wrecker's Daughter; Thalaba.
    C.—Born to Good Luck; Married Daughter; Turn Out.
10.   W.—Thalaba; Hofer.
    C.—Speed the Plough; The Picnic.
11.   W.—The Spirit of the Rhine *: *Huntley*—Conner, *Ignatius*—

Hadaway, *Irma*—Mrs. Willis; Thalaba.

C.—O'Flannigan and the Fairies; More Blunders than One.

13. *Monday:*

W.—North Pole *: *Montague*—J. G. Porter, *Ned*—Conner, *Cato*—Proctor, *Dip*—Watson, *Amelia*—Mrs. Watson, *Betty*—Mrs. Willis; ZaZeZiZoZu *: *ZaZeZiZoZu*— Hadaway, *ZiZi*—Mrs. Willis, *ZoZu*—Mrs. Watson, *ZuZu*—Miss S. Packard, *ZaZa*—Miss Packard, *Grosbac* —Porter.

C.—Pirate Boy *: *Francisco*—Miss Watson, *Cain*—Hamilton, *Hawkhurst*—Walton, *Templemore*—Pearson; Raising the Wind.

14. W.—North Pole; ZaZeZiZoZu.

C.—Pirate Boy; Picnic.

15. W.—Wrecker's Daughter; North Pole.

C.—La Sonnambula; Rendezvous.

16. W.—Thalaba; Spirit of the Rhine.

C.—Pirate Boy; Fire and Water.

17. W.—Thalaba; Lilian, the Show Girl.

C.—Pirate Boy; Rendezvous.

18. W.—Star Spangled Banner *: *Howard*—Vache, *Madison*—J. G. Porter, *Go-a-head*—Conner, *Israel*—Greene, *Rimenito* —Clarke, *Hugh*—Porter, *Julia*—Mrs. Watson, *Rose*— Mrs. Willis; Ion, Travestie *: *Ion*—Walton, *Medon*— Porter, *Ctesiphon*—J. G. Porter, *Cassander*—McConachy, *Adrastus*—Greene, *Chemanthe*—Mrs. Willis; Lover's Quarrels.

C.—Pirate Boy; Gretna Green.

20. *Monday:*

W.—Prophet of St. Paul's *: *Brandon*—Conner, *Dorset*— Wemyss, *Louis XII.*—McConachy, *Francis I.*—Proctor, *Andrel*—Hadaway, *Mary*—Mrs. Greene, *Stella*—Mrs. Willis; Tom Cringle.

C.—Pirate Boy; Spoiled Child.

21. W.—Prophet of St. Paul's; Star Spangled Banner; Ion, Travestie.

C.—Guy Mannering; Wandering Minstrel.

22. W.—Which is the Man?; Swiss Cottage; The Middy Ashore *: *Moreton*—McConachy, *Cringle*—Proctor, *Tonnish*— Conner, *Harry*—Mrs. Willis.

C.—Pirate Boy; Cinderella.

23. W.—Ion; Ion, Travestie.

C.—La Sonnambula; Scape Goat.

24. W.—Damon and Pythias; The Robber Chieftain *: *Jack*— Proctor, *Tim*—J. Greene, *Danvers*—McConachy, *Ellen* —Mrs. Willis.

C.—La Sonnambula; Comfortable Service.
25. W.—The Hut of the Red Mountain; Spirit of the Rhine; Middy Ashore.
C.—La Sonnambula; The Grenadier *: *Fanny, Grenadier, Mrs. Popps*—three rôles—Mrs. Gibbs, *Doughty*—Walton, *Will*—Burton.
27. *Monday:*
W.—Siege of Missolonghi *: *Miaulis*—Conner, *Ibrahim*—Proctor, *Beppo*—Hadaway, *Nimbo*—Watson, *Bauclis*—Greene, *Phedora*—Mrs. Greene; Irishman in London.
C.—La Sonnambula; Grenadier.
28. W.—Wrecker's Ashore; Star Spangled Banner.
C.—La Sonnambula; Forty Winks.
29. W.—Marmion; Hit or Miss.
C.—La Sonnambula; State Secrets.
30. W.—Three and the Deuce; Mummy; Thalaba.
C.—Cinderella.
31. W.—Siege of Missolonghi; Lilian, the Show Girl.
C.—Der Freischutz; Grenadier.

APRIL

1. *Saturday:*
W.—Kate Kearney; Robert the Devil; Irishman in London.
C.—One O'Clock *: *Rupert*—Pearson, *Hardyknute*—Hamilton, *Willikind*—Burton, *Rolph*—Walton, *Adriel*—Mrs. Walstein, *Clothilda*—Mrs. Maywood, *Una*—Mrs. Rowbotham; Scape Goat.
3. *Monday:*
W.—Siege of Missolonghi; Kate Kearney. Last night of the season.
C.—One O'Clock; Make your Wills.
4. C.—Damon and Pythias; Black Eyed Susan.
5. C.—One O'Clock; Mummy.
6. C.—One O'Clock; John Jones.
7. C.—One O'Clock; Forty Winks.
8. C.—One O'Clock; Pleasant Neighbors.
10. *Monday:*
C.—Laugh when you Can; Three and the Deuce.
11. C.—Cure for the Heart Ache; Pleasant Neighbors; Raising the Wind.
12. C.—Poor Gentleman; A Roland for an Oliver.
13. C.—Wild Oats; Twenty-Three John Street.
14. C.—Fontainbleau; Joe Miller *: *Taciturn*—Balls, *Joe*—Walton, *Bob*—Burton, *Lucy*—Mrs. Walstein; Three and the Deuce.

[173]

15. C.—One O'Clock; The Mummy.
17. *Monday:*
C.—Much Ado about Nothing; Pleasant Neighbors.
18. C.—Stranger; State Secrets.
19. C.—As You Like It; The Daughter; Pleasant Neighbors.
20. C.—Ion; Make your Wills.
21. C.—The Wonder; Youthful Queen.
22. C.—Ion; John Jones.
24. *Monday:*
C.—Ion; Man about Town.
25. C.—Provoked Husband; Barrack Room *: *Marquis*—Faulkner, *Colonel*—Lindsay, *Bernard*—Burton, *Captain*—Thayer, *Clarisse*—Miss Tree.
26. C.—Belle's Stratagem; Perfection.
27. C.—Honey Moon; A Roland for an Oliver.
28. C.—Pleasant Neighbors; The Ransom; Youthful Queen.
29. C.—Ion; Barrack Room. Last night of the season.

MAY

1. *Monday:*
A.—Paul Pry; May Queen.
2. A.—House Room *: *Major*—Burton, *Cinnamon*—Watson, *Gustavus*—Lindsay, *Mrs. Dandleby*—Mrs. Brood; Sweethearts and Wives; Quadrupeds.
3. A.—Second Thoughts; May Queen; Quadrupeds.
4. A.—The Young Quaker; Tom Thumb; Quadrupeds.
5. A.—The Hunchback; Turning the Tables.
6. A.—House Room; No!; The Deep, Deep Sea.
8. *Monday:*
A.—John Bull; Cheap Boarding.
9. A.—Henri Quatre; Deep, Deep Sea.
10. A.—Rivals; Omnibus; No!
11. A.—Pizarro; Therese.
12. A.—Nervous Man; Review; Rendezvous.
13. A.—Irish Ambassador; Omnibus.
15. *Monday:*
A.—St. Patrick's Eve; Scape Goat.
16. A.—May Queen; No!; Black Eyed Susan.
17. A.—Nervous Man; Gretna Green; State Secrets.
18. A.—Speculation; The Old Oak Chest.
19. A.—Irish Ambassador; Is He Jealous?; Comfortable Service.
20. A.—Born to Good Luck; More Blunders than One.
22. *Monday:*
A.—Hamlet; High Life below Stairs.
23. A.—Macbeth; Cheap Boarding.

24. A.—Speed the Plough; Wandering Minstrel.
25. A.—Richard III; Scape Goat.
26. A.—Brigand; Spring and Autumn.
27. A.—My Aunt; Rent Day; The Wolf and the Lamb.
29. *Monday:*
    A.—Lucille; Loan of a Lover.
30. A.—Farmer's Story; 'Twas I.
31. A.—Lucille; Twice Killed *: *Facile*—Keeley, *Fanny*—Mrs. Keeley.

JUNE

1. *Thursday:*
    A.—Hide and Seek; Swiss Cottage; Twice Killed.
2. A.—Julie *: *Morrisseau*—Keeley, *Regent*—R. Hamilton, *Duke*—Thayer, *Adrian*—Lindsay, *Julie*—Mrs. Keeley; Loan of a Lover.
3. A.—Julie; Swiss Cottage.
5. *Monday:*
    A.—Honeymoon; Pleasant Neighbors.
6. A.—Ion; Wandering Minstrel.
7. A.—Stranger; The Lady of the Lake *: *Fitzjames*—Lindsay, *Roderick Dhu*—R. Hamilton, *Graeme*—Brunton, *Ellen*—Miss Fisher, *Blanche*—Mrs. Rowbotham.
8. A.—Wrecker's Daughter; State Secrets.
9. A.—Belle's Stratagem; Barrack Room.
10. A.—Wrecker's Daughter; Pleasant Dreams.
12. *Monday:*
    A.—As You Like It; Youthful Queen.
13. A.—Wrecker's Daughter; Perfection.
14. A.—Romeo and Juliet; Kill or Cure.
15. A.—Wonder!; Barrack Room.
16. A.—The Dumb Belle; French Spy; Twice Killed.
17. W.—Richard III; Swiss Cottage.
    A.—Twelfth Night; One Hour *: *Swiftly*—Lindsay, *O'Leary*—Faulkner, *Julia*—Miss Tree, *Mrs. Bevit*—Mrs. Brood.
19. *Monday:*
    W.—Fazio; Spoiled Child.
    A.—Cinderella; Luke the Laborer.
20. W.—French Spy; Hunting a Turtle.
    A.—Paul Pry; Vol-Au-Vent; Three Gladiators.
21. W.—Richard III; Turn Out.
    A.—Sweethearts and Wives; Godenski.
22. W.—French Spy; Welsh Girl.
    A.—Deaf as a Post; Bedouin Arabs; Dumb Belle.
23. W.—Black Brig of Bermuda; Spoiled Child.

A.—Cinderella; Cheap Boarding.

24. W.—Black Brig of Bermuda; Welsh Girl.

A.—Fire and Water; Bedouin Arabs; The Four Lovers; Ladies' Man.

26. *Monday:*

W.—Black Eyed Susan; New Way To Pay Old Debts, fifth act; Jane Shore, fifth act; Comfortable Service; Winning a Husband.

A.—Married Bachelor; Monsieur de Chaluman; Jocko.

27. W.—Manager in Distress; John Bull; Nature and Philosophy.

A.—La Sonnambula; Charles VII.

28. W.—Othello; Swiss Cottage.

A.—Kill or Cure; La Fete Champetre; The Death of Abel; Scape Goat.

29. W.—Virginius; Welsh Girl.

A.—Idiot Witness; Petticoat Government; Forty Thieves.

30. W.—Vision of the Sun *: *King*—Rice, *Oratzuma*—J. G. Porter, *Koran*—Conner, *Warriors*—J. Greene, Kent, Collingbourne, Crouta, Vache, W. Warren, Wilks, Clemens, McConachy, *Tacmar*—Porter, *Oultampac*—Proctor, *Tycobra*—Hadaway, *Genie of the Harp*—Miss Brittenham, *Genius of the Ebon Wand*—J. Addams, *Zacateczas*—Kirby, *Ocelot*—Myers, *Imps of Oultampac*—Joseph, Jackson, Collingbourne, S. Collingbourne, *Rumac*—Mrs. Proctor, *Cassana*—Mrs. Kent, *Ocella*—Miss M. A. Warren, *Guiseppa*—Miss Chester, *Elise*—Mrs. Smith, *Oreana* —Miss Watson, *Frivola*—Miss Hichie, *Anniolo*—Miss Parker, *Cora*—Mrs. Willis, *Matall*—Miss Angelica; Comfortable Service.

A.—Petticoat Government; Comfortable Service; Italian Brigands.

JULY

1. *Saturday:*

W.—Vision of the Sun; Swiss Cottage.

A.—Is He Jealous?; Monsieur de Chaluman; Bedouin Arabs; Petticoat Government.

3. *Monday:*

W.—Vision of the Sun; Agreeable Surprise.

A.—Ellen Wareham; The Ship Launch *: *Bunks*—Burton, *Stevens*—Pearson, *Polly*—Mrs. Walstein; Two Thompsons.

4. W.—Star Spangled Banner; Vision of the Sun.

A.—Actor of all Work; French Spy; Ship Launch.

5. W.—Vision of the Sun; Star Spangled Banner.

A.—Maid of Cashmere, the opera; Ship Launch.
6. W.—Vision of the Sun; Star Spangled Banner.
A.—Maid of Cashmere, the opera; Crossing the Line; Make your Wills.
7. W.—Vision of the Sun; Rival Pages *: *Louis*—Rice, *Marquis*— J. G. Porter, *Victoire*—Mrs. Kent, *Julie*—Mrs. Proctor.
A.—Maid of Cashmere; Animal Magnetism.
8. W.—Vision of the Sun; Presumptive Evidence.
A.—Wept of Wish-Ton-Wish; Wizard Skiff. Last night of the season.
10. *Monday:*
W.—Hamlet; Farmer's Son *: *Chopstick*—Walbourne, *Tom*— Davis, *Jaws*—Taylor, *Billy*—Jackson, *Margaret*—Miss Angelica.
11. W.—Richard III; Farmer's Son.
12. W.—New Way To Pay Old Debts; Farmer's Son.
13. W.—Macbeth; Farmer's Son.
14. W.—Apostate; Farmer's Son.
15. W.—Richard III; Mayor of Garrat.
17. *Monday:*
W.—Tom and Jerry; L'Amour; Rival Pages.
18. W.—The Navy Forever; Vision of the Sun.
19. W.—Othello; The Navy Forever.
20. W.—Venice Preserved; The Navy Forever.
A.—The Roses of Baron de Malesherbes; The Bride; U.A.W.G.
21. W.—Julius Caesar; Rival Pages.
22. W.—King Lear; Review.
24. *Monday:*
W.—Peculiar Position *: *Champignon*—Hadaway, *Carlo*— Conner, *Countess*—Mrs. Herring; *Thalaba;* Queer Subject.
A.—The Conjuration; The Widow and the Riding Horse; The Straight Way is the Best.
25. W.—Othello; Queer Subject.
26. W.—Douglass; Queer Subject.
27. W.—Damon and Pythias; Spoiled Child.
A.—Dissipated Invalids; Nante the Porter; Watchman. Last performance.
28. W.—Pizarro; Infidelity.
29. W.—Walder, the Revenger; Comfortable Service; Adopted Child.
31. *Monday:*
W.—Pickwick Club *: *Pickwick*—Porter, *Tupman*—Kent, *Snodgrass*—Rice, *Winkle*—Addams, *Veller*—Hadaway, *Fat Boy*—Conner, *Slumkey*—Proctor, *Jingle*—Stiggins,

[177]

Fitzmarshall—three rôles—Wemyss, *Emily*—Mrs. Proctor, *Biddy*—Mrs. Kent; Welsh Girl.

AUGUST

1. *Tuesday:*
   W.—Pickwick Club; Comfortable Service.
2. W.—Pickwick Club; Infidelity.
3. W.—Pickwick Club; Queer Subject.
4. W.—Tom and Jerry; Farmer's Son.
5. W.—Thalaba; Pickwick Club.
7. *Monday:*
   W.—Star of Seville *: *Carlos*—A. H. Bannister, *Pedro*—Proctor, *Alphonso*—Addams, *Hyacinth*—Hadaway, *Estrella*—Mrs. Proctor, *Florilla*—Mrs. Kent; Spoiled Child.
8. W.—Star of Seville; Children in the Wood.
9. W.—Star of Seville; Queer Subject.
10. W.—Thalaba; Children in the Wood.
11. W.—Hypocrite, second and fifth acts; Wandering Boys.
12. W.—La Fitte; Rival Pages.
14. *Monday:*
    W.—Crichton; Comfortable Service.
15. W.—Crichton; Rival Pages.
16. W.—Crichton; Welsh Girl.
17. W.—Crichton; Queer Subject.
18. W.—Crichton; Rival Pages.
19. W.—Crichton; Married Yesterday.
    C.—Every one has his Fault; Wandering Minstrel.
21. *Monday:*
    W.—Gladiator; Wild Boy of Bohemia.
    C.—Charles II; One O'Clock.
22. W.—French Spy; Wild Boy of Bohemia.
    C.—Education; Two Thompsons.
23. W.—Coriolanus; Jack Brag.
    C.—Point of Honor; May Queen.
24. W.—George Barnwell; Vision of the Sun.
    C.—Paul Pry; Ladies' Man.
25. W.—Chamber of Death; Vision of the Sun.
    C.—School of Reform; Raising the Wind.
26. W.—The Whistler; Catching an Heiress.
    C.—Married Life; The Picnic.
28. *Monday:*
    W.—Brian Boroihme; Rival Pages.
    C.—Castle of Andalusia; No Song, No Supper.
29. W.—Brian Boroihme; Chamber of Death.
    C.—Foundling of the Forest; Happiest Day of my Life.

30.   W.—Bronze Horse; Mob, the Outlaw.
      C.—Cinderella; Pleasant Neighbors.
31.   W.—Gaulantus *: *Gaulantus*—Proctor, *Baranicus*—Conner, *Mauclus*—Porter, *Laticus*—Mrs. Proctor; Tom Cringle.
      C.—Mons. Mallet; Kentuckian; Two Thompsons.

SEPTEMBER

1. *Friday:*
      W.—The Wizard of the Moor; Black Eyed Susan.
      C.—La Sonnambula; Turn Out.
2.   W.—Alvardo of Spain; La Sonnambula, Travestie *: *Elvino*—Rice, *Rodolpho*—Conner, *Alessio*—Herbert, *Notary*—Myers, *Amina*—Hadaway, *Liza*—Mrs. Kent, *Terese*—Mrs. Herbert; Spoiled Child. Last night of the season. Recess to introduce gas light.
      C.—Rip Van Winkle; Jonathan in England.
4. *Monday:*
      C.—La Sonnambula; Mummy.
5.   C.—Marriage of Figaro; John Jones.
6.   C.—Cinderella; Abon Hassan.
7.   C.—La Sonnambula; Masaniello, second and third acts.
8.   C.—Castle of Andalusia; Masaniello.
9.   C.—Jonathan Doubikins; Make your Wills; Forest Rose.
11. *Monday:*
      C.—Knight of the Golden Fleece; Forty and Fifty; Forest Rose.
12.   C.—Who wants a Guinea?; Green Mountain Boy.
13.   C.—Jonathan Doubikins; Forty and Fifty; Yankee Pedlar.
14.   C.—Kaspar Hauser; Yankee Pedlar; Dumb Belle.
15.   C.—Knight of the Golden Fleece; Speculations *: *Wheeler*—Hill, *Ledger*—Watson, *Ellen*—Mrs. Walstein; Twice Killed.
16.   C.—Kaspar Hauser; A Down East Bargain *: *Makepeace*—Hill, *Earnest*—Thayer, *Mrs. Missletoe*—Mrs. Brood; Speculations; Yankee Pedlar.
18. *Monday:*
      C.—The Rivals; Of Age Tomorrow.
19.   C.—Wild Oats; Raising the Wind.
20.   C.—A Cure for the Heart Ache; Turning the Tables.
21.   C.—The Way to get Married; Haunted Inn.
22.   C.—Every one has his Fault; Sleeping Draught.
23.   C.—Road to Ruin; Robert Macaire.
25. *Monday:*
      C.—The Wife; Barrack Room.
26.   C.—As You Like It; Twice Killed.
27.   C.—Ion; Married Bachelor.

28. C.—Much Ado about Nothing; Youthful Queen.
29. C.—Stranger; Perfection.
30. C.—Honeymoon; Wrecker's Daughter.

OCTOBER

2. *Monday:*
     C.—Duchess de LaValliere *: *Duchess*—Miss Tree, *De Lau-
     zune*—Lindsay, *Grammont*—Thayer, *De Bragelone*—
     Wood, *Madame de la Valliere*—Mrs. Maywood, *Ma-
     dame de Vallancour*—Mrs. Walstein; Scape Goat.
3.   C.—Duchess de LaValliere; Cheap Boarding.
     P.—Hedwig.
4.   C.—Duchess de LaValliere; Married Life.
5.   C.—Hunchback; Pleasant Neighbors.
6.   C.—Ion; Ladies' Man.
7.   C.—Wonder; Wrecker's Daughter.
9.   *Monday:*
     C.—Coriolanus; Wandering Minstrel.
10. C.—La Sonnambula; Deep, Deep Sea.
11. C.—Macbeth; No Song, No Supper.
12. C.—Coriolanus; Deep, Deep Sea.
13. C.—Cinderella; Animal Magnetism.
14. C.—Othello; John Jones.
16. *Monday:*
     C.—Cato; Turn Out.
17. C.—Fra Diavolo; Loan of a Lover.
18. C.—King Lear; Two Thompsons.
19. C.—Confusion *: *Neville*—Lindsay, *Stilton*—Burton, *Jack*—
     Thayer, *Ellen*—Mrs. Walstein, *Sally*—Mrs. Brood; Twa
     Ghaists; The Barbers at Court *: *Maximus*—Burton,
     Magnus—Thayer, *Charles II.*—Harrington, *Rochester*—
     Lindsay, *Queen*—Mrs. Walstein, *Catharine*—Miss Fisher.
20. C.—Cato; The Barbers at Court.
21. C.—Hamlet; The Liar.
23. *Monday:*
     C.—The Barbers at Court; Peacock and the Crow; Twice
     Killed.
24. C.—Ladies' Man; Peacock and the Crow; Forty Winks.
25. C.—Jim Crow in London *: *Crow*—Rice, *Hector*—Lindsay,
     Skinflint—Watson, *Pop*—Thayer, *Holdfast*—Eberle,
     Ellen—Miss Fisher; Confusion.
26. C.—Jim Crow in London; The Barbers at Court; Black and
     White *: *Sambo*—Rice, *Canova*—Watson, *Julia*—Mrs.
     Walstein.

27. C.—Sweethearts and Wives; Jim Crow in London; Black and White.
28. C.—Virjinny Mummy; Twa Ghaists; Jim Crow in London.
30. *Monday:*
C.—Rob Roy; Peculiar Position.
31. C.—Richard III; Married Bachelor.

NOVEMBER

1. *Wednesday:*
C.—Provost of Bruges; Peculiar Position.
2. C.—Hamlet; Tom Cringle.
3. C.—La Sonnambula; Barbers at Court.
4. C.—Fra Diavolo; A Gentleman in Difficulties.
6. *Monday:*
C.—Don Juan *: *Don Juan*—Horn, *Leporello*—Brough, *Masetto*—Walton, *Octavio*—Pearson, *Zerlina*—Miss Horton, *Elvira*—Mrs. R. Hamilton, *Anna*—Miss Morgan; John Jones.
7. C.—Don Juan; Scape Goat.
8. C.—Don Juan; Spoiled Child.
9. C.—Don Juan; Peculiar Position.
10. C.—Love in a Village; The Father and Son *: *Marcello*—Wood, *Uberti*—Brough, *Madame Laurenti*—Mrs. Maywood.
11. C.—Love in a Village; Father and Son.
13. *Monday:*
C.—La Sonnambula; Abon Hassan.
14. C.—Fra Diavola; Turn Out.
15. W.—Hamlet; Welsh Girl.
C.—Othello; Black Eyed Susan.
16. W.—Richard III; Rival Pages.
C.—King Lear; Pleasant Neighbors.
17. W.—A New Way To Pay Old Debts; Infidelity.
C.—Damon and Pythias; Turning the Tables.
18. W.—Macbeth; Mayor of Garrat.
C.—Virginius; My Own Ghost *: *Button*—Burton, *Clipper*—Harrington, *Mrs. Button*—Mrs. Brood, *Mrs. Clipper*—Mrs. Walstein.
20. *Monday:*
W.—Destruction of Jerusalem *: *Jewantus*—Proctor, *Fustavis*—Rice, *Judas*—Bannister, *Felix*—Jackson, *Titus*—Kent, *Canino*—Hadaway, *Amanthe*—Mrs. Proctor, *Areana*—Mrs. Kent; Middy Ashore.
C.—Hamlet; The Mummy.
21. W.—Destruction of Jerusalem; Adventures of a Sailor.

C.—Richard III; Weather Cock.

22. W.—The Destruction of Jerusalem; Welsh Girl.
   C.—Brutus; The Barbers at Court.

23. W.—The Destruction of Jerusalem; Captain's not a Miss.
   C.—Macbeth; Animal Magnetism.

24. W.—Destruction of Jerusalem; Infidelity.
   C.—William Tell; My Own Ghost.

25. W.—Faith and Falsehood *: *Pereaux*—Rice, *Jukes*—Wemyss, *Graves*—Bannister, *Dobbs*—Hadaway, *Jane*—Mrs. Proctor, *Arabella*—Mrs. Kent; Destruction of Jerusalem.
   C.—Pizarro; Twice Killed.

27. *Monday:*
   W.—Faith and Falsehood; La Fitte.
   C.—Broker of Bogota; Ladies' Man.

28. W.—Pleasant Neighbors; Faith and Falsehood; Gretna Green.
   C.—Broker of Bogota; Pleasant Neighbors.

29. W.—Faith and Falsehood; Skeleton Robber.
   C.—Gladiator; Cheap Boarding.

30. W.—Faith and Falsehood; Paul Jones, the Pilot.
   C.—Gladiator; Dumb Belle.

DECEMBER

1. *Friday:*
   W.—Gaulantus; Highways and Byeways.
   C.—Gladiator; Peculiar Position.

2. W.—Battle of Sedgemoor *: *Monmouth*—Rice, *Kirk*—Proctor, *Fillerton*—Bannister, *Trombone*—Hadaway, *Aquilia*—Mrs. Proctor, *Tabitha*—Mrs. Kent; Captain's not a Miss.
   C.—Gladiator; Bold Dragoons.

4. *Monday:*
   W.—The Demon of the Desert; Catching an Heiress.
   C.—Othello; Forty Winks.

5. W.—The Demon of the Desert; Queer Subject.
   C.—Richard III; Wandering Minstrel.

6. W.—Demon of the Desert; Pleasant Neighbors.
   C.—Metamora; Animal Magnetism.

7. W.—Demon of the Desert; Battle of Sedgemoor.
   C.—Metamora; Make your Wills.

8. W.—Demon of the Desert; Love Laughs at Locksmiths.
   C.—Metamora; Whirligig Hall.

9. W.—The Tiger at Large; The Demon of the Desert.
   C.—Metamora; Sleeping Draught.

11. *Monday:*

W.—Richard III; Demon of the Desert.

C.—Marino Faliero *: *Marino Faliero*—E. S. Conner.

12.   W.—Apostate; Demon of the Desert.

C.—Mountaineers; No!; Weathercock.

13.   W.—Othello; Demon of the Desert.

C.—Marino Faliero; Promissory Note.

14.   W.—King Lear; Love Laughs at Locksmiths.

C.—Two Figaros *: *Cherubino*—H. Wallack, *Almaviva*—Pearson, *Figaro*—Walton, *Susanetta*—Miss Turpin, *Susanna*—Mrs. R. Hamilton; Dumb Belle; Married Bachelor.

15.   W.—Richard III; My Husband's Ghost.

C.—Old English Gentleman *: *Broadlands*—H. Wallack, *Horace*—Thayer, *George*—Lindsay, *Guard*—Hathwell, *Fanny*—Mrs. R. Hamilton, *Sophy*—Mrs. Walstein; Two Figaros.

16.   W.—Riches; Review.

C.—Old English Gentleman; Two Figaros.

18.   *Monday:*

W.—The Tiger at Large; Rural Felicity *: *Layton*—Rice, *Unit*—Wemyss, *Twaddle*—Porter, *Simon*—Hadaway, *Mrs. Colpepper*—Mrs. Kent, *Cecilia*—Mrs. Proctor; The Beehive.

C.—Guy Mannering; Old English Gentleman.

19.   W.—Battle of Sedgemoor; Rural Felicity.

C.—Rob Roy; Two Figaros.

20.   W.—Sam Patch; Rural Felicity.

C.—Love in a Village; Old English Gentleman.

21.   W.—Forest Rose; Sam Patch.

C.—Fazio; Ladies' Man.

22.   W.—Who wants a Guinea?; Sam Patch.

C.—Apostate; Sleeping Draught.

23.   W.—The Saxon Girl *: *William II.*—Rice, *Prince*—Smith, *Walter*—Proctor, *Robert*—Percival, *Tassal*—Hadaway, *Ghita*—Mrs. Bannister, *Editha*—Mrs. Proctor, *Margaret*—Mrs. Kent; The Tiger at Large.

C.—Stranger; Dead Shot.

25.   *Monday:*

W.—Koeuba *: *Diego*—Vache, *Donald*—Rice, *Mat*—Kent, *Isabella*—Miss White, *Frosine*—Mrs. Proctor; Set a Beggar on Horseback *: *Selim*—Addams, *Sadi*—Hadaway, *Gulnare*—Mrs. Kent; My Husband's Ghost.

C.—Zembuca; State Secrets; May Queen.

26.   W.—No newspapers printed.

C.—No newspapers printed.

27.   W.—Fire Raiser *: *White*—Proctor, *Hal*—Kent, *John*—Hadaway, *Joey*—Herbert, *Ruth*—Mrs. Proctor, *Catherine*—Miss White; Masquerade; Sam Patch.

      C.—Bianca Viscounti *: *Bianca*—Miss Clifton, *Guellio*—Miss Fisher, *Francisco*—Wood, *Sarpelloni*—Conner, *Rosana*—Harrington, *Pasqueli*—Burton; Twice Killed.

28.   W.—La Fitte; Demon of the Desert.

      C.—The Wife; My Own Ghost.

29.   W.—El Hyder; Warlock of the Glen.

      C.—Bianca Viscounti; Perfection.

30.   W.—Fire Raiser; Masquerade.

      C.—Maid of Cashmere, opera; State Secrets.

JANUARY 1838

1. *Monday:*

      W.—Margaret's Ghost *: *William*—Bannister, *Solomon*—Hadaway, *Ben*—Kent, *Madeline*—Mrs. Bannister, *Catharine*—Mrs. Proctor; King's Command *: *Edward IV.*—Rice, *Simon*—Hadaway, *Edith*—Mrs. Proctor, *Lucy*—Mrs. Kent; A Match in the Dark *: *Clements*—Proctor, *Courtney*—Rice, *Ellen*—Mrs. Proctor.

      C.—Maid of Cashmere, the opera; Scotch Cooper; Barbers at Court.

2.   W.—The Maiden's Vow *: *Jacob*—Marble, *George*—Bannister, *Charles*—J. Addams, *Emily*—Mrs. Proctor, *Peggy*—Mrs. Kent; King's Command.

      C.—Old English Gentleman; Jim Crow in London.

3.   W.—Maiden's Vow; Sam Patch.

      C.—Maid of Cashmere, the opera; Bold Dragoons.

4.   W.—Maiden's Vow; Virginia Mummy.

      C.—Maid of Cashmere, the opera; Turning the Tables.

5.   W.—Who want's a Guinea?; Oh! Hush; Sam Patch.

      C.—Maid of Cashmere, the opera; Ladies' Man.

6.   W.—Margaret's Ghost; Bone Squash Diavolo.

      C.—Maid of Cashmere, the opera; The Two Ghosts.

8. *Monday:*

      W.—The Love Chase *: *Wildlove*—Porter, *Wildrake*—Wemyss, *Trueworth*—J. Rice, *Wallen*—Bannister, *Widow Green*—Mrs. Bannister, *Constance*—Mrs. Proctor; Faith and Falsehood.

      C.—Maid of Cashmere, the opera; State Secrets.

9.   W.—Othello; A Match in the Dark.

      C.—Maid of Cashmere, the opera; The Strange Gentleman *: *Gentleman*—Burton, *Charles*—Lindsay, *Tom*—Walton, *Mary*—Mrs. Walstein.

10.   W.—Tiger at Large; Will Watch, the Bold Smuggler *: *Hugh* —Proctor, *Will Watch*—Kent, *Levi*—Hadaway, *Mary* —Mrs. Proctor; Abon Hassan.

       C.—La Sonnambula; Wandering Minstrel.

11.   W.—Love Chase; King's Command.

       C.—Married Life; No Song, No Supper.

12.   W.—Love Chase; Will Watch.

       C.—Maid of Cashmere, the opera; Adopted Child.

13.   W.—Margaret's Ghost; Abon Hassan.

       C.—Maid of Cashmere, the opera; Castle of Andalusia.

15. *Monday:*

       W.—Syracusan Brothers *: *Lucinius*—Bannister, *Manacles*—J. Rice, *Dionysius*—Proctor, *Naxeus*—Porter, *Clothinia*— Mrs. Bannister; Life in Philadelphia *: *Homo*—Bannister, *Mrs. Homo*—Mrs. Bannister; Delicate Attentions.

       C.—Love Chase; Good Husbands Make Good Wives *: *Gadfly*—Wood, *Faithful*—Burton, *Sidney*—Walton, *Mrs. Gadfly*—Miss Fisher, *Miss Careful*—Mrs. Brood.

16.   W.—Syracusan Brothers; Bee Hive.

       C.—Maid of Cashmere, the opera; Perfection.

17.   W.—Comedy of Errors; Sweethearts and Wives.

       C.—Richard III; Strange Gentleman.

18.   W.—Love Chase; Gulliver in Lilliput.

       C.—Love Chase; Good Husbands Make Good Wives.

19.   W.—Margaret's Ghost; Gulliver in Lilliput.

       C.—Gladiator; Mummy.

20.   W.—Comedy of Errors; Gulliver in Lilliput; Spoiled Child.

       C.—Damon and Pythias; William Tell.

22. *Monday:*

       W.—Lilliputians in Kentucky; Gulliver in Lilliput; Sweethearts and Wives.

       C.—Coriolanus; Married Bachelor.

23.   W.—Scotch Clans and Irish Chieftains; A Match in the Dark.

       C.—King Lear; Promissory Note.

24.   W.—Scotch Clans and Irish Chieftains; Pleasant Neighbors.

       C.—Gladiator; Waterman.

25.   W.—Scotch Clans and Irish Chieftains; Industry Must Prosper.

       C.—Coriolanus; Dumb Belle.

26.   W.—Scotch Clans and Irish Chieftains; Delicate Attentions.

       C.—Othello; Therese.

27.   W.—Scotch Clans and Irish Chieftains; Infidelity.

       C.—Charles II; Masaniello.

29. *Monday:*

       W.—Law of the Land *: *Platitude*—Porter, *Robson*—J. Addams, *Dodsworth*—Bannister, *Snail*—Hadaway, *Lucy*—

Mrs. Proctor, *Florence*—Mrs. Kent; Scotch Clans and Irish Chieftains.

C.—Metamora; The Liar.

30. W.—Virginius; Star Spangled Banner.

C.—Wild Oats; Crossing the Line.

31. W.—Othello, second and fourth acts; Richard III, fifth act; Scotch Clans and Irish Chieftains.

C.—Macbeth; Pleasant Neighbors.

FEBRUARY

1. *Thursday:*

W.—Koeuba; Set a Beggar on Horseback.

C.—Damon and Pythias; Tom Cringle.

2. W.—The Review; Gaulantus.

C.—Virginius; Barbers at Court.

3. W.—Deserted Village; Richard III, fourth and fifth acts.

C.—William Tell; Therese.

5. *Monday:*

W.—Guy Mannering; Brigand.

C.—Coriolanus; Metamora.

6. W.—Romeo and Juliet; Delicate Attentions.

C.—May Queen; Zembuca.

7. W.—Fazio; William Tell.

C.—Old English Gentleman; Bold Dragoons.

8. W.—School for Scandal; State Secrets.

C.—Maid of Cashmere, the opera; The Liar.

9. W.—Macbeth; Queen Subject.

C.—Paul Pry; Ladies' Man.

10. W.—Hunchback, omitting first act; Fazio, the mad scene; William Tell.

C.—Maid of Cashmere, the opera; Forty Winks.

12. *Monday:*

W.—Wallace; La Fitte.

C.—Barber of Seville; State Secrets.

13. W.—Closed to prepare for new drama: "The Installation of the Knights of the Garter."

C.—Maid of Cashmere, the opera; Good Husbands Make Good Wives.

14. W.—Closed.

C.—Love in a Village; Scape Goat.

15. W.—Richard III; Delicate Attentions.

C.—Maid of Cashmere, the opera; Botheration.

16. W.—Riches; Queer Subject.

C.—Cinderella; Barbers at Court.

17. W.—Apostate; Mayor of Garret.

C.—Promissory Note; Robert le Diable, one scene; The Picnic; Botheration.

19. *Monday:*

W.—The Battle of Poictiers *: *Black Prince*—J. Addams, *Salisbury*—Bannister, *Audley*—Rice, *Force*—Kent, *Blunt*—Proctor, *Simple*—Hadaway, *France*—Vache, *Ribemont*—Warren, *Beaufleur*—Porter, *Joan*—Mrs. Bannister, *Mignette*—Mrs. Proctor; Swiss Cottage.

C.—Barber of Seville; Wandering Minstrel.

20. W.—Battle of Poicters; Agreeable Surprise.

C.—Dumb Belle; Robert le Diable, one scene; Good Husbands Make Good Wives; Cheap Boarding.

21. W.—Battle of Poictiers; Weathercock.

C.—Cinderella; John Jones.

22. W.—Battle of Poictiers; Swiss Cottage.

C.—Make your Wills; Robert le Diable, one scene; Fish out of Water; Happiest Day of my Life.

23. W.—Battle of Poictiers; My Husband's Ghost.

C.—Confusion; Zembuca.

24. W.—Battle of Poictiers; Soldier's Wife and Soldier's Widow *: *Martin*—Carpenter, *Soldier*—Dickenson, *Husband*—Vache, *Wife*—Mrs. Barrymore, *Sisters*—Misses Packard and A. Packard.

C.—Botheration; Pleasant Neighbors; Miller and his Men.

26. *Monday:*

W.—Impulse *: *Impulse*—Rice, *Cabbage*—Hadaway, *Thornton*—Porter, *Sophia*—Mrs. Rice; Soldier's Wife and Soldier's Widow; A Match in the Dark.

C.—La Sonnambula; Fish out of Water.

27. W.—Soldier's Wife and Soldier's Widow; Swiss Cottage; Impulse.

C.—Maid of Cashmere, the opera; Masaniello.

28. W.—Scotch Clans and Irish Chieftains; Impulse.

C.—La Sonnambula; Bold Dragoons.

MARCH

1. *Thursday:*

W.—Jonathan and his Apprentices; Soldier's Wife and Soldier's Widow; Battle of Poictiers.

C.—Maid of Cashmere, the opera; Masaniello.

2. W.—Jonathan and his Apprentices; Queer Subject.

C.—La Sonnambula; Scape Goat.

3. W.—The Two Conquerors on the Plains of Palestine; The Lady and the Devil.

C.—Wallace; How to Die for Love! !

5. *Monday:*
   W.—Hofer; Star Spangled Banner.
   C.—Barber of Seville; Mummy.
6. W.—Fire Raiser; Will Watch.
   C.—Love Chase; Samuel Slick, Esq *: by the Cooke family.
7. W.—Thalaba; Black Eyed Susan.
   C.—La Sonnambula; Fish out of Water.
8. W.—Jonathan and his Apprentices; The Secret.
   C.—Sweethearts and Wives; Wallace.
9. W.—Mob, the Outlaw; La Fitte.
   C.—Good Husbands Make Good Wives; Miller and his Men.
10. W.—Clandare *: *Clandare*—Proctor, *Alvin*—Mrs. Proctor,
   Blackcliff—J. Addams, *Killoch*—Kent, *Ronald*—Hadaway, *Lady Lomond*—Mrs. Bannister; Unfinished Gentle-
   man; Lady of the Lake.
   C.—Fra Diavolo; Barbers at Court.
12. *Monday:*
   W.—Lodoiska; Impulse.
   C.—Man and Wife; Robert Macaire.
13. W.—Wallace; Therese.
   C.—Love Chase; May Queen.
14. W.—Gilderoy; Hunting a Turtle.
   C.—She Would and She Would Not; The Invincibles.
15. W.—Wallace; The Picnic.
   C.—Pizarro; Lover's Quarrels.
16. W.—Bronze Horse; How to Die for Love.
   C.—Confusion; The Invincibles.
17. W.—Brian Boroihme; Bronze Horse.
   C.—Dew Drop *: *Hela*—Brough, *Donald*—Walton, *Christie*
   —Thayer, *Morna*—Crowley, *Bailie*—Hathwell, *Ivy*—
   Miss Armstrong, *Jessamine*—Mrs. Lee, *Honeysuckle*—
   Mrs. Harrington, *Dew Drop*—La Petite Augusta May-
   wood; Fish out of Water.
19. *Monday:*
   W.—Forest of Rosenwald; Plot and Counterplot; Sentinel.
   C.—Dew Drop; Forty Winks.
20. W.—Faith and Falsehood; Hunting a Turtle; Black Eyed
   Susan.
   C.—She Would and She Would Not; The Invincibles.
21. W.—Poor Gentleman; Courtship of Slick of Slickville.
   C.—Dew Drop; Botheration.
22. W.—Damon and Pythias; Black Eyed Susan. Last night of the
   season.
   C.—Man and Wife; The Strange Gentleman.
23. C.—Dew Drop; Ladies' Man.
24. C.—Dew Drop; Turning the Tables.

[188]

26. *Monday:*
    C.—Dew Drop; Twice Killed.
27.   C.—Paul Pry; Invincibles.
28.   C.—Dew Drop; Wandering Minstrel.
29.   C.—Good Husbands Make Good Wives; A Quiet Day*:
      Somerday—Burton,   *Brian*—Lindsay,   *Emma*—Miss
      Fisher; May Queen.
30.   C.—Dew Drop; Make your Wills.

APRIL

2. *Monday:*
    W.—Mazeppa*: *Castellan*—Amherst, *Rudzloff*—Foster, *Olin-
    ska*—Mrs. Cole, *Abder Khan*—Rodney, *Mazeppa*—Wool-
    ford, *Premislaus*—Cooke, Jr., *Drolinski*—Gates, *Zemila*
    Mrs. Herring; Pleasant Neighbors.
    C.—Jonathan Doubikins; A Quiet Day; Yankee Pedlar.
3.   W.—Mazeppa; Pleasant Neighbors.
    C.—Green Mountain Boys; Forest Rose; Invincibles.
4.   W.—Mazeppa; Pleasant Neighbors.
    C.—Kaspar Hauser; Victorine.
5.   W.—Mazeppa; Gretna Green.
    C.—Knight of the Golden Fleece; Jonathan Doubikins.
6.   W.—Mazeppa; Gretna Green.
    C.—Kaspar Hauser; Green Mountain Boy.
7.   W.—Mazeppa; Gretna Green.
    C.—Peaceful Pelton; Yankee Pedlar; Speculations.
9. *Monday:*
    W.—Mazeppa; Courtship of Slick of Slickville.
    C.—A Quiet Day; Kentuckian; Monsieur Tonson
10.   W.—Mazeppa; Courtship of Slick of Slickville.
    C.—Jonathan in England; Mons. Mallett; Barbers at Court.
11.   W.—Mazeppa; Henri and Louise*: Characters by Messrs.
    Rodney, Percival, Gates, and Mrs. Herring.
    C.—Rip Van Winkle; Job Fox; Fish out of Water.
12.   W.—Mazeppa; Henri and Louise.
    C.—Weathercock; Jonathan Doubikins; Mons. Tonson.
13.   W.—Mazeppa; Henri and Louise.
    C.—Henry IV; Mons. Mallett; Kentuckian.
14.   W.—Mazeppa; Henri and Louise.
    C.—Castle Spectre; Cramond Brig; Spitfire.
16. *Monday:*
    W.—Mazeppa; Little Red Riding Hood.
    C.—Castle Spectre; Spitfire; Quadrupeds.
17.   W.—Mazeppa; Little Red Riding Hood.
    C.—Confusion; Spitfire; Quadrupeds.

18.   W.—An afternoon performance at two o'clock of Mazeppa; Little Red Riding Hood. No evening performance.
      C.—Stranger; Cinderella; My Young Wife and my Old Umbrella *: *Gregory*—Burton, *Dinah*—Mrs. Walstein.

19.   W.—Mazeppa; Little Red Riding Hood.
      C.—Good Husbands Make Good Wives; My Young Wife and my Old Umbrella; Spitfire.

20.   W.—Mazeppa; Little Red Riding Hood.
      C.—Stranger; Two Queens *: *Magnus*—Burton, *George*—Walton, *Christine*—Miss A. Fisher, *Margaret*—Mrs. Thayer; Swiss Cottage.

21.   W.—Mazeppa; Little Red Riding Hood.
      C.—Fazio; Spitfire.

23. *Monday:*
      W.—Napoleon Bonaparte; The Rich Poor Man!
      C.—Fazio; Swiss Cottage.

24.   W.—Napoleon Bonaparte; The Rich Poor Man!
      C.—Castle Spectre; Family Jars.

25.   W.—Napoleon Bonaparte; High Road to Marriage.
      C.—Romeo and Juliet; Turning the Tables.

26.   W.—Where does the Money Come from?; Napoleon Bonaparte.
      C.—Heir at Law; Two Queens.

27.   W.—Where does the Money Come from?; Napoleon Bonaparte.
      C.—Hamlet; Spitfire.

28.   W.—Cataract of the Ganges.
      C.—Cato; The Mummy.

30. *Monday:*
      W.—Cataract of the Ganges.
      C.—Macbeth; Twice Killed.

MAY

1. *Tuesday:*
      W.—Cataract of the Ganges.
      C.—Henry VIII; Perfection.

2.   W.—Cataract of the Ganges.
      C.—Coriolanus; Hunter of the Alps.

3.   W.—Mazeppa.
      C.—Wonder; Ransom.

4.   W.—Mazeppa.
      C.—Wives as they Were; Mons. Mallet; Job Fox.

5.   W.—Mazeppa. End of season.
      C.—Sam Weller; Spitfire.

7. *Monday:*
    C.—Sam Weller; Scape Goat.
8.   C.—Sam Weller; Twice Killed.
9.   C.—Sam Weller; Mr. and Mrs. Pringle.
10.   C.—Sam Weller; The Spitfire.
11.   C.—Sam Weller; Dumb Belle.
12.   C.—Sam Weller; Popping the Question; Bengal Tiger.
14. *Monday:*
    C.—Paul Pry; Barbers at Court.
15.   C.—Magpie and Maid; May Queen.
16.   C.—Wild Oats; Robert Macaire.
17.   C.—Speed the Plough; Deaf as a Post.
18.   C.—Road to Ruin; Victorine.
19.   C.—Virginius; Family Jars.
21. *Monday:*
    C.—The Way to get Married; Robert Macaire.
22.   C.—William Tell; Black Eyed Susan.
23.   C.—Englishmen in India; Sam Weller.
24.   C.—Old English Gentleman; Of Age Tomorrow; Raising the Wind.
25.   C.—School of Reform; Maid of Croissy.
26.   C.—Busy Body; Spitfire.
28. *Monday:*
    C.—Maid of Croissy; Unfinished Gentleman; The Critic.
29.   C.—Castle of Andalusia; State Secrets.
30.   C.—Ion; No Song, No Supper.
31.   C.—Battle of Algiers; Masaniello.

JUNE

1. *Friday:*
    C.—Richard III; Dumb Belle.
2.   C.—Lady of Lyons *: *Beausant*—Harrington, *Glavis*—Lindsay, *Damas*—Faulkner, *Melnotte*—Wood, *Madame Deschappelles*—Mrs. Thayer, *Pauline*—Miss Fisher, *Widow Melnotte*—Mrs. Brood; Rosina.
4. *Monday:*
    C.—Lady of Lyons; No Song, No Supper.
5.   C.—Dew Drop; Guns without Shot.
6.   C.—Dew Drop; Fish out of Water.
7.   C.—Lady of Lyons; Spitfire.
8.   C.—Paul Pry; Masaniello, last two acts.
9.   C.—Maid of Cashmere, the opera; Irish Tutor.
11. *Monday:*
    C.—Richard III, three acts; Manager's Daughter *: *Jane*—

Miss Davenport, *Dictator*—Lindsay, *Crogs*—Eberle, *Shanks*—Jones, *Miss Grand*—Mrs. Walstein.

12. C.—Dumb Belle; Manager's Daughter; Haunted Inn.
13. C.—No! Spoiled Child; Black Eyed Susan.
14. C.—Fire and Water; Manager's Daughter; Family Jars.
15. C.—Merchant of Venice; Spoiled Child.
16. C.—Dumb Boy of Manchester; Manager's Daughter.
18. *Monday:*
C.—Hunchback; Second Thoughts.
19. C.—Wild Oats; Spitfire.
20. C.—Lover's Quarrels; Lady of Lyons; Dancing Barber *:
Barber—Burton, *Lord*—Lindsay, *Lady*—Miss Fisher.
21. C.—Dumb Belle; Folly as it Flies; Amateur Actors
22. C.—Lady of Lyons; Barbers at Court.
23. W.—Comedy of Errors; Jim Crow in London.
C.—Fire and Water; Point of Honor; My Aunt.
25. *Monday:*
W.—The Last Pardon; Bone Squash Diavolo.
C.—Lady of Lyons; Married Rake.
26. W.—Oh! Hush!!; Sarcophagus.
C.—Damon and Pythias; Forty Winks.
27. W.—Honeymoon; Jim Crow in London.
C.—Poor Soldier; Idiot Witness; The Quaker.
28. W.—The Last Pardon; Bone Squash Diavolo.
C.—Haunted Inn; Married Rake; Master's Rival.
29. W.—Syracusan Brothers; Black and White.
C.—The Wife; Spoiled Child.
30. W.—Black and White; Sylvester Daggerwood; Bone Squash Diavolo.
C.—A Cure for the Heart Ache; Idiot Witness.

JULY

2. *Monday:*
W.—Leila *: *Muza*—Bannister, *Almamen*—Porter, *Boabdil*—Davenport, *Ferdinand*—J. Rice, *Leila*—Mrs. Bannister, *Isabella*—Miss White; Oh! Hush!!
C.—Lady of Lyons; Married Rake; Wandering Minstrel.
3. W.—Leila; Black and White.
C.—Lady of Lyons; Poor Soldier.
4. W.—Cradle of Liberty; La Masque.
C.—She Would be a Soldier; John Jones.
5. W.—Macbeth; My Husband's Ghost.
C.—No newspapers published today, and no advance notice given of program for Chesnut.
6. W.—Pizarro; Sudden Thoughts.

C.—Lady of Lyons; The Quaker.

7. W.—Othello; No!
C.—Dancing Barber; Does Your Mother Know You're Out *: *Mizzle*—Burton, *Mrs. Stichly*—Mrs. Thayer; The Original *: *Jack*—Burton, *Emily*—Mrs. Walstein; Spitfire. Last night of season.

9. *Monday:*
W.—King Lear; State Secrets.

10. W.—New Way To Pay Old Debts; Every Body's Husband.

11. W.—Apostate; Cad of the Buss.

12. W.—Julius Caesar; Black Eyed Susan.

13. W.—Venice Preserved; Turnpike Gate.

14. W.—Richard III; Wife; Mayor of Garret.

16. *Monday:*
W.—P.P., or the Man and the Tiger; My Aunt; The Review.

17. W.—Jonathan in England; Black Eyed Susan.

18. W.—Sam Patch; Sprigs of Laurel.

19. W.—Luke the Laborer; Forest Rose.

20. W.—Maiden's Vow; Turnpike Gate.

21. W.—Sam Patch; Turn Out.

23. *Monday:*
W.—No Song, No Supper; Forest Rose.

24. W.—Virginius; The Bush Whacker *: *Slanter*—Marble, *Rover*—Bannister, *Moll*—Mrs. Bannister.

25. W.—Lady of Lyons; Spitfire.

26. W.—The Last Pardon; Rosina.

27. W.—Rosina; Spitfire.

28. W.—Wallace.

30. *Monday:*
W.—Lady of Lyons; Pilot of the Ocean.

31. W.—Othello; Frank Fox Phipps.

AUGUST

1. *Wednesday:*
W.—Damon and Pythias; Hundred-Pound Note.

2. W.—La Fitte; State Secrets.

3. W.—Richard III; Spitfire.

4. W.—Douglas; Mob, the Outlaw.

6. *Monday:*
W.—Does Your Mother Know You're Out?; Simpson and Company; Adopted Child; Promissory Note.

7. W.—Luke the Laborer; Does Your Mother Know You're Out?

8. W.—The Jesuit's Colony *: *Victor Ralle*—Porter, *Ravillac*—Davenport, *Voorn*—Bannister, *Outalissi*—Pickering, *Pray*

—Hadaway, *Adnee*—Mrs. Rice, *Woika*—Miss White; A Roland for an Oliver.

9. W.—My Husband's Ghost; Rosina.
10. W.—Coronation of Queen Victoria, a pageant *; Sudden Thoughts; Our Mary Ann.
11. W.—Coronation of Queen Victoria; Our Mary Ann; A Roland for an Oliver.
13. *Monday:*
    W.—Coronation of Queen Victoria; State Secrets; Poor Soldier.
14. W.—Coronation of Queen Victoria; Sentinel; Does Your Mother Know You're Out?
15. W.—Coronation of Queen Victoria; Poor Soldier; Sentinel.
16. W.—Coronation of Queen Victoria; The Gentleman of Lyons *: *Julian*—Bannister, *Dupuis*—Wemyss, *Valcour*—Porter, *Ernestide*—Mrs. Bannister, *Bridget*—Mrs. La Forest.
17. W.—Coronation of Queen Victoria; Sentinel; Does Your Mother Know You're Out?
18. W.—Coronation of Queen Victoria; Rory O'More.
20. *Monday:*
    W.—Coronation of Queen Victoria; Rory O'More.
21. W.—Coronation of Queen Victoria; Rory O'More.
22. W.—Coronation of Queen Victoria; Rory O'More.
23. W.—Coronation of Queen Victoria; Rory O'More.
24. W.—Coronation of Queen Victoria; Rory O'More.
25. W.—Boat Builder's Hovel *: *Jack*—Hadaway, *Miers*—Porter, *Maria*—Pickering, *Broadhead*—Vache, *Fanny*—Mrs. La Forest; Rory O'More.
    C.—Maids as they Are; Ladies' Man.
27. *Monday:*
    W.—Caius Silius *: *Caius*—Parsons, *Labantus*—La Forest, *Carteantus*—J. G. Hall, *Rulus*—Pickering, *Leonbel*—Porter, *Florena*—Mrs. Bannister; Confounded Foreigners.
    C.—Perfection; John Jones; Twice Killed.
28. W.—Caius Silius; Spitfire.
    C.—Master's Rival; Botheration; Family Jars.
29. W.—Nick of the Woods; Confounded Foreigners.
    C.—Ransom; Dumb Belle; Deaf as a Post.
30. W.—King Lear; Nick of the Woods.
    C.—Charles II; Raising the Wind.
31. W.—Macbeth; Nick of the Woods.
    C.—A Roland for an Oliver; The Mummy.

SEPTEMBER

1. *Saturday:*
    W.—Othello; Nick of the Woods.

       C.—Sweethearts and Wives; Married Rake.
3. *Monday:*
       W.—Oranska; Paul Jones.
       C.—Young Widow; Of Age Tomorrow.
4.   W.—Tom Cringle; Nick of the Woods.
       C.—Youthful Queen; Perfection.
5.   W.—Brutus; Nick of the Woods.
       C.—Fire and Water; Rip Van Winkle; Job Fox.
6.   W.—Oranska; Woman's the Devil.
       C.—Jonathan Doubikins; Kentuckian; Dumb Belle.
7.   W.—Julius Caesar; Woman's the Devil.
       C.—Jonathan in England; Mons. Tonson.
8.   W.—Lady of the Lake; Paul Jones.
       C.—Henry IV; Monsieur Mallet; Militia Training.
10. *Monday:*
       W.—Rienzi; Woman's the Devil.
       C.—Richard III; Of Age Tomorrow.
11.   W.—Coriolanus; Nick of the Woods.
       C.—New Way To Pay Old Debts; Spitfire.
12.   W.—La Fitte; Weathercock.
       C.—Othello; Dancing Barber.
13.   W.—The Stranger.
       C.—King Lear; Wandering Minstrel.
14.   W.—Wallace.
       C.—Hamlet; Ladies' Man.
15.   W.—Hofer.
       C.—Weak Points *: *Wheedle*—Burton, *Bocker*—Watson, *Jolly*—Faulkner, *Miss Agnes*—Mrs. Walstein; Gemini *: *Edmond, Andre*—two rôles—Burton, *Tisserand*—Walton, *McQuehlon*—Watson, *Sophia*—Mrs. Walstein; Comfortable Lodgings.
17. *Monday:*
       W.—Rory O'More.
       C.—Irish Ambassador; Omnibus; No!
18.   W.—Black Eyed Susan; Swiss Cottage.
       C.—Nervous Man; Teddy the Tiler; Wandering Minstrel.
19.   W.—Athenian Captive; Star Spangled Banner.
       C.—St. Patrick's Eve; Irish Lion *: *Moore*—Power, *Squabs*—Watson, *Dixon*—Lindsay, *Mrs. Fitzjig*—Mrs. Sharpe; John Jones.
20.   W.—Rory O'More.
       C.—Born to Good Luck; Irish Lion; No.
21.   W.—Athenian Captive; Irish Lion.
       C.—Irish Ambassador; Irish Lion.
22.   W.—Soldier and Sailor *: *Bombshell*—Vache, *Binnacle*—Hield, *Botch*—Hadaway, *Barbara*—Miss White; Irish Lion.

C.—Born to Good Luck; Irish Lion.

24. *Monday:*
    W.—La Bayadere; Swiss Cottage.
    C.—Rory O'More; Weak Points.

25.   W.—La Bayadere; Woman's the Devil.
    C.—Rory O'More; Ladies' Man.

26.   W.—State Secrets; Spitfire; Catharine and Petruchio.
    C.—Rory O'More; Irish Lion.

27.   W.—La Bayadere; Day after the Wedding.
    C.—Englishmen in India; Swiss Cottage.

28.   W.—La Sonnambula; Swiss Cottage.
    C.—Rory O'More; Turn Out.

29.   W.—La Sonnambula; Catharine and Petruchio.
    C.—Rory O'More; Omnibus.

OCTOBER

1. *Monday:*
    W.—La Bayadere; State Secrets.
    C.—Born to Good Luck; Irish Tutor; Highland Reel.

2.   W.—Mob, the Outlaw; Mischief Making.
    C.—White Horse of the Peppers *: *Pepper*—Power, *Hano*—Burton, *Chesham*—Harrington, *Darby*—Faulkner, *Phelim*—Walton, *Magdalene*—Mrs. Walstein, *Agatha*—Miss De Barr; Fish out of Water.

3.   W.—Timour the Tartar; Infidelity; Yankee Duellist *: *Jeremiah Hector*—Dr. Valentine, *Betsy*—Miss White.
    C.—White Horse of the Peppers; Irish Lion.

4.   W.—Rory O'More; Mischief Making.
    C.—White Horse of the Peppers; Irish Tutor; Perfection.

5.   W.—La Bayadere; The Lady and the Unknown.
    C.—White Horse of the Peppers; Irishman in London; Weathercock.

6.   W.—La Bayadere; Why did you Die?
    C.—Irish Ambassador; Rory O'More.

8. *Monday:*
    W.—La Bayadere; Why did you Die?
    C.—One Hour; Loan of a Lover; He Would be an Actor.

9.   W.—La Bayadere; Jenny Jones.
    C.—One Hour; Loan of a Lover; He Would be an Actor.

10.   W.—The Avenger of Blood! *: *Richard*—Hield, *John*—Burgress, *Beauty*—Hadaway, *Matthew*—Pickering, *Maude*—Miss Lee.
    C.—Barrack Room; He Would be an Actor; Swiss Cottage.

11. W.—The Avenger of Blood; Virginia Mummy; Miller and his Men.
    C.—Barrack Room; He Would be an Actor; Swiss Cottage.
12. W.—Richard III; Jim Crow in London; No Song, No Supper.
    C.—Handsome Husband; One Hour; Too Late for Dinner.
13. W.—Hamlet; Bone Squash Diavolo.
    C.—One Hour; Handsome Husband; Too Late for Dinner.
15. *Monday:*
    W.—Othello; Our Mary Ann.
    C.—Know your own Mind; Patter Versus Clatter *: *Patter*—
        C. Matthews, *Parker*—Watson, *Polly*—Miss Armstrong;
        Loan of a Lover.
16. W.—Damon and Pythias; Loan of a Lover.
    C.—Barrack Room; Love in a Cottage; Patter versus Clatter.
17. W.—Lady of Lyons; Why did you Die?
    C.—Love in a Cottage; Handsome Husband; Patter versus
        Clatter.
18. W.—Macbeth; How do you Manage?
    C.—Know your own Mind; Patter versus Clatter.
19. W.—Metamora; How do you Manage?
    C.—Love in a Cottage; Welsh Girl; He Would be an Actor.
20. W.—Metamora; How do you Manage?
    C.—Welsh Girl; Patter versus Clatter; Handsome Husband;
        One Hour.
22. *Monday:*
    W.—Lady of Lyons; William Tell.
    C.—St. Mary's Eve *: *Wentworth*—Murdock, *Vaughan*—
        Lindsay, *Baggs*—Walton, *Chalk*—Faulkner, *Sharpe*—
        Harrington, *Dame Mayfield*—Mrs. Brood, *Mary*—Miss
        De Barr, *Madeline*—Mlle. Celeste; Pleasant Neighbors.
23. W.—Metamora; Our Mary Ann.
    C.—St. Mary's Eve; John Jones.
24. W.—Gladiator; Why did you Die?
    C.—St. Mary's Eve; French Spy.
25. W.—Lady of Lyons; Trick for Trick *: *Tweezer*—Porter,
        Trivet—Hield, *Wigler*—Hadaway, *Clidper*—Mrs. La
        Forest.
    C.—St. Mary's Eve; French Spy.
26. W.—Gladiator; Trick for Trick.
    C.—St. Mary's Eve; French Spy.
27. W.—Richard III; Monsieur Jacques.
    C.—Child of the Wreck; St. Mary's Eve.
29. *Monday:*
    W.—Gladiator; Therese.
    C.—Child of the Wreck; Indian Girl.

30. W.—Virginius; Rent Day.
C.—Child of the Wreck; Indian Girl.
31. W.—Ion; Youthful Queen.
C.—Susanne; Child of the Wreck.

NOVEMBER

1. *Thursday:*
W.—Hamlet; Trick for Trick.
C.—Susanne; St. Mary's Eve.
2. W.—Woman's Wit; Why did you Die?
C.—Child of the Wreck; St. Mary's Eve.
3. W.—Woman's Wit; Heart of Midlothian.
C.—The Mother *: *Mother*—Celeste, *Captain*—Murdock, *Fringella*—Miss Fisher; French Spy.
5. *Monday:*
W.—Love Chase; Agnes de Vere.
C.—Rory O'More; Perfection.
6. W.—Avenger of Blood; Our Mary Ann.
C.—St. Patrick's Eve. Irish Lion.
7. W.—Agnes de Vere; Avenger of Blood.
C.—Irish Ambassador; Omnibus; Rendezvous.
8. W.—Boat Builder's Hovel; Avenger of Blood.
C.—White Horse of the Peppers; Teddy the Tiler; Weathercock.
9. W.—Agnes de Vere; Boat Builder's Hovel.
C.—Nervous Man; Irish Lion; Turn Out.
10. W.—Avenger of Blood; Naval Engagements.
C.—Rory O'More; More Blunders than One.
12. *Monday:*
W.—Heart of Midlothian; Naval Engagements.
C.—Irish Ambassador; Nervous Man; Rendezvous.
13. W.—Avenger of Blood; Naval Engagements.
C.—Born to Good Luck; More Blunders than One; No!
14. W.—Dumb Boy of Manchester; Spoiled Child.
C.—A Roland for an Oliver; Of Age Tomorrow.
15. W.—Dumb Boy of Manchester; Manager's Daughter.
C.—The Ransom; Young Widow.
16. W.—Dumb Boy of Manchester; Manager's Daughter.
C.—Youthful Queen; No Song, No Supper.
17. W.—School for Scandal; Richard III; Actress of all Work.
C.—Rendezvous; Perfection.
19. *Monday:*
W.—Amilie *: *Amilie*—Madame Otto, *General*—Brough, *Gervais*—Bishop; Naval Engagements.
C.—Wandering Minstrel; Weak Points.

20.   W.—Amilie; Trick for Trick.
      C.—Comfortable Lodgings; Turning the Tables.
21.   W.—Amilie; How do you Manage?
      C.—State Secrets; Highland Reel.
22.   W.—Amilie; Our Mary Ann.
      C.—Deaf as a Post; Katharine and Petruchio.
23.   W.—Amilie; Loan of a Lover.
      C.—Married Rake; Fish out of Water.
24.   W.—Amilie; No Song, No Supper.
      C.—Pleasant Neighbors.
26.   *Monday:*
      W.—Amilie; No!
      C.—Stranger.
27.   W.—Amilie; Jenny Jones.
      C.—Wonder.
28.   W.—Amilie; Swiss Cottage.
      C.—Lady of Lyons; Ladies' Man.
29.   W.—Amilie; Catching an Heiress.
      C.—Velasco *: *Velasco*—Murdock, *Ferdinand*—Walton, *Julio*
      —Wood, *Carlos*—Miss Fisher; *Isadora*—Mrs. Sharpe;
      U and I *: *Dick*—Murdock, *Puff*—Burton, *Dial*—Lind-
      say, *Lydia*—Miss Fisher.
30.   W.—Amilie; Who's the Murderer?
      C.—Honey Moon; U and I.

DECEMBER

1.   *Saturday:*
      W.—Amilie; Miller and his Men.
      C.—Rob Roy; Don Giovanni.
3.   W.—Damon and Pythias; Youthful Queen.
      C.—St. Mary's Eve; French Spy.
4.   W.—Lady of Lyons; Therese.
      C.—Child of the Wreck; Indian Girl.
5.   W.—Metamora; Rosina.
      C.—Susanne; Child of the Wreck.
6.   W.—Virginius; Swiss Cottage.
      C.—The Mother; Maid of Cashmere.
7.   W.—Gladiator; Blind Boy.
      C.—The Mother; Maid of Cashmere.
8.   W.—Metamora; Catharine and Petruchio.
      C.—Wizard Skiff; Maid of Cashmere.
10.   *Monday:*
      W.—Lady of Lyons; William Tell.
      C.—Indian Girl; Wizard Skiff.
11.   W.—Foundling of the Forest; Hunter of the Alps.

[199]

C.—Child of Air *: *Agloe*—Mlle. Celeste; Turning the Tables.

12. W.—Maid of Mariendorpt *: *Metta*—Mrs. Shaw, *General*—Porter, *Baron*—Hall, *Joseph*—Burgess, *Hans*—Pickering, *Rudolph*—La Forest, *Ahab*—Vache, *Adolpha*—Mme. La Trust; Agnes de Vere.
    C.—Child of Air; Sleeping Draught.

13. W.—Dream of Fate; Uncle Sam.
    C.—Child of Air; Fish out of Water.

14. W.—Tom and Jerry; Miller's Murder.
    C.—Child of Air; Whirligig Hall.

15. W.—The Mountain King; Lear of Private Life.
    C.—Star of the Forest; Child of Air.

17. *Monday:*
    W.—Virginius; Hamlet; My Neighbor's Wife.
    C.—Star of the Forest; Child of Air.

18. W.—Six Degrees of Crime!; The Romp.
    C.—Star of the Forest; Child of Air.

19. W.—Fazio; Open House.
    C.—Moorish Page; Child of Air.

20. W.—Miller's Murder; Dream of Fate.
    C.—Child of Air; Moorish Page.

21. W.—Lear of Private Life; My Neighbor's Wife.
    C.—Wizard Skiff; French Spy.

22. W.—Devil's Bridge; Broken Sword.
    C.—La Tentation; St. Mary's Eve.

24. *Monday:*
    W.—Friar's Oak *: *Darnley*—Pickering, *Dunleavy*—La Forest, *Margaret*—Mrs. Hield, *Ellen*—Mrs. Knight; Open House.
    C.—Bride of Lammermoor; Tom Noddy's Secret *: *Ormond*—Lindsay, *Noddy*—Burton, *Mary*—Mrs. Walstein, *Gabrielle*—Miss De Barr.

25. W.—Friar's Oak; Tom and Jerry.
    C.—Blue Beard; Tom Noddy's Secret; Spitfire.

26. W.—My Neighbor's Wife; Golden Farmer.
    C.—Velasco; Tom Noddy's Secret.

27. W.—Friar's Oak; Golden Farmer.
    C.—Englishmen in India; Blue Beard.

28. W.—Golden Farmer; Open House.
    C.—Velasco; Whirligig Hall.

29. W.—Golden Farmer; Swiss Cottage; Catching an Heiress.
    C.—Love and Murder *: *Jubb*—Burton, *Mrs. Frigid*—Mrs. Sharpe, *Mrs. Jumble*—Mrs. Thayer, *Laffet*—Miss De Barr; My Friend the Governor.

31. *Monday:*

W.—Zameo *: *Tomac*—Burgess, *Zameo*—Pickering, *Celestine* —Mrs. Knight; He's not A-Miss; Golden Farmer.
C.—Macbeth; Spitfire.

JANUARY 1839

1. *Tuesday:*
   W.—Oliver Twist *: *Oliver*—Mrs. Knight, *Burns*—Burgess, *Fagin*—Porter, *Claypole*—La Forest, *Sykes*—Pickering, *Nancy*—Mrs. Hield; Broken Sword.
   C.—Brigand; Wolf and the Lamb; Tom Noddy's Secret.
2. W.—Oliver Twist; Swiss Cottage.
   C.—The Scholar *: *Bookworm*—J. Wallack, *Hans*—Burton, *Fred*—Lindsay, *Mrs. Wurtzburg*—Mrs. Brood, *Helen*— Miss Fisher; Brigand.
3. W.—Devil's Bridge; Friar's Oak.
   C.—Wives as they Were; Husband at Sight.
4. W.—Dream of Fate; Tom and Jerry.
   C.—The Wife; Wolf and the Lamb.
5. W.—Don Pedro, The Cruel; Oliver Twist.
   C.—The Scholar; Rent Day.
7. *Monday:*
   W.—Don Pedro, The Cruel; Broken Sword.
   C.—Pizarro; My Aunt.
8. W.—Indian Prophecy *: *Washington*—Porter, *Bishop*— Kemble, *Woodford*—Rice, *Menalva*—Pickering, *Marietta* —Mrs. Hield; Spoiled Child; Volunteer.
   C.—Maid of Mariendorpt; Rival Valets.
9. W.—A Lesson for Ladies *: *St. Val*—Wemyss, *Mathieu*— Kemble, *M'lle. Dellreux*—Mrs. Hield; Don Pedro, the Cruel.
   C.—Maid of Mariendorpt; Rival Valets.
10. W.—Dumb Man of Manchester; Lesson for Ladies; Foulah Slave.
    C.—Bride of Lammermoor; Whirligig Hall.
11. W.—Dumb Man of Manchester; Foulah Slave.
    C.—Paul Pry; Spitfire.
12. W.—Wild Boy of Bohemia; The Disowned and his Poor Dog Tray.
    C.—Merry Wives of Windsor; Mons. Mallett; Perfection.
14. *Monday:*
    W.—A Lesson for Ladies; Irish Tutor; Children in the Wood.
    C.—La Sonnambula; Katharine and Petruchio.
15. W.—The Last Nail; Is He Jealous?; Illustrious Stranger.
    C.—La Sonnambula; Spitfire.
16. W.—Maid of Mariendorpt; Smuggler of Bootle Bay.

C.—La Sonnambula; State Secret.
17. W.—Wild Boy of Bohemia; Smuggler of Bootle Bay.
C.—La Sonnambula; Wandering Minstrel.
18. W.—Dumb Girl of Genoa; The Disowned and his Poor Dog Tray.
C.—Amilie; Fish out of Water.
19. W.—Valentine and Orson; Irish Lion.
C.—Amilie; Mummy.
21. *Monday:*
W.—Henriette; Cherokee Chief.
C.—La Sonnambula.
22. W.—Forest of Bondy; Valentine and Orson.
C.—Amilie; Dead Shot.
23. W.—Dumb Slave; Obi.
C.—Amilie; My Friend the Governor.
24. W.—Dumb Man of Manchester; The Disowned and his Poor Dog Tray.
C.—Amilie; Spitfire.
25. W.—Dumb Slave; Valentine and Orson.
C.—La Sonnambula; Comfortable Service.
26. W.—Hamlet; A Maiden's Fame.
C.—Amilie; Fish out of Water.
28. *Monday:*
W.—Charming Polly *: *Nat*—Hadaway, *Pierce*—Mossop, *Farmer*—Grierson, *Betty*—Mrs. La Forest; Joan of Arc.
C.—La Sonnambula.
29. W.—Melmoth, the Doomed; Castle of Paluzzi.
C.—Fra Diavolo; My Friend the Governor.
30. W.—Titus Andronicus *: *Saturnius*—Burgess, *Bassanius*—Rice, *Titus*—Bannister, *Aaron*—Pickering, *Marcus Antonius*—Porter, *Clown*—Hadaway, *Young Lucius*—Miss Lee, *Tamora*—Mrs. Hield, *Lavinia*—Mrs. Bannister; A Lesson for Ladies.
C.—Fra Diavolo; Barbers at Court.
31. W.—Titus Andronicus; Charming Polly.
C.—Fra Diavolo; Mummy.

FEBRUARY

1. *Friday:*
W.—Titus Andronicus; Maidens Beware; Mischief Making.
C.—Fra Diavolo; Comfortable Service.
2. W.—Titus Andronicus; The Lady and the Devil.
C.—Fra Diavolo; Turning the Tables.
4. *Monday:*
W.—Evil Day *: *Pierce*—Mossop, *Elliott*—Porter, *Hubert*—

J. B. Rice, *Nicholas*—Hadaway, *Henry*—Burgess, *Jane*—
Mrs. Knight, *Margery*—Mrs. La Forest; Rory O'More.
C.—La Sonnambula; Perfection.

5. W.—Joan of Arc; My Neighbor's Wife; Irish Tutor.
C.—Cinderella; Katharine and Petruchio.

6. W.—Wood Demon; Venus in Arms.
C.—Cinderella.

7. W.—Joan of Arc; Poor Soldier.
C.—Cinderella; Young Widow.

8. W.—Rent Day; Charming Polly.
C.—Guy Mannering; Day after the Wedding.

9. W.—Forty Thieves; My Neighbor's Wife.
C.—Cinderella.

11. *Monday:*
W.—Forty Thieves; Irish Tutor.
C.—Maid of Cashmere; Dead Shot.

12. W.—Forty Thieves; Venus in Arms.
C.—Maid of Cashmere; May Queen.

13. W.—Forty Thieves; Irish Lion.
C.—Sweethearts and Wives; Spitfire.

14. W.—Forty Thieves; My Neighbor's Wife.
C.—Maid of Cashmere; Comfortable Lodgings.

15. W.—Forty Thieves; The Lady and the Devil.
C.—Honey Moon; Wandering Minstrel.

16. W.—El Hyder; Poor Soldier.
C.—Rent Day; Mummy.

18. *Monday:*
W.—El Hyder; Spoiled Child.
C.—Maid of Cashmere; Cramond Brig.

19. W.—El Hyder; Swiss Cottage.
C.—Jealous Wife; Barbers at Court.

20. W.—El Hyder; Catching an Heiress.
C.—Maid of Cashmere; State Secrets.

21. W.—El Hyder; Poor Soldier.
C.—Paul Pry; Spitfire.

22. W.—Forty Thieves; Review.
C.—Married Life; Comfortable Lodgings.

23. W.—Timour the Tartar; Is He Jealous?
C.—Maid of Cashmere; Rival Valets.

25. *Monday:*
W.—Timour the Tartar; Nicholas Nickleby.
C.—Soldier's Daughter; My Friend the Governor.

26. W.—Timour the Tartar; Nicholas Nickleby.
C.—Ransom; A Roland for an Oliver.

27. W.—Timour the Tartar; Nicholas Nickleby.
C.—Wives as they Were; Young Widow.

28.   W.—Timour the Tartar; Nicholas Nickleby.
      C.—Laugh when you Can; Married Rake.

MARCH

1. *Friday:*
      W.—Timour the Tartar; Nicholas Nickleby.
      C.—Guy Mannering; No Song, No Supper.
2.   W.—Forty Thieves; Timour the Tartar.
      C.—Rob Roy; Rosina.
4. *Monday:*
      W.—The Cataract of the Ganges; Review.
      C.—Isabella; Fish out of Water.
5.   W.—The Cataract of the Ganges; Nicholas Nickleby.
      C.—Lady of Lyons; Master's Rival.
6.   W.—The Cataract of the Ganges; Catching an Heiress.
      C.—The Stranger; Deaf as a Post.
7.   W.—The Cataract of the Ganges; Poor Soldier.
      C.—Jealous Wife; Family Jars.
8.   W.—The Cataract of the Ganges; Billy Button.
      C.—Jane Shore; Dead Shot.
9.   W.—The Cataract of the Ganges; Billy Button.
      C.—Maid of Mariendorpt; Fish out of Water.
11. *Monday:*
      W.—The Cataract of the Ganges; Agreeable Surprise.
      C.—Lady of Lyons; Victorine.
12.   W.—The Cataract of the Ganges; Turnpike Gate.
      C.—Isabella; Deaf as a Post.
13.   W.—The Cataract of the Ganges; Billy Button; Spoiled Child.
      C.—Gamester; Family Jars.
14.   W.—Forty Thieves; Agreeable Surprise.
      C.—The Stranger; Dead Shot.
15.   W.—The Cataract of the Ganges; Irish Tutor.
      C.—Jane Shore; Master's Rival.
16.   W.—Lodoiska; Tom and Jerry.
      C.—Venice Preserved; A Day after the Fair.
18. *Monday:*
      W.—Lodoiska; Tom and Jerry.
      C.—The Deformed; The Invincibles.
19.   W.—Lodoiska; Agreeable Surprise.
      C.—The Wife; Young Widow.
20.   W.—El Hyder; Lodoiska.
      .—Julietta Gordini *: *Julietta*—Miss Hildreth, *Gordini*—
      Harrington, *Careffa*—Lindsay, *Lenoi*—Thayer, *Russell*—
      Davenport, *Agnes*—Mrs. Thayer; Dead Shot.
21.   W.—Gaspardo the Gondolier; Lodoiska.

C.—Julietta Gordini; Married Rake.
22. W.—Gaspardo the Gondolier; Lodoiska.
C.—Hunchback; A Day after the Wedding.
23. W.—Gaspardo the Gondolier; Blue Beard.
C.—Gaspardo; Souter Johnnie *: *Allan*—Walton, *Baillie*—
Watson, *Johnnie*—Maywood, *Marian*—Miss Bunjie.
25. *Monday:*
W.—Blue Beard; Gaspardo.
C.—Dramatist; Gaspardo.
26. W.—Blue Beard; Gaspardo.
C.—Laugh when you Can; Gaspardo.
27. W.—Blue Beard; The Tiger Horde.
C.—Road to Ruin; Rafael, the Libertine *: *Rafael*—J. S.
Balls, *Maria*—Miss A. Fisher.
28. W.—The Tiger Horde; Gaspardo.
C.—Rafael; Perfection.
29. W.—El Hyder; Gaspardo.
C.—Way to get Married; Dancing Barber.
30. W.—Blue Beard; Forty Thieves.
C.—Fontainbleau; Three and the Deuce.

APRIL

1. *Monday:*
W.—Peter the Great *: *Dunder*—Burton, *Peter*—Pickering,
Baron—Rice, *Stanmitz*—Hadaway, *Bertha*—Mrs. Knight;
Killing no Murder.
C.—La Sonnambula; Touch and Take.
2. W.—Peter the Great; Killing no Murder; Love, Law and
Physic.
C.—Fra Diavolo; Fortune's Frolic.
3. W.—Rake's Progress; Love, Law and Physic.
C.—La Sonnambula; Married Rake.
4. W.—Rake's Progress; Lottery Ticket; X. Y. Z.
C.—Fra Diavolo; The Secret.
5. W.—Comedy of Errors; X. Y. Z.
C.—La Sonnambula; A Day after the Wedding.
6. W.—Comedy of Errors; Lottery Ticket; Two Gregories.
C.—Fra Diavolo; Dumb Belle.
8. *Monday:*
W.—Plot and Counterplot; Hundred-Pound Note; Peter the
Great.
C.—Marriage of Figaro; Raising the Wind.
9. W.—Lady of Lyons; Forest Rose.
C.—Marriage of Figaro; Fortune's Frolic.
10. W.—Killing no Murder; Brian Boroihme.

C.—Marriage of Figaro.

11. W.—The Sentinel; Spitfire; Golden Farmer.
C.—Gaspardo; Perfection.

12. W.—Plot and Counterplot; Lottery Ticket; X. Y. Z.
C.—Conquest of Taranto; My Aunt.

13. W.—William Tell; The Pilot.
C.—Marriage of Figaro; The Secret.

15. *Monday:*
W.—Peter the Great; 'Tis all a Farce; Mummy.
C.—Cinderella; Married Rake.

16. W.—Forest Rose; Therese; Unfinished Gentleman.
C.—Cinderella; 'Twas I.

17. W.—The School of Reform; Honest Thieves.
C.—Cinderella; Weathercock.

18. W.—Richard III; Forest Rose.
C.—Amilie; Rival Valets.

19. W.—Virginius; Mons. Tonson.
C.—Young Quaker; The Critic.

20. W.—Mr. Greenfinch; Here she Goes, There she Goes; Fire and Water; Nicholas Nickleby.
C.—Amilie; 'Twas I.

22. *Monday:*
W.—La Bayadere; Mr. Greenfinch.
C.—Love in a Village; La Sonnambula, first act.

23. W.—La Bayadere; Here she Goes, There she Goes; Mons. Tonson.
C.—Amilie; The Waterman.

24. W.—La Bayadere; Mr. Greenfinch.
C.—Marriage of Figaro; Unfinished Gentleman.

25. W.—Turn Out; La Bayadere.
C.—Wheel of Fortune; Turn Out.

26. W.—Loan of a Lover; Vermont Wool Dealer; New Way To Pay Old Debts; Fire Raiser.
C.—Rent Day; Rival Valets.

27. W.—La Bayadere; Here she Goes, There she Goes; Dead Shot.
C.—La Sonnambula; Cramond Brig.

29. *Monday:*
W.—Heir at Law; Bombastes Furioso; Chaos is come Again.
C.—Lady of Lyons; Chaos is come Again.

30. W.—Wild Oats; Rafael, the Libertine.
C.—Golden Farmer; Chaos is come Again.

MAY

1. *Wednesday:*
W.—Julie; Why did you Die?; Gil Blas.

C.—School for Scandal; The Crown Prince.
2.   W.—Lady of Lyons; He's not A-Miss.
    C.—Cure for the Heart Ache; The Crown Prince.
3.   W.—Golden Farmer; Mob, the Outlaw.
    C.—Busy Body; Rafael, the Libertine.
4.   W.—Irish Ambassador; Robber's Wife; Rory O'More, last act.
    C.—Know your own Mind; William Tell.
6. *Monday:*
    W.—Mob, the Outlaw, first part; Three Hunchbacks; Frightened to Death.
    C.—Deserted Daughter; My Fellow Clerk; Man and the Tiger.
7.   W.—Wallace; Black Eyed Susan.
    C.—Lady of Lyons; The Pilot.
8.   W.—Poor Gentleman; Two Gregories.
    C.—School for Scandal; Abon Hassan.
9.   W.—Rent Day; Adopted Child.
    C.—Poor Gentleman; Abon Hassan.
10.   W.—The Yankee Servant; Militia Training; One, Two, Three, Four, Five; Forest Rose.
    C.—Gretna Green; Dumb Belle; Raising the Wind.
11.   W.—High Life below Stairs; Frightened to Death; Bombastes Furioso.
    C.—Cinderella; Barrack Room.
13. *Monday:*
    W.—As You Like It; Ella Rosenberg.
    C.—Richelieu *: *Louis XIII*—Lindsay, *Richelieu*—Harrington, *Baradas*—Davenport, *Beringhen*—Thayer, *Julie*—Mrs. Sharpe; Katharine and Petruchio.
14.   W.—Hofer; Review.
    C.—Maid of Cashmere; Married Rake.
15.   W.—Wallace; The Pilot of the German Ocean.
    C.—Maid of Cashmere; Raising the Wind.
16.   W.—The Stranger; Gilderoy.
    C.—La Sonnambula; Weathercock.
17.   W.—Paul Pry; X. Y. Z.
    C.—La Sonnambula; Barrack Room.
18.   W.—The Gambler's Fate; Jack's the Lad *: *Jack*—Conner, *Polly*—Mrs. La Forest.
    C.—Maid of Cashmere; Dumb Belle; Two Words.
20. *Monday:*
    W.—John Jones; Hundred-Pound Note; Jack's the Lad.
    C.—La Sonnambula; Dead Shot.
21.   W.—Romeo and Juliet; Militia Training; Mob, the Outlaw.
    C.—Richelieu; My Aunt.
22.   W.—Peter the Great; Perfection; Mummy.

C.—Ion; A Day after the Wedding.
23. W.—Hunchback; Fortune's Frolic.
C.—Love Chase; Youthful Queen.
24. W.—Lady of Lyons; Tom Cringle.
C.—Lady of Lyons; Perfection.
25. W.—Tom and Jerry; Therese.
C.—As You Like It; Barrack Room.
27. *Monday:*
W.—Rochester; John Jones.
C.—Evadne; Dead Shot.
28. W.—Rochester; High Life below Stairs.
C.—The Stranger; Deaf as a Post.
29. W.—Heir at Law; Mob, the Outlaw.
C.—Hunchback; Hercules, King of Clubs.
30. W.—Oliver Twist; Mummy.
C.—Jane Shore; Hercules, King of Clubs.
31. W.—Oliver Twist; 'Tis all a Farce.
C.—Hunchback; A Day after the Fair.

JUNE

1. *Saturday:*
W.—Golden Farmer; The Monarch, the Minister, and the Mimic; Oliver Twist.
C.—Evadne; A Day after the Wedding; Hercules, King of Clubs.
3. *Monday:*
W.—Tekeli; Richard III.
C.—Olympic Devils; Weathercock; Fortune's Frolic.
4. W.—Maid of Orleans; La Pie Voluse.
C.—The Magpie and Maid; The Critic.
5. W.—Virginius; Gambler's Fate.
C.—My Aunt; 'Twas I; Olympic Devils.
6. W.—Paul Pry; Mons. Jacques.
C.—Dumb Belle; The Emerald Isle; Olympic Devils.
7. W.—Hypocrite; Chaos is come Again; Peter, my Pipkin.
C.—Married Rake; Abon Hassan.
8. W.—Grace Darling; Two Thompsons; Hypocrite.
C.—The Emerald Isle; Olympic Devils.
10. *Monday:*
W.—Grace Darling; Hundred-Pound Note; One Hundred and Two.
C.—La Sylphide, second act; Midnight Hour; Gretna Green.
11. W.—Mons. Jacques; Tam O'Shanter; Grace Darling.
C.—La Sylphide; Barrack Room.

12. W.—Wallace; Grace Darling.
    C.—La Sylphide; The Secret; Midnight Hour.
13. W.—Gilderoy; Irish Tutor.
    C.—Lady of Lyons; Spoiled Child.
14. W.—The Pilot; Weathercock.
    C.—Perfection; Fire and Water; My Fellow Clerk.
15. W.—Grace Darling; Jack's the Lad; Jamie of Aberdeen.
    C.—Youthful Queen; La Sylphide; Wedding Day.
17. *Monday:*
    W.—Black Eyed Susan; Cabin Boy.
    C.—My Little Adopted; La Petite Chaperon Rouge.
18. W.—Hofer; Jamie of Aberdeen.
    C.—Love Chase; Gaspardo.
19. W.—Grace Darling; Cabin Boy; Jamie of Aberdeen.
    C.—John of Paris; Waterman.
20. W.—Tortesa the Usurer *: *Angelo*—E. S. Conner, *Tortesa*—
    Jackson, *Isabella*—Mrs. Cramer; Floating Beacon.
    C.—Hundred-Pound Note; Charles II; La Petite Chaperon
    Rogue.
21. W.—Iron Chest; The Dream at Sea.
    C.—Much Ado about Nothing; Victoria.
22. W.—Richard III; Loan of a Lover.
    C.—The Lady of the Lake; A Hasty Conclusion. Last night
    of the season.
24. *Monday:*
    W.—Richard III; Mayor of Garrat.
25. W.—King Lear; Chaos is come Again.
26. W.—Othello; Weathercock.
27. W.—Merchant of Venice; Jack's the Lad.
28. W.—Hamlet; Irish Tutor.
29. W.—New Way To Pay Old Debts; Amateurs and Actors.

JULY

1. *Monday:*
   W.—Hamlet; Hide and Seek.
2. W.—Othello; Raising the Wind.
3. W.—Apostate; Review.
4. W.—Richard III; Plains of Chippewa.
5. W.—Iron Chest; Wallace.
6. W.—Brutus; Review.
8. *Monday:*
   W.—Closed.
9. W.—Pizarro; Perfection.
10. W.—Isabella; Swiss Cottage.
11. W.—Bold Stroke for a Husband; Therese.

12. W.—Katharine and Petruchio; The Broken Sword; A Day after the Wedding.
13. W.—Englishmen in India; Raymond and Agnes.
15. *Monday:*
     W.—Tortesa the Usurer; A Day in Paris.
16. W.—Loan of a Lover; Rob Roy; Bath Road.
17. W.—Virginius; Lucile.
18. W.—Honest Thieves; Chaos is come Again.
19. W.—Turning the Tables; The Queen's Horse.
20. W.—The Idiot Witness; The Queen's Horse.
22. *Monday:*
     W.—Damon and Pythias; The Robber's Wife.
23. W.—Spitfire; Jamie of Aberdeen.
24. W.—Mischief Making; Monsieur Tonson.
25. W.—Turning the Tables; Irish Tutor.
26. W.—Spitfire; The Queen's Horse.
27. W.—Monsieur Tonson; Vol Au Vent.
29. *Monday:*
     W.—Loan of a Lover; The Lion King.
30. W.—Turn Out; The Lion King.
31. W.—Perfection; The Lion King.

AUGUST

1.   *Thursday:*
     W.—Weathercock; The Lion King.
2.   W.—The Lady and the Invisible; The Lion King.
3.   W.—Black Eyed Susan; The Lion King.
5.   *Monday:*
     W.—Is she a Woman?; The Lion King.
6.   W.—Is she a Woman?; The Lion King.
7.   W.—Turn Out; The Lion King.
8.   W.—Wallace; The Lion King.
9.   W.—Pizarro; State Secrets; Man about Town; Star Spangled Banner.
10. W.—Town and Country; A Roland for an Oliver.
12. *Monday:*
     W.—Castle of St. Aldobrand; La Fitte.
13. W.—Joan of Arc; Therese.
14. W.—Omreah; Star Spangled Banner.
15. W.—William Tell; Dream at Sea.
16. W.—La Fitte; Waterman.
17. W.—Rent Day; Hunting a Turtle; Don Juan.
19. *Monday:*
     W.—Romanzo *: *Romanzo*—E. S. Conner, *Alphonzo*—T. Matthews, *Alonzo*—N. Johnson, *Italia*—Mrs. Hunt.

20. W.—Romanzo; Perfection.
21. W.—Romanzo; Irish Tutor.
22. W.—Romanzo; Monsieur Tonson.
23. W.—Romanzo; Loan of a Lover.
24. W.—Romanzo; The Conquering Game.
    C.—The Soldier's Daughter; The Rent Day.
26. *Monday:*
    W.—Hamlet; The Conquering Game.
    C.—St. Mary's Eve; The Critic.
27. W.—Pizarro; The Conquering Game.
    C.—Indian Girl; St. Mary's Eve.
28. W.—Tortesa, the Usurer; Catching an Heiress.
    C.—Child of the Wreck; French Spy.
29. W.—Tortesa, the Usurer; The Conquering Game.
    C.—Child of the Wreck; Wizard Skiff.
30. W.—Pizarro; The Rum Old Commodore.
    C.—Indian Girl; Wizard Skiff.
31. W.—Romanzo; Star Spangled Banner.
    C.—The Force of Love; Child of Air.

SEPTEMBER

2. *Monday:*
    W.—Capt. Kyd; Swiss Cottage.
    C.—Child of the Wreck; Child of Air.
3. W.—Capt. Kyd; Rum Old Commodore.
    C.—Child of Air; French Spy.
4. W.—Capt. Kyd; Nipped in the Bud.
    C.—Maid of Cashmere; My Little Adopted; The Secret.
5. W.—Capt. Kyd; Romanzo.
    C.—Maid of Cashmere; Youthful Queen; Tom Noddy's Secret.
6. W.—Capt. Kyd; Romanzo.
    C.—Child of the Wreck; Wizard Skiff.
7. W.—Capt. Kyd; Bandit Dost.
    C.—La Tentation; St. Mary's Eve.
9. *Monday:*
    W.—Tortesa, the Usurer; Raising the Wind.
    C.—Lady of Lyons; Turn Out.
10. W.—Ann Boleyn; Last Man.
    C.—Hunchback; Rival Valets.
11. W.—Englishmen in India; Miller and his Men.
    C.—Belle's Stratagem; Weathercock.
12. W.—Capt. Kyd; Youthful Queen; Last Man.
    C.—Stranger; Adopted Child.
13. W.—Perfection; Last Man; Romanzo.

C.—Romeo and Juliet; Tom Noddy's Secret.
14. W.—Ann Boleyn; Youthful Queen.
C.—Much Ado about Nothing; Luke the Laborer.
16. *Monday:*
W.—Virginius; Nipped in the Bud.
C.—La Sonnambula; Gretna Green.
17. W.—Gladiator; Ask no Questions.
C.—La Sonnambula; Perfection.
18. W.—Damon and Pythias; Padlock.
C.—Fra Diavolo; The Secret.
19. W.—Metamora; The Conquering Game.
C.—Cinderella; Wedding Day.
20. W.—Gladiator; Rum Old Commodore.
C.—Fra Diavolo; Rival Valets.
21. W.—Metamora; Padlock.
C.—Cinderella; Chaos is come Again.
23. *Monday:*
W.—Othello; Therese.
C.—Marriage of Figaro; Luke the Laborer.
24. W.—Richelieu; Love Laughs at Locksmiths.
C.—Love in a Village; Married Rake.
25. W.—Richelieu; Nipped in the Bud.
C.—Marriage of Figaro; Chaos is come Again.
26. W.—Richelieu; Ask no Questions.
C.—Native Land.
27. W.—Richelieu; Padlock.
C.—Native Land; Spoiled Child.
28. W.—Richelieu; The Conquering Game.
C.—Fra Diavolo; Cramond Brig.
30. *Monday:*
W.—Richelieu; William Tell.
C.—Hamlet; Shocking Events.

OCTOBER

1. *Tuesday:*
W.—Metamora; Rum Old Commodore.
C.—Wheel of Fortune; Shocking Events.
2. W.—Mazeppa; The Romp.
C.—New Way To Pay Old Debts; Chaos is come Again.
3. W.—Blanche of Navarre *: *Count*—Conner, *Philip*—N. Johnson, *Isabel*—Miss Murray, *Blanche*—Mrs. Hunt; Freemason.
C.—King Lear; Gretna Green.
4. W.—Mazeppa; The Romp.

C.—New Way To Pay Old Debts; A Hasty Conclusion.

5.   W.—Paul Pry; Sweethearts and Wives.

C.—Richard III; The Secret.

7. *Monday:*

W.—His First Champagne; Peter the Great.

C.—Macbeth; Shocking Events.

8.   W.—Peter the Great; Mayor of Garratt.

C.—Merchant of Venice; The King and the Mimic.

9.   W.—Plots; His First Champagne.

C.—Othello; The King and the Mimic.

10.   W.—Plots; State Secrets.

C.—Hamlet; A Hasty Conclusion.

11.   W.—Nipped in the Bud; His First Champagne; The Mummy.

C.—The Iron Chest; Tom Noddy's Secret.

12.   W.—Whigs and Democrats *: *Major*—Burton; Peeping Tom of Coventry.

C.—Lady of Lyons; The King and the Mimic.

G.N.—Humoristiche Studien; Der Schauspieler Wider Willen; Der Alte Teldherr.

14. *Monday:*

W.—Emigrant; Peeping Tom of Coventry.

C.—Belle's Stratagem; Luke the Laborer.

15.   W.—Robinson Crusoe; Wandering Minstrel; Murder at the Inn.

C.—Conquest of Taranto; Barrack Room.

16.   W.—Paul Pry; John Jones.

C.—Cinderella; Chaos is come Again.

17.   W.—Whigs and Democrats; Wandering Minstrel.

C.—Cinderella; The King and the Mimic.

18.   W.—Sweethearts and Wives; Irish Tutor; State Secrets.

C.—La Sonnambula; Gretna Green.

19.   W.—But However!; Der Wachter; Love, Law and Physic.

C.—La Sonnambula; Shocking Events.

21. *Monday:*

W.—Knight of the Golden Fleece; New Notions.

C.—Fidelio; A Hasty Conclusion.

22.   W.—Knight of the Golden Fleece; Jonathan in England; New Notions.

C.—Fidelio; The King and the Mimic.

23.   W.—Knight of the Golden Fleece; Forest Rose.

C.—Fidelio; Agreeable Surprise.

24.   W.—Loan of a Lover; A Wife for a Day *: *Nathan*—Hill; New Notions.

C.—Fidelio; Perfection.

25.   W.—A Wife for a Day; Yankee Pedlar.

[213]

C.—La Sonnambula; Waterman.

26.   W.—Seth Slope *: *Seth*—Hill, *Belmont*—Lennox; Nipped in the Bud; A Wife for a Day.
C.—Fidelio; Agreeable Surprise.

28.   *Monday:*
W.—Man and Wife; Yankee Pedlar.
C.—La Gazza Ladra; The Secret.

29.   W.—Cramond Brig; Forest Rose; Seth Slope.
C.—La Gazza Ladra; Agreeable Surprise.

30.   W.—Kaspar Hauser; Nipped in the Bud; Seth Slope.
C.—La Gazza Ladra; Blue Devils.

31.   W.—The Tourists; Lady of Munster; Jonathan in England.
C.—La Gazza Ladra; Turn Out.

NOVEMBER

1.   *Friday:*
W.—Kaspar Hauser; A Wife for a Day.
C.—La Gazza Ladra; The Crown Prince.

2.   W.—New Notions; Seth Slope; Lady of Munster; Yankee Pedlar.
C.—La Gazza Ladra; Barrack Room.

4.   *Monday:*
W.—Der Freischutz; Clari.
C.—Country Girl; The Widow Wiggins; Blue Devils.

5.   W.—Der Freischutz; Cramond Brig.
C.—The Will; The Widow Wiggins.

6.   W.—Der Freischutz; The Will.
C.—Country Girl; The Widow Wiggins; Fire and Water.

7.   W.—Der Freischutz; The Warlock of the Glen.
C.—Irish Widow; The Widow Wiggins; Spoiled Child.

8.   W.—Der Freischutz; The Secret.
C.—The Will; Dead Shot.

9.   W.—Marriage of Figaro; Der Freischutz.
C.—Englishmen in India; The Widow Wiggins.

11.   *Monday:*
W.—Marriage of Figaro; Der Freischutz.
C.—Man and Wife; Mischief Making; Fire and Water.

12.   W.—Cinderella; Loan of a Lover; Der Freischutz.
C.—Englishmen in India; Mischief Making.

13.   W.—Cinderella; The Secret.
C.—Single Life; The Widow Wiggins.

14.   W.—Cinderella; No Song, No Supper.
C.—Man and Wife; Dead Shot.

15.   W.—Fra Diavolo; Swiss Cottage.

[214]

	C.—Single Life; Irish Widow.
16.	W.—Fra Diavolo; Cramond Brig.
	C.—Country Girl; Widow Wiggins; Mischief Making.
18.	*Monday:*
	W.—Marriage of Figaro; Fra Diavolo; Charles XII.
	C.—Hunchback; Chaos is come Again.
19.	W.—Battle of Austerlitz; Loan of a Lover.
	C.—Cato; Turning the Tables.
20.	W.—Battle of Austerlitz; The Warlock of the Glen.
	C.—Hunchback; The King and the Mimic.
21.	W.—Innkeeper's Daughter; Battle of Austerlitz.
	C.—Richelieu; Gretna Green.
22.	W.—Is He Jealous?; Battle of Austerlitz; Idiot Witness.
	C.—The Stranger; Turning the Tables.
23.	W.—Jacques Strop *: *Macaire*—Lennox, *Jacques*—Hadaway, *Duval*—Harrison; Doctor Dilworth.
	C.—Richelieu; The King and the Mimic.
25.	*Monday:*
	W.—Richelieu; Doctor Dilworth.
	C.—Ion; The Liar.
26.	W.—Richelieu; Dead Shot.
	C.—Virginius; Shocking Events.
27.	W.—Macbeth; Hunting a Turtle.
	C.—Richelieu; Chaos is come Again.
28.	W.—Metamora; Jacques Strop.
	C.—Romeo and Juliet; The Secret.
29.	W.—Hamlet; Dead Shot.
	C.—Hamlet; Blue Devils.
30.	W.—Metamora; William Tell.
	C.—The Wife; Katharine and Petruchio.

DECEMBER

2.	*Monday:*
	W.—Gladiator; My Neighbor's Wife.
	C.—Coriolanus; Clari.
3.	W.—Richelieu; Robber's Wife.
	C.—The Wife; The King and the Mimic.
4.	W.—King Lear; Gretna Green.
	C.—Brutus; Married Rake.
5.	W.—Gladiator; Robber's Wife.
	C.—Damon and Pythias; Lottery Ticket.
6.	W.—Lady of Lyons; My Neighbor's Wife.
	C.—Richelieu; Spoiled Child.
7.	W.—Richelieu; Therese.

[215]

       C.—Wives as they Were; Merchant of Venice.
9. *Monday:*
       W.—Sea Captain *: *Norman*—Kirby, *Lady Arundel*—Mrs. W. Sefton, *Onslow*—Neafie; Bachelor's Buttons.
       C.—Pizarro; Dr. Dilworth.
10.   W.—Cramond Brig; Forty Thieves; Bachelor's Buttons.
       C.—Town and Country; Dr. Dilworth.
11.   W.—Loan of a Lover; Forty Thieves.
       C.—Othello; Lottery Ticket.
12.   W.—Black Eyed Susan; Forty Thieves.
       C.—New Way To Pay Old Debts; The Secret.
13.   W.—Cramond Brig; Forty Thieves.
       C.—Iron Chest; The King and the Mimic.
14.   W.—Love *: *Duke*—Powell, *Catharine*—Mrs. W. Sefton; Forty Thieves.
       C.—Child of Nature; Lucile; Dead Shot.
16. *Monday:*
       W.—Marmion; Dead Shot.
       C.—Damon and Pythias; Doctor Dilworth.
17.   W.—Love; Marmion.
       C.—Rent Day; Black Eyed Susan.
18.   W.—Marmion; The Daring Man.
       C.—Love; A Roland for an Oliver.
19.   W.—Love; Marmion.
       C.—Love; Lottery Ticket.
20.   W.—Love; Marmion.
       C.—Lady of Lyons; Mountaineers.
21.   W.—Love; Marmion.
       C.—The Deformed; Lady of Lyons.
23. *Monday:*
       W.—Jacques Strop; Secret Mine.
       C.—Love; L'Automate.
24.   W.—Black Eyed Susan; Secret Mine.
       C.—Lucille; Harlequin and Mother Goose.
25.   W.—Secret Mine; Mother Shipton.
       C.—Snow Storm; Harlequin and Mother Goose.
26.   W.—Secret Mine; Mother Shipton.
       C.—Snow Storm; Harlequin and Mother Goose.
27.   W.—Secret Mine; Mother Shipton.
       C.—Snow Storm; Harlequin and Mother Goose.
28.   W.—Secret Mine; Mother Shipton.
       C.—Napoleon Bonaparte's Invasion of Russia; Harlequin and Mother Goose.
30. *Monday:*
       W.—Two Drovers; Siege of Tripoli.
       C.—Richard III; Chaos is come Again.

31.   W.—Two Drovers; Siege of Tripoli.
        C.—Hamlet; A Day after the Wedding.

JANUARY 1840

1. *Wednesday:*
    W.—Kenilworth; Billy Button.
    C.—King John; Agreeable Surprise.
2.   W.—Kenilworth; Billy Button.
    C.—Pizarro; The Crown Prince.
3.   W.—Kenilworth; Billy Button.
    C.—Town and Country; The Little Back Parlor *: *Tubbs*—
        T. Placide, *Snooks*—Thayer, *Lucy*—Miss A. Fisher.
4.   W.—Rob Roy; Is the Philadelphian Dead? *: *Perkins*—Had-
        away.
    C.—Macbeth; The Little Back Parlor.
6. *Monday:*
    W.—Woman's Wit; Forty Thieves.
    C.—Child of the Wreck; Indian Girl.
7.   W.—Siege of Tripoli; Is the Philadelphian Dead?
    C.—St. Mary's Eve; Child of the Wreck.
8.   W.—Pizarro; The Adopted Child.
    C.—The Lost Battle; Indian Girl.
9.   W.—George Barnwell; Secret Mine.
    C.—The Lost Battle; French Spy.
10.   W.—Jane Shore; Secret Mine.
    C.—The Lost Battle; French Spy.
11.   W.—Der Wachter; Mummy.
    C.—Soldier's Dream; Mons. Jacques; St. Mary's Eve.
13. *Monday:*
    W.—Hunchback; Amateurs and Actors.
    C.—Soldier's Dream; Child of Air.
14.   W.—Love; Perfection.
    C.—Soldier's Dream; Child of Air.
15.   W.—Rory O'More; Hofer.
    C.—Child of the Wreck; French Spy.
16.   W.—Tekeli; Is the Philadelphian Dead?
    C.—Maid of Cashmere; The Lost Battle.
17.   W.—Luke the Laborer; Tekeli.
    C.—Maid of Cashmere; St. Mary's Eve.
18.   W.—Luke the Laborer; Rory O'More.
    C.—Wizard Skiff; La Tentation.
20. *Monday:*
    W.—Blue Beard; Don Juan.
    C.—Country Girl; Widow Wiggins; The Little Back Parlor.
21.   W.—Jack Sheppard, the House Breaker; Dead Shot.

C.—Englishmen in India; Mischief Making; Lottery Ticket.
22.   W.—Sweethearts and Wives; Peter the Great.
C.—Man and Wife; Widow Wiggins.
23.   W.—Forest Rose; Yankee Bill Sticker *: *Bill*—Bowman, *Mrs. Ledger*—Mrs. Wilks.
C.—Heart of Midlothian; The Middy Ashore.
24.   W.—La Bayadere; Dr. Dilworth.
C.—Irish Widow; Foreign Airs and Native Graces; Fire and Water.
25.   W.—Wallace; Golden Farmer. Last night of performing until Monday, February 3.
C.—Love; The Crown Prince.
A.—The Seven Female Soldiers; Die Schleichhandler.
27. *Monday:*
C.—Irish Widow; Foreign Airs and Native Graces; Fire and Water.
28.   C.—The Country Girl; Foreign Airs and Native Graces; The Secret.
29.   C.—The Pet of the Petticoats; Widow Wiggins; The Weathercock.
30.   C.—The Pet of the Petticoats; Foreign Airs and Native Graces; Married Rake.
31.   C.—Heart of Midlothian; The Pet of the Petticoats.

FEBRUARY

1. *Saturday:*
C.—Irish Widow; Foreign Airs and Native Graces; The Middy Ashore.
3. *Monday:*
W.—Sadak and Kalasrade *: *Sadak*—Mrs. W. Sefton, *Semaek*—Neafie, *Mustapha*—Barry, *Amurath*—Matthews, *Misnar*—Powell, *Dum Dum*—Kirby, *Mahoud*—McBride, *Smutta*—Hadaway, *Rainbow*—Lennox, *Sentinel*—Plumer, *Gheber*—La Forest, *Kezlar*—Burgess, *Kalasrade*—Mrs. Hunt, *Adehl*—Miss Matthews, *Fairy*—Miss Lee, *Hobaddan*—Mrs. Wilks, *Odez*—Miss Price, *Murad*—Wilks.
C.—Comedy of Errors; Children in the Wood; Naval Engagements.
4.   W.—Sadak and Kalasrade.
C.—Lovers' Vows; Child of Nature.
5.   W.—Sadak and Kalasrade.
C.—Romantic Widow *: *Marquis*—Ranger, *Albright*—W. F. Johnson, *Ernestine*—Mrs. Sharpe; Dead Shot; Naval Engagements.

6. W.—Sadak and Kalasrade.
   C.—Romantic Widow.
7. W.—Sadak and Kalasrade.
   C.—Romantic Widow.
8. W.—Sadak and Kalasrade.
   C.—La Sonnambula; Dead Shot.
10. *Monday:*
    W.—Sadak and Kalasrade; Jack Sheppard.
    C.—La Sonnambula; Waterman.
    A.—Die Brilleninsel *; Die Reise von Berlin nach Potsdam.
11. W.—Sadak and Kalasrade; Jack Sheppard.
    C.—Maid of Cashmere; St. Mary's Eve.
12. W.—Sadak and Kalasrade; Jack Sheppard.
    C.—Wizard Skiff; La Tentation.
13. W.—Sadak and Kalasrade; Jack Sheppard.
    C.—Soldier's Dream; Indian Girl.
14. W.—Sadak and Kalasrade; Jack Sheppard.
    C.—The Lost Battle; Child of Air.
15. W.—Sadak and Kalasrade; Dew Drop.
    C.—Irish Widow; Foreign Airs and Native Graces; The Little Back Parlor.
17. *Monday:*
    W.—Sadak and Kalasrade; Dew Drop.
    C.—The Frontier Maid *: *Natalie, Neataluk, Sam Rivers—three rôles*—Mlle. Celeste; French Spy.
    A.—Die Brilleninsel; Herr und Sclave.
18. W.—The Happy Man; Loan of a Lover; Dew Drop.
    C.—The Frontier Maid; French Spy.
19. W.—Sadak and Kalasrade; Dew Drop.
    C.—The Frontier Maid; Child of the Wreck.
20. W.—Sadak and Kalasrade; Dew Drop.
    C.—St. Mary's Eve; Naval Engagements.
21. W.—Sadak and Kalasrade; Dew Drop.
    C.—Soldier's Dream; Wizard Skiff.
22. W.—The White Eagle; Dew Drop.
    C.—Flying Dutchman; Susanne; The Frontier Maid.
    A.—The Seven Female Soldiers; Die Schleichhandler.
24. *Monday:*
    W.—The White Eagle; Is the Philadelphian Dead?
    C.—School for Scandal; Naval Engagements.
25. W.—Jacques Strop; The Happy Man; Two Drovers.
    C.—The Faithful Page; The Ransom.
26. W.—Jack Sheppard; Negro Doorkeeper.
    C.—Richelieu; Turning the Tables.
27. W.—Therese; Irish Tutor.
    C.—The Wife; A Roland for an Oliver.

28. W.—Alice Gray; Paddy Murphy's Weather Almanac; Review.
    C.—The Stranger; The King and the Mimic.
29. W.—The Lear of Private Life; Who's the Murderer?
    C.—Love; Agreeable Surprise.

MARCH

2. *Monday:*
    W.—Alice Gray; Paddy Murphy's Weather Almanac.
    C.—Ion; Maid of Croissy.
3. W.—The White Eagle; Death Token.
    C.—Provoked Husband; Maid of Croissy.
4. W.—Jacques Strop; The Happy Man.
    C.—Cato; Lady of Lyons.
5. W.—The Rivals; The Siamese Twins.
    C.—Hunchback; Chaos is come Again.
6. W.—The Chain of Guilt; La Fitte.
    C.—Richelieu; Dead Shot.
7. W.—School of Reform; Hunters of the Pyrenees.
    C.—Love; The Roman Actor; No!
9. *Monday:*
    W.—Henri Quatre; Philadelphia Fireman *: *Old Grubs*—La
    Forest.
    C.—La Sonnambula; Cramond Brig.
10. W.—Six Degrees of Crime; Damon and Pythias.
    C.—The Faithful Page; Mrs. White; Rival Valets.
11. W.—Brother and Sister; Handsome Husband; Sadak and Ka-
    lasrade.
    C.—The Crown Prince; Roof Scrambler; Mrs. White.
12. W.—Richard III; Damon and Pythias.
    C.—Maid of Croissy; Roof Scrambler; Mrs. White.
13. W.—Hamlet; Dead Shot.
    C.—Lady of the Lake; No!; Roof Scrambler.
14. W.—Cradle of Liberty; Cherry and Fair Star.
    C.—Maid of Croissy; Roof Scrambler; Mrs. White.
16. *Monday:*
    W.—Richard III; Cherry and Fair Star.
    C.—Speed the Plough; Naval Engagements.
17. W.—Othello; Bachelor's Buttons.
    C.—Romantic Widow; A Day after the Wedding; Roof
    Scrambler.
18. W.—Jacques Strop; Loan of a Lover.
    C.—Romantic Widow; Rival Valets; Mrs. White.
19. W.—Therese; A Quiet Day.

C.—Le Preux Chevalier *: *Chevalier*—Ranger, *Frederick*—
Davenport, *Priscilla*—Mrs. Brood; Romantic Widow.

20. W.—Sadak and Kalasrade; A Quiet Day.
C.—Artist's Wife; Poor Gentleman.
21. W.—Ambrose Gwinett; Joan of Arc.
C.—The Gentleman and the Upstart; Artist's Wife.
23. *Monday:*
W.—Battle of Austerlitz; Warlock of the Glen.
C.—Der Freischutz, in German; Roof Scrambler.
24. W.—Romanzo; Old Oak Chest.
C.—Der Freischutz; Mrs. White.
25. W.—Battle of Austerlitz; A Quiet Day.
C.—Der Freischutz; Roof Scrambler.
26. W.—Ambrose Gwinett; Old Oak Chest.
C.—Der Freischutz; My Fellow Clerk.
27. W.—Paul Jones; Brutus.
C.—Der Freischutz; Roof Scrambler.
28. W.—Pizarro.
C.—Der Freischutz; A Roland for an Oliver.
30. *Monday:*
W.—Snakes in the Grass; Irish Lion; Joan of Arc.
C.—Maid of Croissy; The Weathercock.
31. W.—Old Oak Chest; Dew Drop.
C.—Merchant of Venice; The Foundling; Roof Scrambler.

APRIL

1. *Wednesday:*
W.—Point of Honor; The Exile.
C.—Tom Noddy's Secret; The King and the Mimic.
2. W.—Rob Roy; Warlock of the Glen.
C.—Married Rake; Lottery Ticket.
3. W.—Richard III; Black Eyed Susan.
C.—Soldier's Daughter; The Roof Scrambler.
4. W.—Monsieur Jacques; My Neighbor's Wife; Rum Old Com-
modore.
C.—Shipwreck; Simpson and Company.
6. *Monday:*
W.—The Light Ship; But, However!
C.—Charles I; Bachelor's Buttons; Naval Engagements.
7. W.—The Light Ship; Wandering Minstrel.
C.—Maid of Croissy; A Roland for an Oliver.
8. W.—The Light Ship; Humbug *: *Manager*—Burton.
C.—Dramatist; Happy Man; The Foundling.
9. W.—The Light Ship; Humbug.

C.—Shipwreck; My Fellow Clerk.

10.
W.—The Light Ship; Humbug.
C.—New Way To Pay Old Debts; The Roof Scrambler.

11.
W.—Emigration *: *Ned*—Burton, *Boyce*—Lennox, *Jack*—Neafie, *Leighton*—Edwards, *Mary*—Mrs. W. Sefton; My Neighbor's Wife; Humbug.
C.—Goblin Page; Mrs. White.

13. *Monday:*
W.—Begone Dull Care; A Good Night's Rest; Humbug.
C.—Goblin Page; Chaos is come Again.

14.
W.—Emigration; Begone Dull Care.
C.—Cure for the Heart Ache; Naval Engagements.

15.
W.—The Light Ship; A Quiet Day; Humbug.
C.—Hamlet; No!

16.
W.—Emigration; A Good Night's Rest; Humbug.
C.—Merchant of Venice; 'Twas I.

17.
W.—Rum Old Commodore; The Dark Lady *: *Winkey*—Burton; A Good Night's Rest.
C.—Richard III; Agreeable Surprise.

18.
W.—Stag Hall; Little Sins and Pretty Sinners; The Dark Lady.
C.—Iron Chest; Lady of Lyons.

20. *Monday:*
W.—Paul, the Patriot; The Maniac Lover.
C.—Postillion of Lonjumeau *: *Chapelon*—Wilson, *Biju*—Ginbeli, *Madelaine*—Miss Shireff; Dumb Belle.

21.
W.—The Maniac Lover; Charles XII; Cramond Brig; Napoleon Bonaparte's Invasion of Russia.
C.—Postillion of Lonjumeau; The Little Back Parlor.

22.
W.—Damon and Pythias; A Good Night's Rest.
C.—Postillion of Lonjumeau; Mrs. White.

23.
W.—Gladiator; What Have I Done?
C.—Postillion of Lonjumeau; My Uncle John.

24.
W.—The Lady of Lyons; Bold Dragoons.
C.—Postillion of Lonjumeau; A Day after the Wedding.

25.
W.—Virginius; Bold Dragoons.
C.—Postillion of Lonjumeau; Maid of Croissy.

27. *Monday:*
W.—Metamora; Paul Jones.
C.—Postillion of Lonjumeau; Touch and Take.

28.
W.—Damon and Pythias; What Have I Done?
C.—Fra Diavolo; Turning the Tables.

29.
W.—Richelieu; Gladiator.
C.—La Sonnambula; My Uncle John.

30.
W.—Metamora; The Little Back Parlor.
C.—Postillion of Lonjumeau; Loan of a Lover.

MAY

1. *Friday:*
   W.—Richelieu; A Good Night's Rest.
   C.—Postillion of Lonjumeau; Midas.
2. W.—Othello; The Little Back Parlor.
   C.—Postillion of Lonjumeau; Cramond Brig.
4. *Monday:*
   W.—King Lear; Pizarro.
   C.—Happiest Day of my Life; Midas.
5. W.—The Maniac Lover.
   C.—Wives as they Were; Naval Engagements.
   A.—The Swiss Family.*
6. W.—Ugolino; Children in the Wood; Adopted Child.
   C.—The Rivals; The Roof Scrambler; My Uncle John.
7. W.—Ambrose Gwinett; Bold Dragoons.
   C.—Laugh when you Can; The King and the Mimic.
8. W.—Caswallon; Ugolino.
   C.—Die Schweitzer Familie, by the German Company; Is He Jealous; The Roof Scrambler.
9. W.—Faint Heart never won Fair Lady; Nipped in the Bud; If the Cap fits you, wear it.
   C.—The Dropping Well of Knaresborough; The Married Rake.
11. *Monday:*
    W.—His Last Legs; Love's Frailities; Fortunate Couple.
    C.—Ellen Wareham; The Crown Prince.
12. W.—Robert Macaire; Jacques Strop.
    C.—Country Girl; Widow Wiggins; No
13. W.—Robert Macaire; Jacques Strop.
    C.—The Soldier's Daughter; Foreign Airs and Native Graces; Fortune's Frolic.
14. W.—Edgard the Idiot; My Young Wife and my Old Umbrella.
    C.—Irish Widow; Mischief Making; Naval Engagements.
15. W.—Edgard, the Idiot; A Good Night's Rest.
    C.—As You Like It; Wedding Day.
16. W.—Victoire; Frightened to Death; Turning the Tables.
    C.—Bold Stroke for a Husband; Fire and Water.
18. *Monday:*
    W.—Perfection; Black Eyed Susan; Winning a Husband.
    C.—Irish Widow; Curiosity Cured *: five rôles by Mrs. Fitzwilliam; Touch and Take.
19. W.—Edgard, the Idiot; Swiss Cottage.
    C.—Ladies' Club; Curiosity Cured; The Dead Shot.
20. W.—The Man in the Iron Mask; Winning a Husband.
    C.—Ladies' Club; Widow Wiggins; Latin, Love and War.

21. W.—The Man in the Iron Mask; Swiss Cottage.
C.—The Soldier's Daughter; Mischief Making; No!
22. W.—Corsair's Revenge; Disguise; The Miller's Maid.
C.—Bold Stroke for a Husband; Curiosity Cured.
23. W.—Country Girl; Nicholas Nickleby; Corsair's Revenge.
C.—Ladies' Club; Foreign Airs and Native Graces; Widow Wiggins.
25. *Monday:*
W.—Iron Chest; William Tell.
C.—Jonathan in England; Middy Ashore; Loan of a Lover.
26. W.—The Sentinel; Six Degrees of Crime.
C.—Secrets Worth Knowing; Love Laughs at Locksmiths.
27. W.—The Giant of Palestine.
C.—Heir at Law; Honest Thieves.
28. W.—The Giant of Palestine; If the Cap fits you, wear it; Nipped in the Bud.
C.—Touch and Take; Kentuckian; Mons. Mallet.
29. W.—Faint Heart never won Fair Lady; The Giant of Palestine.
C.—Rip Van Winkle; Job Fox; My Fellow Clerk.
30. W.—The Giant of Palestine.
C.—Merry Wives of Windsor; Kentuckian.

JUNE

1. *Monday:*
W.—If the Cap fits you, wear it; Little Back Parlor; Sorcerer.
C.—Henry IV; Mons. Mallet; Fortune's Frolic.
2. W.—Bold Dragoons; Sorcerer.
C.—Midnight Hour; Roof Scrambler.
3. W.—Faint Heart never won Fair Lady; Marco Bombo.
C.—Master's Rival; The Critic.
4. W.—Nipped in the Bud; Rum Old Commodore; Marco Bombo.
C.—The King and the Mimic; My Aunt.
5. W.—Truth; Sorcerer.
C.—'Twas I; Agreeable Surprise.
6. W.—Little Back Parlor; Cramond Brig; Gig Gig.
C.—Dramatist; Charles II.
8. *Monday:*
W.—Henriette; The Vampire.
C.—Lucille; Bengal Tiger.
9. W.—No Advertisement.
C.—Castle Spectre; No Song, No Supper.
10. W.—Richard III; Omnibus.
C.—Wild Oats; Master's Rival.

11.   W.—Henriette; Devil's Daughters.
       C.—Lady of Lyons; Roof Scrambler.
12.   W.—No Bill Received.
       C.—George Barnwell; A Good Night's Rest; Little Back Parlor.
13.   W.—The Falls of Clyde; Hamlet, Travestie; Bleeding Nun of Lindenberg.
       C.—Laugh when you Can; A Good Night's Rest.
15.   *Monday:*
       W.—Hamlet; Loan of a Lover.
       C.—Closed in preparation for engagement of Mlle. Fanny Elssler.
16.   W.—New Way To Pay Old Debts; Pleasant Neighbors.
       C.—Closed.
17.   W.—Richard III; My Neighbor's Wife.
       C.—A Good Night's Rest; La Tarentule *: *Lauretta*—Mlle. Elssler, *Luidgi*—Mons. Silvain.
18.   W.—The Stranger; Perfection.
       C.—A Good Night's Rest; La Tarentule.
19.   W.—The Apostate; Dead Shot.
       C.—My Uncle John: La Tarentule.
20.   W.—Othello; Mayor of Garratt.
       C.—The Secret; La Tarentule.
22.   *Monday:*
       W.—King Lear; Lovers' Quarrels.
       C.—No!; La Tarentule.
23.   W.—Distressed Mother; Rain, Old Commodore.
       C.—L'Amour.
24.   W.—Oroonoko; Little Back Parlor.
       C.—Fire and Water; L'Amour.
25.   W.—Richard III; Nipped in the Bud.
       C.—Mrs. White; L'Amour.
26.   W.—Douglas; Two Greens.
       C.—Mrs. White; L'Amour.
27.   W.—Merchant of Venice, first act; Mountaineers, cavern scene; Richelieu, first act; Review.
       C.—Wedding Day; L'Amour.
29.   *Monday:*
       W.—Ladder of Love; Comfortable Service; Valentine and Orson.
       C.—Day after the Wedding; L'Amour.
30.   W.—Conquest of Taranto; The Purse.
       C.—No Advertisement.
       A.—Die Humoristichen Studien.

JULY

1. *Wednesday:*
   W.—Adelgitha; Wreck Ashore.
   C.—Chaos is come Again; La Sylphide, ballet.
2. W.—William Tell; La Fitte.
   C.—Dumb Belle; La Sylphide.
3. W.—Mountaineers; Black Eyed Susan.
   C.—Dumb Belle; La Sylphide.
4. W.—Dying Gift; Patriotism.
   C.—Is He Jealous?; La Sylphide.
6. *Monday:*
   W.—Closed.
   C.—Is He Jealous?; La Sylphide.
7. W.—Closed.
   C.—Closed.
8. W.—Closed.
   C.—Closed.
9. W.—Dying Gift; Pleasant Neighbors.
   C.—Is He Jealous?; La Sylphide.
10. W.—Patriotism; Two Greens.
    C.—Closed for the season.
11. W.—Death Token *: *Felix*—Percival, *Belair*—Kirby, *Martelle* —Miss Murray, *Justine*—Miss Mathews; My Neighbor's Wife.
13. *Monday:*
    W.—Hunter of the Pyrenees; Lovers' Quarrels.
14. W.—Idiot Witness; Two Greens.
15. W.—The White Farm; Affair of Honor.
16. W.—Miller and his Men; Oh! Hush!!
17. W.—Hunter of the Pyrenees; The Secret.
18. W.—The Inn-Keeper of Abbeville; Oh! Hush!!
20. *Monday:*
    W.—The Evil Eye; Tom and Jerry, Cribb's scene; Dumb Girl of Genoa.
21. W.—The Inn-Keeper of Abbeville; Bombastes Furioso.
22. W.—Matheo Falcone; The Little Tiger; Bee Hive.
23. W.—Wild Oats; Bombastes Furioso; Two Brothers.
24. W.—Alpine Hunters; The Pet of the Admiral; The Little Tiger.
25. W.—Floating Beacon; Turnpike Gate. Last night of the season.
29. Coates St. Theatre.—Warlock of the Glen; Young Widow; Love in Humble Life. Benefit of Mrs. St. Clair.

AUGUST

19. *Wednesday;*
    Coates St. Theatre.—Rented by T. Placide to produce the grand national drama, The Battle of Tippecanoe *: *Harrison*—Pickering, *Harry*—Thoman, *David*—Placide, *Heartwell*—H. Eberle, *O'Prattle*—Kelly, *Beck*—Eberle, *Clarinda* Mrs. La Forest, *Sally*—Mrs. Thoman; Two Gregories.
20. Coates.—*Id.*
21. Coates.—*Id.*
29. C.—School for Scandal; Popping the Question.
31. *Monday:*
    N.—The Rivals; A Roland for an Oliver.
    C.—Weak Points; A Kiss in the Dark; Turning the Tables.

SEPTEMBER

1. *Tuesday:*
    N.—Patrician and Parvenu; Swiss Cottage.
    C.—Married Life; A Kiss in the Dark; Chaos is come Again.
2. N.—Tom Noddy's Secret; Married Rake; Wandering Minstrel.
    C.—Weak Points; Our Mary Ann!; Perfection.
3. N.—Lady of Lyons; A Roland for an Oliver.
    C.—Single Life; Our Mary Ann!; Fire and Water.
4. N.—Tom Noddy's Secret; Swiss Cottage; Married Rake.
    C.—Single Life; Married Life.
5. N.—Oliver Twist; Dumb Belle.
    C.—Rural Felicity; A Kiss in the Dark; Ladder of Love.
7. *Monday:*
    N.—Much Ado about Nothing; Lottery Ticket.
    C.—The Duke's Bride; Lottery Ticket; Ladder of Love.
    A.—The Provost of Paris *: *Emanuel*—Mathews, *Zuroc*—Kirby, *Hugues*—Hunt, *Eric*—Percival, *Zabina*—Mrs. Hunt, *Clotilde*—Miss Hudson; Young Widow.
8. N.—Oliver Twist; Dumb Belle.
    C.—Rural Felicity; Fashionable Friends; Uncle John.
    A.—Provost of Paris; Virginia Mummy.
9. N.—Oliver Twist; Married Rake.
    C.—Single Life; Married Life.
    A.—Provost of Paris; Oh! Hush!!
10. N.—Lady of Lyons; Tom Noddy's Secret.
    C.—The Duke's Progress; Fashionable Friends; The Conquering Game.
    A.—Provost of Paris; Bone Squash Diavolo.
11. N.—The Wife; More Blunders than One.

[227]

C.—Weak Points; Our Mary Ann; Simpson and Company.
A.—Young Widow; Bone Squash Diavolo; Virginia Mummy.

12. N.—Nicholas Nickleby; The Poor Soldier.
C.—Poor Jack *: *Tim*—Buckstone.
A.—Bone Squash Diavolo; Jim Crow in London.

14. *Monday:*
N.—Henry IV; Swiss Cottage.
C.—Conquering Game; The Magpie.
A.—The Sixes *: *Rudolph*—Kirby, *Elfina*—Mrs. La Forest;
Two Gregories.

15. N.—The Wife; More Blunders than One.
C.—King John; Scan. Mag.
A.—The Sixes; Pleasant Neighbors.

16. N.—Henry IV; Mons. Mallet.
C.—Comfortable Service; Simpson and Co.
A.—The Sixes; My Neighbor's Wife.

17. N.—King Lear; Kentuckian.
C.—Nicholas Nickleby; Perfection; Scan. Mag.
A.—Turning the Tables; Perfection; Nipped in the Bud.

18. N.—Venice Preserved; More Blunders than One.
C.—The Innkeeper of Calais, in the French language; Popping
the Question; Uncle John.
A.—Provost of Paris; The Sixes.

19. N.—King Lear; Nicholas Nickleby.
C.—Therese; Nicholas Nickleby.
A.—Now closed until after election, while preparations were
in progress to fit this house as a melodramatic theatre.

21. *Monday:*
N.—Othello; The Critic.
C.—Richelieu; Comfortable Service.

22. N.—King Lear; Nicholas Nickleby.
C.—Damon and Pythias; Scan. Mag.

23. N.—Hunchback; Susanne.
C.—Lady of Lyons; Master's Rival.

24. N.—Merry Wives of Windsor; Jonathan in England.
C.—Metamora; Lottery Ticket.

25. N.—Julius Caesar; Nicholas Nickleby.
C.—Richard III; A Good Night's Rest.

26. N.—King Lear; Militia Training; Kentuckian.
C.—Gladiator; Popping the Question; Ladder of Love.

28. *Monday:*
N.—Poor Jack; Englishmen in India.
C.—Broker of Bogota; Animal Magnetism.

29. N.—Victorine; A Kiss in the Dark; My Young Wife and my
Old Umbrella.
C.—Broker of Bogota; Turn Out.

30.   N.—Married Life; Poor Jack.
C.—Richelieu; Gladiator.

OCTOBER

1. *Thursday:*
   N.—Heir at Law; Out of Luck.
   C.—Wild Oats; Nicholas Nickleby.
2. N.—Victorine; The Christening.
   C.—Jealous Wife; Scan. Mag.
3. N.—Isabelle; Old Guard.
   C.—Love; The Storm.
5. *Monday:*
   N.—A Dream at Sea; Isabelle.
   C.—Irish Ambassador; Irish Tutor; Dead Shot.
6. N.—Susanne; Nicholas Nickleby; A Roland for an Oliver.
   C.—Nervous Man; Irish Lion; The Storm.
7. N.—Virginius; Cameleon.
   C.—How to pay Rent; Irish Lion; Scan. Mag.
8. N.—Washington; Susanne.
   C.—Born to Good Luck; Irish Tutor; Animal Magnetism.
9. N.—Washington; Cameleon.
   C.—How to pay Rent; Omnibus; Turn Out.
10. N.—Washington; Married Rake.
    C.—His Last Legs; Omnibus; My Aunt.
12. *Monday:*
    N.—Water Party; Nicholas Nickleby, first act; Washington.
    C.—His Last Legs; Irish Lion; Is He Jealous?
13. N.—Paul Pry; A Dream at Sea.
    C.—John Bull; Master's Rival.
14. N.—Richard III; Susanne.
    C.—Irish Ambassador; Teddy the Tiler; Ladder of Love.
    W.—The Honey Moon; A Roland for an Oliver.
15. N.—Poor Soldier; Water Party.
    C.—Rory O'More; Lottery Ticket.
    W.—Honey Moon; A Roland for an Oliver.
16. N.—Romantic Widow; Artist's Wife.
    C.—His Last Legs; Paddy Carey.
    W.—School for Scandal; Winning a Husband.
17. N.—Patrician and Parvenu; A Dream at Sea.
    C.—St. Patrick's Eve; How to pay Rent.
    W.—Faint Heart never won Fair Lady; The Rivals.
19. *Monday:*
    N.—John di Procida *: *Procida*—J. R. Scott, *Fernando*—
    Richings, *Guiscardo*—Graham, *Governor*—C. S. Porter,
    Isoline—Miss Cushman; Budget of Blunders.

C.—Irish Attorney; Paddy Carey.
W.—Faint Heart never won Fair Lady; Laugh when you Can.

20. N.—Le Preux Chevalier; Oliver Twist.
C.—Born to Good Luck; Omnibus.
W.—Othello; Family Jars.

21. N.—Father and Daughter; Budget of Blunders.
C.—Irish Attorney; Irish Lion.
W.—Married Rake; Wives as they Were.

22. N.—John di Procida; Le Preux Chevalier.
C.—His Last Legs; Irish Tutor.
W.—Paul Pry; Faint Heart never won Fair Lady.

23. N.—Romantic Widow; Mons. Tonson.
C.—Irish Attorney; Happy Man.
W.—Belle's Stratagem; Review.

24. N.—The Lover Husband; Humbug.
C.—Rory O'More; Irish Haymakers.
W.—Laugh when you Can; The Innkeeper's Daughter.

26. *Monday:*
N.—Lady of Lyons; Blue Devils.
C.—La Sonnambula; Popping the Question.
W.—Romeo and Juliet; Sprigs of Laurel.

27. N.—Jane Shore; Humbug.
C.—Cinderella; Married Rake.
W.—Foundling of the Forest; Family Jars.

28. N.—The Stranger; Place Hunter.
C.—La Sonnambula; Simpson and Company.
W.—Comedy of Errors; Charles II.

29. N.—The Wife; Humbug.
C.—Fra Diavolo; Scan. Mag.
W.—Innkeeper's Daughter; Comedy of Errors.

30. N.—Pizarro; Katharine and Petruchio.
C.—Lucille; Irish Haymakers.
W.—Perfection; Sprigs of Laurel.

31. N.—Swiss Swains; Master Humphrey's Clock.
C.—Guy Mannering; My Neighbor's Wife.
W.—Love and Madness; Sweethearts and Wives.

NOVEMBER

2. *Monday:*
N.—Maid of Mariendorpt; Solomon Smink *: *Solomon—Buckstone.*
C.—Fra Diavolo; The Christening.
W.—Seven's the Main; Last Man.

3. N.—Swiss Cottage; Victorine.
C.—Maid of Judah; Dead Shot.

W.—Hunting a Turtle; The Last Man.
4.   N.—Wreck Ashore; A Kiss in the Dark.
    C.—La Sonnambula; Poor Soldier.
    W.—Faint Heart never won Fair Lady; Last Man.
5.   N.—Solomon Smink; Le Dieu et la Bayadere.
    C.—Maid of Judah; The Quaker.
    W.—Loan of a Lover; Last Man.
6.   N.—Wreck Ashore; Le Dieu et la Bayadere.
    C.—Lady of Lyons; No Song, No Supper.
    W.—Last Man; High Life below Stairs.
7.   N.—Peter Bell, the Wagoner *: *Peter*—Burton, *Martin*—
      Buckstone; Othello.
    C.—Fra Diavolo; The Waterman.
    W.—Laugh when you Can; The Last Man.
9. *Monday:*
    N.—Ups and Downs *: *Felix*—Burton; Le Dieu et la Baya-
      dere, first act.
    C.—Englishmen in India; The Roof Scrambler.
    W.—George Barnwell; Deaf as a Post.
10. N.—John di Procida; Wreck Ashore.
    C.—La Tarentule; The Christening.
    W.—Last Man; Laugh when you Can.
11. N.—More Blunders than One; Le Dieu et la Bayadere.
    C.—Closed.
    W.—Of Age Tomorrow; Mr. and Mrs. Peter White.
12. N.—Rob Roy; Pleasant Neighbors.
    C.—La Sylphide; Popping the Question.
    W.—Sailor's Revenge; A Roland for an Oliver.
13. N.—Ups and Downs; Master Humphrey's Clock.
    C.—Closed.
    W.—Sweethearts and Wives; Married Rake.
14. N.—Rob Roy; Peter Bell.
    C.—La Sylphide; Dead Shot.
    W.—George Barnwell; Sprigs of Laurel.
16. *Monday:*
    N.—Irish Ambassador; Irish Tutor.
    C.—La Tarentule; Shocking Events.
    W.—The Prize; Deaf as a Post.
17. N.—Nervous Man; Irish Lion; Susanne.
    C.—Closed.
    W.—Faint Heart never won Fair Lady; Innkeeper's Daughter.
18. N.—O'Flannigan and the Fairies.
    C.—Nathalie; Young Widow.
    W.—Perfection; Black Eyed Susan.
19. N.—O'Flannigan and the Fairies; Place Hunter.
    C.—Closed.

W.—Winning a Husband; A Day after the Wedding.
20. N.—Nervous Man; Wags of Windsor.
C.—Popping the Question; Tom Noddy's Secret.
W.—Is He Jealous?; The Lady and the Devil.
21. N.—O'Flannigan and the Fairies; Happy Man.
C.—Nathalie; The Christening.
W.—Honey Moon; Ship Wreck.
23. *Monday:*
N.—White Horse of the Peppers; Happy Man.
C.—Othello; Petticoat Government.
W.—Broken Sword; Shipwreck.
24. N.—His Last Legs; Irish Lion.
C.—Metamora; Tom Noddy's Secret.
W.—Broken Sword; Shipwreck.
25. N.—White Horse of the Peppers; His Last Legs.
C.—Virginius; Mr. and Mrs. Pringle.
W.—Archibald of the Wreck; Speed the Plough.
26. N.—O'Flannigan and the Fairies; Happy Man.
C.—Gladiator; She would be a Soldier.
W.—Demon Dwarf; Laugh when you Can.
27. N.—Irish Attorney; Omnibus.
C.—Richelieu; The Christening.
W.—Rob Roy; Is He Jealous?
28. N.—Irish Attorney; Irish Ambassador.
C.—Lady of Lyons; Mr. and Mrs. Pringle.
W.—Hunting a Turtle; Comfortable Service.
30. *Monday:*
N.—Guy Mannering; Place Hunter.
C.—King Lear; Shocking Event.
W.—Speed the Plough; Demon Dwarf.

DECEMBER

1. *Tuesday:*
N.—Devil's Bridge; My Sister Kate.
C.—Damon and Pythias; Happiest Day in my Life.
W.—Archibald of the Wreck; Demon Dwarf.
A.—Jonathan in England; O. K.
2. N.—Love in a Village; Waterman.
C.—Macbeth; Therese.
W.—Goblin Page; Married Rake.
A.—New Notions; A Wife for a Day.
3. N.—Guy Mannering; More Blunders than One.
C.—Marco Bombo; Tom Noddy's Secret.
W.—Charles II; Goblin Page.
A.—Jonathan in England; The Secret.

4.   N.—Masaniello; Blue Devils.
      C.—Wild Oats; Flying Dutchman.
      W.—Romeo and Juliet; Goblin Page.
      A.—Done for a Hundred; Hypocrite.
5.   N.—Masaniello; Tom Noddy's Secret.
      C.—Popping the Question; Dead Shot.
      W.—Of Age Tomorrow; Spoiled Child.
      A.—Cut and come Again; New Notions.
7. *Monday:*
      N.—Masaniello.
      C.—My Fellow Clerk; Fire and Water.
      W.—Simpson and Company; Three and Deuce.
      A.—Rail Road Depot; Lion of the Sea.*
8.   N.—Devil's Bridge; Dumb Belle.
      C.—Naval Engagements; Nicholas Nickleby.
      W.—Stranger; Agreeable Surprise.
      A.—Cut and come Again; Lion of the Sea.
9.   N.—Masaniello; More Blunders than One.
      C.—Day after the Wedding; My Fellow Clerk.
      W.—Agnes deVere; Turn Out.
      A.—Knight of the Golden Fleece; Dead Shot.
10.   N.—Siege of Belgrade; Wandering Minstrel.
      C.—Popping the Question; Ice Witch and Sun Spirit *: *Har-
         old*—Murdock, *Gruthioff*—Henkins, *Seveno*—Davenport.
      W.—Heir at Law; Woman's the Devil.
      A.—Knight of the Golden Fleece; New Notions.
11.   N.—Siege of Belgrade; Swiss Cottage.
      C.—Ice Witch; Mr. and Mrs. Pringle.
      W.—Nature and Philosophy; A Wife for a Day.
      A.—Ben the Boatswain *: *Dionysius*—Flynn, *Dame*—Mrs.
         Judah, *Palmyra*—Mrs. Cantor; True Hearts.
12.   N.—The Slave; Masaniello, first act.
      C.—Ice Witch and the Sun Spirit.
      W.—Green Mountain Boy; Agreeable Surprise.
      A.—Richard III; Secret.
14. *Monday:*
      N.—The Cabinet; The Slave.
      C.—Ice Witch and the Sun Spirit.
      W.—Jonathan in England; Jumbo Jim.
      A.—Richard III; Highlander's Faith.
15.   N.—Dutch Burgomaster; Merchant of Venice.
      C.—Ice Witch; Turn Out.
      W.—Cut and come Again; Foreign Prince.
      A.—Hamlet; Dead Shot.
16.   N.—Brutus; State Secrets.
      C.—Ice Witch; La Sonnambula.

[233]

W.—Whew! Here's a Go!; Wife for a Day.
A.—New Way To Pay Old Debts; Sudden Thoughts.

17. N.—Lady of Lyons; Dutch Burgomaster.
C.—Bride of Abydos; Ice Witch.
W.—Seth Slope; Uncle Pop.
A.—Richelieu; Ben the Boatswain.

18. N.—Closed.
C.—Englishmen in India; Ice Witch.
W.—Virginny Mummy; Green Mountain Boy.
A.—Hamlet; True Hearts.

19. N.—The Naiad Queen *: *Rupert*—Shaw, *Almagro*—Boulard,
Greenwald—Owens, *Amphiboo*—Oakey, *Queen*—Miss
Cushman; My Sister Kate.
C.—Bold Stroke for a Husband; Ladies' Club.
W.—Jonathan in England; Bone Squash Diavolo.
A.—Richard III; Mayor of Garratt.

21. *Monday:*
N.—Naiad Queen; The Sleigh Driver.
C.—Irish Widow; Perfection.
W.—Knight of the Golden Fleece; Richard III.
A.—Norman Leslie; Ben the Boatswain.

22. N.—Naiad Queen; More Blunders than One.
C.—Mr. and Mrs. Pringle; Christening.
W.—Knight of the Golden Fleece; New Notions.
A.—Norman Leslie; Highlander's Fate.

23. N.—Naiad Queen; Swiss Cottage.
C.—Banished Star; Tom Noddy's Secret.
W.—New Way To Pay Old Debts; Loan of a Lover.
A.—Convict's Child; Lion of the Sea.

24. N.—Virginius; Joan of Arc.
C.—Single Life; Fortune's Frolic.
W.—Hamlet; A Day in Paris.
A.—Convict's Child; Lion of the Sea.

25. N.—Naiad Queen; Dancing Scotchman.
C.—A Kiss in the Dark; Widow Wiggins.
W.—Richard III.
A.—Norman Leslie; The Secret.

26. N.—Naiad Queen; Dancing Scotchman.
C.—Ice Witch and the Sun Spirit.
W.—No advertisement.
A.—Convict's Child; Like Father, Like Son.

28. *Monday:*
N.—Naiad Queen; The Deserter.
C.—Town and Country; Nipped in the Bud.
W.—Norman Leslie.
A.—Poor Dog Tray; Tom and Jerry.

29. N.—Naiad Queen; The Deserter.
     C.—Lucille; Therese.
     W.—Norman Leslie.
     A.—Poor Dog Tray; True Hearts.
30. N.—Naiad Queen; The Sleigh Driver.
     C.—Castle Spectre; Agreeable Surprise.
     W.—Norman Leslie.
     A.—Dumb Man of Manchester; Serpent Lady.
31. N.—Town and Country; Der Nacht Wachter.
     C.—Rural Felicity; Valentine and Orson.
     W.—Norman Leslie.
     A.—Dumb Man of Manchester; Serpent Lady.

JANUARY 1841

1. *Friday:*
     W.—George Barnwell; Norman Leslie.
     A.—Phillip Quarl and his Monkey; The Sailor's Return.
     N.—The Naiad Queen.
     C.—Bride of Abydos; Ice Witch.
2. W.—Norman Leslie.
     A.—Dumb Man of Manchester; Serpent Lady.
     N.—The Naiad Queen; Mother Goose.
     C.—Ice Witch; Valentine and Orson.
4. *Monday:*
     W.—Norman Leslie.
     A.—Siege of Janina; Tom Thumb.
     N.—The Naiad Queen; The King's Word.
     C.—Hints for Husbands; Rural Felicity.
5. W.—Norman Leslie.
     A.—Siege of Janina; Black Eyed Susan.
     N.—Naiad Queen; Mother Goose.
     C.—Closed.
6. W.—Norman Leslie; George Barnwell.
     A.—Wild Boy of Bohemia; Forest of Bondy.
     N.—Naiad Queen; Mother Goose.
     C.—Closed.
7. W.—Romeo and Juliet; Forty Thieves.
     A.—Wild Boy of Bohemia; Forest of Bondy.
     N.—Naiad Queen; Mother Goose.
     C.—Closed.
8. W.—Stars and Stripes; Philadelphia as it Is.
     A.—Smuggler's Dog; Tomb Thumb.
     N.—Foundling of the Forest; Wreck Ashore.
     C.—Closed.
9. W.—Laugh when you Can; Philadelphia as it Is.

A.—Siege of Janina; Don Juan.
N.—Maurice the Woodcutter; Mother Goose.
C.—Closed.

11. *Monday:*
    W.—Carpenter of Rouen; Philadelphia as it Is.
    A.—Grateful Lion; Death Struggle.
    N.—Norma; More Blunders than One.
    C.—Norma.

12. W.—Carpenter of Rouen; Philadelphia as it Is.
    A.—Forest of Bondy; Don Juan.
    N.—Norma; Place Hunter.
    C.—Norma.

13. W.—Carpenter of Rouen; Catching an Heiress.
    A.—Forest of Bondy; Don Juan.
    N.—Norma, King's Word.
    C.—Norma.

14. W.—Carpenter of Rouen; Philadelphia as it Is.
    A.—The Foulah Slave; Jack Robinson.
    N.—Norma; The Sleigh Driver.
    C.—Norma.

15. W.—Carpenter of Rouen; P.P.P.P.
    A.—The Foulah Slave; Jack Robinson.
    N.—Norma; Wandering Minstrel.
    C.—Norma.

16. W.—Laugh when you Can; Carpenter of Rouen.
    A.—Clandare; A Night in the Pyrenees.
    N.—Norma; Monster's Fate.
    C.—Norma.

18. *Monday:*
    W.—Mazeppa; Turn Out.
    A.—French Spy; Grateful Lion.
    N.—Ataxerxes; Monster's Fate.
    C.—Norma.

19. W.—Mazeppa; Turn Out.
    A.—Courier of the Ocean; Is He Jealous?
    N.—Artaxerxes; Monster's Fate.
    C.—Closed.

20. W.—Mazeppa; P.P.P.P.
    A.—Hazard of the Die; Tom Cringle.
    N.—Norma; Loan of a Lover.
    C.—Closed.

21. W.—Mazeppa; P.P.P.P.
    A.—Courier of the Ocean; A Night in the Pyrenees.
    N.—Norma; Yankee Valet.
    C.—Closed.

22.
    W.—Mazeppa; Like Father, Like Son.
    A.—Dumb Man of Manchester; Tom Cringle.
    N.—Norma; John Jones.
    C.—Closed.

23.
    W.—Mazeppa; Carpenter of Rouen.
    A.—Courier of the Ocean; Grateful Lion.
    N.—Norma; Rob Roy.
    C.—Closed.

25. *Monday:*
    W.—Mazeppa; Carpenter of Rouen.
    A.—Richard Turpin; Cherokee Chief.
    N.—Money; Mummy.
    C.—Norma.

26.
    W.—Mazeppa; Carpenter of Rouen.
    A.—Richard Turpin; Cherokee Chief.
    N.—Mazeppa; Carpenter of Rouen.
    C.—Norma.

27.
    W.—Mazeppa; Carpenter of Rouen.
    A.—Brazen Drum; Venus in Arms.
    N.—Rent Day; State Secrets.
    C.—Norma.

28.
    W.—Douglas; P.P.P.P.
    A.—Brazen Drum; Venus in Arms.
    N.—A Grand Ball, no play.
    C.—Norma.

29.
    W.—Mazeppa; Carpenter of Rouen.
    A.—The Foundling; Easy Joe Bruce.
    N.—A Promenade Concert, no play.
    C.—Norma.

30.
    W.—Mazeppa; Golden Farmer.
    A.—The Foundling; Lion of the Sea.
    N.—The Exile; Merchant of Venice, the trial scene.
    C.—Norma.

FEBRUARY

1. *Monday:*
    W.—Kate Kearney; Flying Dutchman.
    A.—Bridge of Terror; Tommy Tit in Trouble.
    N.—Money; Killing no Murder.
    C.—Norma.

2.
    W.—Kate Kearney; Flying Dutchman.
    A.—Bridge of Terror; Tommy Tit in Trouble.
    N.—Rochester; 1841 and 1891.
    C.—Norma.

3. W.—Kate Kearney; Flying Dutchman.
   A.—No advertisement.
   N.—Killing no Murder; 1841 and 1891
   C.—Norma.

4. W.—Kate Kearney; Flying Dutchman.
   A.—No advertisement.
   N.—Money; 1841 and 1891.
   C.—Norma.

5. W.—Kate Kearney; Jonathan in England.
   A.—No advertisement.
   N.—Rochester; 1841 and 1891.
   C.—No advertisement.

6. W.—Ransom; Flying Dutchman.
   A.—No advertisement.
   N.—Fireman's Life; 1841 and 1891.
   C.—No advertisement.

8. *Monday:*
   W.—Rail Road Depot; Zembrica.
   N.—Fireman's Life; 1841 and 1891.

9. W.—Bride of Abydos; Lilian.
   N.—School for Scandal; 1841 and 1891.

10. W.—Wallace; The Foundling of the Forest.
    N.—Money; 1841 and 1891.
    C.—Wheel of Fortune; King and the Mimic.

11. W.—Ransom; Philadelphia as it Is.
    N.—Young Napoleon and his Father; Yankee Valet.
    C.—Soldier's Daughter; Turning the Tables.

12. W.—George Barnwell; Tom and Jerry.
    N.—Young Napoleon and his Father; 1841 and 1891.
    C.—No advertisement.

13. W.—The King and the Deserter; Rail Road Depot.
    N.—Charles II; Tekeli.
    C.—No advertisement.

15. *Monday:*
    W.—Like Father, Like Son; French Spy.
    N.—Uncle John; Young Napoleon and his Father.

16. W.—Like Father, Like Son; French Spy.
    N.—Secret Service; Young Napoleon and his Father.

17. W.—Zembrica; French Spy.
    N.—The Rivals; Young Napoleon and his Father.

18. W.—Bride of Abydos; Pirate of the Atlantic.
    N.—Village Doctor; Young Napoleon and his Father.

19. W.—Bride of Abydos; Pirate of the Atlantic.
    N.—Village Doctor; Agreeable Surprise.
    C.—School for Scandal; Ice Witch.

20. W.—The Convict's Child; Pirate of the Atlantic.

N.—Speed the Plough; Rival Soldiers.
C.—The Honey Moon; How to Die for Love.
22. *Monday:*
W.—The Stranger; Mob, the Outlaw.
N.—Merry Wives of Windsor; Bandit Merchant.
C.—Heir at Law; Ice Witch.
23. W.—Tale of Blood; Convict's Child.
N.—Sweethearts and Wives; Mummy.
C.—Bride of Lammermoor; Katharine and Petruchio.
24. W.—Rory O'More; Kate Kearney.
N.—Nervous Man; Happy Man.
C.—No advertisement.
25. W.—Carpenter of Rouen; Pirate of the Atlantic.
N.—His Last Legs; Teddy the Tiler.
C.—Brian Boroihme; Roof Scrambler.
26. W.—Carpenter of Rouen; Stranger.
N.—Born to Good Luck; Irish Lion.
C.—Bride of Lammermoor; Roof Scrambler.
27. W.—Carpenter of Rouen; Mazeppa.
N.—The Rivals; His Last Legs.
C.—Laugh when you Can; Ice Witch.

MARCH

1. *Monday:*
W.—Lilian; Mazeppa.
N.—Grand Ball in the theatre.
C.—School for Scandal; Last Man.
2. W.—White Horse of the Peppers; Mazeppa.
N.—Jane Shore; Tekeli.
C.—Poor Gentleman; Gustavus III.
3. W.—New Way To Pay Old Debts; Four Sisters.
N.—Hunchback; Yankee Valet.
C.—No advertisement.
4. W.—Hamlet; Widow's Victim.
N.—Fazio; Bandit Merchant.
C.—No advertisement.
5. W.—Mountaineers; Carpenter of Rouen.
N.—Love Chase; Joan of Arc.
C.—No advertisement.
6. W.—Richard III; Mob, the Outlaw.
N.—The Wife; Rake's Progress.
C.—No advertisement.
8. *Monday:*
W.—Pizarro; Rail Road Depot.

N.—Rake's Progress; 1841 and 1891.
9.   W.—Carpenter of Rouen; Like Father, Like Son.
N.—Merry Wives of Windsor; Mons. Mallet.
10.   W.—Closed in preparation for performance of Rook Wood.
N.—King Lear; Kentuckian.
11.   N.—Hamlet; But However.
12.   N.—Horse-Shoe Robinson; 1841 and 1891.
13.   W.—Rookwood *: *Turpin*—La Forest, *Tom*—Russell, *Titus*—Charles Luke Fredericks, *Jerry*—Hadaway, *Sybil*—Mrs. Flynn, *Hanassah*—Mrs. La Forest, *Barbara*—Mrs. Charles, *Lady Rookwood*—Mrs. Plumer.
N.—Rip Van Winkle; Horse-Shoe Robinson.
15.   *Monday:*
W.—Rookwood.
N.—Henry IV; Horse-Shoe Robinson.
16.   W.—Rookwood.
N.—Forty Winks; 1841 and 1891.
17.   W.—Rookwood.
N.—The Genoese; Gil Blas.
18.   W.—Rookwood.
N.—Man and Wife; Gil Blas.
19.   W.—Rookwood.
N.—Forty Winks; Sweethearts and Wives.
20.   W.—Rookwood.
N.—Night and Morning; Loan of a Lover.
22.   *Monday:*
W.—Rookwood.
N.—Night and Morning; State Secrets.
23.   W.—Rookwood.
N.—Night and Morning; My Friend the Governor.
24.   W.—Rookwood.
N.—The New President *: *Bambino*—Burton; Spitfire.
25.   W.—Rookwood.
N.—Night and Morning; New President.
26.   W.—Rookwood.
N.—Night and Morning; Turnpike Gate.
27.   W.—Rookwood.
N.—Night and Morning; Money.
29.   *Monday:*
W.—Rookwood.
N.—Wrecker's Daughter; Oliver Twist.
30.   W.—Rookwood.
N.—Delusion; Spitfire.
31.   W.—Cataract of the Ganges; Widow's Victim.
N.—The Quadroone; Forty Winks.

APRIL

1. *Thursday:*
   W.—Cataract of the Ganges; Widow's Victim.
   N.—Naiad Queen; 1841 and 1891.
2. W.—Cataract of the Ganges; Like Father, Like Son.
   N.—Naiad Queen; Loan of a Lover.
3. W.—Cataract of the Ganges; Rail Road Depot.
   N.—Naiad Queen; My Friend the Governor.
5. *Monday:*
   W.—Fortune Teller; El Hyder.
   N.—Naiad Queen; State Secrets.
   A.—Lady of Lyons; Deaf as a Post.
6. W.—Fortune Teller; El Hyder.
   N.—Naiad Queen; Turnpike Gate.
   A.—Macbeth; Pleasant Neighbors.
7. W.—Fortune Teller; El Hyder.
   N.—Naiad Queen; But However.
   A.—Damon and Pythias; Popping the Question.
8. W.—Fortune Teller; Timour the Tartar.
   N.—Lady of Lyons; Turning the Tables.
   A.—Richard III; A Nabob for an Hour.
9. W.—Fortune Teller; Timour the Tartar.
   N.—Therese; Dead Shot.
   A.—Richelieu; Pleasant Neighbors.
10. W.—El Hyder; Timour the Tartar.
    N.—Tippoo Saib.
    A.—Metamora; Village Gossip.
12. *Monday:*
    W.—Mazeppa; Carpenter of Rouen.
    N.—Tippoo Saib.
    A.—Gladiator; Turning the Tables.
13. W.—Mazeppa; Carpenter of Rouen.
    N.—Tippoo Saib.
    A.—Richelieu; Irishman in London.
14. W.—Black Castle of the Desert; P.P.P.P.
    N.—Caswallon; Light Ship.
    A.—Othello; Village Gossip.
15. W.—Black Castle of the Desert; P.P.P.P.
    N.—Tippoo Saib.
    A.—Virginius; My Aunt.
16. W.—Black Castle of the Desert; Widow's Victim.
    N.—Tippoo Saib.
    A.—Hamlet; Mr. and Mrs. Pringle.
17. W.—Black Castle of the Desert; Ransom.

N.—Tippoo Saib.
A.—Pizarro; Deaf as a Post.

19. *Monday:*
W.—Black Castle of the Desert; Gambler's Fate.
N.—Tippoo Saib; The Enchanted Chinese.
A.—Venice Preserved; William Tell.

20. W.—Theatres closed in respect to memory of President Harrison, on day of funeral procession.

21. W.—Ransom; Mazeppa.
N.—Tippoo Saib; The Enchanted Chinese.
A.—Broker of Bogota; Village Gossip.

22. W.—Kate Kearney; Loan of a Lover.
N.—The Invasion of Russia.
A.—Gladiator; Married Rake.

23. W.—Damon and Pythias; King and the Deserter.
N.—The Invasion of Russia.
A.—Lady of Lyons; Therese.

24. W.—Seven Voyages of Sinbad the Sailor; Rail Road Depot.
N.—The Invasion of Russia.
A.—Damon and Pythias; Buckle of Brilliants.

26. *Monday:*
W.—Seven Voyages of Sinbad the Sailor; How to pay Rent.
N.—Closed in preparation for new play.
A.—Coriolanus; Adopted Child.

27. W.—Seven Voyages; How to pay Rent.
A.—Richelieu; Gladiator.

28. W.—Seven Voyages; Like Father, Like Son.
A.—Money; Naval Engagements.

29. W.—Seven Voyages; Like Father, Like Son.
A.—Wild Oats; Brutus.

30. W.—Lady of Lyons; Wandering Boys.
A.—Money; Deaf as a Post.

MAY

1. *Saturday:*
W.—Rookwood; Oh! Hush!
C.—La Gazza Ladra; Delusion.
A.—Stranger; Popping the Question.

3. *Monday:*
W.—Rookwood.
C.—La Gazza Ladra; H. B.
A.—New Way To Pay Old Debts; Black Eyed Susan.

4. W.—Rookwood.
C.—Don Giovanni; H. B.
A.—Speed the Plough; Irish Tutor.

5.   W.—Rum Old Commodore; Kate Kearney.
     C.—Don Giovanni.
     A.—Rent Day; Last Man.

6.   W.—Rookwood; Rum Old Commodore.
     C.—Don Giovanni.
     A.—Henry IV; Fashionable Friends.

7.   W.—Rookwood; Launch of the Mississippi.
     C.—Don Giovanni; Maid of Cashmere.
     A.—Last Man; Fashionable Friends.

8.   W.—Avenger; Launch of the Mississippi.
     N.—Seven Champions of Christendom.
     C.—L'Elsire d'Amore; Maid of Cashmere.
     A.—Wonder; Love, Law and Physic.

10. *Monday:*
     W.—Avenger; Launch of the Mississippi.
     N.—Seven Champions of Christendom.
     C.—L'Elsire d'Amore; My Sister Kate.
     A.—Wandering Minstrel; Denouncer.

11.   W.—Avenger; Pizarro.
     N.—Seven Champions of Christendom.
     C.—L'Elsire d'Amore; Maid of Cashmere.
     A.—'Twas I; Denouncer.

12.   W.—Avenger; Launch of the Mississippi.
     N.—Seven Champions of Christendom.
     C.—Zampa.
     A.—Laugh when you Can; Last Man.

13.   W.—Avenger; Pizarro.
     N.—Seven Champions of Christendom.
     C.—Zampa.
     A.—Denouncer; Mr. and Mrs. Pringle.

14.   W.—Damon and Pythias; Review.
     N.—No advertisement.
     C.—Zampa.
     A.—Denouncer; Last Man.

15.   No newspapers published. National Fast Day in memory of President Harrison.

17. *Monday:*
     W.—Avenger; Carpenter of Rouen.
     C.—Zampa; My Sister Kate.
     A.—Guy Mannering; Loan of a Lover.

18.   W.—Black Eyed Susan. Review.
     C.—Zampa; Married Rake.
     A.—Turn Out; Buckle of Brilliants.

19.   W.—Virginius; Pet of the Petticoats.
     C.—Zampa; La Bayadere.
     A.—Rob Roy; My Aunt.

20.   W.—Damon and Pythias; Pet of the Petticoats.
       C.—L'Elsire d'Amore; Close Siege.
       A.—Englishman in India; Spirit of the Clyde.
21.   W.—Othello; Adopted Child.
       C.—La Gazza Ladra; Close Siege.
       A.—Guy Mannering; Barrack Room.
22.   W.—Damon and Pythias; Black Eyed Susan.
       C.—Zampa; La Sylphide.
       A.—Lady of Lyons; Pizarro.
24. *Monday:*
       W.—King Lear; Rail Road Depot.
       C.—Fra Diavolo; La Sylphide.
       A.—Red Mask; Loan of a Lover.
25.   W.—Hamlet; Lady of Lyons.
       C.—L'Elsire d'Amore; La Sylphide.
       A.—Heir at Law; Swiss Cottage.
26.   W.—Love Laughs at Locksmiths; Avarice.
       C.—Zampa.
       A.—Lady of Lyons; Black Eyed Susan.
27.   W.—Adopted Child; Dumb Belle.
       C.—Cinderella.
       A.—Richelieu; Swiss Cottage.
28.   W.—No advertisement.
       C.—Cinderella.
       A.—Romeo and Juliet; Siege of Stralsund.
29.   W.—Lady of the Lake; Fish out of Water.
       C.—Fra Diavolo; Faint Heart never won Fair Lady.
31. *Monday:*
       W.—Lady of the Lake; How to Die for Love.
       C.—La Sonnambula; Midas.
       A.—Sea Captain; Wallace.

JUNE

1. *Tuesday:*
       W.—Lady of the Lake; Fish out of Water.
       C.—La Bayadere; My Sister Kate.
       A.—The Pilot; Sea Captain.
2.   W.—Lady of the Lake; How to Die for Love.
       C.—Closed.
       A.—Money; Star Spangled Banner.
3.   W.—Lady of the Lake; Unfinished Gentleman.
       A.—Damon and Pythias; Pilot.
4.   W.—Lady of the Lake; Maurice the Wood Cutter.
       C.—Fra Diavolo; Midas.
       A.—Virginius; Star Spangled Banner.

5.   W.—Lady of the Lake; Maurice the Wood Cutter.
      C.—Fra Diavolo; Midas.
      A.—Simpson and Co.; La Fitte.

7. *Monday:*
      W.—Ugolino; Mathilde.
      C.—Norma.
      A.—Richelieu; Irishman in London.

8.   W.—Lady of the Lake; Love Laughs at Locksmiths.
      C.—Norma.
      A.—Gladiator; Irish Tutor.

9.   W.—Mathilde; Maurice the Wood Cutter.
      C.—Norma.
      A.—Metamora; Irishman in London.

10.   W.—Ugolino; Fish out of Water.
      C.—Norma.
      A.—Money; Review.

11.   W.—Rob Roy; Unfinished Gentleman.
      C.—Wives as they Were; Roof Scrambler.
      A.—No performance.

12.   W.—Mathilde; How to Die for Love.
      N.—Buy-It-Dear—'Tis Made of Cashmere; Cat's in the Larder.
      C.—Norma.
      A.—La Tour de Nesle; La Fitte.

14. *Monday:*
      W.—Wm. Tell; Unfinished Gentleman.
      N.—Buy It Dear; Cat's in the Larder.
      C.—Norma.
      A.—Aylmere; Irish Tutor.

15.   W.—Lady of Lyons; Rail Road Depot.
      N.—Buy It Dear; Turned Head.
      C.—Charles II; Victorine.
      A.—Aylmere; Buckle of Brilliants.

16.   W.—Mathilde; The Pilot.
      N.—Humpback; Turned Head.
      C.—Norma.
      A.—Aylmere.

17.   W.—Pizarro; Black Eyed Susan.
      N.—Humpback; Unfortunate Miss Bailey.
      C.—Money; Faint Heart never won Fair Lady.
      A.—Aylmere; Pleasant Neighbors.

18.   W.—Iron Chest; The Pilot.
      N.—Humpback; Puss in Boots.
      C.—Norma.
      A.—Aylmere; Irishman in London.

19.   W.—La Tour de Nesle; Star Spangled Banner.

   N.—Poor Gentleman; Humpback.
   C.—Norma; Midas.
   A.—Aylmere; Swiss Cottage.
21. *Monday:*
   W.—Unfinished Gentleman; The Flying Dutchman.
   N.—Puss in Boots; Sam Parr.
   C.—Norma; Last night of the season.
   A.—Aylmere; Married Rake.
22. W.—Sweethearts and Wives; Star Spangled Banner.
   N.—Puss in Boots; Sam Parr.
   A.—Ion; Loan of a Lover.
23. W.—Sudden Thoughts; Nicholas Nickleby.
   N.—Sam Parr; Puss in Boots.
   A.—Aylmere; The Irish Tutor.
24. W.—Soldier's Son; Turning the Tables.
   N.—Puss in Boots; Sam Parr.
   A.—Mrs. Nomer; Pleasant Neighbors.
25. W.—Paul Pry; X.Y.Z.
   N.—Buy It Dear; Sam Parr.
   A.—Mrs. Nomer; Presumptive Evidence.
26. W.—School for Scandal; Four Sisters.
   N.—Sam Parr; Mrs. Normer.
   A.—Mrs. Nomer; Irish Lion.
28. *Monday:*
   W.—Irish Lion; Mrs. Normer.
   N.—Stars in Phila.; Mrs. Normer.
   A.—Isabelle; Mrs. Normer.
29. W.—Dream at Sea; Mischief Making.
   N.—Mrs. Normer; Humpback.
   A.—No bill received.
30. W.—Irish Lion; Dream at Sea.
   N.—Stars in Phila.; Mrs. Normer.
   A.—Jonathan in England; Wandering Minstrel.

JULY

1. *Thursday:*
   W.—Death Token; Unfinished Gentleman.
   N.—Sam Parr; Mrs. Normer. Last night of Olympic Company.
   A.—No bill received.
2. W.—Dream at Sea; How to Die for Love.
   A.—No bill received.
3. W.—Death Token; Shipwreck.
   A.—No bill received.
5. *Monday:*
   W.—Glory of Columbus; Shipwreck.

N.—Austerlitz; Love will have its Way.

A.—Honey Moon; Faint Heart never won Fair Lady.

6. —No newspapers published.

7. W.—Simpson and Co.; Shipwreck.

8. W.—Monsieur Tonson; Jack Robinson and his Monkey.

9. W.—Love, Law, and Physic; Jack Robinson.

10. W.—Day Well Spent; Shipwreck.

12. *Monday:*

W.—Waterman.

13. W.—Waterman; Jocko.

14. W.—Widow's Victim; Jocko.

15. W.—Village Lawyer; Hofer.

21. W.—Irish Tutor; Perfection.

AUGUST

10. *Tuesday:*

A.—Therese; Black Eyed Susan.

11. A.—Stranger; Fish out of Water.

12. A.—Pizarro; Dumb Belle.

13. A.—Pilot; Two Gregories.

14. A.—Robert Macaire; Frightened to Death.

16. *Monday:*

A.—No advertisement.

18. A.—Maid of Croissy; Hide and Seek.

19. A.—Forty and Fifty; Jacque Strop.

20. A.—Forty and Fifty; Jacque Strop.

21. A.—Robert Macaire; La Bayadere.

N.—Money; Faint Heart never won Fair Lady.

23. *Monday:*

A.—Forty and Fifty; La Bayadere.

N.—Damon and Pythias; Faint Heart never won Fair Lady.

24. A.—Maid of Croissy; La Bayadere.

N.—Lady of Lyons; Love's Victory.

25. A.—Yellow Kids; Nabob for an Hour.

N.—Othello; Married Rake.

26. A.—Damon and Pythias; Too Late for Dinner.

N.—Metamora; Turnpike Gate.

27. A.—Yellow Kids; Othello.

N.—Virginius; Wandering Minstrel.

28. W.—Water Queen; Dead Shot.

N.—Gladiator; Animal Magnetism.

A.—King Lear; Two Gregories.

C.—Much Ado about Nothing; Faint Heart never won Fair Lady.

30. *Monday:*
    W.—Water Queen; Young Widow.
    N.—Kentuckian; Monsieur Mallet.
    A.—Virginius; Tekeli.
    C.—Wife; Louise.
31.   W.—Water Queen; Happy Man.
    N.—Jonathan in England.
    A.—Hamlet; Therese.
    C.—Hamlet; Uncle John.

SEPTEMBER

1. *Wednesday:*
    W.—Water Queen; Catching an Heiress.
    N.—Henry IV.
    A.—King Lear; Tekeli.
    C.—Faint Heart never won Fair Lady; Nathalie.
2.   W.—Water Queen; Pleasant Neighbors.
    N.—Rip Van Winkle; Animal Magnetism.
    A.—William Tell; Fish out of Water.
    C.—Hamlet; Shocking Events.
3.   W.—Water Queen; Catching an Heiress.
    N.—Perfection; Home Squadron.
    A.—Merchant of Venice; How to pay Rent.
    C.—La Sylphide; Shocking Events.
4.   W.—Pizarro; Water Queen.
    N.—My Fellow Clerk.
    A.—Water Witch; Two Gregories.
    C.—Othello; Shocking Events.
6. *Monday:*
    W.—Water Queen; Blue Jackets.
    N.—Raphael's Dream; Home Squadron.
    A.—Water Witch; How to pay Rent.
    C.—Two Queens; Nathalie.
7.   W.—Pizarro; Water Queen.
    N.—Raphael's Dream; Home Squadron.
    A.—Blind Boy; Water Witch.
    C.—John di Procida; Two Queens.
8.   W.—Lady of Lyons; Water Queen.
    N.—Rent Day; Black Eyed Susan.
    A.—Blind Boy; Water Witch.
    C.—La Tarentula; Shocking Events.
9.   W.—Rob Roy; Water Queen.
    N.—Raphael's Dream; Home Squadron.
    A.—Charles II; Water Witch.
    C.—John di Procida; Nabob for an Hour.

10.   W.—Blue Jackets; Water Queen.
        N.—No advertisement.
        A.—No advertisement.
        C.—Maid of Cashmere; No!
11.   W.—Richard III; My Aunt.
        N.—Heir at Law; Harlequin's Olio.
        A.—Rookwood; Dick Turpin.
        C.—Maid of Cashmere; Nabob for an Hour.
13. *Monday:*
        W.—King Lear; Blue Jackets.
        N.—Valsha, the Saxon Serf; Winning a Husband.
        A.—Rookwood; Dick Turpin.
        C.—Maid of Cashmere; Dumb Belle.
14.   W.—Rob Roy; Iron Chest.
        N.—Valsha; Winning a Husband.
        A.—Rookwood; Dick Turpin.
        C.—Revenge; Is He Jealous?
15.   W.—Richard III; Carpenter of Rouen.
        N.—Valsha; Spoiled Child.
        A.—Rookwood; Dick Turpin.
        C.—La Tarentula; My Sister Kate.
16.   W.—Othello; My Aunt.
        N.—Valsha; Spoiled Child.
        A.—Rookwood; Dick Turpin.
        C.—Wonder; My Sister Kate.
17.   W.—Ugolino; Carpenter of Rouen.
        N.—Valsha; Home Squadron.
        A.—Rookwood; Dick Turpin.
        C.—Nathalie; The Secret.
18.   W.—Giovanni in Phila.; Red Riding Hood.
        N.—Valsha; Nick of the Woods.
        A.—Rookwood; Young Widow.
        C.—No advertisement.
20. *Monday:*
        W.—Giovanni in Phila.; My Aunt.
        N.—Valsha; Nick of the Woods.
        A.—Sixteen Years Ago *: *Count*—Watson, *Farmer*—Myers,
            Josephine—Mrs. La Forest, *Therese*—Miss M. Price;
            Bank Monster.
21.   W.—Giovanni in Phila.; The Happy Man.
        N.—Nick of the Woods; A Day in New York.
        A.—Sixteen Years Ago; Bank Monster.
        C.—Nathalie; A Roland for an Oliver.
22.   W.—Council of Ten; Bibboo.
        N.—Nick of the Woods; A Day in New York.
        A.—Forest Rose; Masquerade.

[249]

C.—Youthful Queen; Zembrica.
23. W.—Council of Ten; Bibboo.
N.—No performance.
A.—Forest Rose; Masquerade.
C.—Simpson and Co.; La Gipsey—two scenes.
24. W.—George Barnwell; Hypochondriac.
N.—Valsha; A Speck of War.
A.—Jonathan in England; Bank Monster.
C.—The Wife; A Roland for an Oliver.
25. W.—Council of Ten; Giovanni in Phila.
N.—The Ocean Child *: *Manderville*—Roberts, *Sturdy*—
Sherman, *Harry*—E. S. Conner, *Dennis*—E. Shaw, *Jock*—
Miss A. Fisher, *Mary*—Mrs. G. Jones; Valsha, first act.
A.—Bank Monster; Jonathan in England.
C.—School for Scandal; My Sister Kate.
27. *Monday:*
W.—Naiad Queen; Happy Man.
N.—Ocean Child; Barnaby Rudge *: *Geoffery*—Roberts, *Barn-
aby*—Miss A. Fisher.
A.—Wool Dealer; Hypocrite, last act.
C.—Barnaby Rudge; Shocking Events.
28. W.—Naiad Queen; Dead Shot.
N.—Ocean Child; Barnaby Rudge.
A.—Charles II; Black Ghost.
C.—Barnaby Rudge; Youthful Queen.
29. W.—Naiad Queen; Pleasant Neighbors.
N.—Ocean Child; Rent Day.
A.—Mrs. White; Black Ghost.
C.—Barnaby Rudge; Dumb Belle.
30. W.—Naiad Queen; Adopted Child.
N.—Ocean Child; Rent Day.
A.—Bank Monster; Black Ghost.
C.—Barnaby Rudge; Nabob for an Hour.

OCTOBER

1. *Friday:*
W.—Naiad Queen; Adopted Child.
N.—Barnaby Rudge; Ocean Child.
A.—Two Gregories; Young Reefer.
C.—No advertisement.
2. W.—Michael Erl; Naiad Queen.
N.—Douglas; Ocean Child.
A.—Young Reefer; Sam Slick.
C.—Fazio; Barnaby Rudge.

4. *Monday*
    W.—Naiad Queen; Rail Road Depot.
    N.—Money; Ocean Child.
    A.—New Way To Pay Old Debts; Idiot Witness.
    C.—Werner *: *Werner*—Charles Mason, *Ulric*—Richings, *Ida*—Mrs. Lambert.
5.   W.—Naiad Queen; My Aunt.
    N.—One Glass More; Ocean Child.
    A.—Richard III; Young Reefer.
    C.—Provoked Husband; Valet de Sham.
6.   W.—Napoleon and the Patriot; Naiad Queen.
    N.—One Glass More; Ocean Child.
    A.—Hunchback; Broken Sword.
    C.—Charles XII; Valet de Sham.
7.   W.—Napoleon and the Patriot; Naiad Queen.
    N.—One Glass More; Ocean Child.
    A.—The Wife; Bill Stickers and the Jersey Girl *: *William*—W. H. Smith, *Marie*—Mrs. Harrison.
    C.—Jealous Wife; Lottery Ticket.
8.   W.—Giovanni in Phila.; Naiad Queen.
    N.—Paul Pry; One Glass More.
    A.—Othello; Bill Stickers.
    C.—Rent Day; Pizarro.
9.   W.—Bill Stickers; Naiad Queen.
    N.—Cabinet Secrets; Billy Taylor.
    A.—Richard III, fifth act; Bill Stickers.
    C.—Honey Moon; Fish out of Water.
11. *Monday:*
    W.—Seth Slope; Bill Stickers.
    N.—Cleopatra, Serpent of the Nile.
    A.—Miller's Maid; Bill Stickers.
    C.—Money; Brother Ben.
12.   W.—Jonathan in England; Wife for a Day.
    N.—No advertisement.
    A.—Richard III, fifth act; Bill Stickers.
    C.—Venice Preserved; Dumb Belle.
13.   W.—Green Mountain Boy; Yankee Pedlar.
    N.—Cabinet Secrets; Billy Taylor.
    A.—Stranger; Bill Stickers.
    C.—Money; Aldgate Pump.
14.   W.—Knight of the Golden Fleece; Wife for a Day.
    N.—My Fellow Clerk; Black Eyed Susan.
    A.—Hamlet; How to pay Rent.
    C.—School for Scandal; Mr. H.
15.   W.—New Notions; Hypocrite.

N.—Alexander the Great; Osceola.
A.—Evadue; Blue Devils.
C.—Hunchback; Fish out of Water.

16. W.—New Notions; Hypocrite.
N.—Money; Nick of the Woods.
A.—Julius Caesar; Rival Lovers.
C.—No performance.

18. *Monday:*
W.—Surgeon of Paris; Is He Jealous?
N.—Lady of Lyons; Cabinet Secrets.
A.—First Fleet and the First Flag *: *Tom*—W. H. Smith; Idiot Witness.
C.—Two Gentlemen of Verona; Pleasant Neighbors.

19. W.—Surgeon of Paris; Young Widow.
N.—Richelieu; Turning the Tables.
A.—First Fleet and the First Flag; Idiot Witness.
C.—Two Gentlemen of Verona; Animal Magnetism.

20. W.—Surgeon of Paris; Blue Jackets.
N.—Richelieu; My Fellow Clerk.
A.—Miller's Maid; Ella Rosenberg.
C.—Shocking Events; Vol-Au-Vent.

21. W.—Surgeon of Paris; Carpenter of Rouen.
N.—Othello; Weather Cock.
A.—Woodman's Hut; Blind Boy.
C.—Pleasant Neighbors; Godenski.

22. W.—Surgeon of Paris; Carpenter of Rouen.
N.—Gladiator; Wandering Minstrel.
A.—Ella Rosenberg; Woodman's Hut.
C.—Aldgate Pump; Venetian Carnival.

23. W.—Surgeon of Paris; Siege of Boston *: *Sam*—J. S. Jones.
N.—Metamora; Pizarro.
A.—Jane of the Hatchet; Lilian.
C.—Animal Magnetism.

25. *Monday:*
W.—Siege of Boston; Wife for a Day.
N.—Jack Cade; Katharine and Petruchio.
A.—Jane of the Hatchet; Lilian.
C.—A Roland for an Oliver; Invisible Harlequin.

26. W.—Jonathan in England; Siege of Boston.
N.—Jack Cade; Ocean Child.
A.—Victorine; Jane of the Hatchet.
C.—Aldgate Pump.

27. W.—The Aethiop; My Aunt.
N.—Jack Cade; Black Eyed Susan.
A.—Victorine; Lilian.
C.—No Gamester; New Notions; Last night of the season.

28.   W.—Green Mountain Boy; Surgeon of Paris.
       N.—Jack Cade; Weather Cock.
       A.—Rory O'More; Victorine.
29.   W.—A Roland for an Oliver; Perfection.
       N.—Jack Cade; Raising the Wind.
       A.—No advertisement.
30.   W.—Jersey Girl; Rail Road Depot.
       N.—King Lear; Ocean Child.
       A.—No advertisement.

NOVEMBER

1. *Monday:*
       W.—Yankees in China; Siege of Boston.
       N.—Hamlet; Gladiator.
       A.—Paris and London; Irish Tutor.
2.   W.—Yankees in China; Jonah.
       N.—Out of Place; Nick of the Woods.
       A.—Paris and London; Two Gregories.
3.   W.—Two Gregories; Jersey Girl.
       N.—Snapping Turtles; Raising the Wind.
       A.—Paris and London; How to pay Rent.
4.   W.—Two Gregories; Charles XII.
       N.—Out of Place; My Old Woman.
       A.—Irish Ambassador; Paris and London.
5.   W.—Yankees in China; Charles XII.
       N.—Irish Widow; Widow Higgins.
       A.—No bill received.
6.   W.—London Assurance *: *Dazzle*—Richings, *Max*—W. B.
       Wood, *Sir Haricourt*—Lambert, *Spanker*—Chapman,
       Charles—Davenport, *Cool*—Russel, *Lady Gay*—Mrs.
       Flynn, *Grace*—Miss Wood, *Pert*—Miss Ayres; Rail Road
       Depot.
       N.—Out of Place; My Old Woman.
       A.—Paris and London; Bone Squash Diavola.
8. *Monday:*
       W.—London Assurance; A Roland for an Oliver.
       N.—Banished Star; Snapping Turtles.
       A.—Bone Squash Diavola; Tom and Jerry.
9.   W.—London Assurance; Animal Magnetism.
       N.—Heir at Law; Foreign Airs and Native Graces.
       A.—Foreign Prince; Irish Ambassador.
10. W.—London Assurance; Animal Magnetism.
       N.—Irish Widow; Widow Higgins.
       A.—Jim Crow in London; Irish Tutor.
11. W.—London Assurance; Pleasant Neighbors.

N.—My Old Woman; Wandering Minstrel.
A.—Lost Son; Don Juan.
12. W.—London Assurance; Wife for a Day.
N.—Scotch Widow; Snapping Turtles.
A.—Foreign Prince; Lost Son.
13. W.—London Assurance; Animal Magnetism.
N.—Irish Widow; Out of Place.
A.—No bill received.
15. *Monday:*
W.—London Assurance; Widow's Victim.
N.—London Assurance; Mr. and Mrs. Pringle.
A.—Military Execution; Blue Beard.
16. W.—Kate Kearney; Gambler's Fate.
N.—London Assurance; Mr. and Mrs. Pringle.
A.—Maniac Lover; Strange Gentleman.
17. W.—London Assurance; The Critic.
N.—London Assurance; Mr. and Mrs. Pringle.
A.—Military Execution; Don Juan.
18. W.—London Assurance; Gambler's Fate.
N.—Tom Noddy's Secret; Ocean Child.
A.—Rookwood.
19. W.—London Assurance; The Critic.
N.—London Assurance; Popping the Question.
A.—Rookwood.
20. W.—Kate Kearney; The Critic.
N.—Jonathan Bradford; Lottery Ticket.
A.—Rookwood.
22. *Monday:*
W.—Weather Cock; Gambler's Fate.
N.—London Assurance; Popping the Question.
A.—Rookwood; Loan of a Lover.
23. W.—Fire Raiser; Warlock of the Glen.
N.—London Assurance; Mr. and Mrs. Pringle.
A.—Rookwood; Irish Tutor.
24. W.—Demon Fire Fly; A Roland for an Oliver.
N.—London Assurance; The Lady and the Devil.
A.—Mazeppa; My First Night in a Strange Bed Chamber.
25. W.—Demon Fire Fly; The Stranger.
N.—London Assurance; Mischief Making.
A.—Mazeppa; My First Night in a Strange Bed Chamber.
26. W.—Weather Cock; Faint Heart never won Fair Lady.
N.—London Assurance; Middy Ashore.
A.—Mazeppa; Two Gregories.
27. W.—George Barnwell; Bibboo.
N.—Valsha; Mummy.
A.—Rookwood; Mazeppa.

[254]

29. *Monday:*
    W.—Gilderoy; Sprigs of Laurel.
    N.—La Tour de Nesle; Othello, Travestie.
    A.—Mazeppa; Two Friends.
30.   W.—Jane Shore; Love Laughs at Locksmiths.
    N.—London Assurance; Maid of Croissy.
    A.—Conancheotah; The Omnibus.

DECEMBER

1. *Wednesday:*
    W.—Jewess; Harlequin Nuptials.
    N.—Dutch Burgomaster; State Secrets.
    A.—Conancheotah; Two Friends.
2.   W.—Jewess; Mountaineers.
    N.—London Assurance; Romeo and Juliet.
    A.—Conancheotah; Two Friends.
    C.—London Assurance; My Sister Kate.
3.   W.—Jewess; Hunter of the Alps.
    N.—School for Scandal; Hunter of the Alps.
    A.—Timour the Tartar; Military Execution.
    C.—London Assurance; My Sister Kate.
4.   W.—Jewess; Warlock of the Glen.
    N.—Mable's Curse; Robert Macaire.
    A.—Mazeppa; Timour the Tartar.
    C.—London Assurance; The Secret.
6. *Monday:*
    W.—Christening; Murders of Messina.
    N.—Mabel's Curse; Wanted, a Wife.
    A.—Philadelphia Assurance *: *Squire*—Thompson, *Charles*—
        Thoman, *Flax*—Mills, *Mizzle*—Myers, *Nick*—Wil-
        liams, *Grease*—Mrs. Sexton, *Fatty*—Mrs. Thoman.
    C.—London Assurance; The Secret.
7.   W.—Christening; Murders of Messina.
    N.—Wreck Ashore; Ladies' Man.
    A.—Philadelphia Assurance; Swiss Cottage.
    C.—London Assurance; Married Rake.
8.   W.—Christening; Gustavus III.
    N.—Evadue; Ruffian Boy.
    A.—Phila. Assurance; Swiss Cottage.
    C.—London Assurance; How to pay Rent.
9.   W.—Mr. Midshipman Easy; Christening.
    N.—Too Late for Dinner; Jacque Strop.
    A.—Phila. Assurance; Clandare.
    C.—London Assurance; Weather Cock.
10.   W.—Murderers of Messina; Gustavus III.

N.—The Dream at Sea; Wallace.
A.—Phila. Assurance; Clandare.
C.—London Assurance; How to pay Rent.

11. W.—Mr. Midshipman Easy; Gustavus III.
N.—Jane Shore; Sweethearts and Wives.
A.—Phila. Assurance; Oh! Hush!
C.—London Assurance; Oliver Twist.

13. *Monday:*
W.—Rookwood.
N.—Othello; John Jones.
A.—Joan of Arc; Hunting a Turtle.
C.—The Rivals; Lady of the Lake.

14. W.—Wallace; Black Eyed Susan.
N.—Richard III; Ladies' Man.
A.—Phila. Assurance; Joan of Arc.
C.—School for Scandal; Lady of the Lake.

15. W.—Rookwood.
N.—King Lear; State Secrets.
A.—Phila. Assurance; Maniac Lover.
C.—Road to Ruin; My Sister Kate.

16. W.—Rookwood; My Companion in Arms.
N.—Hamlet; Jonathan Bradford.
A.—Phila. Assurance; Clandare.
C.—School for Scandal; The Secret.

17. W.—Rookwood; Christening.
N.—Coriolanus; Katharine and Petruchio.
A.—How to pay Rent; Oh! Hush!!
C.—Poor Gentleman; How to pay Rent.

18. W.—Rookwood; Tom Cringle's Log.
N.—Macbeth; Mr. and Mrs. Pringle.
A.—Joan of Arc; Oh! Hush!!
C.—Speed the Plough; Lady of the Lake.

20. *Monday:*
W.—Mazeppa; Black Eyed Susan.
N.—Venice Preserved; Coriolanus, second act.
A.—Floating Beacon; Dumb Belle.
C.—What will the World Say?

21. W.—Foundling of the Forest; Is He Jealous?
N.—Richelieu; Wags of Windsor.
A.—Last Nail; Luke the Laborer.
C.—What will the World Say?

22. W.—Mazeppa; Rum Old Commodore.
N.—Money; Tom Cringle's Log.
A.—Closed.
C.—West Indian; Wicklow Gold Mines.

23.   W.—Mazeppa; Turnpike Gate.
      N.—Closed.
      A.—Closed.
      C.—What will the World Say?
24.   W.—Mazeppa; Turnpike Gate.
      N.—Brutus; Maurice the Woodcutter.
      A.—Bronze Horse; Harlequin of the Giants' Isle.
      C.—What will the World Say?
25.   W.—Marion; Marco Bombo.
      N.—Cleopatra.
      A.—Bronze Horse; Harlequin of the Giants' Isle.
      C.—What will the World Say?
27. *Monday:*
      W.—Marion; Marco Bombo.
      N.—Cleopatra.
      A.—Bronze Horse; Mother Goose.
      C.—What will the World Say?
28.   W.—Marion; Old Ironsides.
      N.—Cleopatra.
      A.—Bronze Horse; Harlequin of the Giants' Isle.
      C.—What will the World Say?
29.   W.—Blue Beard; Old Ironsides.
      N.—Cleopatra.
      A.—Bronze Horse; Harlequin of the Giants' Isle.
      C.—Hamlet; Maid of Croissy.
30.   W.—Blue Beard; Old Ironsides.
      N.—Cleopatra.
      A.—Bronze Horse; Harlequin of the Giants' Isle.
      C.—Macbeth; Manager's Daughter.
31.   W.—Mr. Midshipman Easy; Is He Jealous?
      N.—Town and Country; Lottery Ticket.
      A.—Bronze Horse; Harlequin of the Giants' Isle.
      C.—The Stranger; What will the World Say?

JANUARY 1842

1. *Saturday:*
      N.—(Afternoon) William Penn; Home Squadron. (Evening) The Magic Head; Ocean Child.
      C.—(Afternoon) Aladdin; Robinson Crusoe. (Evening) Macbeth; Robinson Crusoe.
      W.—(Afternoon) Dew Drop; Old Hickory. (Evening) Siege of Boston; Old Ironsides.
      A.—(Afternoon and Evening) Descart; Harlequin or the Fair One with the Golden Locks.

3. *Monday:*
    N.—William Penn; The Magic Head.
    C.—Merchant of Venice; What will the World Say?
    W.—Gilderoy; Warning Dream.
    A.—Descart; The Two Smiths.

4.
    N.—William Penn; The Magic Head.
    C.—The Avenger; Robinson Crusoe.
    W.—Dew Drop; La Sylphide.
    A.—Timour the Tartar; The Two Smiths.

5.
    N.—William Penn; The Magic Head.
    C.—What will the World Say?; Maid of Croissy.
    W.—Gilderoy; Warning Dream.
    A.—No advertisement.

6.
    N.—Paul Pry; Valsha.
    C.—Wives as they Were; A Roland for an Oliver.
    W.—Warning Dream; Marion.
    A.—No advertisement.

7.
    N.—Paul Pry; Valsha.
    C.—What will the World Say?; Manager's Daughter.
    W.—Kate Kearney; Warning Dream.
    A.—No advertisement.

8.
    N.—The Wife; Peter Bell.
    C.—No advertisement.
    W.—Tom and Jerry; Battle of New Orleans.
    A.—No advertisement.

10. *Monday:*
    N.—The Rivals; The Spitfire
    C.—Washington *: *Washington*—Richings; What will the World Say?
    W.—Zanthe; Loan of a Lover.

11.
    N.—Popping the Question; The Spitfire.
    C.—Romeo and Juliet; Washington.
    W.—Zanthe; Blue Jackets.

12.
    N.—Popping the Question; The Spitfire.
    C.—The Devil's Bridge; Washington.
    W.—Faith and Falsehood; Don Juan.

13.
    N.—The Robbers; La Tour de Nesle.
    C.—Romeo and Juliet; A Roland for an Oliver.
    W.—Mr. Midshipman Easy; Don Juan.

14.
    N.—Luke the Laborer; The Clown and the Cat.
    C.—A Cure for the Heartache; Devil's Bridge.
    W.—Lady of Lyons; Lost Heir.

15.
    N.—The Stranger; Ocean Child.
    C.—Manager's Daughter; Sergeant of Austerlitz.
    W.—The Stranger; The Pilot.

17. *Monday:*
    N.—Speed the Plough; Sleep Walker.
    C.—White Milliner; My Sister Kate.
    W.—Romeo and Juliet; Lost Heir.

18.   N.—Douglas; Wild Boy of Bohemia.
    C.—White Milliner; Mrs. White.
    W.—Merchant of Venice; Brigand.

19.   N.—Sweethearts and Wives; Wandering Minstrel.
    C.—Wives as they Were; Boarding School.
    W.—Gilderoy; Star Spangled Banner.

20.   N.—Charles O'Malley *: *Charles*—J. Smith, *Monsoon*—W. Jones, *Webber*—Burton, *Power*—Wallach, *Free*—E. Shaw, Spitfire.
    C.—White Milliner; Our House at Home.
    W.—Wallace; The Pilot.

21.   N.—Charles O'Malley; Blind Boy.
    C.—White Milliner; Our House at Home.
    W.—Iron Chest; Star Spangled Banner.

22.   N.—The Exile; The Prize.
    C.—Clari; The Brigand.
    W.—The Robbers; La Tour de Nesle.

24. *Monday:*
    N.—Wild Oats; Family Jars.
    C.—Robert Kyd; White Milliner.
    W.—La Tour de Nesle; Golden Farmer.

25.   N.—Honey Moon; Fish out of Water.
    C.—Clari; Robert Kyd.
    W.—Lost Heir; Thalaba.

26.   N.—Charles O'Malley; Two Gregories.
    C.—Irish Ambassador; Brigand.
    W.—La Tour de Nesle; Thalaba.

27.   N.—The Rise of the Rothschilds *: *Rothschild*—W. Jones, *Timothy*—Burton; Charles O'Malley.
    C.—Sergeant of Austerlitz; Mrs. White.
    W.—Woman's the Devil; Thalaba.

28.   N.—A Cure for the Heartache; Mummy.
    C.—The Secret; Manager's Daughter.
    W.—The Stranger; Thalaba.

29.   N.—The Green Eyed Monster; Miller's Maid. Last night of the season.
    C.—What will the World Say?; Victorine.
    W.—Thalaba; La Fitte.

31. *Monday:*
    C.—My Sister Kate; How to pay Rent.
    W.—Nature and Philosophy; The Carpenter of Rouen.

FEBRUARY

1. *Tuesday:*
   C.—Faint Heart never won Fair Lady; The Brigand.
   W.—Agnes de Vere; Tom and Jerry.
2. C.—Faint Heart never won Fair Lady; The Review.
   W.—Pizarro.
3. C.—The Ransom; My Wife's Dentist *: *Dick*—Richings.
   W.—The Carpenter of Rouen; Phila., as it Is.
4. C.—Faint Heart never won Fair Lady; My Wife's Dentist.
   W.—Rob Roy; Love and Madness.
5. C.—Sergeant of Austerlitz; My Wife's Dentist.
   W.—The Brigand; The Jersey Girl.
7. *Monday:*
   C.—Rent Day; The Secret.
   W.—Rail Road Depot; Warlock of the Glen.
8. C.—No performance.
   W.—The White Farm; Day after the Wedding.
9. C.—Nina Sforza *: *Nina*—Mrs. Seymour, *Doria*—Richings,
   Ugone—Wood, *D'Estalo*—Charles, *Brigitta*—Mrs.
   Thayer; Faint Heart never won Fair Lady.
   W.—Two Gregories; Spoiled Child.
10. C.—Nina Sforza.
    W.—Two Gregories; Spoiled Child.
11. C.—Nina Sforza; The Secret.
    W.—Loan of a Lover; Rail Road Depot.
12. C.—Guy Mannering; A Maiden's Fame.
    W.—Poor Soldier; Sudden Thoughts.
14. *Monday:*
    C.—Nina Sforza; Maid of Munster.
    W.—The Robbers.
15. C.—Nina Sforza; A Roland for an Oliver.
    W.—The Robbers.
16. C.—Nina Sforza; Fashionable Arrivals.
    W.—The Young Widow; Tom Cringle's Log.
17. C.—School for Scandal; Fashionable Arrivals.
    W.—Sudden Thoughts; The Dream at Sea.
18. C.—Fashionable Arrivals; Oliver Twist.
    W.—Fox and Wolf; The Dream at Sea.
19. C.—Fashionable Arrivals; Boarding School.
    W.—La Fitte.
21. *Monday:*
    C.—Clari; A Maiden's Fame.
    W.—The Last Days of Pompeii.
22. C.—My Wife's Dentist; Oliver Twist.
    W.—The Last Days of Pompeii.

23.   C.—Home, Sweet Home; Oliver Twist.
       W.—The Last Days of Pompeii.
24.   C.—Nina Sforza; Home, Sweet Home.
       W.—Richelieu.
25.   C.—Guy Mannering; Simpson and Co.
       W.—The Last Days of Pompeii.
26.   C.—My Wife's Dentist; Green Eyed Monster.
       W.—Richard III; Lo Zingaro.
28. *Monday:*
       C.—Home, Sweet Home; Boarding School.
       W.—Skeleton Witness.

MARCH

1. *Tuesday:*
       C.—No play. Dr. Lardner's lectures on the moon.
       W.—Skeleton Witness.
2.   C.—No advertisement.
       W.—Wallace.
       A.—Die Eifersuchtige Frau; Der Nachtwachter; Die Helden.
3.   C.—Dr. Lardner's lectures.
       W.—Wallace.
4.   C.—My Wife's Dentist; Loan of a Lover.
       W.—Last Days of Pompeii; Manfredi.
5.   C.—Dr. Lardner's lectures.
       W.—Last Days of Pompeii.
7. *Monday:*
       C.—Love Chase; My Wife's Dentist.
       W.—Manfredi.
8.   C.—Dr. Lardner's lectures.
       W.—Surgeon of Paris; Irish Tutor.
9.   C.—Nicholas Nickleby; The Waterman.
       W.—The Secret; The Dead Shot.
10.   C.—Dr. Lardner's lectures.
       W.—Surgeon of Paris.
11.   C.—Love Chase; Robber's Wife.
       W.—Manfredi.
12.   C.—Dr. Lardner's lectures.
       W.—Werner; Nick of the Woods.
14. *Monday:*
       C.—Love; Youthful Queen.
       W.—Damon and Pythias; The Pilot.
15.   C.—Richard III; My Wife's Dentist.
       W.—William Tell.
16.   C.—Nicholas Nickleby; My Wife's Dentist.
       W.—Virginius.

[261]

17. C.—Dr. Lardner's lectures.
     W.—Pizarro.
18. C.—Dr. Lardner's lectures.
     W.—The Young Widow; Skeleton Witness.
19. C.—Dr. Lardner's lectures.
     W.—Nick of the Woods.
21. *Monday:*
     C.—Dr. Lardner's lectures.
     W.—Nick of the Woods; Last Days of Pompeii.
22. C.—Closed. To be opened March 23 by L. T. Pratt and W. E.
         Burton and their two companies.
     W.—Nick of the Woods.
23. C.—Money; State Secrets.
     W.—Rail Road Depot; St. George and the Dragon.
24. W.—The Patrician and the Parvenu; Rent Day.
     W.—St. George and the Dragon; Nick of the Woods.
25. C.—Hunchback; His First Champagne.
     W.—St. George and the Dragon; Nick of the Woods.
26. C.—Paul Pry; Charles O'Malley.
     W.—El Hyder; Nick of the Woods.
28. *Monday:*
     C.—Money; Innkeeper's Daughter.
     W.—Sherwood Forest; Therese.
     A.—Lady of Lyons; La Tour de Nesle.
29. C.—Henry IV; Wandering Minstrel.
     W.—Sherwood Forest; William Tell.
     A.—Damon and Pythias; Black Eyed Susan.
30. C.—Jonathan in England; Kentuckian.
     W.—Richard III; Rail Road Depot.
     A.—Pizarro; Raising the Wind.
31. C.—Rip Van Winkle; Mons. Mallet.
     W.—No bill received.
     A.—Virginius; My Neighbor's Wife.

APRIL

1. *Friday:*
    C.—King Lear; His First Champagne.
    W.—Othello; Pleasant Neighbors.
    A.—Hofer; Family Jars.
2. C.—Merry Wives of Windsor; His Last Legs.
    W.—Hamlet; Dead Shot.
    A.—Hofer; Hazard of the Die.
4. *Monday:*
    C.—Past and Present; Pickwick Club.
    W.—New Way To Pay Old Debts; Spitfire.

A.—Hazard of the Die; Married Rake.
5. C.—Charles O'Malley; Mr. and Mrs. Pringle.
W.—King Lear; Spitfire.
A.—The Robbers; Married Rake.
6. C.—Past and Present; Charles O'Malley.
W.—Richard III; The Review.
A.—Charles II; Nick of the Woods.
7. C.—My Aunt; Ten Thousand a Year *: *Aubrey*—Wood, *Titmouse*—Burton, *Kate*—Mrs. G. Jones.
W.—Sergeant's Wife; The Omnibus.
A.—The Robbers; Nick of the Woods.
8. C.—Ten Thousand a Year; Pickwick Club.
W.—Spitfire; Bear Hunters of the Pyrenees.
A.—Wallace; The Purse.
9. C.—The Groves of Blarney; Rosina.
W.—The Omnibus; New Notions.
A.—The Warrior of the Wave; The Carpenter of Rouen.
11. *Monday:*
C.—Lady of Lyons; Pickwick Club.
W.—Sergeant's Wife; Yankee Pedlar.
A.—Warrior of the Wave; Married Rake.
12. C.—Macbeth; Three Hats.
W.—Jonathan in England; Wife for a Day.
A.—Warrior of the Wave; My Neighbor's Wife.
13. C.—Jack Cade; My Wife's Dentist.
W.—Sergeant's Wife; New Notions.
A.—Richelieu; The Purse.
14. C.—Richelieu; His First Champagne.
W.—Green Mountain Boy; The Hypocrite.
A.—Amaldi *: *Amaldi*—E. S. Conner, *Celestina*—Miss Porter; Blue Devils.
15. C.—King Lear; Rosina.
W.—Jonathan in England; Seth Slope.
A.—Amaldi; Spitfire.
16. C.—Damon and Pythias; Metamora.
W.—Jonathan in England; Seth Slope.
A.—Robber's Wife; Spitfire.
18. *Monday:*
C.—Jack Cade; Pickwick Club.
W.—Richard III; Robin Hood.
A.—Rent Day; Pleasant Neighbors.
19. C.—Gladiator; My Fellow Clerk.
W.—Bertram; Turn Out.
A.—Carpenter of Rouen; What Have I Done?
20. C.—Othello; Mummy.
W.—Macbeth; Pleasant Neighbors.

A.—Amaldi; Irish Lion.
21. C.—Jack Cade; Gladiator.
  W.—The Apostate; Poor Soldier.
  A.—Wallace; Irish Lion.
22. C.—Ten Thousand a Year; Groves of Blarney.
  W.—Merchant of Venice; Mountaineers.
  A.—Heir at Law; The Robber's Wife.
23. C.—Romeo and Juliet.
  W.—Bertram; Nick of the Woods.
  A.—Sardanapalus; Miser of Southwark Ferry.
25. *Monday:*
  C.—The Bubbles of the Day; Hobbs, Dobbs, and Stubs *:
   Hobbs—Burton.
  W.—Sweethearts and Wives; Skeleton Witness.
  A.—Iron Chest; Oh! Hush!!
26. C.—The Bubbles of the Day.
  W.—The Haunted Inn; Hunting a Turtle.
  A.—Richard III; Oh! Hush!!
27. C.—Sweethearts and Wives; Hobbs, Dobbs, and Stubs.
  W.—Hunting a Turtle; Golden Farmer.
  A.—Othello; Bank Monster.
28. C.—Paul Pry; Black Eyed Susan.
  W.—Haunted Inn; Golden Farmer.
  A.—The Robbers; Phila. Assurance.
29. C.—Wild Oats; Tom Noddy's Secret.
  W.—The Padlock; Golden Farmer.
  A.—New Way To Pay Old Debts; Blue Devils.
30. C.—Secrets Worth Knowing; Poor Soldier.
  W.—George Barnwell; Two Gregories.
  A.—Richard III; The Purse.

MAY

2. *Monday:*
  C.—Zanoni; Irish Tutor.
  W.—Golden Farmer; Surgeon of Paris.
  A.—Damon and Pythias; Pleasant Neighbors.
3. C.—Zanoni; Irish Tutor.
  W.—Tom and Jerry; Mob, the Outlaw.
  A.—Carpenter of Rouen; Turnpike Gate.
4. C.—Young Quaker; Turnpike Gate.
  W.—Golden Farmer; Mob, the Outlaw.
  A.—Lucille; Our Mary Ann.
5. C.—Zanoni; Young Widow.
  W.—Rogueries of Thomas; Floating Beacon.
  A.—Damon and Pythias; Swiss Cottage.

6.   C.—Zanoni; Young Widow.
       W.—Charlotte Temple; Valentine and Orson.
       A.—King Lear; Pleasant Neighbors.
7.   C.—Foundling of the Forest; Turning the Tables.
       W.—Boz; Kate Kearney. Last night of the season.
       A.—Lady of Lyons; Dead Shot.
9. *Monday:*
       C.—Tom Noddy's Secret; Turning the Tables.
       A.—Six Degrees of Crime; Minerali.
10.   C.—Poor Gentleman; Ladies' Man.
       A.—Six Degrees of Crime; Minerali.
11.   C.—No bill received.
       A.—William Tell; Six Degrees of Crime.
12.   C.—No advertisement.
       A.—Bear Hunters of the Pyrenees; A Day in Paris.
13.   C.—No advertisement.
       A.—Golden Farmer; Swiss Cottage.
       W.—Mary, Queen of Scots; Boz.
14.   A.—Six Degrees of Crime; La Tour de Nesle.
       W.—Mary, Queen of Scots; Boz.
16. *Monday:*
       A.—The Heir and Highwayman; Actress of all Work.
       W.—Stewart's Capture; Ninth Statue.
17.   A.—Heir and Highwayman; Actress of all Work.
       W.—Stewart's Capture; The Vagrant.
18.   A.—Heir and Highwayman; Kabri.
       W.—Stewart's Capture; The Vagrant.
19.   A.—Lochinvar; Heir and Highwayman.
       W.—Stewart's Capture; Mary, Queen of Scots.
20.   A.—Six Degrees of Crime; Married Rake.
       W.—Stewart's Capture; Mary, Queen of Scots.
21.   A.—Hunchback; Faith and Falsehood.
       W.—Stewart's Capture; Ninth Statue.
23. *Monday:*
       A.—Walter Lynch *: *Walter*—E. S. Conner, *Roderick*—C.
       Porter, *Dominic*—Gann, *Anastacia*—Miss Porter; A Ro-
       land for an Oliver.
       W.—Damon and Pythias; Stewart's Capture.
24.   A.—Walter Lynch; A Roland for an Oliver.
       W.—Othello; The Floating Beacon.
25.   A.—Six Degrees of Crime; Faith and Falsehood.
       W.—William Tell; Apostate.
26.   A.—Richard III; Pleasant Neighbors.
       W.—Damon and Pythias; Stewart's Capture.
27.   A.—Six Degrees of Crime; A Father by Chance.
       W.—Pizarro; Stewart's Capture.

28.   A.—La Fitte; Nick of the Woods.
        W.—New Way To Pay Old Debts, fifth act; Clandare.

30. *Monday:*
        A.—La Fitte; Nick of the Woods.
        W.—Virginius; Therese.

31.   A.—Faith and Falsehood; La Fitte.
        W.—Floating Beacon; Boz.

JUNE

1. *Wednesday:*
        A.—La Fitte; Turnpike Gate.
        W.—Iron Chest; Hamlet, third act.

2.   A.—Columbus; Black Eyed Susan.
        W.—Ninth Statue; Stewart's Capture.

3.   A.—Columbus; A Father by Chance.
        W.—Boz; How To Pay Rent.

4.   A.—Rob Roy; Honest Thieves.
        W.—Robert Macaire; Stewart's Capture.

6. *Monday:*
        A.—Forest Fiend; Weathercock.
        W.—Maid of Croissy; Bombastes Furioso.

7.   A.—Forest Fiend; Comfortable Service.
        W.—Robert Macaire; Good Night's Rest.

8.   A.—Lovers' Quarrels; Wives as they Were.
        W.—My Young Wife; Stewart's Capture.

9.   A.—Perfection; Comfortable Service.
        W.—Maid of Croissy; My Wife's Dentist.

10.   A.—Alfonso; Irish Tutor.
        W.—Forty and Fifty; My Wife's Dentist.

11.   A.—Pizarro; Irishman in London.
        W.—Robert Macaire; Jacques Strop.

13. *Monday:*
        A.—Alfonso; King and the Deserter.
        W.—Victorine; My Wife's Dentist.

14.   A.—Comfortable Service; The Pilot.
        W.—Rob Roy; Hunting a Turtle.

15.   A.—The Pilot.
        W.—Wizard of the Heath; Tom and Jerry.

16.   A.—Adelgitha; Irishman in London.
        W.—Boz; Wizard of the Heath.

17.   A.—Rob Roy.
        W.—Two Gregories; Haunted Inn.

18.   A.—Point of Honor; Middy Ashore.
        W.—Raymond and Agnes; Oh! Hush!!

20. *Monday:*
    A.—Adelgitha; Catching an Heiress.
    W.—Quadrupeds; Stewart's Capture.
21.   A.—Merchant of Venice, trial scene; Robert Emmet.
    W.—What will the World Say?; Quadrupeds.
22.   A.—Honey Moon; Hunting a Turtle.
    W.—Mary Tudor; Hunting a Turtle.
23.   A.—Robert Emmet; He Lies like Truth.
    W.—Mary Tudor; Pleasant Neighbors.
24.   A.—Raising the Wind; Brian Boroihme.
    W.—What will Mrs. Jones Say?; Mary Tudor.
25.   A.—Adopted Child.
    W.—Jamie of Aberdeen; Mary Tudor.
27. *Monday:*
    A.—Robber's Wife; Horse and Widow.
    W.—Town and Country; Stewart's Capture.
28.   A.—Brian Boroihme; Horse and Widow.
    W.—Wizard of the Heath; Jamie of Aberdeen.
29.   A.—Hunchback; Three Simpsons.
    W.—New Way To Pay Old Debts; A Chip of the Old Block.
30.   A.—Alfonso; Three Simpsons.
    W.—Mungo Park *: *Karfa*—Drisbach, *Mungo*—Davenport;
    Haunted Inn.

JULY

1. *Friday:*
    A.—The Pilot; Swiss Cottage.
    W.—Mungo Park; Haunted Inn.
2.   A.—Alexander the Great; Star Spangled Banner.
    W.—The Daughter; Mungo Park.
4. *Monday:*
    A.—Hero of the North; Vagaries of the Day.
    W.—Mungo Park; Marco Bombo.
5.   A.—Frederick the Great; Star Spangled Banner.
    W.—My Companion in Arms.
6.   A.—A Roland for an Oliver; Perfection.
    W.—Turn Out; Lion of the Desert.
7.   A.—Military Execution; Fortune's Frolic.
    W.—Young Widow; Lion of the Desert.
8.   A.—Six Degrees of Crime; Middy Ashore.
    W.—Lion of the Desert; Two Gregories.
9.   A.—Sweethearts and Wives; Nick of the Woods.
    W.—Lady and the Devil; Lion of the Desert.
11. *Monday:*
    A.—Money; Hundred-Pound Note.

W.—Lion of the Desert; Mungo Park.
12.   A.—Englishman in India; A Roland for an Oliver.
W.—Lion of the Desert; Mungo Park.
13.   A.—School for Scandal; Wandering Minstrel.
W.—Lion of the Desert; Mungo Park.
14.   A.—Money; Gretna Green.
W.—Idiot Witness; The Beacon of Death.
15.   A.—Charles II; Englishman in India.
W.—Swiss Cottage; A Day in Paris.
16.   A.—Rose of Arragon; Promissory Note.
W.—Barrack Room; Snapping Turtle.
18. *Monday:*
  A.—Rake's Progress; Humbug.
  W.—My Little Hotel; Joseph Bragg.
19.   A.—Rake's Progress; A Roland for an Oliver.
W.—My Old Woman; Belle of the Hotel.
20.   A.—Ion; No Song, No Supper.
W.—My Little Adopted; Joseph Bragg.
21.   A.—Charles II; The Pilot.
W.—Two Gregories; Out of Place.
22.   A.—Alexander the Great; Promissory Note.
W.—A Kiss in the Dark; Out of Place.
23.   A.—Adrian and Orrilla; Tom and Jerry.
W.—Ladies' Club; Belle of the Hotel.
25. *Monday:*
  A.—Romeo and Juliet; Irish Tutor.
  W.—Fashionable Friends; Married Yesterday.
26.   A.—Black Brig of Bermuda; Three Simpsons.
W.—Ladies' Club; Widow Wiggins. Last night of the season.
27.   A.—The Rivals; No Song, No Supper.
28.   A.—Emilia; Weathercock.
29.   A.—No advertisement.
30.   A.—Firemen of Phila.; Jersey Girl.

AUGUST

1. *Monday:*
  A.—Country Girl; Broken Sword.
2.   A.—Nervous Man; My Poll and my Partner Joe.
3.   A.—La Tour de Nesle; Stewart's Triumph.
4.   A.—Gambler's Fate; My Poll and my Partner Joe.
5.   A.—Emilia; Weathercock.
6.   A.—Two Foscari; Sailor's Dream.
8. *Monday:*
  A.—Six Degrees of Crime; Miller and his Men.

9.   A.—Patrician and the Parvenu; Animal Magnetism.
10.   A.—Dutch Burgomaster; May Queen.
11.   A.—Man and Wife; Wreck Ashore.
12.   A.—Paul Pry; Patrician and the Parvenu.
13.   A.—Pickwick Club; Quaker Girls.
15.   *Monday:*
      A.—Much Ado about Nothing; The Vampire.
16.   A.—Macbeth; The Secret.
17.   A.—Richelieu; Horse and Widow.
18.   A.—Richard III; The Secret.
19.   A.—Shoemaker of Toulouse; Irish Tutor.
20.   A.—Ugolino; Shoemaker of Toulouse.
22.   *Monday:*
      A.—Shoemaker of Toulouse; Adopted Child.
23.   A.—Magpie and the Maid; Irish Valet.
24.   A.—Gambler's Fate; Dead Shot.
25.   A.—Two Firemen; Monday Baptist.
26.   A.—Sea Captain; White Scarf.
27.   A.—Kill or Cure; Quaker Girls. Last night of the season.

SEPTEMBER

10.   *Saturday:*
      A.—Louise; Spitfire.
12.   *Monday:*
      A.—Virginius; Crowded Houses.
13.   A.—Maurice, the Woodcutter; Adopted Child.
14.   A.—Maurice, the Woodcutter; Children in the Wood.
15.   A.—Venice Preserved; Simpson and Company.
16.   A.—Macbeth; Dead Shot.
17.   A.—Othello; Day after the Wedding.
      C.—Man of the Wood; Borrowed Feathers.
19.   *Monday:*
      A.—John Jones; My Master's Rival.
      C.—Lady of Lyons; A Lover by Proxy.
20.   A.—Peter Bell; De Nacht Wachter.
      C.—Wives as they Were; Luke the Laborer.
21.   A.—Belle's Stratagem; Too Late for Dinner.
      C.—Rob Roy; A Lover by Proxy.
22.   A.—Road to Ruin; Green Eyed Monster.
      C.—Bride of Lammermoor; The New Footman.
      W.—Belle's Stratagem; Nabob for an Hour.
23.   A.—She Stoops to Conquer; Robert Macaire.
      C.—Man of the World; New Footman.
      W.—School for Scandal; A Roland for an Oliver.

24.   A.—Old English Gentleman; Victorine.
       C.—Belford Castle; New Footman.
       W.—Rivals; Dumb Belle.

26. *Monday:*
       A.—Love, Law, and Physic; Woman's Life.
       C.—Belford Castle; New Footman.
       W.—Macbeth; Windmill.

27.   A.—Charcoal Burner; Therese.
       C.—Belford Castle; My Wife's Dentist.
       W.—Hunchback; Windmill.

28.   A.—Is He Jealous?; Dead Shot.
       C.—Peter and Paul *: *Paul*—Andrews, *Peter*—Maywood;
         New Footman.
       W.—Gwinneth Vaughan; Windmill.

29.   A.—The Taming of the Shrew; Shoemaker of Toulouse.
       C.—Peter and Paul; A Lover by Proxy.
       W.—Gwinneth Vaughan; Windmill.

30.   A.—Village Coquette; La Sylphide, ballet.
       C.—Closed.
       W.—Cape May Will; The Review.

OCTOBER

1. *Saturday:*
       A.—Mysterious Visitor; Nathalie.
       C.—Closed.
       W.—Barrack Room; Cape May Will.

3. *Monday:*
       A.—Three Weeks after Marriage; Nathalie.
       C.—Dr. Lardner's lectures upon the French Revolution.
       W.—Sixteen String Jack; Agreeable Surprise.

4.   A.—Wreck Ashore; Mummy.
       C.—Dr. Lardner on French Revolution.
       W.—Sixteen String Jack; Golden Farmer.

5.   A.—Pizarro; Sudden Thoughts.
       C.—Dr. Lardner on Physical Science.
       W.—Sixteen String Jack; Dream of the Future.

6.   A.—Grumbling; Cheap Boarding.
       C.—Dr. Lardner, on French Revolution.
       W.—Sixteen String Jack; Dream of the Future.

7.   A.—Ugolino; Four Sisters.
       C.—Dr. Lardner, on Physical Science.
       W.—Sixteen String Jack; Golden Farmer.

8.   A.—The Pilot; Jersey Girl.
       C.—Dr. Lardner, on French Revolution.
       W.—Oliver Twist; Mob, the Outlaw.

10. *Monday:*
    A.—The Gondolier; Ben the Boatswain.
    C.—Dr. Lardner, on French Revolution.
    W.—Hamlet; Lady of Lyons, musical burlesque.
11.   A.—No advertisement.
    · C.—Lady of Lyons; Borrowed Feathers.
    W.—Much Ado about Nothing; Oliver Twist.
12.   A.—Agnes de Vere; Perfection.
    C.—Peter and Paul; A Lover by Proxy.
    W.—Hamlet; Golden Farmer.
13.   A.—Louise; Agnes de Vere.
    C.—Abduction; Peter and Paul.
    W.—Richard III; Sixteen String Jack.
14.   A.—Michael Earl; Loan of a Lover.
    C.—Abduction; My Wife's Dentist.
    W.—The Wife; Mob, the Outlaw.
15.   A.—A Dream at Sea; Fire Raiser.
    C.—Loan of a Lover; Abduction.
    W.—Lady of Lyons; Pizarro.
17. *Monday:*
    A.—Retribution; A Dream at Sea.
    C.—Marie du Cange *: *Marie*—Mlle. Celeste; Swiss Swains.
    W.—Othello; Rail Road Depot.
18.   A.—Damon and Pythias; Gondolier.
    C.—Marie du Cange; French Spy.
    W.—Damon and Pythias; Twin Sisters.
19.   A.—Retribution; Maniac Lover.
    C.—Marie du Cange; French Spy.
    W.—Macbeth; Twin Sisters.
20.   A.—Richelieu; Young Widow.
    C.—Marie du Cange; St. Mary's Eve.
    W.—Vagrant; Twin Sisters.
21.   A.—Rob Roy; A Lover by Proxy.
    C.—Marie du Cange; St. Mary's Eve.
    W.—Nick of the Woods; Pretty Girls of Stilberg.
22.   A.—Capt. John Rock; Milford Castle.
    C.—Foreign Affairs *: *Baron*—Andrews, *Count*—Mlle. Celeste; Marie du Cange.
    W.—Oliver Twist; Incendiary.
24. *Monday:*
    A.—Court Fool; Capt. John Rock.
    C.—The Banker *: *Maxwell*—Maywood, *Clara*—Miss Maywood; Youthful Queen.
    W.—Metamora; Pretty Girls of Stilberg.
25.   A.—Blood Red Knight; The Vampire.
    C.—The Banker; Aladdin.

       W.—Richelieu; Pretty Girls of Stilberg.

26.   A.—Fair Philadelphia; Blood Red Knight.
       C.—Foreign Affairs; Wept of Wish-Ton-Wish.

27.   A.—House Room; New Footman.
       C.—Foreign Affairs; French Spy.
       W.—Metamora; Pretty Girls of Stilberg.

28.   A.—Stranger; Simpson and Company.
       C.—Wept of Wish-Ton-Wish; Wizard Skiff.
       W.—Jack Cade; Pretty Girls of Stilberg.

29.   A.—Fate of Calas; Miller and his Men.
       C.—Child of the Wreck; Wizard Skiff.
       W.—King Lear; Pizarro.

31. *Monday:*
       A.—Jane Shore; Fate of Calas.
       C.—School for Scandal; Irish Lion.
       W.—Jack Cade; Pretty Girls of Stilberg.

NOVEMBER

1. *Tuesday:*
       A.—The Vampire; Sudden Thoughts.
       C.—The Rivals; Teddy the Tiler.
       W.—Lady of Lyons; Pretty Girls of Stilberg.

2.   A.—Dumb Belle; Blue Devils.
       C.—London Assurance; Red Gauntlet *: *Peter*—Maywood, *Joshua*—Andrews.
       W.—Virginius; Pretty Girls of Stilberg.

3.   A.—Dream at Sea; Melmoth.
       C.—London Assurance; Irish Tutor.
       W.—Richelieu; Gladiator.

4.   A.—Bellamira; Tom and Jerry.
       C.—Born to Good Luck; Irish Tutor.
       W.—Jack Cade; Therese.

5.   A.—Soldier's Daughter; Zembuca.
       C.—Wonder; Irish Lion.
       W.—Road to Ruin; Meet me by Moonlight.

7. *Monday:*
       A.—Stag Hall; Kill or Cure.
       C.—Love Chase; Born to Good Luck.
       W.—King O'Neil; Green Eyed Monster.

8.   A.—Begone Dull Care; My Own Ghost.
       C.—Irish Ambassador; Married Rake.
       W.—The West End; Meet me by Moonlight.

9.   A.—Old English Gentleman; Stag Hall.
       C.—Hunchback; His Last Legs.
       W.—The West End; Oliver Twist.

10.   A.—Something Original *: *Jack*—Burton, *Solomon*—Owens; Ladies' Man.
    C.—Love Chase; Irish Ambassador.
    W.—The West End; Agreeable Surprise.

11.   A.—Drunkard's Progress *: *Vernon*—J. G. Porter, *Patty*—Mrs. Altemus; Irish Lion.
    C.—Jealous Wife; Enthusiasm.
    W.—She Would and she Would Not; Uncle John.

12.   A.—Love's Disguises; Happy Man.
    C.—Honey Moon; Omnibus.
    W.—Speed the Plough; The Anatomist.

14. *Monday:*
    A.—Fate of Calas; His Last Legs.
    C.—Richard III; Three Lovers.
    W.—London Assurance; Teddy the Tiler.

15.   A.—Zembuca; Omnibus.
    C.—New Way To Pay Old Debts; Three Lovers.
    W.—As You Like It; Irish Lion.

16.   A.—No advertisement.
    C.—King Lear; Revolt of the Arabs.
    W.—London Assurance; Married Rake.

17.   A.—No advertisement.
    C.—Hamlet; Revolt of the Arabs.
    W.—London Assurance; Anatomist.

18.   A.—No advertisement.
    C.—Youthful Queen; Revolt of the Arabs.
    W.—London Assurance; Sharratah.

19.   A.—Jonathan Bradford; Falls of Clyde.
    C.—Richard III; Mayor of Garrat.
    W.—London Assurance; Rory O'More.

21. *Monday:*
    A.—Jonathan Bradford; Lover's Revenge.
    C.—Englishmen in India; Life in the Clouds.
    W.—Love Chase; Robert le Diable, incantation scene.

22.   A.—Ocean Child; Jonathan Bradford.
    C.—The Banker; My Wife's Dentist.
    W.—Wonder; Omnibus.

23.   A.—Charles O'Malley; Ocean Child.
    C.—Provoked Husband; Life in the Clouds.
    W.—Money; La Bayadere.

24.   A.—Falls of Clyde; Ocean Child.
    C.—Foreign Graces; Aladdin.
    W.—Six Degrees of Crime; Pretty Girls of Stilberg.

25.   A.—No advertisement.
    C.—Life in the Clouds; Flying Dutchman.
    W.—London Assurance; Rory O'More.

26.   A.—Natty Bumpo; Ocean Child.
       C.—Inheritance; Youthful Queen.
       W.—Love's Sacrifice; Omnibus.

28. *Monday:*
       A.—Natty Bumpo; Grumbler.
       C.—Miller's Maid; Flying Dutchman.
       W.—Henry IV; Devil's Bridge.

29.   A.—Natty Bumpo; Incendiary.
       C.—Inheritance; Phila. Assurance.
       W.—Jonathan in England; Kentuckian.

30.   A.—Clandare; Natty Bumpo.
       C.—No advertisement.
       W.—Henry IV; Rail Road Depot.

DECEMBER

1. *Thursday:*
       A.—No bill received.
       C.—No advertisement.
       W.—Rip Van Winkle; Mons. Tonson.

2.   A.—No bill received.
       C.—No advertisement.
       W.—Richard III; A Roland for an Oliver.

3.   A.—No bill received.
       C.—No advertisement.
       W.—Merry Wives of Windsor; Mons. Tonson.

5. *Monday:*
       C.—First night of the opera season, La Sonnambula; A Day in
          Paris.
       W.—London Assurance; Love Laughs at Locksmiths.

6.   C.—La Sonnambula; A Day in Paris.
       W.—Rob Roy; Oliver Twist.

7.   C.—Barber of Seville; Familiar Friend.
       W.—No advertisement.

8.   C.—Barber of Seville; Familiar Friend.
       W.—No advertisement.

9.   C.—Barber of Seville; La Sonnambula, third act.
       W.—No advertisement.

10.   C.—Postilion of Lonjumeau; Familiar Friend.
       W.—No advertisement.

12. *Monday:*
       C.—Postilion of Lonjumeau; A Day in Paris.

13.   C.—Postilion of Lonjumeau; Familiar Friend.
       W.—John Overy; Pretty Girls of Stilberg.

14.   C.—Postilion of Lonjumeau; Familiar Friend.
       W.—John Overy; Black Raven of the Tombs.

15.   C.—Closed.
      W.—John Overy; Black Raven of the Tombs.
16.   C.—Israelites in Egypt.
      W.—John Overy; Black Raven of the Tombs.
17.   C.—Israelites in Egypt.
      W.—Sarah, the Jewess; Black Raven of the Tombs.
19.   *Monday:*
      C.—Israelites in Egypt.
      W.—Sarah the Jewess; Black Raven of the Tombs.
20.   C.—Israelites in Egypt.
      W.—Sentinel; Black Raven of the Tombs.
21.   C.—Israelites in Egypt.
      W.—Sentinel; Black Raven of the Tombs.
22.   C.—Israelites in Egypt.
      W.—Sentinel; Black Raven of the Tombs.
23.   C.—Fra Diavolo; Olympic Revels.
      W.—No Song, No Supper; Black Raven of the Tombs.
24.   C.—Inheritance; Faint Heart never won Fair Lady.
      W.—Black Raven of the Tombs; Richard III.
26.   *Monday:*
      C.—Cinderella; Faint Heart never won Fair Lady.
      W.—Carpenter of Rouen; Black Raven of the Tombs.
27.   C.—Cinderella; My Wife's Dentist.
      W.—Love Laughs at Locksmiths; Black Raven of the Tombs.
28.   C.—Barber of Seville; Familiar Friend.
      W.—No advertisement.
29.   C.—Cinderella; A Day in Paris.
      W.—Carpenter of Rouen; Black Raven of the Tombs.
30.   C.—Norma; Youthful Queen.
      W.—Pleasant Dreams; Black Raven of the Tombs.
31.   C.—Warden of Galway; Lady of the Lake.
      W.—Surgeon of Paris; Black Raven of the Tombs.

JANUARY 1843

2.   *Monday:*
      C.—Warden of Galway; Lady of the Lake.
      W.—Surgeon of Paris; Black Raven of the Tombs.
3.   C.—No performance.
      W.—Surgeon of Paris; Black Raven of the Tombs.
4.   C.—No performance.
      W.—Love's Frailty; Black Raven of the Tombs.
5.   C.—Guy Mannering; No!
      W.—Love's Frailty; Black Raven of the Tombs.
6.   C.—Rob Roy; No Song, No Supper.
      W.—Love's Frailty; Black Raven of the Tombs.

7.   C.—Devil's Bridge; No!
    W.—Mutiny of the Nore; Black Raven of the Tombs.

9.   *Monday:*
    C.—Norma; Olympic Revels.
    W.—Conjuror; Alice Gray.
    O.—H-ll on Earth; Kill or Cure.

10.   C.—Norma Rendezvous.
    W.—Richard III; Seth Slope.
    O.—H-ll on Earth; Is She Married?

11.   C.—Norma; Rendezvous.
    W.—La Tour de Nesle; Pretty Girls of Stilberg.
    O.—Ladies' Man; H-ll on Earth.

12.   C.—Lady of Lyons; Riever's Ransom.
    W.—New Way To Pay Old Debts; Green Mountain Boy.
    O.—Christening; H-ll on Earth.

13.   C.—Norma; Olympic Revels.
    W.—Town and Country; Wife for a Day.
    O.—Christine of Sweden; H-ll on Earth.

14.   C.—Rendezvous; Ice Witch.
    W.—Mountaineers; Yankee Pedlar.
    O.—Jack Sheppard; H-ll on Earth.

16.   *Monday:*
    C.—Norma; Ice Witch.
    W.—Hamlet; People's Lawyer.
    O.—Abelard and Heloise; Jack Sheppard.

17.   C.—Cinderella; Ice Witch.
    W.—Iron Chest; People's Lawyer.
    O.—Abelard and Heloise; Dead Shot.

18.   C.—La Sonnambula; Olympic Revels.
    W.—Carpenter of Rouen; Carli.
    O.—Sergeant's Wife; Abelard and Heloise.

19.   C.—Israelites in Egypt; Familiar Friend.
    W.—Paul Pry; also, esquestrian troupe.

20.   C.—Masaniello; Rendezvous.
    W.—Pleasant Dreams; Conjuror.

21.   C.—Masaniello; Olympic Revels.
    W.—Alice Gray.

23.   *Monday:*
    C.—Masaniello; Ice Witch.
    W.—Alice Gray.

24.   C.—Closed.
    W.—Surgeon of Paris; Dr. Dilworth.

25.   C.—Marriage of Figaro; Masaniello.
    W.—Lucky Stars; Secret Mine.

26.   C.—Marriage of Figaro; Masaniello.
    W.—Paul Pry; Secret Mine.

27.   C.—Stabat Mater.
       W.—Secret Mine; What will Mrs. Jones Say?
28.   C.—Fra Diavolo; John of Paris.
       W.—Love Chase; Omnibus.
30. *Monday:*
       C.—Fra Diavolo; John of Paris.
       W.—Love's Sacrifice; Irish Lion.
31.   C.—Fra Diavolo; Masaniello.
       W.—Love's Sacrifice; Omnibus.

FEBRUARY

1. *Wednesday:*
       C.—Norma; The Waterman.
       W.—Hunchback; Married Rake.
2.   C.—Marriage of Figaro; The Waterman.
       W.—Alma Mater; Irishman's Fortune.
3.   C.—Der Freischutz; Familiar Friend.
       W.—Alma Mater; Irishman's Fortune.
4.   C.—Der Freischutz; Rendezvous.
       W.—Irish Ambassador; Alma Mater.
6. *Monday:*
       C.—Blanche of Jersey.
       W.—Alma Mater; Shakespeare's Dream.
7.   C.—Blanche of Jersey; Fra Diavolo.
       W.—Money; Two Gregories.
8.   C.—Blanche of Jersey; Der Freischutz.
       W.—Ion; His Last Legs.
9.   C.—Fra Diavolo; Foreign Graces.
       W.—Alma Mater; Shakespeare's Dream.
10.   C.—La Sonnambula; Foreign Graces.
       W.—Money; Shakespeare's Dream.
11.   C.—Norma; Rendezvous.
       W.—Bubbles of the Day; Love Chase.
13. *Monday:*
       C.—Zampa; Cramond Brig.
       W.—Broken Heart; Twice Killed.
14.   C.—Zampa; Cramond Brig.
       W.—Paul Pry; Curiosities.
15.   C.—Zampa; Faint Heart never won Fair Lady.
       W.—The Race Course; Lottery Ticket.
16.   C.—Zampa; Faint Heart never won Fair Lady.
       W.—The Race Course; Sweethearts and Wives.
17.   C.—Norma; Zampa.
       W.—The Race Course; Broken Heart.
18.   C.—Closed. End of operatic season.

W.—Merchant and Mechanic; Wreck Ashore.

20. *Monday:*

W.—Merchant and Mechanic; Boots at the Swan.

21. W.—Surgeon of Paris; Earthquake.

22. W.—Wreck Ashore; Earthquake.

23. W.—Married Life; Oliver Twist.

24. W.—Carpenter of Rouen; Earthquake.

25. W.—Naval Engagements; Black Raven of the Tombs.

27. *Monday:*

W.—Naval Engagements; Black Raven of the Tombs.

28. W.—Married Life; Black Raven of the Tombs.

MARCH

1. *Wednesday:*

W.—Married Life; Black Raven of the Tombs.

2. W.—Black Raven of the Tombs; American Enterprise.

3. W.—Alice Gray; Black Raven of the Tombs.

4. W.—American Enterprise; Black Raven of the Tombs.

A.—Eugene Aram; Maid of Munster.

6. *Monday:*

W.—Brandywine Springs; Black Raven of the Tombs.

A.—School for Scandal; Spoiled Child.

7. W.—The Sentinel; Black Raven of the Tombs.

A.—Eugene Aram; A Roland for an Oliver.

8. W.—Blanche Heriot; Black Raven of the Tombs.

A.—Steam Dentist; White Horse of the Peppers.

9. W.—Blanche Heriot; Black Raven of the Tombs.

A.—Victorine; Ostler, Robber and Inn-Keeper.

10. W.—Blanche Heriot; Black Raven of the Tombs.

A.—Victorine; Spoiled Child.

11. W.—Lucky Stars; Black Raven of the Tombs.

A.—No advertisement.

13. *Monday:*

W.—Blanche Heriot; Hunters of the Pyrenees.

A.—No advertisement.

14. W.—Blanche Heriot; Hunters of the Pyrenees.

A.—Steam Dentist; Rugantino.

15. W.—Blanche Heriot; Stratagem.

A.—St. Cuthbert's Abbey; Bandit of Corsica.

16. W.—Blanche Heriot; Black Raven of the Tombs.

A.—St. Cuthbert's Abbey; Jack Robinson and his Monkey.

17. W.—La Tour de Nesle; Black Raven of the Tombs.

A.—Climbing Boy; Benevolent Tar.

18. W.—Inch Cape Bell; Six Degrees of Crime.

A.—St. Cuthbert's Abbey; Bandit of Corsica.

20. *Monday:*
    W.—Hunchback; Inch Cape Bell.
    A.—Tempter; Forest Rose.
21.   W.—Irish Ambassador; Born to Good Luck.
    A.—Hamlet; Richard III; fourth and fifth acts.
22.   W.—Honey Moon; His Last Legs.
    A.—Hypocrisy Detected; Don Juan.
23.   W.—Married Life; Irish Tutor.
    A.—No advertisement.
24.   W.—Irish Ambassador; Youthful Queen.
    A.—No advertisement.
25.   W.—Irish Ambassador; Tom and Jerry.
    A.—Land of Washington; Our Old House at Home.
27. *Monday:*
    W.—Conquest of Toronto; Twin Sisters.
    A.—Therese; Robber's Wife.
28.   W.—Irish Lion; Tom and Jerry.
    A.—Richard III; Tempter.
29.   W.—Brutus; Inch Cape Bell.
    A.—No advertisement.
30.   W.—Merry Monarch; Twice Killed.
    A.—Wraith of the Lake; Tempter.
31.   W.—Englishmen in India; Kill or Cure.
    A.—Wraith of the Lake; Land of Washington.

APRIL

1. *Saturday:*
    W.—The Race Course; Peter Bell.
    A.—Robber's Wife; Bombastes Furioso.
3. *Monday:*
    W.—Twin Sisters; Comedy of Errors.
    A.—Vision of Home; Benevolent Tar.
4.   W.—Merchant and Mechanic; Kill, or Cure.
    A.—Richard III; Two Gregories.
5.   W.—Comedy of Errors; Twice Killed.
    A.—No advertisement.
6.   W.—Recruiting Officer; Peter Bell.
    A.—Masaniello; Queer Subject.
7.   W.—Recruiting Officer; X.Y.Z.
    A.—Masaniello; Two Gregories.
8.   W.—Comedy of Errors; Oliver Twist.
    A.—Masaniello; Queer Subject.
10. *Monday:*
    W.—Ask no Questions; Two Barbers.
    A.—Rugantino; Dumb Girl of Genoa.

11. W.—Rivals; Loan of a Lover.
      A.—No advertisement.
12. W.—Brutus; Dumb Man of Manchester.
      A.—No advertisement.
13. W.—Macbeth; Dumb Man of Manchester.
14. W.—Bride of Abydos; Dumb Man of Manchester.
15. W.—Bride of Abydos; Smuggler of Bootle Bay.
17. *Monday:*
      W.—Bride of Abydos; Forest of Bondy.
18. W.—Richard III; Smuggler of Bootle Bay.
19. W.—King Lear; Mayor of Garrat.
20. W.—Julius Caesar; Wandering Minstrel.
21. W.—Forest of Bondy; A Roland for an Oliver.
22. W.—Dumb Man of Manchester; Exile of Erin.
24. *Monday:*
      W.—Muleteer of Palermo; Trial by Battle.
      A.—Richard III; Two Gregories.
25. W.—Muleteer of Palermo; Trial by Battle.
      A.—Therese; Forest Rose.
26. W.—Much Ado about Nothing; Muleteer of Palermo.
      A.—Champion of Cordova; Day after the Wedding.
27. W.—Greek Patriots; Phantom Pilot.
      A.—Champion of Cordova; Day after the Wedding.
28. W.—Hamlet; Scan Mag.
      A.—Champion of Cordova.
29. W.—Rob Roy; Pizarro.
      A.—Iron Chest; Assassin King.

MAY

1. *Monday:*
     W.—Rule a Wife and Have a Wife; Scan Mag.
     A.—Grace Huntley; Dumb Girl of Genoa.
2. W.—Suspicious Husband; Katharine and Petruchio.
     A.—Charles II; Wreck Ashore.
3. W.—Suspicious Husband; Day after the Wedding.
     A.—Yankee Land; Forest Rose.
4. W.—Romeo and Juliet; Rule a Wife and Have a Wife.
     A.—Wool Pedlar; Yankee Land.
5. W.—No advertisement.
     A.—Speculation; Yankee Abroad.
6. W.—Scan Mag; Peter Wilkins.
     A.—Richard III; Wool Pedlar.
8. *Monday:*
     W.—Scan Mag; Peter Wilkins.

A.—Nick of Time *: *Obediah*—J. S. Silsbee, *Lucy*—Mrs. Thoman; Jonathan in England.

9.   W.—Scan Mag; Peter Wilkins.
      A.—Yankee Land; Forest Rose.
10.   W.—Speed the Plough; Peter Wilkins.
      A.—No advertisement.
11.   W.—Peter Wilkins; Sam Patch in France *: *Sam*—Marble, *Farmer*—Philips.
      A.—No advertisement.
12.   W.—She Stoops to Conquer; Peter Wilkins.
13.   W.—Sam Patch in France; Vermont Wool Dealer.
15.   *Monday:*
      W.—Yankee Land; Yankee in Time.
16.   W.—Mummy; Peter Wilkins.
17.   W.—Market Street Merchant *: *Harford*—Philips, *Mapleton*—Wheatley; *Kit*—Burton; Ladies' Man.
18.   W.—Market St. Merchant; Foundling of an Apple Orchard.
19.   W.—Peter Wilkins; Vermonter.
20.   W.—Market St. Merchant; Yankee Farmers.
22.   *Monday:*
      W.—Comfortable Lodgings; Wool Pedlar.
23.   W.—Boston Tea Party; Jonathan in England.
24.   W.—Man and Wife; Forest Rose.
25.   W.—Comfortable Lodgings; X.Y.Z.
26.   W.—Market St. Merchant; Mummy.
27.   W.—Woman's Life; Cousin Lambkin.
29.   *Monday:*
      W.—Brutus; Scan Mag.
30.   W.—Richelieu; Boarding School.
31.   W.—Jack Cade; Dumb Belle.

JUNE

1.   *Thursday:*
      W.—Metamora; Wags of Windsor.
2.   W.—Jack Cade; Young Widow.
3.   W.—Gladiator; Therese.
5.   *Monday:*
      W.—Patrician's Daughter; Abon Hassan.
6.   W.—Patrician's Daughter; Boarding School.
7.   W.—Othello; Valet de Sham.
8.   W.—Patrician's Daughter; Valet de Sham.
9.   W.—Jack Cade; Lucky Stars.
10.   W.—Lady of Lyons; Pizarro.
12.   *Monday:*
      W.—Love's Sacrifice; Oliver Twist.

13. W.—Stranger; Star Spangled Banner.
14. W.—Six Degrees of Crime; Lucky Stars.
15. W.—Rob Roy; Woman's Life.
16. W.—She Stoops to Conquer; Valet de Sham.
17. W.—Tour de Nesle; Star Spangled Banner.
19. *Monday:*
    W.—Thalaba; Pretty Girls of Stilberg.
20. W.—Skeleton Witness; Black Eyed Susan.
21. W.—Thalaba; La Fitte.
22. W.—Paul Jones; La Fitte.
23. W.—Last Days of Pompeii; Scan Mag.
24. W.—Wallace; Nicholas Nickleby.
26. *Monday:*
    W.—Married Life; Blanche Heriot.
27. W.—Last Days of Pompeii; Bombastes Furioso.
28. W.—Town and Country; Pretty Girls of Stilberg.
29. W.—Last Days of Pompeii; Bombastes Furioso.
30. W.—Belle's Stratagem; Two Barbers.

JULY

1. *Saturday:*
    W.—Comedy of Errors; Wager.
3. *Monday:*
    W.—Siege of Boston; Pretty Girls of Stilberg.
4. W.—Glory of Columbia; American Enterprise.
5. W.—Heir at Law; Wager.
6. W.—Der Nacht Wachter; Sweethearts and Wives.
7. W.—Wild Oats; Green Eyed Monster.
8. W.—Begone, Dull Care; Charles O'Malley.
10. *Monday:*
    W.—Cure for the Heartache; Spitfire. Last night of the season.
15. C.—Lucia di Lammermoor.
    W.—Truth; Black Raven of the Tombs.
17. *Monday:*
    C.—Lucia di Lammermoor.
    W.—Binks, the Bagman; Black Raven.
18. C.—Lucia di Lammermoor.
    W.—Binks, the Bagman; Black Raven.
19. C.—Lucia di Lammermoor.
    W.—Our Mary Ann; Black Raven.
20. C.—Lucia di Lammermoor.
    W.—Our Mary Ann; Black Raven.
21. C.—Lucia di Lammermoor.
    W.—Woman's Failing; Black Raven.

22.   C.—Il Puritani.
        W.—Woman's Failing; Three Lovers.
24. *Monday:*
        C.—Il Puritani.
        W.—Binks, the Bagman; The Three Lovers.
25.   C.—Norma.
        W.—Black Raven; Married Maid.
26.   C.—Norma.
        W.—Valet de Sham; Married Rake.
27.   C.—Norma.
        W.—Woman's Failing; Black Raven.
28.   C.—Culprit; Faint Heart never won Fair Lady.
        W.—Our Mary Ann; Three Lovers.
29.   C.—Belisario.
        W.—Lancers; Vol-Au-Vent.
31. *Monday:*
        C.—Norma. Last night of the Italian opera.
        W.—Lancers; Harlequin and the Ocean Imp *: *Leonardo*—
           Smith, *Firebrand*—Barnes, *Fireface*—Parsloe, *Clorinda*—
           Miss Walters.

AUGUST

1. *Tuesday:*
        W.—Lancers; Harlequin and the Ocean Imp.
2.   W.—Binks, the Bagman; Harlequin and the Ocean Imp.
3.   W.—Inquisitive Yankee; Harlequin and the Ocean Imp.
4.   W.—Inquisitive Yankee; Harlequin and the Ocean Imp.
5.   W.—Frolics of Thomas; Harlequin and the Ocean Imp.
7. *Monday:*
        W.—Irish Lion; Harlequin and the Ocean Imp.
8.   W.—Clandare; Gold Bug *: *Friendling*—Charles, *Legrand*—
           Thompson, *Jupiter*—J. H. White, *Old Martha*—Mrs.
           Knight.
9.   W.—Frolics of Thomas; Three Lovers.
10.   W.—Frolics of Thomas; Harlequin and the Ocean Imp.
        A.—Patrician and Parvenu; P.P.
11.   W.—Irish Lion; Harlequin and the Ocean Imp.
        A.—School of Reform; Boots at the Swan.
12.   W.—Our Mary Ann; Black Raven. Last night of the season.
        A.—Woman's Life; Sam Weller.
14. *Monday:*
        A.—Money; Three Lovers.
15.   A.—Othello; Vagrant.
16.   A.—No advertisement.

17. A.—Hawks of Hawk Hollow; Fire Raiser.
18. A.—Hamlet; Rendezvous.
19. A.—Virginius; Vagrant.
21. *Monday:*
     A.—King Lear; Two Gregories.
22. A.—Hamlet; Secret.
23. A.—The Stranger.
24. A.—Soldier's Daughter.
25. A.—Lady of Lyons; Secret.
26. A.—Patrick Lyon.
28. *Monday:*
     A.—Pizarro; Patrick Lyon.
29. A.—Honey Moon; Patrick Lyon.
30. A.—Damon and Pythias; Jack Robinson and his Monkey.
31. A.—William Tell; Rip Van Winkle.

SEPTEMBER

1.   *Friday:*
     A.—Othello; Patrick Lyon.
2.   A.—Patrick Lyon; Spectre Bridegroom.
4.   *Monday:*
     A.—Robbers; Patrick Lyon.
5.   A.—Black Eyed Susan; King's Gardner.
6.   A.—Richard III; Weathercock.
7.   A.—New Way To Pay Old Debts; Sudden Thoughts.
     C.—Man and Wife; Lover by Proxy.
8.   A.—Italian Bride; Patrick Lyon.
     C.—Speed the Plough; Married Rake.
9.   A.—Iron Chest; Raising the Wind.
     C.—Wild Oats; Valet de Sham.
11. *Monday:*
     A.—Six Degrees of Crime; Tour de Nesle.
     C.—She Stoops to Conquer; Boots at the Swan.
12. A.—Macbeth; Turning the Tables.
     C.—Laugh when you Can; Boots at the Swan.
13. A.—Othello; Poor Soldier.
     C.—Woman's Life; Valet de Sham.
14. A.—Julius Caesar; Fortune's Frolic.
     C.—L'Ambassadrice.
     W.—Laugh when you Can; Woman's Life.
15. A.—King Lear; Romp.
     C.—L'Ambassadrice.
     W.—Rivals; Artful Dodger.
16. A.—No advertisement.
     C.—L'Ambassadrice.

W.—Swiss Cottage; Gabrielle *: *Chevalier*—Field; *Gabrielle*—
Miss C. Cushman.

18. *Monday:*
C.—L'Ambassadrice.
W.—Gabrielle; The Last Man.

19. A.—Brutus; Mayor of Garratt.
C.—L'Ambassadrice.
W.—King's Gardner; Gabrielle.

20. A.—Virginia Mummy; Jumbo Jim.
C.—L'Ambassadrice.
W.—Gabrielle; Artful Dodger.

21. A.—Jim Crow in London; Virginia Mummy.
C.—L'Ambassadrice.
W.—Binks, the Bagman; Gabrielle.

22. A.—Damon and Pythias; Oh! Hush!!
C.—Les Diamans de la Couronne.
W.—Boots at the Swan; Carpenter of Rouen.

23. A.—Dutch Governor; Mountaineers.
C.—Les Memoires du Diable.
W.—Gabrielle; Artful Dodger.
N.—Honey Moon; Perfection.

25. *Monday:*
A.—Surgeon of Paris; Shoemaker of Toulouse.
C.—La Fille du Regiment.
W.—Gabrielle; Valet de Sham.
N.—Pizarro; My Aunt.

26. A.—Six Degrees of Crime; Bone Squash Diavolo.
C.—Les Diamans de la Couronne.
W.—Antony and Cleopatra; Pretty Girls of Stilberg.
N.—No bill received.

27. A.—Pizarro; Jumbo Jim.
C.—Les Diamans de la Couronne.
W.—Married Rake; Artful Dodger.
N.—Hamlet; Young Widow.

28. A.—Richard III; Mummy.
C.—No advertisement.
W.—Carpenter of Rouen; Simpson and Co.
N.—Merchant of Venice; Children in the Wood.

29. A.—Dutch Governor; Douglass.
C.—Le Postillion de Lonjumeau.
W.—King's Gardner; Gabrielle.
N.—Richard III; Irish Tutor.

30. A.—Water Witches; Rake's Progress.
C.—La Grace de Dieu.
W.—Captain Charlotte; Blue Anchor.
N.—Pizarro; My Aunt.

OCTOBER

2. *Monday:*
    A.—A Wife for a Day; Iron Chest.
    C.—Les Diamans de la Couronne.
    W.—Boots at the Swan; Blue Anchor.
    N.—Wild Oats; His Last Legs.

3.   A.—Seth Slope; Michael Erle.
    C.—Le Domino Noir.
    W.—Lady of Lyons; Blue Anchor.
    N.—Stranger; Irish Tutor.

4.   A.—Caius Silius; Golden Farmer.
    C.—Le Domino Noir.
    W.—Hamlet; Captain Charlotte.
    N.—Town and Country; Young Widow.

5.   A.—Stranger; Wife for a Day.
    C.—Le Grace de Dieu.
    W.—Henry IV; Artful Dodger.
    N.—Honey Moon; Village Lawyer.

6.   A.—Virginius; Green Mountain Boy.
    C.—La Fille du Regiment.
    W.—Venice Preserved; Thumping Legacy.
    N.—Stranger; His Last Legs.

7.   A.—Mary Stuart; Jonathan in England.
    C.—Anna Bolena.
    W.—Day after the Wedding; Surgeon of Paris.
    N.—Macbeth; Irish Tutor.

9. *Monday:*
    A.—Julius Caesar; Knight of the Golden Fleece.
    C.—Anna Bolena.
    W.—Wife; Blue Anchor.
    N.—Ruby Rings *: *Arundale*—Matthews, *Francis*—Faulkner,
        Motley—Winnans, *Adeline*—Mrs. Abbott; Sergeant's
        Wedding.

10.   A.—Richard III; Jackets of Blue.
    C.—Le Domino Noir.
    W.—Hunchback; Thumping Legacy.
    N.—Ruby Ring; Sergeant's Wedding.

11.   A.—Hamlet; Raising the Wind.
    C.—Le Domino Noir.
    W.—Suspicious Husband; Blue Anchor.
    N.—Ruby Ring; Sergeant's Wedding.

12.   A.—Othello; Irishman in London.
    C.—Anna Bolena.
    W.—Lady of Lyons; Little Devil's Share.
    N.—Ruby Ring; Sergeant's Wedding.

13.   A.—Town and Country; Weathercock.
       C.—Anna Bolena.
       W.—Katharine and Petruchio; Little Devil's Share.
       N.—Ruby Ring; Sergeant's Wedding.

14.   A.—King John; Forest Rose.
       C.—Polichinel; Le Gamin du Paris.
       W.—Macbeth; My Wife's Second Floor.
       N.—Sergeant's Wedding; My Valet and I.

16. *Monday:*
       A.—Distressed Mother; Apostate.
       C.—Acteon.
       W.—Henry IV; La Sylphide, ballet.
       N.—Othello; My Wife's Second Floor.

17.   A.—Golden Fleece; Yankee Pedlar.
       C.—La Perruche.
       W.—Married Life; Last Days of Pompeii.
       N.—Metamora; My Valet and I.

18.   A.—Julius Caesar; Tom and Jerry.
       C.—Le Pre aux Clercs.
       W.—Little Devil's Share; Pretty Girls of Stilberg.
       N.—Hamlet; My Wife's Second Floor.

19.   A.—Romeo and Juliet; Green Mountain Boy.
       C.—Le Postillion de Lonjumeau.
       W.—Wife; Little Devil's Share.
       N.—Gladiator; My Wife's Second Floor.

20.   A.—Jonathan in England; Black Eyed Susan.
       C.—Les Diamans de la Couronne.
       W.—Married Life; Day after the Wedding.
       N.—Damon and Pythias; My Valet and I.

21.   A.—Macbeth; Wife for a Day.
       C.—Acteon; La Fille du Regiment.
       W.—Love's Sacrifice; My Little Adopted.
       N.—King Lear; Gladiator, first two acts.

23. *Monday:*
       A.—Open until end of week but not advertised.
       C.—Macbeth; King's Gardner.
       W.—Charles II; Is He Jealous?
       N.—Jack Cade; My Wife's Second Floor.

24.   C.—Hamlet; Married Rake.
       W.—Suspicious Husband; Little Devil's Share.
       N.—Macbeth; Widow and Horse.

25.   C.—Hamlet; Married Rake.
       W.—Hunter of the Alps; Charles II.
       N.—Metamora; My Wife's Second Floor.

26.   C.—Werner; My Wife's Second Floor.
       W.—George Barnwell; Secret.

       N.—Jack Cade; My Valet and I.

27.   C.—Richelieu; My Wife's Second Floor.
       W.—Laugh when you Can; Carpenter of Rouen.
       N.—Hamlet; Sergeant's Wedding.

28.   C.—Richelieu; My Wife's Second Floor.
       W.—Simpson and Co.; Oh! Hush!!
       N.—Richelieu; Double-Bedded Room.
       A.—Scape Goat; A Kiss in the Dark.

30. *Monday:*
       C.—Hamlet; My Wife's Second Floor.
       W.—Mountaineers; Sweethearts and Wives.
       N.—Tour de Nesle; Golden Farmer.

31.   C.—Hamlet; My Wife's Second Floor.
       W.—Mountaineers; Sweethearts and Wives.
       N.—Tour de Nesle; Golden Farmer.

NOVEMBER

1. *Wednesday:*
       C.—Othello; Daughter.
       W.—Maid of Croissy; Hundred-Pound Note.
       N.—Black Eyed Susan; My Wife's Second Floor.

2.   C.—Richelieu; Daughter.
       W.—No advertisement.
       N.—Richelieu; John Jones.

3.   C.—Virginius; Capt. Charlotte.
       W.—No advertisement.
       N.—Robert Bruce; Golden Farmer.

4.   C.—Werner; Little Devil's Share.
       W.—Occupied by Howe's circus.
       N.—Robert Bruce; Nick of the Woods.

6. *Monday:*
       C.—Macbeth; Boots at the Swan.
       N.—Robert Bruce; Swiss Cottage.

7.   C.—Othello; Black Eyed Susan.
       N.—Stranger; Is He Jealous?

8.   C.—Much Ado about Nothing; Little Devil's Share.
       N.—Widow and Horse; My Valet and I.

9.   C.—Love's Sacrifice; Boots at the Swan.
       N.—Night Hag; John Jones.

10.   C.—Lady of Lyons; My Wife's Second Floor.
       N.—Robbers; Weathercock.

11.   C.—Speed the Plough; Little Devil's Share.
       N.—Stranger; Is He Jealous?

13. *Monday:*
       C.—Norma, with Italian Opera Co.

N.—Mysteries of Paris.
14. C.—Passion; Good Looking Fellow.
N.—Mysteries of Paris.
15. C.—Lucia di Lammermoor.
N.—Mysteries of Paris.
16. C.—Hunchback; Boots at the Swan.
N.—Mysteries of Paris.
17. C.—Belisario.
N.—Mysteries of Paris; Weathercock
18. C.—Belisario.
N.—Mysteries of Paris; Robert Bruce.
20. *Monday:*
C.—Il Puritani.
N.—Jonathan in England; Mysteries of Paris.
21. C.—Il Puritani.
N.—Yankee Land; Mysteries of Paris.
22. C.—Lucia di Lammermoor.
N.—Forest Rose; Mysteries of Paris.
23. C.—Il Puritani.
N.—Wool Pedlar; Mysteries of Paris.
24. C.—Richard III; My Wife's Second Floor.
N.—Red Wood; Mysteries of Paris.
26. *Monday:*
C.—Gemma di Vergy.
N.—Yankee Land; Boston Tea Party.
27. C.—Gemma di Vergy.
N.—Happy Man; King of the Mist.
28. C.—Il Puritani. Last night of Italian Opera Co.
N.—Happy Man; King of the Mist.
29. C.—Much Ado about Nothing; Adopted Child.
N.—Happy Man; King of the Mist.
30. C.—The Wife; The Brigand.
N.—My Wife's Second Floor; King of the Mist.

DECEMBER

1. *Friday:*
C.—Pizarro; The Wolf and the Lamb.
N.—Our Old House at Home; King of the Mist.
2. C.—Wild Oats; The Brigand.
N.—Wallace; King of the Mist.
4. *Monday:*
C.—My Wife's Second Floor; The Valet de Sham.
N.—Wallace; King of the Mist.
5. C.—Henry IV; Boots at the Swan.
N.—Our Old House at Home; King of the Mist.

6.   C.—Monsieur Mallet; His Last Legs.
        N.—King of the Mist; His Last Legs.
7.   C.—Irish Lion; Married Rake.
        N.—Hofer; King of the Mist.
8.   C.—Merry Wives of Windsor; A Companion in Arms.
        N.—Hofer; King of the Mist.
9.   C.—A Companion in Arms; Lucky Stars.
        N.—Old Virginia; Six Degrees of Crime.
11.   *Monday:*
        C.—Man of the World; His Last Legs.
        N.—Wallace; King of the Mist.
        A.—Honey Moon; Family Jars.
12.   C.—Laugh when you Can; A Companion in Arms.
        N.—Irish Attorney; King of the Mist.
        A.—Virginius; My Fellow Clerk.
13.   C.—Carpenter of Rouen; A Companion in Arms.
        N.—Happy Man; King of the Mist.
        A.—Stranger; Bob Short.
14.   C.—Surgeon of Paris; Valet de Sham.
        N.—Jane Shore; King of the Mist.
        A.—The Wife; Bob Short.
15.   C.—Catching an Heiress; Rail Road Depot.
        N.—Rob Roy; King of the Mist.
        A.—Merchant of Venice; Rent Day.
16.   C.—Rose of Killarney; Carpenter of Rouen.
        N.—Blud-Da-Nowns; King of the Mist.
        A.—John Bull; A Nabob for an Hour.
18.   *Monday:*
        C.—Werner; Catching an Heiress.
        N.—King of the Mist; Blud-Da-Nowns.
        A.—Rebel Chief; Luke the Laborer.
19.   C.—The Bridal; Secret Service.
        N.—Blud-Da-Nowns; King of the Mist.
        A.—Rebel Chief; Bob Short.
20.   C.—The Bridal; Secret Service.
        N.—Hercules of Brittany; King of the Mist.
        A.—Rebel Chief; A Roland for an Oliver.
21.   C.—Hamlet; Irish Lion.
        N.—Hercules of Brittany; King of the Mist.
        A.—Rebel Chief; George Barnwell.
22.   C.—No program.
        N.—Weathercock; Hercules of Brittany.
        A.—Rebel Chief; The Denouncer.
23.   C.—The Bridal; Rose of Killarney.
        N.—Gilderoy; Hercules of Brittany.
        A.—Rebel Chief; Family Jars.

25. *Monday:*
    C.—George Barnwell; Sun Spirit.
    N.—Hercules of Brittany; Santa Claus.
    A.—Rebel Chief; Crime and Repentance.
26.   C.—No advertisement.
    N.—Hercules of Brittany; Santa Claus.
    A.—Pizarro; Crime and Repentance.
27.   C.—No advertisement.
    N.—Hercules of Brittany; Double-Bedded Room.
    A.—Damon and Pythias; Hide and Seek.
28.   C.—No advertisement.
    N.—Skeleton Hand; Two Murderers.
    A.—Lady of Lyons; My Fellow Clerk.
29.   C.—No advertisement.
    N.—Romeo and Juliet; The Wren Boys.
    A.—The Bohemians; A House Divided.
30.   C.—Closed.
    N.—Gilderoy; Santa Claus.
    A.—The Bohemians; Mons. Jacques.
    W.—The Bohemians; Valet de Sham.

JANUARY 1844

1. *Monday:*
    W.—Bohemians; Boots at the Swan.
    N.—Handy Andy *: *Andy*—Winnans, *Squire*—Gann, *Nancy*—
       Mrs. Lewis, *Bridget*—Mrs. A. Knight; Santa Claus.
    A.—Animal Magnetism; Bohemians.
2.   W.—Lady of Lyons; Bohemians.
    N.—Handy Andy; Santa Claus.
    A.—Rebel Chief; Bohemians.
3.   W.—Bohemians; A Roland for an Oliver.
    N.—Handy Andy; Santa Claus.
    A.—Hunchback; Bohemians.
4.   W.—Bohemians; Perfection.
    N.—Bayonet; Handy Andy.
    A.—The Wife; Turtles.
5.   W.—Bohemians; Rose of Killarney.
    N.—Bayonet; Handy Andy.
    A.—Stranger; Bleeding Nun.
6.   W.—Married Life; Bohemians.
    N.—Murder of the Quarry; Handy Andy.
    A.—Husband's Revenge; Mons. Jacques.
8. *Monday:*
    W.—Sleeping Beauty; Secret Service.
    N.—Osceola; Double-Bedded Room.

A.—Love Chase; Married Rake.

9. W.—Sleeping Beauty; A Roland for an Oliver.
    N.—Osceola; Handy Andy.
    A.—Perfection; King's Gardner.

10. W.—Sleeping Beauty; Rose of Killarney.
    N.—Murder of the Quarry; Handy Andy.
    A.—Barrach Room; Chamber of Death.

11. W.—Sleeping Beauty; Naval Engagements.
    N.—Murder of the Quarry; The Wren Boys.
    A.—Stranger; Married Rake.

12. W.—Sleeping Beauty; Midnight Hour.
    N.—The Wren Boys; Kriss Kringle's Visit.
    A.—Charles XII; Black Eyed Susan.

13. W.—The Rivals; Sleeping Beauty.
    N.—Iron Chest; King of the Mist.
    A.—Charles XII; Ruffian Boy.

15. *Monday:*
    W.—Giaffer; Sleeping Beauty.
    N.—My Wife's Second Floor; The Hercules of Brittany.
    A.—A Lesson for Ladies; Charles II.

16. W.—Giaffer; Sleeping Beauty.
    N.—My Wife's Second Floor; The Hercules of Brittany.
    A.—Othello; Irish Tutor.

17. W.—New Way To Pay Old Debts; The Pink of Politeness.
    N.—Double-Bedded Room; The Flying Machine.
    A.—Apostate; Jumbo Jim.

18. W.—Hamlet; The Pink of Politeness.
    N.—Double-Bedded Room; Flying Machine.
    A.—Damon and Pythias; Sarcophagus.

19. W.—Stranger; Brigand.
    N.—George Barnwell; Flying Machine.
    A.—Merchant of Venice; Foreign Prince.

20. W.—Richard III; Sleeping Beauty.
    N.—Valentine and Orson; Loan of a Lover.
    A.—Jumbo Jim; Rendezvous.

22. *Monday:*
    W.—Julius Caesar; Place Hunter.
    N.—Wood Wolf of the Black Mountains; Valentine and Orson.
    A.—New Way To Pay Old Debts; Animal Magnetism.

23. W.—Macbeth; Poor Soldier.
    N.—Ruby Ring; Valentine and Orson.
    A.—Mountaineers; Stranger.

24. W.—King Lear; The Review.
    N.—Stranger; Fairly Hit and Fairly Missed.
    A.—Iron Chest; Raymond and Agnes.

25. W.—Richard III; Place Hunter.

N.—London 'Prentices; Fairly Hit and Fairly Missed.
A.—Ambrose Gwinette; Self Accusation.
26. W.—Mountaineers; Sleeping Beauty.
N.—London 'Prentices; Yankee Dentist.
A.—El Hyder; Valentine and Orson.
27. W.—Apostate; American Valor.
N.—Mysteries of New York; London 'Prentices.
A.—Sailor's Home; Tour de Nesle. Last night of the season.
29. *Monday:*
W.—Brutus; Festival of St. Michael.
N.—Metamora; Mysteries of New York.
30. W.—Apostate; Sleeping Beauty.
N.—Gladiator; Mysteries of New York.
31. W.—Othello; Mayor of Garrat.
N.—Jack Cade; Mysteries of New York.

FEBRUARY

1. *Thursday:*
W.—Merchant of Venice; The Lancers.
N.—Ruby Ring; London 'Prentices.
2. W.—Iron Chest; Boarding School.
N.—Murder of the Glen; Yankee Dentist.
3. W.—King John; Mayor of Garrat.
N.—Enchanted Lake and the Hall of Fate.
5. *Monday:*
W.—Town and Country; Oliver Twist.
N.—Enchanted Lake; Mysteries of New York.
6. W.—Belle's Stratagem; Sleeping Beauty.
N.—Enchanted Lake; London 'Prentices.
7. W.—Perkin Warbeck; Lover by Proxy.
N.—Enchanted Lake; My Wife's Second Floor.
8. W.—Perkin Warbeck; Brigand.
N.—Repeal; Enchanted Lake.
9. W.—School for Scandal; Rugantino.
N.—Repeal; Enchanted Lake.
10. W.—Repeal; Life in Philadelphia.
N.—Charles II; Enchanted Lake.
12. *Monday:*
W.—Married Life; Faith and Falsehood.
N.—Fazio; Bayonet.
A.—Spy of St. Marc's; Kehama.
13. W.—School for Scandal; Rubber of Life.
N.—Wren Boys; Enchanted Lake.
A.—Spy of St. Marc's; Battle of Austerlitz.
14. W.—Hunchback; Oliver Twist.

[293]

       N.—Charles II; Enchanted Lake.

       A.—Spy of St. Marc's; Battle of Austerlitz.

15.   W.—Wife; Last Days of Pompeii.

       N.—Frankenstein; Enchanted Lake.

       A.—Spy of St. Marc's; Two Murderers.

16.   W.—She Stoops to Conquer; Last Man.

       N.—Frankenstein; Enchanted Lake.

       A.—The Avenger; Nature and Philosophy.

17.   W.—Poor Gentleman; Perkin Warbeck.

       N.—Frankenstein; Enchanted Lake.

       A.—The Avenger; Spy of St. Marc's.

19. *Monday:*

       W.—Every one has his Fault; Laugh when you Can.

       N.—Hercules of Brittany; Enchanted Lake.

       A.—Gold Seekers; Kehama.

20.   W.—Poor Gentleman; Rubber of Life.

       N.—Enchanted Lake; Frankenstein.

       A.—No advertisement.

21.   W.—Every one has his Fault; Wanted, a Wife.

       N.—Enchanted Lake; Frankenstein.

       A.—No advertisement.

22.   W.—Money; Ben the Boatswain.

       N.—Land of Washington; Enchanted Lake.

       A.—No advertisement.

23.   W.—Speed the Plough; Ben the Boatswain.

       N.—Hercules of Brittany; Honest Thieves.

       A.—No advertisement.

24.   W.—Honey Moon; The Ostler and the Robber.

       N.—Alexander the Great; French Spy.

       A.—No advertisement.

26. *Monday:*

       W.—Black Raven of the Tombs; Secret Service.

       N.—Grecian Queen; Charles II.

27.   W.—Black Raven of the Tombs; Pretty Girls of Stilberg.

       N.—French Spy; Honest Thieves.

28.   W.—Black Raven of the Tombs; Place Hunter.

       N.—Honest Thieves; French Spy.

29.   W.—Black Raven of the Tombs; The Little Devil's Share.

       N.—Closed.

MARCH

1. *Friday:*

       W.—No advertisement.

       N.—Closed.

2.   W.—Black Raven of the Tombs; Maid of Orleans.

N.—Yara, the Gipsy *: *Count*—Matthews, *Yara*—Mrs. Lewis; Katharine and Petruchio.

4. *Monday:*
W.—Honey Moon; Black Raven of the Tombs.
N.—Yara; Ben the Boatswain.

5. W.—Irish Lion; Black Raven.
N.—Yara; Ben the Boatswain.

6. W.—Wives as they Were; Black Raven.
N.—Yara; Ben, the Boatswain.

7. W.—Foundling of the Forest; Black Raven.
N.—Yara; Jack's the Lad.

8. W.—Heir at Law; Black Raven.
N.—Richelieu; Yara.

9. W.—Faith and Falsehood; Black Raven.
N.—Pride of the Ocean; Yara.

11. *Monday:*
W.—Naval Glory; A Roland for an Oliver.
N.—Yara; Pride of the Ocean.

12. W.—Naval Glory; Married Rake.
N.—Yara; Pride of the Ocean.

13. W.—Naval Glory; Wanted, a Wife.
N.—Yara; Luke the Laborer.

14. W.—Naval Glory; Simpson and Co.
N.—Yara; Luke the Laborer.

15. W.—Naval Glory; High Life below Stairs.
N.—Katharine and Petruchio; Yara.

16. W.—Married Life; Naval Glory.
N.—Evil Eye; Yara.

18. *Monday:*
W.—King John; Boarding School.
N.—Esmerelda; Yara.

19. W.—New Way To Pay Old Debts; The Pink of Politeness.
N.—Esmerelda; Robinson Crusoe.

20. W.—Richard III; Agreeable Surprise.
N.—Esmerelda; Falls of Clyde.

21. W.—Town and Country; Lancers.
N.—Mazeppa; Imp of the Elements.

22. W.—Hamlet; Rendezvous.
N.—Mazeppa; Imp of the Elements.

23. W.—Cymbeline; Mayor of Garrat.
N.—Mazeppa; Imp of the Elements.

25. *Monday:*
W.—Macbeth; Mr. and Mrs. White.
N.—Linda; Two Queens.

26. W.—Apostate; Little Devil's Share.
N.—Mazeppa; Lochinvar *: *Lochinvar*—Wareham.

[295]

27.   W.—Iron Chest; Money.
      N.—Linda; Thumping Legacy.
28.   W.—Cymbeline; Wanted, a Wife.
      N.—Linda; Robinson Crusoe.
29.   W.—Julius Caesar; Binks, the Bagman.
      N.—Imp of the Elements; Mazeppa.
30.   W.—Richard III; Rubber of Life.
      N.—Wallace; Ladder of Love.

APRIL

1. *Monday:*
      W.—Beaux Stratagem; Oliver Twist.
      N.—French Spy; Plains of Chippewa.
      C.—Postillion of Lonjumeau.
2.   W.—Pink of Politeness; Yankee in France.
      N.—Rookwood; Columbia's Son.
      C.—La Sonnambula.
3.   W.—King Lear; Yankee in Tune.
      N.—Rookwood; Columbia's Son.
      C.—La Sonnambula.
4.   W.—Richard II; Yankee in France.
      N.—Rookwood; Columbia's Son.
      C.—Barber of Seville.
5.   W.—1777; Turnpike Gate.
      N.—Rookwood; Two Queens.
      C.—Fra Diavolo.
6.   W.—School for Scandal; Sleeping Beauty.
      N.—Rookwood; Harlequin Statue.
      C.—Fra Diavolo.
8. *Monday:*
      W.—Wheel of Fortune; Oliver Twist.
      N.—Robert Emmet; Rookwood.
      C.—La Sonnambula.
9.   W.—Honey Moon; Swiss Cottage.
      N.—Robert Emmet; Fall of Algiers.
      C.—Cinderella.
10.   W.—John Buzzby; Maid of Croissy.
      N.—Robert Emmet; Fall of Algiers.
      C.—Cinderella.
11.   W.—Every one has his Fault; Twice Killed.
      N.—Robert Emmet; Fall of Algiers.
      C.—Anna Bolena.
12.   W.—As You Like It; Wandering Minstrel.
      N.—Robert Emmet; Wool Pedlar.
      C.—Anna Bolena.

13.   W.—Rivals; Comedy of Errors.
      N.—Infidelity; Ben the Boatswain.
      C.—No performance.
15. *Monday:*
      W.—Man and Wife; Blind Man's Buff.
      N.—Burning of the Caroline; Bumps.
      C.—No performance.
16.   W.—Heir at Law; Mummy.
      N.—Othello; Tom, Jerry and Logic's Visit to Philadelphia.
      C.—Anna Bolena.
17.   W.—Paul Pry; Comedy of Errors.
      N.—Stranger; Tom, Jerry, and Logic's Visit to Philadelphia.
      C.—Anna Bolena.
18.   W.—Money; Blind Man's Buff.
      N.—Virginius; Tom, Jerry, and Logic's Visit to Philadelphia.
      C.—Anna Bolena.
19.   W.—As You Like It! Wreck Ashore.
      N.—Damon and Pythias; Infidelity.
      C.—Anna Bolena.
20.   W.—Secrets Worth Knowing; Nicholas Nickleby.
      N.—Jane Shore; Robert Emmet.
      C.—Norma.
22. *Monday:*
      W.—A Cure for the Heart Ache; Blind Man's Buff.
      N.—Doom of the Drinker; Two Queens.
      C.—Fra Diavolo.
23.   W.—Englishman in India; Green Eyed Monster.
      N.—Doom of the Drinker; Two Queens.
      C.—Norma; last night of operas.
24.   W.—Sweethearts and Wives; Married Rake.
      N.—Doom of the Drinker; Two Queens.
25.   W.—Secrets Worth Knowing; My Master's Rival.
      N.—Timour the Tartar; Gammon and Galvanism.
26.   W.—Begone, Dull Care; A Kiss in the Dark.
      N.—Lady of Lyons; Gammon and Galvanism.
27.   W.—Married Life; Broken Hearted.
      N.—Hamlet; Hope and Fears. Last night of the season.
29. *Monday:*
      W.—Much Ado about Nothing; Brigand.
30.   W.—School for Scandal; Boots at the Swan.

MAY

1. *Wednesday:*
      W.—Wives as they Were; Wanted, a Wife.
2.   W.—Love's Sacrifice; Pretty Girls of Stilberg.

3.   W.—Love Chase; New Footman.
4.   W.—Road to Ruin; Haunted Hulk.
6.   *Monday:*
      W.—London Assurance; Valet de Sham.
7.   W.—London Assurance; My Wife's Second Floor.
8.   W.—London Assurance; Swiss Cottage.
9.   W.—London Assurance; Lancers.
10.   W.—No advertisement.
11.   W.—London Assurance; Valet de Sham.
      N.—Wedding Breakfast; Fortunio and his Seven Gifted Servants.
13.   *Monday:*
      W.—Heir at Law; Maid of Croissy.
      N.—Wedding Breakfast; Fortunio.
14.   W.—Young Quaker; Yankee Land.
      N.—Wedding Breakfast; Fortunio.
15.   W.—Speed the Plough; Tom Cringle.
      N.—Wedding Breakfast; Fortunio.
16.   W.—Castle Spectre; Hunter of the Alps.
      N.—Wedding Breakfast; Fortunio.
17.   W.—Laugh when you Can; Female Blue Beard.
      N.—Wedding Breakfast; Fortunio.
18.   W.—Female Blue Beard; Ben the Boatswain.
      N.—Wedding Breakfast; Fortunio.
20.   *Monday:*
      W.—Rivals; Tom Cringle.
      N.—Fortunio; Antony and Cleopatra.
21.   W.—Money; Carpenter of Rouen.
      N.—Fortunio; Antony and Cleopatra.
22.   W.—The Will; Tom Cringle.
      N.—Fortunio; Curiosities of Literature.
23.   W.—She Stoops to Conquer; Black Eyed Susan.
      N.—Mischief Making; Antony and Cleopatra.
24.   W.—Lady of Lyons; The Pirate Dey.
      N.—Boots at the Swan; Wedding Breakfast.
25.   W.—Hypocrite; Pirate Dey.
      N.—Water Party; Married and Settled.
      C.—Norma.
27.   *Monday:*
      W.—Paul Pry; Middy Ashore.
      N.—No performance.
      C.—Gustavus III, opera.
28.   W.—Young Scamp; Star Spangled Banner.
      N.—Closed.
      C.—Gustavus III, opera.

29. W.—The Ocean of Life; Young Scamp.
     N.—Closed.
     C.—Gustavus III, opera.
30. W.—The Ocean of Life; Young Scamp.
     N.—Hamlet; Irish Tutor.
     C.—Gustavus III, opera.
31. W.—Bold Stroke for a Husband.
     N.—No advertisement.
     C.—Gustavus III, opera.

JUNE

1. *Saturday:*
     W.—Richard III; Rendezvous.
     C.—Gustavus III, opera.
     A.—A Chapter of Accidents; A Kiss in the Dark.
3. *Monday:*
     W.—New Way To Pay Old Debts; Grandfather Whitehead.
     C.—La Sonnambula.
     A.—Rent Day; So She Married.
4. W.—Bertram; Last Man.
     C.—Fra Diavolo.
     A.—City Wives; The Stranger.
5. W.—Apostate; Irish Lion.
     C.—Closed.
     A.—Sonnambulist; City Wives.
6. W.—Town and Country; Faint Heart never won Fair Lady.
     A.—Intemperate; City Wives.
7. W.—Riches; Pretty Girls of Stilberg.
     A.—Intemperate; Widow's Victim.
8. W.—Oliver Twist; Hercules of Brittany.
     A.—Heir at Law; Spirit of the Fountain.
10. *Monday:*
     W.—School of Reform; Bold Dragoons.
     A.—Rob Roy; Spirit of the Fountain.
11. W.—Married Life; Hercules of Brittany.
     A.—She Stoops to Conquer; Spirit of the Fountain.
12. W.—Bold Stroke for a Husband; Married Rake.
     A.—Light Ship; Spirit of the Fountain.
13. W.—Man and Wife; Hercules of Brittany.
     A.—Rob Roy; Spirit of the Fountain.
14. W.—Fazio; Bold Dragoons.
     A.—Pizarro; Maid or Wife.
15. W.—King John; Young Scamp.
     A.—Macbeth; Light Ship.

17. *Monday:*
    W.—Much Ado about Nothing; Brigand.
    A.—Shipwreck of the Medusa; Widow's Victim.
18.   W.—Othello; A Roland for an Oliver.
    A.—Shipwreck of the Medusa; Bathing.
19.   W.—Julius Caesar; A Day after the Wedding.
    A.—No advertisement.
20.   W.—Brutus; Wonder.
    A.—Siamese Twins; Shipwreck of the Medusa.
21.   W.—Stranger; Mountaineers.
    A.—Siamese Twins; Confounded Foreigners.
22.   W.—King John; Married Rake.
    A.—Confounded Foreigners; Shipwreck of the Medusa.
24. *Monday:*
    W.—Merchant of Venice; Honey Moon.
    A.—New Actress; Light Ship.
25.   W.—Spring and Autumn; Iron Chest.
    A.—Bathing; Mummy.
26.   W.—King John; Married Rake.
    A.—New Actress; Wedding Night.
27.   W.—Richard III; My Aunt.
    A.—Wedding Night; Confounded Foreigners.
28.   W.—Jane Shore; Grandfather Whitehead.
    A.—Arabian Night's Entertainment; Billy Taylor.
29.   W.—Bertram; Pizarro.
    A.—Floating Beacon; Siamese Twins.

JULY

1. *Monday:*
    W.—Othello; Youthful Queen.
    A.—Beauty and the Beast; Sold to the Devil.
2.   W.—No record.
    A.—Beauty and the Beast; Mother's Pets.
3.   W.—Fazio; Bold Dragoons.
    A.—Widow's Victim; Beauty and the Beast.
4.   W.—Beauty and the Beast; Yankee Land.
    A.—Beauty and the Beast; Native American.
5.   W.—No newspapers published today.
    A.—No newspaper.
6.   W.—Beauty and the Beast; Wept of Wish-Ton-Wish.
    A.—Beauty and the Beast; Fazio.
8. *Monday:*
    W.—Beauty and the Beast; Grandfather Whitehead.
    A.—Printer's Apprentice; Confounded Foreigners.

9. W.—No advertisement.
    A.—No advertisement.
10. W.—Black Raven; Irish Lion.
    A.—No advertisement.
11. W.—Black Raven; Lancers.
    A.—Printer's Apprentice; Sold to the Devil.
12. W.—Black Raven; A Day after the Wedding.
    A.—Printer's Apprentice; Sold to the Devil.
13. W.—Black Raven; Perfection.
    A.—Bathing; Printer's Apprentice.
15. *Monday:*
    W.—Black Raven; Young Scamp.
    A.—Woman's Life; Beauty and the Beast.
16. W.—Black Raven; Faint Heart never won Fair Lady.
    A.—Printer's Apprentice; Ocean Child, first act.
17. W.—Black Raven; Place Hunter.
    A.—Printer's Apprentice; Ocean Child, first act.
18. W.—Wept of Wish-Ton-Wish; Naval Engagements.
    A.—Heart of Midlothian; Spectre Bridegroom.
19. W.—Wept of Wish-Ton-Wish; Naval Engagements.
    A.—Woman's Life; Ocean Child, first act.
20. W.—Young Scamp; Washington.
    A.—Printer's Apprentice; Heart of Midlothian.
22. *Monday:*
    W.—Soldier's Daughter; Vol-Au-Vent.
    A.—Dream at Sea; John Jones.
23. W.—The Will; Mad as a March Hare.
    A.—Arabian Night's Entertainment; Widow Bewitched.
24. W.—A Roland for an Oliver; Black Raven.
    A.—School for Scandal; Wool Dealer.
25. W.—Closed.
    A.—John Bull; Ocean Child, first act.
26. W.—Closed.
    A.—Dream at Sea; A Tragedy Rehearsed.
27. W.—Munchausen *: *Munchausen*—Wells, *Tombsamtifigaleo*
    —Barnes, *Pantaloon*—C. Foster, *Columbine*—Mrs. How-
    ard; The Lancers.
    A.—Richelieu in Love; Sea Serpent.
29. *Monday:*
    W.—Munchausen.
    A.—Richelieu in Love; Sea Serpent.
30. W.—Munchausen.
    A.—Richelieu in Love; Sea Serpent.
31. W.—Munchausen.
    A.—Richelieu in Love; Sea Serpent.

AUGUST

1. *Thursday:*
   W.—Munchausen; Perfection.
   A.—John Bull; Sea Serpent.
2. W.—Munchausen; Perfection.
   A.—Beauty and the Beast; A Tragedy Rehearsed.
3. W.—Munchausen; Young Scamp.
   A.—Love Gift *: *Peter*—Burton, *Mike*—Burke, *Mary*—Mrs. Burke; Wool Dealer.
5. *Monday:*
   W.—Munchausen; Young Scamp.
   A.—Deserter; A Tale of Mystery.
6. W.—Munchausen; Place Hunter.
   A.—Lady of Lyons; Love Gift.
7. W.—Munchausen; Place Hunter.
   A.—Beauty and the Beast; Partners and Friends.
8. W.—Munchausen; Irish Lion.
   A.—Victorine; Rake's Progress.
9. W.—Munchausen; Rendezvous.
   A.—Love Gift; Robert Macaire.
10. W.—Munchausen; Dumb Belle.
    A.—Smuggler's Son; Border Beagles.
12. *Monday:*
    W.—Munchausen; Napoleon Bonaparte.
    A.—Smuggler's Son; Wild Oats.
13. W.—Munchausen; Napoleon Bonaparte.
    A.—Honey Moon; Robert Macaire.
14. W.—Munchausen; Napoleon Bonaparte.
    A.—Rivals; Border Beagles.
15. W.—Munchausen; Napoleon Bonaparte.
    A.—Speed the Plough; Smuggler's Son.
16. W.—Munchausen; George Barnwell.
    A.—Romeo and Juliet; Partners and Friends.
17. W.—Munchausen; A Wife's First Lesson.
    A.—Simpson and Co.; Devil's Head.
19. *Monday:*
    W.—Love in Disguise; Naiad Queen, the demon fight.
    A.—Smuggler's Son; Devil's Head.
20. W.—Rule a Wife and Have a Wife; William Tell, second act.
    A.—Quid Pro Quo; Widow Bewitched.
21. W.—The Wife; Middy Ashore.
    A.—Quid Pro Quo; Who owns the Hand.
22. W.—Hunchback; Love in Disguise.
    A.—Quid Pro Quo; Smuggler's Son.
23. W.—Fazio; Black Eyed Susan.

	A.—Quid Pro Quo; Smuggler's Son.
24.	W.—Romeo and Juliet; Love in Disguise.
	A.—Ambrose Gwinett; Devil's Head.
26.	*Monday:*
	W.—Othello; The Pass Word.
	A.—Open Sesame; Smuggler's Son.
27.	W.—Metamora; The Pass Word.
	A.—Open Sesame; Apostate.
28.	W.—Richelieu; Young Scamp.
	A.—Open Sesame; Foundling of the Forest.
29.	W.—Gladiator; Grandfather Whitehead.
	A.—Open Sesame; Deserter.
30.	W.—Richard III; Perfection.
	A.—Banker's Clerk; Devil's Head.
31.	W.—Jack Cade; A Roland for an Oliver.
	A.—Coroner's Inquest; Open Sesame.

SEPTEMBER

2.	*Monday:*
	W.—Closed.
	A.—Romeo and Juliet; Open Sesame.
3.	A.—Rob Roy; Open Sesame.
4.	A.—Grist to the Mill; Open Sesame.
5.	A.—Grist to the Mill; Open Sesame.
6.	A.—New Way To Pay Old Debts; Honey Moon.
7.	W.—Damon and Pythias; New Footman.
	A.—La Tour de Nesle; Open Sesame.
9.	*Monday:*
	W.—Hamlet; Man about Town.
	A.—Hamlet; Three Weeks after Marriage.
10.	W.—Jack Cade; Valet de Sham.
	A.—Lady of Lyons; Lottery Ticket.
11.	W.—Metamora; Stranger.
	A.—Stranger; His Last Legs.
12.	W.—William Tell; Therese.
	A.—Merchant of Venice; Spectre Bridegroom.
13.	W.—Richelieu; Horatio Sparkins.
	A.—Love Gift; Grist to the Mill.
14.	W.—Macbeth; Gladiator.
	A.—Werner; Amateur and Actors.
16.	*Monday:*
	W.—Heir at Law; Sprigs of Laurel.
	A.—Lady of Lyons; Young Widow.
17.	W.—Speed the Plough; Review.
	A.—Macbeth; Papa Jerome.

[303]

18. W.—Honey Moon; Sprigs of Laurel.
    A.—Hamlet.
19. W.—Pizarro; Robert Macaire.
    A.—Lady of Lyons; Smuggler's Son.
20. W.—Money; Robert Macaire.
    A.—Othello.
21. W.—Putnam *: *Washington*—J. Wallack, Sr., *Zomoni*—Mrs.
    Wallack; Perfection.
    A.—Richard III; Papa Jerome.
23. *Monday:*
    W.—Putnam; Young Scamp.
    A.—Putnam.
24. W.—Putnam; Young Scamp.
    A.—Putnam.
25. W.—Putnam.
    A.—Putnam.
26. W.—Putnam; New Footman.
    A.—Putnam.
27. W.—Putnam; Valet de Sham.
    A.—Putnam; Coroner's Inquest.
28. W.—Putnam; Man about Town.
    A.—Putnam; Fickle One.
30. *Monday:*
    W.—Putnam; New Footman.
    A.—Putnam; Coroner's Inquest.

OCTOBER

1. *Tuesday:*
   W.—Putnam; Pleasant Neighbors.
   A.—Putnam; Turning the Tables.
2. W.—Putnam; Pleasant Neighbors.
   A.—Putnam; Outillissi.
3. W.—Putnam; A Roland for an Oliver.
   A.—Putnam; Beauty and the Beast.
4. W.—Putnam; A Roland for an Oliver.
   A.—Putnam; Beauty and the Beast.
5. W.—Putnam; Beauty and the Beast.
   A.—Putnam; Yellow Dwarf.
7. *Monday:*
   W.—Putnam; Beauty and the Beast.
   A.—Putnam; Yellow Dwarf.
8. W.—Putnam; Beauty and the Beast.
   A.—Yellow Dwarf; Beauty and the Beast.
9. W.—Putnam; Beauty and the Beast.
   A.—Yellow Dwarf; Beauty and the Beast.

10.   W.—Putnam; Love's Sacrifice.
        A.—Yellow Dwarf; Beauty and the Beast.
11.   W.—Putnam; Poor Soldier.
        A.—Yellow Dwarf; Beauty and the Beast.
12.   W.—Putnam; Three Wives of Madrid.
        A.—Putnam; Jonathan in England.
14.   *Monday:*
        W.—Putnam; Three Wives of Madrid.
        A.—Sam Slick; Border Beagles.
        C.—Mountain Sylph.
15.   W.—Putnam; Three Wives of Madrid.
        A.—Sam Slick; Wool Dealer.
        C.—Robert Macaire; Blue Domino.
16.   W.—Putnam; Merchant of Venice.
        A.—Sam Slick; Border Beagles.
        C.—Mountain Sylph; Blue Domino.
17.   W.—Putnam; Iron Chest.
        A.—American Farmer; The Field of Forty Footsteps.
        C.—Mountain Sylph; Blue Domino.
18.   W.—Putnam; Adelgitha.
        A.—Yankee Land; Yankee Magnetism.
        C.—Young Widow; Christine of Sweden.
19.   W.—Putnam; Richard III.
        A.—Field of Forty Footsteps; Bumps.
        C.—Country Girl; Blue Domino.
21.   *Monday:*
        W.—Putnam; Othello.
        A.—Grist to the Mill; Smuggler's Son.
        C.—Nature and Philosophy; Robber's Wife.
22.   W.—Putnam; New Way To Pay Old Debts.
        A.—Rob Roy; Last Day.
        C.—Black Eyed Susan; Loan of a Lover.
23.   W.—Putnam; Bertram.
        A.—School for Scandal; Grist to the Mill.
        C.—Country Girl; Our Old House at Home.
24.   W.—Putnam; Richard III.
        A.—The Dancing Feather *: *Morris*—G. S. Conner, *Blanche*—
          Mrs. Booth; My Friend, the Captain.
        C.—Lady of Lyons; Bamboozling.
25.   W.—Putnam.
        A.—Dancing Feather; My Friend, the Captain.
        C.—Christine of Sweden; Bamboozling.
26.   W.—Putnam; Brutus.
        A.—Dancing Feather; Yellow Dwarf.
        C.—He is not A-Miss; Judith of Mont Blanc.
28.   *Monday:*

W.—Putnam; Married Life.
A.—Dancing Feather; Yellow Dwarf.
C.—Othello; Grandfather Whitehead.

29. W.—Closed.
A.—Exchange no Robbery; Yellow Dwarf.
C.—Othello; Grandfather Whitehead.

30. W.—Knights of the Dark Ages.
A.—One Glass More; La Fitte.
C.—Bone Squash Diavolo; Otello.

31. W.—Knights of the Dark Ages.
A.—Whigs and Democrats; One Glass More.
C.—Patrician's Daughter; Otello.

NOVEMBER

1. *Friday:*
W.—Knights of the Dark Ages.
A.—Whigs and Democrats; Yellow Dwarf.
C.—Otello; Patrician's Daughter.

2. W.—Knights of the Dark Ages.
A.—Yellow Dwarf; La Fitte.
C.—Otello; Macbeth.

4. *Monday:*
W.—Knights of the Dark Ages.
A.—Exchange no Robbery; Yellow Dwarf.
C.—Otello; Grandfather Whitehead.

5. W.—Knights of the Dark Ages.
A.—Voice of Nature; Dancing Feather.
C.—Otello; Bone Squash Diavolo.

6. W.—Knights of the Dark Ages.
A.—One Glass More; City Wives and City Husbands.
C.—Otello; Lady of Lyons.

7. W.—Knights of the Dark Ages; Mummy.
A.—Vampire; Dunn Brown.
C.—Otello; Virginia Mummy.

8. W.—Knights of the Dark Ages; New Footman.
A.—City Wives and City Husbands; Voice of Nature.
C.—Stranger; Mons. Jacque.

9. W.—Knights of the Dark Ages; Putnam.
A.—City Wives and City Husbands; Vampire.
C.—Richard III; Le Chapeau du General.

11. *Monday:*
W.—Knights of the Dark Ages; Putnam.
A.—Henry IV; Nymphs of the Red Sea.
C.—Grandfather Whitehead; The President Incog.; He is not A-Miss.

12.   W.—Knights of the Dark Ages; Putnam.
       A.—Kentuckian; Lady of Lyons.
       C.—Macbeth; Blue Domino.

13.   W.—Knights of the Dark Ages; Putnam.
       A.—Henry III; Nymphs of the Red Sea.
       C.—Judith of Mont Blanc; The President Incog.

14.   W.—Clandare; Putnam.
       A.—Rip Van Winkle; Nymphs of the Red Sea.
       C.—Pizarro; Irish Tutor.

15.   W.—Clandare; Putnam.
       A.—Man of the World; Nymphs of the Red Sea.
       C.—Virginius; Lottery Ticket.

16.   W.—Warning; Putnam.
       A.—Rip Van Winkle; Kentuckian.
       C.—George Barnwell; Golden Farmer.

18. *Monday:*
       W.—Horatio Sparkins; Putnam.
       A.—Merry Wives of Windsor; Mons. Mallet.
       C.—School for Scandal; Simpson and Co.

19.   W.—Rivals; Ton Quewaschen.
       A.—Werner; Nymphs of the Red Sea.
       C.—Dumb Boy of the Pyrenees; The Stranger.

20.   W.—Rookwood.
       A.—Merry Wives of Windsor; Nymphs of the Red Sea.
       C.—Fazio; Hunting a Turtle.

21.   W.—Rookwood.
       A.—Rip Van Winkle; Kentuckian.
       C.—Romeo and Juliet; Sleep Walker.

22.   W.—Rookwood.
       A.—King Lear; Nymphs of the Red Sea.
       C.—Hunchback; The President Incog.

23.   W.—Rookwood; Rascal Jack.
       A.—Murder in the First Degree; Mons. Tonson.
       C.—Therese; Aladdin.

25. *Monday:*
       W.—Rookwood; Rascal Jack.
       A.—Open Sesame; City Wives.
       C.—Hamlet; Catching an Heiress.

26.   W.—Rookwood; Sketches in India.
       A.—Werner; Murder in the First Degree.
       C.—Lady of Lyons; Blue Domino.

27.   W.—Rookwood; Sketches in India.
       A.—Open Sesame; Partners and Friends.
       C.—Macbeth; Sleep Walker.

28.   W.—Rookwood; Richard ye Thirde.
       A.—Nymphs of the Red Sea; Dunn Brown.

C.—Much Ado about Nothing; The President Incog.
29. W.—Rookwood; Richard ye Thirde.
A.—Vampire; Coroner's Inquest.
C.—Lady of Lyons; Sleeping Draught.
30. W.—Rookwood; Richard ye Thirde.
A.—Momentous Question; Drunkard's Progress.
C.—Patrician's Daughter; Wags of Windsor.

DECEMBER

2. *Monday:*
W.—Jack Cade; Mrs. Singleton.
A.—Magic Lamp in a New Light; A Momentous Question.
C.—Othello; John Jones.
3. W.—Othello; New Footman.
A.—Magic Lamp; A Momentous Question.
C.—Patrician's Daughter; Sleeping Draught.
4. W.—Richelieu; Horatio Sparks.
A.—Magic Lamp; Momentous Question.
C.—Lady of Lyons; Catching an Heiress.
5. W.—Metamora; Grandfather Whitehead.
A.—Magic Lamp; Momentous Question.
C.—Stranger; Lottery Ticket.
6. W.—Jack Cade; Man about Town.
A.—Magic Lamp.
C.—Lady of Lyons; Grandfather Whitehead.
7. W.—Gladiator; Mrs. Singleton.
A.—Magic Lamp; Robinson Crusoe.
C.—Ion; Honey Moon.
9. *Monday:*
W.—King Lear; Wandering Minstrel.
A.—Magic Lamp; Robinson Crusoe.
C.—Sixteen String Jack; Golden Farmer.
10. W.—Macbeth; Mummy.
A.—Magic Lamp; Robinson Crusoe.
C.—Laugh when you Can; G. T. T.
11. W.—Brutus; Married Life.
A.—Magic Lamp; Robinson Crusoe.
C.—Catharine and Petruchio; G. T. T.
12. W.—Jack Cade; A Roland for an Oliver.
A.—Magic Lamp; Yellow Dwarf.
C.—Bamboozling; G. T. T.
13. W.—Gladiator; Rival Pages.
A.—Money; Wool Dealers.
C.—Bamboozling; Robert Macaire.

[308]

14.   W.—Hamlet; Damon and Pythias, fourth and fifth acts.
      A.—Magic Lamp; Three Degrees of Loafing.
      C.—Wags of Windsor; Otello.

16. *Monday:*
      W.—Jack Cade; Married Life.
      A.—Bohemian Girl, opera; Magic Lamp.
      C.—Otello; Sleeping Draught.

17.   W.—Money; Beauty and the Beast.
      A.—Bohemian Girl; Magic Lamp.
      C.—Wags of Windsor; Otello.

18.   W.—Bohemian Girl; New Footman.
      A.—Magic Lamp; Bohemian Girl.
      C.—Dumb Girl of Genoa; Jim Crow in London.

19.   W.—Bohemian Girl, drama; Horatio Sparks.
      A.—Bohemian Girl; Sauve qui Peut.
      C.—Bone Squash Diavolo; Catching an Heiress.

20.   W.—Bohemian Girl, drama; Mummy.
      A.—Bohemian Girl, opera; Sauve qui Peut.
      C.—Bohemian Girl, opera.

21.   W.—Bohemian Girl, drama; Irish Lion.
      A.—Bohemian Girl, opera; Mad Anthony *: *Anthony Wayne*
        —Paullin, *Caroline*—Mrs. Burke.
      C.—Bohemian Girl, opera.

23. *Monday:*
      W.—Bohemian Girl; Valet de Sham.
      A.—Mad Anthony; Robinson Crusoe.
      C.—Bohemian Girl.

24.   W.—Bohemian Girl; Middy Ashore.
      A.—Doom of the Spy; Vermonter.
      C.—Bohemian Girl.

25.   W.—Bohemian Girl; Harlequin and the Silver Tower.
      A.—Doom of the Spy; Wife's First Lesson.
      C.—Bohemian Girl.

26.   W.—No advertisement.
      A.—Doom of the Spy; Two Murderers.
      C.—Bohemian Girl.

27.   W.—No advertisement.
      A.—Doom of the Spy; Coiner's Cane.
      C.—Bohemian Girl.

28.   W.—Bohemian Girl; Harlequin and the Silver Tower.
      A.—Doom of the Spy; The Conscripts.
      C.—Bohemian Girl.

30. *Monday:*
      W.—No advertisement.
      A.—Black Wreckers; Harlequin's Festival.

    C.—Bohemian Girl.

31.   W.—Bohemian Girl; Harlequin and the Silver Tower.
    A.—The Light Ship; Harlequin's Festival.
    C.—Bohemian Girl.

JANUARY 1845

1. *Wednesday:*
    W.—Rubber of Life; Harlequin and the Silver Tower.
    A.—Black Wrecker; Harlequin's Festival.
    C.—Bohemian Girl.

2.   W.—Rubber of Life; Harlequin and the Silver Tower.
    A.—The Conscript; Ole Bull.
    C.—Bohemian Girl.

3.   W.—Bohemian Girl, drama; Harlequin and the Silver Tower.
    A.—Dumb man of the Rocks; Harlequin's Festival.
    C.—Bohemian Girl.

4.   W.—Cesar de Bazan; Harlequin and the Silver Tower.
    A.—Grumbling; State Secrets. Last night of the season.
    C.—Bohemian Girl.

6. *Monday:*
    W.—Cesar de Bazan; Harlequin and the Silver Tower.
    C.—Fra Diavolo.

7.   W.—Cesar de Bazan; Richard ye Thirde.
    C.—Bohemian Girl.

8.   W.—Cesar de Bazan; Richard ye Thirde.
    C.—La Sonnambula.

9.   W.—Cesar de Bazan; Richard ye Thirde.
    C.—Bohemian Girl.

10.   W.—Maldichina; Kabri.
    C.—Fra Diavolo.

11.   W.—Cesar de Bazan; Richard ye Thirde.
    C.—La Sonnambula.

13. *Monday:*
    W.—Cesar de Bazan; Black Eyed Susan.
    C.—People's Lawyer; Green Mountain Boy.

14.   W.—Cesar de Bazan; Robert Macaire.
    C.—People's Lawyer; A Wife for a Day.

15.   W.—Cesar de Bazan; Sketches in India.
    C.—Green Mountain Boy; Yankee Pedlar.

16.   W.—Cesar de Bazan; Sketches in India.
    C.—Jonathan in England; A Wife for a Day.

17.   W.—Cesar de Bazan; Black Eyed Susan.
    C.—Seth Slope; A Wife for a Day.

18.   W.—Honey Moon; Cupid.
    C.—Jonathan Doubikins; Yankee Pedlar.

20. *Monday:*
    W.—Old Heads and Young Hearts*: *Littleton*—Wheatley, *Countess*—Mrs. W. R. Blake; Mrs. Singleton.
    C.—Seth Slope; New Notions.
21.   W.—Old Heads and Young Hearts; Mummy.
    C.—Green Mountain Boy; Wife for a Day.
22.   W.—Old Heads and Young Hearts; Man about Town.
    C.—Old Heads and Young Hearts; Perfection.
23.   W.—Old Heads and Young Hearts; Wandering Minstrel.
    C.—Old Heads and Young Hearts; Perfection.
24.   W.—Old Heads and Young Hearts; The River God.
    C.—Old Heads and Young Hearts; Shocking Events.
25.   W.—Old Heads and Young Hearts; Milliner's Holiday.
    C.—Old Heads and Young Hearts; Fortunio.
27. *Monday:*
    W.—Old Heads and Young Hearts; Milliner's Holiday.
    C.—Old Heads and Young Hearts; Fortunio.
28.   W.—School for Scandal; River God.
    C.—Old Heads and Young Hearts; Fortunio.
29.   W.—Old Heads and Young Hearts; New Footman.
    C.—Old Heads and Young Hearts; Fortunio.
30.   W.—Wives as they Were; Cesar de Bazan.
    C.—Busy Body; Fortunio.
31.   W.—Old Heads and Young Hearts; Horatio Sparkins.
    C.—Fortunio; Young Widow.

FEBRUARY

1. *Saturday:*
    W.—Jealous Wife; White Sergeant.
    C.—Fortunio; Christmas Carol.
3. *Monday:*
    W.—Old Heads and Young Hearts; Milliner's Holiday.
    C.—Hunchback; Christmas Carol.
4.   W.—Every one has his Fault; The Little Devil's Share.
    C.—Old Heads and Young Hearts; Christmas Carol.
5.   W.—Isabella; Rivals.
    C.—Rob Roy; Born to Good Luck.
6.   W.—Isabella; Rivals.
    C.—Wonder.
7.   W.—Soldier's Daughter; Cesar de Bazan.
    C.—Lady of Lyons; A Roland for an Oliver.
8.   W.—Bold Stroke for a Husband; Foundling of the Forest.
    C.—No advertisement.
10. *Monday:*
    W.—Old Heads and Young Hearts; Satan in Paris.

C.—Love's Sacrifice; Perfection.
11. W.—Bold Stroke for a Husband; Satan in Paris.
C.—Love's Sacrifice; Dumb Girl of Genoa.
12. W.—Satan in Paris; Simpson and Co.
C.—Love's Sacrifice; Dumb Girl of Genoa.
13. W.—Provoked Husband; Maid of Croissy.
C.—Love's Sacrifice; Dumb Girl of Genoa.
14. W.—Satan in Paris; Foundling of the Forest.
C.—No advertisement.
15. W.—Fazio; Satan in Paris.
C.—No advertisement.
17. *Monday:*
W.—Fazio; Married Life.
18. W.—Stranger; White Sergeant.
19. W.—All in the Wrong; Day after the Wedding.
20. W.—Cure for the Heartache; Polkamania.
21. W.—Lady of Lyons; Polkamania.
22. W.—Polkamania; Washington.
24. *Monday:*
W.—Othello; New Footman.
25. W.—My Wife and I; Satan at Home.
26. W.—Cure for the Heartache.
27. W.—Town and Country; Wife for a Day.
28. W.—Old Heads and Young Hearts; Polkamania.

MARCH

1. *Saturday:*
W.—Cesar de Bazan; River God.
3. *Monday:*
W.—Poor Gentleman; Satan in Paris.
4. W.—Old Heads and Young Hearts; Matrimony.
5. W.—Single Life; Hamlet, Travestie.
6. W.—Cesar de Bazan; Satan in Paris.
7. W.—London Assurance; Loan of a Lover.
8. W.—Single Life; Matrimony.
10. *Monday:*
W.—Revolt of the Harem; Horatio Sparkins.
11. W.—Revolt of the Harem; Dumb Belle.
12. W.—Revolt of the Harem; Milliner's Holiday.
13. W.—Revolt of the Harem.
14. W.—Revolt of the Harem; New Footman.
15. W.—Revolt of the Harem; Robert Macaire.
17. *Monday:*
W.—Revolt of the Harem; Satan in Paris.
18. W.—Revolt of the Harem; The Rubber of Life.

19.   W.—Revolt of the Harem; Cesar de Bazan.
20.   W.—Revolt of the Harem; Ostler and the Robber.
21.   W.—Revolt of the Harem; Rose of Killarney.
22.   W.—Revolt of the Harem; Rose of Killarney.
      A.—Emigrant's Daughter; The Lone Star.
24. *Monday:*
      W.—Speed the Plough; Lise et Colin.
      A.—Heir at Law; Lone Star.
25.   W.—Faint Heart never won Fair Lady; Lise et Colin.
      A.—Three Degrees of Loafing; Lone Star.
26.   W.—London Assurance; Lise et Colin.
      A.—Green Bushes; His own Ghost.
27.   W.—Bertram; Lise et Colin.
      A.—Green Bushes; His own Ghost.
28.   W.—Town and Country; Lise et Colin.
      A.—Green Bushes; Yellow Dwarf.
29.   W.—Pizarro; Lise et Colin.
      A.—Green Bushes; Charles O'Malley.
31. *Monday:*
      W.—Richard III; Mummy.
      A.—Martin Chuzzlewit; Otello.

APRIL

1. *Tuesday:*
      W.—Hamlet; Man about Town.
      A.—Martin Chuzzlewit; Lone Star.
2.   W.—New Way To Pay Old Debts; Loan of a Lover.
      A.—Mysterious Stranger; Charles O'Malley.
3.   W.—King Lear; Dumb Belle.
      A.—Lawyer's Victim; Wilful Murder.
4.   W.—No advertisement.
      A.—Ireland's Curse; Mysterious Stranger.
5.   W.—Richard III; Perfection.
      A.—Putnam; Ireland's Curse.
7. *Monday:*
      W.—Othello; Married Rake.
      A.—Secrets Worth Knowing; Exchange no Robbery.
8.   W.—Old Heads and Young Hearts; Young Scamp.
      A.—Welsh Girl; Yankee Lad.
9.   W.—Heir at Law; Robert Macaire.
      A.—Putnam; Welsh Girl.
10.   W.—Battle of Germantown *: *Washington*—Richings *Maria*—
      Miss A. Fisher; Single Life.
      A.—Putnam; Welsh Girl.
11.   W.—River God; Battle of Germantown.

A.—Putnam; Thimble Rig.

12. W.—Castle of Linburg; Battle of Germantown.
    A.—Putnam; Bohea-Man's Gal.

14. *Monday:*
    W.—Closed.
    A.—Bohea-Man's Gal; Beauty and the Beast.

15. W.—Closed.
    A.—Bohea-Man's Gal; Beauty and the Beast.

16. W.—Fashion *: *Adam*—W. R. Blake, *Count*—Wheatley, *Seraphina*—Miss S. Cushman; Pleasant Neighbors.
    A.—Dunn Brown; Vermonter.

17. W.—Fashion; Matrimony.
    A.—Macbeth; Bohea-Man's Gal.

18. W.—Fashion; River God.
    A.—Rivals; Bohea-Man's Gal.

19. W.—Fashion; Dumb Belle.
    A.—Rob Roy; Bohea-Man's Gal.

21. *Monday:*
    W.—Fashion; Irish Lion.
    A.—Love's Sacrifice; Beauty and the Beast.

22. W.—Fashion; Rendezvous.
    A.—Fashion, or How to Write a Comedy *: *Author*—Thayer, *Manager*—Burton; Pizarro.

23. W.—Fashion; Young Scamp.
    A.—Fashion, or How to Write a Comedy; Merchant of Venice.

24. W.—Fashion; River God.
    A.—Rent Day; Green Bushes.

25. W.—Fashion; New Footman.
    A.—Maid's Tragedy; Fashion, or How to Write a Comedy.

26. W.—Fashion; Wandering Minstrel.
    A.—Romeo and Juliet; Fashion, or How to Write a Comedy.
    C.—Green Mountain Boy; New Notions.

28. *Monday:*
    W.—Fashion; Perfection.
    A.—Hamlet; Thimble Rig.
    C.—Youthful Queen; Wife for a Day.
    N.—Tower of Nesle; A Mother's Murder.

29. W.—Fashion; P. P.
    A.—Lady of Lyons; Fashion, or How to Write a Comedy.
    C.—Kaspar Hauser; Wife for a Day.
    N.—Tower of Nesle; A Mother's Murder.

30. W.—Fashion; P. P.
    A.—Richard III; His own Ghost.
    C.—Old Manor House; New Notions.
    N.—Werner; A Mother's Murder.

MAY

1. *Thursday:*
   W.—Fashion; Loan of a Lover.
   A.—Richard III; Welsh Girl.
   C.—Kaspar Hauser; Yankee Pedlar.
   N.—Stranger; A Mother's Murder.
2. W.—Fashion; Loan of a Lover.
   A.—Money; Bewitched.
   C.—American Farmer; Seth Slope.
   N.—No advertisement.
3. W.—Damon and Pythias; American Enterprise.
   A.—Lady of Lyons; Taming the Shrew.
   C.—People's Lawyer; Cut and Come Again.
   N.—Robbers; Anthony Wayne.
5. *Monday:*
   W.—Virginius; Black Eyed Susan.
   A.—Hamlet; Welsh Girl.
   C.—The Roué; Wife for a Day.
   N.—Robbers; Anthony Wayne.
6. W.—Money; Binks, the Bagman.
   A.—Money; Yankee Lad.
   C.—Roué; New Notions.
   N.—Deceiver Deceived; Gipsy King.
7. W.—Othello; Valet de Sham.
   A.—Elder Brother; Matrimony.
   C.—Hypocrite; Rob Roy.
   N.—Rob Roy; Outalissi.
8. W.—Richelieu; Midshipman Easy.
   A.—Wandering Jew; Loan of a Lover.
   C.—Fall of Kessichack; Cut and Come Again.
   N.—Corsair's Revenge; Married Rake.
9. W.—Secrets Worth Knowing; American Enterprise.
   A.—Wandering Jew; Swiss Cottage.
   C.—Fall of Kessichack; Cut and Come Again.
   N.—Gipsy King; Weather Cock.
10. W.—Pizarro; Ben, the Boatswain.
    A.—Wandering Jew; Lone Star.
    C.—Fall of Kessichack; American Farmer.
    N.—Richard III; Corsair's Revenge.
12. *Monday:*
    W.—Douglas; Carpenter of Rouen.
    A.—Wandering Jew; Sealed Sentence.
    C.—New Notions; Yankee Pedlar.
    N.—No advertisement.

13.   W.—Gamester; Ben, the Boatswain.
      A.—Innkeeper's Daughter; Sealed Sentence.
      C.—Charles II; Broken Sword.
      N.—No advertisement.

14.   W.—Brutus; Rob Roy.
      A.—Wallace; Innkeeper's Daughter.
      C.—No advertisement.
      N.—No advertisement.

15.   W.—Sylvius; Adopted Child.
      A.—Hofer; Sealed Sentence.

16.   W.—Richelieu; The Old and Young Salt.
      A.—Hofer; Wallace.

17.   W.—Evadne; Old and Young Salt.
      A.—Merchant of Venice; Taming of the Shrew.

19.   *Monday:*
      W.—School for Scandal; P. P.
      A.—Hack Driver; Exciseman of Winchester.
      C.—Bohemian Girl.

20.   W.—Emelie Plater; The Old and Young Salt.
      A.—Simpson and Co.
      C.—Bohemian Girl.

21.   W.—Henry IV; Emelie Plater.
      A.—Sweethearts and Wives.
      C.—Bohemian Girl.

22.   W.—Carpenter of Rouen; Emelie Plater.
      A.—The Jibbenainosay.
      C.—Bohemian Girl.

23.   W.—New Way To Pay Old Debts; Emelie Plater.
      A.—Heir at Law.
      C.—Bohemian Girl.

24.   W.—Richard III; Polkamania.
      A.—Victorine.
      C.—Bohemian Girl.

26.   *Monday:*
      W.—King Lear; American Enterprise.
      A.—Jealous Wife; Fazio.
      C.—Postillion of Lonjumeau.

27.   W.—Julius Caesar; Ben, the Boatswain.
      A.—Soldier's Daughter; Sweethearts and Wives.
      C.—Postillion of Lonjumeau.

28.   W.—Hamlet; Mummy.
      A.—Race Course; Victorine.
      C.—Bohemian Girl.

29.   W.—Bertram; Dumb Belle.
      A.—Venice Preserved; John Jones.
      C.—Fra Diavolo.

30.   W.—Richard III; Milliner's Holiday.
        A.—Jane Shore; Wreck Ashore.
        C.—Fra Diavolo.
31.   W.—Brutus; Mayor of Garrat.
        A.—Children in the Woods; Nick of the Woods.
        C.—Postillion of Lonjumeau.

JUNE

2. *Monday:*
        W.—Time Works Wonders; New Footman.
        A.—Last Days of Pompeii; Deaf as a Post.
3.   W.—Time Works Wonders; Horatio Sparkins.
        A.—Last Days of Pompeii; Deaf as a Post.
4.   W.—Time Works Wonders; River God.
        A.—Paul Pry; Race Course.
        C.—Leonora.
5.   W.—Time Works Wonders; Perfection.
        A.—Time Works Wonders; Children in the Wood.
        C.—Leonora.
6.   W.—Time Works Wonders; Wandering Minstrel.
        A.—Time Works Wonders; Oregon *.
        C.—Leonora.
7.   W.—Shoemaker of Toulouse; Pleasant Neighbors.
        A.—Bronze Horse; Oregon.
        C.—Leonora.
9. *Monday:*
        W.—Bronze Horse; Adopted Child.
        A.—Bronze Horse; Oregon.
10.   W.—Cesar de Bazan; Bronze Horse.
        A.—Bronze Horse; Oregon.
        C.—Leonora.
11.   W.—Cesar de Bazan; Bronze Horse.
        A.—Bronze Horse; Oregon.
        C.—Leonora.
12.   W.—Young Napoleon and his Father; Bronze Horse.
        A.—Hofer; Oregon.
        C.—Leonora.
13.   W.—Young Napoleon and his Father; Bronze Horse.
        A.—Wallace; Oregon.
        C.—Leonora.
14.   W.—Ugolino; Bronze Horse.
        A.—Oregon; Bronze Horse.
        C.—Leonora.
16. *Monday:*
        W.—Irish Lion; Bronze Horse.

[317]

A.—Antigone; Oregon.
C.—Leonora.

17. W.—Bronze Horse; Polkamania.
A.—Antigone; Star Spangled Banner.
C.—Leonora.

18. W.—Speed the Plough; Bronze Horse.
A.—Sheriff of the County; Charles O'Malley.
C.—No advertisement.

19. W.—Bronze Horse; Lancers.
A.—No advertisement.
C.—No advertisement.

20. W.—Young America; Golden Farmer.

21. W.—Young America; Matrimony.

23. *Monday:*
W.—Lady of Lyons; Young America.
C.—Fra Diavolo.

24. W.—Lady of Lyons; New Footman.
C.—Bohemian Girl.

25. W.—Honey Moon; Mummy.
C.—Leonora.

26. W.—Soldier's Daughter; Battle of Germantown.
C.—Bohemian Girl.

27. W.—Young America; Bride of Lammermoor.
C.—No advertisement.

28. W.—Bride of Lammermoor; Day after the Wedding.
C.—Norma.

30. *Monday:*
W.—Fashion; Young America.
C.—Norma.

JULY

1. *Tuesday:*
W.—Rural Felicity; Battle of Austerlitz.
C.—Norma.

2. W.—Golden Farmer; Last Nail.
C.—Dramatist.

3. W.—Cure for the Heartache; Last Nail.
C.—A Veteran *: *Gunshot*—Richings, *Josephine*—Mrs. A. Knight.

4. W.—Young America; Freedom's Last Martyr *.
C.—A Veteran; Traitor.
A.—My Wife's Out; Lovers' Quarrels.

5. W.—Rendezvous; Freedom's Last Martyr.
C.—Veteran; Traitor.
A.—Wandering Minstrel; Miller's Maid.

7. *Monday:*
    W.—Henrietta; Freedom's Last Martyr.
    C.—No advertisement.
    A.—Loan of a Lover; Broken Heart.

8.   W.—Robert Macaire; Freedom's Last Martyr.
    A.—Our Flag is Nailed to the Post; Love, Law and Physic.

9.   W.—Henrietta; Battle of Germantown.
    A.—Pleasant Neighbors; Loan of a Lover.

10.   W.—Rural Felicity; White Sergeant.
    A.—The Seamstress; My Wife's Out.

11.   W.—Naiad Queen; P. P.
    A.—The Seamstress; Young Widow.

12.   W.—Naiad Queen; Young America.
    A.—Bank Clerk; The Seamstress.

14. *Monday:*
    W.—Naiad Queen; Young America.
    A.—The Seamstress; No!

15.   W.—Naiad Queen.
    A.—Bank Clerk; No Song, No Supper.

16.   W.—Naiad Queen; Perfection.
    A.—The Seamstress; Devil to Pay.

17.   W.—Naiad Queen; Horatio Sparkins.
    A.—No Song, No Supper; Devil to Pay.

18.   W.—Bottle Imp; Dumb Belle.
    A.—No Song, No Supper; Devil to Pay.

19.   W.—Bottle Imp; Rural Felicity.
    A.—The Death Fetch; Golden Farmer.

21. *Monday:*
    W.—Bottle Imp.
    A.—Maid and Magpie; Widow Bewitched.

22.   W.—Bottle Imp.
    A.—Death Fetch; Maid and Magpie.

23.   W.—Hunchback; Polkamania.
    A.—Fair Star; Stranger.

24.   W.—Macbeth; Rendezvous.
    A.—Foundling of the Forest; Fair Star.

25.   W.—Pizarro; Battle of Germantown.
    A.—Maid and Magpie; Fair Star.

26.   W.—Romeo and Juliet; Middy Ashore.
    A.—Death Fetch; Fair Star.

28. *Monday:*
    W.—Bridal; Asmodeus.
    A.—Buccaneer's Barque; Does your Mother Know you're
    Out?

29.   W.—Bridal; Young America.
    A.—Buccaneer's Barque; Sealed Sentence.

30.   W.—Rob Roy; Young Napoleon and his Father.
       A.—Spy of St. Marc; Ole Bull.
31.   W.—Coriolanus; Love Chase.
       A.—Spy of St. Marc; Death Fetch.

AUGUST

1. *Friday:*
       W.—Fazio; Bohemian Girl.
       A.—Spy of St. Marc; Mizzle, Bolt, and Cutaway.
2.   W.—William Tell; Black Eyed Susan.
       A.—Flying Dutchman; Spy of St. Marc.
4. *Monday:*
       W.—Young Quaker; Polkamania.
       A.—Flying Dutchman; Maid of Palaiseau.
5.   W.—Hamlet; Rendezvous.
       A.—Fair Star; Flying Dutchman.
6.   W.—Stranger; Sweethearts and Wives.
       A.—Dumb Man of Manchester; Flying Dutchman.
7.   W.—Merchant of Venice; Charles II.
       A.—Smuggler of Bootle Bay; Spy of St. Marc.
8.   W.—Honey Moon; Dumb Belle.
       A.—Dumb Man of Manchester; Murdered Waterman.
9.   W.—Bertram; Brigand.
       A.—Faustus; Cherokee Chief.
11. *Monday:*
       W.—Romeo and Juliet; Young America.
       A.—Vow of Silence; Cherokee Chief.
12.   W.—Soldier's Daughter; Paul Jones.
       A.—Ambrose Gwinett; Hunting a Turtle.
13.   W.—Wild Oats; Paul Jones.
       A.—Dumb Man of Manchester; Foulah Slave.
14.   W.—Belle's Stratagem; Battle of Germantown.
       A.—Rob Roy; My Poor Dog Tray.
15.   W.—Old Heads and Young Hearts; Cesar de Bazan.
       A.—My Poor Dog Tray; Flying Dutchman.
16.   W.—Bridal; Paul Jones.
       A.—Wife of Seven Husbands; Tom and Jerry.
18. *Monday:*
       W.—Coriolanus; Rural Felicity.
       A.—Fire Raiser; Therese.
19.   W.—Pizarro; Henriette.
       A.—Judgment of Solomon; Macbeth, fifth act.
20.   W.—William Tell; Black Eyed Susan.
       A.—Dream at Sea; Mrs. Caudle's Curtain Lectures.
21.   W.—Old Heads and Young Hearts; New Footman.

A.—Margaret Catchpole; Mrs. Caudle's Curtain Lectures.
22. W.—Fashion; Brigand.
A.—Margaret Catchpole; Mrs. Caudle's Curtain Lectures.
23. W.—Macbeth; Young America.
A.—Margaret Catchpole; Mrs. Caudle's Curtain Lectures.
25. *Monday:*
W.—Hunchback; Horatio Sparkins.
A.—Margaret Catchpole; Mrs. Caudle's Curtain Lectures.
26. W.—Mountaineers; My Aunt.
A.—Margaret Catchpole; Mrs. Caudle's Curtain Lectures.
27. W.—Merchant of Venice; Robber's Wife.
A.—Speed the Plough; Margaret Catchpole.
28. W.—Dumb Belle; Robber's Wife.
A.—Margaret Catchpole; Ambrose Gwinett.
29. W.—Point of Honor; Soldier's Daughter.
A.—Adelgitha; Margaret Catchpole.
30. W.—Fazio; Rob Roy.
A.—Margaret Catchpole; Wild Boy of Bohemia.
C.—Sheriff of the County; No!

SEPTEMBER

1. *Monday:*
W.—Lady of Lyons; Black Eyed Susan.
A.—Margaret Catchpole; Wild Boy of Bohemia.
C.—The Wife; Welsh Girl.
2. W.—Fashion; Valet de Sham.
A.—Margaret Catchpole; My Poor Dog Tray.
C.—Honey Moon; Used Up.
3. W.—Fashion; My Aunt.
A.—Margaret Catchpole; Murdered Waterman.
C.—Lady of Lyons; Used Up.
4. W.—Bridal; Young Scamp.
A.—Margaret Catchpole.
C.—Romeo and Juliet; Irish Tutor.
5. W.—Romeo and Juliet; Pass Word.
A.—Margaret Catchpole.
C.—Faint Heart never won Fair Lady; A Day after the Wedding.
6. W.—Point of Honor; Mountaineers. Last night of the season.
A.—Margaret Catchpole.
C.—School for Scandal; Irish Tutor.
8. *Monday:*
A.—Red Cross Knights.
C.—Henry IV; Welsh Girl.
9. A.—Red Cross Knights.

[321]

   C.—Kentuckian; Who Is He?
10. A.—Red Cross Knights; Margaret Catchpole.
   C.—Yankee in England; Critic.
11. A.—Forest of Bondy; Margaret Catchpole.
   C.—Merry Wives of Windsor; Who Is He?
12. A.—Forest of Bondy.
   C.—Kentuckian; His Last Legs.
13. A.—Bill Jones; Forest of Bondy.
   C.—Rip Van Winkle; Mons. Mallet.
15. *Monday:*
   A.—Bill Jones; Dog of Montargis.
   C.—Gamester; No!
16. A.—Bill Jones; Dog of Montargis.
   C.—Much Ado about Nothing; Gardner's Wife.
17. A.—Richelieu; Lady of Lyons.
   C.—Stranger; Pleasant Neighbors.
18. A.—Dog of Montargis.
   C.—Wonder; Gardner's Wife.
19. A.—Bill Jones; Margaret Catchpole.
   C.—As You Like It; Married Bachelor.
20. A.—Dog of Montargis; Ole Bull.
   C.—Merchant of Venice; Irish Tutor.
22. *Monday:*
   A.—Wife of Seven Husbands; Margaret Catchpole.
   C.—Much Ado about Nothing; Peter White.
23. A.—Dream at Sea; Love Gift.
   C.—Money; Wicked Widow.
24. A.—Jack Sheppard; Ole Bull.
   C.—As You Like It; Secret.
25. A.—Jack Sheppard; Hunting a Turtle.
   C.—Money; Welsh Girl.
26. A.—Jack Sheppard; Hunting a Turtle.
   C.—Gamester; Loan of a Lover.
27. A.—Jack Sheppard; Oregon.
   C.—Stranger; Honey Moon.
29. *Monday:*
   A.—Rip Van Winkle; Oregon.
   C.—La Favorite.
30. A.—Kentuckian; Jack Sheppard.
   C.—Les Premiéres Armés de Richelieu.

OCTOBER

1. *Wednesday:*
   W.—School for Scandal; Young Widow.
   A.—His Last Legs; Jack Sheppard.

C.—La Fille du Regiment.
2. W.—Wife; Young Widow.
   A.—Yankee in England; Jack Sheppard.
   C.—Robert le Diable.
3. W.—Macbeth; Mummy.
   A.—Merry Wives of Windsor; Mons. Tonson.
   C.—Le Domino Noir.
4. W.—Merchant of Venice; Wonder.
   A.—Rip Van Winkle; Jack Sheppard.
   C.—Merchant of Venice; Wonder.
6. *Monday:*
   W.—Romeo and Juliet; Black Eyed Susan.
   A.—Julius Caesar; Mariner and his Monkey.
   C.—La Muette de Portici.
7. W.—Cure for the Heartache; Thimble Rig.
   A.—Damon and Pythias; Mariner and his Monkey.
   C.—Vicomte de l'Etorieres.
8. W.—Bridal; Thimble Rig.
   A.—Evadne; Pilot.
   C.—L'Ambassadrice.
9. W.—Speed the Plough; Robber's Wife.
   A.—Pizarro; Mariner and his Monkey.
   C.—La Júme.
10. W.—Point of Honor; William Tell.
   A.—Douglass; Shoemaker of Toulouse.
   C.—Les Hugenots.
11. W.—Soldier's Daughter; Rob Roy.
   A.—Shoemaker of Toulouse; Loan of a Lover.
   C.—Les Hugenots.
13. *Monday:*
   W.—Old Heads and Young Hearts; Poor Soldier.
   A.—Jane Shore; Jumbo Jim.
   C.—La Sonnambula; Mr. and Mrs. White.
14. W.—Bertram; High Life below Stairs.
   A.—Jack Sheppard; Sarcophagus.
   C.—Hunchback; Gardener's Wife.
15. W.—Hamlet; Thimble Rig.
   A.—Margaret Catchpole; Jim Crow in London.
   C.—La Sonnambula; King and I.
16. W.—Lady of Lyons; Agreeable Surprise.
   A.—Otello; Wife of Seven Husbands.
   C.—Fra Diavolo; King and I.
17. W.—Stranger; Deaf as a Post.
   A.—Grist to the Mill; Jumbo Jim.
   C.—Stranger; Irish Tutor.
18. W.—Coriolanus; High Life below Stairs.

A.—Otello; Alexander the Great.
C.—Der Freischutz; King and I.

20. *Monday:*
W.—West Indian; Deaf as a Post.
A.—Change Makes Change *: *Madeline*—Mrs. Mowatt, *Vanquish*—Crisp; Raising the Wind.
C.—Der Freischutz; John Jones.

21. W.—Macbeth; High Life below Stairs.
A.—Change Makes Change; Grist to the Mill.
C.—Der Freischutz; No Song, No Supper.

22. W.—Fazio; Wonder.
A.—Change Makes Change; Marriage Squabbles.
C.—Fra Diavolo; Married Rake.

23. W.—Heir at Law; William Tell.
A.—Change Makes Change; Used Up.
C.—Der Freischutz; Waterman.

24. W.—Bridal; Robber's Wife.
A.—Change Makes Change; Stranger.
C.—Therese; Why don't she Marry?

25. W.—Bohemian Girl; Young Widow.
A.—Change Makes Change; Robert Macaire.
C.—Der Freischutz; Cinderella, second act.

27. *Monday:*
W.—Fatal Dowry; Agreeable Surprise.
A.—Bride of Lammermoor; Used Up.
C.—Lady of Lyons; King and I.

28. W.—Fatal Dowry; Poor Soldier.
A.—Bellamira; Flying Dutchman.
C.—Hamlet; 23 John Street.

29. W.—Bohemian Girl; opera; Deaf as a Post.
A.—Bellamira; Jack Sheppard.
C.—Othello; Two Queens.

30. W.—Maid of Croissy; Wonder.
A.—Alexander the Great; Jack Sheppard.
C.—Love, Two Queens.

31. W.—West Indian; High Life below Stairs.
A.—Muleteer of Palermo; Jack Sheppard.
C.—Macbeth; Gardener's Wife.

NOVEMBER

1. *Saturday:*
W.—Fatal Dowry; Deaf as a Post.
A.—Bill Jones; Obi.
C.—Much Ado about Nothing; Peter White.

3. *Monday:*
    W.—Hamlet; Young America.
    A.—Sam Slick; Obi.
    C.—Love; Two Queens.

4.   W.—Lady of Lyons; Mummy.
    A.—Yankee Land; Sam Slick.
    C.—Romeo and Juliet; Follies of a Night.

5.   W.—Much Ado about Nothing; P. P.
    A.—Agnes de Vere; Courting in Connecticut.
    C.—Hamlet; Secret.

6.   W.—Othello; Young Widow.
    A.—Zanonah; Yankee Land.
    C.—Macbeth; Chapter of Accidents.

7.   W.—Lady of Lyons; Wandering Minstrel.
    A.—Agnes de Vere; A Hard Subject.
    C.—Stranger; Follies of a Night.

8.   W.—Macbeth; A Roland for an Oliver.
    A.—Zanonah; Doolittle Family.
    C.—No performance.

10. *Monday:*
    W.—Romeo and Juliet; Mr. and Mrs. Pringle.
    A.—Jonathan Bradford; Fortune Teller.
    C.—Il Puritani, in English.

11.   W.—Venice Preserved; My Aunt.
    A.—Jonathan Bradford; Fortune Teller.
    C.—Puritans; Two Queens.

12.   W.—Lady of Lyons; Mr. and Mrs. Pringle.
    A.—Redwood; Yankee Abroad.
    C.—Puritans; Two Queens.

13.   W.—Stranger; Faint Heart never won Fair Lady.
    A.—Nervous Man; Irish Lion.
    C.—Puritans; Secret.

14.   W.—Hamlet; Faint Heart never won Fair Lady.
    A.—Declaration of Independence *: *Ebenezer*—Brougham; Jonathan Bradford.
    C.—La Sonnambula; Irish Tutor.

15.   W.—Wild Oats; Therese.
    A.—Tour de Nesle; Cherokee Chief.
    C.—Norma; Irish Dragoon.

17. *Monday:*
    W.—Wedding Day; Mountain Drover.
    A.—King and the Deserter; Cherokee Chief.
    C.—Bohemian Girl; Irish Dragoon.

18.   W.—Uncle John; Mountain Drover.
    A.—Tour de Nesle; Idiot of the Shannon.

C.—Norma; Two Queens.

19. W.—Ben the Boatswain; Omandhaun.
A.—Napoleon; Tour de Nesle.
C.—Bohemian Girl; Irish Dragoon.

20. W.—Nabob for an Hour; Omandhaun.
A.—Dumb Man of Manchester; Napoleon.
C.—Love Spell; Love, Law and Physic.

21. W.—Secret Panel; Mountain Drover.
A.—New Way To Pay Old Debts; Philip Quarl and his Monkey.
C.—Bohemian Girl; Irish Dragoon.

22. W.—Forest of Bondy; Uncle Sam.
A.—Napoleon; Murrell, the Land Pirate *.
C.—Norma, first act; Fra Diavolo.

24. *Monday:*
W.—Simpson and Co.; A Roland for an Oliver.
A.—Murrell, the land Pirate.
C.—Eva, the Page *: *Eva*—Miss Nelson, *Guilderschoff*—Brougham; Born to Good Luck.

25. W.—Charles II; Faint Heart never won Fair Lady.
A.—Murrell.
C.—Rob Roy, opera; John Jones.

26. W.—Secret Panel; La Bayadere.
A.—Buried Alive; Nature and Philosophy.
C.—Eva, the Page; Sweethearts and Wives.

27. W.—Charles II; La Bayadere.
A.—False and True.
C.—Town and Country; Tom More.

28. W.—La Bayadere; Mr. and Mrs. Pringle.
A.—Jerry Murphy; Young Widow.
C.—Card Drawer; Rent Day.

29. W.—Raising the Wind; La Bayadere.
A.—Pilot; Irish Stratagem.
C.—Grandfather Whitehead; Matrimony.

DECEMBER

1. *Monday:*
W.—Animal Magnetism; La Bayadere.
A.—Maid of Frankfort; Wags of Windsor.
C.—Venice Preserved; Love, Law and Physic.

2. W.—Cesar de Bazan; Animal Magnetism.
A.—Maid of Frankfort; A Convenient Distance.
C.—Julius Caesar; Tom and Jerry in America.

3. W.—Simpson and Co.; La Sylphide, ballet.
A.—Buried Alive; Irish Stratagem.

C.—Othello; Honey Moon.
4.   W.—Wedding Day; Raising the Wind.
A.—Emerelda Isle; Irish Tutor.
C.—Grandfather Whitehead; Married Bachelor.
5.   W.—La Bayadere; Uncle John.
A.—Maid of Frankfort; King and the Deserter.
C.—Lady of Lyons; Black Hugh, the Outlaw.
6.   W.—Lady of Lyons; Swiss Cottage.
A.—Felon's Last Dream; Macbeth, second and fifth acts.
C.—A Cure for the Heartache; Tom and Jerry in America.
8. *Monday:*
W.—Venice Preserved; Animal Magnetism.
A.—Felon's Last Dream; Dancing Mad.
C.—Theatre features a magician.
9.   W.—Charles II; Family Jars.
A.—Felon's Last Dream; Love, Law, and Physic.
10.   W.—Stranger; Family Jars.
A.—Hamlet; Dancing Mad.
11.   W.—Lady of Lyons; Abstraction.
A.—King Lear; Dancing Mad.
12.   W.—No!; Abstraction.
A.—Virginius; Budget of Blunders.
13.   W.—No!; Young Napoleon and his Father.
A.—Macbeth; Budget of Blunders.
15. *Monday:*
W.—Bridal; P. P.
A.—Damon and Pythias, drama; Damon and Pythias, comedy.
16.   W.—Bertram; Family Jars.
A.—Foundling of the Forest; High Life below Stairs.
C.—Bohemian Girl; Irish Lion.
17.   W.—Fazio; Young Napoleon and his Father.
A.—Virginius; Tom and Jerry in America.
18.   W.—Old Heads and Young Hearts; Mummy.
A.—Pizarro; Mummy.
19.   W.—Macbeth; Abstraction.
A.—Brutus; Mountain Devil.
20.   W.—Monseigneur *: *Monseigneur*—Richings, *La Barre*—
Wemyss; Jonathan in England.
A.—Richard III; Tom and Jerry in America.
22. *Monday:*
W.—Monseigneur; High, Low, Jack, and the Game.
A.—Green Monster; Irish Tutor.
23.   W.—Monseigneur; High, Low, Jack, and the Game.
A.—Green Monster; Irish Tutor.
24.   W.—Monseigneur; High, Low, Jack, and the Game.
A.—Poor Gentleman; Green Monster.

25.   W.—George Barnwell; Monseigneur.
      A.—Dancing Mad; Green Monster.
26.   W.—Monseigneur; Young Widow.
      A.—Poor Gentleman; Green Monster.
27.   W.—High, Low, Jack, and the Game; Naiad Queen.
      A.—George Barnwell; Green Monster.
29. *Monday:*
      W.—Fatal Dowry; La Bayadere.
      A.— A Wife's Revenge; Green Monster.
      C.—Ion; Charles II.
30.   W.—Rent Day; Bohemian Girl.
      A.—George Barnwell; Green Monster.
      C.—Twelfth Night; Gardener's Wife.
31.   W.—High, Low, Jack and the Game; Bohemian Girl.
      A.—Tour de Nesle; Green Monster.
      C.—Hunchback; Railway Mania.

JANUARY 1846

1. *Thursday:*
      W.—Speed the Plough; The Spell of the Cloud King.
      A.—Artisan of Lyons; Fancy Stocks.
      C.—Much Ado about Nothing; Tom and Jerry.
2.   W.—Coriolanus; Bronze Horse.
      A.—Damon and Pythias; Artisan of Lyons.
      C.—Twelfth Night; Railroad Mania.
3.   W.—Prairie Bird *: *War Eagle*—J. Wallack, Jr., *Mahega*—
      Leman, *Prairie Bird*—Mrs. J. Wallack, Jr.; Glorious Mi-
      nority.
      A.—William Tell; Artisan of Lyons.
      C.—Ion; Honey Moon.
5. *Monday:*
      W.—Prairie Bird; Dumb Belle.
      A.—Hamlet; Khut Yer Styk.
      C.—Arcade *: *O'Slack*—Brougham, *Wigton*—Owens, *Miss
      Moss*—Mrs. Thayer; Venus and Adonis.
6.   W.—Prairie Bird; P.P.
      A.—Bertram; Green Monster.
      C.—Fleur de Marie; Arcade.
7.   W.—Prairie Bird; Fiend of the Golden Rock.
      A.—Stranger; Green Monster.
      C.—Nervous Man; Tom and Jerry in America.
8.   W.—Freedom's Martyrs; Prairie Bird.
      A.—Brutus; Dog of Montargis.
      C.—The Rivals; Venus and Adonis.
9.   W.—Battle of Germantown; Prairie Bird.

A.—Ion; Widow's Victim.
C.—Fleur de Marie; The Rival Fakirs.

10. W.—Cure for the Heart Ache; Pizarro. *
A.—Virginius; The Felon's Last Dream.
C.—Cure for the Heartache; Rival Fakirs.

12. *Monday:*
W.—Romeo and Juliet; Prairie Bird.
A.—Macbeth; Therese.
C.—Poor Gentleman; Rival Fakirs.

13. W.—Old Heads and Young Hearts; George Barnwell.
A.—Susan Hopley; Widow's Victim.
C.—John Bull; Rival Fakirs.

14. W.—Lady of Lyons; Abstraction.
A.—Susan Hopley; Ion.
C.—Seven Castles; Arcade.

15. W.—Money; Robert Macaire.
A.—Artisan of Lyons; Susan Hopley.
C.—Heir at Law; Seven Castles.

16. W.—Stranger; Black Eyed Susan.
C.—Nervous Man; Seven Castles.
A.—Jack Sheppard; Irish Dragoon.

17. W.—Venice Preserved; My Aunt.
A.—Susan Hopley; Abd-El Kader.
C.—Franklin; Seven Castles.

19. *Monday:*
W.—The Deformed; Loan of a Lover.
A.—Jack Sheppard; Abd-El Kader.
C.—Franklin; Seven Castles.

20. W.—Money; Swiss Cottage.
A.—Jack Sheppard; Abd-El Kader.
C.—Franklin; Irishman in London. Last night of the season.

21. W.—Much Ado about Nothing; School for Scandal.
A.—Susan Hopley; Abd-El Kader.

22. W.—Hamlet; Loan of a Lover.
A.—Timour the Tartar; Irish Dragoon.

23. W.—Laugh when you Can; Perfection.
A.—Timour the Tartar; Bank Clerk.

24. W.—Laugh when you Can; Elder Brother.
A.—Tom Cringle's Log; Widow's Victim.

26. *Monday:*
W.—Henry IV; Young Widow.
A.—Closed.

27. W.—Lady of Lyons; Rent Day.
A.—Closed.

28. W.—Elder Brother; His Last Legs.
A.—Closed.

29.   W.—Fazio; Heir at Law.
        A.—Closed.
30.   W.—Coriolanus; High Life below Stairs.
        A.—French Spy; Jumbo Jim.
31.   W.—Rendezvous; The Enchantress.
        A.—French Spy; Jumbo Jim.

FEBRUARY

2. *Monday:*
        A.—Death Token; Sarcophagus.
3.   W.—The Enchantress.
        A.—Death Token; Bone Squash Diavolo.
4.   W.—The Enchantress.
        A.—Otello; Mountain Devil.
5.   W.—The Enchantress.
        A.—Otello; Zelina.
6.   W.—The Enchantress.
        A.—Zelina; Bone Squash Diavolo.
7.   W.—The Enchantress.
        A.—Otello; Highland Whistler.
9. *Monday:*
        W.—The Enchantress.
        A.—Red Riven; Jim Crow in London.
10.   W.—The Enchantress.
        A.—Highland Whistler; Bone Squash Diavolo.
11.   W.—The Enchantress.
        A.—Otello; Clari.
12.   W.—The Enchantress.
        A.—Blind Boy; Sarcophagus.
13.   W.—The Enchantress.
        A.—Clari; The Rival Jim Crows.
14.   W.—The Enchantress.
        A.—Esmerelda; Foreign Prince.
16. *Monday:*
        W.—The Enchantress.
        A.—Esmerelda; Maurice, the Wood-Cutter.
17.   W.—Surgeon of Paris; Rogantino.
        A.—Richard III; Esmerelda.
18.   W.—Richard III; Dumb Belle.
        A.—Foundling of the Forest; Beacon of Death.
19.   W.—Hamlet; Loan of a Lover.
        A.—Cricket on the Hearth; Maurice, the Wood-Cutter.
20.   W.—The Way To Pay Old Debts; High Life below Stairs.
        A.—Cricket on the Hearth; Beacon of Death.
21.   W.—Othello; Deaf as a Post.

A.—Cricket on the Hearth; Seven Castles of the Passions.
23. *Monday:*
    W.—King John; Perfection.
    A.—Our Native Land; Broken Heart.
24.   W.—Riches; Therese.
    A.—Beacon of Death; Seven Castles.
25.   W.—Richard III; Agreeable Surprise.
    A.—Woman's Fate; Bear Hunters.
26.   W.—Venice Preserved; Swiss Cottage.
    A.—Ocean Child; Broken Heart.
27.   W.—Julius Caesar; Young Widow.
    A.—Irish Dragoon; Ocean Child.
28.   W.—Damon and Pythias; Mountaineers.
    A.—Peter Wilkins; Ocean Child.

MARCH

2. *Monday:*
    W.—The Enchantress.
    A.—Peter Wilkins; Sam Slick.
3.   W.—The Enchantress.
    A.—Dutch Burgomaster; Ambrose Gwinnett.
4.   W.—The Enchantress.
    A.—She Stoops to Conquer; The Celestial Empire.
5.   W.—The Enchantress.
    A.—Dumb Man of Manchester; Peter Wilkins.
6.   W.—The Enchantress.
    A.—Woman's Fate; The Celestial Empire.
7.   W.—The Enchantress.
    A.—Cricket on the Hearth; Celestial Empire.
9. *Monday:*
    W.—The Enchantress; Midnight Hour.
    P.M.—Kate Kearney; Young Widow.
    A.—Nick of Time; Wizard of the Wave.
10.   W.—The Enchantress; Rent Day.
    A.—Honey Moon; Wreck Ashore.
    P.M.—Kate Kearney; Young Widow.
11.   W.—The Enchantress; The Last Man.
    A.—Stranger; Wizard of the Wave.
    P.M.—Kate Kearney; Love in Humble Life.
12.   W.—The Enchantress; The Last Man.
    A.—Valsha; Cricket on the Hearth.
    P.M.—Kate Kearney; Dutchman in Love.
13.   W.—Enchantress; Laugh when you Can.
    A.—Oranaska; Valsha.
    P.M.—Kate Kearney; Ole Bull.

14.   W.—Bertram; Enchantress.
     A.—Valsha; Nick of the Woods.
     P.M.—Kate Kearney; Simpson and Co.
16. *Monday:*
     W.—Enchantress.
     A.—Valsha; Nick of the Woods.
     P.M.—Agnes de Vere; Dutchman in Love.
17.   W.—Enchantress.
     A.—Crockett in Texas; Valsha.
     P.M.—Agnes de Vere; Ole Bull.
18.   W.—Enchantress.
     A.—Golden Farmer; Broken Heart.
     P.M.—Grandfather Whitehead; Simpson and Co.
19.   W.—Heir at Law; Rent Day.
     A.—Oranaska; Valsha.
     P.M.—Cricket on the Hearth; Love in Humble Life.
20.   W.—Surgeon of Paris.
     A.—Yankee in Jersey; Charles O'Malley.
     P.M.—Cricket on the Hearth; Spectre Bridegroom.
21.   W.—Bohemian Girl, drama.
     A.—Kiss in the Dark; Wizard of the Wave.
     P.M.—Cricket on the Hearth; Pleasant Neighbors.
23. *Monday:*
     W.—Every one has his Fault; Mr. Singleton.
     A.—Paul Pry; Actress and the Artist.
     P.M.—Cricket on the Hearth; Rendezvous.
24.   W.—Enchantress.
     A.—Maiden Aunt; Zanoni.
     P.M.—Cricket on the Hearth; Spectre Bridegroom.
25.   W.—Paul Pry; Jacques Strop.
     A.—Maiden Aunt; Zanoni.
     P.M.—Cricket on the Hearth; Dead Shot.
26.   W.—Gisippus; Jacques Strop.
     A.—Maiden Aunt; Sweethearts and Wives.
     P.M.—Cricket on the Hearth; Young Reefer.
27.   W.—Virginius; Jacques Strop.
     A.—Cricket on the Hearth; Twice Killed.
     P.M.—Grandfather Whitehead; Kate Kearney.
28.   W.—Othello; Agreeable Surprise.
     A.—Emigrant's Daughter; Crimson Crimes *: *Fright*—Burton.
     P.M.—Maid of Croissy; Cricket on the Hearth.
30. *Monday:*
     W.—Werner; Laugh when you Can.
     A.—Three Degrees of Loafing; Crimson Crimes.
     P.M.—Maid of Croissy; Dumb Belle.
31.   W.—Macbeth; Mr. Singleton.

A.—Poor Gentleman; Fairy of the Golden Wheat Sheaf.
P.M.—Sweethearts and Wives; Dead Shot.

APRIL

1. *Wednesday:*
   W.—Enchantress; Lady of the Lake.
   A.—Swamp Fox *: *Marion*—Becom, *Mrs. Motte*—Mrs. Greene; Crimson Crimes.
   P.M.—Orphan Madelene; Simpson and Co.
2. W.—King Lear; Poor Soldier.
   A.—Swamp Fox; Crimson Crimes.
   P.M.—Orphan Madelene; You can't Marry your Grandmother.
3. W.—Enchantress; Battle of Germantown.
   A.—Swamp Fox; Cricket on the Hearth.
   P.M.—Orphan Madelene; Cricket on the Hearth.
4. W.—Pizarro; Lady of the Lake.
   A.—Swamp Fox; Fairy of the Golden Wheat Sheaf.
   P.M.—Lucille; Lady of the Lions.
6. *Monday:*
   W.—Venice Preserved; Robert Macaire.
   A.—Swamp Fox; Miseries of Human Life.
   P.M.—Two Queens; Lucille.
7. W.—Brutus; Stranger.
   A.—Swamp Fox; Miseries of Human Life.
   P.M.—Cricket on the Hearth; Two Queens.
8. W.—London Assurance; The Mill of St. Aldervon.
   A.—Swamp Fox; Miseries of Human Life.
   P.M.—Sweethearts and Wives; Spectre Bridegroom.
9. W.—Gisippus; Mill of St. Aldervon.
   A.—Swamp Fox; Miseries of Human Life.
   P.M.—Cricket on the Hearth; Orphan Madelene.
10. W.—Werner; Soldier's Daughter.
    A.—Swamp Fox; Charles O'Malley.
    P.M.—Cricket on the Hearth; Ole Bull.
11. W.—London Assurance; Glorious Minority.
    A.—Swamp Fox; Broken Heart.
    P.M.—Cricket on the Hearth; Two Queens.
13. *Monday:*
    W.—Enchantress; Swiss Cottage.
    A.—Swamp Fox; Mother Goose and the Golden Egg.
    P.M.—Kate Kearney; Cricket on the Hearth.
14. W.—Enchantress; Loan of a Lover.
    A.—No bill received.
    P.M.—No advertisement.
15. W.—Giselle; Glorious Minority.

A.—Swamp Fox; Mother Goose.

P.M.—Maidens, Beware!; Cricket on the Hearth.

16.   W.—Griselle; Glorious Minority.

A.—Ernest Maltravers.

P.M.—Maidens, Beware!; Cricket on the Hearth.

17.   W.—Giselle; Mummy.

A.—Ernest Maltravers.

P.M.—Loan of a Lover; Paul Pry.

18.   W.—Giselle; Perfection.

A.—Swamp Fox; John di Procida.

P.M.—Cricket on the Hearth; Two Queens.

20.   *Monday:*

W.—Giselle; Midnight Hour.

A.—Jack Sheppard; Ella Rosenberg.

P.M.—Fate of Ambrose; Dumb Belle.

21.   W.—La Sonnambula; Glorious Minority.

A.—Monseigneur; Jack Sheppard.

P.M.—Fate of Ambrose; Maidens, Beware!

22.   W.—Giselle; Mr. Singleton.

A.—William Tell; Swamp Fox.

P.M.—Cricket on the Hearth; Perfection.

23.   W.—La Bayadere; Robert Macaire.

A.—Cesar de Bazan; Avenger.

P.M.—Paul Pry; Maidens, Beware!

24.   W.—La Bayadere; Deaf as a Post.

A.—Mother Goose; Swamp Fox.

P.M.—Cricket on the Hearth; Perfection.

25.   W.—La Bayadere; Secret Service.

A.—Anaconda; Crimson Crimes.

P.M.—Grandfather Whitehead; Dumb Belle.

27.   *Monday:*

W.—Lady of Lyons; Jacques Strop.

A.—Lady of Lyons; Anaconda.

P.M.—Brewer of Preston; Paul Pry.

C.—Don Pasquale; A Kiss in the Dark.

28.   W.—Money; Rent Day.

A.—Town and Country; Anaconda.

P.M.—Brewer of Preston; Maid of Croissy.

C.—Don Pasquale; A Kiss in the Dark.

29.   W.—The Stranger; Laugh when you Can.

A.—Money; Anaconda.

P.M.—Brewer of Preston; The Cricket on the Hearth.

C.—Don Pasquale; Miseries of Human Life.

30.   W.—Elder Brother; My Aunt.

A.—Rob Roy; Anaconda.

P.M.—Blind Father and his Daughter; My Aunt.
C.—Don Pasquale; Miseries of Human Life.

MAY

1. *Friday:*
   W.—Lady of Lyons; Elder Brother.
   A.—She Stoops to Conquer; Stranger.
   P.M.—Maidens, Beware!; Cricket on the Hearth.
   C.—Don Pasquale; Scape Goat.
2. W.—Pizarro; Heir at Law.
   A.—Romeo and Juliet; Tom Cringle's Log.
   P.M.—Blind Father and his Daughter; You can't Marry your
   Grandmother.
   C.—Bohemian Girl.
4. *Monday:*
   W.—Witchcraft; Deaf as a Post.
   A.—Gamester; Tom Cringle's Log.
   P.M.—Lovers, Wife and Friend; Loan of a Lover.
   C.—Bohemian Girl.
5. W.—Witchcraft; Perfection.
   A.—Cherry and Fair Star; Tom and Jerry.
   P.M.—Cricket on the Hearth; Hunting a Turtle.
6. W.—Witchcraft; Young America.
   A.—Virginius; Lady of Lyons.
   P.M.—Lovers, Wife and Friend; Two Queens.
   C.—Brewer of Preston, opera.
7. W.—Witchcraft; P.P.
   A.—Cricket on the Hearth; Cherry and Fair Star.
   P.M.—Lovers, Wife and Friend; Love in Humble Life.
   C.—Brewer of Preston.
8. W.—Romeo and Juliet; School for Scandal.
   A.—Deeds of Dreadful Note; Cherry and Fair Star.
   P.M.—Cricket on the Hearth; Lovers, Wife and Friend.
   C.—Brewer of Preston.
9. W.—Macbeth; Young America.
   A.—Woman's Life; Black Brig of Bermuda.
   P.M.—Love in Humble Life; Cricket on the Hearth.
   C.—Brewer of Preston.
11. *Monday:*
    W.—Othello; New Footman.
    A.—Ups and Oowns; Greek Fire.
    P.M.—The Chimes; Swiss Cottage.
    C.—Brewer of Preston.
12. W.—Richard III; Mill of St. Aldervon.

A.—Rent Day; Cricket on the Hearth.

P.M.—The Chimes; Turning the Tables.

C.—Brewer of Preston.

13. W.—Apostate; Young America.

A.—Damon and Pythias; Did you ever Send your Wife to Germantown? *: *Mr. Chesterfield Honeybun*—Burton.

P.M.—The Chimes.

C.—Brewer of Preston.

14. W.—Merchant of Venice; Pizarro.

A.—Card Drawer; Did you ever Send your Wife to Germantown?

P.M.—Cricket on the Hearth; Turning the Tables.

C.—Brewer of Preston.

15. W.—Richard III; New Footman.

A.—The Mountaineers; Did you ever Send your Wife to Germantown?

P.M.—Cricket on the Hearth; Hunting a Turtle.

C.—Bohemian Girl.

16. W.—Venice Preserved; Did you ever Send your Wife to Germantown?

A.—Card Drawer; Did you ever Send your Wife to Germantown?

P.M.—Paul Pry.

C.—Elixir of Love; John of Paris.

18. *Monday:*

W.—Old Heads and Young Hearts; Rory O'More.

A.—Rent Day; Cabin Boy.

P.M.—Kate Kearney.

C.—Norma, first act; Don Pasquale, second act; Brewer of Preston, second act.

19. W.—Werner; Did you ever Send your Wife to Germantown?

A.—New Way To Pay Old Debts; Cabin Boy.

P.M.—The Chimes.

20. W.—Old Heads and Young Hearts; Did you ever Send your Wife to Burlington? *: *Honeybun*—Chapman.

A.—Beggar on Horseback; Cabin Boy.

P.M.—The Chimes.

21. W.—Jealous Wife; New Footman.

A.—A Father's Malediction; Cherokee Chief.

P.M.—Violet; Hunting a Turtle.

22. W.—School for Soldiers; Therese.

A.—Beggar on Horseback; Father's Malediction.

P.M.—Violet; Turning the Tables.

23. W.—Cure for the Heart Ache; Black Eyed Susan.

A.—Bombardment of Matamoras; Card Drawer.

P.M.—The Chimes.

25. *Monday:*
   W.—Werner; Did you ever Send your Wife to Burlington?
   A.—Bombardment of Matamoras; Black Brig of Bermuda.
   P.M.—The Chimes; Perfection.
26. W.—Monkey; Rent Day.
   A.—Tom Crinkle's Log; Cabin Boy.
   P.M.—Somnambulist; Cricket on the Hearth.
27. W.—Fashion; Did you ever Send your Wife to Burlington?
   A.—Bombardment of Matamoras; Irish Tutor.
   P.M.—The Chimes; Maidens, Beware!
28. W.—Fashion; Did you ever Send your Wife to Burlington?
   A.—Bohemians; Golden Farmer.
   P.M.—The Chimes; Mr. and Mrs. Peter White.
29. W.—Fashion; New Footman.
   A.—Cricket on the Hearth; Jack Sheppard.
   P.M.—Somnambulist; Cricket on the Hearth.
30. W.—Campaign of the Rio Grande; Merchant of Venice.
   A.—Marcus Curtius; Cabin Boy.
   P.M.—The Deserter; Lady of Lyons.

JUNE

1. *Monday:*
   W.—Campaign of the Rio Grande; Lady of Lyons.
   A.—Marcus Curtius; Honest Thieves.
   P.M.—Day in Paris; He's not A-Miss.
   C.—Don Pasquale.
2. W.—Campaign of the Rio Grande; Fazio.
   A.—Marcus Curtius; Father's Malediction.
   P.M.—He's not A-Miss; Hunting a Turtle.
3. W.—Fashion; Campaign of the Rio Grande.
   A.—Bohemians; Ella Rosenberg.
   P.M.—John Jones; Kate Kearney.
4. W.—Bridal; Campaign of the Rio Grande.
   A.—Robert Emmett; Hunting a Turtle.
   P.M.—Catching an Heiress; Two Queens.
5. W.—Fashion; Campaign of the Rio Grande.
   A.—Robert Emmett; Bohemians.
   P.M.—My Neighbor's Wife; Mr. and Mrs. Peter White.
6. W.—Romeo and Juliet; Campaign of the Rio Grande.
   A.—Margaret Catchpole; Irish Tutor.
   P.M.—My Neighbor's Wife; Cricket on the Hearth.
8. *Monday:*
   W.—Wyoming.
   A.—Margaret Catchpole; Father's Malediction.
   P.M.—Brewer of Preston, drama; Irish Tutor.

9.   W.—Wyoming.
      A.—Margaret Catchpole; Murdered Boatman. Last night of
      the season.
      P.M.—Catching an Heiress; The Trumpeter's Daughter.

10.   W.—Wyoming.
      P.M.—Trumpeter's Daughter; He's not A-Miss.

11.   W.—Wyoming.
      P.M.—A Day in Paris; Who's your Friend?

12.   W.—Laugh when you Can; La Bayadere, ballet.
      P.M.—Who's your Friend? Madelon.

13.   W.—Douglas; Wyoming.
      A.—Rookwood; Dead Shot.
      P.M.—Who's your Friend?; King's Command.

15. *Monday:*
      W.—Enchantress; Yankee Wool Dealer.
      A.—Rookwood; Honest Thieves.
      P.M.—Irish Tutor; 'Twas I.

16.   W.—Enchantress; Spectre Bridegroom.
      A.—Rookwood; Swiss Cottage.
      P.M.—Married Rake; Two Gregories.

17.   W.—Enchantress; Mother and Child are Doing Well.
      A.—Margaret Catchpole; Bombardment of Paris.
      P.M.—Perfection; Frightened to Death.

18.   W.—Wyoming.
      A.—Spy of St. Marc; Bombardment of Matamoras.
      P.M.—'Twas I; Married Rake.

19.   W.—Wyoming; Mother and Child are Doing Well.
      A.—Spy of St. Marc; Robert Emmett.
      P.M.—Nature and Philosophy; Frightened to Death.

20.   W.—Lessons for Lovers; Campaign of the Rio Grande.
      A.—Rebel Chief; Spy of St. Marc.
      P.M.—Dumb Belle; Rendezvous.

22. *Monday:*
      W.—Fashion; Campaign of the Rio Grande.
      A.—King Eagle.
      P.M.—Married Rake; Alpine Maid.

23.   W.—Wild Oats; Pocahontas.
      A.—King Eagle.
      P.M.—Blue Domino; Vaudeville Sketches of India.

24.   W.—Douglas; Lessons for Lovers.
      A.—King Eagle.
      P.M.—Blue Domino; Sketches of India.

25.   W.—Werner; La Bayadere.
      A.—King Eagle; Spy of St. Marc.
      P.M.—Lancers; Irishman in London.

26.   W.—As You Like It; Joan of Arc.
        A.—Peter Wilkins; Rebel Chief.
        P.M.—Lancers; Alpine Maid.
27.   W.—George Barnwell; Lady of Lyons.
        A.—Rookwood; Married Rake.
        P.M.—One Hour; Frightened to Death.
29. *Monday:*
        W.—Rivals; Robert Macaire.
        A.—Enchanter; Dumb Man of Manchester.
        P.M.—One Hour; Widow's Victim.
30.   W.—Fatal Dowry; Lady of the Lions.
        A.—Rookwood; Dead Shot.
        P.M.—Blue Domino; Faint Heart never won Fair Lady.

JULY

1. *Wednesday:*
        W.—Smiles and Tears; Devil's Bridge.
        P.M.—Faint Heart never won Fair Lady; Widow's Victim.
2.   W.—Charles XII; Forty Thieves.
        A.—Enchanter; Mountain Minstrel Boy.
        P.M.—Lancers; Beauty and the Beast.
3.   W.—Bears not Beasts; Wyoming.
        A.—Rookwood; Hole in the Wall.
        P.M.—Faint Heart never won Fair Lady.
4.   W.--Enchantress.
        A.—Felon's Last Dream; Philip Quarl.
        P.M.—Alpine Maid; Sketches of India.
6. *Monday:*
        W.—Speed the Plough; Bears not Beasts.
        A.—Swamp Fox; Enchanter.
        P.M.—Lottery Ticket; Beauty and the Beast.
7.   W.—Gisippus; Joan of Arc. Last night of the season.
        A.—Felon's Last Dream; Secret.
        P.M.—Zephyrina; Beauty and the Beast.
8.   A.—Macbeth; Married Rake.
        P.M.—Sketches in India; Beauty and the Beast.
9.   A.—Pizarro; Dumb Girl of Genoa.
        P.M.—A Roland for an Oliver; Beauty and the Beast.
10.   A.—The Wife; Honest Thieves.
        P.M.—Widow's Victim; Beauty and the Beast.
11.   A.—Richard III; Perfection.
        P.M.—My Wife's Second Floor; The Cricket on the Hearth.
13. *Monday:*
        W.—Putnam; Dumb Belle.

A.—Macbeth; Irish Post.

P.M.—Alpine Maid; Lend Me Five Shillings.

14. W.—Putnam; Lesson for Lovers.

A.—Shoemaker of Toulouse; Oh! Hush!!

P.M.—Lend Me Five Shillings; Brother and Sister.

15. W.—Putnam; Matrimony.

A.—Richelieu; Irish Post.

P.M.—Brother and Sister; Secret.

16. W.—Child of Nature; Putnam.

A.—Shoemaker of Toulouse; Perfection.

P.M.—My Wife's Out; Deaf as a Post.

17. W.—Child of Nature; Putnam.

A.—Stranger; Tom Cringle's Log.

P.M.—John of Paris; Secret.

18. W.—Honey Moon; Putnam.

A.—Brutus; Oh! Hush!!

P.M.—Paul Pry; Seeing Holland.

20. *Monday:*

W.—Bold Stroke for a Husband; Satan in Paris.

A.—Presumption; Paul Pry.

P.M.—Seeing Paris; Asmodeus in Paris.

21. W.—London Assurance; Young Scamp.

A.—Presumption; Enchanter.

P.M. –Asmodeus in Paris; Lend Me Five Shillings.

22. W.—Satan in Paris; Somebody Else.

A.—Bohemians.

P.M.—Home Again; Governor's Wife.

23. W.—She Stoops to Conquer; Somebody Else.

A.—Flying Dutchman; Planter and his Dog.

P.M.—Governor's Wife; Deaf as a Post.

24. W.—Old Heads and Young Hearts; The Eton Boy.

A.—Merchant of Venice; The Review.

P.M.—Asmodeus in Paris; The House Dog.

25. W.—London Assurance; Eaton Boy.

A.—Burglar; Captain Stevens.

P.M.—Cabinet Question; The House Dog.

27. *Monday:*

W.—Macbeth; Lessons for Lovers.

P.M.—Secret; An Object of Interest.

28. W.—Apostate; Bears not Beasts.

P.M.—An Object of Interest; Did you ever Send your Wife to Bristol?

29. W.—Hunchback; Husband at Sight.

P.M.—Cabinet Question; Did you ever send your Wife to Bristol?

30. W.—Richelieu; Cesar de Bazan.
     P.M.—John of Paris; New Footman.
31. P.M.—Lend Me Five Shillings; New Footman.

AUGUST

1. *Saturday:*
    W.—Lady of Lyons; Comedy of Errors.
    P.M.—Golden Farmer; Married Bachelor.
3. *Monday:*
    W.—Henry IV; A Husband at Sight.
    P.M.—Naval Engagements; Perfection.
4. W.—Rip Van Winkle; His Last Legs.
    P.M.—Charles II; Widow's Victim.
5. W.—Yankee in England; Married Rake.
    P.M.—Naval Engagements; My Fellow Clerk.
6. W.—Yankee in England; Married Rake.
    P.M.—Naval Engagements; My Fellow Clerk.
7. W.—Merry Wives of Windsor; Comedy of Errors.
    P.M.—Matrimony; A Roland for an Oliver.
8. W.—Rip Van Winkle; Comedy of Errors.
    P.M.—Loan of a Lover; One Hour.
10. *Monday:*
    W.—School for Scandal; Young Widow.
    P.M.—Matrimony; Beauty and the Beast.
11. W.—Married Life; Mother and Child Doing Well.
    P.M.—Married Rake; Beulah Spa!
12. W.—Yankee in Mississippi; The Chimes.
    P.M.—Young Scamp; A Roland for an Oliver.
13. W.—Yankee in Mississippi; Child of Nature.
    P.M.—Young Scamp; Of Age Tomorrow.
14. W.—Poor Gentleman; Wizard of the Wave.
    P.M.—A Day after the Wedding; Beauty and the Beast.
15. W.—Wizard of the Wave; Comedy of Errors.
    P.M.—Of Age Tomorrow; Beulah Spa.
17. *Monday:*
    W.—Wizard of the Wave; Lend Me Five Shillings.
    P.M.—Emigration; Charles II.
18. W.—The Rivals; Lend Me Five Shillings.
    P.M.—Luke the Laborer; My Fellow Clerk.
19. W.—Wizard of the Wave; Lend Me Five Shillings.
    P.M.—Mysterious Lady; My Neighbor's Wife.
20. W.—Speed the Plough; A Husband at Sight.
    P.M.—Turning the Tables; The Two Thompsons.
21. W.—Honey Moon; Irish Lion.

P.M.—Naval Engagements; Widow's Victim.
22.   W.—Wizard of the Wave; Did you ever Send your Wife to Burlington?
P.M.—Grist to the Mill; Too Late for Dinner.
24. *Monday:*
    W.—Bold Stroke for a Husband; Last Man.
P.M.—My Wife's Second Floor; Swiss Swains.
25.   W.—Did you ever Send your Wife to Burlington?; Wizard of the Wave.
P.M.—Victorine; Young Widow.
26.   W.—Closed.
    A.—Charles II; John Jones.
P.M.—Faint Heart never won Fair Lady.
27.   A.—Der Nacht Wachter; Wandering Minstrel.
P.M.—My Wife's Second Floor; Two Queens.
28.   A.—Der Nacht Wachter; Dumb Belle.
P.M.—Colin; The Truth a Lie.
29.   W.—Town and Country; Therese.
    A.—Nervous Man; Paul Pry.
P.M.—Rival Pages; Sketches in India.
31. *Monday:*
    W.—Nervous Man; Teddy the Tiler.
    A.—French Spy; Dumb Belle.
P.M.—Two Friends; Young Widow.

SEPTEMBER

1. *Tuesday:*
    W.—His Last Legs; How to Pay Rent.
    A.—Nervous Man; French Spy.
P.M.—Loan of a Lover; Fortunio.
2.   W.—Irish Ambassador; Young Scamp.
    A.—Lady of Lyons; Raising the Wind.
P.M.—Two Friends; Fortunio.
3.   W.—Irish Ambassador; Irish Post.
    A.—Werner; Hunting a Turtle.
P.M.—My Fellow Clerk; Fortunio.
4.   W.—A Husband at Sight; Born to Good Luck.
    A.—Stranger; Actress of all Work.
P.M.—Raising the Wind: Fortunio.
5.   W.—Irish Attorney; Born to Good Luck.
    A.—Fazio; Of Age Tomorrow.
P.M.—Gretna Green; Fortunio.
7. *Monday:*
    W.—Hamlet; Lend Me Five Shillings.
    A.—King of the Commons *: *James V*—J. Wallack, Jr.,

Madeleine—Mrs. J. Wallack, Jr.; Actress of all Work.

P.M.—Dr. Dilworth; Fortunio.

8.   W.—Lady of Lyons; Married Rake.

A.—King of the Commons; Hunting a Turtle.

P.M.—Is He Jealous?; Fortunio.

9.   W.—Honey Moon; Deaf as a Post.

A.—King of the Commons; Of Age Tomorrow.

P.M.—Dr. Dilworth; Fortunio.

10.   W.—The Stranger; Weathercock.

A.—King of the Commons; Of Age Tomorrow.

P.M.—Married Bachelor; Mr. and Mrs. White.

11.   W.—The Inconstant; Lady of Lyons.

A.—King of the Commons; Poor Soldier.

P.M.—Swiss Swains; Cricket on the Hearth.

12.   W.—The Inconstant; My Aunt.

A.—King of the Commons; Poor Soldier.

P.M.—My Neighbor's Wife; Cricket on the Hearth.

14. *Monday:*

W.—Gamester; Lend Me Five Shillings.

A.—King of the Commons; Ladies, Beware.

P.M.—Dr. Dilworth; Fortunio.

15.   W.—Much Ado about Nothing; Deaf as a Post.

A.—King of the Commons; Beauty and the Beast.

P.M.—Married Rake; Married Alive.

16.   W.—Hunchback; Pleasant Neighbors.

A.—King of the Commons; Beauty and the Beast.

P.M.—Rival Pages; Cricket on the Hearth.

17.   W.—Gamester; Lend Me Five Shillings.

A.—King of the Commons; Beauty and the Beast.

P.M.—Secret; Married Life.

18.   W.—The Stranger; Honey Moon.

A.—King of the Commons; Actress of all Work.

P.M.—Gretna Green; Fortunio.

19.   W.—Stranger; Honey Moon.

A.—The Stranger; Lady of Lyons.

P.M.—Mr. and Mrs. White; Married Life.

21. *Monday:*

W.—As You Like It; A Man without a Head.

A.—Richard III.

P.M.—Paul Pry; Widow's Victim.

22.   W.—Merchant of Venice; Wonder.

A.—Richard III.

P.M.—Who's Your Friend?; Bamboozling.

23.   W.—Jealous Wife; Man without a Head.

A.—Richard III.

P.M.—Married Life; Bamboozling.

24. W.—Ion; Man without a Head.
     A.—Richard III.
     P.M.—Paul Pry; Ladder of Love.
25. W.—Hunchback; Follies of a Night.
     A.—Richard III.
     P.M.—Married Life; Ladder of Love.
26. W.—Ion; Follies of a Night.
     A.—Richard III.
     P.M.—It's all very Fine, Mr. Ferguson; The Golden Farmer.
28. *Monday:*
     W.—Much Ado about Nothing; My Aunt.
     A.—Richard III.
     P.M.—Maid of Croissy; 2, 4, 5, o!
29. W.—Wonder; My Aunt.
     A.—Romeo and Juliet; Poor Soldier.
     P.M.—Hue and Cry; Secret.
30. W.—Man without a Head; Ernestine.
     A.—King John; Gardner's Wife.
     P.M.—Woman's a Wonder; 2, 4, 5, o!

OCTOBER

1. *Thursday:*
    W.—Cesar de Bazan; Ernestine.
    A.—Richard III.
    P.M.—Catharine and Petruchio; Woman's a Wonder.
2. W.—Married Rake; Cesar de Bazan.
    A.—King of the Commons; Hunting a Turtle.
    P.M.—Maid of Croissy; Dumb Belle.
3. W.—Cesar de Bazan; Ernestine.
    A.—Macbeth; Of Age Tomorrow.
    P.M.—Saturday Night; Woman's a Wonder.
5. *Monday:*
    W.—Romeo and Juliet; Irish Tutor.
    A.—Is He Jealous?; Irish Tutor.
    P.M.—Wandering Boys; True Use of Riches.
6. W.—Love's Sacrifice; His Last Legs.
    A.—Married Rake.
    P.M.—Wandering Boys; Mr. and Mrs. White.
7. W.—Fazio; Born to Good Luck.
    A.—The Lady and the Devil.
    P.M.—Wandering Boys; Omnibus.
8. W.—Fashion; Happy Man.
    A.—Dumb Belle.
    P.M.—Welsh Girl; Dumb Belle.
9. W.—Evadne; Irish Attorney.

A.—Actress of all Work.
P.M.—The Welsh Girl; Hue and Cry.
10. W.—Fashion; Irish Tutor.
A.—Raising the Wind; Invisible Harlequin.
P.M.—Wandering Boys; Irish Tutor.
12. *Monday:*
W.—Hamlet; Deaf as a Post.
A.—Lady and the Devil.
P.M.—Maid and Magpie; Colin.
13. W.—Lady of Lyons; Man without a Head.
A.—Rob Roy; Wandering Minstrel.
P.M.—Maid and Magpie; Colin.
14. W.—King of the Commons; New Footman.
A.—Wild Oats; Beauty and the Beast.
P.M.—Maid and Magpie; Family Jars.
15. W.—King of the Commons; Married Rake.
A.—The Wife; Is he a Ghost?
P.M.—Happy Man; Irish Lion.
16. W.—Othello; Faint Heart never won Fair Lady.
A.—Brigand; Rent Day.
P.M.—Born to Good Luck; Irish Tutor.
17. W.—King of the Commons; Elder Brother.
A.—Pizarro; Rent Day.
P.M.—Born to Good Luck; Hundred-Pound Note.
19. *Monday:*
W.—Hamlet; A Day after the Wedding.
A.—Ernestine; Spring and Autumn.
P.M.—Emerald Isle; Dumb Belle.
20. W.—Othello; New Footman.
A.—Brigand; Spring and Autumn.
P.M.—Emerald Isle; Irish Tutor.
21. W.—Macbeth; Pleasant Neighbors.
A.—Invisible Harlequin; Grandfather Whitehead.
P.M.—Bashful Irishman; Irish Tutor.
22. W.—Richelieu; Did you ever Send your Wife to Burlington?
A.—Hunting a Turtle.
P.M.—Emerald Isle; Bashful Irishman.
23. W.—King Lear; Did you ever Send your Wife to Burlington?
A.—Of Age Tomorrow.
P.M.—Welsh Girl; Married Rake.
24. W.—Gladiator; Deaf as a Post.
A.—Is He Jealous?; Dumb Belle.
P.M.—Cricket on the Hearth; Dr. Dilworth.
26. *Monday:*
W.—Damon and Pythias; Lend Me Five Shillings.
A.—Cesar de Bazan; Ernestine.

[345]

P.M.—Ransom; Uncle Sam.

27. W.—Metamora; Wandering Minstrel.
A.—Cesar de Bazan; Spring and Autumn.
P.M.—Ransom; Day after the Wedding.

28. W.—Gladiator; Faint Heart never won Fair Lady.
A.—The Violet; Cesar de Bazan.
P.M.—Cricket on the Hearth; Welsh Girl.

29. W.—Jack Cade; Married Rake.
A.—Violet; Ernestine.
P.M.—Miseries of Human Life; Dead Shot.

30. W.—Jack Cade; Pleasant Neighbors.
A.—Stranger; Wonder.
P.M.—Miseries of Human Life; Tom Grig, the Lamplighter.

31. W.—No performance.
A.—Richard III; Siege of Monterey.
P.M.—Cricket on the Hearth; 2, 4, 5, 0!

NOVEMBER

2. *Monday:*
W.—Bohemian Girl; Man without a Head.
A.—Rob Roy; Siege of Monterey.
P.M.—Sergeant's Wife; A Kiss in the Dark.

3. W.—Bohemian Girl.
A.—Iron Chest; Siege of Monterey.
P.M.—Sergeant's Wife; Married Bachelor.

4. W.—Brewer of Preston.
A.—Hamlet; Siege of Monterey.
P.M.—Maid and Magpie; Pleasant Neighbors.

5. W.—Brewer of Preston.
A.—Grandfather Whitehead.
P.M.—Causes and Effects; Uncle Sam.

6. W.—Don Pasquale.
A.—Too Late for Dinner.
P.M.—Causes and Effects; Hunting a Turtle.

7. W.—Bohemian Girl.
A.—Agnes de Vere.
P.M.—Sergeant's Wife; Toothache.

9. *Monday:*
W.—Maritana.
A.—Cricket on the Hearth.
P.M.—Faint Heart never won Fair Lady; Toothache.

10. W.—Maritana; Wandering Minstrel.
A.—Dumb Belle.
P.M.—Two Friends; A Kiss in the Dark.

11. W.—Maritana; Lend Me Five Pounds.

  A.—Hunting a Turtle; Spectre Bridegroom.
  P.M.—Asmodeus; Dr. Dilworth.
12. W.—Maritana; Lottery Ticket.
  A.—Gardner's Wife.
  P.M.—Good Genius of the Attic; Hunting a Turtle.
13. W.—Norma; Maritana.
  A.—Rob Roy; Ladies, Beware.
  P.M.—Good Genius of the Attic; Rendezvous.
14. W.—Norma; Maritana.
  A.—Lady of the Lions; Deserter.
  P.M.—Cricket on the Hearth; Toothache.
16. *Monday:*
  W.—Irish Ambassador; Teddy the Tiler.
  A.—Lady of the Lions; Spitfire.
  P.M.—Paul Pry; My Neighbor's Wife.
17. W.—Irish Post; How to pay Rent.
  A.—Hamlet; Lady of the Lions.
  P.M.—Kate Kearney; What have I Done?
18. W.—Maid of Croissy; My Sister Kate.
  A.—Macbeth; Lady of the Lions.
  P.M.—Fortunio; Bamboozling.
19. W.—Born to Good Luck; How to pay Rent.
  A.—Love's Sacrifice; Lady of the Lions.
  P.M.—Kate Kearney; Miseries of Human Life.
20. W.—Soldier of Fortune; Irish Post.
  A.—Stranger; Honey Moon.
  P.M.—Cricket on the Hearth; What Have I Done?
21. W.—Soldier of Fortune; Irish Ambassador.
  A.—Tour de Nesle; Weathercock.
  P.M.—Married Life; Sayings and Doings.
23. *Monday:*
  W.—Midnight Hour.
  A.—Lady of Lyons.
  P.M.—Lady of Lyons.
24. W.—Did you ever Send your Wife to Burlington?
  A.—Hunchback; Lady of the Lions.
  P.M.—Cricket on the Hearth; My Sister Kate.
25. W.—Child of Nature.
  A.—Douglas; The Stranger.
  P.M.—Honey Moon; My Little Adopted.
26. W.—Pleasant Neighbors; Lottery Ticket.
  A.—Fazio; Wallace.
  P.M.—Beauty and the Beast; Rendezvous.
27. W.—A Child of Nature.
  A.—Love's Sacrifice; Soldier's Daughter.
  P.M.—No record.

28.   W.—Robert Macaire.
        A.—Heir at Law; Mysteries of Odd Fellowship.
        P.M.—Kate Kearney; My Little Adopted.
30. *Monday:*
        W.—Man without a Head; Deaf as a Post.
        A.—Tour de Nesle; Magic Pills.
        P.M.—Lucille; The Watch-House.

DECEMBER

1. *Tuesday:*
        W.—Artist's Wife; New Footman.
        A.—Wallace; Magic Pills.
        P.M.—Beauty and the Beast; All in the Dark.
2.   W.—Lady of Lyons.
        A.—Wallace; Magic Pills.
        P.M.—Cricket on the Hearth; Our Mary Ann.
3.   W.—Pizarro.
        A.—Therese; Magic Pills.
        P.M.—Lady of Lyons.
4.   W.—Midnight Hour.
        A.—Charles XII; Hundred-Pound Note.
        P.M.—Augustus Durance; A Roland for an Oliver.
5.   A.—Charles XII; Magic Pills.
        P.M.—May Queen; False Pretences.
7. *Monday:*
        W.—Maritana; Lottery Ticket.
        A.—Coriolanus; Wallace.
        P.M.—Grist to the Mill; Eton Boy.
8.   W.—Leonora; Man without a Head.
        A.—Richelieu; Lady of Lyons.
        P.M.—Soldier's Daughter; Four Sisters.
9.   W.—Leonora; Happiest Day of my Life.
        A.—Honey Moon; Weathercock.
        P.M.—Satan in Paris; Loan of a Lover.
10.   W.—Leonora; Lend Me Five Pounds.
        A.—Therese; Aladdin.
        P.M.—Satan in Paris; Eton Boy.
11.   W.—Leonora; Our Mary Ann.
        A.—Taming the Shrew; Aladdin.
        P.M.—Love Chase; Somebody Else.
12.   W.—Bohemian Girl; Our Mary Ann.
        A.—Ella Rosenberg; Aladdin.
        P.M.—Agnes de Vere; Fortunio.
14. *Monday:*
        W.—Maritana; Robert Macaire.

A.—She Stoops to Conquer; French Spy.
P.M.—Augustus Durance; False Pretences.
15. W.—Fra Diavolo; Our Mary Ann.
A.—Fazio; Irish Helps.
P.M.—Stranger.
16. W.—Luli; Lottery Ticket.
A.—Taming the Shrew; Dumb Man of Manchester.
P.M.—Cricket on the Hearth; Peter Smink.
17. W.—Luli; Robert Macaire.
A.—Ella Rosenberg; Siege of Monterey.
P.M.—Therese; 'Twas I.
18. W.—Luli; Wandering Minstrel.
A.—Volunteer; La Fitte.
P.M.—May Queen; Bamboozling.
19. W.—Luli; William Thompson.
A.—La Fitte; Volunteer.
P.M.—Lady of Lyons; Peter Smink.
21. *Monday:*
W.—Richelieu; Man without a Head.
A.—Wandering Minstrel; The Roll of the Drum.
P.M.—Jewess; Watch-House.
22. W.—Metamora; William Thompson.
A.—Roll of the Drum; Volunteer.
P.M.—Jewess; Our Mary Ann.
23. W.—Jack Cade; Our Mary Ann.
A.—Montezuma; Black Eyed Susan.
P.M.—Asmodeus; Dunn Brown.
24. W.—Pizarro; Young Scamp.
A.—Montezuma; Lady of the Lions.
P.M.—Wandering Boys; Cricket on the Hearth.
25. W.—Young Scamp; Robert Macaire.
A.—Gulliver; Montezuma.
P.M.—Christmas Morn; George Barnwell.
26. W.—Artist's Wife; Happiest Day of my Life.
A.—Gulliver; Montezuma.
P.M.—Christmas Morn.
28. *Monday:*
W.—Julius Caesar; Lend Me Five Pounds.
A.—Gulliver; Montezuma.
P.M.—Christmas Morn; One Hour.
29. W.—Ion; Wandering Minstrel.
A.—Gulliver; Montezuma.
P.M.—Christmas Morn; 'Twas I.
30. W.—King John; Man without a Head.
A.—King Lear; Gulliver.
P.M.—Christmas Morn; Venus in Arms.

31. W.—Lady of Lyons; Two Thompsons.
    A.—Gulliver; Village Lawyer.
    P.M.—Christmas Morn; Cricket on the Hearth.

JANUARY 1847

1. *Friday:*
    P.M.—Young Scamp; New Year's Morn.
    A.—The Chimes; Aladdin.
    W.—Alexander the Great; Money.
2. P.M.—Dunn Brown; New Year's Morn.
    A.—Oliver Twist; Gulliver.
    W.—Robbers; Did you ever Send your Wife to Burlington?
4. *Monday:*
    P.M.—Kabri; Venus in Arms.
    A.—The Slave; Blue Beard.
    W.—Gladiator; Pleasant Neighbors.
5. P.M.—Faint Heart never won Fair Lady; Kabri.
    A.—Oliver Twist; The Chimes.
    W.—Richelieu; Highways and Byways.
6. P.M.—What will my Wife Say?; Asmodeus.
    A.—Closed.
    W.—Jack Cade; Highways and Byways.
7. P.M.—What will my Wife Say?; Mr. and Mrs. White.
    W.—Macbeth; Happiest Day of my Life.
    A.—Closed.
8. P.M.—Look before you Leap; Peter Smink.
    W.—Damon and Pythias; Therese.
    A.—Beauty and the Beast; The Three Lovers.
9. P.M.—The Cricket on the Hearth; Kriss Kringle.
    W.—William Tell; Metamora.
    A.—Oliver Twist; The Chimes.
11. *Monday:*
    P.M.—Look before you Leap.
    W.—Broker of Bogota; Highways and Byways.
    A.—Oliver Twist; Jack Robinson and his Monkey.
12. P.M.—Look before you Leap.
    W.—Gladiator; Robert Macaire.
    A.—Dumb Man of Manchester; La Perouse.
13. P.M.—Charles II; Two Queens.
    W.—Broker of Bogota; House Dog.
    A.—Hunchback; Jack Robinson and his Monkey.
14. P.M.—Look before you Leap.
    W.—Jack Cade; House Dog.
    A.—Stranger; Black Eyed Susan.

15. P.M.—Look before you Leap.
    W.—Broker of Bogota; Pizarro.
    A.—Lady of Lyons.

16. P.M.—Look before you Leap.
    W.—Richard III; House Dog.
    A.—Hunchback.

18. *Monday:*
    P.M.—Heir at Law; A Kiss in the Dark.
    W.—Ion; Deaf as a Post.
    A.—Love's Sacrifice.

19. P.M.—What will my Wife Say?; Gretna Green.
    W.—Jealous Wife; Man without a Head.
    A.—Soldier's Daughter.

20. P.M.—Peter and Paul; 2, 4, 5, o!
    W.—Wife's Secret; Two Thompsons.
    A.—Jane Shore; Dumb Man of Manchester.

21. P.M.—Peter and Paul; The Secret.
    W.—Wife's Secret; Lend Me Five Shillings.
    A.—She Stoops to Conquer; French Spy.

22. P.M.—Welsh Girl; Dead Shot.
    W.—Wife's Secret; Follies of a Night.
    A.—As You Like It; Stranger.

23. P.M.—Asmodeus; Venus in Arms.
    W.—Wife's Secret; Follies of a Night.
    A.—Katharine and Petruchio; Actress of all Work.

25. *Monday:*
    P.M.—The Son of Temperance.
    W.—Wife's Secret; Robert Macaire.
    A.—Soldier's Daughter; Hunting a Turtle.

26. P.M.—The Son of Temperance.
    W.—Wife's Secret; Artist's Wife.
    A.—The Chimes; Village Lawyer.

27. P.M.—The Son of Temperance.
    W.—Hunchback; Midnight Hour.
    A.—Agnes de Vere; Gardener's Wife.

28. P.M.—The Son of Temperance.
    W.—Wife's Secret; Two Thompsons.
    A.—Cricket on the Hearth; Spectre Bridegroom.

29. P.M.—Look before you Leap.
    W.—Gamester; The Wonder.
    A.—Roll of the Drum; Lady of the Lions.

30. P.M.—Kate Kearney; Cricket on the Hearth.
    W.—Merchant of Venice; The Wonder.
    A.—Oliver Twist.

FEBRUARY

1. *Monday:*
    P.M.—Wolf and the Lamb; Toothache.
    W.—Born to Good Luck; House Dog.
    A.—Look before you Leap; Ole Bull.

2. P.M.—Faint Heart never won Fair Lady; Love and Misanthropy.
    W.—Irish Ambassador; Teddy the Tiler.
    A.—Family Jars; Richard III.

3. P.M.—The Battle of Life; Loan of a Lover.
    W.—Born to Good Luck; Irish Post.
    A.—Lady of the Lions; Richard III.

4. P.M.—The Battle of Life; Loan of a Lover.
    W.—Irish Attorney; Teddy the Tiler.
    A.—Look before you Leap; Of Age Tomorrow.

5. P.M.—The Battle of Life; Venus in Arms.
    W.—Soldier of Fortune; Irish Post.
    A.—Look before you Leap; Village Lawyer.

6. P.M.—Battle of Life; All in the Dark.
    W.—Soldier of Fortune; His Last Legs.
    A.—Infidelity; Nicholas Nickleby.

8. *Monday:*
    P.M.—Pet of the Petticoats; No Song, No Supper.
    W.—Irish Attorney; Happy Man.
    A.—Poor Gentleman; Wreck Ashore.

9. P.M.—Battle of Life; 2, 4, 5, 0!
    W.—Nervous Man; Battle of Life.
    A.—Infidelity; Nicholas Nickleby.

10. P.M.—Battle of Life; You can't Marry your Grandmother.
    W.—Irish Ambassador; Wife Hunters.
    A.—Old Morgan; Dumb Belle.

11. P.M.—Pet of the Petticoats; Cricket on the Hearth.
    W.—Born to Good Luck; How to pay Rent.
    A.—Old Morgan; Raising the Wind.

12. P.M.—Swiss Cottage; Lady of Lyons.
    W.—King O'Neil; Wife Hunters.
    A.—Old Morgan; Raising the Wind.

13. P.M.—Battle of Life; Golden Farmer.
    W.—King O'Neil; Wife Hunters.
    A.—Nicholas Nickleby; Old Morgan.

15. *Monday:*
    P.M.—You can't Marry your Grandmother; Uncle Sam.
    W.—Romeo and Juliet; Happiest Day of my Life.
    A.—The Philadelphia Merchant; Oliver Twist.

16. P.M.—Asmodeus; Alpine Maid.

W.—The Wife; Highways and Byways.
A.—Phila. Merchant; Mummy.
17. P.M.—The Chimes; Ole Bull.
W.—Fazio; Robert Macaire.
A.—Closed.
18. P.M.—The Chimes; Spectre Bridegroom.
W.—Jealous Wife; Spring Gardens.
19. P.M.—Sweethearts and Wives; Village Lawyer.
W.—Hunchback; Perfection.
20. P.M.—A Day in Paris; Lady of the Lions.
W.—Fazio; Laugh when you Can.
22. *Monday:*
P.M.—Sweethearts and Wives; Lady of the Lions.
W.—Richard III; Spring Gardens.
23. P.M.—Wife's Revenge; All in the Dark.
W.—Richard III; Two Thompsons.
24. P.M.—Emerald Isle; Ole Bull.
W.—Richard III; Lend Me Five Shillings.
25. P.M.—Heir at Law; Young Widow.
W.—Jealous Wife; Lottery Ticket.
26. P.M.—The Rivals; Village Lawyer.
W.—Richard III; Man without a Head.
27. P.M.—Married Life; False Pretences.
W.—Richard III; Wandering Minstrel.

MARCH

1. *Monday:*
P.M.—Cricket on the Hearth; Spectre Bridegroom.
W.—Richard III; House Dog.
2. P.M.—Cricket on the Hearth; Mesmerism.
W.—Richard III; Too many Cooks Spoil the Broth.
3. P.M.—Kate Kearney; Mesmerism.
W.—Wife's Secret; Wonder.
4. P.M.—Cricket on the Hearth; Kate Kearney.
W.—Battle of Life; Young Scamp.
5. P.M.—Cricket on the Hearth; Kate Kearney.
W.—Weak Points; Irish Footman.
6. P.M.—The Chimes; Mesmerism.
W.—Weak Points; Cesar de Bazan.
8. *Monday:*
P.M.—Poor Smike; Omnibus.
W.—What will the World Say?; School for Soldiers.
9. P.M.—Poor Smike; A Kiss in the Dark.
W.—What will the World Say? Cesar de Bazan.
10. P.M.—Poor Smike; Naval Engagements.

W.—Jack Cade; Too many Cooks Spoil the Broth.

11. P.M.—Poor Smike; Mesmerism.
W.—Bold Stroke for a Husband; Battle of Germantown.

12. P.M.—Poor Smike; Mesmerism.
W.—Lady of Lyons; Gwynneth Vaughn.

13. P.M.—Poor Smike; Hunting a Turtle.
W.—Werner; Gwynneth Vaughn.

15. *Monday:*
P.M.—The Chimes; Dew Drop, ballet.
W.—Metamora; Too many Cooks Spoil the Broth.

16. P.M.—Kate Kearney; Dew Drop.
W.—Jack Cade; House Dog.

17. P.M.—Poor Smike; Irishman in London.
W.—Gladiator; Two Thompsons.

18. P.M.—Poor Smike; Mesmerism.
W.—Broker of Bogota; Wind Mill.

19. P.M.—Battle of Life; Cricket on the Hearth.
W.—Richelieu; Pizarro.

20. P.M.—Battle of Life; Beauty and the Beast.
W.—Virginius; Therese.

22. *Monday:*
P.M.—Naval Engagements; A Day in Paris.
W.—The Wind Mill; Two Thompsons.

23. P.M.—Two Friends; Beauty and the Beast.
W.—Man without a Head; Young Scamp.

24. P.M.—Beauty and the Beast; The King and I.
W.—Weak Points; Our Mary Ann.

25. P.M.—Poor Smike; King and I.
W.—Deaf as a Post; New Footman.
A.—Dutch Burgomaster; Wandering Minstrel.

26. P.M.—Dew Drop; Battle of Life.
W.—Wandering Minstrel; Too many Cooks Spoil the Broth.
A.—Charles II; Loan of a Lover.

27. P.M.—Beauty and the Beast; Boots at the Swan.
W.—Faint Heart never won Fair Lady; Mr. and Mrs. Peter White.
A.—Second Thoughts; Dumb Belle.

29. *Monday:*
P.M.—The Chimes; Boots at the Swan.
W.—A Day after the Wedding; Happiest Day of my Life.
A.—Second Thoughts; Dutch Burgomaster.

30. P.M.—The Cricket on the Hearth; Naval Engagements.
W.—Pleasant Neighbors; Lend Me Five Shillings.
A.—Stag Hall; Ladies' Man.

31. P.M.—Battle of Life; The King and I.
W.—Faint Heart never won Fair Lady; Young Scamp.

APRIL

1. *Thursday:*
   P.M.—Poor Smike; Boots at the Swan.
   A.—Soldier's Return; Second Thoughts.
   W.—Nature and Philosophy; My Sister Kate.
2. P.M.—Beauty and the Beast; Ba! Ba! Ba!
   A.—Blue Devils; Broken Heart.
   W.—Did you ever Send your Wife to Burlington?; Lottery Ticket.
3. P.M.—Kate Kearney; Hunting a Turtle.
   A.—Rake's Progress; Charles O'Malley.
   W.—Perfection; Wind Mill.
5. *Monday:*
   P.M.—The Fair One of the Golden Locks; The Two Friends.
   A.—Blue Devils; Charles O'Malley.
   W.—Highways and Byways; Deaf as a Post.
   C.—Norma.
6. P.M.—The Fair One of the Golden Locks; Naval Engagements.
   A.—Rake's Progress; Two Thompsons.
   W.—Nature and Philosophy; Too many Cooks Spoil the Broth.
   C.—Fra Diavolo.
7. P.M.—The Fair One of the Golden Locks; Boots at the Swan.
   A.—The Lady and the Devil; Broken Heart.
   W.—My Wife's Dentist; Loan of a Lover.
   C.—Postillion of Lonjumeau.
8. P.M.—The Fair One of the Golden Locks; Born to Good Luck.
   A.—Merchant of Venice; Billy Taylor.
   W.—My Wife's Dentist; Married Rake.
   C.—La Sonnambula.
9. P.M.—The Fair One of the Golden Locks; Born to Good Luck.
   A.—Hunchback; Ladies' Man.
   W.—Man without a Head; Valet de Sham.
   C.—Maritana.
10. P.M.—Born to Good Luck; Iron Lion.
    A.—Fazio; Paul Pry.
    W.—Lend Me Five Shillings; Virginia Mummy.
    C.—Brewer of Preston.
12. *Monday:*
    P.M.—Snow Storm; Irish Tutor.
    A.—King of the Commons; Lost Letter.
    W.—Old Guard; Loan of a Lover.
    C.—Norma.
13. P.M.—Voice of Nature; The Review.
    A.—Lady of Lyons; Mysteries of Odd Fellowship.
    W.—Old Guard; Virginia Mummy.

> C.—Fra Diavolo.

14. P.M.—The Snow Storm; The Review.
    A.—King of the Commons; Shocking Events.
    W.—Swiss Cottage; Valet de Sham.
    C.—Postillion of Lonjumeau.

15. P.M.—Card Player; Irish Post.
    A.—Bertram; Sketches in India.
    W.—Somebody Else; Did you ever Send your Wife to Burlington?
    C.—La Sonnambula.

16. P.M.—The Fair One of the Golden Locks; The Attick Story.
    A.—Werner; Shocking Events.
    W.—Old Guard; Wandering Minstrel.
    C.—Maritana.

17. P.M.—Fair One of the Golden Locks; Grandfather Whitehead.
    A.—William Tell; Soldier's Daughter.
    W.—My Wife's Dentist; Lottery Ticket.
    C.—Brewer of Preston.

19. *Monday:*
    P.M.—Maid and Magpie; Cricket on the Hearth.
    A.—Our Flag is Nailed to the Mast; Paul Pry.
    W.—New Way to Pay Old Debts; Somebody Else.
    C.—Fra Diavolo.

20. P.M.—Two Queens; Ransom.
    A.—School for Scandal; Our Flag is Nailed to the Mast.
    W.—King John; Sam Patch in France.
    C.—Bohemian Girl.

21. P.M.—Maid and Magpie; Hunting a Turtle.
    A.—King of the Commons; Sketches in India.
    W.—Richard III; American Farmer.
    C.—Don Pasquale.

22. P.M.—Maid and Magpie; Hunting a Turtle.
    A.—The Rivals; The Lost Letter.
    W.—Apostate; Backwoodsman.
    C.—Norma.

23. P.M.—Faint Heart never won Fair Lady.
    A.—Bridal; Dumb Girl of Genoa.
    W.—Venice Preserved; Mayor of Garrat.
    C.—Bohemian Girl.

24. P.M.—The Two Friends.
    A.—Pizarro; Dumb Girl of Genoa.
    W.—Macbeth; Backwoodsman.
    C.—Maritana.

26. *Monday:*
    P.M.—Closed in preparation for a new series of dramas.
    A.—Honey Moon; Pizarro.

W.—Lady of Lyons; Somebody Else.
C.—Bohemian Girl.
27. A.—Feudal Times; Young Widow.
W.—Hamlet; Loan of a Lover.
C.—La Sonnambula.
28. A —Feudal Times; The King and I.
W.—Gamester; Highways and Byways.
C.—Masaniello.
29. A.—Feudal Times; The King and I.
W.—Inconstant; My Aunt.
C.—Don Pasquale.
30. A.—Feudal Times; The Mummy.
W.—Stranger; Wild Oats.
C.—Masaniello.

MAY

1. *Saturday:*
A.—Feudal Times; The Deserter.
W.—Stranger; Inconstant.
C.—Cinderella.
3. *Monday:*
A.—Gizelle; Hunting a Turtle.
W.—Rienzi; Miller's Maid.
C.—Masaniello.
P.M.—Crock of Gold; Loan of a Lover.
4. P.M.—Crock of Gold; The Omnibus.
A.—Gizelle; Young Widow.
W.—Rienzi; Old Guard.
C.—Cinderella.
5. P.M.—Crock of Gold; Pleasant Neighbors.
A.—Dumb Man of Manchester.
W.—Fashion; The Wind Mill.
C.—Elixir of Love.
6. P.M.—Crock of Gold; Day after the Wedding.
A.—The Illustrious Stranger.
W.—Town and Country; Campaign of the Rio Grande.
C.—Bohemian Girl.
7. P.M.—Crock of Gold; False Pretences.
A.—Hunting a Turtle.
W.—Old Heads and Young Hearts; La Fille du Regiment.
C.—Masaniello.
8. P.M.—Crock of Gold; Cricket on the Hearth.
A.—Oliver Twist; Illustrious Stranger.
W.—Gwynneth Vaughan; Robert Macaire.
C.—Marriage of Figaro.

10. P.M.—Battle of Life; Pleasant Neighbors.
    A.—Tom Noddy's Secret; Gizelle.
    W.—Jack Cade; Loan of a Lover.
    C.—Der Freyschutz.
11. P.M.—Our Flag is Nailed to the Mast; Boots at the Swan.
    A.—Tom Noddy's Secret; La Sylphide.
    W.—Brutus; House Dog.
    C.—Fra Diavolo.
12. P.M.—Isabelle; Windmill.
    A.—Young Widow; La Sylphide.
    W.—Gladiator; Highways and Byways.
    C.—No performance.
13. P.M.—Crock of Gold; Dr. Dilworth.
    A.—John Jones.
    W.—Oralloosa; Somebody Else.
    C.—Maid of Çashmere.
14. P.M.—Isabelle; 'Twas I.
    A.—Ole Bull; La Sylphide.
    W.—Richelieu; William Tell.
    C.—Marriage of Figaro.
15. P.M.—Isabelle; All in the Dark.
    A.—Adventures of an Umbrella; Pleasant Neighbors.
    W.—Oralloosa; Valet de Sham.
    C.—Maid of Cashmere.
17. *Monday:*
    P.M.—Blanche of Brandywine; Valet de Sham.
    A.—Hamlet; State Secrets.
    W.—Oralloosa; Cesar de Bazan.
    C.—Maid of Cashmere.
18. P.M.—Blanche of Brandywine; Day after the Wedding.
    A.—Robert Macaire; Adventures of an Umbrella.
    W.—Jack Cade; Loan of a Lover.
    C.—Elixir of Love.
19. P.M.—Blanche of Brandywine; Bamboozling.
    A.—Adventures of an Umbrella; Artful Dodger.
    W.—Metamora; Young Scamp.
    C.—Maid of Cashmere.
20. P.M.—Isabelle; Loan of a Lover.
    A.—Jack Sheppard; Artful Dodger.
    W.—Virginius; Robert Macaire.
    C.—La Sonnambula.
21. P.M.—Isabelle; The Secret.
    A.—Poor Gentleman; Artful Dodger.
    W.—Broker of Bogota; Pizarro.
    C.—Maid of Cashmere.
22 P.M.—Crock of Gold; Bamboozling.

    A.—Jack Sheppard; Drunken Corporal.
    W.—Damon and Pythias; Oralloosa.
    C.—Maid of Cashmere.

24. *Monday:*
    P.M.—Blanche of Brandywine; Tom Thumb.
    A.—Telemachus; Drunken Corporal.
    W.—King of the Commons; Somebody Else.
    C.—Zampa.

25. P.M.—Christmas Carol; Cricket on the Hearth.
    A.—The Jewess.
    W.—Fazio; Weak Points.
    C.—Zampa.

26. P.M.—Ransom; Tom Thumb.
    A.—The Jewess.
    W.—Hunchback; Too many Cooks Spoil the Broth.
    C.—Zampa.

27. P.M.—Christmas Carol; Tom Thumb.
    A.—Telemachus; Jack Sheppard.
    W.—Jealous Wife; House Dog.
    C.—Zampa.

28. P.M.—Battle of Life; Our Mary Ann.
    A.—Six Degrees of Crime; Drunken Corporal.
    W.—Lady of Lyons; Youthful Queen.
    C.—Zampa.

29. P.M.—Card Drawer; 'Twas I.
    A.—The Jewess.
    W.—Feudal Times; Merchant of Venice.
    C.—Zampa.

31. *Monday:*
    P.M.—Paul Pry; Bamboozling.
    A.—Native Nobility; The Deserter.
    W.—Windmill; House Dog.
    C.—Mountain Sylph.

JUNE

1. *Tuesday:*
    P.M.—Card Drawer; My Neighbor's Wife.
    A.—Native Nobility; Invisible Prince.
    W.—Man without a Head; Deaf as a Post.
    C.—Mountain Sylph.

2. P.M.—You can't Marry your Grandmother; Alpine Maid.
    A.—Native Nobility; Invisible Prince.
    W.—New Footman; Did you ever Send your Wife to Burlington?
    C.—La Sonnambula.

3. P.M.—Disowned; Boots at the Swan.
   A.—Jack Sheppard; Invisible Prince.
   W.—Somebody Else; Lottery Ticket.
   C.—Zampa.

4. P.M.—Sweethearts and Wives; Tom Thumb.
   A.—Jemmy Twitcher in America; Cerro Gordo *: *Joe*—
   Burke, *Haus*—Burton.
   W.—Loan of a Lover; Pleasant Neighbors.
   C.—No advertisement.

5. P.M.—Kate Kearney; Our Mary Ann.
   A.—Invisible Prince; Cerro Gordo.
   W.—Highways and Byways; Valet de Sham.
   C.—Norma. Last night of the season.

7. *Monday:*
   P.M.—Three Eras in a Woman's Life; Miseries of Human Life.
   A.—Jemmy Twitcher in America; Invisible Prince.
   W.—Somebody Else; Wind Mill.

8. P.M.—School for Scheming; Day after the Wedding.
   A.—Native Nobility; Invisible Prince.
   W.—Lend Me Five Shillings; Rendezvous.

9. P.M.—School for Scheming; Married Rake.
   A.—Laid up in Port; Invisible Prince.
   W.—Loan of a Lover; Two Thompsons.

10. P.M.—School for Scheming; Pleasant Neighbors.
    A.—Laid up in Port; Invisible Prince.
    W.—Happiest Day of My Life; Valet de Sham.

11. P.M.—Soldier's Daughter; Welsh Girl.
    A.—Speed the Plough; Mischief Making.
    W.—Lottery Ticket; House Dog.
    C.—Das Goldene Kreutz; No. 777.

12. P.M.—Sweethearts and Wives; The Secret.
    A.—Laid up in Port; Invisible Prince.
    W.—No advertisement.

14. *Monday:*
    P.M.—Roof Scrambler; You can't Marry your Grandmother.
    A.—Uncle John; Tom and Jerry.
    W.—Born to Good Luck; Irish Post.

15. P.M.—Son of Temperance; Married Rake.
    A.—Drunkard's Fate; Invisible Prince.
    W.—Irish Ambassador; Somebody Else.

16. P.M.—Roof Scrambler; Welsh Girl.
    A.—Drunkard's Fate; Mischief Making.
    W.—Nervous Man; Teddy the Tiler.

17. P.M.—Roof Scrambler; Faint Heart never won Fair Lady.
    A.—Tit for Tat; Invisible Prince.
    W.—Soldiers of Fortune; Young Scamp.

18. P.M.—Roof Scrambler; Two Friends.
    A.—Uncle John; Loan of a Lover.
    W.—Irish Attorney; Omnibus.
19. P.M.—Wedding Day; Roof Scrambler.
    A.—Jemmy Twitcher in America; Tom and Jerry.
    W.—Born to Good Luck; Wife Hunters.
21. *Monday:*
    P.M.—Farmer and the Baronet; The Most Unfortunate Man
       in the World.
    A.—Tit for Tat; Picnic.
    W.—King O'Neil; Omnibus.
22. P.M.—Naval Engagements; Roof Scrambler.
    A.—Margaret Catchpole; Spoiled Child.
    W.—Nervous Man; Happy Man.
23. P.M.—Golden Farmer; Alpine Maid.
    A.—Tit for Tat; Illustrious Stranger.
    W.—School for Scandal; How to pay Rent.
24. P.M.—Married Life; Widow's Victim.
    A.—Yellow Dwarf; Nicholas Nickleby.
    W.—Fashion; Rendezvous.
25. P.M.—Honey Moon; Blue Domino.
    A.—Secret Pamphlet *; Crimson Crimes.
    W.—London Assurance; Pleasant Neighbors.
26. P.M.—Golden Farmer; Dr. Dilworth.
    A.—Margaret Catchpole; Yellow Dwarf.
    W.—Pizarro; Somebody Else.
28. *Monday:*
    P.M.—Golden Farmer; Sketches of India.
    A.—Yellow Dwarf; Monsieur de Chalumeau.
    W.—Married Life; Miller's Maid.
29. P.M.—Golden Farmer; Three Clerks.
    A.—Illustrious Stranger.
    W.—House Dog; Last Days of Pompeii.
30. P.M.—Two of the B'hoys; Robert Macaire.
    A.—Pleasant Neighbors.
    W.—Pleasant Neighbors; Last Days of Pompeii.

JULY

1. *Thursday:*
    P.M.—Kate Kearney; Sketches of India.
    A.—Pleasant Neighbors.
    W.—Heir at Law; Last Days of Pompeii.
2. P.M.—Poor Gentleman.
    A.—Three Faced Frenchman.
    W.—Speed the Plough; Robert Macaire.

3.   P.M.—Our Mary Ann; Cherokee Chief.
      A.—Ole Bull.
      W.—Comedy of Errors; Triumphs in Mexico.

5. *Monday:*
      P.M.—Loan of a Lover; Cherokee Chief.
      A.—Hunting a Turtle.
      W.—Pocahontas; Washington.

6.   P.M.—Dumb Man of Manchester; Welsh Girl.
      A.—Young Widow.
      W.—Last Days of Pompeii; Washington.

7.   P.M.—Sketches of India; Philip Quarl and his Monkey.
      A.—Hunting a Turtle.
      W.—Robert Macaire; Washington. Last night of the season.

8.   P.M.—Dumb Man of Manchester; Pleasant Neighbors.
      A.—The King and I.

9.   P.M.—'Twas I; Raphael's Dream.
      A.—Young Widow.

10.   P.M.—Shipwrecked Orphan; First Fratricide.
      A.—King and I; Mons. de Chalumeau.

12. *Monday:*
      P.M.—Bleeding Nun; Naval Engagements.
      A.—Invisible Prince.
      W.—Saffo.

13.   P.M.—Wind Mill; Alpine Maid.
      A.—Two of the B'hoys; Don Juan.
      W.—Hernani.

14.   P.M.—Cricket on the Hearth; Dead Shot.
      A.—Secret Pamphlet; Invisible Prince.
      W.—Hernani.

15.   P.M.—Wind Mill; Our Mary Ann.
      A.—Secret Pamphlet; Beauty and the Beast.
      W.—Hernani.

16.   P.M.—Home Sweet Home; Virginia Mummy.
      A.—Dream at Sea; A Kiss in the Dark.
      W.—Hernani.

17.   P.M.—Sudden Thoughts; Printer's Devil.
      A.—Woman's Life; Two of the B'hoys.
      W.—Lombards at the First Crusade.

19. *Monday:*
      P.M.—No drama.
      A.—Laugh when you Can; Dutch Burgomaster.
      W.—Two Foscari.

20.   A.—Sudden Thoughts; Blue Devils.
      W.—La Sonnambula.

21.   A.—Dream at Sea; Actor and the Heiress *: *Jack Carter*—
      J. S. Bonsall.

W.—La Sonnambula.
22. A.—Lady of Lyons; Nipped in the Bud.
W.—No performance.
23. A.—Hunchback; Will Brore.
W.—Norma.
24. A.—Fazio; Honey Moon.
W.—La Sonnambula.
26. *Monday:*
A.—Jane Shore; Will Brore.
W.—Lombards at the First Crusade.
27. A.—No advertisement.
W.—Norma.
28. A.—Hunchback; Will Brore.
W.—Linda de Chamounix.
29. A.—School for Scandal; Raphael's Dream.
W.—No advertisement.
30. A.—Money; Mischief Making.
31. A.—Dream at Sea; Will Brore.

AUGUST

2. *Monday:*
A.—Poor Gentleman; Catching an Heiress.
W.—Norma.
3. A.—Speed the Plough; Peter White.
W.—Hernani.
4. A.—Heir at Law; Young America.
5. A.—Jack Sheppard; Catching an Heiress.
W.—Norma.
6. A.—White Farm; X.Y.Z.
W.—Romeo and Juliet, opera.
7. A.—Jack Sheppard; White Farm.
W.—Speed the Plough; Swiss Cottage.
9. A.—Voice of Nature; Rascal Jack.
W.—Heir at Law; Loan of a Lover.
10. A.—Peter White; Rascal Jack.
W.—Poor Gentleman; Our Mary Ann.
11. A.—Jane Shore; Rascal Jack.
W.—Child of Nature; Robert Macaire.
12. A.—Richelieu; Rascal Jack.
W.—Our Mary Ann; Juan Romiro.
13. A.—Hunchback; Lady of Lyons.
W.—Swiss Cottage; Juan Romiro.
14. A.—Joe the Orphan; Lucky Stars.
W.—Man without a Head; Loan of a Lover.

16. *Monday:*
    A.—Romeo and Juliet; Lucky Stars.
    W.—Rivals; Gambler's Fate.
17.
    A.—Pizarro; Joe the Orphan.
    W.—Heir at Law; Robert Macaire.
18.
    A.—Love's Sacrifice; Sketches in India.
    W.—Deaf as a Post; Point of Honor.
19.
    A.—Honey Moon; Richard ye Thirde.
    W.—Rendezvous; Gambler's Fate.
20.
    A.—The Wife; Golden Farmer.
    W.—Wonder; Orphan of Blockley.
21.
    A.—Rascal Jack; Joe the Orphan.
    W.—Pocahontas; Orphan of Blockley.
23. *Monday:*
    A.—Jack Sheppard; Dumb Girl of Genoa.
    W.—Binks the Bagman; French Spy.
24.
    A.—Wept of Wish-Ton-Wish; Jack Sheppard.
    W.—Man without a Head; French Spy.
25.
    A.—Wept of Wish-Ton-Wish; Dumb Girl of Genoa.
    W.—Wonder; French Spy.
26.
    A.—Nick of the Woods; Artful Dodger.
    W.—Bold Stroke for a Husband; French Spy.
27.
    A.—Six Degrees of Crime; Nick of the Woods.
    W.—Asmodeus; Gambler's Fate.
28.
    A.—Bride's Journey; Artful Dodger.
    W.—Maidens, Beware; French Spy.
30. *Monday:*
    A.—Bride's Journey; Telemachus.
    W.—Country Girl; Mischief Making.
31.
    A.—Bride's Journey; Nick of the Woods.
    W.—Lucille; Binks, the Bagman.

SEPTEMBER

1. *Wednesday:*
    A.—Bride's Journey; Mysteries of Paris.
    W.—Country Girl; French Spy.
2.
    A.—Bride's Journey; Mysteries of Paris.
    W.—Lucille; Mischief Making.
3.
    A.—Bride's Journey; Light Ship.
    W.—Binks, the Bagman; Asmodeus.
4.
    A.—Bride's Journey; Artful Dodger.
    W.—Maidens, Beware; Mischief Making.
6. *Monday:*
    A.—Stranger; State Secrets.

W.—Married Rake; Irish Lion.
7.   A.—Romeo and Juliet; Mummy.
W.—Husband at Sight.
8.   A.—Road to Ruin; Catharine and Petruchio.
W.—Somebody Else.
9.   A.—Jane Shore; Married Life.
W.—King's Gardener.
10.   A.—Blue Devils; Wreck Ashore.
W.—Mischief Making.
11.   A.—Hunchback; An Object of Interest.
W.—Maidens, Beware!
13.   *Monday:*
      A.—Lucille; Scape Goat.
      W.—Haunted Inn.
14.   A.—Irish Attorney; Smuggler's Son and the Exciseman's
        Daughter.
      W.—Asmodeus.
15.   A.—Wife's Revenge; Smuggler's Son and the Exciseman's
        Daughter.
      W.—Somebody Else.
16.   A.—Lucille; Smuggler's Son and the Exciseman's Daughter.
      W.—Day after the Wedding; King's Gardener.
17.   A.—Wife's Revenge; Raphael's Dream.
      W.—A Husband at Sight.
18.   A.—Undine; Raphael's Dream.
      W.—Wandering Minstrel.
20.   *Monday:*
      A.—Undine; The Wife.
      W.—Werner; Married Life.
21.   A.—Love's Sacrifice; Undine.
      W.—Othello; King's Gardener.
22.   A.—Gamester; Undine.
      W.—Macbeth; My Wife's Second Floor.
23.   A.—Lucrece Borgia; Undine.
      W.—King of the Commons; Maidens, Beware.
24.   A.—Evadne; Undine.
      W.—Richard III; Mischief Making.
25.   A.—Lucrece Borgia; Undine.
      W.—Merchant of Venice; French Spy.
27.   *Monday:*
      A.—Stranger; Lucrece Borgia.
      W.—Irish Ambassador; Teddy the Tiler.
28.   A.—Richelieu; Lucrece Borgia.
      W.—Born to Good Luck; How to pay Rent.
29.   A.—Loan of a Lover.

W.—Irish Attorney; Irish Post.

30.   A.—X.Y.Z.

W.—Soldier's Fortune; Wife Hunters.

OCTOBER

1. *Friday:*
   A.—An Object of Interest.
   W.—Wrong Passenger *: *Dennis McCarthy*—Collins; Happy Man.
2. A.—You can't Marry your Grandmother.
   W.—Wrong Passenger; Happy Man.
4. *Monday:*
   A.—You can't Marry your Grandmother.
   W.—Nervous Man; Wrong Passenger.
5. A.—Loan of a Lover; An Object of Interest.
   W.—Born to Good Luck; Irish Post.
6. A.—Raising the Wind; Miseries of Human Life.
   W.—Irish Attorney; Husband at Sight.
7. A.—You can't Marry your Grandmother.
   W.—Irish Ambassador; Wrong Passenger.
8. A.—Raising the Wind; High Life below Stairs.
   W.—King O'Neil; Teddy the Tiler.
9. A.—Loan of a Lover; High Life below Stairs.
   W.—King O'Neil; Teddy the Tiler.
11. *Monday:*
   A.—Lady of Lyons; X.Y.Z.
   W.—Bohemian Girl, opera; Angel of the Attic.
12. A.—Hamlet; Two Queens.
   W.—Norma; Mischief Making.
13. A.—Inconstant; Stranger.
   W.—La Sonnambula; Pleasant Neighbors.
14. A.—Macbeth; My Aunt.
   W.—Norma; Our Mary Ann.
15. A.—Loan of a Lover; Agnes de Vere.
   W.—Barber of Seville.
16. A.—Dream at Sea; State Secrets.
   W.—Barber of Seville; Waterman.
18. *Monday:*
   A.—Miseries of Human Life; Smuggler's Son.
   W.—Cinderella; Masaniello.
19. A.—Two Queens; Miseries of Human Life.
   W.—Postilion of Lonjumeau; Masaniello.
20. A.—Naval Engagements; Antony and Cleopatra, the interlude.
   W.—Postilion of Lonjumeau.

21.   A.—Man without a Head; Wedding Day.
        W.—La Gazza Ladra; Did you ever Send your Wife to Burlington?
22.   A.—Kill or Cure; Man without a Head.
        W.—Fra Diavolo; Olympic Revels.
23.   A.—An Object of Interest; Man without a Head.
        W.—Fra Diavolo; Olympic Revels.
25. *Monday:*
        A.—Henry IV; Captain of the Watch.
        W.—Feudal Times; Somebody Else.
26.   A.—London Assurance; Raising the Wind.
        W.—Bridal; Old Guard.
27.   A.—London Assurance; Three Weeks after Marriage.
        W.—Werner; My Wife's Dentist.
28.   A.—Who's the Composer? *: *Carina*—Miss Clarke; Lioness of the North.
        W.—Feudal Times; A Roland for an Oliver.
29.   A.—London Assurance; My Friend, the Captain.
        W.—King of the Commons; Rent Day.
30.   A.—London Assurance; Captain of the Watch.
        W.—The Wife; French Spy.

NOVEMBER

1. *Monday:*
        A.—Hamlet; Turning the Tables.
        W.—King Lear; Did you ever Send your Wife to Burlington?
2.   A.—Old English Gentleman; Humpback.
        W.—Damon and Pythias; A Roland for an Oliver.
3.   A.—Gamester; Snake Chief.
        W.—Jack Cade; Valet de Sham.
4.   A.—Richelieu; Snake Chief.
        W.—Othello; Pleasant Neighbors.
5.   A.—Merchant of Venice; Snake Chief.
        W.—Richelieu; Lottery Ticket.
6.   A.—Wife's Revenge; Lucille.
        W.—Metamora; Robert Macaire.
8. *Monday:*
        A.—Macbeth; Guerilla Chief and his Son.
        W.—Jack Cade; Perfection.
9.   A.—Wild Oats; Guerilla Chief and his Son.
        W.—Othello; Lottery Ticket.
10.   A.—Hamlet; Guerilla Chief and his Son.
        W.—Gladiator; Jacobite.
11.   A.—Honor; Ladies, Beware.
        W.—Macbeth; Jacobite.

12.   A.—Honor; Ladies, Beware.
        W.—Lady of Lyons; Pizarro.
13.   A.—Lady of Lyons; Laugh when you Can.
        W.—Jack Cade; Jacobite.
15. *Monday:*
        A.—Gamester; Inconstant.
        W.—Broker of Bogota; How to Settle Accounts with your Washerwoman.
16.   A.—Lady of Lyons; Laugh when you Can.
        W.—Metamora; Dead Shot.
17.   A.—Pizarro; Honey Moon.
        W.—Jack Cade; Mischief Making.
18.   A.—Stranger; Oliver Twist.
        W.—Broker of Bogota; Jacobite.
19.   A.—Money; Deformed.
        W.—Venice Preserved; Therese.
20.   A.—Richard III; Ladies, Beware.
        W.—Gladiator; Unfinished Gentleman.
22. *Monday:*
        A.—New Way To Pay Old Debts; Spoiled Child.
        W.—Norma; King's Gardener.
23.   A.—King Lear; Ladies, Beware.
        W.—La Sonnambula; Dead Shot.
24.   A.—Iron Chest; Woman's Life.
        W.—Linda of Chamouni; A Day after the Wedding.
25.   A.—Othello; Bottle.
        W.—Linda of Chamouni; A Day after the Wedding.
26.   A.—Town and Country; Bottle.
        W.—La Sonnambula; Did you ever Send your Wife to Burlington?
27.   A.—Richard III; Bottle.
        W.—Linda of Chamouni; Perfection.
29. *Monday:*
        A.—Hamlet; Bottle.
        W.—Lucrezia Borgia; Our Mary Ann.
30.   A.—The Cavalier *: *Hargrave*—Pitt, *Mrs. Hargrave*—Mrs. Burke; Bottle.
        W.—Linda of Chamouni; Lottery Ticket.

DECEMBER

1. *Wednesday:*
        A.—Virginius; Guerrilla Chief.
        W.—Hunchback; Robert Macaire.
2.   A.—Cavalier; Katharine and Petruchio.
        W.—Lucrezia Borgia; Our Mary Ann.

3.   A.—Dutch Burgomaster; Bottle.
     W.—Linda of Chamouni, first two acts; Anna Bolena, last act.
4.   A.—Macbeth; Trial by Battle.
     W.—Norma; Lottery Ticket.
6. *Monday:*
     A.—Merchant of Venice; Lady of Lyons.
     W.—Lucrezia Borgia.
7.   A.—Evadne; Trial by Battle.
     W.—Linda of Chamouni; Dead Shot.
8.   A.—Lucrece Borgia, the drama; Ladies, Beware.
     W.—Born to Good Luck; How to pay Rent.
9.   A.—Love Chase; Lucille.
     W.—Nervous Man; Teddy the Tiler.
10.   A.—Lucrece Borgia; Ransom.
     W.—Irish Ambassador; His Last Legs.
11.   A.—Mary Tudor; Ransom.
     W.—Wrong Passenger; Deaf as a Post.
13. *Monday:*
     A.—Adelgitha; Mary Tudor.
     W.—Rory O'More; A Roland for an Oliver.
14.   A.—Love Chase; Ransom.
     W.—Rory O'More; Valet de Sham.
15.   A.—Romeo and Juliet; Barrack Room.
     W.—Rory O'More; Unfinished Gentleman.
16.   A.—Adelgitha; Youthful Queen.
     W.—Soldier's Fortune; Teddy the Tiler.
17.   A.—Blue Devils; Dream at Sea.
     W.—Irish Ambassador; Irish Post.
18.   A.—Fatal Marriage; Lucrece Borgia.
     W.—Rory O'More; Happy Man.
20.   A.—Richard III.; Smuggler's Son.
     W.—White Horse of the Peppers; How to pay Rent.
21.   A.—Othello; Two Queens.
     W.—White Horse of the Peppers; Happy Man.
22.   A.—William Tell; Trial by Battle.
     W.—King O'Neil; My Wife's Dentist.
23.   A.—Naiad Queen.
     W.—Soldier of Fortune; My Wife's Dentist.
24.   A.—Naiad Queen; Loan of a Lover.
     W.—White Horse of the Peppers; Irish Ambassador.
25.   A.—Naiad Queen; Loan of a Lover.
     W.—Fatal Curiosity; Young America.
27. *Monday:*
     A.—Naiad Queen; Swiss Cottage.
     W.—Linda of Chamouni; Jacobite.
28.   A.—Naiad Queen; Sudden Thoughts.

W.—La Sonnambula; Pleasant Neighbors.
29. A.—Naiad Queen; Sudden Thoughts.
W.—Maid of Artois; Turning the Tables.
30. A.—Naiad Queen; Sudden Thoughts.
W.—Linda of Chamouni; Jacobite.
31. A.—Naiad Queen; Sudden Thoughts.
W.—Lucrezia Borgia; Turning the Tables.

JANUARY 1848

1. *Saturday:*
A.—Mother and Child are Doing Well; Naiad Queen.
3. *Monday:*
A.—Mother and Child are Doing Well; Naiad Queen.
W.—Norma; Used Up.
4. A.—Mother and Child are Doing Well; Naiad Queen.
W.—Love Spell; Used Up.
5. A.—Naiad Queen; Miseries of Human Life.
W.—Lucrezia Borgia; Jacobite.
6. A.—Miseries of Human Life; Naiad Queen.
W.—Love Spell.
7. A.—Naiad Queen; Smuggler's Son.
W.—Merchant of Venice; Used Up.
8. A.—Eighth of January * Naiad Queen.
W.—Pizarro; Glory of Columbia.
10. *Monday:*
A.—Eighth of January; Naiad Queen.
W.—Macbeth; Miller's Maid.
11. A.—Pride of the Market *: *Marton*—Mrs. Booth; Naiad Queen.
W.—Belle's Stratagem; Luke the Laborer.
12. A.—Naiad Queen.
W.—Gisippus; Box and Cox *: *Box*—Andrews, *Cox*—Chapman.
13. A.—Pride of the Market; Naiad Queen.
W.—Stranger; Box and Cox.
14. A.—Naiad Queen; Box, Cox, and Knox *: *Box*—Burton.
W.—A Cure for the Heart Ache; Robert Macaire.
15. A.—Pride of the Market; Box, Cox, and Knox.
W.—Gisippus; French Spy.
17. *Monday:*
A.—Cavalier; Katharine and Petruchio.
W.—Used Up; Box and Cox.
18. A.—Richard III; Seeing the Elephant.
W.—Day after the Wedding; Dumb Belle.

19.   A.—Lady of Lyons; Honey Moon.
      W.—Old Guard; Perfection.
20.   A.—Money; Two Gregories.
      W.—Box and Cox; Emigrant's Dream.
21.   A.—New Way To Pay Old Debts; Youthful Queen.
      W.—White Horse of the Peppers; Emigrant's Dream.
22.   A.—Macbeth; Seeing the Elephant.
      W.—Old Guard; White Horse of the Peppers.
24. *Monday:*
      A.—Werner; Rule a Wife and Have a Wife.
      W.—P.P.; Macarthy More.
25.   A.—Stranger; Rule a Wife and Have a Wife.
      W.—Macarthy More; Old Guard.
26.   A.—King's Gardener; Animal Magnetism.
      W.—Macarthy More; Emigrant's Dream.
27.   A.—Lucille; Two Gregories.
      A.—Dream at Sea; Spoiled Child.
28.   W.—Macarthy More; Happy Man.
      W.—Macarthy More; Happy Man.
      W.—Dumb Belle; Happy Man.
29.   A.—Iron Chest; Somebody Else.
      W.—Macarthy More; Fair One with the Golden Locks.
31.   A.—Hunchback; Somebody Else.
      W.—Oberon; Jacobite.

FEBRUARY

1. *Tuesday:*
      A.—Evadne; Where Shall I Dine?
      W.—Oberon; Young America.
2.   A.—Genevieve *: *Genevieve*—Miss C. Wemyss, *Arthur*—
      Roberts; Kill or Cure.
      W.—Oberon; Mischief Making.
3.   A.—Genevieve; Kill or Cure.
      W.—Oberon; Love, Law, and Physic.
4.   A.—Iron Chest; Loan of a Lover.
      W.—Oberon; Box and Cox.
5.   A.—Lucille; Dream at Sea.
      W.—Oberon; Fair One with the Golden Locks.
7. *Monday:*
      A.—Lady of Lyons; Box and Cox.
      W.—Hunchback; Fair One with the Golden Locks.
8.   A.—Romeo and Juliet; Black Eyed Susan.
      W.—Romeo and Juliet; Fair One with the Golden Locks.
9.   A.—Richelieu; Tom Cringle's Log.

W.—Lucrece Borgia; Robert Macaire.

10.   A.—Octavia Bragaldi *: *Francesco*—Conner, *Octavia*—Mrs. Conner; Weathercock.

W.—Jane Shore; Faint Heart never won Fair Lady.

11.   A.—Octavia Bragaldi; The Stranger.

W.—Honey Moon; Lucrece Borgia.

12.   A.—Octavia Bragaldi; The Pilot.

W.—Jane Shore; Fair One with the Golden Locks.

14. *Monday:*

A.—Douglass; Jumbo Jim.

W.—Douglass; French Spy.

15.   A.—The Forest Princess *: *Powhatan*—Conner, *Pocahontas* —Mrs. Conner; Virginia Mummy.

W.—No advertisement.

16.   A.—Forest Princess; Jumbo Jim.

W.—Pizarro; Fair One with the Golden Locks.

17.   A.—Forest Princess; Otello.

W.—Love's Sacrifice; Kill or Cure.

18.   A.—Otello; Tour de Nesle.

W.—Jane Shore; Genevieve.

19.   A.—Man and Wife; Wallace; Bone Squash Diavolo.

W.—Love Chase; Genevieve.

C.—Gemma di Vergy.

21. *Monday:*

A.—Naiad Queen; Seeing the Elephant.

W.—Coriolanus; Love, Law, and Physic.

C.—Gemma di Vergy.

22.   A.—Naiad Queen; Spoiled Child.

W.—Werner; Fair One with the Golden Locks.

C.—Gemma di Vergy.

23.   A.—Naiad Queen; Sudden Thoughts.

W.—Heir at Law; Last of the Fairies.

C.—Gemma di Vergy.

24.   A.—Naiad Queen; Animal Magnetism.

W.—Cesar de Bazan; Oberon.

C.—Gemma di Vergy.

25.   A.—Naiad Queen; Omnibus.

W.—Hypocrite; Oberon.

C.—Gemma di Vergy.

26.   A.—Naiad Queen; Farmer's Daughter.

W.—House Dog.

28. *Monday:*

A.—My Boy Tom; The Lonely Man of the Ocean.

W.—Mischief Making; P.P.

29.   A.—My Boy Tom; The Lonely Man of the Ocean.

W.—House Dog.

MARCH

1. *Wednesday:*
   A.—Lonely Man of the Ocean; Foreign Prince.
   W.—P.P.; Mischief Making.
   C.—Lucia di Lammermoor.
2.   A.—My Boy Tom; Otello.
   W.—Mischief Making; P.P.
   C.—No advertisement.
3.   A.—Breach of Promise; Otello.
   W.—Used Up; Perfection.
   C.—Lucia di Lammermoor.
4.   A.—Lonely Man of the Ocean; Oh! Hush!!
   W.—Young America; Fair One with the Golden Locks.
   C.—Lucia di Lammermoor.
6. *Monday:*
   A.—The Secret Order; Oh! Hush!!
   W.—Day after the Wedding; Perfection.
   C.—Lucia di Lammermoor.
7.   A.—Secret Order; Jim Crow in London.
   W.—House Dog; Pleasant Neighbors.
8.   A.—Secret Order; Jim Crow in London.
   W.—Angel of the Attic; Spoiled Child.
   C.—Lucrezia Borgia.
9.   A.—Breach of Promise; Oh! Hush!!
   W.—How to pay Rent; Oberon.
10.   A.—Exiles of Erin *: *Pat*—B. Williams; The Limerick Boy.
    W.—Young Scamp; Oberon.
    C.—Lucrezia Borgia.
11.   A.—Richard III; Sprigs of Ireland *: *Jerry*—B. Williams.
    W.—Richard III; His Last Legs.
    C.—Lucrezia Borgia.
13. *Monday:*
    A.—Othello; Teddy the Tiler.
    W.—King of the Commons; Waterman.
    C.—Lucia di Lammermoor.
14.   A.—Brutus; Rake's Progress.
    W.—Hunchback; Wandering Boy.
15.   A.—King Lear; Tom More.
    W.—Bertram; Point of Honor.
    C.—Ernani.
16.   A.—Apostate; Wags of Windsor.
    W.—Faint Heart never won Fair Lady; Old and Young.
    C.—Lucia di Lammermoor.
    P.M.—Isabelle; Two Gregories.
17.   A.—Irish Post; Born to Good Luck.

W.—Romeo and Juliet; Old and Young.
C.—Ernani.
P.M.—Two Queens; Rendezvous.
18.   A.—Virginius; Rake's Progress.
W.—William Tell; Soldier's Daughter.
C.—Ernani.
P.M.—Cricket on the Hearth; Box, Cox, and Knox.
20. *Monday:*
A.—The Wife; Barrack Room.
W.—Faint Heart never won Fair Lady; P.P.
C.—Il Giuramento.
P.M.—Lucille; An Object of Interest.
21.   A.—Horatii and the Curiatii *; Nothing.
W.—A Roland for an Oliver.
C.—Lucia di Lammermoor.
P.M.—Agnes de Vere; My Neighbor's Wife.
22.   A.—Horatii and the Curiatii; Nothing.
W.—A Gentleman in Difficulties; Wandering Minstrel.
C.—Il Giuramento.
P.M.—Loan of a Lover; My Fellow Clerk.
23.   A.—Horatii and the Curiatii; Seeing the Elephant.
W.—Old Guard; Gentleman in Difficulties.
C.—Lucrezia Borgia.
P.M.—Isabelle; Crossing the Line.
24.   A.—Horatii and the Curiatii; Seeing the Elephant.
W.—Did you ever Send your Wife to Burlington?; Robert Macaire.
C.—Il Giuramento.
P.M.—Married Life; Hunting a Turtle.
25.   A.—Horatii and the Curiatii; Doings in France.
W.—Did you ever Send your Wife to Burlington?; Robert Macaire.
P.M.—Maid and Magpie; My Neighbor's Wife.
27. *Monday:*
A.—Stranger; Horatii and the Curiatii.
W.—La Bayadere; Jacobite.
P.M.—Pride of the Market; Box, Cox, and Knox.
28.   A.—Rob Roy Macgregor; Box, Cox, and Knox.
W.—La Bayadere; Jacobite.
P.M.—Pride of the Market; Charles II.
29.   A.—Horatii and the Curiatii; Cork Leg.
W.—La Bayadere; Gentleman in Difficulties.
P.M.—Pride of the Market; 'Twas I.
30.   A.—Love Chase; Horatii and the Curiatii.
W.—La Bayadere; P.P.

[374]

P.M.—Pride of the Market; Widow's Victim.
31.   A.—Macbeth; Honey Moon.
    W.—Did you ever Send your Wife to Burlington?; La Bayadere.
    P.M.—Theresa's Vow; Spectre Bridegroom.

APRIL

1. *Saturday:*
    A.—Lady of Lyons; Lucrece Borgia.
    W.—Did you ever Send your Wife to Burlington?
    P.M.—Idiot Witness; Turning the Tables.
3.   A.—Henry IV; Seeing the Elephant.
    W.—Hamlet; Gentleman in Difficulties.
    P.M.—Robber's Wife; A Nabob for an Hour.
4.   A.—Pizarro; Mountaineers.
    W.—Lady of Lyons; A Roland for an Oliver.
    P.M.—Robert Macaire; Widow's Victim.
5.   A.—Lady of Lyons; William Tell.
    W.—The Robbers; Perfection.
    P.M.—Jacobite; Young Widow.
6.   A.—Hamlet; Beauty and the Beast.
    W.—King of the Commons; Fair One with the Golden Locks.
    P.M.—Nabob for an Hour; Irish Tiger.
7.   A.—Wild Oats; Beauty and the Beast.
    W.—Merchant of Venice; Lady of Lyons.
    P.M.—Bottle; Irish Tiger.
8.   A.—Venice Preserved; Billy Taylor.
    W.—Othello; Deaf as a Post.
    P.M.—Bottle; Irish Tiger.
10. *Monday:*
    A.—A Cure for the Heart Ache; Swiss Swains.
    W.—Glencoe; Lottery Ticket.
    P.M.—Follies of a Night; Kill or Cure.
11.   A.—Lady of Lyons; Paul Pry.
    W.—Macbeth; Windmill.
    P.M.—Grist to the Mill; Man without a Head.
12.   A.—A Cure for the Heart Ache; Billy Taylor.
    W.—Lady of Lyons; Loan of a Lover.
    P.M.—Asmodeus; Kill or Cure.
13.   A.—Jacob Leisler; Swiss Swains.
    W.—Stranger; Pizarro.
    P.M.—Follies of a Night; An Object of Interest.
14.   A.—Jacob Leisler; Beauty and the Beast.

        W.—Glencoe; Money.

        P.M.—Grist to the Mill; My Little Adopted.

15.   A.—Jacob Leisler; Dumb Belle.

        W.—Robbers; Gentleman in Difficulties.

        P.M.—Boots at the Swan; Kill or Cure.

17. *Monday:*

        A.—Jacob Leisler; A Roland for an Oliver.

        W.—Julius Caesar; A Husband at Sight.

        P.M.—School for Scandal; Pet of the Petticoats.

18.   A.—Jacob Leisler; Deep, Deep Sea.

        W.—Hunchback; Windmill.

        P.M.—Pet of the Petticoats; Boots at the Swan.

19.   A.—Jacob Leisler; Deep, Deep Sea.

        W.—Stranger; Pizarro.

        P.M.—Charles XII; Captain of the Watch.

20.   A.—Jacob Leisler; Honey Moon.

        W.—Eudocia; Valet de Sham.

        P.M.—My Little Adopted; An Object of Interest.

21.   A.—Jacob Leisler; Inconstant.

        W.—Eudocia; Fair One with the Golden Locks.

        P.M.—Charles XII; Kill or Cure.

22.   A.—Jacob Leisler; Lady of Lyons.

        W.—Jane Shore; Genevieve.

        P.M.—London Assurance; Down among the Dead Men *: *Tompkins*—Walcot.

24. *Monday:*

        A.—Poor Gentleman; Turnpike Gate.

        W.—Fazio; Genevieve.

        P.M.—Tom More; The Limerick Boy.

25.   A.—A Glance at Philadelphia *: *Jakey*—Ownes; Deep, Deep Sea.

        W.—Evadne; Lady of Lyons.

        P.M.—Sprigs of Ireland; Robber's Wife.

26.   A.—A Glance at Philadelphia; This House to be Sold.

        W.—Werner; Ernestine.

        P.M.—Born to Good Luck; Limerick Boy.

27.   A.—A Glance at Philadelphia; This House to be Sold.

        W.—Gisippus; Dumb Belle.

        P.M.—Irish Post; Happy Man.

28.   A.—Heir at Law; Spectre Bridegroom.

        W.—Othello; Love, Law, and Physic.

        P.M.—Irish Lion; Irish Tutor.

29.   A.—Dumb Belle; A Glance at Philadelphia.

        W.—Cavalier; Mountaineer.

        P.M.—Irish Ambassador; Born to Good Luck.

MAY

1. *Monday:*
   A.—A Glance at Philadelphia; Swiss Cottage.
   W.—Cavalier; Money.
   P.M.—Charles II; Omnibus.
2. A.—Pride of the Market; A Glance at Philadelphia.
   W.—Iron Chest; Honey Moon.
   P.M.—Weathercock; Irish Tutor.
3. A.—Pride of the Market; A Glance at Philadelphia.
   W.—Cavalier; Hunter of the Alps.
   P.M.—Cricket on the Hearth; Teddy the Tiler.
4. A.—Spoiled Child; A Glance at Philadelphia.
   W.—Romance and Reality *: *Jack*—Brougham, *Barbara*—
   Mrs. Winstanley, *Blossom*—Mrs. Brougham; Maidens,
   Beware.
   P.M.—Irish Tiger; Citizen and the Royalist.
5. A.—Spoiled Child; A Glance at Philadelphia.
   W.—Romance and Reality; Gentlemen in Difficulties.
   P.M.—Exile of Erin; Irish Ambassador.
6. A.—A Glance at Philadelphia; Omnibus.
   W.—Romance and Reality; Fair One with the Golden Locks.
   P.M.—Exile of Erin; Married Rake.
8. *Monday:*
   A.—A Glance at Philadelphia; Raising the Wind.
   W.—Romance and Reality; Valet de Sham.
   P.M.—Cavalier; Faint Heart never won Fair Lady.
9. A.—Welsh Girl; A Glance at Philadelphia.
   W.—Romance and Reality; Old Guard.
   P.M.—Isabelle; Fashionable Society.
10. A.—A Glance at Philadelphia; This House to be Sold.
    W.—Romance and Reality; Barrack Room.
    P.M.—Stranger; Young Widow.
11. A.—A Glance at Philadelphia; This House to be Sold.
    W.—Romance and Reality; Barrack Room.
    P.M.—Therese; Faint Heart never won Fair Lady.
12. A.—A Glance at Philadelphia; Swiss Cottage.
    W.—Romance and Reality; Metamora, a burlesque.
    P.M.—Honey Moon; Fashionable Society.
13. A.—Waterman; A Glance at Philadelphia.
    W.—Romance and Reality; Metamora, a burlesque.
    P.M.—Cavalier; Captain of the Watch.
15. *Monday:*
    A.—A Roland for an Oliver; A Glance at Philadelphia.
    W.—Irish Ambassador; Teddy the Tiler.

P.M.—Three Poisons; Weathercock.
16.   A.—Barrack Room; A Glance at Philadelphia.
W.—Nervous Man; How to pay Rent.
P.M.—Dumb Girl of Genoa; Some Things can be Done as well as Others *: *Belton*—Paul.
17.   A.—A Glance at Philadelphia; Dumb Belle.
W.—Irish Attorney; Carbonari.
P.M.—Maid of Croissy; Some Things can be Done as well as Others.
18.   A.—Lady and the Devil; Dumb Girl.
W.—Born to Good Luck; Carbonari.
P.M.—Laugh when you Can; Captain of the Watch.
19.   A.—Welsh Girl; Mother and Child are Doing Well.
W.—Irish Ambassador; Wrong Passenger.
P.M.—Stranger; Box, Cox, and Knox.
20.   A.—Dead Shot; Welsh Girl.
W.—Dead Shot; Wrong Passenger.
P.M.—Laugh when you Can; Barrack Room.
22. *Monday:*
A.—King's Gardener; A Glance at Philadelphia.
W.—Maidens, Beware; King O'Neil.
O.—Ein Deutscher Krieger; Royalty in Distress.
23.   A.—A Glance at Philadelphia; Guerilla Chief.
W.—Irish Attorney; Blacksmith of Hesse Cassel.
24.   A.—A Glance at Philadelphia; Guerilla Chief.
W.—Soldier of Fortune; Wrong Passenger.
O.—Hinko; Two Candidates.
25.   A.—A Glance at Philadelphia; The Bee and the Orange Tree.
W.—King O'Neil; Happy Man.
O.—Hinko; Two Candidates.
26.   A.—The Bee and the Orange Tree; A Glance at Philadelphia.
W.—Nervous Man; How to pay Rent.
27.   A.—Dead Shot; A Glance at Philadelphia.
W.—Irish Post; Happy Man.
O.—Lola Montes; Griseldis.
29. *Monday:*
A.—The Subterraneous; A Glance at Philadelphia.
W.—Wrong Passenger; Teddy the Tiler.
O.—Five in One; Maid of Lorette.
30.   A.—The Subterraneous; A Glance at Philadelphia.
W.—Enchantress; Love, Law, and Physic.
31.   A.—The Subterraneous; A Glance at Philadelphia.
W.—Enchantress; Hypocrite.

JUNE

1. *Thursday:*
   W.—Enchantress; Fair One with the Golden Locks.
   A.—Subterraneous; A Glance at Philadelphia.
2. W.—Enchantress; New Footman.
   A.—Subterraneous; A Glance at Philadelphia.
3. W.—Enchantress.
   A.—Pride of the Market; A Glance at Philadelphia.
5. *Monday:*
   W.—The Windmill.
   A.—Nervous Man; Metamora, burlesque.
6. W.—Love, Law, and Physic.
   A.—John Bull; Metamora, Burlesque.
   C.—La Sonnambula.
7. W.—Two Thompsons.
   A.—Mother and Child are Doing Well; Metamora, burlesque.
   C.—La Sonnambula.
8. W.—A Gentleman in Difficulties.
   A.—Irish Dragoon; Metamora, burlesque.
   C.—La Sonnambula.
9. W.—Maidens, Beware.
   A.—Irish Dragoons; Metamora, burlesque.
   C.—La Sonnambula.
10. W.—King's Gardener.
    A.—Old Guard; Metamora, burlesque.
    C.—La Sonnambula.
12. *Monday:*
    W.—A Roland for an Oliver.
    A.—Irish Tiger; Tom and Jerry in America.
    C.—Lucia di Lammermoor.
13. W.—Jacobite.
    A.—Tom and Jerry in America; Sketches in India.
    C.—Lucia di Lammermoor.
14. W.—Poor Soldier.
    A.—Old Guard; Boots at the Swan.
    C.—No advertisement.
15. W.—My Master's Rival.
    A.—Rivals; Tom and Jerry in America.
16. W.—A Gentleman in Difficulties.
    A.—Fortune Teller; Astrologer.
17. W.—The Windmill.
    A.—Astrologer; Metamora, burlesque.
19. *Monday:*
    W.—Enchantress.
    A.—Jack Sheppard; Richard ye Thirde.

20. W.—Enchantress.
   A.—Jack Sheppard; Richard ye Thirde.
21. W.—Enchantress.
   A.—Golden Farmer; Richard ye Thirde.
22. W.—Enchantress.
   A.—Dramatist; Whites and the Browns.
23. W.—Enchantress.
   A.—Lady of Lyons; Boots at the Swan.
24. W.—Enchantress.
   A.—Stranger; Jack Sheppard.
26. *Monday:*
   W.—Mose's Visit to Philadelphia *: *Mose*—Chapman, *Sykessy*—Nagle, *Lize*—Miss Fisher; My Master's Rival.
   A.—Macbeth; That Rascal Jack.
27. W.—Mose's Visit to Philadelphia; Dumb Belle.
   A.—Honey Moon; Jack Sheppard.
28. W.—Mose's Visit to Philadelphia; Lancers.
   A.—Romeo and Juliet; Whites and the Browns.
29. W.—Mose's Visit to Philadelphia; Did you ever Send your Wife to Burlington?
   A.—Romeo and Juliet; O'Donoghue *: *Dan*—J. Dunn, *Kate*—Mrs. Burke.
30. W.—Mose's Visit to Philadelphia; Rob Roy.
   A.—Lady of Lyons; Dramatist.
   C.—Spectre Bridegroom; Born to Good Luck.

JULY

1. *Saturday:*
   W.—Robert Macaire; Mose's Visit to Philadelphia.
   A.—Pizarro; O'Donoghue.
   C.—William Tell; Waterman.
   P.M.—Cricket on the Hearth; Which is the Man?
3. *Monday:*
   W.—Warlock of the Glen; Mose's Visit to Philadelphia.
   A.—Merchant of Venice; A Glance at Philadelphia.
   C.—Irish Lion; Four Mowbrays.
   P.M.—Cricket on the Hearth; The Model of a Wife.
4. W.—Enchantress; Mose's Visit to Philadelphia.
   A.—Smuggler's Son; Philip Quarl.
   C.—A Day in Paris; Happy Man.
   P.M.—Model of a Wife; Day after the Wedding.
5. W.—Masaniello; A Glance at Philadelphia.
   A.—Hunchback; Jakey's Marriage with Lize.
   C.—Swiss Cottage; Irish Tutor.
   P.M.—Model of a Wife; Day after the Wedding.

6.   W.—Masaniello; A Glance at Philadelphia.
     A.—Hamlet; Jakey's Marriage with Lize.
     C.—Irish Tutor; Four Mowbrays.
     P.M.—Dead Shot; Spectre Bridegroom.
7.   W.—Masaniello; A Glance at Philadelphia.
     A.—Rebel Chief; Jakey's Marriage.
     C.—Bath Road; Box and Cox.
     P.M.—Boots at the Swan; Spectre Bridegroom.
8.   W.—Masaniello; A Glance at Philadelphia.
     A.—Rebel Chief; Jakey's Marriage.
     C.—Waterman; Oh! Hush!!
     P.M.—Sudden Thoughts; My Neighbor's Wife.
10. *Monday:*
     W.—Artful Dodger; Bronze Horse.
     A.—Guerilla Chief; A Glance at Philadelphia.
     C.—Spoiled Child; Box and Cox.
     P.M.—Our Mary Ann; My Neighbor's Wife.
11.   W.—Artful Dodger; Bronze Horse.
     A.—Mischief Making; Jakey's Marriage.
     C.—Richard III; Waterman.
     P.M.—Sudden Thoughts; Spectre Bridegroom.
12.   W.—Indian Girl; A Glance at Philadelphia.
     A.—Mischief Making; Jakey's Marriage.
     C.—Spoiled Child; Oh! Hush!!
     P.M.—Boots at the Swan; Perfection.
13.   W.—Indian Girl; A Glance at Philadelphia.
     A.—Sudden Thoughts; Jakey's Marriage.
     C.—Happy Man; Love in Humble Life.
     P.M.—No advertisement.
14.   W.—Bride's Journey; A Glance at Philadelphia.
     A.—Somebody Else; Jakey's Marriage.
     C.—Golden Farmer; Swiss Cottage.
     P.M.—No advertisement.
15.   W.—Nick of the Woods; Bride's Journey.
     A.—Jakey's Marriage; Forty Winks.
     C.—Richard III; Waterman.
     P.M.—No advertisement.
17. *Monday:*
     W.—Old Heads and Young Hearts; A Roland for an Oliver.
     A.—Macbeth.
     C.—Spectre Bridegroom; His Last Legs.
18.   W.—School for Scandal; P.P.
     A.—Othello.
     C.—Boots at the Swan; Four Mowbrays.
19.   W.—London Assurance; New Footman.
     A.—Damon and Pythias; Indian Girl.

C.—Box and Cox; Our Mary Ann.

20.   W.—Old Heads and Young Hearts; A Gentleman in Difficulties.
A.—Pizarro; Indian Girl.
C.—Therese; Young Scamp.

21.   W.—London Assurance; Lancers
A.—The Wife.
C.—Spectre Bridegroom; Irish Tutor.

22.   W.—Laugh when you Can; Grandfather Whitehead.
A.—Shoemaker of Toulouse.
C.—Venice Preserved; Black Eyed Susan.

24. *Monday:*
W.—Speed the Plough; Volunteers' Departure and Return *.
A.—Shoemaker of Toulouse.
C.—No advertisement.

25.   W.—Rivals; Volunteers' Departure and Return.
A.—Shoemaker of Toulouse.
C.—Hamlet; Irish Footman.

26.   W.—Heir at Law; Volunteers' Departure and Return.
A.—Luke the Laborer; A Glance at Philadelphia.
C.—Fortune of War; Siege of Vera Cruz.

27.   W.—Poor Gentleman; A Gentleman in Difficulties.
A.—Sudden Thoughts; A Glance at Philadelphia.
C.—Damon and Pythias; Pizarro.

28.   W.—Mr. and Mrs. White; Abou Hassan.
A.—Jack Sheppard; A Glance at Philadelphia.
C.—Spectre Bridegroom; A Glance at Philadelphia.

29.   W.—Mr. and Mrs. White; Old Heads and Young Hearts, Last night of the season.
A.—Jack Sheppard; A Glance at Philadelphia.
C.—Irish Footman; Young Widow.

31. *Monday:*
A.—Old Guard; A Glance at Philadelphia.
C.—Maid of Croissy; A Glance at Philadelphia. Last night of the season.

AUGUST

1. *Tuesday:*
A.—Old Guard; Jack Sheppard.

2.   A.—Sweethearts and Wives; Miller's Maid.

3.   A.—Paul Pry; Love's Changes.

4.   A.—Cesar de Bazan; Bamboozling.

5.   A.—The Prophecy; Mr. and Mrs. White.

7. *Monday:*
A.—The Prophecy; Bamboozling.

8. A.—The Prophecy; Used Up.
9. A.—Richard III; Raising the Wind.
10. A.—New Way To Pay Old Debts; A Day after the Wedding.
11. A.—Cesar de Bazan; Robert Macaire.
12. A.—The Dream at Sea; Windmill.
14. *Monday:*
    A.—Smuggler's Son.
    W.—Il Barbiere di Siviglia.
15. A.—Old Guard.
16. A.—Valet de Sham.
    W.—Il Barbiere di Siviglia.
17. A.—Smuggler's Son; Sudden Thoughts.
18. A.—Valet de Sham.
    W.—Il Barbiere di Siviglia.
19. A.—Dancing Barber; Jocko.
21. *Monday:*
    A.—Windmill; Monsieur de Chalumeau.
    W.—Il Barbiere di Siviglia, first act; Lucia di Lammermoor, third act.
22. A.—Vol-au-Vent; Death of Abel.
    W.—Il Barbiere di Siviglia.
23. A.—Miseries of Human Life; Monsieur de Chalumeau.
    W.—Il Barbiere di Siviglia.
24. A.—Jenny Lind at Last; Harlequin Invisible.
    W.—Ernani, third act; Il Barbiere di Siviglia, second act.
25. A.—Ladies, Beware; Vol-au-Vent.
    W.—Ernani, third act; Il Barbiere di Siviglia, second act.
26. A.—Windmill; Jocko.
    W.—Il Barbiere di Siviglia.
28. *Monday:*
    A.—Robert Macaire; Harlequin Invisible.
    W.—The Millionaire *: *Marston*—Wheatley, *Would Be*—Richings, *Swift*—Chapman, *Sinclair*—Leman, *Mrs. Lofty*—Mrs. Blake; No!
29. A.—Raising the Wind.
    W.—The Millionaire; Two Thompsons.
30. A.—Turning the Tables; A Glance at Philadelphia.
    W.—The Millionaire; Love, Law and Physic.
31. A.—Used Up.
    W.—The Millionaire; Katharine and Petruchio.

SEPTEMBER

1. *Friday:*
    A.—Faint Heart never won Fair Lady; Jocko.
    W.—The Millionaire; Therese.

2.   A.—Monsieur de Chalumeau; Faint Heart never won Fair Lady.
    W.—The Millionaire; Robert Macaire.

4. *Monday:*
    A.—Cesar de Bazan.
    W.—John Savile of Haysted *: *Savile*—J. Wallack, Jr.; A Roland for an Oliver.

5.   A.—Cesar de Bazan.
    W.—John Savile of Haysted; A Husband at Sight.

6.   A.—Miseries of Human Life; Used Up.
    W.—John Savile of Haysted; Dead Shot.

7.   A.—Miseries of Human Life; Used Up.
    W.—Fatal Dowry; Ladies, Beware.

8.   A.—Laugh when you Can.
    W.—John Savile of Haysted; Ladies, Beware.

9.   A.—Vol-au-Vent; Weathercock.
    W.—William Tell; Bohemian Girl, opera.

11. *Monday:*
    A.—Lady of Lyons; Smuggler's Son.
    W.—Born to Good Luck; Ladies, Beware.

12.   A.—Cesar de Bazan; Death Struggle.
    W.—Nervous Man; Happy Man.

13.   A.—Old Honesty *: *Toby*—Raymond, *Dame Bradshaw*— Mrs. Hughes; Smuggler's Son.
    W.—Irish Attorney; Irish Post.

14.   A.—Dombey and Son *: *Dombey*—Henkins, *Susan*—Mrs. Booth; Old Honesty.
    W.—Irish Ambassador; Box and Cox.

15.   A.—Dombey and Son; Sweethearts and Wives.
    W.—Soldier of Fortune; How to pay Rent.

16.   A.—Dombey and Son; Old Honesty.
    W.—Rory O'More; Lucille.

18. *Monday:*
    A.—Dombey and Son; Old Honesty.
    W.—Soldier of Fortune; Last Man.

19.   A.—Dombey and Son; Old Honesty.
    W.—Irish Ambassador; Abou Hassan.

20.   A.—Dombey and Son; Old Honesty.
    W.—Wrong Passenger; Ladies, Beware.

21.   A.—Dombey and Son; A Glance at Philadelphia.
    W.—Irish Attorney; Zembuca.

22.   A.—Dombey and Son; A Glance at Philadelphia.
    W.—King O'Neil; Happy Man.

23.   A.—Old Honesty; A Glance at Philadelphia.
    W.—King O'Neil; Zembuca.

25. *Monday:*
    A.—Dombey and Son; Poor Pillicoddy *: *Peter*—Burton.
    W.—Bohemian Girl; Ladies, Beware.
26. A.—Dombey and Son; Poor Pillicoddy.
    W.—Norma; Box and Cox.
27. A.—Dombey and Son; Poor Pillicoddy.
    W.—Maritana; Poor Pillicoddy.
28. A.—Ladies, Beware; Two Queens.
    W.—Fra Diavolo; Poor Pillicoddy.
29. ^.—Married Bachelor; Smuggler's Son.
    W.—Bohemian Girl; Poor Pillicoddy.
30. A.—Old Guard; Spoiled Child.
    W.—Fra Diavolo; Poor Pillicoddy.

OCTOBER

2. *Monday:*
   A.—Faint Heart never won Fair Lady; Miseries of Human Life.
   W.—Daughter of the Regiment; Poor Pillicoddy.
3. A.—Dream at Sea; Old Guard.
   W.—Daughter of the Regiment; Box and Cox.
4. A.—Luke the Laborer; Blue Devils.
   W.—La Sonnambula; Ladies, Beware.
   C.—Norma.
5. A.—Romeo and Juliet; Love in Humble Life.
   W.—L'Elisire d'Amore; Bohemian Girl, third act.
6. A.—Stranger; Tom Cringle's Log.
   W.—Daughter of the Regiment.
   C.—L'Elisire d'Amore.
7. A.—Mary Tudor; Pizarro.
   W.—Daughter of the Regiment.
9. *Monday:*
   A.—Hunchback; Raising the Wind.
   W.—A Roland for an Oliver.
   C.—L'Elisire d'Amore.
10. A.—Lady of Lyons; Tom Cringle's Log
    W.—Ladies, Beware.
    C.—Norma.
11. A.—Adelgitha; Boots at the Swan.
    W.—Poor Pillicoddy.
    C.—L'Elisire d'Amore.
12. A.—Gamester; Lucrece Borgia.
    W.—Therese.
13. A.—Adelgitha; Mary Tudor.

[385]

W.—Poor Pillicoddy.
C.—Norma.
14. A.—Wife's Revenge; Lucrece Borgia.
W.—Abou Hassan.
C.—Lucrezia Borgia.
16. *Monday:*
A.—Evadne; The Pilot.
W.—Jack O'Both Sides.
C.—Lucrezia Borgia.
17. A.—The Stranger; Bold Stroke for a Husband.
W.—Jack O'Both Sides.
18. A.—Lady of Lyons; Honey Moon.
W.—Box and Cox.
C.—Lucrezia Borgia.
19. A.—Hunchback; Barrack Room.
W.—Jack O'Both Sides.
20. A.—Black Eyed Susan; A Glance at Philadelphia.
W.—A Day after the Wedding.
C.—Lucrezia Borgia.
21. A.—The Fireman's Daughter *: *Barney O'Boodle*—Fenno, *Marie Merrythought*—Mrs. Howard; Rake's Progress.
W.—Jack O'Both Sides.
C.—Lucia di Lammermoor.
23. *Monday:*
A.—Welsh Girl; Jenny Lind.
W.—Love's Martyr *: *Casimir*—J. Wallack, Jr., *Mariella*— Miss A. Fisher; Poor Pillicoddy.
C.—Lucia di Lammermoor.
24. A.—Nipped in the Bud; Old Guard.
W.—Love's Martyr; Jack O'Both Sides.
C.—Lucrezia Borgia.
25. A.—Married Rake; The Secret.
W.—Love's Martyr; Love, Law, and Physic.
C.—Lucia di Lammermoor.
26. A.—Welsh Girl; Trumpeter's Daughter.
W.—Love's Martyr; Post of Honor.
27. A.—Windmill; Dumb Belle.
W.—Love's Martyr; Post of Honor.
28. A.—Jenny Lind; Raising the Wind.
W.—Bridal; Lady of the Lake.
C.—Linda di Chamounix. Last night of the season.
30. *Monday:*
A.—Alpine Maid; A Day after the Wedding.
W.—Werner; Lady of the Lake.
31. A.—Paul Pry; Jack Sheppard.
W.—Fatal Dowry; Lady of the Lake.

NOVEMBER

1. *Wednesday:*
   A.—An Object of Interest; Turnpike Gate.
   W.—Dead Shot; Poor Pillicoddy.
2.   A.—Welsh Girl; The Lady and the Devil.
   W.—Jack O'Both Sides; No!
3.   A.—Faint Heart never won Fair Lady; Dead Shot.
   W.—Box and Cox; Two Thompsons.
4.   A.—Black Eyed Susan; Love in Humble Life.
   W.—Jack O'Both Sides; Post of Honor.
6. *Monday:*
   A.—Naval Engagements; Secret.
   W.—Post of Honor; Poor Pillicoddy.
7.   A.—Naval Engagements; An Object of Interest.
   W.—Two Thompsons; Jacobite.
8.   A.—Simpson and Co.; Jack Sheppard.
   W.—Loan of a Lover; Post of Honor.
9.   A.—Of Age Tomorrow; Two Queens.
   W.—Matrimony; Irish Lion.
10.   A.—Black Eyed Susan; Married Bachelor.
    W.—Nature and Philosophy; Wandering Minstrel.
11.   A.—Jack Sheppard; Jenny Lind.
    W.—Jacobite; Irish Lion.
13. *Monday:*
    A.—Nervous Man; Married Bachelor.
    W.—Lady of Lyons; Jack O'Both Sides.
14.   A.—Irish Ambassador; Welsh Girl.
    W.—Stranger.
15.   A.—Irish Ambassador; Paddy Carey.
    W.—Inconstant.
16.   A.—Nervous Man; Paddy Carey.
    W.—Mountaineers; Wild Oats.
17.   A.—St. Patrick's Eve; The Secret.
    W.—Richelieu; Honey Moon.
18.   A.—St. Patrick's Eve; Paddy Carey.
    W.—Inconstant; Pizarro.
20. *Monday:*
    A.—Macbeth; Welsh Girl.
    W.—Macbeth; Post of Honor.
21.   A.—Stranger; John Jones.
    W.—Metamora; Matrimony.
22.   A.—Othello; The Secret.
    W.—Othello; Jack O'Both Sides.
23.   A.—Werner; Dumb Belle.
    W.—Damon and Pythias; Jacobite.

24.   A.—Merchant of Venice; Swiss Swains.
       W.—Gladiator; Poor Pillicoddy.

25.   A.—Richelieu; Jenny Lind.
       W.—Richelieu; Irish Lion.

27. *Monday:*
       A.—King Lear; Trumpeter's Daughter.
       W.—King Lear; No!

28.   A.—The Stranger; Of Age Tomorrow.
       W.—Gladiator; Two Thompsons.

29.   A.—Virginius; Faint Heart never won Fair Lady.
       W.—Virginius; Wild Oats.

30.   A.—Henry VIII; Blue Devils.
       W.—Jack Cade; Matrimony.

DECEMBER

1. *Friday:*
       A.—Lady of Lyons; Cesar de Bazan.
       W.—Richelieu; Blanche of Paris.

2.   A.—Hamlet; A Day after the Fair.
       W.—Hamlet; Blanche of Paris.

4. *Monday:*
       A.—Macbeth; The Woman Hater.
       W.—Jack Cade; Box and Cox.

5.   A.—Henry IV; Old Honesty.
       W.—Metamora; Wild Oats.
       C.—Linda di Chamounix.

6.   A.—Merry Wives of Windsor; The Woman Hater.
       W.—Jack Cade; Poor Pillicoddy.

7.   A.—Damon and Pythias; Two Queens.
       W.—Gladiator; Deaf as a Post.
       C.—Linda di Chamounix.

8.   A.—Brutus; Windmill.
       W.—Jack Cade; Post of Honor.

9.   A.—Evadne; Dumb Belle.
       W.—Broker of Bogota; Pizarro.
       C.—Lucia di Lammermoor.

11. *Monday:*
       A.—Love's Sacrifice.
       W.—Jack O'Both Sides; Two Thompsons.

12.   A.—Hunchback.
       W.—Post of Honor; Deaf as a Post.
       C.—Norma.

13.   A.—Evadne.
       W.—Jacobite; P.P.

14.   A.—The Wife.
     W.—New Footman; Wandering Minstrel.
     C.—Norma.

15.   A.—Wrecker's Daughter; Katharine and Petruchio.
     W.—Bombastes Furioso; Poor Pillicoddy.

16.   A.—Jane Shore; Faint Heart never won Fair Lady.
     W.—Bombastes Furioso; P.P.
     C.—Norma.

18. *Monday:*
     A.—Poor Gentleman; California Gold Mines.
     W.—Jacobite; Virginia Mummy.

19.   A.—Sweethearts and Wives; California Gold Mines.
     W.—Robert Macaire; Jumbo Jim.
     C.—Ernani.

20.   A.—Welsh Girl; Spectre Bridegroom.
     W.—Post of Honor; Otello.

21.   A.—Gilderoy; California Gold Mines.
     W.—Otello; Virginia Mummy.
     C.—Ernani.

22.   A.—Gilderoy; California Gold Mines.
     W.—Otello; Foreign Prince.

23.   A.—Rag Picker of Paris *: *Rag Picker*—W. Marshall, *Dress-maker*—Mrs. Howard; Ole Bull.
     W.—Deaf as a Post; A Glance at Philadelphia.
     C.—Ernani.

25. *Monday:*
     A.—Rag Picker of Paris; Philadelphia in Spots *: *Sam*—C. Burke.
     W.—Bohemian Girl; Lady of the Lake.
     C.—Lucrezia Borgia.
     Ath.—Soldier's Daughter; Dead Shot.

26.   A.—No advertisement.
     W.—Bohemian Girl; Lady of the Lake.
     Ath.—Lady of Lyons; Swiss Swains.

27.   A.—Rag Picker of Paris; Philadelphia in Spots.
     W.—Blanche of Paris; Cesar de Bazan.
     Ath.—Stranger; Spectre Bridegroom.

28.   A.—Rag Picker of Paris; Philadelphia in Spots.
     W.—Lady of the Lake; Bone Squash Diavolo.
     Ath.—Love's Sacrifice; Dumb Belle.
     C.—I Lombardi.

29.   A.—Adopted Child; Philadelphia in Spots.
     W.—Hofer; Bone Squash Diavolo.
     Ath.—Lucretia Borgia; Siege of Stralsund.

30.   A.—Rag Picker of Paris; Philadelphia in Spots.

W.—Three Eras in Washington's Life *; Virginia Mummy.
Ath.—Therese; Robert Macaire.
C.—I Lombardi.

JANUARY 1849

1. *Monday:*
   A.—Rag Picker of Paris; Philadelphia in Spots.
   W.—Three Eras of Washington's Life; Hofer.
   Ath.—Lucretia Borgia; A Ghost in Spite of Himself.
   C.—Il Barbiere di Siviglia.
2. A.—Rag Picker of Paris; Philadelphia in Spots.
   W.—Three Eras in Washington's Life; Hofer.
   Ath.—Bold Stroke for a Husband; Village Lawyer.
3. A.—Rag Picker of Paris; Philadelphia in Spots.
   W.—Three Eras in Washington's Life; Bohemian Girl.
   Ath.—Golden Farmer; Box and Cox.
   C.—Il Barbiere di Siviglia; Last night of the season.
4. A.—Rag Picker of Paris; Philadelphia in Spots.
   W.—Three Eras in Washington's Life; Lady of the Lake.
   Ath.—Rent Day; Sudden Thoughts.
5. A.—Hunting a turtle; Philadelphia in Spots.
   W.—Court and City *: *Scruple*—Richings; Three Eras in
   Washington's Life.
   Ath.—Money; My Neighbor's Wife.
6. A.—The Crock of Gold *: *Sarah*—Mrs. Howard; Philadelphia
   in Spots.
   W.—Court and City; Post of Honor.
   Ath.—Deserter; Our Mary Ann.
8. *Monday:*
   A.—The Crock of Gold; Slasher and Crasher *: *Slasher*—
   Burke, *Crasher*—Robinson.
   W.—Court and City; An Irish Engagement.
   Ath.—Animal Magnetism; Our Mary Ann.
9. A.—Slasher and Crasher; Crock of Gold.
   W.—Jacobite; An Irish Engagement.
   Ath.—Maid of Croissy; Mother and Child are Doing Well.
10. A.—Lavater, the Physiognomist *: *Lavater*—Thayer; Slasher
    and Crasher.
    W.—Madelaine *; Laugh when you Can.
    Ath.—Wolf and Lamb; My Wife's Second Floor.
11. A.—Rob Roy Macgregor; Lady of the Lions.
    W.—Wild Oats; Loan of a Lover.
    Ath.—Bold Stroke for a Husband; My Wife's Second Floor.
12. A.—Masaniello; Slasher and Crasher.
    W.—Court and City; Madelaine.

Ath.—Cesar de Bazan; Dead Shot.
13.   A.—Haunted Man; A Glance at Philadelphia.
W.—Madelaine; The Chiffonier.
Ath.—Midnight Watch; Rendezvous.
15. *Monday:*
A.—Richard III; Haunted Man.
W.—Madelaine; Chiffonier.
Ath.—She Stoops to Conquer; Wilful Murder.
16.   A.—Pizarro; Swiss Cottage.
W.—Blanche of Paris; Chiffonier.
Ath.—Cricket on the Hearth; John Jones.
17.   A.—John di Procida; Jack Sheppard.
W.—Laugh when you Can; Deaf as a Post.
Ath.—Point of Honor; The Secret.
18.   A.—John di Procida; Jack Sheppard.
W.—Poor Pillicoddy; Madelaine.
Ath.—Iron King; John Jones.
19.   A.—Ella Rosenberg; Avenger.
W.—Box and Cox; Post of Honor.
Ath.—Honey Moon; Animal Magnetism.
20.   A.—Warlock of the Glen; Jack Sheppard.
W.—Matrimony; Djim-Kro-Ryce.
Ath.—Speed the Plough; Dumb Belle.
22. *Monday:*
A.—Masaniello; Warlock of the Glen.
W.—Jack O' Both Sides; Madelaine.
Ath.—Poor Gentleman; Poor Pillicoddy.
23.   A.—Lavater, the Physiognomist; Crock of Gold.
W.—Two Thompsons; Box and Cox.
Ath.—Paul Pry; Crimson Crimes.
24.   A.—Count of Monte Cristo *: *Dantes*—W. Marshall.
W.—Count of Monte Cristo *.
Ath.—Pride of the Market; Poor Pillicoddy.
25.   A.—Count of Monte Cristo.
W.—Count of Monte Cristo.
Ath.—Pride of the Market; Lottery Ticket.
26.   A.—Count of Monte Cristo.
W.—Count of Monte Cristo.
Ath.—Golden Farmer; A Kiss in the Dark.
27.   A.—Count of Monte Cristo.
W.—Count of Monte Cristo.
Ath.—Merchant and his Clerks; John Jones.
29. *Monday:*
A.—Count of Monte Cristo.
W.—Count of Monte Cristo.
Ath.—No legitimate drama.

30.   A.—Count of Monte Cristo.
        W.—Count of Monte Cristo.
31.   A.—Count of Monte Cristo.
        W.—Count of Monte Cristo.

FEBRUARY

1. *Thursday:*
        A.—Count of Monte Cristo.
        W.—Count of Monte Cristo.
2.   A.—Count of Monte Cristo.
        W.—Count of Monte Cristo.
3.   A.—Count of Monte Cristo.
        W.—Count of Monte Cristo.
5. *Monday:*
        A.—Count of Monte Cristo.
        W.—Count of Monte Cristo.
6.   A.—Count of Monte Cristo.
        W.—Count of Monte Cristo.
7.   A.—Count of Monte Cristo.
        W.—Count of Monte Cristo.
8.   A.—Count of Monte Cristo.
        W.—Count of Monte Cristo.
9.   A.—Count of Monte Cristo.
        W.—Count of Monte Cristo.
10.   A.—Count of Monte Cristo.
        W.—Count of Monte Cristo.
12. *Monday:*
        A.—Maniac Lover; A Glance at Philadelphia.
        W.—Count of Monte Cristo.
13.   A.—Maniac Lover; A Glance at Philadelphia.
        W.—Count of Monte Cristo.
14.   A.—Midnight Watch; A Glance at Philadelphia.
        W.—Count of Monte Cristo.
15.   A.—Midnight Watch; A Glance at Philadelphia.
        W.—Count of Monte Cristo.
16.   A.—Midnight Watch; A Glance at Philadelphia.
        W.—Count of Monte Cristo.
17.   A.—Adopted Child; A Glance at Philadelphia.
        W.—Count of Monte Cristo.
19. *Monday:*
        A.—Wacousta; Monte Cristy *: *Dantes*—Robinson.
        W.—Slasher and Crasher; Tom and Jerry.
20.   A.—Wacousta; Monte Cristy.
        W.—Slasher and Crasher; Tom and Jerry.
21.   A.—Wacousta; Monte Cristy.

W.—Slasher and Crasher; Tom and Jerry.
22.   A.—Wacousta; Monte Cristy.
W.—Slasher and Crasher; Tom and Jerry.
23.   A.—Wacousta; Monte Cristy.
W.—Post of Honor; Tom and Jerry.
24.   A.—Wacousta; Charles II.
W.—Slasher and Crasher; Arabs of the Desert.
26.   *Monday:*
A.—Dombey and Son; Poor Pillicoddy.
W.—Arabs of the Desert; No!
27.   A.—Dombey and Son; Slasher and Crasher.
W.—Arabs of the Desert; Madelaine.
28.   A.—Dombey and Son; Katharine and Petruchio.
W.—Arabs of the Desert; Madelaine.

MARCH

1.   *Thursday:*
A.—Dombey and Son; Poor Pillicoddy.
W.—Tom and Jerry; Arab of the Niger.
2.   A.—Dombey and Son; How to Pay your Washerwoman.
W.—Madelaine; Arab of the Niger.
3.   A.—Dombey and Son; Your Life's in Danger.
W.—Tom and Jerry; Arab of the Niger.
5.   *Monday:*
A.—Carpenter of Rouen; The Twin Brothers of the Blood
Red Cross *: *Wild Man of the Mountain*—Canfield,
DeLancy—Brandon, *Bertha*—Mrs. Burke.
W.—Elder Brother; Wine Does Wonders.
6.   A.—Carpenter of Rouen; Twin Brothers.
W.—Lady of Lyons; My Aunt.
7.   A.—Seven Clerks; Twin Brothers.
W.—Stranger; Wild Oats.
8.   A.—Seven Clerks; Twin Brothers.
W.—Walter Raymond *: *Walter*—Murdock, *Okeama*—Mrs.
Blake; Founded on Facts.
9.   A.—Walter Brand; Twin Brothers.
W.—Walter Raymond; Wine Does Wonders.
10.   A.—Paul Pry; Twin Brothers.
W.—Walter Raymond; Wine Does Wonders.
12.   *Monday:*
A.—Crimson Crimes; A Glance at Philadelphia.
W.—Walter Raymond; Honey Moon.
13.   A.—A Glance at Philadelphia; Jack Sheppard.
W.—Walter Raymond; Elder Brother.

14. A.—Physiognomist; Jakey's Visit to California *: *Jakey*—J. Owens, *Lize*—Mrs. Booth.
     W.—Walter Raymond; Laugh when you Can.
15. A.—Two Queens; Jakey's Visit to California.
     W.—Lady of Lyons; Wine Works Wonders.
16. A.—Queer Dilemmas; Jakey's Visit to California.
     W.—Money; Dramatist.
17. A.—Queer Dilemmas; Jakey's Visit to California.
     W.—Venice Preserved; Mountaineers.
19. *Monday:*
     A.—Stranger; Bold Stroke for a Husband.
     W.—Henry IV; Slasher and Crasher.
20. A.—Hunchback; Faint Heart never won Fair Lady.
     W.—Kentuckian; His Last Legs.
21. A.—Jane Shore; Lucrece Borgia.
     W.—Man of the World; Kentuckian.
22. A.—Love's Sacrifice; Barrack Room.
     W.—Rip Van Winkle; His Last Legs.
23. A.—Jane Shore; Lucrece Borgia.
     W.—Merry Wives of Windsor; Monsieur Mallet.
24. A.—Venetian *: *Bravo*—Marshall, *Theodora*—Mrs. Farren; Pizarro.
     W.—Henry IV; Kentuckian.
26. *Monday:*
     A.—Evadne; Venetian.
     W.—Romeo and Juliet; Laugh when you Can.
27. A.—Venetian; Soldier's Daughter.
     W.—Lady of Lyons; My Aunt.
28. A.—Venetian; Time Tries All *: *Laura*—Mrs. Farren, *Bates*—Baker.
     W.—Robbers; Founded on Facts.
29. A.—Venetian; Time Tries All.
     W.—Money; Dramatist.
30. A.—Remorse *: *Dorival*—Farren, *Madame Dorival*—Mrs. Farren; Venetian.
     W.—Stranger; Wild Oats.
31. A.—Remorse; Venetian.
     W.—Robbers; Slasher and Crasher.

APRIL

2. *Monday:*
    A.—Remorse; Mary Tudor.
    W.—Much Ado about Nothing; Cure for the Heart Ache.
3. A.—Remorse; Time Tries All.
    W.—Millionaire; Gambler's Fate.

4.   A.—Macbeth; Therese.
       W.—Julius Caesar; Djim-Kro-Ryce.
5.   A.—Jane Shore; Perfection.
       W.—Poor Gentleman; Madelaine.
6.   A.—Walter Brand; Undine.
       W.—Wild Oats; Dramatist.
7.   A.—Dombey and Son; Carpenter of Rouen.
       W.—Romeo and Juliet; Wine Works Wonders.
9. *Monday:*
       A.—Richard III; Hunting a Turtle.
       W.—Irish Ambassador; My Wife's Come.
10.   A.—Hamlet; Widow's Victim.
       W.—Born to Good Luck; How to pay Rent.
11.   A.—Merchant of Venice; Lady of Lyons.
       W.—Nervous Man; My Wife's Come.
12.   A.—Othello; Widow's Victim.
       W.—Irish Attorney; Mary Melvyn *.
13.   A.—Werner; Katharine and Petruchio.
       W.—Rory O'More; How to pay Rent.
14.   A.—Macbeth; Antony and Cleopatra, farce.
       W.—Born to Good Luck; Mary Melvyn.
16. *Monday:*
       A.—Revenge; Ladies' Club.
       W.—Soldier of Fortune; My Wife's Come.
17.   A.—Much Ado about Nothing; The Brigand.
       W.—King O'Neil; Irish Post.
18.   A.—Cavalier; Brigand.
       W.—Soldier of Fortune; Wrong Passenger.
19.   A.—School of Reform; Brigand.
       W.—Irish Ambassador; Nervous Man.
20.   A.—Gamester; The Delusion *: *Harleigh*—Pitt, *Marion*—
          Mrs. Pitt.
       W.—King O'Neil; Teddy the Tiler.
21.   A.—Cavalier; School of Reform.
       W.—Irish Attorney; Witch of Windemere.
23. *Monday:*
       A.—Eagle Eye *: *Otahontas*—J. H. Hall; *LeBeau*—Bernard,
          Coquese—Mrs. Burke; Hunting a Turtle.
       W.—Enchantress.
24.   A.—Eagle Eye; Weather Cock.
       W.—Enchantress.
25.   A.—Eagle Eye; Done on Both Sides.
       W.—Enchantress.
       P.M.—Linda; Somebody Else.
26.   A.—Eagle Eye; Done on Both Sides.
       W.—Enchantress.

[395]

P.M.—Linda; Handsome Husband.
27.　　A.—Eagle Eye; Loan of a Lover.
W.—Enchantress.
P.M.—Linda; Handsome Husband.
28.　　A.—Eagle Eye; Adopted Child.
W.—Enchantress.
P.M.—No advertisement.
30. *Monday:*
　　A.—Putnam; Katharine and Petruchio.
　　W.—Fra Diavolo; Witch of Windermere.
　　P.M.—Milliner's Holiday; Four Sisters.

MAY

1. *Tuesday:*
　　A.—Putnam; Done on Both Sides.
　　W.—Bohemian Girl.
　　P.M.—Milliner's Holiday; Four Sisters.
2.　　A.—Putnam; Wreckers of Norway.
W.—Enchantress.
P.M.—Lola Montes; Fashionable Arrivals.
3.　　A.—Putnam; Maniac Lover.
W.—La Sonnambula; My Wife's Come.
P.M.—Lola Montes; Fashionable Arrivals.
4.　　A.—Rookwood; Putnam.
W.—Daughter of the Regiment; Enchantress, second act.
P.M.—Linda; Swiss Swains.
5.　　A.—Rookwood; Putnam.
W.—Bohemian Girl; Witch of Windermere.
P.M.—Linda; Swiss Swains.
7. *Monday:*
　　A.—Money; Ringdoves.
　　W.—Dramatist; Day after the Wedding.
　　P.M.—White Farm; Wedding Breakfast.
8.　　A.—Rookwood; Ringdoves.
W.—Strangers; Wine Works Wonders.
P.M.—White Farm; Wedding Breakfast.
9.　　A.—Horse of the Prairie *: *Matalaki*—J. H. Hall, *Capt. Howard*—Mortimer; Ringdoves.
W.—Robbers; Witch of Windermere.
P.M.—Roll of the Drum; Pat Lyon.
10.　　A.—Horse of the Prairie; Ask no Questions.
W.—Romeo and Juliet; My Aunt.
P.M.—Roll of the Drum; Handsome Husband.
11.　　A.—Horse of the Prairie; Wallace.
W.—Much Ado about Nothing; Lady of Lyons.

P.M.—Attic Story; Wedding Breakfast.
12.   A.—Horse of the Prairie; Rookwood.
W.—Wild Oats; Pizarro.
P.M.—Attic Story; Wedding Breakfast.
14.   A.—Miseries of Human Life; My Husband's Ghost.
W.—Money; Mountaineers.
P.M.—Duchess de la Vaubaliere; Windmill.
15.   A.—Dumb Belle; My Husband's Ghost.
W.—Madelaine; Witch of Windermere.
P.M.—Duchess de la Vaubaliere; Windmill.
16.   A.—Katharine and Petruchio; Mr. and Mrs. White.
W.—Werner; Dead Shot.
P.M.—American Farmers; Crimson Crimes.
17.   A.—Everybody's Husband; Dead Shot.
W.—Richelieu; King's Gardener.
P.M.—Flowers of the Forest *: *Lavrock*—Tidmarsh, *Alfred*—Crocker, *Cheap John*—Jefferson, *Cynthia*—Mrs. Bowers.
18.   A.—Everybody's Husband.
W.—School of Reform; Hunter of the Alps.
P.M.—Flowers of the Forest.
19.   A.—Maniac Lover.
W.—Cavalier; Antony and Cleopatra, farce.
P.M.—Flowers of the Forest.
21. *Monday:*
A.—Midnight Watch.
W.—Hamlet; Ladies' Club.
P.M.—Flowers of the Forest.
22.   A.—Ask no Questions.
W.—As You Like It; Ladies' Club.
P.M.—Flowers of the Forest.
23.   A.—Three Wives of Madrid *: *Moreno*—Thayer, *Beatrice*—Mrs. Winstanley.
W.—Money; Iron Chest.
P.M.—American Farmers; Somebody Else.
24.   A.—Three Wives of Madrid.
W.—Wives as they Were; Victorine.
P.M.—American Farmers; Somebody Else.
25.   A.—Dr. Dilworth; My Husband's Ghost.
W.—Everyone has his Fault; Witch of Windermere.
P.M.—Who Speaks First; Spectre Bridegroom.
26.   A.—Wallace; Double Bedded Room.
W.—Count of Monte Cristo.
P.M.—Who Speaks First; Spectre Bridegroom.
28.   A.—Born to Good Luck; Double Bedded Room.
W.—Othello; King's Gardener.
P.M.—Mental Electricity *.

29.   A.—Irish Tutor; Double Bedded Room.
      W.—Stranger; Wild Oats.
      P.M.—Mental Electricity.
30.   A.—Rory O'More; Ringdoves.
      W.—Much Ado about Nothing; Perfection.
      P.M.—Four Sisters.
31.   A.—His Last Legs; Happy Man.
      W.—Money; Dramatist.
      P.M.—Handsome Husband.

JUNE

1. *Friday:*
      A.—Born to Good Luck; Irish Dragoon.
      W.—Count of Monte Cristo; Irish Lion.
      P.M.—My Wife's Out; Spectre Bridegroom.
2.   A.—Teddy the Tiler; Irish Dragoon.
      W.—Othello; Who Speaks First?
      P.M.—Who Speaks First?; Milliner's Holiday.
4. *Monday:*
      A.—Irish Attorney; Mabel's Curse.
      W.—Richelieu; Who Speaks First?
      P.M.—Beauty and the Beast; Four Sisters.
5.   A.—Rory O'More; Happy Man.
      W.—Gladiator; Poor Pillicoddy.
      P.M.—Beauty and the Beast; Who Speaks First?
6.   A.—Rag Picker of Paris; A Glance at Philadelphia.
      W.—Jack Cade; Who Speaks First?
      P.M.—Who Speaks First?; My Neighbor's Wife.
7.   A.—Rag Picker of Paris; A Glance at Philadelphia.
      W.—Metamora; Witch of Windermere.
      P.M.—No legitimate drama.
8.   A.—Carpenter of Rouen; Ask no Questions.
      W.—Broker of Bogota; My Wife's Come.
9.   A.—Children in the Wood; Double Bedded Room.
      W.—Jack Cade; Who Speaks First?
11. *Monday:*
      A.—Chloroform *: *Aminabab*—Logan, *Pink Patter*—Mrs.
      Winstanley; Mr. and Mrs. Macbeth *: *Macbeth*—
      Brougham, *Lady Macbeth*—Burton.
      W.—Box and Cox.
12.   A.—Chloroform; Mr. and Mrs. Macbeth.
      W.—Slasher and Crasher.
13.   A.—Chloroform; Where's Barnum? *: *Mr. Smiler*—Broug-
      ham, *Spriggles*—Burton.
      W.—Who Speaks First?

14.   A.—Chloroform; Where's Barnum?
       W.—King's Gardener.
15.   A.—Chloroform; Where's Barnum?
       W.—My Wife's Come.
16.   A.—Chloroform; Where's Barnum?
       W.—Witch of Windermere.
18. *Monday:*
       A.—John Bull; Where's Barnum?
       W.—Bridal; Victorine.
19.   A.—Love's Sacrifice; Chloroform.
       W.—Venice Preserved; Robert Macaire.
20.   A.—Jane Shore; A Glance at Philadelphia. Last night of the season.
       W.—Rob Roy; Witch of Windermere.
21.   W.—Bertram; Wonder.
22.   W.—William Tell; House Dog.
23.   W.—Much Ado about Nothing; Merchant of Venice, fourth act. Last night of the season.
27.   P.M.—Faint Heart never won Fair Lady; Rival Pages.
28.   P.M.—*Id.,* June 27.
29.   P.M.—Asmodeus; Rival Pages.
30.   P.M.—A Husband at Sight; My Little Adopted.

JULY

2.   *Monday:*
       P.M.—Widow's Victim; Artful Dodger.
3.   P.M.—Did you ever Send your Wife to Germantown?; Artful Dodger.
4.   P.M.—Robert Macaire; Did you ever Send your Wife to Germantown?
5.   P.M.—Slasher and Crasher; Spirit of the Fountain.
6.   P.M.—*Id.,* July 5.
7.   P.M.—One Hour; Eton Boy.
9.   *Monday:*
       P.M.—Pierre Gamouche *: *Pierre*—De Bar; Sketches in India.
10.   P.M.—His Last Legs; Loan of a Lover.
11.   P.M.—State Secrets; Did you ever Send your Wife to Germantown?
12.   P.M.—Agnes de Vere; Eton Boy.
13.   P.M.—Honey Moon; Married Rake.
14.   P.M.—Faint Heart never won Fair Lady; Eton Boy.
16.   P.M.—Soldier's Return; Jenny Lind.
17.   P.M.—Dumb Belle; Jolly Cobbler.
18.   P.M.—Sketches in India; Chloroform.
19.   P.M.—*Id.,* July 18.

20. P.M.—Founded on Facts; Chloroform.
21. P.M.—Uncle Sam; Chloroform.
23. *Monday:*
    P.M.—Iron Chest; King's Gardener.
24. P.M.—Therese; King's Gardener.
25. P.M.—William Tell; My Fellow Clerk.
26. P.M.—Pride of the Market; A Glance at Philadelphia.
27. P.M.—Cricket on the Hearth; Pride of the Market.
28. P.M.—Eton Boy; Artful Dodger. Last night of the season.

AUGUST

15. *Wednesday:*
    A.—Adopted Child; John Dobbs *: *Paternoster*—Burton, *Dobbs*—Baker.
    C.—Black Eyed Susan.
16. A.—As You Like It; John Dobbs.
    C.—Day after the Wedding; Glance at Philadelphia.
17. A.—Stranger; That Rascal Jack.
    C.—Two Gregories.
18. A.—Love's Sacrifice; Mr. and Mrs. White.
    C.—Agnes de Vere.
20. *Monday:*
    A.—Lady of Lyons; Taken in and Done for *: *Pewitt*—Dunn.
    C.—Lady of Lyons.
21. A.—Katharine and Petruchio; Taken in and Done for.
    C.—Love in Humble Life; John Bull in France.
22. A.—Richelieu; Catching an Heiress.
    C.—Stranger.
23. A.—Hunchback; Gentleman in Difficulties.
    C.—Ambrose Gwinett.
24. A.—She Stoops to Conquer; Poor Pillicoddy.
    C.—A Glance at Philadelphia.
25. A.—Pizarro; Taken in and Done for.
    C.—Two Gregories; A Glance at Philadelphia.
27. *Monday:*
    A.—Honey Moon; A Wonderful Woman *: *Crepin*— J. Dunn, *Hortense*—Mrs. Winstanley.
    C.—Shipwrecked Mariner.
28. A.—Romeo and Juliet; A Wonderful Woman.
    C.—Old Guard; Jakey's Visit to his Aunts. Last night of the season.
29. A.—Love Chase; Taken in and Done for.
30. A.—Faint Heart never won Fair Lady; A Wonderful Woman.
31. A.—Cesar de Bazan; Adopted Child.

SEPTEMBER

1. *Saturday:*
   A.—Idiot of the Mill *: *Lendormie*—Miss Wallack, *Franval*
   —Thayer, *Simon*—J. Dunn; Soldier and the Peasant.
   C.—Lady of Lyons; Mr. and Mrs. White.
3. *Monday:*
   A.—Idiot of the Mill; Luke the Laborer.
   C.—Lady of Lyons; Bobby Breakwindow.
4. A.—Idiot of the Mill; Richard ye Thirde.
   C.—My Poll and my Partner Joe; Faint Heart never won
   Fair Lady.
5. A.—Idiot of the Mill; Mammon and Gammon *: *Smudge*—
   J. Dunn.
   C.—My Poll and my Partner Joe; A Kiss in the Dark.
6. A.—Idiot of the Mill; Mammon and Gammon.
   C.—My Poll and my Partner Joe; Loan of a Lover.
7. A.—Cesar de Bazan; Idiot of the Mill.
   C.—My Poll and my Partner Joe; Turning the Tables.
8. A.—Wardock Kennilson *: *Ramble*—Thayer, *Wardock*—
   Mrs. Winstanley; Idiot of the Mill.
   C.—My Poll and my Partner Joe; The Miser of Philadelphia *: *Nat*—C. Foster.
10. *Monday:*
    A.—Brian Boroihme; Wardock Kennilson.
    C.—Love's Sacrifice; Miser of Philadelphia.
    W.—Soldier of Fortune; Born to Good Luck.
11. A.—Wardock Kennilson; Cesar de Bazan.
    C.—Hunchback; Miser of Philadelphia.
    W.—Nervous Man; Witch of Windermere.
12. A.—Brian Boroihme; Taken in and Done for.
    C.—Honey Moon; Miser of Philadelphia.
    W.—Irish Attorney; Perfection.
13. A.—Romeo and Juliet; Wreckers of Norway.
    C.—My Poll and my Partner Joe; Miser of Philadelphia.
    W.—O'Grady, the Irish Guardsman *: *O'Grady*—Collins;
    His Last Legs.
14. A.—She Stoops to Conquer; Idiot of the Mill.
    C.—Hamlet; Poor Pillicoddy.
    W.—O'Grady; How to pay Rent.
15. A.—Brian Boroihme; Warlock of the Glen.
    C.—Richard III; Omnibus.
    W.—O'Grady; Teddy the Tiler.
17. *Monday:*
    A.—Strathmore *: *Strathmore*—Marshall, *Katharine*—Miss
    Wallack; Everybody's Husband.

[401]

C.—Macbeth; Slasher and Crasher.
W.—O'Grady; Teddy the Tiler.

18. A.—Strathmore; Lawyer's Practice.
C.—Pizarro; Make Your Wills.
W.—O'Grady; His Last Legs.

19. A.—Surgeon of Paris; Tom Cringle's Log.
C.—Richard III; Slasher and Crasher.
W.—Born to Good Luck; Irish Post.

20. A.—Widow's Victim; Mose in California.
C.—Richelieu; Golden Farmer.
W.—Soldier of Fortune; Irish Attorney.

21. A.—Widow's Victim; Mose in California.
C.—Sea King's Vow; My Poll and my Partner Joe, first and third acts.
W.—Nervous Man; Wonderful Woman.

22. A.—Widow's Victim; Mose in California.
C.—Infidelity; Sea King's Vow.
W.—O'Grady.

24. *Monday:*
A.—Adopted Child; New York as it Is.
C.—The Fighting Brothers of Rome; A Day after the Wedding.
W.—Irish Ambassador; Wonderful Woman.

25. A.—Black Eyed Susan; New York as it Is.
C.—Fighting Brothers of Rome; Omnibus.
W.—King O'Neil; Who Speaks First?

26. A.—Jonathan Bradford; Omnibus.
C.—Fighting Brothers of Rome; Philadelphia as it Is.
W.—Irish Ambassador; Irish Post.

27. A.—Jonathan Bradford; Irish Tutor.
C.—Fighting Brothers of Rome; Philadelphia as it Is.
W.—Rory O'More; His Last Legs.

28. A.—Faint Heart never won Fair Lady; New York as it Is.
C.—Fighting Brothers of Rome; Philadelphia as it Is.
W.—Irish Ambassador; Teddy the Tiler.

29. A.—Widow's Victim; New York as it Is.
C.—Fighting Brothers of Rome; A Glance at Philadelphia.
W.—Born to Good Luck; Irish Post.

OCTOBER

1. *Monday:*
A.—Poor Gentleman; My Sister Kate.
C.—Faithful Slave; Crimson Crimes.
W.—La Fille du Regiment; Separate Maintenance.

2.   A.—Speed the Plough; The Empire of Hayti *: *Faustin I.*—
    J. Dunn.
    C.—Paul Pry; A Glance at Philadelphia.
    W.—The Bravo.

3.   A.—Mysteries and Miseries of New York *: *Mose*—T. B.
    Johnston, *Tobin*—Hadaway, *Jack*—Dunn; Empire of
    Hayti.
    C.—Fighting Brothers of Rome; Water Witches.
    W.—La Fille du Regiment; Wonderful Woman.

4.   A.—Mysteries and Miseries of New York; Empire of Hayti.
    C.—Fighting Brothers of Rome; Water Witches.
    W.—The Bravo; Slasher and Crasher.

5.   A.—Mysteries and Miseries of New York; Double Bedded
    Room.
    C.—A New Way To Pay Old Debts; Make your Wills.
    W.—La Fille du Regiment; Witch of Windermere.

6.   A.—Mysteries and Miseries of New York; Idiot of the Mill.
    C.—Richard III; Water Witches.
    W.—The Bravo; House Dog.

8. *Monday:*
    A.—Mammon and Gammon; Mose and Jakey *: *Jakey*—
    T. B. Johnston.
    C.—Hamlet; A Kiss in the Dark.
    W.—Norma; Who Speaks First?
    N.—Mysteries and Miseries of New York; Mose and Jakey in
    Philadelphia *.

9.   A.—*Id.,* Oct. 8.
    C.—Merchant of Venice; Faithful Slave.
    W.—Bohemian Girl; Separate Maintenance.
    N.—*Id.,* Oct 8.

10.   A.—Young America; Mose and Jakey.
    C.—Apostate; Miser of Philadelphia.
    W.—Norma; House Dog.
    N.—*Id.,* Oct. 8.

11.   A.—Love in Humble Life; Mysteries and Miseries of New
    York.
    C.—Richard III; Water Witches.
    W.—Norma; Bohemian Girl, second and third acts.
    N.—Foreign Prince; Mose and Jakey.

12.   A.—White Farm; Virginia Mummy.
    C.—Hunchback; Chloroform.
    W.—Don Giovanni; Wonderful Woman.
    N.—Virginia Mummy; Mose and Jakey.

13.   A.—Comedy of Errors; Slasher and Crasher.
    C.—Romeo and Juliet; Chloroform.

W.—Don Giovanni.

15. *Monday:*
    A.—Cesar de Bazan; Who's your Friend?
    C.—Lady of Lyons; Chloroform.
    W.—Born to Good Luck; Irish Lion.

16.   A.—Luck's All; Black Eyed Susan.
    C.—The Wife; Chloroform.
    W.—King O'Neil; Wonderful Woman.

17.   A.—Who's your Friend?; Robert Macaire.
    C.—Love's Sacrifice; Chloroform.
    W.—Rory O'More; How to pay Rent.

18.   A.—Post of Honor; Mrs. Harris.
    C.—Romeo and Juliet; Chloroform.
    W.—Knight of Arva *: *Connor*—Hudson; Irish Lion.

19.   A.—Gilderoy; Maniac Lover.
    C.—School for Scandal; Simpson and Co.
    W.—Nervous Man; Irish Secretary *: with Hudson.

20.   A.—Who's your Friend?; Maniac Lover.
    C.—Pizarro; Honey Moon.
    W.—Knight of Arva; Perfection.

22. *Monday:*
    A.—Gilderoy; A Day after the Fair.
    C.—Ion; Uncle Sam.
    W.—O'Flannigan and the Fairies; Box and Cox.

23.   A.—Merchant of Venice; The Sphinx.
    C.—Poor Gentleman; Married Life.
    W.—Knight of Arva; Nervous Man.

24.   A.—Hamlet; Black Eyed Susan.
    C.—Benj. Franklin *: *Washington*—Bayley, *Franklin*—Cartlick; A Kiss in the Dark.
    W.—St. Patrick's Eve; Irish Diplomacy.

25.   A.—Surgeon of Paris; Joe the Orphan.
    C.—Benjamin Franklin; Omnibus.
    W.—O'Flannigan and the Fairies; Witch of Windermere.

26.   A.—Rag Picker of Paris; Faint Heart never won Fair Lady.
    C.—Benj. Franklin; Forty Thieves.
    W.—Knight of Arva; Irish Diplomacy.

27.   A.—Surgeon of Paris; The Sphinx.
    C.—Benj. Franklin; Ups and Downs of a Student's Life.
    W.—O'Flannigan and the Fairies; St. Patrick's Eve.

29. *Monday:*
    A.—Stranger; Lucrece Borgia.
    C.—Benj. Franklin; Ups and Downs of a Student's Life.
    W.—Stranger; Jacobite.

30.   A.—Evadne; Lucrece Borgia.
    C.—Benj. Franklin; Ups and Downs of a Student's Life.

[404]

W.—As You Like It; Box and Cox.
31.   A.—Jane Shore; World Changed.
     C.—Hearts are Trumps; Forty Thieves.
     W.—Macbeth; Poor Pillicoddy.

NOVEMBER

1. *Thursday:*
     A.—Hunchback; World Changed.
     C.—Pizarro; Hearts are Trumps.
     W.—Money; John Dobbs.
2.   A.—Mary Tudor; World Changed.
     C.—Infidelity; Hearts are Trumps.
     W.—Hunchback; Jacobite.
3.   A.—Venetian; Daughter of the Regiment, drama.
     C.—Mose in China *; Black Raven of the Tombs.
     W.—Macbeth; John Dobbs.
5. *Monday:*
     A.—Romeo and Juliet; World Changed.
     C.—Mose in China; Black Raven of the Tombs.
     W.—Hunchback; Witch of Windermere.
6.   A.—Maid of Mariendorpt; World Changed.
     C.—Mose in China; Black Raven of the Tombs.
     W.—Guy Mannering; Poor Pillicoddy.
7.   A.—Hunchback; World Changed.
     C.—Mose and Jakey's Visit to the Chesnut *; Mose in China.
     W.—Guy Mannering; School of Reform.
8.   A.—Maid of Mariendorpt; World Changed.
     C.—Black Raven of the Tombs; Mose in China.
     W.—Guy Mannering; Laugh when you Can.
9.   A.—Love Chase; World Changed.
     C.—Hamlet; Jack Sheppard.
     W.—Stranger; Honey Moon.
10.   A.—The Wife; Wreckers of Norway.
     C.—Miner of Pottsville; Harlequin and Mother Goose.
     W.—Guy Mannering; Katharine and Petruchio.
12.   A.—Love; Ask no Questions.
     C.—Miner of Pottsville; Mose in China.
     W.—Macbeth; Dead Shot.
13.   A.—Love Chase; Adopted Child.
     C.—Miner of Pottsville; Mose in China.
     W.—Henry VIII; John Dobbs.
14.   A.—Love; How to Pay your Washerwoman.
     C.—The Pride of the Ocean; Mose in China.
     W.—Henry VIII; P.P.
15.   A.—The Wife; Mammon and Gammon.

C.—Female Forty Thieves; Harlequin and Mother Goose.

W.—Wild Oats; Cesar de Bazan.

16. A.—Lady of Lyons; Ringdoves.

C.—Female Forty Thieves; Mose in China.

W.—Much Ado about Nothing; Robert Macaire.

17. A.—Evadne; White Farm.

C.—The Brigadier's Horse; Female Forty Thieves.

W.—Guy Mannering; Loan of a Lover.

19. *Monday:*

A.—Sam Patch in France; Robert Macaire.

C.—Brigadier's Horse; Naiad Queen.

W.—Ion; Perfection.

20. A.—Rag Picker of Paris; White Farm.

C.—Brigadier's Horse; Naiad Queen.

W.—Ion; John Dobbs.

21. A.—Carpenter of Rouen; Soldier and the Peasant.

C.—Brigadier's Horse;. Naiad Queen.

W.—Lady of Lyons; Honey Moon.

22. A.—Hand of Cards *: *Joe*—Marshall, *Lawson*—Baker, *Bill* —Clarke; Weathercock.

C.—Brigadier's Horse; Naiad Queen.

W.—Honey Moon; Cesar de Bazan.

23. A.—Sam Patch in France; Hand of Cards.

C.—Brigadier's Horse; Naiad Queen.

W.—Much Ado about Nothing; Second Thoughts.

24. A.—Sam Patch in France; Drunkard.

C.—Naiad Queen; Mad Anthony Wayne.

W.—Lady of Lyons; Wild Oats.

26. *Monday:*

A.—Ireland as it Is; Rosina Meadows.

C.—Lola Montes; Richard ye Thirde.

W.—Daughter of the Regiment; Cesar de Bazan.

27. A.—Ireland as it Is; Rosina Meadows.

C.—His Last Legs; Richard ye Thirde.

W.—Fra Diavolo; Wandering Minstrel.

28. A.—Rosina Meadows; Limerick Boy.

C.—Spectre Bridegroom; Lola Montes.

W.—Daughter of the Regiment; Young Scamp.

29. A.—The Match Woman of Philadelphia *: *Horace*—J. P. Addams, *Skipper*—Marshall, *Frank*—Watkins, *Catharine*—Mrs. J. P. Addams; Born to Good Luck.

C.—Asmodeus; Rascal Jack.

W.—Bohemian Girl.

30. A.—Match Woman of Philadelphia; Mose in California.

C.—Asmodeus; Swamp Steed.

W.—Norma; House Dog.

DECEMBER

1. *Saturday:*
   A.—Match Woman of Philadelphia; Mose in California.
   C.—Swamp Steed; Lola Montes.
   W.—Don Giovanni; Separate Maintenance.
3. *Monday:*
   A.—Match Woman of Philadelphia; Drunkard.
   C.—Old Guard; Joe, the Orphan.
   W.—Norma; Box and Cox.
4. A.—*Id.,* December 3.
   C.—*Id.,* December 3.
   W.—Masaniello; Jacobite.
5. A.—Orange Girl of Venice *: *Galliano*—Marshall, *Uberone*
   —Clarke, *Eugenia*—Miss Wood; Wallace.
   C.—Swamp Steed; Sketches in India.
   W.—Masaniello.
6. A.—Orange Girl of Venice; Drunkard.
   C.—The Jewess; A Ghost in Spite of Himself.
   W.—Daughter of the Regiment.
7. A.—*Id.,* December 6.
   C.—Night Dancers; The Jewess.
   W.—Gustavus III, opera; John Dobbs.
8. A.—Orange Girl of Venice; Hand of Cards.
   C.—Night Dancers; Swamp Steed.
   W.—Gustavus III.
10. *Monday:*
    A.—Darnley; Promissory Note.
    C.—Mountain Devil; Night Dancers.
    W.—Knight of Arva; Irish Secretary.
11. A.—Darnley; Hand of Cards.
    C.—No advertisement.
    W.—White Horse of the Peppers; John Dobbs.
12. A.—Closed.
    C.—No advertisement.
    W.—More Blunders than One; St. Patrick's Eve.
13. W.—Knight of Arva; Loan of a Lover.
14. W.—Soldier of Fortune; Irish Recruit.
15. W.—*Id.,* December 14.
    A.—Soldier and Peasant; Darnley.
17. *Monday:*
    W.—Henry IV; Poor Pillicoddy.
    A.—Richard III; Antony and Cleopatra, comedietta.
18. W.—Rip Van Winkle; Mons. Tonson.
    A.—School of Reform; Katharine and Petruchio.
19. W.—Rip Van Winkle; Kentuckian.

[407]

A.—Hamlet; Hunting a Turtle.
20.　W.—Man of the World; Mons. Tonson.
A.—Ion; Dead Shot.
21.　W.—Merry Wives of Windsor; Monsieur Mallet.
A.—Macbeth; An Object of Interest.
22.　W.—Merry Wives of Windsor; Kentuckian.
A.—Othello; Antony and Cleopatra, burletta.
24.　*Monday:*
W.—Money; My Aunt.
A.—Serious Family *: *Torrens*—Watkins, *Mrs. Torrens*—
Mrs. Nicholls; Jack Sheppard.
25.　W.—Stranger; Wild Oats.
A.—Serious Family; Wreckers of Norway.
26.　W.—Lady of Lyons; Honey Moon.
A.—Douglass; Rule a Wife.
27.　W.—Wine Works Wonders; Dramatist.
A.—Poor Gentleman; Your Life's in Danger.
28.　W.—Much Ado about Nothing; The Critic.
A.—Heir at Law; Poor Pillicoddy.
29.　W.—The Robbers; P.P.
A.—Kriss Kringle; Philadelphia Directory *: *Piccadilly*—
Hadaway, *Brown*—Thayer.
31.　*Monday:*
W.—Walter Raymond; Laugh when you Can.
A.—Gilderoy; Bird of Passage.

JANUARY 1850

1.　*Tuesday:*
A.—Philadelphia Directory; Maniac Lover.
W.—Lady of Lyons; Dramatist.
C.—Giselle.
2.　A.—She Stoops to Conquer; Philadelphia Directory.
W.—Romeo and Juliet; Wine Works Wonders.
C.—The Vampire; Harlequin and the Monster of St. Michael.
3.　A.—No advertisement.
W.—Cure for the Heart Ache; The Critic
C.—Bird of Passage; Harlequin and the Monster of St.
Michael.
4.　A.—No advertisement.
W.—Elder Brother; Wild Oats.
C.—Dancing Bears of Cashmere; Harlequin and the Monster
of St. Michael.
5.　A.—No advertisement.
W.—Venice Preserved; My Aunt.
C.—Giselle; Harlequin and the Monster of St. Michael.

7. *Monday:*
    W.—Richard III; Swiss Cottage.
    C.—Midshipman Easy; Monster Harlequin.
8.   W.—Macbeth; Spoiled Child.
    C.—Somnambulist; Monster Harlequin.
9.   W.—Perfection; Richard III, fifth act.
    C.—Bird of Passage; Monster Harlequin.
10.   W.—Four Mowbrays; Wonderful Woman.
    C.—Midshipman Easy; Monster Harlequin.
11.   W.—Hunter of the Alps; Swiss Cottage.
    C.—Tiger Horde; Monster Harlequin.
12.   W.—Macbeth, trial scene; Bombastes Furioso.
    C.—Marmion; Monster Harlequin.
14. *Monday:*
    W.—Loan of a Lover.
    C.—Marmion; Monster Harlequin.
15.   W.—John Dobbs.
    C.—Marmion; Monster Harlequin.
16.   W.—Pleasant Neighbors.
    C.—Will Watch; Cesar de Bazan.
17.   W.—Our Mary Ann.
    C.—Will Watch; Bird of Passage.
18.   W.—Dumb Belle.
    C.—Cesar de Bazan; Monster Harlequin.
19.   W.—Dumb Belle.
    C.—Philadelphia Fireman *; Will Watch.
21. *Monday:*
    W.—Witch of Windermere.
    C.—Philadelphia Fireman; Morgan, the Jersey Wagoner *.
22.   W.—Witch of Windermere.
    C.—Philadelphia Fireman; Morgan.
23.   W.—Our Mary Ann.
    C.—Philadelphia Fireman; Morgan.
24.   W.—Box and Cox.
    C.—Rake's Progress; Philadelphia Fireman.
25.   W.—Cousin Cherry.
    C.—Morgan; Philadelphia Fireman.
26.   W.—Cousin Cherry.
    C.—Morgan; Philadelphia Fireman.
28. *Monday:*
    W.—Pleasant Neighbors.
    C.—The Three Guardsmen; Philadelphia Fireman.
29.   W.—Pleasant Neighbors.
    C.—The Three Guardsmen; Philadelphia Fireman.
30.   W.—Cousin Cherry.
    C.—The Three Guardsmen; Philadelphia Fireman.

31.   W.—Lottery Ticket.
       C.—The Three Guardsmen; Philadelphia Fireman.

FEBRUARY

1. *Friday:*
       W.—State Secrets.
       C.—The Three Guardsmen; Philadelphia Fireman.
2.   W.—Mummy.
       C.—The Three Guardsmen; Philadelphia Fireman.
4. *Monday:*
       W.—Irish Lion.
       C.—Lucrezia Borgia; French Spy.
5.   W.—Cousin Cherry.
       C.—Lucrezia Borgia; French Spy.
6.   W.—Wandering Minstrel.
       C.—Pizarro; Wept of Wish-Ton-Wish.
7.   W.—Lend Me Five Shillings.
       C.—Romeo and Juliet; Indian Girl.
8.   W.—State Secrets.
       C.—The Three Guardsmen; Will Watch.
9.   W.—Lend Me Five Shillings.
       C.—Esmeralda; Black Brig of Bermuda.
11. *Monday:*
       W.—Lottery Ticket.
       C.—Esmerelda; Jack Sheppard.
       A.—Othello; Limerick Boy.
12.   W.—No!
       C.—Esmerelda; Black Brig of Bermuda.
13.   W.—Irish Lion.
       C.—Esmerelda; Life in Alabama.
14.   W.—Rendezvous.
       C.—Richard III; Captain of the Watch.
15.   W.—No!
       C.—The Spectre Pilot; The Three Guardsmen.
16.   W.—It's Only My Aunt.
       C.—Tour de Nesle; The Whistler.
18. *Monday:*
       W.—It's only my Aunt.
       C.—Tour de Nesle; The Whistler.
19.   W.—Rendezvous.
       C.—Zelina; Philadelphia Fireman.
20.   W.—Sudden Thoughts.
       C.—Ivanhoe; The Three Guardsmen.
21.   W.—Day after the Wedding.
       C.—Rob Roy; Philadelphia Fireman.

22.   W.—Sudden Thoughts.
        C.—Ivanhoe; Morgan.
23.   W.—Old Guard.
        C.—Serious Family; Siege of Comorn.
        A.—Othello, third act; Venice Preserved, first act; The Wife, fourth act.
25. *Monday:*
        W.—Rascal Jack.
        C.—Serious Family; Madeline.
26.   W.—Rascal Jack.
        C.—Sadak and Kalasrade; Whose is It?
27.   W.—Boots at the Swan.
        C.—Leap Year *: *Walker*—Baker; Serious Family.
28.   W.—Sudden Thoughts.
        C.—Born to Good Luck; Leap Year.

MARCH

1. *Friday:*
        W.—Boots at the Swan.
        C.—Madeline; Limerick Boy.
2.   W.—Spectre Bridegroom.
        C.—Rory O'More; Sprigs of Ireland.
4. *Monday:*
        W.—No!
        C.—Paddy's Trip to America *; Ireland as it Is.
        A.—School for Scandal; New Footman.
5.   W.—Spectre Bridegroom.
        C.—Ireland as it Is; Teddy the Tiler.
        A.—The Stranger; Crossing the Line.
6.   W.—Day after the Wedding.
        C.—Rory O'More; Happy Man.
        A.—Lady of Lyons; Family Jars.
7.   W.—Rendezvous.
        C.—Paddy's Trip to America; Irish Post.
        A.—Richelieu; Nipped in the Bud.
8.   W.—Boots at the Swan.
        C.—Irish Ambassador; Irish Lion.
        A.—Lucille; The Captive.
9.   W.—Rascal Jack.
        C.—Robber's Wife; Irish Tiger.
        A.—The Loving Woman; Tour de Nesle.
11. *Monday:*
        W.—Ladies, Beware.
        C.—Catching an Heiress; The Limerick Boy.
        A.—The Loving Woman; Mike Martin.

12.   W.—Spectre Bridegroom.
      C.—Asmodeus; Omnibus.
      A.—The Loving Woman; Mike Martin.
13.   W.—Ladies, Beware.
      C.—The Robber's Wife; Emerald Isle.
      A.—The Loving Woman; Mike Martin.
14.   W.—No legitimate drama.
      C.—Irish Farmer; Sudden Reformation.
      A.—The Loving Woman; Mike Martin.
15.   W.—No legitimate drama.
      C.—Irish Farmer; In and Out of Place.
      A.—Crossing the Line; Mike Martin.
16.   W.—No legitimate drama.
      C.—Lucrezia Borgia; Zelina.
      A.—The Stranger; Kit Karson *.
18.   *Monday:*
      W.—Hunchback; Ladies, Beware.
      C.—Zindel *: *Zindel*—C. Foster, *Doubar*—Clark, *Behran*—
          Young, *Arianthe*—Miss Mowbray, *Sylvane*—Mrs.
          Walker; Faint Heart never won Fair Lady.
      A.—Rookwood; Kit Karson.
19.   W.—Lady of Lyons; Richard ye Thirde.
      C.—Zindel; Serious Family.
      A.—Rookwood; Kit Karson
20.   W.—The Stranger; Richard ye Thirde.
      C.—Zindel; Serious Family.
      A.—Rookwood; Kit Karson.
21.   W.—The Wife; Soldier's Daughter.
      C.—Zindel; Serious Family.
      A.—Siege of Corinth; Kit Karson.
22.   W.—The Love Chase; Honey Moon.
      C.—Zindel; Serious Family.
      A.—Siege of Corinth; Kit Karson.
23.   W.—Lady of Lyons; Richard ye Thirde.
      C.—Zindel; Serious Family.
      A.—Tour de Nesle; Siege of Corinth.
25.   *Monday:*
      W.—Extremes *: *Mark*—Richings, *Augustus*—Wheatley, *Patrick*—Dunn, *Mrs. Crosby*—Miss Fisher; No!
      C.—Zindel; Grist to the Mill.
      A.—Belle's Stratagem; Wild Ducks.
26.   W.—Extremes; Lend Me Five Shillings.
      C.—Zindel; Leap Year.
      A.—Richelieu; Wild Ducks.
27.   W.—Extremes; Rendezvous.
      C.—Zindel; Leap Year.

A.—Loving Woman; Stranger.
28. W.—Extremes; State Secrets.
C.—Zindel; Serious Family.
A.—Black Eyed Susan; New Footman.
29. W.—Extremes; Box and Cox.
C.—Zindel; Seven Clerks.
A.—Wild Ducks; Sisters of Charity.
30. W.—Extremes; Rascal Jack.
C.—Zindel.
A.—Sisters of Charity; Personation.

APRIL

1. *Monday:*
   W.—Extremes; John Dobbs.
   C.—Zindel; Valsha.
   A.—Wallace; Jack Robinson.
2. W.—Extremes; Richard ye Thirde.
   C.—Zindel; Valsha.
   A.—Jane Shore; Lucrezia Borgia.
3. W.—Extremes; Slasher and Crasher.
   C.—Zindel; Valsha.
   A.—Evadne; Lucrezia Borgia.
4. W.—Extremes; P.P.
   C.—Dumb Man of Manchester, first and second acts; Zindel.
   A.—Hunchback; Mary Tudor.
5. W.—Extremes; Uncle Sam.
   C.—Zindel; Serious Family.
   A.—Lady of Lyons; Mary Tudor.
6. W.—Extremes; Lend Me Five Shillings.
   C.—Grub Mudge and Co.*: *Grub Mudge*—Ellsler, *Delia Mudge*—Miss E. Eberle; The Launch of the Susquehanna *: *Cotton*—Ellsler, *Harriet Ferguson*—Miss E. Eberle.
   A.—Venetian; Daughter of the Regiment.
8. *Monday:*
   W.—Extremes; Spectre Bridegroom.
   C.—Launch of the Susquehanna; El Melechor *: *Faulkner*— C. Foster, *Diana*—Mrs. Clarke.
   A.—Gamester; Venetian.
9. W.—Extremes; House Dog.
   C.—Launch of the Susquehanna; El Melechor.
   A.—Wallace; Black Eyed Susan.
10. W.—Extremes; Uncle Sam.
    C.—El Melechor; Launch of the Susquehanna.
    A.—Youthful Queen; Jenny Lind in Philadelphia.

[413]

11.   W.—Extremes.
       C.—El Melechor; Launch of the Susquehanna.
       A.—Blind Man's Buff; Barrack Room.
12.   W.—Extremes; Alarming Sacrifice.
       C.—Serious Family; Alarming Sacrifice.
       A.—Blind Man's Buff; Personation.
13.   W.—Extremes; Alarming Sacrifice.
       C.—Hernani; Alarming Sacrifice.
       A.—Black Eyed Susan.
15. *Monday:*
       W.—Hunchback; Alarming Sacrifice.
       C.—Who Speaks First?; Maseppa.
       A.—Youthful Queen.
16.   W.—Romeo and Juliet; Alarming Sacrifice.
       C.—Serious Family; Maseppa.
       A.—Barrack Room.
17.   W.—Love; No!
       C.—Trumpeter's Wedding *: *Tallboy*—Baker, *Lady Mary Montague*—Miss A. Eberle; Maseppa.
       A.—Loving Woman.
18.   W.—The Stranger; Ladies, Beware.
       C.—Trumpeter's Wedding; Maseppa.
       A.—Wallace.
19.   W.—Love; Jacobite.
       C.—Mazeppa.
       A.—Blind Man's Buff.
20.   W.—Lady of Lyons; Corporal's Wedding.
       C.—Winning a Husband; Mazeppa.
       A.—The Stranger.
22. *Monday:*
       W.—Maid of Mariendorpt; Corporal's Wedding.
       C.—Changes *; Married Rake.
       A.—An Object of Interest; King Rene's Daughter *.
23.   W.—The Wife; Alarming Sacrifice.
       C.—Changes; Trumpeter's Wedding.
       A.—King Rene's Daughter.
24.   W.—Maid of Mariendorpt; Separate Maintenance.
       C.—Changes; High Life in Philadelphia.*
       A.—King Rene's Daughter; Tour de Nesle.
25.   W.—Belle's Stratagem; Ladies, Beware.
       C.—Changes; Alarming Sacrifice.
       A.—Loving Woman; King Rene's Daughter.
26.   W.—Gamester; Love Chase.
       C.—Changes; Mazeppa.
       A.—King Rene's Daughter; Dumb Man of Manchester.
27.   W.—Love; Alarming Sacrifice.

C.—Changes; Pizarro.

A.—Crossing the Line; Struggle for Life and Death *: *Clarence Clevedon*—E. S. Conner.

29. *Monday:*

W.—Irish Ambassador; No Song, No Supper.

C.—Reprobate; Mechanic and the Queen.

A.—Forest Princess; Struggle for Life and Death.

30. W.—Born to Good Luck; My Precious Betsy.

C.—Changes; Will Watch.

A.—King Rene's Daughter; Otello.

MAY

1. *Wednesday:*

W.—Nervous Man; Irish Post.

C.—Knight of the Lion Heart *: *Henry VIII*—Clarke, *Francis I*—Reynolds, *Heartly*—Harrison, *Richard*—Baker, *Lady Constance*—Mrs. Myers; A Quiet Day.

A.—Jack Robinson and his Monkey; Otello.

2. W.—Irish Attorney; His Last Legs.

C.—Knight of the Lion Heart; Quiet Day.

A.—Dumb Man of Manchester; Jumbo Jim.

3. W.—King O'Neil; Wrong Passenger.

C.—The Luprechaun; Changes.

A.—Forest Princess; Foreign Prince.

4. W.—King O'Neil; Happy Man.

C.—Knight of the Lion Heart; Gentleman Harry, the Terror of the Road.

A.—La Fitte; Mummy.

6. *Monday:*

W.—Irish Honor *: with Collins; How to pay Rent.

C.—Gentleman Harry; Quiet Day.

A.—La Fitte; Bone Squash Diavolo.

7. W.—Irish Honor; Wrong Passenger.

C.—Gentleman Harry.

A.—La Fitte; Bone Squash Diavolo.

8. W.—Irish Honor; Happy Man.

C.—Gentleman Harry.

A.—La Fitte; Peacock and Crow.

9. W.—Irish Honor; His Last Legs.

C.—Who is It?; Wilful Murder.

A.—La Fitte; Oh! Hush!

10. W.—Soldier of Fortune; Irish Honor.

C.—Who is It?; Wilful Murder.

A.—Damon and Pythias; Mysterious Knockings.

11. W.—Irish Ambassador; Irish Honor.

   C.—Hunter of the Pyrenees; Wilful Murder.
   A.—Virginius; Mysterious Knockings.
13. *Monday:*
   W.—Serious Family; National Guard.
   C.—Hunter of the Pyrenees; Quiet Day.
   A.—Damon and Pythias; Mysterious Knockings.
14. W.—Serious Family; National Guard.
   C.—My Poll and my Partner Joe; Leap Year.
   A.—Cesar de Bazan; Adopted Child.
15. W.—Serious Family; National Guard.
   C.—An Awful Verdict; Knight of the Lion Heart.
   A.—Pizarro; Mysterious Knockings.
16. W.—Serious Family; Laugh when you Can.
   C.—An Awful Verdict; Knight of the Lion Heart.
   A.—Brutus; Shoemaker of Toulouse.
17. W.—Extremes; John Dobbs.
   C.—Serious Family; Things in the Next Century.
   A.—A New Way To Pay Old Debts; Mysterious Knockings.
18. W.—Serious Family; Somnambulist.
   C.—Knight of the Lion Heart, first and second acts; Last Nail.
   A.—Richard III; Mysterious Knockings.
20. *Monday:*
   W.—Soldier of Fortune; Irish Lion.
   C.—Last Nail; Sleeping Beauty.
   A.—Othello; Mysterious Knockings.
21. W.—Knight of Arva; Irish Secretary.
   C.—Henriette; Pet of the Petticoats.
   A.—Apostate; Lager Beer.
22. W.—Serious Family; Alarming Sacrifice.
   C.—Leap Year; Sleeping Beauty.
   A.—Iron Chest; Lager Beer.
23. W.—Serious Family; How to pay Rent.
   C.—William Tell; Pet of the Petticoats.
   A.—Dumb Girl of Genoa; Lager Beer.
24. W.—Serious Family; Irish Recruit.
   C.—Henrietta; Things in the Next Century.
   A.—Honey Moon; Mysterious Knockings.
25. W.—Serious Family; Irish Recruit.
   C.—Soldier's Progress; The Flying Highwayman.
   A.—Trial by Battle; The Stranger.
27. *Monday:*
   W.—Love.
   C.—Soldier's Progress; Queen of the Abruzzi.
   A.—Fazio; An Object of Interest.
28. W.—Belle's Stratagem.

C.—Queen of the Abruzzi; Soldier's Progress.
A.—Guy Mannering; Mysterious Knockings.
29. W.—Virginia *: *Virginius*—Richings, *Virginia*—Miss Davenport; National Guard.
C.—Soldier's Progress; No. 333 Locust Street *.
A.—Macbeth; Jenny Lind at Last.
30. W.—Lady of Lyons; Amazing Sacrifice.
C.—Soldier's Progress; No. 333 Locust Street.
A.—Romeo and Juliet; Jenny Lind at Last.
31. W.—Virginia; Witch of Windermere.
C.—Mysteries and Miseries of Philadelphia *; No. 333 Locust Street.
A.—School for Scandal; Simpson and Co.

JUNE

1. *Saturday:*
    W.—Love; My Precious Betsy.
    C.—Mysteries and Miseries of Philadelphia; Tom and Jerry.
    A.—Guy Mannering; Nature and Philosophy.
3. *Monday:*
    W.—Maid of Mariendorpt; John Dobbs.
    C.—Wrong Flue; Queen of the Abruzzi.
    A.—School for Scandal; Simpson and Co.
4. W.—Gamester; My Precious Betsy.
    C.—Mysteries and Miseries of Philadelphia; Tom and Jerry.
    A.—Romeo and Juliet; My Sister Kate.
5. W.—Love; Witch of Windermere.
    C.—Duke's Wager *; Delicate Ground *.
    A.—London Assurance; Nature and Philosophy.
6. W.—Lady of Lyons; Alarming Sacrifice.
    C.—Hunchback; Post of Honor.
    A.—London Assurance; My Sister Kate.
7. W.—Adrienne, the Actress *: *Maurice*—Wheatley, *Adrienne* —Miss Davenport; Honey Moon.
    C.—Pizarro; A Ghost in Spite of Himself.
    A.—As You Like It; Henry VIII, fourth act.
8. W.—Adrienne, the Actress; Slasher and Crasher.
    C.—Blanch Heriot; No. 333 Locust St.
    A.—Guy Mannering; Honey Moon.
10. *Monday:*
    W.—Extremes; Lend Me Five Shillings.
    C.—Zanthe; Blanch Heriot.
    A.—Mountaineers; Paul Pry.
11. W.—Serious Family; Madelaine.
    C.—Duke's Wager; Romance and Burlesque.

[417]

A.—Lady of Lyons; Robinson Crusoe.
12. W.—Extremes; My Precious Betsy.
    C.—Delicate Ground; Romance and Burlesque.
    A.—Merchant of Venice; Robinson Crusoe.
13. W.—Extremes; Nature and Philosophy.
    C.—How to Die for Love; Romance and Burlesque.
    A.—Rake's Progress; Artist's Wife.
14. W.—Serious Family.
    C.—Married Bachelor; A Coroner's Verdict.
    A.—Othello; Katharine and Petruchio.
15. W.—Serious Family; A Wonderful Woman.
    C.—Duke's Wager; Romance and Burlesque.
    A.—Paul Jones; Is he Jealous?
17. *Monday:*
    W.—Othello; Nature and Philosophy.
    C.—Devil's Ducat; Romance and Burlesque.
    A.—Vicar of Wakefield; Paul Jones.
18. W.—Macbeth; Ladies, Beware.
    C.—Wilful Murder; Whose is It?
    A.—Vicar of Wakefield; Dream at Sea.
19. W.—The Stranger; Jacobite.
    C.—Devil's Ducat; Out on a Lark.
    A.—Bride's Journey; Island Ape.
20. W.—Merchant of Venice; Madelaine.
    C.—Cure for the Heart Ache; Out on a Lark.
    A.—Vicar of Wakefield; Bride's Journey.
21. W.—London Assurance; House Dog.
    C.—Rent Day; Mysteries and Miseries of Philadelphia.
    A.—Lady of the Lake; Turning the Tables.
22. W.—London Assurance; P.P.
    C.—Out on a Lark; His Last Legs.
    A.—Guy Mannering; Lady of the Lake.
24. *Monday:*
    W.—Masaniello; Somnambulist.
    C.—Rory O'More; Teddy the Tiler.
    A.—Tom Cringle; A Glance at Philadelphia.
25. W.—Masaniello; Somnambulist.
    C.—Maharajah Surovy Seing *: *Lanty Leary*—Macarthy;
        Irish Tutor.
    A.—Golden Farmer; Virginia Mummy.
26. W.—Extremes; Rascal Jack.
    C.—Thalaba; Irish Wager.
    A.—Jack Sheppard; Lola Montes.
27. W.—Catspaw *: *Burgonet*—Wheatley, *Appleface*—Dunn,
        Mrs. Peachdown—Miss A. Fisher; Ladies, Beware.
    C.—Irish M. D.; Thalaba.

A.—Lola Montes; A Glance at Philadelphia.
28. W.—Serious Family; Wonderful Woman.
C.—Thirty Years of a Woman's Life; Ladies' Man.
A.—Vicar of Wakefield; Jack Sheppard.
29. W.—Catspaw; Rascal Jack.
C.—Pat Rooney; Mose in China.
A.—Born to Good Luck; Irish Lion.

JULY

1. *Monday:*
W.—Extremes; My Precious Betsy.
C.—King O'Neil; Honor and Honesty.
A.—His Last Legs; Happy Man.
2. W.—Serious Family; Maid of Croissy.
C.—Isabelle; Who's the Father?
A.—Rory O'More; A Glance at Philadelphia.
3. W.—Laugh when you Can; Madelaine.
C.—Devil's Ducat; Queen of the Abruzzi.
A.—Irish Lion; A Glance at Philadelphia.
4. W.—Serious Family; Gen. Washington. Last night of the
season.
C.—Philadelphia Boys and Girls in 1776; World Reformed.
A.—Born to Good Luck.
5. C.—Phila. Boys and Girls in 1776; World Reformed.
A.—Robber's Wife; Irish Post.
6. C.—Damon and Pythias; Phila. Boys and Girls in 1776.
A.—Robber's Wife; Star Spangled Banner.
8. *Monday:*
C.—Rob Roy; World Reformed.
A.—Michael Earle; Irish Post.
9. C.—Nick of the Woods; A Glance at Philadelphia.
A.—Brian Boroihme; A Kiss in the Dark.
10. C.—William Tell; Phila. Boys and Girls in 1776.
A.—Rory O'More; Irish Post.
11. C.—Nick of the Woods; A Glance at Philadelphia.
A.—Brian Boroihme; A Kiss in the Dark.
12. C.—Damon and Pythias; World Reformed.
A.—St. Patrick's Eve; Invincible.
13. C.—Iron Chest; Nick of the Woods.
A.—Democracy and Aristocracy *: *Robert Rattle*—Brelsford;
Invincible.
15. *Monday:*
C.—Rose of Ettrick Vale *: *Steenie*—McMillan.
A.—Democracy and Aristocracy; Delicate Ground.
16. C.—Rose of Ettrick Vale.

[419]

A.—Damon and Pythias; Democracy and Aristocracy.

17.   C.—Red Riever; Tipperary Legacy *: *Lanty*—R. Ryan.
A.—The Wife; Democracy and Aristocracy.

18.   C.—Wizard of the Moor; Tipperary Legacy.
A.—Pizarro; Democracy and Aristocracy.

19.   C.—Rose of Ettrick Vale; Irish Dragoon.
A.—Faint Heart never won Fair Lady; Adopted Child.

20.   C.—Bride of Lammermoor; Irish Dragoon.
A.—Richard III; Star Spangled Banner.

22.   *Monday:*
C.—Rob Roy; Eddystone Elf *.
A.—Julius Caesar; Sudden Thoughts.

23.   C.—His Last Legs; My Fellow Clerk.
A.—Lola Montes; Spirit of the Fountain.

24.   C.—Pizarro; Jakey in California.
A.—Spirit of the Fountain; Charles II.

25.   C.—Evadne; Jakey in California.
A.—Brutus; Alpine Maid.

26.   C.—Nick of the Woods; A Glance at Philadelphia.
A.—Dumb Belle; Esmerelda.

27.   C.—William Tell; Spectre Bridegroom.
A.—Maurice the Woodcutter; Esmerelda.

29.   *Monday:*
C.—The Robbers; Ole Bull.
A.—Delicate Ground; Fairy Lake.

30.   C.—Forty Years of Life; A Glance at Philadelphia.
A.—Cesar de Bazan; Maurice the Woodcutter.

31.   C.—School for Scandal; Friend Waggles; Last night of the
season.
A.—Therese; My Poll and my Partner Joe.

AUGUST

1.   *Thursday:*
A.—Ambrose Gwinett; Captain of the Watch.

2.   A.—No advertisement.

3.   A.—The Drunkard; Dumb Belle.

5.   *Monday:*
A.—Sweethearts and Wives; Spectre Bridegroom.

6.   A.—Paul Pry; Ole Bull.

7.   A.—Grandfather Whitehead; Faint Heart never won Fair
Lady.

8.   A.—The Drunkard; Spectre Bridegroom.

9.   A.—People's Lawyer; Slasher and Crasher.

10.   A.—Murrell, the Land Pirate; Lady of the Lions.

12. *Monday:*
    A.—Slasher and Crasher; Ole Bull.
13.   A.—People's Lawyer; Ship Carpenter of Kensington *: *Didler*
      —Baker, *Blair*—Brelsford.
14.   A.—Jacobite; Ship Carpenter of Kensington.
15.   A.—Right must Win at Last; Ship Carpenter of Kensington.
16.   A.—Rip Van Winkle; Buried Alive.
17.   A.—Jacobite; Buried Alive.
19. *Monday:*
    A.—Rip Van Winkle; Mose in China.
    W.—As You Like It; John Dobbs.
    B.—Retribution.
20.   A.—Grandfather Whitehead; Mose in California.
    W.—Belle's Stratagem; P.P.
21.   A.—Sweethearts and Wives; Irish Tutor.
    W.—Leap Year; Katharine and Petruchio.
22.   A.—New York as it Is; Widow's Victim.
    W.—Leap Year; Wonderful Woman.
23.   A.—Jonathan Bradford; New York as it Is.
    W.—Leap Year; Lend Me Five Shillings.
24.   A.—Idiot Witness; Murrell.
    W.—Passing Cloud; Leap Year.
26. *Monday:*
    A.—Mysteries and Miseries of New York; Omnibus.
    W.—Hunchback; Ladies Beware.
    B.—During the week: Broken Sword; Our Mary Ann; Not
      to be Done; My Sister Kate; Married Life.
27.   A.—Revolution; Mysteries and Miseries of New York.
    W.—Passing Cloud; Honey Moon.
28.   A.—A Kiss in the Dark; Mysteries and Miseries of New York.
    W.—Retribution *: *Briarly*—McMillan, *Alice*—Miss Wal-
      lack; Something Else.
29.   A.—Revolution; Irish Dragoon.
    W.—Retribution; Our Mary Ann.
30.   A.—Model of a Wife; Widow's Victim.
    W.—Extremes; Somebody Else.
31.   A.—Golden Farmer; People's Lawyer.
    W.—Retribution; Eton Boy.

SEPTEMBER

2. *Monday:*
    A.—Yankee Land; One Dollar on the Bank of Kentucky.
    W.—Hamlet; Eton Boy.
    B.—School for Scandal.
3.   Performance by candle light:

       A.—Sam Slick; Yankee in China.

       W.—No performance. City in darkness from tremendous flood which put the gas works on the river out of running order.

       B.—School for Scandal. House brilliantly lighted by Barnum's Drummond light.

4.   A.—Walter Tyrrel; The Vermonter.

       W.—Stranger; Wine Works Wonders.

       B.—Lady of Lyons.

5.   A.—Sam Patch's First Visit to Europe; Yankee Pedlar.

       W.—Lady of Lyons; My Aunt.

       B.—Lady of Lyons.

6.   A.—Green Mountain Boy; Jonathan in England.

       W.—Gamester; Wonder.

       B.—Hunchback.

7.   A.—Damon and Pythias; American Farmer.

       W.—Money; Dramatist.

       B.—Hunchback.

9. *Monday:*

       A.—Wives as they Were; Presumptive Evidence.

       W.—Adrienne; Eton Boy.

       B.—Cricket on the Hearth; Sudden Thoughts.

10. A.—Virginius; Somebody Else.

       W.—Adrienne; Somebody Else.

       C.—Norma.

       B.—Cricket on the Hearth; Sudden Thoughts.

11. A.—Jane Shore; Trumpeter's Daughter.

       W.—Love; Jacobite.

       C.—Lucrezia Borgia.

       B.—Drunkard.

12. A.—Six Degrees of Crime; Secret.

       W.—Hunchback; Ladies, Beware.

       B.—Broken Sword; Loan of a Lover.

13. A.—Six Degrees of Crime; Walter Tyrrel.

       W.—Apostate; Katharine and Petruchio.

       C.—Lucia di Lammermoor.

       B.—Hunchback.

14. A.—Six Degrees of Crime; Trumpeter's Daughter.

       W.—Love; House Dog.

       C.—Ernani.

       B.—Drunkard.

16. *Monday:*

       A.—Somebody Else; My Friend the Captain.

       W.—Apostate; Poor Pillicoddy.

       C.—Saffo.

       B.—Cricket on the Hearth; Paul Pry.

17. A.—Secret; Presumptive Evidence.

W.—Romeo and Juliet; My Wife's Come.
C.—Lucia di Lammermoor.
B.—Cricket on the Hearth; Paul Pry.
18. A.—The Drunkard.
W.—Lady of Lyons; A Nabob for an Hour.
C.—Norma.
B.—Merchant of Venice; Swiss Cottage.
19. A.—The Drunkard.
W.—Love; My Wife's Come.
B.—Merchant of Venice; Swiss Cottage.
20. A.—Idiot Witness.
W.—Love's Sacrifice; Youthful Queen.
C.—I Puritani.
B.—Young Scamp; Paul Pry.
21. A.—Six Degrees of Crime; Gold Seekers.
W.—Stranger; Youthful Queen.
B.—Young Scamp; Paul Pry.
23. *Monday:*
A.—Six Degrees of Crime.
W.—Apostate; Poor Pillicoddy.
C.—Lucrezia Borgia.
B.—Four Mowbrays; Cricket on the Hearth.
24. A.—Gold Seekers.
W.—Adrienne, the Actress; Spectre Bridegroom.
C.—La Favorita!
B.—Four Mowbrays; Cricket on the Hearth.
25. A.—Macbeth; Young Widow.
W.—The Betrothal *: *Count Jurdino*—Wheatley, *Salvator*—
Richings, *Marsio*—Couldock, *Constanza*—Miss F. Wal-
lack, *Filippia*—Miss K. Horn, *Marchioness*—Mrs. Kin-
lock; Ladies, Beware.
B.—Macbeth; Cricket on the Hearth.
26. A.—Stranger; Poor Cousin Walter.
W.—Betrothal; Slasher and Crasher.
B.—Macbeth; Cricket on the Hearth.
27. A.—Poor Cousin Walter; Loan of a Lover.
W.—Betrothal; Alarming Sacrifice.
B.—Sweethearts and Wives; Agnes de Vere.
28. A.—The Robbers; Cold Stricken.
W.—Betrothal; House Dog.
B.—Drunkard.
30. A.—Othello; My Precious Betsy.
W.—Betrothal; Eton Boy.
B.—Pride of Birth *: *Ernest*—Goodall, *Grelier*—Baker,
Bouquet—Rogers, *Emeline*—Miss Fisher; Chaos is come
Again.

[423]

OCTOBER

1. *Tuesday:*
   A.—Damon and Pythias; My Precious Betsy.
   W.—Betrothal; Alarming Sacrifice.
   B.—Pride of Birth; Chaos is come Again.
2. A.—Nick of the Woods; Poor Cousin Walter.
   W.—Betrothal; Friend Waggles.
   B.—Honey Moon.
3. A.—Cold Stricken; Nick of the Woods.
   W.—Betrothal; Friend Waggles.
   B.—The Pride of Birth.
4. A.—Carpenter of Rouen; Nick of the Woods.
   W.—Betrothal; Slasher and Crasher.
   B.—The Pride of Birth.
5. A.—Avenger's Vow; Nick of the Woods.
   W.—Betrothal; Friend Waggles.
   B.—Miller and his Men; Swiss Cottage.
7. *Monday:*
   A.—Stranger; Lucretia Borgia.
   W.—The Wife; Friend Waggles.
   B.—Miller and his Men; Barrack Room.
8. A.—Jane Shore; Lucretia Borgia.
   W.—Retribution; Daughter of the Stars.
   B.—Miller and his Men; The Daughter.
9. A.—Evadne; Lucretia Borgia.
   W.—Jealous Wife; Daughter of the Stars.
   B.—Miller and his Men; The Daughter.
10. A.—Gamester; Lucretia Borgia.
    W.—Retribution; Daughter of the Stars.
    B.—Miller and his Men; Turn Out.
11. A.—Hunchback; Venetian.
    W.—Lady of Lyons; Honey Moon.
    B.—Miller and his Men; Turn Out.
12. A.—Venetian; Lucretia Borgia.
    W.—Venice Preserved; Daughter of the Stars.
    B.—The Pride of Birth.
14. *Monday:*
    A.—Remorse; Daughter of the Regiment.
    W.—Irish Fortune Hunter *: *Gerald*—Collins, *Alice*—Miss Horn; Teddy the Tiler.
    B.—Masaniello; Man without a Head.
15. A.—Gamester; Venetian.
    W.—Irish Fortune Hunter; His Last Legs.
    B.—Masaniello; Man without a Head.
16. A.—Remorse; Bold Stroke for a Husband.

W.—Irish Fortune Hunter; How to pay Rent.
B.—Masaniello; Chaos is come Again.
17. A.—Tour de Nesle; Venetian.
W.—Irish Fortune Hunter; Irish Post.
C.—Mademoiselle Jenny Lind, the Swedish Nightingale, to present her first Grand Concert.
B.—Masaniello; Chaos is come Again.
18. A.—Wrecker's Daughter; Mary Tudor.
W.—Serious Family; Irish Fortune Hunter.
B.—Honey Moon.
19. A.—Bride of Lammermoor; Daughter of the Regiment.
W.—Serious Family; Irish Fortune Hunter.
B.—Drunkard.
21. *Monday:*
A.—Six Degrees of Crime; Two Galley Slaves.
W.—Extremes; Friend Waggles.
B.—The Pride of Birth.
22. A.—Poor Gentleman; A Glance at Philadelphia.
W.—Extremes; Daughter of the Stars.
B.—Cricket on the Hearth.
23. A.—One Hundred and Two; Poor Pillicoddy.
W.—Clari; Cesar de Bazan.
B.—Caught in a Trap.
24. A.—Paul Pry; A Glance at Philadelphia.
W.—Extremes; Eton Boy.
B.—Caught in a Trap.
25. A.—Serious Family; A Glance at Philadelphia.
W.—School of Reform.
B.—Money.
26. A.—Serious Family; A Glance at Philadelphia.
W.—Serious Family; Charles XII.
B.—Drunkard.
28. *Monday:*
A.—Serious Family; Jakey's Marriage.
W.—Lady of Lyons; Mysterious Family.
B.—Brigand; Caught in a Trap.
29. A.—Serious Family; Drunkard.
W.—Stranger; Mysterious Family.
B.—Brigand; Caught in a Trap.
30. A.—Serious Family; Crimson Crimes.
W.—As You Like It; My Precious Betsy.
B.—School of Reform.
31. A.—Serious Family; Jakey's Marriage.
W.—Hunchback; Mysterious Family.
B.—Money.

NOVEMBER

1. *Friday:*
    A.—Rake's Progress; Live Indian *: with J. Owens in three characters.
    W.—Money; Daughter of the Stars.
    B.—Brigand; Cricket on the Hearth.
2.   A.—Rake's Progress; Live Indian.
    W.—Venice Preserved; Mysterious Family.
    B.—Drunkard.
4. *Monday:*
    A.—Macbeth; Forest Rose.
    W.—Macbeth; My Precious Betsy.
    B.—Madeline; Turn Out.
5.   A.—Carpenter of Rouen; Nick of the Woods.
    W.—Romeo and Juliet; Friend Waggles.
    B.—Madeline; Turn Out.
6.   A.—Avenger's Vow; Nick of the Woods.
    W.—London Assurance; Eton Boy.
    B.—David Copperfield.
7.   A.—Gaulantus; Nick of the Woods.
    W.—London Assurance; Friend Waggles.
    B.—David Copperfield.
8.   A.—William Tell; Carpenter of Rouen.
    W.—Henry VIII; Honey Moon.
    B.—David Copperfield.
9.   A.—Gaulantus; Oua Cousta.
    W.—Romeo and Juliet; Slasher and Crasher.
    B.—David Copperfield.
11. *Monday:*
    A.—Roman Tribute *: *Anthemius*—Conner, *Attila*—Johnston, *Endocia*—Mrs. Conner; Forest Rose.
    W.—Love; Ladies, Beware.
    B.—Forty Thieves; Barrack Room.
12.   A.—Roman Tribute; Two Galley Slaves.
    W.—Guy Mannering; Mysterious Family.
    B.—Forty Thieves; Barrack Room.
13.   A.—Roman Tribute; Loan of a Lover.
    W.—Romeo and Juliet; My Precious Betsy.
    B.—Forty Thieves; Valet de Sham.
14.   A.—Roman Tribute; Drunkard.
    W.—Guy Mannering; Daughter of the Stars.
    B.—Forty Thieves; Valet de Sham.
15.   A.—Six Degrees of Crime; Rosina Meadows.
    W.—Stranger; Much Ado about Nothing.

B.—Forty Thieves; Simpson and Co.
16.   A.—Roman Tribute; Virginia Mummy.
W.—Guy Mannering; Eton Boy.
B.—Forty Thieves; Simpson and Co.
18. *Monday:*
A.—Ireland as it Is; Limerick Boy.
W.—Fazio; Platonic Attachment *: *Thistledown*—Chapman,
Mary—Miss Miles.
B.—Forty Thieves; Faint Heart never won Fair Lady.
19.   A.—Rory O'More; Irish Lion.
W.—Lady of Lyons; Platonic Attachment.
B.—Forty Thieves; Faint Heart never won Fair Lady.
20.   A.—Born to Good Luck; Sprigs of Ireland.
W.—Lady of Lyons; Alarming Sacrifice.
B.—Forty Thieves; Robert Macaire.
21.   A.—Ireland as it Is; Teddy the Tiler.
W.—No advertisement.
B.—Forty Thieves; Robert Macaire.
22.   A.—Paddy the Piper; Kate Kearney.
W.—Daughter of the Stars; Used Up.
B.—Forty Thieves; Robert Macaire.
23.   A.—Paddy the Piper; Kate Kearney.
W.—Platonic Attachment; Rough Diamond.
B.—Drunkard.
25. *Monday:*
A.—Paddy the Piper; Irish Tiger.
W.—Serious Family; Poor Pillicoddy.
B.—Forty Thieves; Grist to the Mill.
26.   A.—Irish Post; Paddy the Piper.
W.—Serious Family; Rough Diamond.
B.—Forty Thieves; Grist to the Mill.
27.   A.—Irish Farmer; Broken Sword.
W.—Used Up; Jacobite.
B.—Fair One with the Golden Locks; Barrack Room.
28.   A.—Irish Farmer; Alive and Kicking.
W.—Alarming Sacrifice; Rough Diamond.
B.—Fair One with the Golden Locks; Cricket on the Hearth
29.   A.—Paddy's Trip to America; Happy Man.
W.—Single Life; Rough Diamond.
B.—Fair One with the Golden Locks; Simpson and Co.
30.   A.—Paddy the Piper; Broken Sword.
W.—Single Life; Poor Pillicoddy.
B.—Fair One with the Golden Locks; Valet de Sham.

DECEMBER

2. *Monday:*
    A.—People's Lawyer; Buried Alive.
    W.—Single Life; Used Up.
    B.—Drunkard; Cricket on the Hearth.
3. A.—Sweethearts and Wives; Paddy the Piper.
    W.—Box and Cox; Rough Diamond.
    B.—Cesar de Bazan; David Copperfield.
4.   A.—Irish Farmer; Ole Bull.
    W.—Serious Family; Alarming Sacrifice.
    B.—Cure for the Heart Ache.
5.   A.—Breach of Promise; Sprigs of Ireland.
    W.—Single Life; Giralda *: *Gil*—Chapman, *Giralda*—Miss
        Anderson.
    B.—Rent Day.
6.   A.—People's Lawyer; Wool Dealer.
    W.—Used Up; Giralda.
    B.—Faint Heart never won Fair Lady; Swiss Swains.
7.   A.—Murrell; Ole Bull.
    W.—Jacobite; Rough Diamond.
    B.—Drunkard; Man without a Head.
9. *Monday:*
    A.—Retribution; Widow's Victim.
    W.—Extremes; My Precious Betsy.
    B.—Fair One with the Golden Locks; Valet de Sham.
10.   A.—Retribution; Adopted Child.
    W.—Riches, or the City Madam; School of Reform.
    B.—Sudden Thoughts; Barrack Room.
    C.—Lucia di Lammermoor.
11.   A.—Retribution; Shoemaker of Toulouse.
    W.—Wreck Ashore; Giralda.
    B.—My Sister Kate; Swiss Swains.
12.   A.—Richard III; Giralda.
    W.—Friend Waggles; Giralda.
    B.—The Daughter; No Song No Supper.
13.   A.—Damon and Pythias; Ugolino.
    W.—Platonic Attachments; Giralda.
    B.—Nettlewig Hall *: *Nettlewig*—Thayer, *Emily*—Miss
        Mortimer; Perfection.
    C.—Don Giovanni.
14.   A.—Ugolino; Giralda.
    W.—Mysterious Family; Eton Boy.
    B.—Hop o' my Thumb; Simpson and Co.
16. *Monday:*
    A.—Giralda; Wizard of the Wave.

W.—Wreck Ashore; Giralda.
B.—Nettlewig Hall.
17.   A.—Giralda; Wizard of the Wave.
W.—Child of Air; Ladies, Beware.
B.—Nettlewig Hall.
C.—Ernani.
18.   A.—Giralda; Wizard of the Wave.
W.—Child of Air; School of Reform.
B.—Hop o' my Thumb; Man without a Head.
19.   A.—Giralda; Wizard of the Wave.
W.—Giralda; Child of Air.
B.—Hop o' my Thumb; Man without a Head.
20.   A.—Mischief Making; Wizard of the Wave.
W.—Child of Air; My Precious Betsy.
B.—Hop o' my Thumb; Nettlewig Hall.
C.—Lucrezia Borgia.
21.   A.—A Poor Girl's Story; Wizard of the Wave.
W.—Child of Air; Rascal Jack.
B.—Hop o' my Thumb; No Song No Supper.
C.—Lucrezia Borgia.
23.   *Monday:*
A.—A Poor Girl's Story; Wizard of the Wave.
W.—Money; Daughter of the Stars.
B.—Hop o' my Thumb; Hypochondriac.
C.—Norma.
24.   A.—Mischief Making; Wizard of the Wave.
W.—Lady of Lyons; Slasher and Crasher.
B.—Cherry and Fair Star.
25.   A.—Wizard of the Wave; Harlequin and the Fairy of the
    Golden Wheatsheaf.
W.—Dramatist; Mountaineers.
B.—Cherry and Fair Star.
26.   A.—A Poor Girl's Story; Harlequin and the Fairy of the
    Golden Wheatsheaf.
W.—Wine Works Wonders; Riches.
B.—Cherry and Fair Star.
C.—Ernani.
27.   A.—Wizard of the Wave; Harlequin and the Fairy of the
    Golden Wheatsheaf.
W.—Stranger; Wild Oats.
B.—Young Scamp; Cherry and Fair Star.
28.   A.—Wizard of the Wave; David and Goliath.
W.—The Robbers; Friend Waggles.
B.—Cherry and Fair Star; Charles II.
C.—Gemma di Vergy.

30. *Monday:*
    A.—Wandering Boys; David and Goliath.
    W.—Much Ado about Nothing; My Aunt.
    B.—Cherry and Fair Star; Married Man.
    C.—Norma.
31.   A.—Country Girl; David and Goliath.
    W.—The Robbers; Rascal Jack.
    B.—Cherry and Fair Star; Married Man.

JANUARY 1851

1. *Wednesday:*
    W.—Money; Honey Moon.
    A.—Fire Raiser; Harlequin and the Fairy.
    B.—Kiss in the Dark; Cherry and Fair Star.
2.   W.—Wine Works Wonders; Mountaineer.
    A.—Fire Raiser; Harlequin and the Fairy.
    B.—Matrimony; Cherry and Fair Star.
    C.—Lucrezia Borgia.
3.   W.—Lady of Lyons; Cure for the Heart Ache.
    A.—La Fitte; Miser of Southwark Ferry.
    B.—Matrimony; Cherry and Fair Star.
4.   W.—Venice Preserved; Giralda.
    A.—Drunkard; Harlequin and the Fairy.
    B.—Hop o' my Thumb; Cherry and Fair Star.
    C.—Parisina.
6. *Monday:*
    W.—Katharine and Petruchio.
    A.—Sketches in India; Harlequin and the Fairy.
    B.—Two Friends; Cherry and Fair Star.
    C.—Parisina.
7.   W.—Daughter of the Stars.
    A.—Broken Sword; Harlequin and the Fairy.
    B.—Two Friends; Cherry and Fair Star.
8.   W.—Charles XII.
    A.—La Fitte; Broken Sword.
    B.—Cricket on the Hearth; Cherry and Fair Star.
    C.—Il Giuramento.
9.   W.—Jacobite; My Precious Betsy.
    A.—A Poor Girl's Story; Harlequin and the Fairy.
    B.—Caught in a Trap; Cherry and Fair Star.
10.   W.—Box and Cox; Spectre Bridegroom.
    A.—Mob, the Outlaw; Eighth of January.
    B.—Married Man; Cherry and Fair Star.
    C.—Ernani.
11.   W.—Charles XII.

      A.—Country Girl; Tour de Nesle.
      B.—Wandering Boys; Cherry and Fair Star.
      C.—Il Giuramento.

13. *Monday:*
      W.—Giralda.
      A.—Carpenter of Rouen; Sketches in India.
      B.—Soldier's Daughter; Cherry and Fair Star.
      C.—La Favorita.

14. W.—Dead Shot; Slasher and Crasher.
      A.—Surgeon of Paris; Spectre Bridegroom.
      B.—Soldier's Daughter; Cherry and Fair Star.
      C.—Don Giovanni.

15. W.—Mysterious Family; Rascal Jack.
      A.—Surgeon of Paris; Katharine and Petruchio.
      B.—Lover by Proxy; Cherry and Fair Star.
      C.—Ernani.

16. W.—Cure for the Heart Ache.
      A.—Shoemaker of Toulouse; Adopted Child.
      B.—Not to be Done; Cherry and Fair Star.

17. W.—Wild Oats.
      A.—Captain Kyd; Maniac Lover.
      B.—Wandering Boys; Cherry and Fair Star.
      C.—La Sonnambula.

18. W.—Mysterious Family.
      A.—Captain Kyd; Maniac Lover.
      B.—Young Widow; Cherry and Fair Star.
      C.—La Favorita.

20. *Monday:*
      W.—Calaynos *: *Calaynos*—Murdock, *Don Luis*—Richings,
         Oliver—Wheatley, *Don Miguel*—A'Becket, *Donna Alda*
         —Miss Anderson; P.P.
      A.—Rag Picker of Paris; Whites and Browns.
      B.—Honey Moon; Aristocracy and Democracy.
      C.—Il Giuramento, third act; I Lombardi, third act.

21. W.—Calaynos; Friend Waggles.
      A.—Rag Picker of Paris; Wandering Boys.
      B.—The Wonder; Deep, Deep Sea.

22. W.—Calaynos; John Dobbs.
      A.—Rag Picker of Paris; Weathercock.
      B.—Cricket on the Hearth; Deep, Deep Sea.

23. W.—Calaynos; Poor Pillicoddy.
      A.—Rag Picker of Paris; Black Eyed Susan.
      B.—Wonder!; Deep, Deep Sea.

24. W.—Calaynos; My Aunt.
      A.—Brian Boroihme; Gilderoy.
      B.—Two Friends; Charles II.

[431]

25.   W.—Calaynos; Rascal Jack.
        A.—Brian Boroihme; Gilderoy.
        B.—Wives as they Were; King's Gardener.

27. *Monday:*
        W.—Calaynos; Lend Me Five Shillings.
        A.—Satan in Paris; Whites and Browns.
        B.—Vicar of Wakefield; Young Widow.

28.   W.—Calaynos; My Precious Betsy.
        A.—Satan in Paris; Whites and Browns.
        B.—Vicar of Wakefield; Young Widow.

29.   W.—School for Scandal; Rough Diamond.
        A.—Love and Charity; Satan in Paris.
        B.—Vicar of Wakefield; Poor Pillicoddy.

30.   W.—Calaynos; Spectre Bridegroom.
        A.—Satan in Paris; Eton Boy.
        B.—Vicar of Wakefield; Poor Pillicoddy.
        C.—Doctor Wespe, in German.

31.   W.—Calaynos; A Nabob for an Hour.
        A.—Youthful Days of Richelieu; Used Up.
        B.—Vicar of Wakefield; Gentleman in Difficulties.
        C.—Doctor Wespe.

FEBRUARY

1. *Saturday:*
        W.—Calaynos; Honey Moon.
        A.—Youthful Days of Richelieu; Rough Diamond.
        B.—Vicar of Wakefield; Gentleman in Difficulties.
        C.—Doctor Wespe.

3. *Monday:*
        W.—My Friend in the Straps *; Box and Cox.
        A.—Ireland as it Is; Jenny Lind in America.
        B.—London Assurance.
        C.—Wilhelm Tell, in German.

4.   W.—My Friend in the Straps; Sent to the Tower *.
        A.—Irish Farmer; Jenny Lind in America.
        B.—Wives as they Were; Married Rake.

5.   W.—*Id.,* Feb. 4.
        A.—Wallace; The Secret.
        B.—Gamester; Widow's Victim.

6.   W.—Mysterious Family; Sent to the Tower.
        A.—Fortune's Whim; Jenny Lind in America.
        B.—Vicar of Wakefield; Simpson and Co.
        C.—Der Pariser Taugenichts; Die Selbstmoerder.

7.   W.—Jacobite; Sent to the Tower.
        A.—Paddy's Trip to America; Limerick Boy.

B.—Cricket on the Hearth; Valet de Sham.
8. W.—Rascal Jack; Sent to the Tower.
A.—*Id.,* Feb. 7.
B.—Old Heads and Young Hearts; Nature and Philosophy.
10. W.—The Daughter of the Stars.
A.—Presumptive Evidence; Bashful Irishman.
B.—Israelites in Egypt.
C.—Der Wirrwar.
11. W.—A Wonderful Woman.
A.—Irish Farmer; Paddy the Piper.
B.—Israelites in Egypt.
12. W.—The Husband of my Heart.
A.—Shandy Maguire; Jenny Lind in America.
B.—Israelites in Egypt.
13. W.—The Husband of my Heart.
A.—Shandy Maguire; Our Gal.
B.—Israelites in Egypt.
14. W.—Box and Cox.
A.—Born to Good Luck; Sprigs of Ireland.
B.—Israelites in Egypt.
15. W.—Platonic Attachment.
A.—Shandy Maguire; Sketches in India.
B.—Israelites in Egypt.
17. *Monday:*
W.—Fazio; David Copperfield.
A.—Ireland as it Is; Irish Post.
B.—Israelites in Egypt.
18. W.—Husband of my Heart; David Copperfield.
A.—Court Fool; Irish Lion.
B.—La Sonnambula.
19. W.—Fazio; David Copperfield.
A.—Shandy Maguire; Irish Tiger.
B.—Bohemian Girl.
20. W.—Love; David Copperfield.
A.—Richelieu; Broken Sword.
B.—La Sonnambula.
21. W.—Extremes; Giralda.
A.—Born to Good Luck; Eton Boy.
B.—Bohemian Girl.
22. W.—Love; David Copperfield.
A.—Shandy Maguire; Irish Tiger.
B.—La Gazza Ladra.
C.—Apostate; Momentous Question.
24. *Monday:*
W.—Nervous Man; Rascal Jack.
A.—Stranger; Wallace.

   B.—La Gazza Ladra.
25. W.—Irish Ambassador; How to pay Rent.
   A.—Iron Chest; Ella Rosenberg.
   B.—Der Freischutz.
26. W.—Rory O'More; Wife Hunters.
   A.—Six Degrees of Crime; Wandering Boys.
   B.—Der Freischutz.
   C.—Das Kaetchen von Heilbronn.
27. W.—Irish Ambassador; His Last Legs.
   A.—Tour de Nesle; The Pilot.
   B.—Bohemian Girl.
   C.—*Id.,* Feb. 26.
28. W.—King O'Neil; Born to Good Luck.
   A.—Templar; A Kiss in the Dark.
   B.—Child of the Regiment.

MARCH

1. *Saturday:*
   W.—King O'Neil; Born to Good Luck.
   A.—Templar; Pleasant Neighbors.
   B.—Child of the Regiment.
3. *Monday:*
   W.—Serious Family; Irish Post.
   A.—Templar; Spectre Bridegroom.
   B.—Richard III.
   C.—Hunchback; Forty and Fifty.
4. W.—Serious Family; Irish Attorney.
   A.—Wives as they Were; Widow's Victim.
   B.—New Way To Pay Old Debts.
   C.—Love's Sacrifice; Dumb Belle.
5. W.—Serious Family; Wrong Passenger.
   A.—Templar; Broken Sword.
   B.—Iron Chest.
   C.—Wife; Sketches in India.
6. W.—Serious Family; Friend Waggles.
   A.—She Would be a Soldier; Idiot Witness.
   B.—Hamlet.
   C.—Love's Sacrifice; Forty and Fifty.
7. W.—Soldier of Fortune; Nervous Man.
   A.—Rent Day; Virginia Mummy.
   B.—Merchant of Venice.
   C.—Adrienne, the Actress; Sketches in India.
8. W.—Irish Guardian; Happy Man.
   A.—Richard III; A Glance at Philadelphia.
   B.—Richard III.

      C.—Evadne; Raising the Wind.
10. *Monday:*
      W.—Love Chase; Katharine and Petruchio.
      A.—Sam Patch in France; My Precious Betsy.
      B.—Hamlet.
      C.—Love; My Uncle John.
11.   W.—Old Love and the New *: *Camilla*—Julia Bennett,
        Courtown—Couldock; My Uncle John.
      A.—Green Mountain Boy; A Wife for a Day.
      B.—Othello.
      C.—Love Chase; My Uncle John.
12.   W.—Belle's Stratagem; Betsy Baker.
      A.—Yankee in Time; Idiot Witness.
      B.—Othello.
      C.—Lady of Lyons; Day after the Wedding.
13.   W.—Old Love and the New; Mysterious Family.
      A.—Yankee Land; Wool Dealer.
      B.—Apostate.
      C.—Adrienne; Forty and Fifty.
14.   W.—All that Glitters is not Gold; Dead Shot.
      A.—Seth Slope; Yankee Abroad.
      B.—Merchant of Venice.
      C.—Belle's Stratagem; Youthful Queen.
15.   W.—All that Glitters is not Gold; Loan of a Lover.
      A.—Forest Rose; Seth Slope.
      B.—Richard III.
      C.—Gamester; Dumb Belle.
17. *Monday:*
      W.—Housekeeper; All that Glitters is not Gold.
      A.—People's Lawyer; His Last Legs.
      B.—King Lear.
      C.—No advertisement.
18.   W.—All that Glitters is not Gold; Loan of a Lover.
      A.—Charlotte Corday; Forest Rose.
      B.—The Stranger.
      C.—Charlotte Corday; My Uncle John.
19.   W.—*Id.,* Mar. 17.
      A.—Charlotte Corday; Sam Slick.
      B.—Macbeth.
      C.—No advertisement.
20.   W.—All that Glitters is not Gold; A Roland for an Oliver.
      A.—Charlotte Corday; Yankee Land.
      B.—Brutus.
      C.—Charlotte Corday; Faint Heart never won Fair Lady.
21.   W.—All that Glitters is not Gold; Belphegor.
      A.—Kaspar Hauser; Sam Patch.

B.—Richard III.
C.—Love; Promissory Note.

22. W.—*Id.,* Mar. 21.
A.—Charlotte Corday; Yankee Pedlar.
B.—Merchant of Venice.
C.—Charlotte Corday; Wedding Ring.

24. *Monday:*
W.—Stranger; All that Glitters is not Gold.
A.—Charlotte Corday; Fire Raiser.
B.—Macbeth.
C.—Hunchback; Serious Family.

25. W.—Wife; All that Glitters is not Gold.
A.—Hamlet; Laughing Hyena.
B.—Othello.
C.—Adrienne; Naval Engagements.

26. W.—Hunchback; Rascal Jack.
A.—Fazio; Robert Macaire.
B.—Hamlet.
C.—Centurion's Daughter; Dr. Dilworth.

27. W.—Fazio; My Precious Betsy.
A.—Robbers; Widow's Victim.
B.—Lady of Lyons.
C.—Evadne; Promissory Note.

28. W.—Lady of Lyons; Allow Me to Apologize.
A.—Gambler's Fate; Ugolino.
B.—Money.
C.—Maid of Mariendorpt; Rough Diamond.

29. W.—Romeo and Juliet; Honey Moon.
A.—Hamlet; Waterman.
B.—Richelieu.
C.—Love; Naval Engagements.

31. *Monday:*
W.—Evadne; Allow Me to Apologize.
A.—Stranger; Lucretia Borgia.
B.—King of the Commons.
C.—School for Scandal; Virginia Mummy.

APRIL

1. *Tuesday:*
W.—Love Chase; All that Glitters is not Gold.
A.—Jane Shore; Lucretia Borgia.
B.—Richelieu; Pleasant Neighbors.
C.—Adrienne; Wedding Ring.

2. W.—Duke's Wager; Allow Me to Apologize.

    A.—Lady of Lyons; Daughter of the Regiment.

    B.—King of the Commons.

    C.—No advertisement.

3.   W.—Duke's Wager; Sent to the Tower.

    A.—Romeo and Juliet; Rough Diamond.

    B.—School of Reform.

4.   W.—Duke's Wager; Faint Heart never won Fair Lady.

    A.—Philip de France and Marie de Meranie *: *Marie*—Mrs. Farren; Daughter of the Regiment.

    B.—Rob Roy.

5.   W.—Duke's Wager; Betsy Baker.

    A.—Venetian; Lucretia Borgia.

    B.—Pizarro; Katharine and Petruchio.

7. *Monday:*

    W.—*Id.,* April 2.

    A.—Philip of France and Marie de Meranie; My Precious Betsy.

    B.—Husband of my Heart; Luke the Laborer.

    C.—The Robbers.

8.   W.—Duke's Wager; Box and Cox.

    A.—Gamester; Venetian.

    B.—Husband of my Heart; Luke the Laborer.

9.   W.—Indian Queen *: *Ino*—Miss Julia Dean, *Zagreus*—Couldock, *Candaides*—McMillan, *Gyges*—Dyott; Friend Waggles.

    A.—Evadne; Venetian.

    B.—Husband of my Heart; Raymond and Agnes.

10.   W.—Indian Queen; Twice Killed.

    A.—Venetian; Lucretia Borgia.

    B.—Love in a Maze *: *Col. Buckthorne*—Germon, *Mrs. Buckthorne*—Miss Fisher; Virginia Mummy.

11.   W.—Hunchback; Love Chase.

    A.—Wrecker's Daughter; Mary Tudor.

    B.—Love in a Maze.

12.   W.—Indian Queen; Faint Heart never won Fair Lady.

    A.—Bride of Lammermoor; Mary Tudor.

    B.—Love in a Maze.

14. *Monday:*

    W.—Old Heads and Young Hearts; Jacobite.

    A.—Six Degrees of Crime; School for Tigers *: *Kiteflyer*—Davenport, *Stiff*—T. Wemyss, *Panels*—Worrell, *Fibber*—Justice, *Stiff*—J. S. Baker, *Crop*—Mrs. Conner, *Alexander*—Miss Kinlock.

    B.—Romeo and Juliet.

15.   W.—Betrothal; Twice Killed.

A.—Richelieu; My Precious Betsy.
B.—Belphegor.

16.   W.—Betrothal; Allow Me to Apologize.
A.—Macbeth; Luke the Laborer.
B.—Belphegor.

17.   W.—Betrothal; Spectre Bridegroom.
A.—Cure for the Heart Ache; Tour de Nesle.
B.—Belphegor; Virginia Mummy.

18.   W.—Betrothal; An Object of Interest.
A.—Charlotte Corday; School for Tigers.
B.—Belphegor.

19.   W.—Betrothal; Rascal Jack.
A.—*Id.,* April 18.
B.—Honey Moon; No!

21.   *Monday:*
W.—The World a Mask *: *Galldove*—Couldock, *Teresa*—Mad. Ponisi; An Object of Interest.
A.—Harry Burnham; Swiss Cottage.
B.—Bronze Horse; Twice Killed.

22.   W.—The World a Mask; Betsy Baker.
A.—Harry Burnham; Loan of a Lover.
B.—Bronze Horse; Twice Killed.

23.   W.—The World a Mask; Twice Killed.
A.—Harry Burnham; School for Tigers.
B.—Bronze Horse; Platonic Attachments

24.   W.—The World a Mask; Box and Cox.
A.—*Id.,* April 22.
B.—*Id.,* April 23.

25.   W.—*Id.,* April 21.
A.—*Id.,* April 23.
B.—*Id.,* April 23.

26.   W.—The World a Mask; The Teacher Taught *.
A.—*Id.,* April 23.
B.—*Id.,* April 23.

28.   *Monday:*
W.—*Id.,* April 26.
A.—Harry Burnham; The World's Fair.
B.—Bronze Horse; Love, Law, and Physic.

29.   W.—*Id.,* April 26.
A.—*Id.,* April 28.
B.—*Id.,* April 28.

30.   W.—Retribution; All that Glitters is not Gold.
A.—No Song no Supper; That Odious Captain Cutter.
B.—Bronze Horse; Presented at Court.

MAY

1. *Thursday:*
    W.—*Id.,* April 30.
    A.—Tour de Nesle; That Odious Captain Cutter.
    B.—*Id.,* April 30.
2. W.—Riches; The Day of Reckoning.
    A.—Pet of the Petticoats; World's Fair.
    B.—Bronze Horse.
3. W.—Merchant of Venice; Robert Macaire.
    A.—Carpenter of Rouen; World's Fair.
    B.—Bronze Horse.
5. *Monday:*
    W.—Hamlet; Teacher Taught.
    A.—Shandy Maguire; Irish Tiger.
    B.—Bronze Horse; Barrack Room.
6. W.—Stranger; Wonder.
    A.—Ireland as it Is; Limerick Boy.
    B.—*Id.,* May 5.
7. W.—Money; Katharine and Petruchio.
    A.—Fortune's Whim; Sprigs of Ireland.
    B.—Bronze Horse; Cricket on the Hearth.
8. W.—Much Ado about Nothing; My Aunt.
    A.—Irish Farmer; Our Gal.
    B.—*Id.,* May 7.
9. W.—Town and Country; Dramatist.
    A.—Shandy Maguire; Paddy the Piper.
    B.—Duke's Wager; Bronze Horse.
10. W.—*Id.,* May 7.
    A.—Happy Man; Limerick Boy.
    B.—The Drunkard.
12. *Monday:*
    W.—Calaynos; Box and Cox.
    A.—Born to Good Luck; Brian O'Lynn.
    B.—All that Glitters is not Gold.
13. W.—Town and Country; Cure for the Heart Ache.
    A.—Hamlet; Irish Tutor.
    B.—*Id.,* May 12.
14. W.—Lady of Lyons; All that Glitters is not Gold.
    A.—Fortune's to Him; Brian O'Lynn.
    B.—*Id.,* May 12.
15. W.—School for Scandal; Teacher Taught.
    A.—Ireland as it Is; Our Gal.
    B.—*Id.,* May 12.
16. W.—Wine Works Wonders; Wild Oats.

A.—Card Drawer; Irish Lion.

B.—All that Glitters is not Gold; Man without a head.

17. W.—Venice Preserved; My Aunt.

A.—*Id.,* May 16.

B.—*Id.,* May 16.

19. *Monday:*

W.—Noble Heart; Patrician and Parvenu.

A.—Virgin of the Sun; Rough Diamond.

B.—*Id.,* May 12.

20. W.—Love; Betsy Baker.

A.—Virgin of the Sun; Swiss Cottage.

B.—Wild Oats.

21. W.—Rob Roy; Robert Macaire.

A.—Truand Chief; Nick of the Woods.

B.—Lady of the Lake.

22. W.—Richard III; Teacher Taught.

A.—Virgin of the Sun; Loan of a Lover.

B.—*Id.,* May 21.

23. W.—New Way To Pay Old Debts.

A.—Virgin of the Sun; Pizarro.

B.—*Id.,* May 21.

24. W.—*Id.,* May 22.

A.—Day of Reckoning; Virgin of the Sun.

B.—Lady of the Lake; Bronze Horse.

26. *Monday:*

W.—Faustus; Ladies, Beware.

A.—Hamlet; I'll be your Second.

B.—Married Life; A Morning Call.

27. W.—Faustus; Jacobite.

A.—New Way To Pay Old Debts; My Fellow Clerk.

B.—Idiot Witness; Mr. and Mrs. Peter White.

28. W.—Faustus; Rascal Jack.

A.—Virginius; Perfection.

B.—Drunkard; A Morning Call.

29. W.—Faustus; Friend Waggles.

A.—Gisippus; My Fellow Clerk.

B.—*Id.,* May 28.

30. W.—Faustus; Spectre Bridegroom.

A.—Julius Caesar; Did you ever Send your Wife to Frankford.

B.—Old Heads and Young Hearts.

31. W.—Faustus; My Precious Betsy.

A.—Gisippus; Ocean Child.

B.—All that Glitters is not Gold.

JUNE

2. *Monday:*
    W.—Faustus; Box and Cox.
    A.—Evadne; State Prisoner.
    B.—Negro Fidelity; Life in Alabama.
3.   W.—Faustus; Poor Pillicoddy.
    A.—Romeo and Juliet; State Prisoner.
    B.—Cricket on the Hearth; Twice Killed.
4.   W.—Faustus; Faint Heart never won Fair Lady.
    A.—Lady of Lyons; Chloroform.
    B.—A Morning Call; Soldier's Daughter.
5.   W.—Faustus; An Alarming Sacrifice.
    A.—Fazio; Chloroform.
    B.—A Morning Call; Husband of my Heart.
6.   W.—Faustus; Adopted Child.
    A.—Astarte; Chloroform.
    B.—Cricket on the Hearth; Simpson and Co.
7.   W.—Faustus; Boots at the Swan.
    A.—Lady of Lyons; Chloroform.
    B.—Married Life; Sudden Thoughts.
9. *Monday:*
    W.—Faustus; Allow Me to Apologize.
    A.—Sweets and Wives; Captive.
    B.—Paul Pry; Your Life's in Danger.
10.   W.—Faustus; Sent to the Tower.
    A.—People's Lawyer; A Kiss in the Dark.
    B.—My Poll and my Partner Joe.
    C.—Lady of Lyons; The Review.
11.   W.—Faustus; Rascal Jack.
    A.—Grandfather Whitehead; Buried Alive.
    B.—*Id.,* June 10.
12.   W.—Faustus; My Precious Betsy.
    A.—Breach of Promise; Lady of the Lions.
    B.—*Id.,* June 10.
13.   W.—Faustus; Without Incumbrances.
    A.—Murrell; Rip Van Winkle.
    B.—Speed the Plough.
14.   W.—*Id.,* June 13.
    A.—Spectre Bridegroom; Rip Van Winkle.
    B.—Cricket on the Hearth; Your Life's in Danger.
16. *Monday:*
    W.—Macbeth; Betsy Baker.
    A.—Day of Reckoning; Revolution.
    B.—Hamlet.
17.   W.—Guy Mannering; Without Incumbrances.

[441]

    A.—Revolution; Rough Diamond.

    B.—Speed the Plough.

18.   W.—School for Scandal; Teacher Taught.

    A.—People's Lawyer; Rough Diamond.

    B.—Paul Pry.

19.   W.—Guy Mannering; Adopted Child.

    A.—Josey the Spartan; Young Widow.

    B.—Lady of Lyons.

20.   W.—Henry VIII; London Assurance, last three acts.

    A.—Poor Gentleman; Wool Dealer.

    B.—Valet de Sham; Magic Trumpet.

21.   W.—Romeo and Juliet; Ladies, Beware.

    A.—Murrell; Ocean Child.

    B.—*Id.*, June 20.

23. *Monday:*

    W.—Hamlet; Box and Cox.

    A.—Othello; Young Widow.

    B.—Young Widow; Magic Trumpet.

24.   W.—Othello; Alarming Sacrifice.

    A.—No advertisement.

    B.—*Id.*, June 23.

25.   W.—Caecinna *: *Caecinna*—Buchannan, *Claudius*—McMillan, *Aria*—Mad. Ponisi; Without Incumbrances.

    A.—Azael; Somebody Else.

    B.—Twice Killed.

26.   W.—Caecinna; Lend Me Five Shillings.

    A.—Azael; Young Widow.

    B.—*Id.*, June 25.

27.   W.—Othello; A Morning Call.

    A.—Azael; Somebody Else.

    B.—No legitimate drama.

28.   W.—Lady of Lyons; A Morning Call.

    A.—Azael; Rough Diamond.

    B.—No legitimate drama.

30. *Monday:*

    W.—Paris and London.

    A.—Azael; Ocean Child.

    B.—Cricket on the Hearth; David Copperfield.

JULY

1. *Tuesday:*

    W.—Paris and London.

    A.—Azael; Swiss Swains.

    B.—Simpson and Co.

2.   W.—Paris and London.

A.—Lady of Lyons; Azael.
B,—Faint Heart never won Fair Lady.

3. W,—*Id.,* June 2.
A,—Azael; Six Degrees of Crime.
B.—*Id.,* June 2.
C.—Hunchback; Hickety Pickety.

4. W.—*Id.,* June 2.
A.—Pleasant Neighbors; Thalaba.
B.—No legitimate drama advertised.
C,—Romeo and Juliet.

5. W.—*Id.,* June 2.
A.—Azael; Thalaba.
C.—Honey Moon.

7. *Monday:*
W.—Closed.
A.—Azael; Guy Mannering.
C.—No advertisement.

8. A.—Lady of Lyons; Azael.

9. A.—All that Glitters is not Gold; Azael.

10. A.—Lady of Lyons; Tour de Nesle.

11. A.—All that Glitters is not Gold; Widow's Victim.

12. A.—All that Glitters is not Gold; Broken Sword.
C.—Romeo and Juliet.

14. *Monday:*
A.—School for Scandal; Sketches in India.

15. A.—Crimson Crimes; Life in Phila.
N.—Elshie; Rake's Progress.

16. A.—Lady of Lyons; Used Up.
N.—Michael Erle; Elshie.

17. A.—No play advertised.
N,—Somebody Else; Elshie.

18. A.—Broken Sword; Perfection.
N.—Mischief Making; Court Fool.

19. A.—Lady of Lyons; Michael Erle.
N.—Heart of Midlothian; Elf of the Rock.

21. *Monday:*
A.—People's Candidate; Michael Erle.
N.—Truand Chief; Tom and Jerry.

22. A.—People's Candidate; Serious Family.
N.—*Id.,* July 19.

23. A.—All that Glitters is not Gold; The Maiden's Vow.
N.—The Huntsman and the Spy; Tom and Jerry.

24. A.—Family Ties; Maiden's Vow.
N.—Your Life's in Danger; Ivanhoe.

25. A.—Douglas; Hugh and Cry.
N.—Ivanhoe; Rough Diamond.

26.   A.—Family Ties; Hugh and Cry.
        N.—The Huntsman and the Spy; Koeuba.
28. *Monday:*
        A.—Family Ties; Sam Patch in France.
        N.—No advertisement.
29.   A.—Carpenter of Rouen; Life in Alabama.
        N.—Ella Rosenberg; Koeuba.
30.   A.—Tour de Nesle; Life in Phila.
        N.—The Wraith of the Lake; Koeuba.
31.   A.—Richelieu; The Secret.
        N.—Ambrose Gwinett; The Wraith of the Lake.

AUGUST

1. *Friday:*
        A.—No advertisement.
        N.—Dark Doings; Swamp Fox.
2.   A.—No advertisement.
        N.—Cramond Brig; Carpenter of Rouen.
4. *Monday:*
        N.—Pride of the Market; Margaret Catchpole.
5.   N.—Iron Chest; Rose of Ettrick Vale.
6.   N.—Isabelle; Black Sea Gull.
7.   N.—John Overy; Black Eyed Susan.
8.   N.—Peerless Pool; William Tell.
9.   N.—Rob Roy; Dark Doings.
11. *Monday:*
        N.—The Captain is not A-Miss; Rory O'More.
12.   N.—Bronze Horse; Philadelphia Fireman.
13.   N.—Charles XII; My Poll and my Partner Joe.
14.   N.—Laid up in Port; Dumb Man of Manchester.
15.   N.—Liberty, Equality, and Fraternity; The Saxon's Oath.
16.   N.—Carpenter of Rouen; Peerless Fool. Last night of the season.
18. *Monday:*
        W.—La Sonnambula.
        C.—Azael; Loan of a Lover.
19.   W.—Fra Diavolo; Poor Pillicoddy.
        C.—Azael; Loan of a Lover.
20.   W.—La Sonnambula; Loan of a Lover.
        C.—Azael; A Kiss in the Dark.
21.   W.—Fra Diavolo; Rough Diamond.
        C.—*Id.,* August 20.
22.   W.—Elixir of Love; Truand Chief.
        C.—Azael; Rendezvous.
23.   W.—Rob Roy; Truand Chief.

C.—*Id.,* August 22.

25. *Monday:*
 W.—Elixir of Love; All that Glitters is not Gold.
 C.—Azael; Day after the Wedding.

26. W.—Pauline; Loan of a Lover.
 C.—*Id.,* August 25.

27. W.—Daughter of the Regiment; Rough Diamond.
 C.—Azael; Ladies, Beware.

28. W.—Pauline; Poor Pillicoddy.
 C.—*Id.,* August 27.

29. W.—Cinderella; Slasher and Crasher.
 C.—Azael; Lottery Ticket.

30. W.—Pauline; Grimshaw, Bagshaw, and Bradshaw.
 C.—*Id.,* August 29.
 A.—Woman's Wit; Somebody Else.

SEPTEMBER

1. *Monday:*
 W.—Irish Ambassador; Grimshaw, Bagshaw, and Bradshaw.
 C.—Azael; The Secret.
 A.—Woman's Wit; My Precious Betsy.
 B.—Linda.

2. W.—Nervous Man; Irish Post.
 C.—Azael; The Secret.
 A.—All that Glitters is not Gold; Floating Beacon.
 B.—Linda.

3. W.—King O'Neil; His Last Legs.
 C.—Poor Gentleman; Forty and Fifty.
 A.—All that Glitters is not Gold; Black Eyed Susan.
 B.—Linda.

4. W.—Serious Family; How to pay Rent.
 C.—Rivals; Ladies, Beware.
 A.—Printer's Apprentice; Ole Bull.
 B.—Linda.

5. W.—Soldier of Fortune; Happy Man.
 C.—Serious Family; My Uncle John.
 A.—All that Glitters is not Gold; Young Widow.
 B.—Linda.

6. W.—King O'Neil; How to pay Rent.
 C.—Azael; The Secret.
 A.—Printer's Apprentice; My Precious Betsy.
 B.—Linda.

8. *Monday:*
 W.—Wild Oats; Angelo.
 C.—Romeo and Juliet; A Kiss in the Dark.

  A.—Madelaine; Spectre Bridegroom.
  B.—Woman's Trails; My Husband's Ghost.

9. W.—Money; Angelo.
  C.—Adrienne; Ladies, Beware.
  A.—Madelaine; Golden Farmer.
  B.—*Id.,* Sept. 8.

10. W.—Stranger; Daughter of the Regiment.
  C.—Love; Forty and Fifty.
  A.—Peeping in at 6 P. M.; Ole Bull.
  B.—Happiest Day of my Life; Hypochondriasis.

11. W.—Wonder; Cinderella.
  C.—Lady of Lyons; Lottery Ticket.
  A.—Isabelle; Peeping in at 6 P. M.
  B.—*Id.,* Sept. 10.

12. W.—Lady of Lyons; My Aunt.
  C.—Love's Sacrifice; Pleasant Neighbors.
  A.—Isabelle; Grimshaw.
  B.—Woman's Trials; Three Shaws.

13. W.—Pizarro; Fra Diavolo.
  C.—Apostate; Day after the Wedding.
  A.—Lucretia Borgia; Cousin Joe.
  B.—*Id.,* Sept. 12.

15. *Monday:*
  W.—Much Ado about Nothing; Three Shaws.
  C.—Adrienne; Mr. and Mrs. White.
  A.—Married Rake.
  B.—Grace Huntley.

16. W.—Wine Works Wonders; Love Spell.
  C.—Much Ado about Nothing; Ladies, Beware.
  A.—Cousin Joe.
  B.—*Id.,* Sept. 15.

17. W.—Money; La Sonnambula.
  C.—Love; Twice Killed.
  A.—Three Shaws.
  B.—*Id.,* Sept. 15.

18. W.—Dramatist; Rob Roy.
  C.—School for Scandal; Mr. and Mrs. Peter White.
  A.—John Dobbs.
  B.—*Id.,* Sept. 15.

19. W.—School for Scandal; Katharine and Petruchio.
  C.—Valeria *: *Valeria*—Miss Davenport, *Claudius*—Gilbert,
   Sillius—Taylor; Twice Killed.
  A.—Married Rake.
  B.—*Id.,* Sept. 15.

20. W.—Venice Preserved; Daughter of the Regiment.
  C.—Apostate; Day after the Wedding.

      B.—*Id.*, Sept. 15.

22. *Monday:*
      W.—La Bayadere; Soldier's Daughter.
      C.—Valeria; Forty and Fifty.
      A.—Mysterious Stranger.
      B.—Poor Cousin Walter; Bloomers out in Force.

23.   W.—Delicate Ground; La Bayadere.
      C.—Love's Sacrifice; Box and Cox.
      A.—*Id.*, Sept. 22.
      B.—*Id.*, Sept. 22.

24.   W.—La Bayadere; A Wonderful Woman.
      C.—Valeria; Sketches in India.
      A.—Lucretia Borgia.
      B.—*Id.*, Sept. 22.

25.   W.—La Bayadere; Wonder.
      C.—*Id.*, Sept. 22.
      A.—Agnes de Vere.
      B.—*Id.*, Sept. 22.

26.   W.—Delicate Ground; Who Speaks First?
      C.—Valeria; My Uncle John.
      A.—Three Shaws; A Morning Call.
      B.—*Id.*, Sept. 22.

27.   W.—Naval Engagements; Three Shaws.
      C.—Merchant of Venice; Sketches in India.
      A.—*Id.*, Sept. 26.
      B.—*Id.*, Sept. 22.

29. *Monday:*
      W.—Lover by Proxy; Rough Diamond.
      C.—Lady of Lyons; Twice Killed.
      A.—Fall of Algiers; The Chisel *: *Chisel*—Burke.
      B.—The Maniac Lover.

30.   W.—Loan of a Lover; Poor Pillicoddy.
      C.—Stranger; Wine Works Wonders.
      A.—*Id.*, Sept. 29.
      B.—*Id.*, Sept. 29.

OCTOBER

1. *Wednesday:*
      W.—Naval Engagements; Who Speaks First?
      C.—Hamlet; Mr. and Mrs. Peter White.
      A.—Cesar de Bazan; People's Lawyer.
      B.—Fire Eater.

2.   W.—All that Glitters is not Gold.
      C.—Town and Country; My Aunt.
      A.—Printer's Apprentice; Three Shaws.

B.—*Id.,* Oct 1.

3.   W.—Katharine and Petruchio.

C.—Much Ado about Nothing; A Cure for the Heart Ache.

A.—Poor Gentleman; Young Widow.

B.—Paul Pry.

4.   W.—Honey Moon.

C.—Hamlet; Sketches in India.

A.—Murrell; New Footman.

B.—Paul Pry.

6.   *Monday:*

W.—Damon and Pythias; Delicate Ground.

C.—Hunchback; Ladies, Beware.

A.—Damon and Pythias; My Young Wife.

B.—Faint Heart never won Fair Lady.

7.   W.—Richelieu; Faint Heart never won Fair Lady.

C.—Romeo and Juliet; Dr. Dilworth.

A.—Othello; Fire Eater.

B.—*Id.,* Oct. 6.

8.   W.—Macbeth; Who Speaks First?

C.—Love Chase; Twice Killed.

A.—Virginius; New Footman.

B.—Adopted Child.

9.   W.—Damon and Pythias; A Lover by Proxy.

C.—Lady of Lyons; Dr. Dilworth.

A.—Pizarro; Spectre Bridegroom.

B.—Adopted Child.

10.   W.—Richelieu; Asmodeus.

C.—Ion; Forty and Fifty.

A.—Student of Morlaix *: *Eugene*—Scott, *Hortense*—Mrs. A. F. Baker; Charles II.

B.—All that Glitters is not Gold.

11.   W.—Macbeth; Asmodeus.

C.—Stranger; Honey Moon.

A.—Student of Morlaix; Adopted Child.

B.—*Id.,* Oct. 10.

13.   *Monday:*

W.—Othello; Your Life's in Danger.

C.—As You Like It; Dr. Dilworth.

A.—Richard III; A Kiss in the Dark.

B.—*Id.,* Oct. 10.

14.   W.—Jack Cade; Your Life's in Danger.

C.—Ion; Sketches in India.

A.—Hamlet; A Man without a Head.

B.—*Id.,* Oct. 10.

15.   W.—King Lear; Naval Engagements.

C.—Armand *: *Blanche*—Mrs. Mowatt, *Armand*—Taylor;

A Kiss in the Dark.
A.—Rob Roy; Children in the Wood.
B.—*Id.*, Oct. 10.

16.   W.—Jack Cade; A Lover by Proxy.
C.—Love Chase; Lottery Ticket.
A.—Damon and Pythias; Wool Dealer.
B.—*Id.*, Oct. 10.

17.   W.—Gladiator; Asmodeus.
C.—Armand; Faint Heart never won Fair Lady.
A.—Brutus; Shoemaker of Toulouse.
B.—*Id.*, Oct. 10.

18.   W.—Jack Cade; Mysterious Family.
C.—*Id.*, Oct. 17.
A.—Maurice; Michael Erle.
B.—*Id.*, Oct. 10.

20. *Monday:*
W.—Gladiator; Betsy Baker.
C.—Irish Lion; His Last Legs.
A.—Golden Farmer; New Footman.
B.—Child of Nature.

21.   W.—Metamora; My Precious Betsy.
C.—Irish Lion; His Last Legs.
A.—The Chimes; Somebody Else.
B.—Child of Nature.

22.   W.—Jack Cade; Your Life's in Danger.
C.—Crown of Diamonds; Forty and Fifty.
A.—Cesar de Bazan; People's Lawyer.
B.—Child of Nature.

23.   W.—Metamora; Crown Prince.
C.—St. Patrick's Eve; Irish Secretary.
A.—Fall of Algiers; Rough Diamond.
B.—Bloomers out in Force; Perfection.

24.   W.—Gladiator; Asmodeus.
C.—Crown of Diamonds; Mr. and Mrs. White.
A.—Le Diable a Paris; Buried Alive.
B.—*Id.*, 23.

25.   W.—Richard III; Crown Prince.
C.—St. Patrick's Eve; Twice Killed.
A.—Joan d' Arc; Ben, the Boatswain.
B.—*Id.*, Oct. 23.

27. *Monday:*
W.—Patrician's Daughter; Three Shaws.
C.—Crown of Diamonds; A Day after the Wedding.
A.—Rip Van Winkle; Ben, the Boatswain.
B.—Midnight Watch; Four Sisters.

28.   W.—Love's Sacrifice; Crown Prince.

  C.—Knight of Arva; Forty and Fifty.
  A.—Serious Family; Monsieur Jacques.
  B.—Midnight Watch; Miseries of Woman's Life.
29. W.—Jealous Wife; Wonderful Woman.
  C.—Crown of Diamonds; My Sister Kate.
  A.—Serious Family; Joan d' Arc.
  B.—*Id.,* Oct. 28.
30. W.—Patrician's Daughter; All that Glitters is not Gold.
  C.—St. Patrick's Eve; His Last Legs.
  A.—Henriette; Cool as a Cucumber.
  B.—*Id.,* Oct. 28.
31. W.—Jealous Wife; Honey Moon.
  C.—Crown of Diamonds; Sketches in India.
  A.—Isabelle; Three Shaws.
  B.—*Id.,* Oct. 28.

NOVEMBER

1. *Saturday:*
  W.—Jane Shore; Asmodeus.
  C.—Knight of Arva; My Sister Kate.
  A.—Revolution; Madelaine.
  B.—*Id.,* Oct. 28.
3. *Monday:*
  W.—Mary Stuart; Rough Diamond.
  C.—Child of the Regiment; My Sister Kate.
  A.—Cool as a Cucumber; Fortune's Whims.
  B.—Stage-Struck Yankee.
4. W.—Mary Stuart; Mysterious Family.
  C.—Serious Family; Irish Secretary.
  A.—Ireland as it Is; Brian O'Lynn.
  B.—*Id.,* Nov. 3.
5. W.—*Id.,* Nov. 1.
  C.—*Id.,* Nov. 3.
  A.—Shandy Maguire; Cousin Joe.
  B.—*Id.,* Nov. 3.
6. W.—Evadne; Delicate Ground.
  C.—Irish Ambassador; Betsy Baker.
  A.—Ireland as it Is; Our Gal.
  B.—*Id.,* Nov. 3.
7. W.—Hunchback; A Figure of Fun.
  C.—Child of the Regiment; Betsy Baker.
  A.—Irish Tiger; Teddy the Tiler.
  B.—*Id.,* Nov. 3.
8. W.—Mary Stuart; A Figure of Fun.
  C.—Knight of Arva; Betsy Baker.

A.—*Id.*, Nov. 7.

B.—*Id.*, Nov. 3.

10. *Monday:*

W.—Green Bushes; My Precious Betsy.

C.—Henry VIII; Betsy Baker.

A.—The Pilgrim of Love; Yacht Race.

B.—A Countess for an Hour.

11. W.—*Id.*, Nov. 10.

C.—Macbeth; Jenny Lind.

A.—Pilgrim of Love; Alive and Kicking.

B.—*Id.*, Nov. 10.

12. W.—French Spy; Crown Prince.

C.—Jealous Wife; Jenny Lind.

A.—Irish Farmer; Pilgrim of Love.

B.—*Id.*, Nov. 10.

13. W.—French Spy; Asmodeus.

C.—Hunchback; Mr. and Mrs. White.

A.—Shandy Maguire; Our Gal.

B.—*Id.*, Nov. 10.

14. W.—French Spy; All that Glitters is not Gold.

C.—Winter's Tale; Jenny Lind.

A.—Born to Good Luck; Tim Moore, The Lion of the Day.

B.—*Id.*, Nov. 10.

15. W.—Marie du Cange; French Spy.

C.—Macbeth; Jenny Lind.

A.—Rory O'More; Cousin Joe.

B.—*Id.*, Nov. 10.

17. *Monday:*

W.—*Id.*, Nov. 15.

C.—Winter's Tale; Lola Montes.

A.—Madelaine; Revolution.

B.—Louise.

18. W.—Your Life's in Danger; Poor Pillicoddy.

C.—*Id.*, Nov. 17.

A.—Rip Van Winkle; Married Rake.

B.—*Id.*, Nov. 17.

19. W.—Delicate Ground; Rough Diamond.

C.—Ingomar, the Barbarian *: *Parthenia*—Mrs. Warner, *Polydor*—C. Hill; Lola Montes.

A.—Isabelle; Cool as a Cucumber.

B.—*Id.*, Nov. 17.

20. W.—Marie du Cange; Taming a Tartar.

C.—Ingomar; Dr. Dilworth.

A.—Henriette; My Young Wife and my Old Umbrella.

B.—*Id.*, Nov. 17.

21. W.—French Spy; Taming a Tartar.

      C.—Ingomar; Honey Moon.
      A.—Sixteen String Jack; Buried Alive.
      B.—*Id.*, Nov. 17.

22.   W.—Harvest Home *: *Amy*—Mad. Celeste, *Popjoy*—Rich-
        ings; Taming a Tartar.
      C.—Winter's Tale; Jenny Lind.
      A.—Sixteen String Jack; Every Inch a Sailor.
      B.—*Id.*, Nov. 17.

24. *Monday:*
      W.—*Id.*, Nov. 22.
      C.—Richard III; Sketches in India.
      A.—*Id.*, Nov. 22.
      B.—Midnight Watch; Four Sisters.

25.   W.—Harvest Home; French Spy.
      C.—Love's Sacrifice; Jenny Lind.
      A.—Robber's Wife; Wool Dealer.
      B.—Sweethearts and Wives.

26.   W.—Wept of Wish-Tom-Wish; Taming a Tartar.
      C.—Crown of Diamonds; Sketches in India.
      A.—Jonathan Bradford; A Man without a Head.
      B.—*Id.*, Nov. 25.

27.   W.—Wept of Wish-Ton-Wish; French Spy.
      C.—Knight of Arva; How to pay Rent.
      A.—George Barnwell.
      B.—Separate Maintenance.

28.   W.—*Id.*, Nov. 22.
      C.—Virginius; Jenny Lind.
      A.—Wallace; Forty Thieves.
      B.—*Id.*, Nov. 27.

29.   W.—Harvest Home; Cabin Boy.
      C.—Rob Roy; Mr. and Mrs. White.
      A.—Jonathan Bradford; Wallace.
      B.—All That Glitters is not Gold.

DECEMBER

1. *Monday:*
      W.—Calaynos; Three Shaws.
      C.—Macbeth; Betsy Baker.
      A.—Female Guard; Honest Thieves.
      B.—Handsome Husband.

2.   W.—Amilie; Betsy Baker.
      C.—Guy Mannering; Omnibus.
      A.—Female Guard; Adopted Child.
      B.—*Id.*, Dec. 1.

3.   W.—Calaynos; Your Life's in Danger.

C.—Lady of Lyons; A Kiss in the Dark.
A.—Female Guard; Robber's Wife.
B.—Woman's Trials.

4. W.—Amilie; All that Glitters is not Gold.
C.—*Id.,* Dec. 2.
A.—Female Guard; Michael Erle.
B.—*Id.,* Dec. 3.

5. W.—Betrothal; Robert Macaire.
C.—Romeo and Juliet; A Kiss in the Dark.
A.—Female Guard; Black Eyed Susan.
B.—Yankee Watchman.

6. W.—Fra Diavolo; Rob Roy.
C.—The Stranger; Honey Moon.
A.—Female Guard; Bottle Imp.
B.—*Id.,* Dec. 5.

8. *Monday:*
W.—Bohemian Girl; Your Life's in Danger.
C.—Actress of Padua; Promissory Note.
A.—Love's Sacrifice; Female Guard.
B.—Bold Stroke for a Husband.

9. W.—Bohemian Girl; Slasher and Crasher.
C.—Hamlet; Promissory Note.
A.—The Wife; Female Guard.
B.—*Id.,* Dec. 8.

10. W.—Extremes; Pass Word.
C.—Actress of Padua; Omnibus.
A.—Romeo and Juliet; Female Guard.
B.—Separate Maintenance.

11. W.—Betrothal; Poor Pillicoddy.
C.—Actress of Padua; Promissory Note.
A.—Female Guard; Honey Moon.
B.—*Id.,* Dec. 10.

12. W.—Child of the Regiment; Robert Macaire.
C.—As You Like It; Betsy Baker.
A.—Female Guard; Bottle Imp.
B.—Happiest Day of my Life.

13. W.—Venice Preserved; Masaniello.
C.—Guy Mannering; Jenny Lind.
A.—Female Guard; Carpenter of Rouen.
B.—*Id.,* Dec 12.

15. W.—Cinderella; Three Shaws.
C.—School for Scandal; Turning the Tables.
A.—Six Degrees of Crime; Jack's the Lad.
B.—Stage-Struck Yankee.

16. W.—Extremes; Poor Pillicoddy.
C.—Rob Roy; Turning the Tables.

A.—Six Degrees of Crime; Evil Eye.

B.—*Id.,* Dec. 15.

17. W.—Der Freischutz; Masaniello, first and second acts.

C.—Guy Mannering; Jenny Lind.

A.—Lucille; Every Inch a Sailor.

B.—*Id.,* Dec. 15.

18. W.—Bohemian Girl; Der Freischutz, the incantation scene.

C.—Henry VIII; Simpson and Co.

A.—Luke the Laborer; Michael Erle.

B.—Four Sisters.

19. W.—Extremes; Three Cuckoos *: *Col. Cranky*—McKeon.

C.—Banker's Wife; Actress of Padua.

A.—Hut of the Red Mountain; Bottle Imp.

B.—*Id.,* Dec. 18.

20. W.—School of Reform; Robert Macaire.

C.—Banker's Wife; London Assurance.

A.—Hut of the Red Mountain; Jack's the Lad.

B.—*Id.,* Dec. 18.

22. *Monday:*

W.—Serious Family; All that Glitters is not Gold.

C.—Azael; Loan of a Lover.

A.—Barrack Room; Wallace.

B.—Major Jones' Courtship *.

23. W.—Retribution; Serious Family.

C.—*Id.,* Dec. 22.

A.—A Morning Call; Cabin Boy.

B.—*Id.,* Dec. 22.

24. W.—Your Life's in Danger; Swedish Patriotism.

C.—Azael; Promissory Note.

A.—Evil Eye; Land Sharks and Sea Gulls.

B.—*Id.,* Dec. 22.

25. W.—Extremes; Swedish Patriotism.

C.—Lady of Lyons; Azael.

A.—False Colors; Cabin Boy.

B.—*Id.,* Dec. 22.

26. W.—Pauline; Swedish Patriotism.

C.—Hamlet; Jenny Lind.

A.—Carpenter of Rouen; Swan of Beauty.

B.—*Id.,* Dec. 22.

27. W.—*Id.,* Dec. 26.

C.—Stranger; Honey Moon.

A.—Warlock of the Glen; Black Eyed Susan.

B.—*Id.,* Dec. 22.

29. *Monday:*

W.—Hunchback; Three Cuckoos.

C.—Stranger; Honey Moon.

A.—John Overy; Crossing the Line.
B.—*Id.*, Dec. 22.
30. W.—Love Chase; Deeds of Dreadful Note.
C.—Money; Katharine and Petruchio.
A.—Wallace; Warlock of the Glen.
B.—*Id.*, Dec. 22.
31. W.—Lady of Lyons; Deeds of Dreadful Note.
C.—The Robbers; Rough Diamond.
A.—The Mummy; Jumbo Jim.
B.—*Id.*, Dec. 22.

JANUARY 1852

1. *Thursday:*
W.—Love.
A.—Columbia's Son; The Mummy.
C.—Money; Katharine and Petruchio.
2. W.—Duke's Wager; Rough Diamond.
A.—Pirate's Legacy; Jim Crow in London.
C.—Romeo and Juliet; Cricket on the Hearth.
3. W.—Duke's Wager.
A.—*Id.*, Jan. 2.
C.—The Robbers; Forty and Fifty.
5. *Monday:*
W.—New Way To Pay Old Debts; Lend Me Five Shillings.
A.—No regular drama during engagement of Macallister the magician.
C.—Hamlet; Turning the Tables.
6. W.—Hamlet; Three Shaws.
C.—Town and Country; Cure for the Heart Ache.
7. W.—New Way To Pay Old Debts; Domestic Economy.
C.—Lady of Lyons; Dramatist.
8. W.—Merchant of Venice; All that Glitters is not Gold.
C.—Elder Brother; Cure for the Heart Ache.
9. W.—Othello; Domestic Economy.
C.—Stranger; Wild Oats.
10. W.—Richard III; Caught in his own Trap.
C.—Inconstant; Elder Brother.
12. *Monday:*
W.—Pizarro; Caught in his own Trap.
C.—Henry IV; My Uncle John.
13. W.—Othello; Caught in his own Trap.
C.—Wild Oats; Dramatist.
14. W.—William Tell; School of Reform.
C.—Richard III; Rough Diamond.
15. W.—Hamlet; Fire-Eater.

C.—Venice Preserved; Honey Moon.

16. W.—Hunchback; His Last Legs.
C.—Hamlet; Turning the Tables.

17. W.—Macbeth; Fire-Eater.
C.—Apostate; Jenny Lind.

19. *Monday:*
W.—Naval Engagements; Caught in his own Trap.
C.—Julius Caesar; My Aunt.

20. W.—Asmodeus; Domestic Economy.
C.—New Way To Pay Old Debts; Jenny Lind.

21. W.—Mysterious Family; Deeds of Dreadful Note.
C.—Betram; Omnibus.

22. W.—Katharine and Petruchio; Three Cuckoos.
C.—Richard III; Day after the Wedding.

23. W.—Charles XII; Fire-Eater.
C.—Othello; A Kiss in the Dark.

24. W.—Robert Macaire; Three Shaws.
C.—Macbeth; My Uncle John.

26. *Monday.*
W.—Miller's Maid; Caught in his own Trap.
C.—Venice Preserved; Forty and Fifty.

27. W.—All that Glitters is not Gold; Your Life's in Danger.
C.—Iron Chest; Wild Oats.

28. W.—Charles XII; Two Bonnycastles.
C.—Julius Caesar; Omnibus.

29. W.—Delicate Ground; Two Bonnycastles.
C.—King John; Betsy Baker.

30. W.—Miller's Maid; Two Bonnycastles.
C.—Brutus; Dramatist.

31. W.—School of Reform; Two Bonnycastles.
C.—Iron Chest; Stranger.

FEBRUARY

2. *Monday:*
W.—Extremes; Two Bonnycastles.
C.—Shandy Maguire; Pilgrim of Love.

3. W.—Heir at Law; Pride of the Market.
C.—Shandy Maguire; Limerick Boy.

4. W.—Fashion; Life in Alabama.
C.—Ireland as it Is; Irish Lion.

5. W.—Wild Oats; Robert Macaire.
C.—Ireland as it Is; Pilgrim of Love.

6. W.—Extremes; Caught in his own Trap.
C.—Born to Good Luck; Rough Diamond.

7. W.—Retribution; Bamboozling.

C.—*Id.*, Feb. 6.

9. *Monday:*
W.—Child of the Regiment; Pride of the Market.
C.—Ireland and America; Our Gal.

10. W.—Child of the Regiment; Charles VII.
C.—*Id.*, Feb. 9.

11. W.—L'Elisire d' Amore; Two Bonnycastles.
C.—Ireland and America; It's the Custom of the Country *

12. W.—L'Elisire d' Amore; Three Cuckoos.
C.—Ireland as it Is; It's the Custom of the Country.

13. W.—La Sonnambula; Naval Engagements.
C.—It's the Custom of the Country; In and Out of Place.

14. W.—La Sonnambula; Deeds of Dreadful Note.
C.—*Id.*, Feb. 13.

16. *Monday:*
W.—Linda di Chamounix; Domestic Economy.
C.—Crown of Diamonds; Betsy Baker.

17. W.—Linda di Chamounix; Delicate Ground.
C.—School for Scandal; Knight of Arva.

18. W.—Linda di Chamounix; Caught in his own Trap.
C.—Crown of Diamonds; Irish Secretary.

19. W.—Linda di Chamounix; Two Bonnycastles.
C.—John Bull; How to pay Rent.

20. W.—Norma; Three Shaws.
C.—Daughter of the Regiment; Irish Secretary

21. W.—Norma; Slasher and Crasher.
C.—John Bull; How to pay Rent.

23. *Monday:*
W.—Paul Clifford; Poor Pillicoddy.
C.—Daughter of the Regiment; His Last Legs.

24. W.—Paul Clifford; Two Bonnycastles.
C.—Love; Knight of Arva.

25. W.—Paul Clifford; Three Cuckoos.
C.—Black Domino; 102!

26. W.—Paul Clifford; House Dog.
C.—St. Patrick's Eve; My Uncle John.

27. W.—Paul Clifford; Momentous Question.
C.—Black Domino; Forty and Fifty.

28. W.—Paul Clifford; I've Eaten my Friend *.
C.—St. Patrick's Eve; His Last Legs.
A.—Otello; Virginia Mummy.

MARCH

1. *Monday:*
W.—Serious Family; I've Eaten my Friend.

C.—Black Domino; 102!
A.—Momentous Question; Charcoal Burner.
2. W.—Nervous Man; I've Eaten my Friend.
C.—Knight of Arva; Irish Lion.
A.—The Devil and the Deserter; Broken Sword.
3. W.—Soldier of Fortune; His Last Legs.
C.—Black Domino; Pleasant Neighbors.
A.—Truand Chief; Charcoal Burner.
4. W.—King O'Neil; House Dog.
C.—Richelieu; Tour de Nesle.
A.—Broken Sword; Idiot Witness.
5. W.—Happy Man; Born to Good Luck.
C.—Crown of Diamonds; How to pay Rent.
A.—Artist's Wife; Lion of the Sea.
6. W.—Id., Mar. 5.
C.—Knight of Arva; Katharine and Petruchio.
A.—Carpenter of Rouen; Lion of the Sea.
8. Monday:
W.—As You Like It; Caught in his own Trap.
C.—Evadne; Married Rake.
A.—Two Bonnycastles; Mother's Blessing.
9. W.—School for Scandal; Loan of a Lover.
C.—Love's Sacrifice; Married Rake.
A.—Artist's Wife; Hall of Fate and the Enchanted Lake.
10. W.—She Stoops to Conquer; Delicate Ground.
C.—Fazio; Cesar de Bazan.
A.—Two Bonnycastles; Hall of Fate.
11. W.—Much Ado about Nothing; Loan of a Lover.
C.—Lady of Lyons; Honey Moon.
A.—Momentous Question; Hall of Fate.
12. W.—Ladies' Battles*: Countess—Julia Bennett, Gustavus—
Richings; All that Glitters is not Gold.
C.—Lucretia Borgia; Chloroform.
A.—Two Bonnycastles; Hall of Fate.
13. W.—Ladies' Battle; Somebody Else.
C.—Id., Mar. 12.
A.—Maid of Switzerland; Hall of Fate.
15. Monday:
W.—Ladies' Battle; Queensbury Fete.
C.—Fazio; Faint Heart never won Fair Lady.
A.—Damon and Pythias; Donation Concerts.
16. W.—Id., Mar. 15.
C.—Romeo and Juliet; Chloroform.
A.—Othello; Donation Concerts.
17. W.—Ladies' Battle; Fair One of the Golden Locks.

      C.—Hunchback; Gentleman in Difficulties.

      A.—Virginius; Donation Concerts.

18.   W.—Much Ado about Nothing; Fair One with the Golden Locks.

      C.—Ion; Faint Heart never won Fair Lady.

      A.—Macbeth; Donation Concerts.

19.   W.—Twelfth Night; Fair One of the Golden Locks.

      C.—Love; Simpson and Co.

      A.—Ingomar; Student of Morlaix.

20.   W.—*Id.*, Mar. 19.

      C.—Adelgitha; Chloroform.

      A.—Ingomar; Shoemaker of Toulouse.

22. *Monday:*

      W.—The Painter of Brienne *: *Napoleon*—Couldock, *Clotilde*—Miss Wemyss; Robert Macaire.

      C.—School for Scandal; Gentleman in Difficulties.

      A.—Pizarro; Charles II.

23.   W.—Painter of Brienne; All that Glitters is not Gold.

      C.—School for Scandal; Forty and Fifty.

      A.—Richelieu; Maid of Switzerland.

24.   W.—Comedy of Errors; Painter of Brienne.

      C.—School for Scandal; Married Rake.

      A.—Helos, the Helot *: *Helos*—J. R. Scott; Two Bonny-castles.

25.   W.—Rivals; Painter of Brienne.

      C.—Much Ado about Nothing; Gentleman in Difficulties.

      A.—Helos; Charcoal Burner.

26.   W.—She Stoops to Conquer; Serious Family.

      C.—Love's Sacrifice; Pleasant Neighbors.

      A.—Helos; Charles XII.

27.   W.—Twelfth Night; Somebody Else.

      C.—Love's Sacrifice; 102!

      A.—Helos; Adopted Child.

29. *Monday:*

      W.—Othello; Box and Cox.

      C.—Lady of Lyons; Day after the Wedding.

      A.—Forest of Bondy; Ourang Outang.

30.   W.—New Way To Pay Old Debts; Lend Me Five Shillings.

      C.—Lady of Lyons; Dr. Dilworth.

      A.—Butcher's Dog of Ghent. Ourang Outang.

31.   W.—Macbeth; Domestic Economy.

      C.—Much Ado about Nothing; Queen's Husband.

      A.—Forest of Bondy; Three Thieves.

APRIL

1. *Thursday:*
   W.—Iron Chest; Caught in his own Trap.
   C.—Patrician's Daughter; Pleasant Neighbors.
   A.—Butcher's Dog of Ghent; Three Thieves.
2. W.—Hamlet; House Dog.
   C.—Love's Sacrifice; School for Scandal.
   A.—Cross of Death; Planter's Pest.
3. W.—Serious Family; Comedy of Errors.
   C.—Lady of Lyons; Dr. Dilworth.
   A.—*Id.,* Apr. 2.
5. *Monday:*
   W.—Corsican Brothers; Three Shaws.
   C.—Patrician's Daughter; Queen's Husband.
   A.—Soldier's Return; Old Toll-House.
6. W.—Corsican Brothers; Poor Pillicoddy.
   C.—Ingomar; Simpson and Co.
   A.—John Jones; Omadhaun.
7. W.—Corsican Brothers; House Dog.
   C.—*Id.,* Apr. 6.
   A.—Jack Robinson and his Monkey; 102!
8. W.—Corsican Brothers; A Duel in the Dark *.
   C.—Wild Oats; My Uncle John.
   A.—Jack Robinson and his Monkey; Omadhaun.
9. W.—*Id.,* April 8.
   C.—Stranger; Katharine and Petruchio.
   A.—Bloodhounds; Two Bonnycastles.
10. W.—Corsican Brothers; Tender Precautions.
    C.—Cure for the Heart Ache; Dramatist.
    A.—Bloodhounds; Angel of the Attic.
12. *Monday:*
    W.—*Id.,* Apr. 10.
    C.—Hamlet; Betsy Baker.
    A.—Maid of Switzerland; Ourang Outang.
13. W.—*Id.,* Apr. 8.
    C.—Money; My Aunt.
    A.—Stranger; Napoleon.
14. W.—*Id.,* Apr. 8.
    C.—Lady of Lyons; Simpson and Co.
    A.—Forest of Bondy; Planter's Pest.
15. W.—Corsican Brothers; Two Bonnycastles.
    C.—Elder Brother; Cure for the Heart Ache.
    A.—Knights of the Cross; Momentous Question.
16. W.—Corsican Brothers; His Last Legs.
    C.—Macbeth; Forty and Fifty.

A.—Dumb Slave; Sentinel.
17. W.—Corsican Brothers; All that Glitters is not Gold.
C.—Stranger; Elder Brother.
A.—Knights of the Cross; Sentinel.
19. *Monday:*
W.—Macbeth; Tit for Tat.
C.—De Soto *: *De Soto*—Murdock, *Ulah*—Miss Anderton; A Kiss in the Dark.
A.—Hamlet; Sentinel.
20. W.—School for Scandal; A Duel in the Dark.
C.—De Soto; Queen's Husband.
A.—Richard III; Sentinel.
21. W.—Guy Mannering; Tit for Tat.
C.—De Soto; Queen's Husband.
A.—Mohammed; Spitfire.
22. W.—As You Like It; Caught in his own Trap.
C.—De Soto; Great Western.
A.—*Id.,* Apr. 21.
23. W.—Henry VIII; Honey Moon.
C.—De Soto; Queen's Husband.
A.—Mohammed; Carpenter of Rouen.
24. W.—*Id.,* Apr. 21.
C.—De Soto; A Kiss in the Dark.
A.—Court Fool; Innkeeper's Daughter.
26. *Monday:*
W.—Romeo and Juliet; Three Shaws.
C.—Love; Matrimonial Prospectuses.
A.—The Unknown; Spitfire.
27. W.—Guy Mannering; All that Glitters is not Gold.
C.—Belle's Stratagem; Matrimonial Prospectuses.
A.—The Unknown; Innkeeper's Daughter.
28. W.—Lady of Lyons; Duel in the Dark.
C.—As You Like It; Matrimonial Prospectuses.
A.—The Unknown; Paul Pry.
29. W.—Actress of Padua; Two Bonnycastles.
C.—Valeria; A Kiss in the Dark.
A.—The Unknown; Haunted Inn.
30. W.—Banker's Wife; Actress of Padua.
C.—Adrienne; Matrimonial Prospectuses.
A.—Maid of Switzerland; Haunted Inn.

MAY

1 *Saturday:*
W.—Banker's Wife; London Assurance.
C.—Valeria; Matrimonial Prospectuses.

A.—Edith *; Philadelphia Fireman.

3. *Monday:*
W.—Extremes; A Duel in the Dark.
C.—Charlotte Corday; P.P.
A.—*Id.,* May 3.

4. W.—Corsican Brothers; Naval Engagements.
C.—Maid of Mariendorpt; Queen's Husband.
A.—*Id.,* May 3.

5. W.—Faint Heart never won Fair Lady; Robert Macaire.
C.—Charlotte Corday; Dead Shot.
A.—Edith; Guy Mannering.

6. W.—Extremes; Domestic Economy.
C.—Love's Sacrifice; P.P.
A.—Gilman's Wedding; Family Jars.

7. W.—Norma; A Duel in the Dark.
C.—Ingomar; Rough Diamond.
A.—Lady of Lyons; Gilman's Wedding.

8. W.—Corsican Brothers; Katharine and Petruchio.
C.—Ingomar; Dr. Dilworth.
A.—Broken Sword; Harlequin Margery Daw.

10. W.—Harvest Home; Caught in his own Trap.
C.—Bianca Visconti; P.P.
A.—Flying Dutchman; Perfection.

11. W.—French Spy; Delicate Ground.
C.—Adrienne; Matrimonial Prospectuses.
A.—Family Jars; Flying Dutchman.

12. W.—Taming a Tartar; A Duel in the Dark.
C.—Ingomar; Forty and Fifty.
A.—Truand Chief; Flying Dutchman.

13. W.—French Spy; House Dog.
C.—Adrienne; A Kiss in the Dark.
A.—Wild Boy of Bohemia; Carpenter of Rouen.

14. W.—Wept of Wish-Ton-Wish; Taming a Tartar.
C.—London Assurance; Clari.
A.—No advertisement.

15. W.—French Spy; Taming a Tartar.
C.—Apostate; P.P.
A.—The Seven Escapes; Dumb Man of Manchester.

17. *Monday:*
W.—St. Mary's Eve; Domestic Economy.
C.—De Soto; Queen's Husband.
A.—No advertisement.

18. W.—St. Mary's Eve; Forest Rose.
C.—De Soto; Matrimonial Prospectuses.

19. W.—Marie du Cange; Forest Rose.
C.—*Id.,* May 18.

20. W.—St. Mary's Eve; All that Glitters is not Gold.
     C.—Much Ado about Nothing; Chloroform.
21. W.—La Bayadere; Wonderful Woman.
     C.—De Soto; Dramatist.
22. W.—La Bayadere; Forest Rose.
     C.—De Soto; Queen's Husband.
     N.—Dumb Man of Manchester; Adopted Child.
24. *Monday:*
     W.—Willow Copse; Deeds of Dreadful Note.
     C.—De Soto; Double-Bedded Room.
     N.—Truand Chief; Frederick the Great.
25. W.—Willow Copse; The Duel in the Dark.
     C.—Henry IV; Queen's Husband.
     N.—Idiot Witness; Dumb Man of Manchester.
26. W.—Masaniello; Forest Rose.
     C.—De Soto; Chloroform.
     N.—Ambrose Gwinett; Don Juan. Last night of the season.
27. W.—Masaniello; Three Cuckoos.
     C.—Dramatist; Swiss Cottage.
28. W.—Willow Copse; La Bayadere.
     C.—The Inconstant; Elder Brother.
29. W.—*Id., May 28.*
     C.—Henry IV; My Aunt.
31. *Monday:*
     W.—Lola Montez in Bavaria; Deeds of Dreadful Note.
     C.—Pizarro; Faint Heart never won Fair Lady.

JUNE

1. *Tuesday:*
    W.—Lola Montez in Bavaria; Three Shaws.
    C.—Lady of Lyons; A Day in Paris.
2. W.—Lola Montez in Bavaria; Domestic Economy.
    C.—Money; Lucretia Borgia.
3. W.—Lola Montez in Bavaria; Caught in his own Trap.
    C.—Honey Moon; Double-Bedded Room.
4. W.—Lola Montez in Bavaria; Two Bonnycastles.
    C.—School for Scandal; Faint Heart never won Fair Lady.
5. W.—Lola Montez in Bavaria; A Kiss in the Dark.
    C.—Adelgitha; Wild Oats.
7. *Monday:*
    W.—Pizarro; Your Life's in Danger.
    C.—Gamester; William Tell.
8. W.—Willow Copse; Deeds of Dreadful Note.
    C.—Stranger; My Aunt.
9. W.—Richelieu; A Kiss in the Dark.

C.—Inconstant; Lucretia Borgia.
10. W.—Jack Cade; House Dog.
C.—London Assurance; Pizarro.
11. W.—Damon and Pythias; Lend Me Five Shillings.
C.—London Assurance; Dramatist.
12. W.—Jack Cade; Who Stole the Pocket-Book?*: *Tipthorp*—
Chapman, *Fanny*—Miss Gougenheim.
C.—Douglas; Chloroform.
14. *Monday:*
W.—Othello; Who Stole the Pocket-Book?
C.—London Assurance; Waterman.
15. W.—Willow Copse; Who Stole the Pocket-Book?
C.—Stranger; His Last Legs.
16. W.—Broker of Bogota; Caught in his own Trap.
C.—Double-Bedded Room; Why don't she Marry?
17. W.—Jack Cade; Duel in the Dark.
C.—A Kiss in the Dark; Irishman's Fortune.
18. W.—Virginius; Deeds of Dreadful Note.
C.—Rory O'More; Spoiled Child.
19. W.—Metamora; A Kiss in the Dark.
C.—Rory O'More; Rough Diamond; Last night of the
Season.
21. *Monday:*
W.—Hamlet; Who Stole the Pocket-Book?
22. W.—Richelieu; Three Shaws.
23. W.—Gladiator; Our Clerks *.
24. W.—Metamora; Our Clerks.
25. W.—Hamlet; Two Bonnycastles.
26. W.—Gladiator; Our Clerks.
28. *Monday:*
W.—No legitimate drama.

JULY

12. *Monday:*
N.—Three Guardsmen; Come at Last.
C.—Love's Sacrifice; Rough Diamond.
13. N.—*Id.,* July 12.
C.—The Wife; Wandering Boys.
14. N.—Three Guardsmen; Spitfire.
C.—Hunchback; Nix, the Cabman.
15. N.—Six Fighting Brothers; Lola Montez.
C.—Ion; Nix, the Cabman.
16. N.—Six Fighting Brothers; Your Life's in Danger.
C.—Romeo and Juliet; Wandering Boys.
17. N.—Six Fighting Brothers; Mose in China.

C.—Pizarro; Rough Diamond.
19. *Monday:*
    N.—Tour de Nesle; Faithful Slave.
    C.—Fazio; Climbing Boy.
20. N.—*Id.,* July 17.
    C.—Douglas; Little Devil.
21. N.—Three Guardsmen; Lola Montez.
    C.—Honey Moon; Young Scamp.
22. N.—Robert Kyd; Your Life's in Danger.
    C.—Climbing Boy; Youth who never Saw a Woman *.
23. N.—*Id.,* July 22.
    C.—Romeo and Juliet; King's Gardener.
24. N.—No advertisement.
    C.—Lady of Lyons; Jack Sheppard.
26. *Monday:*
    N.—Red Rover; Tom and Jerry.
    C.—The Wife; Wandering Boys.
27. N.—The Drunkard; Black Mummy.
    C.—Gil Blas; Jack Sheppard.
28. N.—My Poll and my Partner Joe; Catching an Heiress.
    C.—Gil Blas; Young Scamp.
29. N.—Rake's Progress; Faithful Slave.
    C.—Lady of Lyons; Youth who never Saw a Woman.
30. N.—Yankee Jack; Things in the Next Century.
    C.—Fazio; Blind Boy.
31. N.—Philadelphia Locksmith; Tom and Jerry.

AUGUST

2. *Monday:*
    N.—Valsha; Make your Wills.
    C.—Hamlet; Rough Diamond.
3. N.—Witch Fiend of Hurlgate; A Kiss in the Dark.
    C.—Nervous Man; Irish Lion.
4. N.—Pat Lyon; Yankee Jack.
    C.—Dombey and Son; Bamboozling.
5. N.—Ivanhoe; Jenny Lind in Town.
    C.—Dombey and Son; Wife for an Hour.
6. N.—Ivanhoe; Black Mummy.
    C.—Dombey and Son; Great Mistake.
7. N.—Miser of Philadelphia; Ivanhoe.
    C.—Dombey and Son; Stage-Struck Irishman.
9. *Monday:*
    N.—Greek Slave; Wallace.
    C.—Dombey and Son; Serious Family.

10.   N.—William Tell; Handsome Bachelors and Pretty Girls of Philadelphia.
      C.—Irish Emigrant and the Philadelphia Carman; Serious Family.
11.   N.—Lucretia Borgia; Miser of Philadelphia.
      C.—*Id.*, Aug. 10.
12.   N.—Bull-Fighter of Spain; Handsome Bachelors.
      C.—David Copperfield; Irish Emigrant and the Philadelphia Carman.
13.   N.—*Id.*, Aug. 12.
      C.—*Id.*, Aug. 12.
14.   N.—Greek Slave; Ball of Death.
      C.—The Fast Man *: *Edward*—J. Brougham, *Kate*—Miss Celia Logan; David Copperfield.
16.   *Monday:*
      N.—Enchantress.
      C.—Fast Man; Bamboozling.
17.   N.—Enchantress.
      C.—Dombey and Son; David Copperfield.
18.   N.—Enchantress.
      C.—Rendezvous; Rough Diamond.
19.   N.—Enchantress.
      C.—Crowded Houses; Fortune's Frolic.
20.   N.—Enchantress.
      C.—Mr. and Mrs. White; My Neighbor's Wife.
21.   N.—Enchantress.
      C.—Spitfire; Wandering Minstrel.
      A.—The Wonder; Who do they Take me for?
23.   *Monday:*
      N.—Enchantress.
      C.—Our Mary Ann; Midnight Hour.
      A.—Romeo and Juliet; Two Bonnycastles.
24.   N.—Enchantress.
      C.—Young Widow; How to Die for Love.
      A.—Jane Shore; Queen's Own.
25.   N.—Enchantress.
      C.—Ingomar; Chloroform.
      A.—The Wonder; Robber's Wife.
26.   N.—Enchantress; Scott and Pierce *: *Scott*—Burnett.
      C.—The Italian Wife.
      A.—Wine Does Wonders; Faint Heart never won Fair Lady.
27.   N.—Philadelphia Fireman; Scott and Pierce.
      C.—She Would and she Would Not; Miseries of Human Life.
      A.—Love; Agnes de Vere.
28.   N.—Swamp Fox; French Spy.

C.—*Id.,* Aug. 27.
A.—Pizarro; French Spy.
30. *Monday:*
    N.—Uncle Tom's Cabin; Swamp Fox.
    C.—Old Heads and Young Hearts; Eton Boy.
    A.—Hamlet; Double-Bedded Room.
    W.—Ireland as it Is; Limerick Boy.
31. N.—*Id.,* Aug. 30.
    C.—*Id.,* Aug. 27.
    A.—Lady of Lyons; French Spy.
    W.—Ireland as it Is; In and Out of Place.

SEPTEMBER

1. *Wednesday:*
    N.—*Id.,* Aug. 30.
    C.—*Id.,* Aug. 30.
    A.—Drunkard; More Blunders than One.
    W.—Shandy Maguire; Haunted Chamber.
2. N.—Uncle Tom's Cabin; Mose in China.
    C.—Love's Sacrifice; Miseries of Human Life.
    A.—Drunkard; Broken Sword.
    W.—Shandy Maguire; Our Gal.
3. N.—Julius Caesar; Napoleon.
    C.—The Wife; Nature and Philosophy.
    A.—Dream at Sea; Broken Sword.
    W.—It's the Custom of the Country; Haunted Chamber.
4. N.—Rookwood; Napoleon.
    C.—Romeo and Juliet; Wandering Boys.
    A.—Damon and Pythias; Widow's Victim.
    W.—*Id.,* Sept. 3.
6. *Monday:*
    N.—Buried Alive; Rookwood.
    C.—Hamlet; An Irish Engagement.
    A.—Italian Wife; Widow's Victim.
    W.—Godenski; Four Sisters.
7. N.—*Id.,* Sept. 6.
    C.—Othello; An Irish Engagement.
    A.—Honey Moon; Ugolino.
    W.—Bamboozling.
8. N.—Wool Dealer; Rookwood.
    C.—New Way To Pay Old Debts; Irish Tutor.
    A.—Joan of Arc; Idiot Witness.
    W.—Two Bonnycastles.
9. N.—Naiad Queen; Wool Dealer.
    C.—Merchant of Venice; An Irish Engagement.

A.—Venice Preserved; Boots at the Swan.
W.—Box and Cox.

10. N.—Naiad Queen; Spectre Bridegroom.
C.—Town and Country; Irish Tutor.
A.—Macbeth; Joan of Arc.
W.—Poor Pillicoddy.

11. N.—Naiad Queen; People's Lawyer.
C.—Merchant of Venice; An Irish Engagement.
A.—Drunkard; Widow's Victim.
W.—Bamboozling; Robert Macaire.

13. *Monday:*
N.—Naiad Queen; Handsome Widow.
C.—Corsican Brothers.
A.—Othello; Who do you Take me for?
W.—Three Shaws.

14. N.—Naiad Queen; Ole Bull.
C.—*Id., Sept.* 13.
A.—Richelieu; Wandering Minstrel.
W.—Naval Engagements.

15. N.—Naiad Queen; Lady of the Lions.
C.—*Id., Sept.* 13.
A.—Rob Roy; Adopted Child.
W.—A Kiss in the Dark.

16. N.—*Id., Sept.* 15.
C.—*Id., Sept.* 13.
A.—Maurice; Double-Bedded Room.
W.—Four Sisters.

17. N.—Naiad Queen; A Ghost in Spite of Himself.
C.—*Id., Sept.* 13.
A.—Damon and Pythias; Charles II.
W.—House Dog.

18. N.—Toodles; Jonathan Bradford.
C.—Corsican Brothers; Sketches in India.
A.—Rob Roy; Tom Cringle's Log.
W.—Deeds of Dreadful Note.

20. *Monday:*
N.—The Stranger; Tour de Nesle.
C.—Child of the Regiment; Naval Engagements.
A.—Masaniello; Used Up.
W.—Three Shaws.

21. N.—Six Degrees of Crime; Mariette.
C.—She Would and she Would Not; Good for Nothing.
A.—Masaniello; State Secrets.
W.—Poor Pillicoddy.

22. N.—Wallace; Black Eyed Susan.
C.—Crown Diamonds; Good for Nothing.

A.—Cross of Gold; Masaniello.
W.—Your Life's in Danger; Robert Macaire.
23. N.—Stranger; Tour de Nesle.
C.—Road to Ruin; Taking by Storm.
A.—Macbeth; Children in the Wood.
W.—Two Bonnycastles.
24. N.—Richelieu; Lady of Lyons.
C.—Crown Diamonds; Taking by Storm.
A.—Nick of the Woods; Review.
W.—Three-Faced Frenchman.
25. N.—La Fitte; Nick of the Woods.
C.—Henry IV; Good for Nothing.
A.—Carpenter of Rouen; Nick of the Woods.
W.—Three-Faced Frenchman.
27. *Monday:*
N.—Wild Boy of Bohemia; Forty Thieves.
C.—Black Domino; Sketches in India.
A.—Wizard of the Wave; Wandering Minstrel.
W.—Nervous Man; Your Life's in Danger.
28. N.—Mary Tudor; Forty Thieves.
C.—School for Scandal; Miseries of Human Life.
A.—Wizard of the Wave; Queen's Own.
W.—Soldier of Fortune; Young Couple.
29. N.—Wild Boy of Bohemia; Jack Sheppard.
C.—Black Domino; An Irish Engagement.
A.—Wizard of the Wave; Boots at the Swan.
W.—Irish Ambassador; Young Couple.
30. N.—Manfredoni; Mary Tudor.
C.—Lady of Lyons; Good for Nothing.
A.—Wacousta; Shoemaker of Toulouse.
W.—Why don't she Marry?; Wrong Passenger.

OCTOBER

1. *Friday:*
N.—Manfredoni; French Spy.
C.—Enchantress; Valet de Sham.
A.—Self-Accusation; Seeing Hemple.
W.—Irish Post; Happy Man.
2. N.—Manfredoni; Jack Sheppard.
C.—Stranger; Cesar de Bazan.
A.—Surgeon of Paris; Carpenter of Rouen.
W.—Irish Post; Happy Man.
4. *Monday:*
N.—Count of Monte Cristo.
C.—*Id.,* Oct. 1.

A.—Stranger; Lucretia Borgia.
W.—Old School and the New; Three Shaws.

5. N.—*Id.,* Oct. 4.
C.—Money; Alarming Sacrifice.
A.—Evadne; Bold Stroke for a Husband.
W.—Old School and the New; Young Couple.

6. N.—*Id.,* Oct. 4.
C.—Daughter of the Regiment; Alarming Sacrifice.
A.—Stranger; Lucretia Borgia.
W.—Merchant of Venice; Loan of a Lover.

7. N.—*Id.,* Oct. 4.
C.—School for Scandal; Valet de Sham.
A.—Lady of Lyons; Love Chase.
W.—Merchant of Venice; His Last Legs.

8. N.—*Id.,* Oct. 4.
C.—Crown Diamonds; Good for Nothing.
A.—Wrecker's Daughter; The Venetian.
W.—How to pay Rent; Young Couple.

9. N.—*Id.,* Oct. 4.
C.—Love's Sacrifice; Katharine and Petruchio.
A.—The Venetian; Lucretia Borgia.
W.—Wife Hunter; Young Couple.

11. *Monday:*
N.—Mazeppa; Count of Monte Cristo, fourth and fifth acts.
C.—Lola Montez in Bavaria; Sketches in India.
A.—Hunchback; Love Chase.
W.—Very Suspicious.

12. N.—Mazeppa; Beauty and the Beast.
C.—Lola Montez in Bavaria; Taking by Storm.
A.—Wrecker's Daughter; Lucretia Borgia.
W.—Very Suspicious.

13. N.—*Id.,* Oct. 12.
C.—Lola Montez in Bavaria; Delicate Ground.
A.—Jane Shore; The Venetian.
W.—Novel Expedient.

14. N.—*Id.,* Oct. 12.
C.—Charlotte Corday; Delicate Ground.
A.—Hunchback; Love Chase.
W.—Novel Expedient.

15. N.—*Id.,* Oct. 12.
C.—Charlotte Corday; Forty and Fifty.
A.—Jane Shore; Mary Tudor.
W.—Four Sisters.

16. N.—*Id.,* Oct. 12.
C.—Charlotte Corday; Uncle John.
A.—Bride of Lammermoor; Mary Tudor.

W.—Novel Expedient.
18. *Monday:*
 N.—Ship Carpenter of Philadelphia; Terror of the Road.
 C.—Charlotte Corday; Alarming Sacrifice.
 A.—Ingomar; A Morning Call.
 W.—Pilgrim of Love; Haunted Chamber.
19. N.—*Id.,* Oct. 18.
 C.—Maritana; Uncle John.
 A.—Stranger; Venetian.
 W.—Ireland as it Is; Brian O'Lynn.
20. N.—Seven Escapes; Mad Anthony Wayne.
 C.—Maritana; Taking by Storm.
 A.—Ingomar; Lucretia Borgia.
 W.—Shandy Maguire; Brian O'Lynn.
21. N.—Mad Anthony Wayne; Monster of St. Michael.
 C.—Maritana; Lola Montez in New York.
 A.—Mary Tudor; Venetian.
 W.—Ireland as it Is; Irish Lion.
22. N.—Three Guardsmen; Spoiled Child.
 C.—Lola Montez in Bavaria; Lola Montez in New York.
 A.—Bankrupt's Wife; Ingomar.
 W.—Irish Broom Maker; Brian O'Lynn.
23. N.—Mad Anthony Wayne; Tom and Jerry.
 C.—Lola Montez in Bavaria; Charlotte Corday.
 A.—Adelgitha; Tour de Nesle.
 W.—Irish Broom Maker; Our Gal.
25. *Monday:*
 N.—The Triumphs of Rough and Ready; Three Guards-
  men.
 C.—Kill or Cure.
 A.—Bankrupt's Wife; Love Chase.
 W.—Postillion of Lonjumeau; Naval Engagements.
26. N.—Closed.
 C.—Sketches in India.
 A.—Love's Sacrifice; Dombey and Son.
 W.—Postillion of Lonjumeau; Novel Expedient.
27. C.—*Id.,* Oct. 26.
 A.—Jane Shore; Ingomar.
 W.—Louise Muller; Bamboozling.
28. C.—Good for Nothing.
 A.—Gamester; Lucretia Borgia.
 W.—Louise Muller; Two Bonnycastles.
29. C.—Valet de Sham.
 A.—Fazio; Husband at Sight.
 W.—Louise Muller; House Dog.
30. C.—No legitimate drama advertised.

A.—Wrecker's Daughter; Husband at Sight.
W.—Louise Muller; Three Shaws.

NOVEMBER

1. *Monday:*
 C.—Valet de Sham.
 A.—The Stranger; Jane Shore.
 W.—Henri Quatre; Novel Expedient.
2. C.—Tender Precautions.
 A.—Adelgitha; A Morning Call.
 W.—Henri Quatre; Box and Cox.
3. C.—Delicate Ground.
 A.—Romeo and Juliet; Ingomar.
 W.—Florine; House Dog.
4. C.—Kill or Cure.
 A.—Apostate; Orphan's Dream.
 W.—Florine; Two Bonnycastles.
5. C.—Tender Precautions.
 A.—Romeo and Juliet; London Assurance.
 W.—Linda di Chamounix; Novel Expedient.
6. C.—Good for Nothing.
 A.—Isabella; Serjeant's Wife.
 W.—Linda di Chamounix; Robert Macaire.
8. *Monday:*
 C.—Much Ado about Nothing; An Irish Engagement.
 A.—Macbeth; Double-Bedded Room.
 W.—Richelieu; Three Shaws.
9. C.—Wild Oats; Tender Precautions.
 A.—Hamlet; Queen's Own.
 W.—Damon and Pythias; Novel Expedient.
10. C.—Cure for the Heart Ache; Irish Lion.
 A.—Werner; Used Up.
 W.—Jack Cade; Miller of Whetstone.
11. C.—Lady of Lyons.
 A.—Lady of Lyons; Rob Roy.
 W.—Macbeth; Miller of Whetstone.
12. C.—Money.
 A.—Merchant of Venice; Pizarro.
 W.—Hamlet; Miller of Whetstone.
13. C.—Belle's Stratagem.
 A.—Richard III; Carpenter of Rouen.
 W.—Jack Cade; Miller of Whetstone.
15. *Monday:*
 C.—Perfection; Delicate Ground.

A.—King of the Commons; A Husband at Sight.
W.—Gladiator; Domestic Economy.

16.   C.—Wedding Day; Good for Nothing.
A.—King of the Commons; Black Eyed Susan.
W.—Richelieu; Sent to the Tower.

17.   C.—Alarming Sacrifice; Wedding Day.
A.—Maid's Tragedy; Wandering Minstrel.
W.—Gladiator; Bamboozling.

18.   C.—Delicate Ground; Tom Noddy's Secret.
A.—Werner; Carpenter of Rouen.
W.—Jack Cade; Betsy Baker.

19.   C.—Irish Lion; Tender Precautions.
A.—King Lear; Honey Moon.
W.—Damon and Pythias; Our New Lady's Maid.

20.   C.—Perfection; Tom Noddy's Secret.
A.—Bertram; Double-Bedded Room.
W.—Gladiator; Our New Lady's Maid.

22. *Monday:*
C.—Swiss Swains; Tom Noddy's Secret.
A.—Gaspardo; Wallace.
W.—Metamora; Naval Engagements.

23.   C.—Naval Engagements; Swiss Swains.
A.—Rag Picker of Paris; Cramond Brig.
W.—Hamlet; Novel Expedient.

24.   C.—Ask no Questions; Swiss Swains.
A.—Rag Picker of Paris; Warlock of the Glen.
W.—Othello; Miller of Whetstone.

25.   C.—Naval Engagements; Good for Nothing.
A.—*Id.,* Nov. 23.
W.—Metamora; Jacobite.

26.   C.—Ask no Questions; An Irish Engagement.
A.—Rosina Meadows; Wallace.
W.—King Lear; Betsy Baker.

27.   C.—Tender Precautions; Swiss Swains.
A.—Iron Chest; Robert Macaire.
W.—Broker of Bogota; New Footman.

29. *Monday:*
C.—As You Like It; Somebody Else.
A.—Green Mountain Boy; Gaspardo.
W.—Richard III; Who Speaks First?

30.   C.—Romeo and Juliet; Slasher and Crasher.
A.—Churubusco; Green Mountain Boy.
W.—Virginius; Miller of Whetstone.

DECEMBER

1. *Wednesday:*
   C.—Love's Sacrifice; Somebody Else.
   A.—Yankee Land; Churubusco.
   W.—Jack Cade; New Footman.
2. C.—Hunchback; Banker's Wife.
   A.—Hermit of the Rocks; Yankee Land.
   W.—Brutus; Domestic Economy.
3. C.—Stranger; Honey Moon.
   A.—Yankee Duellist; Green Mountain Boy.
   W.—Bertram; Three Cuckoos.
4. C.—Actress of Padua; Banker's Wife.
   A.—Stage-Struck Yankee; Wallace.
   W.—Lady of Lyons; Jacobite.
6. *Monday:*
   C.—School of Reform; Slasher and Crasher.
   A.—Fireman's Daughter; Siege of Monterey.
   W.—Linda of Chamounix; Who Speaks First?
7. C.—Heir at Law; Tender Precautions.
   A.—Rosina Meadows; Fire Raiser.
   W.—Lucy of Lammermoor; Three Cuckoos.
8. C.—School of Reform; Swiss Swains.
   A.—Solomon Swop; Fire Raiser.
   W.—Linda of Chamounix; Day after the Wedding.
9. C.—Miller's Maid; Irish Tutor.
   A.—Hermit of the Rocks; Yankee Pedlar.
   W.—Lucy of Lammermoor; Jacobite.
10. C.—Miller's Maid; Good for Nothing.
    A.—Telula; Solomon Swop.
    W.—Martha; New Footman.
11. C.—Honey Moon; Fortune's Frolics.
    A.—Telula; Fireman's Daughter.
    W.—Martha; Domestic Economy.
13. *Monday:*
    C.—Dombey and Son; Sketches in India.
    A.—People's Lawyer; Toodles.
    W.—Martha; Ladies, Beware.
14. C.—Dombey and Son; A Row at the Chesnut *.
    A.—Sweethearts and Wives; Wool Dealer.
    W.—Martha; The Republican.
15. C.—David Copperfield; A Row at the Chesnut.
    A.—Box and Cox Married and Settled; Toodles.
    W.—Martha; Ladies, Beware.
16. C.—Romance and Reality.
    A.—Jonathan Bradford; Ole Bull.

W.—Martha; The Woman I Adore.
17.   C.—Romance and Reality; A Row at the Chesnut.
    A.—Rip Van Winkle; Murrell.
    W.—*Id.,* Dec. 16.
18.   C.—*Id.,* Dec. 17.
    A.—Revolution; Robert Macaire.
    W.—*Id.,* Dec. 16.
20. *Monday:*
    C.—Robert Macaire; Uncle John.
    A.—The Rivals; Yankee in England.
    W.—Martha; Rough Diamond.
21.   C.—Henry IV; Irish Emigrant.
    A.—Lucretia Borgia; Child of the Regiment.
    W.—Martha; Novel Expedient.
22.   C.—Maid of Croissy; Irish Tutor.
    A.—Honey Moon; Stage-Struck Yankee.
    W.—La Sonnambula; Your Life's in Danger.
23.   C.—Simpson and Co.; Forty and Fifty.
    A.—Drunkard; Widow's Victim.
    W.—Linda of Chamounix; The Woman I Adore.
24.   C.—Last Man; Frightened to Death.
    A.—Rough and Ready; Yankee Footman.
    W.—La Sonnambula; Three Cuckoos.
25.   C.—Knight of Arva; Robert Macaire.
    A.—Rough and Ready; Stage-Struck Yankee.
    W.—Martha; Jacobite.
27. *Monday:*
    C.—Black Domino; Mr. and Mrs. White.
    A.—Fireman's Bride; Sketches in India.
    W.—Lucrezia Borgia; The Woman I Adore.
28.   C.—Ingomar; Knight of Arva.
    A.—Fireman's Bride; Forest Rose.
    W.—Lucrezia Borgia; Ladies, Beware.
29.   C.—Carlo, the Minstrel; Naval Engagements.
    A.—Captain Kyd.
    W.—Lucrezia Borgia; Two Bonnycastles.
30.   C.—Irish Secretary; Alarming Sacrifice.
    A.—*Id.,* Dec. 29.
    W.—Linda of Chamounix; A Nabob for an Hour.
31.   C.—Carlo, the Minstrel; Tender Precautions.
    A.—Forest Rose; Rival Chieftains in Mexico.
    W.—Martha; Betsy Baker.

JANUARY 1853

1. *Saturday:*
   C.—School for Scandal; Delicate Ground.
   A.—Yankee Land; Rough and Ready.
   W.—Lucy of Lammermoor; Mad. Anna Bishop in the Provinces *.
3. *Monday:*
   C.—Daughter of the Regiment; Irish Secretary.
   A.—Jonathan Bradford; Toodles.
   W.—Belle's Stratagem; Naval Engagements.
4. C.—Satan in Paris; Irish Emigrant.
   A.—Isabelle; Sweethearts and Wives.
   W.—Love Chase; The Woman I Adore.
5. C.—Carlo, the Minstrel; Irish Emigrant.
   A.—Paul Pry; Sixteen-Stringed Jack.
   W.—Much Ado about Nothing; The Three Cuckoos.
6. C.—Road to Ruin; Slasher and Crasher.
   A.—Breach of Promise; Buried Alive.
   W.—She Stoops to Conquer; Who Speaks First?
7. C.—The Devil's in It; Somebody Else.
   A.—Revolution; Fairy Dew-Drop.
   W.—No advertisement.
8. C.—School for Scandal; Valet de Sham.
   A.—Gilderoy; Sixteen-Stringed Jack.
   W.—Novel Expedient; Jacobite.
10. *Monday:*
   C.—Crown Diamonds; Knight of Arva.
   A.—Used Up; Spectre Pilot.
   W.—Honey Moon; Alarming Sacrifice.
11. C.—Giant of the Cave; Delicate Ground.
   A.—Town and Country; The Arch in an Uproar.
   W.—Soldier's Daughter; Domestic Economy.
12. C.—Merry Wives of Windsor; Married Life.
   A.—Richard III; Spectre Pilot.
   W.—She Stoops to Conquer; Alarming Sacrifice.
13. C.—Giant of the Cave; Slasher and Crasher.
   A.—Adopted Child; Frederick the Great.
   W.—She Would and she Would Not; The Woman I Adore.
14. C.—Wives as they Were; Satan in Paris.
   A.—All that Glitters is not Gold; Fireman's Bride.
   W.—She Would and she Would Not; A Nabob for an Hour.
15. C.—Golden Farmer; Good for Nothing.
   A.—Dumb Man of Manchester; Gilderoy.
   W.—Honey Moon; Deeds of Dreadful Note.

17. *Monday:*
    C.—*Id.,* Jan. 15.
    A.—Closed for the season.
    W.—She Would and she Would Not; Your Life's in Danger.
18.   C.—He's not A-Miss; Golden Farmer.
    W.—Katharine and Petruchio; Rough Diamond.
19.   C.—Jemmy Twitcher in France; Sketches in India.
    W.—She Would and she Would Not; A Kiss in the Dark.
20.   C.—Two of the B'hoys; Jemmy Twitcher in France.
    W.—A Roland for an Oliver; Jacobite.
21.   C.—Woman's Rights; He's not A-Miss.
    W.—The Rivals; Betsy Baker.
22.   C.—St. Mary's Eve; Two of the B'hoys.
    W.—Katharine and Petruchio; Robert Macaire.
24. *Monday:*
    C.—St. Mary's Eve; Woman's Rights.
    W.—Daughter of the Stars; All that Glitters is not Gold.
25.   C.—Irish Emigrant; Two of the B'hoys.
    W.—School for Scandal; The Woman I Adore.
26.   C.—Handy Andy; Siamese Twins.
    W.—The Rivals; Three Shaws.
27.   C.—Handy Andy; Review.
    W.—An Alarming Sacrifice.
28.   C.—Siamese Twins; St. Mary's Eve.
    W.—Katharine and Petruchio.
29.   C.—Merry Wives of Windsor; Irish Tutor.
    W.—A Day after the Wedding.
    A.—Giraldi Fazio; Rough Diamond.
31. *Monday:*
    C.—Married Life; Two of the B'hoys.
    W.—Henry IV; Day after the Wedding.
    A.—Romeo and Juliet; Wool Dealer.

FEBRUARY

1. *Tuesday:*
    C.—Merry Wives of Windsor.
    W.—Simpson and Co.; Mons. Mallet.
    A.—The Wife; Stage-Struck Yankee.
2.   C.—Wept of Wish-Ton-Wish; An Object of Interest.
    W.—Henry IV; New Footman.
    A.—Hunchback; Stage-Struck Yankee.
3.   C.—Wept of Wish-Ton-Wish; Dr. Dilworth.
    W.—Simpson and Co.; Kentuckian.
    A.—Lady of Lyons; Battle of Buena Vista.

4. C.—Ask no Questions; A Nabob for an Hour.
  W.—Merry Wives of Windsor; Novel Expedient.
  A.—Stranger; Honey Moon; Wool Dealer.

5. C.—Wept of Wish-Ton-Wish; Dead Shot.
  W.—Merry Wives of Windsor; Kentuckian.
  A.—Charcoal Burner; Battle of Buena Vista.

7. *Monday:*
  C.—Lady of Lyons; Nature and Philosophy.
  W.—Advocate; Three Cuckoos.
  A.—Damon and Pythias; Philadelphia Fireman.

8. C.—Romeo and Juliet; Wandering Boys.
  W.—Advocate; Ladies, Beware.
  A.—Carpenter of Rouen; Adopted Child.

9. C.—Love's Sacrifice; Young Scamp.
  W.—Jacobite; Gemini.
  A.—Ingomar; Charles II.

10. C.—No advertisement.
  W.—Advocate; Gemini.
  A.—Rob Roy; Black Eyed Susan.

11. C.—Hunchback; Little Devil.
  W.—Novel Expedient; Alarming Sacrifice.
  A.—Willow Copse; Pizarro.

12. C.—The Wife; Little Devil.
  W.—Mysterious Family; The Woman I Adore.
  A.—Willow Copse; Wallace.

14. *Monday:*
  C.—Maid of Honor; Wandering Boys.
  W.—Sink or Swim; Domestic Economy.
  A.—Willow Copse; Shoemaker of Toulouse.

15. C.—Maid of Honor; Forest Rose.
  W.—Sink or Swim; Mysterious Family.
  A.—Willow Copse; Good for Nothing.

16. C.—Mattheo Falcone; Honey Moon.
  W.—Two Bonnycastles; Friend Waggles.
  A.—Willow Copse; Dumb Belle.

17. C.—Lady of Lyons; Little Devil.
  W.—Ladies, Beware; Three Cuckoos.
  A.—Willow Copse; Swiss Swains.

18. C.—Douglas; Nature and Philosophy.
  W.—My Precious Betsy.
  A.—Willow Copse; Charcoal Burner.

19. C.—Ion; Rob Roy.
  W.—'Tis all a Farce.
  A.—Willow Copse; Jack Sheppard.

21. *Monday:*
  C.—Hamlet; Dead Shot.

W.—Hunchback; Sink or Swim.
A.—She Would and she Would Not; Irish Emigrant.
22.   C.—Wild Oats; Katharine and Petruchio.
W.—Fazio; My Precious Betsy.
A.—Robber's Wife; Jack Sheppard.
23.   C.—Elder Brother; Dramatist.
W.—The Wife; 'Tis all a Farce.
A.—Satan in Paris; Irish Emigrant.
24.   C.—The Stranger; My Aunt.
W.—Hunchback; Friend Waggles.
A.—Born to Good Luck; Lady of the Lake.
25.   C.—Gamester; A Cure for the Heart Ache.
W.—School for Scandal; The Jenkinses.
A.—Rory O'More; A Thumping Legacy.
26.   C.—The Robbers; Dead Shot.
W.—Macbeth; The Jenkinses.
A.—Lady of the Lake; Rory O'More.
28. *Monday:*
C.—Money; Katharine and Petruchio.
W.—La Figlia del Regimento; The Jenkinses.
A.—Ion; Rory O'More.

MARCH

1. *Tuesday:*
C.—Inconstant; Dramatist.
W.—Advocate; School of Reform.
A.—Satan; Irish Tutor.
2.   C.—Robbers; Ladder of Love.
W.—La Cencrentola; My Precious Betsy.
A.—Agnes de Vere; Born to Good Luck.
3.   C.—De Soto; Ladder of Love.
W.—Iron Chest; Mysterious Family.
A.—Isabelle; A Thumping Legacy.
4.   C.—Town and Country; Pizarro.
W.—La Sonnambula; Sent to the Tower.
A.—Sea and Land *: *Poppy*—J. Drew, *Meg*—Mrs. J. Drew;
Irish American *: *Larry*—J. Drew.
5.   C.—De Soto; Ladder of Love.
W.—No advertisement.
A.—*Id.,* March 4.
7. *Monday:*
C.—Hamlet; Hunting a Turtle.
W.—Il Barbiere di Siviglia; Novel Expedient.
A.—Wild Oats; Irish American.
8.   C.—Stranger; Elder Brother.

[479]

W.—Heir at Law; Sink or Swim.
A.—Much Ado about Nothing; Irish American.

9.   C.—De Soto; Hunting a Turtle.
W.—La Cenerentola; Three Cuckoos.
A.—Cure for the Heart Ache; Irish American.

10. C.—Laugh when you Can; New Footman.
W.—Corsican Brothers; Robert Macaire.
A.—Money; Irish American.

11. C.—Henry IV; Dead Shot.
W.—Norma; An Alarming Sacrifice.
A.—Lady of Lyons; Irish Tutor.

12. C.—Ladder of Love; Uncle Sam.
W.—Willow Copse; Philadelphia Fireman.
A.—Laugh when you Can; William Tell.

14. *Monday:*
C.—Dr. Dilworth; Spectre Bridegroom.
W.—White Slave of England *: *Manly*—Jordan, *Mary*—
Mrs. Duffield; The Jenkinses.
A.—Belle's Stratagem; Sea and Land.

15. C.—The Veteran; Hunting a Turtle.
W.—White Slave of England; Sent to the Tower.
A.—As You Like It; Alarming Sacrifice.

16. C.—Veteran; New Footman.
W.—White Slave of England; Friend Waggles.
A.—The Wife; Irish Tutor.

17. C.—Evadne; Ladder of Love.
W.—Drumming *: *Roger*—McKeon, *Madelaine*—Mrs. Duf-
field; White Slave of England.
A.—St. Patrick's Eve; Omnibus.

18. C.—Love's Sacrifice; Our Mary Ann.
W.—Drumming; Serious Family.
A.—Much Ado about Nothing; Irish Emigrant.

19. C.—Fazio; Walter Tyrrel.
W.—*Id.,* March 17.
A.—Serious Family; Jack Sheppard.

21. *Monday:*
C.—Love; Our Mary Ann.
W.—Go-To-Bed Tom; Prima Donna.
A.—Poor Gentleman; Two of the B'hoys.

22. C.—Ingomar; The Veteran.
W.—Drumming; Serious Family.
A.—Love; Irish Engagement.

23. C.—Ion; Lady and the Devil.
W.—Corsican Brothers; Drumming.
A.—Wild Oats; Alarming Sacrifice.

24. C.—Lucretia Borgia; Clandare.

W.—Love; Our Country Cousin.
A.—Bold Stroke for a Husband; Delicate Ground.
25. C.—Lady of Lyons; Hunting a Turtle.
W.—Willow Copse; Our Country Cousin.
A.—Cure for the Heart Ache; St. Patrick's Eve.
26. C.—Richard III; New Footman.
W.—Heir at Law; House Dog.
A.—Laugh when you Can; St. Patrick's Eve.
28. *Monday:*
C.—The Bridal; Forty and Fifty.
W.—Nymphs of the Red Sea; All that Glitters is not Gold.
A.—The Rivals; Gilderoy.
29. C.—Macbeth; Spectre Bridegroom.
W.—Nymphs of the Red Sea; Advocate.
A.—Sea and Land; William Tell.
30. C.—Werner; Ladder of Love.
W.—Hypocrite; Nymphs of the Red Sea.
A.—Bold Stroke for a Husband; Irish American.
31. C.—Stranger; Veteran.
W.—Nymphs of the Red Sea; Wandering Minstrel.
A.—Money; Born to Good Luck.

APRIL

1. *Friday:*
C.—Gisippus; Honey Moon.
W.—Heir at Law; Nymphs of the Red Sea.
A.—Belle's Stratagem; Gilderoy.
2. C.—King of the Commons; Dead Shot.
W.—Corsican Brothers; Nymphs of the Red Sea.
A.—Giralda; Gilderoy.
4. *Monday:*
C.—Othello; Wind Mill.
W.—Cesar de Bazan; Undine.
A.—Giralda; Gilderoy.
5. C.—King of the Commons; Betsy Baker.
W.—Money; Undine.
A.—Giralda; World's Fair.
6. C.—Merchant of Venice; Pizarro.
W.—*Id.,* Apr. 4.
A.—Giralda; Jack Sheppard.
7. C.—Henry IV; Betsy Baker.
W.—Writing on the Wall; Undine.
A.—Giralda; Gilderoy.
8. C.—Wind Mill; William Tell.
W.—Richelieu; Undine.

A.—Giralda; Jonathan Bradford.

9.   C.—Love Chase; Grandfather Whitehead.
W.—Clari; Undine.
A.—Presumptive Evidence; Giralda.

11.   *Monday:*
C.—George Barnwell; Jenny Lind.
W.—Our Country Cousin; Go-To-Bed Tom.
A.—As You Like It; Presumptive Evidence.

12.   C.—My Little Adopted; Forest of Bondy.
W.—'Tis all a Farce; Friend Waggles.
A.—St. Patrick's Eve; Good for Nothing.

13.   C.—Jenny Lind; The Cattle Stealer.
W.—Ladies, Beware; Your Life's in Danger.
A.—She Stoops to Conquer; An Irish Emigrant.

14.   C.—Forest of Bondy; Three Thieves.
W.—Novel Expedient.
A.—She Would and she Would Not; An Irish Emigrant.

15.   C.—Butcher's Dog; Three Thieves.
W.—Two Bonnycastles.
A.—Ladies' Battle; Giralda.

16.   C.—My Poor Dog Tray; Don Juan.
W.—Our Country Cousin; Wandering Minstrel.
A.—She Stoops to Conquer; Jonathan Bradford.

18.   *Monday:*
C.—Cross of Death; Murdered Boatman.
W.—Henry IV; Betsy Baker.
A.—New Way To Pay Old Debts; Dumb Belle.

19.   C.—Love Chase; Swiss Swains.
W.—Jacobite; Mons. Mallet.
A.—Willow Copse; P.P.

20.   C.—Myra Alwynn *: *Myra*—Miss Kimberly, *Hastings*—Roys; Cross of Death.
W.—*Id.,* April 18.
A.—Irish Engagement; Ladies' Battle.

21.   C.—Myra Alwynn; Forest of Bondy.
W.—Three Shaws; Kentuckian.
A.—Willow Copse; Dumb Belle.

22.   C.—Love's Sacrifice; My Poor Dog Tray.
W.—Merry Wives of Windsor.
A.—Willow Copse; Perfection.

23.   C.—Pauline; Dog of the Ferry House.
W.—Merry Wives of Windsor.
A.—Willow Copse; P.P.

25.   *Monday:*
C.—Actress of Padua; Little Jockey.
W.—Merry Wives of Windsor; Wandering Minstrel.

A.—John Bull; P.P.
26.   C.—Pauline; Butcher's Dog of Kent.
W.—Writing on the Wall.
A.—Shoemaker of Toulouse; Ladies' Battle.
27.   C.—Pauline; Napoleon.
W.—Henry IV; Alarming Sacrifice.
A.—John Bull; Alarming Sacrifice.
28.   C.—Pauline; Napoleon.
W.—Merry Wives of Windsor; Friend Waggles.
A.—Road to Ruin; Irish Lion.
29.   C.—Maid of Honor; Dog of the Ferry House.
W.—The Jenkinses; Mons. Mallet.
A.—Road to Ruin; Rough Diamond.
30.   C.—Banker's Wife; Dogs of Mount St. Bernard.
W.—Rip Van Winkle; Kentuckian.
A.—Rag Picker of Paris; Giralda.

MAY

2. *Monday:*
C.—Born to Good Luck; Irish Swan.
W.—Writing on the Wall; Drumming.
A.—Rag Picker of Paris; Ladies' Battle.
3.   C.—Lord Barney; Limerick Boy.
W.—Extremes; Good for Nothing.
A.—Rag Picker of Paris; Irish Lion.
4.   C.—Ireland as it Is; Our Gal.
W.—Ingomar; Washington.
A.—Rule a Wife and Have a Wife; An Object of Interest.
5.   C.—Irish Assurance and Yankee Modesty; Brian O'Lynn.
W.—Delicate Ground; Robert Macaire.
A.—Rule a Wife and Have a Wife; Ladies' Battle.
6.   C.—In and Out of Place; Happy Man.
W.—Harvest Home; Box and Cox.
A.—Shoemaker of Toulouse; Charles II.
7.   C.—Ireland as it Is; Haunted Chamber.
W.—Betrothal; Betsy Baker.
A.—Hunchback; Carpenter of Rouen.
9. *Monday:*
C.—Uncle Pat's Cabin; Our Jemima.
W.—Hunchback; Good for Nothing.
A.—Bold Stroke for a Husband; Laugh when you Can.
10.   C.—Uncle Pat's Cabin; Happy Man.
W.—Love; Our Country Cousin.
A.—Husband of my Heart; Rory O'More.
11.   C.—Uncle Pat's Cabin; Irish Tutor.

W.—Evadne; House Dog.

A.—Much Ado about Nothing; An Object of Interest.

12. C.—Uncle Pat's Cabin; Irish Assurance.

W.—Lady of Lyons; Wandering Minstrel.

A.—Belle's Stratagem; Husband of my Heart.

13. C.—Uncle Pat's Cabin; Irish Lion.

W.—Ingomar; Faint Heart never won Fair Lady.

A.—St. Patrick's Eve; Husband of my Heart.

14. C.—Uncle Pat's Cabin; Sprigs of Ireland.

W.—Madelaine; Jacobite.

A.—Rag Picker of Paris; Gilderoy.

16. *Monday:*

C.—Crown Diamonds; My Little Adopted.

W.—Madelaine; The Woman I Adore.

A.—Follies of a Night; Wallace.

17. C.—Knight of Arva; Cavaliers and Roundheads.

W.—Love Chase; Sent to the Tower.

A.—Heir at Law; Charles II.

18. C.—Black Domino; Cavaliers and Roundheads.

W.—Duke's Wager; The Jenkinses.

A.—Cesar de Bazan; Follies of a Night.

19. C.—Sea Captain; Raising the Wind.

W.—Lady of Lyons; Deeds of Dreadful Note.

A.—Willow Copse; Husband of my Heart.

20. C.—Daughter of the Regiment; Hunting a Turtle.

W.—Duke's Wager; Rough Diamond.

A.—Wild Oats; Irish Emigrant.

21. C.—School for Scandal; Jenny Lind.

W.—*Id.,* May 20; Last night of the season.

A.—Rule a Wife and Have a Wife; Follies of a Night.

23. *Monday:*

C.—Enchantress; Betsy Baker.

A.—Old Heads and Young Hearts; Faint Heart never won Fair Lady.

24. C.—Nervous Man; 'Tis all a Farce.

A.—Damon and Pythias; A Roland for an Oliver.

25. C.—Carlo, the Minstrel; Windmill.

A.—Old Heads and Young Hearts; A Roland for an Oliver.

W.—Farewell benefit to P. Richings, stage manager; A Hopeless Passion; A Roland for an Oliver.

26. C.—Town and Country; Who Speaks First?

A.—Town and Country; Faint Heart never won Fair Lady.

27. C.—Daughter of the Regiment; His Last Legs.

W.—Willow Copse; Charles II.

28. C.—St. Patrick's Eve; Swiss Swains.

A.—Nick of the Woods; Gilderoy.

30. *Monday:*
    C.—Black Domino; The Secret.
    A.—School for Scandal.
    W.—Othello; Friend Waggles.
31.   C.—Knight of Arva; The Secret.
    A.—London Assurance; Irish Blunders of Handy Andy.
    W.—Richelieu; Precious Betsy.

JUNE

1. *Wednesday:*
    C.—Pride of the Market; My Little Adopted.
    W.—Hamlet; Rough Diamond.
    A.—Much Ado about Nothing; Pizarro.
2.   C.—The Gamester; All the World's a Stage.
    W.—New Way To Pay Old Debts; Wandering Minstrel.
    A.—Wonder; Nick of the Woods.
3.   C.—Daughter of the Regiment; Nervous Man.
    W.—The Stranger; Black-Eyed Susan.
    A.—Married Life; Box and Cox.
4.   C.—No advertisement.
    W.—Othello; Black-Eyed Susan.
    A.—Macbeth; Black-Eyed Susan.
6. *Monday:*
    C.—Crown Diamonds; Who Speaks First?
    W.—Serious Family; Your Life's in Danger.
    A.—Harvest Home; Weathercock.
7.   C.—The Rivals; Forty and Fifty.
    W.—Writing on the Wall; Ladies, Beware.
    A.—Harvest Home; A Roland for an Oliver.
8.   C.—Carlo; the Minstrel; Knight of Arva.
    W.—She Stoops to Conquer; Betsy Baker.
    A.—Six Degrees of Crime; Siege of Stralsund.
9.   C.—Ingomar; Rival Pages.
    W.—Honey Moon; Mysterious Family.
    A.—Heir at Law; Virginia Mummy.
10.   C.—No advertisement.
    W.—Heir at Law; Our Country Cousin.
    A.—Giralda; Rory O'More.
11.   C.—Rob Roy; Philadelphia Fireman.
    W.—Soldier's Daughter; Limerick Boy.
    A.—London Assurance; Robert Macaire.
13. *Monday:*
    C.—Hamlet; Who Speaks First?
    W.—No advertisement.
    A.—Closed for the season.

14.   C.—The Stranger; My Aunt.
       W.—The Jenkinses; Siamese Twins.
15.   C.—Elder Brother; Cure for the Heart Ache.
       W.—No advertisement.
16.   C.—No advertisement.
       W.—Wept of Wish-Ton-Wish; Who Speaks First?
17.   C.—Wild Oats; Katharine and Petruchio.
       W.—The Woman I Adore; Two of the B'hoys.
       A.—Omnibus; Drunkard.
18.   C.—The Robbers; Rival Pages.
       W.—Golden Farmer; Two of the B'hoys.
       A.—Rake's Progress; A Glance at Philadelphia.
20. *Monday:*
       C.—Wine Works Wonders; Dramatist.
       W.—St. Mary's Eve; Sketches in India.
21.   C.—Town and Country; My Aunt.
       W.—A Nabob for an Hour; Your Life's in Danger.
22.   C.—De Soto.
       W.—Heir at Law; Sketches in India.
23.   C.—De Soto.
       W.—St. Mary's Eve; A Kiss in the Dark.
24.   C.—No advertisement.
       W.—A Nabob for an Hour; A Kiss in the Dark.
25.   C.—No advertisement.
       W.—She Stoops to Conquer; Irish Tutor.
       A.—Dumb Belle; A Glance at Philadelphia.
27. *Monday:*
       C.—No advertisements in the newspapers.
28.   C.—Laugh when you Can; Faint Heart never won Fair
       Lady.
29.   C.—Cesar de Bazan; Irish Lion.
30.   C.—Sweethearts and Wives; Dumb Belle.

JULY

1.   *Friday:*
       C.—Lucille; A Roland for an Oliver.
       A.—The Stranger; Ruffian Boy.
2.   C.—Robert Macaire; Used Up.
       A.—Married Rake; Irish Tutor.
4.   *Monday:*
       C.—Declaration of Independence; Bamboozling.
5.   C.—Declaration of Independence; A Wife for an Hour.
6.   C.—Declaration of Independence; A Wife for an Hour.
7.   C.—Fast Man; Maid of Munster.
8.   C.—Dombey and Son; Irish Emigrant.

9.   C.—Dombey and Son; Dumb Belle.
11.   *Monday:*
       C.—David Copperfield; Perfection.
12.   C.—Serious Family; Row at the Chesnut.
13.   C.—David Copperfield; Stage-Struck.
14.   C.—Romance and Reality; Dead Shot.
15.   C.—Dombey and Son; His Last Legs.
16.   C.—Romance and Reality; A Row at the Chesnut.
       A.—Veteran of Austerlitz; Eton Boy.
18.   *Monday:*
       C.—Ireland as it Is; Yankee Gal.
19.   C.—Ireland as it Is; Irish Assurance.
20.   C.—Paddy the Piper; Irish Assurance.
21.   C.—Good for Nothing; Yankee Gal.
22.   C.—Shandy Maguire; Mischievous Annie.
23.   C.—Siamese Twins; Mischievous Annie.
       A.—Irish Tutor; Born to Good Luck.
25.   *Monday:*
       C.—No advertisement.
       N.—The Lost Ship; The Shadow.
26.   N.—Black Rangers; Irish Artist.
27.   N.—No advertisement.

AUGUST

12.   *Friday:*
       C.—Adrienne, the Actress; Loan of a Lover; Lola Montez.
20.   A.—Money; Widow's Victim.
22.   *Monday:*
       A.—Old Heads and Young Hearts; Miseries of Human Life.
       C.—Lucretia Borgia; Lady of Lyons.
23.   A.—Married Life; Giralda.
24.   A.—Speed the Plough; Miseries of Human Life.
25.   A.—*Id.,* Aug. 20.
26.   A.—Heir at Law; Taking by Storm.
27.   A.—Romeo and Juliet; Taking by Storm.
29.   *Monday:*
       A.—School for Scandal; Irish Emigrant.
       W.—A Wife for a Day; Ladies, Beware.
30.   A.—Married Life; Irish Emigrant.
       W.—Yankee Land; A Wife for a Day.
       C.—Poor Gentleman; Box and Cox.
31.   A.—John Bull; P.P.
       W.—Yankee Pedlar; Forest Rose.
       C.—She Stoops to Conquer; Rough Diamond.

SEPTEMBER

1. *Thursday:*
   A.—Poor Gentleman; Taking by Storm.
   W.—Yankee Land; Yankee in China.
   C.—The Rivals; My Mamma's Pets.
2. A.—The Rivals; Giralda.
   W.—Love and Larnin'; New Notions.
   C.—Belle's Stratagem; Love Chase.
3. A.—Lady of Lyons; Irish Dragoon.
   W.—The Vermonter; Yankee Pedlar.
   C.—Merry Wives of Windsor; Eton Boy.
5. *Monday:*
   A.—Comedy of Errors; Irish Dragoon.
   W.—Hunchback; Box and Cox Married and Settled.
   C.—Daughter of the Regiment; My Precious Betsy.
6. A.—Comedy of Errors; White Horse of the Peppers.
   W.—Romeo and Juliet; Poor Pillicoddy.
   C.—Man of Nerve; My Precious Betsy.
7. A.—Comedy of Errors; My Friend in the Straps.
   W.—The Stranger; Practical Man.
   C.—Black Domino; Eton Boy.
8. A.—*Id.,* Sept. 6.
   W.—Lady of Lyons; Box and Cox Married and Settled.
   C.—Knight of Arva; La Bayadere.
9. A.—Comedy of Errors; Irish Ambassador.
   W.—Love; Betsy Baker.
   C.—Crown Diamonds; Cousin Joe.
10. A.—Comedy of Errors; Rory O'More
    W.—Fazio; Box and Cox Married and Settled.
    C.—St. Patrick's Eve; La Bayadere.
12. *Monday:*
    A.—Comedy of Errors; Irish Ambassador.
    W.—Love; Maid of the Milking Pail.
    C.—Bohemian Girl; Young Widow.
13. A.—*Id.,* Sept. 6.
    W.—Lady of Lyons; Valet de Sham.
    C.—Serious Family; La Bayadere.
14. A.—*Id.,* Sept. 10.
    W.—*Id.,* Sept. 5.
    C.—Bohemian Girl; Good for Nothing.
15. A.—Comedy of Errors; Irish Tutor.
    W.—Ingomar; Domestic Economy.
    C.—Soldier of Fortune; La Bayadere.
16. A.—Comedy of Errors; A.S.S.

W.—Macbeth; Morning Call.
C.—Bohemian Girl; Spectre Bridegroom.
17. A.—Comedy of Errors; Taking by Storm.
W.—Ingomar; To Paris and Back for Five Pounds.
C.—Masaniello; Spectre Bridegroom.
19. *Monday:*
A.—*Id.,* Sept. 16.
W.—Adrienne, the Actress; To Paris and Back for Five Pounds.
C.—Bohemian Girl; Faint Heart never won Fair Lady.
20. A.—*Id.,* Sept. 7.
W.—The Gamester; Practical Man.
C.—St. Patrick's Eve; My Precious Betsy.
21. A.—*Id.,* Sept. 16.
W.—Ingomar; Miller of Whetstone.
C.—Fra Diavolo; Eton Boy.
22. A.—Comedy of Errors; May Queen.
W.—*Id.,* Sept. 19.
C.—Irish Secretary; Spectre Bridegroom.
23. A.—*Id.,* Sept. 22.
W.—Camille *: *Camille*—Miss Davenport; *Armand*—Perry; *Gustave*—Eytinge; Ingomar; second and fifth acts.
C.—Fra Diavolo; Young Widow.
24. A.—The Stranger; May Queen.
W.—Camille; Miseries of Human Life.
C.—Daughter of the Regiment; Knight of Arva.
26. *Monday:*
A.—Paul Pry; All that Glitters is not Gold.
W.—Fazio; Miseries of Human Life.
C.—Uncle Tom's Cabin *: *Tom*—J. Gilbert, *Harris*—Fenno, *Cute*—J. Jefferson; *Legree*—Mason, *Topsy*—Lizzie Weston, *Eva*—Little Louisa Parker.
27. A.—Romeo and Juliet; A.S.S.
W.—Evadne; Two Bonnycastles.
C.—Uncle Tom's Cabin.
28. A.—Paul Pry; May Queen.
W.—Ingomar; Obstinate Family.
C.—Uncle Tom's Cabin.
29. A.—Old Heads and Young Hearts; Simpson and Co.
W.—Duke's Wager; To Paris and Back for Five Pounds.
C.—Uncle Tom's Cabin.
30. A.—Speed the Plough; P.P.
W.—Much Ado about Nothing; Obstinate Family.
C.—Uncle Tom's Cabin.

OCTOBER

1. *Saturday:*
    A.—Paul Pry; White Horse of the Peppers.
    W.—Jealous Wife; Box and Cox Married and Settled.
    C.—Uncle Tom's Cabin.
3. *Monday:*
    A.—Hamlet; Omnibus.
    W.—Leonor de Guzman *: *Leonor*—Miss Dean, *Don Pedro*—Perry, *Don Enrique*—Wheatleigh, *Don Juan*—Adams; Obstinate Family.
    C.—Uncle Tom's Cabin.
4. A.—Point of Honor; Rory O'More.
    W.—Leonor de Guzman; Turning the Tables.
    C.—Uncle Tom's Cabin.
5. A.—Pauline; Irish Ambassador.
    W.—Leonor de Guzman; Sergeant's Wedding.
    C.—Uncle Tom's Cabin.
6. A.—Pauline; Bashful Irishman.
    W.—Leonor de Guzman; Domestic Economy.
    C.—Uncle Tom's Cabin.
7. A.—Pauline; Thumping Legacy.
    W.—Leonor de Guzman; Follies of a Night.
    C.—Uncle Tom's Cabin.
8. A.—*Id.,* Oct. 7.
    W.—*Id.,* Oct. 7.
    C.—Uncle Tom's Cabin.
10. *Monday:*
    A.—Pauline; Irish Valet.
    W.—Richelieu; Going to the Races *: *Twiddle*—Chapman.
    C.—Uncle Tom's Cabin.
11. A.—*Id.,* Oct. 10.
    W.—Damon and Pythias; Sergeant's Wedding.
    C.—Uncle Tom's Cabin.
12. A.—Pauline; Family Jars.
    W.—Hamlet; Morning Call.
    C.—Uncle Tom's Cabin.
13. A.—Pauline; May Queen.
    W.—Macbeth; Box and Cox Married and Settled.
    C.—Uncle Tom's Cabin.
14. A.—Comedy of Errors; Pauline.
    W.—Pizarro; Ladies, Beware.
    C.—Uncle Tom's Cabin.
15. A.—Married Life; More Blunders than One.
    W.—Jack Cade; Going to the Races.

C.—Uncle Tom's Cabin.
17. *Monday:*
    A.—Serious Family; All that Glitters is not Gold.
    W.—Othello; To Paris and Back for Five Pounds.
    C.—Uncle Tom's Cabin.
18.   A.—Serious Family; Family Jars.
    W.—Richelieu; Miseries of Human Life.
    C.—Uncle Tom's Cabin.
19.   A.—Serious Family; First Night.
    W.—Gladiator; Ladies, Beware.
    C.—Uncle Tom's Cabin.
20.   A.—Serious Family; Giralda.
    W.—Jack Cade; Betsy Baker.
    C.—Uncle Tom's Cabin.
21.   A.—Serious Family; Aline.
    W.—Metamora; Going to the Races.
    C.—Uncle Tom's Cabin.
22.   A.—*Id.,* Oct. 21.
    W.—Gladiator; Jacobite.
    C.—Uncle Tom's Cabin.
24. *Monday:*
    A.—Serious Family; Laugh when you Can.
    W.—Uncle Pat's Cabin; Barney, the Baron.
    C.—Uncle Tom's Cabin; Ireland as it Is.
25.   A.—Serious Family; Aline.
    W.—Uncle Pat's Cabin; Irish Assurance.
    C.—Irish Assurance; Uncle Tom's Cabin.
26.   A.—Serious Family; White Horse of the Peppers.
    W.—Uncle Pat's Cabin; Shandy Maguire.
    C.—Yankee Gal; Uncle Tom's Cabin.
27.   A.—Serious Family; Comedy of Errors.
    W.—Uncle Pat's Cabin; Born to Good Luck.
    C.—Ireland as it Is; Uncle Tom's Cabin.
28.   A.—Point of Honor; Serious Family.
    W.—Law for Ladies; Paddy Carey.
    C.—Irish Brogue Maker; Uncle Tom's Cabin.
29.   A.—Comedy of Errors; Serious Family.
    W.—No advertisement.
    C.—Shandy Maguire; Uncle Tom's Cabin.
31. *Monday:*
    A.—*Id.,* Oct. 29.
    W.—Dick, the Newsboy *: *Dick*—B. Williams; Limerick Boy.
    C.—Uncle Tom's Cabin.

NOVEMBER

1. *Tuesday:*
   A.—Comedy of Errors; Serious Family.
   W.—*Id.,* Oct. 31.
   C.—*Id.,* Oct. 31.
2.   A.—*Id.,* Nov. 1.
   W.—Dick, the Newsboy; Irish Tiger.
   C.—*Id.,* Oct. 31.
3.   A.—*Id.,* Nov. 1.
   W.—Ireland and America; Uncle Pat's Cabin.
   C.—*Id.,* Oct. 31.
4.   A.—*Id.,* Nov. 1.
   W.—Ireland as it Is; Ireland and America.
   C.—*Id.,* Oct. 31.
5.   A.—Hamlet; Family Jars.
   W.—Ireland as it Is; Irish Assurance.
   C.—Uncle Tom's Cabin.
7. *Monday:*
   A.—Bleak House *: *Carstone*—W. Wheatley, *Inspector*—J. Drew, *Lady Dedlock*—Mrs. Bowers; A.S.S.
   C.—Nervous Man; Going to the Races.
8.   A.—Bleak House; Taking by Storm.
   W.—Wrong Passenger; Teddy the Tiler.
   C.—Magic Well; Faint Heart never won Fair Lady.
9.   A.—Bleak House; P.P.
   W.—Irish Guardian; How to pay Rent.
   C.—Magic Well; Eton Boy.
10.   A.—Bleak House; Thumping Legacy.
    W.—Irish Ambassador; Two Bonnycastles.
    C.—She Stoops to Conquer; Magic Well.
11.   A.—Bleak House.
    W.—Irish Genius; Jacobite.
    C.—Married Life; Magic Well.
12.   A.—Bleak House; Irish Emigrant.
    W.—Irish Genius; Born to Good Luck.
    C.—*Id.,* Nov. 11.
14. *Monday:*
    A.—Cure for the Heart Ache; Bleak House.
    W.—Irish Genius; Irish Guardian.
    C.—Uncle Tom's Cabin.
15.   A.—Wild Oats; Bleak House.
    W.—Irish Genius; Happy Man.
    C.—Uncle Tom's Cabin.
16.   A.—Laugh when you Can; Bleak House.
    W.—Irish Genius; Teddy the Tiler.

C.—Uncle Tom's Cabin.

17.   A.—Madelaine; Serious Family.
     W.—Irish Ambassador; Irish Genius.
     C.—Uncle Tom's Cabin.

18.   A.—*Id.*, Nov. 17.
     W.—Fortune Hunter; Wrong Passenger.
     C.—Uncle Tom's Cabin.

19.   A.—Paul Pry; Madelaine.
     W.—Fortune Hunter; Soldier of Fortune.
     C.—Uncle Tom's Cabin.

21.   *Monday:*
     A.—Speed the Plough; Madelaine.
     W.—Hamlet; Box and Cox.
     C.—Uncle Tom's Cabin.

22.   A.—Married Life; Madelaine.
     W.—Lady of Lyons; Obstinate Family.
     C.—Uncle Tom's Cabin.

23.   A.—Heir at Law; Madelaine.
     W.—Othello; Done on Both Sides.
     C.—Uncle Tom's Cabin.

24.   A.—*Id.*, Nov. 17.
     W.—Ingomar; Spirit Rappings and Table Movings.
     C.—Uncle Tom's Cabin.

25.   A.—Rory O'More; Madelaine.
     W.—Lady of Lyons; Done on both Sides.
     C.—Uncle Tom's Cabin.

26.   A.—Comedy of Errors; Serious Family.
     W.—Richard III; To Paris and Back for Five Pounds.
     C.—Uncle Tom's Cabin; Water Witches.

28.   *Monday:*
     A.—Nationalities *: *Carlton*—Thayer, *Francis*—Wheatley, *Frederick*—Shewell, *John*—Drew, *Clarissa*—Mrs. Nelson; How to pay Rent.
     W.—Ingomar; Going to the Races.
     C.—Uncle Tom's Cabin.

29.   A.—Nationalities; Irish Ambassador.
     W.—Civilization; Spirit Rappings.
     C.—Uncle Tom's Cabin.

30.   A.—Nationalities; His Last Legs.
     W.—Civilization; Domestic Economy.
     C.—Uncle Tom's Cabin.

DECEMBER

1.   *Thursday:*
     A.—Nationalities; Thumping Legacies.

[493]

  W.—Lady of Lyons; Sentinel.

  C.—Curate's Daughter *: *Abel*—J. Gilbert, *Fanny*—Lizzie Weston, *Grace*—Miss Cappell; My Precious Betsy.

2. A.—Nationalities; An Object of Interest.

  W.—Civilization; Matrimony.

  C.—Curate's Daughter; Three Cuckoos.

3. A.—Nationalities; White Horse of the Peppers.

  W.—*Id.,* Dec. 2.

  C.—Curate's Daughter; Asmodeus.

5. *Monday:*

  A.—Nationalities; Time Tries All.

  W.—Robbers; Sentinel.

  C.—Curate's Daughter; Mother and Child are Doing Well.

6. A.—*Id.,* Dec. 5.

  W.—Robbers; Alarming Sacrifice.

  C.—Curate's Daughter.

7. A.—Nationalities; Aline.

  W.—Elder Brother; Box and Cox Married and Settled.

  C.—A Cure for Coquettes *: *Sarcasm*—J. Gilbert, *Count*—H. A. Davenport, *Lilly*—Lizzie Weston; Curate's Daughter.

8. A.—The Road to Ruin; Born to Good Luck.

  W.—Robbers; Going to the Races.

  C.—*Id.,* Dec. 7.

9. A.—Money; Madelaine.

  W.—Elder Brother; Two Bonnycastles.

  C.—*Id.,* Dec. 7.

10. A.—The Gamester; Born to Good Luck.

  W.—Robbers; The Sea Fight.

  C.—A Cure for Coquettes; Mother and Child are Doing Well.

12. *Monday:*

  A.—The Road to Ruin; More Blunders than One.

  W.—King of the Commons; The Sea Fight.

  C.—A Cure for Coquettes; Lah-Buy-It-Dear.

13. A.—A Cure for the Heart Ache; Serious Family.

  W.—Lady of Lyons; Alarming Sacrifice.

  C.—Married Life; Lah-Buy-It-Dear.

14. A.—Comedy of Errors; Serious Family.

  W.—King of the Commons; Whitebait at Greenwich *: *Buzzard*—A'Becket, *Small*—Chapman.

  C.—Lady of Lyons; La Som-Am-Bull-Ah.

15. A.—The Gamester; Irish Attorney.

  W.—The Stranger; Morning Call.

  C.—Poor Gentleman; La Som-Am-Bull-Ah.

16. A.—Lady of Lyons; White Horse of the Peppers.

W.—Damon and Pythias; Wonder.
C.—A Roland for an Oliver; Happy Uncle Tom's Cabin.
17. A.—Paul Pry; Irish Emigrant.
W.—Damon and Pythias; Katharine and Petruchio.
C.—To Paris and Back for Five Pounds.
19. *Monday:*
A.—Love Chase; First Night.
W.—Naval Engagements; Whitebait at Greenwich.
C.—Adrienne, the Actress; To Paris and Back for Five Pounds.
20. A.—Love Chase; His Last Legs.
W.—Corsican Brothers; Honey Moon.
C.—Maid of Mariendorpt; Mother and Child are Doing Well.
21. A.—Love Chase; First Night.
W.—Daughter of the Regiment; Robert Macaire.
C.—Love's Sacrifice; Spectre Bridegroom.
22. A.—Love Chase; Madelaine.
W.—Cesar de Bazan; A Roland for an Oliver.
C.—Adrienne, the Actress; Jacobite.
23. A.—Love Chase; Delicate Ground.
W.—Louise Muller; Whitebait at Greenwich.
C.—Camille; Eton Boy.
24. A.—Love Chase; Good for Nothing.
W.—Daughter of the Regiment; Robert Macaire.
C.—Camille; To Paris and Back for Five Pounds.
26. *Monday:*
A.—Paris and London.
W.—Extremes; Two Buzzards.
C.—Lady of Lyons; Student of Oxford.
27. A.—*Id.,* Dec. 26.
W.—Extremes; Going to the Races.
C.—Camille; Three Cuckoos.
28. A.—*Id.,* Dec. 26.
W.—School for Scandal; Robert Macaire.
C.—Camille; To Paris and Back for Five Pounds.
29. A.—*Id.,* Dec. 26.
W.—Extremes; Two Buzzards.
C.—Camille; My Precious Betsy.
30. A.—*Id.,* Dec. 26.
W.—Daughter of the Regiment; Corsican Brothers.
C.—Masks and Faces; School for Scandal.
31. A.—*Id.,* Dec. 26.
W.—Twelve Labors of Hercules; Corsican Brothers.
C.—Camille; Spectre Bridegroom.

JANUARY 1854

2. *Monday:*
    A.—Paris and London.
    W.—Debutante.
    C.—Camille; Three Cuckoos.
3.   A.—*Id.,* Jan. 1.
    W.—*Id.,* Jan. 1.
    C.—Love; Box and Cox.
4.   A.—*Id.,* Jan. 1.
    W.—*Id.,* Jan. 1.
    C.—Hunchback; My Precious Betsy.
5.   A.—*Id.,* Jan. 1.
    W.—*Id.,* Jan. 1.
    C.—Adrienne, the Actress; Eton Boy.
6.   A.—*Id.,* Jan. 1.
    W.—*Id.,* Jan. 1.
    C.—Masks and Faces; Evadne.
7.   A.—Paris and London; A Roland for an Oliver.
    W.—*Id.,* Jan. 1.
    C.—Masks and Faces; Hole in the Wall.
9. *Monday:*
    A.—Paris and London; Irish Attorney.
    W.—*Id.,* Jan. 1.
    C.—Hot Corn *: *Eugene*—A. H. Davenport, *Kate*—Little Louisa Parker, *Eleanor*—Lizzie Weston; Sudden Thoughts.
10.   A.—Wild Oats; Emigrant.
    W.—*Id.,* Jan. 1.
    C.—*Id.,* Jan. 9.
11.   A.—Serious Family; Paris and London.
    W.—*Id.,* Jan. 1.
    C.—Hot Corn; Cure for Coquettes.
12.   A.—Comedy of Errors; London and Paris.
    W.—*Id.,* Jan. 1.
    C.—*Id.,* Jan. 11.
13.   A.—Love Chase; Serious Family.
    W.—*Id.,* Jan. 1.
    C.—Hot Corn; A Roland for an Oliver.
14.   A.—Stranger; Honey Moon.
    W.—*Id.,* Jan. 1.
    C.—Hot Corn; Golden Farmer.
16. *Monday:*
    A.—Paul Pry; Serious Family.
    W.—He's not A-Miss.

C.—Hot Corn; Lady of Lyons.
17. A.—Money; More Blunders than One.
W.—He's not A-Miss.
C.—A Legend of the Chesnut St. Theatre *: Mother and Child are Doing Well.
18. A.—Twelfth Night; Good for Nothing.
W.—Obstinate Family.
C.—A Legend of the Chesnut St. Theatre; Hot Corn.
19. A.—Twelfth Night; Delicate Ground.
W.—*Id.*, Jan. 18.
C.—The Rivals; All that Glitters is not Gold.
20. A.—Twelfth Night; P.P.
W.—Who Speaks First?
C.—*Id.*, Jan. 18.
21. A.—Twelfth Night; A Day Well Spent.
W.—He's not A-Miss.
C.—Paul Pry; Hot Corn.
23. *Monday:*
A.—Twelfth Night; Tender Precautions.
W.—Who Speaks First?
C.—Perfection; Golden Farmer.
24. A.—Twelfth Night; More Blunders than One.
W.—Obstinate Family.
C.—Faint Heart never won Fair Lady; All that Glitters is not Gold.
25. A.—Twelfth Night; Married Rake.
W.—Delicate Ground.
C.—Paul Pry; Hot Corn.
26. A.—*Id.*, Jan. 23.
W.—Delicate Ground.
C.—A Legend of the Chesnut St. Theatre; Slasher and Crasher.
27. A.—Speed the Plough; Irish Emigrant.
W.—Eton Boy.
C.—The Rivals; Slasher and Crasher.
28. A.—Twelfth Night; Paul Pry.
W.—Eton Boy.
C.—Romeo and Juliet; Raising the Wind.
30. *Monday:*
A.—Twelfth Night; Serious Family.
W.—Robert Macaire; Wandering Minstrel.
C.—People's Lawyer; Robert Macaire.
31. A.—Love Chase; Honey Moon.
W.—To Paris and Back for Five Pounds.
C.—Toodles; Robert Macaire.

FEBRUARY

1. *Wednesday:*
   A.—Heir at Law; White Horse of the Peppers.
   W.—Delicate Ground.
   C.—Sweethearts and Wives; Golden Farmer.
2. A.—She Stoops to Conquer; Giralda.
   W.—To Paris and Back for Five Pounds.
   C.—People's Lawyer; Raising the Wind.
3. A.—Wild Oats; Irish Emigrant.
   W.—*Id.,* Feb. 2.
   C.—Rip Van Winkle; Maid of Munster.
4. A.—School for Scandal; P.P.
   W.—Wandering Minstrel.
   C.—Revolution; Buried Alive.
6. *Monday:*
   A.—Comedy of Errors; Paul Pry.
   W.—Two Bonnycastles.
   C.—Woman's Life; Ole Bull.
7. A.—Love Chase; Serious Family.
   W.—*Id.,* Feb. 2.
   C.—Poor Gentleman; Hole in the Wall.
8. A.—Hunchback; Sketches in India.
   W.—The Woman I Adore.
   C.—Sweethearts and Wives; Wool Dealer.
9. A.—*Id.,* Feb. 8.
   W.—*Id.,* Feb. 8.
   C.—Jonathan Bradford; Hunter of the Alps.
10. A.—The Rivals; P.P.
    W.—Lend Me Five Shillings.
    C.—Dumb Man of Manchester; Toodles.
11. A.—Jane Shore; Rory O'More.
    W.—*Id.,* Feb. 10.
    C.—Murrell; Eton Boy.
13. *Monday:*
    A.—Jane Shore; Laugh when you Can.
    W.—Who Speaks First?
    C.—Uncle Tom's Cabin.
14. A.—Comedy of Errors; All that Glitters is not Gold.
    W.—Alarming Sacrifice.
    C.—*Id.,* Feb. 13.
15. A.—Twelfth Night; Comedy of Errors.
    W.—Trying it on *.
    C.—*Id.,* Feb. 13.
16. A.—Jane Shore; Born to Good Luck.
    W.—Miseries of Human Life.

C.—*Id.,* Feb. 13.

17.   A.—She Stoops to Conquer; Madelaine.
W.—*Id.,* Feb. 15.
C.—*Id.,* Feb. 13.

18.   A.—Hunchback; A Roland for an Oliver.
W.—Betsy Baker.
C.—*Id.,* Feb. 13.

20.   *Monday:*
A.—John Bull; Tender Precautions.
W.—Lend Me Five Shillings.
C.—*Id.,* Feb. 13.

21.   A.—Twelfth Night; Comedy of Errors.
W.—The Woman I Adore.
C.—*Id.,* Feb. 13.

22.   A.—Hypocrite; A Day Well Spent.
W.—A Soldier's Courtship.
C.—*Id.,* Feb. 13.

23.   A.—Jane Shore; White Horse of the Peppers.
W.—'Twas I.
C.—*Id.,* Feb. 13.

24.   A.—Hunchback; P.P.
W.—To Paris and Back for Five Pounds.
C.—*Id.,* Feb. 13.

25.   A.—Hypocrite; All that Glitters is not Gold.
W.—Trying it on.
C.—*Id.,* Feb. 13.

27.   *Monday:*
A.—Hypocrite; Irish Ambassador.
W.—Alarming Sacrifice.
C.—Aethiop; Hole in the Wall.

28.   A.—Hypocrite; Wandering Minstrel.
W.—Friend Waggles.
C.—Aethiop; Hunter of the Alps.

MARCH

1.   *Wednesday:*
A.—Hypocrite; Madelaine.
W.—Trying it on.
C.—Aethiop; Robert Macaire.

2.   A.—Hypocrite; Wandering Minstrel.
W.—Friend Waggles.
C.—Speed the Plough; Irish Tutor.

3.   A.—Hypocrite; P.P.
W.—Eton Boy.
C.—Aethiop; Sweethearts and Wives.

[499]

4.   A.—Hypocrite; Time Tries All.
    W.—Lend Me Five Shillings.
    C.—Aethiop; My Neighbor's Wife.

6. *Monday:*
    A.—Much Ado about Nothing; Omnibus.
    W.—Pleasant Neighbor.
    C.—Aethiop; Maid of Croissy.

7.   A.—Much Ado about Nothing; Thumping Legacy.
    W.—Pleasant Neighbors.
    C.—London Assurance; Tom and Jerry.

8.   A.—Much Ado about Nothing; Tender Precautions.
    W.—Delicate Ground.
    C.—Speed the Plough; Tom and Jerry.

9.   A—Much Ado about Nothing; Time Tries All.
    W.—To Paris and Back for Five Pounds.
    C.—Love in a Convent; Nicholas Nickleby.

10.   A.—Much Ado about Nothing; Good for Nothing.
    W.—The Double-Bedded Room.
    C.—Henry IV; Love in a Convent.

11.   A.—Much Ado about Nothing; All that Glitters is not Gold.
    W.—Double-Bedded Room.
    C.—Drunkard; Nicholas Nickleby.

13. *Monday:*
    A.—Lady of Lyons; Delicate Ground.
    W.—A Soldier's Courtship; Double-Bedded Room.
    C.—Romeo and Juliet; My Neighbor's Wife.

14.   A.—Hypocrite; Madelaine.
    W.—Pleasant Neighbors; Double-Bedded Room.
    C.—Lady of Lyons; Bombastes Furioso.

15.   A.—Soldier's Daughter; All that Glitters is not Gold.
    W.—Wandering Minstrel.
    C.—Ingomar; Maid of Croissy.

16.   A.—Hypocrite; Good for Nothing.
    W.—Trying it on.
    C.—Ion; Bombastes Furioso.

17.   A.—Jane Shore; Laugh when you Can.
    W.—Debutante.
    C.—Armand; Faint Heart never won Fair Lady.

18.   A.—Soldier's Daughter; Rory O'More.
    W.—Double-Bedded Room.
    C.—Armand; Honey Moon.

20. *Monday:*
    A.—Hamlet; Irish Tutor.
    W.—Debutante.
    C.—Love Chase; Pet of the Petticoats.

21.   A.—Comedy of Errors; Serious Family.

W.—Friend Waggles.
C.—Camille; Young Widow.

22. A.—Romeo and Juliet; Born to Good Luck.
W.—Debutante.
C.—Love; My Neighbor's Wife.

23. A.—Much Ado about Nothing; An Object of Interest.
W.—Double-Bedded Room.
C.—London Assurance; Eton Boy.

24. A.—Twelfth Night; His Last Legs.
W.—Pleasant Neighbors.
C.—Adrienne, the Actress; Bombastes Furioso.

25. A.—Romeo and Juliet; More Blunders than One.
W.—Debutante.
C.—Masks and Faces; Golden Farmer.

27. *Monday:*
A.—Jealous Wife; Four Sisters.
W.—To Parents and Guardians.
C.—The Wife; Perfection.

28. A.—Jealous Wife; Time Tries All.
W.—*Id., March 27.*
C.—Valeria; My Neighbor's Wife.

29. A.—Belle's Stratagem; Irish Emigrant.
W.—*Id., March 27.*
C.—Ingomar; Young Widow.

30. A.—Jealous Wife; Toodles.
W.—Pet of the Public.
C.—Hunchback; Maid of Croissy.

31. A.—Belle's Stratagem; Toodles.
W.—*Id., March 30.*
C.—Colombe's Birthday *: *Colombe*—Miss Davenport; Adrienne, the Actress.

APRIL

1. *Saturday:*
A.—Jealous Wife; Toodles.
W.—To Parents and Guardians.
C.—The Stranger; Rough Diamond.

3. *Monday:*
A.—As You Like It; Toodles.
W.—Pet of the Public.
C.—Apostate; Three Shaws.

4. A.—*Id., April 3.*
W.—Wandering Minstrel.
C.—Love's Sacrifice; To Paris and Back for Five Pounds.

5. A.—*Id., April 3.*

W.—John Jones.

C.—Fazio; Three Shaws.

6.   A.—As You Like It; Poor Cousin Walter.

W.—The Man about Town.

C.—Masks and Faces; Honey Moon.

7.   A.—*Id.,* Apr. 6.

W.—The Man about Town.

C.—Wallace; Camille.

8.   A.—As You Like It; Serious Family.

W.—John Jones.

C.—The Gamester; Pizarro.

10. *Monday:*

A.—Belle's Stratagem; Poor Cousin Walter.

W.—The Man about Town.

C.—Milly; My Neighbor's Wife.

11.   A.—The Wife; Toodles.

W.—Double-Bedded Room.

C.—Milly; Three Shaws.

12.   A.—Jealous Wife; Wandering Minstrel.

W.—Friend Waggles.

C.—Andy Blake; John Jones.

13.   A.—Fazio; Irish Lion.

W.—To Parents and Guardians.

C.—Andy Blake; Bob Nettles.

14.   A.—Poor Cousin Walter; Toodles.

W.—Box and Cox Married and Unsettled.

C.—Bob Nettles; Young Actress.

15.   A.—The Wife; Irish Lion.

W.—*Id.,* Apr. 14.

C.—Milly; Young Widow.

17. *Monday:*

A.—Fazio; Follies of a Night.

W.—Morning Call.

C.—Forty and Fifty; Invisible Prince.

18.   A.—Jane Shore; Comedy of Errors.

W.—Trying it on.

C.—*Id.,* Apr. 17.

19.   A.—Douglas; Satan in Paris.

W.—The Three-Faced Frenchman.

C.—Andy Blake; Invisible Prince.

20.   A.—Satan in Paris; Paul Pry.

W.—*Id.,* Apr. 19.

C.—A Day after the Wedding; Invisible Prince.

21.   A.—Hypocrite; Madelaine.

W.—*Id.,* Apr. 19.

C.—Loan of a Lover; Milly.

22.   A.—Stranger; Honey Moon.
        W.—*Id.*, Apr. 19.
        C.—Eton Boy; Devil's in it.
24. *Monday:*
        A.—As You Like It; Irish Emigrant.
        W.—No ligitimate drama.
        C.—Poor Pillicoddy; Cupid in a Convent.
25.   A.—Douglas; Satan in Paris.
        W.—No legitimate drama.
        C.—*Id.*, Apr. 24.
26.   A.—Lady of Lyons; The School for Tigers.
        W.—The Three-Faced Frenchman.
        C.—A Day after the Wedding; Bob Nettles.
27.   A.—Follies of a Night; The School for Tigers.
        W.—No legitimate drama. Continuation of the Ravel Family
           in ballets.
        C.—Loan of a Lover; Andy Blake.
28.   A.—She Stoops to Conquer; The School for Tigers.
        W.—Morning Call.
        C.—Young Widow; Invisible Prince.
29.   A.—Douglas; The School for Tigers.
        W.—Double-Bedded Room.
        C.—The Fox Hunt; Young Actress.

MAY

1. *Monday:*
        A.—Plot and Passion *: *DeNeuville*—Wheatley, *Desmarets*—
           Thayer, *Marquis*—D. P. Bowers, *Madame de Fontanges*
           —Mrs. D. P. Bowers; Cousin Cherry.
        W.—Life in the West *: *Sharpe*—Chapman, *Eva*—Mrs. Duf-
           field, *Fanny*—Mrs. John Sefton; A Storm in a Tea-
           Cup *: *Summerly*—Perry, *Jane*—Mrs. Hackurt.
        C.—Fox Hunt; Young Actress.
2.   A.—Plot and Passion; Laugh when you Can.
        W.—Poor Gentleman; Toodles.
        C.—Fox Hunt; Milly.
3.   A.—*Id.*, May 1.
        W.—*Id.*, May 1.
        C.—*Id.*, May 1.
4.   A.—Ion; The Lancers.
        W.—Ingomar; Toodles.
        C.—Prima Donna; Milly.
5.   A.—Plot and Passion; Married Rake.
        W.—School for Scandal; A Storm in a Tea-Cup.
        C.—Heir at Law; Nicholas Nickleby.

6.   A.—Plot and Passion; Satan in Paris.
       W.—Life in the West; Debutante.
       C.—Forty and Fifty; All that Glitters is not Gold.

8. *Monday:*
       A.—Ion; Irish Tutor.
       W.—Extremes; Betsy Baker.
       C.—Nicholas Nickleby; Why don't she Marry?

9.   A.—Romeo and Juliet; Wandering Minstrel.
       W.—Cabin and Parlor *: *Walworth*—Eytinge, *Aunt*—Mrs.
         Langdon; Lone Star.
       C.—Eton Boy; Three Shaws.

10.   A.—Wives as they Were; Black-Eyed Susan.
       W.—Golden Farmer; Two of the B'hoys.
       C.—Heir at Law; Turned Head.

11.   A.—Plot and Passion; Toodles.
       W.—Cabin and Parlor; Delicate Ground.
       C.—Turned Head; Alpine Maid.

12.   A.—Maids as they Were; Black-Eyed Susan.
       W.—Wild Oats; All that Glitters is not Gold
       C.—Paul Pry; Alpine Maid.

13.   A.—Romeo and Juliet; Born to Good Luck.
       W.—Cabin and Parlor; Toodles.
       C.—Katharine and Petruchio; Bombastes Furioso.

15. *Monday:*
       A.—Love; Miseries of Human Life.
       W.—Born to Good Luck; Barney the Baron.
       C.—Katharine and Petruchio; Black-Eyed Susan.

16.   A.—Wives as they Were; Black-Eyed Susan.
       W.—Irish Assurance; Limerick Boy.
       C.—Honey Moon; Black-Eyed Susan.

17.   A.—Sweethearts and Wives; Teddy the Tiler.
       W.—Shandy Maguire; Barney the Baron.
       C.—Poor Gentleman; An Alarming Sacrifice.

18.   A.—Hypocrite; Irish Emigrant.
       W.—Uncle Pat's Cabin; Happy Man.
       C.—Heir at Law; My Precious Betsy.

19.   A.—*Id.,* May 17.
       W.—Paddy Carey; Brian O'Lynn.
       C.—Faint Heart never won Fair Lady; Turned Heads.

20.   A.—Sweethearts and Wives; Black-Eyed Susan.
       W.—*Id.,* May 19.
       C.—Paul Pry; Luke the Laborer.

22. *Monday:*
       A.—Love; Teddy the Tiler.
       W.—John Bull; Irish Assurance.
       C.—Naval Engagements; Uncle John.

23.   A.—Giralda; Rory O'More.
      W.—Shandy Maguire; Uncle Pat's Cabin.
      C.—An Alarming Sacrifice.
24.   A.—Love's Sacrifice; Rough Diamond.
      W.—Ireland as it Is; Limerick Boy.
      C.—To Paris and Back for Five Pounds.
25.   A.—Jealous Wife; Irish Lion.
      W.—John Bull; Connecticut Courtship.
      C.—Katharine and Petruchio.
26.   A.—Man and Wife; Serious Family.
      W.—Asmodeus; Irish Lion; Irish Tutor.
      C.—My Precious Betsy.
27.   A.—Man and Wife; Gilderoy.
      W.—Asmodeus; Robber's Wife.
      C.—Eton Boy.
29. *Monday:*
      A.—Love's Sacrifice; Delicate Ground.
      W.—Rory O'More; Teddy the Tiler.
      C.—A Kiss in the Dark.
30.   A.—Everyone has his Fault; Gilderoy.
      W.—Ireland and America; Omnibus.
      C.—No advertisement.
31.   A.—Hunchback; Toodles.
      W.—Ireland as it Is; Brian O'Lynn.
      C.—No advertisement.

JUNE

1. *Thursday:*
      A.—Everyone has his Fault; Miseries of Human Life.
      W.—Mrs. Williams at Home; Barney the Baron.
2.   A.—Nationalities; Kate Kearney.
      W.—Review; Irish Thrush and Swedish Nightingale.
3.   A.—*Id.,* June 2.
      W.—*Id.,* June 2.
      N.—Drunkard; Widow's Victim.
5. *Monday:*
      A.—Hamlet; A Day Well Spent.
      W.—Ireland and America; Bashful Irishman.
      N.—Lady of Lyons; A Kiss in the Dark.
6.   A.—Stranger; Honey Moon.
      W.—Kate Kearney; Irish Thrush and Swedish Nightingale.
      N.—Hamlet; A Day after the Wedding.
      C.—La Sonnambula.
7.   A.—Rule a Wife and Have a Wife; Ladies' Battle.
      W.—Dick, the Newsboy; Kate Kearney.

N.—Broken Sword; Luke the Laborer.
C.—*Id.*, June 6.

8.   A.—John Bull; Sketches in India.
W.—Irish Yankee *: *Ebenezer O'Donohoo*—B. Williams; Irish Lion.
N.—Rake's Progress; Rough Diamond.
C.—No advertisement.

9.   A.—Isabelle; Momentous Question.
W.—Irish Yankee; Alive and Kicking.
N.—Drunkard; Spectre Bridegroom.

10.   A.—Rule a Wife and Have a Wife; Momentous Question.
W.—Dick, the Newsboy; Irish Yankee.
N.—Floating Beacon; Black-Eyed Susan.

12. *Monday:*
A.—Wives as they Were; Black-Eyed Susan.
W.—Willow Copse; Laugh when you Can.
N.—Ugolino; Dream at Sea.
C.—*Id.*, June 6.

13.   A.—Plot and Passion; Ladies' Battle.
W.—Hunchback; Eton Boy.
N.—Dream at Sea; American Farmer.
C.—*Id.*, June 6.

14.   A.—Secrets Worth Knowing; Black-Eyed Susan.
W.—All that Glitters is not Gold; Debutante.
N.—Broken Sword; Forty Winks.
C.—Child of the Regiment.

15.   A.—*Id.*, June 14.
W.—Heir at Law; Bamboozling.
N.—Idiot Witness; Family Jars.
C.—Spectre Bridegroom; Married Rake.

16.   A.—She Stoops to Conquer; The Momentous Question.
W.—Macbeth; Double-Bedded Room.
N.—How to Rule a Wife; The Rogueries of Thomas.
C.—Our Man; Loan of a Lover.

17.   A.—Road to Ruin; The Momentous Question.
W.—Willow Copse; Robert Macaire.
N.—Pizarro; Broken Sword.
C.—The Secret; Irish Lion.

19. *Monday:*
A.—Rule a Wife and Have a Wife; Gilderoy.
W.—Closed.
N.—Rookwood; Family Jars.
C.—School of Reform; Bridegroom.

20.   A.—Lucretia Borgia; Paul Pry.
W.—Closed.
N.—*Id.*, June 19.

C.—Speed the Plough; Rough Diamond.
21. A.—Comedy of Errors; Serious Family.
W.—The Rivals; No. 1 Round the Corner.
N.—Mazeppa; The Secret.
C.—Loan of a Lover; A Kiss in the Dark.
22. A.—The Wonder; Madelaine.
W.—Poor Gentleman; To Paris and Back for Five Pounds.
N.—*Id.,* June 21.
C.—School of Reform; Perfection.
23. A.—Lucretia Borgia; Hypocrite.
W.—Old Heads and Young Hearts; Bamboozling.
N.—Putnam; Two Fathers.
C.—Cure for the Heart Ache; Betsy Baker.
24. A.—The Wonder; Lucretia Borgia.
W.—Old Heads and Young Hearts; Friend Waggles.
N.—Putnam; Mazeppa.
C.—A Kiss in the Dark; a Nabob for an Hour.
26. *Monday:*
A.—Venice Preserved; How to pay Rent.
W.—Game of Life; Sergeant's Wedding.
N.—Putnam; Mountain Robber.
C.—Love's Frailties; Betsy Baker.
27. A.—Bold Stroke for a Husband; Too many Cooks Spoil the Broth.
W.—Game of Life; A Storm in a Tea-Cup.
N.—*Id.,* June 26.
C.—Yorkshire Brothers; Jacobite.
28. A.—Jealous Wife; Lucretia Borgia.
W.—Game of Life; Stage-Struck Tailor.
N.—Renegade's Horse; Mountain Robber.
C.—Miller's Maid; Luke the Laborer.
29. A.—Sweethearts and Wives; Honey Moon.
W.—Game of Life; Pet of the Public.
N.—*Id.,* June 28.
C.—The Maniac; The Jacobite.
30. A.—Love Chase; P.P.
W.—Old Heads and Young Hearts; Obstinate Family.
N.—Kit Carson; Valentine and Orson.
C.—Othello; Heir at Law.

JULY

1. *Saturday:*
A.—Venice Preserved; White Horse of the Peppers.
W.—School for Scandal; No. 1 Round the Corner.
N.—*Id.,* June 30.

C.—Yorkshire Brothers; A Phenomenon in a Smock Frock.

3. *Monday:*
    A.—Lady of Lyons; Cousin Cherry.
    W.—The West End; Last Man.
    N.—El Hyder; Mat o' the Glen.
    C.—Speed the Plough; Betsy Baker.

4.   A.—Soldier's Daughter; Lucretia Borgia; Last night of the season.
    W.—The West End; Going to the Races. Last night of the season.
    N.—Putnam; Raymo..d and Agnes.
    C.—Maniac; A Roland for an Oliver.

5.   N.—No advertisement. Theatre totally destroyed by fire the night before.
    C.—Love's Frailties; Fortune's Frolic.

6.   C.—Jacobite; Yorkshire Brothers.

7.   C.—School of Reform; A Phenomenon in a Smock Frock.

8.   C.—Miller's Maid; Fortune's Frolic.

10. *Monday:*
    C.—Green Mountain Boy; True Love never Runs Smooth.

11.   C.—Green Mountain Boy; Betsy Baker.

12.   C.—Maid of Croissy; Box and Cox.

13.   C.—Wife for a Day; Stage-Struck Yankee.

14.   C.—Therese; Forest Rose.

15.   C.—Hermit of the Rocks; Loan of a Lover.

17. *Monday:*
    C.—Cabin and Parlor; Day after the Wedding.

18.   C.—No advertisement.

19.   C.—*Id.,* July 17.

20.   C.—Negro Fidelity; Nature and Philosophy.

21.   C.—Faithful Slave; My Cousin Joe.

22.   C.—Negro Fidelity; Day after the Wedding.

24. *Monday:*
    C.—Ireland as it Is; Mischievous Annie.

25.   C.—Irish Assurance; Lord Flanagan.

26.   C.—Paddy the Piper; Limerick Boy.

27.   C.—Ireland as it Is; Good for Nothing.

28.   C.—Sprig of Shillelah; Lola Montez.

29.   C.—Irish Lion; Lord Flanagan.

31. *Monday:*
    C.—Pet of the Petticoats; Rival Pages.

AUGUST

1. *Tuesday:*
    C.—Pet of the Petticoats; Spectre Bridegroom.

2.   C.—Taking by Storm; Dumb Belle.
3.   C.—Pride of the Market; Woman's Wit.
4.   C.—Pride of the Market; Married Bachelor.
5.   C.—The Little Devil's Share; Woman's Wit.
7. *Monday:*
    C.—Born to Good Luck; A Day in Paris.
8.   C.—Who's the Composer?; The First Night.
9.   C.—His Last Legs; Irish Lion.
10.   C.—Dombey and Son; Peggy Green.
11.   C.—Fast Man; Yankee Heiress.
12.   C.—David Copperfield; Sketches in India.
14. *Monday:*
    C.—*Id.,* Aug. 10.
15.   C.—Bachelor of Arts; Family Jars.
16.   C.—Bachelor of Arts; Yankee Heiress.
17.   C.—Fast Man; Peggy Green.
18.   C.—Born to Good Luck; Family Jars.
19.   C.—Money; Yankee Heiress.
    A.—Money; Bobtail and Wagtail.
21. *Monday:*
    C.—Lady of Lyons; Forty Winks.
    A.—Romance and Reality; Bobtail and Wagtail.
22.   C.—Money; Two Gregories.
    A.—Romance and Reality; Three Shaws.
23.   C.—Serious Family; Madelaine.
    A.—*Id.,* Aug. 22.
24.   C.—Madelaine; Irish Tutor.
    A.—Romance and Reality; Swiss Swains.
25.   C.—Hunchback; Toodles.
    A.—*Id.,* Aug. 24.
26.   C.—Lucretia Borgia; Serious Family.
    A.—Romance and Reality; P.P.
28. *Monday:*
    C.—Maria di Rohan.
    A.—She Would and she Would Not; John Dobbs.
29.   C.—Louisa Miller.
    A.—*Id.,* Aug. 28.
    W.—Who's your Friend?; Lover by Proxy.
30.   C.—Love Chase; Rob Roy.
    A.—Rule a Wife and Have a Wife; Three Shaws.
    W.—As You Like It; Grandfather Whitehead.
31.   C.—I Puritani.
    A.—Paul Pry; Black-Eyed Susan.
    W.—Clandestine Marriage; Ganem.

SEPTEMBER

1. *Friday:*
    C.—Lucrezia Borgia.
    A.—Hypocrite; Toodles.
    W.—London Assurance; Ganem.
2.   A.—Satan in Paris; More Blunders than One.
    W.—Lady of Lyons; Ganem.
4. *Monday:*
    A.—The Will; Irish Ambassador.
    W.—Fazio; Married Rake.
    C.—Lucia di Lammermoor.
5.   A.—The Will; Toodles.
    W.—Bertram; Honey Moon
    C.—I Puritani.
6.   A.—She Would and she Would Not; More Blunders than One.
    W.—The Wife; Wandering Minstrel.
    C.—Richard III; Two Gregories.
7.   A.—The Will; Presumptive Evidence.
    W.—Fazio; Eton Boy.
    C.—Masaniello.
8.   A.—Paul Pry; Presumptive Evidence.
    W.—Love; Wandering Minstrel.
    C.—Masaniello.
9.   A.—Hamlet; Swiss Swains.
    W.—Love's Sacrifice; Ganem.
    C.—Lady of Lyons; Black-Eyed Susan.
11. *Monday:*
    A.—Wild Oats; Irish Emigrant.
    W.—Camille.
    C.—No advertisement.
12.   A.—Speed the Plough; First Night.
    W.—Camille.
    C.—La Sonnambula.
    C.M.—Heir at Law; Faint Heart never won Fair Lady.
13.   A.—Rule a Wife and Have a Wife; Toodles.
    W.—Camille.
    C.—Hunchback; Omnibus.
    C.M.—As You Like It; A Kiss in the Dark.
14.   A.—Married Life; Somebody Else.
    W.—Camille.
    C.—Lucia di Lammermoor.
    C.M.—All that Glitters is not Gold; Turning the Tables.
15.   A.—Jealous Wife; My Precious Betsy.
    W.—Camille.

C.—Masaniello.
C.M.—Stranger; Sketches in India.
16.   A.—Apostate; White Horse of the Peppers.
    W.—Camille.
    C.—Forest Rose; Family Jars.
    C.M.—Toodles; Widow's Victim.
18. *Monday:*
    A.—Road to Ruin; Somebody Else.
    W.—Camille.
    C.—Lucia di Lammermoor; Last night of the opera company.
    C.M.—Willow Copse.
19.   A.—Serious Family; Black-Eyed Susan.
    W.—Camille.
    C.M.—Willow Copse.
20.   A.—Apostate; Born to Good Luck.
    W.—Camille.
    C.M.—Willow Copse.
    C.—Soldier's Daughter; Weathercock.
21.   A.—Hypocrite; A Roland for an Oliver.
    W.—Camille.
    C.M.—Honey Moon; Turning the Tables.
    C.—Spectre Bridegroom; Hermit of the Rock.
22.   A.—Serious Family; A Roland for an Oliver.
    W.—Camille.
    C.M.—Debutante; Widow's Victim.
    C.—My Aunt; Green Mountain Boy.
23.   A.—Stranger; Honey Moon.
    W.—Camille.
    C.M.—Robber's Wife; Black-Eyed Susan.
    C.—True Love never did Run Smooth; Lottery Ticket.
25. *Monday:*
    A.—Serious Family; Irish Emigrant.
    W.—Lady of Lyons; Ganem.
    C.M.—Drunkard; An Object of Interest.
    C.—Yankee Land; Wife for a Day.
26.   A.—Serious Family; Paul Pry.
    W.—St. Marc *: *St. Marc*—E. L. Davenport, *Dianora*—Mrs.
      Duffield; Ladies at Home.
    C.M.—Drunkard; Faint Heart never won Fair Lady.
    C.—Rosina Meadows; Deaf as a Post.
27.   A.—Serious Family; Irish Emigrant.
    W.—*Id.,* Sept. 26.
    C.M.—Drunkard; Crimson Crimes.
    C.—Rosina Meadows; Yankee Footman.
28.   A.—*Id.,* Sept. 26.
    W.—St. Marc; Wandering Minstrel.

C.M.—Midnight Watch; Dumb Belle.
   C.—Yankee in England; Loan of a Lover.
29.   A.—Nationalities; Irish Ambassador.
   W.—St. Marc; Eton Boy.
C.M.—Midnight Watch; Perfection.
   C.—Damon and Pythias; Stage-Struck Yankee.
30.   A.—Serious Family; Presumptive Evidence.
   W.—St. Marc; Going to the Races.
C.M.—Toodles; Black-Eyed Susan.
   C.—Rosina Meadows; Rough Diamond.

OCTOBER

2. *Monday:*
   A.—Serious Family; Toodles.
   W.—St. Marc; Ladies at Home.
C.M.—Drunkard; House Dog.
   C.—Love's Sacrifice; Charles II.
3.   A.—Stranger; Born to Good Luck.
   W.—*Id.,* Oct. 2.
C.M.—Drunkard; Virginia Mummy.
   C.—Romeo and Juliet; Dumb Belle.
4.   A.—Belle's Stratagem; Love, Law, and Physic.
   W.—Othello; To Paris and Back for Five Pounds.
C.M.—Drunkard; An Object of Interest.
   C.—Lady of Lyons; Bamboozling.
5.   A.—Serious Family; Love, Law, and Physic.
   W.—Hamlet; Wandering Minstrel.
C.M.—Stranger; Midnight Watch.
   C.—Fazio; Limerick Boy.
6.   A.—Laugh when you Can; Rory O'More.
   W.—The Wife; Black-Eyed Susan.
C.M.—Cricket on the Hearth; Soldier's Return.
   C.—The Wife; Jack Sheppard.
7.   A.—Hamlet; Irish Tutor.
   W.—Brutus; Black-Eyed Susan.
C.M.—Cricket on the Hearth; Turning the Tables.
   C.—Wandering Boys; Jack Sheppard.
9. *Monday:*
   A.—Comedy of Errors; Rory O'More.
   W.—Damon and Pythias; New Footman.
C.M.—Cricket on the Hearth; Naval Engagements.
   C.—First Night; Toodles.
10.   A.—Comedy of Errors; Satan in Paris.
   W.—Pizarro; Ladies at Home.
C.M.—Midnight Watch; Virginia Mummy.

C.—Jack Sheppard; John Jones.
11.   A.—Comedy of Errors; Black-Eyed Susan.
W.—Richelieu; Going to the Races.
C.M.—Naval Engagements; Honey Moon.
C.—Jack Sheppard; Good for Nothing.
12.   A.—Money; White Horse of the Peppers.
W.—Hamlet; Married Rake.
C.M.—Heir at Law; Perfection.
C.—French Spy; First Night.
13.   A.—Jealous Wife; Born to Good Luck.
W.—Macbeth; Double-Bedded Room.
C.M.—Lady of Lyons; Crimson Crimes.
C.—Model of a Wife; New York as it Is.
14.   A.—Comedy of Errors; Cure for the Heart Ache.
W.—Damon and Pythias; A Roland for an Oliver.
C.M.—Eustache, the Condemned; Toodles.
C.—French Spy; Jack Sheppard.
16. *Monday:*
A.—Comedy of Errors; Serious Family.
W.—Othello; Ladies, Beware.
C.M.—Eustache, the Condemned; An Object of Interest.
C.—Lucretia Borgia; Stranger.
17.   A.—Cure for the Heart Ache; Good for Nothing.
W.—Jack Cade; Valet de Sham.
C.M.—Eustache, the Condemned; Virginia Mummy.
C.—The Gamester; Love Chase.
18.   A.—*Id.,* Oct. 16.
W.—Richelieu; Two Buzzards.
C.M.—Eustache, the Condemned; As like as Two Peas.
C.—Jane Shore; Lucretia Borgia.
19.   A.—*Id.,* Oct. 16.
W.—Hamlet; Box and Cox Married and Settled.
C.M.—*Id.,* Oct. 18.
C.—Ingomar; Simpson and Co.
20.   A.—*Id.,* Oct. 16.
W.—Virginius; To Paris and Back.
C.M.—Eustache, the Condemned; Midnight Watch.
C.—Jane Shore; Stranger.
21.   A.—Hypocrite; Laugh when you Can.
W.—Jack Cade; Domestic Economy.
C.M.—Eustache, the Condemned; Cricket on the Hearth.
C.—Bride of Lammermoor; Daughter of the Regiment.
23. *Monday:*
A.—London Assurance.
W.—Gladiator; Ladies at Home.
C.M.—Eustache, the Condemned; Friend Waggles.

    C.—Griselda; Deaf as a Post.
24. A.—*Id.,* Oct. 23.
    W.—King Lear; Going to the Races.
    C.M.—No advertisement.
    C.—Griselda; Lawyer's Clerk.
25. A.—*Id.,* Oct. 23.
    W.—Metamora; A Roland for an Oliver.
    C.M.—*Id.,* Oct. 23.
    C.—Griselda; the Recusant *: *Madelaine*—Mrs. Farren, Major *Wentworth*—Stuart, *Tom*—W. F. Johnson.
26. A.—*Id.,* Oct. 23.
    W.—Gladiator; Wandering Minstrel.
    C.M.—Eustache, the Condemned; Budget of Blunders.
    C.—*Id.,* Oct. 25.
27. A.—*Id.,* Oct. 23.
    W.—Jack Cade; Delicate Ground.
    C.M.—*Id.,* Oct. 26.
    C.—Griselda; Wrecker's Daughter.
28. A.—*Id.,* Oct. 23.
    W.—Richard III; Two Buzzards.
    C.M.—Eustache, the Condemned; Death Struggle.
    C.—Venetian; Sergeant's Wife.
30. *Monday:*
    A.—*Id.,* Oct. 23.
    W.—La Sonnambula; Valet de Sham.
    C.—Griselda; Lucretia Borgia.
    C.M.—Rob Roy; From Village to Court.
31. A.—*Id.,* Oct. 23.
    W.—La Sonnambula; Box and Cox Married and Settled.
    C.M.—Paul Pry; From Village to Court.
    C.—Venetian; Rights of Women.

NOVEMBER

1. *Wednesday:*
    A.—*Id.,* Oct. 23.
    W.—Bohemian Girl; Domestic Economy.
    C.M.—From Village to Court; Friend Waggles; Budget of Blunders.
    C.—Venetian; Phenomenon in a Smock Frock.
2. A.—*Id.,* Oct. 23.
    W.—Bohemian Girl; To Paris and Back.
    C.M.—Simpson and Co.; Dumb Belle.
    C.—Wrecker's Daughter; Bride of Lammermoor.
3. A.—*Id.,* Oct. 23.
    W.—Maritana; Married Rake.

C.M.—A Day after the Wedding; A Day in Paris.
C.—Adelgitha; Rights of Women.
4.   A.—London Assurance; P.P.
W.—Maritana; Pleasant Neighbors.
C.M.—An Object of Interest; Our Gal.
C.—Irish Sibyl and the Rebel Chief *: *Marc Tape*—W. F. Johnson, *Nora*—Mrs. Farren; All that Glitters is not Gold.
6. *Monday:*
A.—London Assurance; Toodles.
W.—Crown Diamonds; Ladies at Home.
C.M.—Rob Roy; From Village to Court.
C.—Live Indian; Toodles.
7.   A.—London Assurance; Good for Nothing.
W.—Crown Diamonds; Double-Bedded Room.
C.M.—Eustache, the Condemned; Toodles.
C.—Live Indian; Poor Gentleman.
8.   A.—London Assurance; Bobtail and Wagtail.
W.—Crown Diamonds; Delicate Ground.
C.M.—Paul Pry; Black-Eyed Susan.
C.—Forty Winks; Faint Heart never won Fair Lady
9.   A.—London Assurance; Three Shaws.
W.—Crown Diamonds; Eton Boy.
C.M.—Cricket on the Hearth; An Object of Interest.
C.—Sketches in India; A Glance at Philadelphia.
10.   A.—London Assurance; Two Great Rascals.
W.—Crown Diamonds; Turning the Tables.
C.M.—Heir at Law; Widow's Victim.
C.—Betsy Baker; A Glance at Philadelphia.
11.   A.—*Id.,* Nov. 10.
W.—Crown Diamonds; New Footman.
C.M.—William Tell; Your Life's in Danger.
C.—Live Indian; A Glance at Philadelphia.
13. *Monday:*
A.—Comedy of Errors; Serious Family.
W.—Maritana; Obstinate Family.
C.M.—A Story of the Heart; Your Life's in Danger.
C.—Soldier's Daughter; Jack Sheppard.
14.   A.—Speed the Plough; Irish Emigrant.
W.—Fra Diavolo; Boots at the Swan.
C.M.—Sweethearts and Wives; Faint Heart never won Fair Lady.
C.—*Id.,* Nov. 13.
15.   A.—Provoked Husband; Ben Bolt.
W.—Beggar's Opera; Married Rake.
C.M.—Coiner's Wife; As like as Two Peas.

C.—Stranger; Jack Sheppard.

16.   A.—Cure for the Heart Ache; A Roland for an Oliver.
W.—Fra Diavolo; To Paris and Back for Five Pounds.
C.M.—William Tell; Irish Tutor.
C.—Rookwood; Limerick Boy.

17.   A.—Comedy of Errors; Serious Family.
W.—Crown Diamonds; Rifle Brigade.
C.M.—A Story of the Heart; A Moving Tale.
C.—Rookwood; Rough Diamond.

18.   A.—Provoked Husband; Black-Eyed Susan.
W.—Beggar's Opera; Boots at the Swan.
C.M.—Robbers; A Moving Tale.
C.—Rookwood; Jack Sheppard.

20. *Monday:*
A.—Jealous Wife; Ben Bolt.
W.—Delicate Ground; Milly.
C.M.—Robbers; Sketches in India.
C.—Lonely Man of the Ocean; Swiss Swains.

21.   A.—Stranger; Irish Ambassador.
W.—Double-Bedded Room; Young Actress.
C.M.—Robbers; Irish Tutor.
C.—Lonely Man of the Ocean; Mr. and Mrs. White.

22.   A.—Othello; Ben Bolt.
W.—Two Buzzards; Milly.
C.M.—Thirty Years of a Gambler's Life; Poor Pillicoddy.
C.—*Id.,* Nov. 21.

23.   A.—Serious Family; Ben Bolt.
W.—Wandering Minstrel; The Devil's in it.
C.M.—Thirty Years of a Gambler's Life; The Devil's in it.
C.—Idiot Witness; Lonely Man of the Ocean.

24.   A.—John Bull; Good for Nothing.
W.—Andy Blake; Fairy Star.
C.M.—Wonderful Woman; Golden Farmer.
C.—Lonely Man of the Ocean; Jack Sheppard.

25.   A.—Othello; Ben Bolt.
W.—Eton Boy; Young Actress.
C.M.—Thirty Years of a Gambler's Life; Black-Eyed Susan.
C.—Drunkard; Lonely Man of the Ocean.

27. *Monday:*
A.—Provoked Husband; Irish Emigrant.
W.—Ladies, Beware; Apollo in New York.
C.M.—Hunchback; Heads or Tails.
C.—Uncle Tom's Cabin.

28.   A.—Road to Ruin; Ben Bolt.
W.—Married Rake; Apollo in New York.
C.M.—The Wife; Sketches in India.

C.—*Id.,* Nov. 27.

29. A.—Single Life; Married Life.
W.—Ladies at Home; Apollo in New York.
C.M.—Love's Sacrifice; Heads or Tails.
C.—*Id.,* Nov. 27.

30. A.—Provoked Husband; Toodles.
W.—Obstinate Family; Apollo in New York.
C.M.—Lady of Lyons; Poor Pillicoddy.
C.—Momentous Question; Warlock of the Glen.

DECEMBER

1. *Friday:*
A.—Point of Honor; Honey Moon.
W.—Used Up; Apollo in New York.
C.M.—Romeo and Juliet; Laughing Hyena.
C.—Honey Moon; Three Shaws.

2. A.—Single Life; Married Life.
W.—A Morning Call; Young Actress.
C.M.—Box and Cox; Robber's Wife.
C.—Uncle Tom's Cabin.

4. *Monday:*
A.—Much Ado about Nothing; Ben Bolt.
W.—Apollo in New York; Young Actress.
C.M.—Hunchback; Laughing Hyena.
C.—Pet of the Petticoats; An Object of Interest.

5. A.—Nationalities; A Day Well Spent.
W.—Apollo in New York; Bob Nettles.
C.M.—Money; As like as Two Peas.
C.—Momentous Question; Middy Ashore.

6. A.—Naval Engagements; Grandfather Whitehead.
W.—Used Up; Young Actress.
C.M.—She Stoops to Conquer; Your Life's in Danger.
C.—No advertisement.

7. A.—Comedy of Errors; Serious Family.
W.—Andy Blake; Bob Nettles.
C.M.—Stranger; Honey Moon.
C.—No advertisement.

8. A.—Money; More Blunders than One.
W.—London Assurance; Bob Nettles.
C.M.—Lucretia Borgia; Loan of a Lover.

9. A.—Romeo and Juliet; A Day Well Spent.
W.—*Id.,* Dec. 8.
C.M.—Lucretia Borgia; Paul Pry.

11. *Monday:*
A.—Single Life; Married Life.

W.—Camille.

C.M.—Fazio; From Village to Court.

12.   A.—Wild Oats; Irish Emigrant.

W.—Camille.

C.M.—She Stoops to Conquer; Faint Heart never won Fair Lady.

13.   A.—Rule a Wife and Have a Wife; Black-Eyed Susan.

W.—Camille.

C.M.—Fashion; As Like as Two Peas.

C.—Grandfather Whitehead; Richard III; Family Jars.

14.   A.—Hypocrite; A Roland for an Oliver.

W.—Camille.

C.M.—Fashion; Poor Pillicoddy.

C. —Family Jars.

15.   A.—Wild Oats; P.P.

W.—Masks and Faces; All that Glitters is not Gold.

C.M.—Fashion; Widow's Victim.

C.—*Id.*, Dec. 14.

16.   A.—Gamester; A Dream at Sea.

W.—Masks and Faces; Black-Eyed Susan.

C.M.—Fashion; Robert Macaire.

C.—*Id.*, Dec. 14.

18. *Monday:*

A.—Single Life; Married Life.

W.—Love; Box and Cox Married and Settled.

C.M.—Fashion; Your Life's in Danger.

C.—Mr. and Mrs. White.

19.   A.—School for Scandal; More Blunders than One.

W.—Camille; To Paris and Back.

C.M.—*Id.*, Dec. 16.

C.—*Id.*, Dec. 18.

20.   A.—Belle's Stratagem; Born to Good Luck.

W.—Adrienne, the Actress; Double-Bedded Room

C.M.—Last Man; Therese.

C.—No legitimate drama.

21.   A.—Comedy of Errors; Serious Family.

W.—Masks and Faces; A Storm in a Tea-Cup.

C.M.—Eustache; Our Country Cousin.

C.—No advertisement.

22.   A.—Hypocrite; Sketches in India.

W.—Roman Father; Ladies' Battle.

C.M.—Robbers; Our Country Cousin.

23.   A.—Fortunio and his Seven Gifted Servants; Naval Engagements.

W.—Ingomar; As like as Two Peas.

C.M.—Major Jones' Courtship; Therese.

25. *Monday:*
    A.—Fortunio; Laugh while you Can.
    W.—Hunchback; Eton Boy.
    C.M.—Forty Thieves; Major Jones' Courtship.
26.   A.—Fortunio; Day after the Wedding.
    W.—Love's Sacrifice; House Dog.
    C.M.—*Id.,* Dec. 25.
27.   A.—*Id.,* Dec. 23.
    W.—*Id.,* Dec. 23.
    C.M.—*Id.,* Dec. 25.
28.   A.—Fortunio; Dumb Belle.
    W.—School for Scandal; Morning Call.
    C.M.—*Id.,* Dec. 25.
29.   A.—Fortunio; Perfection.
    W.—Gamester; Lend Me Five Shillings.
    C.M.—*Id.,* Dec. 25.
30.   A.—Fortunio; Married Rake.
    W.—Stranger; Honey Moon.
    C.M.—*Id.,* Dec. 25.

JANUARY 1855

1. *Monday:*
    A.—Fortunio; Laugh when you Can.
    W.—Ladies' Battle; Paul Pry.
    C.M.—Forty Thieves; Major Jones' Courtship.
2.   A.—Fortunio; Faint Heart never won Fair Lady.
    W.—I Puritani.
    C.M.—*Id.,* Jan. 1.
3.   A.—Fortunio; Naval Engagements.
    W.—Rivals; Poor Soldier.
    C.M.—*Id.,* Jan. 11.
4.   A.—Fortunio; P.P.
    W.—Lucrezia Borgia.
    C.M.—*Id.,* Jan. 1.
5.   A.—*Id.,* Jan. 2.
    W.—Lucrezia Borgia.
    C.M.—*Id.,* Jan. 1.
6.   A.—Fortunio; William Tell.
    W.—Norma.
    C.M.—Last Man; Forty Thieves.
8. *Monday:*
    A.—Fortunio; School for Tigers.
    W.—Midsummer Night's Dream; A Pleasant Neighbor.
    C.M.—Vampire; Paul Pry.
9.   A.—Satan in Paris; School for Tigers.

[519]

W.—*Id.*, Jan. 8.
C.M.—Forty Thieves; Vampire.
10.   A.—She Stoops to Conquer; School for Tigers.
W.—Midsummer Night's Dream.
C.M.—Fashion; Vampire.
11.   A.—Wild Oats; Toodles.
W.—*Id.*, Jan. 10.
C.M.—Virginia Mummy; Vampire.
12.   A.—Soldier's Daughter; A Roland for an Oliver.
W.—*Id.*, Jan. 10.
C.M.—His Last Legs; Vampire.
13.   A.—Fortunio; Honey Moon.
W.—*Id.*, Jan. 10.
C.M.—Rob Roy; Vampire.
15. *Monday:*
A.—Fortunio; William Tell.
W.—*Id.*, Jan. 10.
C.M.—Madelaine; His Last Legs.
C.—London Assurance; Cool as a Cucumber.
16.   A.—Fortunio; Honey Moon.
W.—*Id.*, Jan. 10.
C.M.—Madelaine; Faint Heart never won Fair Lady.
C.—*Id.*, Jan. 15.
17.   A.—Comedy of Errors; Fortunio.
W.—*Id.*, Jan. 10.
C.M.—Stranger; Honey Moon.
C.—Foundling of Paris; Loan of a Lover.
18.   A.—Serious Family; Fortunio.
W.—*Id.*, Jan. 10.
C.M.—Jane Shore; Paddy Miles' Boy.
C.—Pet of the Petticoats; Foundling of Paris.
19.   A.—Comedy of Errors; Fortunio.
W.—*Id.*, Jan. 10.
C.M.—Lucretia Borgia; Major Jones' Courtship.
C.—David Copperfield; Michael Erle.
20.   A.—*Id.*, Jan. 18.
W.—*Id.*, Jan. 10.
C.M.—Jane Shore; Robert Macaire.
C.—Hunchback; Rough Diamond.
22. *Monday:*
A.—Single Life; Fortunio.
W.—*Id.*, Jan. 10.
C.M.—Douglas; Black-Eyed Susan.
C.—Corsican Brothers; Lost Son.
23.   A.—*Id.*, Jan. 19.

W.—*Id.,* Jan. 10.
C.M.—Lucretia Borgia; Youthful Days of Richelieu.
C.—Corsican Brothers; Robber's Wife.
24. A.—Apostate; Irish Emigrant.
W.—*Id.,* Jan. 10.
C.M.—Jane Shore; Robert Macaire.
C.—Lady of Lyons; Michael Erle.
25. A.—Wild Oats; Toodles.
W.—*Id.,* Jan. 10.
C.M.—She Stoops to Conquer; Wandering Boys of Switzerland.
C.—Romeo and Juliet; Slasher and Crasher.
26. A.—Cure for the Heart Ache; White Horse of the Peppers.
W.—*Id.,* Jan. 10.
C.M.—Poor Gentleman; Madelaine.
C.—Cricket on the Hearth; Corsican Brothers.
27. A.—Othello; Irish Tutor.
W.—*Id.,* Jan. 10.
C.M.—Romeo and Juliet; Toodles.
C.—Satan in Paris; David Copperfield.
29. *Monday:*
A.—Child of Nature; Fortunio.
W.—*Id.,* Jan. 10.
C.M.—Carpenter of Rouen; Poor Pillicoddy.
C.—Love and Larnin'; Pride of Killarney.
30. A.—Old Heads and Young Hearts; Irish Emigrant.
W.—*Id.,* Jan. 10.
C.M.—*Id.,* Jan. 29.
C.—A Wife for a Day; Love and Larnin'.
31. A.—Money; More Blunders than One.
W.—*Id.,* Jan. 10.
C.M.—*Id.,* Jan. 29.
C.—Backwoodsman; Wife for a Day.

FEBRUARY

1. *Thursday:*
A.—Comedy of Errors; Serious Family.
W.—*Id.,* Jan. 10.
C.M.—Hunchback; Our Country Cousin.
C.—North and South; Backwoodsman.
2. A.—Apostate; Irish Emigrant.
W.—*Id.,* Jan. 10.
C.M.—School for Scandal; Two Drovers.
C.—Sam Patch; North and South.
[521]

3. A.—Ion; Irish Dragoon.
    W.—*Id.*, Jan. 10.
    C.M.—Carpenter of Rouen; Wandering Boys of Switzerland.
    C.—Yankee in Time; Beacon of Death.
5. *Monday:*
    A.—As You Like It; Irish Dragoon.
    W.—*Id.*, Jan. 10.
    C.M.—Marie; Wandering Boys of Switzerland.
    C.—Fashion and Famine; White or Brown.
6. A.—Money; Ben Bolt.
    W.—*Id.*, Jan. 10.
    C.M.—Rob Roy; Perfection.
    C.—Fashion and Famine; Bamboozling.
7. A.—Wives as they Were; Good for Nothing.
    W.—*Id.*, Jan. 10.
    C.M.—Marie; Mons. Jaques.
    C.—Fashion and Famine; Naval Engagements.
8. A.—Cure for the Heart Ache; Married Life.
    W.—*Id.*, Jan. 10.
    C.M.—Stranger; Honey Moon.
    C.—Fashion and Famine; Presumptive Evidence.
9. A.—Hypocrite; William Tell.
    W.—*Id.*, Jan. 10.
    C.M.—Virginius; Spectre Bridegroom.
    C.—Lady's Stratagem; Fashion and Famine.
10. A.—As You Like It; Luke the Laborer.
    W.—*Id.*, Jan. 10.
    C.M.—Honey Moon; Marie.
    C.—Jack Sheppard; Presumptive Evidence.
12. *Monday:*
    A.—Ion; Luke, the Laborer.
    W.—*Id.*, Jan. 10.
    C.M.—Uncle Tom's Cabin.
    C.—Hamlet; Lady's Stratagem.
13. A.—She Stoops to Conquer; Irish Emigrant.
    W.—Oliver Twist; Eton Boy.
    C.M.—*Id.*, Feb. 12.
    C.—Richelieu; To Oblige Benson.
14. A.—She Would and she Would Not; Good for Nothing.
    W.—Willow Copse; Two can Play at That Game.
    C.M.—*Id.*, Feb. 12.
    C.—Willow Copse; To Oblige Benson.
15. A.—Heir at Law; White Horse of the Peppers.
    W.—St. George and the Dragon; Oliver Twist.
    C.M.—*Id.*, Feb. 12.
    C.—King Lear; Good for Nothing.

16.   A.—Apostate; Irish Tutor.
       W.—Willow Copse; House Dog.
       C.M.—*Id.,* Feb. 12.
       C.—Willow Copse; Louis XI.

17.   A.—Hunchback; Toodles.
       W.—Six Degrees of Crime; Lady of the Lake.
       C.M.—*Id.,* Feb. 12.
       C.—Louis XI; All that Glitters is not Gold.

19.   *Monday:*
       A.—Jealous Wife; Black-Eyed Susan.
       W.—Fra Diavolo; Box and Cox Married and Settled.
       C.M.—*Id.,* Feb. 12.
       C.—Lucretia Borgia; Young Scamp.

20.   A.—The Wife; Irish Ambassador.
       W.—Crown Diamonds; Double-Bedded Room.
       C.M.—*Id.,* Feb. 12.
       C.—*Id.,* Feb. 19.

21.   A.—Stranger; Ben Bolt.
       W.—Bohemian Girl; Two Buzzards.
       C.M.—*Id.,* Feb. 12.
       C.—Jack Sheppard; Philadelphia Fireman.

22.   A.—Hypocrite; Luke, the Laborer.
       W.—Beggar's Opera; Domestic Economy.
       C.M.—*Id.,* Feb. 12.
       C.—Uncle Tom's Cabin.

23.   A.—William Tell; Rory O'More.
       W.—Crown Diamonds; Eton Boy.
       C.M.—*Id.,* Feb. 12.
       C.—*Id.,* Feb. 22.

24.   A.—Castle Spectre; P.P.
       W.—Guy Mannering; To Paris and Back.
       C.M.—*Id.,* Feb. 12.
       C.—*Id.,* Feb. 22.

26.   *Monday:*
       A.—Castle Spectre; More Blunders than One.
       W.—Cinderella.
       C.M.—*Id.,* Feb. 12.
       C.—*Id.,* Feb. 22.

27.   A.—Comedy of Errors; Serious Family.
       W.—*Id.,* Feb. 26.
       C.M.—*Id.,* Feb. 12.
       C.—*Id.,* Feb. 22.

28.   A.—School for Scandal; Thumping Legacy.
       W.—*Id.,* Feb. 26.
       C.M.—*Id.,* Feb. 12.
       C.—*Id.,* Feb. 22.

MARCH

1. *Thursday:*
   A.—Wild Oats; Rory O'More.
   W.—*Id.,* Feb. 26.
   C.M.—*Id.,* Feb. 12.
   C.—*Id.,* Feb. 22.
2.   A.—Stranger; Serious Family.
   W.—*Id.,* Feb. 26.
   C.M.—*Id.,* Feb. 12.
   C.—*Id.,* Feb. 22.
3.   A.—Castle Spectre; Ben Bolt.
   W.—*Id.,* Feb. 26.
   C.M.—Fashion and Famine; Laughing Hyena.
   C.—*Id.,* Feb. 22.
5. *Monday:*
   A.—Lady of Lyons; Irish Ambassador.
   W.—*Id.,* Feb. 26.
   C.M.—Fashion and Famine; Maid of Munster.
   C.—*Id.,* Feb. 22.
6.   A.—Hamlet; Irish Tutor.
   W.—*Id.,* Feb. 26.
   C.M.—Fashion and Famine; Mons. Jacques.
   C.—*Id.,* Feb. 22.
7.   A.—Jane Shore; O'Flannigan and the Fairies.
   W.—Cinderella; Obstinate Family.
   C.M.—Fashion and Famine; Poor Pillicoddy.
   C.—*Id.,* Feb. 22.
8.   A.—*Id.,* Mar. 7.
   W.—Cinderella; Maritana, second act.
   C.M.—Fashion and Famine; Spectre Bridegroom.
   C.—*Id.,* Feb. 22.
9.   A.—Rivals; Luke, the Laborer.
   W.—Cinderella; Waterman.
   C.M.—*Id.,* Mar. 6.
   C.—*Id.,* Feb. 22.
10.   A.—*Id.,* Mar. 7.
   W.—*Id.,* Mar. 9.
   C.M.—Little Katy; Our Country Cousin.
   C.—*Id.,* Feb. 22.
12. *Monday:*
   A.—Pizarro; O'Flannigan and the Fairies.
   W.—St. Marc; Box and Cox.
   C.M.—Little Katy; Paddy Miles' Boy.
   C.—*Id.,* Feb. 22.
13.   A.—*Id.,* Mar. 12.

W.—Othello; Married Rake.
C.M.—Little Katy; Toodles.
    C.—*Id.,* Feb. 22.
14.   A.—*Id.,* Mar. 12.
W.—Egyptian *: *Zabdas*—E. L. Davenport, *Zenobia*—Mrs. Muzzy, *Julia*—Mrs. Duffield; Obstinate Family.
C.M.—Little Katy; Our Country Cousin.
    C.—*Id.,* Feb. 22.
15.   A.—Pizarro; More Blunders than One.
W.—Egyptian; Two Buzzards.
C.M.—Lamp-Lighter; Four Sisters.
    C.—*Id.,* Feb. 22.
16.   A.—*Id.,* Mar. 15.
W.—Egyptian; Valet de Sham.
C.M.—*Id.,* Mar. 15.
    C.—*Id.,* Feb. 22.
17.   A.—Pizarro; Laugh when you Can.
W.—Egyptian; Domestic Economy.
C.M.—Fashion and Famine; Lamp-Lighter.
    C.—*Id.,* Feb. 22.
19. *Monday:*
    A.—Castle Spectre; Irish Lion.
W.—Love's Sacrifice; Caught in a Trap.
C.M.—Douglas; Virginia Mummy.
C.—Pilgrim's Progress.
20.   A.—Comedy of Errors; Serious Family.
W.—Much Ado about Nothing; Delicate Ground.
C.M.—Rivals; Faint Heart never won Fair Lady.
    C.—*Id.,* Mar. 19.
21.   A.—Hypocrite; Pizarro.
W.—Hunchback; Going to the Races.
C.M.—Madelaine; Paul Pry.
    C.—*Id.,* Mar. 19.
22.   A.—Stranger; Honey Moon.
W.—Love Chase; Double-Bedded Room.
C.M.—Midshipman Easy; From Village to Court.
    C.—*Id.,* Mar. 19.
23.   A.—Comedy of Errors; Serious Family.
W.—Charity's Love *: *Captain*—E. L. Davenport, *Charity*—Miss Fanny Vinny; Black-Eyed Susan.
C.M.—Lucretia Borgia; Simpson and Co.
    C.—*Id.,* Mar. 19.
24.   A.—Hypocrite; Castle Spectre.
W.—Charity's Love; Honey Moon.
C.M.—Jane Shore; Midshipman Easy.
    C.—*Id.,* Mar. 19.

26. *Monday:*
    A.—Night and Morning; Thumping Legacy.
    W.—As You Like It; To Oblige Benson.
    C.M.—Wild Oats; As like as Two Peas.
    C.—*Id.,* Mar. 19.

27.   A.—Night and Morning; Irish Tutor.
    W.—Hamlet; Wandering Minstrel.
    C.M.—Lady of Lyons; Paddy Miles' Boy.
    C.—*Id.,* Mar. 19.

28.   A.—*Id.,* Mar. 27.
    W.—Love's Sacrifice; To Oblige Benson.
    C.M.—Hamlet; Spectre Bridegroom.
    C.—No advertisement.

29.   A.—*Id.,* Mar. 26.
    W.—Othello; Obstinate Family.
    C.M.—Money; Mons. Jacques.
    C.—No advertisement.

30.   A.—*Id.,* Mar. 26.
    W.—Romeo and Juliet; He's not A-Miss.
    C.M.—Stranger; My Aunt.

31.   A.—Night and Morning; Wandering Minstrel.
    W.—Stranger; Charity's Love.
    C.M.—Richelieu; Midshipman Easy.

APRIL

2. *Monday:*
    A.—*Id.,* Mar. 31.
    W.—Love and Loyalty; As like as Two Peas.
    C.M.—Hamlet; Sketches in India.

3.   A.—Night and Morning; Irish Lion.
    W.—Love and Loyalty; To Oblige Benson.
    C.M.—Town and Country; Four Sisters.

4.   A.—Night and Morning; Irish Lion.
    W.—Love and Loyalty; Two can Play at That Game.
    C.M.—Gamester; From Village to Court.

5.   A.—*Id.,* Mar. 31.
    W.—Hamlet; Wandering Minstrel.
    C.M.—Stranger; Honey Moon.
    C.—Persecuted Dutchman; Vermont Wool Dealer.

6.   A.—Comedy of Errors; Serious Family.
    W.—Love and Loyalty; Faint Heart never won Fair Lady.
    C.M.—Elder Brother; Dramatist.
    C.—Dutchman in Love; Foulah Slave.

7.   A.—Night and Morning; O'Flannigan and the Fairies.
    W.—Macbeth; Day after the Wedding.

C.M.—Robbers; Sketches in India.
C.—Macbeth; Dutch Actor.

9. *Monday:*
A.—Money; O'Flannigan and the Fairies.
W.—Lady of Lyons; Opposite Neighbors.
C.M.—Elder Brother; Dramatist.
C.—Lady of Lyons; Dutchman in Love.

10. A.—Poor Gentleman; Toodles.
W.—Pizarro; Love Chase.
C.M.—Macbeth; Laughing Hyena.
C.—Wallace; Soldier's Daughter.

11. A.—Night and Morning; Irish Lion.
W.—Brutus; Day after the Wedding.
C.M.—Romeo and Juliet; From Village to Court.
C.—Tour de Nesle; Dutchman in Court.

12. A.—Comedy of Errors; Serious Family.
W.—Hamlet; Obstinate Family.
C.M.—Money; Dramatist.
C.—Blind Orphan; Dutch Richard.

13. A.—Rivals; Gilderoy.
W.—Calaynos; Morning Call.
C.M.—Wine Works Wonders; Katharine and Petruchio.
C.—Richelieu; Star-Spangled Banner.

14. A.—Laugh when you Can; Castle Spectre.
W.—Richard III; Faint Heart never won Fair Lady.
C.M.—Macbeth; My Country Cousin.
C.—Dutchman in Love; Tour de Nesle.

16. *Monday:*
A.—Heir at Law; Gilderoy.
W.—Calaynos; St. George and the Dragon.
C.—Six Degrees of Crime; Black-Eyed Susan.
C.M.—Richelieu; As like as Two Peas.

17. A.—Comedy of Errors; Serious Family.
W.—Richard III; My Aunt.
C.M.—Lady of Lyons; My Precious Betsy.
C.—*Id.,* Apr. 16.

18. A.—Town and Country; Robert Macaire.
W.—Othello; To Oblige Benson.
C.M.—*Id.,* Apr. 13.
C.—Persecuted Dutchman; Pilot.

19. A.—Speed the Plough; O'Flannigan and the Fairies.
W.—New Way To Pay Old Debts; Opposite Neighbors.
C.M.—Robbers; As like as Two Peas.
C.—Rosina Meadows; Long Tom Coffin.

20. A.—*Id.,* Apr. 18.
W.—Hamlet; Morning Call.

C.M.—Much Ado about Nothing; Weathercock.
C.—Ambition; Crime, and Retribution; Wallace.
21. A.—Lucretia Borgia; Robert Macaire.
W.—Othello; Box and Cox Married and Settled.
C.M.—Stranger; Dramatist.
C.—Six Degrees of Crime; Dutch Richard.
23. *Monday:*
A.—Town and Country; Irish Emigrant.
W.—Midsummer Night's Dream.
C.—Housebreaker and the Three Jacks; Dutch Actor.
C.M.—The Wife; Mons. Jacques.
24. A.—*Id., Apr. 17.*
W.—*Id., Apr. 23.*
C.M.—Venice Preserved; His Last Legs.
C.—Robert Emmett; Three Jack Sheppards.
25. A.—Knight of Arva; Wreck Ashore.
W.—*Id., Apr. 23.*
C.M.—Wine Works Wonders; Therese.
C.—Robert Emmett; Mr. and Mrs. White.
26. A.—Poor Gentleman; Lucretia Borgia.
W.—*Id., Apr. 23.*
C.M.—Rivals; Serious Family.
C.—Robert Emmett; Dutchman in Love.
27. A.—*Id., Apr. 25.*
W.—*Id., Apr. 23.*
C.M.—Ingomar; Midshipman Easy.
C.—Robert Emmett; Dutch Actor.
28. A.—Lucretia Borgia; Wreck Ashore.
W.—*Id., Apr. 23.*
C.M.—She Stoops to Conquer; Serious Family.
C.—Robert Emmett; Three Jack Sheppards.
30. *Monday:*
A.—Knight of Arva; Black-Eyed Susan.
W.—Masks and Faces; Eton Boy.
C.M.—Adelgitha; Laughing Hyena.
C.—Loan of a Lover; Sixteen-String Jack.

MAY

1. *Tuesday:*
A.—Comedy of Errors; Serious Family.
W.—Man of the World; To Oblige Benson.
C.M.—Evadne; As like as Two Peas.
C.—No advertisement.
2. A.—Ingomar; P.P.
W.—Changes; Opposite Neighbors.

C.M.—Lucretia Borgia; Major Jones' Courtship.
C.—No advertisement.

3. A.—Ingomar; O'Flannigan and the Fairies.
W.—Romeo and Juliet; David Copperfield.
C.M.—Adelgitha; Midshipman Easy.

4. A.—The Way to get Married; Nervous Man.
W.—Love; Valet de Sham.
C.M.—Wrecker's Daughter; Love Chase.

5. A.—Hunchback; Irish Emigrant.
W.—Road to Ruin; Robert Macaire.
C.M.—Venetian; Rights of Woman.

7. *Monday:*
A.—Stranger; Cure for the Heart Ache.
W.—Hunchback; Going to the Races.
C.M.—Jane Shore; Lucretia Borgia.

8. A.—Comedy of Errors; Serious Family.
W.—Fazio; Masks and Faces.
C.M.—Stranger; St. Mary's Eve.

9. A.—The Way to get Married; Knight of Arva.
W.—Love's Sacrifice; Robert Macaire.
C.M.—*Id.,* May 5.

10. A.—*Id.,* May 4.
W.—Stranger; Honey Moon.
C.M.—Wrecker's Daughter; St. Mary's Eve.

11. A.—Bold Stroke for a Husband; Courier of Lyons.
W.—Evadne; Toodles.
C.M.—Gamester; Clari.

12. A.—Wild Oats; Courier of Lyons.
W.—Adrienne, the Actress; To Oblige Benson.
C.M.—Bride of Lammermoor; Daughter of the Regiment.

14. *Monday:*
A.—*Id.,* May 9.
W.—Lucretia Borgia; Bob Nettles.
C.M.—Ingomar; Lucretia Borgia.

15. A.—Comedy of Errors; Serious Family.
W.—Ingomar; Toodles.
C.M.—*Id.,* May 12.

16. A.—Man and Wife; Phantom Ship.
W.—Love's Sacrifice; Wandering Minstrel.
C.M.—Stranger; Mary Tudor.

17. A.—*Id.,* May 16.
W.—Adrienne, the Actress; A Morning Call.
C.M.—Hunchback; Serious Family.

18. A.—Critic; A New Comedy of Errors *.
W.—Romeo and Juliet; He's not A-Miss.
C.M.—Jane Shore; Honey Moon.

19.   A.—Critic; Phantom Ship.
     W.—Lucretia Borgia; Robert Macaire.
     C.M.—Isabella; Barrack Room.
21. *Monday:*
     A.—Critic; Knight of Arva.
     W.—Masks and Faces; All that Glitters is not Gold.
     C.M.—Richard III; An Object of Interest.
22.   A.—Comedy of Errors; Serious Family.
     W.—Pet of the Petticoats; Wandering Minstrel.
     C.M.—Othello; Sketches in India.
23.   A.—Fair American; A New Comedy of Errors.
     W.—Pet of the Petticoats; Toodles.
     C.M.—New Way To Pay Old Debts; Poor Pillicoddy.
24.   A.—Fair American; Irish Lion.
     W.—Money; Eton Boy.
     C.M.—Richelieu; Virginia Mummy.
25.   A.—Lucille; Sweethearts and Wives.
     W.—Masks and Faces; Pet of the Petticoats.
     C.M.—Hamlet; A Kiss in the Dark.
26.   A.—Paul Pry; Dumb Girl of Genoa.
     W.—Rob Roy; Bob Nettles.
     C.M.—*Id.,* May 21.
28. *Monday:*
     A.—Man and Wife; Lucille.
     W.—Macbeth; Married Rake.
     C.M.—Werner; Forty Winks.
29.   A.—Comedy of Errors; Serious Family.
     W.—Robbers; My Aunt.
     C.M.—Macbeth; A Kiss in the Dark.
30.   A.—*Id.,* May 9.
     W.—Speed the Plough; Grist to the Mill.
     C.M.—King Lear; Forty Winks.
31.   A.—Cure for the Heart Ache; Married Life.
     W.—Othello; Perfection.
     C.M.—New Way To Pay Old Debts; Laughing Hyena.

JUNE

1. *Friday:*
     A.—Hypocrite; Child of Nature.
     W.—Jane Shore; Grist to the Mill.
     C.M.—Merchant of Venice; Iron Chest.
2.   A.—Sweethearts and Wives; Dumb Girl of Genoa.
     W.—Hamlet; Used Up.
     C.M.—Richard III; Forty Winks.

4. *Monday:*
    A.—Critic; Knight of Arva.
    W.—Take that Girl away *: *Dangle*—Shewell, *Mrs. Dangle*—
    Miss Bernard; Knight of Arva.
    C.M.—Damon and Pythias; The Crusaders.
5.   A.—Comedy of Errors; Serious Family.
    W.—London Assurance; Wandering Minstrel.
    C.M.—Othello; Charles XII.
6.   A.—Married Life; Lucille.
    W.—Six Degrees of Crime; Take that Girl away.
    C.M.—Honey Moon; Satan in Paris.
7.   A.—Comedy of Errors; Serious Family.
    W.—Cesar de Bazan; Robert Macaire.
    C.M.—Rob Roy; Paddy Miles' Boy.
8.   A.—Way to get Married; Irish Emigrant.
    W.—William Tell; Married Life.
    C.M.—Henry IV; Virginia Mummy.
9.   A.—Wild Oats; Knight of Arva.
    W.—Rob Roy; Take that Girl away.
    C.M.—Virginius; Weathercock.
11. *Monday:*
    A.—As You Like It; Irish Lion.
    W.—Hunchback; Two Buzzards.
    C.M.—Bohemian Girl; Rough Diamond.
12.   A.—Comedy of Errors; Serious Family.
    W.—No advertisement.
    C.M.—Bohemian Girl.
13.   A.—Money; Irish Tutor.
    C.M.—*Id.,* June 2.
14.   A.—John Bull; Toodles.
    C.M.—Daughter of the Regiment; Two Bonnycastles.
    W.—Rivals; Robert Macaire.
15.   A.—*Id.,* June 12.
    C.M.—Daughter of the Regiment; Bohemian Girl, first act.
16.   A.—Stranger; Castle Spectre.
    C.M.—Daughter of the Regiment; Bohemian Girl, second act.
    W.—Andy Blake; Used Up.
18. *Monday:*
    A.—Cure for the Heart Ache; Hypocrite.
    C.M.—Fra Diavolo; Two Bonnycastles.
    W.—Milly; Used Up.
19.   A.—*Id.,* June 12.
    C.M.—Bohemian Girl.
    W.—Love and Money; Andy Blake.
20.   A.—Busy Body; Miseries of Human Life.
    C.M.—Fra Diavolo; Rough Diamond.

W.—Love and Money; Used Up.
21.   A.—*Id.,* June 20.
C.M.—Rob Roy; Hole in the Wall.
W.—Love and Money; Bob Nettles.
22.   A.—Busy Body; Laugh when you Can.
C.M.—Bohemian Girl.
W.—Love and Money; Invisible Prince.
23.   A.—Ingomar; A Roland for an Oliver.
C.M.—Fra Diavolo; Love in all Corners.
W.—Old Guard; Invisible Prince.
25. *Monday:*
A.—Way to get Married; Rory O'More.
C.M.—Fra Diavolo; Bohemian Girl; second and third acts.
W.—Bob Nettles; Invisible Prince.
26.   A.—*Id.,* June 12.
C.M.—Child of the Regiment; Hole in the Wall.
W.—Used Up; Invisible Prince.
27.   A.—Money; Irish Emigrant.
C.M.—Child of the Regiment; Love in all Corners.
W.—Milly; Loan of a Lover.
28.   A.—Irish Ambassador; Hypocrite.
C.M.—Cinderella; Two Bonnycastles.
W.—Swiss Cottage; Betsy Baker.
29.   A.—Heir at Law; Irish Lion.
C.M.—Daughter of the Regiment; Cinderella, first act.
W.—London Assurance; There's Nothing in it.
30.   A.—Perfection; Sketches in India.
C.M.—Wild Oats; Love and Charity.
W.—Young Actress; Andy Blake.

JULY

2. *Monday:*
A.—Nationalities; Who Speaks First?
C.M.—Ireland as it Is; Mischievous Annie.
W.—Maid with the Milking Pail; Old Guard.
3.   A.—Comedy of Errors; Serious Family.
C.M.—Irish Assurance; Mischievous Annie.
W.—Wandering Minstrel; Young Actress.
4.   A.—Nationalities; P.P. Last night of the season.
C.M.—Ireland as it Is; Lessons for Husbands.
W.—Used Up; Young Actress.
5. C.M.—Young Actress; Good for Nothing.
6. C.M.—Shandy Maguire; Mischievous Annie.
7. C.M.—No advertisement.

9. *Monday:*
   W.—An engagement of the Ravel family in ballet.

AUGUST

18. *Saturday:*
    A.—Bold Stroke for a Husband; Toodles.
20. *Monday:*
    A.—Ingomar; Lend Me Five Shillings.
21. A.—Annie Blake *; A Roland for an Oliver.
22. A.—Ingomar; Toodles.
    G.N.—Die Sieben Maecchen in Uniform; Humoristische Studieu.
23. A.—Annie Blake; To Parents and Guardians.
24. A.—Jealous Wife; Sudden Thoughts.
    G.N.—The Prison.
25. A.—Willow Copse; A Roland for an Oliver.
    G.N.—The Circumnavigator against his Will.
27. *Monday:*
    A.—Willow Copse; To Parents and Guardians.
28. A.—Willow Copse; Lend Me Five Shillings.
29. A.—Willow Copse; Sudden Thoughts.
    G.N.—City and Country.
30. A.—Willow Copse; Perfection.
    G.N.—Das Pfefferroisel.
31. A.—Annie Blake; P.P.

SEPTEMBER

1. *Saturday:*
   A.—The Wife; Peggy Green.
3. *Monday:*
   A.—Much Ado about Nothing; Spectre Bridegroom.
4. A.—All that Glitters is not Gold; Laugh when you Can.
5. A.—Hamlet; A Kiss in the Dark.
6. A.—Way to get Married; All that Glitters is not Gold.
   W.—Extremes; Lottery Ticket.
7. A.—Bridal; Sudden Thoughts.
   W.—Sorceress; Lottery Ticket.
8. A.—Bridal; Spectre Bridegroom.
   W.—Blind Man's Daughter; Sorceress.
   C.M.—Married Life; Wanted, One Thousand Milliners.
   G.N.—Richard's Wanderings.
10. *Monday:*
    A.—Bridal; Peggy Green.
    W.—Extremes.

C.M.—Soldier's Daughter; Swiss Swains.
11. A.—Willow Copse; My Neighbor's Wife.
  W.—Star of the North; Three Shaws.
  C.M.—Poor Gentleman; Wanted, One Thousand Milliners.
12. A.—Bridal; My Neighbor's Wife.
  W.—Star of the North; Lottery Ticket.
  C.M.—Married Life; Milliners.
13. A.—Money; Peggy Green.
  W.—Star of the North; Three Shaws.
  C.M.—Soldier's Daughter; Sketches in India.
14. A.—Anne Blake; To Parents and Guardians.
  W.—Magnolia *: *Silvertop*—Richings, *Magnolia*—Miss Richings; Mr. and Mrs. White.
  C.M.—Poor Gentleman; Lottery Ticket.
15. A.—Ingomar; My Neighbor's Wife.
  W.—Love's Sacrifice; Debutante.
  C.M.—David Copperfield; Sketches in India.
17. *Monday:*
  A.—Belle's Stratagem; Rough Diamond.
  W.—Barney, the Baron; Brian O'Lynn.
  C.M.—David Copperfield; How Stout You're Getting.
18. A.—Ion; A Kiss in the Dark.
  W.—Irish Assurance; Our Gal.
  C.M.—*Id.,* Sept. 17.
19. A.—Bold Stroke for a Husband; Love in Livery.
  W.—Patience and Perseverance; Born to Good Luck.
  C.M.—How Stout You're Getting; Milliners.
20. A.—Ion; Scan. Mag.
  W.—Patience and Perseverance; O'Flannigan and the Fairies.
  C.M.—Faint Heart never won Fair Lady; How Stout You're Getting.
21. A.—Cure for the Heart Ache; Satan in Paris.
  W.—Irish Tutor; Patience and Perseverance.
  C.M.—Organic Affection; How Stout You're Getting.
22. A.—Paul Pry; William Tell.
  W.—Shandy Maguire; Patience and Perseverance.
  C.M.—Faint Heart never won Fair Lady; A Glance at Philadelphia.
24. *Monday:*
  A.—Love's Sacrifice; Love in Livery.
  W.—Patience and Perseverance; Brian O'Lynn.
  C.M.—Toodles; A Glance at Philadelphia.
25. A.—Provoked Husband; Satan in Paris.
  W.—Fairy Circle; O'Flannigan and the Fairies.
  C.M.—Forty Winks; A Glance at Philadelphia.
26. A.—Stranger; Honey Moon.

W.—Fairy Circle; Barney, the Baron.
C.M.—Toodles; A Glance at Philadelphia.
27. A.—Merchant of Venice; Scan. Mag.
W.—Fairy Circle; Connecticut Courtship.
C.M.—Poor Gentleman; A Glance at Philadelphia.
28. A.—Annie Blake; All that Glitters is not Gold.
W.—Fairy Circle; Irish Tiger.
C.M.—First Night; A Glance at Philadelphia.
29. A.—Hamlet; Love in Livery.
W.—Much Ado about Nothing; Young Widow.
C.M.—Id., Sept. 28.

OCTOBER

1. *Monday:*
A.—Bridal; Scan. Mag.
W.—Ingomar; Mr. and Mrs. White.
C.M.—Serious Family; A Glance at Philadelphia.
2. A.—Still Waters Run Deep *: *Mildmay*—Conway, *Mrs. Mildmay*—Mrs. Conway; P.P.
W.—Hunchback; Three Shaws.
C.M.—Id., Oct. 1.
3. A.—Still Waters Run Deep; A Thumping Legacy.
W.—Camille.
C.M.—Id., Sept. 28.
4. A.—Still Waters Run Deep; Irish Secretary.
W.—Camille.
C.M.—Heir at Law; A Glance at Philadelphia.
5. A.—Still Waters Run Deep; To Parents and Guardians.
W.—Camille.
C.M.—Toodles; Organic Affection.
6. A.—Still Waters Run Deep; Scan. Mag.
W.—Camille.
C.M.—Paul Pry; A Glance at Philadelphia.
8. *Monday:*
A.—Still Waters Run Deep; My Neighbor's Wife.
W.—Hamlet; Mr. and Mrs. White.
C.M.—Heir at Law; Serious Family.
9. A.—Wild Oats; Scan. Mag.
W.—Richard III; Lottery Ticket.
C.M.—No advertisement.
10. A.—Still Waters Run Deep; A Thumping Legacy.
W.—Francesca da Rimini *: *Malatesta*—B. Young, *Lanciotto* —E. L. Davenport, *Pepe*—Perry, *Guido da Pelenta*— Hield, *Francesca*—Mrs. (J.) Drew, *Paolo*—A. H. Davenport; Three Shaws.

[535]

C.M.—No advertisement.

11. A.—Still Waters Run Deep; John Dobbs.
W.—Francesca da Rimini; Young Widow.
G.N.—Marianna, a Woman of the People.

12. A.—Still Waters Run Deep; Jacobite.
W.—Francesca da Rimini; William Tell.
C.M.—Watchman; Debutante.

13. A.—*Id.,* Oct. 12.
W.—*Id.,* Oct 12.
C.M.—Watchman; A Glance at Philadelphia.

15. *Monday:*
A.—*Id.,* Oct. 12.
W.—Beauty and the Beast; Rough Diamond.
C.M.—No advertisement. Theatre closed one week for redecoration.

16. A.—*Id.,* Oct. 12.
W.—*Id.,* Oct. 15.
G.N.—Hinko.

17. A.—*Id.,* Oct. 6.
W.—Beauty and the Beast; Loan of a Lover.

18. A.—Still Waters Run Deep; Irish Secretary.
W.—Beauty and the Beast; Love and Murder.

19. A.—Still Waters Run Deep; Deaf as a Post.
W.—Beauty and the Beast; Young Widow.

20. A.—Still Waters Run Deep; Sweethearts and Wives.
W.—Beauty and the Beast; Two Gregories.
C.M.—The Wife; Mehittable Ann.

22. *Monday:*
A.—Still Waters Run Deep; Paul Pry.
W.—Beauty and the Beast; Wandering Minstrel.
C.M.—Othello; Mehittable Ann.

23. A.—Still Waters Run Deep; Laugh when you Can.
W.—*Id.,* Oct. 22.
C.M.—Richard III; Lottery Ticket.

24. A.—Still Waters Run Deep; Simpson and Co.
W.—*Id.,* Oct. 19.
C.M.—Werner; Loan of a Lover.

25. A.—*Id.,* Oct. 19.
W.—Beauty and the Beast; Perfection.
C.M.—*Id.,* Oct. 24.

26. A.—*Id.,* Oct. 20.
W.—Faint Heart never won Fair Lady; Day after the Wedding.
C.M.—King of the Commons; Mehittable Ann.

27. A.—*Stranger;* Honey Moon.
W.—My Neighbor's Wife; New Footman.

C.M.—*Id.,* Oct. 26.
29. *Monday:*
  A.—Hamlet; My Neighbor's Wife.
  W.—Still Waters Run Deep; The Two Gregories.
  C.M.—Hamlet; Mehittable Ann.
30. A.—Still Waters Run Deep; Turning the Tables.
  W.—Still Waters Run Deep; Two Gregories.
  C.M.—Hunchback; All the World's a Stage.
31. A.—Werner; Love in Livery.
  W.—Still Waters Run Deep; Married Rake.
  C.M.—Macbeth; All the World's a Stage.

NOVEMBER

1. *Thursday:*
  A.—Still Waters Run Deep; Faint Heart never won Fair Lady.
  W.—Still Waters Run Deep; Mother and Child are Doing Well.
  C.M.—*Id.,* Oct. 31.
2. A.—Werner; Lend Me Five Shillings.
  W.—Still Waters Run Deep; Eton Boy.
  C.M.—Stranger; Pizarro.
3. A.—Werner; Scan. Mag.
  W.—Still Waters Run Deep; Masks and Faces.
  C.M.—King of the Commons; Loan of a Lover.
5. *Monday:*
  A.—Lady of Lyons; Toodles.
  W.—Serious Family; Black-Eyed Susan.
  C.M.—New Way To Pay Old Debts; In and Out of Place.
6. A.—Fazio; Paul Pry.
  W.—Serious Family; Sweethearts and Wives.
  C.M.—Merchant of Venice; In and Out of Place.
7. A.—Hunchback; Irish Secretary.
  W.—Serious Family; Rory O'More.
  C.M.—King Lear; The Secret.
8. A.—The Wife; Jacobite.
  W.—Serious Family; Toodles.
  C.M.—Richelieu; The Secret.
9. A.—Jane Shore; Simpson and Co.
  W.—Knight of Arva; Good for Nothing.
  C.M.—Richard III; All the World's a Stage.
10. A.—Stranger; Honey Moon.
  W.—Knight of Arva; Serious Family.
  C.M.—Richard III; Simpson and Co.

12. *Monday:*
    A.—The Man of many Friends *: *Popples*—J. S. Clarke, *Mrs. Popples*—Mrs. Conway; Time Tries All.
    W.—Naval Engagements; Eton Boy.
    C.M.—Janet Pride; Young Widow.

13.   A.—Man of many Friends; Still Waters Run Deep.
    W.—Masks and Faces; Mother and Child are Doing Well.
    C.M.—Janet Pride; Poor Pillicoddy.

14.   A.—Werner; Thumping Legacy.
    W.—Pet of the Petticoats; Blue Devils.
    C.M.—*Id.,* Nov. 12.

15.   A.—Love's Sacrifice; Sudden Thoughts.
    W.—Grist to the Mill; Mr. and Mrs. White.
    C.M.—Old Heads and Young Hearts; Poor Pillicoddy.

16.   A.—Hunchback; Turning the Tables.
    W.—Time Tries All; Poor Pillicoddy.
    C.M.—Pride of the Market; Bob Nettles.

17.   A.—Jane Shore; Spectre Bridegroom.
    W.—Naval Engagements; Pet of the Petticoats.
    C.M.—Loan of a Lover; First Night.

19. *Monday:*
    A.—Queensbury Fete; Madelaine.
    W.—Les Horaces; Le Depit Amoureux.
    C.M.—Much Ado about Nothing; Lottery Ticket.

20.   A.—Still Waters Run Deep; Madelaine.
    W.—Angelo, the Tyrant of Padua; La Ligne Droite.
    C.M.—Money; Secret.

21.   A.—Queensbury Fete; Man of many Friends.
    W.—Naval Engagements; Les Droits de l'homme.
    C.M.—Hamlet; Mehittable Ann.

22.   A.—*Id.,* Nov. 13.
    W.—Pet of the Petticoats; Les Droits de l'Homme.
    C.M.—Lady of Lyons; Young Widow.

23.   A.—Masks and Faces; Time Tries All.
    W.—Blue Devils; Chapeau d'un Horloger.
    C.M.—Stranger; Katharine and Petruchio.

24.   A.—Richelieu; Sketches in India.
    W.—Masks and Faces; Le Tartuffe.
    C.M.—Romeo and Juliet; Simpson and Co.

26. *Monday:*
    A.—Romeo and Juliet; Turning the Tables.
    W.—No performance.
    C.M.—Hamlet; Young Widow.

27.   A.—*Id.,* Nov. 13.
    W.—Irish Ambassador; Poor Pillicoddy.
    C.M.—Lady of Lyons; My Aunt.

28. A.—*Id.,* Nov. 24.
  W.—Nervous Man; Happy Man.
  C.M.—Robbers; My Fellow Clerk.
29. A.—Masks and Faces; Madelaine.
  W.—Born to Good Luck; How to pay Rent.
  C.M.—Wild Oats; My Fellow Clerk.
30. A.—Macbeth; Four Sisters.
  W.—Irish Genius; Irish Ambassador.
  C.M.—Money; Dramatist.

DECEMBER

1. *Saturday:*
  A.—Macbeth; Four Sisters.
  W.—Irish Genius; Born to Good Luck.
  C.M.—Robbers; Rough Diamond.
3. *Monday:*
  A.—Plot and Passion; Queensbury Fete.
  W.—Nervous Man; Wrong Passenger.
  C.M.—De Soto; My Fellow Clerk.
4. A.—Plot and Passion; Still Waters Run Deep.
  W.—Irish Fortune Hunter; Happy Man.
  C.M.—De Soto; Poor Pillicoddy.
5. A.—School of Reform; Therese.
  W.—Serious Family; Teddy the Tiler.
  C.M.—De Soto; Little Treasure.
6. A.—Love Chase; Therese.
  W.—Paul Pry; Irish Genius.
  C.M.—De Soto; Little Treasure.
7. A.—School of Reform; Plot and Passion.
  W.—Serious Family; Love and Murder.
  C.M,—De Soto; My Aunt.
8, A,—Romeo and Juliet; Alarming Sacrifice.
  W.—Irish Ambassador; Irish Genius.
  C.M.—De Soto; Little Treasure.
10. *Monday:*
  A.—Still Waters Run Deep; Pizarro.
  W.—Othello; Two Gregories.
  C.M.—*Id.,* Dec. 8.
11. A.—Annie Blake; Pizarro.
  W.—Pizarro; Mr. and Mrs. White.
  C.M.—De Soto; Critic.
12. A.—Camille; A Roland for an Oliver.
  W.—Richelieu; Three Shaws.
  C.M.—Hamlet; My Fellow Clerk.
13. A.—Camille; Morning Call.

W.—Hamlet; Love and Murder.
C.M.—Wine Works Wonders; Dramatist.

14.   A.—*Id.,* Nov. 13.
W.—Damon and Pythias; Don't Judge by Appearances.
C.M.—Stranger; Critic.

15.   A.—Damon and Pythias; Toodles.
W.—Pizarro; Don't Judge by Appearances.
C.M.—De Soto; Wine Works Wonders.

17. *Monday:*
A.—Camille; Scan. Mag.
W.—Jack Cade; Poor Pillicoddy.
C.M.—Virginius; Pirate's Legacy.

18.   A.—Richard III; Married Rake.
W.—Jack Cade; Married Rake.
C.M.—Cricket on the Hearth; How Stout You're Getting.

19.   A.—Wild Oats; Queensbury Fete.
W.—Richard III; Don't Judge by Appearances.
C.M.—Janet Pride; Virginia Mummy.

20.   A.—Serious Family; Still Waters Run Deep.
W.—Richelieu; Spectre Bridegroom.
C.M.—No advertisement.

21.   A.—Cure for the Heart Ache; Lucretia Borgia.
W.—Damon and Pythias; Nature and Philosophy.
C.M.—Damon and Pythias; How Stout You're Getting.

22.   A.—Camille; Sudden Thoughts.
W.—Jack Cade; Family Jars.
C.M.—Old Heads and Young Hearts; Rough Diamond.

24. *Monday:*
A.—Corsican Brothers.
W.—Metamora; Family Jars.
C.M.—Ireland as it Is; Irish Tiger.

25.   A.—*Id.,* Dec. 24.
W.—Metamora; Don't Judge by Appearances.
C.M.—Ireland and America; Irish Tiger.

26.   A.—*Id.,* Dec. 24.
W.—Macbeth; Love and Murder.
C.M.—*Id.,* Dec. 25.

27.   A.—*Id.,* Dec. 24.
W.—Gladiator; Young Widow.
C.M.—Ireland and America; Limerick Boy.

28.   A.—*Id.,* Dec. 24.
W.—Virginius; Caught in a Trap.
C.M.—Ireland and America; The Irish Know Nothing.

29.   A.—Corsican Brothers; Alarming Sacrifice.
W.—Gladiator; Family Jars.
C.M.—Irish Assurance; The Irish Know Nothing.

31. *Monday:*
    A.—Corsican Brothers; A Kiss in the Dark.
    W.—Irish Emigrant; Fortunio.
    C.M.—Shandy Maguire; Irish Tiger.

THE PLAY LIST

THE PLAY LIST

THE following list of plays is presented in compact form and therefore has required abbreviation and punctuation which demand explanation.

Parentheses are used to enclose three kinds of recorded material: first, the year of the nineteenth century when the play was performed, (35) representing 1835; second, the name of an author when it is necessary to show that it is not certain whether the author named wrote the play whose performance is recorded, such as (by John Jones); and third, variant spelling of the play-titles, such as *The Mayor of Garrat*(*t*), to signify that the name was spelled in both ways on different occasions.

Quotation marks are used to enclose comments on authorship made by the theatrical advertisements in the newspapers for the day of performance.

Commas and semi-colons are used after the notice of the year to separate days and months, respectively; and semi-colons are used also to separate years. Numerals represent the months of the year. Asterisks note first performances in Philadelphia.

A hypothetical entry will serve best to acquaint the reader with a working knowledge of this system of recording:

The Man of Townl(e)y, or The Season; "adapted from the novel of the same name by a gentleman of this city," comedy (by Brown White). (45) C.-4.10 *, 16, 19; 6.5; W.-8.7; (46) A.-1.10.

Interpreted, this recording means that *Townley* sometimes appeared with one less letter; and that the authorship of the play is uncertain, for the newspapers say only that a gentleman of Philadelphia wrote the work. For good reasons, the present recorder suggests the name of Brown White but makes allowance for the existence of a doubt. We can be sure, however, that a play called *The Man of Townley* appeared for the first time in Philadelphia at the Chesnut Street Theatre, April 10, 1845, remaining for April 16 and 19, and returning to the Chesnut for June 5 and to the Walnut for August 8. Next year, the play appeared at the Arch Street Theatre, January 10.

Abaellino, the Great Bandit; Wm. Dunlap: (35) P.-12.24, 26, 27.

Abd-el Kader, or The French in Algiers: (46) A.-1.17, 19, 20, 21.

Agustus Durance, or The Life of a Gambler: (46) P.M.-12.4, 14.

Aladdin, or The Wonderful Lamp; operatic piece: (35) W.-10.12, 13; (42) C.-1.1; 10.25; 11.24; (44) C.-11.23; (46) A.-12.10, 11, 12; (47) A.-1.1.

Alarming Sacrifice; farce: (50) W.-4.12, 13, 15, 16, 23, 27; C.-4.12, 13, 25; W.-5.22; 6.6; 9.27; 10.1; 11.20, 28; 12.4; (51) W.-6.5, 24; (52) C.-10.5, 6, 18; 11.17; 12.30; (53) A.-1.10, 12, 25; W.-2.11; 3.11; A.-3.15, 23; W.-4.27; A.-4.27; W.-12.6, 13; (54) W.-2.14, 27; C.-5.17, 23; (55) A.-12.8, 29.

Alberti Contradini, or The Dumb Brigand's Revenge; romantic melodrama: (35) W.-4.6.

Aldgate Pump; farce: (41) C.-10.13, 22, 26.

Alexander the Great, or The Rival Queen; tragedy, Lee: (35) W.-9.14; (36) C.-1.16; (41) N.-10.15; (42) A.-7.2, 22; (44) N.-2.24; (45) A.-10.18, 30; (47) W.-1.1.

Alfonso, or The Patriot Father; tragedy: (42) A.-6.10, 13, 30.

Alias La Sonnambula; see *The Roof Scrambler.*

Alice Gray, or The Band of Crime: (40) W.-2.28; 3.2; (43) W.-1.9, 21, 23; 3.3.

Aline; domestic drama: (53) A.-10.21, 22, 25; 12.7.

Alive and Kicking: (50) A.-11.28; (51) A.-11.11; (54) W.-6.9.

All at Coventry, or Love and Laugh: (35) C.-1.4*, 7.

All in the Dark; see *Rendezvous.*

All in the Downs; see *Black Eyed Susan.*

All in the Wrong; farce, Murphy: (35) C.-2.11, 18; 9.29; (36) A.-5.25; (45) W.-2.19.

All that Glitters is not Gold; domestic drama: (51) W.-3.14, 15, 16, 18, 19, 20, 21, 22, 24, 25; 4.1, 30; 5.1, 14; B.-5.12, 13, 14, 15, 16, 31; A.-7.9, 11, 12, 23; W.-8.25; A.-9.2, 3, 65; W.-10.2, 30; B.-10.10, 11, 13, 14, 15, 16, 17, 18; W.-11.14; B.-11.29; W.-12.4, 22; (52) W.-1.8, 27; 3.12, 23; 4.17, 27; 5.20; (53) A.-1.14; W.-1.24; 3.28; A.-9.26; 10.17; (54) C.-1.19, 24; A.-2.14, 25; 3.11, 15; C.-5.6; W.-5.12; 6.14; C.M.-9.14; C.-11.4; W.-12.15; (55) C.-2.17; W.-5.21; A.-9.4, 6, 28.

All the World's a Stage: (35) C.-12.31; (53) C.-6.2; (55) C.M.-10.30, 31; 11.1, 9.

Allow Me to Apologize: (51) W.-3.28, 31; 4.2, 7, 16; 6.9.

Alma Mater: (43) W.-2.2, 3, 4, 6, 9.

Alonzo the Brave and the Fair Imogene, or The Spectre Bride; by T. C. Dibdin: (35) P.-11.21.

Alpine Hunters, or The Fatal Ravine: (40) W.-7.24; (42) W.-4.8; A.-5.12.

Alpine Maid: (46) P.M.-6.22, 26; 7.4, 13; (47) P.M.-2.16; 6.2, 23; 7.13; (48) A.-10.30; (50) A.-7.25; (54) C.-5.11, 12.

Alvardo of Spain; tragedy, A. N. H. Bannister: (37) W.-9.2.

Amaldi, or The Brigand's Daughter; melodrama by James Rees: (42) A.-4.14*, 15, 20.

Amateur Actors: (38) C.-6.21.

Amateurs and Actors: (39) W.-6.29; (40) W.-1.13; (44) A.-9.14.

Amazing Sacrifice: (50) W.-5.30.

The Amazon Sisters, or The Heroines of Mont Blanc: (35) W.-1.7; 3.5.

Ambition, Crime, and Retribution: (55) C.-4.20.

Ambrose Gwinett, or A Tale of the Seaside; melodrama: (35) W.-12.5; (36) W.-2.18, 23; (40) W.-3.21, 26; (36) P.-11.25; (37) P.-1.5; 2.11; (40) W.-5.7; (44) A.-1.25; 8.24;

(45) A.-8.12, 28; (46) A.-3.3; (49) C.-8.23; (50) A.-8.1; (51) N.-7.31; (52) N.-5.26.

American Courage Triumphant; see *Siege of Tripoli.*

American Enterprize, or Yankee Tars Always on Hand: (43) W.-3.2, 4; 7.4; (45) W.-5.3, 9, 26.

American Farmer; see *Yankee in Jersey.*

American Farmers; see *Forest Rose.*

American Manager; see *XYZ.*

American Sea Serpent; see *Deep, Deep Sea.*

American Tar, The; S. H. Rowson: (35) C.-9.30.

The American Tar's Fidelity; see *Star Spangled Banner.*

American Valor: (44) W.-1.27.

Amilie, or The Love Test; opera: (38) W.-11.19, 20, 21, 22, 23, 24, 26, 27, 28, 29, 30; 12.1; (39) C.-1.18, 19, 22, 23, 24, 26; 4.18, 20, 23; (51) W.-12.2, 4.

L'Amour, or Wine No Poison; pantomime ballet: (37) W.-7.17.

Anaconda, or The Serpent of Ceylon: (46) A.-4.25, 27, 28, 29, 30.

The Anatomist; by Edward Ravenscroft: (42) W.-11.12, 17.

Andreas Zell, or The Death Struggle; historical drama: (35) C.-9.17, 19, 20, 21; (41) A.-1.11; (48) A.-9.12.

Andy Blake, or The Irish Diamond; comedy, (D. Boucicault): (54) C.-4.12, 13, 19, 27; W.-11.24; 12.7; (55) W.-6.16, 19, 30.

Angel of the Attic: (47) W.-10.11; (48) W.-3.8; (52) A.-4.10.

Angelo, the Tyrant of Padua; tragedy: (51) W.-9.8, 9; (55) W.-11.20.

Animal Magnetism; farce, by Mrs. Inchbald: (35) C.-5.8, 9.28; (37) C.-1.10, 16; 10.13; A.-7.7, 1; C.-11.23; 12.6; (40) C.-9.28; 10.8; (41) C.-

10.19, 23; (41) N.-8.28; 9.2; W.-11.9, 10, 13; (42) A.-8.9; (44) A.-1.1, 22; (45) W.-12.1, 2, 8; (48) A.-1.26, 2.24; (49) Ath.-1.8, 19.

Ann Boleyn: (39) W.-9.10, 14.

Anna Bolena: (43) C.-10.7, 9, 12, 13; (44) C.-4.11, 12, 16, 17, 18, 19; (47) W.-12.3.

Annie Blake, or The Poor Dependant; (domestic drama), Rev. W. Marston: (55) A.-8.21, 23, 31; 9.14, 28; 12.11.

Anthony Wayne and his Terrific Horse Devildare; (James Rees): (45) N.-5.3, 5.

Antigone: (45) A.-6.16, 17.

Antony and Cleopatra; burletta by J. M. Field: (43) W.-9.26; (44) N.-5.20, 21, 23; (47) A.-10.20; (49) A.-4.14; W.-5.19; A.-12.17, 22.

Apollo in New York; comedy by D. Boucicault: (54) W.-11.27*, 28, 29, 30; 12.1, 4, 5.

The Apostate; tragedy by R. L. Sheil: (35) W.-2.20; 3.20; (36) W.-1.15; 6.1; 9.14; (37) W.-7.14; 12.12; (38) W.-2.17; 7.11; (39) W.-7.3; (37) C.-2.3; 12.22; (40) W.-6.19; (42) W.-4.21; 5.25; (43) A.-10.16; (44) A.-1.17; W.-1.27, 30; 3.26; 6.5; A.-8.27; (46) W.-5.13; 7.28; (47) W.-4.22; (48) A.-3.16; (49) C.-10.10; (50) A.-5.21; W.-9.13, 16; (51) C.-2.22; B.-3.13; C.-9.13, 20; (52) C.-1.17; 5.15; A.-11.4; (54) C.-4.3; A.-9.16, 20; (55) A.-1.24; 2.2, 16.

Arab Chief, or Pirate of the East; melodrama in three acts by H. J. Conway: (35) W.-10.28, 31; 11.6; (36) W.-1.4.

Arabs of the Desert: (49) W.-2.24, 26, 27, 28.

The Arab of the Niger; see *Mungo Park.*

Arabella, or The Discarded Child: (35) C.-3.3.

Arcade; farce, (John Brougham):
(46) C.-1.5, 6, 14.

The Arch in an Uproar: (53) A.-1.11.

*Archibald of the Wreck, or The Press
Gang:* (40) W.-11.25; 12.1.

*Arde(s)chi, or The Gamester of Mi-
lan:* (35) W.-4.8; (36) A.-3.5.

Aristocracy and Democracy: (51) B.-
1.20.

*Armand, or The Peer and the Peas-
ant;* by Mrs. A. C. O. Mowatt
Ritchie: (51) C.-10.15, 17, 18; (54)
C.-3.17, 18.

Artaxerxes: (40) N.-1.18, 19.

Artisan of Lyons: (46) A.-1.1, 2, 3, 15.

Artist's Wife; comedy: (40) C.-3.20,
21; N.-10.16; (46) W.-12.1, 26; (47)
W.1.26; (50) A.-6.13; (52) A.-
3.5, 9.

Artful Dodger; by J. M. Field: (43)
W.-9.15*, 20, 23, 27; 10.5; (47) A.-
5.19, 20, 21; 8.26, 28; 9.4; (48) W.-
7.10, 11; (49) P.M.-7.2, 3, 28.

As like as Two Peas: (54) C.M.-
10.18, 19; 11.15; 12.5, 13; W.-12.23,
27; (55) C.M.-3.26; W.-4.2; C.M.-
4.16, 19; 5.1.

As You Like It; William Shakespeare:
(35) C.-1.28; 5.6; 10.2; (37) C.-1.3;
4.19; 9.26; (39) C.-5.25; (40) C.-
5.15; (37) A.-6.12; (39) W.-5.13;
(42) W.-11.15; (44) W.-4.12, 19;
(45) C.-9.19, 24; (46) W.-6.26;
9.21; (47) A.-1.22; (49) W.-5.22;
A.-8.16; W.-10.30; (50) A.-6.7; W.-
8.19; 10.30; (51) C.-10.13; 12.12;
(42) W.-3.8; 4.22; C.-4.28; 11.29;
(53) A.-3.15; 4.11; (54) A.-4.3, 4,
5, 6, 7, 8, 24; W.-8.30; C.M.-9.13;
(55) A.-2.5, 10; W.-3.26; A.-6.11.

Ask no Questions; farce: (39) W.-
9.17, 26; (43) W.-4.10; (49) A.-5.10,
22; 6.8; 11.12; (52) C.-11.24, 26;
(53) C.-2.4.

Asmodeus; see *The Little Devil's
Share.*

Asmodeus in Paris: (46) P.M.-7.20,
21, 24.

A. S. S.; farce: (53) A.-9.16, 19, 21, 27;
11.7.

Assassin King: (43) A.-4.29.

Astarte: (51) A.-6.6.

Astrologer; farce: (48) A.-6.16, 17.

The Assassin Laborer; see *The White
Farm.*

Athenian Captive; by Sergeant Talfourd: (38) W.-9.19*, 21.

The Attic(k) Story: (47) P.M.-4.16;
(49) P.M.-5.11, 12.

Attila the Hun; see *Roman Tribute.*

The Auberge Des Adrets; see *Robert
Macaire.*

Austerlitz; see *Battle of Austerlitz.*

Avarice: (41) W.-5.26.

*The Avenger, or The Leaguers of
Austria:* (42) C.-1.14.

The Avenger, or The Moor of Sicily;
see *John De Procida:* (44) A.-2.16,
17; (46) A.-4.23; (49) A.-1.19.

*Avenger of Blood, or Richard Hurdis
and the Idiot Girl:* (38) W.-10.10*,
11; 11.6, 7, 8, 10, 13; (41) W.-5.8,
10, 11, 12, 13, 17.

The Avenger's Vow; (C. P. Clinch):
(50) A.-10.5; 11.6.

An Awful Verdict; farce: (50) C.-
5.15, 16.

Aylmere; see *Jack Cade.*

Azael, the Prodigal Son, by C. P.
Ware: (51) A.-6.26, 27, 28, 30; 7.1,
2, 3, 5; C.-8.18, 19, 20, 21, 22, 23, 25,
26, 27, 28, 29, 30; 9.1, 2, 6; 12.22, 23,
24, 25.

Ba! Ba! Ba!; see *The Village Lawyer.*

Bachelor's Buttons; farce: (39) W.-
12.9, 10; (40) W.-3.17; C.-4.6.

Bachelor of Arts; (John Brougham):
(54) C.-8.15, 16.

Backwoodsman: (47) W.-4.22, 24;
(55) C.-1.31; 2.1.

Ball of Death; see *Bull Fighter of Spain.*

Bam Boozling: (44) C.-10.24, 25; 12.12, 13; (46) P.M.-9.22, 23; 11.18; 12.18; (47) P.M.-5.19, 22, 31; (48) A.-8.4, 7; (52) W.-2.7; C.-8.4, 16; W.-9.7, 11; 10.27; 11.17; (53) C.-7.4; (54) W.-6.15, 23; C.-10.4; (55) C.-2.6.

The Band of Crime; see *Alice Gray.*

Bandit Dost, or The Hut in the Swamp: (39) W.-9.7.

The Bandit Merchant; see *Dumb Girl of Genoa.*

Bandit of Corsica: (43) A.-3.18.

The Bandit's Daughter; see *Rinaldo Rinaldini.*

The Bandit's Doom; see *The Lion King.*

Banished Star: (40) C.-12.23; (41) N.-11.8.

The Bank Monster, or Specie vs. Shinplaster; by S. S. Steele: (41) A.-9.20*, 24, 25, 30; (42) A.-4.27.

The Banker, or a Friend in Need; a comedy by the author of *Abduction, Kate Kearney,* and *The Queen's Necklace:* (42) C.-10.24, 25; 11.22.

Bank Clerk: (45) A.-7.12, 15; (46) A.-1.23.

Banker's Clerk: (44) A.-8.30.

Banker's Wife: (51) C.-12.19, 20; (52) W.-4.30; 5.1; C.-12.2, 4.

The Bankrupt's Wife; see *Remorse.*

Barbarossa; tragedy by John Brown: (35) W.-3.19.

Barber of Seville; opera by Rossini: (36) C.-1.26; 2.3; (38) C.-2.12, 19; (36) A.-4.29; (38) A.-3.5; (42) C.-12.7, 8, 9, 28; (44) C.-4.4; (47) W.-10.15, 16.

The Barbers at Court; farce: (37) C.-10.19*, 20, 23, 26; 11.3, 22; (38) C.-1.1, 2.2, 16; 3.10; 4.10; 5.14; 6.22; (39) C.-1.30; 2.19.

Barnaby Rudge: (41) N.-9.27, 28; 10.1; (41) C.-9.27, 28, 29, 30; 10.2.

Barney, the Baron: (53) W.-10.24; (54) W.-5.15, 17; 6.1; (55) W.-9.17, 26.

Barrack Room; farce: (37) C.-4.25*, 29; 9.25; (38) C.-10.10, 11, 16; (39) C.-5.11, 17; (37) A.-6.9, 15; (41) A.-5.21; (39) C.-5.25; 6.11; 10.15; 11.2; (42) W.-7.16; 10.1; (44) A.-1.10; (47) A.-12.15; (48) A.-3.20; W.-5.10, 11; P.M.-5.20; A.-5.16; 10.19; (49) A.-3.22; (50) A.-4.11, 16; B.-10.7; 11.11, 12, 27; 12.10; (51) B.-5.5; A.-12.22; (55) C.M.-5.19.

Bashful Irishman: (46) P.M.-10.21, 22; (51) A.-2.10; (53) A.-10.6; (54) W.-6.5.

Bath Road, or Married Yesterday; see *My Wife and I.*

Bathing: (44) A.-6.18, 25; 7.13.

Battle of Algiers; melodrama: (38) C.-5.31.

The Battle of Austerlitz; melodrama: (39) W.-11.19, 20, 21, 22; (40) W.-3.23, 25; (41) N.-7.5; (44) A.-2.13, 14; (45) W.-7.1.

The Battle of Bosworth Field; see *Richard III.*

Battle of Buena Vista: (53) A.-2.3*, 5.

The Battle of Chippewa; see *She Would be a Soldier.*

The Battle of Flodden Field; see *Marmion.*

The Battle of Germantown, or A Tale of Tracy's Rangers; national drama (by Walter Leman): (45) W.-4.10, 11, 12; 6.26; 7.9, 25; 8.14; (46) W.-1.9; 4.3; (47) W.-3.11.

The Battle of Life: (47) P.M.-2.3, 4, 5, 6, 9, 10, 13; W.-2.9; 3.4; P.M.-3.19, 20, 26, 31; 5.10, 28.

The Battle of New Orleans; (William Dunlap or C. E. Grice): (42) W.-1.8.

The Battle of Poictiers, or The Knights of the Garter; by W. Barrymore:

(38) W.-2.19, 20, 21, 22, 23, 24; 3.1.

The Battle of Sedgemoor, or Days of Kirkwood and Monmouth: (37) W.-12.2, 7, 19.

The Battle of the Thames; see *Tecumseh.*

The Battle of Tippecanoe; by S. S. Steele: (40) P.-8.19*, 20, 21.

Bayonet: (44) N.-1.4, 5; 2.12.

The Beacon of Death, or The Norwegian Wrecker: (42) W.-7.14; (46) A.-2.18, 20, 24; (55) C.-2.3.

The Bear Hunters; by J. B. Buckstone: (46) A.-2.25*.

Bears not Beasts: (46) W.-7.3, 6, 28.

Beauty and the Beast: (44) A.-7.1, 2, 3, 4, 6, 15; W.-7.4, 6, 8; A.-8.2, 7; 10.3, 4, 8, 9, 10, 11; W.-10.5, 7, 8, 9; 12.17; (45) A.-4.14, 15, 21; (46) P.M.-7.2, 3, 6, 7, 8, 9, 10; 8.10, 14; A.-9.15, 16, 17; 10.14; 11.26; 12.1; (47) A.-1.8; P.M.-3.20, 23, 24, 27; 4.2; A.-7.15; (48) A.-4.6, 7, 14; (49) P.M.-6.4, 5; (52) N.-10.12, 13, 14, 15, 16; (55) W.-10.15, 16, 17, 18, 19, 20, 21, 22, 23, 24, 25.

Beaux Stratagem; by George Farquhar: (44) W.-4.1.

Bedouin Arabs; ballet pantomime by the Ravel Family: (36) C.-12.26, 30, 31; (37) C.-1.28; 2.1, 6; A.-6.22, 24; 7.1.

The Bee and the Orange Tree, or The Four Wishes: (48) A.-5.25, 26.

The Beehive, or Industry Must Prosper; operatic farce: (37) W.-12.18; (38) W.-1.16, 25; (40)-7.22.

The Beggar of Bethnal Green; see *The Blind Beggar of Bethnal Green;* by James S. Knowles: (35) A.-2.28.

Beggar of Cripplegate: (35) W.-1.9*, 10.

Beggar on Horseback: (46) A.-5.20, 22.

Beggar's Opera; by John Gay: (54) W.-11.15, 18; (55) W.-2.22.

Begone Dull Care; comedy by Frederick Reynolds: (40) W.-4.13, 14; (42) A.-11.8; (43) W.-7.8; (44) W.-4.26.

Belford Castle, or The Scottish Gold Mine; comedy: (42) C.-9.24, 26, 27.

Belisario: (43) C.-7.29; 11.17, 18.

Bellamira; tragedy (by Sir Charles Sedley): (42) A.-11.4; (45) A.-10.28, 29.

Belle of the Hotel: (42) W.-7.19, 23.

Belle's Stratagem; by Mrs. Cowley: (35) C.-2.4; 4.10; (36) C.-9.10; (37) C.-1.6, 21; (36) A.-5.21; (37) A.-6.9; (37) C.-4.26; (39) C.-9.11; 10.14; (40) W.-10.23; (42) A.-9.21; W.-9.22; (43) W.-6.30; (44) W.-2.6; (45) W.-8.14; (48) W.-1.11; (50) A.-3.25; W.-4.25, 5.28, 8.20; (51) W.-3.12; C.-3.14; (52) C.-4.27; 11.13; (53) W.-1.3; A.-3.14; 4.1; 5.12; (54) A.-3.29, 31; 4.10; 10.4; 12.20; (55) A.-9.17.

Belphegor; romantic drama by B. N. Webster: (51) W.-3.21, 22; B.-4.15, 16, 17, 18.

Ben Bolt: (54) A.-11.15, 20, 22, 23, 25, 28; 12.4; (55) A.-2.6, 21; 3.3.

Ben the Boatswain, or Sailors' Sweethearts; comedy: (40) A.-12.11, 17, 21; (42) A.-10.10; (44) W.-2.22, 23; N.-3.4, 5, 6; 4.13; W.-5.18; (45) W.-5.10, 13, 25; 11.19; (51) A.-10.25, 27.

Benevolent Tar: (43) A.-3.17, 4.3.

Bengal Tiger: (38) C.-5.12; (40) C.-6.8.

Benjamin Franklin, or The Days of 1776: (49) C.-10.24*, 25, 26, 27, 29, 30.

Bertram, or The Castle of St. Aldobrand; a tragedy (by W. G. Simms): (35) C.-9.26; 12.3; (39) W.-8.12; (42) W.-4.19, 23; (44) W.-6.4, 29; 10.23; (45) W.-3.27; 5.29; 8.9; 10.14; 12.16; (46) A.-1.6; W.-3.14;

(47) A.-4.15; (48) W.-3.15; (49) W.-6.21; (52) C.-1.21; A.-11.20; W.-12.3; (54) W.-9.5.

The Betrothal; by G. H. Boker: (50) W.-9.25*, 26, 27, 28, 30; 10.1, 2, 3, 4, 5; (51) W.-4.15, 16, 17, 18, 19; 12.5, 11; (53) W.-5.7.

Betsy Baker; see *My Precious Betsy.*

Beulah Spa: (35) W.-3.5*, 6, 30; 4.4; (46) P.M.-8.11, 15.

Beware a Bad Name; see *Mr. H.*

Bewitched: (45) A.-5.2.

Bianca Visconti, or The Heart Over-tasked; by N. P. Willis: (37) C.-12.27*, 29; (52) C.-5.10.

Bibboo, the Island Ape; pantomime: (41) W.-9.22, 23; 11.27; (50) A.-6.19.

Biena, or The Maid of Cadiz and the Man of Kent: (35) W.-9.16*, 17; (36) W.-11.16.

Bill Jones: (45) A.-9.13, 15, 16, 19; 11.1.

Bill Stickers and the Jersey Girl; domestic drama: (41) A.-10.7*, 8, 9, 11, 12, 13; (41) W.-10.9, 11, 30; 11.3; (42) W.-2.5; A.-7.30, 10.8.

Billy Button, or The Hunted Tailor; farce: (35) Mammoth Circus-1.5, 2.20; (39) W.-3.8, 9, 13; (40) W.-1.1, 2, 3.

Billy Taylor; farce: (41) N.-10.9, 13; (44) A.-6.28; (47) A.-4.8; (48) A.-4.8, 12.

Binks, the Bagman: (43) W.-7.17, 18, 24; 8.2; 9.21; (44) W.-3.29; (45) W.-5.6; (47) W.-8.23, 31; 9.3.

Bird of Passage; farce: (49) A.-12.31; (50) C.-1.3, 9, 17.

The Birthday of Freedom; see *Irish Yankee.*

The Birthright; see *The Sea Captain.*

Black and White, or The Protean Statue; farce: (37) C.-10.26*, 27; (38) W.-6.29, 30; 7.3.

Black and White, or The Mistakes of

a Morning; farce: (35) Mammoth Circus-1.14, 15.

Black Angus, or The Evil Eye; melodrama: (35) W.-11.21, 12.3.

Black Brig of Bermuda, or The Last Words of Bill Jones; melodrama: (37) A.-6.23, 24; (42) A.-7.26; (46) A.-5.9, 25; (50) C.-2.9, 12.

Black Domino; opera by Auber: (52) C.-2.25, 27; 3.1, 3; 9.27, 29; 12.27; (53) C.-5.18, 30; 9.7.

Black Eyed Susan, or All in the Downs, or The Fleet in Harbor; by D. W. Jerrold: (35) C.-10.7; (36) W.-1.2, 6; 6.20, 7.4; P.-12.22, 29; W.-12.24; (37) W.-1.6; 6.26; 9.1; (38) W.-3.7, 20, 22; (37) C.-4.4, 11.5; (38) C.-5.22, 6.13; (39) C.-12.17; (40) C.-7.3; (37) A.-5.16; (41) A.-1.5; 5.3, 26; 8.10; (38) W.-7.12, 17; 9.18; (39) W.-5.7; 6.17; 8.3; 12.12, 24; (40) W.-4.3; 5.18; 11.18; (41) W.-5.18, 22; 6.17; 12.14, 20; (41) N.-9.8; 10.14, 27; (42) A.-3.29; C.-4.28; A.-6.2; (43) W.-6.20; A.-9.5, 10.20; N.-11.1; C.-11.7; (44) A.-1.12; W.-5.23; 8.23; C.-10.22; (45) W.-1.13, 17; 5.5; 8.2, 20; 9.1; 10.6; (46) W.-1.16; 5.23; A.-12.23; (47) A.-1.14; (48) A.-2.8; C.-7.22; A.-10.20; 11.4, 10; (49) C.-8.15; A.-9.25; 10.16, 24; (50) A.-3.28; 4.9, 13; (51) A.-1.23; 9.3; 12.5, 27; (52) N.-9.22; A.-11.16; (53) A.-2.10; W.-6.3, 4; A.-6.4; (54) A.-5.10, 12, 16, 20; C.-5.15, 16; N.-6.10; A.-6.12, 14, 15; 8.31; C.-9.9; A.-9.19; C.M.-9.23, 30; W.-10.6, 7; A.-10.11; C.M.-11.8, 25; A.-11.18; 12.13; W.-12.16; (55) C.M.-1.22; A.-2.19; W.-3.23; C.-4.16, 17; A.-4.30; W.-11.5.

Black Ghost, or The Nigger Turned Physician: (41) A.-9.28, 29, 30.

Black Hugh, the Outlaw: (45) C.-12.5.

Black Mummy: (52) N.-7.27; 8.6.

The Black Rangers, or The Night

Hawks; a legend of the Wissahickon: (53) N.-7.26*.

Black Raven of the Tombs: (42) W.-12.14, 15, 16, 17, 19, 20, 21, 22, 23, 24, 26, 27, 29, 30, 31; (43) W.-1.2, 3, 4, 5, 6, 7; 2.25, 27, 28; 3.1, 2, 3, 4, 6, 7, 8, 9, 10, 11, 16, 17; 7.15, 17, 18, 19, 20, 21, 25, 27; 8.12; (44) W.-2.26, 27, 28, 29; 3.2, 4, 5, 6, 7, 8, 9; 7.10, 11, 12, 13, 15, 16, 17, 24; (49) C.-11.3, 4, 6, 8.

Black Sea Gull: (51) N.-8.6.

Black Ship of the Desert: (41) W.-4.14, 15, 16, 17, 19.

Black Smith of Hesse Cassel: (48) W.-5.23.

Black Wreckers, or A Vision of the Sea: (44) A.-12.30; (45) A.-1.1.

Blackbourne the Avenger; see *Retribution.*

The Blacksmith's Daughter; see *The Light Ship.*

Blacksmith's Hovel; see *Vow of Silence.*

Blanche Heriot, or The Bell of Death; domestic and historical drama: (43) W.-3.8, 9, 10, 13, 14, 15, 16; 6.26; (50) C.-6.8, 9.

Blanche of Brandywine: (47) P.M.-5.17, 18, 19, 24.

Blanche of Jersey: (43) C.-2.6, 7, 8.

Blanche of Nevarre; advertised as taken from "James' novel of *Love*": (39) W.-10.3*.

Blanche of Paris: (48) W.-12.1, 2, 27; (49) W.-1.16.

Bleak House; by John Brougham: (53) A.-11.7*, 8, 9, 10, 11, 12, 14, 15, 16.

Bleeding Nun, or The Spectre of the Convent: (35) P.-11.19*, 22; (36) P.-1.2; (44) A.-1.5; (47) P.M.-7.12.

Bleeding Nun of Lindenberg: (40) W.-6.13.

Blind Bargain, or Hear it Out: (35) C.-1.6, 8.

The Blind Beggar of Bethnal Green; by J. S. Knowles: (35) C.-1.20*, 22, 23; A.-2.28.

Blind Boy, or Sarmatia's Heir; by Wm. Dunlap: (35) C.-10.10; (37) P.-2.1; (38) W.-12.7; (41) A.-9.7, 8; 10.21; (42) N.-1.21; (46) A.-2.12; (52) C.-7.30.

Blind Father and his Daughter: (46) P.M.-4.30; 5.2.

Blind Man's Buff; farce: (44) W.-4.15, 18, 22; (50) A.-4.11, 12, 19.

Blind Man's Daughter: (55) W.-9.8.

Blind Orphan: (55) C.-4.12.

Bloodhounds, or The Orphan's Grave: (52) A.-4.9, 10.

Blood Red Knight: (42) A.-10.25, 26.

Bloomers out in Force; farce: (51) B.-9.22, 23, 24, 25, 26, 27; 10.23, 24, 25.

Blud-Da-Nouns; burletta: (43) N.-12.16, 18, 19.

Blue Anchor: (43) W.-9.30; 10.2, 3, 9, 11.

Blue Beard, or Female Curiosity; by William Dunlap (?): (37) C.-1.16, 17, 18, 19, 20, 21, 30; (38) C.-12.25; (39) W.-3.23, 25, 26, 27, 30; (40) W.-1.20; (41) W.-12.29, 30; A.-11.15; (47) A.-1.4.

Blue Devils, or The Grumbling Englishman; farce: (39) C.-10.30; 11.4, 29; (40) N.-10.26; 12.4; (41) A.-10.15; (42) A.-4.14, 29; 11.2; (47) A.-4.2, 5; 7.20; 9.10; 12.17; (48) A.-10.4; 11.30; (55) W.-11.14, 23.

Blue Domino: (44) C.-10.15, 16, 17, 19; 11.12, 26; (46) P.M.-6.23, 24, 30; (47) P.M.-6.25.

Blue Jackets: (41) W.-9.6, 10, 13; 10.20; (42) W.-1.11.

Blunders in a Bed Room; see *Forty Winks.*

Boarding School; by J. H. Payne (?): (42) C.-1.19*; 2.19, 28; (43) W.-5.30; 6.6; (44) W.-2.2; 3.18.

Boat Builder's Hovel; comedy: (38) W.-8.25*; 11.8, 9.

Bob Nettles; see *To Parents and Guardians.*

Bob Short: (43) A.-12.13, 14, 19.

Bobby Breakwindow: (49) C.-9.3.

Bobtail and Wagtail: (54) A.-8.19, 21; 11.8.

Bohea-Man's-Gal; burlesque: (45) A.-4.12, 14, 15, 17, 18, 19.

The Bohemians, or The Rogues of Paris; melodrama by E. Sterling: (43) A.-12.29*, 30; W.-12.30; (44) A.-1.1, 2, 3; W.-1.1, 2, 3, 4, 5, 6; (46) A.-5.28; 6.3, 5; 7.22.

The Bohemian Girl; opera by Balfe: (44) A.-12.16, 17, 18, 19, 20, 21; C.-12.20, 21, 23, 24, 25, 26, 27, 28, 30, 31; (45) C.-1.1, 2, 3, 4, 7, 9; C.-5.19, 20, 21, 22, 23, 24, 28; 6.24, 26; W.-10.29; C.-11.17, 19, 21; 12.16; W.-12.30, 31; (46) C.-5.2, 4, 15; W.-11.2, 3, 7; 12.12; (47) C.-4.20, 23, 26; 5.6; W.-10.11; (48) W.-9.9, 25, 29; 10.5; (49) W.-1.3; 5.1, 5; 10.9, 11; 11.29; (51) B.-2.19, 21, 27; W.-12.8, 9, 18; (53) C.-9.12, 14, 16, 19; (54) W.-11.1, 2; (55) W.-2.21; C.M.-6.11, 12, 13, 15 (Act 1), 16 (Act 2), 19, 22, 25 (Acts 1 and 2).

The Bohemian Girl; drama: (44) W.-12.18, 19, 20, 21, 23, 24, 25, 28, 31; (45) W.-1.3; 8.1; 10.25; (46) W.-3.21; (48) W.-12.24, 26.

The Bohemian Mother: (35) W.-1.12.

A Bohemian's Revenge; see *Lo Zingaro.*

The Bold Dragoons: (35) C.-5.12; 6.22; 8.27; (37) C.-12.2; (38) C.-1.3; (36) A.-3.25; 4.20, 22; (38) C.-2.7, 28; (40) W.-4.24, 25; 5.7; 6.2; (44) W.-6.10, 14; 7.3.

A Bold Stroke for a Husband; by Mrs. Cowley: (35) C.-2.2; 12.31; (37) C.-1.20; (40) C.-5.16, 22; 12.19; (35) A.-3.9; (39) W.-7.11; (44) W.-5.31; 6.12; (45) W.-2.8, 11; (46) W.-7.20; 8.24; (47) W.-3.11; 8.26; (48) A.-10.17; (49) Ath.-1.2,

11; A.-3.19; (50) A.-10.16; (51) B.-12.8, 9; (52) A.-10.5; (53) A.-3.24, 30; 5.9; 6.27; (55) A.-5.11; 8.18; 9.19.

Bombardment of Paris: (46) A.-6.17.

Bombardment of Matamoras and Repulse of the Mexicans; national drama: (46) A.-5.23, 25, 27; 6.18.

Bombastes Furioso; burlesque: (35) A.-4.3; C.-12.14, 25; (39) W.-4.29; 5.11; (40) W.-7.21, 23; (42) W.-6.6; (43) A.-4.1; W.-6.27, 29; (48) W.-12.15, 16; (50) W.-1.12; (54) C.-3.14, 16, 24; 5.13.

Bone Squash Diavolo; by T. D. Rice: (35) W.-12.1*, 2, 3, 4; (36) W.-5.19, 20, 21, 24; (38) W.-1.6; 10.13; (40) W.-12.19; (38) C.-6.25, 28, 30; (40) A.-9.10, 11, 12; (41) A.-11.6, 8; (43) A.-9.26; (44) C.-10.30; 11.5; 12.19; (46) A.-2.3, 6, 10; (48) A.-2.19; W.-12.28, 29; (50) A.-5.6, 7.

The Bonnie Boy; see *Gilderoy.*

Boots at the Swan: (43) W.-2.20; A.-8.11; C.-9.10, 12, 22; W.-10.2; C.-11.6, 9, 16; 12.5; (44) W.-1.1; 4.30; N.-5.24; (47) P.M.-3.27, 28; 4.1, 7; 5.11; 6.3; (48) P.M.-4.15, 18; A.-6.14, 23; P.M.-7.7, 12; C.-7.18; A.-10.11; (50) W.-2.27; 3.1, 8; (51) W.-6.7; (52) A.-9.9, 29; (54) W.-11.14, 18.

Border Beagles, or The Tale of the Mississippi: (44) A.-8.10, 14; 10.14, 16.

Born to Good Luck, or An Irishman's Fortune: (35) C.-4.27; 5.8; (36) C.-10.4, 13; 11.19; (37) C.-2.13, 22; 3.9; (38) C.-10.1; 11.13; (40) C.-10.8, 20; (37) A.-5.20; (41) C.-2.25; (42) C.-11.4, 7; (43) W.-2.2, 3; 3.21; (45) C.-2.5; 11.24; (46) W.-9.4, 5; 10.7; P.M.-10.16, 17; W.-11.19; (47) W.-2.1, 3, 11; P.M.-4.8, 9, 10; W.-6.14, 19; 9.28; 10.5; 12.8; (48) A.-3.17; P.M.-4.26, 29; W.-

5.18; C.-6.30; W.-9.11; (49) W.-4.10, 14; A.-5.28; 6.1; W.-9.10, 19, 29; 10.15; A.-11.29; (50) C.-2.28; W.-4.30; A.-6.29; 7.4; 11.20; (51) A.-2.14, 21, 28; W.-3.1; A.-5.12; 11.14; (52) C.-2.6, 7; W.-3.5, 6; C.-6.17; (53) A.-2.24; 3.2, 31; C.-5.2; A.-7.23; W.-10.27; 11.12; A.-12.8, 10; (54) A.-2.16; 3.22; 5.13; W.-5.15; C.-8.7, 18; A.-9.20; 10.3, 13; 12.20; (55) W.-9.19; 11.29; 12.1.

Borrowed Feathers: (35) C.-6.15*, 20; (42) C.-9.17; 10.11.

The Boston Boys of '76; see *Liberty Tree.*

Boston in 1775; see *Cradle of Liberty.*

Boston Tea Party: (43) W.-5.23*; N.-11.26.

Botheration, or A Ten Years' Blunder; farce by W. C. Oulton: (35) W.-10.8; 12.8; (36) C.-7.7, 9; (38) C.-2.15, 17, 24; 3.21; 8.28.

Bottle: (47) A.-11.25, 26, 27, 29, 30; 12.3; (48) P.M.-4.7, 8.

Bottle Imp: (45) W.-7.18, 19, 21, 22; (51) A.-12.6, 12, 19.

Box and Cox; farce by J. M. Morton: (48) W.-1.12*, 13, 17, 20; 2.4; A.-2.7; C.-7.7, 10, 19; W.-9.14, 26; 10.3, 18; 11.3; 12.4; (49) Ath.-1.3; W.-3.19, 23; 6.11; 10.22, 30; 12.3; (50) W.-1.24; 3.29; 12.3; (51) W.-1.10; 2.3, 14; 4.8, 24; 5.12; 6.2, 23; C.-9.23; (52) W.-3.29; 9.9; 11.2; (53) W.-5.6; A.-6.3; C.-8.30; W.-11.21; (54) C.-1.3; 7.12; C.M.-12.2; (55) W.-3.12; 4.21.

Box and Cox Married and Settled: (52) A.-12.15; (53) W.-9.5, 8, 10, 14; 10.1, 13; 12.7; (54) W.-4.14, 15; 10.19, 31; 12.18; (55) W.-2.19.

Box, Cox, and Knox; farce by W. E. Burton (?): (48) A.-1.14, 15; P.M.-3.18, 27; A.-3.28; P.M.-5.19.

The Boy of Clogheen; see *Paddy Carey.*

Boz; by W. T. Moncrieff: (42) W.-5.7, 13, 14, 31; 6.3, 16.

Brandywine Springs: (43) W.-3.6.

Bravery Rewarded; see *Philadelphia Fireman.*

The Bravo, or The Red Mask; (by R. P. Smith): (49) W.-10.2, 4, 6.

Bravo of Venice; by W. T. Moncrieff: (35) W.-1.7*, 10, 11, 13.

The Bravo's Oath; see *Venetian.*

The Brazen Drum; by S. S. Steele: (41) A.-1.27*, 28.

The Brazilian Ape; see *Pongo.*

The Breach of Promise; see *Second Thoughts.*

Brewer of Preston: (46) P.M.-6.8.

Brewer of Preston; comic opera by Adolph Adam: (46) P.M.-4.27, 28, 29; C.-5.6, 7, 8, 9, 11, 12, 13, 14, 18; W.-11.4, 5; (47) C.-4.10, 17.

Brian Boroihme, or The Maid of Erin; by J. S. Knowles: (36) W.-5.28; 6.13, 14, 15, 16, 17; (37) W.-8.28, 29; (38) W.-3.17; (39) W.-4.10; (41) C.-2.25; (42) A.-6.24, 28; (49) A.-9.10, 12, 15; (50) A.-7.9, 11; (50) A.-1.24, 25.

Brian O'Lynn; by S. D. Johnson: (51) A.-5.12*, 14; 11.4; (52) W.-10.19, 20, 22; (53) C.-5.5; (54) W.-5.19, 20, 31; (55) W.-9.17, 24.

The Bridal, or Maid's Tragedy; by J. S. Knowles: (43) C.-12.19, 20, 23; (45) W.-7.28, 29; 8.16; 9.4; 10.8, 24; 12.15; (46) W.-6.4; (47) A.-4.23; W.-10.26; (48) W.-10.28; (49) W.-6.18; (52) W.-11.17; (53) C.-3.28; (55) A.-9.7, 8, 10, 12; 10.1.

The Bridal of the Border; see *The Rose of Ettrick Vale.*

The Bridals of Messina; see *John di Procida.*

The Bride; by Theodore Korner: (37) A.-7.20.

Bride of Abydos: (37) W.-1.9, 11, 13; (41) W.-2.9, 18, 19; (40) C.-12.17;

(41) C.-1.1; (43) W.-4.14, 15, 17.

Bride of Lammermoor, or The Last Heir of Ravenwood: (35) C.-4.15; 8.26; (38) C.-12.24; (39) C.-1.10; (41) C.-2.23, 26; (42) C.-9.22; (45) W.-6.28; A.-10.27; (50) A.-10.19; (51) A.-4.12; (52) C.-10.16; (54) C.-10.21; 11.2; (55) C.M.-5.12, 15.

The Bride of the Isles; see *Vampire.*

The Bride's Revenge; see *The Dark Lady.*

A Bridegroom from the Sea; see *The Wreck Ashore.*

The Bride's Journey; melodrama: (47) A.-8.28, 30, 31; 9.1, 2, 3, 4; (48) W.-7.14, 15; (50) A.-6.19, 20.

The Bridge of Terror: (41) A.-2.1, 2.

The Brigadier's Horse, or The Inn of Cervanne; romantic drama (by James Rees): (49) C.-11.17, 19, 20, 21, 22, 23.

The Brigand: (35) C.-9.15, 16; (36) C.-1.12; (39) C.-1.1, 2; (35) W.-11.2, 3, 4; (36) W.-2.17; (38) W.-2.5; (36) A.-3.12; (37) A.-5.26; (36) P.-12.17; (42) W.-2.5; (43) C.-11.30; 12.2; (44) W.-1.19; 2.8; 4.29; 6.17; (45) W.-8.9, 22; (46) A.-10.16, 20; (49) A.-4.17, 18, 19; (50) B.-10.28, 29; 11.1.

The Brigand's Daughter; see *Amaldi.*

The Briton Chief; see *Caswallon.*

The Broken Heart; see *Agnes de Vere.*

The Broken Heart, or A Wife's Revenge: (35) W.-3.12*, 16; (45) A.-7.7; 12.29; (46) A.-2.23, 26; 3.18; 4.11; (47) P.M.-2.23; A.-4.2, 7; 9.15, 17; (48) A.-10.14.

Broken Hearted, or The Farmer's Daughter: (44) W.-4.27.

Broken Sword, or The Dumb Boy of the Mountains: (36) P.-12.3, 23; (38) W.-12.22; (39) W.-1.1, 7; 7.12; (40) W.-11.23, 24; (41) A.-10.6; (42) A.-8.1; (45) C.-5.13;

(50) B.-8.26; 9.12; A.-11.27, 30; (51) A.-1.7, 8; 2.20; 3.5; A.-7.12, 18; (52) A.-3.2, 4; 5.8; 9.2, 3; (54) N.-6.7, 14, 17.

The Broker of Bogota; by R. M. Bird: (37) C.-11.27, 28; (40) C.-9.28, 29; (41) A.-4.21; (47) W.-1.11, 13, 15; 3.18; 5.21; 11.15, 18; (48) W.-12.9; (49) W.-6.8, (52) W.-6.16; 11.27.

Bronze Horse, or The Spell of the Cloud King; a Chinese romance: (36) W.-8.31; 9.1, 2, 3, 5, 6, 7, 8, 9, 10, 12, 13, 14, 15, 16, 17, 19, 20, 21, 22, 23, 24, 26, 27, 28, 29; 10.12 21; 11.14; 12.20, 23; (37) W.-8.30; (38) W.-3.16, 17; (41) A.-12.24, 25, 27, 28, 29, 30, 31; (45) A.-6.7, 8, 10, 11, 14; W.-6.9, 10, 11, 12, 13, 14, 16, 17, 18, 19; (46) W.-1.1, 2; (48) W.-7.10, 11; (51) B.-4.21, 22, 23, 24, 25, 26, 28, 29, 30; 5.1, 2, 3, 5, 6, 7, 8, 9, 24; N.-8.12.

Brother and Sister; comic opera: (37) C.-1.27; (40) W.-3.11; (46) P.M.-7.14, 15.

Brother Ben; farce: (41) C.-10.11.

The Brothers of the Burning Belt; see *Zindel.*

Brothers of the Pyrenees; "adopted to the stage from Miss Pardoe's Tale of that name," by Stevens: (37) W.-1.2*, 3.

Brutus, or The Fall of Tarquin; by J. H. Payne: (35) W.-1.26; 8.26; 11.25; C.-6.22; (36) W.-5.27; A.-6.6; P.-12.20; (38) W.-9.5; (39) C.-12.4; W.-7.6; (40) W.-3.27; N.-12.16; (41) A.-4.29; N.-12.24; (43) W.-3.29; 4.12; 5.29; A.-9.19; (44) W.-1.29; 6.20; 10.26; 12.11; (45) W.-5.14, 31; A.-12.19; (46) A.-1.8; W.-4.7; A.-7.18; (47) W.-5.11; (48) A.-3.14; 12.8; (50) A.-5.16; 7.25; (51) B.-3.20; A.-10.17; (52) C.-1.30; W.-12.2; (54) W.-10.7; (55) W.-4.11.

The Bubbles of the Days; comedy: (42) C.-4.25, 26; (43) W.-2.11.

Buccaneer's Barque: (45) A.-7.28, 29.

The Buckle of Brilliants; see *Crown Prince.*

Budget of Blunders: (37) W.-1.12, 14, 17; (40) N.-10.19, 21; (45) A.-12.12, 13; (54) C.M.-10.26, 27; 11.1.

Bull Fighter of Spain, or Ball of Death; comedy: (52) N.-8.12, 13, 14.

Bumps of Mystery, or Yankee Magnetism: (44) N.-4.15; A.-10.18, 19.

Bunker Hill's Representative; see *Yankee Duellist.*

Burglar, or The Secret League: (46) A.-7.25.

The Burglar's Stronghold; see *The Match-Woman of Philadelphia.*

Buried Alive: (45) A.-11.26; 12.3; (50) A.-8.16; 17; 12.2; (51) A.-6.11; 10.24; 11.21; (52) N.-9.6, 7; (53) A.-1.6; C.-2.4.

Burning of the Caroline: (44) N.-4.15.

The Burning Sword; see *Thalaba.*

The Bushwhacker; by N. H. Bannister: (38) W.-7.24*.

The Busy Body; by Mrs. Susanna Centlivre: (35) C.-11.19; (38) C.-5.26; (39) C.-5.3; (36) W.-3.29; (45) C.-1.30; (55) A.-6.20, 21, 22.

But However!, or Short of Change: (39) W.-10.19; (40) W.-4.6; (41) N.-3.11; 4.7.

Butcher's Dog of Ghent: (52) A.-3.30; 4.1; (53) C.-4.15, 26.

Buy—It—Dear,—'Tis Made of Cashmere: (41) N.-6.12, 14, 15, 25.

Cabin and Parlor, or A Picture on the Other Side of Jordan to Uncle Tom's Cabin; dramatized by B. Young from novel of same name: (54) W.-5.9, 11, 13; C.-7.17, 19.

The Cabin Boy; see *The Monkey who has Seen the World.*

Cabin Boy, or The Devil of Demeraro:

(46) A.-5.18, 19, 20, 26, 30; (51) W.-11.29; A.-12.23, 25.

The Cabinet; opera: (35) C.-12.10; (40) N.-12.14.

Cabinet Question; farce: (46) P.M.-7.25, 29.

Cabinet Secrets; comedy: (41) N.-10.9, 13, 18.

The Cad of the Buss; see *Tiger at Large.*

Caecinna; tragedy by Isaac C. Pray: (51) W.-6.25*, 26.

Caius Silius, or The Slave of Carthage; tragedy by N. H. Bannister: (38) W.-8.27*, 28; (43) A.-10.4.

Calaynos; tragedy by G. H. Boker: (51) W.-1.20*, 21, 22, 23, 24, 25, 27, 28, 30, 31; 2.1; 5.12; 12.1, 3; (55) W.-4.13, 16.

Calderoni, the Castle Burner; see *The Mountain King.*

California Gold Mines: (48) A.-12.18, 19, 21, 22.

Call again Tomorrow: (36) C.-1.2, 6; A.-5.31.

Cameleon; farce: (40) N.-10.7, 9.

Camille, or The Fate of a Coquette; tragedy by John Wilkins: (53) W.-9.23*, 24; C.-12.23, 24, 27, 28, 29, 31; (54) C.-1.2; 3.21; 4.7; W.-9.11, 12, 13, 14, 15, 16, 18, 19, 20, 21, 22, 23; 12.11, 12, 13, 14, 19; (55) W.-10.3, 4, 5, 6; A.-12.12, 13, 14, 17, 22.

Campaign of the Rio Grande, or Triumphs in Mexico: (46) W.-5.30*; 6.1, 2, 3, 4, 5, 6, 20, 22; (47) W.-5.6.

Cape May Will: (42) W.-9.30; 10.1.

Captain Charlotte: (43) W.-9.30; 10.4; C.-11.3.

Captain Kyd, or The Wizard of the Sea; advertised as dramatized by F. C. Wemyss from Ingraham's novel of that name: (39) W.-9.2*, 3, 4, 5, 6, 7, 12; (41) C.-1.24; (42)

C.-1.24, 25; (51) A.-1.17, 18; (52) A.-12.29, 30.

Captain John Rock: (42) A-10.22, 24.

Captain of the Watch: (47) A.-10.25, 30; (48) P.M.-4.19; 5.13, 18; (50) C.-2.14; A.-8.1.

Captain Stevens, or The Poodle Collar: (46) A.-7.25.

Captain's Not A-Miss: (37) W.-11.23; 12.1; (51) N.-8.11.

The Captive; musical piece by Mrs. C. B. Conner: (50) A.-3.8*; (51) A.-6.9.

Carbonari: (48) W.-5.17, 18.

Caradora, or The Exile's Oath; "new American tragedy written expressly for J. E. Murdoch by a gentleman of this city (Phila.)": (36) W.-5.23*, 24; 6.29.

Card Drawer; by J. B. Buckstone: (45) C.-11.28*; (46) A.-5.14, 16, 23; (47) P.M.-5.29; 6.1; (51) A.-5.16, 17.

Card Player: (47) P.M.-4.15.

The Carib Chief; tragedy: (35) C.-12.2.

Carlo, the Minstrel; opera: (52) C.-12.29, 31; (53) C.-1.5; 5.25; 6.8.

The Carnival Ball; see *One Hour.*

The Carpenter of Rouen; by J. S. Jones: (41) W.-1.11*, 12, 13, 14, 15, 16, 23, 25, 26, 27, 29; 2.25, 26, 27; N.-1.26; W.-3.5, 9; 4.12, 13; 5.17; 9.15, 17; 10.21, 22; (42) W.-1.31; 2.3; A.-4.9, 19; 5.3; W.-5.26, 29; (43) W.-1.18; 2.24; 9.22, 28; 10.27; C.-12.13, 16; (44) W.-5.21; (45) W.-5.12, 22; (49) A.-3.5, 6; 4.7; 6.8; 11.21; (50) A.-10.4; 11.5, 8; (51) A.-1.13; 5.3; 7.29; N.-8.2, 16; A.-12.13, 26; (52) A.-3.6; 4.23; 5.13; 9.25; 10.2; 11.13, 18; (53) A.-2.8, 5.7; (55) C.M.-1.29, 30, 31; 2.3.

The Cashmere Shawl; see *My Uncle John.*

Castilian Honor; see *Velasco.*

Castle of Andalusia; comic opera by John O'Keeffe: (37) C.-8.28; 9.8; (38) C.-1.13; 5.29.

Castle of Linburg: (45) W.-4.12.

Castle of Lochleven; see *Mary Stewart.*

Castle of Paluzzi, or The Extorted Oath: (39) W.-1.29.

Castle of St. Aldobrand; see *Bertram.*

Castle Spectre: (36) W.-10.20; (38) C.-4.14, 16, 24; (40) C.-6.9; 12.30; (44) W.-5.16; (55) A.-2.24, 26; 3.3, 19, 24; 4.14; 6.16.

Caswallon, or The British Chief; tragedy: (36) W.-4.1, 2; (40) W.-5.8; (41) N.-4.14.

Cataline, or The Roman Conspiracy: tragedy in five acts: (37) W.-2.4.

Cataract of the Ganges; romantic, equestrian melodrama (by W. T. Moncrieff): (38) W.-4.28, 30; 5.1, 2; (39) W.-3.4, 5, 6, 7, 8, 9, 11, 12, 13, 15; (41) W.-3.31; 4.1, 2, 3.

Catching an Heiress, or O-I-E-O-E; comedy: (35) W.-11.18, 19, 20; 12.21; (37) W.-8.26; 12.4; (35) C.-12.18, 21, 23; (36) A.-3.18, 22; 4.19; (38) W.-11.29; 12.29; (39) W.-2.20; 3.6; 8.28; (41) W.-1.13; 9.1, 3; (42) A.-6.20; (43) C.-12.15, 18; (44) C.-11.25; 12.4, 19; (46) P.M.-6.4, 9; (47) A.-8.2, 5; (49) A.-8.22; (50) C.-3.11; (52) N.-7.28.

Catharine and Petruchio; see *Katharine and Petruchio.*

Cato; by Joseph Addison: (37) C.-10.16, 20; (38) C.-4.28; (39) C.-11.19; (40) C.-3.4.

Cat's in the Larder: (41) N.-6.12, 14.

Catspaw; comedy by D. W. Jerrold: (50) W.-6.27*, 29.

The Cattle Stealer, or The Rover, The Drover, and His Dog: (53) C.-4.13.

Caught in a Trap; (by B. N. Webster): (50) B.-10.23, 24, 28, 29; (51) B.-1.9; (55) W.-3.19; 12.28.

Caught in his own Trap: (52) W.-

1.10, 12, 13, 19, 26; 2.6, 18; 3.8; 4.1, 22; 5.10; 6.3, 16.

Causes and Effects: (46) P.M.-11.5, 6.

The Cavalier: (47) A.-11.30*; 12.2; (48) A.-1.17; W.-4.29; 5.1, 3; P.M.-5.8, 13; (49) A.-4.18, 21; W.-5.19.

Cavaliers and Roundheads: (53) C.-5.17, 18.

The Celestial Empire: (46) A.-3.4, 6, 7.

Centurion's Daughter: (51) C.-3.26.

Cerro Gordo; farce: (47) A.-6.4*, 5.

Cesar de Bazan, or Love and Honor: (45) W.-1.4, 6, 7, 8, 9, 11, 13, 14, 15, 16, 17, 30; 2.7; 3.1, 6, 19; 6.10, 11; 8.15; 12.2; (46) A.-4.23; W.-7.30; 10.1, 2, 3; A.-10.26, 27, 28; (47) W.-3.6, 9; 5.17; (48) W.-2.24; A.-8.4, 11; 9.4, 5, 12; 12.1; W.-12.27; (49) Ath.-1.12; A.-8.31; 9.7, 11; 10.15; W.-11.15, 22, 26; (50) C.-1.16, 18; A.-5.14; 7.30; W.-10.23; B.-12.3; (51) A.-10.1, 22; (52) C.-3.10; 10.2; (53) W.-4.4, 6; A.-5.18; C.-6.29; W.-12.22; (55) W.-6.7.

The Chain of Guilt, or The Inn on the Heath; romantic drama: (40) W.-3.6.

The Chamber of Death; see *Tour de Nesle.*

The Champion of Cordova; by S. S. Steele: (43) A.-4.26*, 27, 28.

Change Makes Change; comedy by Epes Sargent: (45) A.-10.20*, 21, 22, 23, 24, 25.

Changes; comedy by James Rees: (50) C.-4.22*, 23, 24, 25, 26, 27, 30; 5.3; (55) W.-5.2.

Chaos is come again; farce: (39) W.-4.29; 6.7, 25; 7.18; (39) C.-4.29, 30; 9.21, 25; 10.2, 16; 11.18, 27; 12.30; (40) C.-3.5; 4.13; 7.1; 9.1; (50) B.-9.30; 10.1, 16, 17.

Chapeau d'un Horloger, or Clockmaker's Hat: (55) W.-11.23.

A Chapter of Accidents; by Harriet Lee: (44) A.-6.1; (45) C.-11.6.

Charcoal Burner: (42) A.-9.27; (52) A.-3.1, 3, 25; (53) A.-2.5, 18.

Charity's Love: (55) W.-3.23*, 24, 31.

Charles O'Malley, or The Irish Dragoon; comedy by H. J. Conway: (42) N.-1.20*, 21, 26, 27; C.-3.26; 4.5, 6; A.-11.23; (43) W.-7.8; (45) A.-3.29; 4.2; 6.18; C.-11.15, 17, 19, 21; (46) A.-1.16, 22; 2.27; 3.20; 4.10; (47) A.-4.3, 5; (48) A.-6.8; (49) A.-6.1, 2; (50) C.-7.19, 20; A.-8.29; (53) A.-9.3, 5; (55) A.-2.3, 5.

Charles I; tragedy by Mary Russell Mitford: (40) C.-4.6.

Charles the Second; comedy by J. H. Payne and Washington Irving: (35) W.-2.13; A.-3.4; C.-5.6; (36) P.-11.7; 12.2; (37) P.-1.19; C.-8.21; (38) C.-1.27; 8.30; (39) W.-5.27, 28; C.-6.20; (40) W.-10.28; 12.3; C.-6.6; (41) A.-9.9, 28; C.-6.15; N.-2.5, 7, 13; (42) A.-4.6; 7.15, 21; (43) A.-5.2; W.-10.23, 25; (44) A.-1.15; N.-2.10, 14, 26; (45) C.-5.13; W.-8.7; 11.25, 27; 12.9; C.-12.29; (46) P.M.-8.4, 17; A.-8.26; (47) P.M.-1.13; A.-3.26; (48) P.M.-3.28; 5.1; (49) A.-2.24; (50) A.-7.24; B.-12.28; (51) B.-1.24; A.-10.10; (52) A.-3.22; 9.17; (53) A.-2.9; 5.6, 17, 27; (54) C.-10.2.

Charles XII; (37) A.-6.27; (39) W.-11.18; (40) W.-4.21; (41) W.-11.4, 5; C.-10.6; (44) A.-1.12, 13; (46) W.-7.2; A.-12.4, 5; (48) P.M.-4.19, 21; (50) W.-10.26; (51) W.-1.8, 11; N.-8.13; (52) W.-1.23, 28; 2.10; A.-3.26; (55) C.M.-6.5.

Charlotte Corday; by Mrs. C. B. Conner: (51) A.-3.18*, 19, 20, 22, 24; C.-3.18, 20, 22; A.-4.18, 19; (52) C.-5.3, 5; 10.14, 15, 16, 18, 23.

Charlotte Temple: (42) W.-5.6.

Charming Polly, or The Lucky and Unlucky Days; comedy: (39) W.-1.28, 31; 2.8.

The Chasm of Death; see *The Hunters of the Pyrenees.*

Cheap Boarding; see *Man about Town.*

Cherokee Chief; or Dogs of the Wreck: (35) W.-6.8*, 9, 10, 18; 10.2, 3, 8; (36) W.-1.18; 11.7, 9; (37) W.-1.16; P.-1.28; (39) W.-1.21; (41) A.-1.25, 26; (45) A.-8.9, 11; 11.15, 17; (46) A.-5.21; (47) P.M.-7.3, 4.

Cherry and Fair Star, or The Children of Cypress: (40) W.-3.14, 16; (46) A.-5.5, 7, 8; (50) B.-12.24, 25, 26, 27, 28, 30, 31; (51) B.-1.1, 2, 3, 4, 6, 7, 8, 9 10, 11, 13, 14, 15 16, 17, 18.

Cherry Bounce: (35) W.-11.13, 17; 12.24; (36) W.-1.5, 21; 2.24; 4.16, 20.

The Chesnut Street Heiress; see *Philadelphia Fireman.*

The Chiffonier, or The Rogues of Paris: (49) W.-1.13, 15, 16.

Child of Air; romantic fairy drama: (38) C.-12.11, 12, 13, 14, 15, 17, 18, 19, 20; (39) C.-8.31; 9.2, 3; (40) C.-1.13, 14; 2.14; (50) W.-12.17, 18, 19, 20, 21.

A Child of the Delawares; see *Prairie Bird.*

The Child of the Desert; see *Aethiop.*

Child of Nature; comedy: (35) C.-5.25; (39) C.-12.14; (40) C.-2.4; (46) W.-7.16, 17; 8.13; 11.25, 27; (47) W.-8.11; (51) B.-10.20, 21, 22; (55) A.-1.29; 6.1.

Child of the Regiment: (51) B.-2.28; C.-11.3, 5, 7; W.-12.12; (52) W.-2.9, 10; C.-9.20; A.-12.21; (54) C.-6.14; (55) C.M.-6.26, 27.

Child of the Wreck: (38) C.-10.27, 29, 30, 31; 12.4, 5; (39) C.-8.28, 29; 9.2, 6; (40) C.-1.6, 7, 15; 2.19; (42) C.-10.29.

Children in the Wood: (35) C.-9.26; 12.30; (36) P.-12.17; (37) W.-8.8, 10; (39) W.-1.14; (40) W.-5.6; C.-2.3; (42) A.-9.14; (43) N.-9.28;

(45) A.-5.31; 6.5; (49) A.-6.9; (51) A.-10.15; (52) A.-9.23.

The Children of Chittigong, or The Fatal Anacondas: (36) W.-1.25*, 26.

The Children of Cypress; see *Cherry and Fair Star.*

The Chimes: (46) P.M.-5.11, 12, 13, 19, 20, 23, 25, 27, 28; 8.12; (47) A.-1.1, 5, 9, 26; P.M.-2.17, 18; 3.6, 15, 29; (51) A.-10.21.

The Chimney Piece, or Natural Magic: (35) C.-5.21, 25; 6.9, 30; (36) C.-7.8; A.-5.7, 16; 6.8.

A Chip of the Old Block: (42) W.-6.29.

The Chisel; farce: (51) A.-9.29*, 30.

Chloroform; by C. Logan: (49) A.-6.11*, 12, 13, 14, 15, 16, 19; P.M.-7.18, 19, 20, 21; C.-10.12, 13, 15, 16, 17, 18; (51) A.-6.4, 5, 6, 7; (52) C.-3.12, 13, 16, 20; 5.20, 26; 6.12; 8.25.

The Christening: (40) N.-10.2; C.-11.2, 10, 21, 27; 12.22; (41) W.-12.6, 7, 8, 9, 17; (43) O.-1.12.

Christine of Poland; one-act comedy by J. H. Payne: (37) W.-1.23.

Christine of Sweden; see *Youthful Queen.*

Christmas Carol: (45) C.-2.1, 3, 4; (47) P.M.-5.25, 27.

Christmas Gambols; see *Harlequin Hurry Scurry.*

Christmas Morn: (46) P.M.-12.25, 26, 28, 29, 30, 31.

Churus Busco: (52) A.-11.30; 12.1.

Cinderella, or The Fairy and the Little Glass Slipper; opera by Rossini: (35) C.-1.29; 2.19; 12.14, 16; (36) C.-1.25; 2.5; (37) C.-1.25; (38) C.-3.22, 30; (36) A.-4.30; (37) A.-6.19, 23; (37) C.-8.30; 9.6; 10.13; (38) C.-2.16, 21; 4.18; (39) C.-2.5, 6, 7, 9; 4.15, 16, 17; 5.11; 9.19, 21; 10.16, 17, 27; (41) C.-5.27, 28; (39) W.-11.12, 13, 14; (42) C.-12.26, 27, 29; (43) C.-1.17; (44) C.-4.9, 10; (45)

C.-10.25; (47) C.-5.1, 4; W.-10.18;
(51) W.-8.29; 9.11; 12.15; (55) W.-
2.26, 27, 28; 3.1, 2, 3, 5, 6, 7, 8, 9, 10;
C.M.-6.28, 29 (Act 1).

The Circumstances against his Will;
comedy in four parts by Roeder:
(55) G.N.-8.25.

Circumstantial Evidence: (36) W.-
4.29*; 5.10.

Citizen and the Royalist: (48) P.M.-
5.4.

City Wives, or A Lesson for Listners:
(44) A.-6.4, 5, 6; 11.25.

City Wives and City Husbands: (44)
A.-11.6, 8, 9.

*The City and the Country, or The
Drover from Upper Austria:* (55)
G.N.-8.29.

Civilization, or The Haron Chief;
comedy by John Wilkins: (53) W.-
11.29, 30; 12.2, 3.

*Clandare, or The Robber Clans of the
Lochs;* romantic drama by S. S.
Steele: (38) W.-3.10*; (41) A.-1.16;
12.9, 10, 16; (42) W.-5.28; A.-11.30;
(43) W.-8.8; (44) W.-11.14, 15;
(53) C.-3.24.

The Clandestine Marriage; comedy by
George Colman the Elder and David
Garrick: (36) W.-10.3; (54) A.-8.31.

Clari, or The Maid of Milan; by J. H.
Payne: (35) C.-2.13; 4.8; (37) C.-
2.1, 7; (39) C.-12.2; (35) A.-3.7,
13; (36) P.-12.27; (39) W.-11.4;
(42) C.-1.22, 25; 2.21; (43) W.-
1.18; (46) A.-2.11, 13; (50) W.-
10.23; (52) C.-5.14; (53) W.-4.9;
(55) C.M.-5.11.

Cleopatra, Serpent of the Nile: (41)
N.-10.11; 12.25, 27, 28, 29, 30.

Climbing Boy; comedy in three acts by
R. B. Peake: (35) C.-12.24*; (36)
A.-4.23; (43) A.-3.17; (52) C.-
7.19, 22.

The Clock has Struck; see *Wood Demon.*

The Clockmaker's Hat; see *Chapeau
d'un Horloger.*

Close Siege: (41) C.-5.20, 21.

*The Clown and the Cat, or Harle-
quin and the Old Woman:* (42) N.-
1.14.

The Clown's Luncheon: (35) Mam.
C.-1.26, 27; 2.6, 7.

*Coal Black Rose on Horseback, or Zip
Coon's Visit to Philadelphia:* (35)
Mam. C.-1.12, 13; 2.11, 12.

*The Cobbler's Daughter, or All in the
Wrong:* (35) Mam. C.-1.16, 17, 28,
29.

A Cobbler's Flight in an Air Balloon;
see *Mogul Tale.*

The Cockney Afloat; see *The Spitfire.*

The Coiners; see *Robber's Wife.*

Colin: (46) P.M.-8.28; 10.12, 13.

Colombe's Birthday: (54) C.-3.31*.

*The Colonel's Come; or La Femme Sol-
dat:* (35) C.-7.3; (36) C.-1.9.

Columbus, or A World Discovered;
by Thomas Morton: (36) C.-1.1;
(42) A.-6.2, 3.

Columbia's Son: (44) N.-4.2, 3, 4; (52)
A.-1.1.

Come at Last: (52) N.-7.12, 13.

Comedy of Errors: by William Shakespeare: (36) W.-10.27; (38) W.-
1.17, 20; 6.23; (39) W.-4.5, 6; (40)
W.-10.28, 29; C.-2.3; (43) W.-4.3,
5, 8; 7.1; (44) W.-4.13, 17; (46) W.-
8.1, 7, 8, 15; (47) W.-7.3; (49) A.-
10.13; (52) W.-3.24; 4.3; (53) A.-
9.5, 6, 7, 8, 9, 10, 12, 13, 14, 15, 16,
17, 19, 20, 21, 22, 23; 10.14, 22, 29,
31; 11.1, 2, 3, 4, 26; (54) A.-1.12;
2.6, 14, 15, 21; 3.21; 4.18; 6.21; 10.9,
10, 11, 14, 16, 18, 19, 20; 11.13, 17;
12.7, 21; (55) A.-1.17, 19; 2.1, 27;
3.20, 23; 4.6, 12, 17, 24; 5.1, 8, 15,
22, 29; 6.5, 7, 12, 15, 19, 26; 7.3.

*Comfortable Lodgings, or Paris in
1750:* (35) C.-1.2, 22; 5.8; 6.17;
8.25; (36) C.-8.23; (38) C.-9.15;

11.20; (39) C.-2.14, 22; (43) W.-5.22, 25.

Comfortable Service: (36) W.-3.25, 28; 4.1, 27; 6.2, 8; A.-6.10, 14; 6.29; 8.30; 9.7, 20, 28; 10.22, 24; 11.19, 24; 12.23; (37) A.-5.19; 6.30; C.-3.24; (39) C.-1.25; 2.1; (37) W.-6.26, 30; 7.29; 8.1, 14; (40) W.-6.29; 11.28; C.-9.16, 21; (42) A.-6.7, 9, 14.

A Companion in Arms: (43) C.-12.8, 9, 12, 13.

Conancheotah: (41) A.-11.30; 12.1, 2.

Confounded Foreigners; farce: (38) W.-8.27, 29; (44) A.-6.21, 22, 27; 7.8.

Confusion, or The Patrician and The Pretender; new comedy in three acts by the author of Paul Pry: (37) C.-10.19*; (38) C.-2.23; 3.16; 4.17.

Congress Hall, or No Male Visitors Admitted; farce: (35) W.-8.28*, 31.

The Conjuration, or The Deliverance of Switzerland; taken from Schiller's William Tell: (37) A.-7.24.

Conjuror: (43) W.-1.9, 20.

Connecticut Courtship: (54) W.-5.25; (55) W.-9.27.

Conner the Rash; see Knight of Arva.

The Conquering Game; farce: (39) W.-8.24, 26, 27, 29; 9.19, 28; (40) C.-9.10, 14.

Conquest of Taranto, or St. Clara's Eve: (39) C.-4.12; 10.15; (40) W.-6.30; (43) W.-3.27.

The Conscripts, or The Pledge of Truth: (44) A.-12.28; (45) A.-1.2.

The Conspiracy; see Richelieu.

The Convent; see Pet of the Petticoats.

The Convent Ruins; see Father and Son.

A Convenient Distance: (45) A.-12.2.

The Convention; see Lestocq.

The Convict's Child: (40) A.-12.23, 24, 26; (41) W.-2.20, 23.

The Cook and the Secretary; see Fish out of Water.

Cool as a Cucumber: (51) A.-10.30; 11.3, 19; (55) C.-1.15, 16.

Coriolanus: (37) W.-8.23; (38) W.-1.25; 9.11; (37) C.-10.9, 12; (38) C.-1.22; 2.5; 5.2; (39) C.-12.2; (41) A.-4.26; N.-12.17, 20; (45) W.-7.31; 8.18; 10.18; (46) W.-1.2, 30; A.-12.7; (48) W.-2.21.

Cork Leg: (48) A.-3.29.

Coronation of Queen Victoria; a pageant: (38) W.-8.10, 11, 13, 14, 15, 16, 17, 18, 20, 21, 22, 23, 24.

A Coroner's Verdict: (50) C.-6.14.

Coroner's Inquest, or Murder at the Marl Pit: (44) A.-8.31; 9.27, 30; 11.29.

Corporal's Wedding; farce: (50) W.-4.20, 22.

The Corsair's Revenge: (40) W.-5.22, 23; (45) N.-5.8, 10.

The Corsican Brothers; translated from A. Dumas' Les Freres Corses: (51) W.-4.5, 6, 7, 8, 9, 10, 12, 13, 14, 15, 16, 17; 5.4, 8; C.-9.13, 14, 15, 16, 17, 18; (53) W.-3.10, 23; 4.2; 12.20, 30, 31; (55) C.-1.22, 23, 26; A.-12.24, 25, 26, 27, 28, 29, 31.

Council of Ten, or The Venetian Bravo: (41) W.-9.22, 23, 25.

Council of the Inquisition: (36) W.-4.16*, 18, 19, 20, 21, 22, 23, 26, 27, 29.

Count of Monte Cristo; by G. H. Andrews: (49) A.-1.24*, 25, 26, 27, 29, 30, 31; 2.1, 2, 3, 5, 6, 7, 8, 9, 10; W.-1.24*, 25, 26, 27, 29, 30, 31; 2.1, 2, 3, 5, 6, 7, 8, 9, 10, 12, 13, 14, 15, 16, 17; 5.26; 6.1; (52) N.-10.4, 5, 6, 7, 8, 9, 10 (Acts 4 and 5).

A Countess for an Hour: (51) B.-11.10, 11, 12, 13, 14, 15.

Country Girl; comedy by David Garrick: (39) C.-11.4, 6, 16; (40) C.-1.20, 28; 5.12; W.-5.23; (42) A.-

8.1; (44) C.-10.19, 23; (47) W.-8.30; 9.2; (50) A.-12.31; (51) A.-1.11.

Courier of Lyons: (55) A.-5.11, 12.

Courier of the Ocean: (41) A.-1.19, 21, 23.

Court and City; comedy: (49) W.-1.5*, 6, 8, 12.

Court Fool, or King's Jester; by Victor Hugo: (51) A.-2.18; N.-7.18; (52) A.-4.24.

The Court of Love; comedy by James N. Barker: (36) A.-3.26*; 4.27; 5.14.

Courting in Connecticut: (45) A.-11.5.

Courtship of Slick of Slickville; see *Samuel Slick, Esq.*

Cousin Cherry; farce: (50) W.-1.25*, 26, 30; 2.5; (54) A.-5.1; 7.3.

Cousin Joe; farce: (51) A.-9.13, 16; 11.5, 15; (53) C.-9.9; (54) C.-7.21.

Cousin Lambkin: (43) W.-5.27.

Cradle of Liberty, or Boston in 1775; by S. E. Glover: (38) W.-7.4; (40) 3.14.

Cramond Brig, or The Gudeman of Ballangeich; historical Scotch drama: (36) C.-12.5, 30; (38) C.-4.14; (39) C.-2.18; 4.27; 9.28; (39) W.-10.29; 11.5, 16; 12.10, 13; (40) W.-4.21; 6.6; C.-3.9; 5.2; (43) C.-2.13, 14; (51) N.-8.2; (52) A.-11.23, 25.

Crichton, or The Admirable Scot; "historical drama by Coleman of Philadelphia": (36) W.-8.14*, 15, 16, 17, 18, 19.

Cricket on the Hearth: (46) A.-2.19, 20, 21; 3.7, 12.27; P.M.-3.19, 20, 21, 23, 24, 25, 26, 28; A.-4.3; P.M.-4.3, 7, 9, 10, 11, 13, 15, 16, 18, 22, 24, 29; 5.1, 8, 9, 14, 15, 26; A.-5.7, 12, 29; 6.6; 7.11; P.M.-9.11, 12, 16; 10.24, 28, 31; A.-11.9; P.M.-11.14, 20, 24; 12.2, 16, 24, 31; (47) P.M.-1.9, 30; A.-1.28; P.M.-2.11; 3.1, 2, 4, 5, 19, 30; 4.19; 5.8, 25; 7.14; (48) P.M.-

3.18; 5.3; 7.1, 3; (49) Ath.-1.16; P.M.-7.27; (50) B.-9.9, 10, 16, 17, 23, 24, 25, 26; 10.22; 11.1, 28; 12.2; (51) B.-1.8, 22; 2.7; 5.7, 8; 6.3, 6, 14, 30; (52) C.-1.2; (54) C.M.-10.6, 7, 9, 21; 11.9; (55) C.-1.26; C.M.-12.18.

Crime and Repentance: (43) A.-12.25, 26.

Crimson Crimes, or Deeds of Dreadful Note; farce (by W. E. Burton): (46) A.-3.28*, 30; 4.1, 2, 25; 5.8; (47) A.-6.25; (49) ATH.-1.23; A.-3.12; P.M.-5.16; C.-10.1; (50) A.-10.30; (51) A.-7.15; W.-12.30, 31; (52) W.-1.21; 2.14; 5.24, 31; 6.8, 18; 9.18; (53) W.-1.15; 5.19; (54) C.M.-9.27; 10.13.

The Critic, or A Tragedy Rehearsed; by R. B. Sheridan: (35) C.-10.31; 11.23; (38) C.-5.28; (39) C.-4.19; 6.4; 8.26; (36) A.-3.5, 10, 14; (40) C.-6.3; N.-9.21; (41) W.-11.17, 19, 20; (44) A.-7.26; 8.2; (45) C.-9.10; (49) W.-12.28; (50) W.-1.3; (55) A.-5.18, 19, 21; 6.4; C.M.-12.11, 14.

The Crock of Gold; "Tupper's story dramatized by H. M. Ward." (47) P.M.-5.3*, 4, 5, 6, 7, 8, 13, 22; (49) A.-1.6, 8, 9, 23.

Crockett in Texas, or The Lone Star's Glory: (46) A.-3.17.

Cross of Gold: (52) A.-9.22.

Cross of Death, or The Dogs of Salamanca: (52) A.-4.2, 3; (53) C.-4.18, 20.

Crossing the Line, or Crowded Houses: (35) C.-10.12, 15; (36) C.-6.14, 29; 7.8; 11.21; (35) W.-12.15, 19, 21; (37) W.-2.21; (36) A.-5.9; 6.10; (37) A.-7.6; (36) P.-12.8, 28; (37) P.-1.6, 26; (38) C.-1.30; (42) A.-9.12; (48) P.M.-3.23; (50) A.-3.5, 15; 4.27; (51) A.-12.29; (52) C.-8.19.

Crown Diamonds: (53) C.-6.6; 9.9; (54) W.-11.6, 7, 8, 9, 10, 11, 17; (55) W.-2.20, 23.

Crown of Diamonds; comic opera: (51) C.-10.22, 24, 27, 29, 31; 11.26; (52) C.-2.16, 18; 3.5; 9.22; 10.8; (53) C.-1.10; 5.16.

The Crown Prince, or The Buckle of Brilliants; burletta: (39) C.-5.1, 2; 11.1; (40) C.-1.2, 25; 3.11; 5.11; (41) A.-4.24; 5.18; 6.15; (51) W.-10.23, 25, 28; 11.12.

The Crusaders: (55) C.M.-6.4.

Culprit: (43) C.-7.28.

Cupid: (35) A.-3.14*, 17; (36) A.-3.17, 22; 4.18; (35) C.-12.26; (45) W.-1.18.

Cupid in a Convent; see *Pet of the Petticoats.*

Curate's Daughter: (53) C.-12.1*, 2, 3, 5, 6, 7, 8, 9.

A Cure for Coquettes, or The Student of Oxford; comedy by D. Boucicault: (53) C.-12.7*, 8, 9, 10, 12, 26; (54) C.-1.11, 12.

A Cure for the Heartache; "musical comedy," by Thomas Morton: (35) C.-10.14; 11.20; (37) C.-4.11; 9.20; (38) C.-6.30; (36) W.-3.15; (37) P.-1.14; (39) C.-5.2; (40) C.-4.14; (42) C.-1.14; N.-1.28; (43) W.-7.10; (44) W.-4.22; (45) W.-2.20, 26; 7.3; 10.7; C.-12.6; (46) W.-1.10; C.-1.10; 5.23; (48) W.-1.14; A.-4.10, 12; (49) W.-4.2; (50) W.-1.3; C.-6.20; B.-12.4; (51) W.-1.3, 16; A.-4.17; W.-5.13; C.-10.3; (52) C.-1.6; 4.10, 15; 11.10; (53) C.-2.25; A.-3.9, 25; C.-6.15; A.-11.14; 12.13; (54) C.-6.23; A.-10.14, 17; 11.16; (55) A.-1.26; 2.8; 5.7, 31; 6.18; 9.21; 12.21.

Curfew, or Vision of the Dead: (37) P.-1.10.

Curiosity Cured, or Powder For Peeping; farce: (40) C.-5.18, 19, 22.

Curiosities: (43) W.-2.14.

Curiosities of Literature; farce: (44) N.-5.22.

The Custom of the Country: (52) C.-2.11*.

Cut and come Again: (40) A.-12.5, 8; (40) W.-12.15; (45) C.-5.3, 8, 9.

Cymbeline; by William Shakespeare: (44) W.-3.23, 28.

Damon and Pythias, or The Test of Friendship; tragedy by John Banim: (35) W.-1.9, 17, 27; 3.11; 6.25; 7.6; A.-4.4; W.-9.3; 10.9; 11.16; 12.28; C.-10.15; (36) C.-9.5; W.-2.4; P.-12.8; (37) W.-1.4, 25; 3.24; 7.27; C.-4.4; 11.17; P.-2.7; (38) C.-1.20; 2.1; 6.26; 12.3; W.-3.22; 8.1; 10.16; (39) C.-12.5, 16; W.-7.22; 9.18; (40) C.-9.22; 12.1; W.-4.22, 28; (41) A.-4.7, 24; 6.3; 8.26; W.-5.14, 20, 22; N.-8.23; (42) W.-3.14; A.-5.2, 5; C.-4.16; W.-5.23, 26; A.-10.18; W.-10.18; (43) A.-8.30; 9.22; N.-10.20; A.-12.27; (44) A.-1.18; N.-4.19; W.-9.7; 12.14; (45) W.-5.3; A.-10.7; 12.15; (46) A.-1.2; 2.28; 5.13; W.-10.26, (47) W.-1.8; 5.22; 11.2; (48) A.-7.19; C.-7.27; 9.7; 10.1; 12.13; (51) W.-10.6, 9; A.-10.6, 16; (52) A.-3.15; W.-6.11; A.-9.4, 17; W.-11.9, 19; (53) A.-2.7; 5.24, 25; W.-5.25; 10.10; 12.16, 17; (54) C.-9.29; W.-10.9, 14; (55) C.M.-6.4; W.-12.14, 21; A.-12.15; C.M.-12.21.

Damon and Pythias; farce: (40) W.-3.10, 12; (41) W.-4.23; (45) A.-12.15.

Damp Beds; farce: (35) W.-2.7*.

Dancing Barber; farce (by W. E. Burton): (38) C.-6.20*; 7.7; 9.12; (39) C.-3.29; (48) A.-8.19.

Dancing Bears of Cashmere: (50) C.-1.4.

The Dancing Feather, or Secrets of

Life in New York: (44) A.-10.24*, 25, 26, 28; 11.5.

Dancing Mad, or The Christmas Party: (45) A.-12.8, 10, 11, 25.

Dancing Scotchman: (40) N.-12.25, 26.

The Daring Man: (39) W.-12.18.

The Daring Yankee; see *Sam Patch.*

Dark Doings: (51) N.-8.1, 9.

The Dark Lady (of Dooua), *or The Bride's Revenge;* melodrama in two acts by W. E. Burton: (40) W.-4.17*, 18.

Darnley, or The Freebooters of Castle Keep: (49) A.-12.10, 11, 15.

Das Goldene Kreutz, or France in 1812-1815: (47) C.-6.11.

Das Kaetchen von Heilbronn; romantic drama in five acts: (51) C.-2.26, 27.

Das Pfefferroisel, or The Mass in Frankfort in 1297: (55) G.N.-8.30.

The Daughter; domestic drama in three acts by R. P. Smith: (36) W.-5.21*, 27; (37) C.-4.19; (42) W.-7.2; (43) C.-11.1, 2; (50) B.-10.8, 9; 12.12.

The Daughter; "first time in America, founded on Scribe's *La Lectrice,* with Miss Tree in title rôle": (37) C.-1.23*.

The Daughter of Evil; see *Devil's Daughter.*

Daughter of the Regiment, or The Gallant Twenty-First: (48) W.-10.2, 3, 6, 7; (49) W.-5.4; A.-11.3; W.-11.26, 28; 12.6; (50) A.-4.6; 10.14, 19; (51) A.-4.2, 4; W.-8.27; 9.10, 20; (52) C.-2.20, 23; 10.6; (53) C.-1.3; 5.20, 27; 6.3; 9.5, 24; W.-12.21, 24, 30; (54) C.-10.21; (55) C.M.-5.12, 15; 6.14, 15, 16, 29.

Daughter of the Stars: (50) W.-10.8, 9, 10, 12, 22; 11.1, 14, 22; 12.23; (51) W.-1.7; 2.10; (53) W.-1.24.

A Daughter's Love; see *Maid of Mariendorpt.*

David and Goliath; sacred drama by Hannah More: (50) A.-12.28, 30, 31.

David Copperfield; (by John Brougham): (50) B.-11.6*, 7, 8, 9; 12.3; (51) W.-2.17, 18, 19, 20, 22; B.-6.30; (52) C.-8.12, 13, 14, 17; 12.15; (53) C.-7.11, 13; (54) C.-8.12; (55) C.-1.19, 27; W.-5.3; C.M.-9.15, 17, 18.

A Day after the Fair, or My Nervous Debility; a farce: (35) C.-6.1; (36) C.-12.5; (39) C.-3.16; 5.31; (48) A.-12.2; (49) A.-10.22.

Day after the Wedding; comedy: (35) C.-10.26; 11.17; (39) C.-2.8; 3.22; 4.5; 5.22; (37) P.-1.9, 13; 2.17, 18; (38) W.-9.27; (39) W.-7.12; (40) W.-11.19; (39) C.-6.1; 12.31; (40) C.-3.17; 4.24; 6.29; 12.9; (42) W.-2.8; A.-9.17; (43) A.-4.26, 27; W.-5.3; 10.7, 20; (44) W.-6.19; 7.12; (45) W.-2.19; 6.28; C.-9.5; (46) P.M.-8.14; W.-10.19; P.M.-10.27; (47) W.-3.29; P.M.-5.6, 18; 6.8; W.-9.16; 11.24, 25; (48) W.-1.18; 3.6; P.M.-7.4, 5; A.-8.10; W.-10.20; A.-10.30; (49) W.-5.7; C.-8.16; 9.24; (50) W.-2.21; 3.6; (51) C.-3.12; 8.25, 26; 9.13, 20; 10.27; (52) C.-1.22; 3.29; W.-12.8; (53) W.-1.29, 31; (54) C.-4.20, 26; N.-6.6; C.-7.17, 19, 22; C.M.-11.3; A.-12.26; (55) W.-4.7, 11; 10.26.

A Day in New York: (41) N.-9.21, 22.

A Day in Paris; comedy: (35) W.-5.2, 5, 6, 15; (39) W.-7.15; (40) W.-12.24; (42) A.-5.12; W.-7.15; C.-12.5, 6, 12, 29; (46) P.M.-6.1, 11; (47) P.M.-2.20; 3.22; (48) C.-7.4; (52) C.-6.1; (54) C.-8.7; C.M.-11.3.

The Day of Reckoning; by J. R. Planche: (51) W.-5.2; A.-5.24; 6.16.

Day Well Spent; (by John Oxenford): (41) W.-7.10; (54) A.-1.21; 2.22; 6.5; 12.5, 9.

The Days of Kirk and Monmouth; see *Battle of Sedgemoor.*

Days of Old; see *Riever's Ransom.*

The Days of 1776; see *Benjamin Franklin.*

The Dead Shot: (35) A.-3.13; (40) A.-12.9, 15; (35) W.-9.14; (36) C.-11.3, 14; (37) C.-12.23; (39) C.-1.22; 2.11; 3.8, 14, 20; (39) W.-4.27; 11.26, 29; 12.16; (40) W.-1.21; 3.13; 6.19; 8.28; (41) W.-9.28; (39) C.-5.20, 27; 11.8, 14; 12.14; (40) C.-2.5, 8; 3.6; 5.19; 10.5; 11.3, 14; 12.5; (41) N.-4.9; (42) W.-3.9; 4.2; A.-5.7; 8.24; 9.16, 28; (43) O.-1.17; (46) P.M.-3.25, 31; A.-6.13, 30; P.M.-10.29; (47) P.M.-1.22; 7.14; W.-11.16, 23; 12.7; (48) A.-5.20, 27; W.-5.20; P.M.-7.6; W.-9.6; 11.1; A.-11.3; Ath.-12.25; (49) Ath.-1.12; W.-5.16; A.-5.17; W.-11.12; A.-12.20; (51) W.-1.14; 3.14; (52) C.-5.5; (53) C.-2.5, 21, 26; 3.11; 4.2; 7.14.

Deaf as a Post: (36) C.-11.30; (38) C.-5.17; 8.29; 11.22; (39) C.-3.6; 12.5, 28; (37) A.-6.22; (41) A.-4.5, 17, 30; (40) W.-11.9, 16; (45) A.-6.2; 3; W.-10.17, 20, 29; 11.1; (46) W.-2.21; 4.24; 5.4; P.M.-7.16, 23; W.-9.9, 15; 10.12, 24; 11.30; (47) W.-1.18; 3.25; 4.5; 6.1; 8.18; 12.11; (48) W.-4.8; 12.7, 12, 23; (49) W.-1.17; (54) C.-9.26; 10.23; (55) A.-10.19, 25.

The Death of Abel; see *The First Fratricide.*

The Death of the Moor: (35) Mam. C.-1.3, 12, 13.

The Death Fetch: (45) A.-7.19, 22, 26, 31.

Death Plank, or A True Tale of the Sea; by J. B. Buckstone: (35) A.-3.28*; (36) A.-4.7, 8, 13; (35) C.-6.10, 11, 13; 11.4, 5; (36) C.-6.30; 9.20, 21.

The Death Struggle; see *Andreas Zell.*

Death Struggle, or The Dying Gift: (54) C.M.-10.28.

The Death Token, or The Murderer's Fate; melodrama: (40) W.-7.11; C.-3.3*; (41) W.-7.1, 3; (46) A.-2.2, 3.

Debutante: (54) W.-1.2, 3, 4, 5, 6, 7, 9, 10, 11, 12, 13, 14; 3.17, 20, 22, 25; 5.6; 6.14; C.M.-9.22; (55) W.-9.15; C.M.-10.12.

Deceiver Deceived: (45) N.-5.6.

The Deceived Angus; see *Watchman.*

Declaration of Independence; national drama by John Brougham: (45) A.-11.14*; (53) C.-7.4, 5, 6.

Deeds of Dreadful Note; see *Crimson Crimes.*

The Deep, Deep Sea, or The American Sea Serpent, or Perseus and Andromeda: (35) W.-1.1*, 2, 8; A.-2.27, 28; 3.5, 7, 19, 24; (36) A.-3.15, 16; (37) A.-5.6, 9; C.-10.10, 12; (48) A.-4.18, 19, 25; (51) B.-1.21, 22, 23.

The Deformed, or Woman's Trial; by R. P. Smith: (39) C.-3.18; 12.21; (46) W.-1.19; (47) A.-11.19.

Delicate Attentions: (38) W.-1.15, 26; 2.6, 15.

Delicate Ground, or Paris in 1793: (50) C.-6.5, 12; 7.15, 16, 19; (51) W.-9.23, 26; 10.6; 11.6, 19; (52) W.-1.29; 2.16; 3.10; 5.11, 14; C.-10.13, 14; 11.3, 15, 18; (53) C.-1.1, 11; A.-3.24; W.-5.5; A.-12.23; (54) A.-1.19; W.-1.25, 26; 2.1; 3.8; A.-3.11; W.-5.11; A.-5.29; W.-10.27; 11.8, 20; (55) W.-3.20.

The Deliverance of Switzerland; see *The Conjuration.*

Delusion: (41) N.-3.30; C.-5.1.

The Delusion; comedy: (49) A.-4.20*.

Democracy and Aristocracy, or The Rich and Poor of New York: (50) A.-7.13*, 15, 16, 17, 18.

Demon Dwarf, or The Vampire Bat: (40) W.-11.26, 30; 12.1.

Demon Fire Fly: (41) W.-11.24, 25.

The Demon of the Wissahickon; see *Doctor Foster.*

The Demon of the Desert, or The Murderer's Sacrifice: (37) W.-12.4, 5, 6, 7, 8, 9, 11, 12, 13, 28.

The Demon Statue, or The Hand of Klishing: (36) W.-12.24*, 26, 30.

The Denouncer; see *Seven Clerks.*

Der Alte Teldherr; musical drama in one act: (39) A.-10.12.

Der Freischutz; grand opera by Von Weber: (37) C.-3.31; (39) W.-11.4, 5, 6, 7, 8, 9, 11, 12; (40) C.-3.23, 24, 25, 26, 27, 28; (43) C.-2.3, 4, 8; (45) C.-10.18, 20, 21, 23, 25; (47) C.-5.10; (51) B.-2.25, 26; W.-12.17, 18 (Incantation Scene).

Der Pariser Taugenichts, or The Printer's Apprentice; comedy in four acts: (51) C.-2.6.

Der Schauspieler Wider Willen; comedy in one act: (39) A.-10.12.

Der Nacht Wachter; see *Der Wachter.*

Der Wachter, or A Night's Adventures; comedy: (39) W.-10.19; (40) W.-1.11; N.-12.31; (42) A.-3.3; (43) W.-7.6; (46) A.-8.27, 28.

Der Wirrwar, or Confusion in all Corners; comedy in five acts by August von Kotzebue: (51) C.-2.10.

The Deserted Daughter; comedy by Thomas Holcroft: (35) C.-12.28; (36) C.-1.2; (39) C.-5.6.

Descart, the Free Buccaneer: (42) A.-1.1, 3.

Deserted Village: (35) C.-5.13*, 15, 18; 8.29; 9.2; (36) A.-3.23; (38) W.-2.3.

The Deserter; see *The King and the Deserter.*

The Deserter of Naples; domestic drama in one act: (35) A.-4.1*.

De Soto; historical romantic tragedy by G. H. Miles: (52) C.-4.19*, 20, 21, 22, 23, 24; 5.17, 18, 19, 21, 22, 23, 26; (53) C.-3.3, 5, 9; 6.22, 23; (55) C.M.-12.3, 4, 5, 6, 7, 8, 10, 11, 15.

Destruction of Jerusalem; melodrama by N. H. Bannister: (37) W.-11.20*, 21, 22, 23, 24, 25.

The Devil and the Deserter: (52) A.-3.2.

The Devil of Demeraro; see *Cabin Boy.*

The Devil to Pay; farce by Charles Coffey: (36) A.-3.26; 4.5; (45) A.-7.16, 17, 18.

Devil's Bridge; opera by S. J. Arnold: (38) W.-12.22; (39) W.-1.3; (40) N.-12.1, 8; (42) C.-1.12, 14; W.-11.28; (43) C.-1.7; (46) W.-7.1.

The Devil's Daughter; "melodramatic romance in twelve tableaux and two grand acts, translated from Auber's opera *La Tentation*": (35) C.-11.10, 11, 12, 13; (36) C.-6.23, 24, 28; 7.2; 9.14, 15, 17, 19, 23; 12.17; (38) C.-12.22; (39) C.-9.7; (40) C.-1.18; 2.12.

Devil's Daughters: (40) W.-6.11.

Devil's Ducat, or Earth, Air, Fire, and Water; romantic drama: (50) C.-6.17, 19; 7.3.

Devil's Head: (44) A.-8.17, 19, 24, 30.

Devil's in it: (54) C.-4.22; W.-11.23; C.M.-11.23.

The Devil's in the Dice; opera: (53) C.-1.7.

The Devil's in the Dice; see *The Sixes.*

Dew Drop, or La Sylphide; ballet opera with music by Schneitzhofer: (38) C.-3.17*, 19, 21, 23, 24, 26, 28, 30; 6.5, 6; (39) C.-6.10, 11, 12, 15; (40) W.-2.15, 17, 19, 20, 21, 22; 3.31; (41) C.-5.22, 24, 25; (42) W.-1.1, 4; (47) P.M.-3.15, 16, 26.

Diamond Arrow, or The Postmaster's

Wife and The Mayor's Daughter:
(36) W.-1.9, 12, 21, 27; 2.15;
3.21.

Dick, the Apprentice, or The Stage
Struck Apothecary; farce by Arthur
Murphy: (36) W.-6.29; 7.2.

Dick, the Newsboy; "new local drama"; comedy: (53) W.-10.31*; 11.1,
2; (54) W.-6.7, 10.

Dick Turpin; see *Richard Turpin.*

*Did you ever Send your Wife to Bris-
tol?;* farce: (46) P.M.-7.28, 29.

*Did you ever Send your Wife to Bur-
lington?;* farce: (46) W.-5.20*, 25,
27, 28; 8.22, 25; 10.22, 23; 11.24;
(47) W.-1.2; 4.2, 15; 6.2; 10.21;
11.1, 26; (48) W.-3.24, 25, 31; 4.1;
6.29.

*Did you ever Send your Wife to
Frankford?;* farce: (51) A.-5.30.

*Did you ever Send your Wife to Ger-
mantown?;* farce (by W. E. Burton): (46) A.-5.13*, 14, 15, 16;
W.-5.16, 19; (49) P.M.-7.3, 4, 11.

*Die Brilleninsel, [The Isle of Spec-
tacles]*; by August von Kotzebue,
with music by F. Riemann: (40) A.-
2.10*, 17.

Die Helden: (42) A.-3.2.

Die Humoristischen Studien: (40) A.-
6.30.

Die Reise von Berlin nach Potsdam;
comedy in one act: (40) A.-2.10.

Die Schleichhandler [The Smugglers];
comedy in four acts: (40) A.-1.25;
2.22.

Die Schweitzer Familie; see *The Swiss
Family.*

Die Selbstmoerder, or Self Murder:
(51) C.-2.6.

Die Sieben Maedchen in Uniform:
(55) G.N.-8.22.

The Discarded Child; see *Arabella.*

*Discoveries in the Moon, or Herschel
Out Herscheled;* by T. D. Rice: (35)
W.-9.5*, 7, 8, 10.

Disguise: (40) W.-5.22.

The Dishonored Bill; see *House Room.*

The Disowned, or The Prodigals; by
R. P. Smith: (36) W.-4.11; (47)
P.M.-6.3.

*The Disowned and his Poor Dog
Tray;* (39) W.-1.12, 18, 23; (40)
A.-12.28, 29.

Dissipated Child; comedy in one act
by August von Kotzebue: (37) A.-
7.27.

Distressed Mother; by Ambrose Philips: (40) W.-6.23; (43) A.-10.16.

Djim-Kro-Ryce; burlesque: (49) W.-
1.20; 4.4.

Doctor Dilworth; farce: (39) W.-
11.23, 25; C.-12.9, 10, 16; (40) W.-
1.24; (43) W.-1.24; (46) P.M.-9.7,
9, 14; 10.24; 11.11; (47) P.M.-5.13;
6.26; (49) A.-5.25; (51) C.-3.26;
10.7, 9, 13; 11.20; (52) C.-3.30; 4.3;
5.8; (53) C.-2.3; 3.14.

Doctor Wespe; in German, a comedy
in five acts by R. Benedia: (51) C.-
1.30, 31; 2.1.

*The Doctor's Discovery, or Enchanted
Pie:* (35) Mam.C.-1.7.

*Does your Mother Know you are
Out?;* farce (by W. E. Burton):
(38) C.-7.7*; W.-8.6, 7, 14, 17; (45)
A.-7.28.

Dog of the Ferry House: (53) C.-4.23,
29.

Dog of Montargis; see *Forest of
Bondy.*

The Doge of Venice; see *Marino Faliero.*

Dogs of Mount St. Bernard: (53) C.-
4.30.

The Dogs of Salamanca; see *Cross of
Death.*

Doings in France: (48) A.-3.25.

Dombey and Son; domestic drama by
John Brougham: (48) A.-9.14*, 15,
16, 18, 19, 20, 21, 22, 25, 26, 27;
(49) A.-2.26, 27, 28; 3.1, 2, 3; 4.7;

(52) C.-8.4, 5, 6, 7, 9, 17; A.-10.26; C.-12.13, 14; (53) C.-7.8, 9, 15; (54) C.-8.10, 14.

Domestic Economy: (52) W.-1.7, 9, 20; 2.16; 3.31; 5.6, 17; 6.2; 11.15; 12.2, 11; (53) W.-1.11; 2.14; 9.15; 10.6; 11.30; (54) W.-10.21; 11.1; (55) W.-2.22; 3.17.

Don Giovanni; farce: (38) C.-12.1.

Don Giovanni; opera by Wolfgang Mozart: (41) C.-5.4, 5, 6, 7; (49) W.-10.12, 13; 12.1; (50) C.-12.13; (51) C.-1.14.

Don Juan, or The Libertine Destroyed: (35) W.-6.20, 24, 25; (37) W.-1.21; (41) A.-11.11, 17; (42) W.-1.12, 13; (47) A.-7.13; (52) N.-5.26; (53) C.-4.16.

Don Juan; opera by Wolfgang Mozart: (37) C.-11.6*, 7, 8, 9; (39) W.-8.17; (40) W.-1.20; (41) A.-1.9, 12, 13; (43) A.-3.22.

Don Pasquale; opera by Gaetano Donizetti: (46) C.-4.27, 28, 29, 30; 5.1, 18; 6.1; W.-11.6; (47) C.-4.21, 29.

Don Pedro, the Cruel, or The Cobbler of Seville; melodrama: (39) W.-1.5, 7, 9.

Donation Concerts; burletta: (52) A.-3.15, 16, 17, 18.

Done for a Hundred; see *Seth Slope.*

Done on Both Sides: (49) A.-4.25, 26; 5.1; (53) W.-11.23, 25.

Don't Judge by Appearances: (55) W.-12.14, 15, 19, 25.

Doolittle Family; comedy by J. S. Silsbee: (45) A.-11.8*.

Doom of the Drinker; by T. D. English: (44) N.-4.22*, 23, 24.

Doom of the Spy: (44) A.-12.24, 25, 26, 27, 28.

The Doomed Crew; see *Uda and Magnus.*

The Doorkeeper Outwitted; see *Masquerade.*

Double-Bedded Room: (43) N.-10.28; 12.27; (44) N.-1.8, 17, 18; (49) A.-5.26, 28, 29; 6.9; 10.5; (52) C.-5.24; 6.3, 16; A.-8.30; 9.16; A.-11.8, 20; (54) W.-3.10, 11, 13, 14, 18, 23; 4.11, 29; 6.16; 10.13; 11.7, 21; 12.20; (55) W.-2.20; 3.20.

Douglas, or The Noble Shepherd; tragedy by John Home: (35) W.-1.8; (36) W.-1.7; (37) W.-7.26; (38) W.-8.4; (40) W.-6.26; (41) W.-1.28; N.-10.2; (42) N.-1.18; (43) A.-9.29; (45) W.-5.12; A.-10.10; (46) W.-6.13, 24; A.-11.25; (48) A.-2.14; W.-2.14; (49) A.-12.26; (51) A.-7.25; (52) C.-6.12; 7.20; (53) C.-2.18; (54) A.-4.19, 25, 29; (55) C.M.-1.22; 3.19.

Down East among the Dead Men; farce: (48) P.M.-4.22*.

A Down East Bargain, or Love in New York; by W. T. Moncrieff: (37) C.-9.16*.

The Down Easter; see *Kaspar Hauser.*

The Dramatist, or Stop Him who Can; comedy by Frederick Reynolds: (35) A.-4.1; (36) A.-6.2; (35) C.-11.16; (39) C.-3.25; (40) C.-4.8; 6.6; (37) W.-1.23; P.-2.3; (45) C.-7.2; (48) A.-6.22, 30; (49) W.-3.16, 29; 4.6; 5.7, 31; 12.27; (50) W.-1.1; 9.7; 12.25; (51) W.-5.9; 9.18; (52) C.-1.7, 13, 30; 4.10; 5.21, 27; 6.11; (53) C.-2.23; 3.1; 6.20; (55) C.M.-4.6, 9, 12, 21; 11.30; 12.13.

The Dream at Sea, or The Haunted Cave: (36) W.-4.25*, 28; 5.20; 6.17; (39) W.-6.21; 8.15; (40) N.-10.5, 13, 17; (41) N.-12.10; W.-6.29, 30; 7.2; (42) W.-2.17, 18; A.-10.15, 17; 11.3; (44) A.-7.22, 26; (45) A.-8.20; 9.23; (47) A.-7.16, 21, 31; 10.16; 12.17; (48) A.-1.28; 2.5; 8.12; 10.3; (50) A.-6.18; (52) A.-9.3; (54) N.-6.12, 13; A.-12.16.

Dream of Fate, or The Rich Jew of

4.23, 24; 8.23, 25; (48) P.M.-5.16; (50) A.-5.23; (55) A.-5.26; 6.2.

The Dumb Girl of Portici; see *Masaniello.*

The Dumb Girl of the Inn; see *Mountain Devil.*

The Dumb Man of Manchester, or the Felon Heir: (39) W.-1.10, 11, 24; (40) A.-12.30, 31; (41) A.-1.2, 22; (43) W.-4.12, 13, 14, 22; (45) A.-8.6, 8, 13; 11.20; (46) A.-3.5; 6.29; 12.16; (47) A.-1.12, 20; 5.5; P.M.-7.6, 8; (50) C.-4.4; A.-4.26; 5.2; (51) N.-8.14; (52) A.-5.15; N.-5.22, 25; (53) A.-1.15; (54) C.-2.10.

The Dumb Man of the Rocks: (45) A.-1.13.

The Dumb Sailor Boy; see *The Death Plank.*

The Dumb Savoyard and his Monkey: (35) W.-9.17*, 19.

The Dumb Slave, or The Grateful Lion; see *Hyder Ali.*

Dunn Brown; see *My Friend the Captain.*

Dutch Actor: (55) C.-4.7, 23, 27.

Dutch Burgomaster; see *Peter the Great.*

Dutch Governor: (43) A.-9.23, 29.

Dutch Richard: (55) C.-4.12, 21.

Dutchman in Love: (46) P.M.-3.12, 16; (55) C.-4.6, 9, 11, 14, 26.

The Dying Gift; see *Death Struggle.*

The Dying Gift; see *The Minerali.*

Eagle Eye, or The Steed of the Delawares: (49) A.-4.23*, 24, 25, 26, 27, 28.

The Eagle Eye and the Hand of Steel; see *Putnam.*

Earth, Air, Fire, and Water; see *Devil's Ducat.*

Earthquake: (43) W.-2.21, 22, 24.

Easy Joe Bruce; (by H. H. Weld): (41) A.-1.29*.

Eddystone Elf, or The Fiend of the Rock; new national drama: (51) N.-7.19*, 22.

Edgard, the Idiot: (40) W.-5.14, 15, 19.

Edith, or The Fair Maid of Philadelphia: (52) A.-5.1*, 3, 4, 5.

Education, or Friends and Enemies; comedy by Thomas Morton: (35) A.-4.3; (37) C.-8.22.

The Effects of Endorsing; see *The Promissory Note.*

Egyptian; by John Wilkins: (55) W.-3.14*, 15, 16, 17.

1841 and 1891; farce: (41) N.-2.2*, 3, 4, 5, 6, 8, 9, 10, 12; 3.8, 12, 16; 4.1.

Eighth of January; farce by L. A. Wilmer: (48) A.-1.8*, 10; (51) A.-1.10.

Ein Deutscher Krieger: (48) O.-5.22.

Elder Brother, or Love Makes the Man; comedy by John Fletcher: (45) A.-5.7; (46) W.-1.24, 28; 4.30; 5.1; 10.17; (49) W.-3.5, 13; (50) W.-1.4; (52) C.-1.8, 10; 4.15, 17; 5.28; (53) C.-2.23; 3.8; 6.15; W.-12.7, 9; (55) C.M.-4.6, 9.

El Hyder, or Love and Mystery: (37) W.-12.29; (39) W.-2.16, 18, 19, 20, 21; 3.20, 29; (41) W.-4.5, 6, 7, 10; (42) W.-3.26; (44) A.-1.26; (54) N.-7.3.

El Melechor; nautical drama: (50) C.-4.8*, 9, 10, 11.

Elixir of Love; comic opera by Donizetti: (46) C.-5.16; (47) C.-5.5, 18; (51) W.-8.22, 25. *V. L'Elisir D'Amore.*

Ella Rosenberg; by James Kenney: (39) W.-5.13; (41) A.-10.20, 22; (46) A.-4.20; 6.3; 12.12, 17; (49) A.-1.19; (51) A.-2.25; N.-7.29.

Ella Wareham; domestic drama in three acts by W. E. Burton: (37) A.-7.3; (40) C.-5.11.

Elshie, or The Wizard of the Moor: (51) N.-7.15, 16, 17.

Emerelda Isle: (45) A.-12.4.

The Emerald Isle, or The Witch of Killarney; by Mrs. Gibbs: (39) C.-6.6*, 8; (46) P.M.-10.19, 20, 22; (47) P.M.-2.24; (50) C.-3.13.

Emigrant's Daughter: (45) A.-3.22; (46) A.-3.28.

Emigrant's Dream: (48) W   21, 26.

Emigrants, or Englishmen Abroad; comedy: (39) W.-10.14.

Emigration, or The Progress of an Intemperate; domestic drama by W. E. Burton: (40) W.-4.11*, 14, 16; (46) P.M.-8.17.

Emilie Plater, or The Polish Heroine; by S. S. Steele: (45) W.-5.20*, 21, 22, 23.

Emilia, or The Patriot's Wife: (42) A.-7.28; 8.5.

The Empire of Hayti; or Kingcraft in 1852; farce by T. D. English: (49) A.-10.2*, 3, 4.

The Enchanted Chinese, or A Fete at Pekin: (41) N.-4.19, 21.

The Enchanted Isle; see The Tempest.

The Enchanted Lake and the Hall of Fate, or The Wizard Priest: (44) N.-2.3, 5, 6, 7, 8, 9, 10, 13, 14, 15, 16, 17, 19, 20, 21, 22.

The Enchanted Pie; see The Doctor's Discovery.

The Enchanted Trumpet; see Harlequin and the Magic Trumpet.

Enchanter: (46) A.-6.29; 7.2, 6, 21.

The Enchantress; operatic drama in three acts by Balfe: (46) W.-1.31*; 2.3, 4, 5, 6, 7, 9, 10, 11, 12, 13, 14, 16; 3.2, 3, 4, 5, 6, 7, 9, 10, 11, 12, 13, 14, 16, 17, 18, 24; 4.1, 3, 13, 14; 6.15, 16, 17; 7.4; (48) W.-5.30, 31; 6.1, 2, 3, 19, 20, 21, 22, 23, 24; 7.4; (49) W.-4.23, 24, 25, 26, 27, 28; 5.2, 4; (52)

N.-8.16, 17, 18, 19, 20, 21, 23, 24, 25, 26; C.-10.1, 4; (53) C.-5.23.

The Englishman's Fireside; see John Bull.

Englishmen Abroad; see Emigrants.

Englishmen in India; comedy: (35) C.-5.26, 29; 11.19, 26; 12.29; (38) C.-5.23; 9.27; (36) A.-5.30; (41) A.-5.20; (38) C.-12.27; (39) C.-11.9, 12; (40) C.-1.21; 11.9; 12.18; (39) W.-7.13; 9.11; (40) N.-9.28; (42) A.-7.12, 15; C.-11.21; (43) W.-3.31; (44) W.-4.23.

Enthusiasm: (42) C.-11.11.

Ernani; opera by Giuseppe Verdi: (48) C.-3.15, 17, 18; W.-8.24, 25; C.-12.19, 21, 23; (50) C.-9.14; 12.17, 26; (51) C.-1.10, 15.

Ernestine: (46) W.-9.30; 10.1, 3; A.-10.19, 26, 29; (48) W.-4.26.

Ernest Maltravers; by L. H. Medina: (46) A.-4.16, 17.

The Escape of King Charles the Second; see Marie de Montville.

Esmerelda, or The Hunchback of Notre Dame; (by E. Fitzball): (35) C.-1.1; (44) N.-3.18, 19, 20; (46) A.-2.14, 16, 17; (50) C.-2.9, 11, 12, 13; A.-7.26, 27.

Etiquette; see Etiquette Run Mad.

Etiquette Run Mad: (35) C.-5.5.

The Eton Boy; burletta: (46) W.-7.24, 25; P.M.-12.7, 10; (49) P.M-7.7, 12, 14, 28; (50) W.-8.31; 9.2, 9, 30; 10.24; 11.6, 16; 12.14; (51) A.-1.30; 2.21; (52) C.-8.30; 9.1; (53) C.-9.3, 7, 21; 11.9; 12.23; (54) C.-1.5; W.-1.27, 28; C.-2.11; W.-3.3; C.-3.23; 4.22; 5.9, 27; W.-6.13; 9.7, 29; 11.9, 25; 12.25; (55) W.-2.13, 23; 4.30; 5.24; 11.2, 12.

Eudocia, or The Siege of Damascus; tragedy: (48) W.-4.20, 21.

Eugene Aram: (43) A.-3.4, 7.

Eustache, the Condemned: (54) C.M.-

10.14, 16, 17, 18, 19, 20, 21, 23, 25, 26, 27, 28; 11.7; 12.21.

Eva, the Page: (45) C.-11.24*, 26.

Evadne, or The Statue; tragedy by R. L. Sheil: (35) W.-3.13; (39) C.-5.27; 6.1; (41) A.-10.15; N.-12.8; (45) W.-5.17; A.-10.8; (46) W.-10.9; (47) A.-9.24; 12.7; (48) A.-2.1; W.-4.25; A.-10.16; 12.9, 13; (49) A.-3.26; 10.30; 11.17; (50) A.-4.3; C.-7.25; A.-10.9; (51) C.-3.8, 27; W.-3.31; A.-4.9; 6.2; W.-11.6; (52) C.-3.8; A.-10.5; (53) C.-3.17; W.-5.11; 9.27; (54) C.-1.6; (55) C.M.-5.1; W.-5.11.

Everybody's Husband; farce in one act: (36) A.-3.11; (38) W.-7.10; (49) A.-5.17, 18; 9.17.

Every Inch a Sailor: (51) A.-11.22, 24; 12.17.

Everyone has his Fault; comedy by Mrs. Elizabeth Inchbald: (37) C.-8.19; 9.22; (44) W.-2.19, 21; 4.11; (45) W.-2.4; (46) W.-3.23; (49) W.-5.25; (54) A.-5.30; 6.1.

Evil Day: (39) W.-2.4*.

The Evil Eye; by J. B. Phillips: (37) P.-2.4; (40) P.-7.20; (44) N.-3.16; (51) A.-12.16, 24.

Exchange no Robbery, or Who's My Father; comedy: (44) A.-10.29; 11.4; (45) A.-4.7.

Exciseman of Winchester; see *Turning the Tables.*

The Executioner; melodrama: (35) W.-3.14.

The Exile, or The Russian Daughter: (35) W.-10.7, 8; C.-10.29, 30; (36) A.-2.27; 5.4; (40) N.-1.30; W.-4.1; (42) N.-1.22.

Exile of Erin: (43) W.-4.22; (48) P.M.-5.5, 6.

The Exile of Naples; see *Romanzo.*

The Exile's Oath; see *Caradora.*

Exiles of Erin; comedy: (48) A.-3.10*.

The Extorted Oath; see *Castle of Paluzzi.*

Extremes; comedy by J. A. Sperry: (50) W.-3.25*, 26, 27, 28, 29, 30; 4.1, 2, 3, 4, 5, 6, 8, 9, 10, 11, 12, 13; 5.17; 6.9, 12, 13, 26; 7.1; 8.30; 10.21, 22, 24; 12.9; (51) W.-2.21; 12.10, 16, 19, 25; (52) W.-2.2, 6; 5.3, 6; (53) W.-5.3; 12.26, 27, 29; (54) W-5.8; (55) W.-9.6, 10.

Faint Heart never won Fair Lady: (40) W.-5.9, 29; 6.3; 10.17, 19, 22; 11.4, 17; (41) W.-11.26; C.-5.29; 6.17; 8.29; 9.1; A.-7.5; N.-8.21, 23; (42) C.-2.1, 2, 4, 9; 12.24, 26; (43) C.-2.15, 16; 7.28; (44) W.-6.6; 7.16; (45) W.-3.25; C.-9.5; W.-11.13, 14, 25; (46) P.M.-6.30; 7.1, 3; P.M.-8.26; W.-10.16, 28; P.M.-11.9; (47) P.M.-1.5; 2.2; W.-3.27, 31; P.M.-4.23; 6.17; (48) W.-2.10; 3.16, 20; P.M.-5.8, 11; A.-9.1, 2; 10.2; 11.3, 29; 12.16; (49) A.-3.20; P.M.-6.27, 28; 7.14; A.-8.30; C.-9.4; A.-9.28; 10.26; (50) C.-3.18; A.-7.19; 8.7; B.-11.18, 19; 12.6; (51) C.-3.20; W.-4.4, 12; 6.4; B.-7.2, 3; 10.6, 7; C.-10.8, 17, 18; (52) C.-3.15, 18; W.-5.5; C.-5.31; 6.4; A.-8.26; (53) W.-5.13, 23; A.-5.26; C.-6.28; 9.19; 11.8; (54) C.-1.24; 3.17; 5.19; C.M.-9.12, 26; C.-11.8; C.M.-11.14; 12.12; (55) A.-1.2, 5; C.M.-1.16; 3.20; W.-4.6, 14; C.M.-9.20, 22; W.-10.26; A.-11.1.

The Fair American; see *Young Quaker.*

The Fair Maid of Philadelphia; see *Edith.*

The Fair One of the Golden Locks: (47) P.M.-4.5, 6, 7, 8, 9, 10, 17; (48) W.-1.29; 2.5, 7, 8, 12, 16, 22; 3.4; 4.6, 21; 5.6; 6.1; (50) B.-11.27, 28, 29, 30; 12.9; (52) W.-3.17, 18, 19, 20.

Fair Philadelphian; comedy by John O'Keeffe: (42) A.-10.26.

Fair Star: (45) A.-7.23, 24, 25, 26; 8.5.

Fairly Hit and Fairly Missed: (44) N.-1.24, 25.

Fairly Taken in; see *Personation.*

The Fairy and the Little Glass Slipper; see *Cinderella.*

Fairy Circle; legendary drama: (55) W.-9.25, 26, 27, 28.

Fairy Dew Drop: (52) A.-1.7.

Fairy Lake; operatic drama: (50) A.-7.29.

The Fairy of the Golden Wheat Sheaf: (46) A.-3.31; 4.4.

Fairy Star: (54) W.-11.24.

Faith and Falsehood, or The Fate of a Bushranger: (37) W.-11.25*, 27, 28, 29, 30; (38) W.-1.8; 3.20; (42) W.-1.12; A.-5.21, 25, 31; (44) W.-2.12; 3.9.

The Faithful Irishman; see *Honest Thieves.*

The Faithful Page; historical drama: (40) C.-2.25; 3.10.

Faithful Slave, or The Doom of the Fratricide: (49) C.-10.1, 9; (52) N.-7.19, 29; (54) C.-7.21.

Fall of the Alamo, or Texas and Her Oppressors: (36) A.-5.26*.

Fall of Algiers; by J. H. Payne: (44) N.-4.9, 10, 11; (51) A.-9.29, 30; 10.23.

Fall of Kessichack; Eastern drama by General Harlan: (45) C.-5.8*, 9, 10.

The Fall of Tarquin; see *Brutus.*

Falls of Clyde: (35) C.-12.31; (36) W.-10.10; (40) W.-6.13; (42) A.-11.29, 24; (44) N.-3.20.

The Fallen Saved; see *The Deformed.*

False and True: (45) A.-11.27.

False Colors: (51) A.-12.25.

False Pretences, or The Tinker and His Family; farce: (46) P.M.-12.5, 14; (47) P.M.-2.27; 5.7.

Familiar Friend: (42) C.-12.7, 8, 10, 13, 14, 28; (43) C.-1.19; 2.3.

Family Jars: (35) C.-4.25; 5.7; (36) P.-12.21; (38) C.4.24; 5.19; 6.14; 8.28; (39) C.-3.7, 13; (40) W.-10.20, 27; (42) N.-1.24; (42) A.-4.1; (43) A.-12.11, 23; (45) W.-12.9, 10, 16; (46) P.M.-10.14; (47) A.-2.2; (50) A.-3.6; (52) A.-5.6, 11; (53) A.-10.12, 18; 11.5; (54) N.-6.15, 19, 20; C.-8.15, 18; 9.16; 12.13, 14, 15, 16; (55) W.-12.22, 24, 29.

Family Ties, or The Will of Uncle Josh; prize comedy winning five hundred dollars, by J. M. Field and John S. Robb: (51) A.-7.24*, 26, 28.

Fancy Stocks: (46) A.-1.1.

Farmer and the Baronet: (47) P.M.-6.21.

The Farmer's Daughter; see *Mary.*

The Farmer's Daughter; see *Broken Hearted.*

The Farmer's Son, or Harlequin and the Fairy of the Rose: (36) W.-7.10*, 11, 12, 13, 14; 8.4.

The Farmer's Story; drama in three acts by the author of *Lucille* and *A Woman's Faith:* (36) C.-10.27*, 28; (37) A.-5.30.

Fashion, or Life in New York; by A. C. O. M. Ritchie: (45) W.-4.16*, 17, 18, 19, 21, 22, 23, 24, 25, 26, 28, 29, 30; 5.1, 2; 6.30; 8.22; 9.2, 3; (46) W.-5.27, 28, 29; 6.3, 5, 22; 10.8, 10; (47) W.-5.5; 6.24; (52) W.-2.4; (54) C.M.-12.13, 14, 15, 16, 18, 19; (55) C.M.-1.10.

Fashion, or How to Write a Comedy; burlesque (by W. E. Burton): (45) A.-4.22*, 23, 25, 26, 29.

Fashion and Famine; by C. W. Taylor: (55) C.-2.5*, 6, 7, 8, 9; 3.3, 5, 6, 7, 8, 9, 17.

Fashionable Arrivals: (42) C.-2.16, 17, 18, 19; (49) P.M.-5.2, 3.

Fashionable Friends: (40) C.-9.8, 10; (41) A.-5.6, 7; (42) W.-7.25.

Fashionable Society: (48) P.M.-5.9, 12.

The Fast Man; comedy: (52) C.-8.14*, 16; (53) C.-7.7; (54) C.-8.11, 17.

Fatal Anacondas; see *Children of Chittigong.*

Fatal Curiosity; by George Lillo: (47) W.-12.25.

The Fatal Dowry; tragedy by Philip Massinger: (45) W.-10.27, 28; 11.1; 12.29; (46) W.-6.30; (48) W.-9.7; 10.31.

The Fatal Hazard; see *Gabrielle.*

The Fatal Keepsake; see *Military Execution.*

The Fatal Marriage; see *Isabella.*

The Fatal Oath; see *Zanthe.*

Fatal Prophecies, or The Smuggler's Daughter; melodrama in three acts by H. J. Conway: (35) W.-12.5*.

The Fatal Ravine; see *Alpine Hunters.*

The Fate of Ambrose, or The Sea-side Story of the Olden Time: (46) P.M.-4.20, 21.

The Fate of a Bushranger; see *Faith and Falsehood.*

The Fate of a Coquette; see *Camille.*

The Fate of Argos; see *Ion.*

The Fate of Calas, or The Wronged Father; domestic drama: (36) W.-8.27, 29, 30; (42) A.-10.29, 31; 11.14.

The Fate of Haman; see *The Jewess.*

The Fate of the Lily of St. Leonard; see *The Whistler.*

Father and Daughter; by Ranger: (40) N.-10.21.

The Father and Son, or the Convent Ruins; melodrama by Mrs. H. Siddons: (37) C.-11.10*, 11.

A Father by Chance: (42) A.-5.27; 6.3.

A Father's Malediction, or The Mountain Minstrel Boy: (46) A.-5.21, 22; 6.2, 8.

A Father's Return From Slavery; see *Ransom.*

Faustus; grand romantic spectacle: (45) A.-8.9; (51) W.-5.26, 27, 28, 29, 30, 31; 6.2, 3, 4, 5, 6, 7, 9, 10, 11, 12, 13, 14.

Fazio, or The Italian Wife; tragedy by H. H. Milman: (35) C.-1.12; 2.6, 21; 9.2, 28; W.-2.25; 5.28; 9.11; (36) W.-10.13; (37) C.-2.4, 7; 12.21; W.-6.19; (38) C.-4.21, 23; W.-6.19; (38) C.-4.21, 23; W.-2.7, 10; 12.19; (41) C.-10.2; N.-3.4; (44) N.-2.12; W.-6.14; 7.3; A.-7.6; W.-8.23; C.-11.20; (45) W.-2.15, 17; A.-5.26; W.-8.1, 30; 10.22; 12.17; (46) W.-1.29; 6.2; A.-9.5; W.-10.7; A.-11.26; 12.15; (47) W.-2.17, 20; 4.10; 5.25; A.-7.24; (48) W.-4.24; (50) A.-5.27; W.-11.18; (51) W.-2.17, 19; A.-3.26; W.-3.27; A.-6.5; (52) C.-3.10, 15; 7.19, 30; 8.26; A.-9.6; 10.29; (53) W.-2.22; C.-3.19; W.-9.10, 26; (54) C.-4.5; A.-4.13, 17; W.-9.4, 7; C.-10.5; C.M.-12.11; (55) W.-5.8; A.-11.6.

The Felon Heir; see *Dumb Man of Manchester.*

Felon's Last Dream, or Jack Sheppard in France: (45) A.-12.6, 8, 9; (46) A.-1.10; 7.4, 7.

Female Blue-Beard, or Le Morne-au-Diable: (44) W.-5.17, 18.

Female Curiosity; see *Blue Beard.*

Female Forty Thieves; burlesque: (49) C.-11.15, 16, 17.

Female Guard, or Bloomers in China: (51) A.-12.1, 2, 3, 4, 5, 6, 8, 9, 10, 11, 12, 13.

The Female Sailors; see *Home Squadron.*

The Festival of St. Michael, or Wealth a Curse; domestic drama in two acts by Edward Thompson: (44) W.-1.29*.

[575]

Follies of a Night: (45) C.-11.4, 7;
(46) W.-9.25, 26; (47) W.-1.22, 23;
(48) P.M.-4.10, 13; (53) A.-5.16,
18, 21; W.-10.7, 8; (54) A.-4.17, 27.

Folly as it Flies, or Modern Duelling:
(38) C.-6.21.

Fontainbleau, or Our Way in France;
comic opera by John O'Keeffe: (37)
C.-4.14; (39) C.-3.30.

The Force of Love; see *Susanne.*

The Force of Nature; see *The Wild
Boy.*

The Forced Marriage; see *Julie.*

*Foreign Affairs, or The Court of
Queen Anne:* (42) C.-10.22*, 26, 27.

Foreign Airs and Native Graces:
(40) C.-1.24, 27, 28, 30; 2.1, 15; 5.13,
23; (41) N.-11.9.

Foreign Graces: (42) C.-11.24; (43)
C.-2.9, 10.

Foreign Prince: (40) W.-12.15; (41)
A.-11.12; (44) A.-1.19; (46) A.-
2.14; (48) A.-3.1; W.-12.22; (49)
N.-10.11; (50) A.-5.3.

Forest of Bohemia; see *Woodman's
Hut.*

Forest of Bondy, or Dog of Montargis:
(35) W.-6.11, 12, 13; 10.7, 14, 16;
(36) W.-1.23; (37) P.-1.23; W.-
1.24; (39) W.-1.22; (41) A.-1.6, 7,
12, 13; (43) W.-4.17, 21; (45) A.-
9.11, 12, 13, 15, 16, 18, 20; W.-11.22;
(46) A.-1.8; (52) A.-3.29, 31; 4.14;
(53) O.-4.12, 14, 21.

*Forest of Rosenwald, or Raymond and
Agnes;* melodrama by J. Stokes:
(35) W.-4.4; C.-6.2; (38) W.-3.19;
(39) W.-7.13; (42) W.-6.18; (44)
A.-1.24; (51) B.-4.9; (54) N.-7.4.

*Forest Princess, or Two Centuries
Ago;* historical play by Mrs. C. B.
Conner: (48) A.-2.15*, 16, 17; (50)
A.-4.29; 5.3.

Forest Rose, or American Farmers;
"national pastoral comedy" by Sam-

uel Woodworth: (35) W.-5.9, 14;
12.16, 18; C.-9.8, 12; (36) W.-5.6,
11, 16; A.-5.21, 24; (37) C.-9.9;
9.11; W.-12.21; (38) C.-4.3; W.-
7.19, 23; (39) W.-4.9; W.-4.16, 18;
5.10; 10.23, 29; (40) W.-1.23; (41)
A.-9.22, 23; 10.14; N.-11.22; (44) A.-
10.17; (45) C.-5.2, 10; (47) W.-4.21;
(49) P.M.-5.16, 23, 24; (50) A.-11.4,
11; (51) A.-3.15, 18; (52) W.-5.18,
19, 22, 26; A.-12.28, 31; (53) C.-
2.15; W.-8.31; (54) C.-7.14; 9.16.

The Forgotten Friend; see *Gisippus.*

Fortunate Couple: (40) W.-5.11.

*Fortune's Frolic, or The True Use of
Riches, or The Ploughman Turned
Lord:* (35) C.-5.4; W.-5.28; (36)
C.-6.21; W.-3.20; 4.14; (39) C.-4.2,
9; 6.3; (37) W.-2.2; (40) C.-5.13;
(36) A.-3.29; 6.3; P.-11.12, 13;
12.30; (37) P.-2.2; (39) W.-5.23;
(40) C.-6.1; 12.24; (42) A.-7.7; (43)
A.-9.14; (52) C.-8.19; 12.11; (54)
C.-7.5, 8.

Fortune's Whim: (51) A.-2.6; 5.7, 14;
11.3.

Fortune Hunter: (53) W.-11.18, 19.

Fortune of War: (48) C.-7.26.

Fortune Teller: (41) W.-4.5, 6, 7, 8, 9;
(45) A.-10.10; (48) A.-6.16.

*Fortunio, and His Seven Gifted Serv-
ants;* fairy extravaganza in two acts,
being the nursery tale of Countess
D'Anois, dramatized by J. R.
Planché: (44) N.-5.11*, 13, 14, 15,
16, 17, 18, 20, 21, 22; (45) C.-1.25,
27, 28, 29, 30, 31; 2.1; (46) P.M.-
9.1, 2, 3, 4, 5, 7, 8, 9, 14, 18; 11.18;
12.12; (54) A.-12.23, 25, 26, 27, 28,
29, 30; (55) A.-1.1, 2, 3, 4, 5, 6, 8,
13, 15, 16, 17, 18, 19, 20, 22, 23, 29;
W.-12.31.

Forty and Fifty; farce: (36) W.-6.3*,
7, 9, 28; (37) C.-9.11, 13; (41) A.-

8.19, 20, 23; (42) W.-6.10; (51) C.-3.3, 6, 13, 21; 9.3, 10, 22, 25; 10.10, 22, 28; (52) C.-1.3, 26; 2.27; 3.23; 4.16; 5.12; 10.15; 12.23; (53) C.-3.28; 6.7; (54) C.-4.17, 18; 5.6.

Forty Thieves: (35) A.-3.30; (36) W.-12.26; (37) A.-6.29; (39) W.-2.9, 11, 12, 13, 14, 15, 22; 3.1, 14, 30; 12.10, 11, 13, 14; (40) W.-1.6; (41) W.-1.7; (46) W.-7.2; (49) C.-10.26, 31; (50) B.-11.11, 12, 13, 14, 15, 16, 18, 19, 20, 21, 22, 25, 26; (51) A.-11.28; (52) N.-9.27, 28; (54) C.M.-12.25, 26, 27, 28, 29, 30; (55) C.M.-1.1, 2, 3, 4, 5, 6, 9.

Forty Winks, or Blunders in a Bed Room; farce by W. E. Burton: (35) C.-1.3; 5.20; 6.16; 7.1; 8.31; 9.3; A.-3.21; (36) C.-1.15, 25; 2.12; (37) C.-2.25; 3.28; 4.7; 10.24; 12.4; (38) C.-2.10; 3.19; 6.26; (41) N.-3.16, 19, 31; (48) A.-7.15; (54) N.-6.14; C.-8.21; 11.8; (55) C.M.-5.28, 30; 6.2; 9.25.

Forty Years of Life: (50) C.-7.30.

Foulah Slave; melodrama: (39) W.-1.10; (41) A.-1.12, 13; (45) A.-8.13; (55) C.-4.6.

Founded on Facts: (49) W.-3.8, 28; P.M.-7.20.

The Foundling, or Yankee Fidelity; by R. C. McLellan: (40) C.-3.31; 4.8; A.-1.29, 30.

The Foundling of an Apple Orchard; see Yankee Land.

The Foundling of the Forest; play by Diamond: (35) W.-2.18; C.-6.5; (37) C.-8.29; (38) W.-12.11; (40) W.-10.27; (41) W.-2.10; 12.21; N.-1.8; (42) C.-5.7; (44) W.-37; A.-8.28 (45) W.-2.8, 14; A.-7.24; 12.16; (46) A.-2.18.

The Foundling of Paris; see Madelaine.

Four Lovers: (37) C.-1.31; 2.1; A.-6.24.

The Four Mowbrays; see Old and Young.

The Four Sisters: (35) W.-10.5; (41) W.-3.3; 6.26; (42) A.-10.7; (46) P.M.-12.8; (49) P.M.-4.30; 5.1, 30; 6.4; (51) B.-10.27; 11.24; 12.18, 19, 20; (52) W.-9.6, 16; 10.15; (54) A.-3.27; (55) C.M.-3.15, 16; 4.3; A.-11.30; 12.1.

The Four Wishes; see The Bee and the Orange Tree.

Fox and Wolf: (42) W.-2.18.

The Fox Hunt; by Dion Boucicault: (54) C.-4.29*; 5.1, 2, 3.

Fra Diavolo, or The Inn of Terracina; opera: (36) C.-1.22, 29; 2.6; A.-4.25; 5.3; (37) C.-10.17; 11.4, 14; (38) C.-3.10; (39) C.-1.29, 30, 31; 2.1, 2; 4.2, 4, 6, 9.18, 20, 28; W.-11.15, 16, 18; (40) C.-4.28; 10.9; C.-11.2, 7; (41) C.-5.24, 29; 6.4, 5; (42) C.-12.23; (43) C.-1.28, 31; 2.7, 9; (44) C.-4.5; 6.22; 6.4; (45) C.-1.6, 10; 5.29, 30; 6.23; 10.16, 22; (46) W.-12.15; (47) C.-4.6, 13, 19; 5.11; W.-10.22, 23; (48) W.-9.28, 30; (49) W.-4.30; 11.27; (51) W.-8.19, 21; 9.13; 12.6; (53) C.-9.21, 23; (54) W.-11.14, 16; (55) W.-2.19; C.M.-6.18, 20, 23, 25.

France in 1812–1815; see Das Goldene Kreutz.

Francesca da Rimini; romantic tragedy by G. H. Boker: (55) W.-10.10*, 11, 12, 13, 16.

Frank Fox Phipps: (36) W.-6.20; (38) W.-7.31.

Frankenstein, or The Fate of Presumption: (44) N.-2.15, 16, 17, 20, 21.

Franklin; by John Brougham: (46) C.17*, 19, 20.

Freaks and Follies: (36) C.-1.6*, 11.

The Freaks of Love; see Naval Engagements.

Frederick the Great: (42) A.-7.5; (52) N.-5.24; (53) A.-1.13.

The Freebooters of Castle Keep; see *Darnley.*

Freedom's Last Martyr; national drama by W. M. Leman: (45) W.-7.4*, 5, 7, 8; (46) W.-1.8.

Freemason, or The Secret of the Lodge Room; farce: (39) W.-10.3.

The French Spy, or The Wild Arab of the Desert: (35) A.-3.25, 26, 28; C.-6.10, 11, 20; 11.2, 3, 5, 9, 21; (36) A.-3.28, 29; 4.2, 12; 6.4; C.-6.20, 24; 9.12, 13; 12.10, 15; (37) A.-6.16; W.-6.20, 22; 8.22; A.-7.4; (38) C.-10.24, 25, 26; 11.3; 12.3, 21; (39) C.-8.28; 9.3; (40) C.-1.9, 10, 15; 2.17, 18; (41) W.-2.15, 16, 17; A.-1.18; (42) C.-10.18, 19, 27; (44) N.-2.24, 27, 28; 4.1; (46) A.-1.30, 31; 8.31; 9.1; 12.14; (47) A.-1.21; W.-8.23, 24, 25, 26, 28; 9.1, 25; (48) W.-1.15; 2.14; (50) C.-2.4, 5; (51) W.-11.12, 13, 14, 15, 17, 21, 25, 27; (52) W.-5.11, 13, 15; N.-8.28, 31; A.-8.28; 10.1; (54) C.-10.12, 14.

French Washer Woman; comedy: (35) W.-11.3, 7; (36) W.-4.9.

Friar's Oak: (38) W.-12.24*, 25, 27; (39) W.-1.3.

A Friend in Need; see *The Banker.*

Friend Waggles; farce: (50) C.-7.31; W.-10-2, 3, 5, 7, 21; 11.5, 7; 12.12, 28; (51) W.-1.21; 3.6; 4.9; 5.29; (53) W.-2.16, 24; 3.16; 4.12, 28; 5.30; (54) W.-2.28; 3.2, 21; 4.12; N.-6.24; C.M.-10.23; 11.

Friends and Enemies; see *Education.*

Frightened to Death; farce: (39) W.-5.6, 11; (40) W.-5.16; (41) A.-8.14; (46) P.M.-6.17, 19, 27; (52) C.-12.24.

Frolics of Thomas: (43) W.-8.5, 9, 10.

From 6 to 6; an interlude in one act: (35) W.-6.24.

From Village to Court: (54) C.M.-10.30, 31; 11.1, 6; 12.11; (55) C.M.-3.22; 4.4, 11.

The Frontier Maid; "national drama written by M. M. Noah especially for Mlle. Celeste": (40) C.-2.17*, 18, 19, 22.

The Frozen Hand; see *The Ice Witch and the Sun Spirit.*

The Fruits of a Single Error; see *Adelgitha.*

Gabrielle, or the Fatal Hazard; domestic drama by J. M. Field: (43) W.-9.16*, 18, 19, 20, 21, 23, 25, 29.

The Gallant Twenty-First; see *Daughter of the Regiment.*

Gambler's Fate, or A Lapse of Twenty Years, or Trente Ans Ou La Vie D'Un Jouer: (36) A.-6.3; P.-11.14, 17; 12.1, 31; (39) W.-5.18; 6.5; (41) W.-4.19; 11.16, 18, 22; (42) A.-8.4, 24; (47) W.-8.16, 19, 27; (49) W.-4.3; (51) W.-3.28.

Game, Life, Stakes, Death; see *Hand of Cards.*

The Game of Life; comedy in five acts by John Brougham: (54) W.-6.26*, 27, 28, 29.

The Gamester; tragedy by Edward Moore: (35) W.-4.9; 5.22, 27; C.-5.20; 9.23, 28; (36) C.-11.3; A.-3.2; (39) C.-3.13; (41) C.-10.27; (45) W.-5.13; C.-9.15, 26; (46) A.-5.4; W.-9.14, 17; (47) W.-1.29; 4.28; A.-9.22; 11.3, 15; (48) A.-10.12; (49) A.-4.20; (50) A.-4.8; W.-4.26; 6.4; 9.6; A.-10.10, 15; (51) B.-2.5; C.-3.15; A.-4.8; (52) C.-6.7; A.-10.28; (53) C.-2.25; 6.2; W.-9.20; A.-12.10, 15; (54) C.-4.8; 10.17; A.-12.16; W.-12.29; (55) C.M.-4.4; 5.11.

The Gamester of Milan; see *Ardeschi.*

Gammon and Galvinism; by T. D. English: (44) N.-4.25*, 26.

Ganem, or the Slave of Love: (54) W.-8.31; 9.1, 2, 9, 25.

The Gardner's Wife: (45) C.-9.16, 18; 10.14, 31; 12.30; (46) A.-9.30; 11.12; (47) A.-1.27.

Gaspardo, the Gondolier; by J. Butler: (39) W.-3.21*, 22, 23, 25, 26, 28, 29; (39) C.-3.23, 25, 26; 4.11; 6.18; (52) A.-11.22, 29.

Gaulantus, or The Last of the Gauls; by N. H. Bannister: (37) W.-8.31*; 12.1; (38) W.-2.2; (50) A.-11.7, 9.

Gemini, or The Twin Brothers; farce: (38) C.-9.15; (53) W.-2.9, 10.

Gemma di Vergy: (43) C.-11.26, 27; (48) W.-2.19, 21, 22, 23, 24, 25; (50) C.-12.28.

General Washington, or The Traitor Foiled: (50) W.-7.4*.

Genevieve; domestic tragedy: (48) A.-2.2*, 3; W.-2.18, 19; 4.22, 24.

The Genoese, or The Bridge of Genoa; by Epes Sargent: (41) N.-3.17*.

The Gentleman and the Upstart: (40) C.-3.21.

A Gentleman in Difficulties: (35) A.-4.6*, 7; (37) C.-11.4; (48) W.-3.22, 23, 29; 4.3, 15; 5.5; 6.8, 16; 7.20, 27; (49) A.-8.23; (51) B.-1.31; 2.1; (52) C.-3.17, 22, 25.

The Gentleman of Lyons; by N. H. Bannister: (38) W.-8.16*.

Gentleman Harry, the Terror of the Road: (50) C.-5.4, 6, 7, 8.

George Barnwell, or The London Apprentice; tragedy by George Lillo: (35) W.-12.22; (36) W.-12.31; P.-12.28; (37) W.-8.24; (40) W.-1.9; C.-6.12; W.-11.9, 14; (41) W.-1.1, 6; 2.12; 9.24; 11.27; (42) W.-4.30; (43) W.-10.26; A.-12.21; C.-12.25; (44) N.-1.19; W.-8.16; C.-11.16; (45) W.-12.25; A.-12.27, 30; (46) W.-1.13; 6.27; P.M.-12.25; (51) A.-11.27; (53) C.-4.11.

German Farmer; farce: (35) Mam. C.-2.4, 5, 16.

A Ghost in Spite of Himself; see *Spectre Bridegroom.*

Giaffer, or The Fatal Offspring: (44) W.-1.15, 16.

The Giant Mountains; see *The Gnome King.*

The Giant of the Cave: (53) C.-1.11, 13.

The Giant of Palestine: (40) W.-5.27, 28, 29, 30.

Gig Gig; farce: (40) W.-6.6.

Gil Blas: (39) W.-5.1; (41) N.-3.17, 18; (52) C.-7.27, 28.

Gilderoy, the Bonnie Boy, or The Reiver of Perth; melodrama in three acts by W. Barrymore: (36) W.-12.5, 13; (37) W.-2.1; (38) W.-3.14; (39) W.-5.16; 6.13; (41) W.-11.29; (42) W.-1.3, 5, 19; (43) N.-12.23, 30; (48) A.-12.21, 22; (49) A.-10.19, 22; 12.31; (51) A.-1.24, 25; (53) A.-1.8, 15; 3.28; 4.1, 2, 4, 7; 5.14, 28; (54) A.-5.27, 30; 6.19; (55) A.-4.13, 16.

Gilman's Wedding; comedy: (52) A.-5.6, 7.

Giovanni in Philadelphia; musical burletta: (41) W.-9.18, 20, 21, 25; 10.8.

Gips(e)y of Ashburnham Dell: (35) W.-10.31; 11.2; 12.1.

Gipsy King: (45) N.-5.6, 9.

The Gips(e)y's Prophecy; see *Guy Mannering.*

Giralda, or The Miller's Wife, or Who is my Husband?; "Comedy taken from a French opera by (Adolph) Adam": (50) W.-12.5, 6, 11, 12, 13, 16, 19; A.-12.12, 14, 16, 17, 18, 19; (51) W.-1.4, 13; 2.21; (53) A.-4.2, 4, 5, 6, 7, 8, 9, 15, 30; 6.10; 8.23; 9.2; 10.20; (54) A.-2.2; 5.23.

Giraldi Fazio: (53) A.-1.29.

Giselle; ballet: (46) W.-4.15, 16, 17, 18, 20, 22; (50) C.-1.1, 5.

Gizelle: (47) A.-5.3, 4, 10.

Gisippus, the Forgotten Friend; "Gerald Griffin's classical and moral play": (46) W.-3.26; 4.9; 7.6; (48) W.-1.12, 15; 4.27; (51) A.-5.29, 31; (53) C.-4.1.

The Gladiator; by R. M. Bird: (36) C.-9.7, 8, 9; (37) C.-11.29, 30; 12.1, 2; W.-8.21; (38) C.-1.19, 24; W.-10.24, 26, 29; 12.7; (39) W.-9.17, 20; W.-12.2, 5; (40) W.-4.23, 29; C.-9.26, 30; 11.26; (41) A.-4.12, 22, 27; 6.8; N.-8.28; 10.22; 11.1; (42) C.-4.19, 21; W.-6.3; N.-10.19, 21; (44) N.-1.30; W.-8.29; 9.14; 12.7, 13; (46) W.-10.24, 28; (47) W.-1.4, 12; 3.17; 5.12; 11.10, 20; (48) W.-11.24, 28; 12.7; (49) W.-6.5; (51) W.-10.17, 20, 24; (52) W.-6.23, 26; 11.15, 17, 20; (53) W.-10.19, 22; (54) W.-10.23, 26; (55) W.-12.27, 29.

A Glance at Philadelphia, or Life in the Quaker City: (48) A.-4.25*, 26, 27, 29; 5.1, 2, 3, 4, 5, 6, 8, 10, 11, 12, 13, 15, 16, 17, 22, 23, 24, 25, 26, 27, 29, 30, 31; 6.1, 2, 3; 7.3, 10, 26, 27, 28, 29, 31; W.-7.5, 6, 7, 8, 12, 13, 14; C.-7.28, 31; A.-8.30; 9.21, 22, 23; 10.20; W.-12.23; (49) A.-1.13; 2.12, 13, 14, 15, 16, 17; 3.12, 13; 6.6, 7, 20; P.M.-7.26; C.-8.16, 24, 25; 9.29; 10.2; (50) A.-6.24, 27; 7.2, 3; C.-7.9, 11, 26, 30; A.-10.22, 24, 25, 26; (51) A.-3.8; (53) A.-6.18, 25; (54) C.-11.9, 10, 11; (55) C.M.-9.22; 24, 25, 26, 27, 28, 29; 10.1, 2, 3, 4, 6, 13.

A Glass too Much; see *Truth.*

Glencoe, or The Last of the MacDonalds; tragedy by Sergeant Talfourd: (48) W.-4.10, 14.

The Glorious Minority; see *No.*

The Glory of Columbia; by William Dunlap: (41) W.-7.5; (43) W.-7.4; (48) W.-1.8.

The Gnome King, or The Giant Mountains: (36) C.-7.9; 8.20, 22; (37) C.-1.5.

Goblin Page; melodrama: (40) C.-4.11, 13; W.-11, 2, 3, 4.

Godenski, or The Skates of Wilner: (36) C.-12.24, 27; (37) C.-1.28; 2.3; (41) C.-10.21; (37) A.-6.21; (52) W.-9.6.

Going to the Races; farce: (53) W.-10.10*, 15, 21; 11.7, 28; 12.8, 27; (54) W.-7.4; 9.30; 10.11, 24; (55) W.-3.21; 5.7.

The Gold Bug; by S. S. Steele: (43) W.-8.8*.

Gold Seekers, or The Dying Gift; melodrama: (44) A.-2.19; (50) A.-9.21, 24.

The Gold Stricken, or The Widow's Curse; by J. B. Phillips: (42) A.-6.6, 7; (50) A.-9.28; 10.3.

Gold vs. Love; see *Irish Fortune Hunter.*

Golden Days of Chivalry; see *Knight of the Lion Heart.*

Golden Days of Queen Elizabeth; see *Kenilworth.*

The Golden Farmer, or Jemmy Twitcher in England: (35) W.-1.3, 21; 2.4; 5.19; 11.27; (36) W.-3.11; (37) W.-2.2; P.-2.3, 17, 18; (38) W.-12.26, 27, 28, 29, 31; (39) W.-4.11; 5.3; 6.1; C.-4.30; (40) W.-1.25; (41) W.-1.30; (42) W.-1.24; 4.27, 28, 29; 5.2, 4; A.-5.13; W.-10.4, 7, 12; A.-10.4; N.-10.30, 31; 11.3; (44) C.-11.16; 12.9; (45) W.-6.20; 7.2; A.-7.19; (46) A.-3.18; A.-5.28; P.M.-8.1; 9.26; (47) P.M.-6.23, 26, 28, 29; A.-8.20; (48) A.-6.21; C.-7.14; (49) Ath.-1.3, 26; C.-9.20; (50) A.-6.25; 8.31; (51) A.-9.9; 10.20; (53) C.-1.15, 16, 18; W.-6.18; (54) C.-1.14, 23; 2.1; 3.25; W.-5.10; C.M.-11.24.

The Golden Harp; see *Vision of the Sun.*

[581]

The Gondolier: (42) A.-10.10, 18.

Gone to Texas; see *G. T. T.*

Good for Nothing: (52) C.-9.21, 22, 25, 30; 10.8, 28; 11.6, 16, 25; 12.10; (53) C.-1.15, 16; A.-2.15; 4.12; W.-5.3, 9; C.-7.21; 9.14; A.-12.24; (54) A.-1.18; 3.10, 16; C.-7.27; 10.11; A.-10.17; 11.7, 24; (55) A.-2.7, 14; C.-2.15; C.M.-7.5; W.-11.9.

Good Husbands Make Good Wives; comedy in two acts by John Brougham: (38) W.-1.15*, 18; C.-2.13, 20; 3.9, 29; 4.19.

Good Genius of the Attic: (46) P.M.-11.12, 13.

Good-Looking Fellow; farce: (35) W.-1.15, 16, 22; 2.8; 3.27; (43) C.-11.14.

A Good Night's Rest, or Locked Out; farce: (40) W.-4.13, 16, 17, 22; 5.1, 15; C.-6.12, 13, 17, 18; 9.25; (42) W.-6.7.

Go-to-Bed Tom: (53) W.-3.21; 4.11.

Governor's Wife: (46) P.M.-7.22, 23.

Grace Darling, or The Heroine of the Wreck: (39) W.-6.8, 10, 12, 15, 19.

Grace Huntley; melodrama: (43) A.-5.1; (51) B.-9.15, 16, 17, 18, 19, 20.

Grandfather Whitehead: (44) W.-6.3, 28; 7.28; 8.29; C.-10.28, 29; 11.4; W.-12.5; C.-12.6; (45) C.-11.29; 12.4; (46) P.M.-3.18, 27; 4.25; A.-10.21; 11.5; (45) P.M.-4.17; (48) W.-7.22; (50) A.-8.7, 20; (51) A.-6.11; (53) C.-4.9; (54) W.-8.30; A.-12.6; C.-12.13.

The Grateful Lion; see *Hyder Ali.*

Gray Man of Tottenham; melodrama: (35) W.-12.19, 21.

The Great Bandit; see *Abaellino.*

Great Mistake: (52) C.-8.6.

Great Western: (52) C.-4.22

The Grecian Queen; by S. S. Steele: (44) N.-2.26*.

Greek Fire: (46) A.-5.11.

The Greek Patriots; see *The Siege of Missolonghi.*

Greek Slave: (52) N.-8.9, 14.

Green Bushes, or Ireland and America; by J. B. Buckstone: (45) A.-3.26, 27, 28, 29; 4.24; (51) W.-11.10, 11.

Green Man; comedy: (36) C.-12.28; (37) C.-2.28.

The Green Monster, or The Three Knights of Trineomalee: (45) A.-12.22, 23, 24, 25, 26, 27, 29, 30, 31; (46) A.-1.6, 7.

The Green Eyed Monster: (42) N.-1.29; C.-2.26; A.-9.22; W.-11.7; (43) W.-7.7; (44) W.-4.23.

The Green Mountain Boy, or Love and Learning; comedy by J. S. Jones: (35) W.-5.7, 11; 10.20; 12.15; C.-9.9, 11; (36) W.-5.5, 13; A.-5.23, 25; (37) C.-9.12; (38) C.-4.3, 6; (40) W.-12.12, 18; (41) W.-10.13, 28; (42) W.-4.14; (43) W.-1.12; A.-10.6, 19; (45) C.-1.13, 15, 21; 4.26; (50) A.-9.6; (51) A.-3.11; (52) A.-11.29, 30; 12.3; (54) C.-7.10, 11; 9.22.

The Grenadier, or The Savoyard Boy and his Monkey; musical burletta: (37) C.-3.25, 27, 31.

Gretna Green: (35) A.-3.10; W.-5.22; 10.9; C.-6.25; 11.3; (36) A.-4.6; W.-4.30; C.-1.1; 2.2; P.-11.29; 12.15, 28; (37) A.-5.17; W.-11.28; C.-3.18; (38) W.-4.5, 6, 7; (39) C.-5.10; 6.10; 9.16; W.-12.4; C.-10.3, 18; 11.21; (42) A.-7.14; (46) P.M.-9.5, 18; (47) P.M.-1.19.

Grimshaw, Bagshaw, and Bradshaw, or The Three Shaws: (51) W.-8.30; 9.1, 15, 27; A.-9.12, 17, 26, 27; B.-9.12, 13; A.-10.2, 31; W.-10.27; 12.1, 15; (52) W.-1.6, 24; 2.20; 4.5, 26; 6.1, 22; 9.13, 20; 10.4, 30; (53) W.-1.26; 4.21; (54) C.-4.3, 5, 11; (55) W.-9.11, 13; 10.2, 10; 12.12.

Griselda, or The Patient Woman; by J. M. Field: (54) C.-10.23*, 24, 25, 26, 27, 30.

Griseldis: (48) O.-5.27.

Grist to the Mill; comedy: (44) A.-9.4, 5, 13; 10.21, 23; (45) A.-10.17, 21; (46) P.M.-8.22; 12.7; (48) P.M.-4.11, 14; (50) C.-3.25; B.-11.25, 26; (55) W.-5.30; 6.1; 11.15.

The Groves of Blarney: (42) C.-4.9, 22.

Grub, Mudge, and Co.; comedy in one act: (50) C.-4.6*.

Grumbler: (42) A.-11.28.

Grumbling, or the Discontented Englishman; prelude by Coleman (of Philadelphia): (42) A.-10.6; (45) A.-1.4.

The Grumbling Englishman; see *The Blue Devils.*

G. T. T., or Gone to Texas: (44) C.-12.10, 11, 12.

The Guardian Outwitted; see *Love Laughs at Locksmiths.*

The Gudeman of Ballangeich; see *Cramond Brig.*

Gulliver: (46) A.-12.25, 26, 28, 29, 30, 31; (47) A.-1.2.

Gulliver in Lilliput; farce by David Garrick: (38) W.-1.18, 19, 20, 22.

Guerilla Chief: (47) A.-12.1; (48) A.-5.23, 24; 7.10.

Guerilla Chief and his Son: (47) A.-11.8, 9, 10.

Guns without Shot, or Sailors and Taylors: (38) C.-6.5.

Gustavus III; opera: (49) W.-12.7, 8.

Gustavus III, or The Masked Ball; "grand musical and historical drama": (35) C.-1.7, 10, 13, 17, 21, 24; 2.3, 17; 4, 9, 29; 8.28; 9.5; (36) C.-6.17; (41) C.-3.2; W.-12.8, 10, 11; (44) C.-5.27, 28, 29, 30, 31; 6.1.

Guy Mannering, or The Gipsey's Prophecy; opera: (35) A.-3.3; C.-6.2; 12.8; (36) C.-2.9; (37) C.-3.21; (38) W.-2.3; (39) C.-2.8; 3.1; 10.31; (40) N.-11.30; 12.3; (41) A.-5.17, 21; (42) C.-2.12, 25; (43) C.-1.5; (49)

W.-11.6, 7, 8, 10, 17; (50) A.-5.28; 6.1, 8, 22; W.-11.12, 14, 16; (51) W.-6.17, 19; A.-7.7; C.-12.2, 4, 13, 17; (52) W.-4.21, 24, 27; A.-5.5; (55) W.-2.24.

Gwinneth Vaughan; domestic drama: (42) W.-9.28, 29; (47) W.-3, 12, 13.

Hack Driver: (45) A.-5.19.

H. B., or Harry Belasquez: (41) C.-5.3, 4.

The Hall of Fate and the Enchanted Isle; fairy romantic spectacle: (52) A.-3.9, 10, 11, 12, 13.

Hamlet; by William Shakespeare: (35) W.-1.5; 2.24; 8.25; C.-6.4, 30; 10.19; 12.5; (36) W.-1.12; 2.8; C.-9.30; A.-3.1; W.-4.13; 5.28; 6.7; 9.7; P.-12.14; (37) A.-5.22; W.-7.10; C.-10.21; 11.2, 20; W.-11.15; (38) C.-4.27; 9.14; W.-10.13; 11.1; 12.17; (39) C.-9.30; 10.10; 11.29; 12.31; W.-1.26; 6.28; 7.1; 8.26; 11.29; (40) A.-12.15, 18; W.-3.13; 6.15; 12.24; C.-4.15; (41) A.-4.16; 8.31; W.-3.4; 5.25; C.-8.31; 9.2; 12.29; N.-3.11; 11.1; 12.16; (42) W.-4.2; 10.10, 12; C.-11.17; (41) A.-10.14; (42) W.-6.1; (43) W.-1.16; A.-3.21; W.-4.28; A.-8.18, 22; N.-9.27; W.-10.4; A.-10.11; N.-10.18; C.-10.24, 25; N.-10.27; C.-10.30, 31; 12.21; (44) W.-1.18; 3.22; N.-4.27; 5.30; W.-9.9; A.-9.9, 18; C.-11.25; W.-12.14; (45) W.-4.1; A.-4.28; 5.5; W.-2.28; 8.5; 10.15, 28; 11.3, 14; C.-11.5; A.-12.10; (46) A.-1.5; W.-1.22; 2.19; 9.7; 10.12, 19; A.-11.4, 17; (47) W.-4.27; A.-5.17; 10.12; 11.1, 10, 29; (48) W.-4.3; A.-4.6; 7.6; C.-7.25; A.-12.2; W.-12.2; (49) A.-4.10; W.-5.21; C.-9.14; 10.8; A.-10.24; C.-11.9; A.-12.19; (50) W.-9.2; (51) B.-3.6, 10, 26; A.-3.25, 29; W.-5.5; A.-5.13, 26; B.-6.16; W.-6.23; C.-10.1, 4; A.-10.14; C.-12.9, 26; (52) C.-1.5, 16; W.-1.6, 15; 4.2; C.-4.12;

A.-4.19; W.-6.21, 25; C.-8.2; A.-8.30; C.-9.6; A.-11.9; W.-11.12, 23; (53) C.-2.21; 3.7; W.-6.1, 13; A.-10.3; W.-10.12; A.-11.5; W.-11.21; (54) A.-3.20; 6.5; 9.9; W.-10.5, 12, 19; A.-10.7; (55) C.-2.12; A.-3.6; C.M.-3.28; W.-3.27; C.M.-4.2; W.-4.5, 12, 20; C.M.-5.25; W.-6.2; A.-9.5, 29; W.-10.8; A.-10.29; C.M.-10.29; 11.21, 26; 12.12; W.-12.13.

Hamlet, Travestie: (40) W.-6.13; (45) W.-3.5.

Hand of Cards, or Game, Life, Stakes, Death; melodrama: (49) A.-11.22*, 23; 12.8, 11.

The Hand of Klishing; see *The Demon Statue.*

Handsome Bachelors and Pretty Girls of Philadelphia: (52) N.-8.10, 11, 12, 13.

Handsome Husband; farce: (38) C.-10.12, 13, 17, 20; (40) W.-3.11; (49) P.M.-4.26, 27; 5.10, 31; (51) B.-12.1, 2.

Handsome Widow: (52) N.-9.13.

Handy Andy; comedy by T. D. English: (44) N.-1.1*, 2, 3, 4, 5, 6, 9, 10; (53) C.-1.26, 27.

Happiest Day of My Life; farce: (35) A.-4.4; C.-5.23; 6.23; (36) A.-5.3; C.-2.1; 6.13; C.-11.17, 29; 12.22; (37) C.-1.13; 8.29; (38) C.-2.22; (40) 5.4; 12.1; (46) W.-12.9, 26; (47) W.-1.7; 2.15; 3.29; 6.10, 11; (51) B.-12.12, 13.

The Happy Man: (40) W.-2.18, 25; 3.4; C.-4.8; 10.23; N.-11.21, 23, 26; (41) W.-8.31; 9.21, 27; N.-2.24; (42) A.-11.12; (43) N.-11.27, 28, 29; 12.13; (46) W.-10.8; P.M.-10.15; (47) W.-2.8; 6.22; 10.1, 2; 12.18, 21; (48) W.-1.27, 28; P.M.-4.27; W.-5.25, 27; C.-7.4, 13; W.-9.12, 22; (49) A.-5.31; 6.5; (50) C.-3.6; W.-5.4, 8; A.-7.1; A.-11.29; (51) C.-5.6,

10; W.-11.15; (54) W.-5.18; (55) W.-11.28; 12.4.

A Happy New Year; see *A Scotch Cooper.*

Happy Uncle Tom's Cabin: (53) C.-12.16.

A Hard Subject: (45) A.-11.7.

Harlequin and Mother Goose: (39) C.-12.24, 25, 26, 27, 28; (49) C.-11.10, 15.

Harlequin and the Fairy of the Rose; see *Farmer's Son.*

Harlequin and the Fairy of the Golden Wheat Sheaf: (50) A.-12.25, 26, 27; (51) A.-1.1, 2, 4, 6, 7, 9.

Harlequin and the Magic Trumpet: (37) C.-2.4*; (41) C.-10.25; (46) A.-10.10, 21.

Harlequin and the (Red) Monster of St. Michael: (50) C.-1.2, 3, 4, 5, 7, 8, 9, 10, 11, 12, 13, 14, 18.

Harlequin and the Ocean Nymph: (43) W.-7.31*; 8.1, 2, 3, 4, 5, 7, 10, 11.

Harlequin and the Old Woman; see *The Clown and the Cat.*

Harlequin and the Silver Tower: (44) W.-12.25, 28, 31; (45) W.-1.1, 2, 3, 4, 6.

Harlequin Hurry Scurry, or Christmas Gambols: (35) W.-12.25.

Harlequin Invisible: (48) A.-8.24, 28.

Harlequin Margery Daw: (52) A.-5.8.

Harlequin Nuptials: (41) W.-12.1.

Harlequin of the Giants' Isle: (41) A.-12.24, 25, 28, 29, 30, 31.

Harlequin or the Fair One with the Golden Locks: (42) A.-1.1.

Harlequin Shipwreck: (35) W.-4.3.

Harlequin Statue: (44) N.-4.6.

Harlequin Tom the Piper's Son: (36) W.-1.21*, 22, 23.

Harlequin's Festival: (44) A.-12.30, 31; (45) A.-1.1, 3.

Harlequin's Olio: (41) N.-9.11.

The Haron Chief; see *Civilization.*

Harry Bluff: (35) W.-6.5.

Harry Burnham, the Young Continental; by J. Pilgrim: (51) A.-4.21*, 22, 23, 24, 25, 26, 28, 29.

Harvest Home; domestic drama: (51) W.-11.22, 24, 25, 28, 29; (52) W.-5.10; (53) W.-5.6; A.-6.6, 7.

A Hasty Conclusion; farce: (39) C.-6.22; 10.4, 10, 21.

The Haunted Cave; see *A Dream at Sea.*

Haunted Chamber: (52) W.-9.1, 3, 4; 10.18; (53) C.-5.7.

Haunted Inn: (35) C.-1.7; 5.15, 27; (37) C.-9.21; (38) C.-6.12, 28; (42) C.-4.26; W.-4.28; 6.17, 30; 7.1; (47) W.-9.13; (52) A.-4.29, 30.

Haunted Hulk: (44) W.-5.4

The Haunted Man; by John Brougham: (49) A.-1.13*, 14.

The Hawks of Hawk Hollow: (43) A.-8.17*.

The Hazard of the Die: (35) C.-9.17, 19; 12.1; (36) W.-2.20, 22, 24, 27; A.-5.17; (41) A.-1.20; (42) A.-4.2, 4.

He is not A-Miss, or Une Heure de la Vie d'un Soldat: (35) W.-1.19*, 22, 23, 27; 2.6; (38) W.-12.31; (39) W.-5.2; (44) C.-10.26; (46) P.M.-6.1, 2, 10; (53) C.-1.18, 21; (54) W.-1.16, 17, 21; (55) W.-3.30; 5.18.

He Would be an Actor; burletta by Cornelius Mathews: (38) C.-10.8, 9, 10, 11, 19.

Heads or Tails: (54) C.M.-11.27, 29.

Hear it out; see *Blind Bargain.*

Heart of Midlothian, or The Lilly of St. Leonards, or Highland Whistler: (35) C.-4.18; 5.11; 10.6; (36) W.-4.12; 12.12; (38) W.-11.3, 12; (40) C.-1.23, 31; (44) A.-7.18, 20; (46) A.-2.7, 10; (51) N.-7.19, 22.

The Heart Overtasked; see *Bianca Visconti.*

Hearts and Trumps: (49) C.-10.31; 11.1, 2.

Hedwig; by Thomas Korner: (37) P.-10.3.

Heir at Law; comedy by George Colman the Younger: (36) W.-4.13; 10.6; P.-11.8; (37) P.-2.9; (38) C.-4.26; (39) W.-4.29; 5.29; (40) W.-12.10; C.-5.27; N.-10.1; (41) C.-2.22; A.-5.25; N.-9.11; 11.9; (42) A.-4.22; (43) W.-7.5; (44) A.-3.8; W.-4.16; 5.13; A.-6.8; W.-9.16; (45) A.-3.24; W.-4.9; A.-5.23; W.-10.23; (46) C.-1.15; W.-1.29; 3.19; 5.2; A.-11.28; (47) P.M.-1.18; 2.25; W.-7.1; A.-8.4, 9; W.-8.17; (48) W.-2.23; A.-4.28; W.-7.26; (49) A.-12.28; (52) W.-2.3; C.-12.7; (53) W.-3.8, 26; 4.1; A.-5.17; 6.9; W.-6.10, 22; 8.26; A.-11.23; (54) A.-2.1; C.-5.5, 10, 18; W.-6.15; C.-6.30; C.M.-9.12; 10.12; 11.10; (55) A.-2.15; 4.16; 6.29; C.M.-10.4, 8.

He Lies like Truth: (42) A.-6.23.

H—ll on Earth: (43) O.-1.9, 10, 11, 12, 13, 14.

Helos, the Helot, or the Messinian Slave; tragedy: (52) A.-3.24*, 25, 26, 27.

Henri and Louise, or The Two Murderers; melodrama: (38) W.-4.11*, 12, 13, 14; (43) N.-12.28; (44) A.-2.15; 12.26.

Henri Quatre, or Paris in the Olden Times; musical play by Thomas Morton: (35) C.-6.1, 26; 8.24; (37) A.-5.9; (40) W.-3.9.

Henri Quatre; dramatic opera by Sir R. Bishop: (52) W.-11.1, 2.

Henriette, the Forsaken; by J. B. Buckstone: (35) W.-5.30; 6.1; C.-6.29; (36) W.-1.27; 10.27; A.-3.4; (39) W.-1.21; (40) W.-6.8, 11; (45) W.-7.7, 9; 8.19; (50) C.-5.21, 24; (51) A.-10.30; 11.20.

Henry IV; by William Shakespeare: (36) W.-3.21; 4.4; C.-11.9; (37) C.-2.9; (38) C.-4.13; 9.8; (40) C.-6.1; N.-9.14, 16; (41) N.-3.15; 9.1; A.-5.6; (42) C.-3.29; W.-11.28, 30; (43) W.-10.5, 16; C.-12.5; (44) A.-11.11, 13; (45) W.-5.21; C.-9.8; (46) W.-1.26; 8.3; (47) A.-10.25; (48) A.-4.3; 12.5; (49) W.-3.19, 24; 12.17; (52) C.-1.12; 5.25, 29; 9.25; 12.21; (53) W.-1.31; 2.2; C.-3.11; 4.7; W.-4.18, 20, 27; (54) C.-3.10; (55) C.M.-6.8.

Henry VIII; by William Shakespeare: (38) C.-5.1; (48) A.-11.30; (49) W.-11.13, 14; (50) A.-6.7; W.-11.8; (51) W.-6.20; C.-11.10; 12.18; (52) W.-4.23.

Hercules, King of Clubs; farce: (39) C.-5.29, 30; 6, 1.

Hercules of Brittany: (43) N.-12.20, 21, 22, 23, 25, 26, 27; (44) N.-1.15, 16; 2.19, 23; W.-6.8, 11, 13.

Here she Goes, There she Goes, or The Old Clock: (39) W.-4.20, 23, 27.

Hermit of the Rocks, or Happy Results: (52) A.-12.2, 9; (54) C.-7.15; 9.21.

Hermit's Prophecy, or Richard the Lion Hearted: (35) W.-6.15, 16.

Hernani, or The Castilian Noble; opera by Giuseppe Verdi: (47) W.-7.13, 14, 15, 16; 8.3; (50) C.-4.13. See also *Ernani.*

The Hero of Lake George; see *Marion.*

The Hero of Scotland; see *Wallace.*

The Hero of Switzerland; see *William Tell.*

The Hero of Valley Forge; see *Washington.*

The Hero of the North, or The Liberator of His Country; by Benjamin Colman: (35) A.-2.23, 27; (42) A.-7.4.

The Hero of the Prairie; see *Kit Karson.*

The Heroine of the Wreck; see *Grace Darling.*

The Heroines of Mont Blanc; see *The Amazon Sisters.*

Herr und Sclave; drama in two acts: (40) A.-2.17.

Herschel Outhercheled; see *Discoveries in the Moon.*

Hickety Pickety, or Harlequin and My Black Hen: (51) C.-7.3.

Hide and Seek; farce: (36) C.-10.29*; P-11.24; 12.30; (37) A.-6.1; (39) W.-7.1; (41) A.-8.18; (43) A.-12.27.

High Life below Stairs; farce by David Garrick: (35) W.-3.12; (37) C.-1.11; 2.27; A.-5.22; (39) W.-5.11, 28; (40) W.-11.6; (44) W.-3.15; (45) W.-10.14, 18, 21, 31; A.-12.16; (46) W.-1.30; 2.20; A.-10.8, 9.

High Life in Philadelphia; farce: (50) C.-4.24.

High, Low, Jack, and the Game: (45) W.-12.22, 23, 24, 25, 27, 31.

High Road to Marriage: (38) W.-4.25.

Highland Reel; farce by John O'Keeffe: (38) C.-10.1; 11.21.

Highland Whistler; see *Heart of Midlothian.*

Highlander's Faith: (40) A.-12.14, 22.

A Highlander's Revenge; see *Two Drovers.*

Highways and Byeways; comedy: (37) W.-12.1; (47) W.-1.5, 6, 11; 2.16; 4.5, 28; 5.12; 6.5.

The Hindoos of the Cavern; see *The Secret Mine.*

Hinko, or King and Hangman; by Charles Birch Pfeiffer: (48) O.-5.24, 25; (55) G.N.-10.16.

Hints for Husbands: (41) C.-1.4.

His First Champagne, or Wine Works Wonders: (39) W.-10. 7, 9, 11; (42) C.-3.25; 4.1, 14; (49) W.-3.5,

9, 10, 15; 4.7; 5.8; 12.27; (50) W.-1.2; 12.26; (51) W.-1.2; 5.16; 9.16; C.-9.30; (52) A.-8.26; (53) C.-6.20; (55) C.M.-4.13, 18, 25; 12.13, 15.

His Last Legs: (40) W.-5.11; C.-10.10, 12, 16, 22; N.-11.24, 25; (41) N.-2.25, 27; (42) C.-4.2; 11.9; A.-11.14; (43) W.-2.8; 3.22; N.-10.2, 6; C.-12.6; N.-12.6; C.-12.11; (44) A.-9.11; (45) C.-9.12; A.-10.1; (46) W.-1.28; 8.4; 9.1; 10.6; (47) W.-2.6; 12.10; (48) W.-3.11; C.-7.17; (49) W.-3.20, 21; A-5.31; P.M.-7.10; W.-9.13, 18, 27; C.-11.27; (50) W.-5.2, 9; C.-6.22; A.-7.1; C.-7.23; W.-10.15; (51) W.-2.27; A.-3.17; W.-9.3; C.-10.20, 21, 30; (52) W.-1.15; C.-2.23, 28; W.-3.3; 4.16; C.-6.15; W.-10.7; (53) C.-5.27; 7.15; A.-11.30; 12.20; (54) A.-3.24; C.-8.9; (55) C.M.-1.12, 15; 4.24.

His own Ghost: (45) A.-3.26, 27; 4.30.

The History of Tittlebat Titmouse; see *Ten Thousand a Year.*

Hit or Miss; by Isaac Pocock: (37) W.-3.29.

Hobbs, Dobbs, and Stubs, or The Three Temperance Grocers; farce: (42) C.-4.25*, 27.

Hofer, or The Tell of the Tyrol: (37) W.-2.6; 3.10; C.-2.11; (38) W.-3.5; 9.15; (39) W.-5.14; 6.18; (40) W.-1.15; (41) W.-7.15; (42) A.-4.1, 2; (43) N.-12.7, 8; (45) A.-5.15, 16; 6.12; (48) W.-12.29; (49) W.-1.1, 2.

Hole in the Wall; see *Secret.*

Home Again, or The Sisters; domestic drama (by E. Fitzball): (46) P.M.-7.22*.

Home Squadron, or The Female Sailors: (41) N.-9.3, 6, 7, 9, 17; (42) N-1.1.

Home, Sweet Home, or The Ranz des Vache; musical drama: (35) A.-3.12; (42) C.-2.23, 24, 28; (47) P.M.-7.16.

Honest Thieves, or The Faithful Irishman; by Thomas Knight: (35) A.-4.3; (36) W.-5.11; (37) W.-2.24; (39) W.-4.17; 7.18; (40) C.-5.27; (42) A.-6.4; (44) N.-2.23, 27, 28; (46) A.-6.1, 15; 7.10; (51) A.-12.1.

Honey Moon; comedy by John Tobin: (35) C.-4.13; 10.10, 16; W.-5.23; (36) C.-11.15; W.-9.23; (37) C.-1.18; C.-4.27; 9.30; (38) W.-6.27; C.-11.30; (39) C.-2.15; (37) A.-6.5; (40) W.-10.14, 15; 11.21; (41) C.-2.20; 10.9; A.-7.5; (42) N.-1.25; A.-6.22; C.-11.12; (43) W.-3.22; A.-8.29; N.-9.23; 10.5; A.-12.11; (44) W.-2.24; 3.4; 4.9; 6.24; A.-8.13; 9.6; W.-9.18; C.-12.7; (45) W.-1.18; 6.25; 8.8; C.-9.2, 27; 12.3; (46) C.-1.3; A.-3.10; W.-7.18; 8.21; 9.9, 18, 19; A.-11.20; P.M.-11.25; A.-12.9; (47) A.-4.26; P.M.-6.25; A.-7.24; 8.19, 11.17; (48) A.-1.19; W.-2.11; A.-3.31; 4.20; W.-5.2; P.M.-5.12; A.-6.27; 10.18; W.-11.17; (49) Ath.-1.19; W.-3.12; P.M.-7.13; A.-8.27; C.-9.12; 10.20; W.-11.9, 21, 22; (50) W.-3.22; A.-5.24; W.-6.7; A.-6.8; W.-8.27; B.-10.2, 18; W.-10.11; 11.8; (51) W.-1.1; B.-1.20; W.-2.1; 3.29; B.-4.19; C.-7.5; W.-10.4, 31; C.-10.11; 11.21; 12.6, 27, 29; A.-12.11; (52) C.-1.15; 3.11; W.-4.23; C.-6.3; 7.21; A.-9.7; 11.19; C.-12.3, 11; A.-12.22; (53) A.-1.10; W.-1.15; A.-2.4; C.-2.16; 4.1; W.-6.9; 12.20; (54) A.-1.14, 31; C.-3.18; 4.6; A.-4.22; C.-5.16; A.-6.6, 29; W.-9.5; C.M.-9.21; A.-9.23; C.M.-10.11; A.-12.1; C.-12.1; C.M.-12.7; W.-12.30; (55) A.-1.13, 16; C.M.-1.17; 2.8, 10; A.-3.22; W.-3.24; C.M.-4.5; W.-5.10; C.M.-5.18; 6.6; A.-9.26; 10.27; 11.10.

3.22; 5.29, 31; 9.10; 11.18; 20; W.-5.23; (40) W.-1.13; C.-3.5; N.-9.23; (41) A.-10.6; N.-3.3; C.-10.15; (42) C.-3.25; A.-5.21; 6.29; W.-9.27; C.-11.9; (43) W.-2.1; 3.20; 10.10; C.-11.16; (44) A.-1.3; W.-2.14; 8.22; C.-11.22; (45) C.-2.3; W.-7.23; 8.25; C.-10.14; 12.31; (46) W.-7.29; 9.16, 25; A.-11.24; (47) A.-1.13, 16; W.-1.27; 2.19; A.-4.9; W.-5.26; A.-7.23, 28; 8.18; 9.11; W.-12.1; (48) A.-1.31; W.-2.7; 3.14; 4.18; A.-7.5; 10.9, 19; 12.12; (49) A.-3.20; 8.23; C.-9.11; 10.12; A.-11.1, 7; W.-11.2, 5; (50) W.-3.18; A.-4.4; W.-4.15; C.-6.6; W.-8.26; B.-9.6, 7, 13; W.-9.12; A.-10.11; W.-10.31; (51) C.-3.3, 24; W.-3.26; 4.11; C.-7.3; 10.6; W.-11.7; 12.29; (52) W.-1.16; C.-3.17; 7.14; A.-10.11, 14; C.-12.2; (53) A.-2.2; C.-2.11; W.-2.21; 24; A.-5.7; W.-5.9; 9.5, 14; (54). C.-1.4; A.-2.8, 9, 18, 24; C.-3.30; A.-5.31; W.-6.13; C.-8.25; 9.13; C.M.-11.27; 12.4; W.-12.25; (55) C.-1.20; C.M.-12.1; W.-3.21; A.-5.5; W.-5.6; C.M.-5.17; W.-6.11; 10.2; C.M.-10.30; A.-11.7, 16.

The Hunchback of Notre Dame; see *Esmerelda.*

102, or The Veteran and His Progeny: (35) Mam.C.-2.9, 10; C.-6.4; W.-9.22; (39) W.-6.10.

£100 Note; farce: (35) C.-1.16; A.-2.25; (36) W.-10.6; (37) W.-2.23; (38) W.-8.1; (39) C.-6.20; W.-4.8; 5.20; 6.10; (42) A.-7.11; (43) W.-11.1; (46) P.M.-10.17; A.-12.4.

The Hunted Tailor; see *Billy Button.*

The Hunter of the Alps: (35) C.-4.23; 10.2; 11.27; (36) A.-3.2; 5.4; 6.4; (38) C.-5.2; W.-12.11; (41) W.-12.3; N.-12.3; (43) W.-10.25; (44) W.-5.16; (48) W.-5.3; (49) W.-5.18; (50) W.-1.11; (54) C.-2.10, 28.

The Hunter(s) of the Pyrenees, or The

Chasm of Death; by J. B. Buckstone: (40) W.-3.7; 7.13, 17; (43) W.-3.13, 14; (50) C.-5.11, 13.

Hunting a Turtle; farce: (36) W.-1.13, 14, 15, 16, 19; 2.3, 4, 25, 29; 6.22, 25; 11.22; 12.14; P.-12.7; (37) W.-6.20; P.-1.6; 2.4; (38) W.-3.14, 20; 8.17; (39) W.-11.27; (40) W.-11.3, 28; (41) A.-12.13; (42) W.-4.26, 27; 6.14, 22; A.-6.22; (43) A.-1.4; (44) C.-11.20; (45) A.-8.12; 9.25, 26; (46) P.M.-5.5, 15, 21; 6.2; A.-6.4; 9.3, 8; 10.2, 22; 11.6, 11, 12; (47) A.-1.25; P.M.-3.13; 4.3, 21, 22; A.-5.3, 7; 7.5, 7; (48) P.M.-3.24; (49) A.-1.5; 4.9, 23; 12.19; (53) C.-3.7, 9, 15, 25; 5.20.

Hunting Park Jockey: (35) W.-6.24.

The Huntsman and the Spy: (51) N.-7.23, 26.

A Husband at Sight: (35) A.-3.12; (36) W.-6.30; 7.1; P.-11.11, 25; (39) C.-1.3; (46) W.-7.29; 8.3, 20; 9.4; (47) W.-9.7, 17; 10.6; (48) W.-4.17; 9.5; (49) P.M.-6.30; (52) A.-10.29, 30; 11.15.

The Husband of my Heart; comedy by Selby: (51) W.-2.12, 13, 18; B.-4.7, 8, 9; 6.5; (53) A.-5.10, 12, 13, 19.

A Husband's Sacrifice; see *St. Marc.*

The Husband's Return; see *Infidelity.*

A Husband's Revenge: (44) A.-1.6.

The Hut in the Swamp; see *Bandit Dost.*

The Hut of the Red Mountain: (37) W.-3.25; (51) A.-12.19, 20.

Hyder Ali, or The Grateful Lion: (35) W.-10.10, 14; (36) W.-11.8; (37) P.-1.25; (39) W.-1.23, 25; (41) A.-1.11, 18, 23; (52) A.-4.16.

Hypochondriac, or The Two James': (41) W.-9.24; (50) B.-12.23.

Hypochondriasis: (51) B.-9.10, 11.

Hypocrisy Detected: (43) A.-3.22.

Hypocrite; by Isaac Bickestaff: (35) W.-5.9; 9.15; C.-9.11; 12.23; (36)

W.-5.14, 16; 10.7; C.-11.12; (37)
W.-8.11; (39) W.-6.7, 8; (40) A.-
12.4; (41) W.-10.15, 17; A.-9.27;
(42) W.-4.14; (44) W.-5.25; (45)
C.-5.7; (48) W.-2.25; 5.31; (53)
W.-3.30; (54) A.-2.22, 25, 27, 28;
3.1, 2, 3, 4, 14, 16; 4.21; 5.18; 6.23;
9.1, 21; 10.21; 12.14, 22; (55) A.-
2.9, 22; 3.21, 24; 6.1, 18, 28.

I and my Double; see *U and I.*

*Ice Witch and the Sun Spirit, or The
Frozen Hand:* (40) C.-12.10*, 11,
12, 14, 15, 16, 17, 18, 26; (41) C.-1.1,
2; 2.19, 22, 27; (43) C.-1.14, 16, 17,
23; 12.25.

Ida Stephanoff; romantic drama by
H. J. Conway: (36) W.-1.1*, 2, 4.

Idiot of the Mill; melodrama by Edward Sterling: (49) A.-9.1*, 3, 4, 5,
6, 7, 8, 14; 10.6.

Idiot of the Shannon: (45) A.-11.18.

*The Idiot Witness, or A Tale of
Blood:* (35) W.-12.23; (36) P.-
11.22, 23; (37) A.-6.29; (38) C.-
6.27, 30; (39) W.-7.20; 11.22; (40)
W.-7.14; (41) W.-2.23; A.-10.4, 18,
19; (42) W.-7.14; (48) P.M.-4.1;
(50) A.-8.24; 9.20; (51) A.-3.6, 12;
B.-5.27; (52) A.-3.4; N.-5.25; A.-
9.8; (54) N.-6.15; C.-11.23.

If the Cap Fits you, Wear it; farce:
(40) W.-5.9, 28; 6.1.

Il Barbiere di Siviglio; opera by Giacomo Rossini. See *The Barber of
Seville:* (48) W.-8.14, 16, 18, 21,
22, 23, 24, 25, 26; (49) C.-1.1, 3;
(55) W.-3.7.

Il Giuramento [The Oath]; melodramatic opera in three acts, music
by Mercadante and words by
Gaetano Rossi: (48) C.-3.20*, 22,
24; (51) C.-1.8, 11, 20.

I Lombardi: (48) C.-12.28, 30; (51)
C.-1.20.

Il Puritani; opera by Bellini: (43) C.-
7.22, 24; 11.20, 21, 23, 28; (45) C.-
11.10, 11, 12, 13; (50) C.-9.20; (54)
C.-8.31; 9.5; (55) W.-1.2.

I'll be your Second; comedy: (35) W.-
11.9; (36) A.-4.4, 5; 5.2, 18; (51)
A.-5.26.

I'll Sleep on it; see *Victorine.*

*The Illustrious Stranger, or You Must
Be Buried;* farce (by W. E. Burton): (35) W.-9.18; C.-12.9; (36)
C.-1.27; 2.15, 25; A.-3.3; (39) W.-
1.15; (47) A.-5.6, 8; 6.23, 29.

Imp of the Elements: (44) N.-3.21,
22, 23, 29.

Impulse, or Sudden Thoughts; farce:
(38) W.-2.26*, 27, 28; 3.12; 7.6;
8.10; (40) A.-12.16; (41) W.-6.23;
(42) W.-2.12, 17; A.-10.5; 11.1;
(43) A.-9.7; (47) P.M.-7.17; A.-
7.20; 12.28, 29, 30, 31; (48) A.-2.23;
P.M.-7.8, 11; A.-7.13, 27; 8.17;
(49) Ath-1.4; (50) W.-2.20, 22,
28; A.-7.22; B.-9.9, 10; 12.10; (51)
B.-6.7; (54) C.-1.9, 10; (55) A.-
8.24, 29; 9.7; 11.15; 12.22.

In and Out of Place; by S. D. Johnson: (50) C.-3.15*; (52) C.-2.13,
14; W.-8.31; (53) C.-5.6; (55)
C.M.-11.5, 6.

In the Wrong Box; farce: (35) W.-
1.3, 6, 9, 15; 9.2; C.-1.5.

Incendiary: (42) W.-10.22; A.-11.29.

Inch Cape Bell: (43) W.-3.18, 20, 29.

The Inconstant; see *Time Works
Wonders.*

Indian Girl; see *Wept of Wish-Ton-
Wish.*

The Indian Princess; see *Pocahontas.*

*The Indian Prophecy, or The Early
Days of General George Washington;* by G. W. P. Custis: (39) W.-
1.8.

Indian Queen; tragedy: (51) W.-4.9*,
10, 12.

Industry Must Prosper; see *The Bee-hive.*

The Infernal Machine; see *Fieschi.*

The Infidel; by B. H. Brewster: (35) W.-10.24*, 26, 30; 11.27.

Infidelity, or The Husband's Return; farce by N. H. Bannister: (37) W.-7.28*; 8.2; 11.17, 23; (38) W.-1.27; 10.3; (44) N.-4.13, 19; (47) A.-2.6, 9; (49) C.-9.22; 11.2.

Ingomar, the Barbarian, or The Son of the Wilderness; romantic play by Mrs. Lovell: (51) C.-11.19*, 20, 21; (52) A.-3.19, 20; C.-4.6, 7; 5.7, 8, 12; 8.25; A.-10.18, 20, 22, 27; 11.3; C.-12.28; (53) A.-2.9; C.-3.22; W.-5.4, 13; C.-6.9; W.-9.15, 17, 21, 23, 28; 11.24, 28; (54) C.-3.15, 29; W.-5.4; C.-10.19; W.-12.23, 27; (55) C.M.-4.27; A.-5.2, 3; C.M.-5.14; W.-5.15; A.-6.23; 8.20, 22; 9.15; W.-10.1.

The Inheritance; see *Werner.*

Inkle and Yarico; by George Colman, Jr.: (35) C.-5.14, 19.

The Inn Keeper of Abbeville; by J. D. Burk: (40) W.-7.18*, 21.

The Inn Keeper of Calais, or One For Seven: (40) C.-9.18, in French.

The Inn Keeper's Daughter; melodrama: (35) W.-4.6; (37) P.-1.11; (39) W.-11.21; (40) W.-10.24, 29; 11.17; (42) C.-3.28; (45) A.-5.13, 14; (52) A.-4.24, 27.

The Inn of Cervanne; see *Brigadier's Horse.*

The Inn of Terracina; see *Fra Diavolo.*

The Inn on the Heath; see *The Chain of Guilt.*

The Innocent Condemned; see *Ugolino.*

Inquisitive Yankee: (43) W.-8.3, 4.

Installation of the Knights of the Garter; see *Battle of Poictiers.*

The Intemperate, or A Sister's Love; domestic drama in three acts by W. E. Burton: (35) A.-3.14*; (44) A.-6.6, 7.

Intrigue: (36) P.-11.14; 12.16; (37) W.-2.3.

The Invasion of Russia, or The Life of Napoleon Bonaparte: (41) N.-4.22, 23, 24.

The Invincibles: (38) C.-3.14, 16, 20, 27; 4.23; (39) C.-3.18; (50) A.-7.12, 13.

Invisible Harlequin, or The Enchanted Trumpet; see *Harlequin and the Magic Trumpet.*

Invisible Prince: (47) A.-6.1, 2, 3, 5, 7, 8, 9, 10, 12, 15, 17; 7.12, 14; (54) C.-4.17, 18, 19, 20, 28; (55) W.-6.22, 23, 25, 26.

The Invitation Card; see *U.G.W.G.*

Ion, or The Fate of Argos; tragedy by Sergeant Talfourd: (36) W.-12.6, 7, 8, 9, 12; (37) W.-3.23; C.-4.20, 22, 24, 29; 9.27; 10.6; A.-6.6; (38) W.-10.31; C.-5.30; (39) C.-5.22; 11.25; (40) C.-3.21; (41) A.-6.22; (42) A.-7.20; (43) W.-2.8; (44) C.-12.7; (45) C.-12.29; (46) C.-1.3; A.-1.9, 14; W.-9.24, 26; 12.29; (47) W.-1.18; (49) S.-10.22; W.-11.19, 20; A.-12.20; (51) C.-10.10, 14; (52) C.-3.18; 7.15; (53) C.-2.19; A.-2.28; C.-3.23; (54) C.-3.16; A.-5.4, 8; (55) A.-2.3, 12; 9.18, 20.

Ion, Travestie: (37) W.-3.18*, 21, 23.

Ireland and America, or Life in Both; (by James Pilgrim): (52) C.-2.9, 10, 11; (53) W.-11.3, 4; (54) W.-5.30; 6.5; (55) C.M.-12.25, 26, 27, 28.

Ireland and America; see *Green Bushes.*

Ireland as it Is: (49) A.-11.26, 27; (50) C.-3.4, 5; A.-11.18, 21; (51) A.-2.3, 17; 5.6, 15; 11.4, 6; (52) C.-2.4, 5,

12; W.-8.30, 31; 10.19, 21; (53) C.-
5.4, 7, 10.24, 27; W.-11.4, 5; (54)
W.-5.24, 31; C.-7.24, 27; (55) C.M.-
7.2, 4; 12.24.

Ireland's Curse, or The Rebellion of
'98: (45) A.-4.4, 5.

The Irish Ambassador, or A School
for Diplomats; comedy by Tyrone
Power: (35) C.-4.30; 5.9; (36) C.-
9.26; 10.3, 8; 11.17; C.-11.23; (37)
C.-2.16, 24; A.-5.13, 19, 21; (38)
C.-9.17; 10.6; 11.7, 12; (39) W.-
5.4; (40) C.-10.5, 14; N.-11.16, 28;
(41) A.-11.4, 9; (42) C.-1.26; 11.8,
10; (43) W.-2.4; 3.21, 24, 25; 9.2,
3; 11.16, 21; (47) W.-2.2, 10; 6.15;
9.27; 10.7; 12.10, 17, 24; (48)
P.M.-4.29; 5.5; W.-5.15, 19; 9.14;
A.-11.14, 15; (49) W.-4.9, 19; 9.24,
26, 28; (50) C.-3.8; W.-4.29; 5.11;
(51) W.-2.25, 27; 9.1; C.-11.6; (52)
W.-9.29; (53) A.-9.9, 12; 10.5; W.-
11.10, 17; A.-11.29; (54) A.-2.27;
9.4, 29; 11.21; (55) A.-2.20; 3.5;
6.28; W.-11.27, 30; 12.8.

The Irish American; farce: (53) A.-
3.4*, 5, 7, 8, 9, 10, 30.

Irish Artist: (53) N.-7.26.

Irish Assurance and Yankee Modesty:
(53) C.-5.5*, 12; 7.19, 20; A.-10.25;
C.-10.25; W.-11.5; (54) W.-5.16,
22; C.-7.25; (55) C.M.-7.3; W.-
9.18; 12.29.

The Irish Attorney, or Galway Practice; by Tyrone Power: (40) C.-
10.19, 21, 23; N.-11.27, 28; (43) N.-
12.12; (46) W.-9.5; 10.9; (47) W.-
2.4, 8; 6.18; A.-9.14; W.-9.29; 10.6;
(48) W.-5.17, 23; 9.13, 21; (49) W.-
4.12, 21; A.-6.4; W.-9.12, 20; (50)
W.-5.2; (51) W.-3.4; (53) A.-12.15;
(54) A.-1.9.

Irish Blunders of Handy Andy: (53)
A.-5.31.

The Irish Brigade; see King O'Neil.

Irish Brogue Maker: (53) C.-10.28.

Irish Broom Maker: (52) W.-10.22,
23.

The Irish Diamond; see Andy Blake.

Irish Diplomacy: (49) W.-10.24, 26.

The Irish Dragoon; see Charles
O'Malley.

Irish Emigrant and the Philadelphia
Carman; (by John Brougham): (52)
C.-8.10, 12, 13; 12.21; (53) C.-1.4,
5, 25; A.-2.21, 23; 3.18; 4.13, 14;
5.20; C.-7.8; A.-8.29, 30; 11.12;
12.17; (54) A.-1.10, 27; 2.3; 3.29;
4.24; 5.18; 9.11, 25, 27; 11.14, 27;
12.12; (55) A.-1.24, 30; 2.2, 13;
4.23; 5.5; 6.8, 27; W.-12.31.

An Irish Engagement: (49) W.-1.8, 9;
(52) C.-9.6, 7, 9, 11, 29; 11.8, 26;
(53) A.-3.22; 4.20.

Irish Farmer: (50) C.-3.14, 15; A.-
11.27, 28; 12.4; (51) A.-2.4, 11; 5.8;
11.12.

Irish Footman; farce by Henry H.
Pane: (47) W.-3.5; (48) C.-7.25,
29.

The Irish Fortune Hunter, or Gold vs.
Love; comedy by John Brougham:
(50) W.-10.14*, 15, 16, 17, 18, 19;
(55) W.-12.4.

Irish Genius: (53) W.-11.11, 12, 13,
14, 15, 16, 17; (55) W.-11.30; 12.1,
6, 8.

Irish Guardian: (51) W.-3.8; (53)
W.-11.9, 14.

Irish Haymakers: (40) C.-10.24, 30.

Irish Helps: (46) A.-12.15.

Irish Honor, or Dublin Days in 1765;
by L. Bernard: (50) W.-5.6*, 7, 8,
9, 10.

The Irish Know Nothing: (55) C.M.-
12.28, 29.

Irish Lion; farce: (38) C.-9.19*, 20,
21, 22, 26; 10.3, 11.6, 9; W.-9.21, 22;
(39) W.-1.19; 2.13; (40) C.-10.6,
7, 12, 21; W.-3.30; 11.17; N.-11.24;
(41) W.-6.28, 30; N.-2.26; A.-6.26;
(42) A.-4.20, 21; C.-10.31; 11.5; A.-

11.11, 15; (43) W.-1.30; 3.28; 8.7, 11; C.-12.7, 21; (44) W.-3.5; 6.5; 7.10; 8.7; 12.21; (45) W.-4.21; 6.16; A.-11.13; C.-12.16; (46) W.-8.21; P.M.-10.15; (47) P.M.-4.10; W.-9.6; (48) P.M.-4.28; C.-7.3; W.-11.9, 11, 25; (49) W.-6.1; 10.15, 18; (50) W.-2.4, 13; C.-3.8; W.-5.20; A.-6.29; 7.3; 11.19; (51) A.-2.18; 5.16, 17; C.-10.20, 21; (52) C.-2.4; 3.2; 8.3; W.-10.21; C.-11.10, 19; (53) A.-4.28; 5.3; C.-5.13; 6.29; (54) A.-4.13, 15; 5.25; W.-5.26; 6.8; C.-6.17; 7.29; 8.9; (55) A.-3.19; 4.3, 4, 11; 5.24; 6.11, 29.

The Irish M.D.; see *Maharatah Surovy Seing.*

Irish Post: (46) A.-7.13, 15; W.-9.3; 11.17, 20; (47) W.-2.3, 5; P.M.-4.15; W.-6.14; 9.29; 10.5; 12.17; (48) A.-3.17; P.M.-4.27; W.-5.27; 9.13; (49) W.-4.17; 9.19, 26, 30; (50) C.-3.7; W.-5.1; A.-7.5, 8, 10; W.-10.17; A.-11.26; (51) A.-2.17; W.-3.3; 9.2; (52) W.-10.1, 2.

Irish Recruit: (49) W.-12.14, 15; (50) W.-5.24, 25.

Irish Secretary; farce: (49) W.-10.19*; 12.10; (50) W.-5.21; (51) C.-10.23; 11.4; (52) C.-2.18, 20; 12.30; (53) C.-1.3; 9.22; (55) A.-10.4, 18; 11.7.

Irish Sibyl and the Rebel Chief: (54) C.-11.4*.

Irish Stratagem: (45) A.-11.29; 12.3.

Irish Swan: (53) C.-5.2.

Irish Thrush and Swedish Nightingale: (54) W.-6.2, 3, 6.

Irish Tiger: (48) P.M.-4.6, 7, 8; 5.4; A.-6.12; (50) C.-3.9; A.-11.25; (51) A.-2.19, 22; 5.5; 11.7, 8; (53) W.-11.2; (55) W.-9.28; C.M.-12.24, 25, 26, 31.

Irish Tutor, or New Lights; farce: (35) C.-4.28; (36) C.-9.29; 10.6; 11.17; W.-4.11; (37) P.-1.11, 17;

2.7; C.-2.16; 3.4; (38) C.-6.9; 10.1, 4; (39) W.-1.14; 2.5, 11; 3.15; 6.13, 28; 7.25; 8.21; 10.18; (40) C.-10.5, 8, 22; W.-2.27; N.-11.16; (41) W.-7.21; A.-5.4; 6.8, 14, 23; 11.1, 10, 23; (42) W.-3.8; C.-5.2, 3; W.-6.10; A.-7.25; 8.19; C.-11.3, 4; (43) W.-3.23; N.-9.29; 10.3, 7; (44) A.-1.16; N.-5.30; C.-11.14; (45) C.-9.4, 6, 20; 10.17; 11.14; A.-12.4, 23; W.-12.23; (46) A.-5.27; 6.6; P. M.-6.8, 15; A.-10.5; W.-10.5, 10; P.M.-10.10, 16, 20, 21; (47) P.M.-4.12; (48) P.M.-4.28; 5.2; C.-7.5, 6, 21; (49) A.-5.29; 9.27; (50) C.-6.25; A.-8.21; (51) A.-5.13; (52) C.-9.8, 10; 12.9, 22; (53) C.-1.29; A.-3.1, 11, 16; C.-5.11; W. 6.25; A.-7.2, 23; 9.15; (54) C.-3.2; A.-3.20; 5.8; W.-5.26; C.-8.24; A.-10.7; C.M.-11.16, 21; (55) A.-1.27; 2.16; 3.6, 27, 28; 6.13; W.-9.21.

The Irish Valet; see *More Blunders Than One.*

Irish Wager: (50) C.-6.26.

The Irish Widow; by David Garrick: (35) C.-4.20; (39) C.-11.7, 15; (40) C.-1.24, 27; 2.1, 15; (40) C.-5.14, 18; 12.21; (41) N.-11.5, 10, 13.

The Irish Yankee, or The Birthday of Freedom; national play by John Brougham: (54) W.-6.8*, 9, 10.

An Irishman's Fortune; see *Born to Good Luck.*

The Irishman in London; farce by William Macready: (35) C.-5.4; (36) C.-9.28; 10.3, 11; (37) C.-3.8; W.-2.20; 3.27; 4.1; (38) C.-10.5; (41) A.-4.13; 6.7, 9, 18; (42) A.-6.11, 16; 10.12; (46) C.-1.20; P.M.-6.25; (47) P.M.-3.17.

The Iron Chest, or The Mysterious Murder; by George Colman the Younger: (35) W.-1.23; 6.4; C.-5.16; 6.27; (36) W.-1.14; 6.6; A.-6.9; P.-11.29; (37) P.-1.9; 2.8; (39)

C.-10.11; 12.13; W.-6.21; 7.5; (40) C.-4.18; W.-5.25; (41) W.-6.18; 9.14; (42) W.-1.21; A.-4.25; W.-6.1; (43) W.-1.17; A.-4.29; 9.9; 10.2; (44) N.-1.13; A.-1.24; W.-2.2; 3.27; 6.25; 10.17; (46) A.-11.3; (47) A.-11.24; (48) A.-1.29; 2.4; W.-5.2; (49) W.-5.23; P.M.-7.23; (50) A.-5.22; C.-7.13; (51) A.-2.25; B.-3.5; N.-8.5; (52) C.-1.27, 31; W.-4.1; A.-11.27; (53) W.-3.3; (55) C.M.-6.1.

Iron King: (49) Ath.-1.18.

Is he a Ghost?: (46) A.-10.15.

Is he Alive and Merry? see *Is the Philadelphian Dead?*

Is he Jealous?: (35) W.-12.5; (36) W.-5.16; 7.2; C.-10.7, 14; 11.21; P.-12.16, 23; (37) A.-5.19; 7.1; (39) W.-2.23; 11.22; 1.15; (40) C.-5.8; 7.4, 6, 9; 10.12; W.-11.20, 27; (41) C.-9.14; A.-1.19; W.-10.18; 12.21, 31; (42) A.-9.28; (43) W.-10.23; N.11.7, 11; (46) P.M.-9.8; A.-10.5, 24; (50) A.-6.15.

Is she a Woman?: (39) W.-8.5, 6.

Is she Married?: (43) O.-1.10; (44) A.-6.3.

Is the Philadelphian Dead, or Is he Alive and Merry?: (40) W.-1.4*, 7, 16; 2.24.

Isabella, or The Fatal Marriage; tragedy by Thomas Southerne: (35) W.-10.26; (39) W.-7.10; C.-3.4, 12; (45) W.-2.5, 6; (47) A.-12.18; (52) A.-11.6; (53) A.-1.4; (55) C.M.-5.19.

Isabelle; see *A Woman's Life.*

The Island Ape; see *Bibboo.*

Israelites in Egypt, or The Passage of the Red Sea; "scriptural opera": (42) C.-12.16, 17, 19, 20, 21, 22; (43) C.-1.19; (51) B.-2.10, 11, 12, 13, 14, 15, 17.

Italian Bride; tragedy (by J. H. Payne): (43) A.-9.8*.

The Italian Brigands, or The Midnight Assault; tableau vivant: (36) C.-12.29; (37) A.-6.30.

Italian Polichinello; tragi-comedy in one act: (35) scientific saloon-1.1, 2, 3.

The Italian Wife; see *Fazio.*

It's all very Fine, Mr. Furgeson: (46) P.M.-9.26.

It's only my Aunt; farce: (50) W.-2.16, 18.

It's the Custom of the Country; Yankee comedy: (52) C.-2.11, 12, 13, 14; W.-9.3, 4.

Ivanhoe, or The Jew's Daughter: (50) C.-2.20, 22; (51) N.-7.24, 25; (52) N.-8.5, 6, 7.

I've Eaten my Friend; farce: (52) W.-2.28*; 3.1, 2.

Jack Brag; farce: (37) W.-8.23.

Jack Cade, or the Noble Kinsman; tragedy in five acts by R. T. Conrad: (35) W.-12.7*, 9, 11, 12; (36) W.-2.1, 2, 3; (41) N.-10.25, 26, 27, 28, 29; A.-6.14, 15, 16, 17, 18, 19, 21, 23; (42) C.-4.13, 18, 21; W.-10.28, 31; 11.4; (43) W.-5.31; 6.2, 9; N.-10.23 26; (44) N.-1.31; W.-8.31; 9.10; 12.2, 6, 12, 16; (46) W.-10.29, 30; 12.23; (47) W.-1.6, 14; 3.10, 16; 5.10, 18; 11.3, 8, 13, 17; (48) W.-11.30; 12.4, 6, 8; (49) W.-6.6, 9; (51) W.-10.14, 16, 18, 22; (52) W.-6.10, 12, 17; 11.10, 13, 18; 12.1; (53) W.-10.15, 20; (54) W.-10.17, 21, 27; (55) W.-12.17, 18, 22.

Jack o'both Sides; comedietta: (48) W.-10.16, 17, 19, 21, 24; 11.2, 4, 13, 22; 12.11; (49) W.-1.22.

Jack Robinson and his Monkey: (35) W.-10.17; (37) W.-1.17; (41) W.-7.8, 9; (41) A.-1.14, 15; (43) A.-3.16; 8.30; (47) A.-1.11; 13; (50) A.-4.1; 5.1; (52) A.-4.7, 8.

Jack Sheppard, the Housebreaker;

from novel by W. H. Ainsworth:
(40) W.-1.21; 2.10, 11, 12, 13, 14;
2.26; (43) O.-1.14, 16; (45) A.-9.24,
25, 26, 27, 30; 10.1, 2, 4, 14, 29, 30,
31; (46) A.-1.16, 19, 20; 4.20, 21;
5.29; (47) A.-5.20, 22, 27; 6.3; 8.5,
7, 23, 24; (48) A.-6.19, 20, 24, 27;
7.28, 29; 8.1; 10.31; 11.8, 11; (49)
A.-1.17, 18, 20; 3.13; C.-11.9; A.
12.24; (50) C.-2.11; A.-6.26, 28;
(52) C.-7.24, 27; N.-9.29; 10.2; (53)
A.-2.19; 3.19; 4.6; (54) C.-10.6, 7, 10,
11, 14; 11.13, 14, 15, 18, 24; (55) C.-
2.10, 21.

Jack Sheppard in France; see *Felon's
Last Dream.*

Jack's the Lad; "nautical drama written for E. S. Conner by C. Ferrars of
New York": (39) W.-5.18*, 20; 6.15,
27; (44) N.-3.7; (51) A.-12.15, 20.

Jackets of Blue: (43) A.-10.10.

Jacob Faithful: (35) W.-5.2, 4, 5.

Jacob Leisler; historical tragedy by
Cornelius Mathews: (48) A.-4.13*,
14, 15, 17, 18, 19, 20, 21, 22.

Jacobite: (47) W.-11.10, 11, 13, 18;
12.27, 30; (48) W.-1.15, 31; 3.27,
28; P.M.-4.5; W.-6.13; 11.7, 11,
23; 12.13, 18; (49) W.-1.9; 10.29;
11.2; 12.4; (50) W.-4.19; 6.19; A.-
8.14, 17; W.-9.11; 11.27; 12.7; (51)
W.-1.9; 2.7; 4.14; 5.27; (52) W.-
11.25; 12.4, 9, 25; (53) W.-1.8, 20;
2.9; 4.19; 5.14; 10.22; 11.11; C.-
12.22; (54) C.-6.27, 29; 7.6; (55)
A.-10.12, 13, 15, 16; 11.8.

Jacques Strop; melodrama in three
acts: (39) W.-11.23*, 28; 12.23;
(40) W.-2.25; 3.4, 18; 5.12, 13;
(41) A.-8.19, 20; N.-12.9; (42) W.-
6.11; (46) W.-3.25, 26, 27; 4.27.

Jakey's Marriage: (50) A.-10.28, 31.

Jakey's Visit to California; farce by
W. Chapman. See the *Mose* plays:
(49) A.-3.14*, 15, 16, 17; 9.20, 21,
22; 11.30; 12.1; (50) A.-8.20.

Jakey's Visit to his Aunt: (49) C.-
8.28.

Jakey in California: (50) C.-7.24,
25.

Jamie of Aberdeen: (39) W.-6.15, 18,
19; 7.23; (42) W.-6.25, 28.

Jane Shore; tragedy by Nicholas
Rowe: (35) C.-1.6; 10.8; A.-3.6;
W.-10.28; (36) W.-10.15, 25; (37)
W.-6.26; (39) C.-3.8, 15; 5.30; (40)
W.-1.10; N.-10.27; (41) W.-11.30;
N.-3.2; 12.11; (42) A.-10.31; (43)
N.-12.14; (44) N.-4.20; 6.28; (45)
A.-5.30; 10.13; (47) A.-1.20; 7.26;
8.11; 9.9; (48) W.-2.10, 12, 18; 4.22;
A.-12.16; (49) A.-3.21, 23; 4.5;
6.20; 10.31; (50) A.-4.2; 9.11; 10.8;
(51) A.-4.1; W.-11.1, 5; (52) A.-
8.24; 10.13, 15, 27; 11.1; (54) A.-
2.11, 13, 16, 23; 3.17; 4.18; C.-10.18,
20; (55) C.M.-1.18, 20, 24; A.-3.7,
8, 10; C.M.-3.24; 5.7, 18; W.-6.1;
A.-11.9, 17.

*Jane of the Hatchet, or The Siege of
Beauvais;* historical drama: (41)
A.-10.23, 25, 26.

Janet Pride: (55) C.M.-11.12, 13, 14;
12.19.

The Jealous Wife; comedy in five acts
by George Colman, Sr.: (35) C.-1.8;
4.6; 5.23; A.-3.10; (36) C.-6.13;
8.31; (37) C.-1.16; (39) C.-2.19;
3.7; (40) C.-10.2; (41) C.-10.7;
(42) A.-3.2; C.-11.11; (45) W.-2.1;
5.26; (46) W.-5.21; 9.23; (47) W.-
1.19; 2.18, 25; 5.27; (50) W.-10.9;
(51) W.-10.29, 31; C.-11.12; (53)
W.-10.1; (54) A.-3.27, 28, 30; 4.1,
12; 5.25; 6.28; 9.15; 10.13; 11.20;
(55) A.-2.19; 8.24.

Jemmy Twitcher in America: (47)
A.-6.4, 7, 19.

Jemmy Twitcher in England; see *The
Golden Farmer.*

Jemmy Twitcher in France; see *Mob,
the Outlaw.*

The Jenkinses: (53) W.-2.25, 26, 28; 3.14; 4.29; 5.18; 6.14.

Jenny Jones; farce: (38) W.-10.9; 11.27.

Jenny Lind, the Swedish Nightingale, presents her First Grand Concert, 1850, Chesnut, October 17, with tickets at seven, six, and five dollars.

Jenny Lind: (48) A.-10.23, 28; 11.11, 25; (49) P.M.-7.16; (51) C.-11.11, 12, 14, 15, 22, 25; 12.13, 17, 26; (52) C.-1.17, 20; (53) C.-4.11, 13; 5.21.

Jenny Lind at Last: (48) A.-8.24; (50) A.-5.29, 30.

Jenny Lind in America: (51) A.-2.3, 4, 6.

Jenny Lind in Philadelphia; by J. M. Amherst: (50) A.-4.10.

Jenny Lind in Town: (52) N.-8.5.

Jerry Murphy, the Philosopher; farce: (45) A.-11.28.

The Jersey Girl; see *Bill Stickers.*

The Jesuit's Colony, or The Indian's Doom; "new national drama written by a gentleman of Philadelphia": (38) W.-8.8*.

The Jew; comedy by Richard Cumberland: (35) C.-5.14, 18.

The Jew's Daughter; see *Ivanhoe.*

The Jewess, or The Fate of Haman: (36) W.-2.29*; 3.1, 2, 3, 4, 5, 7, 8, 9, 10, 11; 3.17, 21, 22, 24, 26; (41) W.-12.1, 2, 3, 4.

The Jewess, or A Dream of Fate; Q. V.: (46) P.M.-12.21, 22; (47) A.-5.25, 26, 29; (49) C.-12.6, 7.

The Jibbenainosay; melodrama: (45) A.-5.22.

Jim Crow: (35) W.-1.10, 13, 14, 15; 6.23, 27, 29, 30; 7.1, 2, 3, 4. (With T. D. Rice.)

Jim Crow in London: (37) C.-10.25*, 26, 27, 28; (38) C.-1.2; W.-6.23, 27; 10.12; (40) A.-9.11; (41) A.-11.10; (43) A.-9.21; (44) C.-12.18; (45)

A.-10.15; (46) A.-2.9; (48) A.-3.7, 8; (52) A.-1.2, 3.

Joan of Arc: (39) W.-1.28; 2.5, 7; 8.13; (40) W.-3.21, 30; N.-12.24; (41) N.-3.5; A.-12.13, 14, 18; (46) W.-6.26; 7.7; (51) A.-10.25, 29; (52) A.-9.8, 10.

Job Fox, the Yankee Pedlar; "Entire new farce written for Hackett by the author of *The Nervous Man,* and performed these two seasons at the Park." Compare with *The Yankee Pedlar:* (36) W.-3.29, 31; (37) C.-2.10, 14; (38) C.-4.11; 5.4; 9.5; (40) C.-5.29.

Jocko, the Brazilian Ape; melodrama: (35) W.-9.18, 21; (37) A.-6.26; (41) W.-7.13, 14; (48) A.-8.19, 26; 9.1.

Joe the Orphan: (47) A.-8.14, 17, 21; (49) A.-10.25; C.-12.3, 4.

Joe Miller; "a sketch in one act written by a gentleman of Philadelphia": (37) C.-4.14*.

John Bull, or The Englishman's Fireside; comedy by George Colman the younger: (36) C.-9.27; 10.7; 11.18; (37) C.-2.17; A.-5.8; W.-6.27; (40) C.10.13; (43) A.-12.16; (44) A.-7.25; 8.1; (46) C.-1.13; (48) A.-6.6; (49) A.-6.18; (52) C.-2.19, 21; (53) A.-4.25, 27; 8.31; (54) A.-2.20; W.-5.22, 25; A.-6.8; 11.24; (55) A.-6.14.

John Bull in France: (49) C.-8.21.

John Buzzby, or A Day's Pleasure; comedy by Poole: (37) C.-2.25*; (44) W.-4.10.

John di Procida, or The Bridals of Messina: (40) N.-10.19*, 22; 11.10; (41) C.-9.7, 9; (46) A.-4.18; (49) A.-1.17, 18.

John Dobbs; farce: (49) A.-8.15*, 16; W.-11.1, 3, 13, 20; 12.7, 11; (50) W.-1.15; 4.1; 5.17; 6.3; 8.19; (51) W.-1.22; A.-9.18; (54) A.-8.28, 29; (55) A.-10.11.

John Jones; farce: (35) C.-1.10, 29; 2.10; 4.17; 5.29; 6.8, 18; A.-2.27; 3.21, 28; C.-7.4; 8.26; 9.18; 10.9, 26; 11.4, 6, 24; 12.16; (36) A.-3.5; 4.28; C.-1.22; 2.20; 6.17; A.-5.12; C.-9.9; 11.10, 23; 12.30; (37) C.-4.6, 22; 9.5; 10.14; 11.6; (38) C.-2.21; 7.4; 8.27; 10.23; (39) C.-10.16; W.-5.20, 27; (41) N.-1.22; 12.13; (42) A.-9.19; (43) N.-11.2, 9; (44) A.-7.22; C.-12.2; (45) A.-5.29; C.-10.20; 11.25; (46) P.M.-6.3; A.-8.26; (47) A.-5.13; (48) A.-11.21; (49) Ath.-1.16, 18, 27; (52) A.-4.6; (54) W.-4.5, 8; C.-4.12; 10.10.

John Overy; see *The Miser of Southwark Ferry.*

John of Paris; opera: (35) C.-2.4; (36) C.-1.11; (37) C.-1.27; (39) C.-6.19; (43) C.-1.28, 30; (46) C.-5.16; P.M.-6.17, 30.

John Savile of Haysted; domestic drama: (48) W.-9.4*, 5, 6, 8.

Jolly Cobbler: (49) P.M.-7.17.

Jonah, or A Night in Whales; farce: (41) W.-11.2.

Jonathan and his Apprentices; "nautical and domestic drama" by W. Barrymore: (38) W.-3.1, 2, 8.

Jonathan Bradford, or The Murder at the Road-Side Inn: (36) P.-11.23, 24, 26; (39) W.-10.15; (41) N.-11.20; 12.16; (42) A.-11.19, 21, 22; (45) A.-11.10, 11, 14; (49) A.-9.26, 27; (50) A.-8.23; (51) A.-11.26, 29; (52) N.-9.18; A.-12.16; (53) A.-1.3; 4.8, 16; (54) C.-2.9.

Jonathan Doubikins; comedy: (35) W.-5.13; 10.23; C.-9.9, 10; (36) W.-5.7, 16, 23; A.-5.27; (37) C.-9.9; 9.13; (38) C.-4.2, 5, 12; 9.6; (45) C.-1.18.

Jonathan in England; comedy, being "Mr. (J. H.) Hackett's original alteration of *Who Wants a Guinea?:* (35) W.-5.6, 12; 10.21; 11.18; 12.14; C.-9.8; (36) W.-3.28; 5.5, 16; (37) C.-2.11; 9.2; (38) C.-4.10; 9.7; W.-7.17; 13.9; 10.22, 31; (40) C.-5.25; N.-9.24; A.-12.1, 3; W.-12.14, 19; (41) N.-8.31; A.-6.30; 9.24, 25; W.-2.5; 10.12, 26; (42) C.-3.30; W.-4.12, 15, 16; 11.29; (43) A.-5.8, 23; 10.7, 20; N.-11.20; (44) A.-10.12; (45) C.-1.16; W.-12.20; (50) A.-9.6.

Joseph Bragg; comedy: (42) W.-7.18, 20.

Josey the Spartan: (51) A.-6.19.

A Journey to London; see *The Provoked Husband.*

Juan Romiro: (47) W.-8.12, 13.

Judgment of Solomon; domestic drama (by Royall Tyler). This may have been William Dunlap's *The Voice of Nature,* Q. V.: (35) W.-4.2; (37) W.-7.2; (45) A.-8.19.

Judith of Mont Blanc; domestic drama: (44) C.-10.26; 11.13.

Julie, Duchesse de la Vaubaliere; see *The Duke's Bride.*

Julie, or The Forced Marriage: (36) A.-6.2*, 3; (39) W.-5.1.

Julietta Gordini; tragedy by Isaac C. Pray: (39) C.-3.20*, 21.

Julius Caesar; by William Shakespeare: (35) W.-3.18; 9.1; (36) W.-6.8; A.-3.7; (37) W.-1.28; 7.21; (38) W.-7.12; 9.7; (40) N.-9.25; (41) A.-10.16; (43) W.-4.20; A.-9.14; 10.9, 18; (44) W.-1.22; 3.29; 6.19; (45) W.-5.27; A.-10.6; C.-12.2; (46) W.-2.27; 12.28; (48) W.-4.17; (49) W.-4.4; (50) A.-7.22; (51) A.-5.30; (52) C.-1.19, 28; N.-9.3.

Jumbo Jim: (40) W.-12.14; (43) A.-9.20, 27; (44) A.-1.17, 20; (45) A.-10.13, 17; (46) A.-1.30, 31; (48) A.-2.14, 16; W.-12.19; (50) A.-5.2; (51) A.-12.31.

Kabri, or The Magic Mirror; comic fairy tale: (42) A.-5.18; (45) W.-1.10; (47) P.M.-1.4, 5.

Kaspar Hauser, or The Down Easter; by H. J. Finn: (35) W.-12.14*, 15, 18; (36) W.-5.7, 12; A.-5.28; (37) C.-9.14, 16; (38) C.-4.4, 6; (39) W.-10.30; 11.1; (45) C.-4.29; 5.1; (51) A.-3.21.

Kate Kearney (37) W.-4.1, 3; (41) W.-2.1, 3, 4, 5, 24; 4.22; 5.5; 11.16, 20; (42) W.-1.7; 5.7; (46) P.M.-3.9, 10, 11, 12, 13, 14, 27; 4.13; 5.18; 6.3; 11.17, 19, 28; (47) P.M.-1.30; 3.3, 4, 5, 16; 4.3; 6.5; 7.1; (50) A.-11.22, 23; (54) A.-6.2, 3; W.-6.6, 7.

Katharine and Petruchio; by David Garrick, after Shakespeare: (35) C.-1.19; W.-5.27; (38) C.-11.22; W.-9.26, 29; 12.8; (39) C.-1.14; 2.5; 5.13; 11.30; W.-7.12; (40) N.-10.30; (41) N.-10.25; 12.17; C.-2.23; (44) W.-5.2; 10.13; (44) N.-3.2, 15; C.-12.11; (46) P.M.-10.1; (47) A.-1.23; 9.8; 12.2; (48) A.-1.17; W.-8.31; A.-12.15; (49) A.-2.28; 4.13, 30; 5.16; 8.20; W.-11.10; A.-12.18; (50) A.-6.14; W.-8.21; 9.13; (51) W.-1.6; A.-1.15; W.-3.10; B.-4.5; W.-5.7, 10; 9.19; 10.3; C.-12.30; (52) C-1.1; W.-1.22; 3.6; C.-4.9; 5.8; 10.9; (53) W.-1.18, 22, 28; C.-2.22, 28; 6.17; W.-12.17; (54) C.-5.13, 15, 25; (55) C.M.-4.13, 18; 11.23.

Kehama; romantic drama: (44) A.-2.12, 19.

Kenilworth, or The Golden Days of Queen Elizabeth: (40) W.-1.1, 2, 3.

The Kentuckian, or A Trip to New York; revision of *The Lion of the West:* (35) W.-11.18; (36) W.-3.28, 31; (37) C.-2.8, 11; 8.31; (38) C.-4.9, 13; 9.6; (40) N.-9.17, 26; C.-5.28, 30; (41) N.-8.30; W.-3.10; (42) C.-3.30; W.-11.29; (44) A.-11.12, 16, 21; (45) C.-9.9, 12; A.-

9.30; (49) W.-3.20, 21, 24; 12.19, 22; (53) W.-2.3, 5; 4.21, 30.

Kentucky in 1783; see Nick of the Woods.

Khut Yer Styk: (46) A.-1.5.

Kill or Cure; farce: (35) W.-1.24, 26, 28, 29; 2.4, 10; C.-1.26, 28; 2.9; 4.22; 6.15; 8.29; A.-3.18; C.-10.20; 11.2, 10; (36) A.-4.29; C.-1.20; 12.1; W.-10.10; P.-11.10, 16; (37) A.-6.14, 28; (38) C.-1.23; (42) A.-8.27; 11.7; (43) O.-1.9; W.-3.31; 4.4; (47) A.-10.22; (48) A.-2.2, 3; W.-2.17; P.M.-4.10, 12, 15, 21; (52) C.-10.25; 11.4.

Killing no Murder; farce in two acts: (39) W.-4.1, 2, 10; (41) N.-2.1, 3.

The Kind Impostors; see *She Would and she Would not.*

King and Hangman; see *Hinko.*

King and I: (45) C.-10.15, 16, 18, 27; (47) P.M.-3.24, 25, 31; A.-4.28, 29; 7.8, 10.

The King and the Deserter: (40) N.-12.28, 29; (41) W.-2.13; 4.23; (42) A.-6.13; (44) A.-8.5, 29; (45) A.-11.17; 12.5; (46) P.M.-5.30; (47) A.-5.1, 31; (49) Ath.-1.6.

The King and the Mimic: (39) C.-10. 8, 9, 12, 17, 22; 11.20, 23; 12.3, 13; (40) C.-2.28; 4.1; 5.7; 6.4; (41) C.-2.10.

Kingcraft in 1852; see *Empire of Hayti.*

King Eagle, or The Wild Steed of the Desert: (46) A.-6.22, 23, 24, 25.

King John; by William Shakespeare: (35) W.-3.19; (40) C.-1.1; 9.15; (43) A.-10.14; (44) W.-2.3; 3.18; 6.15, 22, 26; (46) W.-2.23; A.-9.30; W.-12.30; (47) W.-4.20; (52) C.-1.29.

King Lear; by William Shakespeare: (35) W.-3.16; 5.21; 6.29; 8.31; 11.30; C.-7.1; (36) W.-6.2; (37) C.-10.18; 11.16; W.-7.22; 12.14;

(38) C.-9.13; W.-7.9; 8.30; (39) C.-10.30; W.-6.24; W.-12.4; (40) C.-11.30; W.-5.4; N.-9.17, 19, 22, 26; (41) W.-3.10; 5.24; 9.13; N.-10.30; 12.15; A.-8.28; 9.1; (42) C.-4.1, 15; W.-4.5; A.-5.6; W.-10.29; C.-11.16; (43) W.-4.19; A.-8.21; 9.15; N.-10.21; (44) W.-1.24; 4.3; A.-11.22; W.-12.9; (45) W.-4.3; 5.26; A.-12.11; (46) W.-4.2; 10.23; A.-12.30; (47) A.-11.23; (48) A.-3.15; 11.27; W.-11.27; (51) B.-3.17; W.-10.15; (52) A.-11.19; W.-11.26; (54) W.-10.24; (55) C.-2.15; C.M.-5.30; 11.7.

King of the Commons; by James White: (46) A.-97*, 8, 9, 10, 11, 12, 14, 15, 16, 17, 18; 10.2; W.-10.14, 15, 17; (47) A.-4.12, 14, 21; W.-5.24; 9.23; 10.29; (49) W.-3.13; 4.6; (51) B.-3.31; 4.2; (52) A.-11.15, 16; (53) C.-4.2, 5; W.-12.12, 14; (55) C.M.-10.26, 27; 11.3.

King O'Neil, or The Irish Brigade; melodrama by Mrs. Gore: (36) C.-11.21*, 22, 24; (37) C.-2.20; (42) W.-11.7; (47) W.-2.13; 6.21; 10.8, 9; 12.22; (48) W.-5.22, 25; 9.22, 23; (49) W.-4.17, 20; 9.25; C.-10.16; (50) W.-5.3, 4; C.-7.1; (51) W.-2.28; 3.1; 9.3, 6; (52) W.-3.4.

King of the Mist, or The Hartz Mountains: (43) N.-11.27, 28, 29, 30; 12.1, 2, 4, 5, 6, 7, 8, 11, 12, 13, 14, 15, 16, 18, 19, 20, 21; (44) N.-1.13.

King Rene's Daughter: (50) A.-4.22*, 23, 24, 25, 26, 30.

The King's Command: (38) W.-1.1*, 2, 11; (46) P.M.-6.13.

The King's Fool: (42) A.-10.24. See The Old Man's Curse.

The King's Gardner: (43) A.-9.5; W.-9.19, 29; C.-10.23; (44) A.-1.9; (47) W.-9.9, 16, 21; 11.22; (48) A.-1.26; 5.22; W.-6.10; (49) W.-5.17,

28; 6.14; P.M.-7.23, 24; (51) B.-1.25; (52) C.-7.23.

The King's Jester; see Court Fool.

The King's Word: (41) N.-1.4, 13.

A Kiss in the Dark; farce: (40) C.-8.31; 9.1, 5; 12.25; N.-9.29; 11.4; (42) W.-7.22; (43) A.-10.28; (44) W.-4.26; A.-6.1; (46) A.-3.21; C.-4.27, 28; P.M.-10.2, 10; (47) P.M.-1.18; 3.9; A.-7.16; (49) Ath.-1.26; C.-9.5; 10.8, 24; (50) A.-7.9, 11; 8.28; (51) B.-1.1; A.-2.28; 6.10; C.-8.20, 21; 9.8; A.-10.13; C.-10.15; 12.3, 5; (52) C.-1.23; 4.19, 24, 29; 5.13; W.-6.5, 9, 19; C.-6.17; N.-8.3; W.-9.15; (53) W.-1.19; 6.23, 24; (54) C.-5.29; N.-6.5; C.-6.21, 24; C.M.-9.13; (55) C.M.-5.25, 29; A.-9.5, 18; 12.31.

Kit Karson, or The Hero of the Prairie; by W. R. Derr: (50) A.-3.16*, 18, 19, 20, 21, 22; (54) N.-6.30; 7.1.

The Knight of Arva, or Conner the Rash; comedy by D. Boucicault: (49) W.-10.18*, 20, 23, 26; 12.10, 13; (50) W.-5.21; (51) C.-10.28; 11.1, 8, 27; (52) C.-2.17, 24; 3.2, 6; 12.25, 28; (53) A.-1.10; 5.17, 31; C.-6.8; 9.8, 24; (55) A.-4.25, 27, 30; 5.9, 14, 21, 30; 6.4, 9; W.-6.4; 11.9, 10.

The Knight of the Bleeding Scarf; see Moorish Page.

The Knight of the Golden Fleece, or The Yankee in Spain; by J. A. Stone: (35) W.-5.11*, 12, 13, 14, 16; 10.19, 21; 12.18; C.-9.11, 12; (36) W.-5.6, 9, 13; A.-5.24, 26; (37) C.-9.11, 15; (38) C.-4.5; (39) W.-10.21, 22, 23; (40) W.-12.21, 22; A.-12.9, 10; (41) W.-10.14; (43) A.-10.9, 17.

The Knight of the Lion Heart, or Golden Days of Chivalry; musical melodrama by J. Foster: (50) C.-5.1*, 2, 4, 15, 16, 18.

The Knight of Snowden; see *The Lady of the Lake.*

Knights of the Cross: (37) W.-1.18, 19; (52) A.-4.15, 17.

Knights of the Dark Ages: (44) W.-10.30, 31; 11.1, 2, 4, 5, 6, 7, 8, 9, 11, 12, 13.

Knights of the Garter; see Battle of Poictiers.

Know your own Mind; comedy by Arthur Murphy: (38) C.-10.15, 18; (39) C.-5.4.

Koeuba, or The Pirate of the Capes: (37) W.-12.25*; (38) W.-2.1; (51) N.-7.26, 29, 30.

Kriss Kringle: (47) P.M.-1.9; (49) A.-12.29.

Kriss Kringle's Visit: (44) N.-1.12.

L'Ambassadrice: (43) C.-9.14, 15, 16, 18, 19, 20, 21; (45) C.-10.8.

L'Amour, or La Rose Animée: (40) C.-6.23, 24, 25, 26, 27, 29.

L'Automate; farce: (39) C.-12.23.

La Bayadere; opera: (38) W.-9.24, 25, 27; 10.1, 5, 6, 8, 9; (39) W.-4.22, 23, 24, 25, 27; (40) W.-1.24; (41) C.-5.19; 6.1; A.-8.21, 23, 24; (42) W.-11.23; (45) W.-11.26, 27, 28, 29; 12.1, 5, 29; (46) W.-4.23, 24, 25; 12.25; (48) A.-3.27, 28, 29, 30, 31; (51) W.-9.22, 23, 24, 25; (52) W.-5.21, 22, 28, 29; (53) C.-9.8, 10, 13, 15.

La Cenerentola; opera by Rossini: (53) W.-3.2, 9.

L'El(i)sire d'Amore; opera by Donizetti. See Elixir of Love: (41) C.-5.8, 10, 11, 20, 25; (48) W.-10.5; C.-10.6, 9, 11; (52) W.-2.11, 12.

La Favorita; opera by Donizetti: (45) C.-9.29; (50) C.-9.24; (51) C.-1.13, 18.

La Femme Soldat; see The Colonel's Come.

La Fête Champêtre; ballet pantomime:

(36) C.-12.29; (37) C.-1.30; A.-6.28.

La Figlia del Reggimento; opera by Donizetti: (53) W.-2.28.

La Fille du Regiment; opera by Donizetti: (43) C.-9.25; 10.6, 21; (45) C.-10.1; (47) W.-5.7; (49) W.-10.1, 3, 5.

La Fille Mal Garde; see Lise et Colin.

La Fitte, or The Pirate's Home; (by Percival): (36) W.-10.28*, 29, 31; 11.1, 2, 3, 4, 5, 7, 8, 9, 10, 11, 12, 17, 18, 19, 30; 12.1, 20, 29; (37) W.-1.26; 8.12; 11.27; 12.28; (38) W.-2.12; 3.9; 8.2; 9.12; (39) W.-8.12, 16; (40) W.-3.6; 7.2; (41) A.-6.5, 12; (42) W.-1.29; 2.19; A.-5.28, 30, 31; 6.1; (43) W.-6.21, 22; (44) A.-10.30; 11.2; (46) A.-12.18, 19; (50) A.-5.4, 6, 7, 8, 9; (51) A.-1.3, 8; (52) N.-9.25.

La Gazza Ladra, or The Maid of Paulaiseur; opera by Rossini: (39) C.-10.28, 29, 30, 31; 11.1, 2; (41) C.-5.1, 3, 21; (47) W.-10.21; (51) B.-2.22, 24.

La Gipsey; ballet: (41) C.-9.23.

La Juive; opera by Jacques Halévy: (45) C.-10.9.

La Ligne Droite: (55) W.-11.20.

La Lutte du Pugilat; see The Three Gladiators.

La Masque; opera: (38) W.-7.4.

La Muette de Portici; opera by François Auber: (45) C.-10.6.

La Perouse; pantomime: (47) A.-1.12.

La Perruche: (43) C.-10.17.

La Petite Chaperon Rouge; ballet opera: (39) C.-6.17, 20.

La Pie Voluse; farce: (39) W.-6.4.

La Rose Animée; see L'Amour.

La Som-Am-Bull-Ah: (53) C.-12.14, 15.

La Sonnambula; opera by Vincenzo Bellini: (36) C.-2.11*, 12, 13, 15, 16, 17, 18, 19, 20, 22, 23, 24, 25, 26;

A.-5.2, 5.7, 9, 10, 12, 13; (37) C.-3.15, 23, 24, 25, 27, 28; 9.1; A.-6.27; C.-9.3, 7; 10.10; 11.3, 13; (38) C.-1.10; 2.26, 28; 3.2, 7; W.-9.28, 29; (39) C.-1.14, 15, 16, 17, 21, 25, 28; 2.4; 4.1, 3, 5, 22, 27; 5.16, 17, 20; 9.16, 17; 10.18, 19, 25; (40) C.-2.8, 10; 3.9; 4.29; 10.26, 28; 11.4; 12.16; (41) C.-5.31; (42) C.-12.5, 6, 9; (43) C.-1.18; 2.10; (44) C.-4.2, 3, 8; 6.3; (45) C.-1.8, 11; 10.13, 15; 11.14; (46) W.-4.21; (47) C.-4.8, 15, 27; 5.20; 6.2; W.-7.20, 21, 24; 10.13; 11.23, 26; 12.28; (48) C.-6.6, 7, 8, 9, 10; W.-10.4; (49) W.-5.3; (51) C.-1.17; B.-2.18, 20; W.-8.18, 20; 9.17; (52) W.-2.13, 14; 12.22, 24; (53) W.-3.4; (54) C.-6.6, 7, 12, 13; 9.12; W.-10.30, 31.

La Sonnambula, Travestie; "the Ethiopian opera": (36) W.-9.2*.

La Sylphide; ballet: (40) C.-7.1, 2, 3, 4, 5, 9; 11, 12, 14; (41) C.-9.3; (42) C.-1.4; A.-9.30; (43) W.-10.16; (45) W.-12.3; (47) A.-5.11, 12, 14. See *Dew Drop.*

La Tarentule; comic ballet in two acts: (40) C.-6.17*, 18, 19, 20, 22; 11.10, 16; (41) C.-9.8, 15.

La Tentation, or The Daughter of Evil. See *The Devil's Daughter.*

La Tour de Nesle; see *The Tower de Nesle.*

Ladder of Love: (40) W.-6.29; C.-9.5, 7, 26; 10.14; (44) N.-3.30; (46) P.M.-9.24, 25; (53) C.-3.2, 3, 5, 12, 17, 30.

Ladies at Home: (54) W.-9.26, 27; 10.2, 3, 10, 23; 11.6, 29.

Ladies' Battle, or Duel en Amour; comedy by Charles Reade: (52) W.-3.12*, 13, 15, 16, 17; (53) A.-4.15, 20, 26; 5.2, 5, 14; (54) A.-6.7, 13; W.-12.22; (55) W.-1.1.

Ladies' Club: (40) C.-5.19, 20, 23;

12.19; (42) W.-7.23, 26; (49) A.-4.16; W.-5.21, 22.

The Ladies' Man; "first time, a new farce, altered and translated by Mr. [W. E.] Burton from the French Vaudeville, *Les Malheurs d'un Joli Garcon*": (35) C.-1.12*, 14, 17; 2.5; 4.6; 8.22; 9.23; A.-3.17, 25; C.-10.22; (36) A.-6.7; C.-1.13; 2.13; W.-2.10; (37) A.-6.24; C.-1.12; 8.24; 10.6, 24; 11.27; 12.21; (38) C.-1.5; 2.9; 3.23; 8.25; 9.14, 25; 11.28; (41) N.-12.7, 14; (42) C.-5.10; 11.10; (43) O.-1.11; W.-5.17; (47) A.-3.30; 4.9; (50) C.-6.28.

The Ladies' Privilege; see *Leap Year.*

The Lady and the Devil; farce in two acts: (36) W.-5.3, 31; 8.30; (38) W.-3.3; (39) W.-2.2, 15; (40) W.-11.20; (41) N.-11.24; (42) W.-7.9; (46) A.-10.7, 12; (47) A.-4.7; (48) A.-5.18; 11.1; (53) C.-3.23.

The Lady and the Invisible: (39) W.-8.2.

The Lady and the Unknown; farce: (38) W.-10.5.

The Lady of the Lake; melodrama: (35) W.-4.9; (38) W.-9.8; (39) C.-6.22; (41) W.-5.29, 31; 6.1, 2, 3, 4, 5, 8; (42) C.-12.31; (43) C.-1.2; (46) W.-4.1, 4; (48) W.-10.28, 30, 31; 12.25, 26, 28; (49) W.-1.4; (50) A.-6.21, 22; (51) B.-5.21, 22, 23, 24; (53) A.-2.24, 26; (55) W.-2.17.

The Lady of the Lake, or The Knight of Snowden; "first time, with music, original romantic drama": (37) A.-6.7*; (38) W.-3.10; (40) C.-3.13; (41) C.-12.13, 14, 18. From this point, it is difficult to know which version of the play, or if both, persisted.

The Lady of Lyons, or Love and Pride; romantic drama by Edward Bulwer-Lytton: (38) C.-6.2*, 4, 7, 20, 22, 25; 7.2, 3, 6; 11.28; W.-7.25,

2.15; (45) A.-6.2, 3; (47) W.-6.29, 30; 7.1, 6. The version of this play used after the above recorded performances of 1835 may have been that of L. H. Medina, but it is likely that all performances at the Walnut issued from the adaptation of W. Barrymore.

The Last Heir of Ravenswood; see *The Bride of Lammermoor.*

The Last Man, or The Miser of Eltham Green; by W. R. Blake: (39) W.-9.10*, 12, 13; (40) W.-11.2, 3, 4, 5, 6, 7, 10; (41) C.-3.1; A.-5.5, 7, 12, 14; (43) W.-9.18; (44) W.-2.16; 6.4; (46) W.-3.11, 12; 8.24; (48) W.-9.18; (52) C.-12.24; (54) W.-7.3; C.M.-12.30; (55) C.M.-1.6.

The Last Nail, or The Drunkard's Doom; melodrama: (36) W.-6.20*, 21, 23, 24; (39) W.-1.15; (41) A.-12.21; (45) W.-7.2, 3; (50) C.-5.18, 20.

The Last of the Fairies: (48) W.-2.23.

The Last of the Gauls; see *Gaulantus.*

The Last of the MacDonalds; see *Glencoe.*

The Last of the Wampanoags; see *Metamora.*

The Last Pardon: (38) W.-6.25, 28; 7.26.

Last Words of Bill Jones; see *Black Brig of Bermuda.*

Latin, Love, and War; farce: (40) C.-5.20.

Laugh when you Can, or The Laughing and Crying Philosopher; by [Frederick] Reynolds: (35) C.-11.17, 24; 12.30; (36) C.-6.16; W.-3.17; A.-6.1; (37) C.-4.10; (39) C.-2.28; 3.26; (40) W.-10.19, 24; 11.7, 10, 26; C.-5.7; 6.13; (41) W.-1.9, 16; A.-5.12; C.-2.27; (43) C.-9.12; W.-9.14; 10.27; C.-12.12; (44) W.-2.19; 5.17; C.-12.10; (46) W.-1.23, 24;

3.13, 30; 4.29; 6.12; (47) W.-2.20; A.-7.19; 11.13, 16; (48) P.M.-5.18, 20; W.-7.22; A.-9.8; (49) W.-1.10, 17; 3.14, 26; 11.8; 12.31; (50) W.-5.16; 7.3; (53) C.-3.10; A.-3.12, 26; 5.9; C.-6.28; A.-10.24; 11.16; (54) A.-2.13; 3.17; 5.2; W.-6.12; A.-10.6, 21; 12.25; (55) A.-1.1; 3.17; 4.14; 6.22; 9.4; 10.23.

The Laughing and Crying Philosopher; see *Laugh when you Can.*

Laughing Hyena: (51) A.-3.25; (54) C.M.-12.1, 4; (55) C.M.-3.3; 4.10, 30; 5.31.

The Launch of the Mississippi: (41) W.-5.7, 8, 10, 12.

The Launch of the Susquehanna, or A Day's Sport at the Navy Yard: (50) C.-4.6*, 7, 9, 10, 11.

Lavater, the Physiognomist; comedy: (49) A.-1.10*, 23.

Law for Ladies: (53) W.-10.28.

The Law of the Land; domestic drama: (38) W.-1.29*.

Lawyer's Clerk: (54) C.-10.24.

Lawyer's Practice: (49) A.-9.18.

Lawyer's Victim: (45) A.-4.3.

Le Chapeau du General: (44) C.-11.9.

Le Depit Amoureux; comedy: (55) W.-11.19.

Le Diable à Paris: (51) A.-10.24.

Le Dieu et la Bayadere; see *The Maid of Cashmere;* opera.

Le Domino Noir: (43) C.-10.3, 4, 10, 11; (45) C.-10.3.

Le Gamin du Paris: (43) C.-10.14.

Le Grace de Dieu: (43) C.-9.30; 10.5.

Le Morne-au-Diable; see *Female Blue Beard.*

Le Postillion de Lonjumeau: (43) C.-9.29; 10.19.

Le Pre aux Clercs: (43) C.-10.18.

Le Preux Chevalier; comedy: (40) C.-3.19*; N.-10.20, 22.

Les Premières Armès de Richelieu: (43) C.-9.30.

Le Tartuffe; comedy by Moliere: (55) W.-11.24.

Leap Year, or The Ladies' Privilege; comedy by J. B. Buckstone: (50) C.-2.27*, 28; 3.26, 27; 5.14, 22; W.-8.21, 22, 23, 24.

The Lear of Private Life, or A Voice from Bedlam: (38) W.-12.15, 21; (40) W.-2.29.

The Learned Men Outwitted; farce: (35) Mam.C.-1.30, 31; 2.13, 14.

The Leaguers of Austria; see *The Avenger.*

The Legend of the Catskill Mountains; see *Rip van Winkle.*

A Legend of the Chesnut Street Theatre; "first time on any stage, a play in five acts by a gentleman of this city": (54) C.-1.17*, 18, 20, 26.

Legion of Honor: (36) W.-10.4.

Leila, or The Siege of Granada: (38) W.-7.2*, 3.

Lend Me Five Shillings: (46) P.M.-7.13, 14, 21, 31; W.-8.17, 18, 19; 9.7, 14, 17; 10.26; (47) W.-1.21; 2.24; 3.30; 4.10; 6.8; (50) W.-2.7, 9; 3.26; 4.6; 6.10; 8.23; (51) W.-1.27; 6.26; (52) W.-1.5; 3.30; 6.11; (54) W.-2.10, 11, 20; 3.4; 12.29; (55) A.-8.20, 28; 11.2.

Lend Me Five Pounds: (46) W.-11.11; 12.10, 28.

Leonora; grand opera by Fry; "first American opera": (45) C.-6.4, 5, 6, 7, 10, 11, 12, 13, 14, 16, 17, 25; (46) W.-12.8, 9, 10, 11.

Leonor de Guzman; historical tragedy by G. H. Boker: (53) W.-10.3*, 4, 5, 6, 7, 8.

Les Diamants de la Couronne: (43) C.-9.22, 26, 27; 10.2, 20.

Les Droits de l'Homme: (55) W.-11.21, 22.

Les Horaces; tragedy in five acts by Corneille: (55) W.-11.19.

Les Hugenots: (45) C.-10.10, 11.

Les Malheurs d'un Joli Garçon; see *The Ladies' Man.*

Les Memoires du Diable: (43) C.-9.23.

A Lesson for Ladies; comedy: (39) W.-1.9*, 10, 14, 30; (44) A.-1.15.

A Lesson for Listners; see *City Wives.*

Lessons for Husbands: (55) C.M.-7.4.

Lessons for Lovers; see *Young Widow.*

Lestocq, or The Convention; romantic drama: (36) W.-11.15*, 21.

The Liar; by Samuel Foote: (37) C.-10.21; (38) C.-1.29; 2.8; (39) C.-11.25.

The Liberation of Rome; see *Virginius.*

The Liberator of his Country; see *The Hero of the North.*

The Libertine Destroyed; see *Don Juan.*

The Libertine's Ship: see *Margaret's Ghost.*

Liberty, Equality, and Fraternity: (51) N.-8.15.

The Liberty Tree, or The Boston Boys of '76; national drama by J. S. Jones: (36) W.-7.4*.

Life among the Lowly; see *Uncle Tom's Cabin.*

Life in Alabama: (50) C.-2.13*; (51) B.-6.2; A.-7.29; (52) W.-2.4.

Life in a Country Town; see *Rural Felicity.*

Life in Both; see *Ireland and America.*

Life in London; see *Tom and Jerry.*

Life in Philadelphia, or The Unfortunate Author; by N. H. Bannister: (38) W.-1.15*; (44) W.-2.10; (51) A.-7.15, 30.

Life in the Clouds: (42) C.-11.21, 23, 25.

Life in the Quaker City; see *A Glance at Philadelphia.*

Life in the Temple; see *Chamber Practice.*

Life in the West, or Playing False;

comedy by J. Austin Sperry: (54) W.-5.1*, 3, 6.

The Life of Napoleon Bonaparte; see *The Invasion of Russia.*

The Light Ship, or The Blacksmith's Daughter: (40) W.-4.6, 7, 8, 9, 10, 15; (41) N.-4.14; (44) A.-6.12, 15, 24; 12.31; (47) A.-9.3.

Like Father, Like Son: (40) A.-12.26; (41) W.-1.22; 2.15, 16; 3.9; 4.2, 28, 29.

Lilian, the Show Girl: (37) W.-2.27*, 28; 3.1, 2, 17, 31; (41) W.-2.9; 3.1; A.-10.23, 25, 27.

Lilliputians in Kentucky, or Little Cause for Jealousy: (38) W.-1.22.

The Lilly of St. Leonards; see *The Heart of Midlothian.*

The Limerick Boy; by James Pilgrim: (48) A.-3.10*; P.M.-4.24, 26; (49) A.-11.28; (50) A.-2.11; C.-3.1, 11; A.-11.18; (51) A.-2.7, 8; 5.6, 10; (52) C.-2.3; W.-8.30; (53) C.-5.3; W.-6.11; 10.31; 11.1; (54) W.-5.16, 24; C.-7.26; 10.5; 11.16; (55) C.M.-12.27.

Linda, or The Pearl of Savoy: (44) N.-3.25, 27, 28; (49) P.M.-4.25, 26, 27; 5.4, 5; (51) B.-9.1, 2, 3, 4, 5, 6.

Linda di Chamounix; opera by Doni-zette: (47) W.-7.28; 11.24, 25, 27, 30; 12.3, 7, 27, 30; (48) C.-10.28; 12.5, 7; (52) W.-2.16, 17, 18, 19; 11.5, 6; 12.6, 8, 23, 30.

The Lion and the Kiss; see *Victoria.*

The Lion King, or The Bandit's Doom: (39) W.-7.29, 30, 31; 8.1, 2, 3, 5, 6, 7, 8.

The Lion of the Desert, or The Conquest of Algiers: (42) W.-7.6, 7, 8, 9, 11, 12, 13.

The Lion of the East: (35) W.-5.15, 16; 10.22, 23; C.-9.12.

The Lion of the Forest; see *Oua Cousta.*

The Lion of the Sea, or Our Infant

Navy; by Silas S. Steele: (40) A.-12.7*, 8, 23, 24; (41) A.-1.30; (52) A.-3.5, 6.

The Lioness of the North: (47) A.-10.28.

The Liquor of Life; see *The Mummy.*

Lise et Colin, or La Fille Mal Garde; comic ballet: (45) W.-3.24, 25, 26, 27, 28, 29.

Little Cause for Jealousy; see *Lilliputians in Kentucky.*

Little Devil: (52) C.-7.20; (53) C.-2.11, 12, 17.

Little Levil's Share, or Asmodeus: (43) W.-10.12, 13, 18, 19, 24; C.-11.4, 8, 11; (44) W.-2.29; 3.26; (45) W.-2.4; 7.28; (46) P.M.-11.11; 12.23; (47) P.M.-1.6, 23; 2.16; W.-8.27; 9.3, 14; (48) P.M.-4.12; (49) P.M.-6.29; C.-11.29, 30; (50) C.-3.12; (51) W.-10.10, 11, 17, 24; 11.1, 5, 13; (52) W.-1.20; (53) C.-12.3; (54) W.-5.26, 27; C.-8.5.

Little Jockey: (53) C.-4.25.

Little Katy; see *Hot Corn.*

Little Red Riding Hood; ballet: (37) W.-2.6; (38) W.-4.16, 17, 18, 19, 20, 21; (41) W.-9.18.

Little Sins and Pretty Sinners; farce: (40) W.-4.18.

The Little Back Parlor; farce: (40) C.-1.3*, 4, 20; 2.15; 4.21; 6.12; W.-4.30; 5.2; 6.1, 6, 24.

The Little Tiger: (40) W.-7.22, 24.

Little Treasure: (55) C.M.-12.5, 6, 8, 10.

Live Indian: (50) A.-11.1*, 2; (54) C.-11.6, 7, 11.

The Loan of a Lover: (35) W.-5.4, 6, 7, 20, 26; 6.9; 10.15; (36) C.-10.15, 17, 19, 24, 28; P.-11.16; 12.26, 29; (37) C.-10.15; P.-2.13; A.-5.29; 6.2; (38) C.-10.8, 9, 15; W.-10.16; 11.23; (39) W.-4.26; 6.22; 7.16, 29; 8.23; 10.24; 11.12, 19; 12.11; (40) W.-2.18; 3.18; 6.15; 11.5; 12.23; C.-

4.30; 5.25; (41) A.-5.17, 24; 6.22;
11.22; W.-4.22; N.-1.20; 3.20; 4.2;
(42) W.-1.10; 2.11; C.-3.4; A.-10.14,
15; (43) W.-4.11; (44) N.-1.20; C.-
10.22; (45) W.-3.7; 4.2; 5.1, 2, 8;
A.-7.7, 9; C.-9.26; A.-10.11; (46)
W.-1.19, 22; 2.19; 4.14; P.M.-4.17;
5.4; 8.8; 9.1; 12.9; (47) P.M.-2.3,
4; A.-3.26; W.-4.7, 12, 27; P.M.-
5.3, 20; W.-5.10, 18; 6.4, 9; A.-6.18;
P.M.-7.5; W.-8.9, 14; A.-9.29; 10.5,
9, 15; 12.24, 25; (48) A.-2.4; P.M.-
3.22; W.-4.12; 11.8; (49) W.-1.11;
A.-4.27; P.M.-7.10; C.-9.6; W.-
11.17; 12.13; (50) W.-1.13; 5.22; C.-
8.18, 19; W.-8.20, 26; 9.30; C.-12.22,
23; (52) W.-3.9, 11; 10.6; (53) C.-
8.12; (54) C.-4.21, 27; 6.16, 21;
7.15; 9.28; C.M.-12.8; (55) C.-1.17;
4.30; W.-6.27; 10.17; C.M.-10.24,
25; 11.3, 17.

Lochinvar; romance: (44) N.-3.26.

Lochinvar, or The Bridal of Netherby:
(40) A.-5.19.

Locked Out; see *A Good Night's Rest.*

Lodoiska, or The Poles and Tartars:
(35) W.-12.24; (38) W.-3.12; (39)
W.-3.16, 18, 19, 20, 21, 22.

*Lola Montez, or Catching a Gov-
ernor:* (48) O.-5.27*; (49) P.M.-
5.2, 3; C.-11.26, 28; 12.1; (50) A.-
6.26, 27; 7.23; (51) C.-11.17, 18, 19.

*Lola Montez, or Countess for an
Hour:* (52) N.-7.15*, 21; (53) C.-
8.12; (54) C.-7.28.

Lola Montez in Bavaria: (52) W.-
5.31; 6.1, 2, 3, 4, 5; C.-10.11, 12, 13,
22, 23.

Lola Montez in New York: (52) C.-
10.21, 22.

Lombards at the First Crusade; opera
by Verdi: (47) W.-7.17, 26.

The London Apprentice; see *George
Barnwell.*

London Assurance; comedy by D.
Boucicault: (41) W.-11.6*, 8, 9, 10,

11, 12, 13, 15, 17, 18, 19; N.-11.15,
16, 17, 19, 22, 23, 24, 25, 26, 30; 12.2;
C.-12.2, 3, 4, 6, 7, 8, 9, 10, 11; (42)
C.-11.2, 3; W.-11.14, 16, 17, 18, 19,
25; 12.5; (44) W.-5.6, 7, 8, 9, 11;
(45) W.-3.7, 26; (46) W.-4.8, 11;
7.21, 25; (47) W.-6.25; A.-10.26,
27, 29, 30; (48) P.M.-4.22; W.-7.19,
21; (50) A.-6.5, 6; W.-6.21, 22;
11.6, 7; (51) B.-2.3; W.-6.20; C.-
12.20; (52) W.-5.1; C.-5.14; 6.10,
11, 14; A.-11.5; (53) A.-5.31; 6.11;
(54) C.-3.7, 23; W.-9.1; A.-10.23,
24, 25, 26, 27, 28, 30, 31; 11.1, 2, 3,
4, 6, 7, 8, 9, 10, 11; W.-12.8, 9;
(55) C.-1.15, 16; W.-6.5, 29.

London in 1796; see *The Flying Highwayman.*

London 'Prentices: (44) N.-1.25, 26,
27; 2.1, 6.

The Lone Star, or Troubles in Texas:
(45) A.-3.22*, 24, 25; 4.1; 5.10; (54)
W.-5.9.

The Lone Star's Glory; see *Crockett
in Texas.*

The Lonely Man of the Ocean: (48)
A.-2.28, 29; 3.1, 4; (54) C.-11.20, 21,
22, 23, 24, 25.

Long Tom Coffin: (55) C.-4.19.

*Look before you Leap, or Wooing
and Wedding:* (47) P.M.-1.8, 11, 12,
14, 15, 16, 29; A.-2.1, 4, 5.

Lord Barney: (53) C.-5.3.

Lord Flanagan: (54) C.-7.25, 29.

The Lord of the Manor; opera: (35)
C.-12.11.

The Lost Battle; see *Marie de Montville.*

*The Lost Heir, or The Tarnal
Yankee:* (42) W.-1.14, 17, 25.

The Lost Letter; farce: (47) A.-4.12,
22.

The Lost Ship: (53) N.-7.25.

The Lost Son: (41) A.-11.11, 12;
(55) C.-1.22.

The Lottery Ticket: (35) W.-4.10;

(36) W.-5.18; P.-11.10; 12.10; (39) W.-4.4, 6, 12; C.-12.5, 11, 19; (40) C.-1.21; 4.2; 9.7, 24; 10.15; N.-9.7; (41) C.-10.7; N.-11.20; 12.31; (43) W.-2.15; (44) A.-9.10; C.-11.15; 12.5; (46) P.M.-7.6; W.-11.12, 26; 12.7, 16; (47) W.-2.25; 4.2, 17; 6.3, 11; 11.5, 9, 30; 12.4; (48) W.-4.10; (49) Ath.-1.25; (50) W.-1.31; 2.11; (51) C.-8.29, 30; 9.11; 10.16; (54) C.-9.23; (55) W.-9.6, 7, 12, 14; 10.8; C.M.-10.23; 11.19.

Louis XI: (55) C.-2.16, 17.

Louise, or The White Scarf: (51) C.-8.30; (42) A.-8.26; 9.10; 10.13; (51) B.-11.17, 18, 19, 20, 21, 22.

Louise Miller; opera by Verdi: (52) W.-10.27, 28, 29, 30; (53) W.-12.23; (54) C.-8.29.

Love; by J. S. Knowles: (39) W.-12.14*, 17, 19, 20, 21; C.-12.18, 19, 23; (40) W.-1.14; C.-1.25; 2.29; 3.7; 10.3; (42) C.-3.14; (45) C.-10.30; 11.3; (49) A.-11.12, 14; (50) W.-4.17, 19, 27; 6.1, 5; 9.11, 14, 19; 11.11; (51) W.-2.20, 22; C.-3.10, 21, 29; W.-5.20; C.-9.10, 17; (52) W.-1.1; C.-2.24; 3.19; 4.26; A.-8.27; (53) C.-3.2; A.-3.24; 5.10; 9.9, 12; (54) C.-1.3; 3.22; A.-5.15, 22; W.-9.8; 12.18; (55) W.-5.4.

Love and Charity: (51) A.-1.29; (55) C.M.-6.30.

Love and Friendship; see *Volunteer.*

Love and Honor; see *Cesar de Bazan.*

Love and Larnin': (53) W.-9.2; (55) C.-1.29, 30.

Love and Laugh; see *Secrets Worth Knowing.*

Love and Learning; see *Green Mountain Boy.*

Love and Loyalty: (55) W.-4.2, 3, 4, 6.

Love and Madness: see *Mountaineers.*

Love and Misanthropy: (47) P.M.-2.2.

Love and Money; by D. Boucicault: (54) W.-6.19*, 20, 21, 22.

Love and Murder; comedy in three acts by John Brougham: (38) C.-12.29*; (55) W.-10.18; 12.7, 13, 26.

Love and Mystery; see *El Hyder.*

Love and Pride; see *Lady of Lyons.*

The Love Chase, or The Widow Green; comedy by J. S. Knowles: (38) W.-1.8*, 11, 12, 18; C.-1.15, 18; 3.6, 13; 11.5; (39) C.-5.23; 6.18; (40) N.-3.5; (42) C.-3.7, 11; 11.7, 10; W.-11.21; (43) W.-1.28; 2.11; (44) A.-1.8; W.-5.3; (45) W.-7.31; (46) P.M.-12.11; (47) A.-12.9, 14; (48) W.-2.19; A.-3.30; (49) A.-8.29; 11.9, 13; (50) W.-3.22; 4.26; (51) W.-3.10; C.-3.11; W.-4.1, 11; C.-10.8, 16; W.-12.30; (52) A.-10.7, 11, 14, 25; (53) W.-1.4; C.-4.9, 19; 5.17; 9.2; A.-12.19, 20, 21, 22, 23, 24; (54) A.-1.13, 31; 2.7; C.-3.20; A.-6.30; C.-8.30; 10.17; (55) W.-3.22; 4.10; 5.4; A.-12.6.

The Love Gift: (44) A.-8.3*, 6., 9; 9.13; (45) A.-9.23.

Love in all Corners: (55) C.M.-6.23, 27.

Love in a Cottage: (38) C.-10.16, 17, 17, 19.

Love in Disguise: (44) W.-8.19, 22, 24.

Love in Humble Life; by J. H. Payne: (40) P.-7.29*; (46) P.M.-3.11, 19; 5.7, 9; (48) C.-7.13; A.-10.5; 11.4; (49) C.-8.21; A.-10.11.

Love in Livery: (55) A.-9.19, 24, 29; 10.31.

Love in a Maze; comedy: (51) B.-4.10*, 11, 12.

Love in a Mist: (36) P.-12.10, 13.

Love in a Mist; see *Coal Black Rose on Horseback.*

Love in a Village; comic opera (by Isaac Bickerstaff): (36) C.-2.2; 10.2; A.-5.6; (37) C.-11.10, 11; 12.20;

(38) C.-2.14; (39) C.-4.22; 9.24; (40) N.-12.2.

Love in all Disguises; see *Plots.*

Love in New York; see *A Down East Bargain.*

Love in the Far, Far West; see *Samuel Slick, Esq.*

Love, Laugh, and Physic; farce: (39) W.-4.2, 3.

Love Laughs at Locksmiths; or The Guardian Outwitted: (35) W.-12.19; (37) W.-12.8, 14; (39) W.-9.24; (40) C.-5.26; (41) W.-5.26; 6.8; 11.30; (42) W.-12.5, 27.

Love, Law, and Physic: (39) W.-10.19; (41) W.-7.9; A.-5.8; (42) A.-9.26; (45) A.-7.8; C.-11.20; 12.1; A.-12.9; (48) W.-2.3, 21; 4.28; 5.30; 6.6; 8.30; 10.25; (51) B.-4.28, 29; (54) A.-10.4, 5.

Love Makes the Man; see *Elder Brother.*

Love Me, Love my Dog: (35) W.-10.5, 6, 9; (36) W.-1.19.

The Love Spell; comic opera by Donizetti: (45) C.-11.20; (48) W.-1.4, 6; (51) W.-9.16.

The Love Test; see *Amilie.*

Love will Have its Way: (41) N.-7.5.

Love's Changes: (48) A.-8.3.

Love's Disguises; see *A Woman's Wit.*

Love's Fascination; see *The Wild Boy of Bohemia.*

Love's Frailties; see *Passion and Repentance.*

Love's Martyr; tragedy by Mayne Reid: (48) W.-10.23*, 25, 26, 27.

Love's Sacrifice: (42) W.-11.26; (43) W.-1.30, 31; 6.12; 10.21; C.-11.9; (44) W.-5.2; 10.10; (45) C.-2.10, 11, 12, 13; A.-4.21; (46) W.-10.6; A.-11.19, 27; (47) A.-1.18; 8.18; 9.21; (48) W.-2.17; A.-12.11; Ath.-12.28; (49) A.-3.22; 6.19; 8.18; C.-9.10; 10.17; (50) W.-9.20; (51) C.-3, 4, 6; 9.12, 23; W.-10.28; C.-11.25;

A.-12.8; (52) C.-3.9, 26, 27; 4.2; 5.6; 7.12; 9.2; 10.9; A.-10.26; C.-12.1; (53) C.-2.9; 3.18; 4.22; 12.21; (54) C.-4.4; A.-5.24, 29; W.-9.9; C.-10.2; C.M.-11.29; W.-12.26; (55) W.-3.19, 28; 5.9, 16; 9.15; A.-9.24; 11.15.

Love's Victory: (41) N.-8.24.

The Lover Husband: (40) N.-10.24.

Lover by Proxy: (42) C.-9.19, 21, 29; 10.12; A.-10.21; (43) C.-9.7; (44) W.-2.7; (51) B.-1.15; W.-9.29; 10.9, 16; (54) W.-8.29.

Lover's Revenge: (42) A.-11.21.

The Lovers of Surnam; see *The Slave.*

Lovers, Wife, and Friend, or The Momentous Question: (46) P.M.-5.4, 6, 7, 8.

Lovers' Quarrels: (35) W.-1.1; 5.8; 6.10; C.-11.4, 13; (37) W.-3.18; P.-1.16; (38) C.-3.15; 6.20; (40) W.-6.22; W.-7.13; (42) A.-6.8; (45) A.-7.4.

Lovers' Vows: (40) C.-2.4. By William Dunlap or by J. H. Payne.

The Loving Woman; by Mark Lemon: (50) A.-3.9, 11, 12, 13, 14, 27; 4.17, 25.

Lowena of Tobolska: (37) W.-1.12, 14.

Lo Zingaro: (42) W.-2.26: see *A Maiden's Fame.*

Lo Zingaro, or A Bohemian's Revenge: (35) W.-9.26*, 28, 30; 10.1, 19; 11.23; (36) P.-11.18, 21.

Lucia di Lammermoor; opera by Donizetti: (43) C.-7.15, 17, 18, 19, 20, 21; 11.15, 22; (48) C.-3.1, 3, 4, 6, 13, 16, 21; 6.12, 13; W.-8.21; C.-10.21, 22; 12.9; (50) C.-9.13, 17; 12.10; (54) C.-9.4, 14, 18.

Lucille, or A Story of the Heart; domestic drama in three acts by the author of *A Farmer's Story* and *A Woman's Faith:* (36) W.-6.22,

23, 24; C.-10.15, 17, 19, 25, 29; (37)
A.-5.29, 31; (39) C.-12.14, 24; (40)
C.-6.8; C.-10.30; 12.29; (42) A.-5.4;
(46) P.M.-4.4, 6; 11.30; (47) W.-
8.31; 9.2; A.-9.13, 16; 11.6; 12.9;
(48) A.-1.27; 2.5; P.M.-3.20; W.-
9.16; (50) A.-3.8; (51) A.-12.17;
(53) C.-7.1; (54) C.M.-11.13, 17;
(55) A.-5.25, 28; 6.6.

Luck in a Name; see *The Two Gregories.*

Luck's All: (49) A.-10.16.

The Lucky and Unlucky Days; see *Charming Polly.*

Lucky Stars: (43) W.-3.11; 6.9, 14;
C.-12.9; A.-8.14, 16.

Lucrece Borgia; drama: (47) A.-9.23,
25, 27, 28; W.-11.29; 12.2, 6.31; A.-
12.8, 10, 18; (48) W.-1.5; 2.9, 11;
A.-4.1; 10.12, 14; (49) A.-3.21, 23;
10.29, 30.

Lucretia Borgia, The Poisoner;
drama by J. Rees: (48) Ath.-12.29;
(49) ATH.-1.1; (50) A.-10.7, 8, 9,
10, 12; (51) A.-3.31; 4.1, 5, 10; 9.13,
24; (52) C.-3.12, 13; 6.2, 9; N.-8.11;
A.-10.4, 6, 9, 12, 20, 28; 12.21; (53)
C.-3.24; 8.22; (54) A.-6.20, 23, 24,
28; 7.4; C.-8.26; 10.16, 18, 30; C.M.-
12.8, 9; (55) C.M.-1.19, 23; C.-2.19,
20; C.M.-3.23; A.-4.21, 26, 28; C.M.-
5.2, 7, 14; W.-5.14, 19; A.-12.21.

Lucrezia Borgia; opera by Donizetti:
(48) C.-3.8, 10, 11, 23; 10.14, 16, 18,
20, 24; 12.25; (50) C.-2.4, 5; 3.16;
A.-4.2, 3; C.-9.11, 23; 12.20, 21;
(51) C.-1.2; (52) W.-12.27, 28, 29;
(54) C.-9.1; (55) W.-1.4, 5.

Lucy of Lammermoor: (52) W.-12.7,
9; (53) W.-1.1.

Luke the Laborer: (35) C.-1.31; 2.14;
9.29; W.-5.23; 6.26; 12.7; (36) A.-
5.25; P.-11.10; (37) A.-6.19; (38)
W.-7.19; 8.7; (39) C.-9.14, 23;
10.14; (40) W.-1.17, 18; (41) A.-
12.21; (42) N.-1.14; C.-9.20; (43)

A.-12.18; (44) N.-3.13, 14; (46)
P.M.-8.18; (48) W.-1.11; A.-7.26;
10.4; (49) A.-9.3; (51) B.-4.7, 8;
A.-4.16; 12.18; (54) C.-5.20; N.-6.7;
C.-6.28; (55) A.-2.10, 11, 22; 3.9.

Luli, or The Switzer's Bride: (46)
W.-12.16, 17, 18, 19. Opera.

Lunar Caustic; see *Moonshine.*

The Luprechaun: (50) C.-5.3.

The Lying Valet; by David Garrick:
(35) W.-9.21; 10.1, 20; 11.4.

Mabel's Curse: (41) N.-12.4, 6; (49)
A.-6.4.

Macbeth; by William Shakespeare:
(35) W.-1.6, 13; 3.9; 7.1; 9.4; 11.19;
C.-9.25; (36) C.-1.13; 11.14; P.-
12.19; W.-1.30; 3.24; 9.10, 15; 10.14;
(37) C.-10.11; A.-5.23; W.-7.13;
11.18; C.-11.23; (38) W.-2.9; 7.5;
8.31; 10.18; C.-1.31; 4.30; 12.31;
(39) W.-11.27; C.-10.7; (40) C.-1.4;
12.2; (41) A.-4.6; N.-12.18; C.-
12.30; (42) C.-1.1; 4.12; W.-4.20;
A.-8.16; 9.16; W.-9.26; 10.19; (43)
W.-4.13; A.-9.12; N.-10.7; W.-10.14;
A.-10.21; C.-10.23; N.-10.24; C.-
11.6; (44) W.-1.23; 3.25; A.-6.15;
W.-9.14; A.-9.17; C.-11.2, 12, 27;
W.-12.10; (45) A.-4.17; W.-7.24;
A.-8.19; W.-8.23; 10.3, 21; C.-
10.31; 11.6; W.-11.8; A.-12.6, 13;
W.-12.19; (46) A.-1.12; W.-3.31;
5.9; A.-7.8, 13; W.-7.27; A.-10.3;
W.-10.21; A.-11.18; (47) W.-1.7;
4.24; 9.22; A.-10.14; 11.8; W.-11.11;
A.-12.4; (48) W.-1.10; A.-1.22;
3.31; W.-4.11; A.-6.26; 7.17; W.-
11.20; A.-11.20; 12.4; (49) A.-4.4,
14; C.-9.17; W.-10.31; 11.3, 12; A.-
12.21; (50) W.-1.8, 12; A.-5.29, W.-
6.18; A.-9.25; B.-9.25, 26; A.-11.4;
W.-11.4; (51) B.-3.19, 24; A.-4.16;
W.-6.16; 10.8, 11; C.-11.11, 15; 12.1;
(52) W.-1.17; C.-1.24; A.-3.18; W.-
3.31; C.-4.16; W.-4.19; A.-9.10, 23;

A.-11.8; W.-11.11; (53) W.-2.26;
C.-3.29; A.-6.4; W.-9.16; 10.13; (54)
W.-6.16; 10.13; (55) W.-4.7; C.-
4.7; C.M.-4.10, 14; W.-5.28; C.M.-
5.29; 10.30; 11.1; A.-11.30; 12.1;
W.-12.26.

Macarthy More: (47) W.-1.24, 25, 26,
27, 29.

*Mad Anthony, or The Pennsylvania
Line:* (44) A.-12.21*, 23.

*Mad Anthony Wayne, or The Mas-
sacre of Paoli:* (49) C.-11.24; (52)
N.-10.20, 21, 23.

Mad as a March Hare: (44) W.-
7.23.

*Madame Anna Bishop in the Prov-
inces:* (53) W.-1.1*.

*Madelaine, or The Foundling of
Paris;* domestic drama: (49) W.-
1.10*, 12, 13, 15, 18, 22; 2.27, 28;
3.2; 4.5; 5.15; (50) W.-6.11, 20;
7.3; (51) A.-9.8, 9; 11.1, 17; (53)
W.-5.14, 16; A.-11.17, 18, 19, 21, 22,
23, 24, 25; 12.9, 22; (54) A.-2.17; 3.1,
14; 4.21; 6.22; C.-8.23, 24; (55)
C.M.-1.15, 16, 26; C.-1.17, 18; C.M.-
3.21; A.-11.19, 20, 29.

*Madeline, the Daughter of the Regi-
ment:* (50) C.-2.25; 3.1; B.-11.4, 5.

Madelon; see *The Trumpeter's
Daughter.*

The Magic Head: (42) N.-1.1, 3, 4, 5.

Magic Lamp in a New Light: (44)
A.-12.2, 3, 4, 5, 6, 7, 9, 10, 11, 12,
14, 16, 17, 18.

The Magic Mirror; see *Kabri.*

Magic Pills, or The Emperor's Gift:
(46) A.-11.30; 12.1, 2, 3, 5.

Magic Trumpet: (51) B.-6.20, 21 23,
24.

Magic Well: (53) C.-11.8, 9, 10, 11,
12.

*Magnolia, or The Child of the
Flower;* Indian legendary drama in
three acts: (55) W.-9.14*.

The Magpie, or The Maid of Palai-

seau; see *The Maid and the Magpie.*

*Maharajah Surovy Seing, or The
Irish M.D.:* (50) C.-6.25*, 27.

The Maid and the Magpie; by J. H.
Payne: (35) W.-6.22; 8.24; (36) C.-
10.18; P.-11.28; (38) C.-5.15; (39)
C.-6.4; (40) C.-9.14; (42) A.-8.23;
(45) A.-7.21, 22, 25; 8.4; (46) P.M.-
10.12, 13, 14; 11.4; (47) P.M.-4.19,
21, 22; (48) P.M.-3.25.

The Maid of Artois: (47) W.-12.29.

*The Maid of Cadiz and The Man of
Kent;* see *Biena.*

The Maid of Cashmere; drama: (36)
W.-11.24*, 25, 26, 28; 12.1; (41)
C.-5.7, 8, 11.

*The Maid of Cashmere, or Le Dieu
et la Bayadere;* ballet opera by
Auber: (36) C.-11.28*, 29, 30; 12.1,
2, 3, 5, 6, 7, 8, 9, 10, 13, 14, 16;
(37) A.-7.5, 6, 7; C.-12.30; (38)
C.-1.1, 3, 4, 5, 6, 8, 9, 12, 13, 16;
2.8, 10, 13, 15, 27; 3.1; 6.9; 12.6,
7, 8; (39) C.-2.11, 12, 14, 18, 20,
23; 5.14, 18; 9.4, 5; (40) C.-1.16,
17; 2.11; N.-11.5, 6, 9, 11; (41) C.-
9.10, 11, 13; (47) C.-5.13, 15, 17, 19,
21, 22.

*The Maid of Croissy, or Theresa's
Vow:* (38) C.-5.25, 28; (40) C.-
3.2, 3, 12, 14, 30; 4.7, 25; (41) C.-
12.29; A.-8.18, 24; N.-11.30; (42)
C.-1.5; W.-6.6, 9; (43) W.-11.1;
(44) W.-4.10; 5.13; (45) W.-2.13;
10.30; (46) P.M.-3.28, 30; 4.28;
9.28; 10.2; W.-11.18; (48) P.M.-
3.31; 5.17; C.-7.31; (49) Ath.-1.9;
(50) W.-7.2; (52) C.-12.22; (54)
C.-3.6, 15, 30; 7.12.

The Maid of Erin; see *Brian Boroihme.*

The Maid of Frankfort: (45) A.-12.1,
2, 5.

The Maid of Genoa; see *The Mountain Devil.*

The Maid of Honor; an adaptation

of Philip Massinger's play by John P. Kemble in 1784: (53) C.-2.14, 15; 4.29.

The Maid of Judah; opera: (36) C.-1.18, 21; 2.1; A.-4.28; (40) C.-11.3, 5.

The Maid of Lorette; melodrama: (48) O.-5.29.

The Maid of Mariendorpt, or A Daughter's Love; by J. S. Knowles: (38) W.-12.12*; (39) W.-1.16; C.-1.8, 9; 3.9; (40) N.-11.2; (49) A.-11.6, 8; (50) W.-4.22, 24; 6.3; (51) C.-3.28; (52) C.-5.4; (53) C.-12.20.

The Maid of Milan; see *Clari.*

The Maid of the Milking Pail: (53) W.-9.12; see *The Maid with the Milking Pail.*

The Maid of Munster; see *Perfection.*

The Maid of Orleans: (36) W.-1.8, 15, 18; 2.9, 13, 16, 23; 4.5; 5.10; (39) W.-6.4; (44) W.-3.2.

The Maid of Palaiseau; see *Maid and Magpie.*

The Maid of Paulaiseur; see *La Gazza Ladra.*

The Maid of Switzerland: (52) A.-3.13, 23; 4.12, 30.

Maid or Wife: (44) A.-6.14.

The Maid's Tragedy, or The Bridal; by Beaumont and Fletcher: (45) A.-4.25; (52) C.-11.17. See *The Bridal.*

Maiden Aunt: (46) A.-3.24, 25, 26.

Maidens, Beware, or Ladies, Beware: (39) W.-2.1; (46) P.M.-4.15, 16, 21, 23; 5.1, 27; A.-9.14; 11.13; (47) W.-8.28; 9.4, 11, 23; A.-11.11, 12, 20, 23; 12.8; (48) W.-1.15, 4, 22; 6.9; A.-8.25; W.-9.7, 8, 11, 20, 25; A.-9.28; W.-10.4, 10; (50) W.-3.11, 13, 18; 4.18, 25; 6.18, 27; 8.26; 9.12, 25; 11.11; 12.17; (51) W.-5.26; 6.21; C.-8.27, 28; 9.4, 9, 16; 10.6; (52) W.-12.13, 15, 28; (53) W.-2.8, 17; 4.13; 6.7; 8.29; 10.14, 19; (54) W.-10.16; 11.27.

A Maiden's Fame, or the Zingaro's Prophecy: (39) W.-1.26; (42) C.-2.12, 21.

The Maiden's Vow, or the Yankee in Time: (38) W.-12*, 3, 4; 7.20; (43) W.-5.15; (44) W.-4.3; (51) A.-3.12; 7.23, 24; (55) C.-2.3.

Maids as they Are; see *Wives as they Are.*

Major Jack Downing: (35) W.-3.12.

Major Jones' Courtship, or Adventures on Christmas Eve: (51) B.-12.22*, 23, 24, 25, 26, 27, 29, 30, 31; (54) C.M. 1-1 12.23, 25; 26, 27, 28, 29, 30; (55) C.M.-1.1, 2, 3, 4, 5, 19; 5.2.

Major Wheeler Abroad; see *Speculations.*

Make your Wills; farce: (36) W.-11.19*, 21, 24, 25; 12.3, 6, 27; C.-12.1, 3, 6; (37) W.-1.31; C.-1.2; 2.13; 4.3, 20; 9.9; 12.7; A.-7.6; (38) C.-2.22; 3.30; (49) C.-9.18; 10.5; (52) N.-8.2.

Maldichina, or The Dumb Boy and his Monkey: (45) W.-1.10.

Mammon and Gammon: (49) A.-9.5*, 6; 10.8, 9, 11.15.

Man about Town, or Cheap Boarding: (36) W.-8.31*; 9.1, 2; 10.13; C.-8.31; 9.1, 5, 21, 24; 10.31; 11.28; P.-11.8; (37) W.-11.29; C.-1.9; 2.9; 4.24; 10.2; A.-5.8, 23; 6.23; (38) C.-2.20; (39) W.-8.9; (42) A.-10.6; (44) W.-9.9, 28; 12.6; (45) W.-1.22; 4.1; (54) W.-4.6, 7, 10.

The Man and the Tiger; see *P.P.*

Man and Wife; (by S. J. Arnold): (38) C.-3.12, 22; (39) C.-11.11, 14; W.-10.28; (40) C.-1.22; (41) N.-3.18; (42) A.-8.11; (43) W.-5.24; C.-9.7; (44) W.-4.15; 6.13; (48) A.-2.19; (54) A.-5.26, 27; (55) A.-5.16, 17, 28.

Manfredi, or The Mysterious Her-

25; W.-11.9, 11, 18; (43) C.-1.25, 26; 2.2; (47) C.-5.8, 14.

Marriage Squabbles; farce: (45) A.-10.22.

Married and Settled: (44) N.-5.25.

Married and Single: (36) W.-10.7.

The Married Bachelor: (35) C.-12.24; (36) A.-3.22; 4.20; (37) A.-6.26; C.-3.1; 9.27; 10.31; 12.14; (38) C.-1.22; (45) C.-9.19; 12.4; (46) P.M.-8.1; 9.10; 11.3; (48) A.-9.29; 11.10, 13; (50) C.-6.14; (54) C.-8.4.

Married Daughter: (37) C.-3.9.

Married Life: comedy by J. B. Buckstone: (35) C.-2.12, 14, 17; 5.1, 28; 6.6; 8.22; 9.7; W.-2.12, 16, 17, 19; 3.31; 5.25; 7.6; A.-4.2; (36) A.-3.19; 5.14; C.-7.8; 8.20; 12.24; (37) C.-8.26; 10.4; (38) C.-1.11; (39) C.-2.22; (40) C.-9.1, 4, 9; (40) N.-9.30; (43) W.-2.23, 28; 3.1, 23; 6.26; 10.17, 20; (44) W.-1.6; 2.12; 3.16; 4.27; 6.11; 10.28; 12.11, 16; (45) W.-2.17; (46) W.-8.11; P.M.-9.15, 17, 19, 23, 25; 11.21; (47) P.M.-2.27; 6.24; 28; A.-9.9; W.-9.20; (48) P.M.-3.24; (49) C.-10.23; (50) B.-8.26; (51) B.-5.26; 6.7; (53) C.-1.12, 31; A.-6.3; 8.23, 30; 10.15; C.-11.11, 12; A.-11.22; C.-12.13; (54) A.-9.14; 11.29; 12.2, 11, 18; (55) A.-2.8; 5.31; 6.6; W.-6.8; C.M.-9.8, 12.

Married Maid: (43) W.-7.25.

Married Man; (by Mrs. Inchbald): (50) B.-12.30; 31; (51) B.-1.10.

Married Rake; farce: (36) W.-5.18*, 20; 6.10; (38) C.-6.25, 28; 7.2; 9.1; 11.23; (39) C.-2.28; 3.21; 4.3, 15; 5.14; 6.7; 9.24; 12.4; (40) W.-10.21; 11.13; 12.2; C.-1.30; 4.2; 5.9; 10.27; N.-9.2, 4, 9; 10.10; (41) C.-5.18; 12.7; N.-8.25; A.-4.22; 6.21; (42) A.-4.4, 5, 11; 5.20; C.-11.8; W.-11.16; (43) W.-2.1; 7.26;

C.-9.8, 27; 10.24, 25; 12.7; (44) A.-1.8, 11; W.-3.12; 4.24; 6.12, 22, 26; (45) W.-4.7; N.-5.8; C.-10.22; (46) P.M.-6.16, 18, 22, 27; A.-7.8; W.-8.5, 6; P.M.-8.11; W.-9.8; P.M.-9.15; W.-10.2, 15, 29; A.-10.6; P.M.-10.23; (47) W.-4.8; P.M.-6.9, 15; W.-9.6; (48) P.M.-5.6; A.-10.25; (49) P.M.-7.13; (50) C.-4.22; (51) B.-2.4; A.-9.15, 19; 11.18; (52) C.-3.8, 9, 24; (53) A.-7.2; (54) A.-1.25; 5.5; C.-6.15; W.-9.4; 10.12; 11.3, 15, 28; A.-12.30; (55) W.-3.13; 5.28; 10.31; A.-12.18; W.-12.18.

Married Yesterday; see *My Wife and I.*

Martha, or The Richmond Market; opera: (52) W.-12.10, 11, 13, 14, 15, 16, 17, 18, 20, 21, 25, 31.

Martin Chuzzlewit: (45) A.-3.31; 4.1.

Mary, or The Farmer's Daughter: (35) W.-1.17, 20; (42) C.-10.13, 14, 15; (48) A.-2.26.

Mary Melvyn: (49) W.-4.12*, 14.

Mary Stewart [or Stuart], *or The Castle of Lochleven:* (35) C.-10.9, 30; (36) W.-12.10.

Mary Stuart, or Queen of the Scots; "translated from the German of Schiller by Laura Addison, and adapted by her to the English stage": (42) W.-5.13, 14, 19, 20; (43) A.-10.7; (51) W.-11.3, 4, 8.

Mary Tudor, or Gilbert the Mechanic; (by E. Flagg): (42) W.-6.22, 23, 24, 25; (47) A.-12.11, 13; (48) A.-10.7, 13; (49) A.-4.2; 11.2; (50) A.-4.4, 5; 10.18; (51) A.-4.11, 12; (52) N.-9.28, 30; A.-10.15, 16, 21; (55) C.M.-5.16.

Masaniéllo, or The Dumb Girl of Portici, or The Fisherman of Naples; opera by Auber: (35) C.-2.19; A.-3.31; (36) C.-1.19, 23, 8.24; 12.17;

A.-4.26; (37) C.-9.7, 8; (38) C.-
1.27; 2.27; 3.1; 5.31; 6.8; (40) N.-
12.4, 5, 7, 8, 12; (43) C.-1.20, 21, 23,
25, 26, 31; A.-4.6, 7, 8; (47) C.-
4.28, 30; 5.3, 7; W.-10.18, 19; (48)
W.-7.5, 6, 7, 8; (49) A.-1.12, 22;
W.-12.4, 5; (50) W.-6.24, 25; B.-
10.14, 15, 16, 17; W.-12.13, 17;
(52) W.-5.26, 27; A.-9.20, 21, 22;
(53) C.-9.17; (54) C.-9.7, 8, 15.

The Masked Ball; see *Gustavus III.*

*Masks and Faces, or Both Sides of the
Curtain;* by Charles Reade: (53) C.-
12.30*; (54) C.-1.6, 7; 3.25; 4.6;
W.-12.15, 16, 21; (55) W.-4.30; 5.8,
21, 25; 11.3, 13, 24; A.-11.23, 29.

*Masquerade, or The Door Keeper
Outwitted:* (37) W.-12.27, 30; (41)
A.-9.22, 23.

The Mass in Frankfort in 1297; see
Das Pfefferroisel.

The Massacre of Paoli; see *Mad Anthony Wayne.*

The Massacre of the Huguenots; see
The Surgeon of Paris.

Master Humphrey's Clock: (40) N.-
10.31; 11.13.

Master's Rival; see *My Master's
Rival.*

Mat o' the Glen: (54) N.-7.3.

Mat of the Iron Hand; see *Tom
Cringle.*

A Match in the Dark: (38) W.-1.1*,
9, 23; 2.26.

*The Matchwoman of Philadelphia,
or The Burglar's Stronghold;* comedy by J. P. Adams: (49) A.-11.29*,
30; 12.1, 3, 4.

Match Making; comedy in one act:
(35) C.-11.28.

Matheo Falcone: (36) P.-12.26; (40)
W.-7.22; (53) C.-2.16.

Mathilde: (41) W.-6.7, 9, 12, 16.

*Matrimony, or The Castle of Lin-
burg;* comedy: (35) C.-1.9; (36)
A.-3.29; 4.25; 6.1; (37) P.-1.13, 20;

(45) W.-3.4, 8; 4.17; A.-5.7; W.-
6.21; C.-11.29; (46) W.-7.15; P.M.-
8.7, 10; (48) W.-11.9, 21, 30; (49)
W.-1.20; (50) B.-1.2, 3; (53) W.-
12.2, 3.

Matrimonial Prospectuses: (52) C.-
4.26, 27, 28, 30; 5.1, 11, 18, 19.

Maurice: (51) A.-10.18; (52) A.-
9.16.

Maurice, the Woodcutter: (41) N.-
1.9; 12.24; W.-6.4, 5, 9; (42) A.-
9.13, 14; (46) A.-2.16, 19; (50) A.-
7.27, 30.

*May Queen, or The Sergeant and the
Tinker:* (36) W.-5.2, 4; 8.27; 10.25;
(37) A.-5.1, 3, 16; C.-8.23; 12.25;
(38) C.-2.6; 3.13, 29; 5.15; (39)
C.-2.12; (42) A.-8.10; (46) P.M.-
12.5, 18; (53) A.-9.22, 23, 24, 28;
10.13.

The Mayor of Garrat(t); farce by
Samuel Foote: (35) W.-9.1; (36)
W.-6.4, 11; (37) W.-1.28; 7.15;
11.18; (38) W.-2.17; 7.14; (39) W.-
6.24; 10.8; (40) W.-6.20; A.-12.19;
(42) C.-11.19; (43) W.-4.19; A.-
9.19; (44) W.-1.31; 2.3; 3.23; (45)
W.-5.31; (47) W.-4.23.

Mazeppa and the Wild Horse; by
Lord Byron: (38) W.-4.2*, 3, 4, 5,
6, 7, 9, 10, 11, 12, 13, 14, 16, 17, 18,
19, 20, 21; 5.3, 4, 6; (39) W.-10.2,
4; (41) W.-1.18, 19, 20, 21, 22, 23,
25, 26, 27, 29, 30; 2.27; 3.1, 2; 4.12,
13, 21; 12.20, 22, 23, 24; N.-1.26; A.-
11.24, 25, 26, 27, 29; 12.4; (44) N.-
3.21, 22, 23, 26, 29; (50) C.-4.15, 16,
17, 18, 19, 20, 26; (52) N.-10.11,
12, 13, 14, 15, 16; (54) N.-6.21, 22,
24.

The Mechanic and his Brother; see
Peter and Paul.

The Mechanic and the Queen: (50)
C.-4.29.

Meet Me by Moonlight; farce: (42)
W.-11.5, 8.

Mehittable Anne: (55) C.M.-10.20, 22, 26, 27, 29; 11.21.

Melmoth the Doomed: (39) W.-1.29; (42) A.-11.3.

Mental Electricity; farce: (49) P.M.-5.28, 29, (49) P.M.-5.28*, 29.

Merchant and his Clerks: (49) Ath.-1.27.

Merchant and Mechanic: (43) W.-2.18, 20; 4.4.

The Merchant of Venice; by William Shakespeare: (35) W.-4.11; 6.5; 7.4; 10.2; C.-4.20; 5.12; (36) C.-9.3; A.-3.11; W.-6.10; 12.16; (37) C.-1.14; (38) C.-6.15; (39) W.-6.27; C.-10.8; 12.7; (40) W.-6.27; C.-3.31; 4.16; N.-12.15; (41) A.-9.3; N.-1.30; (42) C.-1.3, 18; W.-4.22; A.-9.12; W.-10.16; (45) A.-4.23; 5.17; W.-8.7, 27; C.-9.20; W.-10.4; C.-10.4; (46) W.-5.14, 30; A.-7.24; W.-9.22; (47) W.-1.30; A.-4.8; W.-5.29; 9.25; A.-11.5; 12.6; (48) W.-1.7; 4.7; A.-7.3; 11.24; (49) A.-4.11; W.-6.23; C.-10.9; A.-10.23; (50) A.-6.12; W.-6.20; B.-9.18, 19; (51) B.-3.7, 14, 22; W.-5.3; C.-9.27; (52) W.-1.8; C.-9.9, 11; W.-10.6, 7; A.-11.12; (53) C.-4.6; (55) C.M.-6.1; A.-9.27; C.M.-11.6.

The Merry Days of Charles II; see *Charles II.*

The Merry Monarch: (43) W.-3.30.

The Merry Mourners; see *Modern Antiques.*

The Merry Wives of Windsor; by William Shakespeare: (35) A.-3.30; (39) C.-1.12; (40) C.-5.30; N.-9.24; (41) N.-2.22; 3.9; (42) C.-4.2; W.-12.3; (43) C.-12.8; (44) A.-11.18, 20; (45) C.-9.11; A.-10.3; (46) W.-8.7; (48) A.-12.6; (49) W.-3.23; 12.21, 23; (53) C.-1.12, 29; 2.1; W.-2.4, 5; 4.22, 23, 25, 28; C.-9.3.

Mesmerism: (47) P.M.-3.2, 3, 6, 11, 12, 18.

The Messinian Slave; see *Helos the Helot.*

Metamora, or The Last of the Wampanoags; by John A. Stone: (37) C.-12.6, 7, 8, 9; (38) C.-1.29; 2.5; W.-10.19, 20, 23; 12.5, 8; (39) W.-9.19, 21; 10.1; 11.28, 30; (40) C.-9.24; 11.24; W.-4.27, 30; (41) A.-4.10; 6.9; N.-8.26; 10.23; (42) C.-4.16; W.-10.24, 27; (43) W.-6.1; N.-10.17, 25; (44) N.-1.29; W.-8.27; 9.11; 12.5; (46) W.-10.27; 12.22; (47) W.-1.9; 3.15; 9.15; 11.6, 16; (48) W.-11.21; (49) W.-6.7; (51) W.-10.21, 23; (52) W.-6.19, 24; 11.22, 25; (53) W.-10.21; (54) W.-10.25; (55) W.-12.24, 25.

Metamora, or The Last of the Pollywogs: (48) W.-5.12, 13; A.-6.5, 6, 7, 8, 9, 10, 17; 12.5.

Michael Erl; see *The Maniac Lover.*

Midas, burletta; (by Kane O'Hara): (40) C.-5.1, 4; (41) C.-5.31; 6.4, 5, 19.

Middy Ashore; farce: (37) W.-3.22*, 25; 11.20; (40) C.-1.23; 2.1; 5.25; (41) N.-11.26; (42) A.-6.18; 7.8; (44) W.-5.27; 8.21; 12.24; (45) W.-7.26; (54) C.-12.5.

The Midnight Assassin; see *Paul, the Reprobate.*

The Midnight Assault; see *The Italian Brigands.*

The Midnight Hour, or Ruse contra Ruse; by Mrs. Elizabeth Inchbald: (35) C.-4.27, 11.11; (36) P.-11.15; (39) C.-6.10, 12; (40) C.-6.2; (44) W.-1.12; (46) W.-3.9; 4.20; 11.23; 12.4; (47) W.-1.27; (52) C.-8.23.

The Midnight Watch: (49) Ath.-1.13; 2.14, 15, 16; A.-5.21; (51) B.-10.27, 28, 29, 30, 31; 11.1, 24; (54) C.M.-9.28, 29; 10.5, 10, 20.

Midsummer Night's Dream: (55) W.-1.8, 9, 10, 11, 12, 13, 15, 16, 17, 18, 19, 20, 22, 23, 24, 25, 26, 27,

29, 30, 31; 2.1, 2, 3, 5, 6, 7, 8, 9, 10, 12; 4.23, 24, 25, 26, 27, 28.

Mike Martin, or The Bold Irish Robber and Daring Highwayman: (50) A.-3.11, 12, 13, 14, 15.

Milford Castle: (42) A.-10.22.

Military Execution, or The Fatal Keepsake: (36) W.-4.11, 25; (41) A.-11.15, 16; (42) W.-7.7.

Military Training, or A Real Down East Muster: (38) W.-9.8; (39) W.-5.10, 21; (40) N.-9.26.

The Mill of St. Alderon, or The Two Galley Slaves: (46) W.-4.8, 9; 5.12.

The Miller and the Coalman; farce: (35) Mam.C.-1.21, 22; 2.19.

The Miller and his Men; by Isaac Pocock: (35) W.-11.14; 12.2; (36) P.-11.26, 28; 12.1; (37) P.-1.3; (38) C.-2.24; 3.9; (40) W.-7.16; (42) A.-8.8; 10.29; (50) B.-10.5, 7, 8, 9, 10, 11.

The Miller of Whetstone: (52) W.-11.10, 11, 12, 13, 24, 30; (53) A.-9.22.

The Miller's Holiday: (35) Mam.C.-2.21.

The Miller's Maid: (36) P.-11.24, 25; (40) W.-5.22; (41) A.-10.11, 20; (42) N.-1.29; C.-11.28; (45) A.-7.5; (47) W.-5.3; 6.28; (48) W.-1.10; A.-8.2; (52) W.-1.26, 30; C.-12.9, 10; (54) C.-6.28; 7.8.

The Miller's Man and the Chevalier; see *Solomon Smink.*

The Miller's Murder, or The Rose of Corbelle: (38) W.-12.14, 20.

The Miller's Wife; see *Giralda.*

The Milliner's Holiday: (45) W.-1.25, 27; 2.3; 3.12; 5.30; (49) P.M.-4.30; 5.1; 6.2.

The Millionaire; comedy (by Walter Leman): (48) W.-8.28*, 29, 30, 31; 9.1, 2; (49) W.-4.3.

Milly; see *The Maid with the Milking Pail.*

The Miner of Pottsville; melodrama: (49) C.-11.10, 12, 13.

The Minerali, or The Dying Gift: (36) W.-12.13*, 14, 15, 16, 22; (40) W.-7.4, 9; (42) A.-5.9, 10.

Mirth and Music; see *The Wandering Minstrel.*

Mischief Making; farce: (36) P.-12.20, 24, 29; (38) W.-10.2, 4; (39) W.-2.1; 7.24; C.-11.11, 12, 16; (40) C.-1.21; 5.14, 21; (41) W.-6.29; N.-11.25; (44) N.-5.23; (47) A.-6.11, 16; 7.30; W.-8.30; 9.2, 4, 10, 24; 10.12; 11.17; (48) W.-2.2, 28; 3.1, 2; A.-7.11, 12; (50) A.-12.20, 24; (51) N.-7.18.

Mischievous Annie; farce by W. T. Florence: (52) C.-7.22, 23; (54) C.-7.24; (55) C.M.-7.2, 3, 6.

The Miser of Eltham Green; see *Last Man.*

The Miser of Philadelphia: (49) C.-9.8*, 10, 11, 12, 13; 10.10; (52) N.-8.7, 11.

The Miser of Southwark Ferry, or John Overy: (42) A.-4.23; W.-12.13, 14, 15, 16; (50) A.-1.3; (51) N.-8.7; A.-12.29. By Douglas Jerrold.

The Miser's Daughter: (35) W.-6.22.

A Miser's Miseries; farce by H. J. Conway: (35) W.-11.9*, 10, 11, 12; (36) W.-1.4.

Miseries of Human Life: (46) A.-4.6, 7, 8, 9; C.-4.29, 30; P.M.-10.29, 30; 11.19; (47) P.M.-6.7; A.-10.6, 18, 19; (48) A.-1.5, 6; 8.23; 9.6, 7; 10.2; (49) A.-5.14; (52) C.-8.27, 28, 31; 9.2, 28; (53) A.-8.22, 24; W.-9.24, 26; 10.18; (54) W.-2.16; A.-5.15; 6.1; (55) A.-6.20, 21.

The Mistakes of a Morning; see *Black and White.*

The Mistakes of a Night; see *She Stoops to Conquer.*

Mizzle, Bolt, and Cutaway; farce: (45) A.-8.1.

Mob, the Outlaw, or Jemmey Twitcher in France: (36) W.-9.17, 20, 22, 30; 10.1, 8, 11, 21; 11.18; 12.23; (37) W.-2.6; 8.30; (38) W.-3.9; 8.4; 10.2; (39) W.-5.3, 6, 21, 29; (41) W.-2.22; 3.6; (42) W.-5.3, 4; 10.8, 14; (51) A.-1.10; (53) C.-1.19, 20.

The Model of a Wife: (48) P.M.-7.3, 4, 5; (50) A.-8.30; (54) C.-10.13.

Modern Antiques, or The Merry Mourners; by John O'Keeffe: (35) C.-1.9; 2.2.

Modern Duelling; see *Folly as it Flies.*

The Mogul Tale, or A Cobbler's Flight in an Air Balloon; (by Mrs. Inchbald): (35) C.-4.24; 6.18; 9.17.

The Mohawk Chief; see *Oranaska.*

Mohammed; tragedy by G. H. Miles: (52) A.-4.21, 22, 23.

The Momentous Question: (44) A.-11.30; 12.2, 3, 4, 5; (51) C.-2.22; (52) W.-2.27; A.-3.1, 11; 4.15; (54) A.-6.9, 10, 16, 17; C.-11.30; 12.5. See also *Lovers, Wife and Friend.*

The Monarch, the Minister, and the Mimic; farce: (39) W.-6.1.

Monday Baptist, or The Almshouse Festival: (42) A.-8.25.

Money; comedy by Lord Lytton: (41) N.-1.25*; 2.1, 4, 10; 3.27; 8.21; 10.4, 16; 12.22; A.-4.28, 30; 6.2, 10; C.-6.17; 10.11, 13; (42) C.-3.23, 28; A.-7.11, 14; W.-11.23; (43) W.-2.7; 10; A.-8.14; (44) W.-2.22; 3.27; 4.18; 5.21; 9.20; A.-12.13; W.-12.17; (45) A.-5.2, 6; W.-5.6; C.-9.23, 25; (46) W.-1.15, 20; 4.28, 29; (47) W.-1.1; A.-7.30; 11.19; (48) A.-1.20; W.-4.14; 5.1; (49) Ath.-1.5; W.-3.16, 29; A.-5.7; W.-5.14, 23, 31; 11.1; W.-12.24; (50) W.-

9.7; B.-10.25, 31; W.-11.1; 12.23; (51) W.-1.1; B.-3.28; W.-5.7, 10; 9.9, 17; C.-12.30; (52) C.-1.1; 4.13; 6.2; 10.5; 11.12; (53) C.-2.28; A.-3.10, 31; W.-4.5; A.-8.20, 25; 12.9; (54) A.-1.17; C.-8.19, 22; A.-8.19; 10.12; C.M.-12.5; A.-12.8; (55) A.-1.31; 2.6; C.M.-3.29; A.-4.9; C.M.-4.12; W.-5.24; A.-6.13, 27; 9.13; C.M.-11.20, 30.

The Monk, the Mask, and the Murderer; see *Who owns the Hand?*

The Monkey: (46) W.-5.26.

The Monkey and his Double; see *Ourang Outang.*

The Monkey and the Bridegroom; see *The Sorcerer.*

The Monkey who has Seen the World: (35) W.-6.17, 18; (39) W.-6.17, 19.

Monkeyana: (35) W.-6.13, 15, 16; (37) P.-1.25, 26.

Monseigneur, or The Paris Robbers in 1720; comedy: (45) W.-12.20*, 22, 23, 24, 25, 26; (46) A.-4.21.

Monsieur de Chaluman, or Village Holiday; comic ballet pantomime: (37) A.-6.26; 7.1; (47) A.-6.28; 7.10; (48) A.-8.21, 23; 9.2.

Monsieur Jacques; farce: (38) W.-10.27; (39) W.-6.6, 11; (40) W.-4.4; C.-1.11; (43) A.-12.30; (44) A.-1.6; C.-11.8; (51) A.-10.28; (55) C.M.-2.7; 3.6, 9, 29; 4.23.

Monsieur Mallet: (36) W.-3.31; (37) C.-2.8, 11, 14, 8.31; (38) C.-4.10, 13; 5.4; 9.8; (39) C.-1.12; (40) C.-5.28; 6.1; N.-9.16; (41) N.-3.9; 8.30; (42) C.-3.31; (43) C.-12.6; (44) A.-11.16; (45) C.-9.13; (49) W.-3.23; 12.21; (53) W.-2.1; 4.19, 29.

Monsieur Tonson; farce in one act by W. T. Moncrieff: (35) W.-11.18; (36) W.-3.29; (38) C.-4.9, 12; 9.7; (39) W.-4.19, 23; 7.24, 27; 8.22; (40) N.-10.23; (41) W.-7.8; (42)

W.-12.1, 3; (44) A.-11.23; (45) A.-10.3; (49) A.-12.18, 20.

Monster Harlequin; see Harlequin and the Red Monster of St. Michaels.

Monster of St. Michael: (52) N.-10.21.

Monster's Fate: (41) N.-1.16, 18, 19.

Monte Cristy; burlesque: (49) A.-2.19*, 20, 21, 22.

Montezuma; by George Hielge: (46) A.-12.23*, 24, 25, 26, 28, 29.

Moonshine, or Lunar Caustic; by W. E. Burton: (35) C.-9.7, 8, 9, 11.

The Moorish Page, or The Knight of the Bleeding Scarf; "first time in Philadelphia, Milner's new grand Legendary Drama formed on the story of the Page, in the popular fashionable novel of Chantilly, or The Days of France": (35) A.-3.21, 23, 24, 27; C.-6.17, 19; (36) A.-4.2, 4, 7, 12, 14, 15; C.-6.28, 30; 7.1; 9.15; 22; 12.12, 13; (38) C.-12.19, 20.

More Blunders than One, or The Irish Valet: (35) C.-5.7; (36) C.-11.25, 26; (37) A.-5.20; (38) C.-11.10, 13; (40) N.-9.11, 15, 18; 11.11; 12.3, 9, 22; (41) N.-1.11; (42) A.-8.23; (49) W.-12.12; (52) A.-9.1; (53) A.-10.10; 11, 15; 12.12; (54) A.-1.17, 24; 3.25; 9.2, 6; 12.8, 19; (55) A.-1.31; 2.26; 3.15, 16.

Morgan, the Jersey Wagoner: (50) C.-1.21*, 22, 23, 25, 26; 2.22.

A Morning Call: (51) B.-5.26, 28, 29; 6.4, 5; W.-6.27, 28; A.-9.26; 12.23; (52) A.-10.18; 11.2; (53) W.-9.16; 10.12; 12.15; (54) W.-4.17, 28; 12.2, 28; (55) W.-4.13, 20; 5.17; A.-12.13, 14.

Mose and Jakey, or The United Fire Boys in Philadelphia; farce by T. B. Johnston: (49) A.-10.8*, 9, 10; N.-10.8, 9, 10, 11, 12.

Mose and Jakey's Visit to the Chesnut: (49) C.-11.7*.

Mose in California; see Jakey's Visit to California.

Mose in China; (by B. A. Baker): (49) C.-11.3*, 4, 6, 7, 8, 12, 13, 14, 16; (50) C.-6.29; A.-8.19; (52) N.-7.17, 20; 9.2.

Mose's Visit to Philadelphia: (48) W.-6.26*, 27, 28, 29, 30; 7.1, 3, 4; A.-7.5, 6, 7, 8, 11, 12, 13, 14, 15.

The Most Unfortunate Man in the World: (47) P.M.-6.21.

The Mother: (38) C.-11.3*; 12.6, 7.

Mother and Child are Doing Well: (46) W.-6.17, 19; 8.11; (48) A.-12.1, 3, 4; 5.19; 6.7; (49) Ath.-1.9; (54) C.-12.5, 10, 20; (54) C.-1.17; (55) W.-11.1, 13.

Mother Goose: (41) N.-1.2, 5, 6, 7, 9; A.-12.27; (46) A.-4.15, 24.

Mother Goose and the Golden Egg: (46) A.-4.13.

Mother Shipton, or The Pig and the Piper: (39) W.-12.25, 26, 27, 28.

Mother's Blessing, or The New Fanchon; opera: (52) A.-3.8.

Mother's Dream: (36) W.-3.3*, 4.

A Mother's Murder: (45) N.-4.28, 29, 30; 5.1.

Mother's Pets: (44) A.-7.2.

The Mountain Devil, or The Maid of Genoa, or The Dumb Girl of the Inn: (35) W.-10.17; (35) W.-1.17, 20; (45) A.-12.19; (46) A.-2.4; (49) C.-12.10.

Mountain Drover: (45) W.-11.17, 18, 21.

The Mountain King, or Calderoni the Castle Burner: (38) W.-12.15.

The Mountain Minstrel Boy: (46) A.-7.2. See A Father's Malediction.

Mountain Robber: (54) N.-6.26, 27, 28, 29.

Mountain Sylph, or The Magic Scarf;

opera: (36) C.-1.28*, 30; 2.8; (44) C.-10.14, 16, 17; (47) C.-5.31; 6.1.

The Mountain Torrent; see *The First Fratricide.*

The Mountaineer(s), or Love and Madness; by George Colman the Younger: (35) C.-6.25; (36) C.-8.26; W.-1.19; 12.27; (37) C.-12.12; P.-1.7; 2.10; (39) C.-12.20; (40) W.-6.27; 7.3; 10.31; (41) W.-3.5; 12.2; (42) W.-2.4; 4.22; (43) W.-1.14; A.-9.23; W.-10.30, 31; (44) A.-1.23; W.-1.26; 6.21; 8.26; 9.6; (46) W.-2.28; A.-5.15; (48) A.-4.4; W.-4.29; 11.16; (49) W.-3.17; 5.14; A.-6.10; (50) W.-12.25; (51) W.-1.2.

A Moving Tale: (54) C.M.-11.17, 18.

Mr. Greenfinch: (39) W.-4.20, 22, 24.

Mr. H., or Beware a Bad Name: (41) C.-10.14.

Mr. Midshipman Easy: (41) W.-12.9, 11, 31; (42) W.-1.13; (45) W.-5.8; (50) C.-1.7, 10; (55) C.M.-3.22, 24, 31; 4.27; 5.3.

Mr. and Mrs. Jenkins: (36) A.-5.13, 26.

Mr. and Mrs. MacBeth; burlesque: (49) A.-6.11*, 12.

Mr. and Mrs. Pringle: (38) C.-5.9; (40) C.-11.25, 28; 12.11, 22; (41) A.-4.16; 5.13; N.-11.15, 16, 17, 23; 12.18; (42) C.-4.5; (45) W.-11.10, 12, 28.

Mr. and Mrs. Peter White; see *Mrs. White and Mrs. Peter White.*

Mr. and Mrs. White: (44) W.-3.25; (45) C.-10.13; (46) P.M.-9.10; 19; 10.6; (47) P.M.-1.7; (48) W.-7.28, 29; A.-8.5; (49) A.-5.16; 8.18; C.-9.1; (51) C.-9.15; 10.24; 11.13, 29; (52) C.-8.20; 12.27; (54) C.-11.21, 22; 12.18, 19; (55) C.-4.25; W.-9.14; 10.1, 8; 11.15; 12.11.

Mrs. White and Mrs. Peter White; farce: (36) W.-11.4*, 5, 15, 19, 25;

12.2, 5, 17; P.-11.14; (37) W.-1.5, 21; P.-2.4; (40) C.-3.10, 11, 12, 14, 18, 24; 4.11, 22; 6.25, 26; W.-11.11; (41) A.-9.29; (42) C.-1.18, 27; (46) P.M.-5.28; 6.5; (47) W.-3.27; A.-8.3, 10; (51) B.-5.27; C.-9.18; 10.1.

Mrs. Caudle's Curtain Lectures: (45) A.-8.20, 21, 22, 23, 25, 26.

Mrs. Harris: (49) A.-10.18.

Mrs. Nomer: (41) A.-6.24, 25, 26, 28.

Mrs. Normer; burlesque of *Mrs. Nomer:* (41) N.-6.26, 28, 29, 30; 7.1; W.-6.28.

Mrs. Singleton and Mr.: (44) W.-12.2, 7; (45) W.-1.20; (46) W.-3.23, 31; 4.22.

Mrs. Williams at Home: (54) W.-6.1.

Much Ado about Nothing; by William Shakespeare: (35) A.-3.11; W.-5.27; C.-10.26; (?6) A.-3.11; W.-9.16; C.-1.14; (37) C.-1.10; 4.17; 9.28; (39) C.-6.21; 9.14; (40) N.-9.7; (41) C.-8.28; (42) A.-8.15; W.-10.11; (43) W.-4.26; C.-11.8, 29; (44) W.-4.29; 6.17; C.-11.28; (45) C.-9.16, 22; 11.1; W.-11.5; (46) C.-1.1; W.-1.21; 9.15, 28; (49) W.-4.2; A.-4.17; W.-5.11, 30; 6.23; 11.16, 23; 12.28; (50) W.-11.15; 12.30; (51) W.-5.8; 9.15; C.-9.16; 10.3; (52) W.-3.11, 18; C.-3.25, 31; 5.20; 11.8; (53) W.-1.5; A.-3.8, 18; 5.11; A.-6.1; W.-9.30; (54) A.-3.6, 7, 8, 9, 10, 11, 23; 12.4; (55) W.-3.20; C.M.-4.20; A.-9.3; W.-9.3; C.M.-11.19.

The Muleteer of Palermo: (43) W.-4.24, 25, 26; (45) A.-10.31.

The Mummy, or The Liquor of Life; farce by W. E. Burton: (35) C.-1.6; 2.7; 4.11; 5.22; 6.20; 8.24; 9.2; 10.8, 14, 24; 12.25, 28; A.-3.4, 14, 23; (36) A.-3.7; 4.26; C.-1.19; 2.8; 6.16; 9.3, 27; 10.12; 11.9; W.-4.13; A.-6.6; C.-12.14; (37) W.-3.30; P.-2.4, 11;

C.-2.17; 4.5, 15; 9.4; 11.20; (38) C.-1.19; (39) C.-1.19, 31; 2.16; W.-4.15; 5.22, 30; 10.11; (40) W.-1.11; (41) N.-1.25; 2.23; 11.27; (42) N.-1.28; C.-4.20; A.-10.4; (43) W.-5.16, 26; A.-9.28; (44) W.-4.16; A.-6.25; W.-11.7; 12.10, 20; (45) W.-1.21; 3.31; 5.28; 6.25; 10.3; 11.4; 12.18; A.-12.18; (46) W.-4.17; (47) A.-2.16; 4.30; 9.7; (50) W.-2.2; 5.4; (51) A.-12.31; (52) A.-1.1.

Munchausen; pantomime: (44) W.-7.27*, 29, 30, 31; 8.1, 2, 3, 5, 6, 7, 8, 9, 10, 12, 13, 14, 15, 16, 17.

Mungo Park, or The Arab and the Niger: (42) W.-6.30*; 7.1, 2, 4, 11, 12, 13; (49) W.-3.1, 2, 3.

Murder at the Black Farm: (36) W.-9.8*.

Murder at the Inn; see *Jonathan Bradford.*

The Murder at the Marl Pit; see *Coroner's Inquest.*

The Murder at the Road-Side Inn; see *Jonathan Bradford.*

Murder in the First Degree: (44) A.-11.23, 26.

The Murder of the Blind Boy, or The Smuggler and his Dog: (35) W.-10.15; (36) W.-1.20.

The Murder of the Glen: (44) N.-2.2.

The Murder of the Quarry: (44) N.-1.6, 10, 11.

Murdered Putnam: (46) A.-6.9; (53) C.-4.18.

The Murdered Waterman; see *The Smuggler of Bootle Bay.*

The Murderer's Fate; see *The Death Token.*

The Murderer's Sacrifice; see *Demon of the Desert.*

Murderers of Messina: (41) W.-12.6, 7, 10.

Murrell, the Land Pirate; by Charles Burke: (45) A.-11.22*, 24, 25; (50) A.-8.10, 23; 12.7; (51) A.-6.13, 21;

10.4; (52) A.-12.17; (54) C.-2.11.

Mutiny of the Nore: (43) W.-1.7.

My Aunt; (by J. Galt): (35) C.-9.14, 17; 11.30; (36) C.-11.2; W.-2.19, 24; 3.18; (37) A.-5.27; (38) C.-6.23; W.-7.16; (39) C.-1.7; 4.12; 5.21; 6.5; (40) C.-6.4; 10.10; (41) W.-9.11, 16; A.-4.15; 5.19; W.-9.20; 10.5, 27; (42) C.-4.7; (43) N.-9.25, 30; (44) W.-6.27; (45) W.-8.26; 9.3; 11.11; (46) W.-1.17; 4.30; P.M.-4.30; W.-9.12, 28, 29; (47) W.-4.29; A.-10.14; (49) W.-3.6, 27; 5.10; 12.24; (50) W.-1.15; 9.3, 5; 12.30; (51) W.-1.24; 5.8, 17; 9.12; (52) C.-1.19; 4.13; 5.29; 6.8; (53) C.-2.24; 6.14, 21; (54) C.-9.22; (55) C.M.-3.30; W.-4.17; C.M.-11.27; 12.7.

My Boy Tom: (48) A.-2.28, 29; 3.2.

My Companion in Arms: (41) W.-12.16; (42) W.-7.5.

My Country Cousin: (55) C.M.-4.14.

My Fellow Clerk: (35) C.-9.30*; 10.1, 6, 16; (36) C.-7.1; 12.2; A.-3.30; 5.5; 6.7; (39) C.-5.6; 6.14; (40) C.-3.26; 4.9; 5.29; 12.7, 9; (41) N.-9.4; 10.14, 20; (42) C.-4.19; (43) A.-12.12, 28; (46) P.M.-8.5, 6, 18; 9.3; (48) P.M.-3.22; (49) P.M.-7.25; (50) C.-7.23; (51) A.-5.27, 29; (55) C.M.-11.28, 29; 12.3, 12.

My First Night in a Strange Bed Chamber: (41) A.-11.24, 25.

My Friend the Captain, or Dunn Brown: (44) A.-10.24, 25; 11.7, 28; (45) A.-4.16; (46) P.M.-12.23; (47) P.M.-1.2; A.-10.29; (50) A.-9.16.

My Friend the Governor; by W. E. Burton: *(35) A.-3.11, 13, 20; C.-4.16, 22, 30; 6.12; (36) C.-1.16, 30; 2.18; (38) C.-12.29; (39) C.-1.23, 29; 2.25; (41) N.-3.23; 4.3.

My Friend in the Straps: (51) W.-2.3*, 4, 5; (53) A.-9.7.

My Husband's Ghost; farce: (36) C.-

10.25, 26; (37) W.-12.15, 25; (38) W.-2.23; 7.5; 8.9; (49) A.-5.14, 15, 25; (51) B.-9.8, 9.

My Little Adopted: (39) C.-6.17; 9.4; (42) W.-7.20; (43) W.-10.21; (46) P.M.-11.25, 28; (48) P.M.-4.14, 20; (49) P.M.-6.30; (53) C.-4.12; 5.16; 6.1.

My Little Hotel: (42) W.-7.18.

My Mamma's Pets: (53) C.-9.1.

My Master's Rival: (35) C.-2.19; (36) W.-10.3, 5; C.-10.18; (38) C.-6.28; 8.28; (39) C.-3.5, 15; (40) C.-6.3, 10; 9.23; 10.13; (42) A.-9.19; (44) W.-4.25; (48) W.-6.15, 26.

My Neighbor's Wife: (35) W.-6.22, 23; 7.4; 8.22, 26; 9.23; 10.16; 11.5; (36) W.-1.5; 2.8; 3.1; 5.26; P.-11.28; (37) P.-1.3; (38) W.-12.17, 21, 26; (39) W.-2.5, 9, 14; 12.2, 6; (40) W.-4.4, 11; 6.17; A.-9.16; C.-10.31; (42) A.-3.31; A.-4.12; (46) P.M.-6.5, 6; 8.19; 9.12; 11.16; (47) P.M.-6.1; (48) P.M.-3.21, 25; 7.8, 10; (49) Ath.-1.5; P.M.-6.6; (52) C.-8.20; (54) C.-3.4, 13, 22, 28; 4.10; (55) A.-9.11, 12, 15; 10.8, 29; W.-10.27.

My Nervous Debility; see *Day after the Fair.*

My Old Woman: (36) N.-11.4, 6, 11; (42) W.-7.19.

My own Ghost: (37) C.-11.18*, 24; 12.28; (42) A.-11.8.

My Poll and my Partner Joe: (36) W.-2.1*, 2, 11; 3.4; (42) A.-8.2, 4; (49) C.-9.4, 5, 6, 7, 8, 13, 21; (50) C.-5.14; A.-7.31; (51) B.-6.10, 11, 12; N.-8.13; (52) N.-7.28.

My Poor Dog Tray: (45) A.-8.14, 15; 9.2; W.-11.19, 20; (52) A.-4.6 8; (53) C.-4.16, 22.

My Precious Betsy, or Betsy Baker: (50) W.-4.30; 6.1, 4, 12; 7.1; A.-9.30; 10.1; W.-10.30; 11.4, 13; 12.9, 20; (51) W.-1.9, 28; A.-3.10; W.-

3.12, 27; 4.5, 22; A.-4.7, 15; W.-5.20, 31; 6.12, 16; A.-9.1, 6; W.-10.20, 21; C.-11.6, 7, 8, 10; W.-11.10, 11; C.-12.1, 12; W.-12.2; (52) W.-1.21; 2.18, 22; 3.2; C.-4.5, 7; W.-4.18, 20; 5.7, 31; C.-5.23; W.-6.8; C.-9.5, 6, 20; W.-9.9; 10.20; C.-12.1, 29; (54) C.-1.4; W.-2.18; 5.8; C.-5.18, 26; 6.23, 26; 7.3, 11; A.-9.15; C.-11.10; (55) C.M.-4.17; W.-6.28.

My Sister Kate: (40) N.-12.1, 19; (41) C.-5.10, 17; 6.1; 9.15, 16, 20, 25; 12.2, 3, 15; (12) C.-1.17, 31; (46) W.-11.18, 24; (47) W.-4.1; (49) A.-10.1; (50) A.-6.4, 6; B.-8.26; 12.11; (51) C.-10.29; 11.1, 3, 5.

My Two Nephews; see *The Duel.*

My Uncle John, or The Cashmere Shawl: (35) C.-1.13, 15, 20; 5.1; A.-2.24; 3.25; (36) C.-1.18; (40) C.-4.23, 29; 5.6; 6.19; 9.8, 18; (41) C.-8.31; N.-2.15; (42) W.-11.11; (45) W.-11.18; 12.5; (47) A.-6.14, 18; (51) C.-3.10, 11, 18; W.-3.11; C.-9.5, 26; (52) C.-1.12, 24; 2.26; 4.8; 10.16, 19; 12.20; (54) C.-5.22.

My Uncle Toby; see *Tristram Shandy.*

My Valet and I: (43) N.-10.14, 17, 20, 26; 11.8.

My Wife and I, or Married Yesterday: (36) W.-11.1; P.-12.3; (37) P.-1.19; 8.19; (39) W.-7.16; (42) W.-7.25; (45) W.-2.25; (48) C.-7.7.

My Wife's Come: (49) W.-4.9, 11, 16; 5.3; 6.8, 15; (50) W.-9.17, 19.

My Wife's Dentist: (42) C.-2.3*, 4, 5, 22, 26; 3.4, 7, 15; 4.13; W.-6.9, 10, 13; C.-9.27; 10.14; 11.22; 12.27; (47) W.-4.7, 8, 17; 10.27; 12.22, 23.

My Wife's Mother: (35) C.-4.18, 21, 24.

My Wife's Out: (45) A.-7.4, 10; (46) P.M.-7.16; (49) P.M.-6.1.

My Wife's Second Floor: (43) W.-10.14; N.-10.16, 18, 19, 23, 25; C.-

10.26, 27, 28, 30, 31; N.-11.1; C.-11.10; C.-11.24; N.-11.30; C.-12.4; (44) N.-1.15, 16; 2.7; W.-5.7; (46) P.M.-7.11; 8.24, 27; (47) W.-9.22; (49) Ath.-1.10, 11.

My Young Wife and my Old Umbrella: (38) C.-4.18*, 19; (40) W.-5.14; N.-9.29; (42) W.-6.8; (51) A.-10.6; 11.20.

Myr(n)a Alwyn(n); tragedy in five acts: (53) C.-4.20, 21.

The Mysteries of Lurlei Berg; see *The Naiad Queen.*

The Mysteries and Miseries of New York; by Thaddeus W. Meighan: (49) A.-10.3*, 4, 5, 6, 11; N.-10.8, 9, 10; (50) A.-8.26, 27, 28.

The Mysteries and Miseries of Philadelphia: (50) C.-5.31; 6.1, 4, 21.

The Mysteries of New York: (44) N.-1.27, 29, 30, 31; 2.5.

The Mysteries of Odd Fellowship: (46) A.-11.28; (47) A.-4.13.

The Mysteries of Paris; "adapted from book of same name by F. C. Wemyss, James Gann, and John Sefton": (43) N.-11.13*, 14, 15, 16, 17, 18, 20, 21, 22, 23, 24; (47) A.-9.1, 2.

The Mysterious Blunder; see *Savage of the Forest.*

Mysterious Family: (50) W.-10.28, 29, 31; 11.2, 12; 12.14; (51) W.-1.15, 18; 2.6; 3.13; 10.18; 11.4; (52) W.-1.21; (53) W.-2.12, 15; 3.3; 6.9.

The Mysterious Hermit; see *Manfredi.*

The Mysterious Lady; see *Zephyrina.*

Mysterious Knockings: (50) A.-5.10, 11, 13, 14, 17, 18, 20, 24, 28.

Mysterious Stranger: (51) A.-9.22.

Mysterious Visitor: (42) A.-10.1.

A Nabob for an Hour; see *Uncle Sam.*

The Naiad Queen, or The Mysteries of Lurlei Berg: (40) N.-12.19*, 21, 22, 23, 25, 26, 28, 29, 30; (41) N.-1.1, 2, 4, 5, 6, 7; 4.1, 2, 3, 5, 6, 7; W.-9.27, 28, 29, 30; 10.1, 2, 4, 5, 6, 7, 8, 9; (44) W.-8.19; (45) W.-7.11, 12, 14, 15, 16, 17; 12.27; (47) A.-12.23, 24, 25, 27, 28, 29, 30, 31; (48) A.-1.1, 3, 4, 5, 6, 7, 8, 10, 11, 12, 13, 14; 2.21, 22, 23, 24, 25; (49) C.-11.19, 20, 21, 22, 23, 24; (52) N.-9.9, 10, 11, 13, 14, 15, 16, 17.

Nante the Porter; farce by Berkmann: (37) A.-7.27.

Napoleon, or Passage of Mt. St. Bernard: (35) C.-5.26, 27, 29; 6.6, 24; (36) C.-6.14, 15; 7.4, 7; (45) A.-11.19, 20, 22; (52) A.-4.13; N.-9.3, 4.

Napoleon, or The Deserter and His Dog: (53) C.-4.27, 28.

Napoleon and the Patriot: (41) W.-10.6, 7.

Napoleon Bonaparte; by H. J. Amherst: (38) W.-4.23, 24, 25, 26, 27; (44) W.-8.12, 13, 14, 15.

Napoleon Bonaparte's Invasion of Russia: (39) C.-12.28; (40) W.-4.21.

Nathalie; pantomime ballet: (40) C.-11.18, 21; (41) C.-9.1, 6, 7, 21; (42) A.-10.1, 3.

National Guard, or Bride and no Bride; comic opera: (50) W.-5.13, 14, 15, 29.

Nationalities, or John, Jean, and Jonathan; by J. Oakes Pardey: (53) A.-11.28*, 29, 30; 12.1, 2, 3, 5, 6, 7; (54) A.-6.2, 3; 9.29; 12.5; (55) A.-7.2, 4.

The Native American: (44) A.-7.4.

Native Land: (39) C.-9.26, 27; (46) A.-2.23.

Native Nobility; burlesque by L. A. Wilmer: (47) A.-5.31*; 6.1, 2, 8.

Natty Bumpo: (42) A.-11.26, 27, 29, 30.

Natural Magic; see *The Chimney Piece.*

Nature and Philosophy: (35) W.-1.29; 12.8, 23; (36) W.-1.11; 2.20; (37) P.-1.21; W.-6.27; (40) W.-12.11; (42) W.-1.31; (44) A.-2.16; C.-10.21; (45) A.-11.26; (46) P.M.-6.19; (47) W.-4.1, 6; (48) W.-11.10; (50) A.-6.1, 5; W.-6.13, 17; (51) B.-2.8; (52) C.-9.3; (53) C.-2.7, 18; (54) C.-7.20; (55) W.-12.21.

Naval Engagements, or The Freaks of Love; farce: (38) W.-11.10, 12, 13, 19; (40) C.-2.3, 5, 20, 24; 3.16; 4.6, 14; 5.5, 14; 12.8; (41) A.-4.28; (43) W.-2.25, 27; (44) W.-1.11; 7.18, 19; (46) P.M.-8.3, 5, 6, 21; (47) P.M.-3.10, 22, 30; 4.6; 6.22; 7.12; A.-10.20; (48) A.-11.6, 7; (51) C.-3.25, 29; W.-9.27; 10.1, 15; (52) W.-1.19; 2.13; 5.4; 9.14; C.-9.20; W.-10.25; 11.22; C.-11.23; 25; C.M.-10.9, 11; A.-12.6, 23, 27; (55) A.-1.3; C.-2.7; W.-11.12, 17, 21.

Naval Glory, or Decatur's Triumph: (44) W.-3.11*, 12, 13, 14, 15, 16.

The Navy Forever: (37) W.-7.18, 19, 20.

Negro Doorkeeper: (40) W.-12.26.

Negro Fidelity; drama in three acts: (51) B.-6.2; (54) C.-7.20, 22.

The Nervous Man and Man of Nerve; comedy: (35) C.-4.28; 5.7; (36) C.-9.28; 10.5; 11.16; 25; (37) C.-2.15, 21; A.-5.12, 17; (38) C.-9.18; 11.9, 12; (40) C.-10.6; N.-11.17, 20; (41) N.-2.24 (42) A.-8.2; (45) A.-11.13; (46) C.-1.7, 16; A.-8.29; W.-8.31; A.-9.1; (47) W.-2.9; 6.16, 22; 10.4; 12.9; (48) W.-5.16, 26; A.-6.5; W.-9.12; A.-11.13, 16; (49) W.-4.11, 19; 9.11, 21; 10.19, 23; (50) W.-5.1; (51) W.-2.24; 3.7; 9.2; (52) W.-3.2; C.-8.3; W.-9.27; (53) C.-5.24; 6.3;

9.6; 11.7; (55) A.-5.4, 10; W.-11.28; 12.3.

The Net Maker and his Wife; see *Zembuca.*

Nettlewig Hall; farce: (50) B.-12.13, 16, 17, 20.

New Actress: (44) A.-6.24, 26.

A New Comedy of Errors: (55) A.-5.18*, 23.

The New Fanchon; see *Mother's Blessing.*

The New Footman: (42) C.-9.22, 23, 24, 26, 28; A.-10.27; (44) W.-5.3; 9.7, 26, 30; 11.8; 12.3, 18; (45) W.-1.29; 2.24; 3.14; 4.25; 6.2, 24; 8.21; (46) W.-5.11, 15, 21, 29; P.M.-7.30, 31; W.-10.14, 20; 12.1; (47) W.-3.25; 6.2; (48) W.-6.2; 7.19; 12.14; (50) A.-3.4, 28; 10.4, 8, 20; (52) W.-11.27; 12.1, 10; (53) W.-2.2; C.-3.10, 16, 26; (54) W.-10.9; 11.11; (55) W.-10.27.

New Lights; see *Irish Tutor.*

New Notions: (39) W.-10.21, 22, 24; 11.2; (40) W.-12.22; A.-12.2, 5, 10; (41) W.-10.15, 16; C.-10.27; (42) W.-4.9, 13; (45) C.-1.20; 4.26, 30; 5.6, 12.

The New President; farce: (41) N.-3.24*, 25.

A New Way to Pay Old Debts; by Philip Massinger: (35) W.-2.19; 6.3; 8.24; 11.26, 28; C.-6.25; (36) W.-1.13; 5.31; 9.12; 12.19; P.-12.10; (37) W.-6.26; 7.12; 11.17; W.-2.3; (38) C.-9.11; W.-7.10; (39) C.-10.2, 4; 12.12; W.-4.26; 6.29; (40) C.-4.10; W.-6.16; 12.23; A.-12.16; (41) A.-5.3; 10.4; W.-3.3; (42) W.-4.4; A.-4.29; W.-5.28; 6.29; C.-11.15; (43) W.-1.12; A.-9.7; (44) W.-1.17; A.-1.22; 3.19; W.-6.3; A.-9.6; W.-10.22; (45) W.-4.2; 5.23; A.-11.21; (46) W.-2.20; A.-5.19; (47) W.-4.19; A.-11.22; (48) A.-1.21; 8.10; (49) C.-10.5; (50) A.-

5.17; (51) B.-3.4; W.-5.23; A.-5.27; (52) W.-1.5, 7; C.-1.20; W.-3.30; C.-9.8; (53) A.-4.18; W.-6.2; (55) W.-4.19; C.M.-5.23, 31; 11.5.

New Year's Morn: (47) P.M.-1.1, 2.

New York as it Is; by B. A. Baker: (49) A.-9.24*, 25, 28, 29; (50) A.-8.22, 23; (54) C.-10.13.

The Nice Young Man; see *Weak Points.*

Nicholas Nickleby; by E. Sterling: (39) W.-2.25, 26, 27, 28; 3.1, 5; 4.20; (40) W.-5.23; N.-9.12, 19, 22, 25; 10.6, 12; C.-9.17, 19; 10.1; 12.8; (42) C.-3.9, 16; (43) W.-6.24; (44) W.-4.20; (47) A.-2.6, 9; 6.24; (54) C.-3.9, 11; 5.5, 8.

Nick of Time; Yankee drama: (43) A.-5.8*; (46) A.-3.9.

Nick of the Woods, or Kentucky in 1783, or The Jibbenalnosay; melodrama in three acts by L. H. Medina: (38) W.-8.29*, 30, 31; 9.1, 4, 5, 11; (41) N.-9.18, 20, 21, 22; 10.16; 11.2; (42) W.-3.12, 19, 22, 24, 25, 26; A.-4.6, 7; W.-4.23; A.-5.28, 30; 7.9; W.-10.21; (43) N.-11.4; (45) A.-5.31; (46) A.-3.14, 16; (47) A.-8.26, 27, 31; (48) W.-7.15; (50) C.-7.9, 11, 13, 26; A.-10.2, 3, 4, 5; 11.5, 6, 7; (51) A.-5.21; (52) A.-9.24, 25; N.-9.25; (53) A.-5.28; 6.2.

The Nigger turned Physician; see *Black Ghost.*

Night and Morning: (41) N.-3.20, 22, 23, 25, 26, 27.

Night and Morning; by John Brougham: (55) A.-3.26*, 27, 28, 29, 30, 31, 4.2, 3, 4, 5, 7, 11.

Night Dancers: (49) C.-12.7, 8, 10.

Night Hag, or St. Swithin's Chair: (35) W.-1.1, 3; (43) N.-11.9.

The Night Hawks; see *The Black Rangers.*

A Night in the Forest; see *Two Words.*

A Night in the Pyrenees: (41) A.-1.16, 21.

A Night in Whales; see *Jonah.*

A Night of Adventures; see *Vol-au-Vent.*

A Night's Adventures; see *Der Wachter.*

Nina Sforza; tragedy: (42) C.-2.9*, 10, 11, 14, 15, 16, 24.

Ninth Statue, or The Irishman of Bagdad: (42) W.-5.16, 21; 6.2.

Nipped in the Bud; farce: (39) W.-9.4, 16, 25; 10.11, 26, 30; (40) W.-5.9; 28; 6.4, 25; A.-9.17; C.-12.28; (47) A.-7.22; (48) A.-10.24; (50) A.-3.7.

Nix, the Cabman: (52) C.-7.14, 15.

No!, or The Glorious Minority: (35) C.-12.12; (36) C.-10.17; 11.30; W.-1.14; 4.22; P.-11.21, 23; (37) C.-2.8, 20; 3.6; 12.12; A.-5.6, 10, 16; (38) W.-7.7; 11.26; C.-6.13; 9.17; 11.13; (40) C.-3.7, 13; 4.15; 5.12, 21; C.-6.22; (41) C.-9.10; (43) C.-1.5, 7; (45) A.-7.14; C.-8.30; 9.15; W.-12.12, 13; (46) W.-1.3; 4.11, 15, 16, 21; (48) W.-8.28; 11.2, 27; (49) W.-2.26; (50) W.-2.12, 15; 3.4, 25; (51) B.-4.19.

No Male Visitors Allowed; see *Congress Hall.*

No. 1 Round the Corner: (54) W.-6.21; 7.1.

The Noble Shepherd; see *Douglass.*

Noble Heart: (51) W.-5.19.

Non Imprisonment for Debts; see *Fireman of Philadelphia.*

Norma; opera by Bellini: (41) N.-1.11, 12, 13, 14, 15, 16, 20, 21, 22, 23; C.-1.11, 12, 13, 14, 15, 16, 18, 25, 26, 27, 28, 29, 30; C.-2.1, 2, 3, 4, 6, 7, 8, 9, 10, 12, 14, 16, 18, 19, 21; (42) C.-12.30; (43) C.-1.9, 10,

11, 13, 16; 2.1, 11, 17; 7.25, 26, 27, 31; 11.13; (44) C.-4.20, 23; 5.25; (45) C.-6.28, 30; 7.1; 11.15, 18, 22; (46) C.-5.18; W.-11.13, 14; (47) C.-4.5, 12, 22; 6.5; W.-7.23, 27; 8.2, 5; 10.12, 14; 11.22; 12.4; (48) W.-1.3; 9.26; C.-10.4, 10, 13; 12.12, 14, 16; (49) W.-10.8, 10, 11; 11.30; 12.3; (50) C.-9.10, 18; 12.23, 30; (52) W.-2.20, 21; 5.7; (53) W.-3.11; (55) W.-1.6.

Norman Leslie; domestic drama by F. C. Wemyss founded on Fay's novel of that name: (36) W.-3.14*, 15, 16, 18, 19, 22, 25, 26; 6.18; (40) W.-12.28, 29, 30, 31; A.-12.21, 22, 25; (41) W.-1.1, 2, 4, 5, 6.

North and South, or The Pedlar and the Planter; comedy: (55) C.-2.1, 2.

North Pole, or A Tale of the Frozen Sea: (36) W.-3.13*, 14, 15.

No Song no Supper; by Prince Hoare: (35) C.-1.30; 12.7, 15; (36) C.-9.2, 6; (37) C.-8.28; 10.11; (38) C.-5.30; 11.16; W.-7.23; 10.12; 11.24; (36) A.-5.3; (39) W.-11.14; (40) C.-6.9; 11.6; (42) A.-7.20, 27; W.-12.23; (43) C.-1.6; (45) A.-7.15, 17, 18; C.-10.21; (47) P.M.-2.8; (50) W.-4.29; B.-12.12, 21; (51) A.-4.30.

Not to be Done: (50) B.-8.26; (51) B.-1.16.

Note Forger: (35) W.-10.24, 27; 11.10; 12.22.

Nothing: (48) A.-3.21, 22.

Nothing like Wheedling; see *Weak Points.*

No. 33 Locust Street; farce: (50) C.-5.29*, 30, 31; 6.8.

Novel Expedient: (52) W.-10.13, 14, 16, 26; 11.1, 5, 9, 23; 12.21; (53) W.-1.8; 2.4, 11; 3.7; 4.14.

Nymphs of the Red Sea: (44) A.-11.11, 13, 4, 15, 19, 20, 22, 28; (53) W.-3.28, 29, 30, 31; 4.1, 2.

The Oath; see *Il Giuramento.*

Oberon, or The Enchanted Horn: (48) W.-1.31; 2.1, 2, 3, 4, 5, 24, 25; 3.9, 10.

Obi, or Three Fingered Jack; pantomime: (39) W.-1.23; (45) A.-11.1, 3.

Obid and Ovid: (35) W.-5.11.

An Object of Interest: (46) P.M.-7.27, 28; (47) A.-9.11; 10.1, 5.23; (48) P.M.-3.20; 4.13, 20; A.-11.1, 6; 12.21; (50) A.-4.22; 5.27; (51) W.-4.18, 21, 25; (53) C.-2.2; A.-5.4, 11; 12.2; (54) A.-3.23; C.M.-9.25; 10.4, 16; 11.4, 9; C.-12.4; (55) C. M.-5.21, 26.

Obstinate Family: (53) W.-9.28, 30; 10.3; 11.22; (54) W.-1.18, 19, 24; 6.30; 11.13, 30; (55) W.-3, 7, 14, 29; 4.12.

The Ocean Child; melodrama: (41) N.-9.25*, 27, 28, 29, 30; 10.1, 2, 4, 5, 6, 7, 26, 30; 11.18; (42) N.-1.1, 15; A.-11.22, 23, 24, 26; (44) A.-7.16, 17, 19, 25; (46) A.-2.26, 27, 28; (51) A.-5.31; 6.21, 30.

The Ocean of Life: (44) W.-5.29, 30.

Octavia Bragaldi; tragedy by Charlotte M. S. Barnes: (48) A.-2.10*, 11, 12.

O'Donoghue; "new legendary drama": (48) A.-6.29*; 7.1.

O'Flannigan and the Fairies: (37) C.-2.27*; 3.1, 2, 4, 6, 7, 8, 11; (40) N.-11.18, 19, 21, 26; (49) W.-10.22, 25, 27; (55) A.-3.7, 8, 10, 12, 13, 14; 4.7, 9, 19; 5.3; W.-9.20, 25.

O'Grady, the Irish Guardsman: (49) W.-9.13*, 14, 15, 17, 18, 22.

Of Age Tomorrow; musical farce: (36) C.-11.7; (37) C.-9.18; (38) C.-5.24; 9.3, 10; 11.14; (40) W.-11.11; 12.5; (46) P.M.-8.13, 15; A.-9.5, 9, 10; 10.3, 23; (47) A.-2.4; (48) A.-11.9, 28.

Oh! Hush!! or The Verginny Cupids; "Ethiopian opera": (35) W.-1.16; 6.27, 29; 7.4; 9.4, 12; 11.26, 28;

(36) W.-5.23; (38) W.-1.5; 6.26;
7.2; (40) W.-7.16, 18; A.-9.9; (41)
W.-5.1; A.-12, 11, 17, 18; (42) A.-
4.25, 26; W.-6, 18; A.-9.22; W.-10.28;
(46) A.-7.14, 18; (48) A.-3, 4, 6, 9;
C.-7.8, 12; (50) A.-5.9.

O-I-E-O-E; see *Catching an Heiress.*

O. K.: (40) A.-12.1.

*Old and Young, or The Four Mow-
brays:* (35) A.-3.3, 5; W.-3.20;
C.-12.8, 11; (48) W.-3.16, 17; C.-
7.3, 6, 18; (50) W.-1.10; B.-9.23, 24.

The Old and Young Salt: (45) W.-
5.16, 17, 20.

The Old Clock; see *Here she goes,
There she goes.*

Old Drury in an Uproar; see *A Row at
the Chesnut.*

Old English Gentleman; comedy: (37)
C.-12, 15*, 16, 18, 20; (38) C.-1.2;
2.7; 5.24; (42) A.-9.24; 11.9; (47)
A.-11.2.

The Old Gentleman: (35) A.-3.6, 12,
16, 26; C.-5.16; 9.7; (36) W.-4.23,
26; 5.16.

Old Guard: (40) N.-10.3; (47) W.-
4.12, 13, 16; 5.4; 10.26; (48) W.-
1.19, 22, 25; 3.23; 5.9; A.-6.10, 14;
7.31; 8.1, 15; 9.30; 10.3, 24; (49)
C.-8.28; C.-12.3, 4; (50) W.-2.23;
(55) W.-6.23; 7.2.

Old Heads and Young Hearts; comedy
by D. Boucicault: (45) W.-1.20*, 21,
22, 23, 24, 25, 27, 29, 31; C.-1.22, 23,
24, 25 27 28 29; W.-2.3 10, 28; C.-
2.4; W.-3.4; 4.8; 8.15, 21; 10.13;
12.18; (46) W.-1.13; 5.18; 20; 7.24;
(47) W.-5.7; (48) W.-7.17, 20, 29;
(51) B.-2.8; W.-4.14; B.-5.30; (52)
C.-8.30; 9.1; (53) A.-5.23, 25; 8.22;
9.29; (54) W.-6.23, 24, 30; (55)
A.-130; C.M.-11.5; 12.22.

Old Hickory: (42) W.-1.1.

Old Honesty: (48) A.-9.13*, 14, 16, 18,
19, 20, 23; 12.5.

Old Ironsides: (41) W.-12.28, 29, 30;
(42) W.-1.1.

Old Love and the New: (51) W.-3.11*,
13. Comedy.

Old Maid; farce by A. Murphy: (36)
C.-6.16.

Old Manor House; comedy: (45) C.-
4.30.

Old Morgan: (47) A.-2.10, 11, 12, 13.

Old Man's Curse: (35) W.-2.28*; 3.2;
4.3; C.-10.31; (36) A.-2.29; 3.3.

The Old Oak Chest: (37) A.-5.18;
(40) W.-3.24, 26, 31. Melodrama.

Old School and the New: (52) W.-
10.4, 5.

Old Times in Virginia; see *Yankee
Pedlar.*

*Old Toll House, or The Carrier and
his Dogs:* (52) A.-4.5.

Old Virginia, or Southern Chivalry:
(43) N.-12.9.

Ole Bull; farce by Charles Burke: (45)
A.-1.2; 7.30; 9.20, 24; P.M.-3.14,
17; 4.10; (47) A.-2.1; P.M.-2.17, 24;
A.-5.14; 7.3; (48) A.-12.23; (50)
C.-7.29; A.-8.6, 12; 12.4, 7; (51)
A.-9.4, 10; (52) N.-9.14; A.-12.16;
(54) C.-2.6.

*Oliver Twist, or The Almshouse Boy,
or The Parish Boy's Progress:* (39)
W.-1.1*, 2, 5; 5.30, 31; 6.1; (49)
N.-9.5, 8, 9; 10.20; (41) N.-3.29;
C.-12.11; (42) C.-2.18, 22, 23; W.-
10.8, 11, 22; 11.9; 12.6; (43) W.-
2.23; 4.8; 6.12; (44) W.-2.5, 14; 4.1,
8; 6.8; (47) A.-12, 5, 9, 11, 30; 2.15;
5.8; 11.18; (55) W.-2.13, 15.

Olla Podrida: (35) A.-4.1, 4; C.-4.18.

*Olympic Devils, or Orpheus and Eury-
dice:* (39) C.-6.3, 5, 6, 8.

Olympic Revels: (42) C.-12.23; (43)
C.-1.9, 13, 18, 21; (47) W.-10.22, 23.

Omandhaun; see *My Poor Dog Tray.*

Omnibus; comedy: (35) C.-4.30; (36)
C.-10.1, 5, 8; 11.16, 19; (37) C.-2.13,

20, 24; 3.6; (38) C.-9.17, 29; 11.7; (40) C.-10.9, 10, 20; (37) A.-5.10, 13; (41) A.-11.30; (40) W.-6.10; (40) N.-11.27; (42) W.-7.9; C.-11.12; A.-11.15; W.-11.22, 26; (43) W.-1.28, 31; (46) P.M.-10.7; (47) P.M.-3.8; 5.4; W.-6.18, 21; (48) A.-2.25; P.M.-5.1; A.-5.6; (49) C.-9.15, 25; A-9.26; C.-10.25; (50) C.-3.12; A.-8.26; (51) C.-12.2, 4, 10; (52) C.-1.21, 28; (53) A.-3.17; 6.17; 10.3; (54) A.-3.6; W.-5.30; C.-9.13.

Omreah: (39) W.-8.14.

One Dollar on the Bank of Kentucky; farce: (50) A.-9.2.

One for Seven; see *Inn Keeper of Calais.*

One Glass More: (41) N.-10.5, 6, 7, 8; (44) A.-10.30, 31; 11.1.

One Hour, or The Carnival Ball: (37) A.-6.17*; (38) C.-10.8, 9, 12, 13, 20; (46) P.M.-6.27, 29; 8.8; 12.28; (49) P.M.-7.7.

One Hundred and Two, or The Veteran and his Progeny; domestic drama: (50) A.-10.23; (52) C.-2.25; 3.1, 27; A.-4.7. See also under *H,* play called 102.

One O'Clock, or The Knight and the Wood Demon: (37) C.-4.1*, 3, 5, 6, 7, 8, 15; 8.21.

One, Two, Three, Four, Five: (35) C.-12.17, 19, 22, 26; (36) A.-3.19, 21, 25; 4.20, 22; (39) A.-5.10.

Open House; farce: (38) W.-12.19, 24, 28.

Open Sesame: (44) A.-8.26, 27, 28, 29, 31; 9.2, 3, 4, 5, 7; 11.25, 27.

Opposite Neighbors: (55) W.-4.9, 19; 5.2.

Oralloosa; tragedy by R. M. Bird: (47) W.-5.13, 15, 17, 22.

Oranaska, or The Mohawk Chief; tragedy by J. B. Phillips: (38) W.-9.3, 6; (46) A.-3.13, 19.

Orange Girl of Venice: (49) A.-12.5*, 6, 7, 8.

The Order of the Day; see *St. Patrick's Eve.*

Oregon, or The Emigrant's Dream; domestic drama; (by J. M. Field): (45) A.-6.6*, 7, 9, 10, 11, 12, 13, 14, 16; 9.27, 29.

Organic Affection; comedietta: (55) C.M.-9.21; 10.5.

The Original; farce: "first time in America, by the author of *Spitfire*": (38) C.-7.7*.

Oroonoko; by Thomas Southerne: (40) W.-6.24.

Orphan Madelene, or The Child of the Regiment: (46) P.M.-4.1, 2, 3, 9.

The Orphan of Blockley: (47) W.-8.20, 21.

The Orphan of Geneva; see *Therese.*

The Orphan of Russia; see *Yelva.*

Orphan's Dream: (52) A.-11.4.

Orphan's Grave; see *Bloodhounds.*

Orpheus and Eurydice: see *Olympic Devils.*

Osceola, or The Florida War Chief; (by J. H. Sherburne): (41) N.-10.15*; (45) N.-1.8, 9.

Ostler and the Robber: (45) W.-3.20.

Ostler, Robber, and Inn-keeper: (43) A.-3.9; (44) W.-2.24.

Otello; opera: (44) C.-10.28, 29, 30, 31; 11.1, 2, 4, 5, 6, 7; 12.14, 16, 17; (45) A.-3.31; 10.16, 18; (46) A.-2.4, 5, 7, 11; (48) A.-2.17, 18; 3.2, 3; W.-12.20, 21, 22; (50) A.-4.30; 5.1; (52) A.-2.28.

Othello; by William Shakespeare: (35) W.-1.19, 24; 6.23; 8.29; 11.23; C.-7.3; 10.13; (36) C.-9.6; (37) C.-10.14; 11.15; (36) W.-1.20; 5.25; 6.4, 11; 9.21; 10.18; A.-3.11; 6.8; (41) A.-4.14; 8.27; 10.8; (36) P.-12.12; (37) P.-1.12, 24; 2.2, 6; (37) W.-1.5; 6.28; 7.19, 25; (38) W.-

1.9, 31; 7.7, 31; 9.1; 10.15; (37) C.-
12.24; (38) C.-1.26; 9.12; (39) C.-
9.9; 12.11; (40) C.-11.23; (41)
C.-9.4; (39) W.-6.26; 7.2; 9.23; (40)
W.-3.17; 5.2; 6.20; 10.20; (41) W.-
9.16; (40) N.-9.21; 11.7; (41) N.-
5.21; 8.25; 10.21; 12.13; (42) W.-4.1,
20; A.-4.27; W.-10.17; (43) W.-6.7;
A.-8.15; 9.1, 13; 10.12; N.-10.16;
C.-11.1, 7; (44) A.-1.16; W.-1.31;
N.-4.16; W.-6.18; 7.1; 8.26; A.-9.20;
W.-10.21; C.-12.2; W.-12.3; (45)
W.-2.24; 4.7; 5.7; C.-10.29; W.-
11.6; C.-12.3; W.-2.21; 3.28;
5.11; 10.16, 20; (47) W.-9.21; 11.4,
9; A.-11.25; 12.21; (48) A.-3.13;
W.-4.8, 28; A.-7.18; W.-11.22; A.-
11.22; (49) A.-4.12; W.-5.28; 6.2;
A.-12.22; (50) A.-2.11, 23; 5.20;
6.14; W.-6.17; A.-9.30; (51) B.-
3.11; 12.25; A.-6.23; W.-6.24; 27;
A.-10.7; W.-10.13; (52) W.-1.9, 13;
C.-1.23; A.-3.16; W.-3.29; 6.14; C.-
9.7, 13; 11.23; (54) C.-6.30; W.-10.4,
16; A.-11.22, 25; (55) A.-1.27; W.-
3.13, 29; 4.18, 21; C.M.-5.22; W.-
5.31; C.M.-6.5; 10.22; W.-12.10.

Othello, Travestie: (36) C.-8.26*, 27,
29; (41) N.-11.29; (42) N.-5.24;
A.-9.17.

Oua Cousta, or The Lion of the Forest;
national drama by N. H. Bannister:
(50) A.-11.9*.

Our Clerks; farce: (52) W.-6.23*, 24,
26.

Our Country Cousin: (53) W.-3.24,
25; 4.11, 16; A.-5.9; W.-6.10; C.M.-
12.21, 22; (55) C.M.-2.1; 3.10, 14.

Our Flag is Nailed to the Post: (45)
A.-7.8; (47) A.-4.19, 20; P.M.-
5.11.

Our Gal; by S. D. Johnson: (51) A.-
2.13*; 5.8, 15; 11.6, 13; (52) C.-2.9;
W.-10.23; (53) C.-5.4; C.M.-11.4;
(55) W.-9.18.

Our House at Home; domestic drama:

(42) C.-1.20, 21; (43) A.-3.25; N.-
12.15; (44) C.-10.23.

Our Jemima; by H. J. Conway: (53)
C.-5.9*.

Our Mary Ann; farce by J. B. Buckstone: (38) W.-8.10, 11; 10.15, 23;
11.6, 22; (40) C.-9.2, 3, 11; (42) A.-
5.4; (43) W.-7.19, 20, 28; 8.12; (46)
P.M.-12.2, 22; W.-12.11, 12, 15, 23;
(47) W.-3.24; P.M.-5.28; 6.5; 7.3,
15; W.-8.10, 12; 10.14; 11.29; 12.12;
(48) P.M.-7.10, 19; (49) Ath.-1.6, 8;
(50) W.-1.17, 23; B.-8.26; W.-8.29;
(52) C.-8.23; (53) C.-3.18, 21.

Our Nan: (54) C.-6.16.

Our Navy in '76; see *The First Fleet
and the First Flag.*

Our New Lady's Maid: (52) W.-11.19,
20.

Our Way in France; see *Fontainbleau.*

*Ourang Outang, or The Runaway
Monkey, or The Monkey and His
Double:* (35) W.-6.8, 9, 10, 11, 12,
19; 10.6, 10, 12; (36) W.-11.11;
(37) W.-1.18; P.-1.23, 28; (52) A.-
3.29, 30; 4.12.

*The Outlaw Wife, or The Coiner's
Cave:* (44) A.-12.27.

Out of Luck: (40) N.-10.1.

Out of Place: (41) N.-11.2, 4, 6, 13;
(42) W.-7.21, 22.

Out on a Lark: (50) C.-6.19, 20, 22.

*Outallissi, or The Hero of a Hundred
Battles:* (44) A.-10.2; (45) N.-5.7.

Paddy Carey or The Boy of Clogheen;
musical farce in one act: (35) C.-5.5;
(36) C.-10.10; 11.22; (37) C.-2.15,
21; (40) C.-10.16, 19; (48) A.-11.15,
16, 18; (53) W.-10.28; (54) W.-5.19,
20.

Paddy Mile's Boy: (55) C.M.-1.18;
3.12, 27; 6.7.

Paddy Murphy's Weather Almanac:
(40) W.-2.28; 3.2.

Paddy the Piper; by James Pilgrim:

(50) A.-11.22*, 23, 25, 26, 30; 12.3;
(51) A.-2.11; 5.9; (53) C.-7.20; (54)
C.-7.26.

Paddy's Trip to America; (by C. S.
Talbot): (50) C.-3.4*, 7; A.-11.29;
(51) A.-2.7, 8.

Padlock; by Isaac Bickerstaff: (39)
W.-9.18, 21, 27; (42) W.-4.29. Farce.

The Painter of Brienne; romantic play:
(52) W.-3.22*, 23, 24, 25, 26.

Pantodesochoria!: (35) W.-4.2.

Papa Jerome, or Les Petites Amantes:
(44) A.-9.17, 21. Pantomime.

Paris and London; comedy by W. T.
Moncrieff: (41) A.-11.1, 2, 3, 4, 6;
(51) W.-6.30; 7.1, 2, 3, 4, 5, 7, 8,
9; (53) A.-12.26, 27, 28, 29, 30, 31;
(54) A.-1.2, 3, 4, 5, 6, 7, 9, 11, 12.

Paris in 1750; see *Comfortable Lodgings.*

Paris in 1793; see *Delicate Ground.*

Paris in the Olden Times; see *Henri
Quatre.*

The Paris Robbers in 1720; see *Monseigneur.*

Parisina; opera by Donizetti: (51)
C.-1.4, 6.

The Parish Boy's Progress; see *Oliver
Twist.*

Partners and Friends: (44) A.-8.7;
8.16; 11.27.

The Party Wall; see *Queer Neighbors.*

*The Pass Word, or The White Ser-
geant:* (44) W.-8.26, 27; 9.5; (51)
W.-12.10.

The Passage of Mt. St. Bernard; see
Napoleon.

The Passage of the Red Sea; see *Israelites in Egypt.*

Passing Cloud; by W. B. Bernard:
(50) W.-8.24, 27.

Passion: (43) C.-11.14.

*Passion and Repentance, or Love's
Frailties:* (36) W.-1.9; 2.6, 9; 3.5;
(40) W.-5.11; (43) W.-1.4, 5, 6;
(54) C.-6.26; 7.5.

*Past and Present, or The Three Gen-
erations:* (42) C.-4.4, 6.

Pat Rooney: (50) C.-6.29.

Patience and Perseverance; comedy in
one act: (55) W.-9.19, 20, 21, 22, 24.

The Patient Woman; see *Griselda.*

*Patrick Lyon, or The Locksmith of
Philadelphia;* domestic drama by
James Rees: (43) A.-8.26*, 28, 29;
9.1, 2, 4, 8; (52) N.-7.31; 8.4.

Patrician and Parvenu: (35) C.-9.5,
10; (40) N.-9.1; 10.17; (42) C.-3.24;
A.-8.9, 12; (43) A.-8.10; (51) W.-
5.19.

The Patrician and the Pretender; see
Confusion.

The Patrician's Daughter; tragedy in
five acts by J. Westland Marston:
(43) W.-6.5, 6, 8; (44) C.-10.31;
11.1, 30; 12.3; (51) W.-10.27, 30;
(52) C.-4.1, 5.

Patriotism, or The Signal Fire: (40)
W.-7.4, 10.

The Patriot's Wife; see *Emilia.*

Patter versus Clatter; burletta by C. J.
Matthews: (38) C.-10.15*, 16, 17, 18,
20.

Paul Clifford; by B. N. Webster: (52)
W.-2.23, 24, 25, 26, 27, 28.

Paul Jones: (50) A.-6.15, 17. See *The
Pilot.*

Paul Jones, the Pilot; see *the Pilot.*

Paul Pry; comedy by John Brougham:
(35) C.-12.21, 26; (37) C.-8.24; (38)
C.-2.9; 3.27; 5.14; (36) A.-3.17;
4.18; (37) A.-5.1; 6.20; (36) W.-
10.4, 22; (39) W.-5.17; 6.6; 10.5,
16; (40) W.-10.22; (37) P.-2.13;
(38) C.-6.8; (39) C.-1.11; 2.21; (40)
N.-10.13; (41) N.-10.8; W.-6.25;
(42) N.-1.6, 7; C.-3.26; 4.28; A.-
8.12; (43) W.-1.19, 26; 2.14; (44)
W.-4.17; 5.27; (45) A.-5.4; (46)
A.-3.23; W.-3.25; P.M.-4.17, 23, 27;
5.16; 7.18; A.-7.20; 8.29; P.M.-9.21,
24; 11.16; (47) A.-4.10, 19; P.M.-

5.31; (48) A.-4.11; 8.3; 10.31; (49) Ath.-1.23; A.-3.10; C.-10.2, (50) A.-6, 10; 8.6; B.-9.16, 17, 20, 21; A.-10.24; (51) B.-6.9, 18; 10.3, 4; (52) A.-4.28; (53) A.-1.5; 9.26, 28; 10.1; 11.19; 12.17; (54) A.-1.16, 28; C.-1.21, 25; A.-2.6; 4.20; C.-5.12, 20; A.-8.31; 9.8, 26, 28; C.M.-10.31; 11.8; 12.9; (55) W.-1.1; C.M.-1.8; 3.21; A.-5.26; 9.22; C.M.-10.6; A.-10.22; 11.6; 12.6.

Paul, the Patriot: (40) W.-4.20.

Paul, the Reprobate, or The Midnight Assassin; domestic drama: (37) W.-1.4*, 6, 7.

Paul Ulric; by Matson: (36) W.-4.30*; 5.3, 4.

Pauline: (51) W.-8.26, 28, 30; 12.26, 27; (53) C.-4.23, 26, 27, 28; A.-10.5, 6, 7, 8, 10, 11, 12, 13, 14.

Pay for Peeping, or A Woman's Failing: (35) W.-2.5; (43) W.-7.21, 22, 27. Farce.

Peaceful Pelton, or the Vermonter: (38) C.-4.7; (43) W.-5.19; (44) A.-12.24; (45) A.-4.16; (50) A.-9.4; (53) W.-9.3.

The Peacock and the Crow; farce: (37) C.-10.23, 24; (50) A.-5.8.

Peculiar Position; farce: (37) W.-7.24*; C.-10.30; 11.1, 9; 12.1.

The Pedlar and the Planter; see *North and South.*

A Peep at Olympus; see *The Flying Machine.*

Peeping in at 6 P.M.: (51) A.-9.10, 11.

Peeping Tom of Coventry; by John O'Keeffe: (39) W.-10.12, 14. Farce.

The Peer and the Peasant; see *Armand.*

Peerless Pool: (51) N.-8.8.

Peggy Green: (54) C.-8.10, 14, 17; (55) A.-9.1, 10, 13.

The Pennsylvania Line; see *Mad Anthony.*

The People's Candidate: (51) A.-7.21, 22.

The People's Lawyer, or Solomon Shingle; by J. S. Jones: (43) W.-1.16*, 17; (45) C.-1.13, 14; 5.3; (50) A.-8.9, 13, 31; 12.2, 6; (51) A.-3.17; 6.10, 18; 10.1, 22; (52) N.-9.11; A.-12.13; (54) C.-1.30; 2.2.

Perfection, or the Maid of Munster; comedy: (35) C.-2.6; 10.3; (36) C.-7.11; (37) C.-1.14, 21; (35) W.-10.5, 14; 12.11; (36) W.-3.7, 18; 5.25; 10.14; 12.9; (37) W.-12.29; (39) W.-5.22; 7.9, 31; 8.20; (36) P.-12.24, 29; (37) P.-2.16; C.-4.26; 9.29; (38) C.-1.16; 5.1; 8.27; 9.4; 10.4; 11.5, 17; (37) A.-6.13; (40) A.-9.17; (39) C.-1.12; 2.4; 3.28; 4.11; 5.24; 6.14; 9.17; 10.24; (40) C.-9.2, 17; 12.21; (39) W.-9.12; 10.31; 11.2; (40) W.-1.14; 5.18; 6.18; 10.30; 11.18; (41) W.-7.21; N.-9.3; W.-10.29; (42) C.-2.14; A.-6.9; 7.6; 10.12; (43) A.-3.4; N.-9.23; (44) W.-1.4; A.-1.9; 7.13; W.-8.1, 2, 30; 9.21; (45) C.-1.22, 23; 2.10; W.-4.5, 28; 6.5; 7.16; (46) W.-1.23; 2.23; 4.18; P.M.-4.22, 24; W.-5.5; P.M.-5.25; 6.17; A.-7.11, 16; P.M.-8.3; (47) W.-2.19; 4.3; 11.8, 27; (48) W.-1.19; 3.3, 6; 4.5; P.M.-7.12; (49) A.-4.5; W.-5.30; 9.12; 10.20; 11.19; (50) W.-1.9; B.-12.13; (51) A.-5.28; 7.18; B.-10.23, 24, 25; (52) A.-5.10; C.-11.15, 20; (53) A.-4.22; C.-7.7, 11; (54) C.-1.23; 2.3; 3.27; 6.22; C.M.-9.29; 10.12; A.-12.29; (55) C.M.-2.6; 3.5; W.-5.31; A.-6.30; 8.30; W.-10.25.

Perkin Warbeck, or The Impostor: (44) W.-2.7, 8, 17.

Persecuted Dutchman: (55) C.-4.5, 18.

Perseus and Andromeda; see *Deep, Deep Sea.*

Personation, or Fairly Taken in: (35) C.-4.13, 20; 9.28; (36) A.-5.18; W.-10.13, 20; 12.8; (50) A.-3.30; 4.12.

The Pet of the Admiral; farce: (40) W.-7.24.

The Pet of the Petticoats, or The Convent: (35) W.-3.7, 10, 12; 4.3; C.-12.16; (40) C.-1.29, 30, 31; 11.23; (41) W.-5.19, 20; (47) P.M.-2.8, 11; (48) P.M.-4.17, 18; (50) C.-5.21, 23; (51) A.-5.2; (54) C.-3.9, 10, 20; 4.24, 25; 7.31; 8.1; 12.4; (55) C.-1.18; W.-5.22, 23, 25; 11.14, 17, 22.

The Pet of the Public; comedy by Edward Sterling: (54) W.-3.30, 31; 4.3; 6.29.

Peter and Paul, or The Mechanic and His Brother: (42) C.-9.28*, 29; 10.12, 13; (47) P.M.-1.20, 21.

Peter Bell, the Wagoner: (40) N.-11.7*, 14; (42) N.-1.8; A.-9.20; (43) W.-4.1, 6.

Peter my Pipkin; farce: (39) W.-6.7.

Peter Smink; by J. H. Payne: (46) P.M.-12.16, 19; (47) P.M.-1.8.

Peter the Great, and The Dutch Burgomaster: (39) W.-14.1*, 2, 8, 15; 5.22; 10.7, 8; (40) W.-1.22; N.-12.15, 17; (41) N.-12.1; (42) A.-8.10; (46) A.-3.3; (47) A.-3.25, 29; 7.19; 12.3.

Peter White: (45) C.-9.22; 11.1; see also *Mrs. White and Mrs. Peter White.*

Peter Wilkins: (43) W.-5.6, 8, 9, 10, 11, 12, 16, 19; (46) A.-2.28; 3.2, 5; 6.26.

The Petticoat Colonel; see *Venus in Arms.*

Petticoat Government; farce: (37) A.-6.29, 30; 7.1.

The Phantom of the Village; see *Somnambulist.*

The Phantom Pilot: (43) W.-4.27.

The Phantom Ship; see *The Flying Dutchman.*

Phenomenon in a Smock Frock: (54) C.-7.1, 7; 11.1.

The Philadelphia Apprentices; see *Warning Dream.*

Philadelphia as it Is: (41) W.-1.8, 9, 11, 12, 14; 2.11; (42) W.-2.3; (49) C.-9.26, 27, 28.

Philadelphia Assurance; by S. S. Steele: (41) A.-12.6*, 7, 8, 9, 10, 11, 14, 15, 16; (42) A.-4.28; C.-11.29.

Philadelphia Boys and Girls in 1776; national drama: (50) C.-7.4, 5, 6, 10.

Philadelphia Directory; farce: (49) A.-12.29*; (50) A.-1.12.

Philadelphia Fireman, or Bravery Rewarded: (40) W.-3.9*; (51) N.-8.12; (52) A.-5.1, 3, 4; N.-8.27; (53) W.-2.7; 3.12.

Philadelphia Fireman, or The Chesnut Street Heiress: (50) C.-1.19*, 20, 22, 23, 24, 25, 26, 28, 29, 30, 31; 2.1, 2, 19, 21; (53) C.-6.11; (55) C.-2.21.

Philadelphia in Spots; comedy: (48) A.-12.25*, 27, 28, 29, 30; (49) A.-1.1, 2, 3, 4, 5, 6.

Philadelphia Merchant: (47) A.-2.15, 16.

Philip Quarl: (48) A.-7.4.

Philip de France and Marie de Meranie; historical play by J. W. Marston: (51) A.-4.4*, 7.

Phillip Quarl and his Monkey: (41) A.-1.1; (45) A.-11.21; (46) A.-7.4; (47) P.M.-7.7.

Physiognomist: (49) A.-3.14.

Pickwick Club, or The Age we Live in: (37) W.-7.31*; 8.1, 2, 3, 5; (42) A.-8.13; see also *Sam Weller.*

The Picnic, or A Party of Pleasure by Water: (36) C.-12.19*, 21; (37) C.-1.24, 28; 3.10, 14; 8.26; (38) C.-2.17; W.-3.15; (47) A.-6.21.

A Picture on the Other Side of Jordan to Uncle Tom's Cabin; see *Cabin and Parlor.*

Pierre Gamouche, the Duck Vender: (49) P.M.-7.9*.

The Pig and the Piper; see *Mother Shipton.*

The Pilgrim of Love; comedy: (51) A.-11.10, 11, 12; (52) C.-2.2, 5; W.-10.18.

Pilgrim's Progress: (55) C.-3.19, 20, 21, 22, 23, 24, 26, 27.

The Pilot, or A Tale of the Sea, or The Stars and Stripes Triumphant; by W. H. Wallack: (36) W.-11.23, 26; (37) W.-1.25; 11.30; (38) W.-7.30; 9.3, 8; (39) W.-4.13; 5.16; 6.14; C.-5.7; (40) W.-3.27; 4.27; (41) W.-1.8; 6.16; A.-6.1, 3; 8.13; W.-6.18; (42) W.-1.15, 20; 3.14; A.-6.14, 15; 7.1, 21; 10.8; (43) W.-6.22; (45) W.-8.12, 13; A.-10.8; 11.29; (48) A.-2.12; 10.16; (51) A.-2.27; (55) C.-4.18.

The Pilot of the German Ocean; see *The Pilot.*

The Pilot of the Ocean; see *The Pilot.*

The Pink of Politeness: (44) W.-1.17, 18; 3.19; 4.2.

The Pirate Boy; opera, by J. B. Phillips: (37) C.-3.13*, 14, 16, 17, 18, 20, 22.

The Pirate Chief and the Seaman's Daughter; see *Laid up in Port.*

The Pirate Dey, or Freedom's Jubilee: (44) W.-5.24, 25.

The Pirate of the Atlantic: (41) W.-2.18, 19, 20, 25.

The Pirate of the Capes; see *Koeuba.*

The Pirate of the East; see *Arab Chief.*

The Pirate of the Isles; see *Prince Lee Boo.*

The Pirate's Home; see *La Fitte.*

The Pirate's Legacy: (52) A.-1.2, 3; (55) C.M.-12.17.

Pitcairn's Island: (35) W.-9.15, 16, 21.

Pizarro, or The Spaniards in Peru; tragedy by R. B. Sheridan: (35) W.-1.10; 7.3; 9.7; 11.24; 12.30; C.-9.14; 11.30; (36) C.-11.2; W.-1.29; 2.19; 5.17; 10.26; A.-3.12; P.-12.16; (37) C.-11.25; W.-7.28; A.-5.11; (38) C.-3.15; W.-7.6; (39) C.-1.7; 12.9; W.-7.9; 8.9, 27, 30; (40) C.-1.2; W.-1.8; 3.28; 5.4; N.-10.30; (41) A.-4.17; 5.22; 8.12; C.-10.8; W.-3.8; 5.11; N.-10.23; W.-5.13; 6.17; 9.4, 7; (42) W.-2.2; 3.17; A.-3.30; 6.11; W.-5.27; A.-10.5, 15, 29; (43) W.-4.29; 6.10; A.-8.28; N.-9.25; A.-9.27; N.-9.30; C.-12.1, 26; (44) A.-6.14; W.-6.29; 9.19; C.-11.14; (45) W.-3.29; 5.10; 7.25; 8.19; A.-10.9; 12.18; (46) W.-1.10; 4.4; 5.2, 14; A.-7.9; 10.17; W.-12.3, 24; (47) W.-1.15; 3.19; A.-4.24, 26; W.-5.21; 6.26; A.-8.17; 11.12, 17; (48) W.-1.8; 2.16; A.-4.4; W.-4.13, 19; A.-7.1, 20; C.-7.27; A.-10.7; W.-11.18; 12.9; (49) A.-1.16; 3.24; W.-5.12; A.-8.25; C.-9.18; 10.20; 11.1; (50) C.-2.6; 4.27; A.-5.15; C.-6.7; A.-7.18; C.-7.24; (51) B.-4.5; A.-5.23; W.-9.13; A.-10.9; (52) W.-1.12; A.-3.22; C.-5.31; W.-6.7; C.-6.10; 7.17; A.-8.28; (52) A.-11.12; (53) A.-2.11; C.-3.4; 4.6; A.-6.1; W.-10.14; (54) C.-4.8; N.-6.17; W.-10.10; (55) A.-3.12, 14, 15, 16, 17, 21; W.-4.10; C.M.-11.12; A.-12.10, 11; W.-12.11, 15.

The Place Hunter: (40) N.-10.28; 11.19, 30; (41) N.-1.12; (44) W.-1.22, 25; 2.28; 7.17; 8.6, 7.

The Plains of Chippewa: (39) W.-7.4; (44) N.-4.1; see also *The Battle of Chippewa.*

The Planter and His Dogs: (35) W.-6.19, 20; (46) A.-7.23.

Planter's Pest: (52) A.-4.2, 3, 14.

[632]

Platonic Attachment; farce: (50) W.-11.18*, 19, 23; 12.13; (51) W.-2.15; B.-4.23, 24, 25, 26.

Playing False; see *Life in the West.*

Pleasant Dreams; farce: (35) A.-2.26; 3.6, 16; C.-4.14, 28; 6.15; (36) A.-3.28; 4.27; C.-1.26; (37) A.-5.19; (42) W.-12.30; (43) W.-1.20.

Pleasant Neighbors; farce: (37) C.-4.8*, 11, 17, 19, 28; 8.30; 10.5; 11.16, 28; (38) C.-1.31; (37) A.-6.5, 10; (40) A.-9.15; (41) A.-4.6, 9; 6.17, 24; (37) W.-11.28; 12.6; (38) W.-1.24; 4.2, 3, 4; (40) W.-6.16; 7.9; (41) W.-9.2; (38) C.-2.24; 10.22; 11.24; (41) C.-10.18, 21; (40) N.-11.12; (41) W.-9.29; 11.11; (42) W.-4.1; A.-4.18; W.-4.20; A.-5.2, 6; A.-5.26; W.-6.23; (44) W.-10.1, 2; (45) W.-4.16; 5.7; A.-7.9; C.-9.17; (46) P.M.-3.21; W.-9.16; 10.21, 30; P.M.-11.4; W.-11.26; (47) W.-1.4; 3.30; P.M.-5.5, 10; A.-5.15; W.-6.4, 25, 30; P.M.-6.10; A.-6.30; 7.1; P.M.-7.8; W.-10.13; 11.4; 12.29; (48) W.-3.7; (50) W.-1.16, 28, 29; (51) A.-3.1; B.-4.1; A.-7.4; C.-9.12; (52) C.-3.3, 26; 4.1; (54) W.-3.6, 7, 14, 24; 11.4; (55) W.-1.8, 9.

The Pledge of Truth; see *The Conscripts.*

Plot and Counterplot; comedy by Charles Kemble: (38) W.-3.19; (39) W.-4.8, 12.

Plot and Passion; by Tom Taylor: (54) A.-5.1*, 2, 3, 5, 6, 11; 6.13; (55) A.-12.3, 4, 7.

The Plot Discovered; see *Venice Preserved.*

Plots, or Love in All Disguises: (39) W.-10.9, 10.

The Ploughman Turned Lord; see *Fortune's Frolic.*

Pocahontas, or The Indian Princess, or The Settlement of Virginia; by G. W. P. Custis: (36) W.-6.25; 7.1;

(46) W.-6.23; (47) W.-7.5; 8.21.

The Point of Honor; by Charles Kemble: (35) C.-1.27; 4.29; (36) C.-8.24; 12.29; W.-6.18; (37) C.-2.2; 8.23; (38) C.-6.23; (40) W.-4.1; (42) A.-6.18; (45) W.-8.29; 9.6; 10.10; (47) W.-8.18; (48) W.-3.15; (49) Ath.-1.17; (54) A.-10.4, 28; 12.1.

The Poles and Tartars; see *Lodoiska.*

Polichinel: (43) C.-10.14.

The Polish Heroine; see *Emilie Plater.*

Palkamania, or Dancing for a Million: (45) W.-2.20, 21, 22, 28; 5.24; 6.17; 7.23; 8.4. Burletta.

Pongo, or The Brazilian Ape; pantomime: (36) C.-12.30*, 31; (37) C.-2.2.

The Poodle Collar; see *Captain Stevens.*

Poor Cousin Walter; comedy by J. P. Simpson: (50) A.-9.26, 27; 10.2; (51) B.-9.22, 23, 24, 25, 26, 27; (54) A.-4.6, 7, 10, 14.

Poor Dog Tray; see *The Disowned and his Poor Dog Tray.*

Poor Gentleman; by George Colman the Elder: (35) C.-11.25; (36) C.-1.9; 7.11; 11.7; A.-5.28; P.-12.2; (37) C.-4.12; (38) W.-3.21; (39) W.-5.8; C.-5.9; (40) C.-3.20; (41) C.-3.2; 12.17; N.-6.19; (42) C.-5.10; (44) W.-2.17, 20; (45) W.-3.3; A.-12.24, 26; (46) C.-1.12; A.-3.31; W.-8.14; (47) A.-2.8; 5.21; W.-7.2; A.-8.2; W.-8.10; (48) A.-4.24; W.-7.27; A.-12.18; (49) Ath.-1.22; W.-4.5; A.-10.1; C.-10.23; A.-12.27; (50) A.-10.22; (51) A.-6.20; C.-9.3; A.-10.3; (53) A.-3.21; C.-8.30; A.-9.1; C.-12.15; (54) C.-2.7; W.-5.2, 17; 6.22; C.-11.7; (55) C.M.-1.26; A.-4.10, 26; C.M.-9.11, 14, 27.

A Poor Girl's Story: (50) A.-12.21, 23, 26; (51) A.-1.9.

Pride of the Ocean: (44) N.-3.9, 11, 12; (49) C.-11.14.

Prima Donna; comedy by D. Boucicault: (53) W.-3.21*; (54) C.-5.4.

The Prince and the Notary; see *Fleur de Marie.*

Prince Lee Boo, or The Pirate of the Isles; by Milner: (36) A.-4.9, 11; C.-6.25, 27; 9.16.

The Printer's Apprentice: (44) A.-7.8, 11, 12, 13, 16, 17, 20; (51) A.-9.4, 6. See also *Der Pariser Taugenichts,* a separate play.

The Printer's Devil: (47) P.M.-7.17.

The Prison; a comedy in four parts by R. Benedia: (55) G.N.-8.24.

The Prize, or 2538; (by Prince Hoare) (40) W.-11.16; (42) N.-1.22.

The Prodigal Son; see *Azael.*

The Prodigals; see *Disowned.*

The Progress of an Intemperate; see *Emigration.*

The Promissory Note, or The Effects of Endorsing; farce: (35) W.-7.1; (38) W.-8.6; C.-1.23; 2.17; (42) A.-7.16, 22; (49) A.-12.10; (51) C.-3.21, 27; 12.8, 9, 11, 24.

The Proof of the Pudding is the Eating; see *Hotel.*

The Prophecy; by M. B. Fowler: (48) A.-8.5, 7, 8.

The Prophet of St. Paul's; by D. P. Brown: (37) W.-3.20*, 21.

The Prophet of the Haunted Moor; see *Fire-Raiser.*

The Protean Statue; see *Black and White.*

The Provoked Husband, or A Journey to London; comedy by Colley Cibber: (35) C.-1.9; 4.16; 5.25; (37) C.-1.4; 4, 25; (40) C.-3.3; (41) C.-10.5; (42) C.-11.23; (45) W.-2.13; (54) A.-11.15, 18, 27, 30; (55) A.-9.25.

The Provost of Bruges: (36) A.-6.11*; (37) C.-11.1.

The Provost of Paris, or The Truand Chief: (40) A.-9.7*, 8, 9, 10, 18; (51) A.-5.21; N.-7.21; W.-8.22, 23; (52) A.-3.3; 5.12; N.-5.24.

Puritans; see *Il Puritani.*

The Purse; by James C. Cross: (36) W.-1.7, 8; 2.26; C.-10.19; (40) W.-6.30; (42) A.-4.8, 13, 30.

Puss in Boots: (41) N.-6.18, 21, 22, 23, 24.

Putnam, or The Eagle Eye and Hand of Steel; national drama by N. H. Bannister: (44) W.-9.21*, 23, 24, 25, 26, 27, 28, 30; A.-9.23, 24, 25, 26, 27, 28, 30; W.-10.1, 2, 3, 4, 5, 7, 8, 9, 10, 11, 12, 14, 15, 16, 17, 18, 19, 21, 22, 23, 24, 25, 26, 28; A.-10.1, 2, 3, 4, 5, 7, 12; W.-11.9, 11, 12, 13, 14, 15, 16, 18; (45) A.-4.5, 9, 10, 11, 12; (46) W.-7.13, 14, 15, 16, 17, 18; (49) A.-4.30; 5.1, 2, 3, 4, 5; (54) N.-6.23, 24, 26, 27; 7.4.

The Quadroone, or A Legend of Louisiana: (41) N.-3.31.

Quadripeds of Quidlemberg; burlesque: (36) A.-3.25; 4.21, 22; C.-7.7, 9; (37) A.-5.2, 3, 4; (38) C.-4.16, 17; (42) W.-6.20, 21.

The Quaker; musical farce (by Charles Dibdin): (36) C.-1.29; (38) C.-6.27; 7.6; (40) C.-11.5.

Quaker City, or A Romance of Life, Mystery and Crime: (44) C.-11.11*.

Quaker Girls: (42) A.-8.13, 27.

The Queen and the Breeches Maker; see *The Duddlestones.*

Queen of the Abruzzi: (50) C.-5.27, 28; 6.3; 7.3.

Queen of the Scots; see *Mary Stuart.*

The Queen's Horse: (39) W.-7.19, 20, 26.

The Queen's Husband: (52) C.-3.31; 4.5, 20, 21, 23; 5.4, 17, 22, 25.

The Queen's Own: (52) A.-8.24; 9.28; 11.9.

Queen'sbury Fête: (52) W.-3.15, 16; (55) A.-11.19, 21; 12.3, 19.

Queer Dilemmas; comedy: (49) A.-3.16, 17.

Queer Neighbors, or The Party Wall: (35) C.-6.1, 11, 19; (36) C.-2.4; A.-4.30.

Queer Subject; farce: (37) W.-7.24, 25, 26; 8.3, 9, 17; 12.5; (38) W.-2.9, 16; 3.2; (43) A.-4.6, 8.

Quid pro Quo; comedy: (44) A.-8.20, 21, 22, 23.

A Quiet Day; farce (by W. E. Burton): (38) C.-3.29*; 4.2, 9; (40) W.-3.19, 20, 25; 4.15; (50) C.-5.1, 2, 6, 13.

Quite at Home: (36) W.-11.28*; 12.19.

Race Course, or Sporting Made Easy: (43) W.-2.15, 16, 17; 4.1; (45) A.-5.28; 6.4.

Rafael, the Libertine; comedy: (39) C.-3.27*, 28; 4.30; 5.3.

The Rag Picker of Paris: (48) A.-12.23*, 24, 25, 27, 28; (49) A.-1.1, 2, 3, 4; 6.6, 7; 10.26; 11.20; (51) A.-1.20, 21, 22, 23; (52) A.-11.23, 24, 25; (53) A.-4.30; 5.2, 3.

Rail Road Depot: (40) A.-12.7; (41) W.-2.8, 13; 3.8; 4.3, 24; 5.24; 6.15; 10.4, 30; 11.6; (42) W.-2.7, 11; 3.23, 30; 10.17; 11.30; (43) C.-12.15.

Railway Mania: (45) C.-12.31; (46) C.-1.2.

Raising the Wind; comedy: (35) C.-11.17; W.-12.8; (36) C.-9.8; 10.5; W.-3.8; P.-11.7; (37) C.-3.13; P.-1.18; C.-8.25; 9.19; (38) C.-5.24; 8.30; (39) W.-7.2; 9.9; C.-4.8; 5.10; 15; (41) N.-11.3; (42) A.-3.30; 6.24; (43) A.-9.9; 10.11; (45) A.-10.20; W.-11.29; 12.4; (46) A.-9.2; P.M.-9.4; A.-10.10; (47) A.-2.11, 12; 10.6, 8, 26; (48) A.-5.8; 8.9, 29; 10.9, 28; (51) C.-3.8; (53) C.-5.19; (54) C.-1.28; 2.2.

The Rake's Progress, or Three Degrees of Loafing: (35) W.-1.10, 13, 14; (39) W.-4.3, 4; (41) N.-3.6, 8; (42) A.-7.18, 19; (43) A.-9.30; (44) A.-8.8; 12.14; (45) A.-3.25; (46) A.-3.30; (47) A.-4.3, 6; (48) A.-3.14, 18; 10.21; (50) C.-1.24; A.-6.13; 11.1, 2; (51) N.-7.15; (52) N.-7.29; (53) A.-6.18; (54) N.-6.8.

Ransom, or A Father's Return from Slavery: (36) W.-9.3*, 5; C.-10.22, 24, 26; (37) C.-1.3, 4; 4.28; (38) C.-5.3; 8.29; 11.15; (39) C.-2.26; (40) C.-2.25; (41) W.-2.6, 11; 4.17, 21; (42) C.-23; (46) P.M.-10.26, 27; (47) P.M.-4.20; 5.26; A.-12.10, 11, 14.

The Ranz des Vache; see *Home, Sweet Home.*

Raphael's Dream: (41) N.-9.6, 7, 9; (47) P.M.-7.9, 29; A.-9.17, 18.

Rascal Jack; burletta: (44) W.-11.23, 25; (47) A.-8.9, 10, 11, 12, 21; (48) A.-6.26; (49) A.-8.17; C.-11.29; (50) W.-2.25, 26; 3.9, 30; 6.26, 29; 12.21, 31; (51) W.-1.15, 25; 2.8, 24; 4.19; 5.28; 6.11.

Raymond and Agnes; see *Forest of Rosenwald.*

A Real Down East Muster; see *Militia Training.*

Rebel Chief: (43) A.-12.18, 19, 20, 21, 22, 23, 25; (44) A.-1.2; (46) A.-6.20, 26; (48) A.-7.7, 8.

The Rebellion of '98; see *Ireland's Curse.*

Recruiting Officer; by George Farquhar: (43) W.-4.6, 7.

The Recusant: (54) C.-10.25*, 26.

Red Cross Knights: (45) A.-9.8, 9, 10.

The Red Mask; (by John Brougham): (41) A.-5.24. See also *The Bravo.*

Red Riding Hood; see *Little Red Riding Hood.*

Red Gauntlet; national drama: (42) C.-11.2*.

Red Riever: (50) C.-7.17.

Red Riven, or The Freebooter's Ride; melodrama: (46) A.-2.9.

The Red Rover, or The Meeting of the Dolphin; by S. H. Chapman: (52) N.-7, 26.

Redwood; by J. P. Addams: (43) N.-11.24*; (45) A.-11.12.

The Reefer's Log; see *Tom Cringle.*

The Regent of France: (35) W.-3.28; 4.1.

The Reiver of Perth; see *Gilderoy.*

Remorse, or The Bankrupt's Wife; tragedy by J. H. Payne; advertised as new: (49) A.-3.30, 31; 4.2, 3; (50) A.-10.14, 16; (52) A.-10.22, 25.

Removing the Deposites; by H. J. Finn: (3) W.-10.10*.

Rendezvous, or All in the Dark: (35) C.-4.27; 5.13; 6.17; 9.16; 11.10; (36) P.-11.11; (37) C.-3.15, 17; (38) C.-11.7, 12, 17; (37) A.-5.12; (43) C.-1.10, 11, 14, 20; 2.4, 11; A.-8.18; (44) A.-1.20; W.-3.22; 6.1; 8.9; (45) W.-4.22; 7.5, 24; 8.5; (46) W.-1.31; P.M.-3.23; 6.20; 11.13, 26; 12.1; (47) P.M.-2.6, 23; 5.15; W.-6.8, 24; 8.19; (48) P.M.-3.17; (49) Ath.-1.13; (50) W.-2.14, 19; 3.7, 27; (51) C.-8.22, 23; (52) C.-8.18.

Renegade's Horse: (54) N.-6.28, 29.

The Rent Day; by D. W. Jerrold: (35) C.-2.20; 9.15, 18; W.-4.6; (36) C.-1.5, 14; 8.22; W.-2.17; P.-11.9; C.-11.15; (37) A.-5.27; (38) W.-10.30; (39) W.-2.8; C.-1.5; 2.16; 4.26; 8.24; 12.17; W.-5.9; 8.17; (41) C.-10.8; A.-5.5; N.-1.27; 9.8, 29, 30; (42) C.-2.7; 3.24; A.-4.18; (43) A.-12.15; (44) A.-6.3; (45) C.-11.28; W.-12.30; (46) W.-1.27; 3.10, 19; 4.28; A.-5.12, 18, 26; 10.16, 17; (47) W.-10.29; (49) Ath.-1.4; (50) C.-6.21; B.-12.5; (51) A.-3.7.

Repeal, or The Dog Star of Ireland: (44) N.-2.8, 9; W.-2.10.

The Reprobate, or The Death Token: (50) C.-4.29

The Republican: (52) W.-12.14.

Retribution, or Blackbourne the Avenger; tragedy in five acts by George Bennett: (50) W.-8.28, 29, 31; 10.8, 10; A.-12.9, 10, 11; (51) W.-4.30; 5.1; 12.23; (52) W.-2.7.

Retribution, or The Drunkard's Wife: (50) B.-8.19.

The Revenge; tragedy by Edward Young: (41) C.-9.14; (49) A.-4.16.

The Review, or Wags of Windsor; farce by George Colman the younger: (35) C.-1.23; (36) C.-10.13; 11.23; (37) C.-2.22; (35) W.-5.29; 11.13; (37) W.-2.22; 7.22; 12.16; (36) A.-6.11; (37) A.-5.12; (41) A.-6.10; (37) P.-1.24; 2.1; (38) W.-2.2; 7.16; (39) W.-2.22; 3.4; 5.14; 7.3, 6; (40) W.-2.28; 6.27; 10.23; (41) W.-5.14, 18; (40) N.-11.20; (41) N.-12.21; (42) C.-2.2; W.-4.6; 9.30; (43) W.-6.1; (44) W.-1.24; 9.17; C.-11.30; 12.14, 17; (45) A.-12.1; (46) A.-7.24; (47) P.M.-4.13, 14; (48) A.-3.16; (51) C.-6.10; (52) A.-9.24; (53) C.-1.29; (54) W.-6.2, 3.

The Revolt of the Arabs: (42) C.-11.16, 17, 18.

The Revolt of the Harem; grand ballet: (45) W.-3.10, 11, 12, 13, 14, 15, 17, 18, 19, 20, 21, 22.

The Revolution, or The Patriots of '76; (by Charles Burke): (50) A.-8.27*, 29; (51) A.-6.16, 17; 11.1, 17; (52) A.-12.18; (53) A.-1.7; C.-2.4.

Rhyme and Reason: (35) C.-10.17, 23.

The Rich and Poor of New York; see *Democracy and Aristocracy.*

The Rich Jew of Frankfort; see *Dream of Fate.*

The Rich Poor Man: (38) W.-4.23, 24.

Richard Hurdis and the Idiot Girl; see *Avenger of Blood.*

Richard of the Lion Heart; see *Hermit's Prophecy.*

Richard the Lion-Hearted; see *Hermit's Prophecy.*

Richard III, or The Battle of Bosworth Field; by William Shakespeare: (35) W.-2.21; 3.6, 7, 21; 6.2, 6, 25, 26; 8.22, 27; C.-4.21; 7.4; W.-11.7, 21; (37) C.-10.31; 11.21; 12.5; (38) C.-1.17; (36) W.-1.11, 15, 16, 18; 3.30; A.-5.16; W.-5.26; 6.3, 9; 9.9, 13; 10.8; 12.17; P.-12.6, 21; (37) A.-5.25; (40) A.-12.12, 14, 19; (41) A.-4.8; 10.9; (37) P.-1.31; 2.23; (37) W.-1.24; 6.17, 21; 7.11, 15; 11.16; 12.11, 15; (38) W.-1.31; 2.3, 15; 7.14; 8.3; 10.12, 27; 11.17; (39) W.-4.18; 6.3, 22, 24; (38) C.-6.1, 11; 9.10; (39) C.-10.5; 12.30; (40) C.-4.17; 9.25; (39) W.-7.4; (40) W.-3.12, 16; 4.3; 6.10, 17, 25; 12.21, 25; (41) W.-3.6; 9.11; (40) N.-10.14; (41) N.-12.14; W.-9.15; A.-10.12; (42) W.-2.26; 3.30; 4.6, 18; A.-4.26, 30; 5.26; 8.18; W.-10.13; C.-11.14, 19; W.-12.1, 24; (43) W.-1.10; A.-3.21, 28; 4.4; W.-4.18; A.-4.24; 5.6; A.-9.6, 28; N.-9.29; A.-10.10; C.-11.24; W.-10.19, 24; C.-11.9; (45) W.-3.31; 4.5; A.-4.30; 5.1; N.-5.10; W.-5.24, 30; A.-12.20; (46) A.-2.17, 18, 25; W.-5.12, 15; A.-7.11; 9.21, 22, 23, 24, 25, 26, 28; A.-10.1, 31; (47) W.-1.16; A.-2.2, 3; W.-2.22, 23, 24, 26, 27; 3.1, 2; 4.21; 9.24; A.-11.20, 27; 12.20; (48) A.-1.18; 3.11; W.-3.11; C.-7.11, 15; A.-8.9; (49) A.-1.15; 4.9; C.-9.15, 19; 10.6, 11; A.-12.17; (50) W.-1.7, 9; C.-2.14; A.-5.18; 12.12; (51) B.-3.3, 8, 15; A.-3.8; W.-5.22, 24; A.-10.13; W.-10.25; C.-11.24; (52) W.-1.10; C.-1.14, 22; A.-4.20; 11.13; W.-11.29; (53) A.-1.12; C.-3.26; W.-11.26; (54) C.-9.6; W.-10.28; C.-12.13; (55) W.-4.14, 17; C.M.-

5.21, 26; 6.2; W.-10.9; C.M.-10.23; 11.9, 10; A.-12.18; W.-12.20.

Richard Turpin: (41) A.-1.25, 26; 9.11, 13, 14, 15, 16, 17; (42) A.-5.16, 17, 18, 19.

Richard ye Thirde: (44) W.-11.28, 29, 30; (45) W.-1.7, 8, 9, 11; (47) A.-8.19; (48) A.-6.19, 20, 21; (49) A.-9.4; C.-11.26, 27; (50) W.-3.19, 20, 23; 4.2.

Richard's Wanderings; comedy in four parts by Kettel: (55) G.N.-9.8.

Richelieu, or The Conspiracy; by Edward Bulwer-Lytton: (39) C.-5.13*, 21; 11.21, 23, 27; 12.6; (40) C.-2.26; 3.6; 9.21, 30; (39) W.-9.24, 25, 26, 28, 30; 11.25, 26; 12.3, 7; (40) W.-4.29; 5.1; 6.27; C.-11.27; A.-12.17; (41) A.-4.9, 13, 27; 5.27; 6.7; N.-10.19, 20; 12.21; (42) W.-2.24; A.-4.13; C.-4.14; A.-8.17; 10.20; W.-10.20; 11.3; (43) W.-5.30; C.-10.27, 28; N.-10.28; C.-11.2; N.-11.2; (44) N.-3.8; W.-8.28; 9.13; 12.4; (45) W.-5.8, 16; A.-9.17; (46) A.-7.15; W.-7.30; 10.22; A.-12.8; W.-12.21; (47) W.-1.5; 3.19; 5.14; A.-8.12; 9.28; 11.4; W.-11.5; (48) A.-2.9; W.-11.17, 25; A.-11.25; W.-12.1; (49) W.-5.17; 6.4; A.-8.22; C.-9.20; (50) A.-3.7, 26; (51) A.-2.20; B.-3.29; 4.1; A.-4.15; 7.31; W.-10.7, 10; (52) C.-3.4; A.-3.23; W.-6.9, 22; A.-9.14; N.-9.24; A.-11.8; W.-11.16; (53) W.-4.8; 5.31; 10.10, 18; (54) W.-10.11, 18; (55) C.-2.13; C.M.-3.31; C.-4.13; C.M.-4.16; 5.24; 11.8; A.-11.24, 28; W.-12.12, 20.

Richelieu in Love: (44) A.-7.27, 29, 30, 31.

Riches, or The City Madam; by Philip Massinger: (50) W.-12.10, 26; (51) W.-5.2.

Riches, or The Wife and Brother: (37) W.-12.16; (38) W.-2.16; (44) W.-6.7; (46) W.-2.24.

The Richmond Market; see *Martha Rienzi;* by Edward Bulwer-Lytton: (36) W.-2.15, 26; (38) W.-9.10; (47) W.-5.3, 4.

The Riever's Ransom, or Days of Old: (36) C.-12.31; (43) C.-1.12. See also *Gilderoy.*

The Rifle Brigade: (54) W.-11.17.

Right and Wrong; see *Rival Valets.*

Right Must Win at Last: (50) A.-8.15.

Rights of Women: (54) C.-10.31; 11.3; (55) C.M.-5.5, 9.

Rinaldo Rinaldini, or The Bandit's Daughter; (by William Dunlap): (36) P.-11.16, 17, 18, 19; (37) P.-1.2, 6.

Ringdoves: (49) A.-5.7, 8, 9, 30; 11.16.

Rip Van Winkle, or The Legend of the Catskill Mountains; (by John Kerr): (36) W.-3.31; (41) W.-3.13; (37) C.-2.10, 14; 9.2; (38) C.-4.11; 9.5; (40) C.-5.29; (41) N.-9.2; (42) C.-3.31; W.-12.1; (43) A.-8.31; (44) A.-11.14, 16, 21; (45) C.-9.13; A.-9.29; 10.4; (46) W.-8.4, 8; (49) W.-3.22; 12.18, 19; (50) A.-8.16, 19; (51) A.-6.13, 14; 10.27; 11.18; (52) A.-12.17; C.-2.3.

The Rise of the Rothschilds; (by W. E. Burton): (42) N.-1.27*.

The Rival Chieftains in Mexico: (52) A.-12.31*.

The Rival Fakirs: (46) C.-1.9, 10, 12, 13.

The Rival Jim Crows: (46) A.-2.13.

Rival Lovers: (41) A.-10.16.

Rival Pages; farce: (37) W.-7.7*, 17, 21; 8.12, 15, 28; 11.16; (44) W.-12.13; (46) P.M.-8.29; 9.16; (49) P.M.-6.27, 28, 29; (53) C.-6.9, 18; (54) C.-7.31.

The Rivals, or A Trip to Bath; by R. B. Sheridan: (35) C.-5.2; 12.17; (36) C.-9.29; 10.11; 11.8; A.-3.14; (37) A.-5.10; C.-9.18; (40) C.-5.6; W.-3.5; 10.17; N.-8.31; (41) C.-12.13;

N.-2.17, 27; (42) N.-1.10; A.-7.27; W.-9.24; C.-11.1; (43) W.-4.11; 9.15; (44) W.-1.13; 4.13; 5.20; A.-8.14; W.-11.19; (45) W.-2.5, 6; A.-4.18; (46) C.-1.8; W.-6.29; 8.18; (47) P.M.-2.26; A.-4.22; W.-8.16; (48) A.-6.15; W.-7.25; (51) C.-9.4; (52) W.-3.25; A.-12.20; (53) W.-1.21, 26; A.-3.28; C.-6.7; 9.1; A.-9.2; (54) C.-1.19, 27; A.-2.10; W.-6.21; (55) W.-1.3; A.-3.9; C.M.-3.20; A.-4.13; C.M.-4.26; N.-6.14.

The Rival Queens; see *Alexander the Great.*

The Rival Soldiers; see *Sprigs of Laurel.*

The Rival Valets, or Right and Wrong: (39) C.-1.8, 9; 2.23; 4.18, 26; 9.10, 20; (40) C.-3.10, 18.

The River God; farce: (45) W.-1.24, 28; 3.1; 4.11, 18, 24; 6.4.

The Road to Ruin; comedy by Thomas Holcroft: (35) C.-6.3; (36) C.-1.20; 11.11; (37) C.-9.23; (38) C.-5.18; (39) C.-3.27; (41) C.-12.15; (42) A.-9.22; W.-11.5; (44) W.-5.4; (47) A.-9.8; (52) C.-9.23; (53) C.-1.6; A.-4.28, 29; 12.8, 12; (54) A.-6.17; 9.18; 11.28; (55) W.-5.5.

Rob Roy MacGregor; (by Isaac Pocock): (35) C.-12.15; (36) C.-2.4; 8.23; 10.12; P.-12.22; (37) C.-10.30; 12.19; (38) C.-2.1; 3.2; (39) W.-7.16; (40) W.-1.4; 4.2; 11.27; (41) W.-6.11; 9.9, 14; (40) N.-11.12, 14; (41) N.-1.23; A.-5.19; (42) W.-2.4; A.-6.4; W.-6.14; A.-6.17; C.-9.21; A.-10.21; W.-12.6; (43) C.-1.6; W.-4.29; 6.15; N.-12.15; (44) A.-6.10, 13; 9.3; 10.22; (45) C.-2.5; A.-4.19; C.-5.7; N.-5.7; W.-5.14; 7.30; A.-8.14; W.-8.30; 10.11; C.-11.25; (46) A.-4.30; 10.13; 11.2, 13; (48) A.-3.28; W.-6.30; (49) A.-1.11; W.-6.20; (50) C.-2.21; 7.8, 22; (51) B.-4.4; W.-5.21; N.-8.9; W.-8.23; 9.18;

A.-10.15; C.-11.29; W.-12.6; C.-12.16; (52) A.-9.15, 18; 11.11; (53) A.-2.10; C.-2.19; 6.11; (54) C.-8.30; C.M.-10.30; 11.6; (55) C.M.-1.13; 2.6; W.-5.26; C.M.-6.7, 21; W.-6.9.

The Robber Chieftain; "written by a gentleman of Philadelphia": (37) W.-3.24*.

The Robber of the Rhine; see *Schinderhannes.*

The Robber Clans of the Lochs; see *Clandare.*

The Robbers, or The Forest of Bohemia; by Schiller: (42) N.-1.13, 22; W.-2.14, 15; A.-4.5, 7, 28; (43) A.-9.3; N.-11.10; (45) N.-5.3, 5; (47) W.-1.2; (48) W.-4.5, 15; (49) W.-3.28, 31; 5.9; 12.29; (50) C.-7.29; A.-9.28; W.-12.28, 31; (51) A.-3.27; C.-4.7; 12.31; (52) C.-1.3; (53) C.-2.26; 3.2; 6.18; W.-12.5, 6, 8, 10; (54) C.M.-11.18, 20, 21; C.M.-12.22; (55) C.M.-4.7, 19; W.-5.29; C.M.-11.28; 12.1.

The Robber's Wife, or The Coiners; by Isaac Pocock: (35) W.-10.29; (37) P.-2.14; (39) W.-5.4; 7.22; 12.35; (42) C.-3.11; A.-4.16, 22; 6.27; (43) A.-3.27; 4.1; (44) C.-10.21; (45) W.-8.27, 28; 10.9, 24; (48) P.M.-4.3, 25; (50) C.-3.9, 13; A.-7.5, 6; (51) A.-11.25; 12.3; (52) A.-8.25; (53) A.-2.22; (54) W.-5.27; C.M.-9.23; 11.15; 12.2; (55) C.-1.23.

Robert Bruce: (43) N.-11.3, 4, 6, 18.

Robert Emmet, or The Hero of Ireland; by N. H. Bannister: (42) A.-6.21*, 23; N.-4.8, 9, 10, 11, 12, 20; (46) A.-6.4 5, 19; (55) C.-4.24, 25, 26, 27, 28.

Robert Kyd, or The Witch Fiend: (52) N.-7.22, 23.

Robert Kyd, or The Wizard of the Seas; see *Captain Kyd.*

Robert le Diable; opera by Giocomo

Meyerbeer: (38) C.-2.17, 20, 22; (42) W.-11.21; (45) C.-10.2.

Robert Macaire, or The Auberge des Adrets: (37) C.-9.23; (38) C.-2.12; 5.16, 21; (40) W.-5.12, 13; (41) A.-8.14, 21; N.-12.4; (42) W.-6.4, 7, 11; A.-9.23; (44) A.-8.9, 13; W.-9.19, 20; C.-10.15; 12.13; (45) W.-1.14; 3.15; 4.9; 7.8; A.-10.25; (46) W.-1.15; 4.6, 23; 6.29; 11.28; 12.14, 17, 25; (47) W.-1.12, 25; 2.17; 5.8, 20; A.-5.18; P.M.-6.30; W.-7.2, 7; 8.11, 17; 11.6; 12.1; (48) W.-1.14; 2.9; 3.24, 25; P.M.-4.4; W.-6.1; A.-8.11, 28; W.-9.2; 12.19, 30; (49) W.-6.19; P.M.-7.4; A.-10.17; W.-11.16; A.-11.19; (50) B.-11.20, 21, 22; (51) A.-3.26; W.-5.3, 21; 12.5, 12, 20; (52) W.-1.24; 2.5; 3.22; 5.5; 9.11, 22; 11.6; A.-11.27; 12.18; C.-12.20, 25; (53) W.-1.22; 3.10; 5.5; A.-6.11; C.-7.2; W.-12.21, 24, 28; (54) W.-1.30; C.-1.30, 31; 3.1; W.-6.17; C.M.-12.16, 19; (55) C.M.-1.20, 24; A.-4.18, 20, 21; W.-5.5, 9, 19; 6.7, 14.

Robert the Devil: (37) W.-4.1.

Robin Hood; (by Leonard MacNally): (42) W.-4.18.

Robinson Crusoe; (by Isaac Pocock): (36) W.-12.28, 30; (39) W.-10.15; (42) C.-1.1; (44) N.-3.19, 28; A.-12.7, 9, 10, 11, 23; (50) A.-6.11, 12.

Rochester, or The Merry Days of Charles II; see *Charles II.*

The Rogues of Paris; see *The Bohemians.* See also *The Chiffonier.*

Rogueries of Thomas: (42) W.-5.5; (54) N.-6.16.

A Roland for an Oliver; farce: (36) C.-1.8; (37) C.-1.18; 4.12, 27; (38) C.-11.14; W.-8.8, 11, 31; (39) C.-2.26; W.-8.10; C.-12.18; (40) W.-10.14, 15; 11.12; C.-2.27; 3.28; 4.7; N.-8.31; 9.3; 10.6; (41) W.-10.29; C.-9.21, 24; 10.25; W.-11.8, 24; (42)

C.-1.6, 13; 2.15; A.-5.23, 24; 5.6, 12, 19; W.-9.23; 12.1; (43) A.-3.7; W.-4.21; A.-12.20; (44) W.-1.3, 9; 3.11; 6.18; 7.24; 8.31; 10.3, 4; 12.12; (45) C.-2.7; W.-11.8, 24; (46) P.M.-7.9; 8.7, 12; 12.4; (47) W.-10.28; 11.2; 12.13; (48) W.-3.21; 4.4; A.-4.17; 5.15; W.-6.12; 7.17; 9.4; 10.9; (51) W.-3.20; (53) W.-1.20; A.-5.24; 6.7; C.-7.1; 12.16, 22; (54) A.-1.7; C.-1.13; A.-2.18; C.-7.4; A.-9.20, 22; W.-10.14, 25; A.-11.16; 12.14; (55) A.-1.12; 6.23; 8.21, 25; 12.12.

The Roll of the Drum: (46) A.-12.21, 22; (47) A.-1.29; (49) P.M.-5.9, 10.

The Roman Actor; by Philip Massinger: (40) C.-3.7.

The Roman Father; classical tragedy by William Whitehead: (54) W.-12.22.

The Roman Father; see *Virginius.*

The Roman Conspiracy; see *Cataline.*

The Roman Sister; see *Valeria.*

The Roman Tribute, or Attila the Hun; by Mrs. Elizabeth Oakes Smith: (50) A.-11.11*, 12, 13, 14, 16.

Romance and Burlesque: (50) C.-6.11, 12, 13, 15, 17.

Romance and Reality; comedy by John Brougham: (48) W.-5.4*, 6, 8, 9, 10, 11, 12, 13; (52) C.-12.16, 17, 18; (53) C.-7.14, 16; (54) A.-8.21, 22, 23, 24, 25, 26.

A Romance of Life, Mystery and Crime; see *Quaker City.*

The Romantic Widow; comedy: (40) C.-2.5*, 6, 7; 3.17, 18, 19; N.-10.16, 23.

Romanzo, or The Exile of Naples; romantic drama by "A Gentleman of Philadelphia": (39) W.-8.19*, 20, 21, 22, 23, 24, 31; 9.5, 6, 13; (40) W.-3.24.

Romeo and Juliet; by William Shakespeare: (35) W.-1.16; 2.26; 5.29;

9.10; (38) W.-2.6; (35) A.-2.25; (36) A.-3.8; (37) A.-6.14; (41) A.-5.28; (39) W.-5.21; (40) W.-10.26; 12.4; (41) W.-1.7; (35) C.-10.17; (36) C.-1.7; (37) C.-1.11, 30; (38) C.-4.25; (39) C.-9.13; 11.28; (41) N.-12.2; (42) C.-1.11, 13, 17; (42) C.-4.23; A.-7.25; (43) W.-5.4; A.-10.19; N.-12.29; (44) A.-8.16; W.-8.24; A.-9.2; C.-11.21; (45) A.-4.26; W.-7.26; 8.11; C.-9.4; W.-9.5; 10.6; C.-11.4; W.-11.10; (46) W.-1.12; A.-5.2; W.-5.8; 6.6; A.-9.29; W.-10.5; (47) W.-2.15; A.-8.16; 9.7; 12.15; (48) A.-2.8; W.-2.8; 3.17; A.-6.28, 29; 10.5; (49) W.-3.26; 4.7; 5.10; A.-8.28; 9.13; C.-10.13, 18; A.-11.5; (50) W.-1.2; C.-2.7; 4.16; A.-5.30; 6.4; W.-9.17; 11.5, 9, 13; (51) W.-3.29; A.-4.3; B.-4.14; A.-6.3; W.-6.21; C.-7.4, 12; 9.8; 10.7; 12.5; A.-12.10; (52) C.-1.2; 3.16; W.-4.26; C.-7.16, 23; A.-8.23; C.-9.4; A.-11.3, 5; C.-11.30; (53) A.-1.31; C.-2.8; A.-8.27; W.-9.6; A.-9.27; (54) C.-1.28; 3.13; A.-3.22, 25; 5.9, 13; C.-10.3; C.M.-12.1; A.-12.9; (55) C.-1.25; C.M.-10.3; C.M.-12.1; A.-12.9; (55) C.-1.25; C.M.-1.27; W.-3.30; C.M.-4.11; W.-5.3, 18; C.M.-11.24; A.-11.26; 12.8.

Romeo and Juliet; opera by Vincenzo Bellini: (47) W.-8.6.

The Romp; farce by Isaac Bickerstaff: (38) W.-12.18; (39) W.-10.2, 4; (43) A.-9.15.

The Roof Scrambler; farce: (40) C.-3.11, 12, 13, 14, 17, 23, 25, 27, 31; 4.3, 10; 5.6, 8; 6.2, 11; 11.9; (41) C.-2.25, 26; 6.11; (47) P.M.-6.14, 16, 17, 18, 19, 22.

Rookwood; adapted from Ainsworth's book by N. H. Bannister: (41) W.-3.13*, 15, 16, 17, 18, 19, 20, 22, 23, 24, 25, 26, 27, 29, 30; 5.1, 3, 4, 7; 12.13,

15, 16, 17, 18; A.-9.11, 13, 14, 15, 16, 17, 18; 11.18, 19, 20, 22, 23, 27; (44) N.-4.2, 3, 4, 5, 6, 7; W.-11.20, 21, 22, 23, 25, 26, 27, 28, 29, 30; (46) A.-6.13, 15, 16, 27, 30; 7.3; (49) A.-5.4, 5, 8, 12; (50) A.-3.18, 19, 20; (52) N.-9.4, 6, 7, 8; (54) N.-6.19, 20; C.-11.16, 17, 18.

Rory O'More; romantic drama in three acts: (38) W.-8.18, 20, 21, 22, 23, 24; 9.17, 20; 10.4; (39) W.-2.4; 5.4; (38) C.-9.24, 25, 26, 28, 29; 10.6; 11.5, 10; (40) C.-10.15, 24; W.-1.15, 18; (41) W.-2.24; A.-10.28; (42) W.-11.19, 25; (46) W.-5.18; (47) W.-12.13, 14, 15, 18; (48) W.-9.16; (49) W.-4.13; A.-5.30; 6.5; W.-9.27; 10.17; (50) C.-3.2, 6; 6.24; A.-7.2, 10; 11.19; (53) A.-2.25, 26, 28; 5.10; 6.10; 9.10, 14; 10.4; 11.25; (54) A.-2.11; 3.18; 5.23; W.-5.29; A.-10.6, 9; (55) A.-2.23; 3.1; 6.25; W.-11.7.

The Rose of Arragon; by S. B. H. Judah: (42) A.-7.16.

The Rose of Corbelle; see *Miller's Daughter.*

The Rose of Ettrick Vale, or The Bridal on the Border: (50) C.-7.15*, 16; N.-8.5.

The Rose of Killarney: (43) C.-12.16, 23; (44) W.-1.5, 10; (45) W.-3.21, 22.

The Roses of Baron de Malesherbes; by August von Kotzebue: (373 A.-7.20.

Rosina Meadows; domestic drama by C. H. Saunders: (49) A.-11.26*, 27, 28; (50) A.-11.15; (52) A.-11.26; 12.7; (54) C.-9.26, 27, 30; (55) C.-4.19.

Rosina, or The Reapers; by Mrs. Brooke: (36) C.-8.25; 9.26; (38) C.-6.2; W.-7.26, 27; 8.9; 12.5; (39) C.-3.2; (42) C.-4.9, 15.

The Roué: (45) C.-5.5, 6.

Rough and Ready; by J. P. Addams: (52) A.-12.24, 25; (53) A.-1.1.

The Rough Diamond, or Cousin Joe; farce: (50) W.-11.23, 26, 28, 29; 12.3, 7; (51) W.-1.29; A.-2.1; C.-3.28; A.-4.3; 5.9; 6.17, 18, 28; N.-7.25; W.-8.21, 27; 9.29; A.-10.23; W.-11.3, 19; C.-12.31; (52) W.-1.2; C.-1.14; 2.6, 7; 5.7; 6.19; 7.12, 17; 8.2, 18; 12.20; (53) W.-1.18; A.-1.29; 4.29; W.-5.20, 21; 6.1; C.-8.31; (54) C.-4.1; A.-5.24; N.-6.8, 20; C.-9.30; 11.17; (55) C.-1.20; C.M.-6.11, 20; A.-9.17; W.-10.15; C.M.-12.1, 22.

The Rover, the Drover, and his Dog; see *The Cattle Stealer.*

A Row at the Chesnut, or Old Drury in an Uproar; farce: (52) C.-11.14*, 15, 17, 18; (53) C.-7.12, 16.

Royalty in Distress: (48) O.-5.22.

Rubber of Life: (44) W.-2.13, 20; 3.30; (45) W.-1.1, 2; 3.18.

Ruby Ring, or Murder at the Meets; melodrama: (43) N.-10.9*, 10, 11, 12, 13; (44) N.-1.23; 2.1.

Ruffian Boy: (37) W.-1.14; 2.25; (41) N.-12.8; (44) A.-1.13; (53) A.-7.1.

Rugantino: (43) A.-3.14; 4.10; (44) W.-2.9; (46) W.-2.17.

Rule a Wife and Have a Wife: (35) C.-10.24; (36) W.-9.26; (43) W.-5.1, 4; (44) W.-8.20; (48) A.-1.24, 25; (49) A.-12.26; (53) A.-5.4, 5, 21; (54) A.-6.7, 10, 19; 8.30; 9.13; 22.13 "Revived comedy of Beaumont and Fletcher as revised for the modern stage by W. Murry."

The Rum Old Commodore: (39) W.-8.30; 9.3, 20; 10.1; (40) W.-4.4, 17; 6.4, 23; (41) W.-5.5, 6; 12.22.

A Run at Hamstead; see *Hue and Cry.*

The Runaway Monkey; see *Ourang Outang.*

Rural Felicity, or Life in a Country Town; comedy by J. B. Buckstone:

(37) W.-12.18*, 19, 20; (40) C.-9.5, 8; 12.31; (41) C.-1.4; (45) W.-7.1, 10, 19; 8.18.

The Russian Daughter; see *The Exile.*

The Sabre Grinders of Damascus; see *The Three Hunchbacks.*

Sadak and Kalasrade, or The Waters of Oblivion; melodrama: (40) W.- 2.3*, 4, 5, 6, 7, 8, 10, 11, 12, 13, 14, 15, 17, 19, 20, 21; 3.11, 20; (50) C.-2.26.

Saffo; "grand lyrical tragedy in three acts by Giovanni Pocinini": (42) W.- 7.12; (50) C.-9.16.

A Sailor's Dream: (42) A.-8.6.

A Sailor's Home: (44) A.-1.27.

The Sailor's Return; by William Francis: (41) A.-1.1.

The Sailor's Revenge: (40) W.-11.12.

Sailors and Taylors; see *Guns without Shot.*

Sailors' Sweethearts; see *Ben the Boatswain.*

St. Clara's Eve; see *Conquest of Taranto.*

St. Cuthbert's Abbey: (43) A.-3.16, 18.

St. George and the Dragon: (42) W.- 3.23, 24, 25; (55) W.-2.15; 4.16.

St. Marc, or A Husband's Sacrifice; by John Wilkins: (54) W.-9.26*, 27, 28, 29, 30; 10.2, 3; (55) W.-3.12.

St. Mary's Eve; domestic drama: (38) C.-10.22*, 23, 24, 25, 26, 27; 11.1; 12.3, 22; (39) C.-8.26, 27; 9.7; (40) C.- 1.7, 11, 17; 2.11, 20; (42) C.-10.20, 21; (52) W.-5.17, 18, 20; (53) C.- 1.22, 24, 28; W.-6.20, 23; (55) C.M.- 5.8, 10.

St. Patrick's Eve, or The Order of the Day: (35) C.-5.4; (36) C.-10.1, 6; 11.26; (37) A.-5.15; (38) C.-9.19; 11.6; (40) C.-10.17; (48) A.-11.17, 18; (49) W.-10.24, 27; 12.12; (50) A.-7.12; (51) C.-10.23, 24, 30; (52)

C.-2.26, 28; (53) A.-3.17, 25, 26; 4.12; 5.13; C.-5.28; 9.10, 20.

St. Swithin's Chair; see *The Night Hag.*

Sam Parr; vaudeville: (41) N.-6.21, 22, 23, 24, 25, 26; 7.1.

Sam Patch, or The Daring Yankee: (37) W.-12.20, 21, 22, 27; (38) W.- 1.3, 4; 7.18, 21; (55) C.-2.2.

Sam Patch in France, or The Pesky Snake; Yankee comedy by J. P. Addams: (43) W.-5.11*, 13; (47) W.-4.20; (49) A.-11.19, 23, 24; (51) A.-3.10; 7.28.

Sam Patch's First Visit to Europe: (50) A.-9.5.

Sam Slick; see *Samuel Slick, Esq.*

Sam Weller, or The Pickwick Papers; comedy by W. T. Moncrieff: (38) C.-5.5, 7, 8, 9, 10, 11, 12, 23; (42) C.- 4.4, 8, 11, 18; (43) A.-8.12.

Samuel Slick, Esq., or Love in the Far, Far West; comic ballet: (38) C.- 3.6*; W.-3.21; 4.9, 10; (41) A.-10.2; (44) A.-10.14, 15, 16; (45) A.-11.3, 4; (46) A.-3.2; (50) A.-9.3; (51) A.- 3.19, 21.

Sandy and Jenny; ballet of action: (36) P.- 12.3, 8.

Santa Claus; pantomime: (43) C.-12.25, 26; N.-12.30; (44) N.-1.1, 2, 3.

Sarah the Jewess: (42) W.-12.17, 19.

Sarcophagus, or The Two Mummies; farce: (38) W.-6.26; (44) A.-1.18; (45) A.-10.14; (46) A.-2.2, 12.

Sardanapalus; "Lord Byron's tragedy, adapted by Charles Durang": (36) W.-11.23*, 29; (42) A.-4.23.

Sarmatia's Heir; see *Blind Boy.*

Satan: (53) A.-3.1.

Satan at Home: (45) W.-2.25.

Satan in Paris, or The Mysterious Stranger; melodrama: (45) W.-2.10, 11, 12, 14, 15; 3.3, 6, 17; A.-4.2, 4; (46) W.-7.20, 22; P.M.-12.9, 10; (51) A.-1.27, 28, 29, 30; (53) C.-1.4, 14;

A.-2.23; (54) A.-4.19, 20, 25; 5.6; 9.2; 10.10; (55) A.-1.9; C.-1.27; C.M.-6.6; A.-9.21, 25.

Saturday Night, or The Singing Bailiff: (46) P.M.-10.3.

Sauve qui Peut; "ballet d'action": (44) A.-12.19, 20.

The Savage of the Forest, or The Mysterious Blunder: (36) W.-12.29; (37) W.-1.30.

The Savoyard Boy and his Monkey; see *The Grenadier.*

The Saxon Girl, or Walter Tyrrel; tragedy: (37) W.-12.23*; (50) A.-9.4, 13; (53) C.-3.19.

The Saxon's Oath: (51) N.-8.15.

Sayings and Doings, or The Rule of the Contrary: (46) P.M.-11.21.

Scan. Mag., or The Village Gossip; farce: (40) C.-9.15, 17, 22; 10.2, 7, 29; (43) W.-4.28; 5.1, 6, 8, 9, 29; 6.23; (55) A.-9.20, 27; 10.1, 6, 9, 17; 11.3; 12.17.

Scapegoat; farce: (36) W.-10.26*; (37) C.-1.19, 20; 2.6, 10, 23; 3.23; 4.1; 10.2; 11.7; A.-5.15, 25; 6.28; (38) C.-2.14; 3.2; 5.7; (43) A.-10.28; (46) C.-5.1; (47) A.-9.13.

Scene in a Madhouse; "monodrama by M. G. Lewis, Esq.": (36) W.-9.26.

Schinder Hannes, or The Robber of the Rhine: (35) W.-4.11.

The Scholar; comedy: (39) C.-1.2*, 5.

A School for Auctioneers; see *Secrets Worth Knowing.*

A School for Daughters; see *The Will.*

A School for Diplomats; see *Irish Ambassador.*

A School for Grown Children; comedy in five acts by Thomas Morton: (35) C.-12.9; (36) C.-1.27; A.-3.16; 5.19.

The School for Scandal; comedy by R. B. Sheridan: (35) W.-4.11; (36) W.-10.24; (38) W.-2.8; 11.17; (40) W.-10.16; (35) C.-4.17; 9.1, 22; 10.21, 22; (36) C.-11.10; A.-5.18;

(37) C.-1.13; (39) C.-5.1, 8; 2.24; 8.29; (41) C.-2.19; 3.1; 9.25; 10.14; N.-2.9; 12.3; W.-6.26; C.-12.14, 16; (42) C.-2.17; A.-7.13; W.-9.23; C.-10.31; (43) A.-3.6; (44) W.-2.9, 13; 4.6, 30; A.-7.24; 10.23; C.-11.18; (45) W.-1.28; 5.19; C.-9.6; W.-10.1; (46) W.-1.21; 5.8; 8.10; (47) A.-4.20; W.-6.23; A.-7.29; (48) P.M.-4.17; W.-7.18; (49) C.-10.19; (50) A.-3.4; 5.31; 6.3; C.-7.31; B.-9.2, 3; (51) W.-1.29; C.-3.31; W.-5.15; 6.18; A.-6.14; C.-9.18; W.-9.19; C.-12.15; (52) C.-2.17; W.-3.9; C.-3.22, 23, 24; 4.2; W.-4.20; C.-6.4; 9.28; 10.7; (53) C.-1.1, 8; W.-1.25; 2.25; C.-5.21; A.-5.30; 8.29; W.-12.28; C.-12.30; (54) A.-2.4; W.-5.5; 7.1; A.-12.19, 28; (55) C.M.-2.2, 28.

School for Scheming: (47) P.M.-6.8, 9, 10.

School for Soldiers; by William Dunlop: (46) W.-5.22; (47) W.-3.8.

School for Tigers, or The Shilling Hop; farce: (51) A.-4.14*, 18, 19, 23, 25, 26; (54) A.-4.26, 27, 28, 29; (55) A.-1.8, 9, 10.

The School of Reform, or How to Rule a Husband; comedy by Thomas Morton: (35) C.-5.30; (37) C.-8.25; (38) C.-5.24; (36) P.-12.5; (39) W.-4.17; (40) W.-3.7; (43) A.-8.11; (44) W.-6.10; (49) A.-4.19, 21; W.-5.18; 11.7; A.-12.18; (50) W.-10.25; B.-10.30; W.-12.10, 18; (51) B.-4.3; W.-12.20; (52) W.-1.14, 31; C.-12.6, 8; (53) W.-3.1; (54) C.-6.19, 22; 7.7; (55) A.-12.5, 7.

Scotch Clans and Irish Chieftains: (38) W.-1.23, 24, 25, 26, 27, 29, 31; 2.28.

The Scotch Cooper, or A Happy New Year: (37) A.-4.14*, 15; (37) C.-11.12; (38) C.-1.1.

The Scotch Widow: (41) N.-11.12.

Scott and Pierce, or The Champion of Freedom: (52) N.-8.26*, 27.

The Scottish Gold Mine; see *Belford Castle.*

Sea and Land; comedy: (53) A.-3.4*, 5, 14, 29.

The Sea Captain, or The Birthright; by Edward Bulwer-Lytton: (39) W.-12.9*; (41) A.-5.31; 6.1; (42) A.-8.26; (53) C.-5.19.

The Sea Fight: (53) W.-12.10, 12.

The Sea King's Vow: (49) C.-9.21, 22.

The Sea Serpent; by William Crafts: (44) A.-7.27, 29, 30, 31; 8.1.

The Sea-Side Story of the Olden Time; see *The Fate of Ambrose.*

The Sealed Sentence, or The Days of Napoleon: (45) A.-5.12, 13, 15; 7.29.

The Seaman's Log Book; see *Tom Cringle.*

The Seamstress: (49) A.-7.10, 11, 12, 14, 16.

Second Thoughts, or The Breach of Promise: (35) C.-10.28, 29; 12.2; 36) C.-1.23; 2.3; A.-2.29; 3.15; 5.20; (37) A.-5.3; (36) C.-6.17; 7.4; 9.26; 11.4; (37) C.-1.5; (38) C.-6.8; (47) A.-3.27, 29; 4.1; (48) A.-3.3, 9; (49) W.-11.23; (50) A.-12.5; (51) A.-6.12; (53) A.-1.6.

The Secret, or A Hole in the Wall: (35) C.-1.10; 9.22; 10.3; W.-9.18, 22; 10.17; 11.3; 12.25; (36) C.-2.5; (39) C.-4.4, 13; 6.12, 9.4, 18; 10.5, 28; 11.28; 12.12; (36) P.-11.9; 12.1, 31; (37) P.-1.18; (38) W.-3.8; (39) W.-11.8, 13; (40) W.-7.17; (40) C.-1.28; 6.20; (41) C.-9.17; 12.4, 6, 16; (40) A.-12.3, 12, 25; (42) C.-1.28; 2.7, 11; W.-3.9; A.-8.16, 18, 22, 25; (43) W.-10.26; (45) C.-9.24; 11.5, 13; (46) A.-7.3, 7; (48) A.-10.25; 11.6, 17, 22; (49) Ath.-1.17; (50) A.-9.12, 17; (51) A.-2.5; 7.31; C.-9.1, 2, 6; (53) C.-5.30, 31; (54) C.-1.7; 2.7, 27; 6.17; N.-6.21, 22; (55) C.M.-6.21, 26; 11.7, 8, 20.

The Secret, or Frightened to Death: (46) P.M.-7.15, 17, 27; 9.17, 29; (47) P.M.-5.21; 6.12.

The Secret League; see *The Burglar.*

The Secret Mine, or The Hindoos of the Cavern; "Eastern musical spectacle": (39) W.-12.23, 24, 25, 26, 27, 28; (40) W.-1.9, 10; (43) W.-1.26, 27.

The Secret of the Lodge Room; see *Freemason.*

The Secret Order, or The Oath of Silence: (48) A.-3.6, 7, 8.

Secret Pamphlet, or The Ups and Downs of a Printer: (47) A.-6.25*; 7.14, 15.

The Secret Panel; farce: (45) W.-11.21, 26.

Secret Service: (35) W.-9.29; (36) C.-2.19, 23; A.-3.23; (41) N.-2.16; (43) C.-12.19, 20; (44) W.-1.8; 2.26; (46) W.-4.25.

Secrets of Life in New York; see *The Dancing Feather.*

Secrets Worth Knowing, or A School for Auctioneers; by Thomas Morton: (35) C.-11.26; (36) C.-1.4; A.-5.30; (40) C.-5.26; (42) C.-4.30; (44) W.-4.20, 25; (45) A.-4.7; W.-5.9; (54) A.-6.14, 15.

Seeing the Elephant; farce: (48) A.-1.18, 22; 2.21; 3.23, 24; 4.3.

Seeing Hemple: (52) A.-10.1.

Seeing Holland: (46) P.M.-7.18.

Seeing Paris: (46) P.M.-7.20.

Self Accusation: (44) A.-1.25; (52) A.-10.1.

Sent to the Tower; farce: (51) W.-2.4*, 5, 6, 7, 8; 4.3; 6.10; 11.16; (53) W.-3.4, 15; 5.17.

The Sentinel; musical burletta: (38) W.-3.19; 8.14, 15, 17; (39) W.-4.11; (40) W.-5.26; (42) W.-12.20, 21, 22; (43) W.-3.7; (52) A.-4.16, 17, 19, 20; (53) W.-12.1, 5.

Separate Maintenance: (49) W.-10.1,

9; 12.1; (50) W.-4.24; B.-11.27, 28; (51) B.-12.10, 11.

The Sergeant and the Tinker; see *May Queen.*

The Sergeant of Austerlitz: (42) C.-1.15, 27; 2.5.

The Sergeant's Wedding: (43) N.-10.9, 10, 11, 12, 13, 14, 27; (53) W.-10.5, 11; (54) W.-6.26.

The Sergeant's Wife: (42) W.-4.7, 11, 13; (43) O.-1.18; (46) P.M.-11.2, 3, 7; (52) A.-11.6; (54) C.-10.28.

The Serious Family; comedy by Morris Barnett: (49) A.-12.24*, 25; (50) C.-2.23, 25, 27; 3.19, 20, 21, 22, 23, 28; 4.5, 12, 16; W.-5.13, 14, 15, 16, 18, 22, 23, 24, 25; C.-5.17; W.-6.11, 14, 15, 28; 7.2, 4; 10.18, 19, 26; A.-10.25, 26, 28, 29, 30, 31; W.-11.25, 26; 12.4; (51) W.-3.3, 4, 5, 6; C.-3.24; A.-7.22; W.-9.4; C.-9.5; A.-10.28, 29; C.-11.4; W.-12.22, 23; (52) W.-3.1, 26; 4.3; C.-8.9, 10; (53) W.-3.18, 22; A.-3.19; W.-6.6; C.-7.12; 9.13; A.-10.17, 18, 20, 24, 26; 12.13, 14; (54) A.-1.11, 13, 16, 30; 2.7; 3.21; 4.8; 5.26; 6.21; C.-8.23, 26; A.-9.19, 22, 25, 26, 27, 28, 30; 10.2, 5, 16, 18, 19, 20; 11.13, 17, 23; 12.7, 21; (55) A.-1.18, 19, 20, 23; 2.1, 27; 3.2, 20, 23; 4.6, 12, 17, 24; C.M.-4.26, 28; A.-5.1, 8, 15, 22, 29; C.M.-5.17; A.-6.5, 7, 12, 15, 19, 26; 7.3; C.M.-10.1, 2, 8; W.-11.5, 6, 7, 8, 10; 12.5, 7; A.-12.20.

The Serpent Lady: (40) A.-12.30, 31; (41) A.-1.2.

Set a Beggar on Horseback; by John O'Keeffe: (37) W.-12.25*; (38) W.-2.1.

Seth Slope, or Done or a Hundred: (39) W.-10.26* 29, 30; 11.2; (40) W.-12.17; A.-12.4; (41) W.-10.11; (42) W.-4.15, 16; (43) W.-1.10; A.-10.3; (45) C.-1.17, 20; 5.2; (51) A.-3.14. 15.

Seven Castles: (46) C.-1.14, 15, 16, 17, 18; A.-2.24.

Seven Castles of the Passions: (46) A.-2.21.

Seven Champions of Christendom: (41) N.-5.8, 10, 11, 12, 13.

Seven Clerks, or The Denouncer: (35) W.-10.3, 6, 20; 11.11; (41) A.-5.10, 11, 13, 14; (43) A.-12.22; (49) A.-3.7, 8; (50) C.-3.29.

The Seven Escapes, or The Bride's Journey: (52) A.-5.15; N.-10.20.

The Seven Female Soldiers; opera by Angely: (40) A.-1.25; 2.22.

777; farce: (47) C.-6.11.

Seven Voyages of Sinbad the Sailor: (41) W.-4.24, 26, 27, 28, 29.

Seven's the Main; see *Winning a Husband.*

1700 Years Ago: (35) W.-6.3, 4, 5.

1777: (44) W.-4.5.

The Shadow on the Wall: (35) C.-10.3, 5; (37) W.-1.14, 26, 31; (53) N.-7.25.

Shakespeare's Dream; by John Brougham: (43) W.-2.6*, 9, 10.

Shakespeare's Early Days: (37) W.-1.23.

Shandy Maguire; by James Pilgrim: (51) A.-12.12*, 13, 15, 19, 22; 5.5, 9; 11.5, 13; (52) C.-2.2, 3; W.-9.1, 2; 10.20; (53) C.-7.22; W.-10.26; C.-10.29; (54) W.-5.17, 23; (55) C.M.-7.6; W.-9.22; C.M.-12.31.

Sharratah: (42) W.-11.18*.

Sherwood Forest: (42) W.-3.28, 29.

She Stoops to Conquer, or The Mistakes of a Night; comedy by Oliver Goldsmith: (35) C.-8.25; (36) C.-10.20; (42) A.-9.23; (43) W.-5.12; 6.16; C.-9.10; (44) W.-2.16; 5.23; A.-6.11; (46) A.-3.4; 5.1; W.-7.23; A.-12.14; (47) A.-1.21; (49) Ath.-1.15; A.-8.24; 9.14; (50) A.-1.2; (52) W.-3.10, 26; (53) W.-1.6, 12; A.-4.13, 16; W.-6.8, 25; C.-8.31; 11.10; (54)

A.-2.2, 17; 4.28; 6.16; C.M.-12.6, 12; (55) A.-1.10; C.M.-1.25; A.-2.13; C.M.-4.28.

She Would and she Would Not, or The Kind Impostors; comedy by Colley Cibber: (35) W.-3.3; (38) C.-3.14, 20; (42) W.-11.11; (52) C.-8.27, 28, 31; 9.21; (53) W.-1.13, 14, 17, 19; A.-2.21; 4.14; (54) A.-8.28, 29; 9.6; (55) A.-2.14.

She Would be a Soldier, or The Battle of Chippewa; by M. M. Noah: (38) C.-7.4; (40) C.-11.26; (51) A.-3.6.

The Sheriff of the County; comedy by R. B. Peake: (45) A.-6.18; C.-8.30.

The Shilling Hop; see *School for Tigers.*

The Ship Carpenter of Kensington: (50) A.-8.13*, 14, 15.

The Ship Carpenter of Philadelphia: (52) N.-10.18*, 19.

The Ship Launch; farce (by W. E. Burton): (37) A.-7.3*, 4, 5.

Shipwreck, or After the Storm: (40) C.-4.4; W.-11.21, 23, 24; (41) W.-7.3, 5, 7, 10.

The Shipwreck of the Medusa: (44) A.-6.17, 18, 20, 22.

Shipwrecked Mariner: (49) C.-8.27.

Shipwrecked Orphan: (47) P.M.-7.10.

Shocking Events: (39) C.-9.30; 10.1, 7, 19; 11.26; (40) C.-11.16, 30; (41) C.-9.2, 3, 4, 8, 27; 10.20; (45) C.-1.24; (47) A.-4.14, 16.

The Shoemaker of Toulouse; by J. S. Jones: (42) A.-8.19*, 20, 22, 9.29; (43) A.-9.25; (45) W.-6.7; A.-10.10, 11; (46) A.-7.14, 16; (48) A.-7.22, 24, 25; (50) A.-5.16; 12.11; (51) A.-1.16; 10.17; (52) A.-3.20; 9.30; (53) A.-2.14; 4.26; 5.6.

Short of Change; see *But However!*

Siamese Twins; farce: (35) W.-2.14, 18, 20, 26; 3.19, 25; 4.1; 8.27; 11.20; (36) W.-12.2; (40) W.-3.5; (44) A.-

6.20, 21, 29; (53) C.-1.26, 28; W.-6.14; C.-7.23.

The Siege of Beauvais; see *Jane of the Hatchet.*

The Siege of Belgrade; opera: (40) N.-12.10, 11.

The Siege of Boston, or The Sons of the Soil; by J. S. Jones: (41) W.-10.23*, 25, 26; 11.1; (42) W.-1.1; (43) W.-7.3.

The Siege of Comorn: (50) C.-2.23.

The Siege of Corinth: (50) A.-3.21, 22, 23.

The Siege of Damascus; see *Eudocia.*

The Siege of Janina: (41) A.-1.4, 5, 9.

The Siege of Missolonghi, or The Greek Patriots: (37) W.-3.27*, 31; 4.3; (43) W.-4.27.

The Siege of Monterey; by J. Foster: (46) A.-10.31*; 11.2, 3, 4; 12.17; (52) A.-12.6.

The Siege of Montgatz; see *Tekeli.*

The Siege of Stralsund; by J. R. Planché. (41) A.-5.28*; (48) Ath.-12.29; (53) A.-6.8.

The Siege of Tripoli, or American Courage Triumphant; by M. M. Noah: (39) W.-12.30, 31; (40) W.-1.7.

The Siege of Vera Cruz: (48) C.-7.26.

The Signal Fire; see *Patriotism.*

Simple Simon and his Dogs; see *Zenocles and the Greek Chief.*

Simpson and Company; farce: (35) W.-4.4; (38) W.-8.6; (40) W.-12.7; (41) W.-7.7; (40) C.-4.4; 9.11, 16; 10.28; (41) C.-9.23; A.-6.5; (42) C.-2.25; A.-9.15; 10.28; W.-9.28; 10.28; (44) W.-3.14; A.-8.17; C.-11.18; (45) W.-2.12; A.-5.20; W.-12.3; (46) P.M.-3.14, 18; 4.1; (48) A.-11.8; (49) C.-10.19; (50) A.-5.31; 6.3; B.-11.15, 16, 29; 12.14; (51) B.-2.6; 6.6; 7.1; C.-12.18; (52) C.-3.19; 4.6, 7, 14; 12.23; (53) W.-2.1, 3; A.-9.29; (54)

C.-10.19; C.M.-11.2; (55) C.M.-3.23;
A.-10.24; 11.9; C.M.-11.10, 24.

The Singing Bailiff, see *Touch and Take.*

Single Life; comedy by J. B. Buckstone: (39) C.-11.13, 15; (40) C.-9.3, 4, 9; 12.24; (45) W.-3.5; 8; 4.10; (50) W.-11.29, 30; 12.2, 5; (54) A.-11.29; 12.2, 11, 18; (55) A.-1.22.

Sink or Swim: (53) W.-2.14, 15, 21; 3.8.

A Sister's Love; see *The Intemperate.*

The Sisters; see *Home Again.*

Sisters of Charity: (50) A.-3.29, 30.

Six Degrees of Crime, or Wine, Women, Gambling, Theft, Murder, and the Scaffold: (38) W.-12.18; (40) W.-3.10; 5.26; (42) A.-5.9, 10, 11, 14, 20, 25, 27; 7.8; 8.8; W.-11.24; (43) W.-3.18; 6.14; A.-9.10, 26; N.-12.9; (47) A.-5.28; 8.27; (50) A.-9.12, 13, 14, 21, 23; 10.21; 11.15; (51) A.-2.26; 4.14; 7.3; 12.15, 16; (52) N.-9.21; (53) A.-6.8; (55) W.-2.17; C.-4.16, 17, 21; W.-6.6.

The Sixes, or The Devil's in the Dice: (40) A.-9.14*, 15, 16, 18.

Six Fighting Brothers; melodrama: (52) N.-7.15, 16, 17, 20.

Sixteen String Jack: (42) W.-10.3, 4, 5, 6, 7, 13; (44) C.-12.9; (51) A.-11.21, 22, 24; (53) A.-1.5, 8; (55) C.-4.30.

Sixteen Years Ago; domestic drama: (41) A.-9.20*.

The Skaters of Wilner; see *Godenski.*

The Skeleton Hand, or The Demon Statue: (43) N.-12.28.

The Skeleton Robber, or The Smuggler's Son and the Robber's Daughter; by (H. E.) Stevens: (36) W.-10.1*, 11; 12.21; (37) W.-11.29.

The Skeleton Witness: (35) W.-9.12, 24; (42) W.-2.28; 3.1, 18; 4.25; (43) W.-6.30.

Sketches in India; comedy: (44) W.-11.26, 27; (45) W.-1.15, 16; (46) P.M.-6.23, 24; 7.4, 8; 8.29; (47) A.-4.15, 21; P.M.-6.28; 7.1, 7; A.-8.18; (48) A.-6.13; (49) P.M.-7.9, 18, 19; C.-12.5; (51) A.-1.6, 13; 2.15; C.-3.5, 7; A.-7.14; C.-9.24, 27; 10.4, 14, 31; 11.24, 26; (52) C.-9.18; 10.11, 26, 27; 12.13; A.-12.27; (53) C.-1.19; W.-6.20, 22; (54) A.-2.8, 9; 6.8; C.-8.12; C.M.-9.15; C.-11.9; C.M.-11.20, 28; A.-12.22; (55) C.M.-4.2, 7; 5.22; A.-6.30; C.M.-9.13, 15; A.-11.24, 28.

Slasher and Crasher; farce: (49) A.-1.8*, 9, 10, 12; W.-2.19, 20, 21, 22, 24; A.-2.27; W.-3.19, 31; 6.12; P.M.-7.5, 6; C.-9.17, 19; W.-10.4; A.-10.13; (50) W.-4.3; 6.8; A.-8.9, 12; 10.4; 11.9; W.-12.24; (51) W.-1.14; 8.29; 12.9; (52) W.-2.21; C.-11.30; 12.6; (53) C.-1.6, 13; (54) C.-1.26, 27; (55) C.-1.25.

The Slave, or The Lovers of Surinam; opera: (40) N.-12.12, 14; (47) A.-1.4.

The Slave of Carthage; see *Caius Silius.*

The Slave of Love; see *Ganem.*

The Sledge Driver; farcetta: (36) W.-4.4*.

The Sleep Walker; see *Village Phantom.*

Sleeping Beauty, or The Enchanted Wood: (44) W.-1.8, 9, 10, 11, 12, 13, 15, 16, 20, 26, 30; 2.6; 4.6; (50) C.-5.20, 22.

The Sleeping Draught; comedy: (35) C.-1.8; 2.11; 4.7; 5.5; 6.8, 19; A.-3.24; C.-9.24; 11.5; (36) A.-3.30; 5.6; 6.9; C.-1.28; 2.16; 11.29; (37) C.-9.22; 12.9, 22; (38) C.-12.12; (44) C.-11.29; 12.3, 16.

The Sleigh Driver: (40) N.-12.21, 30; (41) N.-1.14.

Smiles and Tears, or The Widow's

Stratagem; by Mrs. Charles Kemble: (46) W.-7.1.

The Smuggler and his Dog; see *The Murder of the Blind Boy.*

The Smuggler of Bootle Bay, or The Murdered Waterman: (39) W.-1.16, 17; (43) W.-4.15, 18; (45) A.-8.7, 8; 9.3.

The Smuggler's Daughter; see *Fatal Prophecies.*

The Smuggler's Dog: (41) A.-1.8.

The Smuggler's Son: (44) A.-8.10, 12, 15, 19, 22, 23, 26; 9.19; 10.21; (47) A.-10.18; 12.20; (48) A.-1.7; 7.4; 8.14, 17; 9.11, 13, 29.

The Smuggler's Son and the Robber's Daughter; see *Skeleton Robber.*

The Smuggler's Son and the Exciseman's Daughter: (47) A.-9.14, 15, 16.

Snake Chief: (47) A.-11.3, 4, 5.

Snakes in the Grass: (40) W.-3.30.

Snapping Turtles: (41) N.-11.3, 8, 12; (42) W.-7.16.

The Snow Storm: (39) C.-12.25, 26, 27; (47) P.M.-4.12, 14.

Sold to the Devil: (44) A.-7.1, 11, 12.

The Soldier and the Peasant: (49) A.-9.1; 11.21; 12.15.

The Soldier of Fortune, or The Irish Settler; comedy: (46) W.-11.20, 21; (47) W.-2.5, 6; 6.17; 9.30; 12.16, 23; (48) W.-5.24; 9.15, 18; (49) W.-4.16, 18; 9.10, 20; 12.14, 15; (50) W.-5.10, 20; (51) W.-3.7; 9.5; (52) W.-3.3; 9.28; (53) A.-9.15; W.-11.19.

The Soldier's Courtship: (54) W.-2.22; 3.13.

The Soldier's Daughter; comedy: (35) C.-2.13, 20; 4.9; 8.27; 10.7; W.-2.27; (36) C.-8.27; W.-4.8; 12.22; P.-12.15; (39) C.-2.25; 8.24; (40) C.-4.3; 5.13, 21; (41) C.-2.11; (42) A.-11.5; (43) A.-8.24; (44) W.-7.22; (45) W.-2.7; A.-5.27; W.-6.26; 8.12,

29; 10.11; (46) W.-4.10; A.-11.27; P.M.-12.8; (47) A.-1.19, 25; 4.17; P.M.-6.11; (48) W.-3.18; Ath.-12.25; (49) A.-3.27; (50) W.-3.21; (51) B.-1.13, 14; 6.4; W.-9.22; (53) W.-1.11; 6.11; (54) A.-3.15, 18; 7.4; C.-9.20; 11.13, 14; (55) A.-1.12; C.-4.10; C.M.-9.10, 13.

The Soldier's Dream: (40) C.-1.11, 13, 14; 2.13, 21.

The Soldier's Progress, or The Honors of War: (50) C.-5.25, 26, 27, 29, 30.

The Soldier's Return: (47) A.-4.1; (49) P.M.-7.16; (52) A.-4.5; (54) C.M.-10.6.

The Soldier's Son: (41) W.-6.24.

Soldier's Wife and Soldier's Widow; pantomime: (38) W.-2.24*, 26, 27; 3.1.

Solomon Smink, or The Miller's Man and the Chevalier; farce by J. B. Buckstone: (40) N.-11.2, 5.

Solomon Swop: (52) A.-12.8, 10.

Somebody Else; burletta: (46) W.-7.22, 23; P.M.-12.11; (47) W.-4.15, 19, 26; 5.13, 24; 6.3, 7, 15, 26; 9.8, 15; 10.25; (48) A.-1.29; 7.14; (49) P.M.-4.25; 5.23, 24; (50) W.-8.28, 30; A.-9.10, 16; W.-9.10; (51) A.-6.25, 27; N.-7.17; A.-8.30; 10.21; (52) W.-3.13, 27; C.-11.29; 12.1; (53) C.-1.7; (54) A.-9.14, 18.

Something Original; comedy: (42) A.-11.10*.

Some Things can be Done as Well as Others; farce by H. H. Paul: (48) P.M.-5.16*, 17.

The Somnambulist, or The Phantom of the Village: (35) W.-2.2; 3.9; 4.1; 5.18; C.-4.13, 15; 6.5; 9.4; 10.9; (36) W.-4.28; 8.29; 10.17, 24; (44) A.-6.5; (46) P.M.-5.26, 29; (50) C.-1.8; W.-5.18; 6.24, 25.

The Son of Temperance, or Christmas Morning: (47) P.M.-1.25, 26, 27, 28; 6.15.

The Son of the Wilderness; see *Ingomar.*

The Sons of the Soil; see *The Siege of Boston.*

The Sorcerer, or The Monkey and the Bridegroom: (40) C.-6.1, 2, 5.

The Sorceress: (55) W.-9.7, 8.

Souter Johnnie: (39) C.-3.23*.

Southern Chivalry; see *Old Virginia.*

Spaniards in Peru; see *Pizarro.*

The Spanish Pirates, or A Union of the Flags; by H. J. Conway: (35) W.-11.14*, 16, 20.

The Speaking Likeness; see *The Maid with the Milking Pail.*

A Speck of War: (41) N.-9.24.

The Spectre Bride; see *Alonzo the Brave and the Fair Imogine.*

The Spectre Bridegroom, or A Ghost in Spite of Himself: (35) C.-5.1; (36) P.-12.5; (43) A.-9.2; (44) A.-7.18; 9.12; (46) P.M.-3.20, 24; 4.8; W.-6.16; A.-11.11; (47) A.-1.28; P.M.-2.18; 3.1; (48) P.M.-3.31; A.-4.28; C.-6.30; P.M.-7.6, 7, 11, 17, 21, 28; A.-12.20; Ath.-12.27; (49) Ath.-1.1; P.M.-5.25, 26; 6.1; C.-11.28; 12.6; (50) W.-3.2, 5, 12; 4.8; C.-6.7; 7.27; A.-8.5, 8; W.-9.24; (51) W.-1.10, 30; A.-1.14; 3.3; W.-4.17; 5.30; B.-6.14; A.-9.8; 10.9; (52) N.-9.10, 17; (53) C.-3.14, 29; 9.16, 17, 22; 12.21, 31; (54) N.-6.9; C.-6.15, 19; 8.1; 9.21; (55) C.M.-2.9; 3.8, 28; A.-9.3, 8; 11.16; W.-12.20.

The Spectre of the Convent; see *The Bleeding Nun.*

The Spectre Pilot: (50) C.-2.15; (53) A.-1.10, 12.

Speculation, or Stopped Payment; comedy in five acts by Frederick Reynolds: (37) A.-5.18.

Speculations, or Major Wheeler Abroad: (37) C.-9.15*, 16; (38) C.-4.7; (43) A.-5.5.

Speed the Plough; comedy by Thomas

Morton: (35) C.-5.19; (36) C.-8.25; (37) C.-3.10; (38) C.-5.17; (37) A.-5.24; (41) A.-5.4; (40) C.-3.16; W.-11.25, 30; (41) C.-12.18; N.-2.20; (42) N.-1.17; W.-11.12; (43) W.-5.10; C.-9.8; 11.11; (44) W.-2.23; 5.15; A.-8.15; W.-9.17; (45) W.-3.24; 6.18; 8.27; 10.9; (46) W.-1.1; 7.6; 8.20; (47) A.-6.11; W.-7.2; A.-8.3; W.-8.7; (48) W.-7.24; (49) Ath.-1.20; A.-10.2; (51) B.-6.13, 17; (53) A.-8.24; 9.30; 11.21; (54) A.-1.27; C.-3.2, 8; 7.3; 9.12; A.-11.14; (55) A.-4.19; W.-5.30.

The Spell of the Cloud King; see *The Bronze Horse.*

The Sphynx; musical burlesque by George Loder: (49) A.-10.23, 27.

The Spirit Bride and the Magi's Daughter: (35) C.-6.13, 15, 16, 17, 18; 11.7, 9, 14; (36) A.-4.5, 6, 13, 16; C.-6.29; 9.24.

The Spirit of Avenel; see *The White Lady.*

The Spirit of '76, or Washington: (35) W.-9.23*, 24, 25, 26, 28, 29, 30; (40) N.-10.8, 9, 10, 12; (45) W.-2.22.

The Spirit of the Black Mantle, or Wenlock of Wenlock: (36) W.-3.25; 4.2, 5.2.

The Spirit of the Clyde: (41) A.-5.20.

The Spirit of the Fountain, or The Student and the Sybil: (44) A.-6.8, 10, 11, 12, 13; (49) P.M.-7.5, 6; (50) A.-7.23, 24.

The Spirit of the Rhine: (37) W.-3.16, 25.

Spirit Rappings and Table Movings: (53) W.-11.24, 29.

The Spitalfield Weaver; see *Fashionable Friends.*

The Spitfire, or The Cockney Afloat: (38) C.-4.14, 16, 17, 19, 21, 27; 5.5, 10, 26; 6.6, 19; 7.7; 9.11; 12.25; W.-7.25, 30; 8.3, 28; 9.26; (39) W.-4.11; 7.23, 26; (38) C.-12.31; (39) C.-1.11,

15; 2.4, 13; 2.21; (41) N.-3.24, 30; (42) N.-1.10, 11, 12, 20; W.-4.4, 5, 8, 15, 16; A.-9.10; (43) W.-7.10; (46) A.-11.16; (52) A.-4.21, 22, 26; N.-7.14; C.-8.21.

The Spoiled Child; farce by Isaac Bickerstaff: (35) W.-2.9, 11; 11.4; A.-3.4; C.-12.10; (37) W.-6.19, 23; 7.27; 8.7; C.-3.20; 11.8; W.-9.2; (38) C.-6.13, 15, 29; W.-1.20; 11.14; (39) W.-1.8; 2.18; 3.13; 12.5; C.-6.13; 9.27; 11.7; 12.6; (41) N.-9.15, 16; (42) W.-2.9, 10; (43) A.-3.6, 10; (47) A.-6.22; 11.22; (48) A.-1.28; 2.22; W.-3.8; A.-5.4, 5; C.-7.10, 12; 9.30; (50) W.-1.8; (52) C.-6.18; N.-10.22.

Sporting Made Easy; see *The Race Course.*

Sprig of Shillelah: (54) C.-7.28.

Sprigs of Ireland; farce: (48) A.-3.11*; P.M.-4.25; (50) C.-3.2; A.-11.20; 12.5; (51) A.-2.14; 5.7; (53) C.-5.14.

Sprigs of Laurel, or The Rival Soldiers, or Humors of Nipperkin: (35) A.-2.23; 3.23; (36) C.-7.4; W.-10.26; (37) P.-1.17, 31; (38) W.-7.18; (40) W.-10.26, 30; 11.14; (41) W.-11.29; N.-2.20; (44) W.-9.16, 18.

Spring and Autumn, or The Bride of Fifty; comedy: (35) C.-9.16, 19; 12.1; (36) C.-11.1; W.-2.27; A.-5.17; (37) A.-5.26; (44) W.-6.25; (46) A.-10.19, 20, 27.

Spring Gardens: (47) W.-2.18, 22.

The Spy of Saint Marc's: (44) A.-2.12, 13, 14, 15, 17; (45) A.-7.30, 31; 8.1, 2, 7; (46) A.-6.18, 19, 20, 25.

Stabat Mater; by Rossini: (43) C.-1.27.

Stag Hall, or Is she a Woman?; translated from the German of Kotzebue, *Der Kohbock;* a comedy in three acts: (36) C.-12.19*, 20, 27; (37) C.-1.31; (40) W.-4.18; (42) A.-11.7, 9; (47) A.-3.30.

Stage Struck, or Clerks on a Spree: (43) C.-7.13.

The Stage Struck Apothecary; see *Dick, the Apprentice.*

The Stage Struck Irishman: (52) C.-8.7.

The Stage Struck Tailor: (54) W.-6.28.

The Stage Struck Yankee; by O. E. Durivage: (51) B.-11.3*, 4, 5, 6, 7, 8; 12.15, 16, 17; (52) A.-12.4, 22, 25; (53) A.-2.1, 2; (54) C.-7.13; 9.29.

The Star of Seville; tragedy by Frances Kemble Butler: (37) W.-8.7*, 8.9.

The Star of the Forest, or A Story of Old Virginia: (38) C.-12.15, 17, 18.

The Star of the North; operatic drama: (55) W.-9.11, 12, 13.

The Stars and Stripes Triumphant; see *The Pilot.*

The Stars in Philadelphia: (41) N.-6.28, 30.

The Star Spangled Banner, or The American Tar's Fidelity: (37) W.-3.18*, 21, 28; 7.4, 5, 6; (38) W.-1.30; 3.5; 9.19; (39) W.-8.9, 14, 31; (41) W.-6.19, 22; A.-6.2, 4; (42) W.-1.19, 21; A.-7.2, 5; (43) W.-6.13, 17; (44) W.-5.28; (45) A.-6.17; (50) A.-7.6, 20; (55) C.-4.13.

The State Prisoner: (51) A.-6.2, 3.

State Secrets, or The Tailor of Tamworth; farce: (36) W.-12.5*, 14; P.-12.6; (38) W.-2.8; 7.9; 8.2, 13; 9.26; 10.1; (39) W.-8.9; (37) C.-1.25, 28; 2.1, 6, 16, 22, 29; 4.18; 12.30; A.-5.15; 6.8; (38) C.-1.8; 2.12; 5.29; 11.21; (39) C.-1.16; 2.20; W.-10.10, 18; (40) N.-12.16; (41) N.-1.27; 3.22; 4.5; 12.1, 15; (42) C.-3.23; (45) A.-1.4; (47) A.-5.17; 9.6; 10.16; (49) P.M.-7.11; (50) W.-2.1, 8; 3.28; (52) A.-9.21.

The Statue; see *Evadne.*

The Steam Dentist: (43) A.-3.8, 14.

Stewart's Capture, or The Captive's Ransom: (42) W.-5.16, 17, 18, 19, 20, 21, 23, 26, 27; 6.2, 4, 8, 20, 27.

Stewart's Triumph: (42) A.-8.3.

Still Waters Run Deep; comedy by Tom Taylor: (55) A.-10.2*, 3, 4, 5, 6, 8, 10, 11, 12, 13, 15, 16, 17, 18, 19, 20, 22, 23, 24, 26, 30; W.-10.29, 30, 31; A.-11.1, 13, 20, 22, 27; W.-11.1, 2, 3; A.-12.4, 10, 20.

Stop Him who Can; see *The Dramatist.*

Stopped Payment; see *Speculation.*

The Storm, or Yankee Tars on Shore: (40) C.-10.3, 6.

A Storm in a Tea Cup; farce: (54) W.-5.1*, 3, 5; 6.27; 12.21.

The Storming of Seringapatam; see *Tipoo Saib.*

A Story of Old Virginia; see *Star of the Forest.*

A Story of the Heart; see *Lucille.*

The Straight Way is the Best; farce in one act by August von Kotzebue: (37) A.-7.24.

The Strange Gentleman; farce in two acts: (38) C.-1.9*, 17; 3.22; (41) A.-11.16.

The Stranger, or Misanthropy and Repentance; domestic drama by William Dunlap: (35) W.-1.2, 22; 2.23; 9.9; C.-1.2, 16; 4.14; 5.21; 9.30; (36) W.-9.6; C.-8.30; 11.1; (37) C.-1.7, 19; 4.18; 9.29; A.-6.7; W.-12.23; (38) W.-9.13; C.-4.18, 20; 11.26; (39) W.-5.16; C.-3.6, 14; 5.28; 9.12; 11.22; (40) W.-6.18; 12.8; C.-2.28; N.-10.28; (41) A.-5.1; 8.11; 10.13; C.-12.31; W.-2.26; 11.25; (42) W.-1.15, 28; A.-10.28; (43) W.-6.13; A.-8.23; N.-10.3; A.-10.5; N.-10.6; W.-11.7, 11; A.-12.13; (44) A.-1.5, 11; W.-1.19; A.-1.23; N.-1.24; 4.16; A.-6.4, 21; W.-9.11; A.-9.11; C.-11.8, 19; 12.5; (45) W.-2.18; N.-5.1; A.-

7.23; W.-8.6; C.-9.17, 27; W.-10.17; C.-10.17; A.-10.24; C.-11.7; W.-11.13; 12.10; (46) A.-1.7; W.-1.16; A.-3.11; W.-4.7, 29; A.-5.1; 7.17; 9.4, 19; W.-9.10, 18, 19; A.-10.30; 11.20, 25; P.M.-5.10, 19; A.-6.24; 10.6, 17; W.-11.14; A.-11.21, 28; Ath.-12.27; (49) W.-3.7, 30; A.-3.19; W.-5.8, 29; A.-8.17; C.-8.22; A.-10.29; W.-10.29; 11.9; 12.25; (50) A.-3.5, 16, 27; W.-3.20; 4.18; A.-4.20; 5.25; W.-6.19; 9.4, 21; A.-9.26; 10.7; W.-10.29; 11.15; 12.27; (51) A.-2.24; B.-3.18; W.-3.24; A.-3.31; W.-5.6; 9.10; C.-9.30; 10.11; 12.6, 27, 29; (52) C.-1.9, 31; 4.9; A.-4.13; C.-4.17; 6.8, 15; N.-9.20, 23; C.-10.2; A.-10.4, 6, 19; 11.1; C.-12.3; (53) A.-7.1; W.-9.7; C.-9.24; W.-12.15; (54) A.-1.14; C.-4.1; A.-4.22; 6.6; C.M.-9.15; A.-9.23; 10.3; C.M.-12.7; W.-12.30; (55) C.M.-1.17; 2.8; A.-2.21; 3.2, 22; C.M.-3.30; W.-3.31; C.M.-4.5, 21; A.-5.7; C.M.-5.8, 16; W.-5.10; A.-6.16; 9.26; 10.27; C.M.-11.2, 23; A.-11.10; C.M.-12.14.

Stratagem: (43) W.-3.15.

Strathmore; tragedy by J. W. Marston: (49) A.-9.17*, 18.

The Strolling Gentleman; see *Wild Oats.*

The Struggle for Life and Death; (by D. Boucicault): (50) A.-4.27*, 29.

The Student of Morlaix; by E. Forrester: (51) A.-10.10*, 11; (52) A.-3.19.

The Student of Oxford; see *A Cure for Coquettes.*

Subterraneans: (48) A.-5.29, 30, 31; 6.1, 2.

Sudden Reformation: (50) C.-3.14.

Sudden Thoughts; see *Impulse.*

The Surgeon of Paris, or The Massacre of the Huguenots; by J. S. Jones: (41) W.-10.18*, 19, 20, 21, 22, 23, 28; (42) W.-3.8, 10; 5.2; 12.31; (43)

W.-1.2, 3, 24; 2.21; A.-9.25; W.-10.7; C.-12.14; (46) W.-2.17; 3.20; (49) A.-9.19; 10.25, 27; (51) A.-1.14, 15; (52) A.-10.2.

Susan Hopley, or The Vicissitudes of a Maid Servant: (46) A.-1.13, 14, 15, 17, 21.

Susanne, or The Force of Love: (38) C.-10.31; 11.1; 12.5; (39) C.-8.31; (40) N.-9.23; 10.6, 8, 14; 11.17.

The Suspicious Husband: comedy by Benjamin Hoadley: (43) W.-5.2, 3; 10.11, 24.

The Swamp Fox, or Marion and his Merry Men: (46) A.-4.1*, 2, 3, 4, 6, 7, 8, 9, 10, 11, 13, 15, 18, 22, 24; 7.6; (51) N.-8.1; (52) N.-8.28, 30, 31; 9.1.

The Swamp Steed, or Marion and his Merry Men of 1776; by H. H. Paul: (49) C.-11.30*; 12.1, 5, 8.

The Swan of Beauty; harlequinade: (51) A.-12.26.

Swedish Patriotism: (51) W.-12.24, 25, 26, 27.

Sweethearts and Wives; comedy in three acts by Poole: (35) C.-8.28; 12.18, 22; (36) A.-3.18; 4.19; (37) C.-10.27; A.-5.2; 6.21; P.-2.15; (38) C.-1.17, 22; 3.8; 9.1; (39) C.-2.13; W.-10.5, 18; (40) W.-1.22; 10.31; 11.13; (41) W.-6.22; N.-2.23; 3.19; 12.11; (42) N.-1.19; W.-4.25; C.-4.27; A.-7.9; (43) W.-2.16; 7.6; 10.30, 31; (44) W.-4.24; (45) A.-5.21, 27; W.-8.6; C.-11.26; (46) A.-3.26; P.M.-3.31; 4.8; (47) P.M.-2.19, 22; 6.4, 12; (48) A.-8.2; 9.15; 12.19; (50) A.-8.5, 21; B.-9.27; A.-12.3; (51) A.-6.9; B.-11.25, 26; (52) A.-12.14; (53) A.-1.4; C.-6.30; (54) C.-2.1, 8; 3.3; A.-5.17, 19, 20; 6.29; C.M.-11.14; (55) A.-5.25; 6.2; 10.20, 26; W.-11.6.

Swiss Cottage, or Why doesn't she Marry?: (36) W.-10.15*, 18, 19,

20, 21, 28; 12.7; C.-10.21, 22, 26, 29; (37) W.-3.22; 6.17; P.-2.9, 15; A.-6.1, 3; W.-6.28; 7.1; (38) C.-4.20, 23; 9.27; 10.10, 11; W.-2.19, 22, 27; 9.18, 24, 28; 11.28; 12.6, 29; (39) W.-2.19; 7.10; 9.2; 11.15; C.-1.2; (40) W.-5.19, 21; N.-9.1, 4, 14; 11.3; 12.11, 23; (42) A.-5.5, 13; 7.1; W.-7.15; (43) W.-9.16; N.-11.6; (44) W.-4.9; 5.8; (45) A.-5.9; C.-10.24; W.-12.6; (46) W.-1.20; 2.26; 4.13; P.M.-5.11; A.-6.16; (47) P.M.-2.12; W.-4.14; 8.7, 13; A.-12.27; (48) A.-5.1, 12; C.-7.5, 14; (49) A.-1.16; (50) W.-1.7, 11; B.-9.18, 19; 10.5; (51) A.-4.21; 5.20; (52) C.-5.27; 6.16; W.-9.30; (54) C.-5.8; (55) W.-6.28.

The Swiss Family; German opera by Weigh: (40) A.-5.5*; C.-5.8.

Swiss Swains, or How to Make Love: (40) N.-10.31; (42) C.-10.17; (46) P.M.-8.24; 9.11; (48) A.-4.10, 13; 11.24; Ath.-12.26; (49) P.M.-5.4, 5; (50) B.-12.6, 11; (51) A.-7.1; (52) C.-11.22, 23, 24, 27; C.-12.8; (53) A.-2.17; C.-4.19; 5.28; (54) A.-8.24, 25; 9.9; C.-11.20; (55) C.M.-9.10.

The Switzer's Bride; see *Luli.*

Sylvester Daggerwood: (35) W.-10.2; (38) W.-6.30.

Sylvius, or The Roman Odd Fellow: (45) W.-5.15.

The Syracusan Brothers; tragedy by N. H. Bannister: (38) W.-1.15*, 16; 6.29.

The Tailor of Tamworth; see *State Secrets.*

Take that Girl away; comedy: (55) A.-6.4*, 6, 9.

Taken in and Done for; farce: (49) A.-8.20*, 21, 25, 29; 9.12.

Taking by Storm: (52) C.-9.23, 24;

10.12, 20; (53) A.-8.26, 27; 9.1, 17; 11.8; (54) C.-8.2.

A Tale of Blood, or The Wizard of the Heath: (42) W.-6.15, 16, 28. See also *The Idiot Witness.*

A Tale of Mantua; see *The Wife.*

A Tale of Mystery, or The Dumb Man of Arpenay: (44) A.-8.5.

A Tale of the American Camp; see *Victoire.*

The Tale of the Mississippi; see *Border Beagles.*

A Tale of the Sea; see *The Pilot:* (36) W.-11.23.

A Tale of the Sea-side; see *Ambrose Gwinett.*

A Tale of Tracy's Rangers; see *The Battle of Germantown.*

The Taming of the Shrew; by William Shakespeare: (42) A.-9.29; (45) A.-5.3, 17; (46) A.-12.11, 16.

Taming a Tartar: (51) W.-11.20, 21, 22, 24, 26, 28; (52) W.-5.12, 14, 15.

Tam O'Shanter: (35) C.-4.10; (36) C.-12.26; (39) W.-6.11.

The Tarnal Yankee; see *The Lost Heir.*

The Teacher Taught; farce: (51) W.-4.26*, 28, 29; 5.5, 15, 22, 24; 6.18.

Tecumseh, or The Battle of the Thames; by Robert Emmons: (36) W.-10.5*.

Teddy the Tiler; farce: (35) C.-5.2; (36) C.-10.4, 14; 11.18, 24; (37) C.-2.18; 3.7; (38) C.-9.18; 11.8; (40) C.-10.14; (41) N.-2.25; (42) C.-11.1; W.-11.14; (46) W.-8.31; 11.16; (47) W.-2.2, 4; 6.16; 9.27; 10.8, 9; 12.9, 16; (48) A.-3.13; P.M.-5.3; W.-5.15, 29; (49) W.-4.20; A.-6.2; W.-9.15, 17, 28; (50) C.-3.5; 6.24; W.-10.14; A.-11.21; (51) A.-11.7, 8; (53) W.-11.8; (54) A.-5.17, 19, 22, 29; (55) W.-12.5.

Tekeli, or The Siege of Montgatz: (36) W.-4.12; (39) W.-6.3; (40)

W.-1.16, 17; (41) N.-2.13; A.-8.30; 9.1.

The Tell of the Tyrol; see *Hofer.*

Telemachus: (47) A.-5.24, 27; 8.30.

Telula, or The Star of Hope; Indian drama by C. H. Saunders: (52) A.-12.10*, 11.

The Tempest, or The Enchanted Isle; by William Shakespeare: (35) C.-1.31; 2.16; (37) C.-2.23, 28.

The Templar: (51) A.-2.28; 3.1, 3, 5.

The Tempter: (43) A.-3.20, 28, 30.

Ten Thousand a Year, or The History of Tittlebat Titmouse; comedy: (42) C.-4.7*, 8, 22.

A Ten Years' Blunder; see *Botheration.*

Tender Precautions; farce: (52) W.-4.10, 11; C.-11.2, 5, 9, 19, 27; 12.7, 31; (54) A.-1.23, 26; 2.20; 3.8.

The Terror of Wallachia; see *Yara the Gipsy.*

The Terror of the Road, or The Flying Highwayman of 1796: (52) N.-10.18, 19.

The Test of Friendship; see *Damon and Pythias.*

Texas and her Oppressors; see *The Fall of the Alamo.*

Thalaba, or The Burning Sword: (37) W.-2.20*, 21, 22, 23, 24, 25, 27, 28; 3.1, 2, 3, 4, 6, 7, 8, 9, 10, 11, 16, 17, 30; 7.24; 8.5, 10; (38) W.-3.7; (42) W.-1.25, 26, 27, 28, 29; (43) W.-6.19, 21; (50) C.-6.26, 27; (51) A.-7.4, 5.

That Odious Captain Cutter: (51) A.-4.30; 5.1.

Theatrical Developments; see *Humbug.*

There's Nothing in it: (55) W.-6.29.

Theresa's Vow; see *Maid of Croissy.*

Therese, or The Orphan of Geneva; by J. H. Payne from the French of Ducange: (35) W.-2.13; 4.8; 5.21; 11.30; (36) P.-11.11, 30; W.-12.2;

(37) P.-1.5; A.-5.11; (38) W.-3.13; 10.29; 12.4; C.-1.26; 2.3; (39) W.-4.16; 5.25; 7.11; 8.13; 9.23; 12.7; (40) C.-9.19; 12.2, 29; W.-2.27; 3.19; (41) A.-4.23; 8.10, 31; N.-4.9; (42) W.-3.28; 5.30; A.-9.27; W.-11.4; (43) A.-3.27; 4.25; W.-6.3; (44) W.-9.12; C.-11.23; (45) A.-8.18; C.-10.24; W.-11.15; (46) A.-1.12; W.-2.24; 5.22; 8.29; A.-12.3, 10; P.M.-12.17; (47) W.-1.8; 3.20; 11.19; (48) P.M.-5.11; C.-7.20; W.-9.1; 10.12; Ath.-12.30; (49) A.-4.4; P.M.-7.24; (50) A.-7.31; (54) C.-7.14; C.M.-12.20, 23; (55) C.M.-4.25; A.-12.5, 6.

Thimble Rig: (45) A.-4.11, 28; W.-10.7, 8, 15.

Things in the Next Century: (50) C.-5.17, 24; (52) N.-7.30.

Thirty Years of a Gambler's Life; by Wm. Dunlap: (54) C.M.-11.22, 23, 25.

This House to be Sold; (by John Brougham): (48) A.-4.26, 27; 5.10, 11.

Three and the Deuce, or Which is Which?: (35) W.-9.22; C.-11.16, 20, 28; (36) C.-1.5, 11; A.-6.2; (37) W.-3.30; C.-4.10, 14; (39) C.-3.30; (40) W.-12.7.

Three Clerks: (47) P.M.-6.29.

Three Cuckoos; farce: (51) W.-12.19*, 29; (52) W.-1.22; 2.12, 25; 5.27; 12.3, 7, 24; (53) W.-1.5; 2.7, 17; 3.9; C.-12.2, 27; (54) C.-1.2.

Three Degrees of Loafing; see *The Rake's Progress.*

Three Eras in Washington's Life: (48) W.-12.30*; (49) W.-1.1, 2, 3, 4, 5.

Three Eras in a Woman's Life: (47) P.M.-6.7.

Three Faced Frenchman; comic vaudeville: (47) A.-7.2; (52) W.-9.24, 25; (54) W.-4.19, 20, 21, 22, 26.

Three Fingered Jack; see *Obi.*

The Three Generations; see *Past and Present.*

Three Gladiators; ballet pantomime: (36) C.-12.20*, 21; (37) A.-6.20.

The Three Guardsmen, or The Three Musketeers, or The Siege of Rochelle; by Lester Wallack: (50) C.-1.28*, 29, 30, 31; 2.1, 2, 8, 15, 20; (52) N.-7.12, 13, 14, 21; 10.22, 25.

Three Hats: (42) C.-4.12.

Three Hunchbacks, or The Sabre Grinders of Damascus: (36) W.-2.6, 16; (39) W.-5.6.

The Three Musketeers; see *The Three Guardsmen.*

Three Jack Sheppards: (55) C.-4.24, 28.

Three Lovers, or Mad as a March Hare: (42) C.-11.14, 15; (43) W.-7.22, 24, 28; 8.9, 14; (47) A.-1.8.

The Three Knights of Trineomalee; see *The Green Monster.*

Three Poisons: (48) P.M.-5.15.

The Three Shaws; see *Grimshaw, Bagshaw, and Bradshaw.*

The Three Simpsons: (42) A.-6.29, 30; 7.26.

The Three Temperance Grocers; see *Hobbs, Dobbs, and Stubs.*

The Three Thieves, or The Monkey of Frankfort: (53) A.-3.31; 4.1; (53) C.-4, 14, 15.

Three Weeks after Marriage; comedy by Arthur Murphy: (35) C.-9.25; (36) C.-11.12; W.-10.20; (42) A.-10.3; (44) A.-9.9; (47) A.-10.27.

Three Wives of Madrid; comedy: (44) W.-10.12*, 14, 15; (49) A.-5.23, 24.

Thumping Legacy: (43) W.-10.6, 10; (44) N.-3.27; (53) A.-2.25; 3.3; 10.7, 8; 11.10; 12.1; (54) A.-3.7; (55) A.-2.28; 3.26, 28, 29, 30; 10.3, 10; 11.14.

The Tiger at Large, or The Cad of the Buss: (37) W.-12.9, 18, 23; (38) W.-1.10; 7.11.

The Tiger Horde, or Dubar the Terrible: (39) W.-3.27, 28; (50) C.-1.11.

Tim Moore, the Lion of the Day; farce: (51) A.-11.14.

Time Tries All; domestic drama: (49) A.-3.28*, 29; 4.3; (53) A.-12.5, 6; (54) A.-3.4, 9, 28; (55) A.-11.12, 16, 23.

Time Works Wonders, or The Inconstant; comedy by D. W. Jerrold: (45) W.-6.2*, 3, 4, 5, 6; A.-6.5, 6; (46) W.-9.11, 12; (47) W.-4.29; 5.1; A.-10.13; 11.15; (48) A.-4.21; W.-11.15, 18; (52) C.-1.10; 5.28; 6.9; (53) C.-3.1.

Timour the Tartar; melodrama: (37) P.-1.30; (38) W.-10.3; (39) W.-2.23, 25, 26, 27, 28; 3.1, 2; (41) W.-4.8, 9, 10; A.-12.3, 4; (42) A.-1.4; (44) N.-4.25; (46) A.-1.22, 23.

The Tinker and his Family; see *False Pretences.*

Tipperary Legacy; farce: (50) C.-7.17*, 18.

Tipoo Saib, or The Storming of Seringapatam: (41) N.-4.10, 12, 13, 15, 16, 17, 19, 21.

'Tis All a Farce: (39) W.-4.15; 5.31; (53) W.-2.19, 24; 4.12; C.-5.24.

Tit for Tat: (47) A.-6.17, 21, 23; (52) W.-4.19, 21, 24.

Titus Andronicus; by William Shakespeare "as altered by [N. H.] Bannister into a beautiful play": (39) W.-1.30, 31; 2.1, 2.

Tom, Jerry, and Logic's Visit to Philadelphia: (44) N.-4.16, 17, 18.

Tom and Jerry, or Life in London; by W. T. Moncrieff: (35) W.-2.9, 10, 12; C.-6.24; (36) W.-3.23; 6.6, 21; A.-3.24; (37) W.-7.17; 8.14; (38) W.-12.14, 25; (39) W.-1.4; 3.16, 18; 5.25; (40) A.-12.28; W.-7.20; (41) A.-11.8; W.-2.12; (42) W.-1.8; 2.1; 5.3; 6.15; A.-7.23; 11.4; (43) W.-

3.25, 28; A.-10.18; (45) A.-8.16; (46) C.-1.1; A.-5.5; (47) A.-6.14, 19; (49) W.-2.19, 20, 21, 22, 23; 3.1, 3; (50) C.-6.1, 4; (51) N.-7.21, 23; (52) N.-7.26, 31; 10.23; (54) C.-3.7, 8.

Tom and Jerry in America: (45) C.-12.2, 6, 17, 20; (46) C.-12.7; (48) A.-6.12, 13, 15.

Tom Cringle, or Mat of the Iron Hand, or The Seaman's Log Book: (35) W.-2.14; 4.10; 5.8; C.-4.25; (36) C.-6.15; (37) W.-3.20; C.-11.2; P.-2.16; W.-8.31; 9.4; (38) C.-2.1; (39) W.-5.24; (41) W.-12.18; A.-1.20, 22; N.-12.22; (42) W.-2.16; (44) W.-5.15, 20, 22; (46) A.-1.24; 5.2, 4, 26; 7.17; (48) A.-2.9; 10.6, 10; (49) A.-9.19; (50) A.-6.24; (52) A.-9.18.

Tom Cringle's Log; see *Tom Cringle.*

Tom Grig, the Lamplighter: (46) P.M.-10.30.

Tom More; farce: (45) C.-11.27; (48) A.-3.15; P.M.-4.24.

Tom Noddy's Secret; farce: (38) C.-12.24*, 25, 26; (39) C.-1.1; 9.5, 13; 10.11; (40) C.-4.1; 11.20, 24; 12.3; N.-9.2, 4, 10, 12.5; C.-12.23; (41) N.-11.18; (42) C.-4.29; 5.9; (47) A.-5.10, 11; (52) C.-11.18, 20, 22.

Tom Thumb the Great; burlesque opera (by Henry Fielding): (35) W.-2.28; 3.3, 4; (36) W.-1.7; C.-7.7; (37) A.-5.4; (41) A.-1.4, 8; (47) P.M.-5.24, 26, 27; 6.4.

Tommy Tit in Trouble: (41) A.-2.1, 2.

The Tongueless Pirate Boy; see *Wizard Skiff.*

Tonquewaschen, or The Terror of Louisiana; pantomime ballet: (44) W.-11.19.

To Oblige Benson: (55) C.-2.13, 14; W.-3.26, 28; 4.3, 18; 5.1, 12.

Toodles; comedy either by Cowley or by W. E. Burton: (52) N.-9.18; A.-12.13, 15; (53) A.-1.3; (54) C.-1.31;

2.10; A.-3.30, 31; 4.1, 3, 4, 5, 11,
14; W.-5.2, 4, 13; A.-5.11, 31; C.-
8.25; A.-9.1, 5, 13; C.M.-9.16, 30;
A.-10.2; C.-10.9; C.M.-10.14; A.-
11.6, 30; C.-11.6; C.M.-11.7; (55)
A.-1.11, 25; C.M.-1.27; A.-2.17;
C.M.-3.13; A.-4.10; W.-5.11, 15, 23;
A.-6.14; 8.18, 22; C.M.-9.24, 26; 10.5;
A.-11.5; W.-11.8; A.-12.15.

The Toothache; (by John Bray): (46)
P.M.-11.7, 9, 14; (47) P.M.-2.1.

Too Late for Dinner; farce: (38) C.-
10.12, 13; (41) A.-8.26; N.-12.9;
(42) A.-9.21; (46) P.M.-8.22; A.-
11.6.

Too Many Cooks Spoil the Broth: (47)
W.-3.2, 10, 15, 26; 4.6; 5.26; (54)
A.-6.27.

*To Parents and Guardians, or Bob
Nettles;* farce: (54) W.-3.27, 28, 29;
4.1, 13; C.-4.13, 14, 26; W.-12.5,
7, 8, 9; (55) W.-5.14, 26; 6.21, 25;
A.-8.23, 27; 9.14; 10.5; C.M.-
11.16.

To Paris and Back for Five Pounds:
(53) W.-9.17, 18, 22, 29; 10.17;
11.26; C.-12.17, 19, 24, 28; (54) W.-
1.31; 2.2, 3, 7, 24; 3.9; C.-4.4; 5.24;
W.-6.22; 10.4, 20; 11.2, 16; 12.19;
(55) W.-2.24.

Tortesa, the Usurer; tragedy by N. P.
Willis: (39) W.-6.20*; 7.15; 8.28,
29; 9.9.

*Touch and Take, or The Singing
Bailiff;* farce: (36) P.-11.26; 12.17;
(37) P.-1.3; (39) C.-4.1; (40) C.-
4.27; 5.18; 28.

The Tourists: (39) W.-10.31.

*Tour de Nesle, or The Chamber of
Death;* by Victor Hugo: (35) W.-
11.5, 6, 9; (36) W.-4.7, 9; (37) W.-
8.25, 29; (41) A.-6.12; W.-6.19; N.-
11.29; (42) N.-1.13; W.-1.22, 24, 26;
A.-3.28; 5.14; 8.3; (43) W.-1.11;
3.17; 6.17; A.-9.10; N.-10.30, 31;
(44) A.-1.10, 27; 9.7; (45) N.-4.28,

29; A.-11.15, 18, 19; 12.31; (46)
A.-11.21, 30; (48) A.-2.18; (50) C.-
2.16, 18; A.-3.9, 23; 4.24; 10.17;
(51) A.-1.11; 2.27; 4.17; 5.1; 7.10,
30; (52) C.-3.4; N.-7.19; 9.20, 23;
A.-10.23; (55) C.-4.11, 14.

Town and Country, or Which is Best;
comedy by Thomas Morton: (35)
W.-1.12; C.-6.23; 7.2; (36) W.-5.18;
(39) W.-8.10; C.-12.10; (40) C.-1.3;
12.28; N.-12.31; (41) N.-12.31; (42)
W.-6.27; (43) W.-1.13; 6.28; N.-
10.4; A.-10.13; (44) W.-2.5; 3.21;
6.6; (45) W.-2.27; 3.28; C.-11.27;
(46) A.-4.28; W.-8.29; (47) W.-
5.6; A.-11.26; (51) W.-5.9, 13; (52)
C.-1.6; 9.10; (53) A.-1.11; C.-3.4;
5.26; A.-5.26; C.-6.21; (55) C.M.-
4.3; A.-4.18, 20, 23.

The Trafalgar Medal; see *Presumptive Evidence.*

A Tragedy Rehearsed; see *The Critic.*

The Traitor: (45) C.-7.4, 5.

The Traitor Foiled; see *General
Washington.*

Trente Ans, ou la Vie d'un Jouer; see
The Gambler's Fate.

Trial by Battle: (36) W.-1.21*; P.-
1.28; (43) W.-4.24, 25; (47) A.-
12.4, 7, 22; (50) A.-5.25.

*Trick for Trick, or The Valet de
Sham:* (38) W.-10.25*, 26; 11.1, 20;
(41) C.-10.5, 6; (43) W.-6.7, 8, 16;
7.26; C.-9.9, 13; W.-9.25; C.-12.4,
14; W.-12.30; (44) W.-5.6, 11; 9.10,
27; 12.23; (45) W.-5.7; 9.2; (47)
W.-4.9, 14; 5.15; P.M.-5.17; W.-6.5,
10; 11.3; 12.14; (48) W.-4.20; 5.8;
A.-8.16, 18; (50) B.-11.13, 14, 30;
12.9; (51) B.-2.7; 6.20, 21; (52)
C.-10.1, 4, 7, 29; 11.1; (53) C.-1.8;
W.-9.13; (54) W.-10.17, 30; (55)
W.-3.16; 5.4.

A Trip to Bath; see *The Rivals.*

A Trip to New York; see *The Kentuckian.*

Tristram Shandy, or My Uncle Toby:
(35) W.-3.11, 13, 17.

The Triumph of Greece: (37) P.-2.14.

Turned Head: (41) N.-6.15, 16; (54)
C.-5.10, 11, 19.

*Turning the Tables, or The Exciseman
of Winchester:* (36) W.-10.10, 29;
11.3; 12.21; C.-12.2, 23; (37) W.-
1.20; C.-9.20; 11.17; P.-2.16; A.-
5.5; (38) C.-1.4; 3.24; 4.25; 11.20;
12.11; (39) C.-2.2; 11.19, 22; W.-
7.19, 25; (40) A.-9.17; C.-2.26; W.-
5.16; C.-4.28; 8.31; (41) A.-4.12;
W.-6.24; C.-2.11; N.-4.8; 10.19; (42)
C.-5.7, 9; (43) A.-9.12; (44) A.-
10.1; (45) A.-5.19; (46) P.M.-5.12,
14, 22; 8.20; (47) A.-11.1; W.-12.29,
31; (48) P.M.-4.1; A.-8.30; (49)
C.-9.7; (50) A.-6.21; (51) C.-12.15,
16; (52) C.-1.5, 16; (53) W.-10.4;
(54) C.M.-9.14, 21; 10.7; W.-11.10;
(55) A.-10.30; 11.16, 26.

The Turnpike Gate; farce: (35) W.-
5.30; 7.2; 11.14; C.-10.13, 19; (36)
W.-3.10; 10.22, 31; (37) P.-2.1, 15;
(38) W.-7.13, 20; (39) W.-3.12;
(40) W.-7.25; (41) W.-12.23, 24;
(41) N.-3.26; 4.6; 8.26; (42) A.-
5.3; C.-5.4; A.-6.1; (44) W.-4.5;
(48) A.-4.24; 11.1.

*The Twa Ghaists, or The Humors of
Mucklestone Manor;* farce: (36) C.-
2.22*, 24, 26; (37) C.-10.28; (38)
C.-1.6.

'Twas I, or Truth a Lie; farce by
J. H. Payne: (36) C.-10.25, 27; (37)
A.-5.30; (39) C.-4.16, 20; 6.5; (40)
C.-4.16; 6.5; (41) A.-5.11; (46)
P.M.-6.15, 18; 8.28; 12.17, 29; (47)
P.M.-5.14, 29; 7.9; (48) P.M.-3.29;
(54) W.-2.23.

Twelfth Night; by William Shakespeare: (37) C.-1.23; A.-6.17; (45)
C.-12.30; (46) C.-1.2; (52) W.-3.19,
20, 27; (54) A.-1.18, 19, 20, 21, 23,
24, 25, 26, 28, 30; 2.15, 21; 3.24.

The Twelve Labors of Hercules;
comedy in two acts: (53) W.-12.31.

23 John Street: (35) C.-6.10; 7.2; 9.1;
10.2, 27; (36) C.-1.6, 21; W.-4.9;
5.28, 30; 6.1, 28; (37) C.-4.13; (45)
C.-10.28.

Twice Killed; farce: (37) A.-5.31*;
6.1, 16; C.-9.15, 26; 10.23, 25; 12.27;
(38) C.-3.26; 4.30; 5.8; 8.27; (43)
W.-2.13; 3.30; 4.5; (44) W.-4.11;
(46) A.-3.27; (51) W.-4.10, 15, 23;
B.-4.22, 23; 6.3, 25, 26; C.-9.17, 19,
29; 10.8, 25.

The Twin Brothers; see *Gemini.*

*The Twin Brothers of the Blood Red
Cross:* (49) A.-3.5*, 6, 7, 8, 9, 10.

The Twin Sisters: (42) W.-10.18, 19,
20; (43) W.-3.27; 4.3.

The Two Barbers: (43) W.-4.10; 6.30.

Two of the B'hoys: (47) P.M.-6.30;
A.-7.3, 17; (53) C.-1.20, 23, 25, 31;
A.-3.21; W.-6.17, 18; (54) W.-5.10.

The Two Bonnycastles; farce: (52)
W.-1.28, 29, 30, 31; 2.11, 19, 24; A.-
3.8, 10, 12, 24; 4.9; W.-4.15, 29; 6.4,
25; A.-8.23; W.-9.8, 23; 10.28; 11.4;
12.29; (53) W.-2.16; 4.15; 9.27;
11.10; 12.9; (54) W.-2.6; (55) C.M.-
6.14, 18, 28.

The Two Brothers: (40) W.-7.23.

The Two Buzzards: (53) W.-12.26,
29; (54) W.-10.18, 28; 11.22; (55)
W.-2.21; 3.15; 6.11.

Two can Play at That Game: (55)
W.-2.14; 4.4.

The Two Candidates; farce: (48) O.-
5.24, 25.

Two Centuries Ago; see *The Forest
Princess.*

*The Two Conquerors on the Plains of
Palestine, or the Wandering Arabs:*
(38) W.-3.3.

*The Two Drovers, or A Highlander's
Revenge:* (39) W.-12.30, 31; (40)
W.-2.25; (55) C.M.-2.2.

The Two Fathers: (54) N.-6.23.

The Two Figaros; comic opera: (37) C.-12.14*, 15, 16, 19.

The Two Firemen: (42) A.-8.25.

2, 4, 5, o!, or *The Lawyer's Clerk;* comedy: (46) P.M.-9.28, 30; 10.31; (47) P.M.-1.20; 2.9.

The Two Foscari; by Lord Byron: (42) A.-8.6.

The Two Foscari; opera by Verdi: (47) W.-7.19.

2538; see *The Prize.*

The Two Friends: (37) P.-1.20, 25; (41) A.-11.29; 12.1, 2; (46) P.M.-8.31; 9.2; 11.10; (47) P.M.-3.23; 4.5, 24; 6.18; (51) B.-1.6, 7, 24.

The Two Galley Slaves, or The Mill of Alderon: (50) A.-10.21; 11.12. See also *The Mill of Alderon.*

Two Gentlemen of Verona; by William Shakespeare: (41) C.-10.18, 19.

The Two Ghosts; see *The Twa Ghaists.*

The Two Great Rascals: (54) A.-11.10.

The Two Greens; farce: (40) W.-6.26; 7.10, 14.

Triumphs in Mexico; see *The Campaign of the Rio Grande.*

The Triumphs of Rough and Ready: (52) N.-10.25.

Troubles in Texas; see *The Lone Star.*

The Truand Chief; see *The Provost of Paris.*

True Hearts: (54) A.-12.11, 18, 29.

True Love never runs Smooth: (54) C.-7.10; 9.23.

A True Tale of the Sea; see *Death Plank.*

The True Use of Riches, or The Singing Cobbler: (46) P.M.-10.5.

The Trumpeter's Daughter: (46) P.M.-6.9, 10, 12; (48) A.-10.26; 11.27; (50) A.-9.11, 14.

The Trumpeter's Wedding; comedy: (50) C.-4.17*, 18, 23.

Truth, or A Glass Too Much: (40) W.-6.5; (43) W.-7.15.

Truth a Lie; see *'Twas I.*

Trying it on; farce: (54) W.-2.15*, 17, 25; 3.1, 16; 4.18.

Turn Out: (35) C.-2.18; 9.21; (36) C.-9.10; P.-12.19, 23; (37) C.-3.2, 9; 9.1; W.-6.21; C.-10.16; 11.14; (38) W.-7.21; C.-9.28; 11.9; (39) W.-4.25; 7.30; 8.7; C.-4.25; 9.9; 10.31; (40) W.-12.9; C.-9.29; 10.9; 12.15; (41) W.-1.18, 19; A.-5.18; (42) W.-4.19; 7.6; (50) B.-10.10, 11; 11.4, 5.

The Two Gregories, or Luck in a Name: (35) W.-4.6; 12.14; (36) P.-11.9, 22, 30; 12.15; (39) W.-4.6; 5.8; (40) A.-9.14; (41) W.-11.3, 4; A.-8.13, 28; 9.4; 10.1; 11.2, 26; (42) N.-1.26; W.-2.9, 10; 4.30; 6.17; 7.8, 21; (43) W.-2.7; A.-4.4, 7, 24; 8.21; (46) P.M.-6.16; (48) A.-1.20, 22; P.M.-3.16; (49) C.-8.17, 25; (54) C.-8.22; 9.6; (55) W.-10.20, 29, 30; 12.10.

The Two James'; see *Hypochondriac.*

The Two Magicians: (35) Mam.C.-1.2, 3, 24.

The Two Mummies; see *Sarcophagus.*

The Two Murderers; see *Henri and Louise.*

The Two Queens; comedy: (38) C.-4.20*, 26; (41) C.-9.6, 7; (44) N.-3.25; 4.5, 22, 23, 24; (45) C.-10.29, 30; 11.3, 11, 12, 18; (46) P.M.-4.6, 7, 11, 18; 5.6; 6.4; 8.27; (47) P.M.-1.13; 4.20; A.-10.12, 19; 12.21; (48) P.M.-3.17; A.-9.28; 11.9; 12.7; (49) A.-3.15.

The Two Smiths: (42) A.-1.3, 4.

The Two Thompsons, or William Thompson; farce: (37) A.-7.3; C.-8.22; 8.31; 10.18; (46) P.M.-8.20; W.-12.19, 22, 31; (47) W.-1.20, 28; 2.23; 3.17, 22; A.-4.6; W.-6.9; (48) W.-6.7; 8.29; 11.3, 7, 28; 12.11; (49) W.-1.23.

Two Words, or A Night in the Forest: (39) C.-5.18.

U and I, or I and my Double: (38) C.-11.29*, 30.

U. A. W. G., or The Invitation Card; farce by August von Kotzebue: (37) A.-7.20.

Uda and Magnus, or The Doomed Crew: (35) W.-12.25, 26, 28, 29, 30, 31; (36) W.-1.5, 6; 2.12.

Ugolino, or The Innocent Condemned; by J. B. Booth: (35) C.-4.22, 24, 25; (36) A.-6.7, 10; P.-12.13; (40) W.-5.6, 8; (41) W.-6.7, 10; 9.17; (42) A.-8.20; 10.7; (45) W.-6.14; (50) A.-12.13, 14; (51) A.-3.28; (52) A.-9.7; (54) N.-6.12.

Uncle John; see *My Uncle John.*

Uncle Pat's Cabin: (53) C.-5.9, 10, 11, 12, 13, 14; (53) W.-10.24, 25, 26, 27; 11.3; (54) W.-5.18, 23.

Uncle Pop: (40) W.-12.17.

Uncle Sam, or A Nabob for an Hour: (35) W.-1.8, 23; 2.3, 23; 3.23; (38) W.-12.13; (41) A.-4.8; 8.25; C.-9.9, 11, 30; (42) W.-9.22; (43) A.-12.16; (45) W.-11.20, 22; (46) P.M.-10.26; 11.5; (47) P.M.-2.15; (48) P.M.-4.3, 6; (49) P.M.-7.21; C.-10.22; (50) W.-4.5, 10; 9.18; (51) W.-1.31; (52) W.-12.30; (53) W.-1.14; C.-2.4; 3.12; W.-6.21, 24; (54) C.-6.24.

Uncle Tom's Cabin, or Life among the Lowly; by G. L. Aiken: (52) N.-8.30*, 31; 9.1, 2; (53) C.-9.26, 27, 28, 29, 30; 10.1, 3, 4, 5, 6, 7, 8, 10, 11, 12, 13, 14, 15, 17, 18, 19, 20, 21, 22, 24, 25, 26, 27, 28, 29, 31; 11.1, 2, 3, 4, 5, 14, 15, 16, 17, 18, 19, 21, 22, 23, 24, 25, 26, 28, 29, 30; (54) C.-2.13, 14, 15, 16, 17, 18, 20, 21, 22, 23, 24, 25; 11.27, 28, 29; 12.2; (55) C.M.-2.12, 13, 14, 15, 16, 17, 19, 20, 21, 22, 23, 24, 25, 27; C.-22, 24, 26, 27, 28; C.M.-3.1, 2; C.-3.1, 2, 3, 5, 6, 7, 8, 9, 10, 12, 13, 14, 15, 16, 17.

Undine: (47) A.-9.18, 20, 21, 22, 23, 24, 25; (49) A.-4.6; (53) W.-4.4, 5, 6, 7, 8, 9.

Une Heure de la Vie d'un Soldat; see *He is not A-Miss.*

Une Passion; vaudeville in French: (37) C.-2.6.

The Unfinished Gentleman; farce by Selby: (35) W.-3.16, 18, 24; 4.1; C.-5.11, 13; (36) A.-3.24; (38) W.-3.10; C.-5.28; (39) W.-4.16; C.-4.24; (41) W.-6.3, 11, 14, 21; 7.1; (47) W.-11.20; 12.15.

The Unfortunate Author; see *Life in Philadelphia.*

The Unfortunate Miss Bailey; Vaudeville: (41) N.-6.17.

A Union of the Flags; see *Spanish Pirates;* see also *Yankees in China.*

The United Fire Boys; see *Mose and Jakey.*

The Unknown; by James Rees: (52) A.-4.26, 27, 28, 29.

Ups and Downs, or The Life of a Cab Driver: (46) A.-5.11.

Ups and Downs, or Felix in Search of a Wife; comedy in three acts by the author of *Paul Pry:* (40) N.-11.9*, 13.

Ups and Downs of a Student's Life: (49) C.-10.27, 28, 30.

Used Up; comedy by Dion Boucicault: (45) C.-9.2*, 3; A.-10.27; (48) W.-1.3, 4, 7, 17; 3.3; A.-8.8, 31; 9.6, 7; (50) W.-11.22, 27; 12.2, 6; (51) A.-1.31; 7.16; (52) A.-9.20; 11.10; (53) A.-1.10; C.-7.2; (54) W.-12.1, 6; (55) W.-6.2, 16, 18, 20, 26; 7.4.

Vagaries of the Day: (42) A.-7.4.

The Vagrant, or His Wife and Family: (42) W.-5.17, 18; 10.20; (43) A.-8.15, 19.

Valentine and Orson, or The Wild Man of the Woods: (36) C.-7.6; (37) W.-1.19, 20; (39) W.-1.19, 22,

25; (40) C.-12.31; W.-6.29; (41)
C.-1.2; (42) W.-5.6; (44) N.-1.20,
22, 23; A.-1.26; (54) N.-6.30; 7.1.

Valeria, or The Roman Sisters;
tragedy: (51) C.-9.19*, 22, 24, 25,
26; (52) C.-4.29; 5.1; (54) C.-3.28.

The Valet de Sham; see *Trick for Trick.*

Valsha, or The Saxon Serf, or The Slave Queen: (41) N.-9.13, 14, 15,
16, 17, 18, 20, 24, 25; 11.27; (42)
N.-1.6, 7; (46) A.-3.12, 13, 14, 16,
17, 19.

Valsha, the Tyrant Queen: (50) C.-
4.1, 2, 3; (52) N.-8.2.

The Vampire, or The Bride of the Isles: (37) P.-1.7, 10, 11, 12, 13, 21;
(40) W.-6.8; (42) A.-8.15; 10.25;
11.1; (44) A.-11.7, 9, 29; (50) C.-
1.2; (55) C.M.-1.8, 9, 10, 11, 12, 13.

The Vampire Bat; see *Demon Dwarf.*

Velasco, or Castilian Honor; tragedy
by Epes Sargent: (38) C.-11.29*;
12.26, 28.

The Venetian, or The Bravo's Oath:
(49) A.-3.24*, 26, 27, 28, 29, 30, 31;
11.3; (50) A.-4.6, 7; 10.11, 12, 15,
17; (51) A.-4.5, 8, 9, 10; (52) A.-
10.8, 9, 13, 19, 21; (54) C.-10.28, 31;
11.1; (55) C.M.-5.5, 9.

The Venetian Bravo; see *Council of Ten.*

Venetian Carnival: (41) C.-10.22.

Venice Preserved, or The Plot Discovered; tragedy by Thomas Otway:
(35) C.-1.1; 4.7; 5.22; 10.23; W.-
3.17; 12.10; (36) C.-1.11; W.-3.23;
5.19; 10.19; (37) W.-7.20; (38) W.-
7.13; (39) C.-3.16; (40) N.-9.18;
(41) C.-10.12; N.-12.20; A.-4.19;
(42) A.-9.15; (43) W.-10.6; (45) A.-
5.29; W.-11.11; C.-12.1; W.-12.8;
(46) W.-1.17; 2.26; 4.6; 5.16; (47)
W.-4.23; 11.19; (48) A.-4.8; C.-
7.22; (49) W.-3.17; 6.19; (50) W.-

1.5; A.-2.23; W.-10.12; 11.2; (51)
W.-1.4; 5.17; 9.20; 12.13; (52) C.-
1.15, 26; A.-9.9; (54) A.-6.26; 7.1;
(55) C.M.-4.24.

Venus and Adonis, or The Handsome Hunter: (46) C.-1.5, 8.

Venus in Arms, or The Petticoat Colonel: (39) W.-2.6, 12; (41) A.-
1.27, 28; (42) P.M.-12.30; (47) P.M.-
1.4, 23; 2.5.

The Verginny Cupids; see *Oh! Hush!!*

The Vermont Wool Dealer; by C. A.
Logan: (39) W.-4.26*; (43) W.-
5.13; (55) C.-4.5.

The Vermonter; see *Peaceful Pelton.*

A Veteran; national drama: (45) C.-
7.3*, 4, 5; (53) C.-3.15, 16, 22, 31.

The Veteran and his Progeny; see *102.*

The Veteran of Austerlitz: (53) A.-
7.16.

Very Suspicious: (52) W.-10.11, 12.

The Vicar of Wakefield: (50) A.-
6.17, 18, 20, 28; (51) B.-1.27, 28, 29,
30, 31; 2.1, 6.

The Vicissitudes of a Maid Servant;
see *Susan Hopley.*

Vicomte de l'Etorieres: (45) C.-10.7.

Victoire, or A Tale of the American Camp: (35) C.-11.14; (40) W.-5.16.

Victoria, or The Lion and the Kiss;
by J. M. Field: (39) C.-6.21.

Victorine, or I'll Sleep on it: (38) C.-
4.4; 5.18; (39) C.-3.11; (40) N.-
9.29; 10.2; 11.3; (41) C.-6.15; A.-
10.26, 27, 28; (42) C.-1.29; W.-6.13;
A.-9.24; (43) A.-3.9, 10; (44) A.-
8.8; (45) A.-5.24, 28; (46) P.M.-
8.25; (49) W.-5.24; 6.18.

The Village Coquette: (42) A.-9.30.

The Village Doctor: (41) N.-2.18, 19.

The Village Gossip: (41) A.-4.10, 14,
21. See also *Scan. Mag.*

The Village Lawyer, or Ba Ba Ba:
(41) W.-7.15; (43) N.-10.5; (46)

A.-12.31; (47) A.-1.26; 2.5; P.M.-
2.19, 26; 4.2; (49) ATH.-1.2.

*The Village Phantom, or The Sleep
Walker:* (37) P.-1.9; (42) N.-1.17;
(44) C.-11.21.

*Violet, or The Father and his Daugh-
ter:* (46) P.M.-5.21, 22; A.-10.28, 29.

The Virgin of the Sun; by William
Dunlap: (35) C.-12.4; (36) C.-1.12;
(51) A.-5.19, 20, 22, 23, 24.

Virginia; tragedy: (50) W.-5.29*, 31.

The Virginia Mummy; farce: (35) W.-
6.30; 7.3, 4; 9.3, 11; (36) W.-5.17,
21; (37) C.-10.28; (38) W.-1.4;
10.11; (40) W.-12.18; A.-9.8, 11;
(42) A.-9.20, 21; (44) C.-11.7; (47)
W.-4.10, 13; P.M.-7.16; (48) A.-
2.15; W.-12.18, 21, 30; (49) A.-
10.12; N.-10.12; (50) A.-6.25; 11.16;
(51) A.-3.7; C.-3.31; B.-4.10, 17;
(52) A.-2.28; (53) A.-6.9; (54)
C.M.-10.3, 10, 17; (55) C.M.-1.11;
3.19; 5.24; 6.8; 12.19.

*Virginius, or The Roman Father, or
The Liberation of Rome;* tragedy by
J. Sheridan Knowles: (35) W.-1.7,
21; 3.14; 5.9, 25; 6.30; 8.28; C.-1.14;
4.23; 6.25; A.-2.26; W.-11.17; 12.4,
31; (36) P.-12.7; W.-1.28; 12.27;
(37) C.-11.18; W.-6.29; (38) W.-
1.30; 7.24; 10.30; 12.6, 17; C.-2.2;
5.19; (39) W.-4.19; C.-11.26; W.-
6.5; 9.16; (40) C.-11.25; W.-4.25;
N.-10.7; 12.24; (41) A.-4.15; 6.4;
8.30; W.-5.19; N.-8.27; (42) W.-
3.16; A.-3.31; W.-5.30; A.-9.12; W.-
11.2; (43) A.-8.19; 10.6; C.-11.3; A.-
12.12; (44) N.-4.18; C.-11.15; (45)
W.-5.5; A.-12.12, 17; (46) A.-1.10;
W.-3.27; A.-5.6; (47) W.-3.20; 5.20;
A.-12.1; (48) A.-3.18; 11.29; W.-
11.29; (50) A.-5.11; 9.10; (51) A.-
5.28; 10.8; C.-11.28; (52) A.-3.17;
W.-6.18; 11.30; (54) W.-10.20; (55)
C.M.-2.9; 6.29; 12.17; W.-12.28.

Vision of the Dead; see *Curfew.*

Vision of Home: (43) A.-4.3.

*Vision of the Sun, or The Golden
Harp:* (37) W.-6.30*; 7.1, 3, 4, 5,
6, 7, 8, 18; 8.24, 25.

A Voice from Bedlam; see *Lear of
Private Life.*

The Voice of Nature; by William
Dunlap, adapted from *Le Jugement
de Solomon* by L. C. Caigniez: (35)
W.-1.31; (44) A.-11.5, 8; (47) P.M.-
4.13; A.-8.9.

*Vol-au-Vent, or A Night of Adven-
tures;* ballet pantomime: (36) C.-
12.20, 21, 28; (37) C.-1.26; 2.6; A.-
6.20; (39) W.-7.27; (41) C.-10.20;
(44) W.-7.22; (48) A.-8.22, 25; 9.9.

Volunteer or Love and Friendship:
(39) W.-1.8; (46) A.-12.18, 19, 22.

Volunteers' Departure and Return:
(48) W.-7.24*, 25, 26.

*The Vow of Silence, or The Black-
smith's Hovel:* (36) W.-11.28*, 29,
30; (45) A.-8.11.

Wacousta, or The Curse; (by N. H.
Bannister): (49) A.-2.19, 20, 21, 22,
23, 24; (52) A.-9.30.

The Wager; farce based on the novel,
Charles O'Malley: (43) W.-7.1, 5.

The Wags of Windsor; see *The Review.*

Walder, the Revenger: (37) W.-7.29.

Wallace, the Hero of Scotland; by W.
Barrymore: (36) W.-11.10, 12, 14,
17, 22; 12.15; (37) W.-1.16; (38)
W.-2.12; 3.13, 15; 7.28; 9.14; C.-
3.3, 8; (39) W.-5.7, 15; 6.12; 7.5;
8.8; (40) W.-1.25; (41) W.-2.10;
12.14; A.-5.31; N.-12.10; (42) W.-
1.20; 3.2, 3; A.-4.9, 21; (43) W.-
6.24; N.-12.2, 4, 11; (44) N.-3.30;
(45) A.-5.14, 16; 6.13; (46) A.-
11.26; 12.1, 2, 7; (48) A.-2.19; (49)
A.-5.11, 26; 12.5; (50) A.-4.1, 9, 18;
(51) A.-2.5, 24; 11.28; 12.22, 30;

(52) N.-8.9; 9.22; A.-11.22, 26; 12.4; (53) A.-2.12; 5.16; (54) C.-4.7; (55) C.-4.10; 20.

Walter Brandt, or The Duel in the Mist: (36) W.-9.24*, 27, 29, 30; (49) A.-3.9; 4.6.

Walter Lynch, or The Warden of Galway: (42) A.-5.23*, 24; C.-12.31; (43) C.-1.2.

Walter Raymond, or The Lovers of Accomac; tragedy: (49) W.-3.8*, 9, 10, 12, 13, 14; 12.31.

Walter Tyrrel; see *The Saxon Girl.*

The Wandering Boys; by M. M. Noah: (35) W.-4.7; (37) W.-8.11; (41) W.-4.30; (46) P.M.-10.5, 6, 7, 10; 12.24; (48) W.-3.14; (50) A.-12.30; (51) B.-1.11, 17; A.-1.21; 2.26; (52) C.-7.13, 16, 26; 9.4; (53) C.-2.8, 14; (54) C.-10.7.

The Wandering Boys of Switzerland: (55) C.M.-1.25; 2.3, 4.

The Wandering Jew, or Ahasuerus the Accused; by N. H. Bannister: (45) A.-5.8, 9, 10, 12.

The Wandering Minstrel, or Mirth and Music: (36) C.-6.18, 21, 30; 11.11, 28; (37) C.-1.7; 2.8, 24; 3.21; 8.19; 10.9; 12.5; A.-5.24; 6.6; (38) C.-2.19; 3.28; 7.2; 9.13, 18; 11.19; (39) C.-1.17; 2.15; W.-10.15, 17; (40) W.-4.7; N.-9.2; 12.10; (41) A.-5.10; 6.30; N.-1.15; 8.27; 10.22; 11.11; (42) N.-1.19; C.-3.29; A.-7.13; (43) W.-4.20; (44) W.-4.12; 12.9; (45) W.-1.23; 4.26; 6.6; A.-7.5; W.-11.7; (46) A.-8.27; 10.13, 27; W.-11.10; 12.18, 29; A.-12.21; (47) W.-2.27; A.-3.25; W.-3.26; 4.16; 9.18; (48) W.-3.22; 11.10; 12.14; (49) W.-11.27; (50) W.-2.6; (52) C.-8.21; A.-9.14, 27; 11.17; (53) W.-3.31; 4.16, 25; 5.12; 6.2; (54) W.-1.30; 2.4; A.-2.28; 3.2; W.-3.15; 4.4; A.-4.12; 5.9; W.-9.6, 8, 28; 10.5, 26; 11.23; (55) W.-3.27; A.-

3.31; 4.2, 5; W.-4.5; 5.16, 22; 6.5; 7.3; 10.22, 23.

The Wandering Piper: (35) W.-4.10; C.-11.8.

Wanted, a Wife, or London, Liverpool, and Bristol: (41) N.-12.6; (44) W.-2.21; 3.13, 28; 5.1.

Wanted, One Thousand Milliners: (55) C.M.-9.8, 11, 12, 19.

The Warden of Galway; see *Walter Lynch.*

Wardock Kennilson, or The Wild Woman of the Village; romantic drama by Edward Fitzball: (49) A.-9.8*, 10, 11.

The Warlock of the Glen: (37) W.-12.29; (39) W.-11.7, 20; (40) W.-3.23; 4.2; (40) P.-7.29; (41) W.-11.23; 12.4; (42) W.-2.7; (48) W.-7.3; (49) A.-1.20, 21; 9.15; (51) A.-12.27, 30; (52) C.-11.24; (54) C.-11.30.

The Warning; domestic drama: (44) W.-11.16.

The Warning Dream, or The Philadelphia Apprentices; domestic drama: (42) W.-1.3, 5, 6, 7.

The Warrior of the Wave: (42) A.-4.9, 11, 12.

Washington, or The Hero of Valley Forge; by James Rees: (42) C.-1.10*, 11, 12; (44) W.-7.20; 7.5, 6, 7; (53) W.-5.4.

Washington; see *The Spirit of '76.*

Washington at Valley Forge; see *Washington, or The Hero of Valley Forge.*

The Watch House, or The Bloodless Duel: (46) P.M.-11.30; 12.21.

The Watchman, or The Deceived Angus: (37) A.-7.27; (55) C.M.-10.12, 13.

The Waterman, or The First of August; comic opera (by C. D. Dibdin): (36) C.-2.9; 10.8, 13; 11.16; (37) C.-2.15; (38) C.-1.24; (39) C.-8.16;

4.23; 6.19; 10.25; (40) C.-2.10; 11.7; N.-12.2; (41) W.-7.12, 13; (42) C.-3.9; (43) C.-2.1, 2; (45) C.-10.23; (47) W.-8.16; (48) W.-3.13; A.-5.13; C.-7.1, 8, 11, 15; (51) A.-3.29; (52) C.-6.14; (55) W.-3.9, 10.

The Water Party: (40) N.-10.12, 15; (44) N.-5.25.

The Water Queen, or The Sprites of Donau: (41) W.-8.23*; 30, 31; 9.1, 2, 3, 4, 6, 7, 8, 9, 10.

The Water Witch; (by J. S. Wallace): (41) A.-9.4, 6, 7, 8, 9; (43) A.-9.30.

The Water Witches, or The Schuyl-kill Rovers; burletta: (49) C.-10.3, 4, 6, 11; (53) C.-11.26.

The Waters of Oblivion; see *Sadak and Kalasrade.*

The Way to get Married; comedy by Thomas Morton: (35) C.-11.23, 27; 12.29; (36) A.-5.31; (37) C.-9.21; (38) C.-5.21; (39) C.-3.29; (55) A.-5.4, 9, 10, 14, 30; 6.8, 25; 9.6.

Weak Points, or The Nice Young Man, or Nothing Like Wheedling; comedy by J. B. Buckstone: (38) C.-9.15*, 24; 11.19; (40) C.-8.31; 9.2, 11; (47) W.-3.5, 6, 24; 5.25.

Wealth a Curse; see *The Festival of St. Michael.*

The Weathercock, or Love alone can Fix Him; farce: (35) W.-3.5; 12.9; C.-11.25; (36) C.-12.22; W.-1.1, 6; A.-2.27; 3.9; (37) C.-3.3; 11.21; 12.12; P.-2.8; (38) W.-2.21; 9.12; C.-4.12; 10.5; 11.8; (39) W.-6.14, 26; 8.1; C.-4.17; 5.16; 6.3; 9.11; (40) C.-1.29; C.-3.30; (41) W.-11.22; C.-12.9; N.-10.21, 28; W.-11.26; (42) A.-6.6; 7.28; 8.5; (43) A.-9.6; 10.13; N.-11.10, 17; 12.22; (45) N.-5.9; (46) W.-9.10; A.-11.21; 12.9; (48) A.-2.10; P.M.-5.2, 15; A.-9.9; (49) A.-4.24; 11.22; (51) A.-1.22; (53) A.-6.6; (54) C.-9.20; (55) C.M.-4.20; 6.9.

The Wedding Breakfast: (44) N.-5.11, 13, 14, 15, 16, 17, 18, 24; (49) P.M.-5.7, 8, 11, 12.

The Wedding Day; (by Mrs. Inchbald): (39) C.-6.15; 9.19; (40) C.-5.15; 6.27; (45) W.-11.17; 12.4; (47) P.M.-6.19; A.-10.21; (52) C.-11.16, 17.

The Wedding Gown; comedy: (35) C.-2.3.

The Wedding Night: (44) A.-6.26, 27.

The Wedding Ring; by Charles Dibdin: (51) C.-3.22; 4.1.

The Weird Woman of the Glen; see *Kenneth.*

The Welsh Girl; farce: (35) W.-2.21, 24; 3.11, 21, 26; 6.25; (37) W.-6.22, 24, 29, 31; 8.16; 11.15, 22; (38) C.-10.19, 20; (45) A.-4.8, 9, 10; 5.1, 5; C.-9.1, 8, 25; (46) P.M.-10.8, 9, 23, 28; (47) P.M.-1.22; 6.11, 16; 7.6; (48) A.-5.9, 19, 20; 10.23, 26; 11.2, 14, 20; 12.20.

Wenlock of Wenlock; see *The Spirit of the Black Mantle.*

The Wept of Wish-Ton-Wish, or The Indian Girl: (35) A.-3.18, 19, 20, 27; (36) A.-3.31; 4.1, 8; (35) C.-6.8, 12, 20; 11.6, 7, 13, 21; (36) C.-6.22, 23; 9.12, 14; 12.7, 8, 9; (38) C.-10.29, 30; 12.4, 10; (37) A.-7.8; (39) C.-8.27, 30; (40) C.-1.6, 8; 2.13; (42) C.-10.26, 28; (44) W.-7.6, 18, 19; (47) A.-8.24, 25; (48) W.-7.12, 13; A.-7.19, 20; (50) C.-2.6, 7; (51) W.-11.26, 27; (52) W.-5.14; (53) C.-2.2, 3, 5; W.-6.16.

Werner, or The Inheritance; tragedy: (41) C.-10.4*; (42) W.-3.12; C.-11.26, 29; 12.24; (43) C.-10.26; 11.4; 12.18; (44) A.-9.14; 11.19, 26; (45) N.-4.30; (46) W.-3.30; 4.10; 5.19, 25; 6.25; A.-9.3; (47) W.-3.13; A.-4.16; W.-9.20; 10. 27; (48) A.-1.24; W.-2.22; 4.26; 10.30; A.-11.23; (49) A.-4.13; W.-5.16; (52) A.-11.10, 18;

(53) C.-3.30; (55) C.M.-5.28; 10.24, 25; A.-10.31; 11.2, 3, 14.

The West End, or The Irish Heiress; comedy by D. Boucicault: (42) W.-11.8*, 9, 10; (54) W.-7.3, 4.

The West Indian; comedy by Richard Cumberland: (36) C.-10.10; (37) C.-2.18; (41) C.-12.22; (45) W.-10.20, 31.

What have I Done?; farce: (40) W.-4.23, 28; (42) A.-4.19; (46) P.M.-11.17, 20.

What will my Wife Say?: (47) P.M.-1.6, 7, 19.

What will Mrs. Jones Say?: (42) W.-6.24; (43) W.-1.27.

What will the World Say?; comedy: (41) C.-12.20, 21, 23, 24, 25, 27, 28, 31; (42) C.-1.3, 5, 7, 9; (42) C.-1.29; W.-6.21; (47) W.-3.8, 9.

The Wheel of Fortune; comedy by R. Cumberland: (35) C.-10.27; (39) C.-4.25; 10.1; (41) C.-2.10; (44) W.-4.8.

Where does the Money Come from?: (38) W.-4.26, 27.

Where shall I Dine?: (35) C.-11.24; (48) A.-2.1.

Where's Barnum?; farce: (49) A.-6.13*, 14, 15, 16, 17.

Whew! Here's a Go!: (40) W.-12.16.

Which is Best?; see *Town and Country.*

Which is the Man?; comedy by Mrs. Cowley: (37) W.-3.22; (48) P.M.-7.1.

Which is Which?; see *Three and the Deuce.*

Whigs and Democrats; comedy by J. E. Heath: (39) W.-10.12*, 17; (44) A.-10.31; 11.1.

Whirligig Hall: (36) C.-12.26; (37) C.-8; (38) C.-12.14, 28; (39) C.-1.10.

The Whistler, or The Fate of the Lily of St. Leonard: (37) W.-8.26; (50) C.-2.16, 18.

White or Brown: (55) C.-2.5.

The White Eagle; melodrama: (40) W.-2.22, 24, 3.3.

The White Farm, or The Assassin Laborer: (40) W.-7.15; (42) W.-2.8; (47) A.-8.6, 7; (49) P.M.-5.7, 8; A.-10.12; 11.17, 20.

The White Horse of the Peppers; comedy: (38) C.-10.2*, 3, 4, 5; 11.8; (40) N.-11.23, 25; (41) W.-3.2; (43) A.-3.8; (47) W.-12.20, 21, 24; (48) W.-1.21, 22; (49) W.-12.11; (53) A.-9.6, 8, 13; 10.1, 26; 12.3, 16; (54) A.-2.1, 23; 7.1; 9.16; 10.12; (55) A.-1.26; 2.15.

The White Lady, or The Spirit of Avenel; opera by J. H. Payne, "from the French, Borieldrius' *La Dame Blanche":* (35) C.-2.5*, 7, 10, 12, 14.

The White Manager: (42) C.-1.17, 18, 20, 21, 24.

The White Scarf; see *Louise.*

The White Sergeant: (45) W.-2.1, 18; 7.10. See also *The Pass Word.*

The White Slave of England; melodrama: (53) W.-3.14*, 15, 16, 17, 19.

The White Warrior; see *Zameo.*

The White Bait at Greenwich; farce: (53) W.-12.14*, 19, 23.

Whites and Browns: (48) A.-6.22, 28; (51) A.-1.20, 27, 28.

Who do they Take me for?: (52) A.-8.21; 9.13.

Who is He?: (45) C.-9.9, 11.

Who is It?: (50) C.-5.9, 10.

Who is my Husband?; see *Giralda.*

Who owns the Hand?, or The Monk, the Mask, and the Murderer: (36) W.-2.10*, 11, 12, 13; 4.5, 18, 14; (44) A.-8.21.

Who Speaks First?: (49) P.M.-5.25, 26; W.-6.2, 4, 6, 9, 13; P.M.-6.2, 5, 6; W.-9.25; 10.8; (50) C.-4.15; (51) W.-9.26; 10.1, 8; (52) W.-11.29; 12.6; (53) W.-1.6; C.-5.26; 6.6, 13;

W.-6.16; (54) W.-1.20, 23; 2.13; (55) A.-7.2.

Who stole the Pocketbook?: (52) W.-6.12*, 14, 15, 21.

Who wants a Guinea?; comedy by George Colman, Jr.: (37) C.-9.12; W.-12.22; (38) W.-1.5. See also *Jonathan in England.*

Who's my Father?; see *Exchange no Robbery.*

Who's the Composer?; comedy: (47) A.-10.28*; (54) C.-8.8.

Who's the Father?: (50) C.-7.2.

Who's the Murderer?: (38) W.-11.30; (40) W.-2.29.

Who's your Friend?: (46) P.M.-6.11, 12, 13; 9.22; (49) A.-10.15, 17, 20; (54) W.-8.29.

Whose is It?: (50) C.-2.26; 6.18.

Why did you Die?; farce: (38) W.-10.6, 8, 17, 24; 11.3; (39) W.-5.1.

Why don't she Marry?; see *Swiss Cottage.*

The Wicked Widow: (45) C.-9.23.

The Wicklow Gold Mines: (41) C.-12.22.

The Widow and the Riding Horse; comedy in one act by August von Kotzebue: (37) A.-7.24; (42) A.-6.27, 28; 8.17; (43) N.-10.24; 11.8.

The Widow Bewitched: (44) A.-7.23; 8.20; (45) A.-7.21.

The Widow Green; see *The Love Chase.*

The Widow Wiggins: (39) C.-11.4, 5, 6, 7, 9, 13, 16; (40) C.-1.20, 22, 29; 5.12, 20, 23; 12.25; (41) N.-11.5, 10; (42) W.-7.26.

The Widow's Curse; see *The Gold Stricken.*

The Widow's Stratagem; see *Smiles and Tears.*

The Widow's Victim; farce: (36) W.-4.6*, 7; (41) W.-3.4, 31; 4.1, 16; 7.14; 11.15; (44) A.-6.7. 17; 7.3; (46) A.-1.9, 13, 24; P.M.-6.29; 7.1,

10; 8.4, 21; 9.21; (47) P.M.-6.24; (48) P.M.-3.30; 4.4; (49) A.-4.10, 12; P.M.-7.2; A.-9.20, 21, 22, 29; (50) A.-8.22, 30; 12.9; (51) B.-2.5; A.-3.4, 27; 7.11; (52) A.-9.4, 6, 11; 12.23; (53) A.-8.20, 25; (54) N.-6.3; C.M.-9.16, 22; 11.10; 12.15.

The Wife, or A Tale of Mantua; by J. Sheridan Knowles: (35) C.-1.3, 19; 5.25; 9.21, 24; (36) C.-9.1; 10.31; (35) W.-1.20; (38) W.-7.14; (35) A.-2.24; (36) A.-3.9; (41) A.-10.7; (37) C.-1.9; 9.25; 12.28; (38) C.-6.29; (39) C.-1.4; 3.19; 11.30; 12.3; (40) C.-2.27; (41) C.-8.30; 9.24; (40) N.-9.11, 15; 10.29; (41) N.-3.6; (42) N.-1.8; W.-10.14; (43) W.-10.9, 19; C.-11.30; A.-12.14; (44) A.-1.4; W.-2.15; 8.21; C.-9.1; W.-10.2; (46) A.-7.10; 10.15; (47) W.-2.16; A.-8.20; 9.20; 10.30; (48) A.-3.20; 7.21; 12.14; (49) C.-10.16; A.-11.10, 15; (50) A.-2.23; W.-3.21; 4.23; A.-7.17; W.-10.7; (51) C.-3.5; W.-3.25; A.-12.9; (52) C.-7.13, 26; C.-9.3; (53) A.-2.1, 12; W.-2.23; A.-3.16; (54) C.-3.27; A.-4.11, 15; W.-9.6; 10.6; C.-10.6; C.M.-11.28; (55) A.2.20; C.M.-4.23; A.-9.1; C.M.-10.20; A.-11.8.

The Wife and Brother; see *Riches.*

A Wife for a Day; comedy: (39) W.-10.24*, 25, 26; 11.1; (40) W.-12.11, 16; (41) W.-10.12, 14, 25; 11.12; (40) A.-12.2; (42) W.-4.12; (43) W.-1.12; A.-10.2, 5, 21; (45) C.-1.14, 16, 17, 21; W.-2.27; C.-4.28, 29; 5.5; (51) A.-3.11; (53) W.-8.29, 30; (54) C.-7.13; 9.25; (55) C.-1.30, 31.

A Wife for an Hour: (52) C.-8.5; (53) C.-7.5, 6.

Wife Hunters, or The Irishman's Umbrella: (47) W.-2.10, 12, 13; 6.19; 9.30; (51) W.-2.26; (52) W.-10.9.

The Wife of Seven Husbands: (45) A.-8.16; 9.22; 10.16.

A Wife's First Lesson: (44) W.-8.17;
A.-12.25.

A Wife's Revenge; see *Broken Heart.*

A Wife's Secret, or A Tale of the Commonwealth: (47) W.-1.20, 21, 22, 23, 25, 26, 28; 3.3.

The Wild Arab of the Desert; see *French Spy.*

The Wild Arabs of the Desert; see *The Hebrew's Son.*

The Wild Boy of Bohemia, or The Force of Nature: (35) W.-10.10, 13; (36) W.-1.22; (37) W.-1.24; 8.21, 22; (39) W.-1.12, 17; (41) A.-1.6, 7; (42) N.-1.18; (45) A.-8.30; 9.1; (52) A.-5.13; N.-9.27, 29.

Wild Ducks; comedy: (50) A.-3.25, 26, 29.

The Wild Man of the Woods; see *Valentine and Orson.*

Wild Oats, or The Strolling Gentleman; comedy by John O'Keeffe: (35) C.-1.21, 26; 5.9; 11.18; (36) W.-3.12; (39) W.-4.30; (40) W.-7.23; (36) A.-5.27; (41) A.-4.29; (37) C.-4.13; 9.19; (38) C.-1.30; 5.16; 6.19; (40) C.-6.10; 10.1; 12.4; (42) N.-1.24; C.-4.29; (43) W.-7.7; C.-9.9; N.-10.2; C.-12.2; (44) A.-8.12; (45) W.-8.13; 11.15; (46) W.-6.23; A.-10.14; (47) W.-4.30; A.-11.9; (48) A.-4.7; W.-11.16, 29; 12.5; (49) W.-1.11; 3.7, 30; 4.6; 5.12, 29; 11.15, 24; 12.25; (50) W.-1.4; 12.27; (51) W.-1.17; 5.16; B.-5.20; W.-9.8; (52) C.-1.9, 13, 27; W.-2.5; C.-4.8; 6.5; 11.9; (53) C.-2.22; A.-3.7, 23; 5.20; C.-6.17; A.-11.15; (54) A.-1.10; 2.3; W.-5.12; A.-9.11; 12.12, 15; (55) A.-1.11, 25; 3.1; C.M.-3.26; A.-5.12; 6.9; C.M.-6.30; A.-10.9; C.M.-11.29; A.-12.19.

The Wild Steed of the Desert; see *King Eagle.*

The Wild Woman of our Village: (35) W.-9.19, 25; 10.1, 22; 11.10.

The Woman of the Village; see *Wardock Kennilson.*

Wilful Murder: (45) A.-4.3; (49) Ath.-1.15; (50) C.-5.9, 10, 11; 6.18.

The Will, or A School for Daughters; comedy (by Frederick Reynolds): (39) C.-11.5, 6, 8; (44) W.-5.22; 7.23; (54) A.-9.4, 5, 7.

Will Brore, or The Miner of the Blind Gap: (47) A.-7.23, 26, 28, 31.

The Will of Uncle Josh; see *Family Ties.*

Will Watch, the Bold Smuggler: (38) W.-1.10*, 12; 3.6; (50) C.-1.16, 17, 19; 2.8; 4.30.

William Penn; by R. P. Smith (42) N.-1.1, 3, 4, 5.

William Tell, or The Hero of Switzerland; by J. Sheridan Knowles: (35) 1.15; 7.2; 9.2; 12.29; C.-1.24; A.-3.2; (36) W.-2.5, 25; 6.22; P.-12.9; (37) C.-11.24; (38) W.-2.10; 10.22; 8.10; C.-1.20; 2.3, 7; 5.22; (39) W.-4.13; 8.15; 9.30; 11.30; C.-5.4; (40) W.-5.25; 7.2; (41) W.-6.14; A.-4.19; 9.2; (42) W.-3.15, 29; A.-5.11, 25; (43) A.-8.31; (44) W.-8.20; 9.12; (45) W.-8.2, 20; 10.10, 23; (46) A.-1.3; 4.22; (47) W.-1.9; A.-4.17; W.-5.14; A.-12.22; (48) W.-3.18; A.-4.5; C.-7.1; W.-9.9; (49) W.-6.22; P.M.-7.25; (50) C.-5.23; 7.10, 27; A.-11.8; (51) N.-8.8, 16; (52) W.-1.14; C.-6.7; N.-8.10; (53) A.-3.12, 29; C.-4.8; (54) C.M.-11.11, 16; (55) A.-1.6, 15; 2.9, 23; W.-6.8; A.-9.22; W.-10.12, 13, 16.

Wilhelm Tell; in German by Schiller: (51) C.-2.3.

William Thompson; see *The Two Thompsons.*

The Willow Copse; a melodrama in five acts by Dion Boucicault: (52) W.-5.24*, 25, 28, 29; 6.8, 15; (53) A.-2.11, 12, 14, 15, 16, 17, 18, 19; W.-3.12, 25; A.-4.19, 21, 22, 23; 5.19,

27; W.-6.12, 17; (54) C.M.-9.18 19, 20; (55) W.-2.14, 16; C.-2.14, 16; A.-8.25, 27, 28, 29, 30; 9.11.

The Windmill; farce: (42) W.-9.26, 27, 28, 29; (47) W.-3.18, 22; 4.3; 5.5, 31; P.M.-5.12; W.-6.7; P.M.-7.13, 15; (48) W.-4.11, 18; 6.5, 17; A.-8.12, 21, 26; 10.27; 12.8; (49) P.M.-5.14, 15; (53) C.-4.4, 8; 5.25.

Win Her and Wear Her; comedy: (35) C.-11.28.

Wine no Poison; see *L'Amour.*

Wine, Women, Gambling, Theft, Murder, and the Scaffold; see *Six Degrees of Crime.*

Wine Works Wonders; see *His First Champagne.*

Winning a Husband, or Seven's the Main; farce: (37) W.-6.26; (40) W.-5.18, 20; 10.16; 11.2, 19; (41) N.-9.13, 14; (50) C.-4.20.

Winter's Tale; by William Shakespeare: (35) C.-2.9; (36) W.-10.17; 12.10; (51) C.-11.14, 17, 18, 22.

The Wirginny Cupids; see *Oh! Hush!!*

Witchcraft; tragedy (by Cornelius Mathews): (46) W.-5.4*, 5, 6, 7.

The Witch Fiend; see *Robert Kyd.*

The Witch Fiend of Hurlgate: (52) N.-8.3.

The Witch of Killarney; see *The Emereld Isle.*

The Witch of Windermere: (49) W.-4.21, 30; 5.5, 9, 15, 25; 6.7, 16, 20; 9.11; 10.5, 25; 11.5; (50) W.-1.21, 22; 5.31; 6.5.

Without Incumbrances: (51) W.-6.13, 14, 17, 25.

Wives as they Were, and Maids as they Are; comedy by Mrs. Elizabeth Inchbald: (35) C.-.30; 4.8; 9.4; 10.12; W.-5.18; (36) W.-9.19; (38) C.-5.4; 8.25; (39) C.-1.3; 2.27; 12.7; (40) W.-10.21; C.-5.5; (41) C.-6.11; (42) C.-1.6, 19; A.-6.8; C.-9.20; (44) W.-3.6; 5.1; (45) W.-1.29; (49) W.-

5.24; (50) A.-9.9; (51) B.-1.25; 2.4; A.-3.4; (53) C.-1.14; (54) A.-5.10, 12, 16; (55) A.-2.7.

The Wizard of the Moor; see *Elshie:* (7) W.-9.1; (50) C.-7.18.

The Wizard of the Sea; see *Captain Kyd.* See also *A Tale of Blood.*

The Wizard of the Seas; see *Robert Kyd.*

The Wizard of the Wave, or The Mighty Man of Garth.

The Wizard Skiff, or The Tongueless Pirate Boy: (35) A.-3.16, 17, 18, 19, 20, 26; C.-6.8, 9, 12, 20; 11.3, 4, 6; (36) A.-3.30, 31; C.-6.21, 22; 7.1; A.-4.1, 9, 11; C.-9.13, 16; 12.12, 16; (37) A.-7.8; (38) C.-12.8, 10, 21; (39) C.-8.29, 30; C.-9.6; (40) C.-1.18; 2.12, 21; (42) C.-10.28, 29.

The Wizard Priest; see *The Enchanted Lake and the Hall of Fate.*

The Wolf and the Lamb; comedy: (35) C.-12.3, 5; (36) C.-1.16; 11.5; W.-2.20, 22; A.-3.8; (37) A.-5.27; (39) C.-1.1, 4; (43) C.-12.1; (47) P.M.-2.1; (49) ATH.-1.10.

The Woman Hater: (48) A.-12.4, 6.

The Woman I Adore: (52) W.-12.16, 17, 18, 23, 27; (53) W.-1.4, 13, 25; 2.12; 5.16; 6.17; (54) W.-2.8, 9, 21.

A Woman Keeps a Secret; see *The Wonder.*

Woman's a Wonder: (46) P.M.-9.30; 10.1, 3.

A Woman's Failing; see *Pay for Peeping.*

Woman's Fate, or The Assassins of the Chateau: (46) A.-2.25; 3.6.

Woman's Life, or The Girl, the Wife, and the Mother: (47) A.-7.17; 11.24; (54) C.-2.6.

Woman's Life, or Isabelle, or Thirty Years of a Woman's Life: (35) W.-9.5*, 8, 9, 11, 12; (36) W.-1.25; (40) N.-10.3, 5; (41) A.-6.28; (42) A.-9.26; (43) W.-5.27; 6.15; A.-8.12;

C.-9.13; W.-9.14; A.-7.15, 19; (46)
A.-5.9; (47) P.M.-5.12, 14, 15, 20,
21; (48) P.M.-3.16, 23; 5.9; (50)
C.-6.28; 7.2; (51) N.-8.6; A.-9.11,
12; B.-10.28, 29, 30, 31; A.-10.31;
B.-11.1; A.-11.19; (53) A.-3.3; (54)
A.-6.9.

Woman's Rights: (53) C.-1.21, 24.

Woman's the Devil: (38) W.-9.6, 7,
10, 24; (40) W.-12.10; (42) W.-1.27.

Woman's Trials: (51) B.-9.8, 9, 12, 13;
12.3, 4.

Woman's Wit: (38) W.-11.2, 3; (40)
W.-1.6; (42) A.-11.12; (51) A.-8.30;
9.1; (54) C.-8.3, 5.

Wonder! A Woman Keeps a Secret;
comedy by Mrs. Susanna Centlivre:
(35) C.-10.5; (36) C.-9.2; 11.4; W.-
2.18; A.-5.20; (37) C.-1.17; 4.21;
10.7; A.-6.15; (38) C.-5.3; 11.27;
(41) A.-5.8; C.-9.16; (42) C.-11.7;
W.-11.22; (44) W.-6.20; (45) C.-
2.6; 9.18; W.-10.4, 22, 30; C.-10.4;
(46) W.-9.22, 29; A.-10.30; (47) W.-
1.29, 30; 3.3; 8.20, 25; (49) W.-6.21;
(50) W.-9.6; (51) B.-1.21, 23; W.-
5.6; 9.11, 25; (52) A.-8.21, 25; (53)
A.-6.2; W.-12.16; (54) A.-6.22, 24.

The Wonderful Lamp; see *Aladdin.*

A Wonderful Woman; farce: (49) A.-
8.27*, 28, 30; W.-9.21, 23; 10.3, 12,
16; (50) W.-1.10; 6.15, 28; 8.22;
(51) W.-2.11; 9.24; 10.29; (52) W.-
5.21; (54) C.M.-11.24.

*The Wood Demon, or The Clock has
Struck;* by J. D. Turnbull: (36) W.-
6.27, 28, 29; (39) W.-2.6.

*The Woodman's Hut, or The Forest of
Bohemia:* (37) W.-1.30, 31; 2.1;
(41) A.-10.21, 22.

*The Wood Wolf of the Black Moun-
tains:* (44) N.-1.22.

Wooing and Wedding; see *Look before you Leap.*

The Wool Dealer: (41) A.-9.27; (43)
A.-5.4, 6, 22; (44) A.-7.24; 8.3;

10.15; 12.13; (50) A.-11.6; (51) A.-
3.13; 6.20; 10.16; 11.25; (52) N.-
9.8, 9; A.-12.14; (54) A.-1.31; 2.4;
(54) C.-2.8, 9.

The Wool Pedlar: (43) N.-11.23; (44)
N.-4.12.

The World a Mask; comedy by G. H.
Boker: (51) W.-4.21*, 22, 23, 24, 25,
26, 28, 29.

*The World Changed, or Female Gov-
ernment:* (49) A.-10.31; 11.1, 2, 5, 6,
7, 8, 9.

A World Discovered; see *Columbus.*

*The World Reformed, or Harlequin's
Trip to Europe:* (50) C.-7.4, 5, 8, 12.

*The World's Fair, or Columbia in the
Clouds:* (51) A.-4.28, 29; 5.2, 3;
(53) A.-4.5.

The Wraith of the Lake: (43) A.-3.30,
31; (51) N.-7.30, 31.

*The Wreck Ashore, or A Bridegroom
from the Sea, or The Rover's Bride:*
(35) A.-4.2; C.-5.30; 12.19, 25; (36)
A.-3.21; 4.21; P.-11.12, 15; 12.20;
(40) W.-7.1; N.-11.4, 6; (41) N.-1.8;
12.7; (42) A.-8.11; 10.4; (43) W.-
2.18, 22; A.-5.2; (44) W.-4.19; (45)
A.-5.30; (46) A.-3.10; (47) A.-2.8;
9.10; (50) W.-12.11, 16; (55) A.-
4.25, 27, 28.

The Wrecker's Daughter; tragedy by
J. S. Knowles: (37) W.-3.6*, 7, 8,
9, 15, 28; A.-6.8, 10, 13; C.-9.30;
10.7; (41) N.-3.29; (48) A.-12.15;
(50) A.-10.18; (51) A.-4.11; (52)
A.-10.8, 12, 30; (54) C.-10.27; 11.2;
(55) C.M.-5.4, 10.

The Wreckers: (35) W.-11.12, 13, 25.

The Wreckers of Norway: (49) A.-
5.2; 9.13; 11.10; 12.25.

The Wren Boys, or Irish Fidelity:
(43) N.-12.29; (44) N.-1.11, 12; 2.13.

The Writing on the Wall: (53) W.-
4.7, 26; 5.2; 6.7.

The Wrong Flue; farce: (50) C.-6.3.

The Wrong Passenger; farce: (47)

W.-10.1*, 2, 4, 7; 12.11; (48) W.-5.19, 20, 24, 29; 9.20; (49) W.-4.18; (50) W.-5.3, 7; (51) W.-3.5; (52) W.-9.30; (53) W.-11.8, 18; (55) W.-12.3.

The Wronged Father; see *The Fate of Calas.*

Wyoming, or The Bride of Liberty: (46) W.-6.8, 9, 10, 11, 13, 18, 19.

Xmas Morning; see *The Son of Temperance.*

XYZ, or The American Manager; farce: (39) W.-4.4, 5, 12; 5.17; (41) W.-6.25; (43) W.-4.7; 5.25; (47) A.-8.6; (47) A.-9.30; 10.11.

The Yacht Race: (51) A.-11.10.

The Yankee Abroad: (43) A.-5.5; (45) A.-11.12; (51) A.-3.14.

The Yankee Bill Sticker; comedy in three acts: (40) W.-1.23*.

The Yankee Dentist: (44) N.-1.26; 2.2.

The Yankee Duellist, or Bunker Hill's Representative; farce by N. H. Bannister: (38) W.-10.3*; (52) A.-12.3.

Yankee Farmers: (43) W.-5.20.

Yankee Fidelity; see *The Foundling.*

The Yankee Footman: (52) A.-12.24; (54) C.-9.27.

The Yankee Gal: (53) C.-7.18; 10.26.

The Yankee Heiress: (54) C.-8.11, 16, 19.

The Yankee in China: (50) A.-9.3; (53) W.-9.1.

The Yankee in England (by David Humphreys): (45) C.-9.10; A.-10.2; (46) P.M.-8.5, 6; (52) A.-12.20; (54) C.-9.28.

The Yankee in France: (44) W.-4.2, 4.

The Yankee in Jersey, or The American Farmer: (46) A.-3.20; (50) A.-9.7; (54) N.-6.13.

The Yankee in Mississippi: (46) W.-8.12, 13.

The Yankee in Spain; see *The Knight of the Golden Fleece.*

The Yankee in Time; see *The Maiden's Vow.*

The Yankee in Tripoli; see *The Adventure.*

Yankee Jack, or The Pride of the Navy; by James Pilgrim: (52) N.-7.30*; 8.4.

Yankee Lad: (45) A.-4.8; 5.6.

Yankee Land, or The Foundling of an Apple Orchard; comedy by C. A. Logan: (37) P.-1.4*; (43) A.-5.3, 4, 9, 15; W.-5.18; N.-11.21, 26; (44) W.-5.14; 7.4; A.-10.18; 11.4, 6; (50) A.-9.2; (51) A.-3.13, 20; (52) A.-12.1, 2; (53) A.-1.1; W.-8.30; 9.1; (54) C.-9.25.

Yankee Magnetism; see *Bumps of Mystery.*

The Yankee Pedlar, or Old Times in Virginia (by Morris Barnett): (35) W.-5.8; 12.17; (36) W.-5.9, 14; (37) C.-9.13, 14, 16; (38) C.-4.2, 7; (39) W.-10.25, 28; 11.2; (41) W.-10.13; (42) W.-4.11; (43) W.-1.14; A.-10.17; (45) C.-1.15, 18; 5.1, 12; (50) A.-9.5; (51) A.-3.22; 12.9; (53) W.-8.31; 9.3.

The Yankee Servant; a comedy in three acts: (39) W.-5.10.

The Yankee Tar; comedy: (36) C.-3.3*.

Yankee Tars on Shore; see *The Storm.*

The Yankee Valet: (41) N.-1.21; 2.11; 3.3.

The Yankee Watchman: (51) B.-12.5, 6.

The Yankee Wool Dealer: (46) W.-6.15.

Yankees in China, or A Union of the Flags: (41) W.-11.1, 2, 5.

Yara the Gipsy, or The Terror of Wallachia: (44) N.-3.2*, 4, 5, 6, 7, 8, 9, 11, 12, 13, 14, 15, 16, 18.

Yard Arm and Yard Arm: (35) W.-3.20.

The Yellow Dwarf; fairy tale: (44) A.-10.5, 7, 8, 9, 10, 11, 26, 28, 29; 11.1, 2, 4; 12.12; (45) A.-3.28; (47) A.-6.24, 26, 28.

The Yellow Kids; farce: (36) W.-1.26*, 28, 29; 2.6, 16; 4.19; (41) A.-8.25, 27.

Yelva, or The Orphan of Russia; advertised as from the French of Casimir Delavigue: (36) A.-4.14*, 15; C.-6.25, 27.

Yelva: (36) C.-9.24. Advertised as from the French of Scribe.

The Yorkshire Brothers; romantic drama by Lysander Thompson: (54) C.-6.27; 7.1, 6.

You can't Marry your Grandmother: (46) P.M.-4.2; 5.2; (47) P.M.-2.10, 15; 6.2, 14; A.-10.2, 4, 7.

You must be Buried; see *The Illustrious Stranger.*

The Young Actress; by Dion Boucicault: (54) C.-4.14*, 29; 5.1; W.-11.21, 25; 12.2, 4, 6; (55) W.-6.30; 7.3, 4; C.M.-7.5.

Young America: (45) W.-6.20, 21, 23, 27, 30; 7.4, 12, 14, 29; 8.11, 23; 11.3; (46) W.-5.6, 9, 13; (47) A.-8.4; W.-12.25; (48) W.-2.1; 3.4; (49) A.-10.10.

The Young Continental; see *Harry Burnham.*

The Young Couple: (52) W.-9.28, 29; 10.5, 8, 9.

Young Napoleon and his Father: (41) N.-2.11, 12, 15, 16, 17, 18; (45) W.-6.12, 13; 7.30; 12.13, 17.

The Young Quaker, or The Fair American; comedy by John O'Keeffe: (37) A.-5.4; (39) C.-4.19; (42) C.-5.4; (44) W.-5.14; (45) W.-8.4; (55) A.-5.23, 24.

The Young Reefer; farce: (35) W.-9.4; 10.30; (41) A.-10.1, 2, 5; (46) P.M.-3.26.

The Young Scamp, or My Grandmother's Pet: (44) W.-5.28, 29, 30, 31; 6.15; 7.15, 20; 8.3, 5, 28; 9.23, 24; (45) W.-4.8, 23; 9.4; (46) W.-7.21; P.M.-8.12, 13; W.-9.2; 12.24, 25; (47) P.M.-1.1; W.-3.4, 23, 31; 5.19; 6.17; (48) W.-3.10; C.-7.20; (49) W.-11.28; (50) B.-9.20, 21; 12.27; (52) C.-7.21, 28; (53) C.-2.9; (55) C.-2.19, 20.

The Young Widow, or Lessons for Lovers: (35) C.-2.21; 11.18; W.-5.19; 9.28; (36) C.-10.4, 15; 11.22; W.-6.27; P.-12.12; (37) P.-1.4; (38) C.-9.3; 11.15; (39) C.-2.7, 27; 3.19; (40) P.-7.29; C.-11.18; A.-9.7, 11; (41) W.-8.30; A.-9.18; W.-10.19; (42) W.-2.16; 3.18; C.-5.5, 6; A.-7.7; 10.20; (43) W.-6.2; N.-9.27; 10.4; (44) A.-9.16; C.-10.18; (45) C.-1.31; A.-7.11; W.-10.1, 2, 25; 11.6; A.-11.28; W.-12.26; (46) W.-1.26; 2.27; P.M.-3.9, 10; W.-6.20, 24; W.-7.14, 27; 8.10, 25, 31; (47) P.M.-2.25; A.-4.27; 5.4, 12; 7.6, 9; (48) P.M.-4.5; 5.10; C.-7.29; (50) A.-9.25; (51) B.-1.18, 27, 28; A.-6.19, 23, 26; B.-6.23, 24; A.-9.5; 10.3; (52) C.-8.24; (53) C.-9.12, 23; (54) C.-3.21, 29; 4.15, 28; (55) W.-9.29; 10.11, 19, 24; C.M.-11.12, 14, 22, 26; W.-12.27.

Your Life's in Danger: (49) A.-3.3; 12.27; (51) B.-6.9, 14; N.-7.24; W.-10.13, 14, 22; 11.18; 12.3, 8, 24; (52) W.-1.27; 6.7; N.-7.16, 22; W.-9.22, 27; 12.22; (53) W.-1.17; 4.13; 6.6, 21; (54) C.M.-11.11; 12.6, 18.

The Youth who never Saw a Woman; farce: (52) C.-7.22*, 29.

Youthful Days of Richelieu: (51) A.-1.31; 2.1; (55) C.M.-1.23.

The Youthful Queen, or Christine of Sweden: (36) W.-4.6; 10.27; P.-

11.29; 12.3, 7; (37) C.-1.6, 17; 4.21, 28; 9.28; A.-6.12; (38) W.-10.31; C.-9.4; 11.16; 12.3; (39) W.-9.12, 14; C.-6.15; 9.5; 5.23; (41) C.-9.22, 28; (42) C.-3.14; 10.24; 11.18, 26; 12.30; (43) O.-1.13; W.-3.24; 7.1; (44) C.-10.14, 18, 25; (45) C.-4.28; (47) W.-5.28; A.-12.16; (48) A.-1.21; (50) A.-4.10, 15; W.-9.20, 21; (51) C.-3.14.

Zameo, or The White Warrior: (38) W.-12.31*.

Zampa, or The Marble Bride; opera: (41) C.-5.12, 13, 14, 17, 18, 19, 22, 26; (43) C.-2.13, 14, 15, 16, 17; (47) C.-5.24, 25, 26, 27, 28, 29; 6.3.

Zanonah: (45) A.-11.6, 8.

Zanoni, or The Actress and the Student: (42) C.-5.2, 3, 5, 6; (46) A.-3.24, 25.

Zanthe, or The Fatal Oath; drama in five acts adapted by W. Barrymore from the French of Victor Hugo: (35) W.-1.28, 29, 30, 31; 2.2, 3, 4, 5, 6, 7, 11, 16, 17, 25, 27; 3.7, 10, 30, 31; 5.26; (36) W.-12.3; (42) W.-1.10, 11; (50) C.-6.10.

ZaZeZiZoZu, or The Chinese Conjurer: (37) W.-3.13, 14.

Zelina, or The Heroine of Grace: (46) A.-2.5, 6; (50) C.-2.19; 3.16.

Zembuca, or The Net Maker and his Wife: (36) W.-12.31; (37) W.-1.2, 3; C.-12.25; (38) C.-2.6, 23; (41) W.-2.8, 17; C.-9.20, 22; (42) A.-11.5, 15; (48) W.-9.21, 23.

Zenocles and the Greek Chief, or Simple Simon and his Dogs: (35) W.-10.17; (36) W.-11.11; (37) P.-1.26.

Zephyrina, or The Mysterious Lady: (46) P.M.-7.7; 8.19.

Zindel, or The Brothers of the Burning Belt: (50) C.-3.18*, 19, 20, 21, 22, 23, 25, 26, 27, 28, 29, 30; 4.1, 2, 3, 4, 5.

The Zingaro's Prophecy; see *A Maiden's Fame.*

Zip Coon's Visit to Philadelphia; see *Coal Black Rose on Horseback.*

Zoological Gardens: (35) A.-3.31.

THE PLAYER LIST

THE PLAYER LIST

THE Player List is an attempt to aid the student of the Philadelphia stage in his effort to follow the actors and actresses in those parts of their careers which touched Philadelphia.

Approximately fifteen hundred players walked the boards of Philadelphia theatres during the twenty-one years between 1835 and 1855 inclusive, and their numbers make it necessary, naturally, to put their careers into a record as compact as possible. Consequently, for the purpose of printing, the present writer has developed a series of abbreviations and punctuation marks in order to preserve space in this list.

The following directions will serve as a guide in reference to the Player List.

If you wish to investigate the career of an actor in Philadelphia between 1835 and 1855, find his name in the Player List. After his name, there will be a word or two of description (tragedian on engagement, opera singer, comedian) if the actor is of sufficient importance to be more than a walking gentleman or minor performer. Next in order comes the year or years of his appearance. The year of 1835, for example, is signified thus: (35). Following the notation of the year, a letter and a series of numbers will be found, to wit: C.10.19 *-8; 11.4-reg. This means that the actor appeared in 1835 at the Chesnut, beginning on the nineteenth day of the tenth month, for an engagement of eight nights; on the fourth day of the eleventh month he returned as a regular member of the stock company. A star (or asterisk), following the day of the month, records a first-night performance of a play. If the reader will look for that identical date under the Annual Chronological Record, he will find the play and the rôle acted by the player on that occasion.

Or again, for further illustration, take the name of A. N. H. Bannister for 1838. We find the following notation: W.1:1 *, 8 *, 15 *; 2:19 *; 3:10 *; 7:2 *, 24 *; 8:16 *, 27 *-reg. We interpret the record to mean that Bannister was a regular stock player at the Walnut for 1838, and that he appeared in the first-nights on the occasions given. Reference to the Annual Chronological Record will give the first-night casts in which he appeared.

Further, if the actor played rôles of any importance, a summary of his

[675]

best rôles will be found opposite his name in the Player List, also. When the rôle which he plays is the same as the title of the play, or when the rôle is Shakespearean and well known, no title of the play is given.

Abbott, tragedian on engagement. (35) C.10: 19-8; (36) C.1: 11-1; 3: 11*-14; (39) C.9: 11-3; (40) N.9: 18-4; (41) W.-5. Hamlet, Charles Surface in *School for Scandal,* Benedick, Daran in *Exile,* Friboulet in *King's Fool.*

Abbott, Mrs. (43) N.-reg.; 10: 9*.

À Becket. (40) N.12:15; (42) W.-reg.; (43) N.-reg.; (44) C.4: 1-18; (46) W.5: 4-reg.; (47) W.-reg.; (48) W.-reg.; (49) W.-reg.; (50) W.-reg.; (51) N.8: 18-reg.; W.1: 20*; (52) W.-reg.; (53) W.12:14*-reg.; (54) W.9: 29-reg.

À Becket, Mrs. (42) W.-reg.; (43) A.8: 10-reg.; N.-reg.; (44) C.4: 1-18; (46) W.5: 4.

Adams, A. J. (48) A.4: 4; (53) W.10: 3*-reg.

Adams, G. J., Elder. Shakespearean actor. (47) A.12: 20-3.

Addams, A. A., star on engagement. (35) W.1: 5-20; W.3: 9-7; W.5: 9-2; W.12: 7*-11; (36) W.-9; (41) W.-5; A.-5; (42) W.5: 23-8; (45) A.12: 10-6; (46) W.1: 2-7; W.2: 26-10. Hamlet, Virginius, Damon in *Damon and Pythias,* Rolla in *Pizarro,* Macbeth, William Tell, Othello, Lear.

Addams, J. P., Yankee comedian on engagement. (37) W.6: 30*; 7: 31*; 12: 25*; (38) W.1: 2*, 29*; 2: 19*; 3: 10*; (49) A.11: 19-7; 11: 29*.

Addams, Mrs. J. P., comedienne. (49) A.11: 29*-4.

Adderton, Miss. (50) W.11: 22. Miriam in *Daughter of the Stars.*

Addis. (44) A.9: 23. Washington in *Putnam.*

Addison, Miss Laura, heroine on engagement. (51) W.10: 27-10.

Albertine, Miss, with Chanfrau. (54) C.10: 9-5.

Alboni, Madame Marietta, opera. (53) W.2: 28-reg.

Albertazzi, Signora M., with Italian Opera Company from Havana, on engagement. (43) C.7: 15-13; C.11: 13-11.

Alexandre, Monsieur, an actor in French. (40) C.9: 18.

Alfred, Madame, with German Opera on engagement. (40) C.3: 23-4. Annchen in *Freischutz.*

Allan, Madame Caradori, an actress and singer, on engagement. (38) C.-8.

Allen. (35) W.5: 24; (48) P.M.-reg.

Altemus, singer and actor. (43) A.4: 6-reg.; A.8: 10-reg.

Altemus, Mrs., in opera. (42) W.5: 16-3; A.11: 11*; (50) A.7: 15-reg.; (54) C.6: 6-6. Namouna in *Ninth Statue,* Pauline in *Delicate Ground.*

Amherst, H. J., with Cooke's Company. (36) W.4: 2*.

Anderson, tragedian on engagement. (44) A.9: 16-6; C.11: 25-12; (45) A.4: 30-10; (48) W.4: 3-12. Hamlet, Macbeth, Claude in *Lady of Lyons.*

Anderson, James. (37) C.12: 16; (42) W.5: 16-3; (43) A.12: 11-reg.; (53) W.11: 20-5. Kilroony in *Ninth Statue.*

Anderson, Mrs. J. (43) A.12: 11-reg.

Anderson, W. (51) A.8: 30-reg.

Anderson, Mrs. Ophelia. (40) C.9: 7.

Anderson, Miss, heroine in stock. (35) W.9: 5*; (36) A.3: 14*; (41) A.12: 6*; (42) A.3: 28-reg; C.-reg; (43) A.5: 8*; (50) W.10: 29-5; W.12: 5*-5; W.1: 20*. Mrs. Haller in *The Stranger.* Later Mrs. Thoman.

Anderson, Miss. (51) C.8:18-reg; A.7:14; (52) C.4:19-reg.

Andrews. (36) A.5:24; (42) C.-reg.; 9:28*; 10:22*; 11:2*.

Andrews, G. H., comedian. (48) W.1:12*-10.

Angelica, Miss. (37) W.6:30*; 7:10*.

Archer, in opera. (41) N.8:27; (42) C.12:5-13; (43) C.1:7-25.

Archer, Miss. (44) C.10:14-reg.

Armstrong, Miss. (37) C.2:27*; (38) C.3:17*; 10:15*; (47) A.2:2. Old Delph in *Family Jars*.

Arnaud, in French opera. (45) C.9:29-12.

Arnold. (46) A.8:26-reg.

Arnoldi, Signor, with Italian Opera Company. (48) C.2:19-23; 6:6-7; 10:4-15; 12:5-12.

Arreline, Mlle., dancer, with Mlle. Celeste, on engagement. (36) C.11:28*-18.

Arthurson, in opera. (47) W.10:11-14.

Ashmer. (47) A.1:13-2; (50) B.10:14-reg.; (54) N.6:3-reg. Wilford in *Hunchback*.

Atkinson. (48) A.3:14. Brutus in *Brutus*.

Augusta, Madame, the Countess St. James, actress and ballet danseuse, on engagement. (38) W.9:24-10; (39) C.-5; (45) W.11:26-5; (46) W.4:15-9. Zoloe in *La Bayadere*.

Austen, Mrs., an actress on engagement. (35) C.1:29; 2:5*-11. Cinderella, Ariel in *The Tempest*, Princess of Navarre in *John of Paris*, Louise in *The White Lady*, Princess in *Masaniello*.

Avignone, Signor, with Italian Opera Company. (50) C.12:10-15.

Ayres, Miss. (41) W.11:6*; (42) C.-reg.; (43) A.3:14-reg.

Badiali, Signor F., with the Italian Opera Company from Havana. (50) C.9:10-10.

Bailey, W. H. (55) C.M.9:8-reg.

Bailey, Mrs. W. H. See Miss Watson, who was married some time between May 13 and May 20, 1837.

Baker, J. (S). (48) P.M.5:1; (49) A.3:28*-reg.; 8:15*; (50) C.2:27*-reg.; 4:17*; 5:1*; B.8:19-reg.; 9:30*; A.8:13*; (51) A.4:14*. Charles II.

Baker, Lewis. (51) A.8:30-reg.; (55) C.1:15-20; C.M.10:20-10.

Baker, Mrs. Lewis. See Miss A. Fisher.

Baker, Mrs. Alexina Fisher. See Miss A. Fisher.

Baker, W. A. (51) C.2:22.

Baker, Miss. (43) C.-reg.

Balls, J. S., in high comedy, on engagement. (35) C.11:28*-15; (36) C.1:2*, 4*-17; (37) C.4:14*-5; (39) C.3:27*-5; (40) C.6:6-10. Vapid in *Dramatist*, George in *Laugh when you Can*, Rover in *Wild Oats*, Splash in *Young Widow*, Marplot in *Busy Body*, Young Rapid in *Cure for the Heartache*, Tangent in *The Way to get Married*, Bramble in *Poor Gentleman*, Frederick in *Crown Prince*.

Balls, Mrs. J. S., in high comedy, on engagement. (35) C.12:25-2; (36) C.3:11*-5. Distafina in *Bombastes Furioso*, Victoria in *Bold Stroke for a Husband*.

Bamford. (48) Ath.12:25-reg.

Bannister, N. H., playwright and actor. (37) W.8:8*; 11:20*-reg.; (38) W.1:1*, 2*, 15*, 29*; 7:2*, 24*; 8:8*, 16*-reg.; (44) N.4:8-11; (47) A.2:6-4.

Bannister, Mrs. N. H., stock actress. (37) W.11:25*; 12:2*, 23*-reg.; (38) W.1:1*, 8*, 15*; 2:19*; 3:10*; 7:2*, 24*; 8:16*, 27*-reg.; (55) C.-reg.

Barber, Miss. (49) A.10:31. Queen Battlehead in *World Changed.*

Barneck, in French Opera Company, on engagement. (43) C.9:14-13.

Barnes, J., comedian on engagement. (36) W.10:26*-5; (40) W.10:16-12. Hardy in *Paul Pry,* Teazle in *School for Scandal,* Pipkin in *May Queen,* Pops in *Scapegoat.*

Barnes, Mrs. J., actress on engagement. (36) W.10:27-4. Mrs. Candour in *School for Scandal,* Alicia in *Jane Shore,* Elvira in *Pizarro,* Rose in *Henriette.*

Barnes, W. J., pantomimist on engagement. (43) W.7:17-10; 7:31*; A.8:14-2; (44) A.2:26; 7:10-18; 12:2-15; W.7:27*; (46) A.11:30-5; (47) A.1:1-4. Noucum in *Black Raven.*

Barnes, Miss, on engagement. (36) W.-4. Lady Teazle in *School for Scandal,* Jane Shore, Cora in *Pizarro,* Henriette.

Barrett, G. (44) A.6:1-reg.; (45) C.-reg.; A-reg.; (50) W.11:6-2. Courtly in *London Assurance.*

Barrett, Mrs. (35) W.4:2; (37) W.3:22.

Barry. (40) W.2:3*.

Barrymore, W. Adapted and directed plays for the Walnut, such as *Zanthe* and *Last Days of Pompeii.*

Barrymore, Mrs. W. First appearance in Philadelphia at her husband's benefit. (38) W.2:24*-4.

Bataglini, L., with Italian Opera Company from Havana. (47) W.7:12-18.

Bateman. (35) C.9:10-reg.; (36) C.-reg.

Bateman, Ellen, at the age of six, on engagement. (50) W.1:7-6; B.9:2-14. Richard III.

Bateman, Kate, at the age of four, on engagement. (50) W.1:7-6; B.9:2-14. Richmond in *Richard III.*

Bathgate. (36) W.9:26.

Bayley. (49) A.10:24*-6; (52) N.7:12-reg. Washington in *Benjamin Franklin.*

Beauvallet, L., with French Opera Company. (55) W.11:19-6.

Beckett, comedian on engagement. (42) A.5:16-11.

Becom. (46) A.4:1*-20. The Stranger, Oranaska, Golden Farmer.

Beechley. (50) A.6:15. Cox in *Box and Cox.*

Belford, Irish comedian. (49) P.M.-reg.

Bell, Mrs. (45) C.8:30-reg.; A.-reg.

Bell, Miss Julia. (43) C.11:16; (44) A.1:3-5. Julia in *Hunchback,* Mrs. Haller in *The Stranger,* Marianna in *The Wife.*

Bellamy. (54) C.11:13-reg.

Bellamy, Mrs. (54) C.11:13-reg.

Bellini, Signora L., with Italian Opera from Havana. (50) C.9:10-10.

Benedetti, Signor, with Italian Opera from Havana. (48) C.2:19-23; 6:6-7; 10:4-15; 12:25-12.

Benevantano, Signor, in Italian Opera. (50) C.12:10-15.

Bennett, Miss Julia, on engagement. (51) W.3:11*-13; (52) W.3:12*-15. Constance in *The Love Chase.*

Bennie, in low comedy. (39) W.12:25; (41) A.-reg. Tom in *Mother Shipton.*

Bennie, Mrs., in low comedy. (39) W.12:25; (41) A.-reg. Rosetta in *Mother Shipton.*

Beraldi, Signor Neri, in Italian Opera. (54) C.8:28-6.

Bernard, in French Opera Company. (43) C.9:14-13.

Bernard. (44) C.10:14-reg.; (49) A.4:23-15. Le Beau in *Eagle Eye.*

Bernard, Miss. (55) W.6:4*-reg.

Berresford. (37) P.2:7.

Bertucca, Signora, with Italian Opera. (50) C.12:10-15; (54) C.8:28-6.

Bihin, Monsieur, the Belgian Giant, on engagement. (40) W.-4. Ali Heirib in *The Giant of Palestine*.

Biscaccianti, Signorina, with Italian Opera Company. (48) C.2:19-23; 6:6-7; 10:4-15; 12:5-12.

Bishop, T., in opera. (38) W.10:1-17; 11:19*; (51) W.8:18-reg. The Unknown in *La Bayadere*, Gervais in *Amelie*.

Bishop, Madame Anna, in opera. (47) W.11:22-18.

Bishop, Little Lavinia, in *Uncle Tom's Cabin*. (55) C.-reg.

Blaike. (35) W.3:16*, 23*.

Blake, W. R. (39) W.9:10; (40) W.-reg.; (43) C.-reg.; (45) W.4:16*; (46) W.8:29-reg.; (48) W.7:18-5; (54) W.6:21. Geoffrey Dale in *Last Man*.

Blake, Mrs. W. R. (39) W.9:13; (40) C.8:29; (45) W.1:20*-reg.; (46) W.8:28*-reg.; (49) W.3:8*-reg. Kate O'Brien in *Perfection*.

Blanchard, Master, appearing with Mr. Cony. (35) W.6:8*, 13*-20; 10:10*, 17*-12; (36) W.-11; (37) W.1:21*-11; (45) W.11:17-6. Monkey in *Monkeyana*, Ourang Outang, Eloi in *Forest of Bondy*.

Bland. (50) A.3:25-reg. Doricourt in *Belle's Stratagem*.

Blankman. (46) A.8:26-reg.

Blankman, Miss, in opera. (51) B.2:10-17.

Boll, in German Opera. (40) C.3:28-4. Zamiel in *Freischutz*.

Bonsall, J. S. (39) W.7:16; (47) A.7:21*. Capt. Rumbleton in *Bath Road*, Jack Carter in *The Actor and the Heiress*.

Booth, Junius Brutus, Senior, tragedian on engagement. (35) W.3:16-6; C.6:27-2; W.8:24-8; (36) W.-34; (37) W.-19; (38) W.-17; (39) W.-13; (40) W.-15; (41) W.-17; (42) W.3:30-12; C.11:14-5; (43) W.1:10-17; A.9:6-16; C.11:24; (44) W.1:17-4; 11:16-8; (45) W.3:31-5; 5:23-7; (46) W.2:18-20; (47) W.4:19-6; A.11:20-7; (48) A.3:11-3; A.8:9-2; (49) C.10:5-6; (50) A.5:17-5; (51) B.3:1-18; 6:16; C.11:24-5; (52) C.1:14-10; drowned in the Mississippi this year. Richard III, Othello, Hamlet, Overreach in *A New Way To Pay Old Debts*, Pescara in *Apostate*, Mortimer in *Iron Chest*, Octavian in *Mountaineer*, Cassius in *Julius Caesar*, Pierre in *Venice Preserved*.

Booth, Junius Brutus, Junior, on engagement. (40) W.6:29. Orson in *Valentine and Orson*.

Booth, Mrs. Junius Brutus Booth, Junior. See Miss De Barr.

Booth, T. G. (50) C.6:1-2; A.6:13. Jimmy Green in *Tom and Jerry*.

Booth, Miss. (35) W.12:5, 14.

Borani, in opera on engagement. (54) W.10:30-16.

Boswell, J. H. (36) W.10:28*; (46) W.8:29-reg.; (51) A.8:30-reg.

Boulard. (40) N.12:19*-reg.

Boulard, Mrs., with Italian Opera Company. (42) C.12:5-2; (48) C.2:19-23; 6:6-7; 10:4-15; 12:5-12.

Bou(r)cicault, Dion, comedian. (55) W.6:16-5. *Used Up.*

Bowers, D. P. (42) C.-reg.; (46) P.M.3:9-reg.; (48) A.10:5-reg.; Ath.12:25-reg.; (49) P.M.4:25-reg.; (50) A.9:10-10; (51) B.9:1-reg.; (52) W.-reg.; (53) A.-reg.; (54) A.5:1*-reg.; C.8:19-reg.; (55) C.M.-manager and reg.

Bowers, Mrs. D. P. (47) W.5:8-reg.; (48) Ath.12:25-reg.; (49) P.M.4:25-reg.; 5:17*; (51) B.9:1-reg.; (52) W.-reg.; (53) A.11:7*-reg.; (54) A.5:1*-reg.; C.8:19-reg.; (55) C.M.-reg.

Bowers, Master. (35) W.-3; (37) P.-3; (38) W.-3. Lump in *Review*, Othello, Richard III.

Bowes, Frank, in low comedy. (49) A.-9:3.

Bowman, Yankee, on engagement. (39) W.4:9; (40) W.1:23*; (43) A.3:20-2. Jonathan in *Forest Rose*.

Bradley. (53) A.-reg.

Bradshaw, appearing with H. P. Grattan. (48) A.7:6. Laertes.

Braham, singer on engagement. (40) N.11:30-12. Belino in *Devil's Bridge*.

Brand. (52) A.3:22-reg.

Brandon, supporting Macready. (48) A.10:20-8; (49) A.3:5*-6.

Brazier. (45) C.8:30-reg.; A.-reg.

Brelsford. (50) C.6:7; A.6:13-6; 7:13*; 8:13-reg. Martin Heywood in *Rent Day*, Rolla in *Pizarro*, Michael Erle.

Brittenham. (35) W.1:17*.

Brittenham, Miss. (35) W.10:17*; (37) W.6:30*.

Brittingham. (42) A.8:2.

Broad, Mrs. (36) C.-reg.; (37) C.-reg.; 2:27*; 5:2*; 6:17*; 9:16*; 10:19*; 11:18*; (38) C.-reg.; 1:15*; 6:2*, 22*; (39) C.1:2*-reg.; (40) C.3:19*-reg.

Brooke, G. V., tragedian on engagement. (52) W.1:5-15; 3:29-10; (53) W.6:2-10. Overreach in *A New Way To Pay Old Debts*, Othello, Shylock, Hamlet, Richard III.

Brookes. (44) N.1:19-reg.

Brough, actor-singer, on engagement. (36) C.1:28*; 2:11*-30; (37) C.11:4*-20; 11:10*; (38) C.2:17*-33; 11:19*; (39) C.-23; (40) C.-9;

(45) C.10:13-10; (47) W.11:22-18.

Dandini in *Cinderella*, Basil in *Barber of Seville*, Hela in *Mountain Sylph*, Cedric in *Maid of Judah*, Pietro in *Masaniello*, Beppo in *Fra Diavolo*, Gabriel in *Guy Mannering*, Rodolpho in *La Sonnambula*, Leparello in *Don Juan*, General in *Amilie*.

Brougham, John, playwright and actor on engagement, particularly in Restoration comedy. (42) W.10:31-20; (43) W.1:28-17; (45) A.11:14*-2; C.11:24*-10; (46) C.1:5*-10; (48) W.5:4*-15; (49) A.6:11*, 13*-7; (51) A.7:14; (52) C.8:14*-5; (53) C.7:4-5; (54) W.6:21; C.8:9-5.

Brougham, Mrs. John, actress on engagement, in Restoration comedy. (42) W.10:31-20; (43) W.1:28-17; (44) W.6:17-12; (48) W.5:4*-15; (52) C.1:24-5; (54) C.8:19-reg.

Brown. (44) N.1:25-reg.; (51) A.-reg.

Brown, F. (37) W.1:23.

Brown, J. M. (35) W.1:1*, 17*; 3:7*, 23*.

Brown, Mrs. J. M. (35) W.1:1.

Brown, P. (51) A.8:30-reg.

Brown, Miss. (37) C.2:27*; (42) W.-reg.

Browne, G. F. (46) A.6:13-5; (48) C.7:12; (49) P.M.-reg.; (51) N.7:15-reg., during summer. Dick Turpin in *Rookwood*, Wilhelm in *Black-Eyed Susan*.

Browne, J. S., comedian on engagement. (37) C.-4; (38) C.-8; (40) N.-4; C.-5; (41) A.-9; N.12:2; (42) W.6:4-8; A.9:22-2. Rover in *Wild Oats*, Alexandre in *Victorine*, Robert Macaire, Goldfinch in *Road to Ruin*, Tangent in *The Way to get Married*, Horace in *Old English Gentleman*, Frederick in *Of Age To-morrow*, Jeremy in *Raising the Wind*, Ferment in *School of Reform*, Austerlitz in *Maid of Croissy,* Marplot in *Busy Body,* Puff in *The Critic,* Jem in *The Unfinished Gentleman.*

Brunton. (36) C.8:26*; 11:28*; (37) C.2:27*; 6:7*; (44) A.10:14-reg.; (45) C.-reg.; (46) W.8:29-reg; (51) N.7:15-reg., in summer; W.8:18-reg.; (52) N.7:12-reg.

Bryant, Miss. (44) C.10:14-reg.

Brydges. (40) W.7:4.

Buchanan, actor on engagement. (50) W.6:17-6; (51) W.6:23-6; 6:25*. Macbeth, Stranger, Shylock.

Buckstone. (40) C.9:12*-18; N.11:2*, 7*; N.-6; (41) N.-5; (42) W.7:16-8. Playwright and comedian on engagement, in his own plays of *Our Mary Ann, Single Life, Married Life, Weak Points,* and *A Kiss in the Dark.*

Bunjie, Miss. (38) C.9:17, 20; (39) C.3:23*.

Burgess. (38) W.10:10*; 12:12*, 31*; (39) W.1:1*; 2:4*; (40) W.2:3. Paul Jones.

Burke, Charles, in low comedy. (44) A.6:1-reg.; 8:3*; (45) A.-reg.; (46) P.M.3:19-reg.; A.8:26-reg.; (47) A.6:4*-reg.; (48) A.12:25*-reg.; (49) A.1:8*; (50) A.8:5-18; 12:2-5; (51) A.6:9-6; C.8:18-reg., as stage manager; (52) A.8:30-reg.; 9:29*; (53) A.1:1-6; (54) A.2:1-5. Wool Dealer.

Burke, Mrs. Charles, in low comedy. (44) A.6:1-reg.; 8:3*; 12:21*; (45) A.-reg.; P.M.3:8-reg.; (47) A.11:30*-reg.; (48) P.M.3:16-reg.; A.6:29*-reg.; 3:5*-6; (49) C.-reg.

Burke, Mrs. M. (51) A.8:30-reg.

Burnes. (42) W.5:18-reg.

Burnett. (52) N.8:26*; N.7:12-reg.

Bussard, C. (51) C.2:22.

Burton, William E., stock actor, prolific playwright of innumerable farces, star on engagement, manager, theatre lessee. (35) C.-reg.; 1:7*, 12*, 13*; 3:11*, 14*, 31*; 4:1*; 5:13*; 6:1*; 9:5*, 7*, 30*; 10:3*, 28*; 11:14*, 28; (36) C.-reg.; 2:6*, 22*; 3:26*; 4:6*, 14*, 16*; 6:15*; 18*; 8:26*; 9?30*; 12:19*; (37) C.-reg.; 1:23*; 2:25*; 4:1*, 14*; 5:2*; 7:3*; 10:19*; 11:18*; 12:27*; (38) C.-reg.; 1:9*, 15*; 3:29*; 4:18*, 20*; 6:20*; 7:7*; 9:15*; 10:2*; 11:29*; 12:24*, 29*; C.1:2*-reg.; W.4:1*-26; 10:12*-14; (40) W.4:8*, 11*, 17*; N.11:7*, 9*; (41) N.3:24*; (42) N.1:20*, 27*; C.4:7*, 25*; 11:2*; (43) O.1:9-reg.; W.1:13-26; 5:17*; A.8:10-6; (44) W.4:10-16; A.6:1-reg.; 8:3*; (45) A.4:22*-reg.; (46) A.-reg.; 3:28*; 5:13*; (47) A.6:4*-reg.; (48) A.1:14*-reg.; 9:25*; (49) A.-reg.; 6:11*, 13*-reg.; 8:15. From the end of 1843 until the beginning of 1849, Burton was the lessee of the Arch. He usually appeared in the leading rôles of the farces which he himself improvised. Other rôles of his were Paul Pry, Dickey in *His First Champagne,* and in *Peter the Great* as Dunder.

Butler, Samuel, classic tragedian on engagement. (41) C.12:30-2; (42) C.1:1-3.

Buts, Joe. (37) W.1:12.

Byrne (S). (44) N.1:19-reg.; (46) P.M.6:25-reg.; (55) C.M.9:8-reg. Trueman in *George Barnewell.*

Cadell, Miss. (44) A.6.:1-reg.

Calladine, J. H. (51) A.8:30-reg.

Calvé, Mlle., on engagement with French Opera Company. (43) C.9:14-13; (45) C.9:29-12.

Candi, Pietro, on engagement with Italian Opera Company from Havana, seventy-two people in number. (47) W.7:12-18.

Canfield, on engagement. Took the rôle of Wild Man in *Twin Brothers*. (49) A.3:5*-6.

Cantor, Mrs. (40) A.-reg.; 12:11*; (42) N.-reg.; (43) N.-reg.

Cappele, Mrs., (also Cappell). (42) A.3:28-reg.; (43) A.8:10-reg.; (45) C.-reg.; A.-8:30-reg.; (53) C.-reg.

Cappell, Miss. (53) C.12:1*-reg.

Carnes. (37) C.2:27*.

Carpenter. (38) W.2:24*-4.

Carson. (51) N.7:15, summer; B.9:1-reg.

Carter. (39) W.7:29. Afghai in *The Lion Ring*.

Cartlich. (49) A.10:24*-6; Benjamin Franklin.

Cartmel. (51) C.2:22.

Casini, Mme., in French Opera. (45) C.9:29-12.

Celeste, Mlle., on engagement; Alexa, Agata, Alexis in *Wizard Skiff;* Hope Gough, Naramattah in *Wept of Wish-Ton-Wish;* Adhel in *Moorish Page;* Mathilde, Henri, Hamet in *French Spy;* Antonio, Victoire in *Death Plank*. (35) A.3:16*, 21*, 28*-12; 6:13*-12; 11:14*-12; (36) 4:9*, 14*, 16*-18, 12; 9:17*-12; 11:28-18; (37) -6; (38) 10:22*; 11:3*, 11; 12:11*-16; (39) -10; (40) 1:8; 2:17*; (42) C.10:17*-9; 10:22*; (51) W.11:10, 22*-5; (52) C.5:10-15.

Chanfrau, as the Yankee type. (49) A.9:20-8; N.10:8-6; (50) A.8:19-8; (54) C.10:9-5.

Chapman, Caroline, Miss. (46) A.8:26 reg.; (51) A.7:14.

Chapman, S. (41) W.11:6*.

Chapman, Mrs. S., one night only, at Jefferson's benefit, imported from Parke Theatre, N. Y. (35) C.4:9.

Chapman, W. B. (44) W.9:17-5; C.10:14-reg.; (45) W.-reg.; (46) W.5:20*-reg.; (47) W.-reg.; (48)

W.-reg.; 1:12*; 6:26*; 8:28*; (49) W.-reg.; (50) W.6:4-reg.; 11:18*; 12:5*; (51) W.8:18-reg.; (52) W.6:12*-reg.; (53) W.10:10*; 12:14*-reg.; (54) W.5:1*-reg.

Chappell, (36) W.10:28*; (37) W.2:20*.

Charles, G. C., Irish comedian. (55) C.M.12:24-6.

Charles, Miss M. A., Irish comedienne. (55) C.M.12:24-6.

Charles, J. S., comedian. (36) W.12:22; (40) W.-reg.; (41) A.3:13*; (42) C.1:24-reg.; 2:9*; W.6:3; (43) O.1:19-reg.; A.3:14-reg.; W.8:8*; A.8:10-reg.

Charles, Mrs. J. S. (40) W.-reg.; (41) W.3:13*; (42) A.3:28-reg.; (43) O.1:9-reg.; A.8:10-reg.

Charnock, Miss. (35) W.1:28*; 11:9*; (36) W.2:29*; 3:14*, 29*; 7:4*; 8:31*; 9:8*; 11:19*; (37) W.1:9*.

Checkini, Mr. and Mrs., and Mlle. Arreline, with Mlle. Celeste. (36) C.11:28*-18.

Cheri, Jr., with French Company. (55) W.11:19-6.

Chester, Miss. (36) P.12:5; (37) W.2:20*, 6:30*.

Chippendale, comedian from Parke Theatre, N. Y. (39) W.8:9; (42) C.2:15-5; (45) C.1:22-reg.; (54) N.6:3-reg. Cosey in *Town and Country*, Chase in *A Roland for an Oliver*.

Chippendale, Miss. (50) W.8:24-2; (51) W.8:18-reg. Linda in *Passing Cloud*.

Clarke, Conrad. (53) A.1:29-reg.; (55) C.M.10:20-reg.

Clarke, Mrs. Conrad. (53) A.1:29-reg.

Clarke, J. S., comedian. (55) A.11:12*-reg.

Clarke, N. B. (35) W.12:25*; (36) W.1:1*; 2:10*; 3:14*; 8:31*; 9:8*; 10:28*; 11:23*; 28*; 12:13*; (37)

W.1:2*, 4*, 7*, 9*; 2:20*; 3:18*; (49) A.-reg.; 12:5*; (50) C.-reg.; 3:18*; 5:1*; (51) A.7:14.

Clarke, Mrs. N. B. (49) A.4:27-reg.; (50) C.-reg.; 4:8*.

Clarke, Miss. (47) A.10:28*; (48) P.M.3:16-reg. Carina in *Who's the Composer?*

Clemens. (36) W.10:28*; (37) W.2:20*; 6:30*.

Clifford, W. S. (51) A.8:30-reg.

Clifton, Miss Josephine, on engagement in support of J. Wallack, and E. Forrest. (36) C.6; (37) C.12:27*-6; (40) N.5; (42) C.4:11-10; (43) W.6:5-7; (44) C.11:27-9. Mariana in *The Wife,* Elvira in *Pizarro,* Mrs. Beverly in *The Gamester,* Violante in *Wonder,* Julia in *Hunchback.*

Cline, T. S. (35) C.-reg.; (36) C.2:6*; 4:9*; 4:16*-reg.; (37) C.10:28*; 11:28*-reg.; (38) W.-engagement of one week during July; (39) C.-reg.; (40) C.5:9.

Coad, Miss. (42) C.12:5-7; (43) C.1:7-6; (46) W.8:29-reg.; in opera.

Coeuriot, Mme. Stephen, in French Opera. (45) C.9:29-12.

Coffee. (51) C.2:22.

Cole, Mrs., with Cooke's Company. (38) W.4:2*.

Coleman, Piccaniny, on engagement. (41) A.9:21-5.

Collingbourne, S. (35) W.8:28*, 10:28*; (36) W.3:25*; 6:20*, 30*; (37) W.6:30*-reg.; (38) W.-reg.; (42) A.3:28-reg.

Collingbourne, Miss. (41) N.12:6; (42) W.-reg.

Collins, J. H., Irish comedian. (35) W.4:11; (36) W.3:14*, 25*; (46) W.11:16-5; (47) W.2:1-35; W.10:1*; (48) W.5:5-10; 9:11-11; (49) W.4:9-12; 9:11-17; 9:13*; (50) C.1:8-1; W.4:29-10; W.5:6*; W.10:14*-5; (51) W.2:24-10; W.9:

10-10; (52) C.2:23-10; (53) C.11:7-10; (55) W.11:27-10. On engagement. Sir Patrick in *Somnambulist.*

Conduit, Mrs. (35) C.3:31*.

Conner, E. S., actor-manager-lessee. (37) C.12:11*-25, on engagement; (38) C.9, performances; (38) C.11, performances; (39) C.5:18*-10; 6:20*-25; 7:19*-10; 10:3*-10; (41) A.10; N.9:25*-reg.; (42) A.4:14*; 5:23*-reg.; (43) W.6:14-9; A.9:4-22; N.10:30-48; (44) A.6:1-reg.; 10:24*; (45) A.5:14-30; N.4:28-15; (46) A.11:18-25; (48) A.2:10*, 15*, 11; (50) A., lessee-4:27*, 11:11*; (51) A.7:14; (52) N.9:20-10; (55) C.4:7-5. Marino Faliero, Iago, Edgar, Pythias in *Damon and Pythias,* Icilius in *Virginius,* Laertes, Richmond, Titus in *Brutus,* Mac-Duff, Michael in *William Tell,* Alonzo in *Pizarro,* Ramon in *Broker of Bogota,* Phasarius in *Gladiator,* Cassio, Fitzarnold in *Metamora.*

Conner, Mrs. E. S. (48) A.2:10*, 15*-11; (50) A.-reg.; 11:11*; (51) A.7:14; 4:14*; (55) C.4:7-5. Pauline in *Lady of Lyons,* Juliet.

Connor, stock actor. (35) W.1:10*, 17*, 28*; 2:21, 28*; 3:7*, 11*, 23*; 4:8*, 11*; 5:11*, 30*; 6:3*, 22*, 27*; 9:5*, 12*, 16*, 19*, 26*, 29*; 10:3*, 5*, 10*, 24*, 28*, 29*, 31*; 11:5*, 7*; 12:14*, 16*, 19*; (36) W.1:1*, 9*, 13*, 25*; 2:1*, 10*, 29*; 3:12*, 14*, 25*; 4:4*, 11*, 16*, 25*, 29*, 30*; 5:23*; 6:13*, 20*, 22*; 7:4*; 8:31*; 9:3*, 8*, 17*, 24*; 10:1*, 15*, 28*; 11:15*, 19*, 23*, 28*; 12:5*, 6*, 24*; (37) W.1:2*, 7*, 9*; 2:20*, 27*; 3:6*, 11*, 13*, 18*; 3:20*, 22*, 27*; 6:30*; 7:24*, 31*; 8:31*; 9:2*; (38) W.-reg.; (41) A.8:10.

Cony, and his dogs, Hector and Bruin. (35) W.6:8*, 19*-20; 10:5*, 10*,

15*, 17*-12; (36) W.11-engagement; (37) W.1:21*-13; (45) W.11:17-6; (52) A.3:29-6; (53) C.4:18-6; (55) C.3:19-5. Cherokee Chief, Landry in *Forest of Bondy,* Conrade in *Hermit's Prophecy,* Cato in *Planter and his Dogs.*

Cony, Master. (52) A.3:29-6; (53) C.4:18-6; (55) C.3:19-5.

Conolly. (37) P.1:19.

Conover. (42) W.-reg.

Conway, F. B., leading man. (50) W.10:29-5; (55) A.10:2*-reg. Stranger.

Conway, Mrs. F. B. (35) W.8:28*; 10:5*, 10*, 15*, 24*, 28*, 31*; 11:9*, 14*; 12:16*, 25*; (55) A.10:2*-reg.; 11:12*.

Cooke, George Frederick. (40) N.-occasionally.

Cooke Family. (38) W.3:6*.

Cooke, Jr. (38) W.4:2*.

Cooke, Mrs. (35) W.6:19*.

Cooper, on engagement, in Restoration Comedy. (35) W.5:18-14; (36) W.-6 performances. Dorillon in *Wives as they Were,* Walter in *Hunchback,* Beverly in *Gamester,* Duke in *Honeymoon,* Virginius, Benedick in *Much Ado about Nothing.*

Cooper, Miss, on engagement, in Restoration Comedy. (35) W.5:18-14; (36) W.-6 performances. Miss Dorillon in *Wives as they Were,* Julia in *Hunchback,* Mrs. Beverly in *Gamester,* Juliana in *Honeymoon,* Virginia in *Virginius,* Beatrice in *Much Ado about Nothing.*

Cooper, Mrs. (51) B.9:1-reg.

Cornish, Miss. (44) C.10:14-reg.

Corsi, Rossi, with Italian Opera Company. (48) C.2:19-23; 6:6-7; 10:4-15; 12:5-12.

Corsini, Signora Ester, with Italian Opera Company from Havana. (43)

C.7:15-13; 11:13-11.

Costini, Signorina Elisa, with Italian Opera Company from Havana. (50) C.9:10-10.

Couldock, with Miss C. Cushman. (49) W.10:29-14; (50) A.5:27-12; W.-reg.; 9:25*; (51) W.8:18-reg.; 3:11*; 4:9*, 15*, 21*; (52) W.3:22*-reg.; (53) W.-reg.; (55) C.2:12-10. Stranger, Jaques.

Couldock, Mrs. (50) W.12:10; (51) W.8:18-reg. Lady Traffic in *City Madame.*

Countess of Lansfeldt. See Mlle. Lola Montez.

Countess St. James. See Mme. Augusta.

Cowell, Joe, comedian on engagement. (36) W.-5 performances; (44) W.4:5. Dromio in *Comedy of Errors,* Paul Pry, Tom in *My Wife and I,* Lazarillo in *The Hotel.*

Craddock. (37) C.2:27*.

Cramer, Mrs. H. (38) C.11:26-4; (39) C.6:20*-reg.; (49) A.4:11-reg.; (50) A.3:4-reg. Mrs. Haller in *Stranger,* Violante in *Wonder,* Pauline in *Lady of Lyons,* Juliana in *Honeymoon,* Portia.

Cramer, Miss F. (50) A.3:4-reg.

Crampton, Miss C. J. See Mrs. Wilkinson.

Crane. (40) A.-reg.

Creswick, from Parke Theatre, N. Y. (40) C.4:6.

Crisp, W. H., on engagement in low comedy. (44) C.12:10-4; (45) A.10:20*-7; W.6:23-5; C.9:2-6; (48) A.8:26-2.

Crocker, from Parke Theatre in N. Y. (45) C.1:22-reg.; (48) Ath.12:25-reg.; (49) P.M.5:17*-5.

Crocker, Miss. (46) W.8:29-reg.

Crouta, the prompter. (36) W.3:14*, 10:28*; (37) 6:30*.

Crowley. (38) C.3:17*.

Cruise, Miss Anna. (55) C.M.9:8-reg.
Cunningham. (37) W.2:20*; (46)
P.M.3:9-reg.; (52) A.8:21-reg.
Curfew, H. A. (38) W.11:28.
Curtis. (43) C.-reg.
Cushman, Miss Charlotte. (40) N.-
reg.-10:19*, 12:19*; (41) C.6:17;
(42) C.2:15-11; (42) W.-reg.; (43)
C.-reg.; W.9:16*; (44) A.-reg.;
(49) W.10:29-17; (50) A.5:27-12;
W.11:4-14; (51) W.6:16-6; C.12:
1-6; 12:18*; (52) W.4:19-6. Mrs.
Haller in *Stranger*, Rosalind.
Cushman, Miss S. (40) C.3:17-5; N.-
reg.; (42) C.2:19; W.-reg.; (43)
C.-reg.; (44) W.9:18; (45) W.4:
16*. Ernestine in *Romantic Widow*,
Lady Clement in *Artist's Wife*,
Mary in *Boarding School*.
Cuvillier, Mrs. (36) W.3:14*.

Da Costa, Mrs. D. See Mrs. Mossop.
Daly, Miss Julia. (48) W.6:1-reg.;
(55) C.-reg.
Darley. (36) C.5:26*; (38) C.5:5.
Davenport, A. H. See Davenport, H. A.
Davenport, E. L. (38) C.7:2*; 8:8*;
(39) C.3:20*; 5:13*; (40) C.3:19*;
(41) W.11:6*; (42) W.6:30*-reg.;
(43) C.-reg.; (45) W.5:5-15; (46)
W.10:15-6; (49) A.11:6-2; (50)
A.12:30-3; (51) W.8:18-reg.; A.4:
14*; (54) W.9:26*-10; (55) W.3:
14*-10; 3:23*; W.10:10*-10. Gener-
al Kleiner in *Maid of Mariendorpt*.
Davenport, Mrs. E. L. (38) W.6:11-5.
Jane in *Dumb Boy of Manchester*,
Lady Teazle in *School for Scandal*.
See Miss Vinny.
Davenport, Miss Jean Margaret. (38)
W.6:11*-12; (49) A.11:5-17; (50)
W.4:15-23; 5:29*; 6:7*; A.9:9-15;
(51) C.3:1-28; 9:19*-10; (52)
C.4:26-10; (53) W.9:23*-10; (54)

C.1:2-10; 3:31*-10. Richard III,
Jane in *Manager's Daughter*, Little
Pickle in *Spoiled Child*, Shylock,
Dumb Boy of Manchester, Teazle in
School for Scandal, Juliet, Meeta in
Maid of Mariendorpt.
Davenport, H. A. (53) C.12:7*-reg.;
(54) C.1:9*-reg.; (55) W.10:10*-
reg.
Davis. (37) W.7:10*-8. Tom in *Farm-
er's Son*, Sol in *Tom and Jerry*.
Davis, Mrs. (45) C.8:30-reg.; (50)
A.11:4. Rose in *Forest Rose*.
Daw(e)s. (44) C.10:14-reg.; (48)
P.M.3:16-reg.
Dawes, Miss Gertrude. (55) C.1:15-
reg.
Dawson. (51) C.8:18-reg.
Dean, E. (48) Ath.12:25-reg.
Dean, Miss Julia. (46) A.11:24-4; (48)
W.2:7-11; A.12:11-5; Ath.12:25-5;
(51) W.3:1-10; 4:9*; (53) W.10:
3*-10; 5:14-10. Julia in *Hunchback*,
Juliet, Lucretia Borgia, Alicia in
Jane Shore.
De Bar. (47) A.5:19-6; 8:24-11; (48)
W.7:5-5; (49) P.M.7:9*-reg. Old
Dodge in *Artful Dodger*, Satisfaction
Skunk in *Indian Girl*.
De Bar, Miss, later Mrs. J. B. Booth,
Jr. (38) C.10:2*, 22*; 12:24*, 29*;
(39) C.-reg.; (40) C.-reg.; (44)
A.6:1-reg.; 10:24*; (47) A.9:11-9;
(48) P.M.3:16-reg.; A.1:11*-reg.,
A.9:14*; (49) A.3:14*; P.M.4:25-
reg.; (50) A.6:15-reg. Helen in
Hunchback, Undine, Kate Plowden in
Paul Jones.
Deering, Mrs. (54) N.6:3-reg.
Deering, Miss E. (54) N.6:3-reg.
DeLarue, tragedian. (35) W.10:2.
De Marguerittes, on engagement in
opera. (54) C.6:6-6.
Delcy, Miss, in opera. (45) C.10:13-10.
Demotte, Garry. (54) C.11:13-10.

Denby. (46) W.8:29-reg.; (51) N.7:15, summer.

Denim, Miss Kate, in support of her sister. (52) C.7:14-5; (53) C.2:7-5.

Denim, Miss Susan. (51) A.12:8; (52) C.7:14-5; (53) C.2:7-5; (54) C.10: 2-5.

Denvil. (36) W.12:13*-5. Martelli in *Minerali,* Shylock, *Richard III,* Overreach in *A New Way To Pay Old Debts.*

Derivage, in low comedy. (35) W.12:19*.

Derr, W. R. (50) A.3:18-6; (54) N.6:3-reg. Dick Turpin in *Rookwood,* Omar in *Siege of Corinth.*

Des Jardins, Mlle. Pauline. (40) C.12:16; (41) C.-15 performances. Singer in *La Sonnambula.*

Diamond, Master. (40) W.7:16; (42) A.4:25-2. Bumbo in *Oh! Hush!!*

Dickenson, G. K. (37) W.12:27; (38) W.2:24*; (51) W.12:1. Oliver in *Calaynos.*

Dieudonne, with French Company. (55) W.11:19-6.

Dinneford. (41) W.4:5.

Dolman. (53) A.4:20-reg.

Don, Sir William, a light comedian. (50) W.11:22-15; (51) W.1:29; C.1:30-3; (53) C.8:31. Sleek in *Serious Family,* Coldstream in *Used Up,* Cousin Joe in *Rough Diamond.*

Donaldson. (54) C.9:13-reg.

D'Ormy, Signora Martini, in opera. (54) C.8:28-6.

Douvry, in French Opera. (45) C.9:29-12.

Downes, Miss. (44) C.10:14-reg.

Drake, Mrs. (45) W.3:29. Elvira in *Pizarro.*

Drisbach. (42) W.6:30*-10. Karfa in *Mungo Park.*

Dowton, comedian from Drury Lane. (36) C.-6 performances. Bramble in *Poor Gentleman,* Sir Anthony in *The*

Rivals, Falstaff in *Henry IV,* Teazle in *School for Scandal,* Dornton in *Road to Ruin,* Cantwell in *Hypocrite.*

Drew, Frank Nelson; comedian. (53) A.-reg.; (54) A.8:19-reg.; (55) A.8:18-reg.

Drew, Mrs. F. Nelson. (53) A.11:28*-reg.; (54) C.7:31-reg.; C.M.9:12-reg.; (55) A.8:18-reg.

Drew, John; comedian, farcist. (52) C.9:8-reg.; (53) A.-Lessee, 3:4*; 11:7*, 28*; (54) A.-reg.; (55) W.-reg., 11:7.

Drew, Mrs. John. (52) C.8:30-reg.; (53) A.-reg., 3:4*; (54) A.-reg.; (55) W.-reg., 10:10*. See Mrs. Hunt.

Drummond. (37) P.1:9; (42) C.3:26-reg.

Duff. (45) C. and A.-reg.; (46) P.M.-reg.; W.8:29-reg.; (50) C.7:24-15.

Duff, Mrs. (35) W.10:29*; (50) C.7:24-5. Elvira in *Pizarro.*

Duff, Miss Mary. (35) W.1:1*, 10*, 17*, 19*, 28*; 2:5*, 7*; 3:5*, 23*; 4:8*, 11*; 5:11*, 15*; 6:2*, 3*, 23*; 9:4*, 12*, 23*, 26*; 10:24*; 12:7*; (36) 2:1*; 3:12*, 14*; (41) N.4:8; (48) C.7:20.

Duffield, Mrs. (53) W.3:14*, 17*-reg.; (54) W.5:1*-reg.; 9:26*; (55) W.3:14*-reg.

Duncan. (37) P.2:4.

Dunham, Mrs. (36) W.4:28.

Dunn, James C. (51) A.7:14.

Dunn, Jno. (44) W.11:24-7; (45) W.1:7-10; A.5:12-3; C.8:30-reg.; (47) A.8:9-12; (48) A.6:29*-20; (49) A.18:16-reg.; 8:20*, 27*; 9:1*, 5*; 10:2*, 3*; (50) W.-reg.; 3:25*; 6:27*. Rascal Jack, Tom Tape in *Sketches in India,* Richard ye Thirde.

Dunn, Mrs. Jno. (45) A.5:12-3.

Durand, Miss Rosalie A., in English opera. (55) C.M.6:11-15.

Durang, Charles. (35) W.6:24, 12:25; (36) W.10:28*.

Durang, Mrs. Charles. (36) W.8:31*; 12:5*; (44) C.11:11*.

Durang, Miss. (42) C.4:15; (43) W.6:5. Rosina, Diana Vernon in *Rob Roy*.

Duret, Miss E. Maria, in support of Dyott. (50) W.3:18-5. Julia in *Hunchback*, Mrs. Haller in *Stranger*, Pauline in *Lady of Lyons*.

Dyott, from Parke Theatre, N. Y. (45) C.1:22-reg.; (50) W.3:19-4; (51) W.4:9*, 15*. Claude Melnotte, Stranger.

Dyott, Mrs. (45) C.1:22-reg.

Eaton, C. H. (35) W.6:3-4; (36) W.-2 performances; (41) A.10:4; (42) A.4:25-10; W.5:23-5; (43) A.4:4-7. Overreach in *A New Way To Pay Old Debts*, Shylock, Mortimer in *Iron Chest*, Richard III.

Eberle, David. (35) C.-infrequently; (36) C.5:28; (37) C.2:27*; 10:25*; (38) C.6:11*; (39) C.-reg.; (42) C.-reg.; (43) A.8:10-reg.; (44) C.-reg.; (45) C. and A.-reg.; (46) W.8:29-reg.; (49) P.M.6:27-reg.; (51) W.8:18-reg.

Eberle, Miss A., in 1851, Mrs. Y. Leonard. (50) C.4:17*; (51) N.7:15, summer; (52) N.5:22-reg.; (54) N.6:3-reg.

Eberle, Miss E. (47) P.M.1:7-reg.; (48) Ath.12:25-reg.; (50) C.4:6*.

Edwards. (40) W.4:11*; (55) C.1:15-reg.

Edwin, from Mitchell's Olympic Company. (41) N.-reg.

Ellis, Miss. (39) C.5:17.

Ellis, Miss Clara, from Parke Theatre, N. Y. (45) C.1:22-reg.

Ellis, Harvey. (50) A.6:10. Octavian in *Mountaineers*.

Ellwell, Mrs. (50) A.2:23-reg.

Elphinstone, Miss. (35) C.1:12; 4:11.

Elssler, J. (47) P.M.2:3-reg.; (50)

C.4:6*-reg.; (51) C.7:3-reg.; N.7:15, summer.

Elssler, Mrs. J. See Mrs. F. S. Myers.

Elssler, Miss Fanny, a dancer. (40) C.6:17*-20; (41) C.-15 performances.

Elssler Brothers, strong men. (43) N.12:20-6; (44) N.1:15-15; W.6:8-5. *Valentine and Orson, Wood Wolf, Flying Machine, Frankenstein*.

Elvins, Miss. (41) N.8:27.

English, Mrs. (42) C.-reg.

English, J. (51) A.8:30-reg.

Eytinge; comedian. (53) C.5:26-reg.; W.9:23*; (54) W.5:9*-reg.

Fannin, J. S. (51) A.8:30-reg.

Farren, Henry. (49) A.3:19-10; 3:30*; 10:29-4; (50) A.4:4; 10:14-2; (54) W.8:29-reg. Don Cesar in *Bold Stroke for a Husband*, Don Alphonzo in *Lucrece Borgia*.

Farren, Mrs. Henry. (47) A.9:20-7; 12:7-10; (48) A.3:20-12; 10:5-10; (49) A.3:24*, 28*, 30*-13; 10:29-4; (50) A.4:2-4; 10:7-10; (51) A.3:31-10; 4:4*; (54) C.10:18-15; 10:25*; 11:4*; (55) C.M.5:10-10. Mariana in *The Wife*, Evadne, Lucrece Borgia, Mary Tudor, Adelgitha.

Faulkner, singer. (35) C.1:8; 8:29; 12:11.

Faulkner. (35) C.4:23*; (36) C.9:30*; (37) C.2:25*; 6:17*; (38) C.6:2*; 9:15*; 10:2*, 22*; (39) C.5:20; (40) C.5:27; (42) C.1:6-reg.; (43) W.-reg.; N.-reg.; 10:9*; (44) A.6:1-reg.; (45) C.1:22-reg.; (46) A.8:26-reg.

Faulkner, Mrs. (39) C.6:20. Her first appearance on any stage, as Mary Capp in *Charles II*.

Faurrest, C. (35) W.3:6.

Felix, Misses Sarah, Lia, and Dinah, with French Company. (55) W.11:19-6.

Fenno, A. W., with Mrs. Farren (48)

A.10:21*-20; (51) C.3:1-28; (52) A.8:21-reg., stage manager; (53) C.9:26*-reg. Hamlet, Stranger, Claude in *Lady of Lyons*.

Ferrai, Miss. (44) C.10:14-reg.

Ferrers, a prompter. (40) W.6:13; N.-reg.

Fest, J., tragedian. (45) W.10:15-8; (47) A.5:17.

Field, J. M., comedian from Tremont Theatre, Boston. (39) W.4:26; (42) A.10:27; (43) C.-reg.; W.9:16*; (48) Ath.12:25-reg. Overreach in *A New Way To Pay Old Debts*.

Finn. (36) W.10:10*-6; (39) W.-4 performances; (40) W.-1 performance. Ogleby in *Clandestine Marriage*, Paul Pry, Richard III, Pangloss in *Heir at Law*, Shatterly in *Married and Single*, Brown in *Kill and Cure*, Paul Pop in *Removing the Deposits*.

Fisher, John, from Parke Theatre, N. Y. (45) C.1:2-reg.; (51) N.7:15, summer; A.8:21-reg.

Fisher, Miss A. (35) W.2:13.

Fisher, Miss Alexina, in 1852 Mrs. Lewis Baker. (35) C.3:23*; 5:11*, 15*; 6:3*, 13*; (36) C.9:17*; (37) C.2:25*, 27*; 6:7*; 10:19*, 25*; 12:27*; (38) C.1:15*; 3:29*; 4:20*; 6:2*, 20*, 27*; 11:3*, 29*; (39) C.1:2*; 3:27*; (40) C.1:3*; (41) N.9:25*, 27*; (42) A.5:5-10; (43) O.1:9-reg.; W.2:21-reg.; A.8: 10-reg.; C.-reg.; (45) W.4:10*; (46) W.8:29-reg.; (47) W.-reg.; (48) W.-reg.; 6:26*; 10:23*; (49) C.9:1-reg.; (50) W.3:25*-reg.; 6.: 27*; (50) B.9:28-reg.; 9:30*; (51) B.4:10*; A.8:30-reg.; (55) C.-1:15-20; C.M.10:20-10.

Fisher, Miss Oceana. (38) C.5:30. Her first appearance on any stage, as Clemanthe in *Ion*.

Fitzgerald. (51) N.7:15, summer; W.8:18-reg.

Fitzjames, Mlle. Nathalie, with Italian Opera Company. (50) C.12:10-2.

Fitzpatrick, Miss Emma. (53) W.1:1-reg.

Fitzwilliam, Mrs., on engagement. (39) C.11:4-12; (40) C.5:18*-20; (41) N.-25 performances; (42) W.7:16-8. Peggy in *Country Girl*, Albina in *The Will*, Irish Widow, Sally in *Englishmen in India*.

Flannigan, Miss. (42) N.1:22. Mrs. Caddy in *The Prize*.

Fleming. (40) C.3:31; 4:10; (43) N.-reg. Shylock, Overreach in *A New Way To Pay Old Debts*.

Florence, W. J. Irish comedian. (53) C.7:18-5; C.10:24-5; (54) C.7:24-5; (55) C.M.7:2-5.

Florence, Mrs. W. J. (53) C.7:18-5; 10:24-5; (54) C.7:24-5; (55) C.M.7:2-5.

Flynn. (40) W.11:27; A.12:11*-reg.; (41) W.10:3; (42) A.10:5-11; (43) A.3:14-reg.

Flynn, Mrs., in support of Vandenhoff. (37) C.-6 performances; (41) 3:13*-W.-reg.; 11:6; (42) W.-reg.; A.10:5-11; (43) A.3:14-reg. Volumnia, Amelia, Cordelia, Ophelia, Marcia in *Cato*.

Fogg, Mrs. M. S. (49) P.M.-reg.

Forbes. (35) W.9:2-6; (43) A.8:25-6. William Tell, Stranger, Romeo, Alexander, Pythias in *Damon and Pythias*, Rolla in *Pizarro*.

Forbes, Mrs. (43) A.8:25. Pauline in *Lady of Lyons*.

Forrest, Edwin: (36) C.-5 performances; (37) C.-22 performances; (38) C.-25 performances; (39) C.-32 performances; (40) W.-10 per. C.-18 per.; (41) A.-20 per.; W.-10 per.; (42) C.-4.11-10; W.-10.17-12; (43) W.-5.29-12; N.-10.16-12; (44) N.-1.29-2; W.-8.26-24; (46) W.-10.19-12; (47) W.-1.4-32; 11.1-17;

(48) W.-10.20-16; (49) W.-6.2-5; (51) W.-10.6-14; (52) W.-6.9-15; W.-10.10-10; (53) W.-10.10-10; (54) W.-10.9-15; (55) W.-12.10-15. Damon in *Damon and Pythias,* Othello, Sparticus in *The Gladiator,* Lear, Virginius, Hamlet, Richard III, Brutus, Macbeth, William Tell, Rolla in *Pizarro,* Febro in *Broker of Bogota,* Claude in *Lady of Lyons,* Richelieu, Aylmere.

Forrest, W.: (44) C.-10.14-reg.

Forrest, Mrs. W.: (44) C.-10.14-reg.

Forti, Signor, with Italian Opera Company: (50) C.-12.10-15.

Foster, Joseph C., from the Adelphi Theatre, London, through Cooke's Company: (38) W.-4.2; (40) W.-4.21; (45) W.-3.10-18; (52) N.-7.12-lessee and reg.

Foster, Mrs. Joseph C.: (52) N.-7.12-reg.

Foster, C.: (40) W.-4.21; (44) W.-7.27*; (45) W.-3.10-18; (46) W.-1.7; (49) C.-9.1-reg.; 9.8*; (50) C.-reg.; 3.18*; 4.8*; (52) N.-7.12-reg. Charles XII.

Fox, Miss: (37) C.-2.27*.

France: (53) W.-reg.

France, Mrs.: (53) W.-reg.

Frary, Mrs.: (48) A.-1.26; (50) A.-10.22-7. Mad Galochard in *King's Gardener.*

Frazer, in opera: (44) C.-12.20-10; (45) C.-5.19-30; 11.10-10; (46) C.-4.27-10; W.-11.2-23; (47) C.-4.5-52.

Fredericks, Williams: (40) W.-reg.; (41) W.-3.13*; (42) W.-7 performances; (45) W.-reg.; C.-8.30-reg.; (49) W.-11.22; (50) W.-reg.; (51) C.-8.18-acting managers; (54) A.-reg.

Freemont: (36) P.-11.25.

Freer: (40) W.-8 performances; (45) N.-4.28-reg. Edgar the Idiot, Gaston in *Man in the Iron Mask.*

Gallagher, J. L.: (44) N.-1.19-reg.; (47) P.M.-reg.; (54) C.M.-9.12-reg. George Barnwell.

Gann, on engagement, in low comedy: (41) W.-9.24-5; (42) C.-1.24-reg.; A.-5.23*-reg.; (43) A.-3.14-reg.; (44) N.-1.1*.

Gann, Miss: (44) N.-1.4-5. Maria in *Bayonet,* Maria in *Murder of the Quarry.*

Gannon, Miss; the Lilliputian wonder: (38) W.-1.19-4.

Gannon, Mary A.: (46) P.M.-3.9-reg.; (49) P.M.-6.27-reg.; Sophia in *Rendezvous.*

Gardner, F., in opera: (45) C.-10.13-10.

Garretson: (47) A.-5.25.

Garry, in French opera: (45) C.-9.29-12.

Garson, T. E.: (38) W.-3.10; 12.13; (39) W.-1.15. Dumpy in *United States.*

Gates, from Bowery Theatre, N. Y., with Cooke's Company: (38) W.-4.2*, 11*.

George: (42) W.-reg.

George, Miss: (42) W.-reg.

Geberding: (37) A.-7.27-6; with German Co. Carl in *Dissipated Invalid,* Zeilig in *Watchman.*

Gerli, Signorina Theodolina, with Italian Opera Company from Havana, 72 in number: (47) W.-7.12-18.

Germon: (36) W.-3.14*; (50) B.-12.5-reg.; (51) B.-4.10*-reg.

Germon, Mrs.: (51) A.-reg.

Gibbons, Mrs.: (46) P.M.-3.9-reg.; W.-8.29-reg.

Gibbs, Mrs.: (37) C.-3.25*; (38) C.-reg.; (39) C.- 6.6*.

Gibson: (36) W.-3.14*.

Gilbert, John, leading man: (51) C.-3.1-reg.; 9.19*, 12.18*; (52) A.-8.21; C.-reg.; (53) C.-9.26*; 12.1*, 7*-reg.

Gilbert, Mrs. John: (52) A.-8.21-reg.; (53) C.-reg.

Giubeli: (39) C.-10.16-15; (40) C.-4.20-15; (41) C.-15 performances. Baron in *Cinderella*, Count in *La Sonnambula*, Don Pizarro in *Fidelio*, Gibo in *Postillion of Lonjumeau*. By engagement in opera.

Gladstone, Mrs. W.: (51) A.-2.20; N.-7.15-summer; (52) N.-7.12-reg. Julie in *Richelieu*.

Glenn, S. W., in Dutch comedy: (55) C.-4.5-15.

Godden: (42) C.-reg.

Gohr, in German opera: (40) C.-3.23. Kuno in *Freischutz*.

Goodall, W. R.: (51) A.-reg.; B.-5.10-reg.; A.-7.14; (54) N.-6.3-reg.

Gordon, Miss Fanny: (50) A.-3.4-reg.

Gordon, G.: (53) W.-1.1.

Gouffe, Mons.: (35) W.-9.17*-4. Monkey in *Dumb Savoyard and his Monkey*.

Gouffe, Mme.: (35) W.-9.17*-4. Pepino in *Dumb Savoyard and his Monkey*.

Goug(h)enheim, Miss A.: (51) W.-8.18-reg.; A.-7.14; (52) W.-6.12*-reg.

Goug(h)enheim, Miss J.: (51) W.-8.8-reg.; A.-7.14.

Gouldock; see Couldock.

Graham: (40) N.-reg.-10.19*; (41) Mitchell's Olympic Company; (44) A.-6.1-reg.

Graham, R. E.: (43) A.-10.2-8. Stranger, Virginius, Mortimer in *Iron Chest*.

Granville, A., in English opera: (54) C.-6.6-6.

Grattan, H. P.: (48) A.-7.3-3. Shylock, Hamlet, Walter in *Hunchback*.

Graziani, Signor, in opera: (54) C.-8.28-6.

Greene, John: (37) W.-3.18*-20; 3.24*, 27*; 6.30*; (41) A.-5 performances; (43) A.-10.12; C.-11.1; A.-12.11-reg.; (45) 8.30-C.-reg. Murtoch in

Irishman in London, Looney in *Review*, O'Schocknessy in *£100 Note*, Teague in *Honest Thieves*, Israel in *Star Spangled Banner*.

Greene, Mrs. John: (37) W.-2.20*; 3.6*-20; 3.20*; 3.27*; (41) A.-2 performances; (43) A.-8.10-reg.; (45) N.-4.28-reg.; C.-8.30-reg.; (46) A.-4.1*. Kawla in *Thalaba*.

Grenick, B.: (40) O.-12.16. A singer, in *La Sonnambula*.

Grierson: (39) W.-1.28*; (44) A.-6.1-reg.; C.-10.14-reg.

Griffiths, G. H.: (54) C.-11.13-reg.; (55) C.-1.15-reg.

Griffiths, Mrs. G. H.: (55) C.-1.15-reg.

Grosvenor: (48) A.-8.11.

Grove, Miss: (37) C.-1.30.

Guissinier, Joaquim, with Italian Opera Company from Havana: (43) C.-7.15-13; 11.13-11.

Hackett, J., portrayer of American character rôles: (35) W.-11.18; (36) W.-3.29*-3; (37) W.-7 performances; (38) W.-11 per.; (40) W.-4 per.; N.-5 per.; (41) N.-10 per.; (42) C.-3.29-5; W.-11.28-6; (43) C.-12.5-4; (44) A.-11.11-10; (45) C.-9.8-6; A.-9.29-6; (46) W.-8.2-6; (48) A.-12.5-2; (49) W.-3.19-6; 12.17-6; (53) W.-2.1-6; W.-4.21-6. Absent in Europe in 1839. Solomon Swop in *Jonathan in England*, Wildfire in *Kentuckian*, Rip Van Winkle, Job Fox.

Hackurt: (42) W.-reg.; (43) C.-reg.

Hackurt, Mrs.: (49) C.-reg.; (51) B.-9.1-reg.; (54) W.-5.1*-reg.

Hadaway: (35) W.-5.11*, 15*; 6.2*, 13*, 22*; 9.5*, 19*; 10.10*, 17*, 24*, 28*, 31*; 11.5*, 9*, 14*, 21*; 12.1*, 19*, 25*; (36) W.-1.1*, 9*, 13*, 25*, 26*, 29*; 3.12*, 14*, 25*; 4.4*, 6*, 11*, 16*, 25*, 29*, 30*; 6.3*, 22*; 7.4*; 8.31*; 9.3*, 8*, 17*, 24*; 10.15*, 28*; 11.4*, 24*; 12.5*, 13*, 24*; (37)

W.-1.7*, 9*; 2.20*, 27*; 3.11*, 13*,
20*, 24*; 6.30*; 7.24*, 31*; 8.8*;
9.2*; 11.20*, 25*; 12.2*, 18*, 23*,
25*, 27*; (38) 1.1*, 10*, 29*; 2.19*,
26*; 3.10*; 8.8*, 25*; 9.22*; 10.10*,
25*; (39) W.-1.28*; 2.4*; 4.1*;
11.23*; (40) W.-14*; 2.3*; (41) W.-
3.13*; (42) W.-reg.; (43) C.-reg.;
(46) W.-3.19; (47) A.-8.2-5; (49)
A.-10.3*-11; 12.29*-5; (51) A.-
7.14.

Hadaway, Miss Polly: (36) W.-12.5.

Haines: (41) W.-reg.; (42) W.-reg.

Hall, J. H., in equestrian drama: (49)
A.-4.23-15; 5.9*. Otahontas in *Eagle
Eye*.

Hall, J. R., coming from Baltimore and
Washington Theatres, in low comedy: (38) W.-8.27*, 12.12*; (40)
W.-reg.; (42) A.-5.2-10; (48) Ath.-
12.25-reg.; (53) A.-reg.; (54) A.-
reg.; (55) A.-reg.

Hall, Mrs.: (53) W.-1.8-reg.

Hall, Miss: (48) Ath.-12.25-reg.

Hall, or Zip Coon, previously appearing at The Mammoth Circus: (35)
W.-3.2.

Hamblin, W. W.: (51) N.-7.15-summer.

Hamblin, Mrs.: (36) W.-12.22-announced as her benefit and last appearance on the stage.

Hamblin, Miss: (38) W.-6.27-announced as her first appearance in
American, direct from Olympic Theatre, London. Juliana in *The
Honeymoon*.

Hamilton, R.: (35) C.-1.7*, 13*; 3.14*;
4.23*; 12.24*; (36) C.-2.6*; (37)
C.-2.25*, 27*; 3.13*; 4.1*; 6.2*; (43)
A.-4.6-reg.; (46) A.-8.26-reg.; (53)
A.-1.29-reg.

Hamilton, Mrs. R.: (37) C.-11.6*;
12.14*, 15*; (38) C.-reg.

Hamilton, Mrs. E. A.: (37) C.-4.10.

Hancker, Miss: (37) A.-7.3.

Hank, in opera: (44) C.-4.1-18.

Harbord, James: (43) A.-3.22-reg.

Harbord, R.: (38) W.-3.21.

Harrington: (37) C.-10.19*; 11.18*;
12.27*; (38) C.-6.2*; 10.2*, 22*; (39)
C.-3.20*; 5.13*; (40) C.-reg.

Harrington, Mrs.: (38) C.-3.17*.

Harris, S. E.: (54) C.-11.13-reg.; (55)
C.-1.15-sole lessee.

Harrison, W., in English opera: (54)
W.-10.30-16.

Harrison: (39) W.-11.23*; (50) C.-
5.1*.

Harrison, Mrs.: (41) A.-10.7*-reg.

Harrison, Miss: (41) W.-reg.

Hathwell: (35) C.-reg.; (36) C.-5.26*-
reg.; (37) C.-2.27*, 12.15*-reg.; (38)
C.-3.17*-reg.

Hathwell, Matilda: (37) W.-2.6.

Hautonville: (39) W.-4.18. Wales in
Richard III.

Hautonville, Mrs.: (39) W.-4.20; (44)
N.-5.11-reg.; C.-10.14-reg. Fanny in
Fire and Water.

Hawke: (44) A.-6.1-reg.

Hazard, Mme.: (39) W.-2.11-in opera.
Fatima in *Maid of Cashmere*.

Hedings, H.: (51) C.-2.22.

Hemphill, T. J.: (51) A.-8.30-lessee;
(52) A.-8.21-lessee.

Hemple, S. H., comedian: (50) A.-
11.16; (52) A.-8.30-10; (54) C.M.-
9.12-reg.; (55) C.M.-10.20-reg. Ginger Blue in *Virginia Mummy*.

Hen(c)kins, H.: (41) W.-reg.; (42)
W.-reg.; (43) C.-reg.; (47) A.-
10.12; (48) A.-9.14*-reg. The Ghost
in *Hamlet*.

Henderson, Charles, tragedian: (54)
C.-9.6-5.

Henry, or Henrie: (42) C.-reg.; (43)
A.-12.11-reg.

Henry, Mrs.: (46) P.M.-3.9-reg.

Herbert: (36) P.-reg.; (37) W.-9.2*;
12.27*-reg.; (38) W.-reg.

Herbert, Mrs.: (36) P.-reg.; (38) W.-
9.2*-reg.; (40) N.-reg.

Herbert, Master: (38) W.-3 performances.

Herbert, Mrs. J.: (39) W.-4.8; (51) A.-8.30-reg.; (53) A.-reg.

Heron Children, in farces: (48) A.-3.6-20; (52) C.-6.16-10.

Heron, Mary Ann: (48) A.-3.6-20; C.-6.30-15.

Heron, Matilda, under tutelage of P. Richings: (51) W.-2.17-4; (53) A.-1.29-reg.; (55) W.-10.3-5. Bianca in Fazio, Camille.

Herring, Mrs., supporting Booth: (36) P.-reg.; (37) W.-7.24*.

Herring, Mrs.: (38) W.-4.2*, 11*-announced as her first dramatic appearance, as Zemila in Mazeppa.

Hichie, Miss: (37) W.-2.20*, 6.30*.

Hichman: (44) A.-6.1-reg.; (45) A.-reg.; (46) A.-8.26-reg.

Hickey, H. P.: (53) A.-1.29-reg.

Hield, on engagement: (38) W.-9.22*-10; 10.10*-6; 10.25*; (42) A.-9.16-6; (55) W.-10.10*-10. Macbeth, Othello, Edgar, Iago, Duncan, Rolla in Pizarro, Malec in Apostate, Brutus in Julius Caesar, Titus in Brutus, Richmond in R. III.

Hield Mrs.: (38) W.-12.24*; (39) W.-1.1*, 8*, 9*; (42) A.-9.16-6. Lady Macbeth,, Desdemona, Volumnia, Tullia in Brutus.

Higham: (51) C.-2.22.

Hildreth: (51) C.-7.3-reg.; N.-7.15-summer.

Hildreth, Miss: (39) C.-3.20*-4; (41) 5 performances; (42) 1.24-reg. Mariana in The Wife, Julietta Gordini, Julia in Hunchback.

Hill, B.: (52) C.-2.5. Thunder in Wild Oats.

Hill, Charles: (41) N.-8.27; (51) C.-11.19*.

Hill, Mrs. Charles: (41) N.-8.27; (51) B.-11.10-5.

Hill, G. H., portrayer of American character rôles: (35) W.-5.11*, 15*-20; C.-9.9-12; W.-12.14*, 16*-6; (36) W.-5.26*-16; (37) W.-9.15*, 16*-7; (38) W.-6 performances; (39) W.-10.24*, 26*-11; (40) A.-4 per.; (41) W.-6 per.; (42) W.-4.9-6; (43) W.-1.10-6; A.-10.2-10; (45) C.-1.3-11; W.-12.20. Solomon Swop in Jonathan in England, Sysaco in Knight of the Golden Fleece, Jonathan Plough Boy in Forest Rose, Obid Bigelow in Obid and Ovid, Jebediah Homebred in Green Mountain Boy, Jonathan Doubikins.

Hill, Miss: (46) A.-5.8; (48) A.-reg. Oliver Twist.

Hilson, Mrs.: (47) A.-1.1-reg.

Hines: (42) C.-reg.

Hirsh: (37) A.-7.27-6, with German Company. Straw Buirbel in Dissipated Invalids.

Holland: (46) P.M.-3.9-reg.

Holman, in opera: (49) W.-4.23-12; 10.1-12; 11.26-12.

Honey, Miss: (37) W.-9.2.

Hood, Miss: (54) C.M.-9.12-reg.

Horn, C. E.: (37) C.-11.4*-16; (44) C.-4.1-18. Felix in Cinderella, Fra Diavolo, Don Juan.

Horn, Miss K.: (50) W.-9.25*; 10.14*. Filippa in The Betrothal.

Horncastle, from National Theatre, N. Y., in opera: (38) W.-9.24-3 (39) W.-13 performances; (41) N.-with Mitchell's Olympic Company. The Unknown in La Bayadere, Adolphe in Freischutz, Count in Marriage of Figaro.

Horton, in opera: (42) C.-12.5.

Horton, Miss, in opera: (37) C.-11.4*-16. Cinderella, Zerlina in Fra Diavolo.

Hough, Mrs. W. H.: (55) C.M.-10.20-reg.

Howard: (40) C.-9.5.

Howard, Charles: (40) W.-reg.; (44)

C.-10.14-reg.; (46) C.-1.20-reg.; P.M.-3.9-reg.; A.-8.26-reg.; (48) A.-reg.

Howard, Mrs., pantomimist: (44) W.-7.27*; (46) C.-1.20-reg.; P.M.-3.9-reg.; A.-8.26-reg.; (48) A.-reg.; 10.21*, 23*; (49) A.-1.6*; (51) C.-2.22.

Howard, Miss Louisa: (54) W.-8.29-reg.

Howard, Miss Virginia: (51) C.-2.22; (52) A.-8.21-reg.

Hows, tragedian: (35) C.-5.12-2. Shylock, Sheva in *The Jew.*

Hudson: (39) W.-4.9. Claude in *Lady of Lyons.*

Hudson, Irish comedian: (49) W.-10.18*, 19*-20; (50) W.-5.20-6; (51) C.-10.20-5; (52) C.-2.7-5; (53) C.-1.1-5; C.-5.17-5.

Hudson, Miss: (40) A.-9.7*-reg. Clotilde in *Provost of Paris.*

Hughes, Mrs.: (44) A.-6.1-reg.; (45) C.-8.30-reg.; (46) A.-8.26-reg.; (48) A.-9.13*-reg.

Hunt, C. W., in low comedy: (49) Ath.-1.15-6. Tony Lumdkin in *She Stoops to Conquer,* Guy Goodluck in *John Jones.*

Hunt: (54) C.-9.13.

Hunt, the singer: (35) C.-2.5*; (40) C.-5.6; A.-9.7*; N.-11.3.

Hunt, Mrs., later Mrs. John Drew: (39) C.-6.21; W.-7.19*; 10.3*; (40) W.-2.3*; A.-9.7*; (41) A.-10 performances; (46) W.-6.20-5. Beatrice in *Much Ado about Nothing,* Elvira in *Pizarro,* Isabella.

Huntley: (35) W.-1.28*.

Hutchings: (40) W.-7.21.

Hutchings, Mrs.: (40) W.-7.21.

Ince, Miss A.: (53) W.-9.6-reg.

Ince, Miss Emma, a dancer: (39) W.-4.22; (40) W.-1.24; (45) W.-3.10-

18; (46) W.-4.15-9; (47) P.M.-3.15-2. Zoloe in *La Bayadere.*

Ingersoll: (35) W.-12.9-4; (37) W.-1 performance. Damon in *Damon and Pythias,* William Tell, Rolla in *Pizarro.*

Inverarity, Miss., see Mrs. Martyn.

Irvin, J.: (51) C.-2.22.

Isherwood: (40) A.-reg.

Jackson: (35) W.-1.10*, 28*; 2.28*; 3.7*, 23*; 4.11*; 6.3*, 22*; (36) P.-reg.-11.16*; (37) P.-1.4*; 2.20*; 3.6*; 6.30*; 11.20*.

Jackson: (37) W.-7.8*-8; (39) W.-6.20*-on engagement. Antoine in *L'Amour.*

Jackson, Mrs.: (36) P.-reg.; (39) C.-5.17.

Jackson, Master; The Young Jim Crow: (35) W.-1.26; (39) W.-1.26. Hamlet.

Jackson, B.: (51) A.-8.30-reg.

Jacques, Miss Rosa, in opera: (49) W.-4.23-12; 10.1-12; 11.26-12.

Jamar, Mrs.: (45) C.-8.30-reg.

James: (45) C.-8.30-reg.

Jamieson, George: (40) N.-10.7; (41) N.-9.29; (43) A.-12.11-reg.; (44) C.-10.14-reg.; (45) C.-2.5-reg.; (46) W.-8.29-reg.

Jarman, Miss Fanny, later Mrs. Ternan: (35) C.-1.28; 2.21; 4.13*-19; 10.3*, 9*-12; (36) C.-12.6*-6. Mrs. Haller in *Stranger,* Lucy in *Bride of Lammermoor,* Lady Townly in *Provoked Husband,* Lady Teazle in *School for Scandal,* Jeanie in *Heart of Midlothian,* Portia, Lady Macbeth, Desdemona, Juliana in *The Honeymoon.*

Jarvis, see Jervis.

Jefferson, Joseph, 2d.: (35) W.-1.9, 31; 2.9; 3.18. Father Philip in *Nature and Philosophy,* Vasquez in *The Voice of Nature,* Old Pickle in *Spoiled Child,*

Lord Totterly in *Unfinished Gentleman.*

Jefferson, Mrs. J.: (35) W.-4.2; 7.25.

Jefferson, Joseph, 3rd: (47) A.-1.1-6; P.M.-2.17-15; A.-12.27; (48) A.-2.23-2; P.M.-7.6-10; Ath.-12.25-reg.; (49) P.M.-4.25-reg.; 5.17*; (51) A.-8.30-reg.; (53) C.-9.26*-reg.; (54) C.-1.14-reg. John Tagby in *The Chimes,* Artful Dodger in *Oliver Twist,* Squeers in *Poor Smike,* Natz in *Swiss Cottage.*

Jefferson, Miss Cornelia: (47) A.-6.22; (51) A.-8.30-reg. Little Pickle in *Spoiled Child.*

Jervis, G. F.: (35) C.-6.27; (39) C.-reg.; (42) C.-1.24-reg; (44) A.-6.1-reg.; (45) A.-reg,; (46) A.-8.26-reg.

Jewell, on engagement: (42) A.-6.4-3. Thornton in "Rob Roy."

Johns, with Mary Duff: (48) C.-7.20. Carwin in *Therese.*

Johnston, N., from Baltimore Theatres: (38) W.-8.6; (39) W.-7.19*; 10.3*; (44) A.-6.1-reg.; (45) N.-4.28-reg.; (47) P.M.-1.1-reg.; (48) P.M.-3.16-reg.; (51) A.-8.30-reg.; (52) N.-7.12-reg.

Johnston, W. F.: (39) C.-reg.; (40) C.-2.5*; (47) P.M.-6.18-reg.; (54) C.-10.25*-reg.; C.-11.4*.

Johnston, R.: (48) Ath.-12.25-reg.; (49) C.-9.1-reg.; (51) C.-7.3-reg.; N.-7.15-summer; W.-8.18-reg.

Johnston, S.: (40) W.-5.25; (45) N.-4.28-reg. William Tell.

Johnston, Thomas B., light comedian: (48) A.-8.17-10; (49) A.-10.3*, 8*-8; (50) A.-11.11*-5; (51) A.-7.14; (52) N.-5.22-reg.; (55) C.M.-9.8-reg. Jack Cabbage in *Sudden Thoughts.*

Jones, E. W.: (50) C.-7.29-Ole Bull, farce.

Jones, George, on engagement: (38) C.-4 performances.

Jones, Mrs. George, tragic actress on engagement: (38) C.-4 performances; (41) N.-9.25*; (42) N.-4.7*-reg.; (43) O.-1.9-reg.; C.-reg.; (48) A.-1.19-reg.; (49) C.-9.1-reg.

Jones, Mrs. Melinda: (49) C.-9.1-reg.; (52) A.-8.21-reg. Hamlet, Jack Sheppard.

Jones, J. S., the playwright: (41) W.-10.23*. Sam in *Siege of Boston,* his own play.

Jones, W. G.: (35) C.-1.12*, 28; 3.6*; 9.5*; 11.28*; (36) C.-1.4*; 2.22*; (37) C.-2.27*; (38) C.-6.11*; (40) C.-8.29; (42) N.-1.20*, 27*; 5.6-reg.-C; (44) N.-3.4-16; W.-5.18-10; A.-6.1-reg.; (51) A.-8.30-reg. Pickwick in *Pickwick Club,* Mr. Primrose in *Popping the Question,* Sir Paul Pagoda in *Bengal Tiger,* Scraggs in *Englishmen in India.*

Jones, Mrs. W. G.: (35) C.-1.12*; (36) C.-6.18*; (37) C.-reg.; (38) C.-5.12; (40) C.-8.29; (51) A.-8.30-reg.

Jones, Miss: (42) C.-reg.

Jordan, H. C.: (44) C.-10.14-reg.; (51) A.-7.14; (53) W.-3.14*-reg.

Jordan, Mrs. H. C.: (44) C.-10.14-reg.

Joseph: (36) W.-10.28*; (37) W.-6.30*; (38) W.-2.8.

Joseph, Master: (37) P.-2.14.

Judah, Mrs.: (40) A.-12.11*-reg.

Justice: (51) A.-4.14*.

Kaiffer, a singer in *La Sonnambula:* (40) C.-12.16.

Kaimes, G.: (49) P.M.-6.27-reg.; C.-9.1-reg.; (50) W.-10.29; (51) N.-7.15-summer; (52) C.-7.16.

Kean, Charles: (39) C.-9.30-11; (40) C.-9 performances; (45) C.-9.15-25;

(46) C.-1.1-3; W.-9.14-11; (47) W.-1.18-21. Hamlet, Lear, Macbeth, Richard III, Shylock, Overreach in *A New Way To Pay Old Debts,* Claude in *A Lady of Lyons.*

Kean, Mrs. Charles, see Miss Ellen Tree.

Keeley, high comedian, on engagement, from Convent Garden Theatre, London: (36) C.-10.25*, 29*-13; (37) C.-5.31*, 6.2*-6. Peter in *Loan of a Lover,* Martin in *Maid and Magpie,* Paul in *My Master's Rival,* Tony in *She Stoops to Conquer,* Hodge in *Love in a Village.*

Keeley, Mrs.: (36) C.-10.29*-13; (37) C.-5.31*, 6.2*-6. Gertrude in *Loan of a Lover,* Annette in *Maid and Magpie,* Tibbie in *My Master's Rival,* Miss Hardcastle in *She Stoops to Conquer,* Madge in *Love in a Village.*

Keller: (45) A.-12.6.

Kellogg: (50) A.-3.26-reg. Baradar in *Richelieu.*

Keenan: (50) A.-2.23-reg.

Kelley: (35) W.-6.2; (42) C.-reg.

Kelly: (37) A.-5.29; (38) A.-4.12.

Kemble, George W.: (54) C.-11.20-5, in melodrama.

Kemble: (38) W.-12.15; (39) W.-1.8*, 9*; (46) P.M.-6.25-reg. Gilbert in *Lear of Private Life.*

Kemble, Mrs.: (38) W.-12.13, 14, 15. Emma in *United States,* Lauretta in *Mountain King,* Justine in *Miller's Murder.*

Kent, W.: (35) W.-2.28*; (37) W.-6.30*; 7.31*, 11.20*, 25*, 27*; (38) W.-1.1*, 10*; 2.19*; 3.10*; (50) A.-6.21. Jack Humphries in *Turning the Tables.*

Kent, Mrs. W.: (35) W.-1.28*; 2.21*; 3.7*, 16*; 4.3*, 8*; 6.8*; (37) W.-6.30*; 7.7*, 21*; 8.8*; 9.2*; 11.20*,

25*; 12.2*, 18*, 23*, 25*; (38) W.-1.1*, 2*, 29*.

Kerr, Miss: (38) W.-9.24-10; (39) C.-5 performances. Fatima in *La Bayadere.*

Kimberley, Miss: (53) C.-4.20*-5.

King, Mrs., in opera: (54) C.-6.6-6.

Kingsmore: (50) A.-2.11-Othello.

Kinlock, Mrs.: (42) W.-reg.; (50) W.-9.25*; (51) W.-8.18-reg.

Kinlock, Miss A., in comedy: (40) W.-reg.; (42) W.-reg.; (51) A.-4.14*.

Kirby, J. H.: (36) P.-12.14; (37) W.-2.20*; 6.30*; (39) W.-12.9*; (40) W.-2.3*; 7.11*; A.-9.7*, 14*; (42) A.-5.2-8; (43) A.-9.22-9. Pythias, Lear.

Kirby, Miss: (43) A.-12.11-reg.; (44) A.-6.1-reg.

Klishing: (35) W.-6 performances. Mammon in *Sorcerer.*

Kneas, Miss: (42) C.-1.24-reg.

Knight, J. P.: (35) W.-10.5*; 11.9*, 11*; (39) C.-reg.

Knight, Mrs. J. P.: (35) W.-8.28*; 9.5*, 16*, 17*, 19*, 29*; 10.3*, 17*, 24*; 11.21*; (38) W.-12.24*, 31*; (39) W.-1.1*; 2.4*; 4.1*.

Knight, Mrs. A., formerly Miss Povey: (38) W.-9.13; (42) A.-11.11; (43) W.-8.8*; A.-8.10-reg.; (44) C.-10.14-reg.; N.-1.1*; (45) C.-7.3*-reg. Mrs. Haller in *Stranger.*

Knight, Mrs. Edward, celebrated vocalist: (35) W.-10.12-4.

Knowles, James Sheridan, the English playwright and actor: (35) C.-1.14 to 1.23; 1.20*; 2.21, recited his own pathetic tale of *The Smuggler;* A.-2.24; A.-4.11; W.-5.25, appeared with Mr. and Miss Cooper in his own play, *Virginius;* 5.28-W.-His Benefit Night. Lord Wilford in *Blind Beggar of Bethnal Green,* Virginius,

Walter in *Hunchback,* Stranger, William Tell, Julian in *The Wife.*

Korsinski, Mlle., in opera, with Mme. A. Bishop: (47) W.-11.22-18.

Kraft, E. B.: (35) W.-4.11.

La Forest: (38) W.-8.27*; 12.12*, 24*; (39) W.-1.1*; (40) W.-2.3*; 3.9*; (41) W.-3.13*; (42) W.-6.4. Welkskeln in *Rory O'More.*

La Forest, Mrs.: (38) W.-8.16*, 25*, 27*; 10.25*; (39) W.-1.28*; 2.4*; 5.18*; (40) W.-reg.; A.-9.14*; (41) W.-3.13*; A.-9.20*; (42) W.-4.27-reg.; (43) A.-8.10-reg. Marian Ramsay in *Turn Out,* Margueretta in *No Song no Supper,* Rosina, Theodore in *La Fitte,* Bridget in *Gentleman of Lyons.*

Lambert: (41) W.-11.6*-reg.

Lambert, Mrs.: (41) C.-10.4*-reg.

Langdon: (51) N.-7.15-summer; W.-8.18-reg.; (54) C.M.-9.12-reg.

Langdon, Mrs.: (54) W.-5.9*-reg.; (55) C.-reg.

Lansfeldt, countess of, see Mlle. Lola Montez.

Larkins: (41) N.-8.27.

Latham: (39) C.-4.24; (41) A.-2 performances. Billy in *The Unfinished Gentleman,* Dominie in *Guy Mannering.*

Latouche, with French Company: (55) W.-11.19-6.

La Petite Bertha: (20) W.-9.12. Youthful Queen.

La Trust, Mme.: (38) W.-12.12*.

Leach, in opera: (49) W.-4.23-12; 10.1-12; 11.26-12.

Leavitt, Master: (37) C.-4.4.

LeCompte, Mme., actress-singer: (38) C.-9 performances; (40) C.-12.16. Zelica in *Maid of Cashmere.*

Lecourt, with French opera Company: (43) C.-9.14-13.

Lecourt, Mme., with French Opera Company: (43) C.-9.14-13.

Lee, Mrs: (37) C.-2.27*; (38) C.-3.17*.

Lee, Miss: (37) C.-2.27*; (38) C.-reg.; (40) N.-reg.; (42) N.-1.29. Miller's maid.

Lee, Miss, dancer on engagement: (38) W.-10.10*-5; (39) W.-5 performances; (40) W.-2.3*-5. Lizette in *Swiss Cottage.*

Lee, Miss Annie: (55) C.M.-9.8-reg.

Leffler: (40) C.-10.29-5. Giacomo in *Fra Diavolo,* Robin Hood in *Maid of Judah.*

Leman, Walter M., from Tremont Theatre, Boston: (43) C.-reg.; (46) W.-1.3*-reg.; (47) W.-reg.; (48) W.-reg.; 8.28*; (50) W.-4.22-3.

Lennox: (39) W.-10.26*; 11.23*; (40) W.-2.3*; 4.11*.

Leonard, J. A., comedian: (46) W.-10.5-6; (48) P.M.-3.16-reg.; (49) C.-reg.; (51) B.-9.1-reg.; (53) A.-1.13. Claude in *Lady of Lyons.*

Leonard, Y.: (51) N.-7.15-summer; (52) N.-5.22-reg.

Leonard, Mrs. Y. See Miss A. Eberle.

Lewellen, G., comedian on engagement: (41) A.-11.30-3; (42) A.-5.16-4. Conancheotah.

Lewis, H.: (40) A.-reg.; (43) A.-3.22-reg.; N.-reg.

Lewis, Mrs. H.: (37) W.-6.19-12; (39) W.-9 performances; (41) W.-15 per.; (43) A.-3.22-reg.; N.-reg.; (44) N.-1.1*; 3.2*; (46) A.-1.30-16; A.-8.26-reg.; (50) C.-2.4-12. Bianca in *Fazio,* Richard III, Bill in *Black Brig of Bermuda,* Henri in *French Spy,* William in *Black-eyed Susan,* Othello, Virginius.

Lind, Mlle. Jenny: (50) C.-10.17-Philadelphia Première.

Linden, H. (or Lindon): (50) C.-7.9-5; (51) C.-7.3-reg. Jakey in *A Glance at Philadelphia.*

Lindsay: (36) C.-8.23; (37) C.-2.27*; 5.2*; 6.2*, 7*, 17*; 10.19*, 25*; 12.15*; (38) C.-1.9*; 3.29*; 6.2*, 11*, 20*; 9.19*; 10.22*; 12.24*; (39) C.-1.2*; 3.20*; 5.13*.

Lingham: (55) C.M.-9.8-reg.

Littell: (49) A.-4.30-5. Washington in *Putnam.*

Locke, G. E., a Yankee comedian: (52) A.-11.29; (54) C.-7.10-10; C.-9.22-10.

Locke, Mrs. G. E.: (54) C.-9.22-10.

Logan, Cornelius A.: (36) P.-reg.; 11.16*; (37) 1.4*; (40) W.-reg.; (45) W.-12.9-10; (49) A.-6.11*-6; C.-9.1-reg.

Logan, Mrs. Cornelius A.: (36) P.-reg.

Logan, Celia. (52) C.3:20; 8:14*. Adelgitha.

Logan, Eliza. (45) C.10:17-7; W.12:9-10; (49) A.6:19; C.9:1-reg.; (51) A.6:2-7; (52) C.3:8-5; (53) C.4:17-5.

Logan, Olive. (54) A.8:19-reg.

Lomas. (54) N.6:3-reg.

Lopez, Miss. (37) C.2:27*.

Lorch, Mlle., in opera. (40) C.3:23. First Bridesmaid in *Freischutz.*

Lorini, Signor Dominico. (50) C.9:10-10. In Italian Opera Company from Havana.

Lovarnay, Mlle., in opera. (54) C.6:6-6.

Lover, a comedian. (48) W.1:17-11.

Ludlow, Kate. (46) P.M.6:1-8. Comedienne in *A Day in Paris.*

Lyn(n)e. (35) W.4:8; (44) N.3:8; (47) W.5:29; (48) A.3:20-12; (51) A.7:14. Richelieu, St. Pierre in *The Wife.*

Lyster, F., in English opera. (55) C.M.6:11-15.

Macarthy, Irish comedian. (50) C.6:25*-6; (55) C.1:15-reg.

Mack, Miss. (44) C.10:14-reg.

Macklin. (47) P.M.1:1-reg.

Macleis. (50) A.2:23-reg.

Maclure, Mrs., in support of E. S. Conner. (44) A.6:2-8. Rachel in *Rent Day.*

Macready, classic tragedian on engagement. (43) C.10:23-21; (44) A.9:9-4; (48) A.10:20-8. Wolsey in *Henry VIII,* Lear, Shylock, Othello, Macbeth, Hamlet.

Maddox, Mrs. (54) C.11:13-reg.

Madison, Mrs. (43) N.-reg.

Maeder, Mrs., formerly Clara Fisher. (35) W.3:3-reg.; (42) W.-reg.

Maharg. (41) N.-with Mitchell's Olymphic Company.

Majocchi, Signora Amalia, with Italian Opera Company from Havana. (43) C.7:15-13; C.11:13-11.

Manvers. (39) C.10;16-15; (40) C.-2 performances; (41) C.-15 performances. In Opera as Prince in *Cinderella,* Elviro in *La Sonnambula,* and Don Florestano in *Fidelio.*

Marble, Dan, in American type rôles. (37) W.3 performances; (38) W.1: 2*-4; 7:24*-5; (43) W.5:11*-3; (44) W.4:2-4; (47) W.4:22-3. Sam Patch, Jonathan in *Forest Rose,* Swop in *Who wants a Guinea?,* Slanter in *The Bush Whacker.*

Marchant, G. F., comedian. (51) W.10:6-6; (52) W.1:6-4. Sangfroid in *Delicate Ground.*

Maretzek, Mme. Bertucca. See Mme. Bertucca.

Marini, Signor Ignazio, with Italian Opera from Havana. (50) C.9:10-10.

Marini, Signorina Sophia, with Italian Opera, Havana. (47) W.7:12-18.

Marozzi, Signora Lorenza, with Italian Opera, Havana. (43) C.7:15-13; C.11:13-11.

Marsden, Mrs. (42) W.-reg.

Marsh. (45) N.4:28-reg.; (46) A.8:26-reg.

Marsh's Juvenile Comedians. (55)
W.10: 15-10. 14 girls, 3 youths, 12
ballet children in *Beauty and the
Beast.*

Marshall, W., tragedian. (48) A.12:
23*-10; (49) A.1:24*, 3:24*-reg.;
9:17*; 12:5*.

Martin. (46) A.8:26-reg.

Martin, a pantomimist. (45) W.3:10-
18.

Martine. (48) P.M.3:16-reg.

Martyn. (39) C.10:16-10. In opera
as Dandini in *Cinderella,* Alessio in
La Sonnambula, and Rocco in *Fidelio.*

Martyn, Mrs., formerly Miss Inverarity. (39) C.10:16-10. In opera,
Cinderella, Amina in *La Sonnambula,* Leonora in *Fidelio.*

Mason, Charles. (41) C.10:4*; (44)
C.10:14-reg.; (53) C.9:26*. Werner.

Mason, Mrs. (45) C.8:30-reg.; (46)
C.-reg.; (47) W.2:15-6. Juliet, Mariana in *The Wife,* Bianca in *Fazio.*

Mason, J. R. (51) C.2:22; 3:1-28.

Mathews, C. (38) C.10:15*-12.
Charles in *One Hour,* Peter in
Loan of a Lover, Motley in *Would
be an Actor,* Mr. Wyndham in
Handsome Husband.

Mathews, Mrs. C., formerly Mme.
Vestris. (38) C.10:8-12. Julia in
One Hour, Gertrude in *Loan of a
Lover,* Mrs. Wyndham in *Handsome
Husband.*

Matthews, T. (39) W.7:19*; (40)
W.2:3*; A.9:7*; (42) C.-reg.; (43)
N.-reg.-10:9*; (44) C.10:14-reg.;
N.3:2*. Carlos in *Isabella,* Rolla
in *Pizarro.*

Matthews, Miss H. (39) W.7:12; (40)
W.2:3*; 7:11*; (42) C.-reg.; (43)
N.-reg. Rosana in *Broken Sword.*

Mayer, Ferdinand, in opera. (54)
C.6:6-6.

Maywood, Robert Campble. (35) C.1:
20*; 4:1*; 10:9*; (36) C.2:22*; 4:
14*; (37) C.1:23*; (38) C.-reg.;
(39) C.3:23*; (42) C.-reg.-9:28*;
10:24; 11:2*.

Maywood, Mrs. R. C. (35) C.1:13*;
3:14*; 10:28*; (36) C.4:14*;
11:21*; 12:19*; (37) C.4:1*;
11:10*; (42) C.-reg.

Maywood, Augusta, a child. (37)
C.12:30*; (38) C.3:17*-17. Dew
Drop, Zelica in *Maid of Cashmere.*

Maywood, Mary Elizabeth. (38)
C.4:14 announced as her first appearance on any stage as Angela in
Castle Spectre; (39) C.8 performances; (42) C.-Lessee-10:24*. Pauline in *Lady of Lyons.*

McBride. (40) W.2:3*; (54) N.6:3-
reg.

McBride, Miss. (44) C.10:14-reg.;
(53) A.-reg.

McConachy. (37) W.2:20*; 3:18*,
20*, 22*, 24*; 6:30*.

McCormick. (38) W.6:26.

M'Cutchen. (37) W.1:5; (39) W.8:9.

McDonough, J. E. (48) A.4:15;
C.7:22; (49) P.M.-reg.; (50) C.7:6-
20; (51) A.6:23-10; C.7:3-reg.;
N.7:15-summer; (53) W.-reg.; (54)
C.M.9:12-reg. Claude in *Lady of
Lyons,* Pierre in *Venice Preserved.*

McDougal. (45) A.9:27-2.

McDowel, J. (39) C.12:20. Octavian
in *Mountaineers.*

McFarland. (53) C.3:17-reg.

McGowan. (51) W.8:18-reg.

McGuire. (37) P.1:17.

McKeon, W. T. (47) W.6:24; 8:20;
(51) N.7:15-summer; W.8:18-reg.;
12:19*; (53) W.3:17*; (54) N.6:3-
reg. Quake in *Rendezvous.*

McLean, Mrs. (or McLane). (45)
N.4:28-reg.; C.8:30-reg.; (46) A.8:
26-reg.; (50) C.2:23.

McMillan, D. (50) C.7:8-reg.; 7:15*;

W.8:28*; (51) W.-reg.; 4:9*, 15*; 6:25*; N.7:15-summer. Bailie in *Rob Roy.*

McMinn. (48) Ath.12:25-reg.

McVicker, Yankee comedian. (51) A.7: 21-5.

Meadows, Miss. (35) W.3:11*.

Meer, Mrs. (37) W.8:7-7. Miss Pickle in *Spoiled Child,* Marguerite in *Crichton.*

Meer, Master R. (37) W.8:7-7. Little Pickle in *Spoiled Child,* Girl in *Children in the Wood,* Mawworm in *Hypocrite,* Paul in *Wandering Boys.*

Meer, Master J. (37) W.8:7-7. Boy in *Children in the Wood,* Justin in *Wandering Boys.*

Megary, Jos. (50) A.2:23-reg.

Melton, Miss. (41) A.-2 performances. Julia in *Guy Mannering.*

Merrifield, Mrs. Rose. (50) A.3:4-reg.; (53) C.-reg.; (55) C.-reg.

Mestayer, Charles. (44) C.10:14-reg.; (45) C.-reg.; (55) C.1:15-reg.; C.M.9:8-reg.

Mestayer, Mrs. Charles. (44) C.10:14-reg.; (45) C.-reg.

Mestayer, J. (35) W.10:17*; (36) W.8:31*; (37) W.2:20*; (43) O.-reg.; 1:9.

Mew, Miss. (37) C.2:27*.

Meyer, in German opera. (40) C.3:23-4; (47) C.10:11-4; (51) B.2: 10-17. Ottakar in *Freischutz.*

Midwinter. (35) C.5:19.

Miles, Miss. (50) W.11:18*. Mary in *Platonic Attachment.*

Millington, Miss. (50) W.9:2; 10:23; (51) W.8:18-reg. Sally in *Eton Boy.*

Mills. (40) A.-reg.; (41) A.12:6*.

Milnor. (45) C.2:11-3.

Mitchell, Miss. (40) W.-reg.

Monier, Miss Virginia. (35) W.2:28*-5. Bianca in *Fazio,* Juliet, Widow Cheerly in *Soldier's Daughter,* Julia in *Hunchback,* Blanche in *Old Man's Curse.*

Montez, Mlle. Lola, the Countess of Lansfeldt, famous dancer. (52) W.5:31-6.

Montgomery, C. (50) A.6:25. Golden Farmer.

Moore, C. (44) C.11:6. Claude in *Lady of Lyons.*

Moorhouse, C. (47) A.10:12-2; (48) P.M.7:1-reg.; (51) C.7:3-reg. Laertes, Henry IV.

Morant, Fanny. (53) W.11:20-5

Morgan, Miss. (36) C.-reg.; (37) C.-2:27*; 11:6*-reg.; (38) C.-reg.

Morley. (38) W.-10:5; (39) W.-2:11-6. Olifour in *Maid of Cashmere.*

Morra, Signor, with Italian Opera Company. (48) C.2:19-23; 6:6-7; 10:4-15; 12:5-12.

Morra, Signorina. (48) C.2:19-23; 6:6-7; 10:4-15; 12:5-12.

Morrell, Mrs. R. (51) A.8:30-reg.

Morris. (44) A.8:30. Charles in *Banker's Clerk.*

Mortimer, light comedian. (48) A.8:9-3; (49) A.5:9*. Fainwood in *Raising the Wind.*

Mortimer, Miss. (49) P.M.-reg.; (50) B.10:2-reg.; 12:13*; (51) B.9:1-reg.

Morton. (36) W.3:14*; 8:31*; 10:28*; 11:23*; (38) W.3:16.

Morton, Mrs. Louisa. (53) A.1:4. Isabella.

Mossop. (39) W.1:28*; 2:4*; (42) A.11:22; (43) N.-reg.; (44) C.10: 14-reg. O'Toole in *Irish Tutor.*

Mossop, Mrs., in 1851 became Mrs. Da Costa. (41) W.9:2; (43) C.-reg.; (46) A.6:13-10; A.8:26-reg.; (51) A.8:30-reg.; (52) A.8:21-reg.

Mowatt, Mrs. (45) A.10:20*-7; W.6: 23-5; C.9:1-6; (46) W.10:5-6; (51) C.10:6-11; (54) C.3:13-10. Pauline in *Lady of Lyons.*

Mowbray, Miss F. (50) C.3:1; 3:18*. Madeline.

Mowbray, Miss Laura. (54) C.11:13-reg.

Mueller, Mrs. (50) B.10:14-reg.; (51) N.7:15-summer.

Mulholland. (45) C.8:30-reg.

Mulligan. (39) C.12:24.

Mulliken. (42) C.-reg.

Murdoch, J. E. (35) C.3:21*; 4:1*; 5:13*; 9:5*, 7*, 17*; went on Southern and Western Circuit for his health.; (36) C.5:18*, 23*; (38) C.10:22*-18; 11:3*, 29*; (39) C.-reg.; (40) C.-acting manager; (41) W.-10 performances; (45) W.11:13-11; (46) W.1:4-25; (47) W.4:26-6; A.10:11-18; (48) A.4:6-25; W.11:13-6; (49) A.3:8*-20; W.12:24-5; (50) W.9:2-6; 12:23-7; (51) W.1:20*-5; 5:5-12; (52) C.4:19*-10; 1:5-10; W.2:5-10; (53) C.2:2-10; 6:14-10; (55) C.M.3:26-15; C.M.11:19-15. Rover in *Wild Oats,* Claude in *Lady of Lyons,* Tom in *Folly as it Flies,* Valcour in *Point of Honour,* Dick in *My Aunt,* Flighty in *Married Rake,* Pythias, Peter in *My Master's Rival,* Young Rapid in *A Cure for the Heart Ache.*

Murdoch, S. K. (55) C.M.6:8-reg. Hotspur in *Henry IV.*

Murray, Miss. (39) W.10:3*; (40) W.7:11*-reg.

Muzzy. (35) W.9:16*; 10:3*, 24*; 11.5*, 14*, 21*; 12:25*; (36) W.2:1*, 10*, 29*; 3:14*, 29*; 4:16*, 25*, 29*, 30*; 6:13*, 20*; 7:4*.

Muzzy, Mrs. (35) W.10:10*, 17*, 24*; 11:11*; (36) W.1:1*, 26*, 29*; 3:14*, 25*; 4:30*; 6:20*; (55) W.3:14*-reg.

Myers, F. S. (36) W.1:23*; 10:28*; (37) W.1:2*; 2:20*; 6:30*; 9:2*; (38) W.-reg.; (39) W.-reg.; (40) W.6:29; (41) A.9:20*; 12:6*;

(42) W.-reg.; (43) O.-reg.; 1:9; (46) A.2:18-10; (48) P.M.-3:16-reg.; (51) C.-2:22.

Myers, Mrs. F. S., in 1851 became Mrs. J. Elssler. (43) A.8:31; (48) P.M.3:16-reg.; (49) C.-reg.; (50) C.-reg. 5:1*; (51) C.7:3-reg.; N.7:15-summer; (52) N.7:12-reg. Albert in *William Tell.*

Nagle, J. E. (48) W.6:26*-reg.; (51) N.7:15-summer; (54) C.8:19-reg.; C.M.9:12-reg.

Neafie. (39) W.12:9; (40) W.2:3*, 4:11*; N.-reg.; 8:31; (48) W.8:31; (52) A.4:19.

Needham. (38) W.9:29. Count St. Rambert in *La Sonnambula.*

Nelson, F. D. See Frank Nelson Drew, who was the brother of John Drew but appeared at Wheatly and Drew's Arch Street Theatre under his middle name of Nelson in order to prevent any rivalry in name.

Nelson, Mrs. F. D. See Mrs. F. N. Drew.

Nelson, Miss. (37) C.10:10; (44) C.10:14-reg.; (45) C.11:24*.

Neville. (44) A.8:6. Claude in *Lady of Lyons.*

Newton. (36) W.10:28*.

Nicholas, Mrs. (46) A.6:17.

Nicholls, H. (39) W.3:8. Billy Button.

Nicholls, Mrs. H. (49) A.12:19-reg.; 12:24*.

Nickinson, with Mitchell's Olympic Company. (41) N.

Norman, Miss. (42) C.-reg.

Oakey (40) N.-reg.; 12:19*; (42) N.-reg.; W.6:4-reg.

O'Brien. (54) C.11:13-reg.

O'Connell, James F., the tattooed man. (39) W.12:18.

O'Flagherty, Brian. (45) C.2:5. Paddy in *Born to Good Luck.*

O'Grath, Mrs. (36) P.11:30*.

Ollier, J. (49) A.3:7-3. Claude in *Seven Clerks,* Sternford in *Walter Brand.*

Olwine, W. (55) C.-reg.

Otto, Madame. (38) C.11:19*-15. Zelica in *Maid of Cashmere,* Amilie.

Owens, John E., comedian. (42) A.11:2*; N.12:19*; (43) A.8:10-reg.; (46) C.1:5*; (48) A.-reg.; 4:25*; (49) A.3:14*; N.10:8-6; (50) A.10:22-9; 11:1*; (51) C.7:3-reg.; (54) C.11:6-reg.; (55) C.M.9:22-20.

Oxley, J. H. (35) W.-reg.; (36) W.-reg.; (37) W.-reg.; (38) W.12:11-reg.; (39) W.4:19; 8:12-reg.; (40) N.10:28.; (43) A.8:18-4; N.-lessee; (51) A.5:26. Count de Calmont in *Foundling of the Forest,* Felix in *Hunter of the Alps.*

Packard, Miss A. (38) W.2:24*.

Packard, Miss E. (37) W.1:21*; 2:20*; 3:13*; (38) W.1:24*.

Packard, Miss S. (37) W.2:20*; 3:13*.

Page, comedian. (55) C.M.9:8-reg.

Palmer, D. S., comedian. (52) A.8:21-reg.; (53) A.1:29-reg.

Palmer, Miss. (44) C.10:14-reg.

Pancoast, S. (51) C.2:22.

Parker, J. S. (37) W.9:2; (43) A.9:28.

Parker, Mrs. J. S. (37) W.9:2.

Parker, Mrs. A. (51) A.8:30-reg.

Parker, Miss. (37) W.6:30*.

Parker, Little Louisa. (53) C.9:26*; (54) C.1:9.

Parodi, Mlle. Teresa, with Italian Opera Company. (50) C.12:10-6.

Parsloe, T. C., pantomimist. (39) W.6:15-4; (40) C.-3 performances; (43) W.7:23; 7:31*; (44) N.3:19-7;

(45) W.3:10-18; (46) W.4:15-9; (47) W.9:17-11. Sandie in *Jamie of Aberdeen,* Monkey in *Cabin Boy.*

Parsons. (38) W.8:27*-12. Caius Silius, Stackpole in *Nick of the Woods,* Lear, Macbeth, Othello, Oranaska, Coriolanus, Brutus in *Brutus.*

Patti, Salvator, with Italian Opera Company. (48) C.2:19-23; 6:6-7; 10:4-15; 12:5-12.

Patti, Signorina Amalia, with Italian Opera Company. (48) C.2:19-23; 6:6-7; 10:4-15; 12:5-12; (50) 10:15.

Patti, Signorina Barili, with Italian Opera Company. (48) C.2:19-23; 6:6-7; 10:4-15; 12:5-12.

Paul, H. H., light comedian. (48) P.M.5:16*-2. Belton in *Some Things can be Done as well as Others,* his own farce.

Paullin. (44) A.12:21*; (53) A.-reg.

Pearman, Murray. (40) W.7:20. Cribb in *Tom and Jerry.*

Pearson, H. G. (37) W.-4 performances. Othello, Glenalvon in *Douglas,* Pythias in *Damon and Pythias,* Rolla in *Pizarro.*

Pearson, Sidney. (36) C.-reg.; (37) C.2:27*; 3:13*; 4:1*; 7:3*; 11:6*; 12:14*-reg.; (38) C.-reg.; (40) C.4:28.

Pearson, Miss. (38) C.6:22.

Pelham, Miss. (35) C.1:7*; 10:9*; 11:28*; 12:24*; (36) C.4:9*; 6:11*, 18*.

Penson, Mrs. (42) W.-reg.; (43) A.-reg.; 12:11; (44) A.-reg.; (47) P.M.1:13-reg.

Percival. (36) W.10:28*; 11:24*; 12:13*; (37) W.12:23*; (38) W.4:11*; (39) W.-reg.; (40) W.7:11*.

Perozzi, Luigi, with Italian Opera, Havana. (43) C.7:15-13; 11:13-11; (47) W.-7:12-18.

Perriner. (39) W.11:22. Belmour in *Is he Jealous?*

Perring. (42) C.-reg.

Perry. (46) W.-reg.; 8.29; (47) P.M.7: 17; (53) W.9:23*; 10:3*; (54) W.5:1*-reg.; (55) W.-reg.; 10:10*. Impulse in *Sudden Thoughts.*

Petrie, Eliza, in 1852 became Mrs. Place. (40) N.-reg.; (46) W.7:13-reg.; (48) A.-reg.; (52) N.7:12-reg.; (53) A.1:29-reg.

Philips, comedian. (43) W.4:6-4; 5:11*, 17*-reg.; A.8:10-reg.; (46) A.8:26-reg.

Phillips, A. J. (43) A.12:11-reg.

Phillips, I. B. (50) A.6:15-reg. Box in *Box and Cox.*

Phillips, Mrs. I. B. (38) W.9:24-7; (44) C.4:1-18; (50) A.3:4-reg.; (52) N.7:12-reg. Ninka in *La Bayadere.*

Phillips, M. S. (43) A.12:11-reg.

Phillips, Miss A. (43) A.3:14-reg.

Phillips, Miss L. A. (35) C.1:1-15; (36) 5:20-6. Belvidera in *Venice Preserved,* Mrs. Haller in *Stranger,* Mariana in *The Wife,* Julia in *The Hunchback,* Jane Shore, Mrs. Oakly in *Jealous Wife,* Lady Townly in *Provoked Husband,* Portia.

Piamon tesi, I, with Italian Opera, Havana. (47) W.7:12-18.

Pickering. (38) W.-reg.; 8:8*, 25*, 27*; 10:10*; 12:12*, 24*, 31*; (39) W.-reg.; 1:1*, 8*; 4:1*. Edmond, Julius Caesar, Buckingham in *Richard III,* Lord Lovel in *A New Way to Pay Old Debts,* Bobby Trot in *Luke the Laborer.*

Pitt, Charles Dibdin. (47) A.11:30*-6; (48) A.1:17-7; W.4:27-6; (49) A.4: 9-12; 4:20*; 12:17-8; (51) B.3: 26-12. Hamlet.

Pitt, Mrs. C. D., comedienne. (49) A.4:9-12; 4:20*; 12:17-8.

Place, Mrs. See Miss Eliza Petrie.

Placide, H. (41) C.12:2-9. Sir Haricourt in *London Assurance,* Uncle John.

Placide, T. (35) C.-reg.; (36) C.-reg.; (38) C.12:18*; (39) C.4:8; (40) C.1:3*; N.-reg.; 8:31; (41) C.12: 2-9; (42) C.-reg.; (48) W.7:18-5. Antonio in *Marriage of Figaro.*

Plucker. (41) N.9:8. Heywood in *Rent Day.*

Plumer. (37) C.3:22; (39) W.8:16; (40) W.2:3*; (43) W.1:9-2; C.1:28-7.

Plumer, Mrs. (40) C.9:5.

Ponisi, Madame. (50) W.10:8-5; (51) W.-reg.; 4:15*, 21*; 6:25*; A.7:14. Alice in *Retribution.*

Poole, Miss. (39) C.10:16-15; (40) C.-4 performances; (41) C.-15 per. Clorinda in *Cinderella,* Liza in *La Sonnambula,* Marceline in *Fidelio,* Apollo in *Midas.*

Pope, Mrs. Coleman. (47) A.1:13-9. Julia in *Hunchback,* Pauline in *Lady of Lyons,* Jane Shore.

Porter, C. S. (35) W.1:3*; 3:16*; 9:12*, 17*, 23*; 10:10*, 24*, 28*, 31*; 11:11*; 12:7*, 14*, 25*; (36) W.1:1*, 9*, 26*; 2:1*; 3:14*; 4:6*, 11*, 25*, 29*; 6:22*; 7:4*; 8:31*; 9:3*, 8*; 10:1*, 28*; 11:4*, 10*, 23*, 24*; 12:24*; (37) W.1:2*, 4*, 7*, 21*; 2:20*, 27*; 3.13*, 18*; 6:30*; 7:21*; 8:31*; (38) W.1:8*, 15*, 29*; 2:19*, 26*; 3:25*; 7:2*; 8:8*, 16*, 25*, 27*; 10:25*; 12:12*; (39) W.1:1*, 8*; 2:4*; (40) N.10:19*; (42) A.5:23*-reg.; (43) A.3:14-reg; 8:10-reg.

Porter, J. G. (35) W.9:23*; 10:17*, 24*; (36) W.4:16*; 5:23*; 6:13*, 20*; 8:31*; 11:15*, 24*; 12:24*; (37) W.1:2*, 7*; 2:20*; 3:6*, 13*, 18*; 6:30*; 7:7*; (42) A.3:28-reg.; 11:11*; (43) A.8:10-reg.

Porter, Mrs. J. G. (42) A.8:24-reg.;
C.-reg. Louisa in *Dead Shot.*

Porter, N. (40) W.-reg.

Porter, the Kentucky Giant. (38)
W.-5 performances.

Porter, Miss S. (38) W.12:17; (41)
W.11:30; (42) W.2:14; A.4:14*;
5:23*-reg.; (43) A.3:14-reg.; A.8:
10-reg. Virginia in *Virginius.*

Potter, Mrs. Estelle. (53) C.8:12; (55)
C.1:15-reg.

Povey, Miss. See Mrs. A. Knight.

Powell. (39) W.12:14*; (40) W.2:3*.

Power, Maurice, Irish comedian. (48)
A.11:13-6. Nervous man.

Power, Tyrone. (35) C.4:27-8; (36)
C.11:21*-25; (37) C.2:27*-26; (38)
C.9:19*, 10:2*-23; (40) C.-30 per-
formances; (41) N.-10 performances.
O'Rafferty in *Born to Good Luck,*
Terry in *Irish Tutor,* O'Plenipo in
Irish Ambassador, Pat in *Omnibus,*
O'Trigger in *The Rivals,* O'Flaherty
in *The West Indian,* Paddy Carey in
Rory O'More.

Preston. (36) W.9:17*; 10:28*.

Preston, Mrs. (36) W.9:17*, 24*;
10.1*, 26*; 11:15*, 23*, 24*; 12:6*,
13*, 24*; (37) W.1:2*, 4*, 9*; (45)
N.4:28-reg.

Price, J. B. (42) W.1:14. Glauis in
Lady of the Lake.

Price, Miss C. (42) C.5:10; (43) C.-
reg.

Price, Miss M. (41) A.9:20*.

Prior, J. J. (55) C.1:15-reg.

Prior, Mrs. J. J. (55) C.1:15-reg.

Pritchard, Mrs., formerly Mrs. Tat-
nall: (35) W.-11.5*; (36) W.-reg.
Madge in *Heart of Midlothian,*
Margaret in *Tour de Nesle.*

Proctor, J.: (37) W.-2.20*, 27*; 3.6*,
13*, 20*, 22*, 24*, 27*; 6.30*; 7.31*;
8.8*, 31*; (38) W.-1.1*, 10*, 15*;
2.19*; 3.10*; (42) W.-3.4-reg.; A.-
11.1-11; (43) A.-8.10-reg.; (50) C.-

6.17-2; A.-9.30-6; A.-11.4-5; (51)
B.-reg.; N.-7.15-Summer.

Proctor, Mrs. J.: (37) W.-6.30*; 7.7*,
31*; 8.8*, 31*; 11.20*, 25*; 12.2*,
18*, 23*, 25*, 27*; (38) W.-1.1*, 2*,
8*, 10*, 29*; 2.19*; 3.10*.

Pyne, Miss, in opera: (54) W.-10.30-
16.

Pyne, Miss Louisa, in opera: (54) W.-
10.30-16.

Quayle: (40) N.-10.15; (51) B.-9.1-
reg.

Radcliffe: (43) W.-2.27-reg.; C.-
reg.; (46) W.-8.29-reg.; (47) W.-
8.21-reg.; (48) W.-reg. Black
Raven.

Radcliffe, Mrs.: (42) W.-reg.

Raffile, C.: (36) W.-10.28*; (37) W.-
2.27*; (42) A.-3.28-reg.

Randolph, Miss E., comedienne: (41)
N.-9.13-6.

Randoux, with French Company: (55)
W.-11.19-6.

Ranger: (40) C.-2.5*; 3.19*-8; N.-7
performances. Marquis in *Romantic
Widow.*

Raphael, Mlle., with French Company: (55) W.-11.19-6.

Rasimi: (35) W.-4.3*.

Ravel Family: (36) C.-12.30*-12;
(37) C.-2.4*-16.

Raymond: (48) A.-9.13*.

Raymond, Miss: (42) A.-6.6.

Rea: (45) C.-8.30-reg.

Reed, D.: (35) W.-reg.-5.30*; 6.13*;
9.4*, 12*, 16*, 23*, 26*, 29*; 10.3*,
10*, 17*, 24*, 29*, 31*; 11.5*, 9*,
14*, 21*; 12.1*; (36) W.-reg.-2.10*;
8.31*; 9.3*, 24*; 10.1*; (38) W.-
1.6-reg.; (42) W.-reg.; (46) W.-
8.29-reg.

Reed, J.: (35) W.-12.16.

Reed, Wm.: (51) W.-8.18-reg.

Reed, Miss E.: (42) W.-reg.: (51) W.-8.18.-reg.

Reed, Master: (38) W.-8.6; (42) W.-reg. Adopted Child.

Rees, W. H., in English Opera: (55) C.M.-6.11-15.

Rees, Mrs. W. H.: (55) C.M.-6.11-15.

Reeve, John, in high comedy: (35) C.-12.17*, 24*-9; (36) C.-13 performances; (42) A.-4.20-2; (44) N.-5.30. Bob in *Rivals*, Billy in *Sweethearts and Wives*, Magog in *Wreck Ashore*, Paul Pry, Mawworm in *Hypocrite*, Sharpe in *Married Bachelor*.

Reeves, W. H., in opera: (47) W.-11.22-18; (48) W.-9.25-12; (49) W.-4.23-12; 10.1-12; 11.26-12.

Reynolds: (50) C.-5.1*.

Reynolds, Miss: (39) W.-10.30; (44) A.-1.10-reg. Kate O'Brien in *Lady of Munster*.

Ribas, Mrs.: (45) C.-8.30; (47) A.-1.13. Isadore in *Jack Robinson*.

Rice, J. B.: (37) W.-6.30*; 7.7*, 31*; 9.2*; 11.20*, 25*; 12.2*, 18*, 23*, 25*; (38) W.-1.1*, 8*, 15*; 2.19*, 26*; 7.2*; 8.8*; (39) W.-1.8*; 2.4*; 4.1.

Rice, Mrs. J. B.: (38) W.-2.26*; 8.8*.

Rice, T. D.: (35) W.-9.5*-12; 12.1*-4; (36) W.-6 performances; (7) W.-10.25*, 26*-6; (38) W.-1.2-10; (40) A.-9.8-5; (41) A.-5 performances; (43) A.-9.20-7; (44) A.-1.17-4; C.-10.28-15; (45) A.-10.13-6; (46) A.-1.30-15; (48) A.-2.14-13; W.-12.18-5; (49) N.-10.8-6; (50) A.-4.30-8; (52) A.-1.1-3. Jim Crow in London, Bone Squash Diavolo, Gumbo Chaff in *Oh Hush,* Ginger Blue in *Sarcophagus*, Sambo in *Black and White,* Sylvester Daggerwood.

Richardson, M. L. B., pantomimist: (48) P.M.-3.16-reg.; (49) C.-11.3-3; (52) N.-7.12-reg.

Richer, in French Opera: (43) C.-9.14-13.

Richer, Madame: (45) C.-9.29-12.

Richings, P.: (40) N.-reg.-10.19*; (41) A.-reg.; C.-10.4*; W.-11.6*; (42) C.-1.10*; 2.3*, 9*-reg.; (43) A.-3.14-reg.; A.-8.10-reg.; (44) C.-4.1-18; (45) W.-4.10*; C.-7.3*; W.-12.20*; (46) W.-8.29-reg.; (47) W.-reg.; (48) W.-reg.; 8.28*; (49) W.-1.5*-reg.; (50) W.-reg.-3.25*; 5.29*; 9.25*; (51) W.-8.18-reg.; W.-1.20*; 4.15*; 11.22*; (52) W.-3.12*-reg.; (55) W.-9.6, 14*-10.

Richings, Caroline, in opera: (52) W.-2.9-10; (55) W.-9.6, 14*-10. Announced as first appearance in *Daughter of the Regiment*.

Riddle, Miss Eliza: (35) W.-4.23*.

Rischler, in German Opera: (40) C.-3.23-4. Kilian in *Freischutz*.

Risley, C. S.: (40) W.-7.16. Sam in *Oh, Hush.*

Roberts, comedian with Mitchell's Olympic Company: (41) N.-9.25*, 27*; (42) A.-5.19-12; (43) A.-3.14-reg.; A.-8.10-reg.; (53) A.-reg. Geoffrey in *Barnaby Rudge,* Mandeville in *Ocean Child.*

Roberts, son of comedian: (35) W.-4.10. Advertised as his first appearance.

Roberts, J. B., with Mrs. Ada Stetson: (47) A.-8.16-5; (48) A.-2.2*-9; (49) C.-9.14-6; (55) C.M.-11.5-6. Romeo, Rolla in *Pizarro,* and Shakespearean rôles in general.

Robertson, Miss Agnes, comedienne: (54) C.-4.10-10; W.-11.20-10; 55.-W.-6.16-10.

Robinson, J. H.: (48) A.-10.5-reg.; (49) A.-1.8*; 2.19*; (51) B.-9.1-reg.

Rock, Miss: (40) W.-reg. Jenny in *Winning a Husband,* Kate in *Perfection.*

[704]

Rockhill: (38) W.-1.9. Othello.

Rodney: (38) W.-4.2*, 11*.

Rogers, the stammering tragedian: (49) A.-10.23. Shylock.

Rogers: (44) N.-3.20.

Rogers, B.: (49) C.-9.1-reg.

Rogers, G.: (50) A.-2.3-reg.; B.-9.28-reg.; 9.30*; (51) N.-7.15-summer; W.-8.18-reg.; (52) N.-7.12-reg.; (54) C.M.-9.12-reg.

Rogers, Mrs., from Edinburgh and Dublin Theatres: (35) C.-9.26. Announced as her first appearance in this country, at Wallack's Benefit; (38) C.-6.30; W.-7.5; (40) C.-6.12; (42) C.-4.27.-reg.; (44) C.-4.1-18; (45) C.-8.30-reg.; (46) A.-8.26-reg.

Rogers, Mrs. E.: (50) B.-10.2-reg.

Rohrman, W.: (51) C.-2.22.

Roland: (37) P.-1.11.

Rose, Miss: (54) C.-9.13.

Rosi, Signor: (48) C.-2.9-23; 6.6-7; 10.4-15; 12.5-12; (50) C.-12.10-15. With Italian Opera Company.

Rottenhaus, Miss: (37) A.-7.27-6. With German Company. Lottechen in *Dissipated Invalids,* Sophia in *Watchman.*

Rowbotham, H. H., a singer: (35) C.-1.20*; 2.5*; (36) C.-4.16*; 5.26*; 6.11*; 8.26*; 11.21*.

Rowbotham, Mrs. H. H.: (35) C.-1.7*; 2.5*; 3.6*, 14*; 4.1*; 5.13*; (36) C.-1.4*, 28*; 2.11*; 4.6*, 14*; 6.15*; 8.26*; 9.30*; 10.25*; 11.21*; 12.19*; (37) C.-2.27*; 4.1*; 6.7*.

Roys: (53) C.-4.20*-reg.

Runeg: (40) C.-3.23-4. In German Opera. Hermit in *Freischutz.*

Russell: (38) W.-9.24-6. Choctar in *La Bayadere.*

Russell, H.: (44) A.-6.1-reg.

Russell, T. B.: (35) W.-reg.; (36) W.-3.14*-reg.; (37) W.-reg.; (38) W.-reg.; (39) W.-reg.; (40) W.-reg.; (41) W.-reg.; 3.13*, 11.6*; (42) W.-reg.; (43) A.-8.10-Lessee.

Russell, Mrs. T. B.: (43) A.-8.10-reg.; (46) P.M.-3.9-reg.; (47) A.-reg.; (48) A.-reg.; P.M.-3.16-reg.

Russell, Mrs. J., comedienne: (49) P.M.-reg.

Ruth, Miss: (35) W.-1.28*.

Ryan, G. C.: (51) C.-7.3-reg.; A.-8.30-reg.

Ryan, Redmond, Irish comedian: (49) A.-5.28-6; (50) A.-7.1-11; C.-7.17*-10.

Ryder, supporting Macready in *Tragedy:* (43) C.-10.23-12; (48) A.-10.28-8.

Ryer: (50) W.-11.22.

Ryner: (54) C.M.-9.12-reg.

Ryner, Mrs.: (54) C.M.-9.12-reg.

Sachse, with German Company: (37) A.-7.27-6. Menghorn in *Dissipated Invalids,* Burgomaster in *Watchman.*

St. Clair, Mrs.: (40) P.-7.29.

St. Clair, Miss: (44) C.-10.14-reg.

St. Luke, Miss: (37) C.-3.3*-4. Ariel in *Tempest,* Arabella.

St. Luke, Master: (37) C.-3.3*-4. Richard III, Harry in *Yankee Tar.*

Sandford, J.: (40) W.-7.16; (42) A.-4.25-2; (46) A.-7.14. Gumbo Chaff in *Oh, Hush.*

Sanford, S. L.: (50) C.-1.8. Hamlet in *Somnambulist.*

Sanford, S. S.: (53) C.-12.12-10.

Sanquirico, Signor, with Italian Opera Company: (50) C.-12.10-15.

Savage: (51) C.-3.1-28; N.-7.15-summer; B.-9.1-reg.; (53) A.-reg.

Scharf: (51) C.-8.18-reg.

Scheidler, Mme., with German Opera: (40) C.-3.23-4. Agathe in *Freischutz.*

Schinnotti: (35) W.-1.9; 3.23.

[705]

Scott, G.: (47) A.-9.11. Walter in *Hunchback.*

Scott, John R.: (35) A.-4.22*-5; (36) A.-4.4*-10; 6.11*; P.-13 performances; (37) A.-13 per.; (38) A.-7 per.; (39) A.-14 per.; (40) A.-3 per.; W.-8 per.; W.-10.19*; N.-8.31-reg.; (41) A.-reg.; W.-8 per.; (42) A.-6.14-23; (44) A.-8.15-10; (45) W.-5.5-15; A.-8.29-10; A.-10.6-5; (46) A.-1.24-acting manager; (47) A.-reg.; (48) A.-7.16-10; A.-12.9-5; (51) A.-10.6-11; (52) A.-3.24*-10; 9.20-10; (53) A.-2.7-10; C.-4.17-10. Richard III, Ugolino, Virginius, Caswallon, Marc Antony in *Julius Caesar,* Julian in *The Wife,* Huon in *Love,* Rob Roy.

Scott, Miss: (36) W.-8.31*.

Seele, Miss: (42) C.-reg.

Sefton, John: (35) W.-manager; (54) W.-reg.

Sefton, Mrs. John: (36) P.-reg.; (37) P.-1.4*; (54) W.-5.1*-reg.

Sefton, Joseph O.: (35) W.-1.1*, 10*, 17*, 19*; 3.7*, 11*, 16*, 23*; (37) P.-2.3; (38) W.-12.26-5; (39) 4.29-16; (42) W.-4.27-7; A.-8 performances; (43) N.-10.30-21; (44) C.-10.14-reg.; (46) P.M.-6.1-reg.; (47) P.M.-1.11-reg.; (51) A.-10.6-5; (53) C.-1.18-10. Jemmy Twitcher in *Golden Farmer,* Teik in *Swiss Cottage,* Tom in *Catching an Heiress,* Prettyman in *He's not A-Miss.*

Sefton, W.: (35) W.-1.1*-2.18.

Sefton, Mrs. W.: (39) W.-8.12, 12.9*-12; 12.14*-4; (40) W.-2.3*; 4.11*; (41) A.-12.6* Imogene in *Castle of St. Aldobrand,* Theodore in *La Fitte,* Louisa in *Dead Shot,* Lady Macbeth, Nahmeokie in *Metamora,* Queen in *Hamlet,* Emma in *William Tell.*

Sefton, Mrs. Ann: (41) A.-12.6*; (42) C.-1.24-reg.

Sefton, Miss Ann: (35) W.-4.10; (41) A.-10.1. Julian in *The Young Reefer.*

Sequin, in opera: (39) C.-1.14-54; (41) C.-15 performances; (42) C.-12.5-17; (43) C.-1.6-34; (44) C.-4.1-18; 12.20-10; (45) C.-5.19-30; 11.10-10; (46) C.-4.27-10; W.-11.2-23; (47) C.-4.5-52; W.-10.11-14; (48) W.-9.25-12; (49) W.-4.23-12; 11.26-12; (51) B.-2.10-17; W.-8.18-reg. Count Rodolpho in *La Sonnambula,* General in *Amilie,* Giacomo in *Fra Diavolo,* Dandini in *Cinderella,* Caspar in *Freischutz,* Basil in *Marriage of Figaro.*

Seguin, Mrs.: (39) W.-11.4-13; (41) C.-15 performances; (42) C.-12.5-17; (43) C.-1.5-35; (44) C.-4.1-18; 12.20-10; (45) C.-5.19-30; 11.10-10; (46) C.-4.27-10; W.-11.2-23; (47) C.-4.5-52; W.-10.11-14; (48) W.-9.25-12; (49) W.-4.23-12; 10.-1-12; 11.26-12; (51) B.-2.10-17; W.-8.18-reg. Linda in *Freischutz,* Countess in *Marriage of Figaro.*

Senior: (35) W.-2.28*.

Seymour, Irish comedian: (49) A.-9.25-5; (50) A.-8.21-8.

Seymour, Mrs.: (41) N.-12.2; (42) C.-2.9*-4. Juliet.

Sharpe: (36) C.-9.28.

Sharpe, Mrs.: (38) C.-reg.; 9.19*; 11.29*; 12.29*; (39) C.-reg.-5.13*; (40) C.-reg.-2.5*; 5.5-advertised as her farewell to the stage. Lady Macbeth, Volumnia, Queen Catharine in *Henry VIII,* Violante in *Wonder,* Paulette in *Ransom,* Miss Dorillon in *Wives as they Were.*

Shaw, E.: (40) N.-reg.; 12.19*; (41) N.-9.25*-reg.; (42) N.-reg.-1.20*; (43) N.-reg.; (45) C.-reg.

Shaw, J. E.: (51) A.-7.14.

Shaw, Mrs.: (36) C.-8.29; 9.10; 9.30; (38) C.-12.12*-15; (42) C.-3.7-3;

(45) C.-2.10-4. Widow in *Soldier's Daughter*, Hamlet, Ion, Hero in *Woman's Wit*, Agnes de Vere.

Sheble: (50) C.-7.13. Wilford in *Iron Chest*.

Shep(h)erd: (51) C.-2.22; (52) N.-7.12-reg.; (54) N.-6.3-reg.

Shelley, Walter: (47) A.-11.1-4. Hamlet, Richelieu, Shylock, Beverly in *Gamester*.

Sherman: (41) N.-9.25*.

Shewell: (53) A.-11.28*; (54) A.-reg.; (55) W.-6.4*-reg.

Shireff, Miss: (39) C.-1.14-50; (40) C.-4.20*-13. Amina in *La Sonnambula*, Amilie, Zerlinain *Fra Diavolo*, Cinderella, Madalaine in *Postillion of Lonjumeau*.

Shrival: (42) C.-12.5-18; (43) C.-1.5-35; (44) C.-4.1-18; W.-10.11-14; (47) W.-10.11-14.

Silsbee, J. S., Yankee comedian: (41) A.-9.21-5; (43) A.-5.8*-12; N.-11.20-6; (44) N.-4.12-2; A.-10.2-7; (45) A.-11.3-9; (46) A.-3.2-7; (48) Ath.-owner-12.25; (50) A.-9.2-6; (51) A.-3.11-12; (53) W.-8.20-11; (55) C.-1.29-12.

Silsbee, Mrs. J. S.: (48) Ath.-12.25-reg.; (50) W.-6.18; (51) W.-8.18-reg. Lady Macbeth.

Silvain, Mons., from Royal Academy of music in Paris, a dancer: (40) C.-6.17*-14; (4) C.-15 performances.

Sinclair: (41) A.-2 performances. Bertram in *Guy Mannering*.

Sinclair, Mrs., supporting Vandenhoff in tragedy: (52) C.-3.23-5.

Sinclair, Miss: (48) A.-7.3. Jenny in *A Glance at Philadelphia*.

Siple, S.: (48) C.-7.22; (51) C.-2.22.

Slack: (37) P.-1.24.

Sloan: (49) C.-11.28-4. A comedian.

Sloan, Mrs.: (49) C.-11.28-4, a comedienne.

Sloman: (39) C.-3.4-8, 6; (41) C.-10.5-

5; (45) W.-2.5-reg. Sam in *Fish out of Water*, Delph in *Family Jars*, Paul in *My Master's Rival*, Tristram in *Deaf as a Post*.

Sloman, Mrs.: (39) C.-3.4-14; (41) C.-10.5-5; (45) W.-1.28-reg. Isabella, Jane Shore, Pauline in *Lady of Lyons*, Mrs. Haller in *The Stranger*, Mrs. Beverly in *Gamester*.

Smead: (50) A.-8.8. Lawyer Cribbs in *Drunkard*.

Smith, C. J.: (44) A.-6.1-reg.; C.-10.14-reg.; (45) C.-reg.; (46) P.M.-6.30-reg.; (51) A.-reg.

Smith, J.: (42) N.-1.20*.

Smith, G.: (44) N.-3.30. Jemmy in *Ladder of Love*.

Smith, J. W.: (41) A.-9.21-5; (43) W.-7.17-23; 7.31*. In American type rôles.

Smith, Sol.: (35) W.-9.15-3. In American type rôles.

Smith, W. H.: (36) P.-reg.; (37) W.-12.23*; (38) W.-reg.; (41) A.-10.7*, 18*.

Smith, Mrs. W. H.: (36) W.-9.3*; 10.28*; P.-11.1-reg.; (37) W.-6.30*; (45) W.-reg.; C.-8.30-reg.; (49) A.-8.23-reg.

Smith, Miss: (42) W.-reg.; (44) C.-10.14-reg.

Solomon: (44) C.-11.14-reg.

Spear: (43) C.-reg.

Spencer: (50) A.-2.23-reg.

Stafford: (40) N.-reg.; (44) C.-10.14-reg.

Stanl(e)y: (35) W.-10.17*; (36) W.-3.14*; (37) W.-2.20*; (42) W.-5.18; A.-5.24-2; C.-reg.

Stearns: (51) B.-9.1-reg.; (54) C.-9.13.

Steele, S. S.: (38) W.-1.31; (53) C.-4.24.

Steele, Miss L.: (53) A.-reg.

Steffenone, Signorina Balbina, with

Italian Opera, Havana: (50) C.-9.10-10.

Stell, T.: (37) W.-2.3; (44) N.-2.8-reg.

Stephan, Mlle., in opera: (39) W.-2.11-6. Zelica in *Maid of Cashmere.*

Stephens, Major, the American dwarf: (38) W.-4 performances-1.22. Tom Thumb. See Major Stevens.

Stephens, H. E. See H. E. Stevens.

Stephens, Mrs.: (50) W.-10.22-reg.; (51) N.-7.15-summer.

Stetson, Mrs. Ada, with J. B. Roberts: (47) A.-8.16-5. Juliet, Elvira in *Pizarro.*

Stevens, Major, the American dwarf: (35) W.-2.28-3.4; then went to American Museum, 3.9.

Stevens, H. E.: (43) O.-reg.-1.9; (46) A.-stage manager; W.-8.29-reg.; (51) A.-7.14.

Stewart, J.: (51) C.-2.22.

Stewart, Miss, with Booth: (50) A.-5.17. Margaret Overreach in *A New Way To Pay Old Debts.*

Stites: (50) A.-2.23-reg.

Stone: (53) A.-1.29-reg.; (55) C.-reg.

Stuart, C.: (47) P.M.-1.1-reg.; (54) C.-9.20-reg.; C.-10.25*.

Studley: (55) C.-reg.

Tatnall, Mrs. See Mrs. Pritchard.

Tasistro, Fitzgerald: (41) C.-9.2-5. Hamlet.

Taylor: (37) W.-7.10-8. Landlord in *Tom and Jerry,* Old Pusang in *L'Amour.*

Taylor, E. F., with the Cony family: (52) A.-3.29-6; (53) C.-4.18-6.

Taylor, J. H.: (35) C.-9.21; (51) C.-7.3-reg.; 9.19*; 10.15*; (52) C.-reg.

Taylor, Mary: (46) P.M.-3.9-reg.

Tedesco, Signorina Fortunata: (47) W.-7.12-18. Italian Opera, Havana.

Tellings: (47) A.-2.1-3. Brandon in *Look before you Leap.*

Ternan: (35) C.-1.28-2.21; 4.13*-19; 10.3*, 9*-12; (36) C.-12.6*-6. Duke in *Honeymoon,* Stranger, Edgar in *Bride of Lammermoor,* Joseph Surface in *School for Scandal,* Staunton in *Heart of Midlothian,* Shylock, Macbeth, Othello, Fazio.

Ternan, Mrs. See Miss Fanny Jarman.

Terry: (51) W.-8.18-reg.

Thames, Bertolama, with Italian Opera, Havana: (43) C.-7.15-13; 11.13-11.

Thayer, E. N.: (35) C.-3.5*; 4.8*; 5.30*; (36) C.-12.19*; (37) A.-6.2*, 7*; C.-9.16*; 10.19*, 25*; 12.15*; (38) C.-3.17*; (39) C.-3.20*; 5.13*; (40) C.-1.3*; (43) O.-reg.-1.9; A.-8.10-reg.; (45) A.-4.22*-reg.; C.-reg.; (47) P.M.-1.21-reg.; (48) A.-reg.; (49) A.-1.10*-reg.; 5.23*; 9.1*, 8*; 12.29*; (50) B.-8.19-reg.; 12.13*; (51) B.-9.1-reg.; (52) N.-5.22-reg.; (53) A.-11.28*-reg.; (54) A.-reg.-5.1*; (55) A.-8.18-reg.

Thayer, Mrs. E. N.: (35) C.-3.11*; 4.23*; 9.5*; (36) C.-4.14*; 9.30*; (37) C.-1.23*; (38) C.-4.20*; 6.2*; 7.7*; 12.29*; (39) C.-3.20*; (40) C.-reg.; (42) C.-2.9*-reg.; A.-3.28-reg.; W.-reg.; (43) C.-reg.; (46) W.-8.29-reg.; C.-1.5*; (49) C.-9.1-reg.; (50) B.-8.19-reg.; (51) B.-9.1-reg.; (54) C.M.-9.12-reg.; (55) A.-8.18-reg.

Thillon, Madame Anna: (51) C.-10.22-5; (52) C.-2.17-5; (53) C.-1.1-5; C.-5.16-5. In comic opera, *Crown of Diamonds.*

Thoman, a singer: (35) C.-9.30*; (36) C.-1.2*; (41) A.-12.6*; (42) A.-3.28-reg.; (43) A.-3.14-reg.

Thoman, Mrs. See Miss Anderson.

Thomas, H. L.: (51) C.-2.22.

Thomas, L. G.: (44) N.-4.27. Hamlet.

Thompson, E.: (36) C.-10.28*; (37)

W.-2.20*, 27*; (38) C.-reg.; (41)
A.-12.6*; (43) A.-3.14-reg.; W.-
8.8*; A.-8.10-reg.; (48) Ath.-12.25-
reg.
Thompson, Mrs.: (46) P.M.-3.9-reg.;
(49) P.M.-reg.
Thompson, Miss: (42) C.-reg.
Thompson, Lysander, a comedian:
(54) C.-6.19-10. Robert Tyke in
School of Reform.
Thorne, C.: (46) A.-4.16-7; (49) 1.15-
6-A. Darville in *Ernest Maltravers,*
Richard III, Rolla in *Pizarro.*
Thorne, Mrs. C.: (46) A.-4.16-7; (49)
A.-1.15-6. Alice in *Ernest Mal-
travers,* Elizabeth in *Richard III,*
Cora in *Pizarro.*
Thorne, J.: (40) N.-reg.; (43) O.-1.9-
reg.
Thorne, R.: (37) W.-1.23.
Thorne, Mrs.: (35) W.-1.3*.
Tidmarsh: (49) P.M.-5.8-reg.; 5.17*.
Tilton, E. L.: (51) A.-7.14.
Timm, Mrs., with Mitchell's Olympic
Company: (41) N.
Town, Mrs.: (43) A.-8.10-reg. Des-
demona.
Tozer: (50) A.-8.1-reg.
Tree, Miss E., from Covent Garden
and English Opera, London: (37)
C.-1.23*-17; 4.25*-11; 6.17*; 10.2*-
12; (39) C.-4 performances; (45)
C.-9.15-25; (46) C.-1.1-3; W.-9.14-
11; (47) W.-1.18-21. Julia in
Hunchback, Portia, Rosalind, Bea-
trice, Juliet, Lady Townly in *Pro-
voked Husband,* Letitia in *Belle's
Stratagem,* Mrs. Haller in *Stranger,*
Mariana in *The Wife,* Lady Teazle
in *School for Scandal,* Mrs. Oakly
in *Jealous Wife,* Violante in *Wonder.*
Truffi, Signora, in Italian opera: (50)
C.-12.10-15.
Truffi, Signorina Teresa: (48) C.-2.19-
23; 6.6-7; 10.4-15; 12.5-12.

Tucket, Capt. Harvey: (47) A.-
10.25-5. Falstaff, Dazzle in *London
Assurance.*
Turnbull, Miss Julia: (41) N.-with
Mitchell's Olympic Company; (50)
A.-7.23-5. Katharine Kloper in *Lola
Montez,* Leoline in *Fairy of the
Fountain.*
Turner, T. V.: (44) N.-4.6.
Turpin, Miss: (37) C.-12.14*-6-a vo-
calist. Susanetta in *Two Figaros,*
Julia in *Guy Mannering,* Diana in
Rob Roy, Rosetta in *Love in a Vil-
lage.*
Tuthill: (41) A.-reg.
Tyrell: (53) C.-5.19-reg. Norman in
Sea Captain.
Tyrell, Mrs.: (53) C.-3.17-reg.
Tyte, Miss: (42) W.-reg.

Vache, W. A.: (35) W.-reg.; (36)
W.-reg.; (37) W.-2.20*; 3.18*;
6.30*; 12.25*; (38) W.-2.19*, 24*;
8.25*; 9.22*; 12.12*; (42) W.-reg.
Valentine, Dr., and his eccentricities,
magic: (35) C.-9.15; (38) W.-10.3.
Vallee, Miss E.: (40) C.-9.5.
Vallee, Mlle. H.: (47) A.-8.24-2; (48)
W.-7.5-2. In support of De Bar.
Narramattah in Indian Girl.
Valtellina, Attilio, with Italian Opera,
Havana: (43) C.-7.15-13; C.-11.13-
11; (47) W.-11.22-18; (48) C.-2.19-
23; 6.6-7; 10.4-15; 12.25-12.
Van Pelt, Miss: (48) P.M.-3.16-reg.
Vandenhoff, G.: (37) C.-6 perform-
ances; (38) C.-5 per.; (39) C.-
11.18-18 per.; (40) C.-10 per.; (42)
W.-10.10-6; (43) W.-4.26-7; W.-
10.3-15; C.-10.26-11; (45) C.-12.1-4;
(52) C.-3.22-5. Hamlet, Cato, Mac-
beth, Coriolanus, Richelieu, Stranger,
Romeo, Wolsey in *Henry VIII,*
Felix in *Hunter of the Alps,*
Adrastus in *Ion.*
Vandenhoff, Miss: (39) C.-11.18-18;

(40) C.-10 performances. Julia in *Hunchback*, Julie in *Richelieu*, Mrs. Haller in *Stranger*, Ion, Juliet, Ophelia, Portia.

Vanhorn: (53) A.-reg.

Vanstavoreen: (40) W.-6.13; A.-12.11*-reg.; (43) W.-2.21-reg.; A.-12.11-reg.; (47) P.M.-6.15.

Vestris, Mme. See Mrs. C. Mathews.

Vincent: (49) A.-11.20.

Vinny or Vining, Miss Fanny, later Mrs. E. L. Davenport: (55) W.-3.23*-10. In support of E. L. Davenport.

Vos, Miss.: (35) C.-8.31-4. Mrs. Haller in *Stranger*, Elvira in *Pizarro*, Juliet, Bianca in *Fazio*.

Wagstaff, Miss: (44) C.-10.14-reg.

Walbourne: (37) W.-7.10*-8. Chopstick in *Farmer's Son*, Bob in *Tom and Jerry*, Jackardo in *Tom and Jerry*. Advertised as having appeared 1995 times in *Tom and Jerry*.

Walcot, in low comedy: (44) N.-5.24; (47) N.-10.26-15; (48) P.M.-4.22*-reg. Courtly in *London Assurance*.

Walker, Mrs.: (50) C.-3.18*.

Wallace, J.: (35) W.-12.10; (37) P.-reg.; (38) P.-2.1.

Wallack, Henry: (37) A.-12.14*, 16*-7; (51) C.-8.18-stage manager. Adam in *Charles XII*, Broadlands in *Old English Gentleman*, Cherubino in *Two Figaros*, Rob Roy.

Wallack, James, Sr.: (35) C.-9.17*-18; (36) C.-45 performances; (37) C.-5 performances; (39) C.-1.2*-11; (41) W.-5 performances; (42) N.-Reg.-1.20*; (43) N.-9.25-12; C.-11.29-3; (44) W.-4.29-14; (46) A.-10.14-6. Rolla in *Pizarro*, Martin Heywood in *Rent Day*, David in *Hazard of the Die*, Michael in *Adopted Child*, Julian in *The Wife*,

Rattle in *Spring and Autumn*, Omreah in *Carib Chief*, Bertram, Rienzi, Don Felix in *Wonder*, Bookworm in *The Scholar*.

Wallack, James, Jr.: (44) W.-8.21-29; 9.21*; (45) A.-4.17-9; W.-7.24-50; (46) W.-1.3*-reg.; A.-9.7*-reg.; (47) W.-reg.; (48) W.-reg.; 9.4*; 10.23!; (53) C.-4.26-10; (55) C.M.-10.20-10.

Wallack, Mrs. James, Jr.: (44) W.-8.21-29; 9.21*; (45) A.-4.17-9; W.-7.24-50; (46) W.-1.3*-reg.; A.-9.7*-reg.; (47) W.-reg.; (48) W.-reg. Marianne in *The Wife*, Julia in *Hunchback*, Juliet, Senona in *Gladiator*, Queen Elizabeth in *Richard III*, Mrs. Haller in *Stranger*.

Wallack, Miss Fanny: (48) W.-7.18-5; (49) A.-reg.-8.16; 9.1*, 17*; (50) W.-8.19-reg.; 8.28*; 9.25*; (51) C.-7.3-reg. Lady Teazle, Lady Spanker in *London Assurance*.

Wallis: (54) W.-8.29-reg.

Walstein: (35) C.-1.7*; 3.14*; 9.5*, 7*; 10.3*; 11.14*.

Walstein, Mrs.: (35) C.-9.5*, 7*, 17*, 30*; (36) C.-1.2*; 2.6*, 22*; 5.26*; 6.11*, 15*; 11.28*; (37) C.-2.25*, 27*; 4.1*, 14*; 7.3*; 9.15*; 10.19*, 26*; 11.18*; 12.15; (38) C.-1.9*; 4.18*; 6.11*; 7.7*; 9.15*; 10.2*; 12.24*.

Walters: (36) W.-10.23; (37) W.-1.28; (39) W.-1.15; (44) A.-6.1-reg.; (45) A.-reg.; (46) A.-8.26-reg.; (48) Ath.-12.25-reg.

Walters, Miss, a pantomimist: (43) W.-7.17-23; 7.31*; (44) W.-2.26; 7.10-18; (45) W.-3.10-18; (46) W.-1.7. Marie in *Black Raven*.

Walton, a singer, in support of Mrs. Austen: (35) C.-2.5*; 3.14*, 31*; 10.3, 9*, 28*; (36) C.-1.4*, 28*; 2.11*; 4.9*; 5.26*; 6.15*; 8.26*; 10.25*; 11.21*; (37) C.-2.27*; 3.13*, 18*; 4.1*, 14*; 11.6*; 12.14*; (38)

C.-1.9*, 15*; 3.17*; 4.20*; 9.15*;
10.2*, 22*; 11.29*; (39) C.-3.23*.

Ward: (35) W.-8.28*-stage manager;
(47) P.M.-7.2; (51) C.-3.1-28; (52)
A.-reg. Lieut. Worthington in *Poor
Gentleman.*

Ward, Mrs.: (52) A.-reg.

Warden: (46) W.-8.29-reg.

Warden, E., in opera: (54) C.-6.6-6.

Wareham: (43) A.-12.11-reg.; (44)
N.-3.26*.

Waring, Ann D.: (35) W.-12.14*, 19*,
25*; (36) W.-1.1*, 9*, 13*; 2.10*,
29*; 3.14, 25*; 4.4*, 6*, 11*, 16*,
25*; 5.18*; 6.3, 13, 20*, 22*.

Warner, Mrs.: (51) C.-11.9-5; 11.19*.

Warren, P.: (35) W.-3.16-treasurer.

Warren, W.: (35) W.-3.16*; (36) W.-
reg.; (37) W.-2.20*; 6.30*-reg.;
(38) W.-1.19*-reg.

Warren, Miss Mary Ann: (37) W.-
6.30*.

Watkins: (49) A.-11.24*.

Watson, C.: (35) C.-12.7*; (36) P.-
reg.-11.16*; (37) C.-1.4*; W.-2.20*,
27*; 3.13*, 27*; A.-5.2*; C.-9.15*;
10.25*, 26*; (38) C.-9.15*, 19*;
10.15*; (39) C.-3.23*; (41) A.-
9.20*; (42) C.-reg.; (43) A.-4.6-
reg.

Watson, Mrs. C.: (35) C.-reg.; (36)
P.-reg.-11.16*; (37) W.-2.20*; 3.13*,
18*; 11.4*; (38) C.-reg.; (39) C.-
reg.; (55) C.M.-9.8-reg.

Watson, Miss, in 1837 became Mrs.
Bailey: (35) A.-reg.; (36) A.-reg.;
(37) A.-3.13*; 6.30*; (40) N.-
11.30-12; (42) C.-12.5-8; (43) C.-
1.5-35; (51) B.-2.10-17; W.-8.18-
reg.

Watson Twins: (37) P.-2.4.

Weaver, John, in light comedies and
farces with Miss Heron: (48) C.-
6.30-15; (50) A.-10.29-6; (54) N.-
6.3-reg.; C.-9.6-reg. Bill Dowton in
The Drunkard.

Weaver, Mrs. John: (54) C.-9.6-reg.

Webb, C.: (35) C.-9.4; W.-11.9; (50)
A.-9.7-reg.; (55) C.-3.19-5. Damon,
Virginius, Stranger.

Wells: (39) C.-12.24; (44) W.-7.27*.

Wells, Master: (38) C.-6.9-6. O'Toole
in *Irish Tutor.*

Wells, Miss: (38) C.-6 performances;
(39) C.-2 per.; (55) C.M.-10.20-
reg. Zoloe in *Maid of Cashmere,*
Rosina, Dew Drop, Margaretta in
No Song no Supper.

Wemyss, Francis C.: (35) W.-lessee
and manager-1.3*, 10*, 17*, 19*;
9.23*; (36) W.-1.13*; 3.14*; 8.31*;
9.17*; 11.4*, 28*; (37) W.-1.7*, 9*;
3.20*; 7.31*; 11.25*; 12.18*; (38)
W.-1.8*; 2.7*; 8.16*; (39) W.-1.9*;
(40) W. and A.-reg.; (43) N.-les-
see; (44) C.-lessee-10.14; 11.11*;
(45) W.-12.20*; (46) W.-3.19-reg.;
(47) A.-7.28-2; (48) A.-1.31-4;
(51) A.-7.14. Modus in *Hunchback.*

Wemyss, T.: (51) A.-4.14*.

Wemyss, Miss C.: (47) A.-7.24-18;
(48) A.-2.2*-4; W.-2.10-7; W.-
4.18-9; (50) C.-6.6; (51) W.-8.18-
reg.; A.-7.14; (52) W.-3.22*-reg.
Bianca in *Fazio,* Jane Shore, Julie
in *Richelieu.*

Wertz, H. C.: (51) C.-2.22.

West: (48) Ath.-12.25-reg.

West, Jenny: (48) Ath.-12.25-reg.

Western, Mrs.: (42) A.-9.27.

Weston, J. M.: (44) A.-6.1-reg.; (52)
W.-1.1-3.

Weston, Miss Lizzie: (53) C.-9.26*;
12.1*, 7*-reg.; (54) C.-1.9*-reg.

Wharton: (37) P.-1.24*.

Wheatleigh: (53) W.-10.3*-reg.

Wheatley, William: (43) W.-5.17*;
(44) W.-1.1-reg.; (45) W.-1.20*-
reg.; (46) W.-reg.; (47) W.-reg.;
(48) W.-reg.-8.28*; (49) W.-reg.;
(50) W.-3.25*-reg.; 6.7*, 27*; 9.25*;
(51) W.-1.20*; (53) A.-lessee-11.7*,

28*; (54) A.-5.1*-reg.; (55) A.-
lessee.

Wheatley, Emma: (35) C.-1.20*;
5.30*; 11.28*; (36) C.-3.26*.

Wheeler, Miss Fanny: (50) A.-3.4-
reg.; C.-7.30. Lize in *A Glance at
Philadelphia*.

White, J. H.: (42) A.-4.25-2; (43)
W.-8.8*.

White, Miss: (37) W.-12.25*, 27*;
(38) W.-7.2*; 8.8*; 9.22*; 10.3*.

Whiting: (40) N.-reg.

Whitney: (39) W.-4.18. Richard III.

Wilhelm: (37) A.-7.27-6-with German Company. Wachtel in *Watchman*.

Wilkinson, Mrs., formerly Miss C. J.
Crampton: (44) C.-11.20-4; (47)
A.-4.2-reg.; (52) A.-8.21-reg. Bianca
in *Fazio*, Juliet, Julia in *Hunchback*.

Wilk(e)s, G. B. S.: (36) C.-5.26*;
8.31*; (36) C.-reg.; (37) C.-2.20*;
6.30*; (38) C.-2.8; (39) W.-reg.;
(40) W.-2.3*.

Wilk(es), Mrs. G. B. S.: (37) W.-
reg.; (39) W. rcg.; (40) W.-1.23*;
2.3*; (46) W.-8.29-reg.; (51) B.-
9.1-reg.; (53) A.-5.20-reg.

Wilks, Miss: (55) A.-8.18-reg.

Williams, Barney: (39) C.-12.24; (40)
W.-reg.; (41) A.-12.6*; (42) A.-
6.18; (46) P.M.-10.15-reg.; (48)-
C.-3.10*, 11*-7; P.M.-4.24-10; (49)
A.-11.26-6; (50) C.-2.28-15; A.-
11.18-15; (51) A.-2.3-15; 5.5-15;
11.3-10; (52) C.-2.2-10; (53) W.-
10.31*-10; C.-5.2-10; (54) W.-5.15-
15; W.-6.8*; (55) W.-9.17-15. In
Irish comic rôles.

Williams, Mrs. Barney: (50) C.-2.28-
15; A.-11.18-15; (51) A.-2.3-15;
5.5-15; 11.3-10; (52) C.-2.2-10;
(53) C.-5.2-10; W.-10.24-10; (54)
W.-5.15-15; (55) C.M.-9.8-15.

Williams, W. H.: (41) N.-2.1; (51)
B.-9.1-reg. Buskin in *Killing no
Murder*.

Williams, Miss: (39) W.-8.28; (53)
A.-reg. Tom Twig in *Catching an
Heiress*.

Willis, Mrs.: (36) W.-4.29*, 30*;
5.25*; 6.20*, 22*; 8.31*; 9.3*, 8*, 24*;
10.1*, 15*, 28*, 11.4*, 15*, 23*, 24*,
28*; 12.13*, 24*; (37) W.-1.4*;
2.20*, 27*; 3.11*, 13*, 18*, 20*, 22*,
24*; 6.30*.

Will(i)s: (38) W.-7.18-4. Nipperkin
in *Sprigs of Laurel,* Luke the Laborer, Crack in *Turnpike Gate,*
Endless in *No Song no Supper*.

Wilson: (39) C.-1.14-21, 20, 11; (40)
C.-4.20*-13. Elvino in *La Sonnam-
bula,* Jose in *Amilie,* Fra Diavolo,
Prince in *Cinderella,* Chapelon in
Postillion of Lonjumeau.

Wilson, Miss: (44) A.-6.1-reg.; C.-
10.14-reg.; (53) A.-5.14-reg.

Win(n)an(s), John, in low comedy:
(38) W.-9.21; (43) A.-9.5-5; N.-
11.20-reg.; 10.9*; (44) N.-1.1*;
(52) C.-7.14-5. Irish Lion, Galochard in *King's Gardener*.

Winstanley, Mrs., in support of the
Broughams: (48) W.-5.4*-8; (49)
A.-reg.; 5.23*; 6.11*; 9.8*.

Wood: (35) C.-1.1, 2, 3, 5, 6, 7. A
singer.

Wood, C. F.: (52) N.-5.22-reg.

Wood, Joseph: (35) C.-1.7*; 3.16*;
4.17*; 5.13*; (36) C.-1.28*; 2.11*;
3.26*; 4.16*; 6.11*, 18*; 12.19*;
(37) C.-2.25*; 11.10*; 12.27*; (38)
C.-1.15*; 6.2*; 11.29*; (40) C.-
10.26; (41) C.-reg.; (42) C.-2.9*;
4.7*-reg.; (44) W.-reg.; (45) C.-
2.7-4.

Wood, Mrs. Joseph: (36) C.-1.28*;
2.11*; (40) C.-10.26-8.

Wood, Wm. B.: (35) W.-6.23; (38)
W.-3.21; (41) W.-6.26; 11.6*; (42)
A.-6.8-3; (43) A.-3.6.

Wood, W., and his wonderful dog, Bruin: (39) W.-1.10-9; (43) W.-4.12-18; (45) A.-8.9-20; (46) A.-1.8-2; A.-7.23-5; A.-8.26-reg.; (47) A.-1.1-6; A.-5.5; P.M.-7.3-5; (50) C.-4.4-5; (51) C.-7.3-reg.; (52) N.-5.22-reg.; (53) A.-1.13. Tom in *Dumb Man of Manchester*, Cato in *Foulah Slave*, Dareall in *Smuggler of Bootle Bay*, Strapado in *Dumb Girl of Genoa*.

Wood, Miss E.: (39) C.-12.14; (40) C.-2.4; (41) W.-11.6*; (42) C.-1.6-reg.; (46) P.M.-3.9-reg.; W.-4.3; (47) C.-1.20-reg.; (48) A.-reg.; (49) P.M.-reg.; A.-reg.-12.5*; (50) C.-reg. Amanthis in *Child of Nature*.

Wood, Master: (47) A.-1.11-3; (52) N.-5.22-reg.

Woodbury: (40) N.-reg.

Woodhull: (36) W.-10.28*; 11.15*.

Woolford: (38) W.-4.2*-with Cooke's Company.

Worrell, T. J., a comedian: (49) A.-10.23-3; (51) A.-reg.; N.-7.15-summer; A.-8.30-reg.; 4.14*; (54) C.M.-9.12-reg.

Wright: (45) C.-8.30-reg.; (46) P.M.-3.9-reg.; A.-8.26-reg.

Young, B.: (42) W.-4.20-reg.; (43) C.-reg.; (46) W.-6.14; (50) C.-1.7-5; 3.18*; (51) W.-8.18-reg.; (52) N.-7.12-reg.; (53) W.-reg.; (54) W.-reg.; (55) W.-reg.-10.10*. Mesty in *Midshipman Easy*.

Young, Miss: (48) Ath.-12.25-reg.

THE PLAYWRIGHT LIST

THE PLAYWRIGHT LIST

THE following list includes more than two hundred and seventy writers for the theatre whose works appeared on the Philadelphia stage from 1835 to 1855 inclusive, and is by no means complete, for custom did not insist that a playwright's name be advertised in connection with the play. Reasons for this indifference were numerous. Three will be enough to suggest the attitude of the theatres: the playwright and his play were so well known at the time that it was unnecessary to mention the author; the playwright was unknown, and it was enough for the producer and manager to hazard an unknown play without the additional burden of an unknown name; and the third reason for not mentioning the author probably was that authors, before copyright protection, were of no importance, unless great favorites.

To interpret the following list, note that parentheses are used to enclose play-titles when it is not certain that the playwright named wrote the Philadelphia-recorded play.

Adam, Adolph: *The Brewer of Preston;* comic opera; *Giralda.*

Addams, J. P.: *The Matchwoman of Philadelphia; Redwood; Rough and Ready; Sam Patch in France.*

Addison, Joseph: *Cato.*

Addison, Laura: *Mary Stuart.*

Aiken, G. L.: *Uncle Tom's Cabin.*

Ainsworth, W. H.: *Jack Sheppard.*

Amherst, H. J.: *Napoleon Bonaparte.*

Amherst, J. M.: *Jenny Lind in Philadelphia.*

Andrews, G. H.: *The Count of Monte Cristo.*

Angely: *The Seven Female Soldiers:* opera.

Arnold, Samuel James: *Man and Wife; The Devil's Bridge.*

Auber, François, all operas: *Black Domino; La Tentation,* V. *The Devil's Daughter; La Muette de Portici; The Maid of Cashmere; Masaniello.*

Baker, B. A.: *Mose in China; New York as it Is.*

Balfe: *The Bohemian Girl:* opera; *The Enchantress:* opera.

Ball, Edward. See Edward Fitzball.

Banim, John: *Damon and Pythias.*

Bannister, N. H.: *Alvardo of Spain; The Bush Whacker; Caius Silius; Destruction of Jerusalem; Gaulantus; The Gentleman of Lyons; Infidelity; Life in Philadelphia; Oua Cousta; Putnam; Robert Emmet; Rookwood; The Syracusan Brothers; Titus Andronicus:* after Shakespeare; *Wacousta,* V. *Oua Cousta; The Wandering Jew; The Yankee Duellist.*

[717]

Barker, James Nelson: *The Court of Love; Marmion.*

Barnett, Morris: *The Serious Family; The Yankee Pedlar.*

Barnes, Charlotte M. S. See Mrs. E. B. Conner.

Barrymore, W.: *The Battle of Poictiers; Gilderoy the Bonnie Boy; Jonathan and his Apprentices; The Last Days of Pompeii; Wallace the Hero of Scotland; Zanthe.*

Beaumont and Fletcher: *The Maid's Tragedy; Rule a Wife and Have a Wife.*

Beethoven: *Fidelio.*

Bellini, Vicenzo: *Il Puritani; La Sonnambula; Norma; Romeo and Juliet:* all operas.

Benedia, R.: *Doctor Wespe; The Prison.*

Bennett, George: *Retribution.*

Berkmann: *Nante the Porter.*

Bernard, L.: *Irish Honor.*

Bernard, William Bayle: *Marie Ducange; The Passing Cloud.*

Birch, Samuel: *The Adopted Child.*

Bickerstaff, Isaac: *The Hypocrite; Love in a Village; The Padlock; The Spoiled Child; The Romp.*

Bird, R. M.: *The Broker of Bogota; The Gladiator; Oralloosa.*

Bishop, Sir R.: *Henri Quatre:* opera.

Blake, W. R.: *The Last Man.*

Boker, George Henry: *The Betrothal; Calaynos; Francesca da Rimini; Leonora de Guzman; The World a Mask.*

Booth, Junius Brutus: *Ugolino.*

Boucicault, D.: *Andy Blake; Apollo in New York; A Cure for Coquettes; The Fox Hunt; The Knight of Arva; London Assurance; Love and Money; Old Heads and Young Hearts; Prima Donna; (The Struggle for Life and Death); Used Up;*

The West End; The Willow Copse; The Young Actress.

Bray, John: *The Toothache.*

Brewster, B. H.: *The Infidel.*

Brooke, Mrs.: *Rosina.*

Brougham, John: *Arcade; The Bachelor of Arts; Bleak House; David Copperfield; The Declaration of Independence; Dombey and Son; Franklin; The Game of Life; Good Husbands Make Good Wives; The Haunted Man; The Irish Emigrant; The Irish Fortune Hunter; The Irish Yankee; Love and Murder; Night and Morning; Paul Pry; (The Red Mask); Romance and Reality; Shakespeare's Dream; This House to be Sold.*

Brown, David Paul: *The Prophet of St. Paul's.*

Brown, John: *Barbarossa.*

Buckstone, John Baldwin: *The Bear Hunters; The Card Drawer; The Death Plank; The Duke's Bride; The Flowers of the Forest; The Green Bushes; Henriette; The Hunter(s) of the Pyrenees; Leap Year; The Maid with the Milking Pail; Married Life; Our Mary Ann; Poor Jack; Rural Felicity; Single Life; Solomon Smink; Weak Points.*

Bulwer-Lytton, Edward: *The Duchess de la Valliere; The Lady of Lyons; Money; Richelieu; Rienzi; The Sea Captain.*

Burk, J. D.: *The Inn Keeper of Abbeville.*

Burke, Charles: *Murrell the Land pirate; Ole Bull; (Revolution).*

Burton, W. E.: *(Box, Cox, and Knox); (Crimson Crimes); (The Dancing Barber); The Dark Lady; (Did you ever Send your Wife to Germantown?); (Does your Mother Know you are Out?); Ella Wareham; Em-*

migration; (Fashion); Forty Winks; (The Illustrious Stranger); The Intemperate; The Ladies' Man; (The Market Street Merchant); Moonshine; The Mummy; My Friend the Governor; (A Quiet Day); (The Rise of the Rothschilds); (The Ship Launch); The Toodles.

Butler, J.: *Gaspardo the Gondolier.*

Byrne, James: *Blue Beard.*

Byron, Lord George Gordon: *Marino Faliero; Mazeppa; Sardanapalus; The Two Foscari.*

Centlivre, Mrs. Susanna: *The Busy Body; Wonder! A Woman Keeps a Secret.*

Chapman, Samuel H.: *Doctor Foster; The Red Rover.*

Chapman, W.: *Jakey's Visit to California.*

Cibber, Colley: *The Provoked Husband; She Would and she Would Not.*

Clinch, C. P.: *The Avenger's Vow.*

Coffey, Charles: *The Devil to Pay.*

Coleman of Philadelphia: *Crichton; Grumbling; XYZ.*

Colman, Benjamin: *The Hero of the North.*

Colman, George the Elder: *The Clandestine Marriage; The Jealous Wife; The Poor Gentleman.*

Colman, George the Younger: *The Heir at Law; Inkle and Yarico; The Iron Chest; John Bull; The Mountaineers; The Review; The Shipwreck; Who wants a Guinea?; Tit for Tat.*

Conner, Mrs. C. B., née Charlotte M. S. Barnes: *The Captain; Charlotte Corday; The Forest Princess; Octavia Bragaldi.*

Conrad, R. T.: *Jack Cade.*

Conway, H. J.: *The Arab Chief; Charles O'Malley; Fatal Prophecies; Ida Stephanoff; A Miser's Miseries; Our Jemima; The Spanish Pirates.*

Corneille: *Les Horaces.*

Cowley: *Toodles.*

Cowley, Mrs.: *The Belle's Stratagem; A Bold Stroke for a Husband; Which is the Man?*

Coyne, Joseph Sterling: *Presented at Court.*

Crafts, William: *The Sea Serpent.*

Cross, James C.: *The Purse.*

Cumberland, Richard: *The Jew; The West Indian; The Shipwreck; The Wheel of Fortune.*

Custis, G. W. P.: *The Indian Prophecy; Pocahontas.*

Dance, Charles: *Horse Shoe Robinson.*

Delavigue, Casimir: *Yelva.*

Deer, W. R.: *Kit Karson.*

Diamond: *Adrian and Orrilla; The Foundling of the Forest.*

Dibdin, Charles: *The Heart of Midlothian; The Quaker; The Waterman; The Wedding Ring.*

Dibdin, Thomas John: *Alonzo the Brave.*

Donizetti, Gaetano, all operas: *Don Pasquale; The Elixir of Love; La Favorita; La Figlia del Reggimento; Linda di Chamounix; The Love Spell; Lucia di Lammermoor; Lucrezia Borgia; Maria di Rohan; Parisina.*

Dumas, A.: *The Corsican Brothers.*

Dunlap, William: *Abaellino; The Battle of New Orleans; The Blind Boy; (Blue Beard); The Flying Dutchman; The Glory of Clumbia; Lovers' Vows; (Rinaldo Rinaldini); The School for Soldiers; The Stranger; Thirty Years of a Gambler's Life; The Virgin of the Sun; The Voice of Nature.*

Durang, Charles: *Marino Faliero:* revision of Byron's work; *Sardanapalus:* revision of Byron's work.

Durivage, O. E.: *The Lady of the Lions; The Stage Struck Yankee.*

Emmons, Robert: *Tecumseh.*

English, T. D.: *The Doom of the Drinker; The Empire of Hayti; Gammon and Galvinism; Handy Andy.*

Farquhar, George: *The Beaux Stratagem; The Recruiting Officer.*

Ferrars, C.: *Jack's the Lad.*

Field, J. M.: *Antony and Cleopatra; The Artful Dodger; Family Ties,* with John S. Robb; *Gabrielle; Griselda; (Oregon); Victoria.*

Fielding, Henry: *Tom Thumb the Great.*

Finn, H. J.: *Kaspar Hauser; Removing the Deposites.*

Fitzball, Edward: *Esmerelda; Home Again; Wardock Kennilson.*

Flagg, E.: *(Mary Tudor).*

Fletcher, John: *The Elder Brother.*

Florence, W. T.: *Mischievous Annie.*

Foote, Samuel: *The Liar; The Mayor of Garrat(t).*

Forrester, E.: *The Student of Morlaix.*

Foster, J.: *The Knight of the Lion Heart; The Siege of Monterey.*

Fowler, M. B.: *The Prophecy.*

Francis, William: *Harlequin Hurry Scurry; The Sailor's Return.*

Fry: *Leonora:* grand opera.

Galt, J.: *(My Aunt).*

Gann, James: *The Mysteries of Paris:* in collaboration with F. C. Wemyss and John Sefton.

Garrick, David: *The Clandestine Marriage:* with G. Colman, Sr.; *The Country Girl; Gulliver in Lilliput; High Life below Stairs; The Irish Widow; Katharine and Petruchio; The Lying Valet.*

Gay, John: *The Beggar's Opera.*

Gibbs, Mrs.: *The Emerald Isle.*

Glover, S. E.: *The Cradle of Liberty.*

Goldsmith, Oliver: *She Stoops to Conquer.*

Gore, Mrs.: *King O'Neil.*

Grice, C. E.: *The Battle of New Orleans.*

Griffin, Gerald: *Gisippus.*

Hackett, J. H.: *Jonathan in England.*

Halévy, Jacques: *La Juive.*

Harlan, General: *The Falls of Kessichack.*

Heath, J. E.: *Whigs and Democrats.*

Hielge, George: *Montezuma.*

Hoadl(e)y, Benjamin: *The Suspicious Husband.*

Hoare, Prince: *No Song no Supper; The Prize.*

Holcroft, Thomas: *The Deserted Daughter; The Road to Ruin.*

Home, John: *Douglas.*

Hugo, Victor: *The Court Fool; The Tour de Nesle; Zanthe.*

Humphreys, David: *The Yankee in England.*

Inchbald, Mrs. Elizabeth: *Animal Magnetism; Everyone has his Fault; The Married Man; The Mogul Tale; The Midnight Hour; The Wedding Day; Wives as they Were and Maids as they Are.*

Irving, Washington: *Charles the Second:* with J. H. Payne.

Jerrold, D. W.: *Black Ey'd Susan; The Catspaw; The Housekeeper; The Miser of Southwark Ferry; The Rent Day; Time Works Wonders.*

Johnson, S. D.: *Brian O'Lynn; In and Out of Place; Our Gal.*

Johnston, T. B.: *Mose and Jakey.*

Jones, J. S.: *The Adventure; The Carpenter of Rouen; The Green Mountain Boy; The Liberty Tree; The People's Lawyer; The Shoemaker of Toulouse; The Siege of Boston; The Surgeon of Paris.*

Judah, S. B. H.: *Rose of Arragon.*

Kemble, Charles: *Plot and Counterplot; The Point of Honor.*

Kemble, Mrs. Charles: *Smiles and Tears.*

Kemble, Frances Ann, later Butler: *The Duke's Wager; The Star of Seville.*

Kemble, John P.: *The Maid of Honor.*

Kenney, James: *Ella Rosenberg.*

Kerr, John: *Rip Van Winkle.*

Kettel: *Richard's Wanderings.*

Knight, Thomas: *The Honest Thieves.*

Knowles, James Sheridan: *The Blind Beggar of Bethnal Green; Brian Boroihme; The Bridal; The Hunchback; John di Procida; Love; The Love Chase; The Maid of Mariendorpt; Virginius; The Wife; William Tell; The Wrecker's Daughter.*

Korner, Theodore: *The Bride.*

Korner, Thomas: *Hedwig.*

Kotzebue, August von: *Der Wirrwar; Die Brilleninsel; The Dissipated Child; The Roses of Baron de Malesherbes; Stag Hall:* i. e., *Der Kohbock; The Straight Way is the Best; U.A.W.G.; The Widow and the Riding Horse.*

Lancaster, Edward: *The Manager's Daughter.*

Lebrun: *Humoristische Studien.*

Lee, Harriet: *A Chapter of Accidents.*

Lee, Nathaniel: *Alexander the Great.*

Leman, Walter M.: *The Battle of Germantown; Freedom; The Last Martyr; The Millionaire; The Prairie Bird.*

Lemon, Mark: *The Loving Woman.*

Lewis, M. G.: *Scene in a Madhouse.*

Lillo, George: *The Fatal Curiosity; George Barnwell.*

Loder, George: *The Sphynx.*

Logan, C. A.: *Chloroform; The Vermont Wool Dealer; Yankee Land.*

Lovell, Mrs.: *Ingomar.*

Lytton, Lord. See Bulwer-Lytton.

Macklin, Charles: *The Man of the World.*

Macnally, Leonard: *Robin Hood.*

Macready, William: *The Irishman in London.*

Mann, Mrs. Sheridan: *Florentine.*

Marston, J. Westland: *The Patrician's Daughter; Philip de France and Marie de Meranie; Strathmore.*

Marston, Rev. W.: *Annie Blake.*

Massinger, Philip: *The Fatal Dowry; The Maid of Honor; A New Way To Pay Old Debts; Riches; The Roman Actor.*

Mathews, Cornelius: *He Would be an Actor; Jacob Leisler; Witchcraft.*

Matson: *Paul Ulric.*

Matthews, Charles James.: *Patter Versus Clatter.*

McLellan, R. C.: *The Foundling.*

Medina, Miss L. H.: *Ernest Maltravers; The Last Days of Pompeii; Nick of the Woods.*

Meighan, Thaddeus W.: *The Mysteries and Miseries of New York.*

Mercadante: *Il Giuramento:* opera.

Meyerbeer, Giacomo: *Robert le Diable:* opera.

Miles, G. H.: *De Soto; Mohammed.*

Milman, H. H.: *Fazio.*

Milner: *The Moorish Page; Prince Lee Boo.*

Mitford, Mary Russell: *Charles I.*

Moliere: *Le Tartuffe.*

Moncrieff, W. T.: *Boz; The Bravo of Venice; The Cataract of the*

Ganges; A Down East Bargain; The Duddlestones; Monsieur Tonson; Paris and London; Sam Weller; Tom and Jerry.

Moore, Edward: *The Gamester.*

More, Hannah: *David and Goliath.*

Morton, James Maddison: *Box and Cox; Done on Both Sides.*

Morton, Thomas: *Columbus; A Cure for the Heartache; Education; Henri Quatre; A School for Grown Children; The School of Reform; Secrets Worth Knowing; Speed the Plough; Town and Country; The Way to get Married.*

Mowatt, Anna C. O. See Mrs. A. C. O. M. Ritchie.

Mozart, Wolfgang: *Don Giovanni; Don Juan; The Marriage of Figaro:* all operas.

Murphy, Arthur: *All in the Wrong; Dick the Apprentice; Know your own Mind; The Old Maid; Three Weeks after Marriage.*

Murry, W.: *Rule a Wife and Have a Wife:* revision of Beaumont and Fletcher's play.

Noah, M. M.: *The Frontier Maid; Marion; She Would be a Soldier; The Siege of Tripoli; The Wandering Boys.*

O'Hara, Kane: *Midas.*

O'Keeffe, John: *The Agreeable Surprise; The Castle of Andulusia; The Fair Philadelphian; Fontainbleau; The Highland Reel; Modern Antiques; Peeping Tom of Coventry; The Poor Soldier; Set a Beggar on Horseback; Wild Oats; The Young Quaker.*

Otway, Thomas: *Venice Preserved.*

Oulton, Walley Chamberlaine: *Botheration.*

Oxenford, John: *A Day Well Spent.*

Pane, Henry H.: *The Irish Footman.*

Pardey, J. Oakes: *Nationalities.*

Paul, H. H.: *Some Things can be Done as Well as Others; The Swamp Steed.*

Payne, J. H.: *Adeline; (The Boarding School); Brutus; Charles the Second,* with W. Irving; *Christine of Poland; Clari; The Fall of Algiers; (The Italian Bride); The Lancers; Love in Humble Life; Lovers' Vows; The Maid and the Magpie; Peter Smink; Remorse; Therese; 'Twas I; The White Lady.*

Peake, R. B.: *The Climbing Boy; The Sheriff of the County.*

Percival: *La Fitte.*

Pfeiffer, Charles Birch: *Hinko.*

Philips, Ambrose: *The Distressed Mother.*

Phillips, J. B.: *The Evil Eye; The Gold Stricken; Oranaska; The Pirate Boy.*

Pilgrim, James: *Harry Burnham; (Ireland and America); The Limerick Boy; Paddy the Piper; Shandy Maguire; Yankee Jack.*

Planché, James Robinson: *The Day of Reckoning; Fortunio; The Siege of Stralsmund.*

Pocinini, Giovanni: *Saffo.*

Pocock, Isaac: *Hit or Miss!; The Miller and his Men; Rob Roy Macgregor; Robinson Crusoe; The Robber's Wife.*

Poole, John: *John Buzzby; Sweethearts and Wives.*

Power, Tyrone: *The Irish Ambassador; The Irish Attorney.*

Pray, Isaac C.: *Caecinna; Julietta Gordini.*

Ranger: *Father and Daughter.*

Ravenscroft, Edward: *The Anatomist.*

Reade, Charles: *The Ladies' Battle;*

Masks and Faces, with Tom Taylor.

Rees, James: *Anthony Wayne; Amaldi; (The Brigadier's Horse); Changes; Lucretia Borgia; Patrick Lyon; The Unknown; Washington.*

Reid, Mayne: *Love's Martyr.*

Reynolds, Frederick: *Begone Dull Care; The Dramatist; The Exile; Laugh when you Can; Speculation; The Will.*

Rice, T. D.: *Bone Squash Diavolo; Discoveries in the Moon.*

Riemann, F. See *Die Brilleninsel.*

Ritchie, Mrs. Anna C. O. Mowatt: *Armand; Fashion.*

Robb, John S.: *Family Ties:* with J. M. Field.

Roeder: *The Circumstances against the Will.*

Rossi, Gaetano: *Il Giuramento:* the liberetto of the opera.

Rossini, Giacomo, operas: *The Barber of Seville; Cinderella; La Cenerentola; La Gazza Ladra; Stabat Mater:* oratorio.

Rowe, Nicholas: *Jane Shore.*

Rowson, S. H.: *The American Tar.*

Sargent, Epes: *Change Makes Change; The Genoese; Velasco.*

Saunders, C. H.: *Rosina Meadows; Telula.*

Schiller, J. C. F. von: *William Tell:* V. *The Conjuration; Wilhelm Tell; The Robbers.*

Schneitzhofer: *Dew Drop.*

Scribe, Eugene: *Yelva.*

Selby: *The Husband of my Heart; The Unfinished Gentleman.*

Sedley, Sir Charles: *Bellamira.*

Sefton, John: *The Mysteries of Paris:* in collaboration with F. C. Wemyss and James Gann.

Shakespeare, William: *As You Like It; The Comedy of Errors; Cymbeline; Hamlet; Henry IV; Henry VIII; Julius Caesar; King John; King Lear; Macbeth; The Merchant of Venice; The Merry Wives of Windsor; Midsummer Night's Dream; Much Ado about Nothing; Othello; Richard III; Romeo and Juliet; The Taming of the Shrew; The Tempest; Titus Andronicus; Twelfth Night; Two Gentlemen of Verona; Winter's Tale.*

Sheil, Richard Lalor: *The Apostate; Evadne.*

Sherburne, J. H.: *Osceola.*

Sheridan, R. B.: *The Critic; Pizarro; The Rivals; The School for Scandal.*

Siddons, Mrs. H.: *The Father and Son.*

Silsbee, J. S.: *The Doolittle Family.*

Simmons, J. W.: *Manfredi.*

Simms, W. G.: *Bertram.*

Simpson, J. R.: *Poor Cousin Walter.*

Smith, Mrs. Elizabeth Oakes: *The Roman Tribute.*

Smith, R. P.: *The Actress of Padua; The Bravo; The Daughter; The Deformed; The Drowned; William Penn.*

Smith, W. H.: *The Drunkard.*

Southerne, Thomas: *Isabella; Oroonoko.*

Sperry, J. Austin: *Drumming; Extremes; Life in the West.*

Steele, Silas S.: *The Bank Monster; The Battle of Tippecanoe; The Brazen Drum; The Champion of Cordova; Clandare; Emilie Plater; The Gold Bug; The Grecian Queen; The Lion of the Sea; Philadelphia Assurance.*

Sterling, Edward: *The Bohemians; The Idiot of the Mill; Nicholas Nickleby; The Pet of the Public.*

Stevens, (H. E.): *The Brothers of the Pyrenees; The Skeleton Robber.*

Stokes, J.: *The Forest of Rosenwald.*

Stone, John A.: *The Knight of the Golden Fleece; Metamora.*

Talbot, C. S.: *(Paddy's Trip to America).*

Talfourd, Sir Thomas Noon: *The Athenian Captive; Glencoe; Ion.*

Tayleure, C. W.: *Hot Corn.*

Taylor, C. W.: *Fashion and Famine.*

Taylor, Tom: *Masks and Faces,* with C. Reade; *Plot and Passion; Still Waters Run Deep.*

Thompson, Edward: *The Festival of St. Michael.*

Thompson, Lysander: *The Yorkshire Brothers.*

Tobin, John: *The Honey Moon.*

Turnbull, J. D.: *The Wood Demon.*

Tyler, Royall: *The Judgment of Solomon.*

Verdi, Giuseppi, operas: *(H)ernani; The Lombards at the First Crusade; Louise Miller; The Two Foscari.*

Wallace, J. S.: *The Water Witch.*

Wallace, Vincent: *Maritana.*

Wallack, Lester: *The Three Guardsmen.*

Wallack, W. H.: *The Pilot.*

Ward, H. M.: *The Crock of Gold.*

Ware, C. P.: *Azael.*

Weber, Carl von: *Der Freischutz.*

Webster, Benjamin Nottingham: *Belphegor; Caught in a Trap; Paul Clifford.*

Weigh: *The Swiss Family.*

Weld, H. H.: *Easy Joe Bruce.*

Wemyss, F. C.: *Captain Kyd; The Mysteries of Paris:* in collaboration with John Sefton and James Gann; *Norman Leslie.*

White, James: *The King of the Commons.*

Whitehead, William: *The Roman Father.*

Wilkins, John: *Camille; Civilization; The Egyptians; St. Marc.*

Willis, N. P.: *Bianca Visconti; Tortesa the Usurer.*

Wilmer, L. A.: *The Eighth of January; Native Nobility.*

Woodworth, Samuel: *The Forest Rose.*

Young, B.: *Cabin and Parlor.*

Young, Edward: *The Revenge.*